RECORD

OF

PENNSYLVANIA MARRIAGES,

PRIOR TO 1810.

VOLUME I.

Baltimore
GENEALOGICAL PUBLISHING CO., INC.
1987

Excerpted and reprinted from
Pennsylvania Archives, Series 2,
Vols. VIII and IX (1880).
Genealogical Publishing Co., Inc.
Baltimore, 1968, 1987.
Library of Congress Catalogue Card Number 67-28626
International Standard Book Number, Volume I: 0-8063-1179-7
Set Number: 0-8063-0214-3
Made in the United States of America

Table of Contents

Volume I

MARRIAGES

RECORDED BY THE REGISTRAR GENERAL

OF THE PROVINCE.

1685–1689.

[In volume II of this series of Archives are contained such records of marriage licenses, issued by the Provincial authorities, as were found in the office of the Secretary of the Commonwealth. Since then, the following paper has come into the hands of the Editors, which affords a fitting preface to the marriage records forming this and the succeeding volume. To the historian and the genealogist, as well as to the people of the State generally, these records will be of great value, and appreciated accordingly.]

1684, ——— —, Thomas Baldwin, and Mary ———, of Chester.

1684–5, Feb. —, William Clayton, and Elizabeth Beazer, both of Chichester, Chester county.

1685, April 15, Andrew Griscome, carpenter, and ——— Dole, of Philadelphia.

1685, May —, David Morris, carpenter, and ——— Philpin, both of Philadelphia.

1683–4, Mar. 4, Jacob Simcock, of Ridley, Chester county.

1685, Sept. 17, Charles Brigham, of Philadelphia, and Hannah Runneger.

1685, Nov. 9, Isaac Pearson, of Philadelphia, blacksmith, and Elizabeth Hall, of the same place.

1685, Nov. 10, Philip Parker, and Hanna Sessions.

1685, Nov. 12, George Emlen, of Philadelphia, husbandman, and Ellener Allen.

1685, Dec. 17, John Marten, of Philadelphia, taylor, and Elizabeth Simms.

1685, Dec: 7, Thomas Masters, of Philadelphia, carpenter, and Hannah Hurd.

1685, Dec. 10, Nathaniel Walton, of Philadelphia, taylor, and Martha Bonell.

1686, April 8, Thomas Harding, of Philadelphia, planter, and Mary Bullon.

1686, April 3, Richard Ormes, of Philadelphia, cordwainer, and Mary Tidder, of Radnor.

1686, May 5, Philip Howell, of Philadelphia, taylor, and Jane Luff.

1686, May 3, Benjamin Chambers, of Philadelphia, yeoman, and Hannab Smith, of the same place.

1686, May 23, John Moon, of Philadelphia, merchant, and Martha Will.

1686, May 24, Jonathan Adams, of Philadelphia, taylor, and Alice Mays, widow.

1686, May 28, Richard Roberts, of Philadelphia, carpenter, and Ellen Holdin, of same place.

1686, June 18, Nathaniel Sikes, of Philadelphia, carpenter, and Eleanor Paine, of the same place.

1686, July 24, George Scotson, of Philadelphia, cooper, and Elizabeth Coombes, of Philadelphia, spinster. At the house of Christopher Taylor, in High street, Philadelphia.

1686, Aug. 5, Robert Kent, of Philadelphia, shoemaker, and Margaret Thompson, of Philadelphia, widow. At public meeting.

1686, Aug. 28, Thomas Langstone, of Philadelphia, bricklyer, and Sarah Header, of the same, widow. At Christopher Taylor's, in Second street.

1686, Sept. 4, Daniel Howell, of West New Jersey, and Hannah Laking, of Philadelphia, spinster. At Isaac Piereson's, in Mulberry street.

1686, Aug. 12, William Hudson, of Philadelphia, bricklayer, and Ann Wayes, of the same. spinster. At the meeting-house.

1686, Nov. 17, Thomas Bowles, of Tinicum Island, gent., and Mary Gibons, of the same, widow. At the house of Robert Tirrill, in Philadelphia.

1686, Nov. 30, Thomas Hooton, sonne of Thomas and Eliza Hooton, of this towne, and Elizabeth Stanley, daughter of Wm Stanley, dec^d. At the meeting-house.

1686, Dec. 8, Philip Oxford, of Philadelphia, cordwainer, and Sarah Jones, daughter of Henry Jones, of Moyamensen. At the house of Henry Jones.

1686, Dec. 7, Zackary, Whitpain, son of Richard Whitpaine, of London, and Sarah Songhurst, dau. of John Songhurst, of this place, carpenter.

1686–7, Jan. 28, Thomas Duckett, of Schulkill, (sic,) and Ruth Wood, widow, widow of Richard Wood.

1686–7, Feb. 4, John Ironmonger, husbandman, and Sarah Lakin, spinster, both of Philadelphia.

1686–7, Feb. 7, William Ffisher, and Bridget Hodgkins, both of Philadelphia county.

———, ——— —, Thomas Maddox, husbandman, and Jane Lee, spinster, both of Philadelphia county.

1686–7, Jan. 16, Daniel Street and Hannah East. At the house of Hannah East.

1686–7, Mar. 3, Abraham Hooper, joyner, and Philitia Greene, spinster. At the house of John Moon, in Philadelphia.

1686–7, Mar. 8, Henry Jones, of Moyamensen, merchant, and Rachel Warner, widow. At the meeting-house.

1686–7, Mar. 9, Henry Labin, husbandman, and Anne Lea, widow.

1687, April 15, Benjamin Howard, cordwainer, and Mary Paine, spinster, both of Philadelphia.

1687, April 27, George Buntin, carpenter, and Anne Lee, spinster, both of Philadelphia. At the house of John Harris.

1687, May 3, Jan du Plouny, baker, and Weyntie Van Janen, both of Philadelphia. At the meeting-house.

1687, May 31, Isaac Rickatt, snuf-maker, and Elizabeth Palmer, spinster, both of Philadelphia. At the meeting-house.

1687, June 27, Jacob Preig, sawyer, and Elizabeth Mayo, spinster, both of Philadelphia. At the house of Edward Smoote.

1687–8, Jan. 3, John Holme, of Philadelphia, and Mary More, widow, of Greenspring, Philadelphia county.

1687–8, Feb. 2, William Bethel, bricklayer, of Amboy, East Jersey, and Helena Claypoole, dau. of James Claypoole, late of Philadelphia.

1687–8, Feb. 2, Thomas Peart, whitesmith, and Anna Wilson, spinster, both of Philadelphia. At the house of Thomas Peart.

1688, April   4, Joshua Tittery, glas-maker, and Cecily Wolley,
              spinster, both of Philadelphia. At the meeting-
              house.

1688, Oct.   11, Francis Cooke, of Newcastle county, and Mary
              Claypoole, of Philadelphia. At the house of
              William Hare, Philadelphia.

1789, April   4, Daniel Hodgson, physician, and Hannah Holme,
              daughter of John Holme. At Green Spring, the
              house of John Holme, Philadelphia county.

1689-90, Jan. 14, William Carver, living near Poetquisink creek,
              Philadelphia county, and Jone (sic) Kinsey, liv-
              ing near Neshaminy creek. Bucks county.

1689, Oct.   18, Francis Rawle, of Philadelphia, merchant, and
              Martha Turner, of the same place, spinster. At
              the meeting-house, Philadelphia.

1693, May   1, Edmund du Castel, and Cristian Boone, both of
              Philadelphia.

MARRIAGE RECORD

OF

CHRIST CHURCH,

PHILADELPHIA.

1709–1806.

CHRIST CHURCH, PHILADELPHIA.

1800, May   15, Aaron, Michael, and Rebecca Smith.
1767, Sept.   4, Aaron, Rachel, and John Kelly.
1797, Feb.   19, Abbot, John, and Jane Oliver.
1751, March 23, Abbot, Mary, and Benjamin Browning.
1798, Nov.   13, Abbott, Edward, and Kitty Strong.
1785, Oct.   20, Abbott, George, and Sarah Brown.
1786, April   20, Abbott, John, and Sarah Brown.
1745, Jan.   2, Abbott, Lydia, and George McCall.
1794, June   5, Abel, James, and Sarah Overturf.
1802, Nov.   11, Abel, Rachel, and Isaac Barnes.
1796, April   6, Abel, Sarah, and John Stokes.
1796, Oct.   17, Abel, Susanna, and William Ferriar.
1753, Nov.   27, Abercrombie, James, and Margaret Bennet.
1783, Oct.   31, Abercrombie, James, and Ann Bannton.
1767, Sept.   26, Abercrombie, Margaret, and Charles Stedman.
1759, Jan.   2, Aberdean, Alexander, and Eleanor Ellis.
1791, Jan.   23, Abernethie, Margaret, and Hugh Morrison.
1722, May   19, Abevan, Evan, and Margaret Griffith.
1758, Feb.   18, Abington, George, and Sarah Wilson.
1754, April   20, Abraham ——— and Rose Usher.
1722, Aug.   23, Ackenhof, David, and Winifred Bradley.
1802, March 30, Acres, James, and Jane Simes.
1791, Aug.   15, Adair, Eliz, and John Farr.
1800, May   31, Adair, Eliz, and Zephaniah Tomlin.
1774, Dec.   22, Adair, Thomas, and Eleanor Jones.
1756, March   3, Adams, Alexander, Mary Holland.
1723, Dec.   11, Adams, Ann, and David Ross.
1798, Dec.   15, Adams, Ann, and David Johnson.
1799, July   20, Adams, Ann, and Luke Usher.
1778, Oct.   18, Adams, Ann, and John Scott.
1794, July   6, Adams, Barbara, and Benjamin Henneen.
1746, Jan.   4, Adams, Comfort, and George Densburgh.
1790, Sept.   7, Adams, David, and Gabella Platt.

1796, Jan.   5, Adams, Edward Hanlin, and Amelia Sophia Mc-
              Pherson.
1800, Dec. 25, Adams, Eliz, and Charles Douglas.
1756, Sept. 27, Adams, Elizabeth, and Daniel Carter.
1786, June   8, Adams, Francis, and Grace Thomas.
1757, Oct. 18, Adams, John, and Jane Fairost.
1758, Sept.   7, Adams, John, and Cornelia England.
1758, May   6, Adams, John, and Hannah Kelly.
1776, Nov. 14, Adams, Margaret, and John Marshall.
1769, March 21, Adams, Margaret, and Samuel Webster.
1785, Oct. 20, Adams, Mary, and William Townsend Donaldson.
1762, Nov.   6, Adams, Rachel, and James Black.
1803, Nov.   2, Adams, Rachel, and George Gray.
1726, Dec. 22, Adams, Rich^d and E. Withers.
1752, Oct. 17, Adams, Robert, and Martha Townsend.
1805, March 28, Adams, Robert, and Martha Levy Jones.
1760, May 29, Adams, Samuel, and Sarah Love.
1774, Jan. 15, Adams, Sarah, and John Millis.
1721, May 17, Adams, William, and Joan Dickinson.
1747, March 11, Adams, William, and Martha Eadarles.
1756, Jan.   5, Adams, William, and Mary Price.
1728, Dec. 26, Adams, W^m, and Rachel Towsend.
1748, Feb.   5, Adamson, Anthony, and Dorothy Hainey.
1755, Jan. 10, Adamson, Dorothy, and James Miller.
1746, Jan. 16, Adamson, Philip, and Frances McCready.
1748, July   8, Adamson, Susannah, and John Parsons.
1738, Feb.   2, Adare, Dinah, and Alexander Miller.
1793, Aug.   5, Adgate, Daniel, and Mary Cochran.
1795, July   7, Affleck, Lewis G., and Ann Potts.
1795, Dec. 24, Affleck, Margaret, and Thomas Newman.
1795, April 2, Affleck, Mary, and Isaac Willis.
1730, Sept. 30, Afflick, Jane, and James Bucksome.
1787, May   5, Afterman, Cath., and James Fisher.
1781, May 30, Ager, Margret, and William Brown.
1770, Oct. 24, Agnew Margaret, and Joseph Price.
1775, April 20, Agnus, John, and Hannah Appowen.
1740, Dec. 23, Aiken, Thomas, and Jane Bairnhill.
1760, Sept. 30, Ainsworth, Ann, and William Howe.
1797, Nov. 30, Akin, James, and Eliza Cox.
1749, Oct. 21, Alaire, Alexander, and Elizabeth Palmer.
1798, Aug.   2, Albertson, Aaron, and Margaret Overturff.
1728, May 17, Albertson, Abraham, and Patience Shew.
1761, Oct. 29, Albertson, Jonathan, and Jemima Thomas.
1787, Dec. 11, Albertson, Mary, and John Ware.
1750, April 3, Albertoon, Richlost, and Mary Coats.
1781, July   1, Albertson, Sarah, and John Price.

1758, June	28, Albright, Margaret, and James Robinson.
1748, Nov.	5, Albrighton, Christiana, and Ezekiel Hicks.
1790, June	5, Alcorn, Charlotte, and John Cartman.
1787, May	10, Alcorn, Robert, and Charlotte Montgomery.
1731, June	16, Aldridge, Anne, and William Glenn.
1758, Nov.	1, Aldridge, David, and Sarah Chew.
1751, May	21, Aldridge, Elizabeth, and Richard Ferrard.
1756, Sept.	2, Aldridge, Timothy, and Catherine Dewee.
1800, Dec.	24, Ale, George, and Ann Kelly.
1768, Dec.	7, Alenby, James, and Elizabeth Snow.
1764, Dec.	6, Alexander, Charles, and Eleanor Johnson.
1794, Sept.	4, Alexander Eliz., and George Story.
1797, Jan.	5, Alexander, James, and Margaret Green.
1797, April	1, Alexander, Mary, and Abraham Penrose.
1787, July	18, Alexander, Mary, and Joseph Brown.
1804, Feb.	14, Alexander, Richard, and Ann Cunning.
1768, May	15, Alexander, William, and Mary Isemaster.
1802, May	20, Alexander, William, and Eliz. Sharpe.
1774, Oct.	19, Alison, Aaron, and Eliz. Phipps.
1805, June	22, Allbright, Frederick, and Mary Talbert.
1803, Jan.	8, Allchin, George Loder, and Lucy Mary Post.
1715, Nov.	27, Alldridge, Peter, and Elizabeth Appleton.
1768, April	21, Allen, Esqr, Andrew, and Sarah Coxe.
1800, April	26, Allen, Ann, and James Greenleaf.
1766, May	31, Allen, Miss Ann, and Honb^le John Penn.
1800, March 13, Allen, Charles, and Sarah Breidenhart.
1730, April	29, Allen, Dorothy, and John Gibbs.
1728, May	14, Allen, Eleanor, and Wm Verschoyle.
1791, June	30, Allen, Eliz, and John Lawrence.
1735, July	8, Allen, Elizabeth, and John Tilla.
1794, March 25, Allen, Eliza, and Adam Mendenhall.
1784, Nov.	25, Allen, Eliz, and William Needless.
1757, Feb.	25, Allen, Febia, and James Moffat.
1748, Jan.	3, Allen, George, and Mary Harding.
1773, Sept.	28, Allen, George, and Esther Bower.
1772, Oct.	8, Allen, Hannah, and Robert Gill.
1769, Dec.	20, Allen, Isaac, and Sarah Campbell.
1720, April	17, Allen, James, and Christian Castill.
1768, March 10, Allen, Esqr, James, and Elizabeth Lawrence.
1769, May	7, Allen, James, and Eliz Hull.
1765, Jan.	15, Allen, James, and Catherine Christy.
1793, May	30, Allen, Jane, and Charles Thomas.
1744, March 26, Allen, John, and Mary Butcher.
1803, June	13, Allen, John Davis, and Eliz Hobart.
1758, Aug.	9, Allen, Joseph, and Mary Hutton.
1753, Dec.	27, Allen, Joseph, and Jane Casedrop.

1794, Aug. 21, Allen, Joseph, and Jane Hayworth.
1784, July   3, Allen, Joseph, and Mary Singleton.
1793, May   20, Allen, Margaret, and George Hammond.
1794, July   1, Allen, Margaret Eliz, and William Tilghman.
1749, April 22, Allen, Marjory, and Ralph Smith.
1783, May   20, Allen, Mary, and Samuel Davis.
1737, June 25, Allen, Mary, and John Aris.
1784, April 20, Allen, Mary, and Thomas McClintock.
1801, Jan. 29, Allen, Mary, James Elliott.
1771, March 2, Allen, Mary, and Thomas Coates.
1796, Nov. 27, Allen, Mary, and Henry Livingston.
1743, Dec. 26, Allen, Pat, and Margaret Marshel.
1768, April 6, Allen Patience, and Josiah Clark.
1780, May   25, Allen, Rebecca, and Joseph Huddle.
1741, April 18, Allen, Richard, and Rebecca Howard.
1786, Feb. 28, Allen, Samuel, and Mary Brown.
1761, June   6, Allen, Sarah, and Thomas Jones.
1742, June 26. Allen, Sarah, and John Jones.
1743, Jan. 15, Allen, Sarah, and Andrew Bankson.
1804, May   17, Allen, Allen, Sidney, and George Goulding.
1734, Feb. 16, Allen, William, Esq., and Mrs. Margaret Hamilton.
1748, April 23, Allen, William, and Jane Reed.
1795, May   28, Allenby, Mary, and William Thackera.
1749, Jan.   1, Allenby, Mary, and Peter Revel.
1804, Sept. 5, Allison, George, and Louisa Cannon.
1797, Aug. 15, Allison, James, and Margaret Belloes.
1769, Feb. 16, Allman, Lawrence, and Hannah Thomas.
1772, July 29, Alloway, Marsena, and Cath. Davis.
1755, Dec. 24, Amber, Mary, and Peter Hunter.
1743, April   9, Ambler, Nathaniel, and Mary Cook.
1714, Feb.   9, Amilton, Jane, and Jacob Tonge.
1792, Dec. 13, Andeison, Sarah, and John Millar.
1796, July 17, Anderson, Abigail, and Michael Foley.
1741, Nov. 12, Anderson, Andrew, and Catherine Brooks.
1732, May   14, Anderson, Barbara, and Henry Reynolds.
1805, May   25, Anderson, Dezia, and Thomas Dorsey.
1785, Dec. 26, Anderson, Eleanor, and John Tice.
1784, Aug. 12, Anderson, Eleanor, and John Scimer.
1773, April 10, Anderson, Eliz, and John Middleton.
1801, March 20, Anderson, Eliz, and David McElroy.
1745, July 25, Anderson, Hannah, and William Denormandie.
1765, Sept. 24, Anderson, Isaac, and Sarah Pearson.
1751, April 16, Anderson, Isaac, and Edith Shute.
1797, July 11, Anderson, James, and Hannah Spiers.
1784, April   2, Anderson, James, and Eliz Green.

1796, June   12, Anderson, Jane, and William Simes.
1751, Nov.   12, Anderson, Jane, and Robert Stokes.
1761, June   20, Anderson, John, and Elizabeth Miller.
1757, Aug.   26, Anderson, John, and Mary Wilson.
1780, Aug.   22, Anderson, John, and Sarah England.
1795, May   28, Anderson, John William, and Mary Shean.
1749, May   11, Anderson, John, and Martha McFarland.
1794, June   4, Anderson, Joyce, and Henry Miles.
1743, Jan.   26, Anderson, Lawrance, and Abigail Ingram.
1772, June   1, Anderson, Lydia, and James Waters.
1770, Nov.   24, Anderson, Martha, and Joshua William.
1774, Dec.   4, Anderson, Mary, and William Knowles.
1751, Oct.   26, Anderson, Mary, and James Woodside.
1730, April   8, Anderson, Mary, and Philip White.
1803, Jan.   1, Anderson, Mary, and John Ferguson.
1796, May   14, Anderson, Mary, and Daniel Gordon.
1759, May   5, Anderson, Mary E., and John Seabrook.
1780, Dec.   11, Anderson, Mary, and Samuel Freeman.
1712, June   13, Anderson, Mary, and Thomas Dyer.
1755, May   10, Anderson, Mary, John Wilkinson, Jr.
1766, Aug.   21, Anderson, Mary, and Jacob Hill.
1748, Dec.   22, Anderson, Patrick, and Hannah Martin.
1796, May   7, Anderson, Robert, and Christiana Burke.
1799, May   4, Anderson, Robert, and Sarah Strong.
1802, May   5, Anderson, Thomas, and Mary Woodruff.
1752, Nov.   1, Anderson, William, and Mary Boyte.
1756, Dec.   21, Anderson, William, and Anne Custard.
1781, Feb.   20, Andrain, Peter, and Margaret Moore.
1767, Nov.   1, Andrews, Ann, and John Cornelius Hay.
1801, May   13, Andrews, George, and Rebecca Stewart.
1773, Aug.   26, Andrews, Joshua, and Esther Hyndes.
1794, Nov.   27, Andrews, Judith, and Joseph Martin.
1801, Sept.   20, Andrews, Martha, and James Linton.
1721, Aug.   24, Andrews, Mary, and Adam Battin.
1772, Nov.   20, Anes, John, and Rachel Clark.
1743, Nov.   12, Angel, Rebecca, and Pat. Bowrne.
1754, July   27, Angelo, Benjamin, and Deborah Helms.
1730, June   2, Angelo, Sarah, and James Boyer.
1753, July   2, Angues, James, and Mary Beisenor.
1723, April   17, Angwin, Frances, and Thomas Phipps.
1737, July   2, Auley Anne, and Robert Thomas.
1751, Dec.   13, Annis, Anne, Josiah Davenport.
1746, Dec.   5, Annis, John, Mary Hollin.
1758, April   13, Annis, Mary, and Enoch Story.
1740, March   1, Annis, Mary, and Samuel Hall.
1753, Feb.   21, Annis, Sarah, and Joseph Kirll.

1751, Dec.   13, Annis, Susannah, and Robert Lindsey.
1742, Oct.   13, Annis, Thomas, and Eliz Thornhill.
1743, Dec.   12, Annis, William, and Susannah Tuttle.
1797, April   22, Anson, Francis, and Madeline Guidar.
1801, March   1, Ansley, John, and Christiana Smith.
1772, Aug.   19, Anson, John, and Sarah Cassel.
1786, Feb.   2, Antom, Charlotte, and John Borden.
1730, May   21, Antrobus, Elizabeth, William Smith.
1785, Dec.   29, Anthony, Joseph, and Henrietta Hilligas.
1796, Dec.   7, Antrim, Parnel, and Ann Farren.
1713, Oct.   26, Apleton, Mary, and Thomas Chase.
1799, Sept.   24, Apowen, Hannah, and Thomas Fisher.
1750, March 19, Apowen, Samuel, and Hannah Cocks.
1727, Feb.   6, Appleton, John, and Alice Heaton.
1806, June   5, Apple, Mary, and John Coates.
1767, June   8, Apple, Sarah, and Thomas Derrick
1782, Jan.   1, Applegate, John, and Sarah Logan.
1715, Nov.   27, Appleton, Elizabeth, and Peter Alldridge.
1737, Sept.   27, Appleton, James, and Elizabeth Smith.
1730, Dec.   29, Appleton, Margaret, and Hugh Thomson.
1729–30, Feb. 5, Appleton Phœbe, and Obadiah Perrey.
1721, Sept.   10, Appleton, Rebecca, and Caleb Cash.
1735, Dec.   30, Appleton, Susannah, and Samuel Rome.
1775, April   20, Appowen, Hannah, and John Agnus.
1775, Feb.   2, Appowen, John, and Mary Mason.
1774, Oct.   27, Appowen, Mary, and William Jackson.
1795, Dec.   24, Arbuckle, John, and Mary Arthur.
1752, Aug.   15, Archdale, Elizabeth, and Francis Robinson.
1734, Dec.   21, Archer, Jacob, and Jane Boon.
1747, Feb.   15, Archer, John, and Sarah Stagleas.
1755, May   30, Archer, Margaret, and Philip Ford.
1756, Jan.   26, Archer, Mary, and James Barton.
1790, March 30, Archer, Sarah, and Abner Kelly.
1782, Aug.   25, Archibald, Elizabeth, and John Hughes.
1803, April   14, Archibald, Sarah, and Robert Grant.
1737, June   25, Aris, John, and Mary Allen.
1796, July   25, Armbruster, Cath., and Charles Nassau.
1796, Jan.   5, Armington, Sarah, and James Perrock.
1779, July   19, Armitt, Mary, and Capt. Thomas Bell.
1751, Nov.   11, Armstrong, Eleanor, and John Clarke.
1784, Oct.   28, Armstrong, Joseph, and Mary Fish.
1713, August 3, Armstrong, Margaret, and Thomas Huggins.
1799, July   22, Armstrong, Margaret, and Galbraith Russel.
1798, Dec.   26, Armstrong, Mary, and Donald McQueen.
1796, August 1, Armstrong, Thomas, and Eliz Skerret.
1763, June   16, Arnan, Jacob, and Mary Lee.

1779, April   8, Arnold, Major General Benedict, and Margaret Shippen.
1787, April   29, Arnold, Margaret, and John Brian.
1794, Nov.   12, Arnold, Thomas, and Catherine Springer.
1749, July   16, Arrel, Richard, and Christian Davis.
1749, March 26, Arrell. William, and Elizabeth Norwood.
1737, Dec.   20, Arrell, William, and Mary Maston.
1785, June   14, Art, William, and Sarah Garwood.
1792, Feb.   16, Arthur, Jane, and Daniel Swetman.
1792, Sept.   16, Arthur, Margaret, and William Perry.
1795, Dec.   24, Arthur, Mary, and John Arbuckle.
1748, Jan.   5, Arts, John, and Elizabeth Gratehouse.
1758, Dec.   5, Arundel, Eleanor, and John Neal.
1756, April   20, Ash, Catherine, and Thomas Trickett.
1760, Nov.   15, Ash, Hannah, and John Marle.
1749, March 25, Ash, Henry, and Rebecca Leech.
1803, Nov.   26, Ash, Hester, and James Crukshank.
1774, Feb.   22, Ash, James, and Mary Lindsay.
1771, May   18, Ash, James, and Sarah Hinchman.
1805, August 5, Ash, James, and Eliz Collings.
1804, March 15, Ash, James, and Rachel Douglas.
1803, Jan.   30, Ash, Joshua, and Urias Brannum.
1761, May   27, Ash, Lawrence, and Martha Nowland.
1795, Oct.   22, Ash, Lettice, and John Jack.
1773, Oct.   26, Ash, Mary, and James Craig.
1752, Aug.   8, Ash, Rebecca, and John Jones.
1743, June   13, Ashbourn, Agnas, and Peter Blaker.
1753, May   8, Ashbourne, Martin, and Mary Betterton.
1778, Nov.   30, Ashbridge, Aaron, and Ann Howell.
1727, Nov.   23, Ashburn, Martin, and E. Bullin.
1737, Oct.   10, Ashburne, Catherine, and William Phillips.
1786, April   13, Ashburner, John, and Abigail Rudrow.
1731, July   22, Ashby, James, and Mary Weston.
1757, Dec.   14, Ashby, William, and Elizabeth O'Neal.
1727, Nov.   9, Ashcton, Mrs. Marg'., and Matt. Hooper.
1767, March 10, Asheton, Frances, and Stephen Watts.
1764, Sept.   17, Asheton, James, and Ann Delavan.
1729, April   8, Asheton, Jane Eliz, and Archibald Cumings.
1794, April   5, Asheton, Mary, and John Claxson.
1744, May   16, Asheton, Thomas, and Rebecca Cotman.
1767, Nov.   14, Asheton, Thomas, and Hannah Flower.
1758, Nov.   4, Asheton, William, and Catherine Easterly.
1795, Aug.   8, Ashford, Mary, and Jacob Bennet.
1798, March 29, Ashford, William, and Eleanor Still.
1799, Feb.   5, Ashley, Mary Ann, and Simon Walker.
1797, Dec.   16, Ashmead, Amelia, and Samuel Bastleson.

1729, Dec. 28, Ashmead, John, and Mary Meekins.
1758, Feb. 13, Ashmead, Joseph, and Lydia Whitman.
1805, Sept. 10, Ashmead, Mary, and Joseph Clay.
1725, Dec. 5, Ashmore, Ed., and Pris. Jones.
1716, March 1, Ashton, Abigail, and John Wheatly.
1789, May 7, Ashton, Eliz, and James Skerret.
1793, June 27, Ashton, Harriet, and Benjamin Morgan.
1767, April 2, Ashton, Isaac, and Rebecca Powell.
1734, Feb. 7, Ashton, John, and Margaret George.
1775, Jan. 1, Ashton, Joseph, and Laetitia Cooper.
1773, April 28, Ashton, Mary, and Jacob Garrigues.
1720, June 23, Ashton, Mrs. Rachael, and Rev. Samuel Monkton.
1725, Aug. 12, Ashton, Robt., and Jane E. Falconier.
1761, July 29, Ashton, William, and Phoebe Hutchinson.
1757, Aug. 21, Askin, Darcas, and Edward Bedford.
1748, April 16, Aspden, Mary, and Henry Harrison.
1729, April 17, Asseton, Ann, and Wm. Crossvit.
1734, Feb. 25, Asshe, Thomas, and Helen Hust.
1716, Nov. 24, Assheton, Ralph, and Susannah Redman.
1716, Oct. 11, Assheton, William, and Elizabeth Herring.
1734, March 30, Aston, Elijah, and Henrietta Trageny.
1796, Oct. 29, Aston, Eliz, and John Harper.
1781, July 12, Atherly, Eliz, and George Price.
1763, Aug. 31, Atlee, William, and Esther Sayre.
1777, May 26, Atkins, Alice, and Matthew Hooker.
1758, Aug. 3, Atkins, Thomas, and Hannah Butler.
1780, Nov. 7, Atkinson, Ann, and William Davis.
1777, Feb. 16, Atkinson, Catherine, and James Purdie.
1799, July 18, Atkinson, Charles, and Barbara Garret.
1756, Aug. 9, Atkinson, George, and Catherine McGinnis.
1769, Nov. 18, Atkinson, John, and Margaret Whitehead.
1737, Oct. 11, Atkinson, Mary, and William Trimble.
1721, July 26, Atkinson, Mary, and John Paynter.
1790, Oct. 16, Atkinson, Mathia, and Ann Miller.
1728, Sept. 16, Atkinson, Wm, and Mary Hugh.
1774, May 11, Atkinson, William, and Ann Lawrence.
1753, Nov. 4, Atkinson, William, and Mary Syce.
1731, Aug. 1, Atkinson, William, and Mary Crowe.
1762, Feb. 11, Audly, Eleanor, and Paul Hemmings.
1802, Jan. 21, Auner, Cath., and Thomas Hape.
1801, April 16, Austin, Eliz, and Thomas Hewitt.
1800, Dec. 24, Austin, James, and Mary Fitzgerald.
1754, Aug. 31, Austin, John, and Joanna Peace.
1806, Feb. 19, Austin, Julia, and Henry Meigs.
1785, Sept. 28, Austin, Mosses, and Mary Brown.
1749, April 1, Austin, Richard, and Lydia Bell.

1727, April   25, Austen, Rich^d and M. Barnett,
1777, July   7, Austin, Sarah, and Capt. John Barry.
1720, Nov.   17, Austin, William, and Hanna Pomfret.
1748, Oct.   6, Autin, Samuel, and Sarah Stilly.
1757, Sept.   2, Avergast, John, and Rebecca Felty.
1780, Feb.   5, Avery, Nicholas, and Eliz Williams.
1773, Aug.   21, Axford, Eliz, and William Wilkins.
1797, Nov.   23, Axford, Samuel, and Mary Palmer.
1753, April   27, Ayers, Eleanor, and John McCoy.
1768, Feb.   7, Aymes, Elizabeth, and Samuel Williams.
1756, Jan.   2, Ayre, Jane, and Robert Wilson.
1759, Dec.   18, Ayres, Catherine, and James Delaplain.
1762, Feb.   23, Ayres, William, and Elizabeth Rush.
1767, Jan.   10, Ayries, Mary, and David Potts.
1766, June   5, Ayries, Sarah, and Philip Benezet.
1784, Dec.   15, Ayrs, Eliz, and Alexander Chambers.
1772, Dec.   12, Baamer, Jane, and Jesse Swaijne.
1791, Nov.   17, Bache, Benjamin Franklin, and Margaret Markoe,
1800, June   28, Bache, Margaret, and William Duane.
1767, Oct.   29, Bache, Richard, and Sarah Franklin.
1805, April   4, Bache, Richard, and Sophia Dallas.
1797, Nov.   28, Bache, William, and Cath. Wistar.
1793, June   22, Bacon, Eleanor, and Philip Linion.
1797, June   21, Badcock, Sarah, and John W. Johnson.
1768, April   23, Badger, Daniel, and Ann Doughty.
1761, Dec.   20, Badger, Edmund, and Margaret Harding.
1773, May   13, Badger, Sarah, and Rev. Thos Coomb.
1796, Nov.   3, Badollet, Paul, and Mary Visdicker.
1756, July   18, Badwin, Margaret, and Jeffery Pour.
1772, Jan.   16, Baggs, Henry, and Mary Flinn.
1796, June   5, Bagingdollar, Frederick, and Ann Titus.
1794, July   10, Bagnall, Benjamin, and Mary Ann Coffee.
1761, Nov.   19, Bagdall, William, and Elizabeth Sutton.
1756, March   2, Bail, George, and Mary Murdock.
1767, Sept.   13, Bailets, Ruth, and John Venn.
1751, June   25, Bailey, Anne, and Hugh Smith.
1758, Nov.   2, Bailey, James, and Elizabeth Ham.
1763, April   18, Bailey, Rebecca, and James Carroll.
1801, Nov.   21, Bailey, Sarah, and Thomas Smith.
1773, July   28, Bailey, Susannah, and Enock Morgan.
1773, April   16, Bailey, William, and Mary Campbell.
1757, Oct.   18, Baily, Arnold, and Mary Cunningham.
1721, Aug.   31, Baily, Frances, and John Kendrick.
1737, Aug.   18, Baily, Hugh, and Grissel Cunningham.
1715, Sept.   26, Baily, Mary, and Richard Cooke.
1731, June   8, Baine, Mordecai, and Mary Teague.

1761, Nov. 22, Baird, Joseph, and Sarah Smith.
1745, May   2, Baird, Thomas, and Anne Cormont.
1797, June 20, Baird, William, and Sarah Reside.
1740, Dec. 23, Bairnhill, Jane, and Thomas Aiken.
1794, Jan.   9, Bakeman, Frances, and John B. Ware.
1710, Jan. 28, Baker, Adam, and Margaret Protheroh.
1785, Dec.   8, Baker, Charlotto Grage, and Robert Jones.
1776, July 17, Baker, Civel, and Thomas Cumpston.
1727, June   5, Raker, E., and Owen Richards.
1735, June 14, Baker, Hannah, and Septimus Robeson.
1769, Nov. 25, Baker, Isaac, and Hannah Pacalock.
1762, Jan. 13, Baker, Jacob, and Mary Miller.
1758, Aug.   9, Baker, Jeremiah, and Ruth Bonham.
1720, Nov. 13, Baker, John, and Ann Mitchell.
1736, June   6, Baker, John, and Catherine Carroll.
1798, April 5, Baker, John Martin, and Harriet Weisenfels.
1737, May   23, Baker, John, and Rebecca Delabar.
1801, Oct.   4, Baker, John, and Sarah Worrall.
1728, March 4, Baker, J., and Rachel Hunter.
1770, Sept. 27, Baker, Lydia, and John Richardson.
1752, Nov.   4, Baker, Mary, and Andrew McCoy.
1785, Oct. 27, Baker, Mary, and Arthur Forsbes.
1801, Oct. 15, Baker, Mary, and John Richards.
1805, April 27, Baker, Nathan, and Helen Claypole.
1733, March 31, Baker, Rachel, and Benjamin Hampton.
1787, April 10, Baker, Richard, and Mary Hannis.
1790, Oct.   6, Baker, Rosanna, & John Bean.
1720, May   29, Baker, Samuel, and Ann Hunter.
1769, July   3, Baker, Samuel, and Susannah Wallace.
1722, June   2, Baker, Sarah, and John Carter.
1794, June   5, Baker, Sarah, and Joseph Landcake.
1802, Oct. 21, Baker, Sarah, and Samuel Ross.
1797, Sept. 5, Baker, Susannah, and John Peter Morel.
1794, May   13, Baker, Thomas, and Hannah Wallace.
1805, Jan.   8, Baker, William J., and Margaret Wager.
1793, March 31, Baker, William, and Sarah Perry.
1726, Nov. 11, Bakerin, M. Cath., and J. Stump.
1784, May   21, Balabriga, Jacob, and Marry Nefford.
1797, April 20, Balan, Andrew, and Eliz Todd.
1800, June   5, Baldesqui, Julianna, and Charles Harris.
1716, Sept. 5, Baldwin, Elizabeth, and Joseph Boud.
1768, March 5, Baldwin, Hannah, and John Marshall.
1775, Nov. 27, Baldwin, Jacob, and Jane Downing.
1773, April 10, Baldwin, Jacob, and Rachel Clifton.
1737, Nov.   4, Baldwin, Joseph, and Rachel Wathell.
1774, April 25, Baldwin, Lawrence, and Mary Harris.

1779, Dec.   25, Baldwin, Mark, and Anne Butcher.
1750, Feb.   1, Baley, John, and Jane Watkins.
1792, April   26, Balfour, George, and Eliz Oswald.
1769, Dec.   28, Balinger, Samuel, and Mary Stiles.
1769, Dec.   26, Ballard, Mary, and Francis Woodward.
1742, July   31, Ballard, William, and Mary Cowan.
1721, Nov.   4, Ballinger, Hester, and John Bartlet.
1757, Oct.   15, Ball, Anna, and John Gibson.
1776, Oct.   10, Ball, Esther, and Samuel Williams.
1731, July   4, Ball, Jane, and Richard Horn.
1733, Oct.   9, Ball, Martin, and Rebecca Wilkinson.
1764, Aug.   22, Ball, Mary, and Andrew May.
1741, Oct.   7, Ball, Rebecca, and Robert Greenaway.
1775, July   20, Ball, Sarah, and John Daniels.
1720, June   5, Balmer, James, and Catherine Pearce.
1751, Oct.   15, Bambridge, Mary, and Thomas Gordon.
1801, Feb.   26, Bandore, Ann, and Valentine Brobst.
1751, May   27, Bane, Mary, and George Charir.
1735, Dec.   27, Bane Nathan, and Mary Cox.
1750, May   26, Banfield, Thomas, and Ruth Maudlin.
1773, Aug.   1, Banks, Joseph, and Catherine Sussex.
1755, Nov.   12, Banks, Richard, and Mary Lindsey.
1759, May   26, Banks, Samuel, and Susannah White.
1763, May   4, Banks, Sarah, and Nathan Dykes.
1767, Nov.   8, Banks, Thomas, and France; Lovekin.
1782, Jan.   3, Banks, William, and Sarah Ghireline.
1771, Oct.   30, Bankson, Jun., Andrew, and Mary Tallman.
1743, Jan.   15, Bankson, Andrew, and Sarah Allen.
1743, May   7, Bankson, Deborah, and John Palmer.
1777, April   16, Bankson, Eleanor, and John Righter.
1760, Nov.   19, Bankson, Eleanor, and Nathaniel Pettit.
1779, Aug.   8, Bankson, Eliz, and Davison Durham.
1767, Dec.   29, Bankson, Hester, and James Channel.
1741, Dec.   5, Bankson, John, and Mary Cowely.
1770, Sept.   13, Bankson, Margaret, and Augustine Talman.
1765, Aug.   17, Bankson, Mary, and Jacob Hanse.
1746, Nov.   24, Bankson, Mary, and John Boid.
1731, May   30, Bankson, Mary, and Swan Bankson.
1743, Oct.   11, Bankson, Peter, and Esther Linn.
1790, July   22, Bankson, Sarah, and Joseph Huddle.
1731, May   30, Bankson, Swan, and Mary Bankson.
1783, Oct.   31, Bannton, Ann, and James Abercrombie.
1805, Sept.   3, Bantom, Moses, and Sarah Woodby.
1747, Dec.   17, Banton, John, and Elizabeth Chevalier.
1714, Aug.   27, Bantost, Thomas, and Elizabeth Everet.
1768, Sept.   22, Barber, Ann, and David Ware.

1764, Oct.   15, Barber, Hannah, and John Huff.
1739, Sept. 12, Barber, Jonathan, and Sarah Dodd.
1753, Sept. 27, Barbold, Anna Maria, and John Wright.
1759, Feb.   8, Barclay, Alexander, and Rebecca Robinson.
1786, Sept. 28, Barclay, George, and Mary Garrette.
1761, Dec.   31, Barclay, Gilbert, and Ann Inglis.
1781, Dec.   11, Barclay, John, and Mary Searle.
1805, Nov.   11, Barclay, Sarah Miles, and William Magee.
1757, Feb.   20, Barefield, John, and Anna Maria Burrow.
1776, Nov.   12, Barge, Eliz, and Philip Marchinton.
1723, Feb.   25, Barger, Elizabeth, and John Beeks.
1723, Nov.   26, Barger, Hannah, and Henry Beeks.
1798, Aug.   23, Baring, Alexander, and Ann Bingham.
1745, Jan.   21, Barker, Ben., and Cath. Trussel.
1748, April 25, Barker, Elinor, and James Pemberton.
1802, Dec.   2, Barker, Hannah, and John Bioren.
1757, Nov.   5, Barker, James, and Dorothy Camby.
1770, July   9, Barker, James, and Mary Wier.
1782, March 31, Barker, Mary, and George Suggs.
1776, Jan.   14, Barker, Mary, and John Miller, Junr.
1772, March 11, Barker, William, and Eleanor Wallace.
1757, Feb.   3, Barlo, James, and Sarah Elexander.
1760, Dec.   2, Barlow, Samuel, and Jane Fallas.
1803, Dec.   29, Barnaby, Joseph, and Eliz Hamilton.
1761, April 22, Barnard, Sarah, and David Bilderback.
1781, March 29, Barndollar, Eliz, and William Brewster.
1805, May   19, Barnes, Ann, and Andrews Williams.
1802, Nov.   11, Barnes, Isaac, and Rachel Abel.
1769, June   24, Barnes, James, and Elizabeth Kennedy.
1804, May   3, Barnes, John, and Eliz Williamson.
1755, Dec.   5, Barnes, John, and Hannah Phips.
1768, June   17, Barnes, Lambert, and Eliz Hay.
1772, Nov.   5, Barnes, Mary, and Benjamin Loxley.
1776, April 18, Barnes, Mary, and John Packard.
1736, Nov.   5, Barnes, Rachel, and Thomas Hutton.
1753, Nov.   2, Barnes, William, and Elizabeth Davis.
1790, June   13, Barnes, William, and Mary Somers.
1771, May   9, Barnet, Hugh, and Margaret Curden.
1736, Dec.   25, Barnett, Josiah, and Esther Mathers.
1727, April 25, Barnett, M., and Rich^d. Austin.
1748, July   8, Barnett, Sarah, and Samuel Crispin.
1771, Oct.   24, Barnet, William, and Eliz Stow.
1745, Aug.   27, Barney, Volentine, and Margaret McMahon.
1768, Sept. 29, Barnitt, John, and Margaret Shepherd.
1711, Dec.   17, Barnott, John, and Ann Wainwright.
1734, Oct.   22, Barnwell, Anne, Robert Mortimore.

1750, March 10, Barr, Zechariah, Martha Cameron.
1772, May   23, Barrell, Francis, and Eliz Harrison.
1780, Nov.   30, Barrett, Francis, and Cath. Jones.
1759, Jan.   8, Barret, John, and Martha Toms.
1768, April 25, Barret, Mary, and John Winter.
1742, May   28, Barrett, Charles, and Hester Harison.
1806, May   21, Barrett, Tobias, and Silvia Dewees.
1784, Aug.   21, Barrett, William, and Alletto Groebe.
1804, June   14, Barrington, Richard, and Ellen Conner.
1797, Aug.   29, Barry, Ann, and Patrick Caldwell.
1777, July   7, Barry, Capt. John, and Sarah Austin.
1765, Jan.   1, Barry, Elizabeth, and William Wild.
1790, March 23, Barry, James, and Eliz McGee.
1796, June   5, Barry, Mary Ann, and George Dean.
1786, July   13, Barry, Mathias, and Susannah Hausld.
1798, June   24, Barry, William, and Cath. Mahon.
1782, Aug.   22, Barry, William, and Sarah Knight.
1743, March 31, Barstler, Cath., and Conrad Price.
1772, May   19, Barthkitt, William, and Cath. Delany.
1744, May   3, Bartholomew, Andrew, and Eliz Beers.
1758, Oct.   4, Bartholomew, Augustine, and Mary Russell.
1771, Oct.   10, Bartholomew, Catherine, and Benjamin Griffith.
1792, March 29, Bartholomew, Eleanor, and Henry Capper.
1738, May   30, Bartholomew, Elizabeth, and Isaac Davies.
1783, Dec.   11, Bartholomew, John, and Mary Milne.
1773, June   19, Bartholomew, Mary, and John Burgum.
1800, Nov.   13, Bartholomew, Sarah, and George Lewis.
1772, June   27, Barthot, Hannah, and Nathaniel Ricketts.
1797, March   2, Bartleson, Mary, and Jacob Seddons.
1797, Dec.   16, Bartleson, Samuel, and Amelia Ashmead.
1770, May   3, Bartlet, Christlet, and Eliz Honogrot.
1721, Nov.   4, Bartlet, John, and Hester Ballingee.
1759, Jan.   2, Bartlet, John, and Sarah Coburn.
1795, Nov.   19, Bartlett, Zaphaniah, and Mary Powers.
1767, Dec.   26, Barton, Elias, and Ann Blair.
1756, Jan.   26, Barton, James, and Mary Archer.
1799, March 18, Barton, Mary, and John Harvey.
1738, Oct.   27, Barton, Robert, and Anne Godfrey.
1768, June   23, Barton, Thomas, and Sarah Benezet.
1750, Nov.   12, Barton, Thomas, and Susannah Cook.
1729, May   17, Barton, Stephen, and Ann Brant.
1784, Nov.   1, Bartow, Cath., and Robert Bazier.
1801, Aug.   1, Bartram, Ann, and Jacob Cart.
1734, April   6, Bartram, Elizabeth, and James Gailbraith.
1767, Dec.   1, Bartram, William, and Mary Fisher.
1784, Dec.   13, Basse, Ambrose, and Sarah Quigg.

1802, Nov.   25, Bass, Anna Maria, and Alexandei J. Miller.
1799, June   8, Bass, Eliz, and Christian Erickson.
1798, July   10, Bass, Eliz, and Samuel Price.
1759, March   9, Bass, Robert, and Cecilia Griffin.
1797, Feb.   15, Bassett, Edward, and Ann Bingham.
1738, May   19, Bassett, Eve, and Joseph Ellis.
1804, June   13, Bassett, Richard, and Clara Hall.
1723, Feb.   20, Bisset, John, and Eve Casselburg.
1752, March   29, Basstick, John, and Elizabeth Fearn.
1764, July   21, Bate, William, and Phoebe Hohne.
1799, March   17, Bates, Ann, and Samuel Crawford.
1727, April   1, Bates, Ann, and T. Griffiths.
1782, June   30, Bates, Benoni, and Mary Fees.
1781, Feb.   3, Bates, Jacob, and Hannah Hopkins.
1785, July   7, Bates, Joseph, and Mary Davis.
1804, Feb.   8, Bates, Margaret, and Samuel Stewart.
1753, Sept.   3. Bates, Mary, and William Harry.
1723, June   20, Bateson, Robert, and Sarah Sympson.
1768, May   19, Batson, Thomas, and Catherine Jones.
1752, May   4, Batson, Thomas, and Elizabeth Boardman.
1750, Nov.   8, Battar, Ineas, and Anne Mason.
1726, Nov.   22, Batt, T., and Rachel Mirick.
1721, Aug.   24, Battin, Adam, and Mary Andrews.
1748, Oct.   29, Battin, Dorothy, and Benjamin Peters.
1768, Aug.   27, Battin, Enoch, and Rebeccah Jones.
1795, Oct.   9, Battin, John, and Eliza Campbell.
1765, June   22, Battle, Susannah, and Phineas Massey.
1728, Oct.   6. Battman, John, and Ann Davies.
1774, May   9, Bavington, Augustina, and Joseph Thomas.
1788, Dec.   23, Baxter, Joseph, and Mary Wharton.
1762, April   8, Baxter, Nancy, and Richard James.
1796, Dec.   8, Bayard, Ami, and Francis Perkins.
1748, April   5, Bay, Rebeccak, and John Windel.
1743, Jan.   11, Bay, Thomas, and Rebecca Robinson.
1736, May   17, Bayle, William, and Mary Davies.
1784, Sept.   9, Bayley, John, and Jane Faithfull.
1736, Oct.   23, Bayley, Joseph, and Mary Richie.
1796, Aug.   25, Bayley, Richard, and Harriet Whitesides.
1786, May   18, Baylor, William, and Cath. Thomas.
1769, Feb.   28, Bayman, Mary, and Anthony Hart.
1773, Dec.   16, Baynton, Eliz, and Abraham Markoe.
1799, Dec.   11, Baynton, Henry, and Susannah Richards.
1780, Nov.   16, Baynton, Peter, and Eliz Bullock.
1759, Dec.   27, Bayte, Hannah, and Charles Swain Drage.
1784, Nov.   1, Bazier, Robert, and Cath. Bartow.
1780, Nov.   2, Beach, Edmund, and Eliz West.

1735, Aug.   23, Beadles, Elisha, and Mary Edwards.
1776, Oct.   18, Beak, Mary, and Lawrence McGennis.
1772, Jan.   31, Beaks, Jane, and Joseph Smith.
1733, April   12, Beale, Rebecca, and Samuel Richie.
1743, July   27, Beaman, William, and Anne Jeans.
1791, March   14, Beamerin, Margaret, and George Linch.
1790, Oct.   6, Bean, John, and Rosanna Baker.
1736, May   13, Beane, Margaret, and Daniel Lavering.
1742, Oct.   22, Beans, James, and Eliz Sands.
1746, Dec.   22, Beany, Nathaniel, and Mary Maxwell.
1740, Dec.   13, Beard, George, and Anne Ellicot.
1756, Nov.   15, Bear, John, and Margaret Reynolds.
1709, July   31, Bears, Mary, and George Page.
1742, Jan.   26, Beasley, William, and Sophia Sharaden.
1758, June   8, Beatsy, Phoebe, and Leonard Philips.
1797, Aug.   26, Beaven, Ann, and Jacob Thomson.
1783, Sept.   3, Beaven, Eliz, and Felix Brisnott.
1801, May   14, Beaven, Mary, and Crook Stevenson.
1771, July   11, Beaven, William, and Mary Greenway.
1786, Feb.   2, Beckett, Thomas Claude, and Sarah Clary.
1799, Nov.   28, Beck, Paul, and Mary Harvey.
1806, May   15, Beck, Susan, and Daniel Lammot.
1776, Feb.   15, Beck, Thomas, and Amelia Vandegrist.
1742, Jan.   30, Beddorne, Joseph, and Ann Jones.
1748, Oct.   16, Beddowe, Joseph, and Elizabeth Sallows.
1743, April   4, Bedford, Ann, and James Coburn.
1757, Aug.   21, Bedford, Edward, and Darcas Askin.
1738, Feb.   12, Bedford, John, and Elanor Smout.
1760, Dec.   24, Bee, Elizabeth, and Andrew Long.
1780, Feb.   26, Beekman, Cath., and Isaac Cox.
1770, Dec.   9, Beekman, John, and Eliz Renaudet.
1723, Nov.   26, Beeks, Henry, and Hannah Barger.
1723, Feb.   25, Beeks, John, and Elizabeth Barger.
1782, Nov.   28, Beere, John, and Mary Jenkins.
1797, Nov.   9, Beering, Charles, and Susan Haywood.
1731-2, Feb. 12, Beer, John, and Ann Edwards.
1744, May   3, Beers, Eliz, and Andrew Bartholomew.
1750, Oct.   15, Beers, Mary, and Gabriel Traut.
1720, Oct.   25, Beeth, Hannah, and William Preston.
1761, March   19, Beezly, John, and Ann Scoghan.
1765, Oct.   31, Beezley, Stephen, and ——— Harrison.
1785, Dec.   1, Begary, Emanuel, and Cath., Slein.
1801, July   28, Bell, Agnes, and John Fisher.
1737, Sept.   27, Bell, Alexander, and Elizabeth Jones.
1805, June   13, Bell, Ann, and Jesse Vogdes.
1774, Jan.   1, Bell, Edward, and Ann Phildy.
        2—Vol. VIII.

1784, April   6, Bell, Eliz, and Edward Roberts.
1751, Nov.   5, Bell, Elizabeth, and George Nicholson.
1741, June   6, Bell, Hannah, and Charles Hartley.
1791, Feb.   15, Bell, Jane, and William O'Brien.
1737, Nov.   21, Bell, Lettice, and Thomas Charlton.
1749, April   1, Bell, Lydia, and Richard Austin.
1753, Jan.   18, Bell, Mary, and Fedidiah Snowden.
1793, Aug.   24, Bell, Peter, and Jane Gray.
1800, Feb.   8, Bell, Peter, and Mary McCarty.
1765, April   11, Bell, Peter, and Mary Williamson.
1795, Jan.   8, Bell, Samuel, and Ann McDaniel.
1779, July   19, Bell, Capt. Thomas, and Mary Armitt.
1791, Aug.   11, Bell, William, and Sarah Ross.
1772, Nov.   4, Belengar, Hannah, and Thomas Naglee.
1771, Jan.   24, Bellamy, William, and Ann Whitebread.
1784, March   22, Bellerose, Louis, and Mary Howell.
1766, May   27, Bellinger, Sarah, and David Logan.
1797, Aug.   15, Belloes, Margaret, and James Allison.
1722, Dec.   9, Bellos, Rebecca, and James Willard.
1795, Dec.   13, Beloe, Peter, and Deborah S. McColloch.
1800, Dec.   18, Belton, Sarah, and Joseph Ford.
1728, Sept.   7, Bemy, Eliz, and William Donilson.
1743, Jan.   21, Benbridge, Isabella, and John McNamar.
1741, June   7, Benbridge, James, and Mary Clark.
1798, April   15, Benezet, Anthony, and Mary Engle.
1745, April   24, Benezet, Dan, and Eliz North.
1747, June   5, Benezet, James, and Anne Hassel.
1775, Oct.   26, Benezet, John, and Hannah Bingham.
1795, Oct.   7, Benezet, Maria, and George Willing.
1766, June   5, Benezet, Philip, and Sarah Ayries.
1768. June   23, Benezet, Sarah, and Thomas Barton.
1783, Nov.   26, Benezett, Hannah, and Rev. Robert Blackwell.
1737, Aug.   13, Benham, William, and Mary Mallard.
1771, Sept.   5, Benjar, Catherine, and James Wiley.
1749, Jan.   9, Bennet, Anne, and John Ford.
1803, May   18, Bennet, Ann, and Raymond Kimbeel.
1767, March   3, Bennet, Catherine, and James Bencle Walker.
1794, Dec.   16, Bennet, Daniel, and Eliz Bruistar.
1751, Nov.   21, Bennet, Daniel, and Mary Felton.
1752. July   27, Bennet, Eleanor, and Isaac Bennet.
1760, Feb.   29, Bennet, Elizabeth, and George Killinger.
1720, Dec.   11, Bennet, Hannah, and John Rugh.
1752, July   27, Bennet, Isaac, and Eleanor Bennet.
1795, August 8, Bennet, Jacob, and Mary Ashford.
1755, Dec.   25, Bennet, John, and Elizabeth Narval.
1729, Dec.   15, Bennet, John, and Mary Smith.

1803, May 22, Bennet, John, and Ruth Cook.
1794, Dec. 11, Bennet, John, and Sarah Robinson.
1753, Nov. 27, Bennet, Margaret, and James Abercrombie.
1760, Oct. 25, Bennet, Martha, and John Hynes.
1752, April 2, Bennet, Mary, and Stephen Gordon.
1773, Sept. 18, Bennet, Thomas, and Cath. Wiley.
1801, Jan. 29, Bennet, William, and Ann Thomson.
1743, Oct. 9, Bennet, William, and Sarah Johnson.
1786, May 29, Bennett, James, and Mary Berry.
1731, April 23, Bennett, John, and Mary Parker.
1786, May 5, Bennett, Stephen, and Sarah Leech.
1770, Oct. 25, Benning, Eliz, and Jonathan Brown.
1753, Nov. 1, Benning, William, and Elizabeth Hagley.
1795, Oct. 20, Bensal, George, and Mary Robeson.
1784, Dec. 3, Bensell, Eleanor, and Jacob Bowers.
1791, Oct. 22, Bensell, George, and Hannah Coomby.
1746, June 14, Benson, Mary, and James Smith.
1804, Nov. 27, Bentley, Michael, and Sarah Lemley.
1791, June 20, Beorne, Mary, and John Burge.
1774, Aug. 28, Bergenhoff, Cath., and John Hughes.
1799, July 10, Berg Hans, and Cath. McMahan.
1716, Jan. 1, Berius, William, and Ann Lovegrove.
1750, Jan. 29, Berkley, Alexander, and Anne Hickman.
1760, Feb. 13, Berkley, Eleanor, and John Chevalier.
1737, Feb. 17, Berkley, Thomas, and Jane Palmer.
1805, May 25, Berkman, John, and Mary Ann Lissran.
1765, April 10, Bern, John, and Mary Brooks.
1800, June 24, Berner, Frederick, and Susannah Thompson.
1775, June 26, Berney, Mary, and Richard Heide.
1765, Oct. 29, Bernhold, Henry, and Anna Nelson.
1795, Oct. 4, Bernondy, Francis, and Molly Clarke.
1726, Dec. 1, Berrie, B., and S. Paxton.
1780, Nov. 9, Berrien, John, and Margaret McPherson.
1781, Sept. 29, Berriman, Ann, and Benjamin Cowen.
1773, Aug. 12, Berry, Eliz, and Benjamin Scull.
1785, March 29, Berry, Garrett, and Anne Carneg.
1793, Jan. 24, Berry, Margaret, and William Crooks.
1783, June 1, Berry, Martin, and Sophia Edwards.
1786, May 29, Berry, Mary, and James Bennett.
1743, Jan. 2, Berry, Peter, and Mary Reirdan.
1750, June 15, Bertholt, Melchoir, and Mary Slaughter.
1731, Sept. 19, Berwick, John, and Elizabeth Smart.
1730, April 7, Berwick, Richard, and Margaret Cunningham.
1794, Nov. 13, Beson, Lewis, and Rebecca Friend.
1769, April 24, Besor, John, and Mary Smith.
1800, Dec. 11, Bess, Eleanor, and Henry Brethoff.

1797, April   8, Bess, John, and Eleanor Sims.
1773, Aug.   9, Best, Margaret, and John Budgin.
1796, Jan.   28, Best, Mary, and Hugh McCarty.
1767, Nov.   30, Beth, Joseph, and Margaret Crawford.
1776, Aug.   5, Bethel, Eliz, and George Ogelsby.
1730, April   2, Bethell, Francis, and Joseph Scull.
1852. Dec.   29, Betson, William, and Elizabeth Davis.
1759, Sept.   6, Betterton, Benjamin, and Rebecca Harvey.
1779, Feb.   20, Betterton, Eliz, and Joshua Collins.
1787, Feb.   8, Betterton, Hannah, and James Rees.
1771, March 28, Betterton, Martha, and Joshua Collins.
1753, May   8, Betterton, Mary, and Martin Ashbourne.
1785, Jan.   13, Betterton, Rebecca, and Joseph Howell.
1800, April   12, Betterton, Rebecca, and Thomas Webb.
1789, May   3, Betterton, Rebecca, and William Greenaway.
1721, July   30, Bettson, Elizabeth, and William Dobbs.
1747, March   9, Betty, Anne, and Joseph Brown.
1730, April   30, Bevan Anne, and Abraham Free.
1734, Nov.   9, Bevan, Anne, and John Lee.
1780, Aug.   26, Bevan, Ann, and Capt. Matthew Lollar.
1768, Jan.   9, Bevan, Mary, and William Forbes.
1726, Oct.   13, Bevan, M., and Griffith Jones.
1766, Nov.   5, Bevan, William, and Margaret Fisher.
1768, May   24, Beverly, Thomas, and Rosanna Smith.
1739, March 29, Bewley, John, and Anne Kimble.
1762, Sept.   14, Beyer, Elizabeth, and Jacob Ommensetter.
1761, March 31, Beyson, James, and Margaret Manson.
1753, Nov.   24, Bezey, *alias* Beaseley, Hannah, and James Cobourn, *alias* Cockburn.
1737, July   24, Bibb, Mary, and Walter Lewis.
1735, June   9, Bibb, Ruth, and B. njamin Flower.
1799, June   8, Bicker, Eliz, and Thomas Hoggard.
1791, Jan.   1, Bicker, Henry, and Eliz McMurray.
1804, Nov.   4, Bickerton, Ann, and John Smith.
1746, Dec.   31, Bickerton, George, and Leah Cannizes.
1783, June   19, Bickerton, Leah, and Edward Mullock.
1798, July   5, Bickham, Ann, and Joseph H. Dill.
1801, April   9, Bickham, Ann, and Lewis Neill.
1776, Jan.   25, Bickham, Caleb, and Mary Hunn.
1797, Dec.   19, Bickham, Christiana, and Washington Lee Finney.
1758, Sept.   28, Bickley, Abraham, and Mary Sewell.
1729-30, Jan. 8, Bickley, Mary, and John Tongue.
1771, June   9, Biddis, Cath., and Frederick Starn.
1743, Nov.   17, Biddison, Robt., and Catherine Murphey.
1765, April   27, Biddle, Abigail, and Nicholas Burhow.
1778, Nov.   12, Biddle, Ann, and Genl. James Wilkinson.

1700, May   21, Biddle, Cath., and George Lux, Esqr.
1753, June   30, Biddle, James, and Frances Marks.
1782, Jan.   9, Biddle, John, and Mary Moore.
1779, Feb.   18, Biddle, Lydia, and Dr. James Hutchinson.
1752, Dec.   3, Biddle, Lydia, and William McFun.
1804, June   25, Biddle, Mary, and Thomas Cadwalader.
1750, March   3, Biddle, Michael, and Rachel Scull.
1766, March   15, Biddle, Sarah, and James Penrose.
1760, April   17, Biddle, Thomas, and Abigail Scull.
1730, April   2, Biddle, William, and Mary Scull.
1757, Dec.   22, Bier, William, and Sarah Dilworth.
1747, June   9, Bigger, Richard, and Susannah Osborn.
1771, Sept.   4, Biggs, Peter, and Sarah Holland.
1792, Oct.   25, Bilderbach, Cath., and Samuel Mecum.
1761, April   22, Bilderbach, David, and Sarah Barnard.
1798, Dec.   6, Bilse, Cath., and Thomas Priest.
1753, July   2, Bilsenor, Mary, and James Angues.
1759, Jan.   8, Bilsonsleane, Catherine, and William Finly.
1743, Feb.   22, Bimb, Mary, and George Listrin.
1734, June   5, Bimrose, Anne, and Abraham Dight.
1798, Aug.   23, Bingham, Ann, and Alexander Baring.
1797, Feb.   15, Bingham, Ann, and Edward Bassett.
1713, Oct.   1, Bingham, Ann, and John Heap.
1775, Oct.   26, Bingham, Hannah, and John Benezet.
1728, June   9, Bingham, Hannah, and John Dexter.
1743, July   23, Bingham, Mary, and Joseph Lokey.
1794, July   28, Bingham, Peter, and Cath. Leonard.
1780, Oct.   26, Brigham, William, and Ann Willing.
1745, Sept.   19, Bingham, William, and Mary Stamper.
1804, April   3, Binney, Horace, and Eliz Cox.
1805, April   2, Binney, Susan, and John B. Wallace.
1772, Sept.   23, Binks, Christopher, and Mary Siddon.
1755, July   21, Binns, John, and Elizabeth Everside.
1806, Sept.   6, Bioren, Mary, and Benjamin Tanner.
1802, Dec.   2, Bioren, John, and Hannah Barker.
1786, May   20, Birck, Mary, and Amariah Peree.
1802, June   1, Birch, Thomas, and Ann Goodwin.
1756, Feb.   15, Bird, Benjamin, and Sarah Peerson.
1720, April   21, Bird, Elizabeth, and Thomas Cole.
1721, July   9, Bird, George, and Mary Green.
1791, April   26, Bird, Jacob, and Cath. Thomas.
1763, Jan.   6, Bird, Mark, and Mary Ross.
1736, March   15, Bird, Mary, and Arthur Burrows.
1763, Jan.   3, Bird, Rebecca, and Peter Turner.
1721, Nov.   5, Bird, Sarah, and William Leder.
1758, July   28, Birret, Grace, and James Harrey.

1739, April   24, Bishop, Samuel, and Hester Trantar.
1767, Sept.   14, Bishop, Sarah, and Joseph Griffith.
1773, Feb.   17, Bissell, John, and Laetitia Philips.
1778, Dec.   10, Bissett, Beulah, and John Brown.
1801, April   19, Bissett, Thomas, and Mary Maxfield.
1801, Jan.   24, Bittle, Martha, and John Lawrence.
1767, Aug.   15, Bizzey, Elizabeth, and Richard Campian.
1797, July   27, Blaadyhough, John, and Ann Mulhollen.
1761, Aug.   15, Black, Abraham, and Catherine Smith.
1788, Oct.   26, Black, Anna, and Joseph Simpson.
1780, Dec.   10, Black, Arthur, and Hannah McGlue.
1762, Nov.   6, Black, James, and Rachel Adams.
1804, Nov.   15, Black, James R., and Maria Eliza Stokes.
1806, Feb.   15, Black, James R., and Maria Eliza Stokes.
1804, June   30, Black, John, and Dorcas Shyne.
1802, Dec.   12, Black, John, and Margaret Phile.
1804, May   10, Black, Joseph, and Eliz Lungren.
1761, Oct.   3, Black, Mary, and Michael Gitts.
1805, Jan.   1, Black, Phillis, and Joseph Haslett.
1796, Aug.   25, Black, Rachel, and Abner Brown.
1755, July   12, Black, Robert, and Anne McCall.
1759, Dec.   18, Black, Robert. and Sarah Cook.
1749, Jan.   9, Black, Sarah, and Garret Bourn.
1751, Nov.   7, Blackfan, Sarah, and Richard Wood.
1757, Jan.   6, Blackford, John, and Anne Hunter.
1737, Jan.   10, Blackham, Mary, and Robert Tuckness.
1757, June   30, Blackledge, Elizabeth, and Thomas Lawrence.
1726, Dec.   26, Blacklidge, Ben., and S. Phillpott.
1782, June   19, Blacklock, Robert, and Elizabeth Howard.
1765, Sept.   12, Blackstone, Presley, and Sarah Warnick.
1800, Nov.   26, Blackwell, Rebecca, and George Willing.
1783, Nov.   26, Blackwell, Rev' Robert, and Hannah Benezett.
1780, Jan.   17, Blackwell, Rev' Rob', and Rebecca Harrison.
1805, Nov.   17, Blackwell, Sarah, and Asaph Stowell.
1792, Dec.   27, Blackwood, Mary, and Samuel Harrison.
1744, May   6, Blainey, Samuel, and Mary Moniss.
1787, Nov.   1, Blair, Alexander, and Priscilla Scull.
1767, Dec.   26, Blair, Ann, and Elias Barton.
1743, Oct.   22, Blair, Ann, and James Tipper.
1750, April   5, Blake, Arthur, and Hannah Hartley.
1750, April   11, Blake, Hannah, and John Dougharty.
1783, Dec.   27, Blake, Sarah, and John Sherry.
1746, Aug.   23, Blake, Sarah, and Joseph Hophar.
1799, Dec.   8, Blake, Thankful, and William Hunt.
1749, Oct.   17, Blake, Thomas, and Elizabeth Jones.
1783, August 6, Blake, William, and Eliz George.

1766, June   1, Blakeley, Lewis, and Jane McCluer.
1753, August 8, Blaker, Judith, and Joseph Ellicut.
1743, June   13, Blaker, Peter, and Agnas Ashbourn.
1733, March 17, Blakey, Susannah, and John Stevenson.
1797, April   27, Blakiston, Martha, and Kenneth Jewell.
1752, June   22, Bland, Elias, and Hannah Stamper.
1717, Jan.   5, Blaxton, Thomas, and Ann Ware.
1712, Nov.   6, Bleak, John, and Margaret Smith.
1737, Nov.   26, Bliss, George, and Anne Harrison.
1798, Feb.   6, Blodget, Maria, and James West.
1792, May   10, Blodget, Samuel, and Rebecca Smith.
1728, Sept.   2, Blood, Peter Young, and Sarah Hand.
1792, April   26, Bloomfield, Sarah, and Omar Boden.
1787, June   9, Blunk, Sarah, and Thomas Broadwax.
1776, Oct.   8, Boardley, John Beale, and Sarah Mifflin.
1752, May   4, Boardman, Elizabeth, and Thomas Batson.
1729, April   16, Boar, Sus'h, and Geo. Foster.
1772, Oct.   5, Boatman, Eliz, and John Small.
1786, June   3, Bochine, John Henry Christian, and Mary Corin.
1796, Jan.   30, Bockins, Eliz, and David Rindt.
1792, April   26, Boden, Omar, and Sarah Bloomfield.
1755, April   2, Boggs, Anna Bella, and John Huddle.
1800, Oct.   18, Boggs, Archibald Hunter, and Eliz Dietz.
1746, July   5, Boggs, James, and Catherine Knoble.
1761, Dec.   2, Boggs, Margaret, and William Watson.
1741, Oct.   28, Boggs, Mary, and Daniel White.
1761, Jan.   15, Boggs, Mary, and Robert Cook.
1766, Sept.   11, Boggs, Rebecca, and Martin Bowers.
1790, July   10, Boggs, Walter, and Mary Kennedy.
1766, July   12, Boggs, William, and Sarah McEntire.
1761, April   20, Bohnan, Mary, and William Kennedy.
1733, Feb.   6, Boice, Margaret, and Aaron Hubberd.
1727, Dec.   15, Boiden, John, and Cath. Whitehall.
1746, Nov.   24, Boid, John, and Mary Bankson.
1776, Sept.   30, Boid, Mary, and Richard Lee.
1728, June   16, Boieles, Esther, and Sam. Winright.
1709, July   31, Boldwin, Mary, and William Wivell.
1763, Oct.   26, Boley, John, and Sophia Shellcock.
1744, March 25, Bolitho, John, Mary Hutchins.
1710, May   12, Boll, John, and Mary Gouin.
1725, Nov.   17, Bollard, Sam., and E. Jones.
1767, Aug.   27, Bollinger, Margaret, and Christian Frederick Post.
1799, Dec.   29, Bollman, Erich, and Eliz Nixon.
1762, Nov.   12, Bolton, Anthony, and Martha Roberts.
1715, Jan.   27, Bolton, Ralph, and Ann Buckley.
1721, Feb.   19, Bolton, Robert, and Ann Clay.

1735, Nov. 22, Bolton, Sarah, and Michael Brown.
1726, Feb. 8, Bolton, S., and Wm Bolton.
1726, Feb. 8, Bolton, W^m, and S. Bolton.
1713, Nov. 1, Bond, Ann, and Charles Read.
1755, Oct. 13, Bond, Benjamin, and Rose Miller.
1765, May 9, Bond, Elizabeth, and John Martin.
1791, March 27, Bond, Eliz, and John Travis.
1805, March 30, Bond, George, and Hester Maxwell.
1738, April 18, Bond, Hannah, and William Boyte.
1754, Feb. 25, Bond, Joseph, and Elizabeth Hodge.
1768, Sept. 22, Bond, Rebeccah, and Thomas Lawrence, Junr.
1793, July 13, Bond, Sarah, and David Easton.
1748, Feb. 13, Bond, Susannah, and William McKnight.
1764, May 10, Bond, Thomas, and Ann Morgan.
1773, Aug. 17, Bonfield, Eliz, and Nicholas Brehant.
1761, March 5, Bonham, Ephraim, and Margaret Jarrat.
1764, Nov. 8, Bonham, Mary, and Robert Harrison.
1758, Aug 9, Bonham, Ruth, and Jeremiah Baker.
1797, Nov. 23, Bonham, Susan, and William Robinson.
1788, Sept. 4, Bonnell, Charles, and Mary Brehault.
1742, Nov. 6, Bonnell, Edward, and Ruth Tompson.
1787, April 5, Bonnell, Jane, and Thomas Cooper.
1779, March 26, Bonnell, Samuel, and Kitty Hughes.
1792, Oct. 21, Booker, Richard, and Eliz Colly.
1728, Nov. 6, Boone, Ann, and Marcus Garret.
1742, March 1, Boon, Catherine, and David Hugh.^{q}
1743, April 9, Boon, Eliz, and Benjamin Simcock.
1750, March 28, Boon, Elizabeth, and John Turner.
1734, Dec. 21, Boon, Jane, and Jacob Archer.
1736, Nov. 4, Boon, Jane, and Thomas Laycock.
1730, Dec. 2, Boon, John, and Elizabeth Hutchins.
1732, June 2, Boon, Rebecca, and Samuel Flower.
1715, March 15, Boon, Sarah, and Jacob Stuber.
1761, June 20, Boon, William, and Elizabeth Williams.
1797, June 17, Boon, William, and Frances Singleton.
1731, July 17, Boore, Andrew, and Gertrude Cox.
1766, Feb. 27, Boore, Elizabeth, and Charles Jervis.
1748, Aug. 8, Boor, Mary, and David Lynn.
1731, July 19, Booreman, James, and Massey Busby.
1790, Oct. 12, Bordeau, Ann, and ———— Thornton.
1768, Sept. 1, Borden, Ann, and Francis Hopkins, Esqr.
1753, June 13, Borden, James, and Jane Stitchbury.
1786, Feb. 2, Borden, John, and Charlotte Antom.
1726, Dec. 27, Borden, Susannah, and Alexander Wordie.
1797, Nov. 28, Bordes, John Marie, and Isabella Osborne.
1795, Sept. 6, Boree, Eliz, and Augustine Jones.

1770, Oct.   18, Borradiall, Susannah, and John Rodman.
1805, July   20, Borrough, Ann, and James McKeever.
1791, March 24, Borrough, John, and Eliz Davis.
1794, Sept.   4, Bosnall, Charles, and Mary Breharelt.
1789, Feb.   23, Bostock, Benjamin, and Harriet Budden.
1720, Oct.   25, Bostock, Joseph, and Mary Handcock.
1794, April   3, Bostwick, Harriot, and Plunket Fleeson Glent-
                   worth.
1758, June   29, Bottomley, John, and Catherine Farra.
1733, Feb.   1, Boucher, John, and Sarah Harper.
1800, Feb.   6, Bouches, Mary, and John Means.
1786, Aug.   25, Bouchin, Charlotte, and Daniel Warren.
1734, April   20, Boude, Deborah, and William Connely.
1745, Nov.   14, Boude, Elizabeth, and John Nigely.
1753, May   10, Boude, Henrietta, and Micheal Hillegas.
1733, Aug.   30, Boude, Henrietta, and Richard Sewell.
1716, Sept.   5, Boud, Joseph, and Elizabeth Baldwin.
1791, April   10, Boue, Margaret, and Francis Ward.
1795, May   14, Boughton, Thomas, and Eliz Draper.
1721, May   17, Bound, John, and Mary Martin.
1804, April   2, Bourdeaux, Ann, and John Crawford.
1798, July   24, Bourden, Mary, and Barney Cousin Dennis.
1805, July   25, Bourdine, James Jacques, and Eliz Gaw.
1767, April   1, Bourk, William, and Elizabeth Tomkins.
1749, Jan.   9, Bourn, Garret, and Sarah Black.
1743, Nov.   12, Bourne, Pat., and Rebecca Angel.
1727, April   2, Bourne, T., and S. Readman.
1781, Dec.   18, Boutcher, Ann, and William Shute.
1721, Sept.   21, Bowan, Ann, and Dennis Salmon.
1797, April   29, Bowden, James, and Mary Donaldson.
1714, Jan.   6, Bowell, William, and Elizabeth Jukesbery.
1796, Aug.   23, Bowen, Ann, and Hugh McGettigen.
1754, May   23, Bowen, Benjamin, and Hannah Collins.
1742, Dec.   3, Bowen, Cornelius, and Rebecca Horsley.
1754, Dec.   14, Bowen, Deborah, and Jonathan Conrad.
1743, May   17, Bowen, Eleanor, and Robert Warpole.
1796, August 2, Bowen, Eliz, and Benjamin Keef.
1805, April   28, Bowen, Eliz, and Henry Skinner.
1786, Sept.   23, Bowen, Eliz, and John More.
1751, June   27, Bowen, Elizabeth, and Thomas Rodger.
1739, March   5, Bowen, Frances, and Theophilus Grew.
1798, Dec.   10, Bowen, George, and Sophia Edwards.
1749, May   2, Bowen, Hannah, and Evan Evans.
1802, Oct.   21, Bowen, Lucy, and Edward Yard.
1806, May   3, Bowen, Mary, and George Erick.
1798, Feb.   22, Bowen, Mary, and Ralph Peacock.

1771, Dec.   28, Bowen, Sabina, and Leonard Wright.
1784, April   24, Bower, Bartholomew, and Mary Buck.
1773, Sept.   28, Bower, Esther, and George Allen.
1796, Feb.   28, Bower, George, and Margaret Hill.
1727, Dec.   1, Bower, M., and John Davis.
1760, May   14, Bower, Valentine, and Hannah Shepperd.
1784, Dec.   3, Bowers, Jacob, and Eleanor Bensell.
1780, May   15, Bowers, Joseph, and Christiana Hedler.
1766, Sept.   11, Bowers, Martin, and Rebecca Boggs.
1778, Oct.   8, Bowers, William, and Sarah Farmer.
1760, Nov.   16, Bowes, Esther, and John Cox.
1767, Nov.   12, Bowes, Mary, and James Montgomery.
1758, Sept.   28, Bowes, Mary, and John Sayre.
1751, April   8, Bowes, Rachel, and John Sayre.
1752, March   9, Bowes, Sarah, and Thomas Smith.
1712, Sept.   10, Boweter, Ann, and William Chandler.
1806, Jan.   2, Bowhay, William, and Jane McMullen.
1778, Oct,   25, Bowker, John, and Helen Murray.
1794, May   29, Bowlby, Edward, and Cath. Wigfall.
1766, Dec.   24, Bowlden, Thomas, and Elizabeth Kemp.
1758, Oct.   21, Bowles, Ann, and Thomas Mullin.
1795, June   27, Bowles, Henry, and Margaret Sharpe.
1787, Oct.   2, Bowles, Henry, and Sarah Dougherty.
1728, Jan.   7, Bowles, S., and Richd Nixon.
1786, June   19, Bowling, Mary, and David Foster.
1731, May   11, Bowling, Thomas, and Lucy Boyte.
1756, Jan.   10, Bowman, Christiana, and William Davison.
1742, Dec.   23, Bowman, Ephraim, and Susannah Jones.
1735, Nov.   18, Bowman, Thomas, and Hester Mitchell.
1737, Nov.   20, Bowne, Cornelius, and Sarah Rivers.
1722, Nov.   28, Bowyer, Lydia, and Job Williams.
1753, Jan.   8, Bowyer, Mary, and David Carpenter.
1722, Aug.   9, Bowyer, Mary, and David Phillips.
1795, Aug.   9, Bowyer, Mary, and Simen Reynolds.
1785, April   17, Bowyer, Sarah, and Thomas Milliard.
1763, Aug.   2, Boxby, George, and Mary Brown.
1736, July   31, Boyard, Jane, and John Hayns.
1788, July   17, Boyce, John, and Mary Dunwick.
1796, Oct.   4, Boyce, Joseph, and Cath. Dunn.
1785, Nov.   30, Boyce, William, and Jane Haines.
1749, April   27, Boyd, Ann, and William Weldon.
1805, June   6, Boyd, Charles, and Jane McAlpine.
1751, April   14, Boyd, Hannah, and Samuel Spencer.
1786, April   10, Boyd, John, and Ann Pearson.
1800, July   11, Boyd, John, and Bridget Quigley.
1733, Dec.   24, Boyd, John, and Hannah Powell.

1770, April 21, Boyd, John, and Mary Ann Griffin.
1759, July 24, Boyd, Lucy, and Thomas Fisher.
1727, July 26, Boyd, Martha, and James Small.
1805, April 23, Boyd, Mary, and John Martin.
1759, April 19, Boyd, Robert, and Sarah Robertson.
1741, April 2, Boyer, Hester, and Philip Boyte.
1732, June 5, Boyer, James, and Dorothy Sprogell.
1730, June 2, Boyer, James, and Sarah Angelo.
1757, Aug. 17, Boyer, Margaret, and Caleb Whiten.
1737, Dec. 28, Boyer, Martha, and Jacob Williamson.
1756, Dec. 18, Boyer, Mary, and William Boyer.
1785, Dec. 27, Boyer, Michael, and Deborah Hall.
1756, Dec. 18, Boyer, William, and Mary Boyer.
1772, Dec. 4, Boyes, Mary, and James McNonght.
1720, Feb. 16, Boyle, Ann, and Thomas Kinston.
1795, July 4, Boyle, Bridget, and John Campbell.
1803, July 19, Boyle, Charles, and Mary Dever.
1800, Nov. 20, Boyle, Daniel, and Mary Ann Simpson.
1767, Sept. 5, Boys, Elias, and Martha Scull.
1734, Oct. 10, Boys, Joseph, and Phoebe Enoch.
1768, Sept. 14, Boyse, Martha, and Cornelius Bryan.
1737, April 9, Boyte, Anne, and John Young.
1768, Feb. 16, Boyte, Hannah, and Joseph Dean.
1731, May 11, Boyte, Lucy, and Thomas Bowling.
1752, Nov. 1, Boyte, Mary, and William Anderson.
1741, April 2, Boyte, Phillip, and Hester Boyer.
1738, April 18, Boyte, William, and Hannah Bond.
1711, Jan. 7, Boyte, William, and Lucy Stokes.
1800, Jan. 9, Boze, Eliz, and William McGinnis.
1770, Sept. 11, Brackell, Richard, and Mary Jones.
1788, Sept. 14, Bradburn, Alice, an dHugh McKage.
1802, Jan. 6, Braddock, Samuel, and Ann Green.
1783, Dec. 22, Braden, Grace, and John Brown.
1744, April 27, Braderick, Jane, and John Ellis.
1801, June 24, Bradfield, Samuel, and Mary Malone.
1788, Jan. 4, Bradford, Riley, and Mary Thomas.
1799, March 7, Bradford, Samuel F., and Abigail Inskeep.
1793, Jan. 1, Bradford, Susannah, and John Smith.
1773, August 4, Bradford, Tace, and Joshua Maddox Wallace.
1768, Nov. 23, Bradford, Thomas, and Mary Fisher.
1749, Nov. 8, Brading, Elizabeth, and William McGee.
1803, Oct. 31, Bradley, Daniel, and Ann Gallagher.
1747, June 5, Bradley, Esther, and Jacob Duche.
1743, Oct. 23, Bradley, George, and Mary Harrison.
1796, Dec. 17, Bradley, James, and Mary Vint.
1722, Aug. 23, Bradley, Winifrey, and David Ackenhof.

1727, June   1, Bradley, Ed., and Esther Flower.
1725, Oct.   31, Bradshaw, T., and Eleanour Phillips.
1799, May   28, Brady, George, and Ann Robinson.
1796, Jan.   31, Brady, John, and Susanna Hersh.
1772, Dec.   19, Brady, Mary, and Thomas Short.
1767, April   11, Brady, Patrick, and Mary Davidson.
1805, Jan.   10, Brady, Richard, and Cath. Riley.
1763, Jan.   7, Brady, Robert, and Mary Trump.
1759, Jan.   20, Bragg, Henry, and Susannah Moon.
1740, Feb.   24, Brain, Mary, and Owen Hughes.
1784, Nov.   18, Bralsford, David, and Mary Gordon.
1785, Jan.   27, Brame, Henry, and Sarah Keybright.
1726, Aug.   28, Bramel, Kath., and Dav. Davies.
1775, Nov.   16, Bramhall, Thomas, and Mary Miller.
1758, March 14, Brampton, William, and Edith Edwards.
1748, Nov.   24, Brand, Mrs. Margaret, and Doct. John Kearsely.
1768, May   2, Branderman, Ann, and James Russell.
1768, June   10, Brandt, John, and Amelia Turner.
1797, Sept.   26, Brandt, Sarah, and Henry Sharer.
1783, Aug.   31, Branham, Ebenezer, and Eliz Funk.
1770, June   6, Brannin, Hannah, and John Torr.
1783, Dec.   11, Brannon, James, and Jane Carter.
1801, July   26, Brannum, Stephen, and Rebecca Cromell.
1803, Jan.   30, Brannum, Urias, and Joshua Ash.
1749, Oct.   27, Branson, Elizabeth, and Lyndford Lardner.
1734, Feb.   25, Bransten, Mary, Bernhard Sanlear.
1729, May   17, Brant, Ann, and Stephen Barton.
1774, March   5, Brathwaite, Eliz, and Robert Threlfal.
1767, Jan.   3, Bratsford, William, and Sarah Brown.
1729, Aug.   27, Brawle, Peter, and Ann Peel.
1759, Jan.   25, Brayman, Hornor, and Thomas Collis.
1786, May   14, Brazinton, Isaac, and Susannah Chester.
1747, July   21, Breding, Elizabeth, and James Collins.
1783, Dec.   24, Brehant, Lydia, and Matthew Vanderen.
1773, Aug.   17, Brehant, Nicholas, and Eliz Bonfield.
1791, Sept.   4, Breharelt, Mary, and Charles Bosnall.
1788, Sept.   4, Brehault, Mary, and Charles Bonnell.
1800, March 13, Breidenhart, Sarah, and Charles Allen.
1771, May   23, Breintnall, Joseph, and Jane Ham.
1752, May   11, Breintnal, Martha, and James Lowther.
1751, July   5, Breintnal, Rebecca, and Edward Weyman.
1712, Jan.   1, Brendly, James, and Mary Wivell.
1784, April   5, Brenton, James, and Mary Buoy.
1800, Dec.   11, Brethoff, Henry, and Eleanor Bess.
1758, Feb.   21, Breton, Ann, and Thomas Brown.
1773, June   6, Brewer, Joseph, and Eliz Caryl.

1732, Nov.   25, Brewer, Lucretia, and John Manly.
1761, June   13, Brewer, Thomas, and Ann Cummings.
1786, June   22, Brewers, Daniel, and Eliz Brown.
1768, June   6, Brewstar, Peter, and Eliz Townsend.
1800, Nov.   15, Brewster, James, and Ann Rindleman.
1781, March 29, Brewster, William, and Eliz Barndollar.
1791, July   3, Brewton, Daniel, and Mary Rudolph.
1795, Feb.   26, Brewton, Eliz, and Robert Forsyth.
1711, July   18, Breyan, Joan, and Darby Grifton.
1787, March 23, Brezy, Henry, and Henry Butler.
1787, April 29, Brian, John, and Margaret Arnold.
1753, Sept. 24, Brice, Thomas, and Elizabeth Murphy.
1784, Feb.   19, Brick, John, and Mercy Hartley.
1794, Sept. 20, Brickall, Caleb, and Sarah Cribbs.
1786, Jan.   1, Brickham, John, and Sarah Jones.
1782, Oct.   27, Brickell, Sarah, and Thomas Willard.
1760, Sept. 13, Brickham, Patience, and Samuel Skill.
1730, Dec.   7, Brickhill, Richard, and Mary Palmer.
1785, Jan.   30, Bridges, Ann, and George Yard.
1790, March 11, Bridges, Cornelia, and Robert Patton.
1804, Feb.   21, Bridges, Culpepper, and Sarah Cliffton.
1759, April   4, Bridges, George, and Margaret Sims.
1804, May   8, Bridges, Harriet, and John Broome Davy.
1783, July   8, Bridges, Mary, and John Sharpe.
1769, Oct.   26, Bridges, Robert, and Jemima Shepherd.
1800, Nov.   30, Briggs, Daniel, and Sarah Ramaje.
1784, Jan.   19, Briggs, Henry, and Esther Locke.
1710, Nov.   13, Briggs, William, and Margaret Cuttler.
1790, Nov.   10, Brigs, Ralph, and Ann Tucker.
1743, Feb.   5, Bright, Anthony, and Jane Hobart.
1739, June   23, Bright, Anthony, and Mary Hemmet.
1750, Dec.   25, Bright, Elizabeth, and John Eton.
1736, April   7, Bright, Mary, and Thomas Burney.
1716, Feb.   6, Bright, Priscilla, and John Justice.
1793, May   9, Bright, Sarah, and Johnson Kelly.
1748, Sept.   5, Brightwel, Joannah, and Tool McCann.
1748, Nov.   27, Brightwel, Rebecca, and Richard Newton.
1795, July   4, Brindley, Ann, and Patrick Lyons.
1715, June   6, Bringhurst, Barbary, and William Morrison.
1786, April 26, Bringhurst, Eliz, and Edward Durant.
1780, July   27, Bringhurst, George, and Ann Clarkson.
1791, Sept. 13, Bringhurst, John, and Mildred Keene.
1803, Jan.   29, Bringhurst, Mary Anna, and Thomas Mifflin Hall.
1801, June   18, Bringhurst, Thomas, and Mary Fraley.
1730, March 26, Brinklowe, John, Jr., and Charity Robeson.
1799, April 15, Brinton, Weldon, and Hester Wilson.

1713, Aug.   6, Brisk, Richard, and Susannah James.
1783, Sept.   3, Brisnott, Felix, and Eliz Beaven.
1800, May   15, Bristol, Eliz, and William Sammons.
1711, June   9, Bristoll, Margaret, and Robert Gerrard.
1759, April   21, Britain, Benjamin, and Mary Pugh.
1753, June   12, Britain, Rachel, and Frederick Fetzer.
1794, June   16, Britton, Ann, and John Mallineux.
1802, Oct.   13, Britton, Benjamin, and Rebecca Smith.
1805, Dec.   10, Britton, Eleanor, and William Dewees.
1767, April   1, Britton, John, and Eleanor Waters.
1800, July   12, Britton, Mary, and William Dewees.
1755, April   15, Britton, Rachel, and Albertson Walton.
1795, Dec.   5, Britton, Sarah, and Standish Ford.
1792, Nov.   23, Britton, Susannah, and George Budd.
1768, Sept.   29, Britton, Thomas, and Catherine Forbes.
1720, Sept.   16, Britton, William, and Elizabeth Northorp.
1739, Dec.   15, Broadgate, Mary, and Peter Snow.
1800, Oct.   29, Broadnax, Amelia, and Adam Menderhall.
1787, June   9, Broadnax, Thomas, and Sarah Blunk.
1762, Aug.   3, Broards, Arthur, and Catherine Rinard.
1801, Feb.   26, Brobst, Valentine, and Ann Bandore.
1722, Feb.   28, Brock, Mercy, and William Smith.
1768, March   3, Brockden, Mary, and Thomas Patterson.
1736, Jan.   11, Brockdon, Mary, and Norton Pryor.
1753, April   25, Brockenberry, Mary, and Francis Griest.
1746, Sept.   10, Brodrick, Daniel, and Hannah Sceen.
1747, Aug.   21, Brodrick, Edmond, and Mary Cahoon.
1780, Oct.   15, Brody, Alexander, and Ann Litchingham.
1742, Dec.   3, Bromwich, William, and Ann Chocolier.
1804, Dec.   4, Bronson, Enos, and Mary White.
1712, Sept.   9, Brook, Charles, and Ann Stroud.
1772, Oct.   15, Brook, Owen, and Eliz Hanimer.
1767, Aug.   23, Brooke, Bowyer, and Hannah Reese.
1795, Dec.   22, Brooke, Eliz, and Philip Reese.
1800, Jan.   18, Brooke, Robert, and Rachel Shee.
1767, July   22, Brookes, Elizabeth, and William Murphin.
1763, Nov.   9, Brookhouse, Samuel, and Mary Duncan.
1780, Oct.   19, Brooks, Benjamin, and Eliz Davis.
1741, Nov.   12, Brooks, Catherine, and Andrew Anderson.
1741, Sept.   30, Brooks, Catherine, and John Murrey.
1786, Aug.   3, Brooks, Cath., and William Tomlinson.
1730, July   12, Brooks, Charles, and Anne Carty.
1803, Jan.   29, Brooks, Eliz, and Jabez Saunders.
1767, Jan.   11, Brooks, Francis, and Elizabeth Sighing.
1776, May   12, Brooks, John, and Catherine Roberts.
1765, April   10, Brooks, Mary, and John Bern.

1712, May   18, Brooks, Matthew, and Ann Evans.
1804, Oct.   11, Brooks, Nathan, and Mary Jones.
1779, Nov.   11, Brooks, Nicholas, and Edith Matthews.
1721, May   16, Brooks, Olivia, and Edward Molley.
1775, Nov.   19, Brooks, William, and Susannah Murphy.
1731, Dec.   23, Broom, Mary, and Daniel Green.
1736, Oct.   17, Broom, Susannah, and Henry Reid.
1712, July   27, Broome, Thomas, and Elizabeth Coley.
1769, Oct.   22, Brothers, William, and Eleanor Quin.
1752, Dec.   25, Broughton, Andrew, and Elizabeth Sandford.
1796, Aug.   25, Brown, Abner, and Rachel Black.
1794, Dec.   22, Brown, Allen, and Christiana McDonald.
1737, Dec.   26, Brown, Amiable, and Samuel Gilbert.
1795, Sept. 27, Brown, Amos, and Barbara Peters.
1732, Aug.   31, Brown, Anne, and John Callander.
1734, Jan.   29, Brown, Anne, and Nehemiah Haynes.
1764, Nov.   8, Brown, Ann, and William Knight.
1736, Jan.   17, Brown, Catherine, and John Harper.
1802, Nov.   21, Brown, Christopher, and Eliz Graham.
1755, Dec.   26, Brown, David, and Catherine Forrester.
1762, April 15, Brown, David, and Susannah Paul.
1786, June   22, Brown, Eliz, and Daniel Brewers.
1715, Oct.   22, Brown, Elizabeth, and James Tonyclifft.
1799, March   3, Brown, Eliz, and John Connover.
1770, March 22, Brown, Elizabeth, and John Pine.
1797, Nov.   30, Brown, Eliz, and Stacy Horner.
1737, April 13, Brown, Elizabeth, and William Collar.
1766, Dec.   17, Brown, Gilbert, and Jane McMullen.
1751, June   5, Brown, Gustavus, and Elizabeth Harper.
1755, Sept. 25, Brown, Hannah, and Edward Smith.
1770, Oct.   29, Brown, James, and Catherine McCormick.
1727, May   18, Brown, James, and Hannah Sharley.
1761, Sept. 13, Brown, James, and Mary Wall.
1716, Feb.   27, Brown, James, and Rachel Froud.
1737, Dec.   31, Brown, Jane, and Richard Ellis.
1779, Dec.   18, Brown, Johanna, and Samuel Powell.
1778, Dec.   10, Brown, John, and Beulah Bissett.
1797, June   29, Brown, John, and Charlotte Hyde.
1768, Dec.   6, Brown, John, and Elizabeth Holloway.
1782, Nov.   22, Brown, John, and Eliz Tanyard.
1783, Dec.   22, Brown, John, and Grace Braden.
1731, May   17, Brown, John, and Hannah Hague.
1757, May   22, Brown, John, and Jane Schofield.
1784, Jan.   8, Brown, John, and Mary Brown.
1795, March   8, Brown, John, and Mary Brown.
1801, May   19, Brown, John, and Mary Polhemus.

1770, Oct.   25, Brown, Jonathar, and Eliz Benning.
1747, March   9, Brown, Joseph, and Anne Betty.
1787, July   18, Brown, Joseph, and Mary Alexander.
1753, April   23, Brown, Joseph, and Polly Leary.
1797, April   1, Brown, Laetitia, and Timothy Cantie.
1761, June   5, Brown, Leah, and John Elliott.
1728, May   30, Brown, Leah, and S. Scott.
1797, Jan.   26, Brown, Lydia, and John Phillips.
1771, Sept.   17, Brown, Margaret, and Dennis Plym.
1756, April   17, Brown, Martha, and William Foukin.
1798, Dec.   4, Brown, Mary Ann, and Peter Didier.
1748, Sept.   4, Brown, Mary, and Edward Williams.
1802, Dec.   18, Brown, Mary, and Francis Winton.
1763, Aug.   2, Brown, Mary, and George Boxby.
1736, April   2, Brown, Mary, and James Calcott.
1784, Jan.   8, Brown, Mary, and John Brown.
1795, March   8, Brown, Mary, and John Brown.
1796, Oct.   23, Brown, Mary, and Joseph Gatty.
1785, Sept.   28, Brown, Mary, and Moses Austin.
1767, Dec.   2, Brown, Mary, and Peter Ridge.
1773, Sept.   24, Brown, Mary, and Richard Hazard.
1786, Feb.   28, Brown, Mary, and Samuel Allen.
1788, July   11, Brown, Mary, and Thomas Evans.
1801, April   14, Brown, Mathew, and Sarah Fox.
1735, Nov.   22, Brown, Michael, and Sarah Bolton.
1804, Aug.   29, Brown, Morris, and Mary Uhle.
1805, July   20, Brown, Peter A., and Harriet Harper.
1781, Oct.   4, Brown, Phillip, and Eleanor Moore.
1748, Oct.   2, Brown, Preserve, and Elizabeth Till.
1755, Aug.   14, Brown, Rebecca, and Joseph Kanny.
1730, Sept.   16, Brown, Richard, and Alice Pain.
1785, Oct.   20, Brown, Sarah, and George Abbott.
1786, April   20, Brown, Sarah, and John Abbott.
1733, Sept.   10, Brown, Sarah, and John Smith.
1761, Aug.   6, Brown, Sarah, and Josse Roe.
1767, Jan.   3, Brown, Sarah, and William Bratsford.
1782, Feb.   5, Brown, Sophia, and James Swaine.
1758, Feb.   21, Brown, Thomas, and Anne Breton.
1775, July   4, Brown, Thomas, and Ann Sherwood.
1744, Oct.   27, Brown, Thomas, and Eliz Fisher.
1758, Dec.   6 Brown, Thomas, and Mary Jones.
1765, Feb.   23, Brown, Thomasine, and John Farns.
1797, April   18, Brown, Stewart, and Sarah Harman.
1790, Dec.   3, Brown, Walter, and Eliz Walker.
1798, Nov.   28, Brown, William, and Ann Siddons.
1781, May   30, Brown, William, and Margret Ager.

1791, June   16, Brown, William, and Mary Knight.
1773, Sept. 16, Browne, John, and Eleanor Saunders.
1799, April 27, Browne, Mary, and Hore Browse Triste.
1729-30, Jan. 29, Browne, Thomas, and Hannah Young.
1801, Dec.   8, Browne, Thomas, and Laetitia Potts.
1734, July   29, Brownley, James, and Anne Costener.
1751, March 23, Browning, Benjamin, and Mary Abbot.
1761, March 16, Browning, Joseph, and Sarah Rownand.
1748, Jan.   21, Browning, William, and Abigail Kostard.
1786, Sept. 13, Brownlow, Mary, and Michael White.
1743, Nov.   24, Brownyard, Hannah, and John Ingram.
1800, Nov.   19, Bruce, Charlotte, and William Curtis.
1748, Sept. 19, Bruce, Isabell and John Pine.
1729, June   15, Bruce, W^m, and Ann Welsh.
1791, Sept. 22, Bruistar, Ann, Peter Stoy.
1794, Dec.   16, Bruistar, Eliz and Daniel Bennet.
1794, Dec.   16, Bruistar, John, and Eliz James,
1805, Oct.   31, Bruistar, Phoebe, and Joseph Kelly.
1779, Aug.   17, Bruister, James, and Ann Cheesman.
1799, Dec.   26, Brum, Christopher, and Lydia Osborne.
1799, Oct.   31, Brum, Nicholas, and Ann Carney.
1740, Dec.   27, Brumley, Mary, and Philip Cole.
1753, April 16, Bruno, Elizabeth, and Richard Cloud.
1761, April 29, Brunnory, Barbary, and George Powell.
1765, Sept.   5, Brusstar, Benjamin, and Rebecca Tatlow.
1791, Jan.   13, Bruster, Mary, and Daniel Stoy.
1768, Jan.   23, Brustrum, Ann, and James Fullerton.
1760, May   7, Brustrum, Mary, and William Stiles.
1760, May   16, Bruxton, Sarah, and John Morris.
1768, Sept. 14, Bryan, Cornelius, and Martha Boyse.
1749, May   2, Bryan, Cornelius, and Mary Roberts.
1793, Aug,   22, Bryan, Eliza, and William Culver.
1785, June   21, Bryan, Guy, and Martha Matlack.
1804, May   25, Bryan, Hannah, and William Hunt.
1762, Jan.   6, Bryan, John, and Elizabeth Cloud.
1747, Feb.   14, Bryan, Joseph, and Jehosheba Wells.
1801, Nov.   26, Bryan, Margaret, and James Phillips.
1762, Oct.   28, Bryan, Mary, and Henry Gill.
1799, Nov.   28, Bryan, Thomas, and Eleanor Scull.
1744, June   9, Bryan, Thomas, and Eliz Waine.
1778, Dec.   3, Bryant, John, and Ann Keating.
1720, May   12, Bryant, John, and Mary Pyke.
1806, July   20, Bryant, Lois, and William Davenport.
1751, Nov.   11, Bryly, Katherine, and Thomas Childs.
1798, April   8, Bryson, Mary, and Cardinal Hoag.
1798, Nov.   15, Buchanan, George, and Cath. Grant.

1803, Oct.   9, Buchanan, George, and Eliz McCutchin.
1752, May   6, Buchannan, James, and Mary Dean.
1766, Nov.   10, Buchanan, John, and ——— ———.
1782, April   19, Buchanan, Rachel, and William Nash.
1784, April   24, Buck, Mary, and Bartholomew Bower.
1774, Sept.   3, Buck, Philip, and Ann Stamp.
1779, Sept.   13, Buckart, Mary, and James Butland.
1715, Jan.   27, Buckley, Ann, and Ralph Bolton.
1748, Oct.   14, Buckley, Jane, and Solomon Helliard.
1760, July   28, Buckley, Thomas, and Mary Turner.
1751, Nov.   18, Buckman, Isaac, and Mary Hilborn.
1753, Dee.   11, Buckman, Thomas, and Elizabeth Carver.
1787, April   24, Bucks, Hannah, and Edmund Mash.
1730, Sept.   30, Bucksome, James, and Jane Afflick.
1747, Dec.   5, Buckston, Rebecca, and William Ghiselin.
1737, June   11, Budd, Elizabeth, and Samuel Bustil.
1792, Nov.   23, Budd, George, and Susannah Britton.
1732, Sept.   10, Budd, John, Rosamund Goseling.
1749, Dec.   30, Budd, Levi, and Elizabeth Edge.
1781, April   5, Budd, Mary, and David Claypoole.
1804, June   4, Budd, Mary Wright, and Oswald Sill.
1731-2, Jan.   6, Budd, Thomas, and Mary Eyre.
1774, Dec.   1, Budd, Thomas, and Sarah Coburn.
1754, March   4, Budden, Elizabeth, and Richard Ward.
1789, Feb.   23, Budden, Harriet, and Benjamin Bostock.
1756, May   30, Budden, Learah, and Cornelius Teel.
1735, July   20, Budden, Richard, and Susannah Carter.
1759, Feb.   24, Budden, William, and Louisa Cuzzins.
1802, Dec.   11, Buddinton, Asa, and Mary Ravel.
1773, Aug.   9, Budgin, John, and Margaret Best.
1763, Jan.   12, Buffington, Jane, and John Deiter.
1750, July   30, Buffington, Peter, and Mary Wilson.
1806, June   5, Bukhorn, Garrel, and Sarah McAllister.
1805, June   27, Bujac, John Lachausec, and Celeste Robin.
1794, May   26, Bulger, Henry, and Mary North.
1797, April   26, Bulkley, Thomas, and Sarah Waln.
1751, April   18, Bull, Elizabeth, and Thomas Rosseter.
1757, Feb.   21, Bull, William, and Mary Melaring.
1776, May   9, Bullin, Edward, and Mary McDonald.
1727, Nov.   23, Bullin, E., and Martin Asiburn.
1764, June   16, Bullman, Frances, and Dunnin Irwin.
1726, Aug.   29, Bullock, Dor., and Abraham Strong.
1728, Sept.   14, Bullock, Ed., and Mary Davenport.
1772, May   25, Bullock, Isabel, and William Wright.
1780, Nov.   16, Bullock, Eliz, and Peter Baynton.
1727, Nov.   7, Bullock, Marg^t, and G. Jones.

1743, April 11, Bullock, Mary, and George Johnson.
1763, April 13, Bullock, Mary, and Thomas Hall.
1803, Dec. 15, Bullock, Rebecca, and Charles Wistar.
1747, April 19, Bullock, Robert, and Catherine Forge.
1800, April 15, Bullus, John, and Charlotte Jane Rumsey.
1762, Jan. 5, Bully, Sarah, and William Sellers.
1728, Dec. 2, Bulman, Robt., and Sarah Sherraid.
1760, June 28, Bulman, Thomas, and Frances Burk.
1768, May 19, Bunbury, Robert, and Mary Iveson.
1780, April 11, Bunn, Eliz, and Joseph Clunn.
1770, Dec. 20, Bunner, Andrew, and Sarah Fisher.
1787, Nov. 1, Bunner, Jacob, and Eliz Good.
1802, May 6, Bunting, Jonathan, and Cath. Keppele.
1760, Feb. 21, Bunting, Marmaduke, and Mary Dislow.
1762, Dec. 29, Bunting, Samuel, and Esther Syng.
1784, April 5, Buoy, Mary, and James Brenton.
1729, June 16, Burch, Mary, and Thomas Stanwell.
1729, Feb. 24, Burchfield, Alice, and John Campbell.
1778, Dec. 17, Burd, Edward, and Eliz. Shippen.
1800, Jan. 9, Burd, Margaret, and Daniel William Coxe.
1732, Oct. 2, Burden, Hannah, and William Cox.
1736, May 31, Burden, John, and Sarah Hopkins.
1735, May 16, Burden, Richard, and Rebecca Hellier.
1753, Nov. 17, Burge, Elizabeth, and Robert Low.
1791, June 20, Burge, John, and Mary Beorne.
1782, Dec. 19, Burgess, Joseph, and Mary Moore.
1785, Oct. 2, Burgess, Ruth, and Godfrey Welsel.
1804, March 3, Burgess, William, and Jane Trisobio.
1795, March 9, Burgess, William, and Sarah Rudd.
1737, Nov. 30, Burgoign, Joseph, and Hannah Price.
1773, June 19, Burgum, John, and Mary Bartholomew.
1765, April 27, Burhow, Nicholas, and Abigail Biddle.
1765, Jan. 29, Burk, Ann, and Philip Ryan.
1727, Nov. 27, Burk, Ben., and Ame. Anne Meekum.
1760, June 28, Burk, Frances, and Thomas Bulman.
1767, April 26, Burk, John, and Ann Hudson.
1761, Jan. 10, Burk, Margaret, and Nicholas Gale.
1743, May 18, Burk, Mary, and Charles Williamson.
1760, Sept. 22, Burk, Mary, and John Marrina.
1797, Aug. 19, Burk, Thomas, and Amy Iveson.
1805, March 3, Burke, Cath., and Isaac Cogill.
1796, May 7, Burke, Christiana, and Robert Anderson.
1804, June 16, Burke, Hannah, and Evan Jones.
1801, Sept. 3, Burke, James, and Ann Miller.
1796, April 24, Burke, John, and Cath. Pancake.
1802, April 30, Burke, Thomas, and Rachel Dare.

1804, May   5, Burke, Thomas, and Sarah Howard.
1763, Jan.   7, Burket, Jacob, and Barbara Fisher.
1800, Aug.   7, Burkit, Mary, and John Thomson.
1762, Oct.   28, Burman, Edward, and Mary Craven.
1784, Dec.   19, Burman, Mary, and Joseph Clinton.
1795, Nov.   4, Burn, Thomas, and Mary Green.
1759, Sept.   21, Burnet, John, and Rebecca Kay.
1736, Feb.   17, Burnett, Daniel, and Grace Lewis.
1730, May   2, Burnett, Mary, and John Plann.
1736, April   7, Burney, Thomas, and Mary Bright.
1748, Nov.   29, Burns, Elizabeth, and Thomas Darling.
1803, Jan.   2, Burns, John, and Penelope Gorton.
1766, Dec.   2, Burns, Joseph, and Jane Lowns.
1786, Juiy   20, Burns, Laurence, and Cath. Fegan.
1786, June   29, Burns, Mary, and William Leo.
1755, April   15, Burr, Henry, and Sarah Hiller.
1767, May   25, Burr, Hudson, and Phoebe Lippencot.
1733, June   24, Burrel, Anne, and William Lane.
1786, June   1, Burrough, Joseph, and Ann Garregues.
1757, Feb.   20, Burrow, Anna Maria, and John Barefield.
1736, March   15, Burrows, Arthur, and Mary Bird.
1763, Oct.   31, Burrows, Arthur, and Mary Morgan.
1768, Aug.   13, Burrows, John, and Margaret Sherlock.
1772, Dec.   14, Burrows, Margaret, and George Willson.
1759, Dec.   1, Burrows, Mary, and George Robotham.
1784, Sept.   1, Burrows, Mary, and John Dickey.
1766, April   7, Burrows, Mary, and John McGibbon.
1771, Feb.   21, Burton, Eliz, and Thomas Shaw.
1776, Feb.   27, Burton, John, and Eliz Mason.
1801, Aug.   14, Busby, Abraham, and Mary Dennis.
1803, June   4, Busby, Eliz, and Peter Summers.
1731, July   19, Busby, Massey, and James Booreman.
1758, Dec.   14, Busel, Grace, and Edmund Fagan.
1796, Dec.   1, Bush, Ann, and William Currie.
1784, Jan.   15, Bush, Mary, and John Gardner.
1797, Nov.   26, Bussier, Daniel, and Cath. Philler.
1737, June   11, Bustil, Samuel, and Elizabeth Budd.
1779, Dec.   25, Butcher, Anne, and Mark Baldwin.
1768, July   25, Butcher, Job, and Mary Shepherd.
1744, March   26, Butcher, Mary, and John Allen.
1734, Aug.   24, Butcher, Mary, and Thomas Cox.
1758, April   29, Butcher, Samuel, and Ann Walton.
1788, May   28, Butcher, Samuel, and Mary Higbee.
1773, Jan.   30, Butcher, William and Ann Hampton.
1779, Sept.   13, Butland, James, and Mary Buckart.
1799, Nov.   16, Butler, Allen, and Martha Herley.

1760, Feb. 13, Butler, Ameron, and Felix Vershon.
1780, April 20, Butler, Anthony, and Eliz. Coates.
1740, Feb. 17, Butler, Bathsheba, and Francis Whitterance.
1803, Dec. 1, Butler, Cath., and Edward Calvery.
1776, Feb. 1, Butler, Daniel, and Martha Fisher.
1758, Aug. 3, Butler, Hannah, and Thomas Atkins.
1787, March 23, Butler, Henry, and ——— Breezy.
1805, Oct. 5, Butler, Jane, and William Caldwell.
1758, Oct. 6, Butler, John, and Rachel Quest.
1801, Jan. 1, Butler, Laurence, and Susanna Mackey.
1767, June 12, Butler, Mary, and Barney Campbell.
1764, June 5, Butler, Matthew, and Sarah Gardner.
1803, Jan. 5, Butler, Penelope, and James Parker.
1800, April 10, Butler, Rachel, and Caleb Coumbs.
1774, May 25, Butler, Richard, and Sarah Mullen.
1729, July 10, Butler, Sarah, and Ed. Denny.
1800, July 3, Butler, Sarah, and James Mease.
1796, Dec. 8, Butler, Sarah, and Nicholas Muniat.
1758, Dec. 23, Butler, Susanna, and Thomas Salter.
1774, Oct. 6, Butler, William, and Ann Griffin.
1767, Dec. 24, Butterworth, Mary, and Alexander Power.
1740, Aug. 20, Buxton, Dorcas, and Jonathan Peesely.
1774, Oct. 19, Bynes, John, and Eliz. Furrow.
1761, Jan. 29, Byrd, Honble William, and Mary Willing.
1742, March 29, Byrn, Margaret, and Conrad Waldocker.
1743, Aug. 14, Byrn, Mary, and Thomas Casey.
1717, March 3, Bywater, Elizabeth, and Robert Fullard.
1761, Nov. 16, Bywater, William, and Margaret Harper.
1761, Sept. 9, Cadman, Anthony, and Ruth Ross.
1796, June 11, Cadwalader, Ann, and Robert Kemble.
1799, Dec. 16, Cadwalader, Fanny, and David Montague Erskine.
1793, May 9, Cadwalader, Lambert, and Mary McCall.
1804, June 25, Cadwalader, Thomas, and Mary Biddle.
1792, May 3, Cadwallader, Eliz., and Archibald McCall.
1772, May 21, Cadwallader, Margaret, and Samuel Meredith.
1792, May 3, Cadwallader, Maria, and Samuel Ringold.
1774, Oct. 20, Cadwallader, Martha, and John Dagworthy.
1767, July 15, Cadwallader, Mary, and Philemon Dickinson.
1804, Sept. 1, Cadwallader, Rebecca, and Philemon Dickinson.
1785, Dec. 29, Caesar, Joseph, and Susannah Jennings.
1764, Jan. 30, Cahaug, Thomas, and Ann Reily.
1730, Dec. 12, Cahoon, Jane, and Andrew Lycan.
1747, Aug. 21, Cahoon, Mary, and Edmond Brodrick.
1795, June 22, Cahoon, Thomas, and Margaret Pearson.
1780, Dec. 27, Cain, Charles, and Jane Moss.
1786, Feb. 2, Cain, Jane, and Joseph Strow.

1783, Nov.   16, Cain, Mary, and William Willis.
1777, March 23, Caine, Patrick, and Mary Haines.
1748, Dec.   1, Calahan, John, and Hannah Welkin.
1747, March 8, Calahan, Mary, and Mathew Welsh.
1780, July   12, Calam, Susannah, and Bartlemy Saley.
1773, Sept. 18, Calbert, Lydia, and David Dunn.
1736, April   2, Calcott, James, and Mary Brown.
1805, June   6, Caldcleugh, Robert, and Rebecca Poyntell.
1789, July   18, Caldeleugh, Margaret, and James Sawyer.
1798, July   29, Caldwell, Ann, and William Hutton.
1799, Jan.   3, Caldwell, Charles, and Eliza Leaning.
1802, June   17, Caldwell, Chew, and Lydia Taylor.
1801, March 19, Caldwell, James, and Ann Thomson.
1797, Aug.   29, Caldwell, Patrick, and Ann Barry.
1783, April 17, Caldwell, Robert, and Agness Douglass.
1805, Oct.   5, Caldwell, William, and Jane Butler.
1740, May   7, Calender, Anne, and William McKinlay.
1806, April 17, Calender, Thomas, and Eliza Bella Wilcox.
1805, Dec.   19, Caley, Mary, and Phineas Lewis.
1756, June   10, Call, Ebenezer, and Margaret Thompson.
1800, May   4, Call, Eliz, and William Roach.
1783, Feb.   24, Callaghan, Cornelius, and Eleanor George.
1761, Jan.   15, Callahan, Dennis, and Elizabeth Wright.
1732, Aug.   31, Callander, John, and Anne Brown.
1803, Dec.   1, Calverly, Edward, and Cath. Butler.
1755, Oct.   29, Calvert, Thomas, and Mary Howard.
1796, Oct.   26, Calvin, Ann, and Benjamin Rogers.
1771, May   4, Calwellin, Mary, and William Hughes.
1728, April 27, Cambridge, Giles, and O. Dehaws.
1757, Nov.   5, Camby, Dorothy, and James Barker.
1765, Aug.   8, Camel, Margaret, and John McCool.
1753, Dec.   2, Camel, Susannah, and William Wright.
1748, Dec.   15, Cameron, John, and Mary Castle.
1763, Nov.   5, Cameron, Elizabeth, and Menan Kennard.
1795, Oct.   5, Cameron, Mary, and John Stapleton.
1788. Aug.   16, Cameron, William, and Mary Reid.
1766, Aug.   30, Cammel, Catherine, and John Preston.
1749, Oct.   19, Cammel, Elizabeth, and Thomas Lackey.
1766, Aug.   7, Cammel, Mary, and Michael Davenport.
1743, June   2, Camp, Wilmouth, and John Rush.
1754, March 28, Campbel, John, and Hannah Smith.
1791, Sept. 12, Campbell, Alexander, and Eliz Kay.
1772, April   1, Campble, Ann, and Hugh Hamilton.
1799, June   12, Campbell, Anthony, and Mary Stewart.
1767, June   12, Campbell, Barney, and Mary Butler.
1770, March 15, Campbell, Catherine, and Evan Whale.

1797, May   1, Campbell, Edward, and Margaret Penrose.
1795, Oct.   9, Campbell, Eliza, and John Battin.
1794, May 24, Campbell, James, and Mary Young.
1763, June 16, Campbell, John, and Lydia Duckeminner.
1729, Feb. 24, Campbell, John, and Alice Burchfield.
1795, July   4, Campbell, John, and Bridget Boyle.
1724, Feb.   6, Campbell, Katherine, and Thomas Hicks.
1802, Aug. 25, Campbell, Margaret, and James Coyles.
1803, Jan. 12, Campbell, Margaret, and George Smith.
1732, Nov. 30, Campbell, Margaret, and James Carr.
1773, April 16, Campbell, Mary, and William Bailey.
1767, Feb. 20, Campbell, Mary, and George McKay.
1796, Jan.   3, Campbell, Naomi, and Isaak Tucker.
1803, Dec. 22, Campbell, Sarah, and Thomas Palmer.
1804, July 14, Campbell, Sarah, and George Davis.
1802, Oct. 21, Campbell, Sarah, and Nicholas Wynkoop.
1769, Dec. 20, Campbell, Sarah, and Isaac Allen.
1747, March 7, Campbell, Thomas, and Tabitha Storke.
1777, Aug. 29, Campbell, William, and Mary Mullen.
1770, July 22, Campbell, William, and Jane Roberts.
1767, Aug. 15, Campian, Richard, and Elizabeth Bizzey.
1750, March 10, Camron, Martha, and Zechariah Barr.
1805, March 2, Canan, John, and Mary Shingle.
1758, Nov. 21, Canby, Martha, and James Steel.
1766, Oct. 23, Candle, Thomas, and Elizabeth Oliver.
1736, Aug.   7, Cane, Anne, and Samuel Leacock.
1774, May 25, Cane, Cath., and Jesse Cart.
1736, March 5, Cane, William, and Rebecca Rutter.
1766, Feb. 25, Cannon, Elizabeth, and Thomas Claxton Pape.
1795, Aug. 16, Cannon, James Ingersoll, and Hannah Gettinger.
1804, Sept. 5, Cannon, Louisa, and George Allison.
1771, Oct. 26, Cannon, Mary, and John Wood.
1742, Sept. 4, Cannon, Mary, and Thomas Smith.
1771, Sept. 23. Cannon, Patrick, and Phœbe Howell.
1728, Feb.   9, Cannon, Stanley, and Dinah Rivers.
1746, Dec. 32, Cannizes, Leah, and George Beckerton.
1720, Sept. 13, Canour, Elizabeth, and Richard Owen.
1749, April 8, Canthan, Mary, and Francis Harding.
1797, April 1, Cantie, Timothy, and Laetitia Brown.
1762, Aug.   2, Capout, Dorothy, and Peter Coupin.
1792, March 29, Capper, Henry, and Eleanor Bartholomew.
1776, April 25, Carberry, William, and Hannah Delahoute.
1784, May 16, Carbord, Joseph, and Mary Powers.
1758, March 30, Card, Samuel, and Elizabeth Lewis.
1801, Aug. 15, Cardiff, Clement, and Ann Goforth.
1784, Feb.   2, Cardiff, Penelope, and Thomas Peirce.

1758, May   31, Cardock, Thales, and Martha Chalkley.
1796, March 22, Care, Ann, and John Devat.
1795, July   8, Care, Sarah, and Asapp Plunket.
1794. Sept.   11, Care, Susannah and Henry Pratt.
1751, April   11, Carew, George, and Elizabeth Sinclair.
1806, June   22, Carey, Francis, and Sarah Long.
1774, Sept.   8, Carey, Esqʳ., John, and Cath. Lawrence.
1782, Oct.   17, Carey, Joshua, and Mary Gibbs.
1796, Sept.   29. Carey, Mary, and David Evans.
1802, Aug.   25, Carleton, George, and Eliz. Plunket.
1729-30, Mar.15, Carleton, Phoebe, and Timothy Spencer.
1742, Feb.   13, Carley, Elizabeth, and Cony Edwards.
1757, Aug.   21, Carley, Jane, and John Woods.
1736, Nov.   15, Carley, Matthew, and Editha Rutherford.
1737, Aug,   13, Carlisle, Sarah, and William Reston.
1727, May   13, Carlow, J., and E. Scay.
1731, Sept.   12, Carlow, Philip, and Elizabeth Pockinhall.
1773, May   3, Carmalt, Martha, and Edward Gabriel.
1733, Feb.   24, Carmalt, Tamar, and Samuel Kinard.
1759, Nov.   22, Carman, Ephraim, and Mary Lisby.
1800, Aug.   19, Carman, Maria, and John Carr.
1710, Jan.   5, Carman, Mary, and John Williams.
1761, Nov.   5, Ca man, Mary, and Sellwood Griffin.
1781, July   9, Carmedy, Eleanor, and Jehu Hoskins.
1784, March   4, Carmick, Anna, and James Horatio Watmough.
1764, Feb.   28, Carmick, Margaret, and John Potts.
1798, Jan.   11, Carmick, Stephen, and Susan Cozens.
1767, March 31, Carncross, William, and Ann Wigmore.
1785, March 29, Carneg, Anne, and Garrett Berry.
1768, April   30, Carnelly, Joanna, and William Selly.
1798, March 25, Carnes, Daniel, and Rachel Stears.
1793, Jan.   1, Carnes, Rebecca, and Timothy Kirby.
1799, Oct.   31, Carney, Ann, and Nicholas Brum.
1796, July   23, Carney, Eleanor, and William Chambers.
1736, Sept.   9, Carney, Rebecca, and Robert Shepherd.
1748, Nov.   3, Carson, John, and Anne Peywel.
1764, Nov.   17, Carpenter, Abraham, and Eleanor Hillyard.
1717, May   13, Carpenter, Ann, and Jonathan Watkins.
1739, Oct.   17, Carpenter, Anne, and Thomas Horner.
1738, Nov.   23, Carpenter, Benjamin, and Mary Harding.
1738, July   20, Carpenter, Benjamin, and Ann Davies.
1753, Jan.   8, Carpenter, David, and Mary Bowyer.
1759, Aug.   11, Carpenter, Jasper, and Mary Clifton.
1743, Dec.   10, Carpenter, Joshua, and Orange Johnson.
1741, Oct.   6, Carpenter, Mary, and George Nicholls.
1795, May   31, Carpenter, Mary, and William Spence.

1772, Aug.   6, Carpenter, Mercy, and Amos Wilkinson.
1754, Oct.   3, Carpenter, Sarah, and Samuel Smith.
1744, May 31, Carpenter, William, and Elizabeth Cummins.
1774, Feb. 28, Carr, Ann Agnes, and John Wright.
1805, Nov.   3, Carr, Edward Wills, and Eliz. Oart.
1743, June 11, Carr, Elizabeth, and Thomas Wilkinson.
1773, June 2, Carr, George, and Eliz. Fitzpatrick.
1739, June 13, Carr, James, and Mary Leadbeater.
1732, Nov. 30, Carr, James, and Margaret Campbell.
1800, Aug. 19, Carr, John, and Maria Carman.
1798, Aug. 5, Carr, John, and Mary Dean.
1749, Feb. 24, Carr, Jonathan, and Deborah Robinson.
1766, Dec. 3, Carr, Magnus, and Isabella Sutor.
1736, Nov. 17, Carr, Mary, and Edward Fowler.
1751, April 23, Carr, Mary, and Joseph Wharton.
1761, Aug. 13, Carr, Sarah, and George Gilbert.
1736, Nov. 23, Carr, Sarah, and Stephen May.
1801, May 1, Carragan, William, and Amelia Clapman.
1742, Dec. 16, Carrall, Rebecca, and Anthony Person.
1804, July 21, Carrell, Ann, and William Knight Gill.
1769, July 2, Carrell, Jacob, and Elizabeth Jemmison.
1806, July 26, Carrell, Mary, and John Kline.
1779, Dec. 31, Carrick, Susannah, and John Singer.
1736, June 6, Carrol, Catherine, and John Baker.
1735, May 31, Carroll, Daniel, and Marjory Gore.
1763, April 18, Carroll, James, and Rebecca Bailey.
1796, Nov. 29, Carruthers, Mary, and Joseph Holmes.
1771, June 22, Carry, Henry, and Eliz. Flick.
1727, April 17, Carry, Roger, and S. Witticker.
1775, April 26, Carson, Ann, and John McFeteridge.
1786, Sept. 20, Carson, Mary, and Patrick Howley.
1758, June 22, Carson, Robert, and Elizabeth Yetton.
1803, Feb. 26, Carson, William, and Margaret Wright.
1769, Aug. 4, Carswell, James, and Elizabeth McCracken.
1801, Aug. 1, Cart, Jacob, and Ann Bartram.
1774, May 25, Cart, Jesse, and Cath. Cane.
1758, Sept. 2, Cart, Susannah, and Jacob Powell.
1721, Dec. 24, Carter, Archibald, and Hester Robinson.
1761, Jan. 12, Carter, Benjamin, and Lucy Colton.
1748, Aug. 13, Carter, Catherine, and Anthony Palmer.
1759, Aug. 20, Carter, Daniel, and Margaret Morfrit.
1756, Sept. 27, Carter, Daniel, and Elizabeth Adams.
1728, March 3, Carter, E., and James Jeffreys.
1726, June 15, Carter, J. and M. Lawrence.
1783, Dec. 11, Carter, Jane, and James Brannon.
1722, June 2, Carter, John, and Sarah Baker.

1711, Oct.   9, Carter, John, and Mary Ripley.
1731, Oct.   14, Carter, John, and Alice Nelson.
1747, June   25, Carter, John, and Prescilla Williams.
1755, June   18, Carter, John, and Edd. Raworth.
1734, July   3, Carter, John, and Elizabeth Spriggs.
1761, May   27, Carter, Margaret, and James Taylor.
1765, Oct.   26, Carter, Rebecca, and David Jones.
1784, Aug.   10, Carter, Sarah, and John Malong.
1773, July   3, Carter, Sarah, and Peter Finnemore.
1735, July   20, Carter, Susannah, and Richard Budden.
1754, March 27, Carter, Thomas, and Elizabeth Farmer.
1761, Dec.   24, Carteret, Daniel, and Elizabeth Jones.
1716, Nov.   20, Carthew, Barthols, and Elizabeth Erett.
1732, Sept.   30, Cartlidge, Edmund, and Anne Hendricks.
1790, June   5, Cartman, John, and Charlotte Alcorn.
1776, Feb.   26, Cartmell, John, and Cath. Fleet.
1768, Aug.   21, Cartwright, Cyrus, and Prudence Dickson.
1798, July   16, Cartwright, Joseph, and Hester Hewit.
1794, May   7, Cartwright, Maria, and William Gordon.
1729, Nov.   20, Cartwright, T., and Cath. Morgan.
1730, July   12, Carty, Anne, and Charles Brooks.
1759, Feb.   13, Carty, Daniel, and Esther Talbot.
1762, June   8, Carty, Isaac, and Rachel Coswell.
1749, Nov.   14, Carty, Patrick, and Jemima Pue.
1753, Dec.   11, Carver, Elizabeth, and Thomas Buckman.
1796, Nov.   24, Carver, John, and Christina Sell.
1760, Nov.   22, Carver, Martha, and Isaac Worthington.
1774, Oct.   8, Carver, Phœbe, and Thomas Tomlinson.
1740, Jan.   27, Carvin, Richard, and Susannah Nelson.
1766, Sept.   2, Cary, Ann, and John McGouish.
1798, Dec.   20, Cary, Mary, and Thomas Porter.
1749, Nov.   25, Cary, Mary, and George Harding.
1747, Dec.   24, Cary, Thomas, and Mary Parker.
1773, June   6, Caryl, Eliz, and Joseph Brewer.
1731-2, Jan. 16, Carwithen, Abigail, and William West.
1772, April   9, Casdrop, Jane, and James Pickering.
1781, Sept.   6, Casdrop, Sarah, and Charles Naglee.
1795, Nov.   17, Case, Henry, and Sophia Wilkinson.
1748, Oct.   19, Case, Jonathan, and Elizabeth Durborow.
1753, Dec.   27, Casedrop, Jane, and Joseph Allen.
1776, Sept.   22, Casey, Adam, and Sarah Kinsey.
1776, Nov.   2, Casey, Jane, and Thomas How.
1739, Sept.   30, Casey, Michael, and Catherine Mullin.
1743, Aug.   14, Casey, Thomas, and Mary Byrn.
1721, Sept.   10, Cash, Caleb, and Rebecca Appleton.
1773, May   11, Cash, Jane, and Simon Murray.

1715, July   3, Cash, Mary, and John Laycock.
1748, Dec.   22, Cash, Rebecca, and Andrew Doz.
1802, Dec.   10, Cason, Patrick, and Eliz. Molloy.
1768, May   3, Cassan, William, and Mary Spencer.
1787, Sept.   20, Cassedy, Eliz., and Richard Ross.
1744, June   5, Cassel, Nicholas, and Mary Fretwell.
1772, Aug.   19, Cassel, Sarah, and John Anson.
1752, July   3, Cassel, Susannah, and Edward Drinker.
1723, Feb.   20, Casselbury, Eve, and John Basset.
1759, May   7, Cassell, John, and Elizabeth Fox.
1763, Oct.   27, Cassell, Joseph, and Mary Evans.
1794, Sept.   25, Cassin, Eliz., and John McDougal.
1720, April   17, Castill, Christian, and James Allen.
1734, July   11, Castle, Anna, and Simon Siron.
1785, May   31, Castle, Mary, and Joseph Paul.
1748, Dec.   15, Castle, Mary, and John Cameron.
1773, Sept.   11, Castle, Thomas, and Margaret Shilling.
1766, Aug.   19, Castle, Thomas, and Margaret Honeygrot.
1785, Dec.   22, Catchem, Mary, and John Farrell.
1768, Nov.   6, Cately, Steward, and Frances Killwell.
1785, Jan.   3, Cater, Ann, and Samuel Dobdell.
1730, March   31, Cathcart, James, and Sarah Miller.
1770, Nov.   13, Cating, Samuel, and Ann Davenport.
1768, Feb.   3, Caton, George, and Mary Hines.
1795, April   2, Caton, Richard, and Sarah Clarke.
1772, June   25, Cattell, Benjamin, and Mary McCall.
1780, Nov.   3, Cattell, David, and Mary Williams.
1780, Nov.   3, Cattell, Jonas, and Sarah Clemens.
1747, July   25, Catts, Christiana Margaretta, and James Murray.
1761, Nov.   30, Cauthorn, David, and Hannah Simpson.
1748, April   20, Cavenaugh, Daniel, and Hannah Damsey.
1799, Aug.   5, Cavenegh, Edward, and Rose McDermot.
1720, July   1, Cawley, Thomas, and Mary Moggrage.
1773, March   11, Cawstring, Samuel, and Hannah Price.
1796, Feb.   25, Celoh, Peter, and Cath. Meloy.
1760, June   1, Cemer, Richard, and Mary England.
1785, June   16, Cermer, Prudence, and Hugh Crawford.
1757, Dec.   22, Chaband, John, and Ann Turner.
1780, Aug.   30, Chaboud, Eliz, and Thomas Earnest.
1738, May   26, Chads, Henry, and Anne Robins.
1714, Feb.   12, Chads, Sarah, and Mordecai Cloud.
1733, Feb.   5, Chafin, Susannah, and James Cooper.
1758, May   31, Chalkley, Martha, and Thales Cardock.
1747, Oct.   9, Chalmler, Isabell, and William Edwards.
1715, Feb.   13, Chalona, Mary, and William Vellecott.
1778, Oct.   8, Chaloner, John, and Ann Simpson.

1767, April   20, Chamber, Mary, and John Kemble.
1783, June   11, Chamberlain, Benjamin, Esqr, and Eliz. Foreman.
1762, Dec.   25, Chamberlain, Benjamin, and Sarah Collins.
1754, Nov.   27, Chamberlain, Isaac, and Elizabeth Thomas.
1768, Aug.   27, Chamberlain, Mary, and Daniel Green.
1786, Nov.   11, Chamberlain, Richard, and Rhody Wright.
1784, Dec.   15, Chambers, Alexander, and Eliz. Ayrs.
1742, Sept.   24, Chambers, Benjamin, and Sarah Patterson.
1770, Nov.   29, Chambers, John, and Deborah Hall.
1796, July   23, Chambers, William, and Elenor Carney.
1782, March   5, Chamney, John, and Mary Fullerton.
1789, Dec.   17, Chancellor, Salome, and Robert Wharton.
1790, June   24, Chancellor, William, and Hannah Wharton.
1749, May   13, Chancelour, Elizabeth, and Alexander Stedman.
1762, Nov.   19, Chancellour, Lethia, and Capt. Benjamin Spring.
1758, Aug.   30, Chandler, Esther, and Isaac Chandler.
1758, Aug.   30, Chandler, Isaac, and Esther Chandler.
1773, Jan.   30, Chandler, John, and Anna Jones.
1768, May   12, Chandler, Margaret, and William Smith.
1731-2, Feb.   8, Chandler, Mary, and Jonathan Price.
1752, March 30, Chandler, Susannah, and Thomas Coates.
1712, Sept.   10, Chandler, William, and Ann Boweter.
1746, July   7, Channel, James, and Rebecca Key.
1767, Dec.   29, Channel, James, and Hester Bankson.
1785, Jan.   8, Channuel, Susannah, and Daniel Tillinhurst.
1770, May   12, Channell, Rebecca, and George Pickering.
1794, Aug.   7, Chapman, George Archer, and Eliza Norton.
1805, Nov.   20, Chapman, Mary, and William Griffith.
1747, Dec.   24, Chapman, Samuel, and Martha Moore.
1731, Dec.   9, Chapman, Susannah, and William Danford.
1767, April   25, Chappel, Elizabeth, and James Miller.
1757, Jan.   22, Chappel, Mary, and Charles Meredith.
1794, July   3, Chardon, Anthony, and Eleanor Rawle.
1751, May   27, Charir, George, and Mary Bane.
1786, Feb.   8, Charles, Rasrol, and Eliz. Long.
1749, Jan.   22, Charleton, William, and Isabella Taylor.
1737, Nov.   21, Charlton, Thomas, and Lettice Bell.
1776, Nov.   27, Chartres, James, and Margaret Early.
1713, Oct.   26, Chase, Thomas, and Mary Apleton.
1727, Oct.   11, Chatam, Ed., and S. Crap.
1770, June   1, Chaterton, Frances, and Joseph Page.
1796, March 28, Chatham, Lewis, and Susan Johnson.
1778, Aug.   23, Chaton, James, and Rebecca Nicholson.
1733, April   16, Chatwin, Timothy, and Elizabeth Harmer.
1803, June   8, Chavres, Mary, and Michael Shields.
1767, Sept.   1, Cheeseman, Mary, and Edward Ireland.

N

1735, March 19, Cheesemond, Abigail, and Patrick Monroe.
1779, Aug. 17, Cheesman, Ann, and James Bruister.
1759, March 22, Cheesman, Bars¹ᵃ, and Jonathan Morgan.
1791, March 24, Cheesman, Benjamin, and Mary Eyre.
1752, Nov. 4, Cheesman, Elizabeth, and Richard Tis.
1786, Feb. 16, Cheesman, Freeman, and Ann Cummings.
1785, Sept. 13, Cheesman, Sarah, and Richard Draper.
1797, May 16, Cherry, Margaret, and James Fulton.
1740, July 7, Chester, Anne, and Alexander Finney.
1736, Oct. 27, Chester, Mary, and Thomas Finney.
1786, May 14, Chester, Susannah, and Isaac Brazinton.
1796, Sept. 20, Chestnut, James, and Mary Coxe.
1801, Oct. 17, Chittenden, Nathaniel, and Cath. Rogers.
1747, Dec. 17, Chevalier, Elizabeth, and John Banton.
1782, Feb. 19, Chevalier, Isabella, and Capt. James Turner.
1760, Feb. 13, Chevalier, John, and Eleanor Berkley.
1735, April 24, Chevalier, Judith, and Joseph Warrell.
1800, Jan. 12, Chevalier, Maria, and John Leonard.
1759, May 16, Chevalier, Peter, and Mary Renaudett.
1721, Dec. 28, Chevars, Adam, and Rebecca Deborax.
1757, Jan. 3, Chever, Abigail, and Thomas Weaver.
1782, Sept. 15, Chew, Anne, and David Wallace.
1757, Sept. 12, Chew, Benjamin, and Elizabeth Oswald.
1764, May, 28, Chew, Edward, and Mary Thomas.
1774, May 26, Chew, Eliz., and Edward Tilghman.
1804, Oct. 28, Chew, Henry, and Mary Curtis.
1760, Oct. 21, Chew, Jesse, and Mary Richards.
1793, April 1, Chew, Juliana, and Philip Nicklin.
1787, May 18, Chew, Margaret, and John Howard.
1768, May 18, Chew, Mary, and Alexander Willcox, Esqr.
1770, Dec. 9, Chew, Michael, and Mary Robinson.
1769, May 23, Chew, Patience, and John Williams.
1786, Oct, 23, Chew, Sarah, and John Galloway.
1758, Nov. 1, Chew, Sarah, and David Aldridge.
1796, Oct. 3, Chew, Sophia, and Henry Philips.
1755, Dec. 26, Cheyne, Thomas, and Mary Taylor.
1742, Dec. 22, Cheyney, Francis, and Sarah Young.
1794, Dec. 26, Cheyney, John H., and Eliz. Johns.
1757, March 18, Cheyney, Mary, and Richard Riley.
1765, Sept. 16, Cheyney, Richard, and Mary Hannum.
1746, Nov. 24, Chievers, Rachel, and Thomas Edwards.
1719, Nov. 30, Chilcoat, T., and Hannah Stone.
1774, Dec. 12, Chilcot, Dorothy, and Edward Stone.
1722, Jan. 30, Chilcot, Elizabeth, and John Keyte.
1761, Dec. 5, Chilcot, George, and Dorothy Talbert.
1767, Nov. 1, Child, Catherine, and John Waters Martindale.

1795, Dec. 24, Child, Hannah, and John Mayberry.
1800, Sept. 29, Chills, Samuel, and Margaret Farill.
1751, Nov. 11, Childs, Thomas, and Katherine Bryly.
1799, July 11, Childs, Thomas, and Mary Smith.
1740, April 15, Chilen, Elizabeth, and George Christopher Peler.
1730, Nov. 3, China, John, and Anne Heickman.
1730, April 20, Chiney, Elizabeth, and Jacob Vernon.
1758, July 20, Chissadee, Charlotte, and Donald Monro.
1729, March 6, Chivers, Rebecca, and John Johnson.
1742, Dec. 3, Chocolier, Ann, and William Bromwich.
1804, Nov. 23, Cholet, David, and Eliz. Leonard.
1777, Jan. 29, Cholones, Charles Christian, and Jane Frances Osborne.
1803, March 24, Christian, Cath., and William Wickham.
1730, Dec. 31, Christian, Elizabeth, and James Downes.
1772, April 30, Christian, Frederick, and Eliz. Hodgkinson.
1781, Feb. 25, Christian, Judith, and Joseph Long.
1753, Sept. 28, Christian, Mary, and Patrick Cunningham.
1801, May 2, Christian, Peter, and Theresa Scull.
1801, Feb. 1, Christian, Thomas, and Ann Essex.
1779, Nov. 25, Christian, William, and Reb. Flood.
1797, April 14, Christie, Robert, and Margaret Cunningham.
1773, Sept. 23, Christopher, Rachel, and Charles Farrier.
1765, Jan. 15, Christy, Catherine, and James Allen.
1764, April 29, Christy, William, and Sarah Laughrey.
1767, Feb. 19, Chrystie, John, and Mary Paine.
1795, Feb. 25, Church, James, and Mary McDermot.
1798, April 19, Church, John, and Cath. Duffield.
1756, Jan. 3, Church, Mary, and Robert Levers.
1805, Feb. 4, Church, Philip Schuyler, and Ann Matilda Stewart.
1725, Oct. 13, Church, S., and T. Goodwin.
1763, March 3, Churchman, Hannah, and John Woods.
1790, Aug. 29, Cirby, Edward, and Hester Gardener.
1792, March 13, Clackner, Cath., and Christopher Miller.
1745, June 25, Clampfert, Margaret, and Peter Ulrich.
1762, Aug. 12, Clampshear, Elizabeth, and Benjamin Ramshear.
1801, May 1, Clapman, Amelia, and William Carragan.
1795, April 14, Clapp, Allen, and Margaret Redman.
1804, March 4, Clark, Abisha, and Rebecca Gibbons.
1760, Jan. 3, Clark, Abner, and Hannah Gilbert.
1772, Nov. 26, Clark, Ann, and Patrick Hamilton.
1767, Nov. 14, Clark, Ann, and Samuel Wilson.
1741, Sept. 9, Clark, Ann, and Thomas Welch.
1756, April 20, Clark, Anne, and Charles Day.
1751, Feb. 14, Clark, Anne, and William Hays.
1763, June 14, Clark, Catherine, and Robert Thicker.

1736, Oct.   31, Clark, Christian, and Benoni Gregory.
1779, April   8, Clark, David, and Mary Walheim.
1716, July   4, Clark, Deborah, and Robert Stacy.
1745, May   14, Clark, Henry, and Anne Jones.
1728, Nov.   3, Clark, James, and Eliz. Parkins.
1790, May   20, Clark, Jane, and William Gurton.
1769, Dec.   28, Clark, Joel, and Phœbe Ward.
1713, May   11, Clark, Jonas, and Mary Long.
1785, June   23, Clark, Joseph, and Mary Masters.
1805, Dec.   30, Clark, Joseph, and Mary Gardner.
1740, July   25, Clark, Joseph, and Alice Morris.
1768, April   6, Clark, Josiah, and Patience Allen.
1740, Dec.   14, Clark, Lydia, and Robert Fox.
1720, June   30, Clark, Mary, and Philip Lenthal.
1773, July   24, Clark, Mary, and James French.
1772, Nov.   20, Clark, Rachel, and John Anes.
1776, Jan.   19, Clark, Richard, and Ann Owen.
1805, July   22, Clark, Samuel, and Eliz. Lecrone.
1764, Dec.   22, Clark, Sylla, and James Davis.
1763, Feb.   23, Clark, Thomas, and Rebecca Clary.
1796, Oct.   28, Clark, William, and Mary Orr.
1742, Dec.   2, Clarke, Ann, and George O'Kill.
1795, Feb.   14, Clarke, Benjamin, and Esther Wayne.
1793, Dec.   31, Clarke, Cath., and Elijah Miller.
1792, Dec.   20, Clarke, Ephraim, and Hannah Claypole.
1794, July   28, Clarke, George, and Eleanor Wright.
1750, Jan.   28, Clarke, Hannah, and Francis Sewer.
1804, Oct.   28, Clarke, Isabella, and Abraham Douglass.
1801, Feb.   1, Clarke, James, and Hannah Cusack.
1794, July   27, Clarke, Jane, and John R. Lynch.
1751, Nov.   11, Clarke, John, and Eleanor Armstrong.
1753, Aug.   13, Clarke, Lydia, and Darby Durel.
1800, July   31, Clarke, Marsh, and Mary Fallon.
1741, June   7, Clarke, Mary, and James Benbridge.
1796, March 13, Clarke, Michael, and Ann White.
1795, Oct.   4, Clarke, Molly, and Francis Bernandy.
1751, July   17, Clarke, Robert, and Bridget Savoy.
1795, April   2, Clarke, Sarah, and Richard Caton.
1796, May   26, Clarke, Sarah, and George Way.
1801, Nov.   16, Clarke, Thomas, and Eliz. Myers.
1795, Aug.   23, Clarke, Thomas, and Jane Ramsey.
1746, May   8, Clarke, William, and Sarah Jones.
1780, July   27, Clarkson, Ann, and George Bringhurst.
1761, May   13, Clarkson, Gerardus, and Mary Flower.
1795, Nov.   28, Clarkson, Jacob, and Jane Stephenson.
1761, June   29, Clarkson, Rachel, and John Mullan.

1785, Nov.   24, Clarkson, Sarah, and Robert Ralston.
1766, Nov.   6, Clare, Elizabeth, and John Perkins.
1755, June   12, Clare, Margaret, and William Williams.
1795, April   26, Claridge, Philip, and Hannah Santloe.
1763, Feb.   23, Clary, Rebecca, and Thomas Clark.
1786, Feb.   2, Clary, Sarah, and Thomas Claude Beckett.
1742, Dec.   23, Class, Humphrey, and Hester Clere.
1738, Sept.   2, Classon, Mary, and George Heap.
1794, April   5, Claxson, John, and Mary Asheton.
1764, Sept.   15, Claxton, Ann, and Richard Sewell.
1803, Nov.   1, Claxton, James, and Lauraher Jackson.
1805, June   6, Claxton, Sarah, and Jesse Elwards.
1721, Feb.   19, Clay, Ann, and Robert Bolton.
1799, July   28, Clay, Ann, and George Mercer.
1768, Nov.   3, Clay, Curtis, and Margaret Wood.
1803, Oct.   22, Clay, Jane, and John Taylor.
1805, Sept.   10, Clay, Joseph, and Mary Ashmead.
1801, April   2, Clay, Margaret, and John Latimer.
1797, April   6, Clay, Robert, and Eliz. Williams.
1795, March   5, Claypole, Ann, and Alex. Mebane.
1783, Nov.   6, Claypole, Cath., and William Fagan.
1756, Oct.   13, Claypole, George, and Mary Parkhouse.
1792, Dec.   20, Claypole, Hannah, and Ephraim Clarke.
1805, April   27, Claypole, Helen, and Nathan Baker.
1742, May   24, Claypole, James, and Rebecca White.
1730, July   30, Claypole, Joseph, and Anne Griffiths.
1756, Oct.   13, Claypole, Joseph, and Mary Wilkinson.
1738, Feb.   13, Claypole, Josiah, and Sarah Jackson.
1794, Oct.   11, Claypole, Mary, and Peter Yorke.
1752, Nov.   2, Claypole, Rebecca, and William Fisher Conwell.
1746, Feb.   2, Claypool, George, and Mary Morris.
1716, April   1, Claypool, Joseph, and Edith Ward.
1781, April   5, Claypoole, David, and Mary Budd.
1763, March   8, Claypoole, James, and Lucia Garwood.
1729, May   1, Claypoole, Rob., and H. Pratt.
1801, April   9, Claypoole, Rebecca, and Joshua Maddox.
1775, Sept.   21, Claypoole, Sarah, and James Withey.
1795, Aug.   27, Clayton, Aaron, and Ann Ford.
1761, Sept.   9, Clayton, Ann, and Ebenezer Harper.
1759, March 22, Clayton, Hannah, and John Fowler.
1801, Oct.   10, Clayton, Margaret, and Lewis Symonds.
1733, June   2, Clayton, Martha, and Solomon Evans.
1754, Feb.   12, Clayton, Philip, and Ruth Mason.
1758, July   25, Clayton, Samuel, and Benjamin Ford.
1772, June   16, Clayton, Thomas, and Mary Walker.
1753, Sept.   8, Cleague Edward, and Rachel Collins.

1727, April   20, Cleaver, Christian, and Wm Molshon.
1715, Feb.   3, Clemens, Hannah, and William Frazier.
1780, Nov.   3, Clemens, Sarah, and Jonas Cattell.
1767, Aug.   20, Clement, John, and Jane Henry.
1742, Dec.   23, Cleve, Hester, and Humphrey Class.
1726, Sept.   18, Cleverly, Sarah, and Jos. Langley.
1726, Sept.   20, Cleverly, W^m, and Alice Joyner.
1804, Feb.   21, Cliffton, Sarah, and Culpepper Bridges.
1735, July   8, Clifton, George, and Mary Collins.
1761, Nov.   14, Clifton, Hannah, and Charles Monk.
1795, Nov.   19, Clifton, John, and Susan Wood.
1759, Aug.   11, Clifton, Mary, and Jasper Carpenter.
1800, Oct.   1, Clifton, Mary, and Franklin Wharton.
1773, April   10, Clifton, Rachel, and Jacob Baldwin.
1763, Aug.   11, Clifton, Thomas, and Martha Jones.
1787, May   23, Cline, Sarah, and John Hungerford.
1775, May   29, Clingham, Barbara, and Thomas Young.
1784, Aug.   12, Clinton, John, and Sarah Harrison.
1784, Dec.   19, Clinton, Joseph, and Mary Burman.
1785, Jan.   13, Clinton, Samuel, and Mary Harrison.
1796, July   14, Cloer, Mary, and Daniel Cornwell.
1740, Feb.   15, Clogas, William, and Sina Thompson.
1769, July   13, Closton, Andrew, and Martha Shockensey.
1720, Oct.   6, Clqud, Anne, and Frederick Ingle.
1762, Jan.   6, Cloud, Elizabeth, and John Bryan.
1771, Dec.   9, Cloud, Mary, and Michael Washington.
1714, Feb.   12, Cloud, Mordecai, and Sarah Chads.
1753, April   16, Cloud, Richard, and Elizabeth Bruno.
1749, Nov.   16, Cloud, Robert, and Magdalen Peterson.
1750, April   15, Cloud, Susannah, and Charles Dougharty.
1710, May   24, Clouter, Ann, and Robert Wallis.
1776, April   18, Clowser, Eliz., and Henry McCormick.
1765, March 18, Clymer, George, and Elizabeth Meredith.
1794, July   9, Clymer, Henry, and Mary Willing.
1794, May   21, Clymer, Margaret, and George McCall.
1742, Jan.   19, Clymer, William, and Ann Judith Robardeau.
1761, Aug.   29, Clugh, Mary, and Lewis Weiss.
1780, April   11, Clum, Joseph, and Eliz. Bunn.
1775, March 25, Coakley, Ann, and James Spencer.
1775, April   20, Coale, Samuel Stringer, and Ann Hopkinson.
1805, Dec.   5, Coarse, Matthias, and Mary Young.
1736, Dec.   4, Coatam, Thomas, and Mary Preston.
1750, June   7, Coates, Abraham, and Susannah Wallace.
1765, Oct.   26, Coates, Alice, and John Langdale, Jr.
1780, April   20, Coates, Eliz., and Anthony Butler.
1788, Aug.   4, Coates, Isaac, and Mary Eyres.

1806, June   5, Coates, John, and Mary Apple.
1803, Oct.   9, Coates, Mary, and Nicholas Leuseur.
1796, May   18, Coates, Mary, and Thomas Robinson.
1731, Oct.   26, Coates, Mary, and Nicholas Crone.
1774, Sept.   7, Coates, Mary, and Robert Cummings.
1771, Oct.   12, Coates, Sarah, and George Moxon.
1793, Sept.   5, Coates, Sarah, and Sampson Levy.
1779, March   9, Coates, Thomas, and Mary Parrish.
1755, Aug.   14, Coates, Thomas, and Marcy Rachford.
1752, March 30, Coates, Thomas, and Susannah Chandler.
1771, March   2, Coates, Thomas, and Mary Allen.
1777, May   11, Coates, Warwick, and Sarah Kelly.
1775, May   11, Coates, William, and Jane Dupuy.
1735, Nov.   10, Coats, Anne, and Henry Goodwin.
1735, Feb.   18, Coats, Daniel, and Mary Lindsey.
1711, June   16, Coats, John, and Mary Hall.
1738, Aug.   17, Coats, John, and Sarah Elford.
1765, April   13, Coats, Lindsay, and Ruth Hughs.
1747, Jan.   4, Coats, Martha, and William Sheed.
1750, April   3, Coats, Mary, and Richlost Alberton.
1745, July   6, Coats, Rachel, and Benjamin Hartley.
1731, Oct.   21, Coats, Sarah, and Thomas Penrose.
1758, May   27, Coatum, Mary, and Thomas Leech.
1755, Aug.   27, Cobb, Eleanor, and Jonas Hopman.
1750, May   26, Cobourn, Job, and Sarah Moore.
1753, Nov.   24, Cobourn, *alias* Cockburn, James, and Hannah
                      Bezey, *alias* Braseley.
1743, April   4, Coburn, James, and Ann Bedford.
1769, April   14, Coburn, Jacob, and Sarah Evans.
1756, Jan.   19, Coburn, John, and Hannah Monro.
1736, Feb.   9, Coburn, Sarah, and John Harris.
1774, Dec.   1, Coburn, Sarah, and Thomas Budd.
1759, Jan.   2, Coburn, Sarah, and John Bartlet.
1790, Dec.   20, Cochran, Alexander, and Eliz. Doyle.
1765, Jan.   15, Cochran, Jane, and Robert York.
1765, Dec.   10, Cochran, Matthew, and Eleanor Gilmore.
1783, Feb.   17, Cochran, Patrick, and Mary Etchews.
1728, Oct.   25, Cockburn, James, and Mary Davies.
1726, Sept.   25, Cockle, Nic., and Margaret Dermod.
1798, Dec.   24, Cockran, Hugh, and Mary Hanna.
1793, Aug.   5, Cockran, Mary, and Daniel Adgate.
1796, Feb.   7, Cockran, Mary, and Patrick Dougherty.
1731-2, Jan. 15, Cockran, Samuel, and Margaret Gilbert.
1800, July   6, Cockrin, James, and Martha Nelson.
1750, March 19, Cocks, Hannah, and Samuel Ap Owen.
1756, March   5, Codd, John, and Mary Fish.

1768, May 29, Coffee, James, and Rebeccah Winterton.
1794, July 10, Coffee, Mary Ann, and Benjamin Bagnall.
1758, April 18, Coffin, Anthony, and Jane Jones.
1772, April 20, Coffin, Mary, and William Walters.
1763, Sept. 13, Coggins, Ann, and Ebenezer Tomlinson.
1805, March 3, Cogill, Isaac, and Cath. Burke.
1715, Oct. 30, Coiffart, Mary, and Peter Voyer.
1773, Sept. 16, Cokley, Mary and Israel Shreve.
1785, Nov. 20, Cole, Ann, and Henry Small.
1743, Oct. 20, Cole, Eliz., and John Wakefield.
1804, May 28, Cole, James, and Mary Smith.
1734, Oct. 24, Cole, John, and Mary Harrad.
1789, Oct. 5, Cole, John, and Eliz. York.
1759, Feb. 15, Cole, Mary, and James Rodgers.
1751, Nov. 12, Cole, Mary, and James Hunter.
1753, July 16, Cole, Mary, and Richard Hancock.
1740, Dec. 27, Cole, Philip, and Mary Brumley.
1783, May 12, Cole, Robert, and Sarah Dilkes.
1793, June 13, Cole, Sarah, and William Exon.
1796, March 30, Cole, Susannah, and John Dreer.
1720, April 21, Cole, Thomas, and Elizabeth Bird.
1795, Aug. 17, Cole, William, and Eleanor Richards.
1800, Aug. 18, Coles, Ann, and Thomas Conner.
1800, July 9, Coleburn, Mary, and Simon Toole.
1798, Dec. 9, Coleman, Ann, and John Walker.
1773, Dec. 9, Coleman, Ann, and Joseph Power.
1766, May 26, Coleman, Jane, and Isaac Quigley.
1786, Dec. 28, Coleman, John, and Margaret Hall.
1715, Jan. 27, Coleman, Joseph, and Mary Pidgeon.
1743, Feb. 12, Coleman, Mary, and Joseph Sharp.
1749, May 11, Coleman, Rebecca, and Thomas Stamper.
1712, July 27, Coley, Elizabeth, and Thomas Broome.
1750, Jan. 1, Colgan, William, and Susannah Heath.
1792, June 2, Colhoun, Gustavus, and Martha Spotswood.
1799, Feb. 14, Colhoun, Hugh, and Maria Taylor.
1748, Oct. 12, Colins, Elizabeth, and John Stockerd.
1737, April 13, Collar, William, and Elizabeth Brown.
1731, Sept. 15, Collet, Hester, and Henry Hickman.
1761, Aug. 29, Collet, Robert, and Hannah Durmady.
1721, Feb. 14, Collet, Winifield, and Giles Gambridge.
1733, Jan. 1, Collet, Mary, and Robert Collier.
1753, Jan. 4, Collier, Elizabeth, and William Fawkes.
1733, Jan. 1, Collier, Robert, and Mary Collett.
1735, May 12, Collier, Sarah, and John Dennis.
1803, Jan. 5, Colliner, John, and Mary Rogay.
1805, Aug. 5, Collings, Eliz., and James Ash.

1802, June　　8, Collings, Stephen, and Ann Hamilton.
1745, April　20, Collins, Abraham, and Rachel Ring.
1748, Nov.　29, Collins, Andrew, and Mary Saunders.
1721, Nov.　12, Collins, Ann, and James Newman.
1787, May　10, Collins, Anne Jane, and Samuel Cummings.
1796, April　23, Collins, Arthur, and Isabella Hastings.
1755, Feb.　19, Collins, Edward, and Elizabeth Naylor.
1763, Jan.　26, Collins, Edward, and Margaret Shovelin.
1716, Aug.　20, Collins, Edward, and Margaret Evans.
1744, Aug.　23, Collins, Eliz., and Thomas Sugar.
1794, June　19, Collins, Eliz., and Richard Bland Lee.
1800, May　　3, Collins, Cath., and Daniel M. Traine.
1770, Oct.　　8, Collins, Charity, and Joseph Garret.
1720, June　　7, Collins, Cornelius, and Mary Watkins.
1754, May　23, Collins, Hannah, and Benjamin Bowen.
1747, July　21, Collins, James, and Elizabeth Breding.
1767, Jan.　18, Collins, James, and Eleanor McDonnel.
1710, Feb.　　7, Collins, Joanna, and Swan Yokam.
1785, Nov.　　2, Collins, John, and Jane Spear.
1755, Sept.　　5, Collins, Joseph, and Diana Pricket.
1779, Feb.　20, Collins, Joshua, and Eliz Betlerton.
1745, June　　3, Collins, Larrance, and Eliz Joyner.
1783, May　　1, Collins, Lydia, and Archibald Shaw.
1735, July　　8, Collins, Mary, and George Clifton.
1800, Dec.　27, Collins, Mary, and Dominic McDeed.
1765, Dec.　　7, Collins, Mercy, and Samuel Thomas.
1753, Sept.　　8, Collins, Rachel, and Edward Cleague.
1762, June　12, Collins, Rachel, and Joseph Falconer.
1772, Dec.　　6, Collins, Rebecca, and Arthur Cuttom.
1748, May　14, Collins, Rebecca, and William Ellis.
1754, Aug.　　3, Collins, Richard, and Esther Zanes.
1794, March　6, Collins, Richard, and Ann Eastlick.
1762, Dec.　25, Collins, Sarah, and Benjamin Chamberlain.
1722, March 28, Collins, Sarah, and William Jameson.
1741, Dec.　　7, Collins, Thomas, and Elizabeth Lynn.
1771, March 28, Collis, Joshua, and Martha Betterton.
1759, Jan.　25, Collis, Thomas, and Hornor Brayman.
1766, Sept.　18, Collister, Elizabeth, and Thomas Tomkins.
1757, July　　2, Collom, Richard, and Hannah Stravery.
1755, Jan.　25, Colly, Alexander, and Abigail Coulston.
1792, Oct.　21, Colly, Eliz., and Richard Booker.
1770, Aug.　　2, Colly, James, and Sarah Lithgow.
1734, Dec.　12, Colly, Mary, and Samuel Man.
1758, Nov.　30, Colston, Ann, and Peter Mark.
1761, Jan.　12, Colton, Lucy, and Benjamin Carter.
1760, Nov.　26, Colton, Mary, and Eleazar Twining.

1753, Oct.   6, Colton, Robert, and Jane Williams.
1759, Aug.   2, Colum, William, and Esther Quee.
1749, Feb. 24, Combs, Anne, and Zachariah Van Leuvenigh.
1787, Sept. 20, Combs, John, and Catherine Heron.
1753, Dec. 29, Comely, Mary, and Benjamin Shoemaker.
1744, April 4, Comeran, Daniel, and Martha Smith.
1727, Jan. 26, Commins, Archable and Ann Finton.
1801, July 10, Compton, Edward, and Sarah Nesbett.
1767, May 21, Comron, Deborah, and George May.
1754, April 10, Comron, Isaac, and Tamazen Gerrard.
1772, April 28, Comron, Mary, and John Shaw.
1767, Oct. 20, Comron, Richard, and Esther Norton.
1763, April 14, Conaroe, Rebecca, and Samuel Conaroe.
1763, April 14, Conaroe, Samuel, and Rebecca Conaroe.
1742, Nov. 17, Condin, Catherine, and Joseph Durell.
1749, Aug. 18, Condon, Honour, and Henry Tisdale.
1757, Sept. 10, Condy, Benjamin, and Elizabeth Lathberry.
1782, Feb.   7, Condy, Lydia, and Cladius Paul Raguet.
1768, March 25, Coney, John, and Mary Jones.
1761, Oct.   5, Coningham, Simpson, and Rachel Lampley.
1761, Nov.   7, Connady, Mary, and Ferguson McGucy.
1760, Oct.   1, Connard, Mary, and Thomas White.
1729, July 21, Connard, Mary, and James Ellwood.
1775, June 15, Connel, Daniel, and Margaret Tobin.
1770, Feb. 16, Connell, Eleanor, and James Kirkpatrick.
1767, April 22, Connell, William, and Sarah Richards.
1803, May 11, Connelly, Jane, and John Riker.
1798, Jan. 20, Connelly, Mary, and William Moore.
1755, Oct. 27, Connely, Margaret, and William Nicholson.
1762, Oct. 14, Connely, Sarah, and Daniel Rees.
1804, June 14, Conner, Ellen, and Richard Barrington.
1771, Aug.   3, Conner, John, and Judith Kennedy.
1768, Jan. 25, Conner, Margaret, and Robert Smith.
1712, Dec. 14, Conner, Margaret, and Andrew Johnson.
1804, March 6, Conner, Mary, and John Spooner.
1800, Aug. 18, Conner, Thomas, and Ann Coles.
1772, Feb. 15, Connoly, Isabella, and James McIlmoyle.
1756, Dec.   9, Connoly, Margaret, and Joseph Martindale.
1734, April 20, Connoly, William, and Deborah Boude.
1734, Sept. 9, Connor, Alice, and John Thomas Humphreys.
1801, Jan.   4, Connor, Eliz., and Robert Wilson.
1781, July   9, Connor, James, and Eliz. Young.
1727, April 20, Connor, John, and Mary Roach.
1799, March 3, Connover, John, and Eliz. Brown.
1744, Oct. 10, Conolly, Deborah, and Henry Elwes.
1801, June 18, Conover, William, and Martha Deihl.

1728, Feb.　27, Conoyhall, Cath., and John Harrison.
1758, Oct.　27, Conrad, Benjamin, aud Margaret Richardson.
1754, Dec.　14, Conrad, Jonathan, and Deborah Bowen.
1804, Jan.　24, Conrad, Joseph, and Sarah Meldrum.
1753, March 16, Conrad, Margaret, and Nicholas Osborn.
1782, Feb.　28, Constable, William, and Ann White.
1752, Nov.　2, Conwell, William Fisher, and Rebecca Claypole.
1730–1, Feb. 28, Conwry, Geinor, and John Heard.
1735, May　19, Conyer, Martha, and Henry Matthews.
1744, Sept.　8, Conyers, Jos., and Mary Rivers.
1756, Jan.　29, Conyers, Mary, and Alexander McGee.
1793, June　16, Conyers, Stephen, and Ann Utes.
1773, Oct.　23, Conyngham, Gustavus, and Ann Hockley.
1806, Oct.　2, Conyngham, Cath., and Ralph Peters.
1798, Aug.　12, Conyngham, George, and Cath. McMahon.
1791, April　29, Conyngham, William, and Eliz. Summers.
1800, May　10, Conynham, Cath., and James Ryan.
1770, Sept.　20, Cook, Amelia, and John Keen.
1735, Oct.　19, Cook, Anne, and Saunders Bartholomew.
1784, Jan.　29, Cook, Edward, and Mary Falconer.
1766, Nov.　25, Cook, Elizabeth, and Frederick Stuber.
1791, Nov.　5, Cook, George, and Hester Long.
1799, June　20, Cook, Hester, and George May.
1800, April　2, Cook, Isaac, and Rebecca Richardson.
1798, Jan.　2, Cook, James, and Margaret Purdon.
1741, July　11, Cook, Jane, and John Thornhill.
1772, Jan.　1, Cook, John, and Sarah Haslett.
1750, June　14, Cook, Joseph, and Mary Skidmore.
1789, July　20, Cook, Maria, and William Morgan.
1745, Feb.　15, Cook, Margaret, and John Jewers.
1720, Oct.　9, Cook, Martha, and William Overthrow.
1761, Jan.　8, Cook, Mary and Nathaniel Ferrisby.
1757, Dec.　14, Cook, Mary, and Archibald Gillaspy.
1801, June　29, Cook, Mary, and John Quin.
1746, Sept.　4, Cook, Nathan, and Mary Rogers.
1801, March 25, Cook, Robert, and Mary Wilson.
1761, Jan.　15, Cook, Robert, and Mary Boggs.
1748, Dec.　26, Cook, Rose, Dennis Ferrel.
1803, May　22, Cook, Ruth, and John Bennet.
1756, Nov.　16, Cook, Rev. Samuel, and —— Kearney.
1779, July　31, Cook, Samuel, and Sarah Price.
1759, Dec.　18, Cook, Sarah, and Robert Black.
1803, April　2, Cook, Spencer, and Barbara Farrier.
1750, Nov.　12, Cook, Susannah, and Thomas Barton.
1717, May　20, Cook, Thomas, and Sarah Nowell.
1804, Jan.　24, Cook, William, and Eliz. Tilgman.

1739, May   17, Cooke, Edward, and Elizabeth Wint.
1736, Sept.   4, Cooke, Jane, and John Meem.
1743, April   9, Cooke, Mary, and Nathaniel Ambler.
1715, Sept. 26, Cooke, Richard, and Mary Baily.
1760, Sept. 30, Cookson, Hannah, and Joseph Galloway.
1768, Aug.   22, Cool, Catherine, and James Judson.
1741, Oct.   31, Coolins, Susannah, and Robert May.
1773, May   13, Coomb, Rev. Tho⁵, and Sarah Badger.
1745, June   25, Coombs, Jane, and James Thomson.
1749, May   22, Coombs, Mary, and Stephen Hains.
1791, Oct.   22, Coomby, Hannah, and George Bensell.
1761, Dec.   2, Cooper, ——, and Moses Long.
1798, Jan.   11, Cooper, Ann, and John McElroy.
1720, Nov.   28, Cooper, Benjamin, and Elizabeth Kelley.
1729, Sept. 22, Cooper, Clement, and Marg⁵ Sherlock.
1744, July   14, Cooper, Edward, and Sarah Presor.
1784, Jan.   28, Cooper, Eliz, and John Thornhill.
1780, Oct.   30, Cooper, George, and Eliz. Shute.
1752, July   25, Cooper, Hannah, and John Mickle.
1793, June   13, Cooper, Hugh, and Jane Knox.
1721, Dec.   16, Cooper, Israel, and Margaret Jenkins.
1769, Sept. 26, Cooper, James, and Elizabeth Morris.
1762, Dec.   15, Cooper, James, and Anne Stewart.
1733, Feb.   5, Cooper, James, and Susannah Chafin.
1750, Sept. 18, Cooper, James, and Hannah Hibbs.
1755, Oct.   23, Cooper, John, and Winneford Linch.
1780, Oct.   19, Cooper, Joseph, and Mary Justice.
1771, Jan.   10, Cooper, Keziah, and Ezekial Cox.
1775, Jan.   1, Cooper, Laetitia, and Joseph Ashton.
1748, Oct.   12, Cooper, Lydia, and Cadwalader Morgan.
1771, Oct.   22, Cooper, Mary, and Robert Maxwell.
1758, June   5, Cooper, Patrick, and Margaret Wilson.
1769, May   3, Cooper, Peter, and Mary Moore.
1760, May   8, Cooper, Robert, and Rachel Glover.
1757, June   10, Cooper, Sarah, and Nathaniel Pelty.
1787, April   5, Cooper, Thomas, and Jane Bonnell.
1796, June   18, Cooper, Thomas, and Susanna Lecoy.
1779, Dec.   25, Coot, Benjamin, and Mary Shoemaker.
1786, May   18, Copeland, Grace, and John McDeermott.
1785, Oct.   12, Copeland, Mary, and Joseph Gray.
1779, Dec.   18, Coperthwaite, Col. Joseph, and Sarah West.
1747, March 17, Copp, Henry, and Susannah Lamplorgh.
1729, Aug.   2, Coppack, Sarah, and T. Wooley.
1797, Aug.   17, Copper, Eliz, and Timothy Matlack.
1782, July   18, Coppock, James, and Jane Reeves.
1768, July   20, Coppock, William, and Eliz. Kenny.

1774, Oct.   27, Coran, Mary, and John Knight.
1743, July   22, Corbet, Elizabeth, and Thomas Swain.
1716, April   7, Corbet, Hannah, and Joseph Kingston.
1737, May   24, Corbet, Lillias, and Robert Johnston.
1747, Aug.   31, Corbet, Patrick, and Anne Dunnavan.
1711, Aug.   12, Corbet, William, and Hannah Holms.
1750, April   23, Corbett, Anne, and James Freeman.
1786, May   21, Corbett, Mary, and Matthew Spilyard.
1771, May   27, Corbett, William, and Sarah Phipps.
1797, Aug.   17, Corbin, George, and Mary Stewart.
1739, Dec.   25, Cordell, Richard, and Maria Barbara Pashe.
1763, May   16, Cordery, Henry, and Mary Wildman.
1753, Aug.   24, Coren, Jeremiah, and Jane Ellis.
1791, May   28, Coren, Sarah, and William Hewlings.
1709, Feb.   16, Corfey, Mary, and John Tilley.
1773, Jan.   21, Corgal, Thomas, and Ann Elliott.
1768, Feb.   18, Corgail, Thomas, and Sarah Hartshorn.
1782, June   30, Coriel, Peter, and Mary McGinnis.
1786, June   3, Corin, Mary, and John Henry Christian Boehme.
1801, April   25, Corl, Ann, and Thomas Davis.
1739, Feb.   22, Corleene, Agnes, and Godfrey Kasbeer.
1799, Oct.   11, Corless, Matthias, and Susanna Harper.
1745, May   2, Cormont, Anne, and Thomas Baird.
1786, Nov.   16, Corn, Michael, and Sarah Mahone.
1806, Jan.   30, Corneau, John Baptiste, and Hannah Lawrence.
1795, June   1, Cornett, Eleanor, and John Jones.
1796, July   14, Cornwell, Daniel, and Mary Cloer.
1758, June   13, Cornwall, Joseph, and Ruth Miller.
1769, Sept.   7, Corren, Elizabeth, and Richard Robertson.
1775, April   20, Corry, Walter, and Bridget Downey.
1806, May   8, Corrigan, John, and Cath. Tagart.
1795, March   7, Corry, Eliz, and Robert Graham.
1769, June   24, Corry, George, and Elizabeth Gordon.
1769, Dec.   24, Corry, Hannah, and Thomas Miles.
1765, April   29, Corse, Jacob, and Hannah Prigg.
1733, April   28, Corslett, William, and Elizabeth Edwards.
1758, March   21, Cosby, Grace, and Daniel Cunningham.
1735, Feb.   9, Cosins, Elizabeth, and Theophilus Grew.
1742, March   12, Cosins, Sarah, and Thomas Stammars.
1747, Dec.   31, Cosster, Samuel, and Ann Thomas.
1762, June   8, Cosswell, Rachel, and Isaac Carty.
1794, June   21, Costa, Joseph, and Ann Tallman.
1731, June   28, Costard, George, and Mary Roads.
1734, July   29, Costener, Anne, and James Brownley.
1794, Dec.   20, Cotman, Rachel, and John Garland.
1744, May   16, Cotman, Rebecca, and Thomas Asheton.

1794, May   22, Cotman, Susannah, and Joseph Harbeson.
1773, March   6, Cotman, Susannah, and John Quee.
1714, June   24, Cotter, Mary, and William Dunwick.
1794, Nov.   18, Cotter, Michael, and Johannah Herring.
1797, April   24, Cottineau, Eloisa Maria Magd. Josephine, and
                   Olando Denny.
1801, Oct.   3, Cottman, Hannah, and Thomas Nightingale.
1801, Oct.   6, Cottman, Hester, and Jesse Hallowell.
1732, Oct.   24, Cottman, Jos., and Hannah Wilmerton.
1804, March   29, Cotman, Joseph, and Sarah Evinger.
1750, Dec.   20, Couch, Daniel, and Phoebe Pollard.
1758, March   21, Coughlin, Elizabeth, and John Middleton.
1755, Jan.   25, Coulston, Abigail, and Alexander Colly.
1760, Jan.   10, Coulston, Sarah, and John Lauderman.
1786, Sept.   7, Coulson, William, and Eve Hooven.
1735, March   13, Coultas, James, and Elizabeth Ewen.
1800, March   20, Coulter, John and Ann Dolby.
1800, Jan.   16, Coulter, Joseph, and Mary Gitts.
1789, Nov.   22, Coultry, Samuel, and Eliz. Pritchard.
1800, April   10, Coumbs, Caleb, and Rachel Butler.
1770, April   12, Coupar, Robert, and Mary Dunlap.
1762, Aug.   2, Coupin, Peter, and Dorothy Capout.
1795, Dec.   10, Courtenay, Sarah, and James Henderson.
1731, Nov.   20, Courtnay, Conway, and Rebecca Lyne.
1804, June   30, Courtney, Harriet, and Peter H. Shenck.
1757, Jan.   13, Couse, Isaac, and Elizabeth Stille.
1779, March   17, Cousin, Nancy, and Benjamin Fordham.
1774, Sept.   27, Covinger, Jane, and John Parke.
1806, May   19, Cowan, Ann, and Benjamin Lincoln.
1792, July   14, Cowan, James, and Anna Whiteman.
1742, July   31, Cowan, Mary, and William Ballard.
1799, March   2, Cowell, Mary, and Patrick Gygham.
1741, Dec.   5, Cowely, Mary, and John Bankson.
1781, Sept.   29, Cowen, Benjamin, and Ann Berriman.
1768, July   25, Cowen, Henry, and Ann Russell.
1732, June   7, Cowen, William, and Susannah Fleming.
1771, Sept.   14, Cowgill, Sarah, and John Walker.
1731, Oct.   2, Cowles, John, and Jane Smith.
1800, Feb.   13, Cowley, John Thomas, and Margaret Craig.
1736, March   8, Cowley, Rebecca, and George Miller.
1742, Jan.   23, Cowley, Sarah, and Thomas Wells.
1756, July   9, Cowman, Atwood, and Mary Morgan.
1772, Nov.   19, Cowper, Eliz, and Edward Taber.
1795, Jan.   29, Cowperthwaite, Hewlings, and Sarah Tallman.
1795, Oct.   23, Cowperthwaite, Mark, and Margaret Jones.
1769, March   30, Cox, Altha, and Peter Wikoff.

1769, April   8, Cox, Ann, and Thomas Marshall.
1765, June   26, Cox, Catherine, and James How.
1783, April   24, Cox, Charles, and Eliz. Huston.
1721, Feb.   1, Cox, Charles, and Ann Wheeler.
1767, March 25, Cox, Elizabeth, and William Moore.
1804, April   3, Cox, Eliz., and Horace Binney.
1797, Nov.   30, Cox, Eliza, and James Akin.
1767, Feb.   4, Cox, Elizabeth, and John Heathcote.
1771, Jan.   10, Cox, Ezekial, and Keziah Cooper.
1735, Nov.   15, Cox, Gabriel, and Eleanor Peterson.
1722, May   27, Cox, Gabriel, and Mary Gill.
1731, July   17, Cox, Gertrude, and Andrew Boore.
1780, Feb.   26, Cox, Isaac, and Cath. Beekman.
1795, March 19, Cox, Jacob, and Eliz. Duffey.
1784, Oct.   21, Cox, James, and Cath. Sitgreaves.
1748, Nov.   24, Cox, Jane, and Thomas Milington.
1756, June   10, Cox, John, and Sarah Edgil.
1760, Nov.   16, Cox, John, and Esther Bowes.
1757, Dec·   14, Cox, Jonathan, and Hannah Parker.
1747, June   21, Cox, Margaret, and Robert Many.
1720, Aug.   6, Cox, Martha, and Walter Griffith.
1766, Jan.   9, Cox, Martha, and Isaac Wikoff.
1735, Dec.   27, Cox, Mary, and Nathan Bane.
1721, April   14, Cox, Mary, and Joseph Platts.
1723, March 13, Cox, Mary, and Michael Harrison.
1759, Jan.   31, Cox, Mary, and Samuel McCall.
1777, July   16, Cox, Mary, and Jacob Morris.
1783, May   1, Cox, Mary, and William Laurence.
1767, Nov.   11, Cox, Rachel, and Francis Illingworth.
1782, Oct.   17, Cox, Rachel, and John Stephens, Esqr.
1763, Dec.   21, Cox, Rebecca, and John Stinson.
1782, Dec.   2, Cox, Rebecca, and William McIlvane.
1749, April   29, Cox, Samuel, and Elizabeth Sprouce.
1801, July   26, Cox, Sarah, and William McDonald.
1773, March 28, Cox, Sarah, and Enous Scalinger.
1737, May   3, Cox, Susannah, and Michael Huling.
1734, Aug.   24, Cox, Thomas, and Mary Butcher.
1732, Oct.   2, Cox, William, and Hannah Burden.
1750, April   10, Cox, William, and Mary Francis.
1792, Dec.   30, Cox, William, and Maria Scull.
1796, July   4, Cox, William, and Sarah White.
1759, Dec.   6, Coxe, Charles, and Rebecca Wells.
1788, Feb.   26, Coxe, Christian, and Peter Stecker.
1800, Jan.   9, Coxe, Daniel William, and Margaret Burd.
1771, June   5, Coxe, Daniel, and Sarah Redman.
1797, June   15, Coxe, Eliz., and Joseph Poole.

1804, Feb.   6, Coxe, Hitty, and John Markoe.
1789, March 26, Coxe, Jacob, and Cath. Hiltzheimer.
1792, May   2, Coxe, John D., and Mary Footman.
1789, Aug. 27, Coxe, John D., and Grace Riche.
1798, March 6, Coxe, John Redman, and Sarah Coxe.
1795, Aug.   2, Coxe, Justice, and Eliz. Paschall.
1797, May 20, Coxe, Margaret, and Constant Freeman.
1771, July 29, Coxe, Martin, and Catherine Smith.
1796, Sept. 20, Coxe, Mary, and James Chestnut.
1788, Oct. 16, Coxe, Rebecca, and John Pew.
1801, Feb. 11, Coxe, Richard, and Thoedosia Henrietta Sayre.
1749, Sept. 13, Coxe, Sarah, and James Wilkinson.
1768, April 21, Coxe, Sarah, and Andrew Allen, Esqr.
1798, March 6, Coxe, Sarah, and John Redman Coxe.
1796, Sept. 29, Coxe, Susan, and Robert Irwin.
1774, Dec. 21, Coxe, Thomas, and Ann Peterson.
1716, Dec.   4, Coxe, William, and Mary Grisley.
1796, July 21, Coy, Ann, and Robert Mercer.
1761, June 22, Coy, Mary, and John Kidd.
1721, Jan. 13, Coyle, Michael, and Margaret Jones.
1796, Dec.   7, Coyles, Edward, and Mary Ireland.
1802, Aug. 25, Coyles, James, and Margaret Campbell.
1802, July 14, Coyles, James, and Margaret McIntire.
1796, Nov.   7, Coyles, Margaret, and Jeremiah Kelly.
1776, March 7, Cozans, Elijah, and Ann Moftat.
1767, Sept. 5, Cozens, Daniel, and Elizabeth Shivers.
1804, Dec.   6, Cozens, Hannah, and John Middleton.
1798, Jan. 11, Cozens, Susan, and Stephen Carmick.
1799, June 10, Cozier, Hannah, and Israel Morton.
1773, Dec. 23, Craddock, William, and Jane Jones.
1793, Feb. 24, Craft, Abigail, and Daniel Skillinger.
1756, Nov.   7, Craft, Charles, and Eleanor Nelson.
1782, Nov. 10, Crafts, Adam, and Susannah Valoiss.
1774, Oct. 15, Crafts, James, and Jemima House.
1752, April 7, Crafts, Mary, and David Gregory.
1785, Oct. 25, Craig, Ann, and Lewis Peter Mirander.
1790, Oct. 11, Craig, Bethiah, and William Dixon.
1759, Sept. 26, Craig, Eleanor, and David McAndrews.
1767, June 5, Craig, Elizabeth, and Charles Molison.
1786, Nov. 27, Craig, Eliz., and Robert Oliver.
1764, July 30, Craig, James, and Elizabeth Wilkinson.
1773, Oct. 26, Craig, James, and Mary Ash.
1790, Oct.   3, Craig, Jared, and Mary Jenings.
1775, March 28, Craig, John, and Ann Driscott.
1760, Nov.   1, Craig, John, and Elizabeth Elder.
1800, Feb. 13, Craig, Margaret, and John Thomas Cowley.

1758, June   13, Craig, Margaret, and William Johnson.
1766, Oct.   29, Craig, Rebeccah, and Hugh Stevenson.
1760, Oct.   30, Craig, Samuel, and Jane Morgan.
1795, Dec.   5, Craig, William, and Hannah Taylor.
1774, April   28, Craig, William, and Mary Johns.
1749, Nov.   1, Crall, Mary, and Daniel Davis.
1793, July   17, Cramond, William, and Sarah Nixon.
1714, June   20, Crampton, Francis, and Ursulah Price.
1742, Nov.   2, Cran, Stephen, and Mary Ryan.
1798, March 4, Crandel, Rachel, and Anthony Pettit.
1771, March 18, Crane, Isabella, and William Iles.
1744, Sept.   8, Cranfield, Michael, and Sarah Warren.
1735, Dec.   19, Crap, Mary, and William Hill.
1727, Oct.   11, Crap, S., and Ed. Chatam.
1721, Aug.   2, Crapp, Jane, and Gibbs Jones.
1731-2, Jan. 9, Crapp, John, and Mary Flower.
1785, Dec.   8, Crarm, John, and Eleanor Dowling.
1791, Sept.   15, Crathorne, Dorothea, and Richard Dale.
1761, March 2, Cratter, Ann, and Alexander French.
1762, Oct.   28, Craven, Mary, and Edward Burman.
1750, Dec.   2, Crawford, Barbara, and William Juniour.
1780, Nov.   16, Crawford, Benjamin, and Sarah Tybout.
1797, March 16, Crawford, Cath., and James Stephenson.
1785, Nov.   14, Crawford, Dan'l, and Thomas Hill.
1766, Aug.   12, Crawford, David, and Lydia Lloyd.
1749, June   4, Crawford, Elizabeth, and Edward Varnum.
1785, June   16, Crawford, Hugh, and Prudence Cermer.
1781, Dec.   20, Crawford, Isaac, and Eliz. Myers.
1730, Nov.   28, Crawford, Jane, and John Lapelly.
1790, July   1, Crawford, Joanna, and John Harper.
1804, April   2, Crawford, John, and Ann Bourdeaux.
1767, Nov.   30, Crawford, Margaret, and Joseph Beth.
1774, Dec.   11, Crawford, Margaret, and John Tare.
1773, Sept.   9, Crawford, Martha, and Robert Dodds.
1803, Aug.   28, Crawford, Mary, and Joseph Harrison.
1781, Dec.   24, Crawford, Mary, and James Foot.
1746, April   5, Crawford, Peter, and Elizabeth Lowdon.
1799, March 17, Crawford, Samuel, and Ann Bates.
1784, July   22, Crawford, Samuel, and Amey Kale.
1735, Sept.   8, Crawford, Sarah, and Solomon Willoughby.
1750, July   25, Crawley, John, and Anne Lennox.
1760, Aug.   16, Craythorne, Jonathan, and Mary Keene.
1785, Nov.   3, Craythorne, Mary, and John Montgomery.
1749, April 30, Crear, Abraham, and Ann Lennington.
1744, Jan.   29, Creear, Abraham, and Rebecca Moyes.
1796, Feb.   6, Creed, Penelop, and William Burnand Johnson.

1799, May   30, Creed, Susanna, and Bartholomew Winder.
1790, Nov.   17, Creed, Susannah, and Jonathan Wade.
1760, Sept.   25, Creighton, Ann, and Cornelius Tucker.
1730–1, Feb. 14, Crew, William, and Rebecca Evans.
1736, June   14, Cribb, Arthur, and Mary Mantle.
1749, May   8, Cribbs, Mary, and Thomas Dodge.
1794, Sept.   20, Cribbs, Sarah, and Caleb Brickall.
1770, Feb.   3, Cridlend, John, and Mary Hurst.
1799, March 16, Crippen, John, and Susanna Johnson.
1795, Nov.   3, Crippin, John, and Susanna Royal.
1767, Sept.   26, Crippin, Thomas, and Elizabeth Midwinter.
1770, Feb.   19, Crispin, Ann, and John Russell.
1776, April   11, Crispin, Eliz., and Simon Sylvester.
1762, Sept.   14, Crispin, Joseph, and Elizabeth Owen.
1786, Feb.   3, Crispin, Lydia, and Daniel Giberson.
1794, Nov.   15, Crispin, Mary, and Peter Lohra.
1748, July   8, Crispin, Samuel, and Sarah Barnett.
1760, Dec.   31, Croce, Adam, and Bab[a] Starts.
1738, May   10, Crockat, Mary, and Jonathan Mason.
1777, April   1, Croghan, Lawrence, and Ann McManus.
1784, June   23, Crohan, Margaret, and Samuel Warner.
1801, July   26, Cromell, Rebecca, and Stephen Bannum.
1785, Feb.   18, Cromwell, Ascheak, and George Gueirn.
1792, Dec.   17, Cromwell, David, and Rebecca Miller.
1795, May   6, Cromwell, Frances, and Peter Gradiner.
1794, Nov.   5, Cromwell, John, and Ann Horner.
1771, Nov.   16, Cromwell, Philip, and Mary Hawning.
1783, Aug.   28, Crone, Jeremiah, and Cath. Parr.
1731, Oct.   26, Crone, Nicholas, and Mary Coates.
1777, April   3, Croney, Ann, and Dennis Toomey.
1727, Aug.   6, Crook, Mary, and W[m] Lowe.
1788, Dec.   24, Crooks, Joseph, and Catherine DeBooke.
1757, Aug.   26, Crooks, Samuel, and Mary Head.
1793, Jan.   24, Crooks, William, and Margaret Berry.
1717, May   11, Crookshank, William, and Mary Robinson.
1744, Oct.   18, Crookshanks, Alex., and Rebecca Hudson.
1742, Dec.   20, Crookshanks, John, and Susannah Harvey.
1766, Sept.   13, Crosby, Jr., John, and Elizabeth Culin.
1798, April   24, Croscup, Sarah, and James Wells.
1731, Aug.   24, Crosdale, Thomas, and Susannah Hamilton.
1737, April   27, Crosier, Robert, and Susannah Woodworth.
1738, Oct.   8, Cross, Adam, and Mary Panham.
1787, Aug.   14, Cross, Westenera, and Eliz. Thompson.
1801, Aug.   16, Crossart, David, and Mary Henry.
1741, Nov.   12, Crossby, Susannah, and John Oliver.
1803, Oct.   16, Crossing, Margaret, and David Teel.

1749, Feb.　　1, Crossley, Elizabeth, and William Malin.
1747, May　 16, Crossley, John, and Alice Mahlin.
1778, Dec.　　3, Crossman, Eliz., and Jeremiah Simmonds.
1757, Sept.　　3, Croston, Edward, and Ann Forbies.
1725, July　 25, Croswit, W^m, and Hannah Ward.
1729, April　17, Crosswit, W^m, and Ann Asseton.
1794, June　 19, Crotto, Eliz., and Joseph Hughes.
1713, Dec.　　1, Crou, Nicholas, and Honor O'Bryan.
1728, Sept.　 22, Crouch, Eliza, and Wm Ellis.
1796, Dec.　 29, Crouding, Peter, and Eliz. Emory.
1731, Aug.　　1, Crowe, Mary, and William Atkinson.
1768, Oct.　 12, Crowley, Daniel, and Mary Lamb.
1767, Oct.　　8, Crowley, Mary, and Robert Martin.
1785, July　 27, Crowley, William, and Cath. Miller.
1805, March 31, Croysdale, Abraham, and Margaret Lambert.
1765, Sept.　 11, Croyston, Margaret, and Henry Naglee.
1783, May　 20, Crozier, John, and Sarah Price.
1774, Feb.　 23, Crozires, Margaret, and Peter Wells.
1785, Nov.　 19, Crugger, Nicholas, and Ann Markoe.
1803, Nov.　 26, Crukshank, James, and Hester Ash.
1774, March　7, Crumbley, Ralph, and Cath. Vanhorn.
1782, April　25, Cubbin, Christiana, and James Stoy.
1797, March 16, Culberson, Mary, and James Lockart.
1710, Feb.　 16, Culf, Mary, and John Tilly.
1797, April　10, Culin, Eliz., and William Johnston.
1766, Sept.　 13, Culen, Elizabeth, and John Crosby, Junr.
1795, Nov.　 26, Cullen, Margaret, and Caleb Foulke.
1801, Jan.　 18, Culnan, Mary, and Thomas Nicholls.
1745, Jan.　　1, Culp, Matthias, and Hannah Evans.
1799, Nov.　 19, Culver, Richard, and Sarah Fennall.
1793, Aug.　 22, Culver, William, and Eliza Bryan.
1729, April　 8, Cumings, Archibald, and Jane Eliz. Asheton.
1748, May　 28, Cumming, David, and Sarah Jobson.
1786, Feb.　 16, Cummings, Ann, and Freeman Cheesman.
1761, June　 13, Cummings, Ann, and Thomas Brewer.
1800, June　 29, Cummings, Charles, and Eliz. Franks.
1722, Feb.　　4, Cummings, Elizabeth, and Thomas Todd.
1748, April　11, Cummings, Jane Elizabeth, and Robert Jermey.
1785, Feb.　 23, Cummings, Jane, and George Morton.
1798, Feb.　　3, Cummings, Jane, and Jesse Ships.
1795, May　　7, Cummings, John, and Mary Ann Harman.
1788, Dec.　 30, Cummings, John, and Margaret Cummings.
1757, Dec.　　2, Cummings, John, and Jane Purser.
1777, July　　8, Cummings, Juliana, and James Dunlap.
1796, Sept.　　4, Cummings, Margaret, and Barnabas McGhy.
1788, Dec.　 30, Cummings, Margaret, and John Cummings.

1748, Jan.   6, Cummings, Matthew, and Hannah Warren.
1788, Jan. 10, Cummings, Robert, and Jane Marshall.
1774, Sept. 7, Cummings, Robert, and Mary Coates.
1787, May 10, Cummings, Samuel, and Anne Jane Collins.
1767, May 30, Cummings, William, and Catherine Jones.
1786, Aug. 20, Cummins, Caesar, and Rose Sanders.
1744, May 31, Cummins, Elizabeth, and William Carpenter.
1802, April 11, Cummins, Jane, and James Shannon.
1795, Nov. 13, Cummins, John, and Jane Stewart.
1763, June 23, Cummins, Mary, and James Marsh.
1727, Sept. 26, Cummins, Timothy, and Agnes Horton.
1776, July 17, Cumpston, Thomas, and Civel Baker.
1734, Sept. 18, Cunditt, Rebecca, and John Stacey.
1804, Feb. 14, Cunning, Ann, and Richard Alexander.
1796, April 14, Cuningham, Margaret, and Robert Christie.
1800, March 13, Cuningham, Mary, and John Lowe.
1744, Oct. 10, Cunningham, Ann, and John Freeston.
1758, March 21, Cunningham, Daniel, and Grace Cosby.
1796, May 28, Cunningham, Eleanor, and Samuel Hunt.
1795, Aug. 13, Cunningham, Eliz., and Alexander Murray.
1737, Aug. 18, Cunningham, Grissel, and Hugh Baily.
1730, April 7, Cunningham, Margaret, and Richard Berwick.
1757, Oct. 18, Cunningham, Mary, and Arnold Baily.
1714, Nov. 1, Cunningham, Matthias, and Katherine Moll.
1753, Sept. 28, Cunningham, Patrick, and Mary Christian.
1744, Feb. 6, Cunningham, William, and Priscilla Owen.
1771, July 15, Cunrad, Samuel, and Susannah Foulkes.
1750, Jan. 13, Cunyingham, Redmond, and Martha Ellis.
1800, Sept. 29, Curby, Eliz., and Daniel Philips.
1771, May 9, Curden, Margaret, and Hugh Barnet.
1786, July 15, Curl, Ann, and James White.
1786, July 18, Curl, Jane, and John Johnson.
1741, June 5, Curll, Mary, and John Fowler.
1794, July 31, Curran, Nathaniel, and Eliza Fullarton.
1756, Jan. 17, Currant, Nathaniel, and Rebecca Dwight.
1771, Aug. 29, Currey, Ann, and Joseph Rice.
1797, July 26, Currie, Margaret, and John Gildea.
1738, Nov. 30, Currie, William, and Margaret Hacket.
1796, Dec. 1, Currie, William, and Ann Bush.
1754, July 27, Curry, David, and Jane Steward.
1735, Nov. 3, Curry, Jane, and George Davis.
1784, Nov. 13, Curry, Eliz., and John Mackey.
1728, Sept. 12, Curry, Mary, and Thomas Wharton.
1784, Dec. 28, Curtain, Eliz., and Samuel Wayne.
1744, Oct. 1, Curtis, Jane, and George Metz.
1752, Dec. 21, Curtis, John, and Elizabeth Smith.

1791, June 16, Curtis, John, and Isabella Dougherty.
1804, Oct. 28, Curtis, Mary, and Henry Chew.
1730-1, Jan. 14, Curtis, Samuel, and Mary Shrieve.
1800, Nov. 19, Curtis, William, and Charlotte Bruce.
1720, Oct. 30, Curwen, Jane, and Ralph Ward.
1801, Feb.   1, Cusack, Hannah, and James Clarke.
1756, Dec. 21, Custard, Anne, and William Anderson.
1799, Jan. 19, Custard, Arnold, and Hannah Manse.
1768, Sept. 16, Custard, Elizabeth, and William Page.
1746, July   7, Custis, George, and Sarah Muckins.
1795, May   2, Cutbush, Edward, and Ann Reynolds.
1785, Dec.   8, Cuthbert, Ann, and Henry Lattimer.
1799, Dec. 19, Cuthbert, Anthony, and Mary Ogden.
1804, Dec.   1, Cuthbert, James, and Frances Lawersweiler.
1752, June 16, Cuthbert, Rebecca, and William Noblett.
1799, March 12, Cuthbert, Ross, and Emily Rush.
1799, Feb. 21, Cuthbert, Sarah, and Joshua Percival.
1744, May   19, Cuthbert, Thomas, and Ann Wilkinson.
1775, March 2, Cuthbert, Anthony, and Sarah Dixon.
1738, April 25, Cutler, William, and Jane Shepherd.
1710, Nov. 13, Cuttler, Margaret, and William Briggs.
1772, Dec.   6, Cuttom, Arthur, and Rebecca Collins.
1759, Feb. 24, Cuzzins, Louisa, and William Budden.
1803, April 7, Dabadie, John, and Rachel Taylor.
1782, June   2, Daccial, Eliz., and Robert Tarrinan.
1737, May   10, Dagg, John, and Abigail Johnson,
1746, Aug.   5, Dagger, Mary, and John Turner.
1789, Sept. 28, Dagnia, William, and Rebecca Millar.
1790, Oct.   9, Dagworthy, Eliz., and William Wells.
1774, Oct. 20, Dagworthy John, and Martha Cadwallader.
1799, June   3, Dailey, Hannah, and Patrick Galagher.
1774, May   18, Daily, Sarah, and Benjamin Leigh.
1747, Jan. 18, Dalbo, Andrew, and Catherine Van Culin.
1751, Nov. 18, Dalbo, Gabriel, and Mary Empson.
1791, Sept. 15, Dale, Richard, and Dorothea Crathorne.
1777, Oct. 15, Dalhton, Sarah, and Alexander Miller.
1805, April 4, Dallas, Sophia, and Richard Bache.
1795, Nov. 10, Dally, Mary, and William Repton.
1772, May   30, Dalrymple, John, and Eleanor Williams.
1759, Feb. 10, Dalton, John, and Catherine Johnson.
1783, Dec. 29, Dame, Thomas, and Mary Smith.
1748, April 20, Damsey, Hannah, and Daniel Cavenaugh.
1743, May   4, Danby, Susannah, and Peter George.
1721, July 11, Dane, Ann, and William Matthews.
1731, Dec.   9, Danford, William, and Susannah Chapman.
1762, July 21, Dangan, Mary, and Henry Wetley.

1732, April 13, Daniel, Catherine, and Charles Spunaway.
1774, July 13, Daniel, Esther, and John Regan.
1760, April 29, Daniel, George, and Elizabeth Hans.
1789, July 30, Daniel, George, and Sarah Holmes.
1781, Feb. 10, Daniel, George, and Abigail Holmes.
1712, Sept. 27, Daniel, James, and Elizabeth Howard.
1794, Oct. 2, Daniel, John, and Mary Nailer.
1801, Nov. 7, Daniel, Thomas, and Mary Gallagher.
1801, April 18, Daniel, Thomas O., and Mary McClane.
1775, July 20, Daniels, John, and Sarah Ball.
1757, Sept. 13, Daulton, Catherine, and John King.
1794, May 22, D'Arch, Mary, and David Lewis.
1780, Dec. 7, Dardis, Cath., and Æneas Urquhart.
1802, April 30, Dare, Rachel, and Thomas Burke.
1756, July 17, Dark, John, and Mary Kees.
1763, Nov. 28, Dark, Mary, and Ralph Moore.
1800, Dec. 4, Darley, John, and Eleanor Westray.
1801, Oct. 4, Darley, William, and Ann Doctor.
1748, Nov. 29, Darling, Thomas, and Elizabeth Burns.
1737, Dec. 3, Darnel, William, and Anne Lassel.
1758, June 9, Darnell, Mary, and Edward Jefferys.
1794, June 1, Daugart, Peter, and Ann Nester.
1728, Nov. 17, Davall, John, and Mary Whittington.
1770, Nov. 13, Davenport, Ann, and Samuel Cating.
1751, Dec. 13, Davenport, Josiah, and Anne Annis.
1774, Aug. 28, Davenport, Margaret, and Maurice Henessy.
1728, Sept. 14, Davenport, Mary, and Ed. Bullock.
1766, Aug. 7, Davenport, Michael, and Mary Cammel.
1791, Sept. 13, Davenport, Rachel, and William Finley.
1806, July 20, Davenport, William, and Lois Bryant.
1743, Aug. 20, Davey, Hugh, and Elizabeth Woodrop.
1772, Nov. 19, Davey, William, and Rachel Snowden.
1768, Oct. 13, David and Eliz. (Tuscaroras.)
1732, Aug. 14, David, Catherine, and Morgan Roberts.
1728, March 1, David, Evan, and Ann Jones.
1748, April 6, David, George, and Elizabeth James.
1728, March 1, David, John, and Mary Vaughan.
1766, Nov. 29, David, John, and Deborah Williams.
1790, Dec. 8, David, Susannah, and Thomas Latimer.
1733, Sept, 30, David, Charlotta, and Thomas Ryan.
1771, June 22, Davidson, Grace, and El^m Stratton.
1761, June 25, Davidson, James, and Mary Simonson.
1800, Nov. 9, Davidson, James, and Eliz. Wallace.
1767, April 11, Davidson, Mary, and Patrick Brady.
1805, June 1, Davidson, Nathan, and Sarah Lane.
1800, June 12, Davidson, Robert, and Margaret Wallington.

1789, March 15, Davidson, William, and Eliz. Pickering.
1774, Oct.   8, Davie, Richard, and Martha Hall.
1728, Oct.   6, Davies, Ann, and John Battman.
1738, July   20, Davies, Ann, and Benjamin Carpenter.
1732, Aug.   19, Davies, Catherine, and James Wood.
1734, Nov.   30, Davies, David, and Lydia Spencer.
1726, Aug.   28, Davies, Dav., and Kath. Bramel.
1728, March 18, Davies, Deb., and James Kierk.
1739, June   18, Davies, Elizabeth, and James Steward.
1735, Sept.   27, Davies, Elizabeth, David Parry.
1738, May   30, Davies, Isaac, and Elizabeth Bartholomew.
1739, July   6, Davies, Jane, and Peter Ganthony.
1735, May   17, Davies, Margaret, and Robert Heaton.
1728, Oct.   25, Davies, Mary, and James Cockburn.
1736, May   17, Davies, Mary, and William Bayle.
1728, Dec.   26, Davies, Rachel, and Wm Lyde.
1734, Nov.   27, Davies, Susannah, and James Fox.
1726, Oct.   15, Davies, W^m, and Deb. Hammer.
1728, Nov.   14, Davies, W^m, and Martha Thomas.
1728, June   13, Davieson, John, and Margt. Pugh.
1748, Dec.   20, Davis, Abigail, and Evan Lloyd.
1769, April   26, Davis, Ann, and John Davis.
1770, May   9, Davies, Ann, and William Weston.
1800, March 24, Davis, Ann, and Robert Deniston.
1727, June   28, Davis, Ann, and Owen Jones.
1727, May   17, Davis, Ann, and Sam. Scorthorn.
1749, April   2, Davis, Ann, and John Peckles.
1756, July   15, Davis, Ann, and John Ruaby.
1769, June   29, Davis, Arthur, and Elizabeth Murray.
1716, Nov.   6, Davis, Bridgett, and Hans Sute.
1793, July   28, Davis, Cath., and Daniel Dolby.
1772, July   29, Davis, Cath., and Marsena Alloway.
1712, April   27, Davis, Catherine, and William Williams.
1735, Oct.   27, Davis, Catherine, and John Whatnell.
1749, July   16, Davis, Christian, and Richard Arrel.
1749, Nov.   1, Davis, Daniel, and Mary Crall.
1764, June   20, Davis, David, and Elizabeth Rambo.
1798, Nov.   27, Davis, Deborah, and William Green.
1717, Jan.   5, Davis, Dorothy, and Edward Pearsall.
1727, Aug.   11, Davis, Ed., and Mary Davis.
1788, Jan.   24, Davis, Elijah, and Ann Pew.
1735, May   10, Davis, Elizabeth, and David Jones.
1763, April   13, Davis, Elizabeth, and Edward Stretcher.
1774, July   25, Davis, Eliz., and Raworth Weldon.
1757, Dec.   7, Davis, Elizabeth, and William Little.
1791, March 24, Davis, Eliz., and John Borrough.

1804, Nov.   10, Davis, Eliz., and Samuel H. Thomson.
1752, Dec.   29, Davis, Elizabeth, and William Betson.
1747, Aug.   18, Davis, Elizabeth, and James Milner.
1753, Nov.   2, Davis, Elizabeth, and William Barnes.
1800, March 21, Davis, Eliz., and Samuel Mifflin.
1780, Oct.   19, Davis, Eliz., and Benjamin Brooks.
1783, June   16, Davis, Eliz., and James Rosbottom.
1771, April 13, Davis, Eliz., and Carpenter Wharton.
1727, Aug.   6, Davis, Evan, and Rebekah Harris.
1734, Nov.   10, Davis, Evan, and Mary Griffith.
1804, July   14, Davis, George, and Sarah Campbell.
1775, April 22, Davis, George, and Ann Vincent.
1735, Nov.   3, Davis, George, and Jane Curry.
1800, April   3, Davis, Hannah, and Jesse Lewis.
1800, March 16, Davis, Hannah, and John Leverly.
1758, Jan.   12, Davis, Hannah, and Jacob Dubre, Jr.
1749, Sept. 13, Davis, Hannah, and Michael Pugh.
1729–30, Jan. 7, Davis, Henry, and Sarah McCary.
1794, Aug.   7, Davis, Hester, and William Jefferies.
1786, May   28, Davis, Isaac, and Hannah Winters.
1734, Nov.   14, Davis, Isabella, and John Cames.
1746, May   22, Davis, James, and Anne Swormey.
1771, June   20, Davis, James, and Eliz. Isabella Parks.
1764, Dec.   22, Davis, James, and Sylla Clark.
1739, March 15, Davis, James, and Mary Davis.
1722, May   15, Davis, Jane, and Thomas James.
1801, Sept.   7, Davis, Jane, and Collin Pullenger.
1801, Oct.   24, Davis, John, and Sarah Thomas.
1769, April 26, Davis, John, and Ann Davis.
1797, June   4, Davis, John, and Mary Grimes.
1800, Aug.   2, Davis, John, and Sarah Neves.
1767, July   9, Davis, John, and Ann Jones.
1776, May   16, Davis, John, and Ann Kemble.
1727, Dec.   1, Davis, John, and Mary Bower.
1749, Oct.   16, Davis, John, and Margaret Lister.
1709, Nov.   14, Davis, Luellen, and Bridgett Jones.
1721, Feb.   16, Davis, Margaret, and James Mortimer.
1786, May   9, Davis, Margaret, and William Williams.
1782, Dec.   26, Davis, Mary, and William Holgate.
1749, Sept. 23, Davis, Mary, and Foster Parks.
1785, July   7, Davis, Mary, and Joseph Bates.
1727, Aug.   11, Davis, Mary, and Ed. Davis.
1765, Dec.   28, Davis, Mary, and Lewis Jerman.
1721, Aug.   14, Davis, Mary, and Owen Evans.
1732, May   6, Davis, Mary, and Thomas King.
1720, Aug.   15, Davis, Mary, and Richard Vaughan.

1739, March 15, Davis, Mary, and James Davis.
1748, Sept. 24, Davis, Mary, and Thomas Magee.
1748, Sept.   5, Davis, Mary, and Thomas Nevil.
1745, Aug.   8, Davis, Meyrick, and Sarah Miles.
1734, Nov.   6, Davis, Rachel, and Joseph Morgan.
1751, June   23, Davis, Rachel, and Andrew Flood.
1747, Nov.   21, Davis, Rebecca, and Joshua Mitchel.
1744, Dec.   23, Davis, Robert, and Margaret O'Neal.
1714, Dec.   5, Davis, Samuel, and Sarah, Sherin.
1783, May   20, Davis, Samuel, and Mary Allen.
1801, March   9, Davis, Samuel W., and Mary G. Thomas.
1769, Dec.   16, Davis, Samuel, and Elizabeth Shaw.
1768, Aug.   17, Davis, Samuel, and Margaret Philips.
1752, Jan.   20, Davis, Samuel, and Margaret Rowan.
1744, May   19, Davis, Sarah, and John Shearle.
1802, April   5, Davis, Sarah, and Apheus Wood.
1771, June   7, Davis, Sarah, and William Shedaker.
1766, April 10, Davis, Sarah, and William Ogilby.
1720, Aug.   15, Davis, Sarah, and David Evans.
1750, March   1, Davis, Sarah, and William Douglas.
1772, April   8, Davis, Susannah, and Abner Evans.
1765, June   26, Davis, Susannah, and John Roberts.
1730, Aug.   27, Davis, Susannah, and George Morgan.
1801, April 25, Davis, Thomas, and Ann Corl.
1730, Oct.   15, Davis, Thomas, and Elizabeth Linter.
1729, Oct.   12, Davis, Thomas, and Eliz. Watson.
1776, June   20, Davis, Thomas, and Rachel Evans.
1710, Jan.   15, Davis, Thomas, and Mary Finnis.
1767, June   28, Davis, Timothy, and Mary Wiitshire.
1750, Oct.   15, Davis, William, and Mary Wilson.
1762, Feb.   15, Davis, William, and Eleanor Smith.
1723, Dec.   12, Davis, William, and Sarah Polson.
1787, Oct.   10, Davis, William, and Eliz. McLean.
1770, Sept. 13, Davis, William, and Ann King.
1781, Jan.   4, Davis, William, and Deborah Yarnall.
1780, Nov.   7, Davis, William, and Ann Atkinson.
1772, Nov.   7, Davis, William, and Mary McNeal.
1776, March 21, Davis, William, and Cath. Whiteman.
1757, April   5, Davis, William, and Elizabeth Ward.
1743, Feb.   28, Davis, William, Esther Owen.
1763, Sept.   6, Davison, Elizabeth, and William Jepson.
1774, Dec.   22, Davison, Thomas, and Ann Read.
1733, Dec.   3, Davison, Thomas, and Susannah Ryall.
1756, Jan.   10, Davison, William, and Christiana Bowman.
1804, May   8, Davy, John Broome, and Harriet Bridges.
1752, Nov.   9, Davy, Thomasin, and Jonathan Hanson.

1805, April 4, Dawes, Eliz., and Thomas Massey.
1747, June 13, Dawes, Geo. Vincent, and Anne Fling.
1757, Oct. 2, Dawkins, Henry, and Percilla Wood.
1788, Sept. 25, Dawkins, John, and Ann Knight.
1721, Nov. 2, Dawson, Edward, and Sarah Griffiths.
1758, Feb. 13, Dawson, Eleanor, and George Rhodes.
1801, Aug. 4, Dawson, Eliz., and Lawrence Humphreys.
1794, Nov. 20, Dawson, Joseph, and Charlotte Green.
1801, April 30, Dawson, Joseph, and Mary Farren.
1761, Dec. 13, Dawson, Mary, and Robert Moore.
1785, July 2, Dawson, Mary, and John McConnell.
1752, Aug. 27, Dawson, Mary, and William Malice.
1839, March 5, Dawson, Robert, and Mary Warner.
1752, May 18, Dawson, Rosamond, and Charles Green.
1728, Nov. 28, Day, Abigail, and Pat. Poe.
1756, April 20, Day, Charles, and Anne Clark.
1769, Aug. 3, Day, Elizabeth, and Moses Smallwood.
1721, Sept. 24, Day, Humphrey, and Jane Oxford.
1801, Nov. 3, Day, James, and Susannah Pearce.
1747, Sept. 7, Day, John, and Jane McSwain.
1750, Nov. 17, Day, John, and Martha Forrest.
1780, April 17, Day, Peter, and Penelope Fisher.
1799, Aug. 14, Day, Samuel, and Margaret Halfpenny.
1714, Sept. 19, Dayly, James, and Catherine Middleton.
1772, Dec. 14, Daymon, Frances, and Ann White.
1769, May 11, Deacon, Mary, and Peter Sutter.
1771, Sept. 12, Deacon, Rebecca, and Joseph Rigby.
1768, Sept. 13, Deacon, Robert, and Sarah Shedaker.
1798, Feb. 18, Deal, Eliz., and James Forrest.
1752, Nov. 27, Dealy, John, and Mary Johnston.
1784, Jan. 15, Dean, Cath., and Robert Willey.
1763, June 22, Dean, Elizabeth, and John McClure.
1796, June 5, Dean, George, and Mary Ann Barry.
1764, Dec. 13, Dean, John, and Mary Rose.
1768, Feb. 16, Dean, Joseph, and Hannah Boyte.
1756, June 5, Dean, Martha, and Samuel Smith.
1752, May 6, Dean, Mary, and James Buchannan.
1798, Aug. 5, Dean, Mary, and John Carr.
1776, Jan. 25, Deason, Eliz., and John Stephenson.
1789, April 25, DeBartholt, David, and Mary Ibetson.
1788, Dec. 24, DeBooke, Catherine, and Joseph Crooks.
1721, Dec. 28, Deborax, Rebecca, and Adam Chevars.
1774, Dec. 20, Decator, Stephen, and Ann Pine.
1735, April 25, DeCow, Anne, and James Richardson.
1798, Dec. 4, Dedier, Peter, and Mary Ann Brown.
1797, March 28, Dedricks, Hester, and Elvington Dixon.

1787, May   29, Deed, William, and Mary Mason.
1804, Sept. 26, DeForrest, Peter, and Ann Wiggins.
1801, Dec.   11, DeFraters, John, and Mary Diegel.
1783, Feb.   27, Dehart, Jacob, and Eliz. Robinson.
1775, April 27, Dehaven, Hugh, and Sarah Holstein.
1763, Jan.   18, Dehaven, Peter, and Elizabeth Knight.
1728, April 27, Dehaws, Sarah, and Giles Cambridge.
1754, July   9, Dehl, Rachel, and Jasper Fetter.
1743, June   16, Deigener, Peter, and Christian Smith.
1801, June   18, Deihl, Martha, and William Conover.
1801, March 31, Deisher, Peter, and Susanna Launville.
1763, Jan.   12, Deiter, John, and Jane Buffington.
1737, May   23, Delabar, Rebecca, and John Baker.
1776, April 25, Delahoute, Hannah, and William Carberry.
1804, June   3, Delanoy, Francis, and Eleanor Johnson.
1772, May   19, Delany, Cath., and William Barthkitt.
1784, May   19, Delany, Eleanor, and Enoch Richardson.
1799, March 28, Delany, Margaret, and Josiah Lewis.
1774, Jan.   20, Delany, Mary, and Richard Johnson.
1787, Oct.   18, Delany, Sarah, and James Moore.
1747, May   2, Delap, James, and Mary Moore.
1760, Dec.   29, Delaplain, Hannah, and John Price.
1748, Feb.   1, Delaplain, Hannah, and Robert Thompson.
1759, Dec.   18, Delaplain, James, and Catherine Ayres.
1768, July   9, Delaplain, Phoebe, and John Knox.
1764, Sept. 17, Delavan, Ann, and James Asheton.
1766, Dec.   25, Delavan, Elizabeth, and James Kain.
1760, Aug.   23, Delavan, Hannah, and William Roberts.
1767, March 18, Delavan, Isaac, and Hannah Grogan.
1794, Jan.   1, Delavan, James, and Eliz. McGill.
1767, Aug.   1, Delavan, Joseph, and Mary Dougherty.
1735, Dec.   17, Delaver, Isaac, and Elizabeth Endicott.
1760, July   28, Delaware, Elizabeth, and William Preston.
1783, May   6, Demeng, Thomas, and Ann Ramsey.
1783, Dec.   11, Dempsey, Magdalen, and Thomas White.
1769, Jan.   26, Dempsy, Jr., Joseph, and Mary Finney.
1784, Aug.   25, Denelly, Owen, and Ann Thomas.
1800, March 24, Deniston, Robert, and Ann Davis.
1773, July   20, Dennis, Ann, and John Scott.
1798, July   24, Dennis, Barney Cousins, and Mary Bourden.
1749, Nov.   9, Dennis, Elizabeth, and Joseph Grassberry.
1720, March 21, Dennis, Elizabeth, and Charles Hargrave.
1805, June   15, Dennis, Hannah, and Richard Garwood.
1735, May   12, Dennis, John, and Sarah Collier.
1806, April 24, Dennis, John, and Maria Read.
1801, Aug.   14, Dennis, Mary, and Abraham Busby.

1743, Jan. 20, Dennis, Bebecca, and Joseph Savage.
1802, Nov. 25, Dennis, Richard, and Harriet Eliza Duffield.
1729, Nov. 22, Dennis, Thomas, and Mary Jones.
1746, Nov. 30, Dennison, Catherine, and William Ramsey.
1761, May 7, Dennison, James, and Mary Sims.
1772, July 28, Denny, Barbary, and Edward Shriver.
1729, July 10, Denny, Ed., and Sarah Butler.
1797, April 24, Denny, Olando, and Eloisa Maria Magdalena Jos[e]
         Cottineau.
1749, Sept. 3, Denormandie, Hannah, and Rev[d] W[m] Sturgeon.
1745, July 25, Denormandie, William, and Hannah Anderson.
1746, Jan. 4, Densburgh, George, and Comfort Adams.
1773, Oct. 13, Dent, Mary, and John Taylor.
1748, July 28, Denton, John, and Mercy Roberts.
1727, July 25, Derborough, J., and Dor. Phillips.
1726, Sept. 25, Dermod, Margaret, and Nic. Cockle.
1769, Dec. 7, Derrick, Frances, and William Johnson.
1767, June 8, Derrick, Thomas, and Sarah Apple.
1777, July 8, Dunlap, James, and Juliana Cummings.
1799, March 17, Devall, Elijah, and Cath. Grenyon.
1796, March 22, Devat, John, and Ann Care.
1734, Nov. 16, Deveney, Martha, and George Gibson.
1803, July 19, Dever, Mary, and Charles Boyle.
1799, Sept. 22, Devereux, John, and Mary Hulton.
1798, Jan. 20, Devine, Dominick, and Kezia Weaver.
1766, Dec. 8, Devo, Benjamin, and Catherine Walker.
1728, Nov. 2, Devonshire, W[m], and Alice McCurry.
1784, Feb. 20, Dewall, Emanuel, and Lucy Lepton.
1756, Sept. 2, Dewee, Catherine, and Timothy Aldridge.
1806, May 21, Dewees, Silvia, and Tobias Barrett.
1800, July 12, Dewees, William, and Mary Britton.
1805, Dec. 10, Dewees, William, and Eleanor Britton.
1748, Oct. 17, Dewer, David, and Susannah Thornhill.
1732, Sept. 17, Dexter, Henry, and Mary Hartley.
1728, June 9, Dexter, John, and Hannah Bingham.
1743, July 16, Dexter, Mary, and Lambert Emerson.
1757, Aug. 24, Deykin, Elizabeth, and Brian Younger.
1739, July 5, Dicas, Randle, and Mary Shute.
1759, June 27, Dick, John, and Ann McGlathery.
1794, Sept. 18, Dick, Philip, and Mary Palmer.
1805, Nov. 9, Dick, Philip, and Mary Ozeas.
1727, Sept. 11, Dickenson, James, and Frances Hall.
1783, Nov. 19, Dickenson, John, and Rebecca Falconer.
1803, Oct. 10, Dickenson, Mary, and George Troa.
1784, Sept. 1, Dickey, John, and Mary Burrows.
1756, May 31, Dickin, Martha, and Andrew Nox.

1768, Jan.   12, Dickinson, Elizabeth, and George Weed.
1721, May   17, Dickinson, Joan, and William Adams.
1789, April   22, Dickinson, Lawrence, and Phoebe Palmer.
1762, Jan.   20, Dickinson, Mary, and Joseph Head.
1767, July   15, Dickinson, Philemon, and Mary Cadwallader.
1804, Sept.   1, Dickinson, Philemon, and Rebecca Cadwallader.
1765, Sept.   19, Dickinson, Thomas, and Mary Lort.
1756, Jan.   25, Dicks, Anne, and John Morris.
1767, Nov.   19, Dickson, Mary, and Samuel Green.
1768, Aug.   21, Dickson, Prudence, and Cyrus Cartwright.
1780. March   4, Dickson, Richard, and Susannah Lewis.
1709, Sept.   18, Dicksey, William, and Eleanor James.
1749, Aug.   28, Dickey, Margaret, and Daniel Marr.
1801, Dec.   11, Diegel, Mary, and John DeFraters.
1800, Oct.   18, Dietz, Eliz., and Archibald Hunter Boggs.
1734, June   5, Dight, Abraham, and Anne Bimrose.
1804, April   15, Dildine, Eliz., and John Richardson.
1783, May   12, Dilkes, Sarah, and Robert Cole.
1798, July   5, Dill, Joseph H., and Ann Bickham.
1795, June   8, Dillintash, Ann, and James Gardiner.
1761, Dec.   23, Dillon, Jonathan, and Mary Yeates.
1790, May   29, Dillon, Martha, and John Hilborn.
1740, Nov.   6, Dilworth, Elizabeth, and William Rigley.
1731-2, Jan.   6, Dilworth, James, and Mary Roberts.
1757, Dec.   22, Dilworth, Sarah, and William Bier.
1804, June   14, Dingey, Daniel, and Mary Fenner.
1804, March   4, Dingey, Jacob, and Eliz. Mittan.
1727, April   14, Dinsie, Esther, and Alex. Grant.
1760, Feb.   21, Dislow, Mary, and Marmaduke Bunting.
1800, April   30, Divine, Pierce, and Barbara Gibson.
1795, April   16, Dixey, Thomas, and Esther Dyche.
1732, May   25, Dixon, Alice, and Tobias Neale.
1768, July   9, Dixon, Ann, and Joseph Weston.
1797, April   23, Dixon, Eliz., and Henry Ransford.
1797, March   28, Dixon, Elvington, and Hester Dedricks.
1794, Nov.   1, Dixon, John, and Lydia Rawson.
1804, Nov.   24, Dixon, Mary, and George Tallman.
1797, Nov.   18, Dixon, Mary, and John Wigglesworth.
1731-2, Feb.   12, Dixon, Mary, and John Wood.
1754, Aug.   6, Dixon, Robert, and Sarah Tuckett.
1735, July   2, Dixon, Robert, and Margaret Hunter.
1775, March   2, Dixon, Sarah, and Anthony Cuthbest
1795, April   26, Dixon, Susannah, and Thomas Norris.
1790, Oct.   11, Dixon, William, and Bethiah Craig.
1738, Nov.   27, Dixsy, William, and Mary Williams
1756, June   2, Doan, Daniel, and Sarah Dyer.

1751, April   8, Doan, Mary, and Thomas Fisher.
1764, Sept.   24, Doan, Sarah, and John Dorland.
1742, Feb.   3, Dobans, Ann, and Pall Tucker.
1785, Jan.   3, Dobdell, Samuel, and Ann Cater.
1763, Jan.   29, Dobins, Joseph, and Mary Forster.
1747, Dec.   5, Dobbins, Martha, and Christopher Finney.
1765, July   18, Dobbins. Rebecca, and George Moore.
1732, April   27, Dobbs, Elizabeth, and Joseph Stynard.
1721, July   30, Dobbs, William, and Elizabeth Bettson.
1800, Feb.   20, Dobson, George, and Sarah Robinson.
1797, Jan.   12, Dobson, Margaret, and James Gallagher.
1801, Oct.   4, Doctor, Ann, and William Darley.
1756, Nov.   29, Dod, Elenor, and Thomas Luven.
1754, Nov.   30, Dodd, Anne, and Jacob Jones.
1729, April   23, Dodd, Hannah, and Ed. Young.
1755, June   28, Dodd, Joseph, and Sarah Whitpain.
1739, Sept.   12, Dodd, Sarah, and Jonathan Barber.
1773, Sept.   29, Dodds, Robert, and Martha Crawford.
1759, June   15, Dodge, ———, and John Hodges.
1749, May   8, Dodge, Thomas, and Mary Cribbs.
1725, Sept.   16. Doeux, Phil., and Martha Gaure.
1721, Nov.   12, Dolby, Abraham, and Sarah Tomlinson.
1788, Aug.   17, Dolby, Abraham, and Ann Robinson.
1800, March 20, Dolby, Ann, and John Coulter.
1795, Oct.   24, Dolby, Eliz., and William James.
1801, May   16, Dolby, Eliz., and Daniel Shute.
1793, July   28, Dolby, Daniel, and Cath. Davis.
1775, June   10, Dolby, Daniel, and Mary Snow.
1774, Dec.   15, Dolby, Martha, and John Earle.
1785, Feb.   20, Dolby, Philip, and Mary Rose.
1795, June   5, Dolman, Peter, and Lucy Green.
1763, June   4, Donald, Jane, and James Truling.
1798, March 10, Donaldly, Mary, and Charles Humphreys.
1763, Sept.   15, Donaldson, Arthur, and Elizabeth Keighan.
1796, July   4, Donaldson, Christiana, and James Seawright.
1785, May   26, Donaldson, Deborah, and Philip Nicolin.
1784, July   12, Donaldson, Eliz., and George Hogg.
1776, July   25, Donaldson, Eliz., and Jacob Spicer.
1798, April   29, Donaldson, John, and Rebecca Wilson.
1751, Aug.   1, Donaldson, Joseph, and Sarah Wilkinson.
1797, April   29, Donaldson, Mary, and James Bowden.
1785, April   12, Donaldson, Sarah, and Walter Roe.
1770, Dec.   31, Donaldson, William, and Sarah Griscome.
1785, Oct.   20, Donaldson, William Townsend, and Mary Adams.
1762, Dec.   17, Donavan, Rachel, and Patrick Flinn.
1804, Aug.   9, Donaven, John, and Sarah Kelly.

1773, Jan.　20, Doncan, Sarah, and Robt. McMekin.
1728, Sept.　7, Donilson, W^m and Eliz. Benny.
1801, Dec.　10, Donnally, Sarah, and Joseph Huckle.
1770, Aug.　20, Donnaughey, Hannah, and Samuel Harper.
1779, Oct.　18, Donnelly, Jane, and John Morie.
1777, May　21, Donohoe, Timothy, and Mary Ryan.
1800, May.　17, Donoldson, Hannah, and David Evans.
1772, July　22, Donovan, Eleanor, and Edward Smith.
1733, Aug.　23, Dony Sarah, and James Stannley.
1779, Nov.　20, Doogan, Michael, and Cath. Matthews.
1750, Jan.　6, Doran, Anne, and Patrick Kirk.
1761, Sept.　8, Doran, John, and Isabella McGorrough.
1764, Sept.　24, Dorland, John, and Sarah Doan.
1766, Sept.　16, Dorrel, Daniel, and Martha Sutton.
1791, Aug.　24, Dorsey, Charles, and Sarah Pleasants.
1785, Oct.　18, Dorsey, John, and Jane Johnston.
1801, Dec.　10 Dorsey, John, and Hannah Moore.
1783, April　3, Dorsey, John, and Rebecca Mannington.
1805, May　25, Dorsey, Thomas, and Dezia Anderson.
1800, Jan.　29, Dorson, Eliz., and Samuel Johnson.
1748, Dec.　28, Dorvil, Joseph, and Anne Shakleton.
1761, Oct.　12, Dorsey, Francis, and Lydia Harmer.
1758, Oct.　28, Dottany, Ann, and John Stoul.
1750, April　15, Dougharty, Charles, and Susannah Cloud.
1760, Oct.　30, Dougharty, Charles, and Sophia Price.
1759, April　2, Dougharty, Henry, and Ann Edgar.
1750, April　11, Dougharty, John, and Hannah Blake.
1802, June　10, Dougherty, Cath., and Daniel Porter.
1774, Jan.　25, Dougherty, Hugh, and Hannah Kelly.
1791, June　16, Dougherty, Isabella, and John Curtis.
1767, June　25, Dougherty, James, and Mary Wilson.
1801, Jan.　19, Dougherty, Mary, and George Taylor.
1767, Aug.　1, Dougherty, Mary, and Joseph Delavan.
1769, Feb.　23, Dougherty, Michael, and Sarah Shilly.
1796, Feb.　7, Dougherty, Patrick, and Mary Cockran.
1796, July　5, Dougherty, Roger, and Terrissa Molony.
1787, Oct.　2, Dougherty, Sarah, and Henry Bowles.
1784, Feb.　19, Doughty, Ann, and John Patton.
1768, April　23, Doughty, Ann, and Daniel Badger.
1793, May　20, Doughty, Eliz., and John Leamy.
1763, Jan.　13, Doughty, Robert, and Elizabeth Garrigues.
1800, Dec.　25, Douglas, Charles, and Eliz. Adams.
1804, Aug.　16, Douglas, Frances, and Samuel Spicer.
1772, Aug.　10, Douglas, John, and Ann Jones.
1804, March 15, Douglas, Rachel, and James Ash.
1799, Feb.　27, Douglas, Sarah, and John Rollington.

1750, March 1, Douglas, William, and Sarah Davis.
1804, Oct.   28, Douglass, Abraham, and Isabella Clarke.
1783, April 17, Douglass, Agness, and Robert Caldwell.
1791, Jan.   1, Douglass, Andrew, and Rachel Morgan.
1757, March 28, Douglass, Ann, and John McFarland.
1747, Oct.   16, Douglass, Margaret, and Patrick Hanigham.
1803, Nov.   28, Douglass, Rebecca, and William Ward.
1762, Sept. 16, Doulkear, Sophia, and George Smith.
1796, Nov.   2, Douty, John, and Frances Hir.
1802, April 18, Dove, John, and Eliz. Mee.
1787, Jan.   2, Dow, Alexander, and Martha Nelson.
1749, July   29, Dowding, Elizabeth, and John Faris.
1776, Nov.   2, Dowdle, Mary, and Thomas Harper.
1743, May   28, Dowell, William, and Mary Tomms.
1762, May   18, Dowell, William, and Grace Peal.
1794, Dec.   4, Dowers, Edward, and Rachel Heyrick.
1736, Aug.   28, Dowers, Edward, and Elizabeth Humphreys.
1764, April 31, Dowers, John, and Mary Thornhill.
1806, Feb.   11, Dowers, Mary, and John Meany.
1761, Aug.   5, Dowins, Francis, and Jane Grimes.
1785, Dec.   8, Dowling, Eleanor, and John Crarm.
1786, Sept. 16, Dowling, James, and Ann Eliz. Hackett.
1769, April 14, Down, Mary, and William Tennant.
1746, Feb.   4, Down, Robert, and Anne Sharpe.
1730, Dec.   31, Downes, James, and Elizabeth Christian.
1775, April 20, Downey, Bridget, and Walter Correy,
1797, July   23, Downey, Eliz., and Thomas Good.
1757, March 27, Downey, James, and Ann McCormack.
1803, Sept. 18, Downey, Terence, and Rebecca Duncan.
1775, Nov.   27, Downing, Jane, and Jacob Baldwin.
1771, April   1, Downs, Benjamin, and Hildah Green.
1757, May   20, Downs, Jonathan, and Mary Wilson.
1775, April   1, Downs, William, and Ann Gerrard.
1766, Dec.   25, Dowthwait, Mary, and Thomas Wall.
1743, June   16, Dowthaite, Sam., and Mary Wilkinson.
1740, Oct.   8, Dowthite, Samuel, and Elizabeth Lynn.
1755, Dec.   10, Doyle, Darby, and Margerie McGee.
1790, Dec.   20, Doyle, Eliz., and Alexander Cockran.
1794, July   17, Doyle, John, and Mary Parker.
1798, June   27, Doyle, Mary, and Mathias Ivory.
1780, Nov.   1, Doyle, Mary Ann, and Peter Wade.
1775, Nov.   1, Doyle, Mary, and John Tipler.
1748, Dec.   22, Doz, Andrew, and Rebecca Cash.
1759, Dec.   27, Drage, Charles Swain, and Hannah Bayte.
1796, Feb.   8, Draper, Elijah, and Martha Mann.
1737, Sept.   4, Draper, James, and Rachel Wilson.

1804, Nov. 6, Draper, Jonathan, and Ann Larkey.
1785, Sept. 13, Draper, Richard, and Sarah Cheesman.
1795, May 14, Draper, Eliz., and Thomas Boughton.
1796, March 30, Dreer, John, and Susannah Cole.
1735, Feb. 21, Drewite, John, and Elizabeth Rosson.
1773, Jan. 24, Drifts, Catherine, and John Moss.
1773, Feb. 18, Drinker, Deborah, and Thomas Harper.
1752, July 3, Drinker, Edward, and Susannah Cassel.
1755, Sept. 6, Drinker, Edward, and Elizabeth Franks.
1775, March 28, Driscott, Ann, and John Craig.
1742, Dec. 19, Drury, Edward, and Sarah Maugridge.
1800, June 28, Duane, William, and Margaret Bache.
1784, Nov. 17, Dubarree, John, and Eliz. Whiteman.
1758, Jan. 12, Dubre, Jr., Jacob, and Hannah Davis.
1761, July 4, Dubre, John, and Marjory Hall.
1788, June 18, Dubuisson, John B., and Henrietta Maria Hemings.
1784, Sept. 16, Duche, Ann, and Thomas Moore.
1763, April 28, Duche, Ann, and John Moyes.
1770, April 24, Duche, Anthony, and Sarah Falconer.
1741, Aug. 15, Duche, Elizabeth, and John Meares.
1799, May 23, Duche, Eliz. Sophia, and John Henry.
1798, Aug. 7, Duche, Esther, and William Hill.
1760, June 19, Duche, Jacob, and Elizabeth Hopkinson.
1747, June 5, Duche, Jacob, and Esther Bradley.
1731, Dec. 12, Duchee, Andrew, and Mary Mason.
1737, May 8, Duchee, James, and Hannah Preston.
1744, Feb. 5, Duchet, Susannah, and William Winkle.
1734, Jan. 13, Duchi, Jacob, and Mary Spence.
1771, Dec. 26, Duck, George, and Eliz. Sutor.
1763, June 16, Duckeminner, Lydia, and John Campbell.
1784, Oct. 28, Ducker, Edward, and Rebecca Reed.
1776, June 20, Duckett, Agness, and Thomas Emerson.
1805, June 29, Dudbridge, Hannah, and Ernest Mason.
1804, Sept. 24, Dudgeon, John, and Margaret Duncan.
1762, Nov. 10, Dudley, Thomas, and Martha Evans.
1801, March 22, Due, Sarah, and Joseph Goring.
1795, April 10, Duer, William, and Hannah Ogden.
1765, Dec. 24, Duff, Hannah, and Simon Meredith.
1742, May 15, Duffeld, Jacob, and Hannah Leech.
1800, May 5, Duffey, Aaron, and Margaret Moore.
1794, Nov. 20, Duffey, Charles, and Dorothy McKean.
1795, March 19, Duffey, Eliz., and Jacob Cox.
1774, Dec. 8, Duffey, Patrick, and Margaret Miller.
1790, Feb. 25, Duffield, Ann, and William Tillyer.
1791, Sept. 29, Duffield, Benjamin, and Rusely Slaughter.
1798, April 19, Duffield, Cath., and John Church.

1751, June 10, Duffield, Edward, and Catherine Parry.
1791, April 11, Duffield, Eliz., and Francis Ingraham.
1733, June 25, Duffield, Elizabeth and Samuel Swift.
1805, Nov. 25, Duffield, Harriet Eliza, and Richard Dennis.
1797, March 23, Duffield, Julianna, and William Ross.
1768, June 16, Duffield, Mary, and Jonathan Gostelow.
1805, Feb. 13, Duffield, Rebecca Grace, and John Selby.
1789, Feb. 8, Duffield, Rhoda, and James Reynolds.
1781, Sept. 10, Duffield, Sarah, and Stacy Hepburn.
1734, Feb. 15, Duffield, Thomas, and Mary Lee.
1801, April 16, Duffield, Thomas W., and Mary Louisa Hassall.
1796, July 7, Duffy, Abigail, and Frederick Holcraft.
1799, April 15, Dugan, Cath., and Samuel Wood.
1786, Jan. 10, Dugan, Cath., and William Rutherford.
1770, Feb. 11, Dugan, Walter, and Jane Thomas.
1745, Jan. 17, Duglass, Eleanor, and John Pick.
1785, June 19, Duguid, Mary, and James Kennedy.
1757, June 23, Duke, Elizabeth, and John Morrison.
1777, Sept. 8, Duke, Sarah, and William Govett.
1766, Aug. 18, Dulany, Sarah, and Hiram Gichon.
1771, Aug. 29, Dunbar, Eleanor, and William Kemble.
1806, June 2, Dunbar, Eliz., and William Rogers.
1781, July 12, Dunbar, Sybil, and Francis Fearis.
1754, Oct. 17, Duncan, Isaac, and Priscilla Stone.
1789, Nov. 28, Duncan, Isaac, and Mary Massey.
1759, March 13, Duncan, James, and Mary Trimble.
1749, May 20, Duncann, John, and Mary Shaw.
1804, Sept. 24, Duncan, Margaret, and John Dudgeon.
1763, Nov. 9, Duncan, Mary, and Samuel Brookhouse.
1730, June 21, Duncan, Patrick, and Rebecca Pritchard.
1803, Sept. 18, Duncan, Rebecca, and Terence Downey.
1755, Aug. 27, Duncan, Sarah, and Thomas Sands.
1776, Feb. 4, Duncan, Thomas, and Eleanor Malone.
1776, April 10, Duncan, William, and Rosanna Gallagher.
1758, Dec. 29, Duncliff, Mary, and James McConnel.
1758, May 11, Dundas, James, and Elizabeth Moore.
1788, Dec. 18, Dundas, Mary, and Frederick William Starrman.
1789, Nov. 14, Dundas, Sarah, and George Scriba.
1785, Oct. 27, Dundas, Eliz., and Henry Pratt.
1742, May 31, Dungan, Elizabeth, and William Reed.
1720, Aug. 28, Dungan, Thomas, and Mary Hart.
1798, Oct. 30, Dunhow, Ann, and George Supple.
1744, July 16, Dunkin, Mary, and Joseph Durborow.
1801, May 28, Dunlap, Eleanor, and Thomas Taylor.
1736, Nov. 4, Dunlap, Elizabeth, and John Dutton.
1773, Feb. 4, Dunlap, John, and Eliz. Ellison.

1805, Dec.   3, Dunlap, Margaret, and John Perit.
1770, April   12, Dunlap, Mary, and Robert Coupar.
1794, Oct.   25, Dunlap, Sarah, and Richard Johnson.
1798, Feb.   1, Dunlap, Sarah, and William Forrest.
1806, Feb.   2, Dunlap, William, and Isabella Strachan.
1775, June   23, Dunn, Archibald, and Mary Maher.
1803, March   12, Dunn, Benjamin, and Hannah Hall.
1796, Oct.   4, Dunn, Cath., and Joseph Boyce.
1769, Nov.   15, Dunn, Catherine, and John Oliver.
1773, Sept.   18, Dunn, David, and Lydia Calbert.
1748, Dec.   5, Dunn, Cartright, and Thomas Greenwood.
1744, March   22, Dunn, Hannah, and Abraham Williamson.
1801, Oct.   29, Dunn, James, and Mary Stewart.
1727, June   20, Dunn, James, and Thamer Jones.
1771, Aug.   17, Dunn, John, and Mary Sowder.
1762, Sept.   8, Dunn, John, and Hannah Hopwell.
1735, Dec.   3, Dunn, Sarah, and Thomas Walmsley.
1748, Aug.   27, Dunn, Susanna, and William Tate.
1747, Aug.   31, Dunnavan, Anne, and Patrick Corbet.
1750, Dec.   20, Dunning, Mary, and William Goforth.
1781, Oct.   11, Dunwick, Hannah, and William Gill.
1788, July   17, Dunwick, Mary, and John Boyce.
1714, June   24, Dunwick, William, and Mary Cotter.
1761, Dec.   8, Dunwick, William, and Catherine Williams.
1802, May   27, Dunwoddy, Martha, and Henry Livingstone.
1741, Nov.   29, Dumber, Martha, and Jacobus Vanoustan.
1788, June   5, Dupuy, Daniel, and Mary Meredith.
1775, May   11, Dupuy, Jane, and William Coates.
1786, April   26, Durant, Edward, and Eliz Bringhurst.
1748, Oct.   19, Durborow, Elizabeth, and Jonathan Case.
1744, July   16, Durborow, Joseph, and Mary Dunkin.
1801, Jan.   23, Durdin, Frances, and William Lewis.
1753, Aug.   13, Durel, Darby, and Lydia Clarke.
1742, Nov.   17, Durell, Joseph, and Katherine Condin.
1756, June   24, Durham, Amy, and William Penny.
1778, Aug.   8, Durham, Davison, and Eliz. Bankson.
1746, Dec.   18, Durham, Stephen, and Jane Wilson.
1761, Aug.   29, Durmady, Hannah, and Robert Collet.
1734, Jan.   23, Durmins, Eleanora, and Cuthbert Story.
1761, June   25, Durmore, Elizabeth, and Jonas Osburn.
1704, Dec.   6, Durnel, Samuel, and Rebecca Hall.
1781, Feb.   27, Durney, Michael, and Margaret Walkeimer.
1764, April   5, Durrows, Jane, and Robert Martin.
1750, Oct.   14, Dutton, Isaac, and Mary Wright.
1751, Jan.   5, Dutton, James, and Hannah Price.
1775, Sept.   23, Dutton, James, and Lydia Kimler.

1736, Nov.   4, Dutton, John, and Elizabeth Dunlap.
1795, May   5, Duval, Gatriel, and Jane Gibbons.
1741, Nov.   3, Dwarihouse, Ann, and Sibe Prier.
1202, April   8, Dwees, William, and Mary Lorain.
1731, Dec.   5, Dwiet, Matthew, and Grace Tinny.
1756, Jan.   17, Dwight, Rebecca, and Nathaniel Current.
1766, Nov.   1, Dwyer, John,·and Mary Riall.
1779, Feb.   4, Dwyer, Thomas, and Jane McCormick.
1795, April 16, Dyche, Esther, and Thomas Dixey.
1795, June   11, Dyer, Dennis, and Mary Mood.
1758, Sept.   7, Dyer, Mary, and Theophilus Gardiner.
1756, June   2, Dyer, Sarah, and Daniel Doan.
1744, July   28, Dyer, Sarah, and Thomas Mitchel.
1712, June   13, Dyer, Thomas, and Mary Anderson.
1799, March   2, Dyghan, Patrick, and Mary Cowell.
1763, May   4, Dykes, Nathan, and Sarah Banks.
1759, June   16, Each, Eleanor, and Isaac Jones.
1747, March 11, Eadarles, Martha, and William Adams.
1750, Jan.   23, Eades, Anne, and Samuel Scolly.
1759, Dec.   15, Eagle, Margaret, and Robert Kennedy.
1731-2, Jan. 31, Eagleton, Mary, and Thomas Woodfield.
1768, March   4, Eaken, Ann, and James Thompson.
1734, Nov.   14, Eames, John, and Isabella Davis.
1758, Sept.   4, Earl, John, and Mary Price.
1774, Dec.   15, Earle, John, and Martha Dolby.
1788, Nov.   19, Earley, John, and Eliz. Hamilton.
1791, May   11, Early, Amos, and Sarah Scott.
1776, Nov.   27, Early. Margaret, and James Chartres.
1794, Nov.   6, Earnest, Jacob, and Stacy McGill.
1780, Aug.   30, Earnest, Thomas, and Eliz. Chaboud.
1731, Oct.   19, Eastborn, Thomas, and Sarah Walmsley.
1731, Nov.   10, Eastburn, Mary, and Richard Studham.
1758, Nov.   4, Easterly, Catherine, and William Asheton.
1794, March   6, Eastlick, Ann, and Richard Collins.
1793, July   13, Easton, David, and Sarah Bond.
1723, Dec.   9, Eastworthy, Thomas, and Ann Moxie.
1804, Nov.   8, Eaton, Daniel, and Mary Warner.
1756, Nov.   9, Eaton, Eleanor, and John Reynolds.
1752, Dec.   11, Eaton, Richard, and Mary Stoakes.
1752, Sept. 25, Eaton, Sarah, and Wilcox Phillips.
1717, May   15, Eaton, Sarah, and John Harris.
1794, Aug.   17, Eaves, Thomas, and Margaret Higgins.
1750, Oct.   7, Eckles, George, and Susannah Holmes.
1761, March   5, Eckleson, Sarah, and George Russell.
1797, Dec.   21, Eddy, Mary, and David Hosack.
1732, Aug.   19, Edgar, Alexander, and Elizabeth Williams.

1759, April   2, Edgar, Ann, and Henry Dougharty.
1761, June 27, Edgar, Elizabeth, and Benjamin Pine.
1731, Dec.   8, Edgar, John, and Lydia Webb.
1729, Feb.   2,.Edgcomb, Nathl., and Sus^h Skinner.
1749, Dec. 30, Edge, Elizabeth, and Levi Budd.
1774, Aug. 15, Edge, Mary, and John Kelly.
1756, June 10, Edgil, Sarah, and John Cox.
1775, May 25, Edminston, Archibald, and Martha Griffin.
1796, May 31, Edmonston, Francis, and Johanna Norris.
1796, Jan.   4, Edmunson, Rebecca, and George Smith.
1759, Nov. 28, Edwards, Amos, and Rachel Pennel.
1731–2, Feb. 12, Edwards, Anne, and John Beer.
1742, May   6, Edwards, Ann, and Richard Finley.
1742, Feb. 13, Edwards, Cony, and Elizabeth Carley.
1758, March 14, Edwards, Edith, and William Brampton.
1713, June 21, Edwards, Eleanor, and Anthony Yealdall.
1785, June 16, Edwards, Eley, and Swaine Warner.
1758, Sept.   9, Edwards, Elizabeth, and Patrick Wolf.
1733, April 28, Edwards, Elizabeth, and William Corslett.
1779, Oct. 26, Edwards, Dr. Enoch, and Frances Gordon.
1735, Dec. 31, Edwards, Hannah, and Stephen Martin.
1727, April   5, Edwards, J., and Frances Torton.
1788, Nov. 22, Edwards, James, and Deborah Pierce.
1782, Nov. 15, Edwards, Jane, and Joshua Hatfield.
1772, March 12, Edwards, Jemima, and Charles Wharton.
1805, June   6, Edwards, Jesse, and Sarah Claxton.
1765, June 19, Edwards, John, and Rachel Gregory.
1746, Jan. 18, Edwards, John, and Elizabeth Saunders.
1761, Nov. 12, Edwards, Joseph, and Hannah Register.
1794, July 21, Edwards, Joseph, and Tacy Ann Johnson.
1805, Nov. 11, Edwards, Margaret, and James Mitchel.
1769, Nov. 17, Edwards, Mary, and Philip Good.
1763, Oct. 31, Edwards, Mary, and George Wright.
1741, Nov. 14, Edwards, Mary, and David Jones.
1756, Jan.   6, Edwards, Mary, and Richard Howison.
1735, Aug. 23, Edwards, Mary, and Elisha Beadles.
1734, Feb. 19, Edwards, Mary, and Thomas Taylor.
1768, July   9, Edwards, Rachel, and John Lukens.
1799, June 17, Edwards, Rebecca, and William Webster.
1798, Dec. 10, Edwards, Sophia, and George Bowen.
1783, June   1, Edwards, Sophia, and Martin Berry.
1734, Nov. 18, Edwards, Susanah, and John Roberts.
1795, Jan.   1, Edwards, Thomas, and Dorothy Vennabel.
1746, Nov. 24, Edwards, Thomas, and Rachel Chievers.
1768, March 14, Edwards, William, and Hannah Hall.
1747, Oct.   9, Edwards, William, and Isabell Chalmler.

1803, Sept.   20, Edwin, David, and Cath. Rogee.
1742, Jan.   11, Efland, Mary, and Thomas Lowne.
1772, March 17, Egan, Nicholas, and Ann Seymore.
1770, Dec.   5, Egglestone, William, and Mary Williamson.
1771, July   15, Eggman, Deborah, and William Vanlone.
1785, Dec.   29, Eglington, Jonathan, and Rebecca Morrell.
1795, Nov.   14, Eislen, Conrad, and Mary Hubley.
1753, April   4, Elbeck, John, and Martha Stapler.
1758, March 27, Elberson, and Dorothy Williams.
1774, June   23, Elden, Joseph, and Ann Folger.
1798, July   22, Elder, Crawford, and Mary Macdonough.
1760, Nov.   1, Elder, Elizabeth, and John Craig.
1783, Sept.   17, Elder, Thomas, and Eliz. Smith.
1804, Feb.   18, Eldridge, Eliz., and Robert Thurston.
1762, Nov.   10, Eldridge, James, and Hannah Evans.
1800, July   21, Eldridge, Joshua, and Rachel Parker.
1761, Nov.   6, Eldridge, William, and Deborah Maylander.
1757, Feb.   3, Elexander, Sarah, and James Barlo.
1732, Sept.   28, Elford, John, and Sarah Lindsey.
1738, Aug.   17, Elford, Sarah, and John Coats.
1795, Dec.   3, Elfrey, Catharine, and Jacob Nonamaker.
1787, July   30, Elfrey, William, and Susannah Fullman.
1791, July   12, Elfry, Margaret, and Robert Leonard.
1753, Dec.   11, Elisson, Margaret, and Joachim Hardeloft.
1768, Oct.   13, Eliz. and David, (Tuscaroras.)
1797, Jan.   14, Elkin, Angel, and Martha Moore.
1709, Oct.   6, Ellen, Margaret, and Nicholas Jones.
1735, Oct.   11, Ellett, Anne, and William Landerman.
1794, Dec.   4, Elleurt, Rachel, and Henry Philips.
1740, Dec.   13, Ellicot, Anne, and George Beard.
1753, Aug.   8, Ellicut, Joseph, and Judith Blaker.
1774, Sept.   15, Elliot, Amy, and Peter Hanwest.
1754, Oct.   31, Elliot, Andrew, and Eleanor McCall.
1772, Nov.   1, Elliot, Binky, and Daniel Hugar, Esq'.
1775, Oct.   10, Elliot, Chloe, and George Forsyth.
1761, June   5, Elliot, John, and Leah Brown.
1744, Nov.   24, Elliot, Martha, and Joseph Sill.
1768, Feb.   23, Elliot, William, and Hannah Linn.
1773, Jan.   21, Elliott, Ann, and Thomas Corgac.
1768, April   9, Elliott, Eliz., and Andrew McCullom.
1769, June   26, Elliott, Elizabeth, and Michael Gold.
1777, May   19, Elliott, James, and Mary Williamson.
1801, Jan.   29, Elliott, James, and Mary Allen.
1782, Sept.   14, Elliott, Thomas, and Ann Swells.
1729, March 10, Ellis, Ann, and Robert Hughes.
1759, Jan.   2, Ellis, Eleanor, and Alexander Aberdean.
        6—VOL. VIII.

1722, July   31, Ellis, Eleanor, and John Hair.
1781, April   16, Ellis, Eliz., and George Franklin.
1725, Dec.   5, Ellis, Everit, and Bridget Knot.
1753, Aug.   24, Ellis, Jane, and Jeremiah Coren.
1745, May   31, Ellis, John, and Eliz. Price.
1744, April   27, Ellis, John, and Jane Braderick.
1714, Nov.   25, Ellis, John, and Sarah Price.
1738, May   19, Ellis, Joseph, and Eve Basset.
1731, Nov.   4, Ellis, Margaret, and Jacob Kollock.
1750, Jan.   13, Ellis, Martha, and Redmond Cunyingham.
1720, Aug.   25, Ellis, Mary, and Willoughby Warder.
1787, Aug.   30, Ellis, Mary, and Joseph Lee.
1777, April   2, Ellis, Mary, and William Knowles.
1800, April   6, Ellis, Nathan, and Celia Farren.
1800, April   10, Ellis, James, and Sarah Holberg.
1764, Aug.   10, Ellis, Reuben, and Hannah Schrack.
1737, Dec.   31, Ellis, Richard, and Jane Brown.
1745, Sept.   8, Ellis, Richard, and Sarah Harris.
1748, May   14, Ellis, William, and Rebecca Collins.
1728, Sept.   22, Ellis, W^m, and Eliza Crouch.
1797, Dec.   23, Ellis, William, and Martha Stern.
1773, Feb.   4, Ellison, Eliz., and John Dunlap.
1802, Nov.   10, Ellison, Margaret, and John Warner.
1733, May   30, Ellitt, Anne, and Zachariah Williams.
1729, July   21, Ellwood, James, and Mary Connard.
1790, Oct.   12, Ellwood, John, and Rebecca Garrigues.
1715, Feb.   24, Ellwood, Richard, and Mary Hasell.
1742, Oct.   16, Elmes, Joseph, and Mary Morton.
1750, March 14, Elton, John, and Mary Hart.
1763, May   6, Elton, Robert, and Margaret Hart.
1774, Nov.   10, Elton, Thomas, and Susannah Wood.
1730, Sept.   30, Ellwell, Hannah, and Robert Jenkins.
1796, Sept.   12, Elwell, Cath. M., and George Fagan.
1759, April   13, Elwell, Joseph, and Margaret Gorvey.
1744, Oct.   10, Elwes, Henry, and Deborah Conolly.
1755, April   21, Elwes, Henry, and Mary Hannis.
1771, Sept.   15, Embrace, Ann, and Asher Jones.
1733, Oct.   13, Emerson, Lambert, and Sarah Lowe.
1743, July   16, Emerson, Lambert, and Mary Dexter.
1776, June   20, Emerson, Thomas, and Agnes Duckett.
1726, Nov.   6, Emit, J., and Jane Harrington.
1801, Aug.   29, Emlen, Ann, and Charles Hare.
1747, Nov.   7, Emmerson, Mary, and James Kappock.
1773, April   20, Emmet, John, and Mary Mitchell.
1796, Dec.   29, Emory, Eliz., and Peter Crouding.
1778, Dec.   7, Emory, Ruth, and George Rogers.

1739, Jan.   20, Empson, Mary, and Joseph Rives.
1751, Nov.   18, Empson, Mary, and Gabriel Dalbo.
1763, May   5, Empson, Thomas, and Elizabeth Soumaine.
1801, Nov.   14, Emrick, Baltis, and Hannah Summers.
1792, April   28, Emslie, Hannah, and Charles Godfrey Palaske.
1763, Jan.   6, Emson, Mary, and Jonathan Hulnis.
1735, Dec.   17, Endicott, Elizabeth, and Isaac Delaver.
1761, Aug.   13, Endt, Mary, and George Miller.
1772, Oct.   20, England, Cornelia, and James King.
1758, Sept.   7, England, Cornelia, and John Adams.
1757, Nov.   8, England, Elizabeth, and Leonard Heiman.
1732, Nov.   16, England, Elizabeth, and Cha⁸ Messer.
1774, Feb.   24, England, Mary, and William Justice.
1760, June   1, England, Mary, and Richard Cremer.
1780, Aug.   22, England, Sarah, and John Anderson.
1798, April   15, Engle, Mary, and Anthony Benezet.
1734, June   22, Englesfield, Anne, and Thomas Heine.
1736, Oct.   16, Englis, John, and Catherine McCall.
1768, Dec.   7, Engram, Elizabeth, and Joseph Gheen.
1745, March   3, Ennis, Eliz.; and Charles Parmale.
1734, Oct.   10, Enoch, Phoebe, and Joseph Boys.
1740, June   15, Enochs, John, and Deborah Evans.
1715, Aug.   26, Enockson, Juliana, and Jonas Yoakhum.
1799, July   25, Enstie, Hannah, and John Philips.
1785, Dec.   29, Entz, Mary, and John Salter.
1768, Aug.   27, Envenson, Richard, and Mary Johnson.
1803, March 12, Erben, Margaret, and John Worrel.
1716, Nov.   20, Erett, Elizabeth, and Barthols Carthew.
1806, May   3, Erick, George, and Mary Bowen.
1799, June   8, Erickson, Christian, and Eliz. Bass.
1799, Dec.   16, Erskine, David Montague, and Fanny Cadwalader.
1775, Dec.   13, Erwin, Alice, and Francis Johnson.
1752, Aug.   29, Erwin, David, and Elizabeth Townsend.
1781, March 16, Erwin, Frances, and Jacob Hammitt.
1799, May   11, Erwin, Jane, and Geoffery Price.
1742, Nov.   13, Erwin, John, and Mary Ramm.
1749, Aug.   20, Erwin, Sarah, and John Tagart.
1801, Oct.   13, Eskit, Robert, and Mary Riley.
1774, Sept.   17, Esler, Henry, and Ann Johns.
1786, Sept.   2, Esley, Phoebe, and Robert Porter.
1794, Oct.   11, Esling, Sarah, and Andrew Fondy.
1741, June   28, Espil, Anne, and Ellis Pugh.
1801, Feb.   1, Essex, Ann, and Thomas Christian.
1734, April   22, Essex, Mary, and Jonas Smith.
1722, Jan.   2, Essleby, Jane, and John Pointsett.
1794, July   6, Estler, Susannah, and John Simpson.

1767, Oct.　27, Esterby, Christopher, and Elizabeth Ryan.
1767, April　29, Estlack, Ann, and Ebenezer Turner.
1763, Aug.　17, Estlack, William, and Diana Shute.
1745, Feb.　7, Estwick, Hannah, and John Harrison.
1783, Feb.　17, Etchews, Mary, and Patrick Cochran.
1743, Oct.　25, Eten, Martha, and William Harris.
1750, Dec.　25, Eton, John, and Elizabeth Bright.
1736, Aug.　21, Eustice, Joseph, and Mary Fortune.
1772, April　8, Evans, Abner, and Susannah Davis.
1712, May　18, Evans, Ann, and Matthew Brooks.
1739, Aug.　31, Evans, Anne, and Samuel King.
1745, April　24, Evans, Anne, and Ebenezer Evans.
1745, Dec.　9, Evans, Anne, and Evan Jones.
1781, Oct.　25, Evans, Benjamin, and Eliz. Russell.
1740, June　15, Evans, Deborah, and John Enochs.
1779, Sept.　1, Evans, Daniel, and Damaris Roney.
1735, May　3, Evans, Dove, and Hugh Hill.
1800, May　17, Evans, David, and Hannah Donoldson.
1780, June　7, Evans, David, and Mary Jones.
1796, Sept.　29, Evans, David, and Mary Carey.
1720, Aug.　15, Evans, David, and Sarah Davis.
1761, Aug.　15, Evans, David, and Mary Hutton.
1747, March　6, Evans, David, and Sarah Yarkess.
1745, April　24, Evans, Ebenezer, and Anne Evans.
1786, Jan.　6, Evans, Edward, and Ann Toomy.
1717, May　17, Evans, Edward, and Elizabeth Finney.
1722, July　1, Evans, Elizabeth, and Nicholas Ghisling.
1742, May　29, Evans, Elizabeth, and George Phillips.
1749, May　2, Evans, Evan, and Hannah Bowen.
1770, March 30, Evans, Ezekial, and Sarah Gardiner.
1804, July　25, Evans, George, and Hannah Lodge.
1720, Feb.　17, Evans, Griffith, and Elizabeth Jones.
1733, Nov.　19, Evans, Gwin, and Reece Jones.
1762, Nov.　10, Evans, Hannah, and James Eldridge.
1763, Aug.　11, Evans, Hannah, and Joseph Huddle.
1745, Jan.　1, Evans, Hannah, and Matthias Culp.
1733, March 12, Evans, Henry, and Sarah Swan.
1774, Jan.　6, Evans, James, and Hannah Fear.
1721, Jan.　1, Evans, James, and Elizabeth Sharlock.
1800, Dec.　4, Evans, John B., and Ann Hawkins.
1739, Aug.　30, Evans, John, and Mary Thomson.
1770, Nov.　27, Evans, Jonathan, and Mary Matthias.
1734, Oct.　29, Evans, Joseph, and Anne Hoops.
1715, Oct.　10, Evans, Julian, and Jonathan Pones.
1801, Nov.　17, Evans, Lewis, and Sarah Evans.
1744, Jan.　21, Evans, Lewis, and Martha Hoskins.

1735, July   21, Evans, Margaret, and Charles Gative.
1716, Aug.   20, Evans, Margaret, and Edward Collins.
1723, June   17, Evans, Mark, and Katherine Thomas.
1734, April   21, Evans, Martha, and John Prichard.
1738, March 16, Evans, Martha, and Stephen Hoopes.
1762, Nov.   10, Evans, Martha, and Thomas Dudley.
1746, Oct.   31, Evans, Mary, and James Scot.
1763, Oct.   27, Evans, Mary, and Joseph Cassell.
1711, Dec.   2, Evans, Mary, and George Gadely.
1720, June   17, Evans, Mary, and James Sturgis.
1774, Sept.   6, Evans, Mary, and Charles Ferguson.
1773, Oct.   20, Evans, Mordecan, and Joseph Hoskins.
1742, May   29, Evans, Morgan, and Hannah Jackson.
1729, April   30, Evans, Nic., and Alice Lewis.
1721, Aug.   14, Evans, Owen, and Mary Davis.
1733, Dec.   31, Evans, Patience, and Warwick Rundle.
1784, Oct.   11, Evans, Phoebe, and Thomas Pugh.
1775, June   10, Evans, Priscilla, and Samuel Thomas.
1776, June   20, Evans, Rachel, and Thomas Davis.
1741, Dec.   8, Evans, Rebecca, and Peter Robinson.
1730-1, Feb. 14, Evans, Rebecca, and William Crew.
1785, May   19, Evans, Rees, and Esther Stretcher.
1802, July   8, Evans, Samuel, and Hannah Oldfield.
1769, April   14, Evans, Sarah, and Jacob Coburn.
1801, Nov.   17, Evans, Sarah, and Lewis Evans.
1729, Jan.   29, Evans, Sarah, and John Peters.
1782, May   5, Evans, Sidney, and John Morrison.
1733, June   2, Evans, Solomon, and Martha Clayton.
1758, Nov.   2, Evans, Susannah, and Lewis Thomas.
1788, July   11, Evans, Thomas, and Mary Brown.
1736, Jan.   22, Evans, Thomas, and Sarah Roberts.
1748, Aug.   17, Evans, Thomas, and Elinor Rees.
1754, Nov.   25, Evans, Thomas, and Hannah Rees.
1729, Jan.   2, Evans, W^m, and Rachel Roberts.
1746, May   20, Evanson, Nathaniel, and Elizabeth Palmer.
1761, Nov.   22, Evanson, Richard, and Sarah Micham.
1768, Oct.   13, Eve and John, (Tuscaroras.)
1744, June   2, Eve, Oswald, and Anne Moore.
1795, Nov.   19, Eveque, Peter L., and Ruth Harding.
1714, Aug.   27, Everet, Elizabeth, and Thomas Bantost.
1771, July   14, Everhart, David, and Eliz. Shetter.
1732, July   8, Everice, Penelope, and Benjamin Gray.
1799, Nov.   14, Everly, John, and Margaret Fletcher.
1755, July   21, Everside, Elizabeth, and John Binns.
1740, Dec.   6, Eves, Abigail, and Samuel Moore.
1804, March 29, Evinger, Sarah, and Joseph Cotman.

1734, Feb.   6, Evrington, John, and Elizabeth Richards.
1735, March 13, Ewen, Elizabeth, and James Coultas.
1767, Oct.   27, Ewer, Ann, and Jenkin Jones.
1750, Feb.   20, Ewing, John, and Sarah Yates.
1714, June   23, Exell, Samuel, and Prudence Myles.
1796. Feb.   23, Exon, Sarah, and William Robinson.
1793, June   13. Exon, William, and Sarah Coles.
1750, June   5, Eyamson, Daniel, and Eleanor Heagan.
1750, Jan.   18, Eyers, Mary, and Jasper Scull.
1805, April   26, Eyre, Eliz., and Charles Quandrill.
1761, Dec.   28, Eyre, Jehu, and Lydia Wright.
1794, Jan.   9, Eyre, Lydia, and Ralph Hunt.
1761, Jan.   8, Eyre, Manuel, and Mary Wright.
1797, July   2, Eyre, Mary, and John Lyster.
1791, March 24, Eyre, Mary, and Benjamin Cheesman.
1744, Dec.   21, Eyre, Mary, and James Price.
1731–2, Jan.   6, Eyre, Mary, and Thomas Budd.
1800, April   8, Eyre, Samuel B., and Hannah Whitehead.
1806, March   8, Eyre, Sarah, and Christopher H. Little.
1753, Jan.   25, Eyres, Anne, and George Mifflin.
1788, Aug.   4, Eyres, Mary, and Isaac Coates.
1758, Dec.   14, Fagan, Edmund, and Grace Busel.
1796, Sept.   12, Fagan, George, and Cath. M. Elwell.
1783, Nov.   6, Fagan, William, and Cath. Claypole.
1712, Dec.   25, Faggin, Thomas, and Elizabeth Syms.
1803, March 14, Fails, Joseph, and Eliz. Quail.
1795, April   5, Fairbanks, George Charles, and Hannah Vernon.
1752, Dec.   30, Fairman, Anne, and William Pearson.
1742, Jan.   23, Fairman, Susannah, and William Hayes.
1757, Oct.   18, Fairost, Jane, and John Adams.
1784, Sept.   9, Faithfull, Jane, and John Bayley.
1800, Aug.   31, Faithful, Sarah, and Joseph Ridick.
1770, April   14, Falconer, Ephraim, and Mary Spafford.
1731, Oct.   16, Falconer, John, and Elizabeth Smith.
1762, June   12, Falconer, Joseph, and Rachel Collins.
1784, Jan.   29, Falconer, Mary, and Edward Cook.
1783, Nov.   19, Falconer, Rebecca, and John Dickenson.
1770, April   24, Falconer, Sarah, and Anthony Duche.
1725, Aug.   12, Falconier, Jane E., and Robt. Ashton.
1760, Dec.   2, Fallas, Jane, and Samuel Barlow.
1779, May   13, Fallon, Dr. James, and Mary Vannost.
1800, July   31, Fallon, Mary, and Marsh Clarke.
1791, Sept.   1, Falkner, Eliz., and George Price.
1759, March 20, Falkner, Nathaniel, and Sarah Pratt.
1762, March 29, Falkner, William, and Hacklace Garrard.
1737, March 19, Falks, Elizabeth, and Joseph Swarfar.

1772, Dec.   3, Fandlin, Barbary, and Samuel Poole.
1771, Jan.   1, Fanning, Joseph, and Lydia Grice.
1734, Dec.   22, Fanington, Mary, and Benjamin Price.
1779, Sept. 11, Fannon, John, and Rachel Horver.
1787, Oct.   11, Fardey, John, and Eliz. Seeds.
1763, April 14, Faries, Francis, and Elizabeth Faulkner.
1800, Sept. 29, Farill, Margaret, and Samuel Childs.
1752, Nov.   29, Faris, Elizabeth, and Samuel Montgomery.
1749, July   29, Faris, John, and Elizabeth Dowding.
1769, April 23, Farley, Thomas, and Elizabeth Fisher.
1801, May   9, Farmer, Ann, and James Prosser.
1734, June   2, Farmer, Edward, and Hannah Morgan.
1754, March 27, Farmer, Elizabeth, and Thomas Carter.
1722, Oct.   25, Farmer, Elizabeth, and John Scull.
1759, Sept. 31, Farmer, Elizabeth, and John Thompson.
1732, Nov.   23, Farmer, Sarah, and Peter Robison.
1778, Oct.   8, Farmer, Sarah, and William Bowers.
1741, Jan.   31, Farmer, Samuel, and Mary Wooling.
1752, Nov.   19, Farmer, Samuel Evans, and Lydia Harry.
1735, July   20, Farmer, William, and Martha Perry.
1765, Feb.   23, Farns, John, and Thomasine Brown.
1786, Aug.   31, Farr, Arabella, and George McCann.
1761, July   29, Farr, John, and Catherine Myers.
1791, Aug.   15, Farr, John, and Eliz. Adair.
1758, June   29, Farra, Catherine, and John Bottomley.
1790, Dec.   7, Farrel, Ann, and Mark West.
1768, March 24, Farrel, Catherine, and Gabriel Simpson.
1747, June   11, Farrel, Robert, and Catherine Welsh.
1746, Dec.   25, Farrel, Michael, and Mary Moran.
1785, Dec.   22, Farrell, John, and Mary Catchem.
1781, Sept. 29, Farrell, John, and Margaret Laurimore.
1787, Sept.   9, Farrell, Mary, and Daniel Marra.
1796, Dec.   7, Farren, Ann, and Parnel Antrim.
1800, April   6, Farren, Celia, and Nathan Ellis.
1801, April 30, Farren, Mary, and Joseph Dawson.
1798, Dec.   9, Farren, Mary, and Peter Johnson.
1743, Oct.   26, Farrey, John, and Isabella Finton.
1803, April   2, Farrier, Barbara, and Spencer Cook.
1773, Sept. 23, Farrier, Charles, and Rachel Christopher.
1748, Aug.   15, Farrington, Elizabeth, and John Stevens.
1794, June   1, Farron, Ann, and Claude Grapin.
1752, July   24, Farron, John, and Hannah Tisdell.
1794, June   12, Farron, Margaret, and Benjamin Kimpton.
1786, July   6, Faston, John, and Eliz. Walters.
1763, April 14, Faulkner, Elizabeth, and Francis Faries.
1785, Feb.   21, Faulkner, Joseph, and Hannah Indigott.

1764, March 1, Faulkner, Lester, and Sarah Penrose.
1787, March 27, Faulkner, Rachel, and Thomas Webb.
1790, June 2, Faulkner, Sarah, and James Owner.
1738, Jan. 25, Fauls, Rebecca, and John Gerich Vanleer.
1773, April 17, Fawkes, John, and Sarah Lane.
1753, Jan. 4, Fawkes, William, and Elizabeth Collier.
1774, Jan. 6, Fear, Hannah, and James Evans.
1781, July 12, Fearis, Francis, and Sybil Dunbar.
1779, April 27, Fearis, Capt. Owen, and Jane Lukens.
1752, March 29, Fearn, Elizabeth, and John Basstick.
1792, April 26, Feble, William, and Margaret Killinger.
1782, June 30, Fees, Mary, and Benoni Bates.
1786, July 20, Fegan, Cath., and Laurence Burns.
1794, Nov. 20, Feinour, Joseph, and Mary McDaniel.
1773, April 1, Feit, Jacob, and Eleanor McCallachan.
1780, Sept. 19, Fell, Ann, and John Wessels.
1758, Jan. 5, Fell, Ann, and Richard Lovelock.
1788, Feb. 3, Fell, Richard, and Eliz. Story.
1785, April 11, Fellers, John, and Mary Rudrow.
1741, May 1, Felstoad, William, and Joyce Weaver.
1742, Sept. 8, Felteas, Erasmus, and Grace Morris.
1756, April 17, Felton, John, and Anne Hurst.
1762, Dec. 24, Felton, Mary, and Benjamin Shoemaker.
1751, Nov. 21, Felton, Mary, and Daniel Bennet.
1771, June 29, Felton, Sarah, and Jacob Souder.
1757, Sept. 2, Felty, Rebecca, and John Avergast.
1734, July 4, Fenbeigh, John, and Mary Lowder.
1759, March 15, Fenimore, Samuel, and Elizabeth Palmer.
1747, Feb. 14, Fenkins, Rachel, and Joseph Street.
1799, Nov. 19, Fennall, Sarah, and Richard Culver.
1801, Nov. 5, Fennell, Thomas, and Mary Kelly.
1786, Jan. 23, Fennemore, Samuel, and Mary Gordon.
1774, Sept. 11, Fenner, Henry, and Mary Ryle.
1804, June 14, Fenner, Mary, and Daniel Dingey.
1749, May 19, Fennimore, Joshua, and Rebecca Pearson.
1769, Sept. 3, Fenton, Robert, and Mary Guy.
1794, Sept. 27, Fenton, Sarah, and John Marr.
1806, May 6, Fenwick, Thomas, and Eliz. Joubert.
1766, May 29, Ferguson, Andrew, and Sarah Harrison.
1774, Sept. 6, Ferguson, Charles, and Mary Evans.
1770, Jan. 11, Ferguson, Charles, and Ann Musgrove.
1796, May 5, Ferguson, Eliz., and John Keys.
1792, June 30, Ferguson, James, and Margaret Kelly.
1803, Jan. 1, Ferguson, John, and Mary Anderson.
1757, Aug. 11, Ferguson, John, and Martha Neale.
1766, June 18, Ferguson, John, and Elizabeth French.

1760, March 12, Ferguson, Joseph, and Mary Jones.
1748, Sept.   8, Ferguson, Joseph, and Martha Walnet.
1796, Aug. 22, Ferguson, Mary, and Matthew Watson.
1798, Jan. 18, Ferguson, Thomas, and Susanna Miller.
1774, Sept.   5, Ferman, Mary, and Patrick McFall.
1751, May 21, Ferrard, Richard, and Elizabeth Aldridge.
1748, Dec. 26, Ferrel Dennis, and Rose Cook.
1796, Oct. 17, Ferriar, William, and Susanna Abel.
1725, Aug.   9, Ferril, T., and E. Stapleton.
1761, Jan.   8, Ferrisby, Nathaniel, and Mary Cook.
1767, Jan. 14, Fester, Hannah, and Jacob Weighter.
1779, Feb. 28, Fester, Mary, and George Savell.
1754, July   9, Fetter, Jaspar, and Rachel Dehl.
1784, Dec. 25, Fetters, Mary, and John Taverner.
1753, June 12, Fetzer, Frederick, and Rachel Britain.
1773, Oct. 14, Few, Eliz., and John McEuen.
1731, Nov. 27, ffaucet, Philip, and Hannah Lewis.
1730, Sept.   2, ffoord, Standish, and Hannah McCarty.
1730, Oct. 25, fframe, Margaret, and Thomas Ingram.
1785, March 29, Field, Christiana, and Samuel McMinn.
1800, March 13, Field, Mary, and William Naff,
1779, Sept.   7, Field, Mary, and Capt. Thomas Read.
1765, Oct. 24, Field, Robert, and Mary Peal.
1750, Feb. 22, Field, Robert, and Rachel Mayberry.
1758, Dec. 13, Fielding, Flora, and Nemo Russell.
1795, Nov.   7, Fielding, Robert, and Hester Lloyd.
1794, May 20, Findley, Diana, and John Thruston Walker.
1804, June 21, Fines, Rebecca, and James Vanholt.
1801, Oct. 22, Finley, Margaret, and Joseph Alexander Houston.
1791, Sept. 13, Finley, William, and Rachel Davenport.
1742, May   6, Finley, Richard, and Ann Edwards.
1765, Oct. 31, Finley, William, and Susanna Skinner.
1759, Jan'y   8, Finly, William, and Catherine Bilsonsleane.
1773, July   3, Finnemore, Peter, and Sarah Carter.
1740, July   7, Finney, Alexander, and Anne Chester.
1754, Sept.   7, Finney, Catherine, and Thomas Smith.
1747, Dec.   5, Finney, Christopher, and Martha Dobbins.
1717, May 17, Finney, Elizabeth, and Edward Evans.
1715, May 15, Finney, Elizabeth, and Thomas Tresse.
1732, Dec. 13, Finney, Elizabeth, and Joseph Toad.
1745, May   9, Finney, John, and Amelia Lindsay.
1769, Jan. 26, Finney, Mary, and Joseph Dempsy, Jr.
1763, March 21, Finney, Rebecca, and John Jones.
1736, Oct. 27, Finney, Thomas, and Mary Chester.
1797, Dec. 19, Finney, Washington Lee, and Christiana Bickham.
1710, Jan. 15, Finnis, Mary, and Thomas Davis.

1795, July 7, Finnix, Christian, and Thomas Williams.
1743, Oct. 8, Finnyman, Martha, and Richard Tucker.
1785, March 12, Finor, George, and Mary Hartley.
1727, Jan. 26, Finton, Ann, and Archable Commins.
1743, Oct. 26, Finton, Isabella, and John Farrey.
1759, Aug. 25, Fish, Eleanor, and James Tay.
1759, May 21, Fish, Elias, and Mary Labony.
1756, March 5, Fish, Mary, and John Codd.
1784, Oct. 28, Fish, Mary, and Joseph Armstrong.
1774, Dec. 7, Fishbourne, Eliz., and Thomas Wharton.
1804, March 2, Fishbourne, Eliz., and George Mifflin.
1767, July 3, Fisher, Ann, and William Watkins.
1763, Jan. 7, Fisher, Barbara, and Jacob Burket.
1761, June 2, Fisher, David, and Margaret Kearney.
1751, Dec. 7, Fisher, Deborah, and James Williams.
1795, Oct. 15, Fisher, Elisha, and Mary Hudson.
1744, Oct. 27, Fisher, Eliz., and Thomas Brown.
1794, May 8, Fisher, Eliz., and Ismael Robinson.
1769, April 23, Fisher, Elizabeth, and Thomas Farley.
1805, June 19, Fisher, George, and Ann Jones.
1728, July 25, Fisher, Isabell, and Jacob Leech.
1802, Oct. 21, Fisher, Jacob, and Ann Haines.
1787, May 5, Fisher, James, and Cath. Afterman.
1801, July 28, Fisher, John, and Agnes Bell.
1743, March 26, Fisher, John, and Mary Follensby.
1806, Jan. 12, Fisher, Joshua, and Eliz. Powell Francis.
1752, April 16, Fisher, Margaret, and Robert Fleming.
1766, Nov. 5, Fisher, Margaret, and William Bevan.
1776, Feb. 1, Fisher, Martha, and Daniel Butler.
1754, Dec. 12, Fisher, Mary, and William Goddard.
1733, Jan. 18, Fisher, Mary, and Joseph Hall.
1768, Nov. 23, Fisher, Mary, and Thomas Bradford.
1767, Dec. 1, Fisher, Mary, and William Bartram.
1780, April 17, Fisher, Penelope, and Peter Day.
1779, Aug. 19, Fisher, Rebecca, and Thomas Leaming.
1770, Dec. 20, Fisher, Sarah, and Andrew Bunner.
1759, July 24, Fisher, Thomas, and Lucy Boyd.
1795, Sept. 24, Fisher, Thomas, and Hannah Ap Owen.
1715, Aug. 26, Fisher, Thomas, and Elizabeth Osborn.
1755, April 23, Fisher, Thomas, and Elizabeth Williamson.
1751, April 8, Fisher, Thomas, and Mary Doan.
1798, Nov. 30, Fisler, Hannah, and Thomas Hess.
1797, Aug. 31, Fiss, James, and Eliz. McBride.
1799, Feb. 3, Fiss, John, and Susanna Ince.
1803, Nov. 17, Fiss, Samuel, and Eleanor Vansant.
1805, Nov. 30, Fiss, William, and Rachel Weston.

1756, Nov.   3, Fitchat, Thomas, and Elizabeth Norwood.
1728, June 29, Fitzakerlin, Henry, and Marg^t Fox.
1783, April 28, Fitzgerald, Ann, and John McHerren.
1777, July 16, Fitzgerald, Eleanor, and John Webster.
1741, Jan. 13, Fitzgerald, John, and Henrietta Russell.
1783, May   1, Fitzgerald, John, and Mary Killinger.
1804, Dec. 24, Fitzgerald, Mary, and James Austin.
1736, Nov. 20, Fitzharris, John, and Marjorie Rousford.
1756, June 23, Fitzhugh, Sarah, and Thomas Rees.
1776, April 13, Fitzpatrick, Daniel, and Margaret Lynch.
1773, June   2, Fitzpatrick, Eliz., and George Carr.
1776, Feb.   8, Fitzpatrick, John, and Eleanor Pryor.
1769, May   4, Fitzpatrick, Margaret, and William Sims.
1752, April 16, Fitzrandal, Edward, and Mary Lowndes.
1760, Dec. 14, Fitzsimmons, Nicholas, and Sarah Goodman.
1781, June   7, Flake, Jacob, and Eliz. Stephenson.
1799, Dec. 26, Flecher, Richard, and Rebecca Vicary.
1753, June 16, Fleeson, Plunket, and Martha Linton.
1776, Feb. 26, Fleet, Cath., and John Cartmell.
1734, Nov.   8, Fleet, Magnis, and Amey Jones.
1805, May   26, Fleming, Ann, and John Williams.
1781, Sept. 10, Fleming, John, and Mary Robinett.
1759, Dec. 14, Fleming, John, and Catherine Shesser.
1767, June 26, Fleming, Mary, and William McClay.
1732, June   7, Fleming, Susannah, and William Cowen.
1752, April 16, Fleming, Robert, and Margaret Fisher.
1796, April 13, Fletcher, James, and Ann Gregory.
1799, Nov. 14, Fletcher, Margaret, and John Everly.
1776, May   16, Fletcher, Samuel, and Eliz. Watson.
1771, June 22, Flick, Eliz., and Henry Carry.
1797, Dec.   3, Flickwir, David, and Rebecca Williamson.
1798, Feb. 28, Fliegener, Sarah Maria, and George Geist.
1747, June 13, Fling, Anne, and Geo. Vincent Dawes.
1774, Dec. 15, Fling, William, and Sarah Vaughan.
1772, Jan. 16, Flinn, Mary, and Henry Baggs.
1762, Dec. 17, Flinn, Patrick, and Rachel Donavan.
1751, June 23, Flood, Andrew, and Rachel Davis.
1758, Oct. 26, Flood, Henry, and Elizabeth Titchet.
1731, Nov. 18, Flood, Patrick, and Mary Towson.
1757, Dec. 17, Flood, Rachel, and John Logan.
1779, Nov. 25, Flood, Reb., and William Christian.
1757, July   2, Flood, William, and Martha Gwinnap.
1765, Nov. 28, Flower, Ann, and Samuel Wheeler.
1735, June   9, Flower, Benjamin, and Ruth Bibb.
1771, Feb.   7, Flower, Benjamin, and Sarah Pickles.
1727, June   1, Flower, Esther, and Ed. Bradly.

1767, Nov.   14, Flower, Hannah, and Thomas Asheton.
1761, May   13, Flower, Mary, and Gerardus Clarkson.
1731-2, Jan.   9, Flower, Mary, and John Crapp.
1769, Dec.   19, Flower, Rachel, and Samuel Saunders.
1762, May   19, Flower, Samuel, and Sarah Ann Williams.
1732, June   2, Flower, Samuel, and Rebecca Boon.
1795, Jan.   8, Flowers, Thomas, and Sarah Page.
1767, May   7, Floyd, Jane, and Neal McEntire.
1750, June   13, Floyd, John, and Mary Latham.
1772, Feb.   17, Flyn, John, and Susannah Tatnall.
1776, Jan.   18, Flynn, Patrick, and Cath. Malaby.
1796, July   17, Foley, Michael, and Abigail Anderson.
1774, June   23, Folger, Ann, and Joseph Elden.
1780, June   8, Folker, Mary, and Thomas Justice.
1734, Aug.   19, Folkers, Phoebe, and Lawrence Williamson.
1743, March   26, Follensby, Mary, and John Fisher.
1753, May   29, Folly, Daniel, and Catherine Walter.
1753, Oct.   25, Folly, Henry, and Mary Griffith.
1794, Oct.   11, Fondy, Andrew, and Sarah Esling.
1781, Dec.   24, Foot, James, and Mary Crawford.
1792, May   2, Footman, Mary, and John D. Coxe.
1768, Sept.   29, Forbes, Catherine, and Thomas Britton.
1760, Nov.   27, Forbes, Hugh, and Mary Mapper.
1764, April   31, Forbes, Margaret, and Thomas York.
1768, Jan.   9, Forbes, William, and Mary Bevan.
1757, Sept.   3, Forbies, Ann, and Edward Croston.
1795, Aug.   27, Ford, Ann, and Aaron Clayton.
1755, May   3, Ford, Anne, and John Ford.
1758, July   25, Ford, Benjamin, and Sarah Clayton.
1750, Sept.   15, Ford, Bridget, and Patrick Gaynor.
1748, Aug.   6, Ford, Charity, and Samuel Wickward.
1783, June   30, Ford, Daniel, and Hannah Gillman.
1796, Oct.   29, Ford, Eliz., and Joseph Norton.
1798, July   5, Ford, Eliz., and Jacob Lawson.
1743, Sept.   15, Ford, Eliz., and Jacob Worrall.
1744, Feb.   5, Ford, Eliz., and Thomas Grant.
1784, Jan.   18, Ford, Eliz., and Baptist William.
1755, May   3, Ford, John, and Anne Ford.
1749, Jan.   9, Ford, John, and Anne Bonnet.
1800, Dec.   18, Ford, Joseph, and Sarah Belton.
1747, Aug.   13, Ford, Mary, and James Waldrick.
1726, Dec.   18, Ford, Mary, and John Robison.
1793, May   16, Ford, Patrick, and Jane Wilson.
1755, May   30, Ford, Philip, and Margaret Archer.
1795, Dec.   5, Ford, Standish, and Sarah Britton.
1737, Aug.   7, Ford, Timothy, and Elizabeth Gardner.

1752, Dec. 30, Fordan, Mary, and Thomas Roberts.
1760, Dec. 14, Fordham, Benjamin, and Catherine Rennion.
1779, March 17, Fordham, Benjamin and Nancy Cousin.
1783, June 11, Foreman, Eliz., and Benjamin Chamberlain, Esqr.
1785, Nov. 23, Foreman, Eliz., and Edward Shippen.
1747, April 19, Forge, Catherine, and Robert Bullock.
1739, Oct. 10, Forneaman, Rebecca, and William White.
1754, Oct. 31, Forrest, Anne, and Nicholas Toy.
1804, Sept. 27, Forrest, Henry, and Mary Shepherd.
1798, Feb. 18, Forrest, James, and Eliz. Deal.
1758, May, 13, Forrest, James, and Mary Revell.
1750, Nov. 17, Forrest, Martha, and John Day.
1771, May, 20, Forrest, May, and John Symes.
1772, Dec. 9, Forrest, Sarah, and Sturges Shoveler.
1770, April 28, Forrest, Thomas, and Ann Whitpaine.
1720, Dec. 8, Forrest, William, and Mary Price.
1794, July 20, Forrest, William, and Martha Rebecca Loarman.
1798, Feb. 1, Forrest, William, and Sarah Dunlap.
1755, Dec. 26, Forrester, Catherine, and David Brown.
1785, Oct. 27, Forsbes, Arthur, and Mary Baker.
1742, June 12, Forster, Barbara, and James Fulloin.
1729, Feb. 13, Forster, John, and Rachel Philpot.
1758, June 17, Forster, Marmaduke, and Ann Murray.
1763, Jan. 29, Forster, Mary, and Joseph Dobins.
1796, Oct. 9, Forsyth, David, and Eliz. Turner.
1775, Oct. 10, Forsyth, George, and Chloe Elliot.
1795, Feb. 26, Forsyth, Robert, and Eliz. Brewton.
1796, Aug. 28, Fortune, Eliz., and James Jones.
1736, Aug. 21, Fortune, Mary, and Joseph Eustice.
1749, March 26, Foster, Content, and John Jones.
1786, June 19, Foster, David, and Mary Bowling.
1794, Sept. 28, Foster, Deborah, and Peter Newlin.
1728, April 16, Foster, Geo., and Susʰ Boar.
1796, Oct. 27, Foster, Margaret, and William Kerr.
1749, Nov. 21, Foster, Salathiel, and Mercy Kirk.
1769, Nov. 21, Foster, William, and Frances Strickland.
1796, Dec. 9, Foster, William, and Mary Lee.
1770, Oct. 17, Fosset, John, and Hannah Ware.
1721, Dec. 29, Fosset, Sarah, and Isaac Lea.
1747, July 30, Fotheringham, John, and Margaret Shoemaker.
1805, March 16, Fouchee, William, and Lucy Lawrence.
1792, April 12, Foudray, William, and Cath. Gamble.
1795, Nov. 26, Foulke, Caleb, and Margaret Cullen.
1735, Sept. 29, Foulke, John, and Margaret Jones.
1771, July 15, Foulkes, Susannah, and Samuel Cunrad.
1799, Jan. 6, Fowler, Cath., and Paul Freneau.

1736, Nov. 17, Fowler, Edward, and Mary Carr.
1741, June   5, Fowler, John, and Mary Curll.
1759, March 22, Fowler, John, and Hannah Clayton.
1798, Dec. 29, Fownes, John, and Sarah Thomas.
1736, Nov. 18, Fox, Anthony, and Joanna Steer.
1759, May   7, Fox, Elizabeth, and John Cassell.
1750, Oct. 14, Fox, Elizabeth, and William Henry.
1741, Dec. 16, Fox, Elizabeth, and Joseph Large.
1751, Aug.   4, Fox, George, and Mary Woods.
1736, Dec. 16, Fox, James, and Mary Wade.
1734, Nov. 27, Fox, James, and Susannah Daviss.
1773, Sept. 26, Fox, John, and Susannah Sheckles.
1740, Dec. 14, Fox, Robert, and Lydia Clark.
1740, Aug.   6, Fox, John, and Mary Johnson.
1742, Aug. 16, Fox, John, and Eliz. Taylor.
1744, March 26, Fox, John, and Catharine Roche.
1728, June 29, Fox, Marg^t, and H. Fitzakerlin.
1743, April 29, Fox, Margaret, and Richard Harris.
1720, Jan.   1, Fox, Mary, and Benjamin Rhodes.
1746, May   29, Fox, Mary, and Timothy Lane.
1806, Feb.   6, Fox, Samuel, and Maria Moylan.
1801, April 14, Fox, Sarah, and Mathew Brown.
1801, March 6, Fox, Sophia, and Charles Goldsmith.
1777, Sept. 14, Fox, Thomas, and Mary Randal.
1748, Aug. 15, Fox, Thomas, and Anne Woodward.
1775, March 26, Foy, John, and Hopper Hersett.
1775, Nov.   3, Fraeme, Eliz., and John Hannah.
1800, Nov. 30, Fraley, John, and Eliza Laskey.
1801, June 18, Fraley, Mary, and Thomas Bringhurst.
1790, Oct. 22, France, John, and Ann White.
1743, Sept. 30, Francis, Anne, and James Tilghman.
1730, April 7, Francis, Arnold, and Elizabeth James.
1750, April 19, Francis, Elizabeth, and John Lawrence.
1806, Jan. 12, Francis, Eliz. Powell, and Joshua Fisher.
1753, Nov. 29, Francis, Margaret, and Edward Shippen, Jr.
1750, April 10, Francis, Mary, and William Cox.
1760, March 3, Francis, Rachel, and John Relfe.
1792, Feb. 15, Francis, Sophia, and George Harrison.
1762, Feb.   8, Francis, Tench, and Ann Willing.
1798, Aug. 23, Francis, Tench, and Hannah Roberts.
1781, June 11, Francis, Thomas, and Martha Williams.
1794, Sept. 25, Francis, Thomas W., and Dorothy Willing.
1751, Feb. 25, Francis, Thomas, and Susannah Turner.
1770, Sept. 27, Francis, Turbutt, and Sarah Mifflin.
1781, April 16, Franklin, George, and Eliz. Ellis.
1767, Oct. 29, Franklin, Sarah, and Richard Bache.

1792, June   28, Franklin, William, and Margaret Mears.
1768, Jan.   6, Franks, Abigail, and Andrew Hamilton.
1755, Sept.   6, Franks, Elizabeth, and Edward Drinker.
1800, June   29, Franks, Eliz., and Charles Cummings.
1760, June   14, Franks, John, and Appelonia Seymour.
1751, June   23, Fraser, Mary, and Cæsar Ghuiselin.
1773, Sept.   16, Frazer, Alice, and Timothy Sloan.
1794, Sept.   13, Frazer, Nabro, and Ann West.
1715, Feb.   3, Frazier, William, and Hannah Clemens.
1746, Aug.   19, Fream, Letitia, and Daniel Taylor.
1771, June   11, Frederick, Alice, and Joseph Neagle.
1723, Dec.   15, Frederick, Henry, and Hannah Parvera.
1743, Dec.   12, Frederick, John, and Abigail Grareway.
1765, April   20, Frederick, Philip, and Alice Kennedy.
1749, Aug.   24, Fredericks, Alice, and Abraham Jessop.
1730, April   30, Free, Abraham, and Anne Bevan.
1758, Jan.   18, Free, William, and Margaret Jones.
1768, Oct.   27, Freeborn, Hill, and Martha Glyn.
1802, July   22, Freed, Sarah, and Peter Cannon Slaughter.
1712, March   18, Freedland, Rebecca, and Charles Reed.
1803, May   13, Freeman, Alpheus, and Mary Parker.
1802, Dec.   23, Freeman, Benjamin, and Ann Mercier.
1795, March   15, Freeman, Charlotte, and John F. Oneal.
1797, May   20, Freeman, Constant, and Margaret Coxe.
1796, Jan.   1, Freeman, Daniel, and Rachel Penington.
1750, April   23, Freeman, James, and Anne Corbett.
1798, Oct.   15, Freeman, Joseph, and Stacy Goodwin.
1798, July   9, Freeman, Margaret, and Absalom Zeigar Vernon.
1780, Dec.   11, Freeman, Samuel, and Mary Anderson.
1766, March   19, Freeman, Sarah, and Thomas Neff.
1761, Nov.   4, Freeman, Sarah, and Lewis Webster.
1777, May   11, Freeman, Thomas, and Sarah Parsons.
1744, Oct.   10, Freeston, John, and Ann Cunningham.
1788, June   5, Freeston, Robert, and Mary Garrison.
1770, Dec.   3, Freight, Ann, and George Liddell.
1790, Oct.   3, French, ——, and Cath. Lawrence.
1761, March   2, French, Alexander, and Ann Cratter.
1783, May   29, French, Charles, and Isabella Stokes.
1766, June   18, French, Elizabeth, and John Ferguson.
1773, July   24, French, James, and Mary Clark.
1805, Dec.   21, French, John, and Mary Voight.
1799, Jan.   6, Freneau, Paul, and Cath. Fowler.
1717, Jan.   5, Fressey, Elizabeth, and Robert Potts.
1744, June,   5, Fretwell, Mary, and Nicholas Cassel.
1738, Nov.   23, Freyers, Eleanor, and James Hale.
1797, June   24, Freytag, Christiana, and Robert Groves.

1735, Oct.　15, Frie, Susannah, and Jacob Seyl.
1781, Jan.　23, Friend, Eliz., and Thomas Phipps.
1726, Nov.　9, Friend, Mary, and Abraham Salvai.
1794, Nov.　13, Friend, Rebecca, and Lewis Beson.
1761, June　17, Frin, Cicily, and William Pett.
1782, March 10, Frinck, Theophilus, and Frances Harrison.
1797, Nov.　15, Fromp, Martha Wilson, and Thomas Quinn.
1716, Feb.　27, Froud, Rachel, and James Brown.
1733, Jan.　7, Frost, Catherine, and Elizabeth Jones.
1729–30, Jan. 13, Frost, John, and Edy Wheeler.
1782, April　16, Froth, Isaac, an Eliz. Lippincott.
1784, Nov.　11, Fruman, Richard, and Rachel Sykes.
1729, Oct.　28, Fruwn, John, and Celia Kelly.
1757, Jan.　5, Fry, John, and Milicent O'Neal.
1773, May　31, Fullan, Philip, and Laetitia Hendricks.
1717, March　3, Fullard, Robert, and Elizabeth Bywater.
1794, July　31, Fullarton, Eliza, and Nathaniel Curran.
1758, Sept.　19, Fuller, Benjamin, and Rebecca Stamper.
1768, Jan.　23, Fullerton, James, and Ann Brustrum.
1739, Feb.　17, Fullerton, Jane, and Hugh Williams.
1768, July　9, Fullerton, Mary, and Robert Pew.
1782, March　5, Fullerton, Mary, and John Chamney.
1746, Aug.　27, Fullerton, Rose, and Edward Maginnis.
1787, July　30, Fullman, Susannah, and William Elfrey.
1742, June　12, Fulloin, James, and Barbara Forster.
1783, Aug.　31, Funk, Eliz., and Ebenezer Branham.
1753, March 10, Furnace, Thomas, and Anne Gibson.
1755, Oct.　15, Fulton, David, and Elizabeth Yeates.
1748, Sept.　17, Fulton, Elizabeth, and William Standley.
1797, May　16, Fulton, James, and Margaret Cherry.
1755, Aug.　20, Fulton, Robert, and Eleanor Wyncoop.
1767, March 17, Furman, Moore, and Sarah White.
1731, May　13, Furnis, Anthony, and Martha Wright.
1774, Oct.　19, Furrow, Eliz., and John Bynes.
1743, March 27, Fusman, Eliz., and Meredith Jones.
1766, May　11, Fustin, Jacob, and Ann Philips.
1756, April　29, Gaae, Grace, and William Nicholson
1773, May　3, Gabriel, Edward, and Martha Carmalt.
1711, Dec.　2, Gadely, George, and Mary Evans.
1738, Dec.　3, Gage, Thomas, and Mary Levett.
1784, Aug.　4, Gagen, Eliz. Gay, and John Harper Hopkins.
1734, April　6, Gailbraith, James, and Elizabeth Bartram.
1759, July　21, Galbraith, Ann, and Paul McLane.
1765, Aug.　28, Galbreath, Samuel, and Margaret Miloy.
1783, Sept.　18, Gale, Eliz. Bella, and Samuel Wilcocks.
1761, Jan.　10, Gale, Nicholas, and Margaret Burk.

1803, Oct.   31, Gallagher, Ann, and Daniel Bradley.
1803, Aug.   14, Gallagher, Daniel, and Eleanor Hart.
1797, Jan.   12, Gallagher, James, and Margaret Dobson.
1794, Dec.   21, Gallagher, John, and Sarah Knowles.
1801, Nov.   7, Gallagher, Mary, and Thomas Daniel.
1799, June   3, Gallagher, Patrick, and Hannah Dailey.
1776, April   10, Gallagher, Rosanna, and William Duncan.
1804, June   25, Gallagher, Sarah, and Peter Lawson.
1801, May   27, Gallant, Narcissus Joseph, and Susanna Shright.
1768, Sept.   29, Galloway, Jenny, and Joseph Shippen, Jr., Esqr.
1786, Oct.   23, Galloway, John, and Sarah Chew.
1760, Sept.   30, Galloway, Joseph, and Hannah Cookson.
1753, Oct.   18, Galloway, Joseph, and Grace Growden.
1759, Dec.   21, Gambier, Samuel, and Eleanor Robinson.
1777, Oct.   11, Gamble, Archibald, and Mary Lisle.
1792, April   12, Gamble, Cath., and William Foudray.
1792, April   5, Gamble, Eliz., and Ezekiel Giberson.
1788, Jan.   24, Gamble, James, and Sarah Morris.
1804, Sept.   1, Gamble, Joseph, and Mary Thompson.
1785, Sept.   1, Gamble, Oliva, and Abraham Gardner.
1764, Nov.   19, Gamble, William, and Ann McDonald.
1721, Feb.   14, Gambridge, Giles, and Winifield Collet.
1715, July   27, Gandoret, Elizabeth, and John Abraham Norman-
                    die.
1761, May   16, Gankins, Barbary, and William Hall.
1779, Aug.   2, Ganthony, Ann, and Nicholas Pickle.
1739, July   6, Ganthony, Peter, and Jane Davies.
1783, Oct.   20, Gantry, John, and Mary Spade.
1751, March   19, Garaway, Charles, and Sarah Montgomery.
1755, July   30, Gard, John, and Elizabeth Tyley.
1790, Aug.   29, Gardener, Hester, and Edward Cirby.
1767, March   13, Gardener, William, and Sarah Houlton.
1795, June   8, Gardiner, James, and Ann Dillintash.
1795, Dec.   10, Gardiner, John, and Mary Servis.
1794, Oct.   4, Gardiner, Mary, and Charles Hutchinson.
1791, Aug.   6, Gardiner, Mary, and Ezekial King.
1770, March   30, Gardiner, Sarah, and Ezekial Evans.
1758, Sept.   7, Gardiner, Theophilus, and Mary Dyer.
1801, May   22, Gardiner, William, and Rebecca Walton.
1785, Sept.   1 Gardner, Abraham, and Oliva Gamble.
1768, Dec.   13, Gardner, Alexander, and Elizabeth Hoover.
1731, Oct.   7, Gardner, Elizabeth, and Thomas Peglar.
1737, Aug.   7, Gardner, Elizabeth, and Timothy Ford.
1764, July   7, Gardner, Elizabeth, and John Morrison.
1790, May   20, Gardner, Hannah, and Thomas Mason.
1784, Jan.   15, Gardner, John, and Mary Bush.

1759, Sept.   7, Gardner, Joseph, and Margaret Henry.
1758, Dec.   5, Gardner, Mary, and George Senniff.
1745, Sept. 30, Gardner, Mary, and Peter Rose.
1805, Dec. 30, Gardner, Mary, and Joseph Clark.
1764, Jan. 16, Gardner, Matthew, and Mary. Little.
1729, April 23, Gardner, Pat., and Mary Osborn.
1764, June   5, Gardner, Sarah, and Matthew Butler.
1756, Jan. 17, Gardner, Sarah, and Anthony King.
1768, Nov.   3, Garland, George, and Ruth Terry.
1794, Dec. 20, Garland, John, and Rachel Cotman.
1765, Nov. 30, Garlin, John, and Mary Smith.
1775, May   7, Garlin, John, and Ann Standford.
1764, Nov. 24, Garner, Joseph, and Hannah Thornhill.
1786, July 20, Garnet, John, and Tracy Thompson.
1762, March 29, Garrard, Hacklace, and William Falkner.
1786, June   1, Garrigues, Ann, and Joseph Burrough.
1799, July 18, Garret, Barbara, and Charles Atkinson.
1770, Oct.   8, Garret, Joseph, and Charity Collins.
1764, March 1, Garret, Lydia, and Edward Hewes.
1728, Nov.   6, Garret, Marcus, and Ann Boone.
1761, Oct. 10, Garrett, Mary, and John Pywell.
1738, June 26, Garret, Valentine, and Rebecca Sweeting.
1728, May 16, Garretson, Mary, and Wm Patterson.
1772, April 16, Garrett, Abraham, and Mary Taylor.
1795, Aug. 13, Garrett, Ann, and John Nelson.
1765, Dec. 23, Garrett, Mary, and Robert Tucker.
1786, Sept. 28, Garrette, Mary, and George Barclay.
1770, Oct. 29, Garrick, Francis, and Sarah Johnson.
1747, June   9, Garrigue, Sarah, and George Howel.
1763, Jan. 13, Garrigues, Elizabeth, and Robert ———.
1747, Jan.   1, Garrigues, Francis, and Mary Knowles.
1801, Oct.   6, Garrigues, Hannah, and Robert Norris.
1773, April 28, Garrigues, Jacob, and Mary Ashton.
1790, Oct. 12, Garrigues, Rebecca, and John Ellwood.
1759, Dec. 24, Garrigues, Sarah, and Charles Woolsall.
1753, Jan. 13, Garrigues, Susannah, and Dennis Sulivan.
1720, Feb.   4, Garrison, Jacob, and Mary Wallen.
1788, June   5, Garrison, Mary, and Robert Freeston.
1795, July 24, Garth, Ann, and John McNeal.
1798, July 23, Gartley, Rebecca, and Joseph Thomson.
1796, June 15, Gartley, William, and Eliz. Woodward.
1783, Dec.   4, Garwin, John, and Eliz. Robinett.
1772, Aug. 15, Garwood, John, and Sarah Neithermark.
1763, March 8, Garwood, Lucia, and James Claypoole.
1805, June 15, Garwood, Richard, and Hannah Dennis.
1785, June 14, Garwood, Sarah, and William Art.

1743, July   11, Garwood, William, and Martha Johnson.
1720, Sept.   1, Gasnold, Thomas, and Mary Hall.
1792, March 13, Gass, George, and Ann Wood.
1735, July   21, Gative, Charles, and Margaret Evans.
1728, Feb.   20, Gative, Mary, and Joshua Maddox.
1755, April   19, Gatline, Rees, and Anne Swane.
1714, March 30, Gatlow, Nicholas, and Mary Ruther.
1796, Oct.   23, Gatty, Joseph, and Mary Brown.
1773, Aug.   5, Gaubert, David, and Mary Walker.
1766, Dec.   8, Gauff, Martha, and John Tufft.
1721, Sept.   10, Gault, Oliver, and Margaret Smith.
1750, Nov.   16, Gaunt, Zebulon, and Esther Woolman.
1725, Sept.   16, Gaure, Martha, and Phil. Doeux.
1805, July   25, Gaw, Eliz., and James Jacques Bourdine.
1720, April   10, Gawcain, John, and Ann Griffith.
1760, Jan.   4, Gay, William, and Mary Rouse.
1750, Sept.   15, Gaynor, Patrick, and Bridget Ford.
1729, Jan.   27, Geals, Jos., and Eleanor Rouse.
1780, Dec.   27, Geary, David, and Eliz. Lumm.
1743, Oct.   24, Geary, Judith, and Patrick McDonnagh.
1763, March   2, Ged, Dougaldus, and Margery Thomas.
1712, June   19, Geesling, Eleanor, and Silvanus Smout.
1783, Sept.   3, Gehry, Ann, and Thomas Pickering.
1798, Feb.   28, Geist, George, and Sarah Maria Fliegener.
1781, Jan.   27, Gemble, James, and Mary Maago.
1735, Dec.   14, Gennet, (or Geimet,) Michael, and Susannah Mor-
                    ton.
1761, Nov.   29, Geogahan, Patrick, and Sarah Robinson.
1734, June   20, George, Abraham, and Anna Richards.
1796, Nov.   15, George, Charles, and Mary Green.
1783, Feb.   24, George, Eleanor, and Cornelius Callaghan.
1783, Aug.   6, George, Eliz., and William Blake.
1742, Dec.   16, George, John, and Susannah Meredith.
1761, Jan.   29, George, Margaret, and Mathew McGlathery.
1734, Feb,   7, George, Margaret, and John Ashton.
1786, Jan.   19, George, Mary, and William King.
1743, May   4, George, Peter, and Susannah Danby.
1781, Dec.   11, George, Peter, and Rebecca Richardson.
1793, April   27, George, Richard, and Mary Reid.
1801, Oct.   12, George, Sarah, and Richard Saunders.
1786, Dec.   14, George, Sarah, and Nicholas Hammond.
1765, June   11, Geraud, Margaret, and James Paulhill.
1768, Sept.   29, Gerhard, Conrad, and Rachel Iselstein.
1721, April   11, German, Benjamin, and Elizabeth Green.
1774, Sept.   3, German, William, and Rebecca Pearce.
1727, Sept.   14, Gerrack, Francis, and Ann Willson.

1770, Jan.　15, Gerrard, Agnes, and Matthew Strong.
1775, April　1, Gerrard, Ann, and William Downs.
1711, June　9, Gerrard, Robert, and Margaret Bristoll.
1754, April　10, Gerrard, Tamazan, and Isaac Comron.
1795, May　28, Getting, Jane, and Conrad Steinmitz.
1795, Aug.　16, Gettinger, Hannah, and James Ingersoll Cannon.
1768, Dec.　7, Gheen, Joseph, and Elizabeth Engram.
1732, Oct.　15, Gheseling, Hannah, and John Panam.
1782, Jan.　3, Ghiseline, Sarah, and William Banks.
1747, Dec.　5, Ghiselin, William, and Rebecca Buckston.
1722, July　1, Ghisling, Nicholas, and Elizabeth Evans.
1720, Oct.　11, Ghristopher, Lurena, and Bracey Warley.
1751, June　23, Ghuiselin, Cæsar, and Mary Fraser.
1797, May　16, Gibbons, Eliz., and Archibald Little.
1782, March 14, Gibbons, James, and Ann Phyle.
1750, Aug.　25, Gibbons, James, and Mary Miller.
1795, May　5, Gibbons, Jane, and Gatriel Duval.
1860, July　22, Gibbons, Mary, and John Hill.
1804, March　4, Gibbons, Rebecca, and Abisha Clark.
1734, Sept.　30, Gibbs, Alexander, and Alice Guff.
1767, Feb.　26, Gibbs, Benjamin, and Elizabeth Nicholson.
1733, Jan.　16, Gibbs, Elizabeth, and James Morris.
1730, April　29, Gibbs, John, and Dorothy Allen.
1790, Sept.　5, Gibbs, Mary, and Jeremiah Nicholson.
1782, Oct.　17, Gibbs, Mary, and Joshua Carey.
1796, Nov.　18, Gibbs, Rebecca, and William Glenn.
1782, Sept.　20, Gibbs, Samuel, and Rachel Rodman.
1785, April　12, Gibbs, Samuel, and Euphemia Willett.
1784, June　3, Gibbs, Sarah, and Gilbert Rodman.
1792, May　17, Gibbs, Thomas, and Ann Morgan.
1786, Feb.　3, Giberson, Daniel, and Lydia Crispin.
1792, April　5, Giberson, Ezekiel, and Eliz. Gamble.
1742, Aug.　15, Gibson, Ann, and Daniel Harrison.
1804, May　31, Gibson, Ann, and William Rex.
1753, March 10, Gibson, Anne, and Thomas Furnace.
1800, April　30, Gibson, Barbara, and Pierce Divine.
1734, Nov.　16, Gibson, George, and Martha Deveney.
1757, Oct.　15, Gibson, John, and Anna Ball.
1801, April　7, Gibson, Sarah, and Peter McCall.
1762, Sept.　4, Gibson, William, and Ruth Johnson.
1766, Aug.　18, Gichon, Hiram, and Sarah Dulany.
1786, Dec.　10, Giden, Susannah, and James Mollineux.
1784, April　9, Giffard, Mary, and William Nash.
1730-1, Feb. 25, Giffin, Joshua, and Jane Wright.
1760, Aug.　17, Gilbert, Benjamin, and Elizabeth Perth.
1775, March 14, Gilbert, Francis, and Margaret Nielson.

1761, Aug.   13, Gilbert, George, and Sarah Carr.
1760, Jan.   3, Gilbert, Hannah, and Abner Clark.
1796, Jan.   17, Gilbert, Henry, and Ann Reading.
1731-2, Jan. 15, Gilbert, Margaret, and Samuel Cockran.
1779, July   22, Gilbert, Mary, and Edward Young.
1775, Dec.   12, Gilbert, Mary, and John Pierce.
1737, Dec.   26, Gilbert, Samuel, and Amiable Brown.
1761, Sept.   1, Gilbert, Sarah, and Daniel Walton.
1797, July   26, Gildea, John, and Margaret Currie.
1760, May   29, Giles, Edward, and Margaret Teas.
1757, Jan.   22, Gilham, John, and Abigail Woodward.
1754, Feb.   27, Gilingham, Sarah, and William Wayn.
1741, Sept.   9, Gill, Edward, and Mary Irwin.
1805, Feb.   9, Gill, Edward, and Ann Hawke.
1762, Oct.   28, Gill, Henry, and Mary Bryan.
1766, Aug.   9, Gill, John, and Sarah Hazell.
1714, Oct.   10, Gill, Juliana, and John Sackeverel.
1722, May   27, Gill, Mary, and Gabriel Cox.
1767, March   23, Gill, Mary, and Jacob Roberts.
1772, Oct.   8, Gill, Robert, and Hannah Allen.
1780, Aug.   24, Gill, Sarah, and Godfrey Stillwell,
1794, July   3, Gill, Sarah, and Alexander Howard.
1781, Oct.   11, Gill, William, and Hannah Dunwick.
1799, April   13, Gill, William, and Eliz. Kennedy.
1804, July   21, Gill, William Knight, and Ann Carrell.
1801, Dec.   9, Gillan, Sarah, and Clotworthy O'Neil.
1757, Dec.   14, Gillaspy, Archibald, and Mary Cook.
1805, May   9, Gillis, Jane, and Andrew Mulcahy.
1746, Dec,   22, Gilliard, Anne, and Joseph Thompson.
1726, Nov.   17, Gillinaur, Rebeccah, and Wm Wright.
1783, June   30, Gillman, Hannah, and Daniel Ford.
1765, Dec.   10, Gilmore, Eleanor, and Matthew Cochran.
1782, April   11, Gilmore, Margaret, and James West.
1777, Aug.   29, Gilpin, ——, and —— Gray.
1736, June   23, Gilpin, Isaac, and Hannah Knight.
1784, July   14, Gilpin, John Bernard, and Ann Woodrop Sims.
1796, Jan.   28, Gist, Rachel, and Joseph Shreeves.
1786, April   8, Githins, Mary, and John Hagarty.
1800, June   19, Gitts, Eliz., and James Selby.
1800, Jan.   16, Gitts, Mary, and Joseph Coulter.
1761, Oct.   3, Gitts, Michael, and Mary Black.
1728, Oct.   10, Gizlin, Mary, and Thomas Rutter.
1802, Jan.   8, Gladden, Samuel, and Eliz. Simkins.
1770, Dec.   5, Gladding, David, and Rebecca Ratcliff.
1770, Aug.   11, Glascow, Jane, and James Harnett.
1751, Aug.   28, Glascow, Jane, and Anthony Pritchard.

1795, June   2, Glen, William, and Margaret Murphy.
1796, Nov.   18, Glenn, William, and Rebecca Gibbs.
1731, June   16, Glenn, William, and Ann Aldridge.
1794, April   3, Glentworth, Plunket Fleeson, and Harriet Bost-
           wick.
1795, May   21, Glentworth, Sarah, and Anthony Simmonds.
1720, May   4, Glentworth, Thomas, and Mary Wilson.
1757, Feb.   10, Glove, Mary, and John Hannis.
1760, May   8, Glover, Rachel, and Robert Cooper.
1780, Aug.   7, Glover, Thomas, and Ann Higgins.
1766, July   19, Glover, William, and Mary Mackinson.
1768, Oct.   27, Glyn, Martha, and Hill Freeborn.
1754, Dec.   12, Godard, William, and Mary Fisher.
1737, April   16, Goddard, Mary, and Shepherd Kollock.
1794, July   12, Godfredy, Edward, and Ann Hamilton.
1738, Oct.   27, Godfrey, Ann, and Robert Barton.
1803, Sept.   8, Godfrey, Charles, and Sarah Wills.
1758, July   1, Godfred, Deborah, and John Stone.
1736, Nov.   25, Godfrey, Eleanor, and John Jones.
1797, May   18, Godfrey, Thomas, and Margaret Mahaffy.
1757, Sept.   7, Godfriend, Catherine, and Henry Showman.
1772, April   17, Goff, Charles, and Eliz. Moore.
1801, Aug.   15, Goforth, Ann, and Clement Cardiff.
1795, March   2, Goforth, Rachel, and Patrick McAllister.
1750, Dec.   20, Goforth, William, and Mary Dunning.
1777, Sept.   9, Goft, Samuel, and Cath. Vance.
1736, March   9, Goin, John, and Anne Warren.
1769, June   26, Gold, Michael, and Elizabeth Elliott.
1802, Aug.   28, Goldsborough, Charles Washington, and Cath.
           Roberts.
1794, Dec.   4, Goldsborough, Eleanor, and Joseph Robertson.
1799, March 25, Goldsborough, Robert, and Sarah Potter.
1801, March   6, Goldsmith, Charles, and Sophia Fox.
1720, Jan.   31, Goldsmith, James, and Eleanor Lewis.
1767, Feb.   25, Golley, Anthony, and Mary McEntire.
1805, Dec.   16, Goudshaw, Paul, and Eliz. Good.
1787, Nov.   1, Good, Eliz., and Jacob Bunner.
1805, Dec.   16, Good, Eliz., and Paul Goudshaw.
1769, Nov.   17, Good, Philip, and Mary Edwards.
1797, July   23, Good, Thomas, and Eliz. Downey.
1753, Jan.   6, Goodin, Anne, and Alexander Kennedy.
1745, Oct.   15, Goodin, Mary, and John McCormick.
1744, Jan.   28, Goodin, Phoebe, and William Hawkins.
1744, Dec.   31, Gooding, John, and Deborah West.
1735, Aug.   27, Goodjohn, Robert, and Rebecca Jonson.
1783, July   15, Goodman, Eliz., and Francis Joseph Lecture.

1760, Dec.   14, Goodman, Sarah, and Nicholas Fitzsimmons.
1741, May   11, Goodman, Walter, and Martha Yarbury.
1731, April   20, Gooldsberry, Robert, and Jane Starke.
1802, June   1, Goodwin, Ann, and Thomas Birch.
1729, April   29, Goodwin, Gartrey, and Theodorus Hall.
1735, Nov.   10, Goodwin, Henry, and Anne Coats.
1772, Dec.   7, Goodwin, John, and Susannah Rockwell.
1733, Oct.   25, Goodwin, John, and Phoebe Williams.
1798, Oct.   15, Goodwin, Stacy, and Joseph Freeman.
1725, Oct.   13, Goodwin, Thomas, and Sarah Church.
1770, Sept.   10, Goodwin, William, and Barbary Vennemore.
1806, March 23, Gordon, Adam, and Aletheia Sparhawk.
1749, June   24, Gordon, Alexander, and Mary Pinder.
1782, Nov.   28, Gordon, Ann, and William McMurtrie, Esqr.
1796, May   14, Gordon, Daniel, and Mary Anderson.
1769, Nov.   30, Gordon, Dorothy, and Lawrence Salter.
1790, Sept.   16, Gordon, Eliz., and John Stewart.
1774, Dec.   29, Gordon, Eliz., and John Salter.
1762, July   15, Gordon, Elizabeth, and Charles Speckman.
1769, June   24, Gordon, Elizabeth, and George Corry.
1779, Oct.   26, Gordon, Frances, and Dr. Enoch Edwards.
1784, Oct.   23, Gordon, Frederick, and Eliz. Pusey.
1762, Jan.   30, Gordon, Harry, and Hannah Meredith.
1774, Feb.   19, Gordon, Henry, and Eliz. Lacy.
1798, Jan.   1, Gordon, Jessey, and Joseph Perevani.
1778, Oct.   1, Gordon, John, and Susannah Head.
1804, July   12, Gordon, Judith, and Israel Lee.
1805, Dec.   12, Gordon, Lewis, and Esther H. Osman.
1750, Jan.   4, Gordon, Lewis, and Mary Jenkins.
1786, Jan.   23, Gordon, Mary, and Samuel Fennemore.
1784, Nov.   18, Gordon, Mary, and David Bralsford.
1804, Sept.   8, Gordon, Mary, and James Snell.
1752, April   2, Gordon, Stephen, and Mary Bennet.
1731-2, Feb. 18, Gordon, Thomas, and Mary Stapleford.
1751, Oct.   15, Gordon, Thomas, and Mary Bambridge.
1788, June   28, Gordon, Thomas, and Margaret Huston.
1794, May   7, Gordon, William, and Maria Cartwright.
1735, May   31, Gore, Marjory, and Daniel Carroll.
1801, March 22, Goring, Joseph, and Sarah Due.
1803, Jan.   2, Gorton, Penelope, and John Burns.
1732, Sept.   10, Goseling, Rosamund, and John Budd.
1754, Aug.   4, Gosline, Anne, and Thomas Scot.
1787, April   20, Gosmer, Mary, and John Probart.
1805, March 10, Gosner, Margaret, and Joseph Small.
1722, Dec.   12, Gosnold, Mary, and Malachi Phelps.
1798, July   20, Gosteloe, Eliz., and Matthew Locke.

1768, June   16, Gostelow, Jonathan, and Mary Duffield.
1789, April   19, Gostelowe, Jonathan, and Eliz. Towers.
1768, Aug.   2, Gottier, Edward, and Mary Wells.
1777, Sept.   5, Goucher, Thomas, and Hannah Hare.
1710, May   12, Gouin, Mary, and John Boll.
1799, April   25, Gould, Josiah, and Eliza Tatmal.
1795, March   4, Gould, Thomas, and Jane Pickering.
1737, April   30, Goulden, Martha, and William McKnight.
1804, May   17, Goulding, George, and Sidney Allen.
1801, June   25, Gourlay, Archibald, and Patience Polton.
1777, Sept.   8, Govett, William, and Sarah Duke.
1759, April   13, Gowey, Margaret, and Joseph Elwell.
1789, Jan.   8, Grace, Mary Ann, and William Murray.
1795, May   6, Gradiner, Peter, and Frances Cromwell.
1748, Jan.   1, Graeme, Anne, and Charles Stedman.
1753, Jan.   27, Graeme, Elizabeth, and Richard Lukens.
1753, Nov.   10, Graeme, Jane, and James Young.
1732, July   10, Grafton, Richard, and Mary Wharton.
1802, Nov.   21, Graham, Eliz., and Christopher Brown.
1768, June   19, Graham, James, and Martha Mason.
1758, Sept.   25, Graham, Joseph, and Elizabeth Lacy.
1786, May   12, Graham, Matthew, and Mary Lovel.
1753, March 13, Graham, Peter, and Elizabeth Ray.
1795, March   7, Graham, Robert, and Eliz. Corry.
1804, April   10, Graham, William, and Jane Robinson.
1764, Oct.   15, Graisbury, James, and Sarah Hart.
1804, July   8, Grant, Alexander, and Amelia Harris.
1727, April   14, Grant, Alex., and Esther Dinsie.
1798, Nov.   15, Grant, Cath., and George Buchanan.
1758, Aug.   13, Grant, Deborah, and John Quandiel.
1794, Nov.   13, Grant, Hannah, and Thomas King.
1731, Sept,   12, Grant, Hester, and Francis Sewers.
1766, Dec,   2, Grant, Isaac, and Martha Hall.
1803, April   14, Grant, Robert, and Sarah Archibald.
1784, May   9, Grant, Tacey, and George Parker.
1774, Feb.   5, Grant, Thomas, and Eliz. Ford.
1728, Jan.   1, Grantum, ———, and Cath. Morton.
1794, June   1, Grapin, Claude, and Ann Farron.
1743, Dec.   12, Grareway, Abigail, and John Frederick.
1720, Oct.   11, Grasbury, Ann, and Daniel Martin.
1776, April   25, Grason, James, and Mary Hoffman.
1749, Nov.   9, Grassberry, Joseph, and Elizabeth Dennis.
1796, Nov.   29, Grasse, John Baptist, and Eliz. Williams.
1748, Jan.   5, Gratehouse, Elizabeth, and John Arts.
1801, Oct.   8, Graves, John, and Ann Ware.
1777, Aug.   29, Gray, ———, and ——— Gilpin.

1800, March 14, Gray, Amelia, and Robert Williams.
1732, July   8, Gray, Benjamin, and Penelope Everice.
1760, Nov. 20, Gray, Elizabeth, and William Killgour.
1800, Nov. 24, Gray, Eliz., and Brittain White.
1778, Nov.   3, Gray, Eliz. Coultas, and Thomas Leiper.
1752, Nov. 25, Gray, George, Jr., and Martha Ibison.
1803, Nov.   2, Gray, George, and Rachel Adams.
1786, Feb.   9, Gray, Hannah, and John Joseph Lintman.
1793, Aug. 24, Gray, Jane, and Peter Bell.
1783, Oct. 12, Gray, Joseph, and Mary Copeland.
1792, Jan.   5, Gray, Martha, and Evan William Thomas.
1780, Nov. 16, Gray, Mary, and Peter Grubb.
1733, Aug. 10, Gray, Mary, and Daniel Syng.
1802, June   1, Gray, Samuel, and Eliz. Young.
1797, Nov. 16, Gray, Sarah, and William Levis.
1796, Oct. 13, Gray, Thomas, and Amelia McDougal.
1747, Nov. 14, Gray, William, and Elizabeth Jones.
1747, Feb. 14, Graydon, Alexander, and Rachel Marks.
1744, Dec. 27, Greathouse, Rebecca, and Leonard Streper.
1750, Feb. 15, Greathouse, William, and Barbara Shatzin.
1785, April 7, Greble, Curtis, and Mary West.
1800, May 15, Greble, Eliz., and Joseph Rapin.
1805, Jan. 19, Greble, Sarah, and Hugh Maxwell.
1793, April 25, Greble, William, and Cath. Yost.
1806, June 21, Green, Ann, and Thomas Wharton.
1802, Jan.   6, Green, Ann, and Samuel Braddock.
1752, May 18, Green, Charles, and Rosamond Dawson.
1794, Nov. 20, Green, Charlotte, and Joseph Dawson.
1805, March 2, Green, Cath., and Richard Merrick.
1731, Dec. 23, Green, Daniel, and Mary Broom.
1768, Aug. 27, Green, Daniel, and Mary Chamberlain.
1757, April 7, Green, Edward, and Elizabeth White.
1721, April 11, Green, Elizabeth, and Benjamin German.
1784, April 2, Green, Eliz., and James Anderson.
1771, April 1, Green, Hildah, and Benjamin Downs.
1787, Jan.   2, Green, John, and Deborah Simpson.
1796, Nov. 29, Green, John, and Susannah Hutchenson.
1765, June 13, Green, John, and Alice Kollock.
1738, April 25, Green, Jonas, and Anne Catherine Hoof.
1795, June   5, Green, Lucy, and Peter Dolman.
1755, Nov. 26, Green, Margaret, and James McMullen.
1765, Aug. 20, Green, Margaret, and Joshua Procter.
1797, Jan.   5, Green, Margaret, and James Alexander.
1744, Nov. 20, Green, Mary, and Henry Vanderborgh.
1796, Nov. 15, Green, Mary, and Charles George.
1795, Nov.   4, Green, Mary, and Thomas Burn.

1714, Oct.   10, Green, Mary, and John Wilson.
1722, Jan.   7, Green, Mary, and Robert Osburn.
1721, July   9, Green, Mary, and George Bird.
1765, Sept.   12, Green, Mary, and William Pollard.
1744, Sept.   13, Green, Pyramus, and Mary Morris.
1742, June   6, Green, Pyramus, and Margaret Pockington.
1783, July   30, Green, Rufus, and Cath. Side.
1767, Nov.   19, Green, Samuel, and Mary Dickson.
1771, Sept.   26, Green, Sarah, and James Irwin.
1786, Feb.   9, Green, Sarah, and Lewis Tousaents.
1733, Nov.   6, Green, Thomas, and Sarah Pegg.
1749, April   5, Green, Thomas, and Ann Lewis.
1798, Nov.   27, Green, William, and Deborah Davis.
1775, July   15, Green, William, and Margaret Grogan.
1781, March   8, Greenaway, Anne, and Bedford Williams.
1782, May   7, Greenaway, Eliz., and Dr. Solomon Halling.
1741, Oct.   7, Greenaway, Robert, and Rebecca Ball.
1789, May   3, Greenaway, William, and Rebecca Betterton.
1773, Jan.   12, Greenland, Sarah, and Edward Jackson.
1800, April   26, Greenleaf, James, and Ann Allen.
1799, June   8, Greenless, Eliz, and Jacob Pope.
1757, April   17, Greenlow, David, and Mary Henderson.
1774, Sept.   4, Greenway, Eliz, and James Ince.
1739, Oct.   14, Greenway, William, and Patience Jackson.
1787, Feb.   13, Greenwood, Barbara, and John Strobunk.
1771, July   11, Greenway, Mary, and William Beaven.
1748, Dec.   5, Greenwood, Thomas, and Gartright Dunn.
1805, Aug.   1, Greer, Margaret, and George Wirling.
1748, Jan.   2, Greesbury, Anne, and Joseph Warner.
1758, Sept.   7, Gregg, Margaret, and John White.
1767, Feb.   28, Gregory, Abraham, and Elizabeth Scott.
1796, April   13, Gregory Ann, and James Fletcher.
1736, Oct.   31, Gregory Benoni, and Christian Clark.
1752, April   7, Gregory, David, and Mary Crafts.
1773, April   29, Gregory, Dougal, and Anne McIlheran.
1773, Aug.   13, Gregory, Eliz, and William Lyell.
1710, Dec.   26, Gregory, Elizabeth, and Edward Ryeles.
1743, Feb.   10, Gregory, Elizabeth, and John Maugridge.
1763, July   17, Gregory, James, and Margaret Lincoln.
1734, March 25, Gregory, Joseph, and Anne Weldon.
1742, Sept.   12, Gregory, Mary, and Ralph Harper.
1740, July   30, Gregory, Mary, and John Williams.
1742, June   29, Gregory, Mary, and Coopman Wildey.
1765, June   19, Gregory, Rachel, and John Edwards.
1753, May   24, Gregory, Thomas, and Rachel Meredith.
1799, March   17, Grenyon, Cath., and Elijah Devall.

1784, March 16, Gressum, Joshua, and Eliz. Hill.
1794, Dec. 13, Greves, Joseph, and Agnes Wallace.
1764, Feb. 9, Grew, Louisa, and Hugh Williams.
1769, Sept. 21, Grew, Peter, and Elizabeth Holkerston.
1739, March 5, Grew, Theophilus, and Frances Bowen.
1735, Feb. 9, Grew, Theophilus, and Elizabeth Cosins.
1785, Jan. 27, Grice, Isaac, and Mary McMichael.
1771, Jan. 1, Grice, Lydia, and Joseph Fanning.
1753, April 25, Griest, Francis, and Mary Brockenberry.
1734, Nov. 10, Griffeth, Mary, and Evan Davis.
1774, Oct. 6, Griffin, Ann, and William Butler.
1759, March 9, Griffin, Cecilia, and Robert Bass.
1750, Dec. 29, Griffin, Elizabeth, and George Rankin.
1779, Nov. 7, Griffin, Hannah, and Andrew Thomson.
1796, April 7, Griffin, John, and Hannah Meade.
1775, May 25, Griffin, Martha, and Archibald Edminston.
1770, April 21, Griffin, Mary Ann, and John Boyd.
1775, April 20, Griffin, Patrick, and Mary Nelson.
1758, Oct. 19, Griffin, Sarah, and Andrew Sleage.
1761, Nov. 5, Griffin, Sellwood, and Mary Carman.
1770, May 16, Griffins, Eliz., and Edward Jones.
1770, May 31, Griffins, John, and Ann Roberts.
1720, April 10, Griffith, Ann, and John Gawcain.
1720, Dec. 7, Griffith, Benjamin, and Sarah Miles.
1771, Oct. 10, Griffith, Benjamin, and Catherine Bartholomew.
1714, Dec. 6, Griffith, Catherine, and Richard Hilton.
1727, June 22, Griffith, Evan, and Mary James.
1768, July 7, Griffith, George, and Rebecca January.
1743, May 29, Griffith, Henry, and Ann White.
1801, Aug. 1, Griffith, Jane, and Jacob Girard Koch.
1730, April 16, Griffith, John, and Anne Mortmore.
1800, May 29, Griffith, Joseph, and Mary Micklejohn.
1767, Sept. 14, Griffith, Joseph, and Sarah Bishop.
1722, May 19, Griffith, Margaret, and Evan Abevan.
1800, Jan. 19, Griffith, Mary Salome, and John Stroubat.
1753, Oct. 25, Griffith, Mary, and Henry Folly.
1730, Feb. 2, Griffith, Methusalem, and Lyky Reece.
1717, May 13, Griffith, Rachel, and Henry Rothwell.
1797, May 22, Griffith, Robert Eaglesfield, and Maria Patterson.
1731, Sept. 6, Griffith, Thomas, and Elizabeth Northon.
1720, Aug. 6, Griffith, Walter, and Martha Cox.
1805, Nov. 20, Griffith, William, and Mary Chapman.
1730, July 30, Griffiths, Anne, and Joseph Claypoole.
1728, Dec. 6, Griffiths, Cath., and Francis Griffiths.
1728, Dec. 6, Griffiths, Francis, and Cath. Griffiths.
1758, March 31, Griffiths, Rachel, and William Thorn.

1721, Nov.   2, Griffiths, Sarah, and Edward Dawson.
1727, April   1, Griffiths, Thomas, and Ann Bates.
1739, Dec.   5, Griffiths, Thomas, and Margaret Rogers.
1775, June   5, Griffiths, Thomas, and Jane Quin.
1737, Sept.   15, Griffiths, William, and Gwin Jones.
1795, Nov.   22, Griffy, Eliz., and Isaak Katz.
1795, Sept.   9, Grift, Martha, and John Baptiste Laplanche.
1711, July   18, Grifton, Darby, and Joan Breyan.
1791, Nov.   10, Griggs, Charlotte, and William Vennable.
1795, May   6, Grim, Peter, and Cath. Sheaffe.
1792, Sept.   8, Grimes, Duncan, and Susannah Long.
1740, May   21, Grimes, Jane, and James Nelly.
1761, Aug.   5, Grimes, Jane, and Francis Dowins.
1800, March   8, Grimes, Marianne, and Isaak Lort.
1797, June   4, Grimes, Mary, and John Davis.
1796, Oct.   15, Grimes, Rosanna, and James Harbeson.
1770, Dec.   31, Griscome, Sarah, and William Donaldson.
1779, May   13, Grise, Jonathan, and Mary Jones.
1716, Dec.   4, Grisley, Mary, and William Coxe.
1784, Aug.   21, Groebe, Alletto, and William Barrett.
1767, March   18, Grogan, Hannah, and Isaac Delavan.
1775, July   15, Grogan, Margaret, and William Green.
1755, Dec.   22, Grogan, Margaret, and John Strickland.
1756, Dec.   9, Grogan, John, and Catherine O'Brian.
1741, Nov.   17, Gronow, John, and Bathsheba Morgan.
1747, April   16, Groom, William, and Rachel Walton.
1739, May   13, Groome, Anne, and Garret Vansandt.
1720, Nov.   10, Grothouse, John, and Amelia Miller.
1784, Aug.   1, Grove, Rosanna, and William Warren.
1796, Oct.   20, Grove, Susanna, and William Thomas.
1797, April   15, Grover, Christiana, and Matthew Outen.
1788, June   26, Grover, Eliz., and William Leeson.
1795, Feb.   8, Groves, Cath., and Elijah Millar.
1760, Feb.   28, Groves, Hagar, and Cæsar Morris.
1753, Aug.   11, Grooves, John, and Jane Mason.
1797, June   24, Groves, Robert, and Christiana Freytag.
1753, Oct.   18, Growden, Grace, and Joseph Galloway.
1781, July   12, Grubb, Isabella, and James Shelley.
1737, Nov.   16, Grubb, Mary, and Robert Moulder.
1780, Nov.   16, Grubb, Peter, and Mary Gray.
1806, April   23, Guarin, Vincent, and Charlotte Ott.
1785, Feb.   18, Gueirn, George, and Ascheah Cromwell.
1755, Aug.   27, Guery Mathias, and Allida Shippen.
1758, Jan.   17, Guest, Simon, and Agnes Salkill.
1761, Sept.   2, Guest, Simon, and Mary Wilcox.
1734, Sept.   30, Guff, Alice, and Alexander Gibbs.

1797, April   22, Guidar, Madeline, and Francis Anson.
1791, Nov.   19, Guiham, James, and Mary Vennable.
1720, May   10, Guilliland, Hugh, and Mary Thomas.
1749, July   18, Guilliot, Mary, and James Shirley.
1742, July   3, Guillot, Elias, and Mary Mason.
1799, June   7, Guin, Andrew, and Mary Jordan.
1760, Jan.   18, Guinet, Rose, and John Quaming.
1781, March   16, Guirey, Ann, and Patrick Walker.
1756, Sept.   9, Guisline, Cæsar, and Elizabeth Rankin.
1771, Oct.   12, Gum, Hannah, and Samuel Snowden.
1734, May   31, Gundey, Alexander, and Anne Williams.
1799, Nov.   30, Gunn, Thomas, and Rebecca Loyd.
1767, July   12, Gunning, Margaret, and Thomas Lee.
1800, May   19, Gunter, Isaac, and Eliz, Humphreys.
1727, Aug.   10, Gurling, George, and Sarah Williams.
1728, June   12, Gurling, W^m, and Ann Webb.
1768, July   7, Gurney, Henry, and Catherine Ross.
1790, May   20, Gurton, William, and Jane Clark.
1740, Aug.   4, Gurwin, John, and Elizabeth Pilcock.
1733, March   9, Guthridge, Anne, and William Phillips.
1797, March   2, Guthrie, John, and Ann Smith.
1752, March   9, Guthry, Anne, and Joseph Hurdith.
1745, June   18, Guttier, Hannah, and Matthew Scot.
1793, Sept.   2, Guy, Catherine, and Jeremiah Holden.
1731, Sept.   4, Guy, Martha, and Benjamin Taylor.
1734, Sept.   3, Guy, Mary, and James Osborn.
1769, Sept.   3, Guy, Mary, and Robert Fenton.
1730, March   25, Guy, Samuel, and Rebecca Kelly.
1731, Dec.   5, Guy, William, and Mary Sewer.
1773, May   8, Gwin, Thomas, and Cath. Sweaver.
1732, Oct.   7, Gwinn, John, and Anne Jones.
1757, July   2, Gwinnap, Martha, and William Flood.
1738, Nov.   30, Hacket, Margaret, and William Currie.
1792, June   24, Hacket, Michael, and Mary Mahoney.
1786, Sept.   16, Hackett, Ann Eliz, and James Dowling.
1725, Oct.   6, Hackney, Mary, and Richd Naylor.
1756, Jan.   5, Haddick, Margaret, and Robert Sanford.
1761, Oct.   9, Hadley, John, and Catherine Maul.
1741, Aug.   8, Hagan, Clarinda, and James Mallaly.
1761, Sept.   1, Hagan, Cornelius, and Mary Potter.
1786, April   8, Hagarty, John, and Mary Githins.
1766, Dec.   18, Hagerty, Chlotilda, and James Wood.
1753, Nov.   1, Hagley, Elizabeth, and William Benning.
1799, Dec.   8, Hagner, Peter, and Sarah Nichols.
1731, May   17, Hague, Hannah, and John Brown.
1773, Sept.   29, Haild, Ruth, and Allen Langley.

1802, Oct. 21, Haines, Ann, and Jacob Fisher.
1767, Dec. 11, Haines, Barzillai, and Hannah Young.
1768, April 28, Haines, Eliz., and Harman Snouder.
1785, Nov. 30, Haines, Jane, and William Boyce.
1777, March 23, Haines, Mary, and Patrick Caine.
1752, Sept. 14, Hains, Elizabeth, and Allen Sharp.
1751, May 4, Hains, Rebecca, and George Owen.
1749, May 22, Hains, Stephen, and Mary Coombs.
1748, Feb. 5, Hainey, Dorothy, and Anthony Adamson.
1743, May 23, Hainey, Eliz, and John Peel.
1722, July 31, Hair, John, and Eleanor Ellis.
1768, April 20, Hair, Mary, and Edward Poole.
1757, Feb. 27, Halbert, Phillip, and Hannah Preston.
1768, July 14, Hale, Alexander, and Frances Yorkson.
1738, Nov. 23, Hale, James, and Eleanor Fryers.
1782, Aug. 31, Hale, Jane, and Thomas Thomas.
1734, Aug. 17, Hale, Samuel, and Sarah Siddels.
1800, May 3, Hale, Thomas, and Mary Myers.
1743, Nov. 17, Hale, Joseph, and Ruth Stephens.
1795, May 14, Hales, Barbara, and Philip Hockburn.
1798, March 24, Hales, Susanna, and John Siddons.
1796, March 12, Haley, Ann, and Sampson Richards.
1749, March 7, Haley, Honours, and John Williams.
1757, Oct. 7, Haley, Jane, and Robert Robson.
1799, Aug. 14, Halfpenny, Margaret, and Samuel Day.
1767, April 2, Hall, Aaron, and Hannah Hallowell.
1749, Oct. 24, Hall, Alice, and Richard Parsons.
1778, Oct. 29, Hall, Ann, and Capt. Herman Stout.
1804, June 13, Hall, Clara, and Richard Basset.
1748, Jan. 7, Hall, David, and Mary Lacock.
1800, March 2, Hall, David, and Margaret Powell.
1770, Nov. 29, Hall, Deborah, and John Chambers.
1785, Dec. 27, Hall, Deborah, and Michall Boyer.
1786, April 13, Hall, Eliz., and Edward Lane.
1749, Feb. 2, Hall, Elizabeth, and John Pettey.
1733, Jan. 4, Hall, Elizabeth, and William West.
1727, Sept. 11, Hall, Frances, and James Dickenson.
1768, March 14, Hall, Hannah, and William Edwards.
1803, March 12, Hall, Hannah, and Benjamin Dunn.
1772, Feb. 11, Hall, James, and Sarah Winn.
1765, Dec. 24, Hall, Jane, and Patrick McGee.
1784, July 4, Hall, John, and Ann Hurd.
1746, May 4, Hall, John, and Margaret McCall.
1746, June 18, Hall, John, and Jane Patterson.
1743, Oct. 24, Hall, John, and Mary Hugg.
1788, Dec. 11, Hall, John, and Sarah Maddox.

1733, Jan. 18, Hall, Joseph, and Mary Fisher.
1759, July 24, Hall, Lyman, and Mary Osborne.
1759, Dec. 26, Hall, Margaret, and Peter Murray.
1786, Dec. 28, Hall, Margaret, and John Coleman.
1861, July 4, Hall, Marjery, and John Dubre.
1774, Oct. 8, Hall, Martha, and Richard Davie.
1766, Dec. 2, Hall, Martha, and Isaac Grant.
1711, June 16, Hall, Mary, and John Coats.
1720, Sept. 1, Hall, Mary, and Thomas Gasnold.
1770, Aug. 26, Hall, Rachel, and Richard Longacre.
1738, Oct. 25, Hall, Rebecca, and George Hughes.
1804, Dec. 6, Hall, Rebecca, and Samuel Durnel.
1730–1, Feb. 25, Hall, Richard, and Anne Phillips.
1740, March 1, Hall, Samuel, and Mary Annis.
1710, May 1, Hall, Sarah, and Alexander Lynsee.
1773, Aug. 5, Hall, Sarah, and Alex. Hunter.
1733, May 2, Hall, Susannah, and Joseph Harvey.
1729, April 29, Hall, Theodorus, and Gartrey Goodwin.
1763, April 13, Hall Thomas, and Mary Bullock.
1803, Jan. 29, Hall, Thomas Mifflin, and Mary Anna Bringhurst.
1754, Oct. 24, Hall, William, and Jane Harvey.
1761, May 16, Hall, William, and Barbary Gankins.
1800, Oct. 8, Hall, William Chandler, and Eliz. Morris.
1782, April 23, Hall, Capt. William, and Ann Willson.
1802, May 24, Halliday, William, and Ruth Lawton.
1773, Jan. 14, Hallam, Lewis, and Eliz. Luke.
1796, May 13, Hallat, William, and Mary Wiggins.
1782, May 7, Halling, Dr. Solomon, and Eliz. Greenaway.
1767, April 2, Hallowell, Hannah, and Aaron Hall.
1801, Oct. 6, Hallowell, Jesse, and Hester Cottman.
1771, Sept. 25, Halton, Mary, and John Meredith.
1758, Nov. 2, Ham, Elizabeth, and James Bailey.
1771, April 20, Ham, James, and Hannah Jones.
1771, May 23, Ham, Jane, and Joseph Breintnall.
1798, Aug. 8, Hamble, Sabra, and John Trump.
1791, March 13, Hamiil, Laetitia and John Hill.
1799, Aug. 9, Hamill, Rebecca, and Samuel Jones.
1741, Dec. 24, Hamilton, Andrew, and Mary Till.
1768, Jan. 6, Hamilton, Andrew, and Abigail Franks.
1760, Dec. 11, Hamilton, Ann, and Robert Howard.
1792, Oct. 17, Hamilton, Ann, and James Lyle.
1794, July 12, Hamilton, Ann, and Edward Godfredy.
1802, June 8, Hamilton, Ann, and Stephen Collings.
1749, June 7, Hamilton, Charles, and Jane Urbaine Voyer.
1803, Dec. 29, Hamilton, Eliz. and Joseph Barnaby.
1759, Jan. 17, Hamilton, Elizabeth, and John Holland.

1788, Nov. 19, Hamilton, Eliz. and John Earley.
1797, Dec.   7, Hamilton, George, and Elizabeth Stout.
1772, April 1, Hamilton, Hugh, and Ann Campbell.
1737, Nov. 22, Hamilton, Jane, and Robert Tilsell.
1790, Aug. 17, Hamilton, John, and Eliz. Ross.
1734, Feb. 16, Hamilton, Mrs. Margaret, and William Allen, Esq
1760, May   6, Hamilton, Margaret, and John White.
1747, Jan.   6, Hamilton, Martha, and Robert Henry.
1760, May   6, Hamilton, Mary, and John Thornton.
1772, Nov. 26, Hamilton, Patrick, and Ann Clark.
1785, Jan. 20, Hamilton, Sidney, and William Redstone.
1731, Aug. 24, Hamilton, Susannah, and Thomas Crosdale.
1761, Aug.   3, Hamilton, Tanerner, and Mary Osburn.
1715, Jan.   2, Hammarsh, John, and Elizabeth Vanbeek.
1726, Oct. 15, Hammer, Deb., and Wm Davies.
1759, Aug. 14, Hammett, Francis, and Ann House.
1781, March 16, Hammitt, Jacob, and Frances Erwin.
1767, March 28, Hammon, Sarah, and Richard West.
1765, Dec. 24, Hammond, Andrew, and Ann Mannahon.
1755, May   8, Hammond, Anne, and Nicholas Nicholson.
1773, May 20, Hammond, George, and Margaret Allen.
1805, Dec. 12, Hammond, Henry, and Evelina Truxton.
1784, July 10, Hammond, Mary, and Capt. Joseph Poole.
1786, Dec. 14, Hammond, Nicholas, and Sarah George.
1782, Nov. 14, Hamper, Sarah, and Major Thos Lloyd Moore.
1795, April 26, Hampton, Ann, and John Satterfield.
1773, Jan. 30, Hampton, Ann, and William Butcher.
1733, March 31, Hampton, Benjamin, and Rachel Baker.
1766, July 26, Hance, Hannah, and George Syng.
1753, July 16, Hancock, Richard, and Mary Cole.
1744, Jan. 25, Hancock, Thomas, and Susannah Symons.
1806, Sept. 13, Hand, John, and Sarah Keen.
1797, Dec.   3, Hand, Lucy, and Thomas Walpole.
1728, Sept.   2, Hand, Sarah, and Peter Young Blood.
1752, Oct.   2, Hand, Thomas, and Mercy Whilding.
1720, Oct. 25, Handcock, Mary, and Joseph Bostock.
1714, Dec. 31, Hancock, Rachel, and Henry Jotue.
1747, Jan. 26, Handlin, Valentine, and Sarah Russel.
1772, Oct. 15, Hanimer, Eliz., and Owen Brook.
1784, Sept. 21, Hanisey, Patience, and Jonathan Hendrickson.
1771, March 14, Hanlon, Edward, and Eliz. Stewart.
1785, Feb.   3, Hanlon, Marmaduke, and Mary Long.
1784, March 11, Hanlon, Patrick, and Hannah Williamson.
1784, July   4, Hanly, Henry, and Mary Stall.
1768, April 14, Hanna, John, and Phoebe Wharton.
1798, Dec. 24, Hanna, Mary, and Hugh Cockran.

1756, Nov.   22, Hannah, John, and Frances Houston.
1775, Nov.   3, Hannah, John, and Eliz. Fraeme.
1737, Sept. 10, Hannas, William, and Mary Rambo.
1721, Feb.   12, Hannis, Andrew, and Sarah Loftus.
1757, Feb.   10, Hannis, John, and Mary Glove.
1757, Dec.   21, Hannis, Margaret, and John Read.
1755, April 21, Hannis, Mary, and Henry Elwes.
1787, April 10, Hannis, Mary, and Richard Baker.
1755, May   17, Hannis, Rachel, and William Jackson.
1759, Dec.   25, Hannon, Margaret, and John Osborn.
1765, Sept. 16, Hannum, Mary, and Richard Cheyney.
1760, April 29, Hans, Elizabeth, and George Daniel.
1765, Aug.   17, Hanse, Jacob, and Mary Bankson.
1786, July   13, Hansld, Susannah, and Mathias Barry.
1797, Dec.   20, Hanson, Frances, and Thomas Moore.
1742, May   28, Hanson, Hester, and Charles Barrett.
1792, May   8, Hanson, James, and Cath. Shyerley.
1752, Nov.   9, Hanson, Jonathan, and Thomasin Davy.
1768, Oct.   23, Hanson, Mary Eliz., and Thomas Robinson, senior.
1804, Dec   6, Hanson, Peter, and Rebecca Johnson.
1777, April 29, Hanson, Samuel, and Mary Key.
1774, Sept. 15, Hanwest, Peter, and Amy Elliot.
1784, Jan.   22, Hapkins, Thomas, and Mary King.
1754, July   30, Harbeson, Benjamin, and Eliphet Harper.
1796, Oct.   15, Harbeson, James, and Rosanna Grimes.
1794, May   22, Harbeson, Joseph, and Susannah Cotman.
1722, May   17, Harbut, John, and Elizabeth Tait.
1756, Nov.   28, Hardcastle, William, and Anne Scully.
1753, Dec.   11, Hardeloft, Joachim, and Margaret Elesson.
1714, Jan.   4, Hardin, Martin, and Hannah Hunt.
1784, Dec.   14, Harding, David, and Eliz. Watts.
1749, April   8, Harding, Francis, and Mary Canthan.
1749, Nov.   25, Harding, George, and Mary Cary.
1760, March 18, Harding, James, and Margaret Usher.
1799, July   30, Harding, Jane, and David Thomas.
1780, March   2, Harding, Lydia, and John Hawkins.
1761, Dec.   20, Harding, Margaret, and Edmund Badger.
1751, Oct.   22, Harding, Margaret, and Abraham Skinner.
1748, Jan.   3, Harding, Mary, and George Allen.
1738, Nov.   23, Harding, Mary, and Benjamin Carpenter.
1795, Nov.   19, Harding, Ruth, and Peter L. Eveque.
1774, July   11, Harding, William, and Jane Taylor.
1776, Nov.   24, Hardwick, Matthias, and Ann Reyley.
1806, Feb.   1, Hardy, Hugh, and Martha Robinson.
1794, Oct.   19, Hardy, Joseph, and Sarah Reader.
1768, Oct.   1, Hare, Agnes, and Philip Terrapin.

1801, Aug.   29, Hare, Charles, and Ann Emlen.
1777, Sept.   5, Hare, Hannah, and Thomas Goucher.
1775, Nov.   16, Hare, Robert, and Margaret Willing.
1793, June   11, Hargisheimer, Barbara, and Jesse Lawton.
1796, April   14, Hargesheimer, John, and Ann Wadman.
1799, March 14, Hargesheimer, Rachel, and Daniel Sulto.
1720, March 21, Hargrave, Charles, and Elizabeth Dennis.
1749, Oct.   19, Hargrave, Sarah, and Isham Randolph.
1769, April   23, Harker, Dominick, and Rachel Knowles.
1728, June   8, Harlinge, Elizabeth, and Wm White.
1775, Nov.   9, Harman, John, and Eliz. Towzer.
1795, May   7, Harman, Mary Ann, and John Cummings.
1797, April   18, Harman, Sarah, and Stewart Brown.
1784, Jan.   8, Harmason, John, and Comfort King.
1733, April   16, Harmer, Elizabeth, and Timothy Chatwin.
1761, Oct.   12, Harmer, Lydia, and Francis Dosey.
1737, Aug.   13, Harmer, Ruth, and James Ingles.
1800, May   31, Harmes, James, and Sarah Siddons.
1795, April   9, Harnet, Eliz., and James Maffett.
1770, Aug.   11, Harnett, James, and Jane Glascow.
1761, Sept.   1, Harper, Deborah, and John Studdert.
1736, Sept.   16, Harper, Deborah, and John Syng.
1761, Sept.   9, Harper, Ebenezer, and Ann Clayton.
1754, July   30, Harper, Eliphet, and Benjamin Harbeson.
1751, June   5, Harper, Elizabeth, and Gustavus Brown.
1763, May   5, Harper, Hannah, and Bryan Kelly.
1805, July   20, Harper, Harriet, and Peter A. Brown.
1785, Aug.   8, Harper, Henry, and Eliz. Mallett.
1736, May   55, Harper, John, and Mary Pain.
1711, May   31, Harper, John, and Deborah Parver.
1790, July   1, Harper, John, and Joanna Crawford.
1796, Oct.   29, Harper, John, and Eliz. Aston.
1736, Jan.   17, Harper, John, and Catherine Brown.
1757, March 31, Harper, Josiah, and Susannah Wey.
1763, Sept.   10, Harper, Josiah, and Catherine Luter.
1761, Nov.   16, Harper, Margaret, and William Bywater.
1793, Jan.   31, Harper, Mary, and John Baptist Roche.
1797, March 22, Harper, Mary, and Charles Quantrill.
1801, Oct.   6, Harper, Mary, and William Shaw.
1799, March 28, Harper, Phœbe, and Patrick Karral.
1742, Sept.   12, Harper, Ralph, and Mary Gregory.
1713, Nov.   8, Harper, Richard, and Jane Smart.
1758, Oct.   10, Harper, Samuel, and Ann Powell.
1770, Aug.   20, Harper, Samuel, and Hannah Donnaughey.
1770, Jan.   30, Harper, Sarah, and Joseph Wager.
1733, Feb.   1, Harper, Sarah, and John Boucher.

1801, Sept. 29, Harper, Sarah, and Jonathan Johnson.
1799, Oct. 11, Harper, Susanna, and Matthias Corless.
1773, Feb. 18, Harper, Thomas, and Deborah Drinker.
1776, Nov. 2, Harper, Thomas, and Mary Dowdle.
1784, Sept. 9, Harper, William, and Jane Murphey.
1734, Oct. 24, Harrad, Mary, and John Cole.
1761, Feb. 24, Harrald, Samuel, and Elizabeth Russell.
1770, Sept. 8, Harran, Ann, and Patrick Stafford.
1742, Nov. 21, Harrard, Ann, and Samuel Sugars.
1790, Nov. 11, Harrell, Thomas, and Penelope Rutter.
1758, July 28, Harrey, James, and Grace Birret.
1747, Oct. 16, Harrighan, Patrick, and Margaret Douglass.
1771, Sept. 14, Harring, Thomas, and Sarah Kirk.
1726, Nov. 6, Harrington, Jane, and John Emit.
1795, Nov. 10, Harriott, Eleanor, and Henry King.
1804, July 8, Harris, Amelia, and Alexander Grant.
1744, July 30, Harris, Ann, and Sam. Vanhist.
1795, Oct. 20, Harris, Catherine, and Andrew Tyrrell.
1800, June 5, Harris, Charles, and Julianna Baldesqui.
1758, Oct. 10, Harris, Francis, and Elizabeth Peal.
1771, Sept. 11, Harris, Isaac, and Mary White.
1793, Nov. 17, Harris, James, and Eliz. Morris.
1776, Nov. 24, Harris, John, and Ruth Taylor.
1717, May 15, Harris, John, and Sarah Eaton.
1735, Dec. 30, Harris, John, and Martha James.
1768, Oct. 13, Harris, John, (Tuscaroras,) and Rachel (Mohawk.)
1736, Feb. 9, Harris, John, and Sarah Coburn.
1774, Nov. 27, Harris, Margary, and Robert McFarland.
1774, April 25, Harris, Mary, and Lawrence Baldwin.
1729, July 20, Harris, Mary, and Stephen Stokes.
1727, Aug. 6, Harris, Rebekah, and Evan Davis.
1743, April 29, Harris, Richard, and Margaret Fox.
1805, March 16, Harris, Robert, and Charlotte Shaw.
1745, Sept. 8, Harris, Sarah, and Richard Ellis.
1800, Sept. 1, Harris, Sayre, and Samuel Plummer.
1796, June 30, Harris, Thankful, and Stephen Symonds.
1743, Oct. 25, Harris, William, and Martha Eten.
1765, Oct. 31, Harrison, ———, and Stephen Beezley.
1777, Feb. 28, Harrison, Ann, and Honble William Paca, Esqr.
1737, Nov. 26, Harrison, Anne, and George Bliss.
1762, April 14, Harrison, Charles, and Esther Shores.
1742, Aug. 15, Harrison, Daniel, and Ann Gibson.
1739, May 26, Harrison, Daniel, and Christian Jones.
1744, Sept. 9, Harrison, Dan, and Ann Veil.
1736, Feb. 28, Harrison, Elizabeth, and Samuel Holt.
1772, May 23, Harrison, Eliz., and Francis Barrell.

1760, June　26, Harrison, Frances, and John Knot.
1790, April　1, Harrison, Francis, and Cath. McLane.
1782, March 10, Harrison, Frances, and Theophilus Frinck.
1792, Feb.　15, Harrison, George, and Sophia Francis.
1748, April　16, Harrison, Henry, and Mary Aspden.
1802, Nov.　27, Harrison, John, and Lydia Leib.
1757, March　1, Harrison, John, and Mary McCoy.
1728, Feb.　27, Harrison, John, and Cath. Conoyhall.
1732, June　15, Harrison, John, and Rachel Lambeth.
1745, Feb.　7, Harrison, John, and Hannah Estwick.
1803, Aug.　28, Harrison, Joseph, and Mary Crawford.
1743, Oct.　23, Harrison, Mary, and George Bradley.
1785, Jan.　13, Harrison, Mary, and Samuel Clinton.
1746, April　17, Harrison, Mary, and Noah Wills.
1724, Jan.　19, Harrison, Mary, and Thomas Kendrick.
1773, Feb.　11, Harrison, Mary, and Wm White.
1723, March 13, Harrison, Michael, and Mary Cox.
1791, Jan.　17, Harrison, Priscilla, and Thomas Wilkins.
1780, Jan.　17, Harrison, Rebecca, and Revr Robt. Blackwell.
1764, Nov.　8, Harrison, Robert, and Mary Bonham.
1792, Dec.　27, Harrison, Samuel, and Mary Blackwood.
1784, Aug.　12, Harrison, Sarah, and John Clinton.
1795, May　12, Harrison, Sarah, and Robert Palethrope.
1766, May　29, Harrison, Sarah, and Andrew Ferguson.
1710, Feb.　21, Harrison, Sarah, and Samuel Shores.
1740, April　17, Harrison, Sarah, and Thomas Sober.
1796, May　31, Harrison, William, and Mary F. Buston.
1756, Dec.　15, Harrle, Anthony, and Anne Valentine.
1804, May　3, Harrod, Joseph, and Jane Lacombe.
1778, Aug.　23, Harrold, ——, and William McDougall.
1773, Sept.　25, Harrow, David, and Rebecca Wilkinson.
1785, June　2, Harrow, Rebecca, and Thomas Holines.
1730, July　7, Harry, David, and Hannah Humphreys.
1751, Aug.　1, Harry, John, and Rachel Saul.
1752, Nov.　19, Harry, Lydia, and Samuel Evans Farmer.
1743, May　14, Harry, Lydia, and Phillip Thomas.
1751, June　4, Harry, Mary, and James Sparks.
1753, Sept.　3, Harry, William, and Mary Bates.
1769, Feb.　28, Hart, Anthony, and Mary Bayman.
1803, Aug.　14, Hart, Eleanor, and Danel Gallaher.
1800, Feb.　20, Hart, Eliz., and Samuel Robinet.
1770, May　20, Hart, John, and Catherine Knowles.
1799, Aug.　8, Hart, John, and Ann Kemble.
1802, July　8, Hart, John, and Mary Shreece.
1763, May　6, Hart, Margaret, and Robert Elton.
1750, March 14, Hart, Mary, and John Elton.

1720, Aug. 28, Hart, Mary, and Thomas Dungan.
1774, June 14, Hart, Mary, and Stephen Porter.
1747, Sept. 21, Hart, Mary, and John Smalwood.
1774, June 12, Hart, Moses, and Sarah McLain.
1762, June 5, Hart, Phoebe, and Robert Vernon.
1764, Oct. 15, Hart, Sarah, and James Graisbury.
1745, July 6, Hartley, Benjamin, and Rachel Coats.
1741, June 6, Hartley, Charles, and Hannah Bell.
1750, April 5, Hartley, Hannah, and Arthur Blake.
1732, Sept. 17, Hartley, Mary, and Henry Dexter.
1768, Sept. 30, Hartley, Mary, and Richard Waddington.
1804, July 21, Hartley, Mary, and Samuel Neal.
1785, March 12, Hartley, Mary, and George Finor.
1784, Feb. 19, Hartley, Mercy, and John Brick.
1771, Feb. 17, Hartley, Richard, and Mary Welsh.
1769, May 9, Hartman, Berry, and Martha Spencer.
1799, Jan. 6, Hartman, Derick, and Eliz. Shannon.
1749, Nov. 11, Hartman, Elizabeth, and William Saunders.
1793, July 7, Hartrick, Margaret, and William Wilson.
1745, March 23, Hartshorne, James, and Cath. McCreagh.
1768, Feb. 18, Hartshorne, Sarah, and Thomas Corgail.
1795, May 9, Hartwell, Eliz., and Richard Peniston.
1748, Nov. 3, Harverd, Rachel, and John Mayhew.
1805, Aug. 1, Harvey, Francis, and Mary McDonald.
1732, April 17, Harvey, Grace, and Samuel Love.
1754, Oct. 24, Harvey, Jane, and William Hall.
1790, April 11, Harvey, Jane, and Joshua Mitchell.
1799, March 18, Harvey, John, and Mary Barton.
1749, Dec. 26, Harvey, John, and Jane Sullivan.
1782, Dec. 5, Harvey, Joseph, and Sarah Williams.
1733, May 2, Harvey, Joseph, and Susannah Hall.
1769, Nov. 14, Harvey, Mary, and John Vicary.
1799, Nov. 28, Harvey, Mary, and Paul Beck.
1759, Sept. 6, Harvey, Rebecca, and Benjamin Betterton.
1784, Nov. 4, Harvey, Sarah, and William Smith.
1762, Oct. 23, Harvey, Susannah, and Daniel Rambo.
1731, July 28, Harvey, Susannah, and James Tomlinson.
1742, Dec. 20, Harvey, Susannah, and John Crookshanks.
1727, Nov. 23, Harwood, Joseph, and Sarah Williams.
1733, Oct. 17, Harwood, Sarah, and Charles Read.
1752, Nov. 2, Hasell, Hannah, and Amos Strettle.
1715, Feb. 24, Hasell, Mary, and Richard Ellwood.
1761, Jan. 19, Hasker, James, and Elizabeth Hawkins.
1805, Jan. 1, Haslett, Joseph, and Phillis Black.
1772, Jan. 1, Haslett, Sarah, and John Cook.
1732, Oct. 30, Hasleum, Apollonia, and Thos Herbert.

1747, June   5, Hassel, Anne, and James Benezet.
1793, Sept. 11, Hassell, Eliz., and William Powell.
1745, Sept. 19, Hassel, Elizabeth, and Alexander Huston.
1801, April 16, Hassall, Mary Louisa, and Thomas W. Duffield.
1757, Nov.   30, Hastings, Hannah, and Thomas Smith.
1796, April 23, Hastings, Isabella, and Arthur Collins.
1785, July   18, Hastings, James, and Mary Higgins.
1800, Sept.   4, Hastings, John, and Rebecca Sanders.
1734, Aug.   5, Hastings, John, and Sarah Powell.
1712, Feb.   20, HaswellLurst, Joshua, and Mary Wall.
1714, Feb.   3, Hatfield, Edward, and Catherine Liekins.
1782, Nov.   15, Hatfield, Joshua, and Jane Edwards.
1792, Jan.   1, Hathaway, Caleb, and Mary Maxwell.
1795, April   2, Hathaway, John, and Cath. Keemle.
1727, April   2, Hatton, Ed., and Mary Steward.
1730, May   26, Hatton, Sarah, and Joseph Weld.
1755, July   1, Haugen, Mary, and Cornelius Sturgis.
1787, May   18, Howard, John, and Margaret Chew.
1786, July   5, Hawk, Josiah, and Hester Stinnyard.
1805, Feb.   9, Hawke, Ann, and Edward Gill.
1795, Jan.   8, Hawke, Mary, and William Wayne.
1800, Dec.   4, Hawkins, Ann, and John B. Evans.
1737, May   8, Hawkins, Elizabeth, and Thomas Poates.
1761, Jan.   19, Hawkins, Elizabeth, and James Hasker.
1767, Sept.   2, Hawkins, Elizabeth, and Jonathan Montgomery.
1735, Sept.   6, Hawkins, Elizabeth, and William Hays.
1735, July   8, Hawkins, Jane, and Oliver Williams.
1711, Aug.   4, Hawkins, John, and Elizabeth Midleson.
1759, Dec.   11, Hawkins, Mary, and Sacheverell Wood.
1799, Jan.   17, Hawkins, Mary, and Swenn Warner.
1750, Sept. 13, Hawkins, Phœbe, and Howell Morgan.
1751, Aug.   17, Hawkins, Rachel, and Edward Turner.
1766, May   8, Hawkins, Sarah, and Joseph Thompson.
1737, June   11, Hawkins, William, and Mary Simmons.
1744, Jan.   28, Hawkins, William, and Phœbe Goodin.
1748, June   9, Hawksworth, Rachel, and John Thomas.
1771, Nov.   16, Hawning, Mary, and Philip Cromwell.
1796, Nov.   17, Hawthorne, Thomas, and Mary Meredith.
1768, June   17, Hay, Eliz., and Lambert Barnes.
1767, Nov.   1, Hay, John Cornelius, and Ann Andrews.
1771, May   29, Haycock, Hannah, and Nicholas Woollis.
1735, July   26, Haycock, Jeremiah, and Mary Thomas.
1783, Dec.   4, Haycock, John, and Esther Pyles.
1758, Dec.   18, Hayes, Ann. and James Reed.
1758, Dec.   16, Hayes, Isabella, and Abraham Liddon.
1780, Dec.   21, Hayes, James, and Ann McIntire.

1781, May 18, Hayes, Mary, and Conrad Young.
1760, Oct. 9, Hayes, Patience, and Edward Moore.
1773, July 28, Hayes, Patrick, and Isabella Patterson.
1742, Jan. 23, Hayes, William, and Susannah Fairman.
1745, Nov. 14, Hayhurst, William, and Rebecca Searle.
1762, July 9, Hayman, Elizabeth, and John Widowfield.
1798, Aug. 15. Haynes, Mary, and Peter York.
1734, Jan. 29, Haynes, Nehemiah, and Anne Brown.
1736, July 31, Hayns, John, and Jane Boyard.
1757, March 26, Hays, Mary, and Samuel Stackhouse.
1795, April 8, Hays, Patrick, and Eliz. Keene.
1751, Feb. 14, Hays, William, and Anne Clark.
1735, Sept. 6, Hays, William, and Elizabeth Hawkins.
1794, July 21, Hayworth, Jane, and Joseph Allen.
1797, Nov. 9, Haywood, Susan, and Charles Beering.
1796, April 11, Hazard, David, and Eliza Johnstone.
1796, Jan. 14, Hazard, Eliz., and Henry Reed.
1773, Sept. 24, Hazard, Richard, and Mary Brown.
1766, Aug. 9, Hazell, Sarah, and John Gill.
1773, Feb. 23, Hazelwood, William, and Rachel Rouse.
1757, Aug. 6, Hazleber, Thomas, and Bridget Miles.
1800, May 2, Hazlehurst, Mary Eliz., and Benjamin Henry La-
            trobe.
1801, Oct. 22, Hazlehurst, Samuel, and Eliz. Markœ.
1730, Dec. 12, Hazlet, Robert, and Elizabeth Parke.
1799, Nov. 11, Hazlet, William, and Eleanor Sullivan.
1729, Dec. 16, Heacock, Margt., and C. Hendsley.
1762, Jan. 20, Head, Joseph, and Mary Dickinson.
1757, Aug. 26, Head, Mary, and Samuel Crooks.
1748, Dec. 20, Head, Samuel, and Mary Womeldorfe.
1778, Oct. 1, Head, Susannah, and John Gordon.
1750, June 5, Heagan, Eleanor, and Daniel Eganson.
1781, Jan. 29, Healey, Morris, and Mary Streaker.
1786, May 9, Heany, John, and Mary Sink.
1738, Oct. 10, Heap, Anne, and Edward Scull.
1738, Sept. 2, Heap, George, and Mary Classon.
1746, Dec. 4, Heap, George, and Mary Jacobs.
1713, Oct. 1, Heap, John, and Ann Bingham.
1731, Feb. 28, Heard, John, and Geinor Conwry.
1755, Nov. 21, Heart, Martha, and John Ivory.
1738, May 2, Heaslum, Margaret, and Anthony Peele.
1729, Feb. 27, Heatcot, John, and Mary Willson.
1764, Jan. 21, Heath, John, and Mary Taylor.
1750, Jan. 1, Heath, Susannah, and William Colgan.
1767, Feb. 4, Heathcote, John, and Elizabeth Cox.
1727, Feb. 6, Heaton, Alice, and John Appelton.

1735, May   17, Heaton, Robert, and Margaret Davies.
1780, Oct.   22, Heavenman, Susannah, and John Kennedy.
1794, Aug.   7, Heavenstreet, Eliz., and John Hendrick Christian
                 Heineker.
1771, March 21, Heblethaite, Middleton, and Margaret Meskell.
1780, May   15, Hedler, Christiana, and Joseph Bowers.
1741, July   11, Heet or Steet, Catherine, and Benjamin Morgan.
1730, Nov.   3, Heickman, Anne, and John John China.
1775, June   26, Heide, Richard, and Mary Berney.
1757, Nov.   8, Heiman, Leonard, and Elizabeth England.
1734, June   22, Heine Thomas, and Anne Englesfield.
1794, Aug.   7, Heineker, John Hendrick Christian, and Eliz.
                 Heavenstreet.
1761, Nov.   12, Heirs, Henry, and Leah Peters.
1798, Jan.   25, Heiss, Cath., and John Markland.
1805, Oct.   10, Heiss, Eliz., and Rebecca Morrell.
1736, April   2, Helborne, Samuel, and Abigail Twining.
1767, Jan.   29, Heligas, Susannah, and William Pitt.
1729, Oct.   7, Hellcoat, John, and Eliz. Smith.
1735, May   16, Hellier, Rebecca, and Richard Burden.
1748, Oct.   14, Helliard, Solomon, and Jane Buckley.
1731, Nov.   11, Hellier, Capt. William, and Sarah Rogers.
1766, April 17, Helm, Elizabeth, and Derrick Kuyper.
1772, March 12, Helm, John, and Eliz. Thomas.
1765, Aug.   29, Helm, Mary and Peter Helm.
1765, Aug.   29, Helm, Peter, and Mary Helm.
1754, July   27, Helms, Deborah, and Benjamin Angelo.
1752, July   4, Helms, Mary, and George Masters.
1788, June   18, Hemings, Henrietta Maria, and John B. Dubuis-
                 son.
1739, June   23, Hemmet, Mary, and Anthony Bright.
1762, Feb.   11, Hemmings, Paul, and Eleanor Audley.
1750, Dec.   26, Hemphill, James, and Elizabeth Wills.
1801, July   17, Hemphill, Sarah, and William Taylor.
1744, Feb.   6, Hemson, John, and Mary Timmerman.
1726, Nov.   3, Hencher, Nic., and Rebecca Smith.
1749, Feb.   27, Hencock, Mary, and Richard Moore.
1738, April 16, Hencock, Richard, and Sarah Marshall.
1731-2, Feb. 22, Henderson, Catherine, and Alexander Howre.
1772, Sept. 24, Henderson, Eliz., and Martin Parkison.
1795, Dec.   10, Henderson, James, and Sarah Courtenay.
1757, April 17, Henderson, Mary, and David Greenlow.
1790, July   10, Henderson, William, and Eliz. Philipson.
1732, Sept. 30, Hendricks, Anne, and Edmund Cartlidge.
1773, March 31, Hendricks, Catharine, and Samuel Long.
1773, May   31, Hendricks, Laetitia, and Philip Fullan.

1726, Aug. 28, Hendrickson, Dinah, and Thomas Stedwell.
1784, Sept. 21, Hendrickson, Jonathan, and Patience Hanisey.
1773, Dec. 28, Hendrickson, Nicholas, and Ann Mains.
1729, Dec. 16, Hendsley, Catharine, and Margt. Heacock.
1774, Aug. 28, Henessy, Maurice, and Margaret Davenport.
1794, July 6, Henneen, Benjamin, and Barbara Adams.
1798, Dec. 9, Hennin, Edward, and Mary Taylor.
1805, Aug. 29, Hennion, David, and Eliz. Keemer.
1803, April 30, Henozey, Thomas, and Cath. Uhl.
1785, April 28, Henry, Ann, and Augustus Morris.
1804, April 20, Henry, Eliz., and John Baptiste Pons.
1774, April 7, Henry, George, and Ann Usher.
1769, May 4, Henry, Hugh, and Phoeby Morris.
1767, Aug. 20, Henry, Jane, and John Clement.
1799, May 23, Henry, John, and Eliz. Sophia Duche.
1801, Sept. 3, Henry, John, and Laetitia York.
1759, Sept. 7, Henry, Margaret, and Joseph Gardner.
1801, Aug. 16, Henry, Mary, and David Crossart.
1764, Dec. 3, Henry, Rebecca, and John Moore.
1747, Jan. 6, Henry, Robert, and Martha Hamilton.
1801, June 6, Henry, Robert, and Eliz. Roberts.
1761, March 7, Henry, Samuel, and Ann Smith.
1799, Feb. 27, Henry, Susanna, and Dominic McCue.
1750, Oct. 14, Henry, William, and Elizabeth Fox.
1742, July 28, Henzey, Sarah, and Zachariah Whitepain.
1781, Sept. 10, Hepburn, Stacy, and Sarah Duffield.
1746, May 24, Herbert, Benjamin, and Grace Walmsley.
1788, March 3, Herbert, John, and Cath. O'Brien.
1732, Oct. 30, Herbert, Thos, and Apollonia Hasleum.
1798, March 29, Heritage, Priscilla, and Thomas Ridge.
1799, Nov. 16, Herley, Martha, and Allen Butler.
1787, Sept. 20, Heron, Catherine, and John Combs.
1716, Oct. 11, Herring, Elizabeth, and William Assheton.
1794, Nov. 18, Herring, Johannah, and Michael Cotter.
1761, April 2, Herring, Capt. Julines, and Mary Inglis.
1801, June 25, Herrington, Eliz., and John Merriman.
1772, June 11, Herse, Rachel, and Godfrey Slyhauff.
1775, March 26, Hersett, Hopper, and John Foy.
1796, Jan. 31, Hersh, Susanna, and John Brady.
1746, Feb. 26, Hertzel, Judith, and George Stuchy.
1751, Aug. 13, Hervey, Precilla, and James Murphy.
1754, Oct. 16, Heselius, Eliz., and Sam. Price.
1798, Nov. 30, Hess, Thomas, and Hannah Fisler.
1730, July 1, Hesselius, Revd Samuel, and Gurtrude Stille.
1803, Aug. 26, Hetherington, Bernard, and Eliz. Middleton.
1768, June 9, Hetkin, Cath. and William Van Bevert.

1766, Oct.   16, Hewes, Caleb, and Deborah Potts.
1764, March 1, Hewes, Edward, and Lydia Garret.
1804, June   27, Hewes, Eliz., and John Walkinhood.
1796, March 27, Hewett, Thomas, and Mary Thoronegood.
1801, April 16, Hewitt, Thomas, and Eliz. Austin.
1803, Nov.   16, Hewitt, Thomas, and Margaretta Way.
1749, Aug.   9, Hewlings Lawrence, and Abigail Walace.
1791, May   28, Hewlings, William, and Sarah Coren.
1733, March 20, Hewit, Aaron, and Judith Yoacum.
1798, July   16, Hewit, Hester, and Joseph Cartwright.
1794, Dec.   4, Heyrick, Rachel, and Edward Dowers.
1792, April 10, Heysham, Ann, and Francis Beawes Sayre.
1756, Jan.   21, Hibbard Hannah, and Abel Moore.
1750, Sept. 18, Hibbs, Hannah, and James Cooper.
1767, April 16, Hibbs, Sarah, and John Wing.
1750, Jan.   29, Hickman, Anne, and Alexander Berkley.
1731, Sept. 15, Hickman, Henry, and Hester Collet.
1769, Nov.   8, Hicks, Edwards, and Hannah Ratten.
1761, March 13, Hicks, Elizabeth, and John Hicks.
1748, Nov.   5, Hicks, Ezekiel, and Christiana Albrighton.
1792, Oct.   20, Hicks, Isaac, and Mary Young.
1761, March 13, Hicks, John, and Elizabeth Hicks.
1805, Aug.   30, Hicks, Joseph Withall, and Judith Hunt.
1749, Feb.   19, Hicks, Mary, and John Searle.
1728, May   15, Hicks, Sarah, and Christian Warner.
1800, Sept. 14, Hicks, Sylvanus, and Ann Williams.
1726, Sept. 15, Hicks, T., and Mary Phenix.
1724, Feb.   6, Hicks, Thomas, and Katherine Campbell.
1758, July   19, Hicks, William, and Francina Jekyll.
1797, Aug.   6, Hider, John, and Sarah Quinlin.
1734, Sept. 26, Hiep, Anne, and Daniel Jones.
1756, Aug.   22, Hifferman, Mary, and William Miles.
1794, Dec.   11, Higbee, Joseph, and Eliz. L. Lewis.
1788, May   28, Higbee, Mary, and Samuel Butcher.
1780, Aug.   7, Higgins, Ann, and Thomas Glover.
1795, Sept. 19, Higgins, George, and Mary Morton.
1794, Aug.   17, Higgins, Margaret, and Thomas Eaves.
1785, July   18, Higgins, Mary, and James Hastings.
1768, Nov.   10, Higgins, Rachel, and James Robinson.
1801, June   13, Higgins, Sarah, and John May.
1777, Aug.   29, Higgins, Thomas, and Martha Sprigg.
1775, June   5, Higgs, Eliz., and John Lee.
1790, May   29, Hilborn, John, and Martha Dillon.
1751, Nov.   18, Hilborn, Mary, and Isaac Buckman.
1774, June   21, Hildebrand, Hannah, and Thomas Till.
1806, June   25, Hill, Archibald, and Margaretta McCleland.

1737, July   23, Hill, Dorothy, and Daniel Smith.
1759, Dec.   8. Hill, Edward, and Catherine Maukin.
1784, March 16, Hill, Eliz., and Joshua Gressum.
1785, Dec.   12, Hill, Eliz., and John Mundy.
1804, July   2, Hill, George, and Kesiah Hopper.
1780, Sept.   5, Hill, George, and Sarah Vanholinger.
1773, June   1, Hill, Esqr., Henry, and Ann Meredith.
1744, Oct.   4, Hill, Hugh, and Mary Hoodt.
1735, May   3, Hill, Hugh, and Dove Evans.
1739, Dec.   17, Hill, Hugh, and Elizabeth Scull.
1791, March   3, Hill, Mumphrey, and Alice Howard.
1766, Aug.   21, Hill, Jacob, and Mary Anderson.
1737, Dec.   17, Hill, James, and Jane Newlin.
1760, July   22, Hill, John, and Mary Gibbons.
1791, March 13, Hill, John, and Laetitia Hamill.
1761, Oct.   8, Hill, Joseph, and Elizabeth West.
1729, April   7, Hill, Lovey, and Ed. Taylor.
1801, Jan.   11, Hill, Margaret, and Paul McLoraine.
1796, Feb.   28, Hill, Margaret, and George Bower.
1758, Aug.   22, Hill, Mary, and George Pierce.
1784, July   20, Hill, Sarah, and Cornelius Moore.
1734, June   6, Hill, Thamar, and Thomas Jones.
1785, Nov.   14, Hill, Thomas, and Dan'l Crawford.
1732, Nov.   2, Hill, Tho⁵, and Elizabeth Mayes.
1747, Nov.   28, Hill, Thomas, and Elizabeth McClellan.
1798, Aug.   7, Hill, William, and Esther Duche.
1760, Dec.   31, Hill, William, and Joanna McCann.
1735, Dec.   19, Hill, William, and Mary Crap.
1793, Sept.   13, Hillar, James, and Agnes McConnell.
1784, Jan.   29, Hillbourne, Eliz., and William West.
1772, Dec.   12, Hillbourne, Mary, and John Wells.
1795, Dec.   3, Hillegas, Deborah, and Henry Kuhl.
1753, May   10, Hillegas, Michael, and Henrietta Boude.
1752, Aug.   18, Hillegas, Susannah, and Samuel Kuhl.
1755, April   15, Hiller, Sarah, and Henry Burr.
1747, Oct.   15, Hillhouse, Mary, and John Reily.
1720, Dec.   13, Hilliard, Margory, and James Jorden.
1737, Jan.   8, Hilliard, Mary, and Evan Morgan.
1785, Dec.   29, Hilligas, Henrietta, and Joseph Anthony.
1793, Oct.   10, Hillman, George, and Ann Wallhelmer.
1793, Jan.   4, Hillman, Mary, and William McConkey.
1764, Nov.   17, Hillyard, Eleanor, and Abraham Carpenter.
1714, Dec.   6, Hilton, Richard, and Catherine Griffith.
1789, March 26, Hiltzheimer, Cath., and Jacob Coxe.
1773, June   22, Himes, Mary, and John McCob.
1727, Jan.   20, Hinchman, Ann, and James Thomas.

1771, May   18, Hinchman, Sarah, and James Ash.
1733, June   14, Hincksman, Phœbe, and William Phillips.
1768, Feb.   3, Hines, Mary, and George Caton.
1773, Sept.   18, Hinton, Lydia, and William Wentworth.
1747, Dec.   5, Hinton, Moses, and Mary Leeds.
1796, Nov.   2, Hir, Frances, and John Douty.
1761, April   25, Hirst, William, and Ann Thomas.
1799, Aug.   4, Hirt, Charles, and Eleanor Magarrld.
1754, Nov.   25, Hitchcock, Joseph, and Mary Pollard.
1799, June   2, Hittner, Henry, and Mary Miller.
1798, April   8, Hoag, Cardinal, and Mary Bryson.
1755, May   3, Hobarart, Enoch, and Hannah Prat.
1737, Oct.   7, Hobard, John, and Margaret Huling.
1803, June   13, Hobart, Eliz., and John Davis Allen.
1743, Feb.   5, Hobart, Jane, and Anthony Bright.
1715, Nov.   27, Hobart, Frances, and Oliver Whitehead.
1795, May   14, Hockburn, Philip, and Barbara Hales.
1773, Jan.   28, Hockenhall, John, and Margaret Walker.
1773, Oct.   23, Hockley, Ann, and Gustavus Conyham.
1791, Jan.   25, Hockley, Eliz., and Josiah Twamley.
1772, June   4, Hockley, Mary, and John Wilcox.
1791, March   2, Hockley, Thomas and Mary Westcott.
1761, Nov.   5, Hockley, Thomas, and Eleanor Rogers.
1754, Feb.   25, Hodge, Elizabeth, and Joseph Bond.
1743, May   29, Hodge, Susannah, and John Williams.
1759, June   15, Hodges, John, and —— Dodge.
1771, Oct.   31, Hodgkinson, Bethanah, and Cath. Simmonds.
1772, April   30, Hodgkinson, Eliz., and Frederick Christian.
1780, July   6, Hodgson, Francis, and Hannah Robbins.
1801, May   12, Hodgson, Robert, and Cath. Walker.
1781, July   16, Hodgson, Samnel, and Mary Paul.
1786, June   1, Hodgson, Thomas, and Mary Tye.
1783, April   8, Hodson, William, and Jannet Jones.
1745, May   30, Hoffety, Mary, and William Race.
1761, July   2, Hoffman, Elizabeth, and Josiah Leech.
1760, Oct.   4, Hoffman, John W., and Elizabeth Weist.
1761, March 17, Hoffman, Mary, and Jacob Slaughter.
1776, April   25, Hoffman, Mary, and James Grason.
1803, Aug.   18, Hoffman, Phoeby, and John Vaughan.
1796, May   10, Hog, John, and Margaret McDougal.
1741, Nov.   10, Hogben, David, and Ann Williams.
1784, July   12, Hogg, George, and Eliz. Donaldson.
1777, Oct.   9, Hogg, Robert, and Ann Williams.
1799, June   8, Hoggard, Thomas, and Eliz. Bicker.
1712, May   28, Hogsflesh, Samuel, and Dorothy James.
1799, May   31, Holaren, Lawrence, and Ann Stewart.

1800, April	10, Holberg, Sarah, and James Ellis.
1796, July	7, Holcraft, Frederick, and Abigail Duffy,
1793, Sept.	2, Holden, Jeremiah, and Catharine Guy.
1795, Oct.	30, Holden, Patrick, and Lowrey Roberts.
1791. March	3, Holden, William, and Mary Isdale.
1803, Jan.	15, Holderness, Jane, and Dockery Smith.
1799, Nov.	21, Holderness, Harriet, and Thomas Price.
1782, Dec.	26, Holgate, William, and Mary Davis.
1799, Dec.	1, Holget, Jane, and John Towell.
1797, Feb.	2, Holiday, Frances, and John Young.
1785, June	2, Holines, Thomas, and Rebecca Harrow.
1769, Sept.	21, Holkerston, Elizabeth, and Peter Grew.
1801, Oct.	7, Holland, Charolette, and William Johnstone.
1801, Aug.	11, Holland, Frances, and Robert Warden.
1758, March	7, Holland, Joanna, and Samuel Potts.
1759, Jan.	17, Holland, John, and Elizabeth Hamilton.
1753, Oct.	6, Holland, Mary, and Abraham Wayne,
1756, March	3, Holland, Mary, and Alexander Adams.
1775, Feb.	26, Holland, Mary, and George McClatchey.
1761, March	26, Holland, Robert, and Jane Price.
1749, Dec.	4, Holland, Samuel, and Elizabeth Scull.
1771, Sept.	4, Holland, Sarah, and Peter Biggs.
1797, Nov.	2, Holland, Syvester, and Frances Ramsey.
1770, May	5, Hollias, William, and Ann McLellan.
1746, Dec.	5, Hollin, Mary, and John Annes.
1756, July	19, Hollingshead, Jacob, and Mary Hollingshead.
1756, July	19, Hollingshead, Mary, and Jacob Hollingshead.
1770, Feb.	20, Hollingshead, Nicholas, and Mary Thompson.
1779, Aug.	31, Hollingshead, Samuel, and Cath. Sobers.
1768, March	10, Hollingsworth, Levi, and Hannah Paschal.
1770, March	1, Hollingsworth, Lydia, and Samuel Wallis.
1755, Jan.	27, Hollington, Hannah, and John Morris.
1768, Dec.	6, Holloway, Elizabeth, and John Brown.
1799, Nov.	25, Holm, Hanse, and Ann Kerney.
1764, July	21, Hohn, Phoebe, and William Bate.
1791, Feb.	10, Holmes, Abigail, and George Daniel.
1742, Nov.	7, Holmes, Elizabeth, and Alexander Keater,
1759, June	6, Holmes, Elizabeth, and James Wright.
1737, Sept.	3, Holmes, Elizabeth, and John Wiar.
1796, Nov.	29, Holmes, Joseph, and Mary Carruthers.
1733, Nov.	17, Holmes, Hannah, and John Merrick.
1791, Nov.	13, Holmes, Henry, and Rebecca Vennable.
1789, July	30, Holmes, Sarah, and George Daniel.
1750, Oct.	7, Holmes, Susannah, and George Eckles.
1711, Aug.	12, Holms, Hannah, and William Corbet.
1760, Sept.	25, Holms, William, and Catherine Martin.

1748, Oct.   31, Holstein, Elizabeth, and Ezekiel Rambo.
1775, April   27, Holstein, Sarah, and Hugh Dehaven.
1742, March 13, Holston, Andrew, and Mary Jones.
1799, July   4, Holston, George, and Mary McGill.
1766, Aug.   13, Holston, Lawrence, and Ann Taylor.
1767, May   5, Holston, Martha, and Joseph Woodfield.
1765, April   28, Holt, Abel, and Mary Ponsonby.
1717, Feb.   7, Holt, Catherine, and Rives Holt.
1797, June   22, Holt, George, and Mary Longfie.
1750, Sept.   8, Holt, Mary, and Joseph Mould.
1754, May   16, Holt, Mordecai, and Elizabeth Loanarn.
1752, Jan.   16, Holt, Rebecca, and Joseph Walton.
1717, Feb.   7, Holt, Rives, and Catherine Holt.
1736, Feb.   28, Holt, Samuel, and Elizabeth Harrison.
1763, Jan.   26, Holwell, Edward, and Eleanor Neason.
1787, Aug.   6, Homassell, Charles Marcel, and Caroline Richard.
1800, April   25, Homesworth, John, and Sophia Wagoner.
1767, Sept.   24, Honey, Christopher, and Catherine Steiner.
1766, Aug.   19, Honeygrot, Mary, and Thomas Castle.
1754, July   26, Honeyman, William, and Mary Wilson.
1770, May   3, Honogrot, Eliz., and Christlet Bartlet.
1804, June   12, Hood, Cath., and William Ramsay.
1783, Oct.   23, Hood, John, and Hannah Meredith.
1742, Sept.   18, Hood, Thomas, and Rebecca Shute.
1742, June   28, Hoods, Elizabeth, and William Trotter.
1744, Oct.   4, Hoodt, Mary, and Hugh Hill.
1738, April   25, Hoof, Anne Catherine, and Jonas Green.
1800, Dec.   7, Hoofman, Mary, and James Rowley.
1800, May   22, Hook, Eliz., and Thomas Howcraft.
1777, May   26, Hooker, Matthew, and Alice Atkins.
1803, Dec.   31, Hooper, Abraham, and Rachel O'Hagan.
1744, Aug.   29, Hooper, Margaret, and John Hyat.
1727, Nov.   9, Hooper, Matt., and Mrs. Marg^t Asheton.
1720, Aug.   15, Hooper, Stephen, and Elizabeth Lewis.
1738, March 16, Hoopes, Stephen, and Martha Evans.
1734, Oct.   29, Hoops, Anne, and Joseph Evans.
1779, March 20, Hoops, Ann, and Thomas Taylor.
1772, Sept.   17, Hoops, Margaret, and Thomas Walker.
1791, Jan.   1, Hoop, Samuel, and Anna Vesmith.
1783, Aug.   16, Hooten, Sarah, and Robert Lawton.
1786, Sept.   7, Hooven, Eve, and William Coulson.
1768, Dec.   13, Hoover, Elizabeth, and Alexander Gardner.
1802, Jan.   21, Hope, Thomas, and Cath. Auner.
1792, June   28, Hopes, Samuel, and Mary Shoures.
1746, Aug.   23, Hophar, Joseph, and Sarah Blake.
1796, June   15, Hopkins, Elisha B., and Sarah Sims.

1731, Aug.   28, Hopkins, Gwin, and Evan Morgan.
1781, Feb.   3, Hopkins, Hannah, and Jacob Bates.
1722, Dec.   6, Hopkins, Capt. John, and Martha Stephens.
1784, Aug.   4, Hopkins, John Harper, and Eliz. Gay Gagen.
1788, March 17. Hopkins, Mary, and William Jackson.
1736, May   31, Hopkins, Sarah, and John Burden.
1789, May   21, Hopkins, Sarah, and Woodrop Sims.
1775, April   20, Hopkinson, Ann, and Samuel Stringer Coale.
1760, June   19, Hopkinson, Elizabeth, and Jacob Duche.
1736, Dec.   30, Hopkinson, Elizabeth, and Alexander Paxton.
1768, Sept.   1, Hopkinson, Esqr, Francis, and Ann Borden.
1794, Feb.   27, Hopkinson, Joseph, and Emily Mifflin.
1765, Sept.   5, Hopkinson, Mary, and Dr John Morgan.
1736, Sept.   9, Hopkinson, Thomas, and Mary Johnson.
1755, Aug.   27, Hopman, Jonas, and Eleanor Cobb.
1733, Oct.   25, Hopper, Cornelius, and Anne Thomas.
1804, July   2, Hopper, Kesiah, and George Hill.
1788, Sept.   27, Hopper, Martha, and David Ross.
1739, March 26, Hopton, William, and Elizabeth Scull.
1762, Sept.   8, Hopwell, Hannah, and John Dunn.
1728, Dec.   19, Hordidge, Rich^d, and Sus^h Parham.
1731, July   4, Horn, Richard, and Jane Ball.
1794, Nov.   5, Horner, Ann, and John Cromwell.
1797, Nov.   30, Horner, Stacy, and Eliz. Brown.
1743, July   2, Horner, Thomas, and Eliz. Waterman.
1739, Oct.   17, Horner, Thomas, and Anne Carpenter.
1752, March 29, Horsey, Elizabeth, and John Jones.
1742, Dec.   3, Horsley, Rebecca, and Cornelius Bowen.
1761, March 4, Horson, Alice, and David Jones.
1727, Sept.   26, Horton, Agnes, and Timothy Cummins.
1779, Sept.   11, Horver, Rachel, and John Fannon.
1797, Dec.   21, Hosack, David, and Mary Eddy.
1725, Oct.   30, Hoskins, Ben., and Mary Lock
1735, Feb.   1, Hoskins, Elizabeth, and Ebenezer Tomlinson.
1781, July   9, Hoskins, Jehu, and Eleanor Carmedy.
1773, Oct.   20, Hoskins, Joseph, and Mordecan Evans.
1744, Jan.   21, Hoskins, Martha, and Lewis Evans.
1756, Jan.   6, Hoster, Rebecca, and Evan Poteus.
1789, Aug.   6, Houch, John, and Barbary Tinaver.
1736, May   20, Hough, Elizabeth, and James Tomlinson.
1757, Nov.   8, Hough, John, and Olive Rogers.
1772, Nov.   28, Houlgate, Samuel, and Susannah Lock.
1740, Feb.   23, Houlston, Elizabeth, and Enoch Story.
1767, March 13, Houlton, Sarah, and William Gardener.
1759, Aug.   14, House, Ann, and Francis Hammet.
1712, Aug.   7, House, Elizabeth, and Thomas Love.

1761, Sept.   29, House, Esther, and Archibald McWattie.
1742, March 27, House, Francis, and Mary Miller.
1774, Oct.   15, House, Jemima, and James Crafts.
1801, Oct.   22, Houston, Joseph Alexander, and Margaret Finley.
1749, Dec.   23, House, Mary, and Morris Morgan.
1772, May   24, Houser, Jacob, and Eliz. Simmerman.
1756, Nov.   22, Houston, Frances, and John Hannah.
1734, Nov.   25, Hoven, Sabel, and Cadwallader Jones.
1765, June   26, How, James, and Catherine Cox.
1751, Aug.   6, How, Mary, and Jacob Stadler.
1776, Nov.   2, How, Thomas, and Jane Casey.
1794, July   3, Howard, Alexander, and Sarah Gill.
1791, March   3, Howard, Alice, and Humphrey Hill.
1755, Dec.   26, Howard, Daniel, and Anne Hutchinson.
1798, Feb.   22, Howard, Deborah, and John F. Malcòlm.
1745, June   15, Howard, Elizabeth, and Peter Johnston.
1732, June   19, Howard, Elizabeth, and Robert Blacklock.
1712, Sept.   27, Howard, Elizabeth, and James Daniel.
1798, April   12, Howard, Francis, and Sarah Wolahorn.
1764, Dec.   28, Howard, John, and Bridget Osborn.
1744, Aug.   9, Howard, John, and Sarah Moet.
1755, Oct.   29, Howard, Mary, and Thomas Calvert.
1741, April   18, Howard, Rebecca, and Richard Allen.
1760, Dec.   11, Howard, Robert, and Ann Hamilton.
1801, April   8, Howard, Samuel, and Ann Taylor.
1804, May   5, Howard, Sarah, and Thomas Burke.
1782, Aug.   22, Howard, Sarah, and Lawrence Salter.
1735, Sept.   2, Howard, Sarah, and John Johnson.
1737, Nov.   16, Howard, Thomas, and Mary Wood.
1800, May   22, Howcraft, Thomas, and Eliz. Hook.
1758, April   6, Howe, Samuel, and Anna Watson.
1760, Sept.   30, Howe, William, and Ann Ainsworth.
1747, June   9, Howel, George, and Sarah Garrigue.
1735, Sept.   27, Howel, Jane, and John Thomas.
1745, May   27, Howel, Jane, and James McSwain.
1753, Oct.   9, Howel, Mary, and William Williamson.
1778, Nov.   30, Howell, Ann, and Aaron Ashbridge.
1721, July   19, Howell, Benjamin, and Catherine Papen.
1785, Jan.   13, Howell, Joseph, and Rebecca Betterton.
1728, March 28, Howell, Jos, and Amy Shepherd.
1730-1, Feb. 23, Howell, Joseph, and Jane Roberts.
1712, Nov.   16, Howell, Mary, and Edward Shaw.
1784, March 22, Howell, Mary, and Louis Bellerose.
1771, Sept.   23, Howell, Phoebe, and Patrick Cannon.
1762, Oct.   19, Howell, Prudence, and James Lucas.
1730, Oct.   29, Howell, Richard, and Lethia Scot.

1770, March 8, Howell, Sarah, and Peter Stretch.
1759, May   21, Howell, Susannah, and Andrew Tybout.
1740, May   31, Howell, Thomas, and Catherine Stuart.
1709, Nov.   15, Howell, Timothy, and Margaret Hughes.
1756, Jan.   6, Howison, Richard, and Mary Edwards.
1780, March 2, Howkins, John, and Lydia Harding.
1786, Sept.   20, Howley, Patrick, and Mary Carson.
1731-2, Feb. 22, Howre, Alexander, and Catherine Henderson.
1792, June   2, Howston, John, and Martha McClenachan.
1747, March 23, Hoy, Elizabeth, and Francis Kelly.
1742, Sept.   16, Hoy, John, and Eliz. Morris.
1735, Sept.   30, Hoy, Rebecca, and Daniel Kelley.
1782, Oct.   8, Hubbard, Rachel, and Nath'l Potts, Esqr.
1794, June   12, Hubbart, John, and Amelia Scot.
1733, Feb.   6, Hubberd, Aaron, and Margaret Boice.
1789, March 18, Huber, Isaac, and Sophia Taylor.
1791, Nov.   17, Hubley, Hannah, and Joseph Marsh.
1785, Nov.   14, Hubley, Mary, and Conrad Eislen.
1755, April   2, Huddle, John, and Anna Bella Boggs.
1790, July   22, Huddle, Joseph, and Sarah Bankson.
1780, May   25, Huddle, Joseph, and Rebecca Allen.
1763, Aug.   11, Huddle, Joseph, and Hannah Evans.
1772, Aug.   15, Huddleston, Henry, and Mary Wilkinson.
1773, Nov.   16, Huddleston, Nathan, and Esther White.
1760, Sept.   18, Hudman, H. C., and Isaac Marshal.
1767, April   26, Hudson, Ann, and John Burk.
1794, Sept.   29, Hudson, Charles, and Sarah Thomas.
1740, Jan.   5, Hudson, Hannah, and James Rork.
1795, Oct.   15, Hudson, Mary, and Elisha Fisher.
1741, Oct.   2, Hudson, Rachel, and John Jorey.
1744, Oct.   18, Hudson, Rebecca, and Alex. Crookshanks.
1805, March 24, Huckle, Cath., and Richard Leach.
1801, Dec.   10, Huckle, Joseph, and Sarah Donnally.
1762, Sept.   15, Huet, Lydia, and George Meyer.
1764, Oct.   15, Huff, John, and Hannah Barber.
1759, May   7, Huff, Richard, and Margaret King.
1762, Jan.   13, Huffman, Mary, and Thomas Whitehead.
1775, Oct.   2, Hufty, Catherine, and Anthony Rue.
1772, Nov.   1, Hugar. Esqr, Daniel, and Binky Elliott.
1774, Aug.   16, Hugg, John, and Sarah West.
1743, Oct.   24, Hugg, Mary, and John Hall.
1757, April   12, Huggard, Jacob, and Hannah Wells.
1783, Oct.   25, Huggins, George, and Rebecca Stoops.
1713, Aug.   3, Huggins, Thomas, and Margaret Armstrong.
1742, March 1, Hugh, David, and Catherine Boon.
1728, Sept.   16, Hugh, Mary, and Wm Atkinson.

1745, Jan.   13, Hugh, Morgan, and Ann Stephens.
1772, March 19, Hughes, Ann, and John Robinson.
1736, Sept. 16, Hughes, Bryan, and Mary Whartonby.
1722, Feb.   2, Hughes, Charles, and Margaret Sutton.
1746, Sept.   6, Hughes, Elias, and Rebecca Wright.
1768, Jan.   9, Hughes, Elizabeth, and John North.
1768, Jan.   21, Hughes, Enoch, and Beersheba Marshal.
1738, Oct.   5, Hughes, George, and Rebecca Hall.
1754, May   18, Hughes, Hugh, and Mary Morris.
1748, Dec.   6, Hughes, Isaac, and Lydia Weldon.
1770, June   4, Hughes, Jacob, and Sarah Richards.
1774, Aug.   28, Hughes, John, and Cath. Bergenhoff.
1782, Aug.   25, Hughes, John, and Eliz. Archibald.
1709, Aug.   15, Hughes, John, and Margaret Pule.
1767, June   11, Hughes, Jr., John, and Margaret Paschal.
1794, June   19, Hughes, Joseph, and Eliz. Crotto.
1768, June   11, Hughes, Judith, and Joseph Pritchard.
1779, March 26, Hughes, Kitty, and Samuel Bonnell.
1709, Nov.   15, Hughes, Margaret, and Timothy Howell.
1712, April   2, Hughes, Mary, and George Pugh.
1767, Nov.   12, Hughes, Mary, and Thomas Wood.
1796, Oct.   19, Hughes, Mary, and Miles McLeveen.
1740, Feb.   24, Hughes, Owen, and Mary Brain.
1801, March 31, Hughes, Rachel, and William Lukins Potts.
1717, May   4, Hughes, Rees, and Mary Jones.
1736, Feb.   28, Hughes, Richard, and Martha McDonald.
1729, March 10, Hughes, Robert, and Ann Ellis.
1713, March 26, Hughes, Sidney, and Thomas Roberts.
1758, Dec.   23, Hughes, Thomas, and Ann Peterson.
1728, July   7, Hughes, Walter, and Ann Phillips.
1771, May   4, Hughes, William, and Mary Calwellin.
1760, Nov.   22, Hughes, William, and Susannah May.
1730, Oct.   30, Hughs, Edward, and Ann Zanes.
1764, Aug.   29, Hughs, David, and Elizabeth McCarnon.
1723, July   8, Hughs, Eleanor, and John Kelly.
1722, Nov.   17, Hughs, James, and Mary Pain.
1720, Nov.   17, Hughs, Margaret, and Benjamin Jones.
1720, Dec.   21, Hughs, Mary, and Isaac Seely.
1766, Dec.   4, Hughs, Matthew, and Jane Rogers.
1765, April 13, Hughs, Ruth, and Lindsay Coats.
1709, Nov.   19, Huit, Susannah, and Joseph Stephenson.
1739, April 14, Hulbeart, Philips, and Hesther Parker.
1738, Nov.   6, Hulbert, Sarah, and John Jacobson.
1737, Oct.   7, Huling, Margaret, and John Hobard.
1737, May   3, Huling, Michael, and Susannah Cox.
1792, May   24, Hulings, Eliz., and William Williams.

1763, Jan.   6, Hulins, Jonathan, and Mary Emson.
1769, May   7, Hull, Eliz., and James Allen.
1734, June   24, Hulm, Naomi, and John Whiteacar.
1799, Sept.   22, Hulton, Mary, and John Devereux.
1742, Nov.   16, Hume, George, and Mary Lacey.
1770, Nov.   13, Hume, Robert, and Cath. McClennan.
1794, Nov.   27, Humes, Isabella, and James White.
1756, May   27, Hummer, William, and Elizabeth Richinson.
1755, Dec.   4, Humphray, Garthenia, and Thomas Wilday.
1772, Dec.   24, Humphreville, Parnel, and Benjamin McVeagh.
1724, Jan.   29, Humphrey, Joanna, and William Young.
1721, Sept.   27, Humphrey, Leaury, and Simon Moon.
1803, Dec.   3, Humphreys, Ann M., and Thomas Potts.
1798, March   10, Humphreys, Charles, and Mary Donaldly.
1736, Aug.   28, Humphreys, Elizabeth, and Edward Dowers.
1801, May   14, Humphreys, Eliz., and Thomas Maxwell.
1800, May   19, Humphreys, Eliz., and Isaac Gunter.
1730, July   7, Humphreys, Hannah, and David Harry.
1789, Oct,   29, Humphreys, Isaac, and Eliz. Montgomery.
1759, Sept.   5, Humphreys, James, and Ann Powell.
1796, July   30, Humphreys, James, and Ann Williams.
1758, Oct.   13, Humphreys, Jonathan, and Ann Moore.
1769, Dec.   27, Humphreys, Joshua, and Elizabeth Stillman.
1801, Aug.   4, Humphreys, Laurence, and Eliz. Dawson.
1724, July   24, Humphreys, Mary, and David Parry..
1721, Aug.   2, Humphreys, Richard, and Mary Ware.
1806, Oct.   6, Humphreys, Sarah, and Haney Killingsworth.
1762, Sept.   6, Humphreys, Sarah, and John Thomas.
1769, Jan.   —, Humphreys, William, and Ann McLaughlin.
1734, Sept.   9, Humphreys, John Thomas, and Alice Connor.
1795, March   11, Humpton, Richard, and Eliz. Morris.
1801, Nov.   12, Hungary, Eliz., and Edward McKegan.
1787, May   23, Hungerford, John, and Sarah Cline.
1776, Jan.   25, Hunn, Mary, and Caleb Bickham.
1805, Nov.   10, Hunneker, Cath., and Richard Miles.
1752, Oct.   17, Hunt, Anne, and George Steward.
1767, May   7, Hunt, Bridget, and Thomas Sutor.
1766, Aug.   5, Hunt, Edward, and Ann Wilson.
1755, May   30, Hunt, Eleanor, and Cornelius Keith.
1714, Jan.   4, Hunt, Hannah, and Martin Hardin.
1767, June   18, Hunt, Isaac, and Mary Shewell.
1761, May   7, Hunt, Joseph, and Ann Triggin.
1805, Aug.   30, Hunt, Judith, and Joseph Withall Hicks.
1786, July   22, Hunt, Mary, and John Nicholson.
1794, Jan.   9, Hunt, Ralph, and Lydia Eyre.
1780, July   4, Hunt, Richard, and Mary Renshaw.

1796, May 28, Hunt, Samuel, and Eleanor Cunningham.
1754, Nov. 6, Hunt, Susannah, and Henry Yeandal.
1799, Dec. 8, Hunt, William, and Thankful Blake.
1804, May 25, Hunt, William, and Hannah Bryan.
1773, Aug. 5, Hunter, Alex., and Sarah Hall.
1764, Aug. 22, Hunter, Alice, and John Jones.
1720, May 29, Hunter, Ann, and Samuel Baker.
1757, Jan. 6, Hunter, Anne, and John Blackford.
1751, Nov. 12, Hunter, James, and Mary Cole.
1735, July 2, Hunter, Margaret, and Robert Dixon.
1775, Dec. 24, Hunter, Peter, and Mary Amber.
1728, March 4, Hunter, Rachel, and John Baker.
1801, April 19, Hunter, Sarah, and William R. Vanleer.
1793, Aug. 27, Hunter, William, and Sarah Perkins.
1784, July 4, Hurd, Ann, and John Hall.
1752, March 9, Hurdith, Joseph, and Anne Guthry.
1757, Nov. 26, Hurley, Mary, and George Kinnard.
1744, June 13, Hurley, Mary, and Peter Powelson.
1756, April 17, Hurst, Anne, and John Felton.
1788, Sept. 9, Hurst, John, and Eliz. Vester.
1770, Feb. 3, Hurst, Mary, and John Cridlend.
1736, Dec. 24, Hurst Thomas, and Rachel Thomson.
1715, June 26, Husbands, John, and Mary Willsear.
1800, Oct. 2, Husler, William, and Charlotte Meade.
1796, March 3, Hussey, Sarah, and Thomas Procter.
1775, Dec. 28, Hussey, Sarah, and William McFadden.
1734, Feb. 25, Hust, Helen, and Thomas Asshe.
1745, Sept. 19. Huston, Alexander, and Elizabeth Hassel.
1772, Dec. 2, Huston, Cath., and James McKenzie.
1748, Nov. 29, Huston, Elinor, and Edmund McVeagh.
1783, April 24, Huston, Eliz., and Charles Cox.
1767, Feb. 26, Huston, James, and Elizabeth Killgore.
1788, June 28, Huston, Margaret, and Thomas Gordon.
1770, Sept. 9, Huston, Patience, and William Stirling.
1730, Dec. 2, Hutchins, Elizabeth, and John Boon.
1744, March 25, Hutchins, Mary, and John Bolitho.
1743, Nov. 1, Hutchins, Sarah, and John Smith.
1742, Dec. 2, Hutchins, Thomas, and Rachel Roberts.
1796, Nov. 29, Hutchenson, Susannah, and John Green.
1755, Dec. 26, Hutchinson, Anne, and Daniel Howard.
1768, Dec. 2, Hutchinson, Catherine, and Benjamin Ramshaw.
1794, Oct. 4, Hutchinson, Charles, and Mary Gardiner.
1779, Feb. 18, Hutchinson, Dr. James, and Lydia Biddle.
1792, June 6, Hutchinson, Jane, and Joseph Whitehead.
1761, July 29, Hutchinson, Phœbe, and William Ashton.
1801, March 8, Hutson, Sarah, and Ainst Ulary.

1780, July   27, Hutton, Benjamin, and Rebecca Plumstead.
1760, Aug.   11, Hutton, George, and Mary Moore.
1749, April   20, Hutton, James, and Mary Weeks.
1759, Aug.   29, Hutton, John, and Susannah Stephens.
1761, Aug.   15, Hutton, Mary, and David Evans.
1758, Aug.   9, Hutton, Mary, and Joseph Allen.
1762, Aug.   13, Hutton, Nathaniel, and Margaret Nuttle.
1736, Nov.   5, Hutton, Thomas, and Rachel Barnes.
1798, July   29, Hutton, William, and Ann Caldwell.
1744, Aug.   16, Hyat, Ann, and Jonas Osburn.
1744, Aug.   29, Hyat, John, and Margaret Hooper.
1797, June   29, Hyde, Charlotte, and John Brown.
1787, Sept.   12, Hyde, Mary, and Jonathan Smith.
1776, Feb.   1, Hyder, Ann, and William Wiles.
1796, June   6, Hyer, William, and Margaret Stuber.
1771, April   10, Hyman, Jane, and Daniel Kinnicott.
1773, Aug.   26, Hyndes, Esther, and Joshua Andrews.
1760, Oct.   25, Hynes, John, and Martha Bennet.
1743, Sept.   1, Hynes, Rachel, and Robert Tempest.
1753, March   8, Ianley, Lidia, and James Scull.
1789, April   25, Ibetson, Mary, and David DeBartholt.
1752, Nov.   25, Ibison, Martha, and George Gray, jr.
1752, March   23, Iddings, Henry, and Mary Winn.
1771, March   18, Iles, William, and Isabella Crane.
1767, Nov.   11, Illingworth, Francis, and Rachel Cox.
1774, Sept.   4, Ince, James, and Eliz. Greenway.
1799, Feb.   3, Ince, Susanna, and John Fiss.
1785, Feb.   21, Indigott, Hannah, and Joseph Faulkner.
1804, Oct.   18, Ingersoll, Charles, and Mary Wilcocks.
1720, Oct.   6, Ingle, Frederick, and Ann Cloud.
1737, Aug.   13, Ingles, James, and Ruth Harmer.
1761, Dec.   31, Inglis, Ann, and Gilber Barclay.
1732, Dec.   23, Inglis, John, and Elizabeth Swift.
1761, April   2, Inglis, Mary, and Capt. Julines Herring.
1760, Nov.   28, Inglis, Rebecca, and John Swaine.
1791, April   11, Ingraham, Francis, and Eliz. Duffield.
1743, Jan.   26, Ingram, Abigail, and Laurance Anderson.
1733, Sept.   4, Ingram, Archibald, and Prisilla Leveritt.
1761, July   28, Ingram, George, and Rachel Talbert.
1743, Nov.   24, Ingram, John, and Hannah Brownyard.
1730, Oct.   25, Ingram, Thomas, and Margaret fframe.
1796, Jan.   8, Innes, David, and Sarah McIntire.
1802, July   15, Innis, George, and Marg. Rivers.
1799, March   7, Inskeep, Abigail, and Samuel F. Bradford.
1767, Sept.   1, Ireland, Edward, and Mary Cheeseman.
1789, Nov.   19, Ireland, Eliz., and Francis Lesher.

1775, July   13, Ireland, Eliz., and George Milward.

1759, Dec.   11, Ireland, Henry, and Mary Stonemetz.

1796, Dec.   7, Ireland, Mary, and Edward Coyles.

1728, May   1, Irish, Ann, and James Welch.

1771, Sept.   26, Irvin, James, and Sarah Green.

1733, May   24, Irvine, George, and Mary Rush.

1803, Aug.   4, Irvine, George, and Sarah McClaskey.

1764, June   16, Irwin, Dunnin, and Frances Bullman.

1765, Jan.   7, Irwin, James, and Elizabeth Yarborough.

1771, Dec.   28, Irwin, Margaret, and James Stawart.

1741, Sept.   9, Irwin, Mary, and Edward Gill.

1796, Sept.   29, Irwin, Robert, and Susan Coxe.

1791, March   3, Isdale, Mary, and William Holden.

1768, Sept.   29, Iselstein, Rachel, and Conrad Gerhard.

1768, May   15, Isemaster, Mary, and William Alexander.

1783, May   6, Ives, Thomas, and Hannah Lloyd.

1797, Aug.   19, Iveson, Amy, and Thomas Burk.

1768, May   19, Iveson, Mary, and Robert Bunbury.

1755, Nov.   21, Ivory, John, and Martha Heart.

1798, June   27, Ivory, Mathias, and Mary Doyle.

1803, June   6, Izard, George, and Eliz. Carter Shippen.

1799, Feb.   23, Izer, Rebecca, and James Moore.

1767, Nov.   23, Izzard, Jane, and Joseph Saunders.

1795, Oct.   22, Jack, John, and Lettice Ash.

1720, Feb.   27, Jack, Mary, and William Macerah.

1748, Oct.   1, Jackman, Thomas, and Elizabeth Stapeler.

1762, May   1, Jackson, Ann, and Joseph Rhoades.

1733, July   24, Jackson, Diana, and Thomas Stamper.

1758, Jan.   27, Jackson, Edith, and John Wainer.

1773, Jan.   12, Jackson, Edward, and Sarah Greenland.

1769, April   25, Jackson, Eleanor, and Jacob Johnson.

1754, Jan.   31, Jackson, Elizabeth, and William Shute.

1797, March   2, Jackson, Eliz., and Charles Reiley.

1742, May   29, Jackson, Hannah, and Morgan Evans.

1795, May   7, Jackson, Isaak H., and Deborah C. Wharton.

1735, Dec.   25, Jackson, Isabell, and Joseph Kellogg.

1783, Jan.   3, Jackson, James, and Mary Tucker.

1796, Nov.   26, Jackson, John, and Mary McClosky.

1767, June   11, Jackson, Joseph, and Ann Kelley.

1781, July   1, Jackson, Joseph, and Diana Sparrow.

1803, Nov.   1, Jackson, Lauraher, and James Claxton.

1781, May   29, Jackson, Lucy, and Henry Kingell.

1799, Dec.   8, Jackson, Martha, and Tauton Mason.

1748, April   14, Jackson, Mary, and Emanuel Rouse.

1784, Nov.   11, Jackson, Mary, and John Storde.

1739, Oct.   14, Jackson, Patience, and William Greenway.

1766, Oct.   9, Jackson, Samuel, and Sarah Voto.
1738, Feb.   13, Jackson, Sarah, and Josiah Claypole.
1752, March 11, Jackson, William, and Abigail Stiles.
1774, Oct.   27, Jackson, William, and Mary App Owen.
1788, March 17, Jackson, William, and Mary Hopkins.
1755, May   17, Jackson, William, and Rachel Hannis.
1795, Nov.   11, Jackson, William, and Eliz. Willing.
1738, Nov.   6, Jacobson, John, and Sarah Hulbert.
1766, Dec.   8, Jacobs, Mary, and Jeremiah Reese.
1746, Dec.   4 Jacobs, Mary, and George Heap.
1709, July   23, Jacobs, Rebecca, and John Newberry.
1804, March 27, Jacobs, Richard, and Margaret McGill.
1805, April   11, Jacques, Gideon, and Martha Smith.
1753, Sept.   13, Jagard, Mary, and John Porch.
1753, Nov.   16, Jahnin, Magdalena, and Ulrich Reinhart.
1774, June   7, James, Ann, and William Nixon.
1757, May   4, James, Ann, and William Thomas.
1712, May   28, James, Dorothy, and Samuel Hogsflesh.
1709, Sept.   18, James, Eleanor, and William Dicksey.
1794, Dec.   16, James, Eliz., and John Bruistar.
1730, April   7, James, Elizabeth, and Arnold Francis.
1748, April   6, James, Elizabeth, and George David.
1763, Sept.   14, James, Jacob, and Christina Ryan.
1786, June   1, James, Jane, and Anthony Murray.
1762, Aug.   13, James, John, and Meldina Kukler.
1735, Dec.   30, James, Martha, and John Hanes.
1727, June   22, James, Mary, and Evan Griffith.
1729, Aug.   30, James, Marg^t, and Jo^s Lewis.
1720, Dec.   8, James, Mary, and Joseph Read.
1757, Nov.   19, James, Mary, and Philip Mendenhall.
1762, April   8, James, Richard, and Nancy Baxter.
1797, Dec.   16, James, Susan, and John Mun.
1713, Aug.   6, James, Susannah, and Richard Brisk.
1747, July   9, James, Thomas, and Mary Syng.
1722, May   15, James, Thomas, and Jane Davis.
1786, Dec.   11, James, Thomas, and Margaret Smith.
1800, May   19, James, William, and Abigail Lauderback.
1795, Oct.   24, James, William, and Eliz. Dolby.
1775, May   4, Jameson, John, and Cath. Osboone.
1722, March 28, Jameson, William, and Sarah Collins.
1783, Jan.   28, Jamison, David, and Eliz. Smith.
1751, July   9, Jamison, John, and Margaret Thompson.
1784, July   29, Janney, Langhorn, and Eleanor Wadman.
1762, April   22, January, Elizabeth, and Benjamin Jenkins.
1768, July   7, January, Rebecca, and George Griffith.
1734, April   16, Janvier, Isaac, and Rebecca Welsh.

1780, Sept. 28, Jarman, Eleanor, and John Taylor.
1761, March 5, Jarrat, Margaret, and Ephraim Bonham.
1730–1, March 2, Jayne, Richard, and Anne Vineing.
1743, July 27, Jeans, Anne, and William Beaman.
1794, Aug. 7, Jefferies, William, and Hester Davis.
1758, June 9, Jefferys, Edward, and Mary Darnell.
1728, March 3, Jeffreys, James, and Elizabeth Carter.
1758, July 19, Jekyll, Francina, and William Hicks.
1734, Oct. 20, Jekyll, John, and Margaret Shippen.
1769, July 2, Jemmison, Elizabeth, and Jacob Carrell.
1790, Oct. 3, Jenings, Mary, and Jared Craig.
1796, Oct. 15, Jenkens, Ezekiel, and Jane Ryan.
1740, July 25, Jenkins, Abigail, and William McGeah.
1772, Feb. 4, Jenkins, Ann, and Thomas McFee.
1762, April 22, Jenkins, Benjamin, and Elizabeth January.
1733, May 20, Jenkins, Catherine, and James Row.
1738, July 19, Jenkins, Catherine, and Charles Maycock.
1721, April 23, Jenkins, Elizabeth, and Francis Powmels.
1733, July 17, Jenkins, Isabella, and Thomas Kirk.
1742, July 3, Jenkins, John, and Rachel Vaughan.
1721, Dec. 16, Jenkins, Margaret, and Israel Cooper.
1782, Nov. 28, Jenkins, Mary, and John Beere.
1750, Jan. 4, Jenkins, Mary, and Lewis Gordon.
1730, Sept. 30, Jenkins, Robert, and Hannah Ellwell.
1767, March 5, Jenkins, William, and Sarah Venables.
1748, April 11, Jenney, Robert, and Jane Elizabeth Cummings.
1797, April 22, Jennings, Henrietta, and Charles Renshaw.
1785, Dec. 29, Jennings, Susannah, and Joseph Cæsar.
1774, July 26, Jennings, William, and Eliz. McAdams.
1780, Nov. 23, Jenny, Sarah, and William Powers.
1763, Sept. 6, Jepson, William, and Elizabeth Davison.
1801, Sept. 24, Jerman, Eleanor, and Jonathan Richards.
1765, Dec. 28, Jerman, Lewis, and Mary Davis.
1742, June 16, Jerman, Martha, and Edmund Wetherby.
1766, Feb. 27, Jervis, Charles, and Elizabeth Boore.
1749, Aug. 24, Jessop, Abraham, and Alice Fredericks.
1762, July 10, Jessup, Samuel, and Elizabeth Neeld.
1797, April 27, Jewell, Kenneth, and Martha Blakiston.
1762, Aug. 21, Jewell, Mary, and Daniel Minanti.
1745, Feb. 15, Jewers, John, and Margaret Cook.
1759, June 28, Jobson, Samuel, and Ann LeDru.
1748, May 28, Jobson, Sarah, and David Cumming.
1768, Oct. 13, John and Eve, (Tuscaroras.)
1786, July 29, John, Eliz, and John Oar.
1774, Sept. 17, Johns, Ann, and Henry Esler.
1794, Dec. 26, Johns, Eliz., and John H. Cheyney.

1767, June   13, Johns, Joseph, and Ann Mears.
1774, April   28, Johns, Mary, and William Craig.
1737, May   10, Johnson, Abigail, and John Dagg.
1712, Dec.   14, Johnson, Andrew, and Margaret Conner.
1803, Dec.   17, Johnson, Ann, and Patrick Shields.
1759, Aug.   22, Johnson, Ann, and Allen Moore.
1800, June   5, Johnson, Ann, and John Read.
1727, Dec.   24, Johnson, Archi^d, and Mary Jones.
1797, April   5, Johnson, Cath., and Scott King.
1758, Dec.   9, Johnson, Catherine, and Robert Younger.
1759, Feb.   10, Johnson, Catherine, and John Dalton.
1798, Dec.   15, Johnson, David, and Ann Adams.
1804, June   3, Johnson, Eleanor, and Francis Delanoy.
1764, Dec.   6, Johnson, Eleanor, and Charles Alexander.
1795, Aug.   29. Johnson, Eliz., and Aquila Ross.
1773, Feb.   11, Johnson, Eliz., and Joseph Philips.
1760, Aug.   6, Johnson, Elizabeth, and James Ranton.
1761, May   12, Johnson, Elizabeth, and Samuel Shimer.
1764, Jan.   21, Johnson, Elizabeth, and James McGill.
1713, Dec.   8, Johnson, Elizabeth, and George Ranton.
1775, Dec.   13, Johnson, Francis, and Alice Erwin.
1787, Jan.   21, Johnson, George, and Jemima Moore.
1743, April   11, Johnson, George, and Mary Bullock.
1799, Jan.   9, Johnson, Gershom, and Ann Stanley.
1752, Nov.   4, Johnson, Hannah, and Peter Thompson.
1805, June   3, Johnson, Henry, and Jane Linscott.
1769, April   25, Johnson, Jacob, and Eleanor Jackson.
1740, Nov.   6, Johnson, James, and Rebecca Rigley.
1735, Sept.   2, Johnson, John, and Sarah Howard.
1799, April   17, Johnson, John, and Martha Small.
1797, June   21, Johnson, John W., and Sarah Badcock.
1786, July   18, Johnson, John, and Jane Curl.
1800, Sept.   14, Johnson, John, and Comfort Till.
1729, March   6, Johnson, John, and Rebecca Chivers.
1760, Feb.   14, Johnson, John, and Margaret Robinson.
1801, Sept.   29, Johnson, Jonathan, and Sarah Harper.
1801, April   2, Johnson, Joseph, and Martha Morris.
1806, March 22, Johnson, Joseph, and Margaret Perry.
1750, Sept.   19, Johnson, Joshua, and Anne Pinyard.
1762, Nov.   15, Johnson, Margaret, and John Reading.
1728, May   30, Johnson, Martha, and Nic. Rimmer.
1743, July   11, Johnson, Martha, and William Garwood.
1768, Aug.   27, Johnson, Mary, and Richard Envenson.
1801, Sept.   24, Johnson, Mary, and Richard Renshaw.
1805, July   28, Johnson, Mary, and Thomas Scarlet.
1712, Nov.   9, Johnson, Mary, and George Perkins.

1736, Sept.   9, Johnson, Mary, and Thomas Hopkinson.
1740, Aug.   6, Johnson, Mary, and John Fox.
1754, June   3, Johnson, Patrick, and Martha Rope.
1798, Dec.   9, Johnson, Peter, and Mary Farren.
1748, April   7, Johnson, Peter, and Sarah Vankirk.
1743, Dec. 10, Johnson, Orange, and Joshua Carpenter.
1804, Dec.   6, Johnson, Rebecca, and Peter Hanson.
1794, Oct. 25, Johnson, Richard, and Sarah Dunlap.
1774, Jan. 20, Johnson, Richard, and Mary Delany.
1796, June   4, Johnson, Ruth, and Benjamin Morris.
1762, Sept.   4, Johnson, Ruth, and William Gibson.
1800, Jan. 29, Johnson, Samuel, and Eliz. Dorson.
1735, April 17, Johnson, Samuel, and Mary Pearce.
1770, Oct. 29, Johnson, Sarah, and Francis Garrick.
1743, Oct.   9, Johnson, Sarah, and William Bennet.
1796, March 28, Johnson, Susan, and Lewis Chatham.
1799, March 16, Johnson, Susanna, and John Crippen.
1794, July 21, Johnson, Tacy Ann, and Joseph Edwards.
1796, Feb.   6, Johnson, William Burnand, and Penelope Creed.
1769, Dec.   7, Johnson, William, and Frances Derrick.
1758, June 13, Johnson, William, and Margaret Craig.
1759, Feb.   3, Johnson, William, and Christiana Knowles.
1763, March 4, Johnson, William, and Margaret Powell.
1730, July 26, Johnson, William, and Mary Kennedy.
1755, May 22, Johnston, Eleanor, and Francis Mountain.
1796, April 11, Johnstone, Eliza, and David Hazard.
1744, March 29, Johnston, Hannah, and Samuel Mason.
1772, Dec. 28, Johnston, James, and Christiana Murray.
1785, Oct. 18, Johnston, Jane, and John Dorsey.
1781, Feb. 22, Johnston, Johanna, and George Thornton.
1769, Dec. 21, Johnston, Joseph, and Sarah Morgan.
1781, July 12, Johnston, Margaret, and William Robinson.
1752, Nov. 27, Johnston, Mary, and John Dealy.
1745, June 15, Johnston, Peter, and Elizabeth Howard.
1782, June   6, Johnston, Richard, and Margaret Lezuleer.
1737, May 24, Johnston, Robert, and Lillias Corbet.
1750, Oct. 11, Johnston, Robert, and Elizabeth Mitchel.
1783, Dec. 24, Johnston, Sarah, and George Vansant.
1794, Sept. 27, Johnston, Sarah, and John Ormrod.
1750, Feb. 19, Johnston, Sarah, and William Prise.
1797, April 10, Johnston, William, and Eliz. Culin.
1801, Oct.   7, Johnstone, William, and Charlotte Holland.
1791, Oct. 23, Johnston, William, and Ann Keer.
1746, June   9, Joiner, Elinour, and Christopher Perry.
1759, Dec.   1, Jolly, Benjamin, and Susannah Robinit.
1783, Dec. 19, Jolly, Eliz., and Thomas McKay.

1740, March 22, Jolly, Stephen, and Rebecca Rees.
1734, Nov.   8, Jones, Amey, and Magnes Fleet.
1773, Jan.   30, Jones, Anna, and John Chandler.
1732, July   30, Jones, Anne, and Charles Mullins.
1732, Oct.   7, Jones, Anne, and John Gwinn.
1745, May   14, Jones, Anne, and Henry Clark.
1745, March 10, Jones, Ann, John Scull.
1742, Jan.   30, Jones, Ann, and Joseph Beddorne.
1805, June   19, Jones, Ann, and George Fisher.
1772, Aug.   10, Jones, Ann, and John Douglas.
1727, Dec.   13, Jones, Ann, and Wm Williams.
1728, March   1, Jones, Ann, and Evan David.
1767, July   9, Jones, Ann, and John Davis.
1771, Sept.   15, Jones, Asher, and Ann Embrace.
1795, Sept.   6, Jones, Augustine, and Eliz. Boree.
1769, July   24, Jones, Benjamin, and Tacy Roberts.
1720, Nov.   17, Jones, Benjamin, and Margaret Hughs.
1709, Nov.   14, Jones, Bridgett, and Luellen Davis.
1734, Nov.   25, Jones, Cadwallader, and Sabel Hoven.
1780, Nov.   30, Jones, Cath., and Francis Barrett.
1767, May   30, Jones, Catherine, and William Cummings.
1768, May   19, Jones, Catherine, and Thomas Batson.
1739, May.   26, Jones, Christian, and Daniel Harrison.
1739, Feb.   21, Jones, Daniel, and Anne Rambo.
1761, June   4, Jones, Daniel, and Jemima Morris.
1734, Sept.   26, Jones, Daniel, and Anne Hiep.
1792, Dec.   16, Jones, David, and Margaret Vance.
1727, Aug.   12, Jones, David, and Ann Thomas.
1761, March   4, Jones, David, and Alice Horson.
1716, March 26, Jones, David, and Joanna Martin.
1765, Oct.   26, Jones, David, and Rebecca Carter.
1741, Nov.   14, Jones, David, and Mary Edwards.
1735, May   10, Jones, David, and Elizabeth Davis.
1793, June   13, Jones, Deborah, and Benjamin Rush.
1725, Nov.   17, Jones, Elizabeth, and Sam. Bollard.
1770, May   16, Jones, Edward, and Eliz. Griffins.
1733, May   23, Jones, Edward, and Margaret Trevoe.
1734, June   15, Jones, Edward, and Elizabeth Paxton.
1774, Dec.   22, Jones, Eleanor, and Thomas Adair.
1779, Oct.   20, Jones, Eliz., and Samuel Wheeler.
1775, Dec.   5, Jones, Eliz., and Thomas Powell.
1747, Nov.   14, Jones, Elizabeth, and William Gray.
1740, Sept.   13, Jones, Elizabeth, and Henry Verney.
1749, Oct.   17, Jones, Elizabeth, and Thomas Blake.
1794, Sept.   21, Jones, Eliz., and William Lindsay.
1745, Aug.   22, Jones, Elizabeth, and Benjamin Levering.

1803, July   21, Jones, Eliz., and John Morgan.
1720, Feb.   17, Jones, Elizabeth, and Griffith Evans.
1761, Dec.   24, Jones, Elizabeth, and Daniel Carteret.
1737, Sept.   27, Jones, Elizabeth, and Alexander Bell.
1733, Jan.   7, Jones, Elizabeth, and Catherine Frost.
1773, July   14, Jones, Ephriam, and Rachel Richardson.
1745, Dec.   9, Jones, Evan, (Niggar), and Anne Evans.
1745, Aug.   14, Jones, Evan, and Diana Thomas.
1729, Feb.   17, Jones, Evan, and Margt. Parry.
1804, June   16, Jones, Evan, and Hannah Burke.
1727, Nov.   7, Jones, G., and Margt. Bullock.
1732, June   15, Jones, George, and Mary Storke.
1721, Aug.   2, Jones, Gibbs, and Jane Crapp.
1726, Oct.   13, Jones, Griffith, and Mary Bevan.
1760, Nov.   29, Jones, Griffith, and Elizabeth Owen.
1720, Nov.   28, Jones, Griffith, and Elizabeth Thomas.
1711, July   2, Jones, Griffith, and Sarah Morris.
1737, Sept.   15, Jones, Gwin, and William Griffiths.
1771, April   20, Jones, Hannah, and James Ham.
1744, May   9, Jones, Hannah, and Joseph Price.
1754, Nov.   23, Jones, Hannah, and John Aplee Manuel.
1759, June   16, Jones, Isaac, and Eleanor Each.
1743, Feb.   13, Jones, Isaac, and Frances Strettell.
1754, Nov.   30, Jones, Jacob, and Anne Dodd.
1796, Aug.   28, Jones, James, and Eliz. Fortune.
1784, June   24, Jones, James Morris, and Arabella Levy.
1733, Dec.   23, Jones, Jane, and William Craddock.
1758, April   18, Jones, Jane, and Anthony Coffin.
1767, Oct.   27, Jones, Jenkin, and Ann Ewer.
1743, Aug.   20, Jones, John, and Sarah Price.
1801, June   27, Jones, John C., and Jane Ross.
1802, Jan.   7, Jones, John, and Rebecca Jones.
1742, June   26, Jones, John, and Sarah Allen.
1730–1, Feb. 15, Jones, John, and Elizabeth Roberts.
1797, Nov.   27, Jones, John, and Phœbe Ryan.
1749, March 26, Jones, John, and Content Foster.
1731, Oct.   21, Jones, John, and Elizabeth Oram.
1764, Aug.   22, Jones, John, and Alice Hunter.
1752, Aug.   8, Jones, John, and Rebecca Ash.
1752, March 29, Jones, John, and Elizabeth Horsey.
1736, Nov.   25, Jones, John, and Eleanor Godfrey.
1795, June   1, Jones, John, and Eleanor Cornett.
1771, Aug.   15, Jones, John, and Mary Rowland.
1763, March 21, Jones, John, and Rebecca Finney.
1717, March   3, Jones, John, and Jane Richards.
1737, Aug.   29, Jones, Joseph, and Margaret Van Niminon.

1730, Oct.   16, Jones, Margaret, and Thomas Morgan.
1732, April 14, Jones, Margaret, and Bryan O'Neal.
1735, Sept. 29, Jones, Margaret, and John Foulke.
1721, Jan.   13, Jones, Margaret, and Michael Coyle.
1795, Oct.   23, Jones, Margaret, and Mark Cowperthwaite.
1758, Jan.   18, Jones, Margaret, and William Free.
1763, Aug.   11, Jones, Martha, and Thomas Clifton.
1805, March 28, Jones, Martha Levy, and Robert Adams.
1801, July   2, Jones, Mary, and Thomas Rowland.
1742, March 13, Jones, Mary, and Andrew Holston.
1717, May   4, Jones, Mary, and Rees Hughes.
1760, March 12, Jones, Mary, and Joseph Ferguson.
1758, Dec.   6, Jones, Mary, and Thomas Brown.
1727, Dec.   24, Jones, Mary, and Arche^d Johnson.
1768, March 25, Jones, Mary, and John Coney.
1770, Sept. 11, Jones, Mary, and Richard Brackell.
1729, Nov.   22, Jones, Mary, and T. Dennis.
1728, Nov.   25, Jones, Mary, and Jo^s Pratt.
1780, June   7, Jones, Mary, and David Evans.
1780, July   1, Jones, Mary, and John Potts.
1779, May   13, Jones, Mary, and Jonathan Grise.
1804, Oct.   11, Jones, Mary, and Nathan Brooks.
1804, April 10, Jones, Mary, and Thomas Wilson.
1744, March 27, Jones, Meredith, and Eliz. Fusman.
1709, Oct.   6, Jones, Nicholas, and Margaret Ellen.
1727, June   28, Jones, Owen, and Ann Davis.
1729, Oct.   17, Jones, Peter, and Sarah Kinner.
1769, March   4, Jones, Peter, and Eliz. Rose.
1747, May   7, Jones, Priscilla and Joshua Wollaston.
1725, Dec.   5, Jones, Pris., and Ed. Ashmore.
1802, Jan.   7, Jones, Rebecca, and John Jones.
1804, Sept. 10, Jones, Rebecca, and Richard Roberts.
1768, Aug.   17, Jones, Rebecca, and Enoch Battin.
1733, Nov.   19, Jones, Reece, and Gwin Evans.
1728, Jan.   10, Jones, Rich^d, and Margt. Williams.
1785, Dec.   8, Jones, Robert, and Charlotto Grage Baker.
1774, March 23, Jones, Robert Strettell, and Ann Shippen.
1744, May   1, Jones, Robert, and Eliz. Rece.
1802, May   23, Jones, Samuel Burgess, and Ann Strable.
1751, Aug.   20, Jones, Samuel, and Rachel Thomas.
1799, Aug.   9, Jones, Samuel, and Rebecca Hamill.
1746, May   8, Jones, Sarah, and William Clarke.
1736, Feb.   18, Jones, Sarah, and William Thomas.
1748, Aug.   13, Jones, Sarah, and David Lewis.
1786, Jan.   1, Jones, Sarah, and John Brickham.
1796, Nov.   26, Jones, Sarah, and Samuel Smith.

1740, Aug.　5, Jones, Susannah, and Belcher Preston.
1742, Dec.　23, Jones, Susannah, and Ephraim Bowman.
1784, Oct.　14, Jones, Susannah, and Samuel Shober.
1729, Dec.　26, Jones, T., and Martha West.
1727, June　20, Jones, Thamer, and James Dunn.
1783, April　8, Jones, Tannet, and William Hodson.
1796, Aug.　11, Jones, Thomas, and Eliz. Tucker.
1761, June　6, Jones, Thomas, and Sarah Allen.
1734, June　6, Jones, Thomas, and Thamar Hill.
1729-30, Mar. 8, Jones, Thomas, and Elizabeth Pughe.
1783, April　29, Jones, William, and Eleanor Young.
1805, Dec.　7, Jones, William, and Phoebe Rowen.
1729-30, Feb. 23, Jones, William, and Mary Porter.
1735, Aug.　27, Jonson, Rebecca, and Robert Goodjohn.
1805, April　21, Jordan, Alex., and Eliz. Shaffer.
1759, Aug.　23, Jordan, James, and Grace Moore.
1749, April　28, Jordan, Jeremiah, and Mary Lewis.
1799, April　4, Jordan, John, and Cath. Van Phul.
1799, June　7, Jordan, Mary, and Andrew Guin.
1720, Dec.　13, Jorden, James, and Margory Hilliard.
1741, Oct.　2, Jorey, John, and Rachel Hudson.
1782, April　4, Josiah, Capt. James, and Eliz. Marsh.
1714, Dec.　31, Jotue, Henry, and Rachel Handcock.
1806, May　6, Joubert, Eliz., and Thomas Fenwick.
1806, April　21, Jovell, John, and Sarah Stevenson.
1726, Sept.　20, Joyner, Alice, and Wm Cleverly.
1745, June　3, Joyner, Eliz., and Larrance Collins.
1769, June　22, Juckness, John, and Elizabeth White.
1787, April　12, Judor, George, and Mary Shute.
1768, Aug.　22, Judson, James, and Catherine Cool.
1714, Jan.　6, Jukesbery, Elizabeth, and William Bowell.
1729, Jan.　1, Jumble, Mary, and John Lowder.
1750, Dec.　2, Juniour, William, and Barbara Crawford.
1728, March 29, Justice, Bridget, and Richd Tison.
1758, June　27, Justice, Christina, and George Morton.
1774, June　2, Justice, James, and Hannah Wayne.
1716, Feb.　6, Justice, John, and Priscilla Bright.
1780, Oct.　19, Justice, Mary, and Joseph Cooper.
1740, Aug.　23, Justice, Moses, and Sarah Longacre.
1776, April　6, Justis, Penelope, and Thomas Rice.
1728, Aug.　25, Justice, Peter, and Anne Monson.
1774, Oct.　27, Justice, Rebecca, and William Meston.
1780, June　8, Justice, Thomas, and Mary Folker.
1774, Feb.　24, Justice, William, and Mary England.
1800, Sept.　21, Kaighn, Mary, and Isaac Sellers.
1782, May　22, Kain, Andrew, and Phœbe Rogers.

1804, Nov.   13, Kain, Cath., and Lewis Mulloney.
1766, Dec.   25, Kain, James, and Elizabeth Delavan.
1784, July   22, Kale, Amey, and Samuel Crawford.
1755, Aug.   14, Kanny, Joseph, and Rebecca Brown.
1752, July   8, Kappock, James, and Catherine Pugh.
1747, Nov.   7, Kappock, James, and Mary Emmerson.
1798, Nov.   14, Karnan, Jane. and James Newton.
1743, June   9, Karnes, David, and Margaret Ovington.
1799, March 28, Karral, Patrick, and Phœbe Harper.
1739, Feb.   22, Kasbeer, Godfrey, and Agnes Corleene.
1769, June   17, Katon, Catherine, and Thomas Willson.
1795, Nov.   22, Katz, Isaak, and Eliz. Griffy.
1791, Sept. 12, Kay, Eliz., and Alexander Campbell.
1794, Sept.   8, Kay, John, and Jane Snelling.
1759, Sept. 21, Kay, Rebecca, and John Burnet.
1773, Sept.   2, Kea, Cath., and Joseph McKee.
1772, April   7, Kearnes, Mary, and Samuel Rogers.
1756, Nov.   16, Kearney, ——, and Rev. Samuel Cook.
1761, June   2, Kearney, Margaret, and David Fisher.
1771, March 24, Kearney, William, and Mary Webster.
1748, Nov.   24, Kearsely, Doct. John, and Mrs. Margaret Brand.
1742, Nov.   7, Keater, Alexander, and Elizabeth Holmes.
1778, Dec.   3, Keating, Ann, and John Bryant.
1796, Aug.   2, Keef, Benjamin, and Eliz. Bowen.
1805, Aug.   29, Keemer, Eliz., and David Hennion.
1795, April   2, Keemle, Cath., and John Hathaway.
1765, Nov.   9, Keen, Hannah, and James Nevill.
1770, Sept. 20, Keen, John, and Amelia Cook.
1768, July   15, Keen, John, and Margaret Relin.
1767, Aug.   29, Keen, Martha, and James Mains.
1795, May   9, Keen, Mary, and Nehemiah Mall.
1780, June   6, Keen, Reynold, and Patience Worrell.
1806, Sept. 13, Keen, Sarah, and John Hand.
1755, Aug.   1, Keen, William, and Anne Shillingsforth.
1756, Nov.   16, Keenan, John, and Mary McDonald.
1795, April   8, Keene, Eliz., and Patrick Hays.
1760, Aug.   16, Keene, Mary, and Jonathan Craythorne.
1791, Sept. 13, Keene, Mildred, and John Bringhurst.
1791, Oct.   23, Keer, Ann, and William Johnston.
1745, Aug.   8, Kees, Andrew, and Deborah Kinner.
1756, July   17, Kees, Mary, and John Dark.
1728, Nov.   10, Kees, Hannah, and Peter Turner.
1740, Jan.   17, Kees, Richard, and Mary Osler.
1728, Dec.   3, Keevan, Ann, and Lawrence Keife.
1715, May   22, Keffett, Samuel, and Alice Smith.
1728, Dec.   3, Keife, Lawrence, and Ann Keevan.

1763, Sept. 15, Keighan, Elizabeth, and Arthur Donaldson.
1775, Aug. 16, Keimer, James, and Sarah King.
1780, Jan. 25, Keimer, James, and Cath. Valentine.
1774, June 16, Keimer, Orpheus, and Martha Stewart.
1794, June 22, Keimley, George, and Susannah Pollard.
1755, May 30, Keith, Cornelius, and Eleanor Hunt.
1762, Sept. 19, Keith, Joseph, and Elizabeth Roberts.
1770, May 31, Keith, William, and Jane Ormes.
1749, Nov. 21, Keller, Catherine, and William Nash.
1767, June 11, Kelley, Ann, and Joseph Jackson.
1720, Nov. 28, Kelley, Elizabeth, and Benjamin Cooper.
1799, Feb. 24, Kelley, John, and Frances Linch.
1732, Dec. 21, Kelley, Mary, and George Newell.
1714, Jan. 9, Kelley, Sarah, and John Wharton.
1806, June 7, Kellinger, Christopher, and Rachel Vaughan.
1735, Dec. 25, Kellogg, Joseph, and Isabell Jackson.
1790, March 30, Kelly, Abner, and Sarah Archer.
1800, Dec. 24, Kelly, Ann, and George Ale.
1752, Dec. 21, Kelly, Bridget, and David Knowles.
1763, May 5, Kelly, Bryan, and Hannah Harper.
1769, May 24, Kelly, Catherine, and John Spear.
1800, Aug. 4, Kelly, Cath., and Thomas McDivitt.
1729, Oct. 28, Kelly, Celia, and John Fruwn.
1764, Oct. 31, Kelly, Charles, and Martha Overend.
1735, Sept. 30, Kelly, Daniel, and Rebecca Hoy.
1800, March 6, Kelly, Eleanor, and Roger McDevitt.
1747, March 23, Kelly, Francis, and Elizabeth Hoy.
1758, May 6, Kelly, Hannah, and John Adams.
1774, Jan. 25, Kelly, Hannah, and Hugh Dougherty.
1776, Nov. 29, Kelly, James, and Mary Kelly.
1796, Nov. 7, Kelly, Jeremiah, and Margaret Coyles.
1774, Aug. 15, Kelly, John, and Mary Edge.
1741, Aug. 11, Kelly, John, and Jane Sullivan.
1752, April 11, Kelly, John, and Rebecca Sutton.
1723, July 8, Kelly, John, and Eleanor Hughs.
1773, Sept. 18, Kelly, John, and Martha Knight.
1767, Sept. 4, Kelly, John, and Rachel Aaron.
1793, May 9, Kelly, Johnson, and Sarah Bright.
1805, Oct. 31, Kelly, Joseph, and Phœbe Bruistar.
1757, Nov. 4, Kelly, Joseph, and Margaret Woods.
1792, June 30, Kelly, Margaret, and James Ferguson.
1801, Nov. 11, Kelly, Mary, and Andrew Tuttle.
1801, Nov. 5, Kelly, Mary, and Thomas Fennell.
1776, Nov. 29, Kelly, Mary, and James Kelly.
1756, Feb. 9, Kelly, Patrick, and Jane Watts.
1730, March 25, Kelly, Rebecca, and Samuel Guy.

1777, May 11, Kelly, Sarah, and Warwick Coates.
1804, Aug. 9, Kelly, Sarah, and John Donaven.
1776, May 16, Kemble, Ann, and John Davis.
1799, Aug. 8, Kemble, Ann, and John Hart.
1763, Dec. 19, Kemble, George, and Elizabeth Robinson.
1752, Nov. 16, Kemble, Hezekiah, and Margaret Willard.
1767, April 20, Kemble, John, and Mary Chamber.
1796, June 11, Kemble, Robert, and Ann Cadwallader.
1740, June 12, Kemble, Rose, and Josiah Wilkinson.
1770, Sept. 26, Kemble, William, and Sarah Worthington.
1771, Aug. 29, Kemble, William, and Eleanor Dunbar.
1798, Dec. 16, Kemp, Eliz., and George Taverner.
1766, Dec. 24, Kemp, Elizabeth, and Thomas Bowlden.
1790, June 9, Kemp, George, and Rebecca Ogilby.
1789, Aug. 29, Kemp, Matthias, and Eliz. Lubey.
1796, June 6, Kemper, Mary, and Samuel Sitgreaves.
1717, March 3, Kemster, Jonathan, and Jane Moore.
1776, April 24, Kenan, Margaret, and Patrick Toury.
1766, June 17, Kendall, James, and Sarah Randall.
1770, Oct. 18, Kendrey Barnabas, and Rachel Thomas.
1721, Aug. 31, Kendrick John, and Frances Baily.
1724, Jan. 19, Kendrick, Thomas, and Mary Harrison.
1763, Nov. 5, Kennard, Menan, and Elizabeth Cameron.
1753, Jan. 6, Kennedy, Alexander, and Anne Goodin.
1765, April 20, Kennedy, Alice, and Philip Frederick.
1783, May 28, Kennedy, Allen, and Mary Winters.
1799, April 13, Kennedy, Eliz., and William Gill.
1769, June 24, Kennedy, Elizabeth, and James Barnes.
1745, June 3, Kennedy, Hannah, and Richard Kennedy.
1785, June 19, Kennedy, James, and Mary Duguid.
1780, Oct. 22, Kennedy, John, and Susannah Heavenman.
1758, Feb. 13, Kennedy, John, and Margaret Walker.
1771, Aug. 3, Kennedy, Judith, and John Conner.
1778, Sept. 23, Kennedy, Margaret, and Hugh McCormick.
1730, July 26, Kennedy, Mary, and William Johnson.
1790, July 10, Kennedy, Mary, and Walter Boggs.
1745, June 3, Kennedy, Richard, and Hannah Kennedy.
1759, Dec. 15, Kennedy, Robert, and Margaret Eagle.
1781, April 20, Kennedy, Thomas, and Deborah Smith.
1761, April 20, Kennedy, William, and Mary Bohnan.
1779, Nov. 20, Kennold, Eliz., and Isaac Marpole.
1797, Nov. 21, Kenney, David, and Mary Mann.
1768, July 20, Kenny, Eliz., and William Coppock.
1799, Jan. 10, Kenney, James, and Bridget McCabe.
1759, Aug. 18, Kenny, John, and Elizabeth Sutton.
1746, Aug. 5, Kenoby, John, and Anne Roe.

1769, June　17, Kenton, Mary, and Joseph Welldon.
1760, Sept.　30, Kenton, Thomas, and Hannah Leech.
1728, May　7, Kenworthy, Elizabeth, and Thomas Reese.
1802, May　6, Keppele, Cath., and Jonathan Bunting.
1797, March 30, Keppele, Kath., and Robert Rainey.
1791, Sept.　1, Kerby, Susannah, and Andrew Stearn.
1801, Jan.　1, Kerlin, Deborah Ann, and William Lynch.
1788, Aug.　21, Kerlin, Hannah, and John Lynch.
1799, Nov.　25, Kerney, Ann, and Hanse Holm.
1796, April　16, Kerr, Alexander, and Ann Whetcroft.
1756, June　2, Kerr, George, and Mary Morgan.
1800, Nov.　27, Kerr, Jane, and Thomas Kirk.
1796, Oct.　27, Kerr, William, and Margaret Foster.
1798, June　27, Kessler, Hannah, and Thomas Shieffelin.
1776, April　10, Kethcart Sarah, and John West.
1796, Dec.　22, Ketland, John, and Henrietta Constantia Meade.
1767, March 27, Key, Joseph, and Judith Lippincot.
1777, April　29, Key, Mary, and Samuel Hanson.
1746, July　7, Key, Rebecca, and James Channel.
1785, Jan.　27, Keybright, Sarah, and Henry Brame.
1796, May　5, Keys, John, and Eliz. Ferguson.
1748, May　7, Keys, John, and Mary Ryon.
1794, April　20, Keys, Mary, and Tabez Stockman.
1745, Aug.　6, Keys, Mary, and Stephen Stephens.
1750, Nov.　5, Keyser, Matthew, and Catherine Midwinter.
1722, Jan.　30, Keyte, John, and Elizabeth Chilcot.
1761, Jan.　11, Kidd, George, and Sarah Leigh.
1772, July　2, Kidd, George, and Mary Wolfe.
1761, June　22, Kidd, John, and Mary Coy.
1728, March 18, Kierk, James, and Deb. Davies.
1734, Oct.　1, Kighley, Hugh Basil, and Mary Roberdeau.
1728, Nov.　26, Kilbright, John, and Dorcus Rody.
1746, Sept.　3, Kilcrease, Anne, and Richard Mosely.
1796, May　24, Killey, John, and Eliza Kinnard.
1760, Nov.　20, Killgour, William, and Elizabeth Gray.
1767, Feb.　26, Killgore, Elizabeth, and James Huston.
1760, Feb.　29, Killinger, George, and Elizabeth Bennet.
1792, April　26, Killinger, Margaret, and William Feble.
1783, May　1, Killinger, Mary, and John Fitzgerald.
1806, Oct.　6, Killingsworth, Haney, and Sarah Humphreys.
1768, Nov.　6, Killwell, Frances, and Steward Cately.
1783, Dec.　18, Kilton, Dorothy, and Joseph Thornhill.
1803, May　18, Kimbeel, Raymond, and Ann Bennet.
1714, Oct.　26, Kimber, Sarah, and James Smith.
1739, March 29, Kimble, Anne, and John Bewley.
1761, March 23, Kimble, Joseph, and Martha Rodgers.

1785, May 24, Kimble, Joseph, and Sarah Witchill.
1783, Oct. 15, Kimble, William, and Eliz. Philips.
1775, Sept. 23, Kimler, Lydia, and James Dutton.
1750, May 5, Kimpson, Samuel, and Susannah Thompson.
1794, June 12, Kimpton, Benjamin, and Margaret Farrow.
1733, Feb. 24, Kinard, Samuel, and Tamar Carmalt.
1727, May 17, King, Ann, and Wm Wood.
1770, Sept. 13, King, Ann, and William Davis.
1734, Feb. 21, King, Anne, and Joseph Topp.
1756, Jan. 17, King, Anthony, and Sarah Gardner.
1784, Jan. 8, King, Comfort, and John Harmason.
1738, June 19, King, Dorothy, and Samuel Read.
1753, Jan. 31, King, Elizabeth, and Andrew Rambo.
1791, Aug. 6, King, Ezekiel, and Mary Gardiner.
1769, Feb. 4, King, Hay, and Hannah Magraw.
1795, Nov. 10, King, Henry, and Eleanor Harriott.
1781, Sept. 24, King, Henry, and Ann Wollard.
1772, Oct. 20, King, James, and Cornelia England.
1757, Sept. 13, King, John, and Catherine Daulton.
1759, May 7, King, Margaret, and Richard Huff.
1774, May 17, King, Margaret, and William Newman.
1733, April 21, King, Mary, and Ralph Lees.
1784, Jan. 22, King, Mary, and Thomas Hopkins.
1731, Dec. 7, King, Rebecca, and John Price.
1739, Aug. 31, King, Samuel, and Anne Evans.
1728, Oct. 28, King, Sarah, and John Redman.
1775, Aug. 16, King, Sarah, and James Klimer.
1797, April 5, King, Scott, and Cath. Johnson.
1794, Nov. 13, King, Thomas, and Hannah Grant.
1732, May 6, King, Thomas, and Mary Davis.
1786, Jan. 19, King, William, and Mary George.
1801, July 30, King, William, and Maria Matilda Ottinger.
1781, May 29, Kingell, Henry, and Lucy Jackson.
1796, Oct. 16, Kingston, Ann, and Alexander Napier.
1716, April 7, Kingston, Joseph, and Hannah Corbet.
1794, Sept. 25, Kingston, Mary, and Andrew McClain.
1725, Sept. 30, Kinman, W^m, and Marg^t Williams.
1796, May 24, Kinnard, Eliza, and John Killey.
1757, Nov. 26, Kinnard, George, and Mary Hurley.
1771, Aug. 12, Kinnard, Sarah, and William White.
1745, Aug. 8, Kinner, Deborah, and Andrew Rees.
1729, Oct. 17, Kinner, Sarah, and Peter Jones.
1771, April 10, Kinnicott, Daniel, and Jane Hyman.
1799, Nov. 25, Kinsey, Ann, and Rev^r Charles H. Wharton.
1712, Aug. 6, Kinsey, John, and Rachel Wilson.
1776, Sept. 22, Kinsey, Sarah, and Adam Casey.

1756, Nov. 29, Kinsil, Hannah, and Isaac Walworth.
1796, April 10, Kinstar, Margaret, and Patrick Learky.
1720, Feb. 16, Kingston, Thomas, and Ann Boyle.
1757, April 25, Kirby, Peter, and Catherine Millard.
1793, Jan.   1, Kirby, Timothy, and Rebecca Carnes.
1736, Dec. 30, Kirk, Isabella, and Thomas Neale.
1785, Nov.   3, Kirk, John, and Rebecca Lukens.
1749, Nov. 21, Kirk, Mercy, and Salathiel Foster.
1750, Jan.   6, Kirk, Patrick, and Anne Doran.
1775, May   24, Kirk, Philip, and Esther Worrell.
1771, Sept. 14, Kirk, Sarah, and Thomas Harring.
1761, Dec. 23, Kirk, Sarah, and William Lofborough.
1800, Nov. 27, Kirk, Thomas, and Jane Kerr.
1733, July 17, Kirk, Thomas, and Isabella Jenkins.
1770, Feb. 16, Kirkpatrick, James, and Eleanor Connell.
1764, Dec. 21, Kirkpatrick, Mary, and Joseph Moore.
1737, May   21, Kirl, Mary, and Bartholomew Penrose.
1753, Feb. 21, Kirll, Joseph, and Sarah Annis.
1768, March 17, Kirthcart, Mary, and Thomas West.
1774, April 9, Kisler, Margaret, and John Taylor.
1804, March 18, Kite, Mary, and William E. Wright.
1805, Aug. 24, Klapp, Joseph, and Anna Milnor.
1806, July 26, Kline, John, and Mary Carrell.
1716, Sept. 19, Knabb, Richard, and Joijel Stevens.
1792, Aug. 18, Knap, John, and Mary Phile.
1788, Sept. 25, Knight, Ann, and John Dawkins.
1779, Nov. 25, Knight, Ann, and Benjamin Miller.
1792, March 1, Knight, Daniel, and Margaret Lowers.
1798, Jan.   2, Knight, Daniel P., and Mary Withy.
1780, March 16, Knight, Deborah, and Joseph Newman.
1763, Jan. 18, Knight, Elizabeth, and Peter Dehaven.
1736, June 23, Knight, Hannah, and Isaac Gilpin.
1774, Oct. 27, Knight, John, and Mary Coran.
1783, Feb. 20, Knight, John, and Mary Rous.
1725, Nov. 24, Knight, Judith, and Ed. Rice.
1789, Dec. 31, Knight, Lydia, and George Ludlam.
1773, Sept. 18, Knight, Martha, and John Kelly.
1791, June 16, Knight, Mary, and William Brown.
1752, June 20, Knight, Peter, and Elizabeth Wilkinson.
1720, March 25, Knight, Sarah, and Joseph Tucker.
1872, Aug. 22, Knight, Sarah, and William Barry.
1726, Oct. 30, Knight, W^m, and Elizabeth Spark.
1764, Nov.   8, Knight, William, and Ann Brown.
1746, July   5, Knoble, Catherine, and James Boggs.
1725, Dec.   5, Knot, Bridget, and Everit Ellis.
1760, June 26, Knot, John, and Frances Harrison.

1758, Dec.   9, Knowles, Ann, and John Smart.
1770, May   20, Knowles, Catherine, and John Hart.
1759, Feb.   3, Knowles, Christiana, and William Johnson.
1752, Dec.   21, Knowles, David, and Bridget Kelly.
1782, Feb.   11, Knowles, Hannah, and Joseph Shallus.
1720, Sept.   10, Knowles, John, and Catherine Wessels.
1783, Nov.   27, Knowles, John, and Sarah Norton.
1782, Nov.   20, Knowles, Mary, and Elias Stoy.
1731, Sept.   28, Knowles Mary, and Peter Taylor.
1747, Jan.   1, Knowles, Mary, and Francis Garrigues.
1769, April   23, Knowles, Rachel, and Dominick Harker.
1794, Dec.   21, Knowles, Sarah, and John Gallagher.
1774, Dec.   4, Knowles, William, and Mary Anderson.
1777, April   2, Knowles, William. and Mary Ellis.
1759. Feb.   16, Knowson, Catherine, and William Webber.
1759, Aug.   21, Knox, Jane, and Robert Knox.
1793, June   13, Knox, Jane, and Hugh Cooper.
1768, July   9, Knox, John, and Phœbe Delaplain.
1800, June   26, Knox, Lætitia, and John Smith.
1759, Aug.   21, Knox, Robert, and Jane Knox.
1750, April   26, Kock, Catherine, and John McEvers.
1801, Aug.   1, Koch, Jacob Gerard, and Jane Griffith.
1765, June   13, Kallock, Alice, and John Green.
1762, Nov.   17, Kollock, Hester, and Robert Saunderson.
1740, Aug.   9, Kollock, Jacob, and Mary Leech.
1731, Nov.   4, Kollock, Jacob, and Margaret Ellis.
1745, Oct.   10, Kollock, Magdalen, and Jasper McCall.
1796, Dec.   8, Kollock, Shepherd, and Mary Stetcher.
1780, April   27, Kollock, Philip, and Jane Wingfield.
1746, Jan.   23, Kollock, Philip, and Hester Leech.
1737, April   16, Kollock, Shepherd, and Mary Goddard.
1801, Oct.   9, Koop, Susan, and Thomas Manning.
1713, Jan.   25, Koseaugins, Nicholas, and Ann Oarum.
1748, Jan.   21, Kostard, Abigail, and William Browning.
1762, Feb.   19, Kuhl, George F., and Susannah Kuhl.
1795, Dec.   3, Kuhl, Henry, and Deborah Hillegas.
1749, Sept.   2, Kuhl, Mary, and Edward Scott.
1752, Aug.   18, Kuhl, Samuel, and Susannah Hillegas.
1762, Feb.   19, Kuhl, Susannah, and George F. Kuhl.
1762, Aug.   13, Kukler, Meldina, and John James.
1752, Nov.   6, Kulans, Catherine, and Patrick McClain.
1803, Feb.   5, Kurtz, Margaret, and Michael Weaver,
1766, April   17, Kuyper, Derrick, and Elizabeth Helm.
1792, Nov.   14, Labbe, John, and Sarah Linn.
1742, Nov.   16, Lacey, Mary, and George Hume.
1749, Oct.   19, Lackey, Thomas, and Elizabeth Cammel.

1804, May   3, Lacombe, Jane, and Joseph Harrod.
1758, Sept.   25, Lacy, Elizabeth, and Joseph Graham.
1774, Feb.   19, Lacy, Eliz., and Henry Gordon.
1757, April   4, Lacy, Mary, and Nathaniel Russel.
1773, May   18, Lake, Catherine, and John Pringle.
1759, Dec.   23, Lake, William, and Elizabeth Simmons.
1798, March   20, Lamb, George, and Jane Sullivan.
1768, Oct.   12, Lamb, Mary, and Daniel Crowley.
1795, Dec.   17, Lamb, Susanna, and Peter Edward Lanenville.
1722, April   13, Lambeth, Lucy, and Thomas Turton.
1732, June   15, Lambeth, Rachel, and John Harrison.
1740, Oct.   31, Lambeth, Ruth, and William White.
1727, Nov.   30, Lambert, Ed., and Frances Palmer.
1805, March   31, Lambert, Margaret, and Abraham Croysdale.
1768, April   4, Lambwood, Mary, and Enoch Yardley.
1806, May   15, Lammot, Daniel, and Susan Beck.
1761, Oct.   5, Lampley, Rachel, and Simpson Coningham.
1747, March   17, Lamplorgh, Susannah, and Henry Copp.
1794, Oct.   23, Lamplugh, Martha, and James McCluney.
1746, June   14, Lamplugh, Martha, and James Steel Thompson.
1785, May   19, Land, Henry, and Cath. Otto.
1784, Oct.   7, Land, Mary, and James Welsh.
1794, June   5, Landcake, Joseph, and Sarah Baker.
1760, Jan.   10, Landerman, John, and Sarah Coulston.
1735, Oct.   11, Landerman, William, and Anne Ellett.
1774, Oct.   3, Lane, Charles, and Susannah McCarrell.
1786, April   13, Lane, Edward, and Eliz. Hall.
1754, Oct.   14, Lane, Edward, and Sarah Richardson.
1721, Oct.   19, Lane, Eleanor, and David Robinson.
1743, June   12, Lane, Joseph, and Ann Pratt.
1805, June   1, Lane, Sarah, and Nathan Davidson.
1773, April   17, Lane, Sarah, and John Fawkes.
1746, May   29, Lane, Timothy, and Mary Fox.
1734, Oct.   8, Lane, William, and Elizabeth Raine.
1733, June   24, Lane, William, and Anne Burrel.
1795, Dec.   17, Lanenville, Peter Edward, and Susanna Lamb.
1799, March   26, Lang, Charles, and Rebecca Newman.
1765, Oct.   26, Langdale, jr., John, and Alice Coates.
1764, April   29, Langhrey, Sarah, and William Christy.
1773, Sept.   29, Langley, Allen, and Ruth Haild.
1761, June   29, Langley, John, and Mary McAwell.
1726, Sept.   18, Langley, Joseph, and Sarah Cleverly.
1730, Nov.   28, Lapelly, John, and Jane Crawford.
1795, Sept.   9, Laplanche, John Baptiste, and Martha Grift.
1789, Dec.   24, Lardner, Jehu, and Margaret Saltor.
1749, Oct.   27, Lardner, Lyndford, and Elizabeth Branson.

1766, May   29, Lardner, Lyndford, and Catherine Lawrence.
1748, Oct.   1, Lardner, Robert, and Elizabeth Piles.
1767, June   4, Laremore, Margaret, and William McMickle.
1728, Sept.   6, Large, Eliza, and Daniel Watkins.
1741, Dec.   16, Large, Joseph, Elizabeth Fox.
1799, June   20, Large, Sarah, and Thomas Miflin.
1804, Nov.   6, Larkey, Ann, and Jonathan Draper.
1797, Nov.   15, Larkey, Margaret, and John Savage.
1731, Oct.   29, Larkins, John, and Hester Shelly.
1791, Sept.   2, Lascum, Ann, and William Spierin.
1800, Nov.   30, Laskey, Eliza, and John Fraley.
1801, Nov.   12, Laskey, Sarah, and William Stokes.
1737, Dec.   3, Lassel, Anne, and William Darnel.
1751, Oct.   26, Lassell, Mary, and Samuel Shaw.
1750, June   13, Latham, Mary, and John Floyd.
1757, Sept.   10, Lathberry, Elizabeth, and Benjamin Condy.
1801, Oct.   1, Latimer, George, and Henrietta Phalan.
1801, April   2, Latimer, John, and Margaret Clay.
1790, Dec.   8, Latimer, Thomas, and Susannah David.
1800, May   2, Latrobe, Benjamin Henry, and Mary Eliz. Hazle-
                   hurst.
1785, Dec.   8, Lattimer, Henry, and Ann Cuthbert.
1803, March 26, Latting, William, and Margaret Montgomery.
1800, May   19, Lauderback, Abigail, and William James.
1789, Aug.   5, Laughlin, Thomas, and Johanna Rakley.
1801, March 31, Launville, Susanna, and Peter Deisher.
1782, Oct.   10, Laurence, Mary, and Richard Powell.
1783, May   1, Laurence, William, and Mary Cox.
1763, Jan.   24, Laurence, William, and Barbara Robinson.
1781, Sept.   29, Laurimore, Margaret, and John Farrell.
1736, May   13, Lavering, Daniel, and Margaret Beane.
1757, Dec.   23, Law, Hugh, and Catherine Yozen.
1782, May   30, Law, Judith, and William Pritchard.
1804, Dec.   1, Lawersweiler, Frances, and James Cuthbert.
1805, April   16, Lawler, Ann, and John Peterson.
1774, May   11, Lawrence, Ann, and William Atkinson.
1774, Sept.   8, Lawrence, Cath., and John Carey, Esqr.
1790, Oct.   3, Lawrence, Cath., and ——— French.
1766, May   29, Lawrence, Catherine, and Lyndford Lardner.
1757, Oct.   23, Lawrence, Charles, and Rachel Molder.
1794, July   23, Lawrence, Diana, and William Swan.
1779, Dec.   13, Lawrence, Col. Elisha, and Rebecca Redman.
1768, March 10, Lawrence, Elizabeth, and James Allen, Esqr.
1775, Sept.   27, Lawrence, Eliz., and Joseph West.
1748, Aug.   2, Lawrence, Giles, and Sarah Thomas.
1806, Jan.   30, Lawrence, Hannah, and John Baptiste Corneau.

1806, Feb.   27, Lawrence, Hannah, and George Bolton Lownes.
1791, June   30, Lawrence, John, and Eliz. Allen.
1801, Jan.   24, Lawrence, John, and Martha Bittle.
1750, April   19, Lawrence, John, and Elizabeth Francis.
1805, March 16, Lawrence, Lucy, and William Fouchee.
1726, June   15, Lawrence, Mary, and John Carter.
1751, Feb.   21, Lawrence, Margaret, and David Malin.
1751, Jan.   19, Lawrence, Martha, and Jenkins Price.
1764, Nov.   10, Lawrence, Martha, and Charles Moore.
1754, Aug.   31, Lawrence, Mary, and William Masters.
1781, March 15, Lawrence, Mary, and John Underwood.
1768, Jan.   7, Lawrence, Rachel, and John Marston.
1768, Sept.   22, Lawrence, Thomas, jr., and Rebeccah Bond.
1757, June   30, Lawrence, Thomas, and Elizabeth Blackledge.
1801, May   11, Lawrenzen, Henry, and Mary Lewis.
1805, July   5, Lawson, Alexander, and Eliz. Scaise.
1798, July   5, Lawson, Jacob, and Eliz. Ford.
1795, May   31, Lawson, John, and Rachel Nash.
1804, June   25, Lawson, Peter, and Sarah Gallagher.
1793, June   11, Lawton, Jesse, and Barbara Hargisheimer.
1783, Aug.   16, Lawton, Robert, and Sarah Hooten.
1802, May   24, Lawton, Ruth, and William Halladay.
1720, Jan.   31, Lawton, William, and Mary Warren.
1715, July   3, Laycock, John, and Mary Cash.
1772, April   21, Laycock, Pamela, and Job Plummer.
1736, Nov.   4, Laycock, Thomas, and Jane Boon.
1721, Dec.   29, Lea, Isaac, and Sarah Fosset.
1787, Sept.   21, Lea, Thomas, and Sarah Shippen.
1789, Oct.   15, Lea, William, and Eliz. Madge.
1774, Feb.   2, Lea, William, and Dorothy Nelson.
1805, March 24, Leach, Richard, and Cath. Huckle.
1748, Jan.   7, Leacock, Mary, and David Hall.
1736, Aug.   7, Leacock, Samuel, and Anne Cane.
1745, April   20, Leacock, Susannah, and James Read.
1746, Feb.   17, Leadbetter, George, and Catherine Thomas.
1767, July   5, Leadbetter, George, and Sarah Wheeler.
1739, June   13, Leadbeater, Mary, and James Carr.
1801, Nov.   2, Leamer, Anthony, and Christiana Parker.
1779, Aug.   19, Leaning, Thomas, and Rebecca Fisher.
1793, May   20, Leamy, John, and Eliz. Doughty.
1799, Jan.   3, Leaning, Eliza, and Charles Caldwell.
1796, April   10, Leasky, Patrick, and Margaret Kinstar.
1797, April   7, Leary, Eliz., and Lewis Madzel.
1753, April   23, Leary, Polly, and Joseph Brown.
1802, April   1, Lecher, George, and Rebecca Statean.
1805, July   22, Lecorne, Eliz., and Samuel Clark.

1796, June   18, Lecoy, Susannah, and Thomas Cooper.
1783, July   15, Lecture, Francis Joseph, and Eliz. Goodman.
1759, June   28, LeDru, Ann, and Samuel Jobson.
1758, Jan.   12, Ledru, Elizabeth, and John Perry.
1801, July   26, Ledru, Eliz., and John Moore.
1762, Nov.   27, Lee, Catherine, and Jacob Shoemaker.
1768, Dec.   6, Lee, Honour, and James Ramsay.
1804, July   12, Lee, Israel, and Judith Gordon.
1757, April   30, Lee, James, and Mary Worrell.
1775, June   5, Lee, John, and Eliz. Higgs.
1750, March 19, Lee, John, and Christiana Tusse.
1734, Nov.   9, Lee, John, and Anne Bevan.
1787, Aug.   30, Lee, Joseph, and Mary Ellis.
1772, Sept.   15, Lee, Martha, and Nicholas Spencer.
1734, Feb.   15, Lee, Mary, and Thomas Duffield.
1763, June   16, Lee, Mary, and Jacob Arnan.
1796, Dec.   9, Lee, Mary, and William Foster.
1748, Dec.   6, Lee, Mary, and Cornelius Vansant.
1782, Oct.   9, Lee, Mary, and Reuben Pownall.
1794, June   19, Lee, Richard Bland, and Eliz. Collins.
1776, Sept.   30, Lee, Richard, and Mary Boid.
1758, Nov.   8, Lee, Susannah, and Archibald Little.
1771, Oct.   4, Lee, Thomas, and Mary Spencer.
1767, July   12, Lee, Thomas, and Margaret Gunning.
1757, May   4, Leech, Alexander, and Mary Ware.
1742, May   15, Leech, Hannah, and Jacob Duffeld.
1760, Sept.   30, Leech, Hannah, and Thomas Kenton.
1765, May   7, Leech, Hannah, and Thomas Wagstaff.
1783, Sept.   13, Leech, Henry, and Henry Standfield.
1746, Jan.   23, Leech, Hester, and Philip Kollock.
1728, July   25, Leech, Jacob, and Isabell Fisher.
1733, April   4, Leech, Jacob, and Eleanor Robison.
1761, July   2, Leech, Josiah, and Elizabeth Hoffman.
1791, Jan.   27, Leech, Mary, and John Long.
1740, Aug.   9, Leech, Mary, and Jacob Kollock.
1743, April   26, Leech, Mary, and John Wilmington.
1726, Dec.   14, Leech, Reb., and Sam. Miles.
1749, March 25, Leech, Rebecca, and Henry Ash.
1745, Jan.   3, Leech, Sarah, and Aeneas Ross.
1786, May   5, Leech, Sarah, and Stephen Bennett.
1758, May   27, Leech, Thomas, and Mary Coatum.
1728, Sept.   2, Leech, Thomas, and Mary Rivers.
1722, July   31, Leech, Thomas, and Ann Moor.
1747, Dec.   5, Leeds, Mary, and Moses Hinton.
1798, Jan.   21, Lees, Philip, and Sophia McIvers.
1733, April   21, Lees, Ralph, and Mary King.

1788, June   26, Leeson, William, and Eliz. Grover.
1803, April 14, Lefferty, Patrick, and Margaret Redy.
1743, Feb.   12, LeGay, Jacob, and Mary Weyman, jr.
1743, Oct.   6, Legay, Ruth, and John Marshall.
1791, March 17, Legens, Dorothy, and Anthony Marckell.
1773, Aug.   16, Lehman, Ann, and William Wallace.
1802, Nov.   27, Leib, Lydia, and John Harrison.
1774, May   18, Leigh, Benjamin, and Sarah Daily.
1761, Jan.   11, Leigh, Sarah, and George Kidd.
1746, April 23, Leipencout, Jacob, and Grace Rudrow.
1746, April   9, Leipencout, Mary, and George Standley.
1778, Nov.   3, Leiper, Thomas, and Eliz. Coultas Gray.
1743, May   28, Leister, Adam, and Ann Watts.
1804, Nov.   27, Lemley, Sarah, and Michael Bentley.
1799, Jan.   10, Lemon, Hugh, and Ann Lewis.
1800, May   13, Lemont, John, and Eliz. McIntire.
1749, April 30, Lennington, Ann, and Abraham Crear.
1779, Aug.   26, Lennox, David, and Tace Lukens.
1732, Aug.   9, Lenny, Peter, and Frances Page.
1720, June   30, Lenthal, Philip, and Mary Clark.
1786, June   29, Leo, William, and Mary Burns.
1794, July   28, Leonard, Cath., and Peter Bingham.
1804, Nov.   23, Leonard Eliz., and David Cholet.
1762, Aug.   21, Leonard, James, and Mary Smith.
1800, Jan.   12, Leonard, John, and Maria Chevalier.
1791, July   12, Leonard, Robert, and Margaret Elfry.
1748, Feb.   1, Leonard, Thomas, and Elizabeth Maugridge.
1799, July   6, Leonard, Timothy, and Eleanor Thornton.
1782, June   20, Le Pellsive, John Francis, and Mary Valois.
1784, Feb.   20, Lepton, Lucy, and Emanuel Dewall.
1789, Nov.   19, Lesher, Francis, and Eliz. Ireland.
1783, June   22, Leslie, Sarah, and John Shindler.
1766, Oct.   30, Lessene, Isaac, and Hannah Noarth.
1770, Aug.   7, Leteliere, John, and Mary Rogers.
1773, July   29, Letellier, Michael Joseph, and Mary Richardson.
1785, May   24, Letzinger, Lydia, and James Pratt.
1743, Dec.   17, Leuellen, Eliz., and George Webster.
1803, Oct.   9, Leuseur, Nicholas, and Mary Coates.
1798, March 22, Levalleau, Sarah, and Abraham Waters.
1785, Oct.   26, Levan, Esqr., Daniel, and Mary Scull.
1745, Aug.   22, Levering, Benjamin, and Elizabeth Jones.
1733, Sept.   4, Leveritt, Prisilla, and Archibald Ingram.
1800, March 16, Leverly, John, and Hannah Davis.
1756, Jan.   3, Levers, Robert, and Mary Church.
1738, Dec.   3, Levett, Mary, and Thomas Gage.
1797, Nov.   16, Levis, William, and Sarah Gray.

1784, June   24, Levy, Arabella, and James Morris Jones.
1793, Sept.   5, Levy, Sampson, and Sarah Coates.
1752, Feb.   15, Lew, Edward, and Harriet Mullan.
1742, May   31, Lewden, Joseph, and Sarah Marshall.
1801, Dec.   21, Lewellen, Hannah, and Zachariah Wood.
1729, April   30, Lewis, Alice, and Nic. Evans.
1799, Jan.   10, Lewis, Ann, and Hugh Lemon.
1749, April   5, Lewis, Ann, and Thomas Green.
1710, Dec.   20, Lewis, Bridgett, and James Rowland.
1748, Aug.   13, Lewis, David, and Sarah Jones.
1794, May   22, Lewis, David, and Mary D'Arch.
1720, Jan.   31, Lewis, Eleanor, and James Goldsmith.
1720, Aug.   15, Lewis, Elizabeth, and Stephen Hooper.
1758, March 30, Lewis, Elizabeth, and Samuel Card.
1794, Dec.   11, Lewis, Eliz. L., and Joseph Higbee.
1801, April   16, Lewis, Evan, and Hannah Trego.
1800, Nov.   13, Lewis, George, and Sarah Bartholomew.
1736, Feb.   17, Lewis, Grace, and Daniel Burnett.
1731, Nov.   27, Lewis, Hannah, and Philip ffauct.
1804, Oct.   11, Lewis, Hannah, and Absalom Trago.
1709, June   10, Lewis, Henry, and Catherine Macarty.
1743, Aug.   25, Lewis, Henry, and Rachel Powel.
1800, April   3, Lewis, Jesse, and Hannah Davis.
1792, June   18, Lewis, John, and Susannah Penrose.
1766, Dec.   3, Lewis, Joseph, and Eleanor Taylor.
1729, Aug.   30, Lewis, Jos, and Margt. James.
1799, March 28, Lewis, Josiah, and Margaret Delany.
1722, Oct.   24, Lewis, Katherine, and Owen Owen.
1748, Feb.   19, Lewis, Lewis, and Elizabeth Reece.
1734, June   8, Lewis, Margaret, and John Remington.
1765, Jan.   12, Lewis, Martha, and Thomas Smith.
1801, May   11, Lewis, Mary, and Henry Lawrenzen.
1749, April   28, Lewis, Mary, and Jeremiah Jordan.
1731, Oct.   4, Lewis, Mary, and Richard Taylor.
1774, March 22, Lewis, Moses, and Elizabeth Owen.
1805, Dec.   19, Lewis, Phineas, and Mary Caley.
1803, July   ·20, Lewis, Phœbe, and John Whitehead.
1800, May   20, Lewis, Susanna, and Simon Spranklin.
1780, March   4, Lewis, Susannah, and Richard Dickson.
1737, July   24, Lewis, Walter, and Mary Bibb.
1726, Sept.   20, Lewis, Walter, and Osilla Young.
1792, April   14, Lewis, Warner, and Courtnay Norton.
1781, Dec.   13, Lewis, William, and Rachel Wharton.
1801, Jan.   23, Lewis, William, and Frances Durdin.
1782, June   6, Lezuleer, Margaret, and Richard Johnston.
1761, July   2, Lichberg, Juliet, and Edward Thomas.

1770, Dec.   3, Liddell, George, and Ann Freight.
1758, Dec.   16, Liddon, Abraham, and Isabella Hayes.
1730, Sept.   1, Liddon, Marjory, and William Neville.
1742, Feb.   4, Liddon, Mary, and Thomas Morris.
1783, Sept.   20, Liege, Peter William, and Eliz. Taylor.
1714, Feb.   3, Liekins, Catherine, and Edward Hatfield.
1798, Dec.   29, Lightcap, Sarah, and John McLane.
1748, Oct.   15, Likens, Rachel, and Tracy Woodal.
1796, Oct.   2, Limote, Lewis, and Ann McGlocklin.
1799, Feb.   24, Linch, Frances, and John Kelley.
1791, March 14, Linch, George, and Margaret Beamerin.
1764, Sept.   10, Linch, Samuel, and Elizabeth Vaniman.
1755, Oct.   23, Linch, Winneford, and John Cooper.
1763, July   17, Lincoin, Margaret, and James Gregory.
1806, May   19, Lincoln, Benjamin, and Ann Cowan.
1746, Dec.   30, Lincon, Isaac, and Mary Shute.
1750, Sept.   19, Lincon, Rebecca, and Joseph Rush.
1745, May   9, Lindsay, Amelia, and John Finney.
1797, Nov.   8, Lindsay, Ann, and William Lithcow.
1774, Feb.   22, Lindsay, Mary, and James Ash.
1794, Sept.   21, Lindsay, William, and Eliz. Jones.
1757, Feb.   9, Lindsey, Cecelia, and Joseph Stafford.
1764, April   29, Lindsey, Margaret, and Robert Porter.
1735, Feb.   18, Lindsey, Mary, and Daniel Coats.
1755, Nov.   12, Lindsey, Mary and Richard Banks.
1751, Dec.   13, Lindsey, Robert, and Susannah Annis.
1732, Sept.   28, Lindsey, Sarah, and John Selford.
1735, July   19, Lindsley, Mary, and Thomas Smith.
1760, Dec.   27, Lington, Margaret, and John Webb.
1793, June   22, Linion, Philip, and Eleanor Bacon.
1800, June   21, Linn, Eliz., and Silas Swaine.
1743, Oct.   11, Linn, Esther, and Peter Bankson.
1768, Feb.   23, Linn, Hannah, and William Elliott.
1792, Nov.   14, Linn, Sarah, and John Labbe.
1715, Jan.   9, Linnex, Mary, and Joseph Stephenson.
1750, July   25, Linnix, Anne, and John Crawley.
1805, June   3, Linscott, Jane, and Henry Johnson.
1730, Oct.   15, Linter, Elizabeth, and Thomas Davis.
1786, Feb.   9, Lintman, John Joseph, and Hannah Gray.
1801, Sept.   20, Linton, James, and Martha Andrews.
1753, June   16, Linton, Martha, and Plunket Fleeson.
1779, Jan.   28, Linton, Robert, and Margaret Tyler.
1782, April   16, Lippincott, Eliz., and Isaac Froth.
1767, May   25, Lippencot, Phœbe, and Hudson Burr.
1786, June   8, Lippencutt, Thomas, and Ann Robertson.
1767, March 27, Lippincot, Judith, and Joseph Key.

1730, Sept. 20, Lipscomb, Ambrose, and Anne Pritchard.
1759, Nov. 22, Lisby, Mary, and Ephriam Carman.
1777, Oct. 11, Lisle, Mary, and Archibald Gamble.
1749, Oct. 16, Lister, Margaret, and John Davis.
1804, Dec. 8, Liston, Esther, and Samuel Stone.
1743, Feb. 22, Listrin, George, and Mary Bimb.
1743, Feb. 22, Listrin, Margaret, and Tobias Weber.
1780, Oct. 15, Litchingham, Ann, and Alexander Brody.
1797, Nov. 8, Lithcow, William, and Ann Lindsay.
1740, June 21, Lithgow, Patrick, and Hannah Vokes.
1770, Aug. 2, Lithgow Sarah, and James Colly.
1758, Nov. 8, Little, Archibald, and Susannah Lee.
1797, May 16, Little, Archibald, and Eliz. Gibbons.
1806, March 8, Little, Christopher H., and Sarah Eyre.
1774, March 24, Little, John, and Mary Williams.
1764, Jan. 16, Little, Mary, and Matthew Gardner.
1757, Dec. 7, Little, William, and Elizabeth Davis.
1796, Nov. 27, Livingston, Henry, and Mary Allen.
1802, May 27, Livingstone, Henry, and Martha Dunwoddy.
1746, March 3, Lloyd, Abigail, and Dennis Monholone.
1748, Dec. 20, Lloyd, Evan, and Abigail Davis.
1783, May 6, Lloyd, Hannah, and Thomas Ives.
1795, Nov. 7, Lloyd, Hester, and Robert Fielding.
1766, Aug. 12, Lloyd, Lydia, and David Crawford.
1774, Oct. 20, Lloyd, Martha, and Daniel Morris.
1759, Jan. 11, Lloyd, Mary, and John Searson.
1772, Jan. 15, Lloyd, Ruth, and Amos Thomas.
1762, Nov. 4, Lloyd, Susannah, and Thomas Wharton.
1732, Oct. 18, Loan, Wᵐ and Mary Stedham.
1754, May 16, Loanarn, Elizabeth, and Mordecai Holt.
1794, July 20, Loarman, Martha Rebecca, and William Forrest.
1725, Oct. 30, Lock, Mary, and Ben. Hoskins.
1772, Nov. 28, Lock, Susannah, and Samuel Houlgate.
1712, March 7, Lock, Thomas, and Sarah Thomas.
1797, March 16, Lockart, James, and Mary Culberson.
1784, Jan. 19, Locke, Esther, and Henry Briggs.
1798, July 20, Locke, Matthew, and Eliz. Gosteloe.
1796, Dec. 3, Lockery, Cath., and Richard Nason.
1735, Dec. 9, Lockhart, George, and Mary Mackey.
1749, Nov. 22, Lockhart, Robert, and Jane McFarson.
1804, July 25, Lodge, Hannah, and George Evans.
1763, Oct. 25, Lodge, Jane, and William Scull.
1761, Dec. 23, Lofborough, William, and Sarah Kirk.
1736, Jan. 20, Loftus, Anne, and Wheldon Simmons.
1721, Feb. 12, Loftus, Sarah, and Andrew Hannis.
1794, Jan. 4, Log, Ann, and William Worrall.

1793, Jan.   3, Log, David, and Cath. Ryan.
1766, May   27, Logan, David, and Sarah Billinger.
1754, Nov.   28, Logan, Jane, and Samuel Yardley.
1757, Dec.   17, Logan, John, and Rachel Flood.
1759, Feb.   1, Logan, John, and Mary Rochford.
1782, Jan.   1, Logan, Sarah, and John Applegate.
1750, Aug.   18, Loghlin, William, and Mary Smith.
1802, April   23, Lohra, Cath., and John Morrell.
1794, Nov.   15, Lohra, Peter, and Mary Crispin.
1803, July   9, Lohra, Peter, and Ruth Potts.
1743, July   23, Lockey, Joseph, and Mary Bingham.
1780, Aug.   26, Lollar, Capt. Matthew, and Ann Bevan.
1804, May   29, Lollar, Mary, and George Starky.
1797, Dec.   19, Lollar, Winnfred, and Jeremiah Much.
1792, Nov.   6, London, Martha, and Patrick McKever.
1804, June   21, Lone, Eleanor, and Samuel Murphy.
1760, Dec.   14, Long, Andrew, and Elizabeth Bee.
1786, Feb.   8, Long, Eliz., and Rasrol Charles.
1791, Nov.   5, Long, Hester, and George Cook.
1783, Nov.   10, Long, James, and Eliz. Reed.
1791, Jan.   27, Long, John, and Mary Leech.
1781, Feb.   25, Long, Joseph, and Judith Christian.
1775, March 13, Long, Martha, and Robert Milner.
1785, Feb.   14, Long, Mary, and James Smith.
1779, March 4, Long, Mary, and Capt. John Wilson.
1785, Feb.   3, Long, Mary, and Marmaduke Hanlon.
1713, May   11, Long, Mary, and Jonas Clark.
1761, Dec.   2, Long, Moses, and ——— Cooper.
1770, Oct.   23, Long, Richard, and Ann Mullemer.
1773, March 31, Long, Samuel, and Catherine Hendricks.
1806, June   22, Long, Sarah, and Francis Carey.
1792, Sept.   8, Long, Susannah, and Duncan Grimes.
1770, May   1, Long, William, and Hannah Maddock.
1770, Aug.   26, Longacre, Richard, and Rachel Hall.
1740, Aug.   23, Longacre, Sarah, and Moses Justice.
1797, June   22, Longfie, Mary, and George Holt.
1730, June   29, Longhust, Henry, and Elizabeth Oliver.
1802, April   8, Lorain, Mary, and William Dwees.
1785, Dec.   27, Lored Mary, and John Rutter.
1781, Nov.   29, Lorkyer, Benjamin, and Susannah Sutton.
1792, March 25, Lort Ann and Patrick McNeill.
1800, March 8, Lort, Isaak, and Marianne Grimes.
1765, Sept.   19, Lort, Mary, and Thomas Dickinson.
1801, March 19, Loscombe, John, and Margaret O'Neil.
1759, Dec.   1, Loughton, William, and Jane Moore.
1729, Jan.   22, Louvin, John, and Ann Parker.

1730-1, Feb. 11, Louvatt Rotchard, and Jane Robinson.
1731, April 17, Love, Samuel, and Grace Harvey.
1760, May 29, Love, Sarah, and Samuel Adams.
1712, Aug. 7, Love, Thomas, and Elizabeth House.
1716, Jan. 1, Lovegrove, Ann, and William Berius.
1714, Jan. 17, Lovegrove, John, and Dorothy Spiller.
1762, July 9, Lovegrove, Mary, and Francis Skiverton.
1769, Sept. 25, Lovegrove, Mary, and Patrick Neave.
1767, Nov. 8, Lovekin, Frances, and Thomas Banks.
1733, March 25, Lovekin, Hannah, and Thomas Thomson.
1786, May 12, Lovel, Mary, and Matthew Graham.
1758, Jan. 5, Lovelock, Richard, and Ann Fell.
1736, Aug. 12, Lovely, Susannah, and Edward Philips.
1754, Jan. 15, Lovett, Charity, and William Wilson.
1796, June 27, Low, Eleanor, and William McConnell.
1775, Dec. 10, Low, Eliz., and Thomas Wade.
1734, May 18, Low, Robert, and Mary Valleott.
1753, Nov. 17, Low, Robert, and Elizabeth Burge.
1801, May 17, Low, Sarah, and Francis Petre.
1757, June 28, Lowcay, Mary, and John Wagg.
1731-2, Jan. 27, Lowden, Esther, and William Morgan.
1729, Jan. 1, Lowder, John, and Mary Jumble.
1734, July 4, Lowder, Mary, and John Fenbeigh.
1746, April 5, Lowdon, Elizabeth, and Peter Crawford.
1800, March 13, Lowe, John, and Mary Cuningham.
1786, Aug. 25, Lowe, Nicholas, and Eleanor Quality.
1733, Oct. 13, Lowe, Sarah, and Lambert Emerson.
1727, June 24, Lowe, Doct. W^m, and Sarah Story.
1727, Aug. 6, Lowe, W^m, and Mary Crook.
1804, Sept. 13, Lower, John, and Sarah Rush.
1752, April 16, Lowndes, Mary, and Edward Fitzrandal.
1742, Jan. 11, Lowne, Thomas, and Mary Efland.
1734, May 21, Lownes, George, and Elizabeth Maddox.
1806, Feb. 27, Lownes, George Bolton, and Hannah Lawrence.
1743, May 27, Lownes, Mary, and Thomas Phillips.
1766, Dec. 2, Lowns, Jane, and Joseph Burns.
1757, Dec. 24, Lownsberry, Benjamin, and Ann Young.
1786, Jan. 1, Lownsburg, Joseph, and Sarah Robinson.
1758, June 24, Lowry, Benjamin, and Ann Robinson.
1782, June 25, Lowry, Jane, and Joseph Vancice.
1777, March 6, Lowry, Jane, and Joseph Wane.
1753, March 20, Lowry, Lasdrass, and Anne Williams.
1752, May 11, Lowther, James, and Martha Breintnal.
1772, Nov. 5, Loxley, Benjamin, and Mary Barnes.
1794, April 13, Loyd, John, and Mary Robinson.
1799, Nov. 30, Loyd, Rebecca, and Thomas Gunn.

1789, Aug.   29, Lubey, Eliz, and Matthias Kemp.
1762, Oct.   19, Lucas, James, and Prudence Howell.
1773, Dec.   15, Lucas, Mary, and Laughlin Maclean.
1774, May   21, Lucas, Robert, and Mary Rowan.
1794, Nov.   26, Lucas, Seth, and Jane Sharpe.
1788, Feb.   5, Lucy, Edward, and Isabella McGraw.
1789, Dec.   31, Ludlam, George, and Lydia Knight.
1757, April   24, Luken, Daniel, and Elizabeth Read.
1779, April   27, Lukens, Jane, and Capt. Owen Fearis.
1768, July   9, Lukens, John, and Rachel Edwards.
1785, Nov.   3, Lukens, Rebecca, and John Kirk.
1753, Jan.   27, Lukens, Richard, and Elizabeth Graeme.
1786, May   11, Lukens, Sarah, and Matthew Tyson.
1783, Sept.   29, Lukens, Susannah, and Joseph Pawling.
1779, Aug.   26, Lukens, Tace, and David Lennox.
1726, Oct.   24, Luker, Dan., and Hester Vane.
1757, Sept.   8, Lum, Elizabeth, and Isaac Midelton.
1762, April   6, Lumley, Rebecca, and Samuel Vickery.
1780, Dec.   27, Lumm, Eliz., and Lavid Geary.
1794, June   10, Lumsden, Charlotte, and Robert Tate.
1758, Feb.   4, Lunsly, Adam, and Eleanor McDonnel.
1794, May   27, Lunden, Joseph, and Mary Wood.
1804, May   10, Lungren, Eliz., and Joseph Black.
1722, Oct.   30, Lunn, William, and Martha Todd.
1769, Dec.   24, Lush, Mary, and John Parker.
1767, July   15, Lush, Thomas, and Mary McKinzey.
1741, Aug.   18, Lushet, John, and Sybilla Slenton.
1763, Sept.   10, Luter, Catherine, and Josiah Harper.
1783, Nov.   27, Lutia, Lawrence, and Lilly Stewart.
1756, Nov.   29, Luven, Thomas, and Elenor Dod.
1779, May   21, Lux, George, Esqr., and Cath. Biddle.
1795, Feb.   4, Lybrand, Susannah, and Benjamin Oldfield.
1730, Dec.   12, Lycan, Andrew, and Jane Cahoon.
1728, Dec.   26, Lyde, W^m, and Rachel Davies.
1773, Aug.   13, Lyell, William, and Eliz. Gregory.
1792, Oct.   17, Lyle, James, and Ann Hamilton.
1776, April   13, Lynch, Margaret, and Daniel Fitzpatrick.
1794, July   27, Lynch, John R., and Jane Clarke.
1788, Aug.   21, Lynch, John, and Hannah Kerlin.
1801, Jan.   1, Lynch, William, and Deborah Ann Kerlin.
1731, Nov.   20, Lyne, Rebecca, and Conway Courtnay.
1784, Aug.   8, Lynn, David, and Mary Boor.
1741, Dec.   7, Lynn, Elizabeth, and Thomas Collins.
1740, Oct.   8, Lynn, Elizabeth, and Samuel Dowthite.
1710, May   1, Lynsee, Alexander, and Sarah Hall.
1802, May   24, Lyon, Patrick, and Cath. Taggart.

1761, July   13, Lyon, Samuel, and Charlotte Minnes.
1755, Nov.   1, Lyons, John, and Elinor Neel.
1771, Aug.   26, Lyons, Patrick, and Mary Nicholson.
1795, July   4, Lyons, Patrick, and Ann Brindley.
1797, July   2, Lyster, John, and Mary Eyre.
1769, May   11, Maag, Ann, and Robert Walker.
1775, Nov.   2, Maag, Henry, and Sarah Plunkett.
1781, Jan.   27, Maago, Mary, and James Gemble.
1802, March   18, Maburry, Lydia, and Francis Potts.
1709, June   10, Macarty, Catharine, and Henry Lewis.
1729, July   12, Maccluire, Anthony, and Rebecca Paxton.
1798, July   22, Macdonough, Mary, and Crawford Elder.
1801, Nov.   12, Mace, Daniel, and Rebecca Sparrowgrove.
1720, Feb.   27, Macerah, William, and Mary Jack.
1756, Dec.   19, Mackay, Elizabeth, and James Turner.
1755, April   19, Mackee, Elizabeth, and Richard Redman.
1754, Dec.   12, Mackenzie, Kenneth, and Mary Thomas.
1803, May   14, Mackie, Alexander, and Jane Trimble,
1802, Jan.   2, Mackie, William, and Eliz. Miller.
1766, July   19, Mackinson, Mary, and William Glover.
1723, March   28, Macklin, Robert, and Elizabeth Robinson.
1783, Nov.   6, Mackey, James, and Susannah Sharpe.
1784, Nov.   13, Mackey, John, and Eliz. Curry.
1735, Dec.   9, Mackey, Mary, and George Lockhart.
1760, Dec.   6, Mackey, Mary, and Robert Rawle.
1801, Jan.   1, Mackey, Susanna, and Lawrence Butler.
1761, July   26, Mackey, William, and Mary Sinclair.
1773, Dec.   15, Maclean, Laughlin, and Mary Lucas.
1806, Jan.   2, Macpherson, Ann, and Samuel Riddle.
1799, Nov.   20, Madden, Margaret, and Peter Peterson.
1770, May   1, Maddock, Hannah, and William Long.
1734, May   21, Maddox, Elizabeth, and George Lownes.
1728, Feb.   20, Maddox, Joshua, and Mary Gative.
1801, April   9, Maddox, Joshua, and Rebecca Claypoole.
1755, Oct.   9, Maddox, Sarah, and Joseph Stamper.
1788, Dec.   11, Maddox, Sarah, and John Hall.
1789, Oct.   15, Madge, Eliz., and William Lea.
1797, April   7, Madzel, Lewis, and Eliz. Leary.
1795, April   9, Maffett, James, and Eliz. Harnet.
1799, Aug.   4, Magarrid, Eleanor, and Charles Hirt.
1748, Sept.   24, Magee, Thomas, and Mary Davis.
1805, Nov.   11, Magee, William, and Sarah Miles Barclay.
1746, Aug.   27, Maginnis, Edward, and Rose Fullerton.
1803, Oct.   20, Magnus, Maria Ann, and John Wilson.
1769, Feb.   4, Magraw, Hannah, and Hay King.
1797, May   18, Mahaffy, Margery, and Thomas Godfrey.

1804, Feb.   1, Mahany, Jane, and Jacob Stille.
1775, June   23, Maher, Mary, and Archibald Dunn.
1743, July   15, Mahery, James, and Mary Smith.
1747, May   16, Mahlin, Alice, and John Crossley.
1798, June   24, Mahon, Cath., and William Barry.
1786, Nov.   16, Mahon, Sarah, and Michael Corn.
1792, June   24, Mahoney, Mary, and Michael Hacket.
1771, June   18, Maine, Eliz, and Anthony Nuss.
1773, Dec.   28, Mains, Ann, and Nicholas Hendrickson.
1767, April 29, Mains, James, and Martha Keen.
1797, Aug.   8, Maise, John, and Mary Simmonds.
1794, May   15, Major, John, and Margaret Worrell.
1776, Jan.   18, Malaby, Cath., and Patrick Flynn.
1765, Oct.   3, Malcom, Moses, and Mary Pillar.
1798, Feb.   22, Malcolm, John F., and Deborah Howard.
1803, June   7, Maley, William, and Ann Service.
1770, Nov.   24, Malice, Eliz., and Walter Manuel.
1752, Aug.   27, Malice, William, and Mary Dawson.
1751, Feb.   21, Malin, David, and Margaret Lawrence.
1761, Nov.   7, Malin, Jane, and Jerman Walker.
1761, Nov.   7, Malin, Randal, and Sarah Walker.
1749, Feb.   1, Malin, William, and Elizabeth Crossley.
1795, May   9, Mall, Nehemiah, and Mary Keen.
1741, Aug.   8, Mallaly, James, and Clarinda Hagan.
1737, Aug.   13, Mallard, Mary, and William Benham.
1785, Aug.   8, Mallett, Eliz., and Henry Harper.
1794, June   16, Mallineux, John, and Ann Britton.
1784, Aug.   10, Malong, John, and Sarah Carter.
1776, Feb.   4, Malone, Eleanor, and Thomas Duncan.
1801, June   24, Malone, Mary, and Samuel Bradfield.
1743, Dec.   20, Malowny, Mary, and James Quin.
1796, Aug.   17, Maltby, Charles, and Sarah Sweers.
1754, Dec.   12, Man, Samuel, and Mary Colly.
1804, Oct.   6, Manchester, John, and Mary Myers.
1768, Oct.   29, Manerlle, Conrad, and Mary Maxwell.
1775, Nov.   29, Manford, Charles, and Rebecca Titchet.
1795, Dec.   8, Mankin, Catherine, and Edward Hill.
1716, Feb.   2, Mankin, Edward, and Margaret Wilkinson.
1732, Nov.   25, Manley, John, and Lucretia Brewer.
1796, Feb.   8, Mann, Martha, and Elijah Draper.
1797, Nov.   21, Mann, Mary, and David Kenney.
1765, Dec.   24, Mannahon, Ann, and Andrew Hammond.
1803, Dec.   29, Manners, Thomas, and Mary Rush.
1744, Dec.   10, Mannin, Robert, and Sarah Mitchel.
1801, Oct.   9, Manning, Thomas, and Susan Koop.
1783, April   3, Mannington, Rebecca, and John Dorsey.

1769, Nov.　2, Mannington, Susannah, and James Sutton.
1761, March 31, Manson, Margaret, and James Beyson.
1771, July　1, Manson, Margaret, and John Taylor.
1759, Feb.　3, Manson, Rachel, and William Terry.
1736, June　14, Mantle, Mary, and Arthur Cribb.
1754, Nov.　23, Manuel, John Aplee, and Hannah Jones.
1770, Nov.　24, Manuel, Walter, and Eliz. Malice.
1737, July　9, Many, Magdalen, and George Moranda.
1736, July　4, Many, Francis, and Mary Moranda.
1747, June　21, Many, Robert, and Margaret Cox.
1752, Aug.　4, Manypenny, Euphemia, and Stephen Williams.
1760, Nov.　27, Mapper, Mary, and Hugh Forbes.
1712, April　8, Marcarty, Catherine, and John Young.
1798, Jan.　27, Marchant, Marie, and Nicholas Poreaux.
1766, Nov.　12, Marchinton, Philip, and Eliz. Barge.
1791, March 17, Marckell, Anthony, and Dorothy Legens.
1730, Dec.　21, Marden, Thomas, and Ann Walmsley.
1779, March 25, Marget, Cath., and Thomas Tucker.
1782, March　5, Mark, John, and Margaret Stoy.
1758, Nov.　30, Mark, Peter, and Ann Colston.
1798, Jan.　25, Markland, John, and Cath. Heiss.
1773, Dec.　16, Markoe, Abraham, and Eliz. Baynton.
1785, Nov.　19, Markoe, Ann, and Nicholas Crugger.
1801, Oct.　22, Markoe, Eliz., and Samuel Hazlehurst.
1804, Feb.　6, Markoe, John, and Hitty Coxe.
1791, Nov.　17, Markoe, Margaret, and Benjamin Franklin Bache.
1753, June　30, Marks, Frances, and James Biddle.
1747, Feb.　14, Marks, Rachel, and Alexander Graydon.
1793, May　23, Markward, Mary, and Hugh Seton.
1760, Nov.　15, Marle, John, and Hannah Ash.
1772, March 19, Maroe, Prudence, and Jacob Row.
1779, Nov.　20, Marpole, Isaac, and Eliz. Kennold.
1749, Aug.　28, Marr, Daniel, and Margaret Dickey.
1794, Sept.　27, Marr, John, and Sarah Fenton.
1787, Sept.　9, Marra, Daniel, and Mary Farrell.
1760, Sept.　22, Marrina, John, and Mary Burk.
1782, April　4, Marsh, Eliz., and Capt. James Josiah.
1734, Aug.　1, Marsh, Henry, and Anne Stewart.
1763, June　23, Marsh, James, and Mary Cummins.
1791, Nov.　17, Marsh, Joseph, and Hannah Hubley.
1797, April　17, Marshall, Abraham, and Susanna Rees.
1737, Nov.　12, Marshal, Alice, and Richard Trimer.
1800, Sept.　18, Marshal, Amos., and Mary Ann Yorkson.
1760, Jan.　30, Marshall, Ann, and Robert Skelton.
1773, Sept.　16, Marshall, Arthur, and Margaret Moore.
1768, Jan.　21, Marshal, Beersheba, and Enoch Hughes.

1798, April 26, Marshall, Charles, and Mary Wallace.
1735, Jan. 3, Marshall, David, and Mary Tenny.
1755, Nov. 18, Marshal, Hannah, and Thomas Walker.
1762, Nov. 6, Marshall, Hannah, and Robert Priest.
1760, Sept. 18, Marshal, Isaac, and H. C. Hudman.
1765, Oct. 6, Marshall, Jacob, and Abigail Wood.
1736, June 13, Marshall, James, and Margaret Miller.
1795, April 10, Marshall, James, and Etty Morris.
1784, Oct. 20, Marshall, James, and Eliz. Neighbour.
1788, Jan. 10, Marshall, Jane, and Robert Cummings.
1743, Oct. 6, Marshall, John, and Ruth Legay.
1776, Nov. 14, Marshall, John, and Margaret Adams.
1768, March 5, Marshall, John, and Hannah Baldwin.
1784, July 3, Marshall, Joseph, and Laetitia Smallwood.
1795, May 28, Marshall, Margaret, and George Smith.
1785, Oct. 2, Marshall, Mary, and George Wood.
1792, Dec. 12, Marshall, Mary, and Lewis Rush.
1797, May 22, Marshall, Mary, and John Thornton.
1763, March 15, Marshall, Moses, and Elizabeth Reinhart.
1763, May 9, Marshall, Ralph, and Mary Wintmore.
1738, April 16, Marshall, Sarah, and Richard Hencock.
1742, May 31, Marshall, Sarah, and Joseph Lewden.
1769, April 8, Marshall, Thomas, and Ann Cox.
1799, Dec. 16, Marshall, Thomas, and Lydia Frances Webb.
1770, April 25, Marshall, William, and Hannah Ridge.
1743, Dec. 26, Marshel, Margaret, and Pat. Allen.
1716, June 18, Marsten, Elizabeth, and John Milton.
1768, Jan. 7, Marston, John, and Rachel Lawrence.
1783, Aug. 21, Martin, Ann, and Thomas Wills.
1766, Sept. 27, Martin, Anthony, and Mary Paine.
1760, Sept. 25, Martin, Catherine, and William Holms.
1720, Oct. 11, Martin, Daniel, and Ann Grasbury.
1795, July 25, Martin, Edward, and Jannet Spiers.
1743, March 1, Martin, Elizabeth, and Joseph Preston.
1748, Dec. 22, Martin, Hannah, and Patrick Anderson.
1782, June 23, Martin, Jane, and Stephen Moore.
1716, March 26, Martin, Joanna, and David Jones.
1765, May 9, Martin, John, and Elizabeth Bond.
1805, April 23, Martin, John, and Mary Boyd.
1800, May 1, Martin, John, and Mary Martin.
1761, Sept. 5, Martin, John, and Ann Tate.
1794, Nov. 27, Martin, Joseph, and Judith Andrews.
1784, Aug. 5, Martin, Joseph, and Eliz. Willoughby.
1762, April 27, Martin, Martha, and Samuel Rogers.
1747, March 10, Martin, Mary, and David Smith.
1721, May 17, Martin, Mary, and John Bound.

1800, May   1, Martin, Mary, and John Martin.
1800, Nov.   6, Martin, Mary, and John Underwood.
1774, July   2, Martin, Patrick, and Mary Right.
1795, June   21, Martin, Phœbe, and Benjamin Scot.
1767, Oct.   8, Martin, Robert, and Mary Crowley.
1764, April   5, Martin, Robert, and Jane Durows.
1756, Sept. 16, Martin, Samuel, and Mary Smith.
1788, June   26, Martin, Sarah, and Thomas Norris.
1735, Dec.   31, Martin, Stephen, and Hannah Edwards.
1767, Nov.   1, Martindale, John Waters, and Catherine Child.
1756, Dec.   9, Martindale, Joseph, and Margaret Connoly.
1789, Oct.   22, Marts, Eliz., and Joseph Moulder.
1787, April 24, Mash, Edmund, and Hannah Bucks.
1761, July   4, Masoer, Frances, and Barnaby McClusky.
1750, Nov.   8, Mason, Anne, and Ineas Battar.
1744, June   23, Mason, Anne, and John Ord.
1745, July   18, Mason, Catherine, and George Smith.
1779, Dec.   2, Mason, Eleanor, and Joseph Quality.
1776, Feb.   27, Mason, Eliz., and John Burton.
1805, June   29, Mason, Ernst and Hannah Dudbridge.
1730-1, Jan. 14, Mason, Jacob, and Mary McVaugh.
1753, Aug.   11, Mason, Jane, and John Grooves.
1785, Sept. 28, Mason, John, and Hannah Young.
1762, April   6, Mason, John, and Deborah Stevens.
1733, May   15, Mason, John, and Margaret Spencer.
1738, May   10, Mason, Jonathan, and Mary Crockat.
1768, June   19, Mason, Martha, and James Graham.
1722, Aug.   10, Mason, Martha, and Gabriel Wood.
1731, Dec.   12, Mason, Mary, and Andrew Duchee.
1775, Feb.   2, Mason, Mary, and John App Owen.
1787, May   29, Mason, Mary, and William Deed.
1720, May   25, Mason, Mary, and William Thomas.
1742, July   3, Mason, Mary, and Elias Guillott.
1802, Nov.   30, Mason, Peter, and Cath. Miller.
1768, March   7, Mason, Richard, and Laetitia Tannagh.
1754, Feb.   12, Mason, Ruth, and Philip Clayton.
1744, March 29, Mason, Samuel, and Hannah Johnston.
1802, April 18, Mason, Solomon, and Jane McCulley.
1730, Sept. 13, Mason, Susannah, and Christopher Tuthill.
1799, Dec.   8, Mason, Tantan, and Martha Jackson.
1790, May   20, Mason, Thomas, and Hannah Gardner.
1766, Oct.   25, Mason, Thomas, and Priscilla Sysom.
1798, Aug.   12, Mason, William, and Eliz. Stine.
1764, April   5, Massey, Eleanor, and George Saunderson.
1788, Nov.   28, Massey, Mary, and Isaac Duncan.
1865, June   22, Massey, Phineas, and Susannah Battle.

1805, April　4, Massey, Thomas, and Eliz. Dawes.
1752, July　4, Masters, George, and Mary Helms.
1785, June　23, Masters, Mary, and Joseph Clark.
1772, May　21, Masters, Mary, and Honble Richard Penn, Esqr.
1761, April　15, Masters, William, and Sarah Morgan.
1754, Aug.　31, Masters, William, and Mary Lawrence.
1737, Dec.　20, Maston, Mary, and William Avrell.
1757, April　11, Mather, Elizabeth, and Nathan Thomas.
1727, Dec.　2, Mather, James, and Marg^t Test.
1743, July　24, Mather, Margaret, and Thomas Watson.
1736, Dec.　25, Mathers, Esther, and Josiah Barnett.
1771, Oct.　14, Matlack, Amos, and Hannah Trager.
1781, Sept.　7, Matlack, Hannah, and John Stafford.
1800, March　8, Matlack, Helen, and Chandler Price.
1773, April　24, Matlack, Jonathan, and Hannah Waln.
1785, June　21, Matlack, Martha, and Guy Bryan.
1766, Nov.　27, Matlack, Seth, and Mary Shute.
1797, Aug.　17, Matlack, Timothy, and Eliz. Copper.
1757, Nov.　19, Matthew, James, and Susannah Shepperd.
1767, Feb.　13, Matthew, Rachel, and Thomas Meredith.
1785, Sept.　23, Matthews, Ann, and John Vicar.
1779, Nov.　20, Matthews, Cath., and Michael Doogan.
1779, Nov.　11, Matthews, Edith, and Nicholas Brooks.
1735, May　19, Matthews, Henry, and Martha Conyer.
1791, Dec.　21, Matthews, James, and Ann Penrose.
1796, Dec.　1, Matthews, James, and Mary Moore.
1768, Feb.　17, Matthews, John, and Hannah North.
1752, June　10, Matthews, John, and Margaret McCreight.
1805, Dec.　3, Matthews, Sarah, and William Scott.
1789, Oct.　28, Matthews, William, and Elector Whitefield.
1721, July　11, Matthews, William, and Ann Dane.
1770, Nov.　27, Matthias, Mary, and Jonathan Evans.
1754, April　16, Mattson, Joseph, and Jane Steers.
1750, May　26, Maudlin, Ruth, and Thomas Banfield.
1748, Feb.　1, Maugridge, Elizabeth, and Thomas Leonard.
1743, Feb.　10, Maugridge, John, and Elizabeth Gregory.
1742, Dec.　19, Maugridge, Sarah, and Edward Drury.
1761, Oct.　9, Maul, Catherine, and John Hadley.
1728, Nov.　12, Maultby, W^m, and Dor. Stegleigh.
1781, March　1, Maus, Matthew, and Charlotte Nichola.
1799, Jan.　19, Mause, Hannah, and Arnold Custard.
1801, April　19, Maxfield, Mary, and Thomas Bissett.
1805, March　30, Maxwell, Hester, and George Bond.
1805, Jan.　19, Maxwell, Hugh, and Sarah Greble.
1766, Nov.　12, Maxwell, Isabell, and Thomas Thompson.
1792, Jan.　1, Maxwell, Mary, and Caleb Hathaway.

1768, Oct.	29, Maxwell, Mary, and Conrad Manerlle.
1746, Dec.	22, Maxwell, Mary, and Nathaniel Beany.
1771, Oct.	22, Maxwell, Robert, and Mary Cooper.
1801, May	14, Maxwell, Thomas, and Eliz. Humphreys.
1764, Aug.	22, May, Andrew, and Mary Ball.
1800, Sept.	21, May, Anna, and George Wright.
1767, May	21, May, George, and Deborah Comron.
1799, June	20, May, George, and Hester Cook.
1801, June	13, May, John, and Sarah Higgins.
1722, April	5, May, Lucila, and William Seltridge.
1741, Oct.	31, Mav, Robert, and Susannah Coolins.
1738, Nov.	6, May, Sarah, and Thomas Prover.
1736, Nov.	23, May, Stephen, and Sarah Carr.
1760, Nov.	22, May, Susannah, and William Hughes.
1795, Dec.	24, Mayberry, John, and Hannah Child.
1750, Feb.	22, Mayberry, Rachel, and Robert Field.
1738, July	19, Maycock, Charles, and Catherine Jenkins.
1773, Jan.	19, Mayer, Charles, and Margaret Wrench.
1732, Nov.	2, Mayes, Elizabeth, and Tho⁵ Hill.
1748, Nov.	3, Mayhew, John, and Rachel Harverd.
1761, Nov.	6, Maylander, Deborah, and William Eldridge.
1781, Dec.	15, Mayney, Thomas, and Mary McCloude.
1739, May	14, McAdam, Hugh, and Elizabeth Vanhust.
1774, July	26, McAdams, Eliz., and William Jennings.
1723, July	—, McAllister, John, and Mary Sullivan.
1795, March	2, McAllister, Patrick, and Rachel Goforth.
1806, June	5, McAllister, Sarah, and Garrel Bukhorn.
1805, June	6, McAlpine, Jane, and Charles Boyd.
1759, Sept.	26, McAndrews, David, and Eleanor Craig.
1761, June	29, McAwell, Mary, and John Langley.
1752, Sept.	19, McBay, Floranna, and John McKenny.
1782, Dec.	15, McBean, Mary, and Joseph Vandergrist.
1797, Aug.	31, McBride, Eliz., and James Fiss.
1764, Feb.	20, McBrier, Jane, and James Robinson.
1799, Jan.	10, McCabe, Bridget, and James Kenney.
1758, April	1, McCadden, Agnes, and Henry McQuad.
1772, Oct.	8, McCadden, Daniel, and Eliz. Pollard.
1747, July	20, McCalister, James, and Mary McGloughlin.
1763, June	9, McCall, Ann, and Thomas Willing.
1796, Sept.	22, McCall, Ann, and William Read.
1755, July	12, McCall, Anne, and Robert Black.
1737, May	28, McCall, Anne, and Samuel McCall.
1792, May	3, McCall, Archibald, and Eliz. Cadwallader.
1736, Oct.	16, McCall, Catherine, and John Englis.
1754, Oct.	31, McCall, Eleanor, and Andrew Elliot.
1745, Jan.	2, McCall, George, and Lydia Abbott.

1794, May　21, McCall, George, and Margaret Clymer.
1745, Oct.　10, McCall, Jasper, and Magdalen Kollock.
1749, May　20, McCall, Magdaline, and John Swift.
1759, Feb.　3, McCall, Margaret, and Joseph Swift.
1746, May　4, McCall, Margaret, and John Hall.
1753, Sept.　27, McCall, Mary, and William Plumsted.
1772, June　25, McCall, Mary, and Benjamin Cattell.
1793, May　9, McCall, Mary, and Lambert Cadwalader.
1801, April　7, McCall, Peter, and Sarah Gibson.
1750, May　16, McCall, Robert, and Catharine Mulica.
1759, Jan.　31, McCall, Samuel, and Mary Cox.
1743, Jan.　29, McCall, Samuel, and Ann Searle.
1737, May　28, McCall, Samuel, and Anne McCall.
1783, Nov.　13, McCalla, John, and Mary Taylor.
1773, April　1, McCallachan, Eleanor, and Jacob Feit.
1759, June　16, McCann, Ann, and Isaac Sweetman.
1785, Nov.　6, McCann, Bridget, and Martin McGra.
1802, Feb.　27, McCann, Cath., and Daniel McKanney.
1786, Aug.　31, McCann, George, and Arabella Farr.
1760, Dec.　31, McCann, Joanna, and William Hill.
1769, Sept.　22, McCann, John, and Elizabeth Sharp.
1748, Sept.　5, McCann, Tool, and Joannah Brightwel.
1764, Aug.　29, McCarnon, Elizabeth, and David Hughs.
1774, Oct.　3, McCarrell, Susannah, and Charles Lane.
1794, June　28, McCartey, Mary, and Samuel Probeit.
1748, Aug.　15, McCarth, Sarah, and John Wessel.
1730, Sept.　2, McCarty, Hannah, and Standish ffoord.
1796, Jan.　28, McCarty, Hugh, and Mary Best.
1792, Dec.　10, McCarty, John, and Sarah McGowan.
1745, June　4, McCarty, Mary, and William Sympson.
1800, Feb.　8, McCarty, Mary, and Peter Bell.
1781, Dec.　6, McCarty, Randolph, and Margaret Welsh.
1729-30, Jan. 7, McCary, Sarah, and Henry Davis.
1766, Dec.　27, McCeman, Margaret, and James McIlharn.
1794, Sept.　25, McClain, Andrew, and Mary Kingston.
1752, Nov.　6, McClain, Patrick, and Catherine Kulans.
1801, April　18, McClane, Mary, and Thomas O'Daniel.
1768, Nov.　5, McClannon, Mary, and Thomas Piercy.
1803, Aug.　4, McClaskey, Sarah, and George Irvine.
1798, March 19, McClasky, Edward, and Ann O'Harra.
1775, Feb.　26, McClatchey, George, and Mary Holland.
1767, June　26, McClay, William, and Mary Fleming.
1749, May　30, McClean, Michael, and Rachel Patterson.
1749, May　16, McClean, William, and Mary Stalker.
1767, Oct.　19, McClear, James, and Jane Sinclair.
1747, Nov.　28, McClellan, Elizabeth, and Thomas Hill.

1806, June   25, McCleland, Margaretta, and Archibald Hill.
1781, April   11, McClenachan, Deborah, and Col. Walter Stewart.
1792, June   2, McClenachan, Martha, and John Howston.
1780, Nov.   25, McClenan, Mary, and Philip McHugh.
1770, Nov.   13, McClellan, Cath., and Robert Hume.
1794, Sept. 22, McCleod, Daniel, and Mary Quingley.
1801, March 12, McClintock, Eliz., and Felix Paschalis.
1803, Dec.   3, McClintock, Margaret, and Isaac Smith.
1784, April   20, McClintock, Thomas, and Mary Allen.
1796, Nov.   26, McClosky, Mary, and John Jackson.
1781, Dec.   15, McCloude, Mary, and Thomas Mayney.
1757, April   12, McCloud, Mary, and John Young.
1763, July   8, McCloy, William, and Margaret McClusky.
1766, June   1, McCluer, Jane, and Lewis Blakeley.
1763, June   22, McClure, John, and Elizabeth Dean.
1740, June   12, McCluer, Rebecaa, and Thomas Venables.
1794, Oct.   23, McCluney, James, and Martha Lamplugh.
1761, July   4, McClusky, Banaby, and Francis Masoer.
1763, July   8, McClusey, Margaret, and William McCloy.
1793, Dec.   14, McCamach, James, and Ann Sharp.
1773, June   22, McCob, John, and Mary Himes.
1793, Jan.   4, McConkey, William, and Mary Hillman.
1793, Sept. 13, McConnell, Agnes, and James Hillar.
1758, Dec.   29, McConnell, James, and Mary Duncliff.
1785, July   2, McConnell, John, and Mary Dawson.
1796, June, 27, McConnell, William, and Eleanor Low.
1769, Oct.   11, McConnelly, Martha, and Andrew Sullivan.
1769, June   23, McCool, Catherine, and Josiah White.
1765, Aug.   8, McCool, John, and Margaret Camel.
1757, March 27, McCormick, Ann, and James Downey.
1798, June   7, McCormick, Ann, and James Welsh.
1770, Oct.   29, McCormick, Catherine, and James Brown.
1794, July   23, McCormick, David, and Sarah Pollard.
1776, April   18, McCormick, Henry, and Eliz. Clowser.
1778, Sept. 23, McCormick, Hugh, and Margaret Kennedy.
1779, Feb.   4, McCormick, Jane, and Thomas Dwyer.
1745, Oct.   15, McCormick, John, and Mary Goodin.
1730, Oct.   25, McCormick, Margaret, and John Ready.
1752, Nov.   4, McCoy, Andrew, and Mary Baker.
1759, Feb.   8, McCoy, Jane, and William Poltis.
1802, April   24, McCoy, John, and Cath. Metts.
1753, April   27, McCoy, John, and Eleanor Ayers.
1803, Sept. 18, McCoy, Margaret, and Michael Perry.
1755, May   1, McCoy, Martha, and John Wallis.
1757, March 1, McCoy, Mary, and John Harrison.
1769, Aug.   4, McCracken, Elizabeth, and James Carswell.

1802, Oct. 17, McCracken, Margaret, and John Woodhouse.
1768, Oct. 26, McCracken, Mary, and Allen Russell.
1746, Jan. 16, McCready, Frances, and Philip Adamson.
1745, March 23, McCreagh, Cath., and James Hartshorne.
1795, June 25, McCredan, Eliz., and Thomas Young.
1752, June 10, McCreight, Margaret, and John Matthews.
1763, Oct. 21, McCrump, Eleanor, and Robert Ross.
1799, Feb. 27, McCue, Dominic, and Susanna Henry.
1802, April 18, McCulley, Jane, and Solomon Mason.
1742, July 27, McCullick, Hugh, and Christian Mullen.
1795, Dec. 13, McCullock, Deborah S., and Peter Belve.
1768, April 9, McCullom, Andrew, and Eliz. Elliott.
1747, Dec. 24, McCullough, James, and Rachel Spence.
1743, Oct. 23, McCullough, Mary, and John Ryan.
1799, Nov. 13, McCully, Hugh, and Cath. McLaughlin.
1728, Nov. 2, McCurry, Alice, and Wm Devonshire.
1737, May 13, McCurry, Jane, and John White.
1803, Oct. 9, McCutchin, Eliz., and George Buchanan.
1795, Jan. 8, McDaniel, Ann, and Samuel Bell.
1799, Feb. 14, McDaniel, Dennis, and Hannah McKimm.
1804, April 12, McDaniel, Mary, and William Mellen.
1794, Nov. 20, McDaniel, Mary, and Joseph Feinour.
1798, Dec. 9, McDavid, Ralph, and Cath. Vincen.
1764, Nov. 19, McDonald, Ann, and William Gamble.
1794, Dec. 22, McDonald, Christiana, and Allen Brown.
1771, Sept. 24, McDonald, Jane, and Thomas Moore.
1736, Feb. 28, McDonald, Martha, and Richard Hughes.
1796, March 1, McDonald, Mary Swasy, and Hamilton Wilson.
1776, May 9, McDonald, Mary, and Edward Bullin.
1756, Nov. 16, McDonald, Mary, and John Keenan.
1805, Aug. 1, McDonald, Mary, and Francis Harvey.
1796, March 11, McDonald, William, and Susannah Sidney.
1801, July 26, McDonald, William, and Sarah Cox.
1739, March 7, McDonall, Mary, and John Price.
1743, Oct. 24, McDonnagh, Patrick, and Judith Geary.
1758, Feb. 4, McDonnel, Eleanor, and Adam Lumsly.
1766, Jan. 18, McDonnel, Eleanor, and James Collins.
1800, Dec. 27, McDeed, Dominic, and Mary Collins.
1786, May 18, McDeermott, John, and Grace Copeland.
1795, Feb. 25, McDermot, Mary, and James Church.
1799, Aug. 5, McDermot, Rose, and Edward Cavenegh.
1800, March 6, McDevitt, Roger, and Eleanor Kelly.
1800, Aug. 4, McDivitt, Thomas, and Cath. Kelly.
1796, Oct. 13, McDougal, Amelia, and Thomas Gray.
1794, Sept. 25, McDougal, John, and Eliz. Cassin.
1797, June 17, McDougal, John, and Susan Niglee.

1796, May   10, McDougal, Margaret, and John Hog.
1778, Aug.   23, McDougal, William, and ——— Harrold.
1801, March 20, McElroy, David, and Eliz. Anderson.
1798, Jan.   11, McElroy, John, and Ann Cooper.
1767, Feb.   25, McEntire, Mary, and Anthony Golley.
1767, May   7, McEntire, Neal, and Jane Floyd.
1766, July   12, McEntire, Sarah, and William Boggs.
1773, Oct.   14, McEuen, John, and Eliz. Few.
1750, April 26, McEvers, John, and Catherine Kock.
1775, Dec.   28, McFadden, William, and Sarah Hussey.
1799, March 28, McFall, Ann, and William Sandford.
1774, Sept.   5, McFall, Patrick, and Mary Ferman.
1766, Dec.   23, McFarlan, Eve, and Solomon McFarlan.
1766, Dec.   23, McFarlan, Solomon, and Eve McFarlan.
1757, March 28, McFarland, John, and Ann Douglass.
1749, May   11, McFarland, Martha, and John Anderson.
1774, Nov.   27, McFarland, Robert and Margary Harris.
1749, Nov.   22, McFarson, Jane, and Robert Lockhart.
1768, Sept. 11, McFee, Daniel, and Sarah Powel.
1776, Feb.   12, McFee, David, and Jane Triggs.
1772, Feb.   4, McFee, Thomas, and Ann Jenkins.
1775, April 26, McFeteridge, John, and Ann Carson.
1805, May   2, McFetrick, Samuel H., and Mary Ann Rolph.
1752, Dec.   3, McFun, William, and Lydia Biddle.
1773, Jan.   5, McFunn, Mary, and Collinson Read.
1765, Oct.   29, McGarvot, Barnaby, and Catherine Mitchell.
1740, July   25, McGeah, William, and Abigail Jenkins.
1756, Jan.   29, McGee, Alexander, and Mary Conyers.
1800, May   28, McGee, Charles, and Eliz. Williams.
1748, Aug.   13, McGee, Elizabeth, and Henry Wright.
1790, March 23, McGee, Eliz., and James Barry.
1755, Dec.   10, McGee, Margerie, and Darby Doyle.
1765, Dec.   24, McGee, Patrick, and Jane Hall.
1749, Nov.   8, McGee, William, and Elizabeth Brading.
1776, Oct.   18, McGennis, Lawrence, and Mary Beak.
1796, Aug.   23, McGettigen, Hugh, and Ann Bowen.
1796, Sept.   4, McGhy, Barnabas, and Margaret Cummings.
1766, April   7, McGibbon, John, and Mary Burrows.
1794, Jan.   1, McGill, Eliz., and James Delavan.
1764, Jan.   21, McGill, James, and Elizabeth Johnson.
1804, March 27, McGill, Margaret, and Richards Jacobs.
1799, July   4, McGill, Mary, and George Halston.
1794, Nov.   6, McGill, Stacy, and Jacob Earnest.
1756, Aug.   9, McGinnis, Catherine, and George Atkinson.
1782, June   30, McGinnis, Mary, and Peter Coriel.
1775, Dec.   5, McGinnis, Mary, and Andrew Nelson.

1790, Sept.   1, McGinnis, Neil, and Margaret Sprowl.
1794, Oct.   26, McGinnis, Phœbe, and Abraham Woodruff.
1800, Jan.   9, McGinnis, William, and Eliz. Boze.
1751, Nov.   4, McGithgan, Bryan, and Anne Toomy.
1767, June   13, McGlashan, Duncan, and Eleanor Walker.
1759, June   27, McGlathery, Ann, and John Dick.
1761, Jan.   29, McGlathery, Mathew, and Margaret George.
1796, Oct.   2, McGlocklin, Ann, and Lewis Limote.
1747, July   20, McGloughlin, Mary, and James McCalister.
1780, Dec.   10, McGlue, Hannah, and Arthur Black.
1761, Sept.   8, McGorrough, Isabella, and John Doran.
1766, Sept.   2, McGouish, John, and Ann Cary.
1804, Dec.   1, McGouran, Mary, and Pierre Tesson.
1792, Dec.   10, McGowan, Sarah, and John McCarty.
1785, Nov.   6, McGra, Martin, and Bridget McCann.
1788, Feb.   5, McGraw, Isabella, and Edward Lucy.
1733, April   10, McGraw, Jane, and Abraham Tustan.
1740, June   16, McGrew, Margaret, and William Williams.
1761, Nov.   7, McGucy, Ferguson, and Mary Connady.
1800, Oct.   23, McGuire, Rosanna, and George Montgomery.
1783, April   28, McHerren, John, and Ann Fitzgerald.
1780, Nov.   25, McHugh, Philip, and Mary McClenan.
1766, Dec.   27, McIlharn, James, and Margaret McCeman.
1773, April   29, McIlheran, Ann, and Dougal Gregory.
1772, Feb.   15, McIlmoyle, James, and Isabella Connoly.
1785, June   16, McIlvaine, Dr. W^m, and Mary Shippen.
1782, Dec.   2, McIlvane, William, and Rebecca Cox.
1797, Aug.   22, McIntire, Andrew, and Cath. McLaughlin.
1780, Dec.   21, McIntire, Ann, and James Hayes.
1769, Nov.   11, McIntire, Charles, and Ann Sullivan.
1800, May   13, McIntire, Eliz., and John Lemont.
1779, Sept.   2, McIntire, Esther, and George Middagh.
1802, July   14, McIntire, Margaret, and James Coyles.
1796, Jan.   8, McIntire, Sarah, and David Innes.
1798, Jan.   21, McIvers, Sophia, and Philip Lees.
1788, Sept.   14, McKage, Hugh, and Alice Bradburn.
1773, March 23, McKahan, Ann, and Gilbert McKillup.
1802, Feb.   27, McKanney, Daniel, and Cath. McCann.
1767, Feb.   20, McKay, George, and Mary Campbell.
1783, Dec.   19, McKay, Thomas, and Eliz. Jolly.
1794, Nov.   20, McKean, Dorothey, and Charles Duffey.
1732, March 21, McKebb, Daniel, and Martha White.
1773, Sept.   2, McKee, Joseph, and Cath. Kea.
1805, April   21, McKee, Sarah, and William Shaw.
1805, July   20, McKeever, James, and Ann Borroughs.
1801, Nov.   12, McKegan, Edward, and Eliz. Hungary.

1806, Oct.   8, McKelway, John, and Eleanor Redman.
1746, Feb.   11, McKenney, John, and Byidget Sullivan.
1752, Sept. 19, McKenny, John, and Floranna McBay.
1772, Dec.   2, McKenzie, James, and Cath. Huston.
1792, Nov.   6, McKever, Patrick, and Martha London.
1780, Feb.   8, McKibsick, John, and Eliz. Thomson.
1773, March 23, McKillup, Gilbert, and Ann McKahan.
1763, Sept.   5, McKillup, Randle, and Jane Miller.
1740, May   7, McKinlay, William, and Anne Calender.
1801, April 19, McKinley, Henry, and Eliz. Sibbet.
1799, Feb.   14, McKinn, Hannah, and Dennis McDaniel.
1767, July   15, McKinzey, Mary, and Thomas Lush.
1756, Nov.   20, McKnight, Martha, and Luke Scanlan.
1748, Feb.   13, McKnight, William, and Susannah Bond.
1737, April 30, McKnight, William, and Martha Goulden.
1774, June   12, McLain, Sarah, and Moses Hart.
1790, April   1, McLane, Cath., and Francis Harrison.
1754, June   17, McLane, Elizabeth, and John Temple.
1798, Dec.   29, McLane, John, and Sarah Lightcap.
1804, Dec.   24, McLane, Mary, and Henry Yates.
1759, July   21, McLane, Paul, and Ann Galbraith.
1769, Jan.   —, McLaughlin, Ann, and William Humphreys.
1797, Aug.   22, McLaughlin, Cath., and Andrew McIntire.
1799, Nov.   13, McLaughlin, Cath., and Hugh McCully.
1799, May   18, McLaughlin, John, and Ann Pennock.
1770, June   7, McLaughlin, Mary, and Daniel Ridge.
1786, June   22, McLaughlin, William, and Margaret McWain.
1787, Oct.   10, McLean, Eliz., and William Davis.
1794, Sept. 11, McLean, Eliz., and John Smith.
1770, May   5, McLellan, Ann, and William Hollias.
1796, Oct.   19, McLeveen, Miles, and Mary Hughes.
1801, Jan.   11, McLoraine, Paul, and Margaret Hill.
1799, July   10, McMahan, Cath., and Hans Berg.
1801, Aug.   5, McMahan, Thomas, and Mary Rowley.
1798, Aug.   12, McMahon, Cath., and George Conyngham.
1744, March 24, McMahon, Hugh, and Agnas Norton.
1745, Nov.   14, McMahon, Jane, and Richard Smith.
1745, Aug.   27, McMahon, Margaret, and Valentine Barney.
1777, April   1, McManus, Ann, and Lawrence Osoghan.
1786, Oct.   25, McMasters, Thomas, and Eliz. Palmer.
1733, Jan.   20, McMekin, Robt. and Sarah Doncan.
1779, June   1, McMichael, Richard, and Eliz. Riddle.
1767, June   4, McMickle, William, and Margaret Laremore.
1785, March 29, McMinn, Samuel, and Christiana Field.
1772, Nov.   12, McMullan, Cath., and John Smith.
1766, Oct.   21, McMullan, Duncan, and Catherine Montgomery.

1755, Nov. 26, McMullen, James, and Margaret Green.
1806, Jan.   2, McMullen, Jane, and William Bowhay.
1766, Dec. 17, McMullen, Jane, and Gilbert Brown.
1785, Oct. 21, McMullen, Joseph, and Rosanna Stewart.
1805, Dec. 28, McMullin, Joseph, and Jane Pierce.
1791, Jan.   1, McMurray, Eliz., and Henry Bicker.
1782, Nov. 28, McMurtrie, Esqr., Wm., and Ann Gordon.
1769, Nov. 23, McMurtry, John, and Margaret Robinson.
1743, Jan. 21, McNamar, John, and Isabella Benbridge.
1805, April 12, McNaughtin, Archibald, and Eliz. Sunsbury.
1795, July 24, McNeal, John, and Ann Garth.
1772, Nov.   7, McNeal, Mary, and William Davis.
1762, Nov. 29, McNeal, Neal, and Elizabeth Stewart.
1792, March 25, McNeill, Patrick, and Ann Lort.
1789, Jan. 22, McNeran, Malcolm, and Mary Sims.
1772, Dec.   4, McNought, James, and Mary Boyes.
1796, Jan.   5, McPherson, Amelia Sophia, and Edward Hanlin
                 Adams.
1782, Nov. 11, McPherson, Hugh, and Eliz. Rose.
1798, Nov. 30, McPherson, John, and Mary Old.
1780, Nov.   9, McPherson, Margaret, and John Berrien.
1803, March 9, McPherson, William, and Eliz. White.
1758, April 1, McQuad, Henry, and Agnes McCadden.
1798, Dec. 26, McQueen, Donald, and Mary Armstrong.
1745, May   27, McSwain, James, and Jane Howel.
1747, Sept. 7, McSwain, Jane, and John Day.
1767, Dec. 10, McTingley, Rebeccah, and James Warden.
1748, Nov. 29, McVagh, Edmund, and Elenor Huston.
1730-1, Jan. 14, McVaugh, Mary, and Jacob Mason.
1772, Dec. 24, McVeagh, Benjamin, and Parnel Humphreville.
1786, June 22, McWain, Margaret, and William McLaughlin.
1761, Sept. 29, McWattie, Archibald, and Esther House.
1800, Oct.   2, Meade, Charlotte, and William Husler.
1800, Nov.   8, Meade, Edward, and Mary Rose.
1796, April 7, Meade, Hannah, and John Griffin.
1796, Dec. 22, Meade, Henrietta Constantia, and John Ketland.
1767, March 3, Meal, Benjamin, and Mary Moore.
1800, Feb.   6, Means, John, and Mary Bouches.
1774, Dec.   3, Means, Margaret, and Joshua North.
1806, Feb. 11, Meany, John, and Mary Dowers.
1741, Aug. 15, Meares, John, and Elizabeth Duche.
1767, June 13, Mears, Ann, and Joseph Johns.
1792, June 28, Mears, Margaret, and William Franklin.
1788, May   8, Mease, Isabella, and Jasper Moylan.
1800, July   3, Mease, James, and Sarah Butler.
1795, March 5, Mebane, Alex., and Ann Claypole.

1792, Oct.　25, Mecum, Samuel, and Cath. Bilderbach.
1784, Oct.　9, Med, Jane, and Edward Moyston.
1736, Sept.　25, Mee, Anne, and John Spafford.
1802, April　18, Mee, Eliz., and John Dove.
1800, April　17, Meek, Ann, and John Newton.
1729, Dec.　28, Meekins, Mary, and John Ashmead.
1727, Nov.　27, Meekum, Ame. Anne, and Ben. Burk.
1736, Sept.　4, Meem, John, and Jane Cooke.
1802, Dec.　25, Meggeson, Thomas H., and Alice Payne.
1806, Feb.　19, Meigs, Henry, and Julia Austin.
1757, Feb.　21, Melaring, Mary, and William Bull.
1780, June　8, Melcher, Esther, and John Vanderen.
1804, Jan.　24, Meldrum, Sarah, and Joseph Conrad.
1804, April　12, Mellen, William, and Mary McDaniel.
1796, Feb.　25, Meloy, Cath., and Peter Celoh.
1713, June　7, Melton, Jane, and John Orton.
1801, Nov.　8, Melvill, Samuel, and Hannah Moulden.
1720, June　7, Melville, Arthur, and Arabella Wyatt.
1800, Oct.　29, Mendenhall, Adam, and Amelia Broadnax.
1794, March　25, Mendenhall, Adam, and Eliza Allen.
1757, Nov.　19, Mendenhall, Philip, and Mary James.
1766, Nov.　18, Menele, Catherine, and Joseph Ornado.
1779, Aug.　1, Meng, Jacob, and Mercy Page.
1799, Jan.　15, Mercer, Ann, and James Sheilds.
1799, July　28, Mercer, George, and Ann Clay.
1758, Nov.　25, Mercer, John, and Elizabeth Miller.
1796, July　21, Mercer, Robert, and Ann Coy.
1802, Dec.　23, Mercier, Ann, and Benjamin Freeman.
1798, May　3, Mercier, Peter, and Margaret Morris.
1800, May　1, Mercier, Sophia, and Washington Perkins.
1773, June　1, Meredith, Ann, and Henry Hill, Esqr.
1757, Jan.　22, Meredith, Charles, and Mary Chappel.
1799, May　30, Meredith, Eliz., and Charles Ogden.
1804, March　5, Meredith, Eliz., and Samuel Weistram.
1765, March　18, Meredith, Elizabeth, and George Clymer.
1779, Feb.　4, Meredith, Eliz., and John Taylor.
1762, Jan.　30, Meredith, Hannah, and Harry Gordon.
1783, Oct.　23, Meredith, Hannah, and John Hood.
1713, Dec.　18, Meredith, John, and Elizabeth Williams.
1771, Sept.　25, Meredith, John, and Mary Holton.
1804, Jan.　21, Meredith, Jonathan, and Sarah Shields.
1796, June　25, Meredith, Martha, and John Read.
1788, June　5, Meredith, Mary, and Daniel Dupuy.
1796, Nov.　17, Meredith, Mary, and Thomas Hawthorne.
1796, Sept.　18, Meredith, Mary, and Edward Stiles.
1753, May　24, Meredith, Rachel, and Thomas Gregory.

1772, May   21, Meredith, Samuel, and Margaret Cadwallader.
1765, Dec.   24, Meredith, Simon, and Hannah Duff.
1742, Dec.   16, Meredith, Susannah, and John George.
1767, Feb.   13, Meredith, Thomas, and Rachel Matthew.
1749, May   1, Merk, Susannah, and Samuel Smith.
1733, Nov.   17, Merrick, John, and Hannah Holmes.
1793, April   1, Merrick, Priscilla, and Stephen Tucker.
1805, March   2, Merrick, Richard, and Cath. Green.
1801, June   25, Merriman, John, and Eliz. Herrington.
1803, Jan.   1, Merry, Ann, and Thomas Wignell.
1771, March 21, Meskell, Margaret, and Middleton Heblethaite.
1732, Nov.   16, Messer, Chas, and Elizabeth England.
1774, Oct.   27, Meston, William, and Rebecca Justice.
1731, April   29, Metcalf, Anne, and John Portlewhait.
1802, April   24, Metts, Cath., and John McCoy.
1744, Oct.   1, Metz, George, and Jane Curtis.
1762, Sept.   15, Meyer, George, and Lydia Huet.
1794, April   26, Michael, Joseph, and Rachel Vandusen.
1785, Jan.   27, Michael, Mary, and Isaac Grice.
1761, Nov.   22, Micham, Sarah, and Richard Evanson.
1720, Feb.   12, Mickle, Archibald, and Mary Wright.
1752, July   25, Mickle, John, and Hannah Cooper.
1800, May   29, Micklejohn, Mary, and Joseph Griffith.
1779, Sept.   2, Middagh, George and Esther McIntire.
1757, Sept.   8, Midelton, Isaac, and Elizabeth Lum.
1714, Sept.   19, Middleton, Catherine, and James Dayly.
1803, Aug.   26, Middleton, Eliz., and Bernard Hetherington.
1780, March 21, Middleton, Eliz., and Henry Truack.
1785, May   11, Middleton, Hannah, and John Nassau.
1758, March 21, Middleton, John, and Elizabeth Conghlin.
1773, April   10, Middleton, John, and Eliz. Anderson.
1804, Dec.   6, Middleton, John, and Hannah Cozens.
1753, Feb.   19, Middleton, Mary, and Bryan O'Harra.
1711, Aug.   4, Middleson, Elizabeth, and Mary Hawkins.
1750, Nov.   5, Midwinter, Catherine, and Matthew Keyser.
1767, Sept.   26, Midwinter, Elizabeth, and Thomas Crippin.
1766, Sept.   5, Midwinter, Sarah, and John Moreton.
1790, Nov.   29, Miercken, Cath. and Richard Potter.
1795, April   16, Miercken, Peter, and Maria Snowden.
1795, March 26, Miercken, Sarah, and John Whitesides.
1749, Sept.   28, Miers, Cornelia, and George Smith.
1795, Jan.   10, Miers, Pamelia, and John Sharpe.
1785, July   21, Mifflin, Benjamin, and Mary Robinson.
1794, Feb.   27, Mifflin, Emily, and Joseph Hopkinson.
1795, April   23, Mifflin, Frances, and Jonathan Mifflin.
1753, Jan.   25, Mifflin, George, and Anna Eyres.

1788, June 18, Mifflin, John, and Clementina Ross.
1795, April 23, Mifflin, Jonathan, and Frances Mifflin.
1800, March 21, Mifflin, Samuel, and Eliz. Davis.
1776, Oct.   8, Mifflin, Sarah, and John Beale Boardley.
1770, Sept. 27, Mifflin, Sarah, and Turbutt Francis.
1804, March 2, Miffling, George, and Eliz. Tishbourne.
1799, June 20, Miflin, Thomas, and Sarah Large.
1757, Aug.   6, Miles, Bridget, and Thomas Hazleber.
1776, March 29, Miles, Edward, and Sarah Wright.
1748, Dec. 31, Miles, Hannah, and William Ogbourn.
1794, June   4, Miles, Henry, and Joyce Anderson.
1787, Aug. 30, Miley, Mary, and John Wood.
1775, Aug.   4, Milet, Nicholas, and Hannah Tremble.
1805, Nov. 10, Miles, Richard, and Cath. Hunneker.
1726, Dec. 14, Miles, Sam., and Reb. Leech.
1745, Aug.   8, Miles, Sarah, and Meyrick Davis.
1720, Dec.   7, Miles, Sarah, and Benjamin Griffith.
1769, Dec. 24, Miles, Thomas, and Hannah Corry.
1732, June   3, Miles, Thomas, and Christian Yocham.
1756, Aug. 22, Miles, William, and Mary Hefferman.
1733, Sept. 1, Mill, Stephen, and Joanna Parker.
1795, Feb.   8, Millar, Elijah, and Cath. Groves.
1769, Oct. 21, Millar, Elizabeth, and Joseph Salsbagg.
1792, Dec. 13, Millar, John, and Sarah Andeison.
1789, Sept. 28, Millar, Rebecca, and William Dagnia.
1757, April 25, Millard, Catherine, and Peter Kirby.
1787, May   13, Millen, James, and Mary Summers.
1799, Jan. 31, Miller, Alexander J., and Margaret Stocker.
1777, Oct. 15, Miller, Alexander, and Sarah Dalhton.
1738, Feb.   2, Miller, Alexander, and Dinah Adam.
1802, Nov. 25, Miller, Alexander J., and Anna Maria Bass.
1720, Nov. 10, Miller, Amelia, and John Grothouse.
1790, Oct. 16, Miller, Ann, and Matthia Atkinson.
1801, Sept. 3, Miller, Ann, and James Burke.
1736, May   18, Miller, Barbara, and John Smith.
1779, Nov. 25, Miller, Benjamin, and Ann Knight.
1785, July 27, Miller, Cath., and William Crowley.
1802, Nov. 30, Miller, Cath., and Peter Mason.
1792, March 13, Miller, Christopher, and Cath. Clackner.
1793, Dec. 31, Miller, Elijah, and Cath. Clarke.
1761, June 20, Miller, Elizabeth, and John Anderson.
1802, Jan.   2, Miller, Eliz., and William Mackie.
1758, Nov. 25, Miller, Elizabeth, and John Mercer.
1761, Aug. 13, Miller, George, and Mary Endt.
1736, March 8, Miller, George, and Rebecca Cowley.
1755, Jan. 10, Miller, James, and Dorothy Adamson.

1767, April 25, Miller, James, and Elizabeth Chappel.
1763, Sept.   5, Miller, Jane, and Randle McKillup.
1791, Nov.   17, Miller, John, and Mary Robinson.
1789, March 5, Miller, John, and Priscilla Seyfert.
1776, Jan.   14, Miller, jun^r, John, and Mary Barker.
1791, Feb.   10, Miller, Joseph T., and Eliz. Whelen.
1756, Sept.   9, Miller, Margaret, and Thomas Alexander Sherlock.
1736, June   13, Miller, Margaret, and James Marshall.
1774, Dec.   8, Miller, Margaret, and Patrick Duffey.
1742, March 27, Miller, Mary, and Francis House.
1750, Aug.   25, Miller, Mary, and James Gibbons.
1762, Jan.   13, Miller, Mary, and Jacob Baker.
1775, Nov.   16, Miller, Mary, and Thomas Bramhall.
1799, June   2, Miller, Mary, and Henry Hittner.
1745, July   18, Miller, Patience, and Samuel Oster.
1792, Dec.   17, Miller, Rebecca, and David Cromwell.
1765, Aug.   13, Miller, Robert, and Prudence Phipps.
1755, Oct.   13, Miller, Rose, and Benjamin Bond.
1758, June   13, Miller, Ruth, and Joseph Cornwall.
1770, March 26, Miller, Ruth, and William Turner.
1730, March 31, Miller, Sarah, and James Cathcart.
1799, Feb.   24, Miller, Sarah, and John Richards.
1798, Jan.   18, Miller, Susanna, and Thomas Ferguson.
1788, April 10, Miller, Thomas, and Esther Ann Palmer.
1730, Aug.   10, Miller, William, and Sarah Quicksey.
1790, Dec.   22, Miller, William, and Juliana Turner.
1741, Aug.   29, Miller, William, and Eleanor Wright.
1786, Sept. 25, Miller, William, and Eliz. Robertson.
1740, Oct.   8, Millhouse, Mauretz, and Dorothy Myer.
1785, April 17, Milliard, Thomas, and Sarah Bowyer.
1774, April 20, Millington, Judith, and Samuel Smith.
1748, Nov.   24, Milington, Thomas, and Jane Cox.
1774, Jan.   15, Millis, John, and Sarah Adams.
1735, Oct.   6, Mills, Anne, and Henry Shokelea.
1732, Nov.   25, Mills, John, and Elizabeth Vernon.
1790, Dec.   23, Mills, Rebecca, and Zaccheus Thorne.
1802, Sept.   2, Mills, Sarah, and Patrick O'Hara.
1793, April   4, Milne, Eliz., and John Russell.
1783, Dec.   11, Milne, Mary, and John Bartholomew.
1747, Aug.   18, Milner, James, and Elizabeth Davis.
1748, June   9, Milner, Martha, and Samuel Rockwell.
1775, March 13, Milner, Robert, and Martha Long.
1805, Aug.   24, Milnor, Anna, and Joseph Klapp.
1785, Nov.   29, Milnor, Isaac, and Hannah Parrish.
1785, Dec.   22, Milnor, Rachel, and Abraham Roberts.
1765, Aug.   28, Miloy, Margaret, and Samuel Galbreath.

1716, June 18, Milton, John, and Elizabeth Marsten.
1775, July 13, Milward, George, and Eliz. Ireland.
1762, Aug. 21, Minanti, Daniel, and Mary Jewell.
1787, June 14, Mindehall, Hannah, and Abram Pistorius.
1794, Feb. 7, Mink, Cath., and Richard Pollard.
1761, July 13, Minnes, Charlotte, and Samuel Lyon.
1737, July 9, Miranda, George, and Anne Magdalen Many.
1736, July 4, Miranda, Mary, and Francis Many.
1785, Oct. 25, Mirander, Lewis Peter, and Ann Craig.
1726, Nov. 22, Mirick, Rachel, and Thomas Batt.
1720, Nov. 13, Mitchell, Ann, and John Baker.
1765, Oct. 29, Mitchel, Catherine, and Barnaby McGarvot.
1797, July 13, Mitchell, Charles, and Sarah Williams.
1794, June 1, Mitchell, Christiana, and William Whitewell.
1722, Sept. 21, Mitchell, Elizabeth, and Richard Stapler.
1750, Oct. 11, Mitchell, Elizabeth, and Robert Johnston.
1800, Jan. 9, Mitchel, Eliza, and William Montgomery.
1735, Nov. 18, Mitchell, Hester, and Thomas Bowman.
1805, Nov. 11, Mitchel, James, and Margaret Edwards.
1767, Dec. 31, Mitchell, John, and Mary Pearson.
1790, April 11, Mitchell, Joshua, and Jane Harvey.
1763, Jan. 15, Mitchel, Joshua, and Sarah Randle.
1747, Nov. 21, Mitchel, Joshua, and Rebecca Davis.
1773, April 20, Mitchell, Mary, and John Emmet.
1804, May 20, Mitchel, Mary, and Owen Roberts.
1791, Nov. 24, Mitchell, Nathaniel, and Hannah Morris.
1763, March 1, Mitchel, Richard, and Rachel Price.
1770, March 29, Mitchell, Sarah, and Jacob Reybold.
1744, Dec. 10, Mitchel, Sarah, and Robert Mannin.
1770, Aug. 22, Mitchell, Thomas, and Mary Young.
1744, July 28, Mitchel, Thomas, and Sarah Dyer.
1804, March 4, Mittan, Eliz., and Jacob Dingey.
1803, Aug. 18, Mode, Ann, and Robert Reed.
1782, Aug. 13, Mode, Eleanor, and John Vanhorn.
1744, Aug. 9, Moet, Sarah, and John Howard.
1757, Feb. 25, Moffat, James, and Febia Allen.
1746, Dec. 15, Moffet, Elizabeth, and Michael Sisk.
1776, March 7, Moftat, Ann, and Elijah Cozans.
1720, July 1, Moggrage, Mary, and Thomas Cawley.
1770, Oct. 23, Molder, Rachel, and Charles Lawrence.
1794, April 21, Molineux, James, and Sarah Shingle.
1767, June 5, Molison, Charles, and Elizabeth Craig.
1714, Nov. 1, Moll, Katherine, and Matthias Cunningham.
1721, May 16, Molley, Edward, and Olivia Brooks.
1786, Dec. 10, Mollineux, James, and Susannah Giden.
1802, Dec. 10, Molloy, Eliz., and Patrick Cason.

1794, June 25, Molong, Daniel, and Mary Smith.
1796, July 5, Molony, Terissa, and Roger Dougherty.
1727, April 20, Molshon, W^m, and Christian Cleaver.
1746, March 3, Monholone Dennis, and Abigail Lloyd.
1761, Nov. 14, Monk, Charles, and Hannah Clifton.
1765, Oct. 13, Monk, James, and Rebecca Price.
1720, June 23, Monkton, Rev. Samuel, and Mrs. Rachel Ashton.
1758, July 20, Monro, Donald, and Charlotte Chissadee.
1756, Jan. 19, Monro, Hannah, and John Coburn.
1735, March 19, Monroe, Patrick, and Abigail Cheesemond.
1771, Dec. 26, Monro, Sarah, and Thomas Roberts.
1766, Oct. 21, Montgomery, Catherine, and Duncan McMullan.
1787, May 10, Montgomery, Charlotte, and Robert Alcorn.
1789, Oct. 29, Montgomery, Eliz., and Isaac Humphreys.
1800, Oct. 23, Montgomery, George, and Rosanna McGuire.
1767, Nov. 12, Montgomery, James, and Mary Bowes.
1785, Nov. 3, Montgomery, John, and Mary Craythorne.
1767, Sept. 2, Montgomery, Jonathan, and Elizabeth Hawkins.
1803, March 26, Montgomery, Margaret, and William Latting.
1752, Nov. 29, Montgomery, Samuel, and Elizabeth Faris.
1751, March 19, Montgomery, Sarah, and Charles Garaway.
1803, Aug. 16, Montgomery, William, and Amelia Moser.
1800, Jan. 9, Montgomery, William, and Eliza Mitchell.
1795, June 11, Mood, Mary, and Dennis Dyer.
1733, Dec. 13, Moon, Elizabeth, and Richard West.
1721, Sept. 27, Moon, Simon, and Leaury Humphrey.
1759, Jan. 20, Moon, Susannah and Henry Bragg.
1722, July 31, Moor, Ann, and Thomas Leech.
1738, Sept. 4, Moor, Charles, and Mary Plunket.
1756, Jan. 21, Moore, Abel, and Hannah Hibbard.
1759, Aug. 22, Moore, Allen, and Ann Johnson.
1790, Nov. 3, Moore, Ann, and Thomas Watson.
1758, Oct. 13, Moore, Ann, and Jonathan Humphreys.
1744, June 2, Moore, Anne, and Oswald Eve.
1756, Dec. 11, Moore, Charles, and Rebecca Pratt.
1764, Nov. 10, Moore, Charles, and Martha Lawrence.
1784, July 20, Moore, Cornelius, and Sarah Hill.
1760, Oct. 9, Moore, Edward, and Patience Hayes.
1770, Aug. 30, Moore, Edward, and Margaret Partridge.
1781, Oct. 4, Moore, Eleanor, and Phillip Brown.
1758, May 11, Moore, Elizabeth, and James Dundas.
1800, Aug. 27, Moore, Eliza, and John Mullen.
1800, Feb. 6, Moore, Eliz., and Joseph Vogdes.
1804, Feb. 1, Moore, Eliza, and Richard Willing.
1772, April 17, Moore, Eliz., and Charles Goff.
1764, April 10, Moore, Esther, and William Potts.

1768, Feb.   27, Moore, Frances, and Edward Saunders.
1765, June   18, Moore, George, and Rebecca Dobbins.
1759, Aug.   23, Moore, Grace, and James Jordan.
1801, Dec.   10, Moore, Hannah, and John Dorsey.
1786, Oct.   26, Moore, James, and Ann Richards.
1787, Oct.   18, Moore, James, and Sarah Delany.
1799, Feb.   23, Moore, James, and Rebecca Izer.
1802, Aug.   28, Moore, James Hamilton, and Sarah Omensetter.
1717, March   3, Moore, Jane, and Jonathan Kemster.
1759, Dec.   1, Moore, Jane, and William Loughton.
1787, Jan.   21, Moore, Jemima, and George Johnson.
1761, Sept.   14, Moore, John, and Sarah Prefontaine.
1797, June   17, Moore, John, and Mary Scott.
1801, July   26, Moore, John, and Eliz. Ledru.
1764, Dec.   3, Moore, John, and Rebecca Henry.
1757, Dec.   14, Moore, John, and Ann O'Neal.
1761, April   8, Moore, Joseph, and Mary Richardson.
1764, Dec.   21, Moore, Joseph, and Mary Kirkpatrick.
1773, Sept.   16, Moore, Margaret, and Arthur Marshall.
1800, May   5, Moore, Margaret, and Aaron Duffey.
1760, Oct.   20, Moore, Margaret, and Thomas Smel.
1781, Feb.   20, Moore, Margaret, and Peter Andrain.
1797, Jan.   14, Moore, Martha, and Angel Elkin.
1747, Dec.   24, Moore, Martha, and Samuel Chapman.
1796, Dec.   1, Moore, Mary, and James Matthews.
1782, Dec.   19, Moore, Mary, and Joseph Burgess.
1782, Jan.   9, Moore, Mary, and John Biddle.
1760, Aug.   11, Moore, Mary, and George Hutton.
1769, May   3, Moore, Mary, and Peter Cooper.
1767, March   3, Moore, Mary, and Benjamin Meal.
1747, May   2, Moore, Mary, and James Delap.
1754, April   11, Moore, Rachel, and David Rees.
1763, Nov.   28, Moore, Ralph, and Mary Dark.
1749, Feb.   27, Moore, Richard, and Mary Hencock.
1761, Dec.   13, Moore, Robert, and Mary Dawson.
1797, May   20, Moore, Samuel, and Mary Taggart.
1740, Dec.   6, Moore, Samuel, and Abigail Eves.
1750, May   26, Moore, Sarah, and Job Cobourn.
1782, June   23, Moore, Stephen, and Jane Martin.
1782, Nov.   14, Moore, Major Tho⁵ Lloyd, and Sarah Hamper.
1797, Dec.   20, Moore, Thomas, and Frances Hanson.
1771, Sept.   24, Moore, Thomas, and Jane McDonald.
1784, Sept.   16, Moore, Thomas, and Ann Duche.
1794, Dec.   4, Moore, Thomas, and Ann Shean.
1798, Jan.   20, Moore, William, and Mary Connelly.
1758, Aug.   16, Moore, William, and Rachel Wright.

1767, March 25, Moore, William, and Elizabeth Cox.
1746, Dec.   25, Moran, Mary, and Michael Farrel.
1786, Sept.   23, More, John, and Eliz. Bowen.
1797, Sept.   5, Morel, John Peter, and Susannah Baker.
1745, Aug.   17, Moreton, Mary, and Thomas Norrington.
1763, Nov.   12, Moreton, George, and Elizabeth Morton.
1766, Sept.   5, Moreton, John, and Sarah Midwinter.
1781, Sept.   16, Morgan, Abigail, and John Thomson.
1792, May   17, Morgan, Ann, and Thomas Gibbs.
1768, Nov.   3, Morgan, Ann, and Revd Alex. Murray.
1764, May   10, Morgan, Ann, and Thomas Bond.
1741, Nov.   17, Morgan, Bathsheba, and John Gronow.
1793, June   27, Morgan, Benjamin, and Harriet Ashton.
1741, July   11, Morgan, Benjamin, and Catherine Heet or Steet.
1748, Oct.   12, Morgan, Cadwalader, and Lydia Cooper.
1729, Nov.   20, Morgan, Cath., and Thomas Cartwright.
1773, July   28, Morgan, Enock, and Susannah Bailey.
1765, June   5, Morgan, Elizabeth, and Buckridge Sims.
1735, Dec.   28, Morgan, Elizabeth, and John Ross.
1740, May   13, Morgan, Elizabeth, and Japhet Woodward.
1801, Sept.   3, Morgan, Eliz., and William Sargeant.
1709, Dec.   1, Morgan, Evan, and Margaret Potts.
1737, Jan.   8, Morgan, Evan, and Mary Hilliard.
1731, Aug.   28, Morgan, Evan, and Gwin Hopkins.
1730, Aug.   27, Morgan, George, and Susannah Davis.
1761, Sept.   10, Morgan, George, and Ann Rumney.
1734, June   2, Morgan, Hannah, and Edward Farmer.
1750, Sept.   13, Morgan, Howel, and Phoebe Hawkins.
1760, Oct.   30, Morgan, Jane, and Samuel Craig.
1765, Sept.   5, Morgan, Dr John, and Mary Hopkinson.
1803, July   21, Morgan, John, and Eliz. Jones.
1759, March 22, Morgan, Jonathan, and Bars^{la} Cheesman.
1734, Nov.   6, Morgan, Joseph, and Rachel Davis.
1722, Feb.   4, Morgan, Margaret, and John Willard.
1728, Dec.   25, Morgan, Marg^t, and James Williams.
1781, July   12, Morgan, Mary, and Rev^r Elhanon Winchester.
1763, Oct.   31, Morgan, Mary, and Arthur Burrows.
1738, Dec.   2, Morgan, Mary, and Rodger Taylor.
1756, June   2, Morgan, Mary, and George Kerr.
1742, Dec.   29, Morgan, Mary, and Thomas Oliphant.
1756, July   9, Morgan, Mary, and Atwood Cowman.
1749, Dec.   23, Morgan, Morris, and Mary House.
1791, Jan.   1, Morgan, Rachel, and Andrew Douglass.
1769, Dec.   21, Morgan, Sarah, and Joseph Johnston.
1761, April   15, Morgan, Sarah, and William Masters.
1741, July   23, Morgan, Sarah, and John Vangozel.

1730, Oct.   16, Morgan, Thomas, and Margaret Jones.
1789, July   20, Morgan, William, and Maria Cook.
1731-2, Jan.   27, Morgan, William, and Lowden Esther.
1759, Aug.   20, Morfrit, Margaret, and Daniel Carter.
1741, Oct.   7, Morgatroy'd, James, and Mary Tresse.
1779, Oct.   18, Morie, John, and Jane Donnelly.
1795, Nov.   30, Morony, Mary Ann, and James Wheelock.
1802, April   23, Morrell, John, and Cath. Lohra.
1805, Oct.   10, Morrell, Rebecca, and Eliza Heisz.
1785, Dec.   29, Morrell, Rebecca, and Jonathan Eglington.
1775, June   7, Morrell, Sarah, and James Taylor.
1728, Sept.   1, Morrice, Faith, and James Sewers.
1740, July   25, Morris, Alice, and Joseph Clark.
1785, April   28, Morris, Augustus, and Ann Henry.
1729, May   13, Morris, B., and Ann Thomas.
1877, June   18, Morris, Benjamin, and Frances Strettell.
1796, June   4, Morris, Benjamin, and Ruth Johnson.
1779, April   8, Morris, Cadwallader, and Ann Strettell.
1760, Feb.   28, Morris, Cæsar, and Hagar Groves.
1774, Oct.   20, Morris, Daniel, and Martha Lloyd.
1727, July   23, Morris, Ed., and Marg\u1d57 Phillips.
1769, Sept.   26, Morris, Elizabeth, and James Cooper.
1793, Nov.   17, Morris, Eliz., and James Harris.
1800, Oct.   8, Morris, Eliz., and William Chandler Hall.
1795, March   11, Morris, Eliz., and Richard Humpton.
1742, Sept.   16, Morris, Eliz., and John Hoy.
1795, April   10, Morris, Etty, and James Marshall.
1748, Dec.   14, Morris, Garret, and Jane Redding.
1742, Sept.   8, Morris, Grace, and Erasmus Felteas.
1791, Nov.   24, Morris, Hannah, and Nathaniel Mitchell.
1761, March   9, Morris, Hannah, and James Ralph.
1777, July   16, Morris, Jacob, and Mary Cox.
1738, Jan.   8, Morris, James, and Elizabeth Silas.
1733, Jan.   16, Morris, James, and Elizabeth Gibbs.
1750, Dec.   15, Morris, Jane, and Joseph Yeates.
1761, June   4, Morris, Jemima, and Daniel Jones.
1756, Jan.   25, Morris, John, and Anne Dicks.
1755, Jan.   27, Morris, John, and Hannah Hollington.
1786, April   20, Morris, John, and Eliz. Murray.
1795, Sept.   16, Morris, John, and Eliz. Philips.
1760, May   16, Morris, John, and Sarah Bruxton.
1743, Feb.   21, Morris, John, and Elizabeth Taylor.
1786, May   9, Morris, Luke, and Ann Willing.
1798, May   3, Morris, Margaret, and Peter Mercier.
1802, March   4, Morris, Maria, and Henry Nixon.
1762, Nov.   16, Morris, Maria, and Robert Olding.

1801, April   2, Morris, Martha, and Joseph Johnson.
1746, Feb.   2, Morris, Mary, and George Claypool.
1749, Dec.   20, Morris, Mary, and William Ranberry.
1754, May   18, Morris, Mary, and Hugh Hughes.
1744, Sept.   13, Morris, Mary, and Pyramus Green.
1744, May   6, Morriss, Mary, and Samuel Blainey.
1769, May   4, Morris, Phœbe, and Hugh Henry.
1769, March   2, Morris, Robert, and Mary White.
1796, May   5, Morris, Robert, and Ann Shoemaker.
1761, March   11, Morris, Ruth, and Jonathan Wells.
1755, Dec.   11, Morris, Samuel, and Rebecca Wistar.
1711, July   2, Morris, Sarah, and Griffith Jones.
1788, Jan.   24, Morris, Sarah, and James Gamble.
1763, March   13, Morris, Sarah, and William Stanbury.
1798, June   23, Morris, States, and Sophia Roberts.
1767, May   28, Morris, Susannah, and Robert Russell.
1742, Feb.   4, Morris, Thomas, and Mary Liddon.
1773, Oct.   18, Morris, William, and Ann Turner.
1804, Dec.   8, Morrison, Arthur, and Margaret Peterson.
1791, Jan.   23, Morrison, Hugh, and Margaret Abernethie.
1764, July   7, Morrison, John, and Elizabeth Gardner.
1757, June   23, Morrison, John, and Elizabeth Duke.
1782, May   5, Morrison, John, and Sidney Evans.
1754, Aug.   10, Morrison, Sarah, and Samuel Williams.
1715, June   6, Morrison, William, and Barbary Bringhurst.
1721, Feb.   6, Mortimer, James, and Margaret Davis.
1734, Oct.   22, Mortimore, Robert, and Anne Barnwell.
1730, April   16, Mortmore, Anne, and John Griffith.
1738, June   18, Morton, Anne, and John Torton.
1728, Jan.   1, Morton, Cath., and ——— Grantum.
1763, Nov.   12, Morton, Elizabeth, and George Moreton.
1800, June   12, Morton, Eliz., and William Tempest.
1758, June   27, Morton, George, and Christina Justice.
1785, Feb.   23, Morton, George, and Jane Cummings.
1799, June   10, Morton, Israel, and Hannah Cozier.
1802, March   18, Morton, Isaac, and Mary Vanculing.
1737, March   16, Morton, Jacob, and Margaret Vanculand.
1765, Feb.   11, Morton, John, and Martha Siver.
1786, Dec.   28, Morton, Margaret, and David Tranor.
1795, Sept.   19, Morton, Mary, and George Higgins.
1742, Oct.   16, Morton, Mary, and Joseph Elmes.
1735, Dec.   14, Morton, Susannah, and Michael Gennet or Geimet.
1801, March   29, Mosely, Mary, and John Thomson.
1746, Sept.   3, Mosely, Richard, and Anne Kilcrease.
1803, Aug.   16, Moser, Amelia, and William Montgomery.
1780, Dec.   27, Moss, Jane, and Charles Cain.

1752, Sept. 1, Moss, Hannah, and Robert Rawlinson.
1773, Jan. 24, Moss, John, and Catherine Drifts.
1739, Aug. 23, Moss, Matthew, and Hannah Tatnal.
1766, June 14, Motley, Walter, and Mary Pawling.
1776, May 23, Mouch, Margaret, and Thomas Wright.
1750, Sept. 8, Mould, Joseph, and Mary Holt.
1801, Nov. 8, Moulden, Hannah, and Samuel Melvill.
1789, Oct. 22, Moulder, Joseph, and Eliz. Marts.
1737, Nov. 16, Moulder, Robert, and Mary Grubb.
1780, Sept. 30, Moulder, Sarah, and Samuel Penrose.
1745, Aug. 3, Moulder, William, and Hannah Smallwoods.
1733, June 4, Mount, Rebecca, and Peter Salter.
1755, May 22, Mountain, Francis, and Eleanor Johnston.
1766, Nov. 29, Mourning, Elizabeth, and William Smith.
1728, Aug. 25, Mouson, Anne, and Peter Justice.
1732, Aug. 3, Mowatt, John, and Sarah Palmer.
1723, Dec. 9, Moxie, Ann, and Thomas Eastworthy.
1771, Oct. 12, Moxon, George, and Sarah Coates.
1788, May 8, Moylan, Jasper, and Isabella Mease.
1806, Feb. 6, Moylan, Maria, and Samuel Fox.
1751, Dec. 12, Moyes, John, and Anne Sheed.
1763, April 28, Moyes, John, and Ann Duche.
1744, Jan. 29, Moyes, Rebecca, and Abraham Creear.
1794, Feb. 7, Moyst, Frederick, and Mary Young.
1784, Oct. 1, Moyston, Edward, and Jane Med.
1797, Dec. 19, Much, Jeremiah, and Winnfred Lollar.
1796, Feb. 27, Mudge, Eleanor, and Jacob Wonters.
1746, July 7, Mukins, Sarah, and George Custis.
1805, May 9, Mulcahy, Andrew, and Jane Gillis.
1797, July 27, Mulhollen, Ann, and John Blaadyhough.
1750, May 16, Mulica, Catherine, and Robert McCall.
1752, Feb. 15, Mullan, Harriet, and Edward Tew.
1761, June 29, Mullan, John, and Rachel Clarkson.
1737, Aug. 5, Mullard, Anne, and William Purdue.
1735, July 22, Mullard, Mary, and Richard Parkhouse.
1770, Oct. 23, Mullemer, Ann, and Richard Long.
1736, July 17, Mullen, Ann, and Richard Swan.
1742, July 27, Mullen, Christain, and Hugh McCullick.
1800, Aug. 27, Mullen, John, and Eliza Moore.
1777, Aug. 29, Mullen, Mary, and William Campbell.
1774, May 25, Mullen, Sarah, and Richard Butter.
1739, Sept. 30, Mullin, Catherine, and Michael Casey.
1758, Oct. 21, Mullin, Thomas, and Ann Bowles.
1732, July 30, Mullins, Charles, and Anne Jones.
1734, Feb. 3, Mullins, Thomas, and Anne Roberts.
1783, June 19, Mullock, Edward, and Leah Bickerton.

1800, Nov. 13, Mulloney, Lewis, and Cath. Kain.
1805, July 6, Mumford, Mary, and John Winters.
1797, Dec. 16, Mun, John, and Susan James.
1774, May 31, Muncuar, James, and Cath. Reagan.
1785, Dec. 12, Mundy, John, and Eliz. Hill.
1796, Dec. 8, Muniat, Nicholas, and Sarah Butler.
1791, Aug. 17, Munyan, Mary, and George Ross.
1756, Aug. 2, Murdock, Mary, and George Bail.
1797, Nov. 30, Murdock, William, and Mary Repton.
1772, May 14, Murgatroyd, Mary, and Richard Rundle.
1743, Nov. 17, Murphey, Catherine, and Robt. Biddison.
1784, Sept. 9, Murphey, Jane, and William Harper.
1729, Aug. 15, Murphey, Martha, and Dan Tracy.
1742, Dec. 4, Murphey, Mary, and William Weldon.
1767, July 22, Murphin, William, and Elizabeth Brookes.
1781, March 20, Murphy, Cath., and Frederick Rankay.
1753, Sept. 24, Murphy, Elizabeth, and Thomas Brice.
1751, Aug. 13, Murphy, James, and Precilla Hervey.
1795, June 2, Murphy, Margaret, and William Glen.
1806, July 1, Murphy, Mary, and Enoch Wheaton.
1804, June 21, Murphy, Samuel, and Eleanor Lone.
1775, Nov. 19, Murphy, Susannah, and William Brooks.
1768, Nov. 3, Murray, Rev[d] Alex., and Ann Morgan.
1795, Aug. 13, Murray, Alexander, and Eliz. Cunningham.
1751, Aug. 25, Murray, Andrew, and Susannah Weaver.
1758, June 17, Murray, Ann, and Marmaduke Forster.
1786, June 1, Murray, Anthony, and Jane James.
1772, Dec. 28, Murray, Christiana, and James Johnston.
1769, June 29, Murray, Elizabeth, and Arthur Davis.
1786, April 20, Murray, Eliz., and John Morris.
1778, Oct. 25, Murray, Helen, and John Bowker.
1747, July 25, Murray, James, and Christiana Margaretta Catts.
1800, Jan. 18, Murray, James, and Sarah Willet.
1796, May 25, Murray, John, and Mary O'Keiff.
1772, April 30, Murray, John, and Eliz. Syng.
1783, Oct. 23, Murray, Margaret, and William Young.
1722, Nov. 11, Murray, Mary, and Christopher ———.
1759, Dec. 26, Murray, Peter, and Margaret Hall.
1786, June 19, Murray, Robert, and Agnes Rodney.
1773, May 11, Murray, Simon, and Jane Cash.
1789, Jan. 8, Murray, William, and Mary Ann Grace.
1783, Sept. 18, Murrell, Mary, and Thomas Patterson.
1795, July 24, Murrell, Patrick, and Eliz. Orr.
1741, Sept. 30, Murrey, John, and Catherine Brooks.
1737, Feb. 17, Murry, Sebastian, and Sarah Parsons.
1770, Jan. 11, Musgrove, Ann, and Charles Ferguson.

1780, March   2, Musgrove, Deborah, and Abraham Shoemaker.
1782, May   30, Musgrove, Rachel, and Samuel Lewis Wharton.
1728, May   17, Musgrove, W^m, and Mary Mussey.
1728, May   17, Mussey, Mary, and Wm Musgrove.
1740, Oct.   8, Myer, Dorothy, and Mauretz Millhouse.
1761, July   29, Myers, Catherine, and John Farr.
1787, Nov.   14, Myers, Catherine, and Benjamin Stagg.
1801, Nov.   16, Myers, Eliz., and Thomas Clark.
1781, Dec.   20, Myers, Eliz., and Isaac Crawford.
1758, Feb.   3, Myers, Hannah, and Jacob Rush.
1772, Oct.   20, Myers, Henry, and Sarah Spencer.
1759, Jan.   24, Myers, Margaret, and James Todd.
1800, May   3, Myers, Mary, and Thomas Hale.
1795, Jan.   19, Myers, Mary, and John Termaine.
1804, Oct.   6, Myers, Mary, and John Manchester.
1798, June   16, Myland, James, and Mary Turner.
1714, June   23, Myles, Prudence, and Samuel Exell.
1800, March   13, Naff, William, and Mary Field.
1781, Sept.   6, Naglee, Charles, and Sarah Casdrop.
1802, Dec.   11, Naglee, Eliz. and George Wakeimer.
1765, Sept.   11, Naglee, Henry, and Margaret Croyston.
1775, Nov.   25, Naglee, Mary, and William Stockton.
1753, Nov.   29, Naglee, Mary, and James Taylor.
1772, Nov.   4, Naglee, Thomas, and Hannah Belenger.
1782, Oct.   29, Naglee, William, and Mary Vanschiver.
1758, Oct.   5, Nailer, Margaret, and Henry Stilfield.
1794, Oct.   2, Nailer, Mary, and John Daniel.
1759, July   12, Nailor, Mary, and Thomas Powell.
1796, Oct.   16, Napier, Alexander, and Ann Kingston.
1755, Dec.   25, Narval, Elizabeth, and John Bennet.
1755, Nov.   8, Nash, Mary, and Benjamin Wells.
1796, Aug.   18, Nash, Page, and Margaret Richardson.
1795, May   31, Nash, Rachel, and John Lawson.
1805, Oct.   30, Nash, Samuel, and Hannah Steel.
1792, April   19, Nash, William, and Rachel Buchanan.
1784, April   9, Nash, William, and Mary Giffard.
1796, Dec.   3, Nason, Richard, and Cath. Lockery.
1796, July   25, Nassau, Charles, and Cath. Armbruster.
1785, May   11, Nassau, John, and Hannah Middleton.
1768, May   27, Nathan, Abraham, and Rachel Wilson.
1781, March   1, Naus, Matthew, and Charlotte Nichola.
1755, Feb.   19, Naylor, Elizabeth, and Edward Collins.
1761, May   6, Naylor, Lane, and Ann Vaughan.
1725, Oct.   6, Naylor, Rich^d, and Mary Hackney.
1771, June   11, Nagle, Joseph, and Alice Frederick.
1796, Sept.   27, Neal, George, and Hannah Plumstead.

1771, June   9, Neal, James, and Eliz. Newel.
1758, Dec.   5, Neal, John, and Eleanor Arundel.
1804, July   21, Neal, Samuel, and Mary Hartley.
1772, Oct.   12, Neal, Thomas, and Ann O'Kell.
1757, Aug.   11, Neale, Martha, and John Ferguson.
1736, Dec.   30, Neale, Thomas, and Isabella Kirk.
1732, May   25, Neale, Tobias, and Alice Dixon.
1763, Jan.   26, Neason, Eleanor, and Edward Holwell.
1769, Sept.   25, Neave, Patrick, and Mary Lovegrove.
1740, Feb.   25, Needham, Richard, and Elizabeth Smallwood.
1784, Nov.   25, Needless, William, and Eliz. Allen.
1762, July   10, Neeld, Elizabeth, and Samuel Jessup.
1766, March 19, Neff, Thomas, and Sarah Freeman.
1784, May   21, Nefford, Mary, and Jacob Balabriga.
1784, Oct.   20, Neighbour, Eliz., and James Marshall.
1755, Nov.   1, Neil, Elinor, and John Lyons.
1764, Sept.   1, Neil, Elizabeth, and Michael Owner.
1801, April   9, Neill, Lewis, and Ann Bickham.
1772, Feb.   17, Neill, Sarah, and Robert Wilson.
1774, Nov.   5, Neils, James, and Sarah Sides.
1747, Feb.   6, Neisman, Rev[d] Gabriel, and Margaretta Rambo.
1765, April   10, Neiss, Catherina, and John Proudfoot.
1772, Aug.   15. Neithermark, Sarah, and John Garwood.
1740, May   21, Nelly, James, and Jane Grimes.
1731, Oct.   14, Nelson, Alice, and John Carter.
1775, Dec.   5, Nelson, Andrew, and Mary McGinnis.
1765, Oct.   29, Nelson, Anna, and Henry Bernhold.
1769, May   2, Nelson, Cath., and James Thomson.
1774, Feb.   2, Nelson, Dorothy, and William Lee.
1756, Nov.   7, Nelson, Eleanor, and Charles Craft.
1802, May   10, Nelson, Jane, and Ebenezer Rogers.
1795, Aug.   13, Nelson, John, and Ann Garrett.
1800, July   6, Nelson, Martha, and James Cockrin.
1787, Jan.   2, Nelson, Martha, and Alexander Dow.
1775, April   20, Nelson, Mary, and Patrick Griffin.
1795, Jan.   11, Nelson, Robert, and Sarah Taylor.
1740, Jan.   27, Nelson, Susannah, and Richard Carvin.
1801, July   10, Nesbett, Sarah, and Edward Compton.
1794, June   1, Nester, Ann, and Peter Daugart.
1800, Aug.   2, Neves, Sarah, and John Davis.
1748, Sept.   5, Nevil, Thomas, and Mary Davis.
1765, Nov.   9, Nevill, James, and Hannah Keen.
1730, Sept.   1, Neville, William, and Marjory Liddon.
1766, Nov.   4, Nevin, Hugh, and Sarah Todd.
1736, Feb.   26, Newberry, Elizabeth, and Joseph Yeates.
1805, May   11, Newbold, Rachel, and Oliver St. John.

1709, July   23, Newberry, John, and Rebecca Jacobs.
1751, Dec.   26, Newel, Dorothy, and Evan Powel.
1771, June   9, Newel, Eliz., and James Neal.
1732, Dec.   21, Newell, George, and Mary Kelley.
1737, Dec.   17, Newlin, Jane, and James Hill.
1804, Dec.   18, Newlin, John, and Lydia Pollard.
1794, Sept.   28, Newlin, Peter, and Deborah Foster.
1794, Nov.   15, Newloold, William, and Mary Smith.
1775, Nov.   28, Newman, Charles, and Ann Robeson.
1747, May   7, Newman, Ester and Thomas White.
1721, Nov.   12, Newman, James, and Ann Collins.
1803, Oct.   6, Newman, Joseph, and Jane Roswell.
1780, March 16, Newman, Joseph, and Deborah Knight.
1799, March 26, Newman, Rebecca, and Charles Lang.
1795, Dec.   24, Newman, Thomas, and Margaret Affleck.
1774, May   17, Newman, William, and Margaret King.
1757, April   15, Newport, Sarah, and John Short.
1738, May   16, Newton, Henry, and Lettice Newtown.
1798, Nov.   14, Newton, James, and Jane Karnan.
1799, June   22, Newton, James, and Martha Wallace.
1800, April   17, Newton, John, and Ann Meek.
1748, Nov.   27, Newton, Richard, and Rebecca Brightwel.
1738, May   16, Newtown, Lettice, and Henry Newton.
1746, Nov.   23, Nice, Anthony, and Mary Packer.
1767, Feb.   16, Nice, Susannah, and William Turner.
1781, March   1, Nichola, Charlotte, and Matthew Naus.
1806, July   17, Nicholas, Jeremiah, and Rosanna Norris.
1741, Oct.   6, Nicholls, George, and Mary Carpenter.
1701, Jan.   18, Nicholls, Thomas, and Mary Culnan.
1734, Sept.   5, Nicholls, William, and Mary Pearom.
1762, Aug.   10, Nichols, Pleasant, and William Vesey.
1799, Dec.   8, Nichols, Sarah, and Peter Hagner.
1772, Sept.   3, Nichols, William, and Brightwed Stout.
1794, Nov.   9, Nicholson, Ann, and Resin Rawlins.
1760, July   22, Nicholson, Edward, and Sarah Vokins.
1767, Feb.   26, Nicholson, Elizabeth, and Benjamin Gibbs.
1751, Nov.   5, Nicholson, George, and Elizabeth Bell.
1790, Sept.   5, Nicholson, Jeremiah, and Mary Gibbs.
1786, July   22, Nicholson, John, and Mary Hunt.
1771, Aug.   26, Nicholson, Mary, and Patrick Lyons.
1792, Nov.   4, Nicholson, Mary, and David Riddle.
1755, May   8, Nicholson, Nicholas, and Anne Hammond.
1778, Aug.   23, Nicholson, Rebecca, and James Chaton.
1755, Oct.   27, Nicholson, William, and Margaret Connely.
1756, April   29, Nicholson, William, and Grace Gaae.
1742, Jan.   10, Nicholson, William, and Mary Williams.

1793, April   1, Nicklin, Philip, and Juliana Chew.
1796, Dec.   22, Nicola, Sarah, and Jacob Webb.
1785, May   26, Nicolin, Philip, and Deborah Donaldson.
1775, March   14, Nielson, Margaret, and Francis Gilbert.
1745, Nov.   14, Nigely, John, and Elizabeth Boude.
1743, July   30, Night, Mary, and John Wilson.
1805, Sept.   10, Nightingale, Thomas, and Janet Stewart.
1801, Oct.   3, Nightingale, Thomas, and Hannah Cottman.
1797, June   17, Niglee, Susan, and John McDougal.
1799, Dec.   29, Nixon, Eliz., and Erick Bollman.
1797, April   22, Nixon, George Washington, and Eliz. Stewart.
1802, March   4, Nixon, Henry, and Maria Morris.
1795, July   30, Nixon, Jane, and Thomas Mayne Willing.
1747, Jan.   24, Nixon, Mary, and John Sutton.
1793, Jan.   10, Nixon, Mary, and Francis West.
1728, Jan.   7, Nixon, Richard, and Sarah Bowles.
1793, July   17, Nixon, Sarah, and William Cramond.
1774, June   7, Nixon, William, and Ann James.
1766, Oct.   30, Noarth, Hannah, and Isaac Lessene.
1737, Nov.   26, Noble, Anthony, and Flower Walker.
1772, Dec.   4, Noble, David, and Anna Powell.
1752, June   16, Noblett, William, and Rebecca Cuthbert.
1801, April   2, Noblit, Dell, and Eliz. Wiall.
1795, Dec.   3, Nonamaker, Jacob, and Catharine Elfrey.
1764, April   9, Norberry, Hannah, and Charles Roberts.
1765, May   20, Norberry, Rebecca, and James Rice.
1715, July   27, Normandie, John Abraham, and Elizabeth Gan-
                   doret.
1745, Aug.   17, Norrington, Thomas, and Mary Moreton.
1805, Jan.   26, Norris, Isaac W., and Mary Vansise.
1796, May   31, Norris, Johanna, and Francis Edmonston.
1802, May   5, Norris, John, and Jane Lear.
1757, May   30, Norris, John, and Mary Wood.
1766, Aug.   7, Norris, Joseph, and Hannah Wood.
1711, Dec.   14, Norris, Mary, and David Walker.
1743, Nov.   17, Norris, Rebecca, and William Rice.
1787, May   11, Norris, Rebecca, and Seth Talbot.
1806, July   17, Norris, Rosanna, and Jeremiah Nicholas.
1801, Oct.   6, Norris, Robert, and Hannah Garrigues.
1795, April   26, Norris, Thomas, and Susannah Dixon.
1788, June   26, Norris, Thomas, and Sarah Martin.
1746, Nov.   17, Norris, Thomas, and Catherine Steward.
1749, Nov.   30, North, Elizabeth, and George Plymm.
1745, April   24, North, Eliz., and Dan Benezet.
1768, Feb.   17, North, Hannah, and John Matthews.
1785, June   2, North, John, and Margaret Price.

1805, May   21, North, John, and Mary Tallman.
1768, Jan.   9, North, John, and Elizabeth Hughes.
1774, Dec.   3, North, Joshua, and Margaret Means.
1794, May   26, North, Mary, and Henry Bulger.
1784, May   8, North, Rebecca, and Benjamin Thornton.
1765, Aug.   24, Northington, Rachel, and John Rice.
1731, Sept.   6, Northon, Elizabeth, and Thomas Griffith.
1720, Sept.   16, Northorp, Elizabeth, and William Britton.
1744, March 24, Norton, Agnas, and Hugh McMahon.
1792, April   14, Norton, Courtney, and Warner Lewis.
1794, Aug.   7, Norton, Eliza, and George Archer Chapman.
1767, Oct.   20, Norton, Esther, and Richard Comron.
1796, Oct.   29, Norton, Joseph, and Eliz. Ford.
1783, Nov.   27, Norton, Sarah, and John Knowles.
1730, June   22, Norway, Margaret, and Peter Patridge.
1723, Jan.   6, Norwood, Anthony, and Elizabeth Stewart.
1749, March 26, Norwood, Elizabeth, and William Arrell.
1750, Nov.   3, Norwood, Elizabeth, and Thomas Fitchat.
1717, May   20, Nowell, Sarah, and Thomas Cook.
1765, Aug.   15, Nowland, Elizabeth, and Jonathan Rose.
1761, May   27, Nowland, Martha, and Lawrence Ash.
1756, May   31, Nox, Andrew, and Martha Dickin.
1771, June   18, Nuss, Anthony, and Eliz. Maine.
1746, July   23, Nut, Abraham, and Elizabeth Sanderson.
1733, May   17, Nutt, Samuel, and Rebecca Savage.
1762, Aug.   13, Nuttle, Margaret, and Nathaniel Hutton.
1785, Jan.   31, Oakes, Samuel, and Hester Pearce.
1787, July   29, Oar, John, and Eliz. Jones.
1805, Nov.   3, Oart, Eliz., and Edward Wills Carr.
1713, Jan.   25, Oarum, Ann, and Nicolas Kaseaugius.
1756, Dec.   9, O'Brian, Catherine, and John Grogan.
1794, March 23, O'Brian, Timothy, and Mercy Pemberton.
1788, March 3, O'Brien, Cath., and John Herbert.
1799, March 31, O'Brien, John, and Ann Simpson.
1791, Feb.   15, O'Brien, William, and Jane Bell.
1713, Dec.   1, O'Bryan, Honor, and Nicholas Cron.
1721, Nov.   3, Oburn, William, and Ann Walter.
1800, Nov.   19, O'Donald, Constantine, and Mary Sanclair Wallace.
1763, Oct.   12, O'Donald, Jane, and Francis Ramsey.
1748, Dec.   31, Ogbourn, William, and Hannah Miles.
1747, Aug.   11, Ogden, Anne, and Robert Stone.
1799, May   30, Ogden, Charles, and Eliz. Meredith.
1797, March 16, Ogden, George, and Deborah Scull.
1795, April   10, Ogden, Hannah, and William Duer.
1799, Dec.   19, Ogden, Mary, and Anthony Cuthbert.
1790, June   9, Ogilby, Rebecca, and George Kemp.

1766, April 10, Ogilby, William, and Sarah Davis.
1776, Aug.   5, Oglesby, George, and Eliz. Bethel.
1803, Dec. 31, O'Hagan, Rachel, and Abraham Hooper.
1798, March 19, O'Harra, Ann, and Edward McClasky.
1753, Feb. 19, O'Harra, Bryan, and Mary Middleton.
1802, Sept. 2, O'Harra, Patrick, and Sarah Mills.
1796, May 25, O'Keiff, Mary, and John Murray.
1772, Oct. 12, O'Kell, Ann, and Thomas Neal.
1742, Dec.   2, O'Kill, George, and Ann Clarke.
1775, Oct. 12, O'Kill, Jane, and Rev. John Stewart.
1798, Nov. 30, Old, Mary, and John McPherson.
1795, Feb.   4, Oldfield, Benjamin, and Susannah Lybrand.
1761, Aug. 18, Oldfield, Hannah, and John Williamson.
1802, July   8, Oldfield, Hannah, and Samuel Evans.
1781, April 18, Oldfield, Sarah, and Jesse White.
1762, Nov. 16, Olding, Robert, and Maria Morris.
1742, Dec. 29, Oliphant, Thomas, and Mary Morgan.
1730, June 29, Oliver, Elizabeth, and Henry Longhust.
1766, Oct. 23, Oliver, Elizabeth, and Thomas Candle.
1797, Feb. 19, Oliver, Jane, and John Abbot.
1741, Nov. 12, Oliver, John, and Susannah Crossby.
1769, Nov. 15, Oliver, John, and Catherine Dunn.
1786, Nov. 27, Oliver, Robert, and Eliz. Craig.
1805, Nov.   9, Oliver, William, and Hannah Step.
1767, Dec. 24, Olson, Thomas, and Mary Wood.
1802, Aug. 28, Omensetter, Sarah, and James Hamilton Moore.
1762, Sept. 14, Ommensetter, Jacob, and Elizabeth Beyer.
1757, Dec. 14, O'Neal, Ann, and John Moore.
1732, April 14, O'Neal, Bryan, and Margaret Jones.
1729, July 27, O'Neal, Cath., and John Ward.
1757, Dec. 14, O'Neal, Elizabeth, and William Ashby.
1796, Nov. 21, O'Neal, John, and Cath. Woodward.
1795, March 15, O'Neal, John F., and Charlotte Freeman.
1754, June 10, O'Neal, Margaret, and Walter Smith.
1744, Dec. 23, O'Neal, Margaret, and Robert Davis.
1757, Jan.   5, O'Neal, Milicent, and John Fry.
1796, June 25, O'Neil, Cath., and James P. Nablow.
1801, Dec.   9, O'Neil, Clotworthy, and Sarah Gillan.
1801, March 19, O'Neil, Margaret, and John Loscombe.
1797, July 29, Oner, Margaret, and William Thorn.
1775, Jan.   1, Openshire, William, and Ann Spier.
1731, Oct. 21, Oram, Elizabeth, and John Jones.
1744, June 23, Ord, John, and Anne Mason.
1775, June   1, Ord, Martha, and William Webb.
1779, Oct. 27, Ore, Reuben, and Eliz. Satchwell.
1767, Dec. 11, Orin, Elizabeth, and John Room.

1770, May   31, Ormes, Jane, and William Keith.
1794, Sept.   27, Ormrod, John, and Sarah Johnson.
1766, Nov.   18, Ornado, Joseph, and Catherine Menele.
1795, July   24, Orr, Eliz., and Patrick Murrell.
1798, April   16, Orr, Isabella, and William Whitby.
1796, Oct.   28, Orr, Mary, and William Clark.
1731, Aug.   9, Orson, Mary, and Joseph Powel.
1713, June   7, Orton, John, and Jane Melton.
1775, May   4, Osboone, Cath., and John Jameson.
1792, March 1, Osborn, Ann, and John Taylor.
1764, Dec.   28, Osborn, Bridget, and John Howard.
1715, Aug.   26, Osborn, Elizabeth, and Thomas Fisher.
1734, Sept.   3, Osborn, James, and Mary Guy.
1759, Dec.   25, Osborn, John, and Margaret Hannon.
1729, April   23, Osborn, Mary, and Pat Gardner.
1759, July   24, Osborne, Mary, and Lyman Hall.
1753, March 16, Osborn, Nicholas, and Margaret Conrad.
1747, June   9, Osborn, Susannah, and Richard Bigger.
1797, Nov.   28, Osborne, Isabella, and John Marie Bordes.
1777, Jan.   29, Osborne, Jane Frances, and Charles Christian
                         Cholones.
1799, Dec.   26, Osborne, Lydia, and Christopher Brum.
1756, Feb.   7, Osborne, Sarah, and Ellis Price.
1737, Nov.   25, Osbourn, Mary, and Robert Tuite.
1722, Oct.   7, Osburn, Amable, and Benjamin Taylor.
1735, Dec.   5, Osburn, George Lucas, and Jane Renaudet.
1761, June   25, Osburn, Jonas, and Elizabeth Durmore.
1744, Aug.   16, Osburn, Jonas, and Ann Hyat.
1761, Aug.   3, Osburn, Mary, and Tanerner Hamilton.
1722, Jan.   7, Osburn, Robert, and Mary Green.
1738, July   13, Oslear, Elizabeth, and Simon Schraik.
1740, Jan.   17, Osler, Mary, and Richard Kees.
1805, Dec.   12, Osman, Esther H., and Lewis Gordon.
1796, June   14, Osman, Mary, and John Skelton.
1745, July   18, Oster, Samuel, and Patience Miller.
1757, Sept.   12, Oswald, Elizabeth, and Benjamin Chew.
1792, April   26, Oswald, Eliz., and George Balfour.
1784, March 21, Oswald, Margaret, and Frederick Smyth, Esqr.
1775, May   22, Otis, James, and Charity Swailes.
1806, April   23, Ott, Charlotte, and Vincent Guarin.
1802, Jan.   7, Ottinger, Harriet, and Frederick Shinkle.
1801, July   30, Ottinger, Maria Matilda, and William King.
1785, May   19, Otto, Cath., and Henry Land.
1802, Dec.   18, Otto, John C., and Eliz. Tod.
1797, April   15, Outen, Mathew, and Christiana Grover.
1764, Oct.   31, Overend, Martha, and Charles Kelly.

1764, Jan.   4, Overend, Thomas, and Martha Powel.
1720, Oct.   9, Overthrow, William, and Martha Cook.
1794, June   5, Overturf, Sarah, and James Able.
1798, Aug.   2, Overturff, Margaret, and Aaron Albertson.
1796, Nov.   9, Overturff, Mary, and Jacob Ware.
1799, May   30, Overy, John, and Sarah Roberts.
1743, June   9, Ovington, Margaret, and David Karnes.
1776, Jan.   19, Owen, Ann, and Richard Clark.
1727, Oct.   1, Owen, Elizabeth, and Andrew Smith.
1762, Sept.   14, Owen, Elizabeth, and Joseph Crispin.
1760, Nov.   29, Owen, Elizabeth, and Griffith Jones.
1716, Nov.   26, Owen, Elizabeth, and John Price.
1774, March   22, Owen, Elizabeth, and Moses Lewis.
1743, Feb.   28, Owen, Esther, and William Davis.
1751, May   4, Owen, George, and Rebecca Hains.
1722, Oct.   24, Owen, Owen, and Katherine Lewis.
1744, Feb.   6, Owen, Priscilla, and William Cunningham.
1720, Sept.   13, Owen, Richard, and Elizabeth Canour.
1800, Jan.   4, Owens, Julia, and William Tilton.
1790, June   2, Owner, James, and Sarah Faulkner.
1730, Oct.   29, Owner, James, and Margaret Pope.
1764, Sept.   1, Owner, Michael, and Elizabeth Neil.
1721, Sept.   24, Oxford, Jane, and Humphrey Day.
1805, Nov.   9, Ozeas, Mary, and Philip Dick.
1771, April   27, Ozier, Eliz., and Richard Thompson.
1766, Jan.   8, Ozier, Sarah, and James Sparks.
1777, Feb.   28, Paca, Honble William, Esqr., and Ann Harrison.
1769, Nov.   25, Pacalock, Hannah, and Isaac Baker.
1790, Nov.   3, Pack, John, and Margaret Urt.
1776, April   18, Packard, John, and Mary Barnes.
1746, Nov.   23, Packer, Mary, and Anthony Nice.
1793, May   9, Page, Ann, and James Pryor.
1732, Aug.   9, Page, Frances, and Peter Lenny.
1709, July   31, Page, George, and Mary Bears.
1770, June   1, Page, Joseph, and Frances Chaterton.
1779, Aug.   1, Page, Mercy, and Jacob Meng.
1795, Jan.   8, Page, Sarah, and Thomas Flowers.
1768, Sept.   16, Page, William, and Elizabeth Custard.
1730, Sept.   16, Pain, Allice, and Richard Brown.
1749, April   2, Pain, Hannah, and Ralph Walker.
1736, May   25, Pain, Mary, and John Harper.
1722, Nov.   17, Pain, Mary, and James Hughs.
1766, Sept.   27, Paine, Mary, and Anthony Martin.
1767, Feb.   19, Paine, Mary, and John Chrystie.
1782, Nov.   24, Paine, William, and Mary Wadman.
1728, March   30, Painter, W^m, and Elizabeth Whitehead.

1792, April 28, Palaske, Charles Godfrey, and Hannah Emslie.
1795, May 12, Palethorpe, Robert, and Sarah Harrison.
1790, June 3, Palmer, Aaron, and Sarah Wilton.
1748, Aug. 13, Palmer, Anthony, and Catherine Carter.
1749, Oct. 21, Palmer, Elizabeth, and Alexander Alaire.
1746, May 20, Palmer, Elizabeth, and Nathaniel Evanson.
1798, Aug. 9, Palmer, Eliz., and John Shaw.
1759, March 15, Palmer, Elizabeth, and Samuel Fennimore.
1785, Dec. 11, Palmer, Eliz., and Thomas Schockuly.
1786, Oct. 25, Palmer, Eliz., and Thomas McMasters.
1788, April 10, Palmer, Esther Ann, and Thomas Miller.
1779, Jan. 18, Palmer, Frances, and George Wilson.
1727, Nov. 30, Palmer, Frances, and Ed. Lambert.
1737, Feb. 17, Palmer, Jane, and Thomas Berkley.
1722, Feb. 5, Palmer, Jane, and William Reach.
1743, May 7, Palmer, John, and Deborah Bankson.
1774, Feb. 17, Palmer, John, and Eliz. Sly.
1730, Dec. 7, Palmer, Mary, and Richard Brickhill.
1794, Sept. 18, Palmer, Mary, and Philip Dick.
1797, Nov. 23, Palmer, Mary, and Samuel Oxford.
1789, April 22, Palmer, Phœbe, and Lawrence Dickinson.
1795, March 12, Palmer, Richard, and Eliz. Parker.
1732, Aug. 3, Palmer, Sarah, and John Mowatt.
1737, Aug. 9, Palmer, Thomas, and Mary Sadiescus.
1803, Dec. 22, Palmer, Thomas, and Sarah Campbell.
1798, Jan. 18, Palmer, William, and Eliz. Peck.
1757, Oct. 29, Palmer, William, and Susannah Wiley.
1796, April 24, Pancake, Cath., and John Burke.
1739, Aug. 16, Pancast, Phœbe, and Richard Ridgway.
1763, Jan. 4, Pander, George, and Mary Steel.
1760, April 23, Pannel, Jane, and Thomas Stroud.
1721, July 19, Papen, Catherine, and Benjamin Howell.
1760, Oct. 11, Papynd, Elizabeth, and Philip Travers.
1754, Nov. 20, Par, Mary, and Thomas Willard.
1721, July 15, Parent, Debora, and Henry Vanhook.
1728, Dec. 19, Parham, Sus^h, and Richd Hordidge.
1730, Dec. 12, Parke, Elizabeth, and Robert Hazlet.
1774, Sept. 27, Parke, John, and Jane Covinger.
1729, Jan. 22, Parker, Ann, and John Louvin.
1797, Aug. 12, Parker, Cath., and William Young.
1789, Dec. 12, Parker, Cath., and John Pike.
1801, Nov. 2, Parker, Christiana, and Anthony Leamer.
1742, Nov. 20, Parker, Elizabeth, and Joseph Redman.
1795, March 12, Parker, Eliz., and Richard Palmer.
1784, May 9, Parker, George, and Tacey Grant.
1799, Feb. 19, Parker, Hannah, and Christopher Sink.

1757, Dec. 14, Parker, Hannah, and Jonathan Cox.
1739, April 14, Parker, Hesther, and Philips Hulbeart.
1799, Jan. 14, Parker, James, and Margaret Stewart.
1803, Jan. 5, Parker, James, and Penelope Butler.
1733, Sept. 1, Parker, Joanna, and Stephen Mill.
1769, Dec. 24, Parker, John, and Mary Lush.
1759, March 7, Parker, Mary, and Isaac Snowden.
1803, May 13, Parker, Mary, and Alpheus Freeman.
1747, Dec. 24, Parker, Mary, and Thomas Cary.
1731, April 23, Parker, Mary, and John Bennett.
1794, July 17, Parker, Mary, and John Doyle.
1767, Dec. 14, Parker, Peter, and Elizabeth Price.
1800, July 21, Parker, Rachel, and Joshua Eldridge.
1736, March 28, Parker, Rebecca, and Budd Robinson.
1796, Sept. 11, Parkeson, Eliz., and Joseph Tervis.
1756, Oct. 13, Parkhouse, Mary, and George Claypole.
1735, July 22, Parkhouse, Richard, and Mary Mullard.
1728, Nov. 3, Parkins, Eliz., and James Clark.
1772, Sept. 24, Parkison, Martin, and Eliz. Henderson.
1771, June 20, Parks, Eliz. Isabella, and James Davis, jun.
1749, Sept. 23, Parks, Foster, and Mary Davis.
1745, March 3, Parmale, Charles, and Eliz. Ennis.
1783, Aug. 28, Parr, Cath., and Jeremiah Crone.
1732, Oct. 15, Parram, John, and Hannah Gheseling.
1738, Oct. 8, Parrham, Mary, and Adam Cross.
1785, Nov. 29, Parrish Hannah, and Isaac Milnor.
1779, March 9, Parrish, Mary, and Thomas Coates.
1751, June 10, Parry, Catherine, and Edward Duffield.
1735, Sept. 27, Parry, David, and Elizabeth Davies.
1724, July 24, Parry, David, and Mary Humphreys.
1790, Aug. 12, Parry, Hannah, and John Spear.
1729, Feb. 17, Parry, Margt., and Evan Jones.
1761, July 23, Parry, Martha, and Richard Pearne.
1754, June 5, Parsons, Alice, and William Sayer.
1728, July 24, Parsons, Cath., and Timothy Tyns.
1749, Oct. 11, Parsons, Hannah, and James Worrel.
1728, Jan. 28, Parsons, James, and Mary Walker.
1710, Feb. 11, Parsons, Jane, and Richard White.
1734, June 25, Parsons, Joanna, and George Shaw.
1748, July 8, Parsons, John, and Susannah Adamson.
1728, Feb. 24, Parson, Mary, and John Perry.
1749, Oct. 24, Parsons, Richard, and Alice Hall.
1737, Feb. 17, Parsons, Sarah, and Sebastian Murry.
1777, May 11, Parsons, Sarah, and Thomas Freeman.
1785, Dec. 6, Parsons, William, and Eliz. Redman.
1770, Aug. 30, Partridge, Margaret, and Edward Moore.

1711, May   31, Parver, Deborah, and John Harper.
1723, Dec.   15, Parvera, Hannah, and Henry Frederick.
1768, April 14, Paschal, Benjamin, and Ann Rudolph.
1751, April   6, Paschal, Hannah, and John Stow.
1768, March 10, Paschal, Hannah, and Levi Hollingsworth.
1767, June   11, Paschal, Margaret, and John Hughes, jr.
1801, March 12, Paschalis, Felix, and Eliz. McClintock.
1795, Aug.   2, Paschall, Eliz., and Justice Coxe.
1771, July   27, Pashall, jun., John, and Rachel Smith.
1739, Dec.   25, Pashe, Maria Barbara, and Richard Cordell.
1757, Oct.   7, Paterson, Sarah, and Joseph Shute.
1730, June   22, Patridge, Peter, and Margaret Norway.
1773, July   28, Patterson, Isabella, and Patrick Hayes.
1746, June   18, Patterson, Jane, and John Hall.
1782, Nov.   8, Patterson, John, and Abigail Raton.
1797, May   22, Patterson, Maria, and Robert Eaglesfield Griffith.
1749, May   30, Patterson, Rachel, and Michael McClean.
1742, Sept. 24, Patterson, Sarah, and Benjamin Chambers.
1783, Sept. 18, Patterson, Thomas, and Mary Murrell.
1768, March   3, Patterson, Thomas, and Mary Brockden.
1728, May   16, Patterson W^m, and Mary Garretson.
1784, Feb.   19, Patton, John, and Ann Doughty.
1795, Aug.   29, Patton, Robert, and Eliz. Peale.
1790, March 11, Patton, Robert, and Cornelia Bridges.
1755, April 29, Patton, Robert, and Catherine Walker.
1781, Dec.   18, Paul, Eliz., and Nathaniel Ranter.
1793, April 11, Paul, Hannah, and John Watson.
1758, Aug.   24, Paul, Jonathan, and Sarah Young.
1758, Feb.   4, Paul, John, and Mary Paul.
1785, May   31, Paul, Joseph, and Mary Castle.
1781, July   16, Paul, Mary, and Samuel Hodgson.
1758, Feb.   4, Paul, Mary, and John Paul.
1790, Feb.   11, Paul, Phœbe, and Jacob Setts.
1802, March 31, Paul, Sarah, and Elisha Smith.
1762, April 15, Paul, Susannah, and David Brown.
1765, June   11, Paulhill, James, and Margaret Geraud.
1783, Sept. 29, Pawling, Joseph, and Susannah Lukens.
1766, June   14, Pawling, Mary, and Walter Motley.
1781, Dec.   18, Payade, Peter Henry, and Ann Smith.
1802, Dec.   25, Payne, Alice, and Thomas H. Meggeson.
1797, Nov.   24, Payne, Barnard, and Ann Peacock.
1803, Sept. 16, Payne, John, and Mary Reed.
1721, July   26, Paynter, John, and Mary Atkinson.
1736, Dec.   30, Paxton, Alexander, and Elizabeth Hopkinson.
1734, June   15, Paxton, Elizabeth, and Edward Jones.
1741, Oct.   13, Paxton, Henry, and Martha Shinn.

1729, July   12, Paxton, Reb., and Anthony Maccluire.
1726, Dec.   1, Paxton, Sarah, and Benjamin Berrie.
1754, Aug.   31, Peace, Joanna, and John Austin.
1797, Nov.   24, Peacock, Anne, and Barnard Payne.
1798, Feb.   22, Peacock, Ralph, and Mary Bowen.
1758, Oct.   10, Peal, Elizabeth, and Francis Harris.
1762, May   18, Peal, Grace, and William Dowell.
1765, Oct.   24, Peal, Mary, and Robert Field.
1795, Aug.   29, Peale, Eliz., and Robert Patton.
1792, Jan.   28, Peale, James, and Cath. Shinney.
1715, Dec.   22, Peale, Thomas, and Ann Richards.
1720, June   5, Pearce, Catherine, and James Balmer.
1740, May   22, Pearce, Elizabeth, and Thomas Robison.
1776, March   6, Pearce, Henry Ward, and Rachel Relfe.
1785, Jan.   31, Pearce, Hester, and Samuel Oakes.
1721, Nov.   30, Pearce, Margaret, and Joseph Yeates.
1711, April   8, Pearce, Mary, and Thomas Tresse.
1744, June   20, Pearce, Mary, and Thomas Pennington.
1735, April   17, Pearce, Mary, and Samuel Johnson.
1774, Sept.   3, Pearce, Rebecca, and William German.
1801, Nov.   3, Pearce, Susanna, and James Day.
1761, July   23, Pearne, Richard, and Martha Parry.
1734, Sept.   5, Pearom, Mary, and William Nicholls.
1717, Jan.   5, Pearsall, Edward, and Dorothy Davis.
1788, Dec.   15, Pease, Adam, and Abigail Zane.
1721, April   27, Pearse, Joseph, and Martha Scaber.
1786, April   10, Pearson, Ann, and John Boyd.
1772, Nov.   19, Pearson, Ann, and James Sparks.
1740, Jan.   1, Pearson, Hannah, and Simon Wyers.
1750, Nov.   17, Pearson, John, and Eleanor Walpole.
1795, June   22, Pearson, Margaret, and Thomas Cahoon.
1765, July   9, Pearson, Mary, and William Symonds.
1771, May   30, Pearson, Mary, and William Thomas.
1767, Dec.   31, Pearson, Mary, and John Mitchell.
1749, May   19, Pearson, Rebecca, and Joshua Fennimore.
1765, Sept.   24, Pearson, Sarah, and Isaac Anderson.
1752, Dec.   30, Pearson, William, and Anne Fairman.
1755, July   3, Peart, Thomas, and Elizabeth Skinner.
1781, June   21, Peart, William, and Susannah Reaves.
1750, Feb.   17, Peaseley, Dorcas, and William Tallert.
1798, Jan.   18, Peck, Eliz., and William Palmer.
1745, Aug.   17, Pedrow, John, and Mary Starn.
1729, Aug.   27, Peel, Ann, and Peter Brawle.
1743, May   23, Peel, John, and Eliz. Hainey.
1751, Dec.   19, Peel, Sarah, and Thomas Riche.
1738, May   2, Peel, Anthony, and Margaret Heaslum.

1729, July   6, Peep, Mary, and John Tinney.
1756, Feb.   15, Pearson, Sarah, and Benjamin Bird.
1740, Aug.   20, Peesely, Jonathan, and Dorcas Buxton.
1733, Nov.   6, Pegg, Sarah, and Thomas Green.
1741, June   20, Pegg, Sarah, and Richard Pigeon.
1731, Oct.   7, Peglar, Thomas, and Elizabeth Gardner.
1784, Feb.   2, Peirce, Thomas, and Penelope Cardiff.
1740, April   15, Peler, George Christopher and Elizabeth Chilen.
1796, Jan.   7, Pelose, Martha, and James Tiffin.
1757, June   10, Pelty, Nathaniel, and Sarah Cooper.
1806, April   24, Pemberton, Eliz., and Henry L. Waddell.
1748, April   25, Pemberton, James, and Elinor Barker.
1773, Sept.   3, Pemberton, John, and Alice Sutton.
1794, March   23, Pemberton, Mercy, and Timothy O'Brian.
1794, Aug.   21, Penington, Isaac, and Rachel Thomson.
1796, Jan.   1, Penington, Rachel, and Daniel Freeman.
1802, April   3, Penington, Sarah, and Joseph Waterford.
1795, May   9, Peniston, Richard, and Eliz. Hartwell.
1743, May   31, Penley, Ann, and Atwood Shute.
1772, May   21, Penn, Hon[ble] Richard, Esqr., and Mary Masters.
1766, May   31, Penn, Hon[ble] John, and Miss Ann Allen.
1759, Nov.   28, Pennel, Rachel, and Amos Edwards.
1744, June   20, Pennington, Thomas, and Mary Pearce.
1799, May   18, Pennock, Ann, and John McLaughlin.
1756, June   24, Penny, William, and Amy Durham.
1797, April   1, Penrose, Abraham, and Mary Alexander.
1791, Dec.   21, Penrose, Ann, and James Matthews.
1737, May   21, Penrose, Bartholomew, and Mary Kirl.
1800, Jan.   16, Penrose, Charles, and Ann Roan.
1782, June   18, Penrose, Isaac, and Ann Smith.
1766, March   15, Penrose, James, and Sarah Biddle.
1797, May   1, Penrose, Margaret, and Edward Campbell.
1766, March   25, Penrose, Mary, and Anthony Wayne.
1780, Sept.   30, Penrose, Samuel, and Sarah Moulder.
1764, March   1, Penrose, Sarah, and Lester Faulkner.
1767, Oct.   15, Penrose, Sarah, and Abraham Robinson.
1776, Aug.   15, Penrose, Sarah, and John Shaw.
1792, June   18, Penrose, Susannah, and John Lewis.
1731, Oct.   21, Penrose, Thomas, and Sarah Coats.
1730, Sept.   30, Penry, Sarah, William Thomson.
1799, Feb.   21, Percival, Joshua, and Sarah Cuthbert.
1786, May   20, Peree, Amariah, and Mary Birck.
1798, Jan.   1, Perevani, Joseph, and Jessey Gordon.
1805, Dec.   3, Perit, John, and Margaret Dunlap.
1796, Dec.   8, Perkins, Francis, and Ami Bayard.
1712, Nov.   9, Perkins, George, and Mary Johnson.

1772, May   14, Perkins, John, and Mary Woodward.
1766, Nov.   6, Perkins, John, and Elizabeth Clare.
1793, Aug.   27, Perkins, Sarah, and William Hunter.
1803, Dec.   13, Perkins, Sarah, and Peter Roberts.
1800, May   1, Perkins, Washington, and Sophia Mercier.
1783, Sept. 18, Perot, John, and Mary Tybout.
1796, Jan.   5, Perrock, James, and Sarah Armington.
1729-30, Feb. 5, Perrey, Obadiah, and Phœbe Appleton.
1746, June   9, Perry, Christopher, and Elinour Joiner.
1758, Jan.   12, Perry, John, and Elizabeth Ledru.
1728, Feb.   24, Perry, John, and Mary Parson.
1806, March 22, Perry, Margaret, and Joseph Johnson.
1735, July   20, Perry, Martha, and William Farmer.
1803, Sept. 18, Perry, Michael, and Margaret McCoy.
1793, March 31, Perry, Sarah, and William Baker.
1792, Sept. 16, Perry, William, and Margaret Arthur.
1742, Dec.   16, Person, Anthony, and Rebecca Carrall.
1760, Aug.   17, Perth, Elizabeth, and Benjamin Gilbert.
1765, May   1, Pesser, Michael, and Elizabeth Simmon.
1795, Sept. 27, Peters, Barbara, and Amos Brown.
1748, Oct.   29, Peters, Benjamin, and Dorothy Battin.
1737, Jan.   22, Peters, Elizabeth, and Henry Tisdal.
1729, Jan.   29, Peters, John, and Sarah Evans.
1761, Nov.   12, Peters, Leagh, and Henry Heirs.
1802, Jan.   6, Peters, Maria Wilhelmina, and William Willing.
1806, Oct.   2, Peters. Ralph, and Cath. Conyngham.
1804, March   1. Peters, Richard, and Abigail Willing.
1776, Aug.   22, Peters, Richard, and Sarah Robinson.
1774, Dec.   21, Peterson, Ann, and Thomas Coxe.
1758, Dec.   23, Peterson, Ann, and Thomas Hughes.
1735, Nov.   15, Peterson, Eleanor, and Gabriel Cox.
1802, March 19, Peterson, Emanuel, and Abigail Sullivan.
1805, April 16, Peterson, John, and Ann Lawler.
1749, Nov.   16, Peterson, Magdalen, and Robert Cloud.
1804, Dec.   8, Peterson, Margaret, and Arthur Morrison.
1799, Nov.   20, Peterson, Peter, and Margaret Madden.
1803, June   10, Peterson, Thomas, and Eliz. Shaw.
1801, May   17, Petre, Francis, and Sarah Low.
1738, Nov.   27, Petre, Philip, and Abigail Powel.
1761, June   17, Pett, William, and Cicily Frin.
1749, Feb.   2, Pettey, John, and Elizabeth Hall.
1798, March   4, Pettit, Anthony, and Rachel Crandel.
1760, Nov.   19, Pettit, Nathaniel, and Eleanor Bankson.
1788, Jan.   24, Pew, Ann, and Elijah Davis.
1788, Oct.   16, Pew, John, and Rebecca Coxe.
1768, July   9, Pew, Robert, and Mary Fullerton.

1748, Nov. 3, Peywel, Anne, and John Carson.
1801, Oct: 1, Phalan, Henrietta, and George Latimer.
1795, Sept. 3, Phelan, Robert, and Henrietta Wagner.
1722, Dec. 12, Phelps, Malachi, and Mary Gosnold.
1726, Sept. 15, Phenix, Mary, and Thomas Hicks.
1774, Jan. 1, Phildy, Ann, and Edward Bell.
1789, Aug. 15, Phile, Eliz., and Ebenezer Stott.
1802, Dec. 12, Phile, Margaret, and John Black.
1792, Aug. 18, Phile, Mary, and John Knap.
1797, Nov. 26, Philler, Cath., and Daniel Bussier.
1728, July 7, Phillips, Ann, and Walter Hughes.
1730-1, Feb. 25, Phillips, Anne, and Richard Hall.
1733, Sept. 26, Phillips, Benjamin, and Catherine Stephen.
1722, Aug. 9, Phillips, David, and Mary Bowyer.
1727, July 25, Phillips, Dor., and John Derborough.
1725, Oct. 31, Phillips, Eleanour, and Thomas Bradshaw.
1742, May 29, Phillips, George, and Elizabeth Evans.
1801, Nov. 26, Phillips, James, and Margaret Bryan.
1797, Jan. 26, Phillips, John, and Lydia Brown.
1727, July 23, Phillips, Marg\u1d57., and Ed. Morris.
1776, Oct. 10, Phillips, Thomas, and Sarah Thompson.
1743, May 27, Phillips, Thomas, and Mary Lownes.
1752, Sept. 25, Phillips, Wilcox, and Sarah Eaton.
1733, June 14, Phillips, William, and Phœbe Hincksman.
1733, March 9, Phillips, William, and Anne Guthridge.
1737, Oct. 10, Phillips, William, and Catherine Ashburne.
1795, March 30, Phillips, Alexander, and Mary Wilson.
1766, May 11, Philips, Ann, and Jacob Fustin.
1754, Nov. 14, Philips, Margaret, and Anthony Stocker.
1773, April 22, Philips, Cath., and John Vandegrist.
1800, Sept. 29, Philips, Daniel, and Eliz. Curby.
1736, Aug. 12, Philips, Edward, and Susannah Lovely.
1795, Sept. 16, Philips, Eliz., and John Morris.
1783, Oct. 15, Philips, Eliz., and William Kimble.
1794, Dec. 4, Philips, Henry, and Rachel Elleurt.
1796, Oct. 3, Philips, Henry, and Sophia Chew.
1781, July 12, Philips, Isabella, and John Staunton.
1766, April 10, Philips, John, and Rebecca Pyewell.
1799, July 25, Philips, John, and Hannah Eustie.
1773, Feb. 11, Philips, Joseph, and Eliz. Johnson.
1773, Feb. 17, Philips, Laetitia, and John Bissell.
1772, Dec. 25, Philips, Leonard, and Cath. Sinclair.
1758, June 8, Philips, Leonard, and Phoebe Beatsy.
1768, Aug. 17, Philips, Margaret, and Samuel Davis.
1787, July 10, Philips, Mary, and Henry Pinkerman.
1750, March 27, Philips, Rebecca, and Erasmus Stevens.

1734, Jan.   23, Philips, Thomas, and Mary Scothern.
1799, April   29, Philips, William, and Anna Smith.
1790, July   10, Philipson, Eliz., and William Henderson.
1726, Dec.   26, Phillpott, Sarah, and Ben. Blacklidge.
1729, Feb.   13, Philpot, Rachel, and John Foster.
1774, Oct.   19, Phipps, Eliz., and Aaron Alison.
1765, Aug.   13, Phipps, Prudence, and Robert Miller.
1771, May   27, Phipps, Sarah, and William Corbett.
1781, Jan.   23, Phipps, Thomas, and Eliz. Friend.
1723, April   17, Phipps, Thomas, and Frances Angwin.
1755, Dec.   5, Phips, Hannah, and John Barnes.
1782, March   14, Phyle, Ann, and James Gibbons.
1792, June   16, Phyle, Charlotte, and Jacob Wicoff.
1745, Jan.   17, Pick, John, and Eleanor Duglass.
1790, Jan.   3, Pickering, Sarah, and Abraham Wilson.
1789, March   15, Pickering, Eliz., and William Davidson.
1770, May   12, Pickering, George, and Rebecca Channell.
1772, April   9, Pickering, James, and Jane Casdrop.
1795, March   4, Pickering, Jane, and Thomas Gould.
1740, Oct.   27, Pickering, John, and Sarah Turner.
1783, Sept.   3, Pickering, Thomas, and Ann Gehry.
1723, July   2, Pickle, John, and Sarah Thomas.
1749, April   2, Pickles, John, and Ann Davis.
1778, Aug.   2, Pickle, Nicholas, and Ann Gauthony.
1771, Feb.   7, Pickles, Sarah, and Benjamin Flower.
1790, June   20, Picks, Mary, and Benjamin Sermon.
1715, Dec.   30, Pidcock, Robert, and Ann Smith.
1715, Jan.   27, Pidgeon, Mary, and Joseph Coleman.
1788, Nov.   22, Pierce, Deborah, and James Edwards.
1722, May   17, Pierce, Elizabeth and John Tiler.
1758, Aug.   22, Pierce, George, and Mary Hill.
1805, Dec.   28, Pierce, Jane, and Joseph McMullin.
1775, Dec.   12, Pierce, John, and Mary Gilbert.
1768, Nov.   5, Piercy, Thomas, and Mary McClannon.
1796, Jan.   24, Pierie, John, and Eve Wauck.
1741, June   20, Pigeon, Richard, and Sarah Pegg.
1789, Dec.   12, Pike, John, and Cath. Parker.
1740, Aug.   4, Pilcock, Elizabeth, and John Gurwin.
1748, Oct.   1, Piles, Elizabeth, Robert Lardner.
1781, Oct.   11, Pilkington, Thomas, and Sarah York.
1865, Oct.   3, Pillar, Mary, and Moses Malcom.
1761, Jan.   15, Pindar, Mary, and Jacob Smith.
1749, June   24, Pinder, Mary, and Alexander Gordon.
1774, Dec.   20, Pine, Ann, and Stephen Decator.
1761, June   27, Pine, Benjamin and Elizabeth Edgar.
1744, March   2, Pine, Ben., and Hannah Stokes.

1772, Nov. 18, Pine, Eliz., and Matthew Whitehead.
1770, March 22, Pine, John, and Elizabeth Brown.
1748, Sept. 19, Pine, John, and Isabell Bruce.
1767, April 2, Piniard, Eleanor, and John Sowder.
1787, July 10, Pinkerman, Henry, and Mary Philips.
1785, June 18, Pinto, Michael, and Mary Shee.
1750, Sept. 19, Pinyard, Anne, and Joshua Johnson.
1767, Nov. 28, Pinyard, Matthias, and Dorcas Swinney.
1787, June 14, Pistorius, Abram, and Hannah Mindehall.
1780, April 6, Pitt, Thomas, and Eliz. Rahnin.
1781, Nov. 1, Pitt, Thomas, and Eliz. Watkins.
1767, Jan. 29, Pitt, William, and Susannah Heligas.
1781, Nov. 28, Plankinhorn, Jacob, and Eliz. Russell.
1730, May 2, Plann, John, and Mary Burnett.
1801, Dec. 13, Planter, Jacob, and Lydia Wansley.
1804, Aug. 3, Platt, Henry, and Phoebe Young.
1790, Sept. 7, Platt, Isabella, and David Adams.
1792, Dec. 21, Platt, Lettice, and Francis Stewart.
1721, April 14, Platts, Joseph, and Mary Cox.
1791, Aug. 24, Pleasants, Sarah, and Charles Dorsey.
1728, July 25, Plinn, George, and Frances Smith.
1759, Sept. 13, Plumley, George, and Hannah ————.
1772, April 21, Plummer, Job, and Pamela Laycock.
1800, Sept. 1, Plummer, Samuel, and Sayre Harris.
1795, Dec. 3, Plumstead, George, and Anna Helena Amelia Ross.
1796, Sept. 27, Plumstead, Hannah, and George Neal.
1780, July 27, Plumstead, Rebecca, and Benjamin Hutton.
1768, July 7, Plumsted, Mary, and James Wilson.
1753, Sept. 27, Plumsted, William, and Mary McCall.
1795, July 8, Plunket, Asapp, and Sarah Care.
1802, Aug. 25, Plunket, Eliz., and George Carleton.
1738, Sept. 4, Plunket, Mary, and Charles Moor.
1775, Nov. 2, Plunkett, Sarah, and Henry Maag.
1805, May 16, Pluright, Lewis, and Hannah Raine.
1771, Sept. 17, Plym, Dennis, and Margaret Brown.
1749, Nov. 30, Plymm, George, and Elizabeth North.
1737, May 8, Poates, Thomas, and Elizabeth Hawkins.
1749, April 17, Pockington, Margaret, and Peter Stilly.
1742, June 6, Pockington, Margaret, and Pyramus Green.
1731, Sept. 12, Pockinhall, Elizabeth, and Philip Carlow.
1728, Nov. 28, Poe, Pat., and Abigail Day.
1722, Jan. 2, Pointsett, John, and Jane Essleby.
1801, May 19, Polhemus, Mary, and John Brown.
1788, April 13, Polk, Margaret Jane, and James Stewart.
1772, Oct. 8, Pollard, Eliz., and Daniel McCadden.
1804, Dec. 18, Pollard, Lydia, and John Newlin.

1754, Nov. 25, Pollard, Mary, and Joseph Hitchcock.
1750, Dec. 20, Pollard, Phœbe, and Daniel Couch.
1794, Feb. 7, Pollard, Richard, and Cath. Mink.
1794, July 23, Pollard, Sarah, and David McCormick.
1794, June 22, Pollard, Susannah, and George Keimley.
1765, Sept. 12, Pollard, William, and Mary Green.
1796, June 25, Pollock, James, and Eliz. Urviler.
1755, Aug. 13, Polson, Andrew, and Mary Shaddock.
1723, Dec. 12, Polson, Sarah, and William Davis.
1801, June 25, Polton, Patience. and Archibald Gourlay.
1759, Feb. 8, Poltis, William, and Jane McCoy.
1781, June 19, Pomeroy, Eliz., and Charles Smith.
1720, Nov. 17, Pomfret, Hannah. and William Austin.
1715, Oct. 10, Pones, Jonathan, and Juliana Evans.
1785, July 30, Pong, Mary, and Michael Smith.
1804, April 20, Pons, John Baptiste, and Eliz. Henry.
1765, April 28, Ponsonby, Mary, and Abel Holt.
1768, April 20, Poole, Edward, and Mary Hair.
1784, July 10, Poole, Capt. Joseph, and Mary Hammond.
1797, June 15, Poole, Joseph, and Eliz. Coxe.
1772, Dec. 3, Poole, Samuel, and Barbary Fandlin.
1745, Aug. 1, Poor, William, and Catherine White.
1799, June 8, Pope, Jacob, and Eliz. Greenless.
1730, Oct. 29, Pope, Margaret, and James Owner.
1754, June 3, Pope, Martha, and Patrick Johnson.
1766, Feb. 25, Pope, Thomas Claxton, and Elizabeth Cannon.
1753, Sept. 13, Porch, John, and Mary Jagard.
1798, Jan. 27, Poreaux, Nicholas, and Marie Marchant.
1801, May 5, Poree, John Baptista, and Alice Matilda Roberts.
1802, June 10, Porter, Daniel, and Cath. Dougherty.
1729–30, Feb. 23, Porter, Mary, and William Jones.
1768, Sept. 28, Porter, Mary, and James Read.
1800, Nov. 23, Porter, Mary, and David Woodroff.
1786, Sept. 2, Porter, Robert, and Phœbe Esiey.
1765, April 29, Porter, Robert, and Margaret Lindsey.
1774, June 14, Porter, Stephen, and Mary Hart.
1798, Dec. 20, Porter, Thomas, and Mary Cary.
1790, July 10, Porterfield, Eliza, and John Smith.
1731, April 29, Portlewhait, John, and Anne Metcalf.
1767, Aug. 27, Post, Christian Frederick, and Margaret Bollinger.
1803, Jan. 8, Post, Lucy Mary, and George Loder Allchin.
1756, Jan. 6, Porteus, Evan, and Rebecca Hoster.
1737, Oct. 5, Potter, Josiah, and Jane Wood.
1861, Sept. 1, Potter, Mary, and Cornelius Hagan.
1790, Nov. 29, Potter, Richard, and Cath. Miercken.
1799, March 25, Potter, Sarah, and Robert Goldsborough.

1795, July   7, Potts, Ann, and Lewis G. Affleck.
1805, May   16, Potts, Benezet, and Margaret Potts.
1759, April 25, Potts, David, and Alice Shull.
1767, Jan.   10, Potts, David, and Mary Ayries.
1766, Oct.   16, Potts, Deborah, and Caleb Hewes.
1802, March 18, Potts, Francis, and Lydia Maburry.
1741, July   23, Potts, Isaac, Mary Topforson.
1780, July   1, Potts, John, and Mary Jones.
1764, Feb.   28, Potts, John, and Margaret Carmick.
1801, Dec.   8, Potts, Laetitia, and Thomas Browne.
1805, May   16, Potts, Margaret, and Benezet Potts.
1709, Dec.   1, Potts, Margaret, and Evan Morgan.
1782, Oct.   8, Potts, Esqr., Nathl., and Rachel Hubbard.
1717, Jan.   5, Potts, Robert, and Elizabeth Fressey.
1803, July   9, Potts, Ruth, and Peter Lohra.
1758, March   7, Potts, Samuel, and Joanna Holland.
1803, Dec.   3, Potts, Thomas, and Ann Mary Humphreys.
1801, March 31, Potts, William Lukins, and Rachel Hughes.
1764, April 10, Potts, William, and Esther Moore.
1793, April 14, Poulnot, Nicholas, and Rosanna Prince.
1756, July   18, Pour, Jeffery, and Margaret Badwen.
1738, Nov.   27, Powel, Abigail, and Philip Petre.
1748, Oct.   5, Powel, Anne, and Joseph Preyor.
1751, Dec.   26, Powel, Evan, and Dorothy Newel.
1758, Sept.   2, Powel, Jacob, and Susannah Cart.
1731, Aug.   9, Powel, Joseph, and Mary Orson.
1731-2, Jan. 4, Powel, Lydia, and Christian Warner.
1764, Jan.   4, Powel, Martha, and Thomas Overend.
1770, Nov.   10, Powel, Martha, and Joseph Smith.
1731, Dec.   21, Powel, Mary, and Peter Worrel.
1743, Aug.   25, Powel, Rachel, and Henry Lewis.
1767, April   2, Powel, Rebecca, and Isaac Ashton.
1769, Aug.   7, Powel, Samuel, and Elizabeth Willing.
1738, May   23, Powel, Sarah, and Michael Rourk.
1768, Sept. 11, Powel, Sarah, and Daniel McFee.
1758, Oct.   10, Powell, Ann, and Samuel Harper.
1759, Sept.   5, Powell, Ann, and James Humphreys.
1772, Dec.   4, Powell, Anna, and David Noble.
1784, Sept. 21, Powell, Anna, and John Conrad Waggoner.
1761, April 29, Powell, George, and Barbary Brunnory.
1768, Oct.   26, Powell, Griffith, and Hannah Thomas.
1733, Dec.   24, Powell, Hannah, and John Boyd.
1717, May   9, Powell, Howell, and Jane Scotson.
1759, July   14, Powell, John, and Mary Webb.
1800, March   2, Powell, Margaret, and David Hall.
1763, March   4, Powell, Margaret, and William Johnson.

1806, July　　8, Powell, Naomi, and Moses Shelly.
1782, Oct.　　10, Powell, Richard, and Mary Laurence.
1779, Dec.　　18, Powell, Samuel, and Johanna Brown.
1734, Aug.　　5, Powell, Sarah, and John Hastings.
1759, July　　12, Powell, Thomas, and Mary Nailor.
1758, Jan.　　27, Powell, Thomas, and Letitia Steward.
1775, Dec.　　5, Powell, Thomas, and Eliz. Jones.
1793, Sept.　　11, Powell, William, and Eliz. Hassell.
1744, June　　13, Powelson, Peter, and Mary Hurley.
1767, Dec.　　24, Power, Alexander, and Mary Butterworth.
1773, Dec.　　9, Power, Joseph, and Ann Coleman.
1795, Nov.　　19, Powers, Mary, and Zaphaniah Bartlett.
1784, May　　16, Powers, Mary, and Joseph Carbord.
1780, Nov.　　23, Powers, William, and Sarah Jenny.
1721, April　　23, Powmels, Francis, and Elizabeth Jenkins.
1782, Oct.　　9, Pownall, Reuben, and Mary Lee.
1805, June　　6, Poyntell, Rebecca, and Robert Caldcleugh.
1800, Oct.　　9, Poyntell, Sarah, and Samuel Relf.
1779, Dec.　　23, Poyntell, William, and Ann Wilcocks.
1755, May　　3, Prat, Hannah, and Enoch Hobarart.
1743, June　　12, Pratt, Ann, and Joseph Lane.
1729, May　　1, Pratt, H., and Reb. Claypoole.
1785, Oct.　　27, Pratt, Henry, and Eliz. Dundass.
1794, Sept.　　11, Pratt, Henry, and Susannah Care.
1785, May　　24, Pratt, James, and Lydia Letzinger.
1728, Nov.　　25, Pratt, Jo^s, and Mary Jones.
1756, Dec.　　11, Pratt, Rebecca, and Charles Moore.
1759, March 20, Pratt, Sarah, and Nathaniel Falkner.
1784, Aug.　　10, Pratt, Thomas, and Mary Shoonover.
1729, Dec.　　7, Pratt, W^m, and Joanna Warner.
1761, Sept.　　14, Prefontaine, Sarah, and John Moore.
1744, July　　14, Presor, Sarah, and Edward Cooper.
1740, Aug.　　5, Preston, Belcher, and Susannah Jones.
1760, Feb.　　18, Preston, Elizabeth, and Robert Shephard.
1757, Feb.　　27, Preston, Hannah, and Phillip Halbert.
1737, May　　8, Preston, Hannah, and James Duchee.
1766, Aug.　　30, Preston, John, and Catherine Cammel.
1743, March 1, Preston, Joseph, and Elizabeth Martin.
1756, Dec.　　18, Preston, Margaret, and William Smith, jr.
1736, Dec.　　4, Preston, Mary, and Thomas Coatam.
1760, July　　28, Preston, William, and Elizabeth Delaware.
1720, Oct.　　25, Preston, William, and Hannah Beeth.
1762, Jan.　　21, Prentice, John, and Priscilla Stille.
1748, Oct.　　5, Preyor, Joseph, and Anne Powel.
1769, Dec.　　30, Price, Ann, and Thomas Wilson.
1734, Dec.　　22, Price, Benjamin, and Mary Fanington.

1794, Dec.   18, Price, Cath., and James Sett.
1800, March 8, Price, Chandler, and Helen Matlack.
1743, March 31, Price, Conrad, and Cath. Barstler.
1747, July   20, Price, Elizabeth, and Edward Smout.
1754, Feb.   14, Price, Elizabeth, and John Rush.
1745, May   31, Price, Eliz., and John Ellis.
1773, May   1, Price, Eliz., and Samuel Purdey.
1767, Dec.   14, Price, Elizabeth, and Peter Parker.
1756, Feb.   7, Price, Ellis, and Sarah Osborne.
1799, May   11, Price, Geoffery, and Jane Erwin.
1791, Sept.   1, Price, George, and Eliz. Falkner.
1781, July   12, Price, George, and Eliz. Atherly.
1758, July   23, Price, Grace, and William Young.
1751, Jan.   5, Price, Hannah, and James Dutton.
1737, Nov.   30, Price, Hannah, and Joseph Burgoign.
1773, March 11, Price, Hannah, and Samuel Cawstring.
1744, Dec.   21, Price, James, and Mary Eyre.
1757, March   3, Price, Jane, and James White.
1761, March 26, Price, Jane, and Robert Holland.
1751, Jan.   19, Price, Jenkins, and Martha Lawrence.
1731-2, Feb. 8, Price, Jonathan, and Mary Chandler.
1758, Dec.   75, Price, Jonathan and Elizabeth Tomlinson.
1731, Dec.   7, Price, John, and Rebecca King.
1739, March   7, Price, John, and Mary McDonall.
1760, Dec.   29, Price, John, and Hannah Delaplain.
1781, July   1, Price, John, and Sarah Albertson.
1716, Nov.   26, Price, John, and Elizabeth Owen.
1796, March 10, Price, John Morgan, and Susan Wistar.
1744, May   9, Price, Joseph, and Hannah Jones.
1770, Oct.   24, Price, Joseph, and Margaret Agnew.
1785, June   2, Price, Margaret, and John North.
1756, Jan.   5, Price, Mary, and William Adams.
1746, Feb.   17, Price, Mary, and James Wells.
1758, Sept.   4, Price, Mary, and John Earl.
1713, June   21, Price, Mary, and Richard Traveller.
1713, Feb.   21, Price, Mary, and William Thomas.
1720, Dec.   8, Price, Mary, and William Forrest.
1763, March   1, Price, Rachel, and Richard Mitchel.
1765, Oct.   13, Price, Rebecca, and James Monk.
1744, Oct.   16, Price, Sam., and Eliz. Heselius.
1798, July   10, Price, Samuel, and Eliz. Bass.
1743, Aug.   20, Price, Sarah, and John Jones.
1779, July   31, Price, Sarah, and Samuel Cook.
1714, Nov.   25, Price, Sarah, and John Ellis.
1783, May   20, Price, Sarah, and John Crozier.
1760, Oct.   30, Price, Sophia, and Charles Dougharty.

1756, Jan.   1, Price, Thomas, and Anne Wood.
1799, Nov.   21, Price, Thomas, and Harriet Holdernesse.
1788, April   24, Price, Thomas, and Pamelia Smothers.
1714, June   20, Price, Ursulah, and Francis Crampton.
1785, March 28, Price, William, and Anne Shute.
1746, March 17, Prichard, Hannah, and Robert Whitehead.
1734, April   21, Prichard, John, and Martha Evans.
1755, Sept.   5, Pricket, Diana, and Joseph Collins.
1741, Nov.   3, Prier, Siber, and Ann Dwarihouse.
1751, April   28, Pritchard, Anthony, and Jane Glascow.
1744, Jan.   9, Pritchard, Martha, and William Sweeting.
1762, Nov.   6, Priest, Robert, and Hannah Marshall.
1798, Dec.   6, Priest, Thomas, and Cath. Biles.
1765, April   29, Prigg, Hannah, and Jacob Corse.
1793, April   14, Prince, Rosanna, and Nicholas Poulnot.
1773, May   18, Pringle, John, and Catherine Lake.
1730, Sept.   20, Pritchard, Anne, and Ambrose Lipscomb.
1789, Nov.   22, Pritchard, Eliz., and Samuel Coulty.
1768, June   11, Pritchard, Joseph, and Judith Hughes.
1730, June   21, Pritchard, Rebecca, and Patrick Duncan.
1782, May   30, Pritchard, William, and Judith Law.
1803, Dec.   10, Pritchett, Rachel, and Nathaniel Sebastian.
1750, Feb.   19, Prise, William, and Sarah Johnston.
1749, Dec.   12, Prisgy, Mary, and George Wells.
1787, April   20, Probart, John, and Mary Gosmer.
1794, June   28, Probeit, Samuel, and Mary McCartey.
1762, Nov.   18, Proby, Jacob, and Anne Steward.
1765, Aug.   20, Procter, Joshua, and Margaret Green.
1767, Jan.   9, Procter, Martha, and William Taylor.
1796, March 3, Procter, Thomas, and Sarah Hussey.
1787, March 1, Procter, William, and Eliz. Stephenson.
1765, April   10, Proudfoot, John, and Catherina Neiss.
1801, May   9, Prosser, James, and Ann Farmer.
1710, Jan.   28, Protheroh, Margaret, and Adam Baker.
1738, Nov.   6, Prover, Thomas, and Sarah May.
1776, Feb.   8, Pryor, Eleanor, and John Fitzpatrick.
1793, May   9, Pryor, James, and Ann Page.
1736, Jan.   11, Pryor, Norton, and Mary Brockdon.
1749, Nov.   14, Pue, Jemima, and Patrick Carty.
1716, Nov.   19, Pugh, Ann, and Joseph Wells.
1752, July   8, Pugh, Catherine, and James Kappock.
1741, June   28, Pugh, Ellis, and Anne Espil.
1712, April   2, Pugh, George, and Mary Hughes.
1720, Dec.   11, Pugh, John, and Hannah Bennet.
1733, July   25, Pugh, John, and Sarah Smith.
1728, June   13, Pugh, Margt., and John Davieson.

1756, May 13, Pugh, Mary, and Cornelius Stevens.
1759, April 21, Pugh, Mary, and Benjamin Britain.
1749, Sept. 13, Pugh, Michael, and Hannah Davis.
1752, July 1, Pugh, Thomas, and Margaret Tucker.
1784, Oct. 11, Pugh, Thomas, and Phoebe Evans.
1729–30, Mar. 8, Pughe, Elizabeth, and Thomas Jones.
1801, Sept. 7, Pullenger, Collin, and Jane Davis.
1758, Sept. 9, Punner, Henry, and Elizabeth Spencer.
1777, Feb. 16, Purdie, James, and Catherine Atkinson.
1773, May 1, Purdey, Samuel, and Eliz. Price.
1798, Jan. 2, Purdon, Margaret, and James Cook.
1737, Aug. 5, Purdue, William, and Anne Mullard.
1730, Sept. 10, Purdy, Charity, and Jacob Warner.
1770, June 2, Purdy, Folliard, and Margaret Slack.
1757, Dec. 2, Purser, Jane, and John Cummings.
1784, Oct. 23, Pusey, Eliz., and Frederick Gordon.
1714, Jan. 10, Putt, Nicholas, and Rachel Williams.
1734, July 2, Pyatt, Jacob, and Jane Young.
1776, April 10, Pyewell, Rebecca, and John Philips.
1735, July 24, Pyewell, William, and Mary Catherine Rutter.
1720, May 12, Pyke, Mary, and John Bryant.
1783, Dec. 4, Pyles, Esther, and John Haycock.
1761, Oct. 10, Pywell, John, and Mary Garret.
1769, Dec. 3, Quackenbus, Peter, and Mary Sheffel.
1803, March 14, Quail, Eliz., and Joseph Fails.
1786, Aug. 25, Quality, Eleanor, and Nicholas Lowe.
1779, Dec. 2, Quality, Joseph, and Eleanor Mason.
1760, Jan. 18, Quaming, John, and Rose Guinet.
1758, Aug. 13, Quandill, John, and Deborah Grant.
1805, April 26, Quandrill, Charles and Eliz. Eyre.
1797, March 22, Quantrill, Charles, and Mary Harper.
1768, June 26, Quay, Abigail, and Robert Slocombe.
1759, Aug. 2, Quee, Esther, and William Colum.
1773, March 6, Quee, John, and Susannah Cotman.
1758, Oct. 6, Quest, Rachel, and John Butler.
1730, Aug. 10, Quicksey, Sarah, and William Miller.
1801, Oct. 20, Quig, Hannah, and Henry Read.
1784, Dec. 13, Quigg, Sarah, and Ambrose Basse.
1800, July 11, Quigley, Bridget, and John Boyd.
1766, May 26, Quigley, Isaac, and Jane Coleman.
1802, Dec. 19, Quin, Andrew, and Eliz. Trimmer.
1802, Dec. 30, Quin, Ann, and John Thornhill.
1769, Oct. 22, Quin, Eleanor, and William Brothers.
1743, Dec. 20, Quin, James, and Mary Malowny.
1775, June 5, Quin, Jane, and Thomas Griffiths.
1801, June 29, Quin, John, and Mary Cook.

1731, Aug. 15, Quinard, Philip, and Martha Stretch.
1794, Sept. 22, Quingley, Mary, and Daniel McCleod.
1797, Aug.   6, Quinlin, Sarah, and John Hider.
1797, Nov. 15, Quinn, Thomas, and Martha Wilson Fromp.
1745, May   30, Race, William, and Mary Hoffety.
1768, Oct. 13, Rachel (Mohawk) and John Harris, (Tuscaroras.)
1755, Aug. 14, Rachford, Marcy, and Thomas Coates.
1782, Feb.   7, Raguet, Cladius Paul, and Lydia Condy.
1780. April 6, Rahnin, Eliz., and Thomas Pitt.
1734, Oct.   8, Raine, Elizabeth, and William Lane.
1805, May   16, Raine, Hannah, and Lewis Pluright.
1797, March 30, Rainey, Robert, and Kath. Keppele.
1789, Aug.   5, Rakley, Johanna, and Thomas Laughlin.
1761, March 9, Ralph, James, and Hannah Morris.
1805, May   2, Ralph, Mary Ann, and Samuel H. McFetrick.
1785, Nov. 24, Ralston, Robert, and Sarah Clarkson.
1800, Nov. 30, Ramaje, Sarah, and Daniel Briggs.
1733, April 30, Ramanage, Rebecca, and Walter Shetford.
1753, Jan. 31, Rambo, Andrew, and Elizabeth King.
1739, Feb. 21, Rambo, Anne, and Daniel Jones.
1762, Oct. 23, Rambo, Daniel, and Susannah Harvey.
1764, June 20. Rambo, Elizabeth, and David Davis.
1775, April 2, Rambo, Eliz., and Isaac Worrell.
1748, Oct. 31, Rambo, Ezekiel, and Elizabeth Holstein.
1752, April 13, Rambo, Gunnar, and Susannah Rambo.
1747, Feb.   6, Rambo, Margaretta, and Rev'd Gabriel Neisman.
1772, June 16, Rambo, Mary, and Joseph Woodfield.
1737, Sept. 10, Rambo, Mary, and William Hannas.
1742, Nov. 13, Ramm, Mary, and John Erwin.
1770, Aug. 29, Rambo, Peter, and Martha Thomas.
1758, March 16, Rambo, Rebecca, and John Walter.
1752, April 13, Rambo, Susannah, and Gunnar Rambo.
1768, Dec.   6, Ramsay, James, and Honour Lee.
1804, June 12, Ramsay, William, and Cath. Hood.
1783, May   6, Ramsey, Ann, and Thomas Demeng.
1795, June 11, Ramsey, Eliz., and Thomas Talbut.
1797, Nov.   2, Ramsey, Frances, and Syvester Holland.
1763, Oct. 12, Ramsey, Francis, and Jane O'Donald.
1762, Dec. 13, Ramsey, Giles, and Mary Rice.
1795, Aug. 23, Ramsey, Jane, and Thomas Clarke.
1735, Jan. 15, Ramsey, Joseph. and Ruth Thomas.
1746, Nov. 30, Ramsey, William, and Catherine Dennison.
1762, Aug. 12, Ramshear, Benjamin, and Elizabeth Clampshear.
1768, Dec.   2, Ramshaw, Benjamin, and Catherine Hutchinson.
1786, June 10, Ramshaw, Christian, and Joseph Williams.
1749, Dec. 20, Ranberry, William, and Mary Morris.

1732, June   16, Ranbury, Jane, and William Sommerset.
1774, Feb.   27, Randall, James, and Pleasant Veasey.
1777, Sept.   14, Randal, Mary, and Thomas Fox.
1766, June   17, Randall, Sarah, and James Kendall.
1774, Aug.   23, Randle, Richard, and Mary Reed.
1763, Jan.   15, Randle, Sarah, and Joshua Mitchel.
1749, Oct.   19, Randolph, Isham, and Sarah Hargrave.
1781, March   20, Rankay, Frederick, and Cath. Murphy.
1756, Sept.   9, Rankin, Elizabeth, and Cæsar Guisline.
1750, Dec.   29, Rankin, George, and Elizabeth Griffin.
1797, April   23, Ransford, Henry, and Eliz. Dixon.
1740, April   12, Ransted, Mary, and James White.
1760, Aug.   6, Ranton, James, and Elizabeth Johnson.
1781, Dec.   18, Ranter, Nathaniel, and Eliz. Paul.
1713, Dec.   8, Ranton, George, and Elizabeth Johnson.
1800, May   15, Rapin, Joseph, and Eliz. Greble.
1770, Dec.   5, Ratcliff, Rebecca, and David Gladding.
1782, Nov.   8, Raton, Abigail, and John Patterson.
1769, Nov.   8, Ratten, Hannah, and Edwards Hicks.
1802, Dec.   11, Ravel, Mary, and Asa Buddinton.
1794, July   3, Rawle, Eleanor, and Anthony Chardon.
1760, Dec.   6, Rawle, Robert, and Mary Mackey.
1786, July   27, Rawlings, George, and Maria Robinett.
1794, Nov.   9, Rawlins, Resin, and Ann Nicholson.
1752, Sept.   1, Rawlinson, Robert, and Hannah Moss.
1758, March   20, Rawlston, John, and Elizabeth Shaw.
1755, June   18, Raworth, Edd, and John Carter.
1794, Nov.   1, Rawson, Lydia, and John Dixon.
1753, March   13, Ray, Elizabeth, and Peter Graham.
1796, Aug.   26, Ray, Mary, and Isaak Stewart.
1802, April   15, Ray, Thomas, and Sarah Tempest.
1772, April   16, Raybold, Mary, and John Rush.
1722, Feb.   5, Reach, William, and Jane Palmer.
1763, Dec.   28, Read, Ann, and Thomas White.
1774, Dec.   22, Read, Ann, and Thomas Davison.
1713, Nov.   1, Read, Charles, and Ann Bond.
1733, Oct.   17, Read, Charles, and Sarah Harwood.
1773, Jan.   5, Read, Collinson, and Mary McFunn.
1725, Aug.   5, Read, Deb., and John Rogers.
1757, April   24, Read, Elizabeth, and Daniel Luken.
1801, Oct.   20, Read, Henry, and Hannah Quig.
1770, Nov.   27, Read, Henry, and Alice Turner.
1768, Sept.   28, Read, James, and Mary Porter.
1745, April   20, Read, James, and Susannah Leacock.
1800, June   5, Read, John, and Ann Johnson.
1757, Dec.   21, Read, John, and Margaret Hannis.

1796, June   25, Read, John, and Martha Meredith.
1720, Dec.   8, Read, Joseph, and Mary James.
1806, April   24, Read, Maria, and John Dennis.
1738, June   19, Read, Samuel, and Dorothy King.
1764, Feb.   2, Read, Samuel, and Mary Weldon.
1779, Sept.   7, Read, Capt. Thomas, and Mary Field.
1796, Sept. 22, Read, William, and Ann McCall.
1794, Oct.   19, Reader, Sarah, and Joseph Hardy.
1796, Jan.   17, Reading, Ann, and Henry Gilbert.
1762, Nov.   15, Reading, John, and Margaret Johnson.
1801, May   9, Reading, Susannah, and John Scott.
1727, April   2, Readman, Sarah, and Thomas Bourne.
1730, Oct.   25, Ready, John, and Margaret McCormish.
1774, May   31, Reagan, Cath., and James Muncuar.
1746, March 27, Real, Israel, and Elizabeth Willes.
1781, June   21, Reaves, Susannah, and William Peart.
1744, May   1, Rece, Eliz., and Robert Jones.
1716, May   27, Receau, Thomas, and Hannah Vander Sloich.
1773, Sept. 14, Redd, Christiana, and James Wharton.
1748, Dec.   14, Redding, Jane, and Garret Morris.
1806, Oct.   8, Redman, Eleanor, and John McKelway.
1785, Dec.   6, Redman, Eliz., and William Parsons.
1790, Oct.   21, Redman, John, and Margaret Tucker.
1728, Oct.   28, Redman, John, and Sarah King.
1782, May   21, Redman, Dr. John, and Rebecca Turner.
1751, April 18, Redman, John, and Mary Sober.
1742, Nov.   20, Redman, Joseph, and Elizabeth Parker.
1758, Dec.   15, Redman, Joseph, and Sidney L. Kee.
1795, April 14, Redman, Margaret, and Allen Clapp.
1779, Dec.   13, Redman, Rebecca, and Col. Elisha Lawrence.
1755, April 19, Redman, Richard, and Elizabeth Mackee.
1771, June   5, Redman, Sarah, and Daniel Coxe.
1716, Nov.   24, Redman, Susannah, and Ralph Assheton.
1791, March 10, Redman, Thomas, and Sarah Riche.
1737, Nov.   20, Redmond, Andrew, and Mary Stephens.
1785, Jan.   20, Redstone, William, and Sidney Hamilton.
1803, April 14, Redy, Margaret, and Patrick Lefferty.
1748, Feb.   19, Reece, Elizabeth, and Lewis Lewis.
1730–1, Feb. 2, Reece, Lyky, and Methusalem Griffith.
1712, March 18, Reed, Charles, and Rebecca Freedland.
1800, April 20, Reed, Dorcas, and Thomas Williams.
1783, Nov.   10, Reed, Eliz., and James Long.
1743, Dec.   29, Reed, Florinda, and George Smith.
1796, Jan.   14, Reed, Henry, and Eliz. Hazard.
1758, Dec.   18, Reed, James, and Ann Hayes.
1748, April 23, Reed, Jane, and William Allen.

1803, Sept. 16, Reed, Mary, and John Payne.
1774, Aug. 23, Reed, Mary, and Richard Randle.
1784, Oct. 28, Reed, Rebecca, and Edward Ducker.
1803, Aug. 18, Reed, Robert, and Ann Mode.
1742, May 31, Reed, William, and Elizabeth Dungan.
1779, Nov. 20, Rees, Abigail, and John Roberts.
1762, Oct. 14, Rees, Daniel, and Sarah Connely.
1754, April 71, Rees, David, and Rachel Moore,
1848, Aug. 17, Rees, Elinor, and Thomas Evans.
1746, Sept. 4, Rees, Evan, and Jane Thomas.
1728, June 17, Rees, Gee, and Ann Robins.
1754, Nov. 25, Rees, Hannah, and Thomas Evans.
1787, Feb. 8, Rees, James, and Hannah Betterton.
1735, Aug. 23, Rees, John, and Mary Shute.
1746, June 18, Rees, Mary, and John Shaw.
1740, March 22, Rees, Rebecca, and Stephen Jolly.
1756, Oct. 11, Rees, Susannah, and John Twiggs.
1797, April 17, Rees, Susannah, and Abraham Marshall.
1754, June 27, Rees, Susannah, and Jonathan Sheen.
1858, July 8, Rees, Thomas, and Ann Thomas.
1756, June 23, Rees, Thomas, and Sarah Fitzhugh.
1728, May 7, Rees, Thomas, and Elizabeth Kenworthy.
1757, Oct. 29, Rees, William, and Martha Thomas.
1798, Feb. 1, Reese, Jacob, and Cath. Sheaff.
1766, Dec. 8, Reese, Jeremiah, and Mary Jacobs.
1767, Aug. 23, Reese, Hannah, and Bowyer Brooke.
1780, June 30, Reese, Laetitia, and William White.
1795, Dec. 22, Reese, Philip, and Eliz., Brooke.
1720, Aug. 11, Reese, Thomas, and Mary Savage.
1780, Oct. 5, Reeves, Absalom, and Hannah Wells.
1782, July 18, Reeves, Jane, and James Coppock.
1773, June 9, Reeves, Mary, and John West.
1774, July 13, Regan, John and Esther Daniel.
1758, May 9, Reger, Samuel, and Barbara Sigfrid.
1761, Nov, 12, Register, Hannah, and Joseph Edwards.
1736, Oct. 17, Reid, Henry, and Susannah Broom.
1736, Sept. 16, Reid, John, and Martha Reid.
1805, June 15, Reid, Joseph, and Maria Watmough.
1736, Sept. 16, Reid, Martha, and John Reid.
1793, April 27, Reid, Mary, and Richard George.
1788, Aug. 16, Reid, Mary, and William Cameron.
1797, March 2, Reiley, Charles, and Eliz. Jackson.
1796, Jan. 1, Reiley, Eliz., and Christopher Tillenghast.
1764, Jan. 30, Reily, Ann, and Thomas Cahaug.
1747, Oct. 15, Reily, John, and Mary Hillhouse.
1765, April 10, Reily, Sarah, and John Ross.

1763, March 15, Reinhart. Elizabeth, and Moses Marshall.
1753, Nov.   16, Reinhart, Ulrich, and Magdalena Jahnin.
1765, Sept. 28, Reinholt, Elizabeth, and William Side.
1743, Jan.   2, Reirdan, Mary, and Peter Berry.
1743, May   11, Reley, William, and Susannah Woods.
1800, Oct.   9, Relf, Samuel, and Sarah Poyntell.
1760, March 3, Relfe, John, and Rachel Francis.
1776, March 6, Relfe, Rachel, and Henry Ward Pearce.
1768, July   15, Relin, Margaret, and John Keen.
1734, June   8, Remington, John, and Margaret Lewis.
1770, Dec.   9, Renaudet, Eliz., and John Beekman.
1735, Dec.   5, Renaudet, Jane, and George Lucas Osburn.
1759, May   16, Renaudett, Mary, and Peter Chevalier.
1741, July   13, Renenedet, Ann, and Townsend White.
1760, Dec.   14, Rennion, Catherine, and Benjamin Fordham.
1756, Nov.   21, Renoret, Barbery, and Henry Sharp.
1796, Sept. 19, Renshaw, Anne, and Edward Thomson.
1797, April 22, Renshaw, Charles, and Henrietta Jennings.
1796, Nov.   12, Renshaw, John, and Eliz. Williams.
1780, July   4, Renshaw, Mary, and Richard Hunt.
1801, Sept. 24, Renshaw, Richard, and Mary Johnson.
1797, Nov.   30, Repton, Mary, and William Murdock.
1795, Nov.   10, Repton, William, and Mary Dally.
1797, June   20, Reside, Sarah, and William Baird.
1737, Aug.   13, Reston, William, and Sarah Carlisle.
1799, July   25, Rethmell, Ruth, and Thomas Spinlove.
1758, May   13, Revell, Mary, and James Forrest.
1749, Jan.   1, Revel, Peter, and Mary Allenby.
1804, May   31, Rex, William, and Ann Gibson.
1770, March 29, Reybold, Jacob, and Sarah Mitchell.
1776, Nov.   24, Reyley, Ann, and Matthias Hardwick.
1804, Oct.   19, Reynard, Jacob, and Mary Walter.
1795, May   2, Reynolds, Ann, and Edward Cutbush.
1801, June 18, Reynolds, Cath., and Thomas Willington.
1738, July   7, Reynolds, Elizabeth, and John Vanlear.
1720, Jan.   1, Reynolds, Elizabeth, and Simon Tillet.
1802, Jan.   23, Reynolds, Hannah, and Thomas Wilkinson.
1732, May   14, Reynolds, Henry, and Barbara Anderson.
1764, March 17, Reynolds, James, and Mary Ross.
1789, Feb.   8, Reynolds, James, and Rhoda Duffield.
1756, Nov.   9, Reynolds, John, and Eleanor Eaton.
1773, March 25, Reynolds, John, and Charlotte Whittle.
1756, Nov.   15, Reynolds, Margaret, and John Bear.
1795, Aug.   9, Reynolds, Simen, and Mary Bowyer.
1720, Jan.   1, Rhodes, Benjamin, and Mary Fox.
1758, Feb.   13, Rhodes, George, and Eleanor Dawson.

1762, May   1, Rhoades, Joseph, and Ann Jackson.
1772, April 11, Rhods, Nathan, and Sarah Stradler.
1738, April 13, Riall, John, and Elizabeth Vincent.
1766, Nov.   1, Riall, Mary, and John Dwyer.
1775, Jan.   5, Rice, Catherine, and Isaac Vanhorn.
1725, Nov.   27, Rice, Ed., and Judith Knight.
1765, May   20, Rice, James, and Rebecca Norberry.
1800, Dec.   26, Rice, John, and Mary White.
1765, Aug.   24, Rice, John, and Rachel Northington.
1771, Aug.   29, Rice, Joseph, and Ann Currey.
1769, April   6, Rice, Joseph, and Sarah Robins.
1762, Dec.   13, Rice, Mary, and Giles Ramsey.
1756, April   8, Rice, Mary, and William Warden.
1784, Sept. 23, Rice, Philip, and Ann Roberts.
1744, April   9, Rice, Sarah, and Henry Williams.
1776, April   6, Rice, Thomas, and Penelope Justis.
1743, Nov.   17, Rice, William, and Rebecca Norris.
1786, Oct.   26, Richards, Ann, and James Moore.
1715, Dec.   22, Richards, Ann, and Thomas Peale.
1734, June   20, Richards, Anne, and Abraham George.
1787, Aug.   6, Richard, Caroline, and Charles Marcel Homassell.
1795, Aug.   17, Richards, Eleanor, and William Cole.
1734, Feb.   6, Richards, Elizabeth, and John Evrington.
1717, March   3, Richards, Jane, and John Jones.
1799, Feb.   24, Richards, John, and Sarah Miller.
1801, Oct.   15, Richards, John, and Mary Baker.
1801, Sept. 24, Richards, Jonathan, and Eleanor Jerman.
1760, Oct.   21, Richards, Mary, and Jesse Chew.
1773, July   29, Richard, Mary, and Michael Joseph Letellier.
1727, June   5, Richards, Owen, and Elizabeth Baker.
1796, March 12, Richards, Sampson, and Ann Haley.
1767, April 22, Richards, Sarah, and William Connell.
1770, June   4, Richards, Sarah, and Jacob Hughes.
1799, Dec.   11, Richards, Susannah, and Henry Baynton.
1714, May   16, Richards, Susannah, and Isaac Smith.
1761, Feb.   10, Richardson, Elizabeth, and William Wellman.
1784, May   19, Richardson, Enoch, and Eleanor Delany.
1735, April 25, Richardson, James, and Anne DeCow.
1758, March 18, Richardson, Jane, and Robert White.
1804, April 15, Richardson, John, and Eliz. Dildine.
1770, Sept. 27, Richardson, John, and Lydia Baker.
1720, May   9, Richardson, Joshua, and Mary Shaw.
1796, Aug.   18, Richardson, Margaret, and Page Nash.
1758, Oct.   27, Richardson, Margaret, and Benjamin Conrad.
1761, April   8, Richardson, Mary, and Joseph Moore.
1773, July   14, Richardson, Rachel, and Ephriam Jones.

1781, Dec. 11, Richardson, Rebecca, and Peter George.
1800, April 2, Richardson, Rebecca, and Isaac Cook.
1754, Oct. 14, Richardson, Sarah, and Edward Lane.
1789, Aug. 27, Riche, Grace, and John D. Coxe.
1791, March 10, Riche, Sarah, and Thomas Redman.
1751, Dec. 19, Riche, Thomas, and Sarah Peel.
1769, Dec. 16, Richey, Adam, and Rebecca Taylor.
1735, Sept. 16, Richey, Francis, and Mary White.
1736, Oct. 23, Richie, Mary, and Joseph Bayley.
1733, April 12, Richie, Samuel, and Rebecca Beale.
1756, May 27, Richinson, Elizabeth, and William Hummer.
1763, Nov. 23, Richison, Sarah, and John Thompson.
1768, May 31, Richmond, Jane, and John Turner.
1733, April 4, Rickets, Margaret, and William Tull.
1757, May 31, Rickets, William, and Rose Robeson.
1772, June 27. Ricketts, Nathaniel, and Hannah Barthot.
1792, Nov. 4, Riddle, David, and Mary Nicholson.
1779, June 1, Riddle, Eliz., and Richard McMichael.
1801, April 16, Riddle, Mary, and Henry Stead.
1806, Jan. 2, Riddle, Samuel, and Ann Macpherson.
1770, June 7, Ridge, Daniel, and Mary McLaughlin.
1729, Nov. 16, Ridge, Eliz., and Jacob Wain.
1770, April 25, Ridge, Hannah, and William Marshall.
1767, Jan. 31, Ridge, John, and Rebeccah White.
1722, March 20, Ridge, Mary, and John Spencer.
1767, Dec. 2, Ridge, Peter, and Mary Brown.
1730, Dec. 23, Ridge, Sarah, and Gabriel Wilkinson.
1798, March 29, Ridge, Thomas, and Priscilla Heritage.
1716, May 27, Ridge, Thomas, and Martha Thornhill.
1776, March 26, Ridgeway, Allen, and Phœbe Ridgeway.
1776, March 26, Ridgeway, Phœbe, and Allen Ridgeway.
1773, April 6, Ridgway, Eliz., and Thomas Wade.
1739, Aug. 16, Ridgway, Richard, and Phœbe Pancast.
1800, Aug. 31, Ridick, Joseph, and Sarah Faithful.
1730, June 15, Ridley, Stephen, and Elizabeth Taylor.
1770, Dec. 30, Riffeth, Phœbe, and Adam Sticker.
1741, July 11, Rigby, Henry, and Sarah Williamson.
1771, Sept. 12, Rigby, Joseph, and Rebecca Deacon.
1774, July 2, Right, Mary, and Patrick Martin.
1777, April 16, Righter, John, and Eleanor Bankson.
1740, Nov. 6, Rigley, Rebecca, and James Johnson.
1740, Nov. 6, Rigley, William, and Elizabeth Dilworth.
1803, May 11, Riker, John, and Jane Connelly.
1805, Jan. 10, Riley, Cath., and Richard Brady.
1801, Oct. 13, Riley, Mary, and Robert Eskit.
1757, March 18, Riley, Richard, and Mary Cheyney.

1728, May   30, Rimmer, Nic., and Martha Johnson.
1762, Aug.   3, Rinard, Catherine, and Arthur Broards.
1800, Nov.   15, Rindleman, Ann, and James Brewster.
1796, Jan.   30, Rindt, David, and Eliz. Bockins.
1801, Dec.   30, Rinedollar, Hester, and William Taylor.
1745, April   20, Ring, Rachel, and Abraham Collins.
1792, May   3, Ringold, Samuel, and Maria Cadwallader.
1711, Oct.   9, Ripley, Mary, and John Carter.
1785, Nov.   10, Ritter, Frederick, and Tacey Underwood.
1728, Feb.   9, Rivers, Dinah, and Stanley Cannon.
1802, July   15, Rivers, Marg., and George Innis.
1728, Sept.   2, Rivers, Mary, and Thomas Leech.
1744, Sept.   8, Rivers, Mary, and Jos. Conyers.
1737, Nov.   20, Rivers, Sarah, and Cornelius Bowne.
1739, Jan.   20, Rives, Joseph, and Mary Empson.
1772, Aug.   17, Rivett, Eliz., and Henry Willkly.
1732, July   24, Rix, Benjamin, and Giles Teyland.
1800, Jan.   16, Roan, Ann, and Charles Penrose.
1727, April   20, Roach, Mary, and John Connor.
1731, June   28, Roads, Mary, and George Costard.
1800, May   4, Roach, William, and Eliz. Call.
1789, July   14, Robbins, Ann, and Benjamin Scott.
1780, July   6, Robbins, Hannah, and Francis Hodgson.
1742, Jan.   19, Roberdeau, Ann Judith, and William Clymer.
1734, Oct.   1, Roberdeau, Mary, and Hugh Basil Kighley.
1785, Dec.   22, Roberts, Abraham, and Rachel Milnor.
1801, May   5, Roberts, Alice Matilda, and John Baptista Poree.
1770, May   31, Roberts, Ann, and John Griffins.
1784, Sept.   23, Roberts, Ann, and Philip Rice.
1734, Feb.   3, Roberts, Anne, and Thomas Mullins.
1755, April   3, Roberts, Aquila, and Mary Sheed.
1776, May   12, Roberts, Catherine, and John Brooks.
1802, Aug.   28, Roberts, Cath., and Charles Washington Golds-
                      brough.
1764, April   9, Roberts, Charles, and Hannah Norberry.
1784, April   6, Roberts, Edward, and Eliz. Bell.
1710, April   11, Roberts, Eleanor, and Abram Smith.
1730-1, Feb.   15, Roberts, Elizabeth, and John Jones.
1721, Jan.   22, Roberts, Elizabeth, and Robert Tait.
1784, Aug.   5, Roberts, Eliz., and Thomas Smith.
1801, June   6, Roberts, Eliz., and Robert Henry.
1762, Sept.   19, Roberts, Elizabeth, and Joseph Keith.
1798, Aug.   23, Roberts, Hannah, and Tench Francis.
1762, Nov.   25, Roberts, Hannah, and John Simpson.
1803, March 10, Roberts, Hugh, and Sarah Smith.
1767, March 23, Roberts, Jacob, and Mary Gill.
1730-1, Feb. 23, Roberts, Jane, and Joseph Howell.

1770, July　22, Roberts, Jane, and William Campbell.
1734, Nov.　18, Roberts, John, and Susanah Edwards.
1765, June　26, Roberts, John, and Susannah Davis.
1795, June　11, Roberts, John, and Eliz. Warner.
1779, Nov.　20, Roberts, John, and Abigail Rees.
1804, March 27, Roberts, Joshua, and Ann Vanholt.
1795, Oct.　30, Roberts, Lowrey, and Patrick Holden.
1752, April　24, Roberts, Margaret, and Jonathan Sturgis.
1762, Nov.　12, Roberts, Martha, and Anthony Bolton.
1749, May　2, Roberts, Mary, and Cornelius Bryan.
1731-2, Jan.　6, Roberts, Mary, and James Dilworth.
1785, March 17, Roberts, Mary, and William Story.
1805, Nov.　6, Roberts, Mary, and John J. Smith.
1728, Feb.　23, Roberts, Matt., and Sarah Walter.
1748, July　28, Roberts, Mercy, and John Denton.
1732, Aug.　14, Roberts, Morgan, and Catherine David.
1803, Dec.　13, Roberts, Peter, and Sarah Perkins.
1804, May　20, Roberts, Owen, and Mary Mitchel.
1742, Dec.　2, Roberts, Rachel, and Thomas Hutchins.
1729, Jan.　2, Roberts, Rachel, and Wm Evans.
1804, Sept.　10, Roberts, Richard, and Rebecca Jones.
1736, Jan.　22, Roberts, Sarah, and Thomas Evans.
1799, May　30, Roberts, Sarah, and John Overy.
1783, Dec.　29, Roberts, Sarah, and Ambrose Williams.
1798, June　23, Roberts, Sophia, and States Morris.
1769, July　24, Roberts, Tacy, and Benjamin Jones.
1730-1, Feb. 10, Roberts, Thomas, and Susannah Thomas.
1752, Dec.　30, Roberts, Thomas, and Mary Fordan.
1713, March 26, Roberts, Thomas, and Sidney Hughes.
1771, Dec.　26, Roberts, Thomas, and Sarah Monro.
1760, Aug.　23, Roberts, William, and Hannah Delavan.
1786, June　8, Robertson, Ann, and Thomas Lippencut.
1786, Sept.　25, Robertson, Eliz., and William Miller.
1794, Dec.　4, Robertson, Joseph, and Eleanor Goldsborough.
1789, June　16, Robertson, Mary, and David Stewart.
1769, Sept.　7, Robertson, Richard, and Elizabeth Corren.
1765, Aug.　16, Robertson, Robert, and Elizabeth Thomas.
1759, April　16, Robertson, Sarah, and Robort Boyd.
1779, Oct.　28, Robeson, Esqr, Andrew, and Mary Stocker.
1775, Nov.　28, Robeson, Ann, and Charles Newman.
1730, March 26, Robeson, Charity, and John Brinklowe, jr.
1795, Jan.　29, Robeson, Jonathan, and Sarah Wharton.
1764, June　5, Robeson, Margaret, and Henry Robinson.
1795, Oct.　20, Robeson, Mary, and George Bensal.
1730, April　14, Robeson, Rachel, and John Royall.
1757, May　31, Robeson, Rose, and William Rickets.

1735, June 14, Robeson, Septimus, and Hannah Baker.
1772, Dec. 2, Robeson, Thomas, and Ann Talbot.
1759, Dec. 1, Robotham, George, and Mary Burrows.
1728, June 17, Robins, Ann, and Gee Rees.
1738, May 26, Robins, Anne, and Henry Chads.
1743, July 30, Robins, Anne, and Thomas Stretch.
1805, June 27, Robin, Celeste, and John Lachausec Bujac.
1735, Feb. 27, Robins, Elizabeth, and William Sutton.
1768, Nov. 29, Robins, Mary, and William Taylor.
1769, April 6, Robins, Sarah, and Joseph Rice.
1767, Oct. 15, Robinson, Abraham, and Sarah Penrose.
1788, Aug. 17, Robinson, Ann, and Abraham Dolby.
1758, June 24, Robinson, Ann, and Benjamin Lowry.
1799, May 28, Robinson, Ann, and George Brady.
1763, Jan. 24, Robinson, Barbara, and William Laurence.
1736, March 28, Robinson, Budd, and Rebecca Parker.
1721, Oct. 19, Robinson, David, and Eleanor Lane.
1749, Feb. 24, Robinson, Deborah, and Jonathan Carr.
1759, Dec. 21, Robinson, Eleanor, and Samuel Gambier.
1773, Sept. 3, Robinson, Eliz., and Nicholas Stackhouse.
1763, Dec. 19, Robinson, Elizabeth, and George Kemble.
1783, Feb. 27, Robinson, Eliz., and Jacob Dehart.
1723, March 28, Robinson, Elizabeth, and Robert Macklin.
1720, March 1, Robinson, Elizabeth, and Henry Rothwell.
1782, Dec. 9, Robinson, Esther, and John Willett.
1752, Aug. 15, Robinson, Francis, and Elizabeth Archdale.
1764, June 5, Robinson, Henry, and Margaret Robeson.
1721, Dec. 24, Robinson, Hester, and Archibald Carter.
1802, Dec. 31, Robinson, Hugh, and Eliz. Seley.
1794, May 8, Robinson, Ismael, and Eliz. Fisher.
1768, Nov. 10, Robinson, James, and Rachel Higgins.
1758, June 28, Robinson, James, and Margaret Albright.
1764, Feb. 20, Robinson, James, and Jane McBrier.
1730–1, Feb. 11, Robinson, Jane, and Rochard Lovatt.
1804, April 10, Robinson, Jane, and William Graham.
1772, March 19, Robinson, John, and Ann Hughes.
1769, Nov. 23, Robinson, Margaret, and John McMurtry.
1760, Feb. 14, Robinson, Margaret, and John Johnson.
1806, Feb. 1, Robinson, Martha, and Hugh Hardy.
1753, Aug. 23, Robinson, Martha, and Charles Smith.
1770, April 26, Robinson, Mary, and Samuel Workman.
1785, July 21, Robinson, Mary, and Benjamin Mifflin.
1787, Nov. 28, Robinson, Mary, and James Smith.
1791, Nov. 17, Robinson, Mary, and John Miller.
1794, April 13, Robinson, Mary, and John Loyd.
1770, Dec. 9, Robinson, Mary, and Michael Chew.

1717, May   11, Robinson, Mary, and William Crookshank.
1765, Sept. 30, Robinson, Mellesim, and James Walker.
1741, Dec.   8, Robinson, Peter, and Rebecca Evans.
1759, Feb.   8, Robinson, Rebecca, and Alexander Barclay.
1766, Nov.   19, Robinson, Rebeccah, and Luke Shields.
1743, Jan.   11, Robinson, Rebecca, and Thomas Bay.
1786, Jan.   1, Robinson, Sarah, and Joseph Lownsburg.
1768, July   21, Robinson, Sarah, and Joseph Trotter.
1800, Feb.   20, Robinson, Sarah, and George Dobson.
1794, Dec.   11, Robinson, Sarah, and John Bennet.
1776, Aug.   22, Robinson, Sarah, and Richard Peters.
1761, Nov.   29, Robinson, Sarah, and Patrick Geogahan.
1768, Oct,   23, Robinson, sen., Thomas, and Mary Eliz. Hanson.
1796, May   18, Robinson, Thomas, and Mary Coates.
1797, Nov.   23, Robinson, William, and Susan Bonham.
1796, Feb.   21, Robinson, William, and Sarah Exon.
1758, Dec.   6, Robinson, William, and Susannah Shead.
1767, Aug.   23, Robinson, William, and Elizabeth Taylor.
1781, July   12, Robinson, William, and Margaret Johnston.
1783, Dec.   4, Robinett, Eliz., and John Garwin.
1786, July   27, Robinett, Maria, and George Rawlings.
1781, Sept. 10, Robinett, Mary, and John Fleming.
1800, Feb.   20, Robinet, Samuel, and Eliz. Hart.
1759, Dec.   1, Robinet, Susannah, and Benjamin Jolly.
1733, April   4, Robison, Eleanor, and Jacob Leech.
1726, Dec.   18, Robison, John, and Mary Ford.
1732, Nov.   23, Robison, Peter, and Sarah Farmer.
1740, May   22, Robison, Thomas, and Elizabeth Pearce.
1757, Oct.   7, Robson, Robert, and Jane Haley.
1744, March 26, Roche, Catharine, and John Fox.
1793, Jan.   31, Roche, John Baptist, and Mary Harper.
1759, Feb.   1, Rochford, Mary, and John Logan.
1748, June   9, Rockwell, Samuel, and Martha Milner.
1772, Dec.   7, Rockwell, Susannah, and John Goodwin.
1751, June   27, Rodger, Thomas, and Elizabeth Bowen.
1759, Feb.   15, Rodgers, James, and Mary Cole.
1784, June   3, Rodman, Gilbert, and Sarah Gibbs.
1770, Oct.   18, Rodman, John, and Susannah Borradiall.
1782, Sept. 20, Rodman, Rachel, and Samuel Gibbs.
1785, Jan.   20, Rodman, William, and Esther West.
1786, June   19, Rodney, Agnes, and Robert Murray.
1728, Nov.   26, Rody, Dorcus, and John Kilbright.
1746, Aug.   5, Roe, Anne, and John Kenoby.
1761, Aug.   6, Roe, Jesse, and Sarah Brown.
1785, April 12, Roe, Walter, and Sarah Donaldson.
1803, Sept. 20, Rogee, Cath., and David Edwin.

1796, Oct.   26, Rogers, Benjamin, and Ann Calvin.
1801, Oct.   17, Rogers, Cath., and Nathaniel Chettenden.
1802, May   10, Rogers, Ebenezer, and Jane Nelson.
1761, Nov.   5, Rogers, Eleanor, and Thomas Hockley.
1778, Dec.   7, Rogers, George, and Ruth Emory.
1725, Aug.   5, Rogers, John, and Deb. Read.
1766, Dec.   4, Rogers, Jane, and Matthew Hughs.
1739, Dec.   5, Rogers, Margaret, and Thomas Griffiths.
1761, March 23, Rogers, Martha, and Joseph Kimble.
1803, Jan.   5, Rogers, Mary, and John Colliner.
1770, Aug.   7, Rogers, Mary, and John Leteliere.
1746, Sept.   4, Rogers, Mary, and Nathan Cook.
1757, Nov.   8, Rogers, Olive, and John Hough.
1782, May   22, Rogers, Phoebe, and Andrew Kain.
1759, June   11, Rogers, Robert, and Mary Talbot.
1772, April   7, Rogers, Samuel, and Mary Kearnes.
1762, April   17, Rogers, Samuel, and Martha Martin.
1731, Nov.   11, Rogers, Sarah, and Capt. William Hellier.
1761, Dec.   11, Rogers, Thomas, and Mary Wilson.
1806, June   2, Rogers, William, and Eliz. Dunbar.
1799, Feb.   27, Rollington, John, and Sarah Douglas.
1735, Dec.   30, Rome, Samuel, and Susannah Appleton.
1779, Sept.   1, Roney, Damaris, and Daniel Evans.
1782, May   8, Rooks, Sarah, and Robert Taylor.
1767, Dec.   11, Room, John, and Elizabeth Orin.
1740, Jan.   5, Rork, James, and Hannah Hudson.
1783, June   16, Rosbottom, James, and Eliz. Davis.
1795, Oct.   25, Rose, Champagne, and Susanna Villgrove.
1769, March   4, Rose, Eliz., and Peter Jones.
1782, Nov.   11, Rose, Eliz., and Hugh McPherson.
1790, Sept.   30, Rose, John, and Ann Walters.
1765, Aug.   15, Rose, Jonathan, and Elizabeth Nowland.
1785, Feb.   20, Rose, Mary, and Philip Dolby.
1764, Dec.   13, Rose, Mary, and John Dean.
1800, Nov.   8, Rose, Mary, and Edward Mende.
1745, Sept.   30, Rose, Peter, and Mary Gardner.
1745, June   4, Ross, Aeneas, and Sarah Leech.
1795, Dec.   3, Ross, Anna Helena Amelia, and George Plumstead.
1795, Aug.   29, Ross, Aquila, and Eliz. Johnson.
1788, Sept.   27, Ross, David, and Martha Hopper.
1723, Dec.   11, Ross, David, and Ann Adams.
1790, Aug.   17, Ross, Eliz., and John Hamilton.
1768, July   7, Ross, Catherine, and Henry Gurney.
1788, June   18, Ross, Clementina, and John Mifflin.
1791, Aug.   17, Ross, George, and Mary Munyan.
1755, April   10, Ross, Jacob, and Jane Sayre.

1801, June 27, Ross, Jane, and John C. Jones.
1735, Dec. 28, Ross, John, and Elizabeth Morgan.
1797, Dec. 16, Ross, John, and Hester Smith.
1765, April 10, Ross, John and Sarah Reily.
1804, Jan. 13, Ross, John D., and Mary Taylor.
1795, June 29, Ross, Margaret, and Anthony Wilson.
1763, Jan. 6, Ross, Mary, and Mark Bird.
1764, March 17, Ross, Mary, and James Reynolds.
1787, Sept. 20, Ross, Richard, and Eliz. Cassedy.
1763, Oct. 21, Ross, Robert, and Eleanor McCrump.
1761, Sept. 9, Ross, Ruth, and Anthony Cadman.
1802, Oct. 21, Ross, Samuel, and Sarah Baker.
1791, Aug. 11, Ross, Sarah, and William Bell.
1797, March 23, Ross, William, and Julianna Duffield.
1751, April 18, Rosseter, Thomas, and Elizabeth Bull.
1735, Feb. 21, Rosson, Elizabeth, and John Drewite.
1803, Oct, 6, Roswell, Jane, and Joseph Newman.
1720, March 1, Rothwell, Henry, and Elizabeth Robinson.
1717, May 13, Rothwell, Henry, and Rachel Griffith.
1738, May 23, Rourk, Michael, and Sarah Powel.
1783, Feb. 20, Rous, Mary, and John Knight.
1736, Nov. 20, Rausford, Marjora, and John Fitzharris.
1729, Jan. 27, Rouse, Eleanor, and Jos Geals.
1748, April 14, Rouse, Emanuel, and Mary Jackson.
1768, Nov. 6, Rouse, Mary, and John Walter.
1760, Jan. 4, Rouse, Mary, and William Gay.
1773, Feb. 23, Rouse, Rachel, and William Hazelwood.
1772, March 19, Row, Jacob, and Prudence Maroe.
1733, May 20, Row, James, and Catherine Jenkins.
1752, Jan. 20, Rowan, Margaret, and Samuel Davis.
1774, May 21, Rowan, Mary, and Robert Lucas.
1743, Oct. 17, Rowe, William, and Ann Taylor.
1805, Dec. 7, Rowen, Phœbe, and William Jones.
1754, April 9, Rowland, Bryan, and Anne Wilson.
1805, May 21, Rowland, Deborah, and William Steel.
1710, Dec. 20, Rowland, James, and Bridgett Lewis.
1771, Aug. 15, Rowland, Mary, and John Jones.
1738, Oct. 24, Rowland, Robert, and Alice Stephens.
1801, July 2, Rowland, Thomas, and Mary Jones.
1800, Dec. 7, Rowley, James, and Mary Hoofman.
1801, Aug. 5, Rowley, Mary, and Thomas McMahan.
1761, March 16, Rownand, Sarah, and Joseph Browning.
1745, Nov. 14, Rowney, Patrick, and Martha Toms.
1730, April 14, Royall, John, and Rachel Robeson.
1795, Nov. 3, Royal, Susanna, and John Crippin.
1756, July 15. Ruaby, John, and Anne Davis.

1756, Sept. 11, Rubee, Jane, and Thomas Smith.
1743, June 18, Rubie, Charles, and Catherine Russell.
1796, Dec. 7, Rudd, Sarah, and Thomas Stanley.
1795, March 9, Rudd, Sarah, and William Burgess.
1768, April 14, Rudolph, Ann, and Benjamin Paschal.
1791, July 3, Rudolph, Mary, and Daniel Brewton.
1786, April 13, Rudrow, Abigail, and John Ashburner.
1746, April 23, Rudrow, Grace, and Jacob Lipencout.
1785, April 11, Rudrow, Mary, and John Fellers.
1771, June 6, Rudulph, Zebulun, and Martha Syng.
1775, Oct. 2, Rue, Anthony, and Catherine Hufty.
1709, Aug. 15, Rule, Margaret, and John Hughes.
1761, Sept. 10, Rumney, Ann, and George Morgan.
1800, April 15, Rumsey, Charlotte Jane, and John Bullus.
1751, May 9, Rundle, Daniel, and Anne Tresse.
1772, May 14, Rundle, Richard, and Mary Murgatroyd.
1733, Dec. 31, Rundle, Warwick, and Patience Evans.
1792, Dec. 19, Ruper, Rebecca, and David Sneider.
1801, Nov. 19, Ruscaman, Gerrat, and Cath. Wheeland.
1768, Oct. 26, Russell, Allen, and Mary McCracken.
1768, July 25, Russell, Ann, and Henry Cowen.
1743, June 18, Russell, Catherine, and Charles Rubee.
1761, Feb. 24, Russell, Elizabeth, and Samuel Harrald.
1781, Oct. 25, Russell, Eliz., and Benjamin Evans.
1781, Nov. 28, Russell, Eliz., and Jacob Plankinhorne.
1799, July 22, Russel, Galbraith, and Margaret Armstrong.
1761, March 5, Russell, George, and Sarah Eckleson.
1741, Jan. 13, Russell, Henrietta, and John Fitzgerald.
1768, May 2, Russell, James, and Ann Branderman.
1787, Feb. 5, Russell, Jemminia Elizabeth, and James Smith.
1770, Feb. 19, Russell, John, and Ann Crispin.
1793, April 4, Russell, John, and Eliz. Milne.
1758, Oct. 4, Russell, Mary, and Augustine Bartholomew.
1757, April 4, Russel, Nathaniel, and Mary Lacy.
1758, Dec. 13, Russell, Nemo, and Flora Fielding.
1767, May 28, Russell, Robert, and Susannan Morris.
1747, Jan. 26, Russell, Sarah, and Valentine Handlin.
1743, Nov. 17, Russell, William, and Sarah Sanders.
1796, May 31, Ruston, Mary F., and William Harrison.
1793, June 13, Rush, Benjamin, and Deborah Jones.
1762, Feb. 23, Rush, Elizabeth, and William Ayres.
1768, June 23, Rush, Eliz., and John Smith.
1799, March 12, Rush, Emily, and Ross Cuthbert.
1743, June 2, Rush, John, and Wilmouth Camp.
1772. April 16, Rush, John, and Mary Raybold.
1754, Feb. 14, Rush, John, and Elizabeth Price.

1750, Sept.　19, Rush, Joseph, and Rebecca Lincon.
1792, Dec.　12, Rush, Lewis, and Mary Marshall.
1733, May　24, Rush, Mary, and George Irvine.
1803, Dec.　29, Rush, Mary, and Thomas Manners.
1761, June　11, Rush, Rebecca, and Thomas Stamper.
1804, Sept.　13, Rush, Sarah, and John Lower.
1766, May　30, Ruth, Francis, and Elizabeth Taylor.
1714, March 30, Ruther, Mary, and Nicholas Gatlow.
1785, Dec.　27, Rutter, John, and Mary Lored.
1735, July　24, Rutter, Mary Catherine, and William Pyewell.
1790, Nov.　11, Rutter, Penelope, and Thomas Harrell.
1800, Aug.　3, Rutter, Phœbe, and William Smith.
1736, March　5, Rutter, Rebecca, and William Cane.
1728, Oct.　10, Rutter, Thomas, and Mary Gizlin.
1758, Aug.　11, Rutherford, Alexander, and Catherine Stewart,
1736, Nov.　15, Rutherford Editha, and Matthew Carley.
1786, Jan.　10, Rutherford, William, and Cath. Dugan.
1749, May　18, Ryall, George, and Mary Worley.
1729–30, Feb. 10, Ryall, Mary, and Edward Wayn.
1733, Dec.　3, Ryall, Susannah, and Thomas Davison.
1793, Jan.　3, Ryan, Cath., and David Log.
1763, Sept.　14, Ryan, Christian, and Jacob James.
1767, Oct.　27, Ryan, Elizabeth, and Christopher Esterby.
1800, May　10, Ryan, James, and Cath. Conynham.
1796, Oct.　15, Ryan, Jane, and Ezekiel Jenkens.
1743, Oct.　23, Ryan, John, and Mary McCullough.
1777, May　21, Ryan, Mary, and Timothy Donohoe.
1742, Nov.　2, Ryan, Mary, and Stephen Cran.
1765, Jan.　29, Ryan, Philip, and Ann Burk.
1797, Nov.　27, Ryan, Phœbe, and John Jones.
1793, Jan.　3, Ryan, Thomas, and Phoebe Young.
1733, Sept.　30, Ryan, Thomas, and Charlotta Davids.
1710, Dec.　26, Ryeles, Edward, and Elizabeth Gregory.
1774, Sept.　11, Ryle, Mary, and Henry Fenner.
1748, May　7, Ryon, Mary, and John Keys.
1758, Feb.　3, Rush, Jacob, and Hannah Myers.
1714, Oct.　10, Sackeverel, John, and Juliana Gill.
1737, Aug.　9, Sadiescus, Mary, and Thomas Palmer.
1720, Aug.　3, Saggerell, James, and Eleanor Scotson.
1789, July　12, Saley, Bartlemy, and Susannah Calam.
1758, Jan.　17, Salkill, Agnes, and Simon Guest.
1748, Oct.　16, Sallows, Elizabeth, and Joseph Beddowe.
1740, May　29, Sallows, Richard, and Elizabeth Stone.
1721, Sept.　21, Salmon, Dennis, and Ann Bowan.
1769, Oct.　21, Salsbagg, Joseph, and Elizabeth Millar.
1774, Dec.　29, Salter, John, and Eliz. Gordon.

1785, Dec.   29, Salter, John, and Mary Entz.
1769, Nov.   30, Salter, Lawrence, and Dorothy Gordon.
1782, Aug.   22, Salter, Lawrence, and Sarah Howard.
1789, Dec.   24, Salter, Margaret, and Jehu Lardner.
1795, Nov.   11, Salter, Maria, and Kearney Wharton.
1733, June   4, Salter, Peter, and Rebecca Mount.
1758, Dec.   23, Salter, Thomas, and Susannah Butler.
1726, Nov.   9, Salvai, Abraham, and Mary Friend.
1800, May   15, Sammons, William, and Eliz. Bristol.
1745, Nov.   15, Sample, William, and Rachel Shanly.
1800, June   26, Samson, Henrietta, and Thomas Sims.
1775, Feb.   5, Samuel, Mary, and Dean Timmons.
1800, Sept.   4, Sanders, Rebecca, and John Hastings.
1786, Aug.   20, Sanders, Rose, and Caeser Cummins.
1743, Nov.   17, Sanders, Sarah, and William Russell.
1746, July   23, Sanderson, Elizabeth, and Abraham Nut.
1752, Dec.   25, Sandford, Elizabeth, and Andrew Broughton.
1799, March 28, Sandford, William, and Ann McFall.
1742, Oct.   22, Sands, Eliz., and James Beans.
1755, Aug.   27, Sands, Thomas, and Sarah Duncan.
1756, Jan.   5, Sanford, Robert, and Margaret Haddick.
1795, April 26, Santloe, Hannah, and Philip Claridge.
1795, Aug.   5, Sapout, William, and Bathsheba Tonkin.
1805, Dec.   27, Sarazin, John B., and Lucretia Scot.
1801, Sept.   3, Sargeant, William, and Eliz. Morgan.
1779, Oct.   27, Satchwell, Eliz., and Rueben Ore.
1795, April 26, Satterfield, John, and Ann Hampton.
1751, Aug.   1, Saul, Rachel, and John Harry.
1735, Oct.   19, Saunders, Bartholomew, and Anne Cook.
1768, Feb.   27, Saunders, Edward, and Frances Moore.
1773, Sept. 16, Saunders, Eleanor, and John Browne.
1746, Jan.   18, Saunders, Elizabeth, and John Edwards.
1803, Jan.   29, Saunders, Jabez, and Eliz. Brooks.
1739, Aug.   4, Saunders, John, and Leah Williams.
1756, Nov.   18, Saunders, John, and Catherine Weaver.
1767, Nov.   23, Saunders, Joseph, and Jane Izzard.
1801, Oct.   12, Saunders, Richard, and Sarah George.
1748, Nov.   29, Saunders, Mary, and Andrew Collins.
1769, Dec.   19, Saunders, Samuel, and Rachel Flower.
1749, Nov.   11, Saunders, William, and Elizabeth Hartman.
1764, April   5, Saunderson, George, and Eleanor Massey.
1762, Nov.   17, Saunderson, Robert, and Hester Kollock.
1797, Nov.   15, Savage, John, and Margaret Larkey.
1743, Jan.   20, Savage, Joseph, and Rebecca Dennis.
1720, Aug.   11, Savage, Mary, and Thomas Reese.
1733, May   17, Savage, Rebecca, and Samuel Nutt.

1779, Feb.　28, Savell, George, and Mary Fester.
1803, Aug.　22, Savin, Samuel, and Deborah Tallman.
1751, July　17, Savoy, Bridget, and Robert Clarke.
1758, Sept.　25, Sawer, John, and Elizabeth Thomas.
1789, July　18, Sawyer, James, and Margaret Caldelengh.
1728, June　7, Saxbye, Elizabeth, and John Waterfield.
1734, June　15, Say, Thomas, and Susannah Sprogle.
1754, June　5, Sayer, William, and Alice Parsons.
1802, Nov.　30, Sayre, Ann, and Hugh Shaw.
1763, Aug.　31, Sayre, Esther, and William Atlee.
1792, April　10, Sayre, Francis Beawes, and Ann Heysham.
1755, April　10, Sayre, Jane, and Jacob Ross.
1751, April　8, Sayre, John, and Rachel Bowes.
1758, Sept.　28, Sayre, John, and Mary Bowes.
1801, Feb.　11, Sayre, Thœdosia Henrietta, and Richard Coxe.
1721, April　27, Scaber, Martha, and Joseph Pearse.
1805, July　5, Scaise, Eliz., and Alexander Lawson.
1773, March 28, Scalinger, Enous, and Sarah Cox.
1756, Nov.　20, Scanlan, Luke, and Martha McKnight.
1805, July　28, Scarlet, Thomas, and Mary Johnson.
1727, May　13, Scay, Elizabeth, and John Carlow.
1746, Sept.　10, Sceen, Hannah, and Daniel Brodrick.
1747, Oct.　8, Schluydhorn, Mary, and Michael Slatter.
1785, Dec.　11, Schockuly, Thomas, and Eliz. Palmer.
1757, May　22, Schofield, Jane, and John Brown.
1764, Aug.　10, Schrack, Hannah, and Reuben Ellis.
1738, July　13, Schraik, Simon, and Elizabeth Oslear.
1784, Aug.　12, Scimer, John, and Eleanor Anderson.
1799, May　5, Scitts, Laurence, and Mary Shiarer.
1749, Feb.　1, Scoggin, Mary, and Joseph Scull.
1761, March 19, Scoghan, Ann, and John Beezly.
1750, Jan.　23, Scolly, Samuel, and Ann Eades.
1727, May　17, Scorthorn, Sam., and Ann Davis.
1794, June　12, Scot, Amelia, and John Hubbart.
1795, June　21, Scot, Benjamin, and Phoebe Martin.
1799, March 11, Scot, Christiana, and George Spence.
1730, Oct.　29, Scot, Lethia, and Richard Howell.
1805, Dec.　27, Scot, Lucretia, and John B. Sarazin.
1746, Oct.　31, Scot, James, and Mary Evans.
1745, June　18, Scot, Matthew, and Hannah Guttier.
1754, Aug.　4, Scot, Thomas, and Anne Gosline.
1734, Jan.　23, Scothorn, Mary, and Thomas Philips.
1720, Aug.　3, Scotson, Eleanor, and James Saggerell.
1717, May　9, Scotson, Jane, and Howell Powell.
1789, July　14, Scott, Benjamin, and Ann Robbins.
1749, Sept.　2, Scott, Edward, and Mary Kuhl.

1767, Feb.   28, Scott, Elizabeth, and Abraham Gregory.
1773, July   20, Scott, John, and Ann Dennis.
1778, Oct.   18, Scott, John, and Ann Adams.
1801, May   9, Scott, John, and Susannah Reading.
1797, June   17, Scott, Mary, and John Moore.
1791, May   11, Scott, Sarah, and Amos Early.
1728, May   30, Scott, Thomas, and Leah Brown.
1805, Dec.   3, Scott, William, and Sarah Matthews.
1789, Nov.   14, Scriba, George, and Sarah Dundas.
1760, April   17, Scull, Abigail, and Thomas Biddle.
1773, Aug.   12, Scull, Benjamin, and Eliz. Berry.
1797, March 16, Scull, Deborah, and George Ogden.
1738, Oct   10, Scull, Edward, and Anne Heap.
1799, Nov.   28, Scull, Eleanor, and Thomas Bryan.
1749, Dec.   4, Scull, Elizabeth, and Samuel Holland.
1739, March 26, Scull, Elizabeth, and William Hopton.
1739, Dec.   17, Scull, Elizabeth, and Hugh Hill.
1766, Oct.   1, Scull, Hester, and Joel Zane.
1753, March 8, Scull, James, and Lidia Ianley.
1721, Feb.   21, Scull, James, and Susannah Siddon.
1745, March 10, Scull, John, and Ann Jones.
1770, Nov.   29, Scull, John, and Mary Shoemaker.
1722, Oct.   25, Scull, John, and Elizabeth Farmer.
1730, April   2, Scull, Joseph, and Frances Bethell.
1749, Feb.   1, Scull, Joseph, and Mary Scoggin.
1750, Jan.   18, Scull, Jasper, and Mary Eyers.
1767, Sept.   5, Scull, Martha, and Elias Boys.
1792, Dec.   30, Scull, Maria, and William Cox.
1747, Oct.   8, Scull, Mary, and Joseph Wood.
1730, April   2, Scull, Mary, and William Biddle.
1785, Oct.   26, Scull, Mary, and Daniel Levan, Esqr.
1732, Oct.   7, Scull, Nicholas, and Rebecca Thomson.
1774, Dec.   13, Scull, Nicholas, and Ann Townsend.
1787, Nov.   1, Scull, Priscilla, and Alexander Blair.
1750, March 3, Scull, Rachel, and Michael Biddle.
1767, April   2, Scull, Susannah, and James Vansandt.
1801, May   2, Scull, Theresa, and Peter Christian.
1763, Oct.   25, Scull, William, and Jane Lodge.
1756, Nov.   28, Scully, Anne, and William Hardcastle.
1759, May   5, Seabrook, John, and Mary E. Anderson.
1798, June   14, Seaman, Thomas, and Margaret Tyson.
1743, Jan.   29, Searle, Anne, and Samuel McCall.
1749, Feb.   19, Searle, John, and Mary Hicks.
1781, Dec.   11, Searle, Mary, and John Barclay.
1745, Nov.   14, Searle, Rebecca, and William Hayhurst.
1801, Sept.   23, Sears, Mary, and James Williams.

1759, Jan.   11, Searson, John, and Mary Lloyd.
1796, July   4, Seawright, James, and Christiana Donaldson.
1803, Dec.   10, Sebastian, Nathaniel, and Rachel Pritchett.
1797, March   2, Seddons, Jacob, and Mary Bartleson.
1723, Dec.   11, Seed, Abigail, and Hugh Sharp.
1787, Oct.   11, Seeds, Eliz., and John Fardey.
1720, Dec.   21, Seely, Isaac, and Mary Hughs.
1770, Nov.   1, Seigman, Susannah, and John Simmons.
1800, June   19, Selby, James, and Eliz. Gitts.
1805, Feb.   13, Selby, John, and Rebecca Grace Duffield.
1802, Dec.   31, Seley, Eliz., and Hugh Robinson.
1796, Nov.   24, Sell, Christina, and John Carver.
1784, Aug.   17, Sell, Margaret, and William Stewart.
1800, Sept. 21, Sellers, Isaac, and Mary Kaighn.
1762, Jan.   5, Sellers, William, and Sarah Bully.
1768, April 30, Selly, William, and Joanna Carnelly.
1722, April   5, Seltridge, William, and Lucila May.
1758, Dec.   5, Senniff, George, and Mary Gardner.
1790, June   20, Sermon, Benjamin, and Mary Picks.
1803, June   7, Service, Ann, and William Maley.
1750, Oct.   11, Seth James, and Anne Wilkinson.
1793, May   23, Seton, Hugh, and Mary Markward.
1794, Dec.   18, Sett, James, and Cath. Price.
1790, Feb.   11, Setts, Jacob, and Phœbe Paul.
1758, Sept. 28, Sewell, Mary, and Abraham Bickley.
1764, Sept. 15, Sewell, Richard, and Ann Claxton.
1733, Aug.   30, Sewell, Richard, and Henrietta Boude.
1750, Jan.   28, Sewer, Francis, and Hannah Clarke.
1731, Dec.   5, Sewer, Mary, and William Guye.
1731, Sept. 12, Sewers, Francis, and Hester Grant.
1728, Sept.   1, Sewers, James, and Faith Morrice.
1789, March   5, Seyfert, Priscilla, and John Miller.
1735, Oct.   15, Seyl, Jacob, and Susannah Frie.
1798, March 10, Seymer, Eleanor, and James Webb.
1772, March 17, Seymore, Ann, and Nicholas Egan.
1760, June   14, Seymour, Appelonia, and John Franks.
1755, Aug.   13, Shaddock, Mary, and Andrew Polson.
1799, May   3, Shade, John, and Mary Simmons.
1805, April 21, Shaffer, Eliz., and Alex. Jordan.
1781, May   28, Shaffis, Richard, and Rosanna Young.
1748, Dec.   28, Shakleton, Anne, and Joseph Dorvil.
1782, Feb.   11, Shallus, Joseph, and Hannah Knowles.
1745, Nov.   19, Shanly, Rachel, and William Sample.
1799, Jan.   6, Shannon, Eliz., and Derick Hartman.
1802, April 11, Shannon, James, and Jane Cummins.
1777, Feb.   9, Shannon, Samuel, and Mary Steuart.

1742, Jan.   26, Sharaden, Sophia, and William Beasly.
1797, Sept.   26, Sharer, Henry, and Sarah Brandt.
1727, May   18, Sharley, Hannah, and James Brown.
1721, Jan.   1, Sharlock, Elizabeth, and James Evans.
1752, Sept.   14, Sharp, Allen, and Elizabeth Hains.
1793, Dec.   14, Sharp, Ann, and James McCamach.
1769, Sept.   22, Sharp, Elizabeth, and John McCann.
1756, Nov.   21, Sharp, Henry, and Barbery Renoret.
1723, Dec.   11, Sharp, Hugh, and Abigail Seed,
1715, June   14, Sharp, Jane, and Robert Taylor.
1743, Feb.   12, Sharp, Joseph, and Mary Coleman.
1771, Jan.   7, Sharp, Mary, and Alexander Tod.
1796, Jan.   13, Sharp, Mary, and William Wood.
1773, July   29, Sharp, Rachel, and Abraham Wynkoop.
1746, Feb.   4, Sharpe, Anne, and Robert Down.
1802, May   20, Sharpe, Eliz., and William Alexander.
1794, Nov.   26, Sharpe, Jane, and Seth Lucas.
1783, July   8, Sharpe, John, and Mary Bridges.
1795, Jan.   10, Sharpe, John, and Pamelia Miers.
1795, June   27, Sharpe, Margaret, and Henry Bowles.
1783, Nov.   6, Sharpe, Susannah, and James Mackey.
1773, Sept.   27, Sharpless, Nathaniel, and Eliz. Wilkinson.
1747, April   30, Sharswood, George, and Anne Topp.
1750, Feb.   15, Shatzin, Barbara, and William Greathouse.
1783, May   1, Shaw, Archibald, and Lydia Collins.
1805, March   16, Shaw, Charlotte, and Robert Harris.
1712, Nov.   16, Shaw, Edward, and Mary Howell.
1769, Dec.   16, Shaw, Elizabeth, and Samuel Davis.
1758, March   20, Shaw, Elizabeth, and John Rawlston.
1783, July   11, Shaw, Eliz., and Edward Swaine.
1803, June   10, Shaw, Eliz., and Thomas Peterson.
1734, June   25, Shaw, George, and Joanna Parsons.
1802, Nov.   30, Shaw, Hugh, and Ann Sayre.
1736, May   31, Shaw, Jane, and Edward Williams.
1746, June   18, Shaw, John, and Mary Rees.
1776, Aug.   15, Shaw, John, and Sarah Penrose.
1772, April   28, Shaw, John, and Mary Comron.
1798, Aug.   9, Shaw, John, and Eliz. Palmer.
1749, May   20, Shaw, Mary, and John Duncann.
1720, May   9, Shaw, Mary, and Joshua Richardson.
1751, Oct.   26, Shaw, Samuel, and Mary Lassell.
1791, Aug.   10, Shaw, Sarah, and Hugh Stephenson.
1771, Feb.   21, Shaw, Thomas, and Eliz. Burton.
1796, May   26, Shaw, Thomas, and Frances Wood.
1805, April   21, Shaw, William, and Sarah McKee.
1801, Oct.   6, Shaw, William, and Mary Harper.

1758, Aug.   19, Shearman, John, and Margaret Sittleton.
1764, May   15, Shea, Walter, and Ann Thompson.
1758, Dec.   6, Shead, Susannah, and William Robinson.
1768, Jan.   19, Shead, William, and Isabella Waddel.
1798, Feb.   1, Sheaff, Cath., and Jacob Reese.
1795, May   6, Sheaffe, Cath., and Peter Grim.
1794, Dec.   4, Shean, Ann, and Thomas Moore.
1795, May   28, Shean, Mary, and John William Anderson.
1767, May   14, Shearcross, Mary, and Joseph Volans.
1744, May   19, Shearle, John, and Sarah Davis.
1773, Sept.   26, Sheckles, Susannah, and John Fox.
1790, Oct.   22, Shedaker, Eliz., and Robert Warnock.
1768, Sept.   13, Shedaker, Sarah, and Robert Deacon.
1771, June   7, Shedaker, William, and Sarah Davis.
1785, June   18, Shee, Mary, and Michael Pinto.
1800, Jan.   18, Shee, Rachel, and Robert Brooke.
1751, Dec.   12, Sheed, Anne, and John Moyes.
1755, April   3, Sheed, Mary, and Aquila Roberts.
1747, Jan.   4, Sheed, William, and Martha Coats.
1754, June   27, Sheen, Jonathan, and Susannah Rees.
1769, Dec.   3, Sheffel, Mary, and Peter Quackenbush.
1799, Jan.   15, Sheilds, James, and Ann Mercer.
1766, Nov.   19, Sheilds, Luke, and Rebeccah Robinson.
1763, Oct.   26, Shellcock, Sophia, and John Boley.
1781, July   12, Shelley, James, and Isabella Grubb.
1773, Sept.   11, Shelling, Margaret, and Thomas Castle.
1731, Oct.   29, Shelly, Hester, and John Larkins.
1806, July   8, Shelly, Moses, and Naomi Powell.
1804, June   30, Shenck, Peter H., and Harriet Courtney.
1726, April   28, Shenton, Nathan, and Eleanour Thomas.
1728, March 28, Shepherd, Amy, and Jos Howell.
1738, April   25, Shepherd, Jane, and William Cutler.
1769, Oct.   26, Shepherd, Jemima, and Robert Bridges.
1768, Sept.   29, Shepherd, Margaret, and John Barnitt.
1768, July   25, Shepherd, Mary, and Job Butcher.
1804, Sept.   27, Shepherd, Mary, and Henry Forrest.
1760, Feb.   18, Shephard, Robert, and Elizabeth Preston.
1736, Sept.   9, Shepherd, Robert, and Rebecca Carney.
1760, May   14, Shepperd, Hannah, and Valentine Bower.
1757, Nov.   19, Shepperd, Susannah, and James Matthew.
1799, May   2, Sherer, Gilbert, and Hannah Thomas.
1714, Dec.   5, Sherin, Sarah, and Samuel Davis.
1768, March 30, Sherlock, Esther, and Samuel Williams.
1768, Aug.   13, Sherlock, Margaret, and John Burrows.
1729, Sept.   22, Sherlock, Margt and Clement Cooper.
1756, Sept.   9, Sherlock, Thomas Alexander, and Margaret Miller

1728, Dec.	2, Sherraid, Sarah, and Robt. Bulman.
1752, Dec.	5, Sherrard, Robert, and Esther Skinner.
1748, Dec.	7, Sherrin, Sarah, and Nicholas Ward.
1783, Dec.	27, Sherry, John, and Sarah Blake.
1775, July	4, Sherwood, Ann, and Thomas Brown.
1759, Dec.	14, Shesser, Catherine, and John Fleming.
1733, April	30, Shetford, Walter, and Rebecca Ramanage.
1771, July	14, Shetter, Eliz., and David Everhart.
1728, May	17, Shew, Patience, and Abraham Albertson.
1767, June	18, Shewell, Mary, and Isaac Hunt.
1799, May	5, Shiarer, Mary, and Laurence Scitts.
1798, June	27, Shieffelin, Thomas, and Hannah Kessler.
1803, June	8, Shields, Michael, and Mary Chavres.
1803, Dec.	17, Shields, Patrick, and Ann Johnson.
1804, Jan.	21, Shields, Sarah, and Jonathan Meredith.
1805, July	14, Shilbread, Eliz., and Jacob Thompson.
1755, Aug.	1, Shillingsforth, Anne, and William Keen.
1769, Feb.	23, Shilly, Sarah, and Michael Dougherty.
1761, May	12, Shimer, Samuel, and Elizabeth Johnson.
1783, June	22, Shindler, John, and Sarah Leslie.
1805, March	2, Shingle, Mary, and John Canan.
1794, April	21, Shingle, Sarah, and James Molineux.
1802, Jane	7, Shinkle, Frederick, and Harriet Ottinger.
1766, Aug.	18, Shinn, Mary, and Richard Sinnet.
1792, Jan.	28, Shinney, Cath., and James Peale.
1767, Sept.	29, Shippen, Abigail, and Edward Spence.
1755, Aug.	27, Shippen, Allida, and Mathias Guery.
1774, March	23, Shippen, Ann, and Robert Strettell Jones.
1730–1, Jan.	21, Shippen, Anne, and Charles Willing.
1760, Dec.	4, Shippen, Catherine, and Richard Wallin.
1785, Nov.	23, Shippen, Edward, and Eliz. Foreman.
1753, Nov.	29, Shippen, Edward, jr., and Margaret Francis.
1803, June	6, Shippen, Eliz. Carter, and George Izard.
1778, Dec.	17, Shippen, Eliz., and Edward Burd.
1768, Sept.	29, Shippen, jr., Esqr., Joseph, and Jenny Galloway.
1734, Oct.	20, Shippen, Margaret, and John Jekyll.
1779, April	8, Shippen, Margaret, and Major General Benedict Arnold.
1785, June	16, Shippen, Mary, and Dr. W^m McIlvaine.
1787, Sept.	21, Shippen, Sarah, and Thomas Lea.
1721, May	4, Shipping, Joseph, and Rose Williams.
1798, Feb.	3, Ships, Jesse, and Jane Cummings.
1749, July	18, Shirley, James, and Mary Guilliot.
1741, Oct.	13, Shirm, Martha, and Henry Paxton.
1767, Sept.	5, Shivers, Elizabeth, and Daniel Cozens.
1773, Sept.	9, Shobel, Eve, and Timothy Wicksted.

1784, Oct.   14, Shober, Samuel, and Susannah Jones.
1769, July   13, Shockensey, Martha, and Andrew Closton.
1780, March 2, Shoemaker, Abraham, and Deborah Musgrove.
1796, May   5, Shoemaker, Ann, and Robert Morris.
1762, Dec.   24, Shoemaker, Benjamin, and Mary Felton.
1753, Dec.   29, Shoemaker, Benjamin, and Mary Comely.
1804, Aug.   13, Shoemaker, Deborah, and Moore Wharton.
1762, Nov.   27, Shoemaker, Jacob, and Catherine Lee.
1736, Sept.   2, Shoemaker, Jacob, and Rebecca Thompson.
1747, July   30, Shoemaker, Margaret, and John Fotheringham.
1779, Dec.   25, Shoemaker, Mary, and Benjamin Coot.
1770, Nov.   29, Shoemaker, Mary, and John Scull.
1804, May   10, Shoemaker, Susan, and Fishbourn Wharton.
1735, Oct.   6, Shokelea, Henry, and Anne Mills.
1784, Aug.   10, Shoonover, Mary, and Thomas Pratt.
1762, April 14, Shore, Esther, and Charles Harrison.
1710, Feb.   21, Shores, Samuel, and Sarah Harrison.
1757, April 15, Short, John, and Sarah Newport.
1772, Dec.   19, Short, Thomas, and Mary Brady.
1792, June   28, Shoures, Mary, and Samuel Hopes.
1777, Dec.   9, Shoveler, Sturges, and Sarah Forrest.
1763, Jan.   26, Shovelin, Margaret, and Edward Collins.
1757, Sept.   7, Showman, Henry, and Catherine Godfriend.
1802, July   8, Shreece, Mary, and John Hart.
1796, Jan.   28, Shreeves, Joseph, and Rachel Gist.
1773, Sept. 16, Shreve, Israel, and Mary Cokley.
1739, Aug.   17, Shrewe, Sarah, and Thomas Shrewe.
1739, Aug.   17, Shrewe, Thomas, and Sarah Shrewe.
1730–1, Jan. 14, Shrieve, Mary, and Samuel Curtis.
1801, May   27, Shright, Susanna, and Narcissus Joseph Gallant.
1772, July   28, Shriver, Edward, and Barbary Denny.
1734, Sept.   5, Shuldren, Mary, and John Smith.
1759, April 25, Shull, Alice, and David Potts.
1773, Jan.   29, Shultzer, Charlotte, and John Temple.
1785, March 28, Shute, Ann, and William Price.
1743, May   31, Shute, Atwood, and Ann Penley.
1801, May   16, Shute, Daniel, and Eliz. Dolby.
1763, Aug.   17, Shute, Diana, and William Estlack.
1751, April 16, Shute, Edith, and Isaac Anderson.
1780, Oct.   30, Shute, Eliz., and George Cooper.
1780, Oct.   24, Shute, Eliz. and Daniel Smith.
1757, Oct.   9, Shute, Joseph, and Sarah Paterson.
1786, Oct.   27, Shute, Martha, and John Ralph Taylor.
1737, July   5, Shute, Mary, and Randle Dicas.
1746, Dec.   30, Shute, Mary, and Isaac Lincon.
1735, Aug.   23, Shute, Mary, and John Rees.

1766, Nov.   27, Shute, Mary, and Seth Matlack.
1720, May   26, Shute, Mary, and Henry Taylor.
1787, April 12, Shute, Mary, and George Judor.
1742, Sept. 18, Shute, Rebecca, and Thomas Hood.
1781, Dec.   18, Shute, William, and Ann Boutcher.
1754, Jan.   31, Shute, William, and Elizabeth Jackson.
1792, May   8, Shyerly, Cath., and James Hanson.
1804, June   30, Shyne, Dorcas, and John Black.
1741, June   20, Sibbald, John, and Rebecca Thornhill.
1776, July   8, Sibbald, Rebecca, and Joseph Snowden.
1801, April 19, Sibbet, Eliz., and Henry McKinley.
1783, July   30, Side, Cath., and Rufus Green.
1765, Sept. 28, Side, William, and Elizabeth Reinholt.
1734, Aug.   17, Siddels, Sarah, and Samuel Hale.
1798, Nov.   28, Siddons, Ann, and William Brown.
1798, March 24, Siddons, John, and Susanna Hales.
1772, Sept. 23, Siddon, Mary, and Christopher Binks.
1800, May   31, Siddons, Sarah, and James Harmes.
1721, Feb.   21, Siddon, Susannah, and James Scull.
1774, Nov.   5, Sides, Sarah, and James Neils.
1796, March 11, Sidney, Susannah, and William McDonald.
1758, May   9, Sigfrid, Barbara, and Samuel Reger.
1767, Jan.   11, Sighing, Elizabeth, and Francis Brooks.
1738, Jan.   8, Silas, Elizabeth, and James Morris.
1792, July   19, Silerue, Mary, and James Whitehill.
1744, Nov.   24, Sill, Joseph, and Martha Elliot.
1804, June   4, Sill, Oswald, and Mary Wright Budd.
1743, April   9, Simcock, Benjamin, and Eliz. Boon.
1737, May   6, Simcock, Samuel, and Sarah Tregoe.
1802, Jan.   8, Simkins, Eliz., and Samuel Gladden.
1772, May   24, Simmerman, Eliz., and Jacob Houser.
1765, May   1, Simmon, Elizabeth, and Michael Pesser.
1795, May   21, Simmonds, Anthony, and Sarah Glentworth.
1771, Oct.   31, Simmonds, Cath., and Bethanah Hodgkinson.
1781, Nov.   29, Simmonds, Eleanor, and John Still.
1778, Dec.   3, Simmonds, Jeremiah, and Eliz. Crossman.
1797, Aug.   8, Simmonds, Mary, and John Maise.
1759, Dec.   28, Simmonds, Elizabeth, and William Lake.
1770, Nov.   1, Simmons, John, and Susannah Seigmen.
1799, May   3, Simmons, Mary, and John Shade.
1737, June   11, Simmons, Mary, and William Hawkins.
1736, Jan.   20, Simmons, Wheldon, and Anne Loftus.
1761, June   25, Simonson, Mary, and James Davidson.
1786, Dec.   20, Simpson, Ambrose, and Mary Wallace.
1799, March 31, Simpson, Ann, and John O'Brien.
1778, Oct.   8, Simpson, Ann, and John Chaloner.

1787, Jan.   2, Simpson, Deborah, and John Green.
1749, June   13, Simpson, Elizabeth, and Revd Thomas Thompson.
1768, March 24, Simpson, Gabriel, and Catherine Farrel.
1761, Nov.   30, Simpson, Hannah, and David Cauthorn.
1794, July   6, Simpson, John, and Susannah Estler.
1762, Nov.   25, Simpson, John, and Hannah Roberts.
1788, Oct.   26, Simpson, Joseph, and Anna Black.
1800, Nov.   20, Simpson, Mary Ann, and Daniel Boyle.
1784, March   7, Simpson, Priscilla, and George Sparks.
1794, Dec.   9, Simpson, Sarah, and Isaac Watson.
1802, March 30, Simes, Jane, and James Acres.
1796, June   12, Simes, William, and Jane Anderson.
1784, July   14, Sims, Ann Woodrop, and John Bernard Gilpin.
1765, June   5, Sims, Buckridge, and Elizabeth Morgan.
1797, April   8, Sims, Eleanor, and John Bess.
1739, Dec.   29, Sims, Joseph, and Anne Woodrop.
1759, April   4, Sims, Margaret, and George Bridges.
1761, May   7, Sims, Mary, and James Dennison.
1789, Jan.   22, Sims, Mary, and Malcolm McNeran.
1767, May   18, Sims, Sarah Wooddrop, and Benjamin Wynkoop.
1796, June   15, Sims, Sarah, and Elisha B. Hopkins.
1802, June   26, Sims, Thomas, and Henrietta Samson.
1769, May   4, Sims, William, and Margaret Fitzpatrick.
1789, May   21, Sims, Woodrop, and Sarah Hopkins.
1772, Dec.   25, Sinclair, Cath., and Leonard Philips.
1751, April   11, Sinclair, Elizabeth, and George Carew
1767, Oct.   19, Sinclair, Jane, and James McClear.
1761, July   26, Sinclair, Mary, and William Mackey.
1794, May   8, Singer, Abraham, and Ann Tress.
1770, Aug.   2, Singer, Eliz., and James Wilson.
1779, Dec.   31, Singer, John, and Susannah Carrick.
1753, Nov.   4, Singer, Robert, and Sarah Williams.
1767, March 30, Singleton, Elizabeth, and Thomas Tresse.
1797, June   17, Singleton, Frances, and William Boon
1784, July   3, Singleton, Mary, and Joseph Allen.
1799, Feb.   19, Sink, Christopher, and Hannah Parker.
1786, May   9, Sink, Mary, and John Heany.
1785, Sept.   26, Sink, Rebecca, and Francis Taylor.
1766, Aug.   18, Sinnet, Richard, and Mary Shinn.
1734, July   11, Siron, Simon, and Anna Castle.
1746, Dec.   15, Sisk, Michael, and Elizabeth Moffet.
1784, Oct.   21, Sitgreaves, Cath., and James Cox.
1796, June   6, Sitgreaves, Samuel, and Mary Kemper.
1758, Aug.   19, Sittleton, Margaret, and John Shearman.
1765, Feb.   11, Siver, Martha, and John Morton.
1758, Dec.   15, Skee, Sidney, and Joseph Redman.

1736, Oct.   23, Skeer, John, and Martha Ward.
1736, Oct.   19, Skeer, John, and Martha Ward.
1796, June   14, Skelton, John, and Mary Osman.
1796, Aug.   1, Skerret, Eliz., and Thomas Armstrong.
1789, May   7, Skerret, James, and Eliz. Ashton.
1750, June   14, Skidmore, Mary, and Joseph Cook.
1760, Sept. 13, Skill, Samuel, and Patience Brickham.
1793, Feb.   24, Skillinger, Daniel, and Abigail Craft.
1760, Jan.   30, Skelton, Robert, and Ann Marshall.
1751, Oct.   22, Skinner, Abraham, and Margaret Harding.
1755, July   3, Skinner, Elizabeth, and Thomas Peart.
1752, Dec.   5, Skinner, Esther, and Robert Sherrard.
1805, April 28, Skinner, Henry, and Eliz. Bowen.
1765, Oct.   31, Skinner, Susannah, and William Finley.
1729, Feb.   2, Skinner, Sus^h, and Nathl Edgcomb.
1762, July   9, Skiverton, Francis, and Mary Lovegove.
1716, May   18, Slack, John, and Frances Tinsley.
1770, June   2, Slack, Margaret, and Folliard Purdy.
1765, March 20, Slator, Elizabeth, and Watson Younger.
1747, Oct.   8, Slatter, Michael, and Mary Schluydhorn.
1761, March 17, Slaughter, Jacob, and Mary Hoffman.
1750, June   15, Slaughter, Mary, and Melchoir Bertholt.
1802, July   22, Slaughter, Peter Cannon, and Sarah Freed.
1791, Sept. 29, Slaughter, Rusely, and Benjamin Duffield.
1758, Oct.   19, Sleage, Andrew, and Sarah Griffin.
1785, Dec.   1, Slein, Cath., and Emanuel Begary.
1741, Aug.   18, Slenton, Sybilla, and John Lushet.
1759, Feb.   21, Sleydorn, Catherine, and John Sutton.
1773, Sept. 16, Sloan, Timothy, and Alice Frazer.
1795, Jan.   29, Sloane, Mary, and Charles Smith.
1768, June   26, Slocombe, Robert, and Abigail Quay.
1774, Feb.   17, Sly, Eliz., and John Palmer.
1722, March   4, Slyfield, George, and Elizabeth Wake.
1772, June   11, Slyhauff, Godfrey, and Rachel Herse.
1785, Nov.   20, Small, Henry, and Ann Cole.
1727, July   26, Small, James, and Martha Boyd.
1772, Oct.   5, Small, John, and Eliz. Boatman.
1805, March 10, Small, Joseph, and Margaret Gosner.
1799, April 17, Small, Martha, and John Johnson.
1740, Feb.   25, Smallwood, Elizabeth, and Richard Needham.
1745, Aug.   3, Smallwood, Hannah, and William Moulder.
1762, July   12, Smallwood, John, and Rebecca Trump.
1784, July   3, Smallwood, Laetitia, and Joseph Marshall.
1769, Aug.   3, Smallwood, Moses, and Elizabeth Day.
1720, Feb.   8, Smallwood, Sarah, and John Thomas,
1747, Sept. 21, Smallwood, John, and Mary Hart.

1731, Sept.   19, Smart, Elizabeth, and John Berwick.
1713, Nov.   8, Smart, Jane, and Richard Harper.
1758, Dec.   9, Smart, John, and Ann Knowles.
1710, April   11, Smith, Abram, and Eleanor Roberts.
1727, Oct.   1, Smith, Andrew, and Elizabeth Owen.
1715, May   22, Smith, Alice, and Samuel Keffett.
1797, March   2, Smith, Ann, and John Guthrie.
1782, May   4, Smith, Ann, and Enoch Taylor.
1781, Dec.   18, Smith, Ann, and Peter Henry Payade.
1782, June   18, Smith, Ann, and Isaac Penrose.
1715, Dec.   30, Smith, Ann, and Robert Pidcock.
1799, April   29, Smith, Anna, and William Philips.
1761, March   7, Smith, Ann, and Samuel Henry.
1805, July   9, Smith, Benjamin, and Mary Ann Walker.
1761, Aug.   15, Smith, Catherine, and Abraham.
1766, June   14, Smith, Catherine, and James Sutton.
1771, July   29, Smith, Catherine, and Martin Coxe.
1795, Jan.   29, Smith, Charles, and Mary Sloane.
1781, June   19, Smith, Charles, and Eliz. Pomeroy.
1753, Aug.   23, Smith, Charles, and Martha Robinson.
1801, March   1, Smith, Christiana, and John Ansley.
1760, Jan.   11, Smith, Christina, and Godfrey Wessell.
1743, June   16, Smith, Christian, and Peter Deigener.
1794, Nov.   8, Smith, Clifford, and Hannah Stephenson.
1737, July   23, Smith, Daniel, and Dorothy Hill.
1780, Oct.   24, Smith, Daniel, and Eliz. Shute.
1747, March   10, Smith, David, and Mary Martin.
1781, April   20, Smith, Deborah, and Thomas Kennedy.
1803, Jan.   15, Smith, Dockery, and Jane Holderness.
1755, Sept.   25, Smith, Edward, and Hannah Brown.
1772, July   22, Smith, Edward, and Eleanor Donovan.
1762, Feb.   15, Smith, Eleanor, and William Davis.
1802, March   31, Smith, Elisha, and Sarah Paul.
1737, Sept.   27, Smith, Elizabeth, and James Appleton.
1731, Oct.   16, Smith, Elizabeth, and John Falconer.
1752, Dec.   21, Smith, Elizabeth, and John Curtis.
1783, Jan.   28, Smith, Eliz., and David Jamison.
1783, Sept.   17, Smith, Eliz., and Thomas Elder.
1729, Oct.   7, Smith, Eliz., and John Hellcoat.
1796, Sept.   1, Smith, Elriah, and Margaret Starke.
1728, July   25, Smith, Frances, and George Plinn.
1784, March   21, Smith, Esqr, Frederick, and Margaret Oswald.
1749, Sept.   28, Smith, George, and Cornelia Miers.
1803, Jan.   12, Smith, George, and Margaret Campbell.
1803, Nov.   28, Smith, George, and Eliz. Westen.
1796, Jan.   4, Smith, George, and Rebecca Edmunson.

1795, May   28, Smith, George, and Margaret Marshall.
1762, Sept. 16, Smith, George, and Sophia Doulkear.
1743, Dec.   29, Smith, George, and Florinda Reed.
1745, July   18, Smith, George, and Catherine Mason.
1754, March 28, Smith, Hannah, and John Campbel.
1797, Dec.   16, Smith, Hester, and John Ross.
1751, June   25, Smith, Hugh, and Anne Bailey.
1803, Dec.   3, Smith, Isaac, and Margaret McClintock.
1714, May   16, Smith, Isaac, and Susannah Richards.
1761, Jan.   15, Smith, Jacob, and Mary Pindar.
1787, Nov.   28, Smith, James, and Mary Robinson.
1785, Feb.   14, Smith, James, and Mary Long.
1714, Oct.   26, Smith, James, and Sarah Kimber.
1787, Feb.   5, Smith, James, and Jemmima E. Russell.
1746, June   14, Smith, James, and Mary Benson.
1731, Oct.   2, Smith, Jane, and John Cowles.
1803, Oct.   4, Smith, Janet, and Paul Smith.
1734, April 22, Smith, Jonas, and Mary Essex.
1787, Sept. 12, Smith, Jonathan, and Mary Hyde.
1794, Sept. 11, Smith, John, and Eliz. McLean.
1790, July   10, Smith, John, and Eliza Poterfield.
1774, Jan.   5, Smith, John, and Cleary Wheely.
1793, Jan.   1, Smith, John, and Susannah Bradford.
1745, July   27, Smith, John, and Mary Thomas.
1804, Nov.   4, Smith, John, and Ann Bickerton.
1734, Sept.   5, Smith, John, and Mary Shuldren.
1743, Nov.   1, Smith, John, and Sarah Hutchins.
1731, Dec.   20, Smith, John, and Christian Warner.
1736, May   18, Smith, John, and Barbara Miller.
1733, Sept. 10, Smith, John, and Sarah Brown.
1768, June   23, Smith, John, and Eliz. Rush.
1805, Nov.   6, Smith, John J., and Mary Roberts.
1772, Nov.   12, Smith, John, and Cath. McMullan.
1800, June   26, Smith, John, and Laetitia Knox.
1770, Nov.   10, Smith, Joseph, and Martha Powel.
1772, Jan.   31, Smith, Joseph, and Jane Beaks.
1712, Nov.   6, Smith, Margaret, and John Bleak.
1721, Sept. 10, Smith, Margaret, and Oliver Gault.
1786, Dec.   11, Smith, Margaret, and Thomas James.
1744, April   4, Smith, Martha, and Daniel Comeran.
1805, April 11, Smith, Martha, and Gideon Jacques.
1799, July   11, Smith, Mary, and Thomas Childs.
1750, Aug.   18, Smith, Mary, and William Loghlin.
1743, July   15, Smith, Mary, and James Mahery.
1762, Aug.   21, Smith, Mary, and James Leonard.
1769, April 24, Smith, Mary, and John Besor.

1765, Nov.   30, Smith, Mary, and John Garlin.
1794, Nov.   15, Smith, Mary, and William Newloold.
1804, May   28, Smith, Mary, and James Cole.
1794, June   25, Smith, Mary, and Daniel Molong.
1756, Sept.   16, Smith, Mary, and Samuel Martin.
1783, Dec.   29, Smith, Mary, and Thomas Dame.
1729, Dec.   15, Smith, Mary, and John Bennet.
1785, July   30, Smith, Michael, and Mary Pong.
1803, Oct.   4, Smith, Paul, and Janet Smith.
1771, July   27, Smith, Rachel, and John Pashall, jun.
1749, April   22, Smith, Ralph, and Marjory Allen.
1726, Nov.   3, Smith, Reb., and Nic. Hencher.
1802, Oct.   13, Smith, Rebecca, and Benjamin Britton.
1800, May   15, Smith, Rebecca, and Michael Aaron.
1792, May   10, Smith, Rebecca, and Samuel Blodget.
1745, Nov.   14, Smith, Richard, and Jane McMahon.
1768, Jan.   25, Smith, Robert, and Margaret Conner.
1768, May   24, Smith, Rosanna, and Thomas Beverly.
1800, June   30, Smith, Roger, and Lydia Strutt.
1749, May   1, Smith, Samuel, and Susannah Merk.
1796, Nov.   26, Smith, Samuel, and Sarah Jones.
1754, Oct.   3, Smith, Samuel, and Sarah Carpenter.
1756, June   5, Smith, Samuel, and Martha Dean.
1774, April   20, Smith, Samuel, and Judith Millington.
1761, Nov.   22, Smith, Sarah, and Joseph Baird.
1735, May   13, Smith, Sarah, and John Woodoth.
1733, July   25, Smith, Sarah, and John Pugh.
1803, March   10, Smith, Sarah, and Hugh Roberts.
1733, Dec.   2, Smith, Simon, and Barbara Spencer.
1742, Sept.   4, Smith, Thomas, and Mary Cannon.
1784, Aug.   5, Smith, Thomas, and Eliz. Roberts.
1801, Nov.   21, Smith, Thomas, and Sarah Bailey.
1790, Dec.   4, Smith, Thomas, and Christiana Wiltenburger.
1765, Jan.   12, Smith, Thomas, and Martha Lewis.
1757, Nov.   30, Smith, Thomas, and Hannah Hastings.
1756, Sept.   11, Smith, Thomas, and Jane Rubee.
1752, March   9, Smith, Thomas, and Sarah Bowes.
1735, July   19, Smith, Thomas, and Mary Lindsley.
1754, Sept.   7, Smith, Thomas, and Catherine Finney.
1754, June   10, Smith, Walter, and Margaret O'Neal.
1768, May   12, Smith, William, and Margaret Chandler.
1798, Oct.   18, Smith, William, and Eliz. Wilson.
1800, Aug.   3, Smith, William, and Phoebe Rutter.
1784, Nov.   4, Smith, William, and Sarah Harvey.
1722, Feb.   23, Smith, William, and Mercy Brock.
1775, Aug.   14, Smith, Wm Drewet, and Margaret Steadman.

1756, Dec.   18, Smith, jr., William, and Margaret Preston.
1766, Nov.   29, Smith, William, and Elizabeth Mourning.
1730, May   21, Smith, William, and Elizabeth Antrobus.
1790, Dec.   28, Smollett, Ann, and Jacob Williams.
1788, April 24, Smothers, Pamelia, and Thomas Price.
1747, July   20, Smout, Edward, and Elizabeth Price.
1738, Feb.   12, Smout, Elanor, and John Bedford.
1712, June   19, Smout, Silvanus, and Eleanor Geesling.
1792, Dec.   19, Sneider, David, and Rebecca Ruper.
1804, Sept.   8, Snell, James, and Mary Gordon,
1794, Sept.   8, Snelling, Jane, and John Kay.
1768, Dec.   7, Snow, Elizabeth, and James Alenby.
1775, June   10, Snow, Mary, and Daniel Dalby.
1739, Dec.   15, Snow, Peter, and Mary Broadgate.
1753, Jan.   18, Snowden, Fedidiah, and Mary Bell.
1759, March   7, Snowden, Isaac, and Mary Parker.
1776, July   8, Snowden, Joseph, and Rebecca Sibbald.
1795, April 16, Snowden, Maria, and Peter Miercken.
1772, Nov.   19, Snowden, Rachel, and William Davey.
1771, Oct.   12, Snowden, Samuel, and Hannah Gum.
1768, April 28, Snouder, Harman, and Eliz. Haines.
1751, April 18, Sober, Mary, and John Redman.
1740, April 17, Sober, Thomas, and Sarah Harrison.
1779, Aug.   31, Sobers, Cath., and Samuel Hollingshead.
1752, Dec.   6, Soley, Alexander, and Phoebe Wiley.
1790, June   13, Somers, Mary, and William Barnes.
1732, June   16, Sommerset, William, and Jane Ranbury.
1801, May   23, Sontag, Mary Wright, and John Craig Wells.
1771, June   29, Souder, Jacob, and Sarah Felton.
1763, May   5, Soumaine, Elizabeth, and Thomas Empson.
1737, Jan.   8, Soumans, Peter, and Barthea Wilson.
1800, Feb.   26, South, John, and Eliz. Willard.
1767, April   2, Sowder, John, and Eleanor Piniard.
1771, Aug.   17, Sowder, Mary, and John Dunn.
1783, Oct.   20, Spade, Mary, and John Gantry.
1736, Sept. 25, Spafford, John, and Anne Mee.
1770, April 14, Spafford, Mary, and Ephraim Falconer.
1806, March 23, Sparhawk, Aletheia, and Adam Gordon.
1726, Oct.   30, Sparke, Elizabeth, and Wm Knight.
1742, Jan.   27, Sparker, Margaret, and Henry Wooleby.
1784, March   7, Sparks, George, and Priscilla Simpson.
1772, Nov.   19, Sparks, James, and Ann Pearson.
1766, Jan.   8, Sparks, James, and Sarah Ozier.
1751, June   4, Sparks, James, and Mary Harry.
1798, April 20, Spain, Richard, and Eleanor Wallace.
1781, July   1, Sparrow, Diana, and Joseph Jackson.

1801, Nov.　12, Sparrowgrove, Rebecca, and Daniel Mace.
1785, Nov.　2, Spear, Jane, and John Collins.
1790, Aug.　12, Spear, John, and Hannah Parry.
1769, May　24, Spear, John, and Catherine Kelly,
1762, July　15, Speckman, Charles, and Elizabeth Gordon.
1767, Sept.　29, Spence, Edward, and Abigail Shippen.
1799, March 11, Spence, George, and Christiana Scot.
1734, Jan.　13, Spence, Mary, and Jacob Duchi.
1747, Dec.　24, Spence, Rachel, and James McCullough.
1786, Sept.　11, Spence, William, and Bridget Tye.
1795, May　31, Spence, William, and Mary Carpenter.
1733, Dec.　2, Spencer, Barbara, and Simon Smith.
1769, July　28, Spencer, Brent, and Martha Thompson.
1758, Sept.　9, Spencer, Elizabeth, and Henry Punner.
1748, Aug.　28, Spencer, Elizabeth, and Robert Warren.
1776, Feb.　18, Spencer, Esther, and John Tawser.
1775, March 25, Spencer, James, and Ann Coakley.
1722, March 20, Spencer, John, and Mary Ridge.
1734, Nov.　30, Spencer, Lydia, and David Davies.
1733, May　15, Spencer, Margaret, and John Mason.
1769, May　9, Spencer, Martha, and Berry Hartman.
1768, May　3, Spencer, Mary, and William Cassan.
1771, Oct.　4, Spencer, Mary, and Thomas Lee.
1772, Sept.　15, Spencer, Nicholas, and Martha Lee.
1751, April　14, Spencer, Samuel and Hannah Boyd.
1722, Aug.　23, Spencer, Sarah, and Joseph Thomas.
1772, Oct.　20, Spencer, Sarah, and Henry Myers.
1729-30,Mar.15, Spencer, Timothy, and Phoebe Carleton.
1776, July　25, Spicer, Jacob, and Eliz. Donaldson.
1804, Aug.　16, Spicer, Samuel, and Frances Douglas.
1775, Jan.　1, Spier, Ann, and William Openshire.
1791, Sept.　2, Spierin, William, and Ann Lascum.
1797, July　11, Spiers, Hannah, and James Anderson.
1795, July　25, Spiers, Jannet, and Edward Martin.
1714, Jan.　17, Spiller, Dorothy, and John Lovegrove.
1786, May　21, Spilyard, Matthew, and Mary Corbett.
1799, July　25, Spinlove, Thomas, and Ruth Rethmell.
1722, May　15, Spinster, Elizabeth Hunter, and Robert Steel.
1720, Jan.　7, Spinster, Mary Lillings, and William Till.
1804, March　6, Spooner, John, and Mary Conner.
1792, June　2, Spotswood, Martha, and Gustavus Calhoun.
1800, May　20, Spranklin, Simon, and Susanna Lewis.
1762, Nov.　19, Spring, Capt. Benjamin, and Lethia Chancellour.
1794, Nov.　12, Springer, Catherine, and Thomas Arnold.
1777, Aug.　29, Sprigg, Martha, and Thomas Higgins.
1734, July　3, Spriggs, Elizabeth, and John Carter.

1732, June 5, Sprogell, Dorothy, and James Boyer.
1792, Sept. 6, Sprogell, Thomas Yorke, and Mary Stretch.
1734, June 15, Sprogle, Susannah, and Thomas Say.
1749, April 29, Sprouce, Elizabeth, and Samuel Cox.
1790, Sept. 1, Sprowl, Margaret, and Neil McGinnis.
1744, March 31, Spruce, Grisel, and John Stephenson.
1732, April 13, Spurraway, Charles, and Catherine Daniel.
1799, Feb. 27, Spurrier, Eleanor, and Philip Taylor.
1734, Sept. 18, Stacey, John, and Rebecca Cunditt.
1745, Jan. 21, Stackhouse, Eliz., and David Wilson.
1757, May 30, Stackhouse, Grace, and John Ware.
1759, Nov. 16, Stackhouse, Lucy, and Richard Yardley.
1764, Sept. 29, Stackhouse, Mary, and John Sutton.
1773, Sept. 3, Stackhouse, Nicholas, and Eliz. Robinson.
1757, March 26, Stackhouse, Samuel, and Mary Hays.
1716, July 4, Stacy, Robert, and Deborah Clark.
1751, Aug. 6, Stadler, Jacob, and Mary How.
1781, Sept. 7, Stafford, John, and Hannah Matlack.
1757, Feb. 9, Stafford, Joseph, and Cecelia Lindsey.
1770, Sept. 8, Stafford, Patrick, and Ann Harran.
1787, Nov. 14, Stagg, Benjamin, and Catherine Myers.
1747, Feb. 15, Stagleas, Sarah, and John Archer.
1757, Dec. 1, Staleop, Mary, and Joshua White.
1749, May 16, Stalker, Mary, and William McClean.
1784, July 4, Stall, Mary, and Henry Hanly.
1742, March 12, Stammars, Thomas, and Sarah Cosins.
1774, Sept. 3, Stamp, Ann, and Philip Buck.
1752, June 22, Stamper, Hannah, and Elias Bland.
1755, Oct. 9, Stamper, Joseph, and Sarah Maddox.
1745, Sept. 19, Stamper, Mary, and William Bingham.
1758, Sept. 19, Stamper, Rebecca, and Benjamin Fuller.
1749, May 11, Stamper, Thomas, and Rebecca Coleman.
1733, July 24, Stamper, Thomas, and Diana Jackson.
1761, June 11, Stamper, Thomas, and Rebecca Rush.
1763, March 13, Stanbury, William, and Sarah Morris.
1783, Sept. 13, Standfield, Henry, and Henry Leech.
1775, May 7, Standford, Ann, and John Garlin.
1746, April 9, Standley, George, and Mary Leipencout.
1770, Sept. 20, Standley, Sarah, and Godfrey Twells.
1748, Sept. 17, Standley, William, and Elizabeth Fulton.
1799, Jan. 9, Stanley, Ann, and Gershom Johnson.
1796, Dec. 7, Stanley, Thomas, and Sarah Rudd.
1733, Aug. 23, Stannley, James, and Sarah Dony.
1729, June 16, Stanwell, Thomas, and Mary Burch.
1731-2, Feb. 18, Stapleford, Mary, and Thomas Gordon.

1748, Oct.　　1, Stapeler, Elizabeth, and Thomas Jackson.
1753, April　　4, Stapler, Martha, and John Elbeck.
1772, Sept.　21, Stapler, Richard, and Elizabeth Mitchell.
1725, Aug.　　9, Stapleton, Elizabeth, and Thomas Ferril.
1795, Oct.　　5, Stapleton, John, and Mary Cameron.
1731, April　20, Starke, Jane, and Roberts Gooldsberry.
1796, Sept.　　1, Starke, Margaret, and Elriah Smith.
1804, May　　29, Starky, George, and Mary Lollar.
1771, June　　9, Starn, Frederick, and Cath. Biddis.
1745, Aug.　17, Starn, Mary, and John Pedrow.
1788, Dec.　18, Starrman, Frederick William, and Mary Dundas.
1760, Dec.　31, Starts, Bab^a, and Adam Croce.
1802, April　　1, Statean, Rebecca, and George Lecher.
1765, Oct.　21, States, Isaac, and Jane Tillyer.
1769, July　21, Statia, Rosanna, and Thomas Taylor.
1781, July　12, Staunton, John, and Isabella Philips.
1771, Dec.　28, Stawart, James, and Margaret Irwin.
1801, April　16, Stead, Henry, and Mary Riddle.
1791, Sept.　　1, Stearn, Andrew, and Susannah Kerby.
1798, March 25, Stears, Rachel, and Daniel Carnes.
1788, Feb.　26, Stecker, Peter, and Christian Coxe.
1732, Oct.　18, Stedham, Mary, and Wm Loan.
1749, May　13, Stedman, Alexander, and Elizabeth Chancelour.
1748, Jan.　　1, Stedman, Charles, and Anne Graeme.
1767, Sept.　26, Stedman, Charles, and Margaret Abercrombie.
1775, Aug.　14, Stedman, Margaret, and Wm Drewet Smith.
1726, Aug.　28, Stedwel, Thomas, and Dinah Hendrickson.
1805, March 30, Steel, Hannah, and Samuel Nash.
1758, Nov.　21, Steel, James, and Martha Canby.
1763, Jan.　　4, Steel, Mary, and George Pander.
1722, May　15, Steel, Robert, and Elizabeth Hunter Spinster.
1783, July　　7, Steel, Timothy, and Lydia Stout.
1805, May　21, Steel, William, and Deborah Rowland.
1736, Nov.　18, Steer, Joanna, and Anthony Fox.
1754, April　16, Steers, Jane, and Joseph Mattson.
1728, Nov.　12, Stegleigh, Dor., and Wm Maultby.
1767, Sept.　24, Steiner, Catherine, and Christopher Honey.
1795, May　28, Steinmitz, Conrad, and Jane Getting.
1785, Jan.　　4, Steinmitz, John, and Grace Watt.
1774, June　16, Stenart, Martha, and Orpheus ———.
1805, Nov.　　9, Step, Hannah, and William Oliver.
1733, Sept.　26, Stephen, Catherine, and Benjamin Phillips.
1738, Oct.　24, Stephens, Alice, and Robert Rowland.
1716, Feb.　14, Stephens, Ann, and John Warren.
1745, Jan.　13, Stephens, Ann, and Morgan Hugh.
1782, Oct.　17, Stephens, John, Esqr., and Rachel Cox.

1722, Dec.   6, Stephens, Martha, and Capt John Hopkins.
1737, Nov.   20, Stephens, Mary, and Andrew Redmond.
1743, Nov.   17, Stephens, Ruth, and Jos. Hale.
1745, Aug.   6, Stephens, Stephen, and Mary Keys.
1759, Aug.   29, Stephens, Susannah, and John Hutton.
1781, June   7, Stephenson, Eliz., and Jacob Flake.
1787, March   1, Stephenson, Eliz., and William Procter.
1794, Nov.   8, Stephenson, Hannah, and Clifford Smith.
1791, Aug.   10, Stephenson, Hugh, and Sarah Shaw.
1797, March 16, Stephenson, James, and Cath. Crawford.
1795, Nov.   28, Stephenson, Jane, and Jacob Clarkson.
1744, March 31, Stephenson, John, and Grisel Spruce.
1776, Jan.   25, Stephenson, John, and Eliz. Deason.
1709, Nov.   19, Stephenson, Joseph, and Susannah Huit.
1715, Jan.   9, Stephenson, Joseph, and Mary Linnex.
1796, Sept. 19, Stephenson, Sarah, and Thomas Woodward.
1797, Dec.   23, Stern, Martha, and William Ellis.
1796, Dec.   8, Stetcher, Mary, and Shepherd Kollock.
1731, Sept. 15, Steuart, Charles, and Hester Todd.
1777, Feb.   9, Steuart, Mary, and Samuel Shannon.
1756, May   13, Stevens, Cornelius, and Mary Pugh.
1750, March 27, Stevens, Erasmus, and Rebecca Philips.
1801, May   14, Stevenson, Crook, and Mary Beavan.
1762, April   6, Stevens, Deborah, and John Mason.
1752, Oct.   25, Stevenson, Edward, and Mary Talman.
1766, Oct.   29, Stevenson, Hugh, and Rebeccah Craig.
1733, March 17, Stevenson, John, and Susannah Blakey.
1748, Aug.   15, Stevens, John, and Elizabeth Farrington.
1716, Sept. 19, Stevens, Joijel, and Richard Knabb.
1742, Sept.   7, Stevenson, Robert, and Rebecca Steward.
1806, April 21, Stevenson, Sarah, and John Jovell.
1762, Nov.   18, Steward, Anne, and Jacob Proby.
1739, June   18, Steward, James, and Elizabeth Davies.
1754, July   27, Steward, Jane, and David Curry.
1758, Jan.   27, Steward, Letitia, and Thomas Powell.
1727, April   2, Steward, Mary, and Ed. Hatton.
1742, Sept.   7, Steward, Rebecca, and Robert Stevenson.
1799, May   31, Stewart, Ann, and Lawrence Holaren.
1805, Feb.   4, Stewart, Ann Matilda, and Philip Schuyler Church.
1762, Dec.   15, Stewart, Anne, and James Cooper.
1734, Aug.   1, Stewart, Anne, and Henry Marsh.
1758, Aug.   11, Stewart, Catherine, and Alexander Rutherford.
1746, Nov.   17, Stewart, Catherine, and Thomas Norris.
1789, June   16, Stewart, David, and Mary Robertson.
1800, Aug.   11, Stewart, Eliz., and William Sweeney.
1797, April 22, Stewart, Eliz., and George Washington Nixon.

1723, Jan.   6, Stewart, Elizabeth, and Anthony Norwood.
1771, March 14, Stewart, Eliz., and Edward Hanlon.
1762, Nov.   29, Stewart, Elizabeth, and Neal McNeal.
1792, Dec.   21, Stewart, Francis, and Lettice Platt.
1752, Oct.   17, Stewart, George, and Anne Hunt.
1796, Aug.   26, Stewart, Isaak, and Mary Ray.
1788. April   13, Stewart, James, and Margaret Jane Polk.
1795, Nov.   13, Stewart, Jane, and John Cummins.
1805, Sept.   10, Stewart, Janet, and Thomas Nightingale.
1775, Oct.   12, Stewart, Rev. John, and Jane O'Kill.
1799, July   2, Stewart, John, and Helen West.
1790, Sept.   16, Stewart, John, and Eliz. Gordon.
1783, Nov.   27, Stewart, Lilly, and Lawrence Lutia.
1799, Jan.   14, Stewart, Margaret, and James Parker.
1801, Oct.   29, Stewart, Mary, and James Dunn.
1799, June   12, Stewart, Mary, and Anthony Campbell.
1797, Aug.   17, Stewart, Mary, and George Corbin.
1752, Aug.   24, Stewart, Mary, and William Williams.
1801, May   13, Stewart, Rebecca, and George Andrews.
1785, Oct.   21, Stewart, Rosanna, and Joseph McMullen.
1804, Feb.   8, Stewart, Samuel, and Margaret Bates.
1781, April   11, Stewart, Col. Walter, and Deborah McClenachan.
1800, March   4, Stewart, William, and Margaret Tipaway.
1784, Aug.   17, Stewart, William, and Margaret Sell.
1770, Dec.   30, Sticker, Adam, and Phoebe Riffeth.
1758, Oct.   5, Stilfield, Henry, and Margaret Nailer.
1752, March 11, Stiles, Abigail, and William Jackson.
1796, Sept.   18, Stiles, Edward, and Mary Meredith.
1749, Nov.   1, Stiles, Henry, and Elizabeth Williams.
1769, Dec.   28, Stiles, Mary, and Samuel Balinger.
1760, May   7, Stiles, William, and Mary Brustrum.
1798, March 29, Still, Eleanor, and William Ashford.
1781, Nov.   29, Still, John, and Eleanor Simmonds.
1757, Jan.   13, Stille, Elizabeth, and Isaac Couse.
1730, July   1, Stille, Gurtrude, and Revᵈ Samuel Hesselius.
1804, Feb.   1, Stille, Jacob, and Jane Mahany.
1762, Jan.   21, Stille, Priscilla, and John Prentice.
1762, Jan.   22, Stille, Sarah, and Edward York.
1780, Aug.   24, Stillwell, Godfrey, and Sarah Gill.
1749, April   17, Stilly, Peter, and Margaret Pockington.
1748, Oct.   6, Stilly, Sarah, and Samuel Autin.
1806, May   14, Stimel, Ann, and Henry Stimel.
1806, May   14, Stimel, Henry, and Ann Stimel.
1798, Aug.   12, Stine, Eliz., and William Mason.
1786, July   18, Stinnyard, Amey, and Edmond West.
1786, July   5, Stinnyard, Hester, and Josiah Hawk.

1763, Dec.   21, Stinson, John, and Rebecca Cox.
1770, Sept.   9, Stirling, William, and Patience Huston.
1753, June 13, Stitchbury, Jane, and James Borden.
1804, May   31, St. John, Mary, and Peter Towell.
1805, May   31, St. John, Oliver, and Rachel Newbold.
1752, Dec.   11, Stoakes, Mary, and Richard Eaton.
1783, July   28, Stock, John, and Mary Thomas.
1754, Nov.   14, Stocker, Anthony, and Margaret Philips.
1799, Jan.   31, Stocker, Margaret, and Alexander J. Miller.
1779, Oct.   28, Stocker, Mary, and Andrew Robeson, Esqr.
1748, Oc·.   12, Stockerd, John, and Elizabeth Colins.
1794, April 20, Stockman, Tabez, and Mary Keys.
1775, Nov.   25, Stockton, William, and Mary Naglee.
1744, March 2, Stokes, Hannah, and Ben. Pine.
1783, May   29, Stokes, Isabella, and Charles French.
1796, April 6, Stokes, John, and Sarah Abel.
1711, Jan.   7, Stokes, Lucy, and William Boyte.
1804, Nov.   15, Stokes, Maria Eliza, and James R. Black.
1806, Feb.   15, Stokes, Maria Eliza, and James R. Black.
1804, Jan.   19, Stokes, Mary, and Caleb Parry Wayne.
1751, Nov.   12, Stokes, Robert, and Jane Anderson.
1729, July   20, Stokes, Stephen, and Mary Harris.
1801, Nov.   12, Stokes, William, and Sarah Laskey.
1774, Dec.   12, Stone, Edward, and Dorothy Chilcot.
1740, May   29, Stone, Elizabeth, and Richard Sallows.
1761, April 21, Stone, Elizabeth, and Peter Story.
1729, Nov.   30, Stone, Hannah, and T. Chilcoat.
1758, July   1, Stone, John, and Doborah Godfred.
1760, Jan.   21, Stone, John, and Mary Walker.
1747, Aug.   11, Stone, Robert, and Anne Ogden.
1804, Dec.   8, Stone, Samuel, and Esther Liston.
1754, Oct.   17, Stone, Priscilla, and Isaac Duncan.
1759, Dec.   11, Stonemetz, Mary, and Henry Ireland.
1783, Oct.   25, Stoops, Rebecca, and George Huggins.
1768, May   11, Stoops, Sarah, and Andrew Tucker.
1784, Nov.   11, Storde, John, and Mary Jackson.
1732, June 15, Storke, Mary, and George Jones.
1747, March 7, Storke, Tabitha, and Thomas Campbell.
1734, Jan.   23, Story, Cuthbert, and Eleanora Durmins.
1788, Feb.   3, Story, Eliz., and Richard Fell.
1758, April 13, Story, Enoch, and Mary Annis.
1740, Feb.   23, Story, Enoch, and Elizabeth Houlston.
1794, Sept.   4, Story, George, and Eliz. Alexander.
1761, April 21, Story, Peter, and Elizabeth Stone.
1727, June 24, Story, Sarah, and Doct. Wm Lowe.
1785, March 17, Story, William, and Mary Roberts.

1789, Aug. 15, Stott, Ebenezer, and Eliz. Phile.
1758, Oct. 28, Stoul, John, and Ann Dottamy.
1772, Sept. 3, Stout, Brightwed, and William Nichols.
1744, Dec. 2, Stout, Cornelius, and Rebecca Till.
1797, Dec. 7, Stout, Elizabeth, and George Hamilton.
1802, Aug. 26, Stout, Hannah, and Peter Thomson.
1778, Oct. 29, Stout, Capt. Herman, and Ann Hall.
1783, July 7, Stout, Lydia, and Timothy Steel.
1743, Jan. 11, Stow, Charles, jr., and Lydia Strowing.
1771, Oct. 24, Stow, Eliz., and William Barnet.
1751, April 6, Stow, John, and Hannah Paschal.
1786, Feb. 2, Stow, Joseph, and Jane Cain.
1805, Nov. 17, Stowell, Asaph, and Sarah Blackwell.
1800, Feb. 10, Stowell, Geo. Wilks, and Barbary Usher.
1791, Jan. 13, Stoy, Daniel, and Mary Bruster.
1772, Nov, 20, Stoy, Elias, and Mary Knowles.
1782, April 25, Stoy, James, and Christiana Cubbin.
1782, March 5, Stoy, Margaret, and John Mark.
1791, Sept. 22, Stoy, Peter, and Ann Bruistar.
1802, May 23, Strable, Ann, and Samuel Burgess Jones.
1806, Feb. 2, Strachan, Isabella, and William Dunlap.
1767, Feb. 25, Stradleman, Catharina, and Jacob Wagenaer.
1772, April 11, Stradler, Sarah, and Nathan Rhods.
1727, Nov. 2, Strange, Jonathan, and Sus. Thomas.
1771, June 22, Stratton, El^m, and Grace Davidson.
1757, July 2, Stravery, Hannah, and Richard Collom.
1781, Jan. 29, Streaker, Mary, and Morris Healey.
1747, Feb. 14, Street, Joseph, and Rachel Fenkins.
1744, Dec. 27, Streper, Leonard, and Rebecca Greathouse.
1731, Aug. 15, Stretch, Martha, and Philip Quinard.
1792, Sept. 6, Stretch, Mary, and Thomas Yorke Sprogell.
1770, March 8, Stretch, Peter, and Sarah Howell.
1743, July 30, Stretch, Thomas, and Anne Robins.
1763, April 13, Stretcher, Edward, and Elizabeth Davis.
1785, May 19, Stretcher, Esther, and Rees Evans.
1794, July 31, Stretcher, Phoenix, and Eliza Todon.
1779, April 8, Strettell, Ann, and Cadwallader Morris.
1743, Feb. 13, Strettell, Frances, and Isaac Jones.
1788, June 18, Strettell, Frances, and Benjamin Morris.
1752, Nov. 2, Strettle, Amos, and Hannah Hasell.
1769, Nov. 21, Strickland, Frances, and William Foster.
1755, Dec. 22, Strickland, John, and Margaret Grogan.
1787, Feb. 13, Strobunk, John, and Barbara Greenwood.
1726, Aug. 29, Strong, Abraham, and Dor. Bullock.
1798, Nov. 13, Strong, Kitty, and Edward Abbott.
1770, Jan. 15, Strong, Matthew, and Agnes Gerrard.

1799, May   4, Strong, Sarah, and Robert Anderson.
1800, Jan.   19, Stroubat, John, and Mary Salome Griffith.
1712, Sept.   9, Stroud, Ann, and Charles Brook.
1760, April   23, Stroud, Thomas, and Jane Pannel.
1743, Jan.   11, Strowing, Lydia, and Charles Strow, jr.
1800, June   30, Strutt, Lydia, and Roger Smith.
1740, May   31, Stuart, Catherine, and Thomas Howell.
1757, April   24, Stuart, Mary, and James Worrell.
1732, March 26, Stuart, Peter, and Mary Vokes.
1766, Nov.   25, Stuber, Frederick, and Elizabeth Cook.
1715, March 15, Stuber, Jacob, and Sarah Boone.
1796, June   6, Stuber, Margaret, and William Hyer.
1746, Feb.   26, Stuchy, George, and Judith Hertzel.
1761, Sept.   1, Studdert, John, and Deborah Harper.
1731, Nov.   10, Studham, Richard, and Mary Eastburn.
1726, Nov.   11, Stump, John, and Mary Cath. Bakerin.
1749, Sept.   3, Sturgeon, Rev^d W^m, and Hannah Denormandie.
1755, July   1, Sturgis, Cornelius, and Mary Haugen.
1720, June   17, Sturgis, James, and Mary Evans.
1752, April   24, Sturgis, Jonathan, and Margaret Roberts.
1733, Jan.   11, Sturk, George, and Rebecca Wright.
1732, April   27, Stynard, Joseph, and Elizabeth Dobbs.
1760, Oct.   5, Suber, George, and Mary Talbert.
1735, Dec.   15, Sugar, Thomas, and Ann Towsend.
1744, Aug.   23, Sugar, Thomas, and Eliz. Collins.
1742, Nov.   21, Sugars, Samuel, and Ann Harrard.
1782, March 31, Suggs, George, and Mary Barker.
1753, Jan.   13, Sulivan, Dennis, and Susannah Garrigues.
1801, March 19, Sullivan, Abigail, and Emanuel Peterson.
1769, Oct.   11, Sullivan, Andrew, and Martha McConnelly.
1769, Nov.   11, Sullivan, Ann, and Charles McIntire.
1746, Feb.   11, Sullivan, Bridget, and John McKenny.
1799, Nov.   11, Sullivan, Eleanor, and William Hazlet.
1741, Aug.   11, Sullivan, Jane, and John Kelly.
1749, Dec.   26, Sullivan, Jane, and John Harvey.
1798, March 20, Sullivan, Jane, and George Lamb.
1723, July   —, Sullivan, Mary, and John McAllister.
1799, March 14, Sulto, Daniel, and Rachel Hargesheimer.
1762, Nov.   13, Sumers, Margaret, and Benjamin Wallis.
1791, April   29, Summers, Eliz., and William Conyngham.
1794, May   21, Summers, George, and Lydia Wright.
1801, Nov.   14, Summers, Hannah, and Baltis Emrick.
1787, May   13, Summers, Mary, and James Millen.
1803, June   4, Summers, Peter, and Eliz. Busby.
1805, April   12, Sunsbury, Eliz., and Archibald McNaughtin.
1798, Oct.   30, Supplee, George, and Ann Dunhow.

1774, Sept. 26, Supplee, John, and Sarah Thomas.
1773, Aug. 1, Sussex, Catherine, and Joseph Banks.
1716, Nov. 6, Sute, Hans, and Bridgett Davis.
1768, June 27, Sutor, Bridget, and Charles Tomkins.
1771, Dec. 26, Sutor, Eliz., and George Duck.
1766, Dec. 3, Sutor, Isabella, and Magnus Carr.
1767, May 7, Sutor, Thomas, and Bridget Hunt.
1769, May 11, Sutter, Peter, and Mary Deacon.
1773, Sept. 3, Sutton, Alice, and John Pemberton.
1759, Aug. 18, Sutton, Elizabeth, and John Kenny.
1761, Nov. 19, Sutton, Elizabeth, and William Bagnall.
1769, Nov. 2, Sutton, James, and Susannah Mannington.
1766, June 14, Sutton, James, and Catherine Smith.
1747, Jan. 24, Sutton, John, and Mary Nixon.
1759, Feb. 21, Sutton, John, and Catherine Sleydorn.
1764, Sept. 29, Sutton, John, and Mary Stackhouse.
1722, Feb. 2, Sutton, Margaret, and Charles Hughes.
1766, Sept. 16, Sutton, Martha, and Daniel Dorrel.
1752, April 11, Sutton, Rebecca, and John Kelly.
1781, Nov. 29, Sutton, Susannah, and Benjamin Lorkyer.
1735, Feb. 27, Sutton, William, and Elizabeth Robins.
1772, Dec. 12, Swaijne, Jesse, and Jane Baamer.
1775, May 22, Swailes, Charity, and James Otis.
1743, July 22, Swain, Thomas, and Elizabeth Corbet.
1783, Aug. 7, Swaine, Ann, and Samuel Wallace.
1783, July 11, Swaine, Edward, and Eliz. Shaw.
1782, Feb. 5, Swaine, James, and Sophia Brown.
1760, Nov. 28, Swaine, John, and Rebecca Inglis.
1700, June 21, Swaine, Silas, and Eliz. Linn.
1765, Oct. 31, Swales, Robert, and Charity Tucker.
1736, July 17, Swan, Richard, and Ann Mullen.
1733, March 12, Swan, Sarah, and Henry Evans.
1794, July 23, Swan, William, and Diana Lawrence.
1755, April 19, Swane, Anne, and Rees Gatline.
1737, March 19, Swarfar, Joseph, and Elizabeth Falks.
1761, Feb. 18, Sweatman, Ann, and Edward Williams.
1773, May 8, Sweaver, Cath., and Thomas Gwin.
1800, Aug. 11, Sweeney, William, and Eliz. Stewart.
1796, Aug. 17, Sweers, Sarah, and Charles Maltby.
1738, June 26, Sweeting, Rebecca, and Valentine Garret.
1744, Jan. 9, Sweeting, William, and Martha Pritchard.
1760, Oct. 20, Swel, Thomas, and Margaret Moore.
1782, Sept. 14, Swells, Ann, and Thomas Elliott.
1792, Feb. 16, Swetman, Daniel, and Jane Arthur.
1759, June 16, Sweetman, Isaac, and Ann McCann.
1732, Dec. 23, Swift, Elizabeth, and John Inglis.

1749, May   20, Swift, John, and Magdaline McCall.
1759, Feb.   3, Swift, Joseph, and Margaret McCall.
1733, June   25, Swift, Samuel, and Elizabeth Duffield.
1746, May   22, Swinney, Anne, and James Davis.
1767, Nov.   28, Swinney, Dorcas, and Matthias Pinyard.
1753, Nov.   4, Syce, Mary, and William Atkinson.
1784, Nov.   11, Sykes, Rachel, and Richard Fruman.
1744, May   5, Sylas, Martha, and John Windridge.
1776, April 11, Sylvester, Simon, and Eliz. Crispin.
1771, May   20, Symes, John, and Mary Forrest.
1801, Oct.   10, Symonds, Lewis, and Margaret Clayton.
1796, June   30, Symonds, Stephen, and Thankful Harris.
1765, July   9, Symonds, William, and Mary Pearson.
1744, Jan.   25, Symons, Susannah, and Thomas Hancock.
1723, June   20, Sympson, Sarah, and Robert Bateson.
1745, June   4, Sympson, William, and Mary McCarty.
1712, Dec.   25, Syms, Elizabeth, and Thomas Faggin.
1733, Aug.   10, Syng, Daniel, and Mary Gray.
1772, April 30, Syng, Elizabeth, and John Murray.
1762, Dec.   29, Syng, Esther, and Samuel Bunting.
1766, July   26, Syng, George, and Hannah Hance.
1736, Sept. 16, Syng, John, and Deborah Harper.
1771, June   6, Syng, Martha and Zebulun Rudulph.
1747, July   9, Syng, Mary, and Thomas James.
1766, Oct.   25, Sysom, Priscilla, and Thomas Mason.
1772, Nov.   19, Taber, Edward, and Eliz. Cowper.
1806, May   8, Tagart, Cath., and John Corrigan.
1749, Aug.   20, Tagart, John, and Sarah Erwin.
1802, May   24, Taggart, Cath., and Patrick Lyon.
1797, May   20, Taggart, Mary, and Samuel Moore.
1722, May   17, Tait, Elizabeth, and John Harbut.
1721, Jan.   22, Tait, Robert, and Elizabeth Roberts.
1761, Dec.   5, Talbert, Dorothy, and George Chilcot.
1760, Oct.   5, Talbert, Mary, and George Suber.
1761, July   28, Talbert, Mary, and Thomas Talbert.
1805, June   22, Talbert, Mary, and Frederick Allbright.
1761, July   28, Talbert, Rachel, and George Ingram.
1761, July   28, Talbert, Thomas, and Mary Talbert.
1772, Dec.   2, Talbot, Ann, and Thomas Robeson.
1767, Dec.   1, Talbot, Elizabeth, and George Williams.
1759, Feb.   13, Talbot, Esther, and Daniel Carty.
1763, Feb.   25, Talbot, Mary, and Henry Williams.
1759, June   11, Talbot, Mary, and Robert Rogers.
1787, May   11, Talbot, Seth, and Rebecca Norris.
1795, June   11, Talbut, Thomas, and Eliz. Ramsey.
1750, Feb.   17, Tallert, William, and Dorcas Peaseley.

1794, June　21, Tallman, Ann, and Joseph Casta.
1803, Aug.　22, Tallman, Deborah, and Samuel Savin.
1804, Nov.　24, Tallman, George, and Mary Dixon.
1801, Nov.　12, Tallman, Mary, and Isaac Waterman.
1805, May　21, Tallman, Mary, and John North.
1771, Oct.　30, Tallman, Mary, and Andrew Bankson, jun.
1795, Jan.　29, Tallman, Sarah, and Huwlings Cowperthwaithe.
1770, Sept.　13, Talman, Augustine, and Margaret Bankson.
1752, Oct.　25, Talman, Mary, and Edward Stevenson.
1768, March　7, Tannagh, Laetitia, and Richard Mason.
1806, Sept.　6, Tanner, Benjamin, and Mary Bivren.
1763, Sept.　14, Tanner, Martha, and Christopher Whitby.
1782, Nov.　22, Tanyard, Eliz., and John Brown.
1774, Dec.　11, Tare, John, and Margaret Crawford.
1782, June　2, Tarrinan, Robert. and Eliz. Dacciol.
1761, Sept.　5, Tate, Ann, and John Martin.
1794, June　10, Tate, Robert, and Charlotte Lumsden.
1748, Aug.　27, Tate, William, and Susannah Dunn.
1765, Sept.　5, Tatlow, Rebecca, and Benjamin Brusstar.
1799, April　25, Tatmal, Eliza, and Josiah Gould.
1739, Aug.　23, Tatnal, Hannah, and Matthew Moss.
1772, Feb.　17, Tatnall, Susannah, and John Flyn.
1798, Dec.　16, Taverner, George, and Eliz. Kemp.
1784, Dec.　25, Taverner, John, and Mary Fetters.
1776, Feb.　18, Tawser, John, and Esther Spencer.
1759, Aug.　25, Tay, James, and Eleanor Fish.
1801, April　8, Taylor, Ann, and Samuel Howard.
1766, Aug.　13, Taylor, Ann, and Lawrence Holston.
1743, Oct.　17, Taylor, Ann, and William Rowe.
1752, Dec.　13, Taylor, Anne, and Thomas Whitelock.
1722, Oct.　7, Taylor, Benjamin, and Amable Osburn.
1731, Sept.　4, Taylor, Benjamin, and Martha Guy.
1746, Aug.　19, Taylor, Daniel, and Letitia Fream.
1729, April　7, Taylor, Ed., and Lovey Hill.
1766, Dec.　3, Taylor, Eleanor, and Joseph Lewis.
1781, Sept.　23, Taylor, Elias, and Ann Wood.
1783, Sept.　20, Taylor, Eliz., and Peter William Liege.
1766, May　30, Taylor, Elizabeth, and Francis Ruth.
1767, Aug.　23, Taylor, Elizabeth, and William Robinson.
1771, Aug.　29, Taylor, Eliz., and John Young.
1730, June　15, Taylor, Elizabeth, and Stephen Ridley.
1743, Feb.　21, Taylor, Elizabeth, and John Morris.
1742, Aug.　16, Taylor, Eliz., and John Fox.
1782, May　4, Taylor, Enoch, and Ann Smith.
1785, Sept.　26, Taylor, Francis. and Rebecca Sink.
1801, Jan.　19, Taylor, George, and Mary Dougherty.

1795, Dec.   5, Taylor, Hannah, and William Craig.
1720, May   26, Taylor, Henry, and Mary Shute.
1749, Jan.   22, Taylor, Isabella, and William Charleton.
1761, May   27, Taylor, James, and Margaret Carter.
1775, June   7, Taylor, James, and Sarah Morrell.
1753, Nov.   29, Taylor, James, and Mary Naglee.
1774, July   11, Taylor, Jane, and William Harding.
1712, Feb.   11, Taylor, Joanna, and Samuel Wells.
1786, Oct.   27, Taylor, John Ralph, and Martha Shute.
1792, March   1, Taylor, John, and Ann Osborn.
1780, Sept.   28, Taylor, John, and Eleanor Jarman.
1803, Oct.   22, Taylor, John, and Jane Clay.
1804, Aug.   18, Taylor, John, and Sarah Williams.
1779, Feb.   4, Taylor, John, and Eliz. Meredith.
1774, April   9, Taylor, John, and Margaret Kisler.
1773, Oct.   13, Taylor, John, and Mary Dent.
1771, July   1, Taylor, John, and Margaret Manson.
1737, Jan.   1, Taylor, John, and Sarah Weekings.
1752, March 29, Taylor, John, and Mary Willis.
1802, June   17, Taylor, Lydia, and Chew Caldwell.
1799, Feb.   14, Taylor, Maria, and Hugh Calhoun.
1783, Nov.   3, Taylor, Martha, and Thomas Wilson.
1798, Dec.   9, Taylor, Mary, and Edward Hennin.
1783, Nov.   13, Taylor, Mary, and John McCalla.
1804, Jan.   13, Taylor, Mary, and John D. Ross.
1764, Jan.   21, Taylor, Mary, and John Heath.
1772, April   16, Taylor, Mary, and Abraham Garrett.
1733, March 25, Taylor, Mary, and Harrie Young.
1755, Dec.   26, Taylor, Mary, and Thomas Cheyne.
1731, Sept.   28, Taylor, Peter, and Mary Knowles.
1799, Feb.   27, Taylor, Philip, and Eleanor Spurrier.
1803, April   7, Taylor, Rachel, and John Dabadie.
1769, Dec.   16, Taylor, Rebecca, and Adam Richey.
1731, Oct.   4, Taylor, Richard, and Mary Lewis.
1782, May   8, Taylor, Robert, and Sarah Rooks.
1715, June   14, Taylor, Robert, and Jane Sharp.
1738, Dec.   2, Taylor, Roger, and Mary Morgan.
1776, Nov.   24, Taylor, Ruth, and John Harris.
1777, Jan.   5, Taylor, Sarah, and John Tennant.
1795, Jan.   11, Taylor, Sarah, and Robert Nelson.
1789, March 18, Taylor, Sophia, and Isaac Huber.
1801, May   28, Taylor, Thomas, and Eleanor Dunlap.
1779, March 20, Taylor, Thomas, and Ann Hoops.
1734, Feb.   19, Taylor, Thomas, and Mary Edwards.
1769, July   21, Taylor, Thomas, and Rosanna Statia.
1801, July   17, Taylor, William, and Sarah Hemphill.

1801, Dec.   30, Taylor, William, and Hester Rinedollar.
1767, Jan.   9, Taylor, William, and Martha Procter.
1768, Nov.   29, Taylor, William, and Mary Robins.
1731, June   8, Teague, Mary, and Mordecai Baine.
1802, May   5, Tear, Jane, and John Norris.
1721, Nov.   5, Teder, William, and Sarah Bird.
1756, May   30, Teel, Cornelius, and Learah Budden.
1803, Oct.   16, Teel, David, and Margaret Crossing.
1743, Sept.   1, Tempest, Robert, and Rachel Hynes.
1802, April   15, Tempest, Sarah, and Thomas Ray.
1800, June   12, Tempest, William, and Eliz. Morton.
1763, Jan.   18, Templar, Mary, and Philip Thomas.
1754, June   17, Temple, John, and Elizabeth McLane.
1773, Jan.   29, Temple, John, and Charlotte Shultzer.
1777, Jan.   5, Tennant, John, and Sarah Taylor.
1728, April   21, Tennant, Sarah, and Thomas Williams.
1769, April   14, Tennant, William, and Mary Down.
1804, Dec.   14, Tennent, Ann, and George Yocum.
1735, Jan.   3, Tenny, Mary, and Daniel Marshall.
1760, May   29, Teos, Margaret, and Edward Giles.
1795, Jan.   19, Termaine, John, and Mary Myers.
1768, Oct.   1, Terrapin, Phillip, and Agnes Hare.
1768, Nov.   3, Terry, Ruth, and George Garland.
1759, Feb.   3, Terry, William, and Rachel Manson.
1796, Sept.   11, Tervis, Joseph, and Eliz. Parkeson.
1795, Dec.   10, Tervis, Mary, and John Gardiner.
1804, Dec.   1, Tesson, Pierre, and Mary McGouran.
1770, May   31, Test, Jane, and Joseph Town.
1727, Dec.   2, Test, Margt., and James Mather.
1768, Feb.   20, Tew, Elizabeth, and Jonathan Williams.
1732, July   24, Teyland, Giles, and Benjamin Rix.
1795, May   28, Thackera, William, and Mary Allenby.
1798, Feb.   7, Tharp, Ann, and Peter Wikoff, jun.
1763, June   14, Thicker, Robert, and Catherine Clark.
1777, March   3, Thierry, Charles, and Eliz. Wrightson.
1772, Jan.   15, Thomas, Amos, and Ruth Lloyd.
1784, Aug.   25, Thomas, Ann, and Owen Denelly.
1729, May   13, Thomas, Ann, and B. Morris.
1747, Dec.   31, Thomas, Ann, and Samuel Cosster.
1758, July   8, Thomas, Ann, and Thomas Rees.
1727, Aug.   12, Thomas, Ann, and David Jones.
1761, April   25, Thomas, Ann, and William Hirst.
1733, Oct.   25, Thomas, Anne, Cornelius Hopper.
1727, May   6, Thomas, Azriah, and Elizabeth Thomas.
1786, May   18, Thomas, Cath., and William Baylor.
1791, April   26, Thomas, Cath., and Jacob Bird.

1746, Feb.   17, Thomas, Catherine, and George Leadbetter.
1793, May   30, Thomas, Charles, and Jane Allen.
1799, July   30, Thomas, David, and Jane Harding.
1745, Aug.   14, Thomas, Diana, and Evan Jones.
1761, July   2, Thomas, Edward, and Juliet Lichberg.
1726, April 28, Thomas, Eleanour, and Nathan Shenton.
1772, March 12, Thomas, Eliz., and John Helm.
1758, Sept. 25, Thomas, Elizabeth, and John Sawer.
1720, Nov.   28, Thomas, Elizabeth, and Griffith Jones.
1727, May   6, Thomas, Elizabeth, and Azriah Thomas.
1765, Aug.   16, Thomas, Elizabeth, and Robert Robertson.
1754, Nov.   27, Thomas, Elizabeth, and Isaac Chamberlain.
1792, Jan.   5, Thomas, Evan William, and Martha Gray.
1786, June   8, Thomas, Grace, and Francis Adams.
1799, May   2, Thomas, Hannah, and Gilbert Sherer.
1794, Nov.   1, Thomas, Hannah, and Robert Thomson.
1769, Feb.   16, Thomas, Hannah, and Lawrence Allman.
1768, Oct.   26, Thomas, Hannah, and Griffith Powel.
1727, Jan.   20, Thomas, James, and Ann Hinchman.
1746, Sept.   4, Thomas, Jane, and Evan Rees.
1746, June   2, Thomas, Jane, and William Wallace.
1770, Feb.   11, Thomas, Jane, and Walter Dugan.
1761, Oct.   29, Thomas, Jemima, and Jonathan Albertson.
1720, Feb.   8, Thomas, John, and Sarah Smallwood.
1762, Sept.   6, Thomas, John, and Sarah Humphreys.
1735, Sept. 27, Thomas, John, and Jane Howel.
1748, June   9, Thomas, John, and Rachel Hawksworth.
1722, Aug.   23, Thomas, Joseph, and Sarah Spencer.
1774, May   9, Thomas, Joseph, and Augustina Bavington.
1723, June   17, Thomas, Katherine, and Mark Evans.
1721, Oct.   21, Thomas, Katherine, and Theophilus Thomas.
1758, Nov.   2, Thomas, Lewis, and Susannah Evans.
1763, March   2, Thomas, Margery, and Dougaldus Ged.
1728, Nov.   14, Thomas, Martha, and Wm Davies.
1757, Oct.   29, Thomas, Martha, and William Reese.
1770, Aug.   29, Thomas, Martha, and Peter Rambo.
1735, July   26, Thomas, Mary, and Jeremiah Haycock.
1745, July   27, Thomas, Mary, and John Smith.
1801, March   9, Thomas, Mary G., and Samuel W. Davis.
1788, Jan.   4, Thomas, Mary, and Riley Bradford.
1783, July   28, Thomas, Mary, and John Stock.
1754, Dec.   12, Thomas, Mary, and Kenneth Mackenzie.
1720, May   10, Thomas, Mary, and Hugh Guilliland.
1764, May   28, Thomas, Mary, and Edward Chew.
1757, April 11, Thomas, Nathan, and Elizabeth Mather.
1730, Aug.   25, Thomas, Owen, and Catherine Wills.

1750, July 28, Thomas, Owen, and Mary Wilson.
1763, Jan. 18, Thomas, Philip, and Mary Templar.
1743, May 14, Thomas, Phillip, and Lydia Harry.
1770, Oct. 18, Thomas, Rachel, and Barnabas Kendrey.
1751, Aug. 20, Thomas, Rachel, and Samuel Jones.
1737, July 2, Thomas, Robert, and Anne Anley.
1784, Oct. 24, Thomas, Rosanna, and John Walley.
1735, Jan. 15, Thomas, Ruth, and Joseph Ramsey.
1775, June 10, Thomas, Samuel, and Priscilla Evans.
1765, Dec. 7, Thomas, Samuel, and Mercy Collins.
1801, Oct. 24, Thomas, Sarah, and John Davis.
1774, Sept. 26, Thomas, Sarah, and John Supplee.
1798, Dec. 29, Thomas, Sarah, and John Fownes.
1712, March 7, Thomas, Sarah, and Thomas Lock.
1723, July 2, Thomas, Sarah, and John Pickle.
1794, Sept. 29, Thomas, Sarah, and Charles Hudson.
1748, Aug. 2, Thomas, Sarah, and Giles Lawrence.
1727, Nov. 2, Thomas, Sus., and Jonathan Strange.
1730–1, Feb. 10, Thomas, Susannah, and Thomas Roberts.
1792, Jan. 7, Thomas, Tabitha, and Samuel Wilson.
1721, Oct. 21, Thomas, Theophilus, and Katherine Thomas.
1782, Aug. 31, Thomas, Thomas, and Jane Hale.
1796, Oct. 20, Thomas, William, and Susanna Grove.
1775, Nov. 18, Thomas, William, and Eliz. Waters.
1757, May 4, Thomas, William, and Ann James.
1720, May 25, Thomas, William, and Mary Mason.
1713, Feb. 21, Thomas, William, and Mary Price.
1771, May 30, Thomas, William, and Mary Pearson.
1736, Feb. 18, Thomas, William, and Sarah Jones.
1764, May 15, Thompson, Ann, and Walter Shea.
1787, Aug. 14, Thompson, Eliz., and Westenera Cross.
1770, Nov. 20, Thompson, Hugh, and Hannah Welch.
1805, July 14, Thompson, Jacob, and Eliz. Shilbread.
1768, March 4, Thompson, James, and Ann Eaken.
1746, June 14, Thompson, James Steel, and Martha Lamplugh.
1772, Jan. 16, Thompson, Jane, and Thomas Wiley.
1763, Nov. 23, Thompson, John, and Sarah Richison.
1759, Sept. 31, Thompson, John, and Elizabeth Farmer.
1766, May 8, Thompson, Joseph, and Sarah Hawkins.
1746, Dec. 22, Thompson, Joseph, and Anne Gilliard.
1756, June 10, Thompson, Margaret, and Ebenezer Call.
1751, July 9, Thompson, Margaret, and John Jamison.
1769, July 28, Thompson, Martha, and Brent Spencer.
1804, Sept. 1, Thompson, Mary, and Joseph Gamble.
1770, Feb. 20, Thompson, Mary, and Nicholas Hollingshead.
1752, Nov. 4, Thompson, Peter, and Hannah Johnson.

1736, Sept.   2, Thompson, Rebecca, and Jacob Shoemaker.
1771, April   27, Thompson, Richard, and Eliz. Ozier.
1748, Feb.   1, Thompson, Robert, and Hannan Delaplain.
1776, Oct.   10, Thompson, Sarah, and Thomas Phillips.
1740, Feb.   15, Thompson, Sina, and William Clogas.
1750, May   5, Thompson, Susannah, and Samuel Kimpson.
1749, June   13, Thompson, Revd Thomas, and Elizabeth Simpson.
1766, Nov.   12, Thompson, Thomas, and Isabell Maxwell.
1786, July   20, Thompson, Tracy, and John Garnet.
1779, Nov.   7, Thomson, Andrew, and Hannah Griffin.
1801, March   19, Thomson, Ann, and James Caldwell.
1801, Jan.   29, Thomson, Ann, and William Bennet.
1796, Sept.   19, Thomson, Edward, and Anne Renshaw.
1780, Feb.   8, Thomson, Eliz., and John McKibrick.
1730, Dec.   29, Thomson, Hugh, and Margaret Appleton.
1797, Aug.   26, Thomson, Jacob, and Ann Beaven.
1769, May   2, Thomson, James, and Cath. Nelson.
1745, June   25, Thomson, James, and Jane Coombs.
1781, Sept.   16, Thomson, John, and Abigail Morgan.
1801, March   29, Thomson, John, and Mary Moseley.
1788, June   15, Thomson, John, and Mary Vicker.
1800, Aug.   7, Thomson, John, and Mary Burkit.
1798, July   23, Thomson, Joseph, and Rebecca Gartley.
1803, Feb.   19, Thomson, Mary, and Samuel Thomson.
1739, Aug.   30, Thomson, Mary, and John Evans.
1802, Aug.   26, Thomson, Peter, and Hannah Stout.
1794, Aug.   21, Thomson, Rachel, and Isaac Penington.
1736, Dec.   24, Thomson, Rachel, and Thomas Hurst.
1732, Oct.   7, Thomson, Rebecca, and Nicholas Scull.
1794, Nov.   1, Thomson, Robert, and Hannah Thomas.
1803, Feb.   19, Thomson, Samuel, and Mary Thomson.
1804, Nov.   10, Thomson, Samuel H., and Eliz. Davis.
1800, June   24, Thomson, Susannah, and Frederick Berner.
1733, March   25, Thomson, Thomas, and Hannah Lovekin.
1730, Sept.   30, Thomson, William, and Sarah Penry.
1796, March   27, Thoronegood, Mary, and Thomas Hewett.
1806, Aug.   9, Thorn, George, and Mary Weaver.
1758, March   31, Thorn, William, and Rachel Griffiths.
1797, July   29, Thorne, William, and Margaret Oner.
1790, Dec.   23, Thorne, Zaccheus, and Rebecca Mills.
1742, Oct.   13, Thornhill, Eliz., and Thomas Annis.
1764, Nov.   24, Thornhill, Hannah, and Joseph Garner.
1741, July   11, Thornhill, John, and Jane Cook.
1802, Dec.   30, Thornhill, John, and Ann Quinn.
1784, Jan.   28, Thornhill, John, and Eliz. Cooper.

1783, Dec.　18, Thornhill, Joseph, and Dorothy Kilton.
1716, May　27, Thornhill, Martha, and Thomas Ridge.
1764, April　31, Thornhill, Mary, and John Dowers.
1741, June　20, Thornhill, Rebecca, and John Sibbald.
1748, Oct.　17, Thornhill, Susannah, and David Dewer.
1790, Oct.　12, Thornton, ——, and Ann Bordeau.
1784, May　8, Thornton, Benjamin, and Rebecca North.
1799, July　6, Thornton, Eleanor, and Timothy Leonard.
1781, Feb.　22, Thornton, George, and Johanna Johnston.
1797, May　22, Thornton, John, and Mary Marshall.
1760, May　6, Thornton, John, and Mary Hamilton.
1774, March　5, Threlfal Robert, and Eliz. Brathwaite.
1804, Feb.　13, Thurston, Robert, and Eliz. Eldridge.
1785, Dec.　26, Tice, John, and Eleanor Anderson.
1796, Jan.　7, Tiffin, James, and Martha Pelrose.
1722, May　17, Tiler, John, and Elizabeth Pierce.
1774, May　26, Tilghman, Edward, and Eliz. Chew.
1743, Sept.　30, Tilghman, James, and Anne Frances.
1794. July　1. Tilghman, William, and Margaret Eliz. Allen.
1804, Jan.　24, Tilgman, Eliz., and William Cook.
1800, Sept.　14, Till, Comfort, and John Johnson.
1748, Oct.　2, Till, Elizabeth, and Preserve Brown.
1741, Dec.　24, Till, Mary, and Andrew Hamilton.
1744, Dec.　2, Till, Rebecca, and Cornelius Stout.
1774, June　21, Till, Thomas, and Hannah Hildebrand.
1720. Jan.　7. Till, William, and Mary Lillings, Spinster.
1783, July　8, Tilla, John, and Elizabeth Allen.
1795, Jan.　1, Tillenghast, Christopher, and Eliz. Reiley.
1720, Jan.　1. Tillet, Simon, and Elizabeth Reynolds.
1709, Feb.　16, Tilley, John, and Mary Corfey.
1785, Jan.　8, Tillinherst, Daniel, and Susannah Channuel.
1710, Feb.　16, Tilly, John, and Mary Culf.
1765, Oct.　21, Tillyer, Jane, and Isaac States.
1798, May　2, Tillyer, Samuel, and Sarah Wright.
1790, Feb.　25, Tillyer, William, and Ann Duffield.
1737, Nov.　22, Tilsell, Robert, and Jane Hamilton.
1800, Jan.　4, Tilton, William, and Julia Owens.
1744, Feb.　6, Timmerman, Mary, and John Hemson.
1775, Feb.　5, Timmons, Dean, and Mary Samuel.
1794, June　14, Timothy, Benjamin Franklin, and Ann Tolfain.
1789, Aug.　6, Tinaver, Barbary, and John Houch.
1729, July　6, Tinney, John, and Mary Peep.
1731, Dec.　5, Tinny, Grace, and Matthew Dwiet.
1716, May　18, Tinsley, Frances, and John Slack.
1800, March　4, Tipaway, Margaret, and William Stewart.
1775, Nov.　1, Tipler, John, and Mary Doyle.

1743, Oct.   22, Tipper, James, and Ann Blair.
1752, Nov.   4, Tis, Richard, and Elizabeth Cheesman.
1737, Jan.   22, Tisdal, Henry, and Elizabeth Peters.
1749, Aug.   8, Tisdale, Henry, and Honour Condon.
1752, July   24, Tisdel, Hannah, and John Farron.
1728, March 29, Tison, Rich⁴, and Bridget Justice.
1805, May   25, Tissran, Mary Ann, and John Berkman.
1758, Oct.   26, Titchet, Elizabeth, and Henry Flood.
1775, Nov.   29, Titchet, Rebecca, and Charles Manford.
1796, June   5, Titus, Ann, and Frederick Bagingdollar.
1732, Dec.   13, Toad, Joseph, and Elizabeth Finney.
1775, June   15, Tobin, Margaret, and Daniel Connel.
1771, Jan.   7, Tod, Alexander, and Mary Sharp.
1802, Dec.   18, Tod, Eliz., and John C. Otto.
1797, April   20, Todd, Eliz., and Andrew Balan.
1731, Sept.   15, Todd, Hester, and Steuart Charles.
1759, Jan.   24, Todd, James, and Margaret Myers.
1722, Oct.   30, Todd, Martha, and William Lunn.
1766, Nov.   4, Todd, Sarah, and Hugh Nevin.
1722, Feb.   4, Todd, Thomas, and Elizabeth Cummings.
1794, July   31, Todon, Eliza, and Phœnix Stretcher.
1793, June   14, Tolfain, Ann, and Benjamin Franklin Timothy.
1768, June   27, Tomkins, Charles, and Bridget Sutor.
1767, April   1, Tomkins, Elizabeth, and William Bourk.
1766, Sept.   18, Tomkins, Thomas, and Elizabeth Collister.
1800, May   31, Tomlin, Zephaniah, and Eliz. Adair.
1763, Sept.   13, Tomlinson, Ebenezer, and Ann Coggins.
1735, Feb.   1, Tomlinson, Ebenezer, and Elizabeth Hoskins.
1758, Dec.   15, Tomlinson, Elizabeth, and Jonathan Price.
1736, May   20, Tomlinson, James, and Elizabeth Hough.
1731, July   28, Tomlinson, James, and Susannah Harvey.
1721, Nov.   12, Tomlinson, Sarah, and Abraham Dolby.
1774, Oct.   8, Tomlinson, Thomas, and Phoebe Carver.
1786, Aug.   3, Tomlinson, William, and Cath. Brooks.
1743, May   28, Tomms, Mary, and William Dowell.
1742, Nov.   6, Tompson, Ruth, and Edward Bonnell.
1759, Jan.   8, Toms, Martha, and John Barret.
1745, Nov.   14, Toms, Martha, and Patrick Rowney.
1714, Feb.   9, Tonge, Jacob, and Jane Amilton.
1729–30, Jan. 8, Tongue, John, and Mary Bickley.
1795, Aug.   5, Tonkin, Bathsheba, and William Sapout.
1776, April   24, Tonry, Patrick, and Margaret Kenan.
1715, Oct.   22, Tonyclifft, James, and Elizabeth Brown.
1800, July   9, Toole, Simon, and Mary Coleburn.
1777, April   3, Toomey, Dennis, and Ann Croney.
1786, Jan.   6, Toomy, Ann, and Edward Evans.

1751, Nov.   4, Toomy, Anne, and Bryan McGithgan.
1741, July   23, Topforson, Mary, and Isaac Potts.
1747, April 30, Topp, Anne, and George Sharswood.
1734, Feb.   21, Topp, Joseph, and Anne King.
1727, April   5, Torton, Frances, and John Edwards.
1738, June   18, Torton, John, and Anne Morton.
1770, June   6, Torr, John, and Hannah Brannin.
1756, April 17, Toukin, William, and Martha Brown.
1786, Feb.   9, Tousaeuts, Lewis, and Sarah Green.
1799, Dec.   1, Towell, John, and Jane Holget.
1804, May   31, Towell, Peter, and Mary St. John.
1789, April 19, Towers, Eliz., and Jonathan Gostelowe.
1792, March   1, Towers, Margaret, and Daniel Knight.
1770, May   31, Town, Joseph, and Jane Test.
1728, Dec.   2, Townsend, Ann, and James Way.
1774, Dec.   13, Townsend, Ann, and Nicholas Scull.
1735, Dec.   15, Townsend, Ann, and Thomas Sugar.
1758, June   6, Townsend, Eliz., and Peter Brewstar.
1752, Aug.   29, Townsend, Elizabeth, and David Erwin.
1759, Dec.   29, Townsend, John, and Isabella Williams.
1752, Oct.   17, Townsend, Martha, and Robert Adams.
1728, Dec.   26, Townsend, Rachel, and W^m. Adams.
1731, Nov.   18, Towson, Mary, and Patrick Flood.
1775, Nov.   9, Towzer, Eliz., and John Harman.
1754, Oct.   31, Toy, Nicholas, and Anne Forrest.
1729, March 15, Tracy, Dan., and Martha Murphey.
1734, March 30, Trageny, Henrietta, and Elijah Aston.
1771, Oct.   14, Trager, Hannah, and Amos Matlack.
1804, Oct.   11, Trago, Absalom, and Hannah Lewis.
1800, May   3, Traine, Daniel M., and Cath. Collins.
1786, Dec.   28, Tranor, David, and Margaret Morton.
1739, April 24, Trantar, Hester, and Samuel Bishop.
1713, June   21, Traveller, Richard, and Mary Price.
1760, Oct.   11, Travers, Philip, and Elizabeth Papynd.
1791, March 27, Travis, John, and Eliz. Bond.
1750, Oct.   15, Traut, Gabriel, and Mary Beers.
1801, April 16, Trego, Hannah, and Evan Lewis.
1737, May   6, Tregoe, Sarah, and Samuel Simcock.
1775, Aug.   4, Tremble, Hannah, and Nicholas Milet.
1733, May   23, Trevoe, Margaret, and Edward Jones.
1794, May   8, Tress, Ann, and Abraham Singer.
1722, Sept. 23, Tress, Mary, and William Ward.
1751, May   9, Tresse, Anne, and Daniel Rundle.
1741, Oct.   7, Tresse, Mary, and James Morgatroy'd.
1711, April   8, Tresse, Thomas, and Mary Pearce.
1767, March 30, Tresse, Thomas, and Elizabeth Singleton.

1715, May   15, Tresse, Thomas, and Elizabeth Finney.
1756, April   20, Trickett, Thomas, and Catherine Ash.
1761, May   7, Triggin, Ann, and Joseph Hunt.
1776, Feb.   12, Triggs, Jane, and David McFee.
1803, May   14, Trimble, Jane, and Alexander Mackie.
1759, March 13, Trimble, Mary, and James Duncan.
1737, Oct.   11, Trimble, William, and Mary Atkinson.
1737, Nov.   12, Trimer, Richard, and Alice Marshal.
1802, Dec.   19, Trimmer, Eliz., and Andrew Quin.
1804, March 3, Trisobio, Jane, and William Burgess.
1799, April   27, Triste, Hore Browse, and Mary Browne.
1803, Oct.   10, Troa, George, and Mary Dickenson.
1713, April   26, Trollup, Elizabeth, and Andrew Yeakum.
1768, July   21, Trother, Joseph, and Sarah Robinson.
1748, Jan.   16, Trotter, Spencer, and Margaret Williams.
1742, June   28, Trotter, William, and Elizabeth Hoods.
1780, March 21, Truack, Henry, and Eliz. Middleton.
1763, June   4, Truling, James, and Jane Donald.
1798, Aug.   8, Trump, John, and Sabra Hamble.
1763, Jan.   7, Trump, Mary, and Robert Brady.
1762, July   12, Trump, Rebecca, and John Smallwood.
1745, Jan.   21, Trussel, Cath., and Ben. Barker.
1805, Dec.   12, Truxton, Evelina, and Henry Hammond.
1768, May   12, Tucker, Andrew, and Sarah Stoops.
1790, Nov.   10, Tucker, Ann, and Ralph Brigs.
1765, Oct.   31, Tucker, Charity, and Robert Swales.
1760, Sept.   25, Tucker, Cornelius, and Ann Creighton.
1796, Aug.   11, Tucker, Eliz., and Thomas Jones.
1796, Jan.   3, Tucker, Isaak, and Naomi Campbell.
1720, March 25, Tucker, Joseph, and Sarah Knight.
1752, July   1, Tucker, Margaret, Thomas Pugh.
1790, Oct.   21, Tucker, Margaret, and John Redman.
1783, Jan.   3, Tucker, Mary, and James Jackson.
1742, Feb.   3, Tucker, Pall, and Ann Dobans.
1743, Oct.   8, Tucker, Richard, and Martha Finnyman.
1765, Dec.   23, Tucker, Robert, and Mary Garrett.
1793, April   1, Tucker, Stephen, and Priscilla Merrick.
1779, March 25, Tucker, Thomas, and Cath. Marget.
1754, Aug.   6, Tuckett, Sarah, and Robert Dixon.
1737, Jan.   10, Tuckness, Robert, and Mary Blackham.
1766, Dec.   8, Tufft, John, and Martha Gauff.
1737, Nov.   25, Tuite, Robert, and Mary Osbourn.
1793, Jan.   14, Tuke, Eliz., and Lewis Hallam.
1765, Jan.   16, Tull, James, and Mary Wood.
1733, April   4, Tull, William, and Margaret Rickets.
1740, July   31, Turnbull, James, and Mary Walker.

1770, Nov. 27, Turner, Alice, and Henry Read.
1768, June 10, Turner, Amelia, and John Brandt.
1757, Dec. 22, Turner, Ann, and John Chaband.
1773, Oct. 18, Turner, Ann, and William Morris.
1767, April 29, Turner, Ebenezer, and Ann Estlack.
1751, Aug. 17, Turner, Edward, and Rachel Hawkins.
1796, Oct. 9, Turner, Eliz., and David Forsyth.
1741, Sept. 9, Turner, George, and Joannah Elizabeth Yanily.
1756, Dec. 19, Turner, James, and Elizabeth Mackay.
1782, Feb. 19, Turner, Capt. James, and Isabella Chevalier.
1746, Aug. 5, Turner, John, and Mary Dagger.
1750, March 28, Turner, John, and Elizabeth Boon.
1768, May 31, Turner, John, and Jane Richmond.
1790, Dec. 22, Turner, Juliana, and William Miller.
1760, July 28, Turner, Mary, and Thomas Buckley.
1798, June 16, Turner, Mary, and James Myland.
1728, Nov. 10, Turner, Peter, and Hannah Kees.
1763, Jan. 3, Turner, Peter, and Rebecca Bird.
1727, Dec. 6, Turner, Peter, and Sarah Wally.
1756, Aug. 17, Turner, Peter, jr., and Sarah Woodrop.
1782, May 21, Turner, Rebecca, and Dr. John Redman.
1740, Oct. 27, Turner, Sarah, and John Pickering.
1751. Feb. 25, Turner, Susannah, and Thomas Francis.
1767, Feb. 16, Turner, William, and Susannah Nice.
1770, March 26, Turner, William, and Ruth Miller.
1722, April 13, Turton, Thomas, and Lucy Lambeth.
1750, March 19, Tusse, Christianna, and John Lee.
1733, April 10, Tustan, Abraham, and Jane McGraw.
1730, Sept. 13, Tuthill, Christopher, and Susannah Mason.
1801, Nov. 11, Tuttle, Andrew, and Mary Kelly.
1743, Dec. 12, Tuttle, Susannah, and William Annis.
1791, Jan. 25, Twamley, Josiah, and Eliz. Hockley.
1770, Sept. 20, Twells, Godfrey, and Sarah Standley.
1756, Oct. 11, Twiggs, John, and Susannah Rees.
1736, April 2, Twining, Abigail, and Samuel Helborne.
1760, Nov. 26, Twining, Eleazar, and Mary Colton.
1759, May 21, Tybout, Andrew, and Susannah Howell.
1783, Sept. 18, Tybout, Mary, and John Perot.
1780, Nov. 16, Tybout, Sarah, and Benjamin Crawford.
1786, Sept. 11, Tye, Bridget, and William Spence.
1786, June 1, Tye, Mary, and Thomas Hodgson.
1779, Jan. 28, Tyler, Margaret, and Robert Linton.
1755, July 30, Tyley, Elizabeth, and John Gard.
1728, July 24, Tynes, Timothy, and Cath. Parsons.
1795, Oct. 20, Tyrrell, Andrew, and Catherine Harris.
1798, June 14, Tyson, Margaret, and Thomas Seaman.

1786, May   11, Tyson, Matthew, and Sarah Lukens.
1803, April   30, Uhl, Cath., and Thomas Henozey.
1804, Aug.   29, Uhle, Mary, and Morris Brown.
1801, March   8, Ulary, Ainst, and Sarah Hutson.
1745, June   25, Ulrich, Peter, and Margaret Clampfert.
1721, Nov.   27, Underwood, John, and Rebecca Vankirk.
1781, March 15, Underwood, John, and Mary Lawrence.
1800, Nov.   6, Underwood, John, and Mary Martin.
1785, Nov.   10, Underwood, Tacey, and Frederick Ritter.
1780, Dec.   7, Urquhart, Æneas, and Cath. Dardis.
1790, Nov.   3, Urt, Margaret, and John Pack.
1796, June   25, Urviler, Eliz., and James Pollock.
1774, April   7, Usher, Ann, and George Henry.
1800, Feb.   10, Usher, Barbary, and Geo. Wilks Stowell.
1799, July   20, Usher, Luke, and Ann Adams.
1760, March 18, Usher, Margaret, and James Harding.
1754, April 20, Usher, Rose, and Abraham.
1793, June   16, Utes, Ann, and Stephen Conyers.
1756, Dec.   15, Valentine, Anne, and Anthony Harrle.
1780, Jan.   25, Valentine, Cath., and James Keimer.
1743, May   26, Vallacott, John, and Eliz. Wade.
1734, May   18, Vallecott, Mary, and Robert Low.
1715, Jan.   2, Vanbeek, Elizabeth, and John Hammarsh.
1768, June   9, Van Bevert, William, and Cath. Hetkin.
1777, Sept.   9, Vancl, Cath., and Samuel Goft.
1792, Dec.   16, Vance, Margaret, and David Jones.
1782, June   25, Vancice, Joseph, and Jane Lowry.
1799, Feb.   17, Vancile, Jonathan, and Mary Wallace.
1737, March 16, Vanculand, Margaret, and Jacob Morton.
1747, Jan.   18, Van Culin, Catharine, and Andrew Dalbo.
1802, March 18, Vanculing, Mary, and Isaac Morton.
1744, Nov.   20, Vanderborgh, Henry, and Mary Green.
1780, June   8, Vanderen, John, and Esther Melcher.
1783, Dec.   24, Vanderen, Matthew, and Lydia Brehaut.
1756, Feb.   17, Vandergrift, Abraham, and Elizabeth Willard.
1776, Feb.   15, Vandegrist, Amelia, and Thomas Beck.
1773, April 22, Vandegrist, John, and Cath. Phillips.
1782, Dec.   15, Vandergrist, Joseph, and Mary McBean.
1776, May   13, Vandermine, Catharine, and Edward Whelline.
1716, May   27, Vander Sloich, Hannah, and Thomas Receau.
1794, April 26, Vandusen, Rachel, and Joseph Michael.
1796, Oct.   28, Vandyke, Sarah, and Thomas Woodfield.
1726, Oct.   24, Vane, Hester, and Dan. Luker.
1741, July   23, Vangozel, John, and Sarah Morgan.
1744, July   30, Vanhist, Sam., and Ann Harris.
1780, Sept.   5, Vanholinger, Sarah, and George Hill.

1804, March 27, Vanholt, Ann, and Joshua Roberts.
1804, June　21, Vanholt, James, and Rebecca Fines.
1721, July　15, Vanhook, Henry, and Debora Parent.
1774, March　7, Vanhorn, Cath., and Ralph Crumbley.
1775, Jan.　5, Vanhorn, Isaac, and Catherine Rice.
1782, Aug.　13, Vanhorn, John, and Eleanor Mode.
1739, May　14, Vanhust, Elizabeth, and Hugh McAdam.
1764, Sept.　10, Vaniman, Elizabeth, and Samuel Linch.
1721, Nov.　27, Vankirk, Rebecca, and John Underwood.
1748, April　7, Vankirk, Sarah, and Peter Johnson.
1734, Feb.　25, Vanlear, Bernhard, and Mary Bransten.
1738, July　7, Vanlear, John, and Elizabeth Reynolds.
1738, Jan.　25, Vanleer, John Gerich, and Rebecca Fauls.
1801, April　19, Vanleer, William R., and Sarah Hunter.
1749, Feb.　24, Van Leuvenigh, Zachariah, and Anne Combs.
1782, June　20, Valois, Mary, and John Francis LePellsive.
1782, Nov.　10, Valoiss, Susannah, and Adam Crafts.
1771, July　15, Vanlone, William, and Deborah Eggman.
1737, Aug.　29, Van Niminon, Margaret, and Joseph Jones.
1779, May　13, Vannost, Mary, and Dr. James Fallon.
1741, Nov.　29, Vanoustan, Jacobus, and Martha Dumber.
1799, April　4, Van Phul, Cath., and John Jordan.
1767, April　2, Vansandt, James, and Susannah Scull.
1739, May　13, Vansandt, Garret, and Anne Groome.
1748, Dec.　6, Vansant, Cornelius, and Mary Lee.
1803, Nov.　17, Vansant, Eleanor, and Samuel Fiss.
1783, Dec.　24, Vansant, George and Sarah Johnson.
1782, Oct.　29, Vansciver, Mary, and William Naglee.
1785, Dec.　25, Vansciver, Sarah, and Samuel Winter.
1805, Jan.　26, Vansise, Mary, and Isaac W. Norris.
1749, June　4, Varnum, Edward, and Elizabeth Crawford.
1761, May　6, Vaughan, Ann, and Lane Naylor.
1752, April　18, Vaughan, Edward, and Anne Wiley.
1803, Aug.　18, Vaughan, John, and Phoebe Hoffman.
1728, March　1, Vaughan, Mary, and John David.
1806, June　7, Vaughan, Rachel, and Christopher Kellinger.
1742, July　3, Vaughan, Rachel, and John Jenkins.
1720, Aug.　15, Vaughan, Richard, and Mary Davis.
1774, Dec.　15, Vaughan, Sarah, and William Fling.
1766, June　20, Vaughan, Thomas, and Mary Zane.
1739, Sept.　17, Vaughan, William, and Sarah Weldon.
1797, July　31, Vaughan, William, and Lydia Ann Wells.
1774, Feb.　27, Veasey, Pleasant, and James Randall.
1744, Sept.　9, Veil, Ann, and Dan. Harrison.
1715, Feb.　13, Vellecott, William, and Mary Chalona.
1767, March　5, Venables, Sarah, and William Jenkins.

1740, June   12, Venables, Thomas, and Rebecca McCluer.
1767, Sept.   13, Venn, John, and Ruth Bailets.
1795 Jan.   1, Vennabel, Dorothy, and Thomas Edwards.
1791, Nov.   19, Vennable, Mary, and James Guiham.
1791, Nov.   13, Vennable, Rebecca, and Henry Holmes.
1791, Nov.   10, Vennable, William, and Charlotte Griggs.
1770, Sept.   10, Vennemore, Barbary, and William Goodwin.
1737, Nov.   15, Verlin, John, and Jane Wilkinson.
1740, Sept.   13, Verney, Henry, and Elizabeth Jones.
1798, June   9, Vernon, Absalom Zeigar, and Margaret Freeman.
1732, Nov.   25, Vernon, Elizabeth, and John Mills.
1795, April   5, Vernon, Hannah, and George Charles Fairbanks.
1730, April 20, Vernon, Jacob, and Elizabeth Chiney.
1762, June   5, Vernon, Robert, and Phoebe Hart.
1760, Feb.   13, Vershon, Felix, and Ameron Butler.
1728, May   14, Verschoyle, W^m, and Eleanor Allen.
1762, Aug.   10, Vesey, William, and Pleasant Nichols.
1791, Jan.   1, Vesmith, Anna, and Samuel Hoop.
1788, Sept.   9, Vester, Eliz., and John Hurst.
1785, Sept.   23, Vicar, John, and Ann Matthews.
1769, Nov.   14, Vicary, John, and Mary Harvey.
1799, Dec.   26, Vicary, Rebecca, and Richard Flecher.
1788, June   15, Vicker, Mary, and John Thomson.
1762, April   6, Vickery, Samuel, and Rebecca Lumley.
1795, Oct.   25, Villgrove, Susanna, and Champagne Rose.
1798, Dec.   9, Vincen, Cath., and Ralph McDavid.
1775, April 22, Vincent, Ann, and George Davis.
1738, April 13, Vincent, Elizabeth, and John Riall.
1730–1, Mar. 2, Vineing, Anne, and Richard Jayne.
1797, Jan.   5, Vining, Henry, and Cath. Williamson.
1796, Dec.   17, Vint, Mary, and James Bradley.
1796, Nov.   3, Visdicker, Mary, and Paul Badollet.
1763, Aug.   2, Vivers, Margaret, and Richard White.
1800, Feb.   6, Vogdes, Joseph, and Eliz. Moore.
1805, June   13, Vogdes, Jesse, and Ann Bell.
1805, Dec.   21, Voight, Mary, and John French.
1740, June   21, Vokes, Hannah, and Patrick Lithgow.
1732, March 26, Vokes, Mary, and Peter Stuart.
1760, July   22, Vokins, Sarah, and Edward Nicholson.
1767, May   14, Volans, Joseph, and Mary Shearcross.
1757, June   20, Von Seeler, Fernandus, and Elenor Winekoop.
1766, Oct.   9, Voto, Sarah, and Samuel Jackson.
1749, June   7, Voyer, Jane Urbaine, and Charles Hamilton.
1715, Oct.   30, Voyer, Peter, and Mary Coiffart.
1794, Feb.   7, Vretenburg, John, and Esther Willet.
1806, April 24, Waddell, Henry L., and Eliz. Pemberton.

1768, Jan. 19, Waddel, Isabella, and William Shead.
1768, Sept. 30, Waddington, Richard, and Mary Hartley.
1743, May 26, Wade, Eliz., and John Vallacot.
1790, Nov. 17, Wade, Jonathan, and Susannah Creed.
1736, Dec. 16, Wade, Mary, and James Fox.
1780, Nov. 1, Wade, Peter, and Mary Ann Doyle.
1775, Dec. 10, Wade, Thomas, and Eliz. Low.
1773, April 6, Wade, Thomas, and Eliz. Ridgway.
1726, Dec. 17, Wade, W^m, and Elizabeth Zean.
1796, April 24, Wadman, Ann, and John Hargesheimer.
1784, July 29, Wadman, Eleanor, and Langhorn Janney.
1782, Nov. 24, Wadman, Mary, and William Paine.
1767, Feb. 25, Wagenaer, Jacob, and Catharina Stradleman.
1770, Jan. 30, Wager, Joseph, and Sarah Harper.
1805, Jan. 8, Wager, Margaret, and William J. Baker.
1757, June 28, Wagg, John, and Mary Lowcay.
1784, Sept. 21, Waggoner, John Conrad, and Anna Powell.
1795, Sept. 3, Wagner, Henrietta, and Robert Phelan.
1800, April 25, Wagoner, Sophia, and John Homesworth.
1765, May 7, Wagstaff, Thomas, and Hannah Leech.
1729, Nov. 16, Wain, Jacob, and Elizabeth Ridge.
1744, June 9, Waine, Eliz., and Thomas Bryan.
1758, Jan. 27, Wainer, John, and Edith Jackson.
1711, Dec. 17, Wainwright, Ann, and John Barnott.
1722, March 4, Wake, Elizabeth, and George Slyfield.
1743, Oct. 20, Wakefield, John, and Eliz. Cole.
1766, Dec. 10, Wakefield, Thomas, and Elizabeth Willard.
1802, Dec. 11, Wakeimer, George, and Eliz. Naglee.
1749, Aug. 9, Walace, Abigail, and Lawrence Hewlings.
1742, March 29, Waldocker, Conrad, and Margaret Byrn.
1747, Aug. 13, Waldrick, James, and Mary Ford.
1779, April 8, Walheim, Mary, and David Clark.
1781, Feb. 27, Walkeimer, Margaret, and Michael Durney.
1801, May 12, Walker, Cath., and Robert Hodgson.
1766, Dec. 8, Walker, Catherine, and Benjamin Devo.
1755, April 29, Walker, Catherine, and Robert Patton.
1711, Dec. 14, Walker, David, and Mary Norris.
1767, June 13, Walker, Eleanor, and Duncan McGlashan.
1790, Dec. 3, Walker, Eliz., and Walter Brown.
1737, Nov. 26, Walker, Flower, and Anthony Noble.
1765, Sept. 30, Walker, James, and Mellesim Robinson.
1767, March 3, Walker, James Buncle, and Catherine Bennet.
1761, Nov. 7, Walker, Jerman, and Jane Malin.
1798, Dec. 9, Walker, John, and Ann Coleman.
1771, Sept. 14, Walker, John, and Sarah Cowgill.
1794, May 20, Walker, John Thruston, and Diana Findley.

1773, Jan.   28, Walker, Margaret, and John Hockenhall.
1758, Feb.   13, Walker, Margaret, and John Kennedy.
17:8, Jan.   28, Walker, Mary, and James Parsons.
1773, Aug.   5, Walker, Mary, and David Gaubert.
1805, July   9, Walker, Mary Ann, and Benjamin Smith.
1760, Jan.   21, Walker, Mary, and John Stone.
1772, June   16, Walker, Mary, and Thomas Clayton.
1740, July   31, Walker, Mary, and James Turnbull.
1781, March 16, Walker, Patrick, and Ann Guirey.
1749, April   2, Walker, Ralph, and Hannah Pain.
1759, Feb.   21, Walker, Rebecca, and Benjamin Willard.
1769, May   11, Walker, Robert, and Ann Maag.
1773, June   17, Walker, Sarah, and Jacob Willson.
1761, Nov.   7, Walker, Sarah, and Randal Malin.
1799, Feb.   5, Walker, Simon, and Mary Ann Ashley.
1772, Sept. 17, Walker, Thomas, and Margaret Hoops.
1755, Nov.   18, Walker, Thomas, and Hannah Marshal.
1804, June   27, Walkinhood, John, and Eliz. Hewes.
1761, Sept. 13, Wall, Mary, and James Brown.
1712, Feb.   20, Wall, Mary, and Joshua Haswellhurst.
1766, Dec.   25, Wall, Thomas, and Mary Dowthwait.
1794, Dec.   13, Wallace, Agnes, and Joseph Greves.
1782, Sept. 15, Wallace, David, and Ann Chew.
1772, March 11, Wallace, Eleanor, and William Barker.
1798, April 20, Wallace, Eleanor, and Richard Spain.
1800, Nov.   9, Wallace, Eliz., and James Davidson.
1794, May   13, Wallace, Hannah, and Thomas Baker.
1805, April   2, Wallace, John B., and Susan Binney.
1773, Aug.   4, Wallace, Joshua Maddox, and Tace Bradford.
1799, June   22, Wallace, Martha, and James Newton.
1799, Feb.   17, Wallace, Mary, and Jonathan Vancill.
1800, Nov.   19, Wallace, Mary Sanclair, and Constantine O'Donald
1798, April 26, Wallace, Mary, and Charles Marshall.
1786, Dec.   20, Wallace, Mary, and Ambrose Simpson.
1783, Aug.   7, Wallace, Samuel, and Ann Swaine.
1769, July   3, Wallace, Susannah, and Samuel Baker.
1750, June   7, Wallace, Susannah, and Abraham Coates.
1773, Aug.   16, Wallace, William, and Ann Lehman.
1746, June   2, Wallace, William, and Jane Thomas.
1720, Feb.   4, Wallen, Mary, and Jacob Garrison.
1784, Oct.   24, Walley, John, and Rosanna Thomas.
1793, Oct.   10, Wallhelmer, Ann, and George Hillman.
1760, Dec.   4, Wallin, Richard, and Catherine Shippen.
1800, June   12, Wallington, Margaret, and Robert Davidson.
1771, May   5, Wallington, Mary, and George West.
1762, Nov.   13, Wallis, Benjamin, and Margaret Sumers.

1755, May   1, Wallis, John, and Martha McCoy.
1710, May 24, Wallis, Robert, and Ann Clouther.
1770, March 1, Wallis, Samuel, and Lydia Hollingsworth.
1727, Dec.   6, Wally, Sarah, and Peter Turner.
1805, March 14, Walm, William, and Mary Wilcocks.
1730, Dec. 21, Walmsley, Ann, and Thomas Marden.
1746, May 24, Walmsley, Grace, and Benjamin Herbert.
1731, Oct. 19, Walmsley, Sarah, and Thomas Eastborn.
1735, Dec.   3, Walmsley, Thomas, and Sarah Dunn.
1773, April 24, Waln, Hannah, and Jonathan Matlack.
1797, April 26, Waln, Sarah, and Thomas Bulkley.
1748, Sept.   8, Walnet, Martha, and Joseph Ferguson.
1750, Nov. 17, Walpole, Eleanor, and John Pearson.
1797, Dec.   3, Walpole, Thomas, and Lucy Hand.
1721, Nov.   3, Walter, Ann, and William Oburn.
1753, May 29, Walter, Catherine, and Daniel Folly.
1786, July   6, Walter, Eliz., and John Faston.
1758, March 16, Walter, John, and Rebecca Rambo.
1768, Nov.   6, Walter, John, and Mary Rouse.
1804, Oct. 19, Walter, Mary, and Jacob Reynard.
1728, Feb. 23, Walter, Sarah, and Matt. Roberts.
1790, Sept. 30, Walters, Ann, and John Rose.
1772, April 20, Walters, William, and Mary Coffin.
1755, April 15, Walton, Albertson, and Rachel Britton.
1758, April 29, Walton, Ann, and Samuel Butcher.
1761, Sept.   1, Walton, Daniel, and Sarah Gilbert.
1752, Jan. 16, Walton, Joseph, and Rebecca Holt.
1747, April 16, Walton, Rachel, and William Groom.
1801, May 22, Walton, Rebecca, and William Gardiner.
1756, Nov. 29, Walworth, Isaac, and Hannah Kinsil.
1777, March 6, Wane, Joseph, and Jane Lowry.
1801, Dec. 13, Wansley, Lydia, and Jacob Planter.
1772, May 28, Ward, Ann, and Benjamin Ward.
1772, May 28, Ward, Benjamin, and Ann Ward.
1716, April 1, Ward, Edith, and Joseph Claypool.
1757, April 5, Ward, Elizabeth, and William Davis.
1762, April 15, Ward, Elizabeth, and James Wilkins.
1791, April 10, Ward, Francis, and Margaret Bone.
1725, July 25, Ward Hannah, and Wm Croswit.
1729, July 27, Ward, John, and Cath. O'Neal.
1736, Oct. 23, Ward, Martha, and John Skeer.
1736, Oct. 19, Ward, Martha, and John Skeer.
1748, Dec.   7, Ward, Nicholas, and Sarah Sherrin.
1769, Dec. 28, Ward, Phoebe, and Joel Clark.
1720, Oct. 30, Ward, Ralph, and Jane Curwen.
1754, March 4, Ward, Richard, and Elizabeth Budden.

1722, Sept.   23, Ward, William, and Mary Tress.
1803, Nov.   28, Ward, William, and Rebecca Douglass.
1767, Dec.   10, Warden, James, and Rebeccah McTingley.
1801, Aug.   11, Warden, Robert, and Frances Holland.
1756, April   8, Warden, William, and Mary Rice.
1720, Aug.   25, Warder, Willoughby, and Mary Ellis.
1729, June   19, Warding, Jane, and Shedack Welsh.
1717, Jan.   5, Ware, Ann, and Thomas Blaxton.
1801, Oct.   8, Ware, Ann, and John Graves.
1768, Sept.   22, Ware, David, and Ann Barber.
1770, Oct.   17, Ware, Hannah, and John Fosset.
1796, Nov.   9, Ware, Jacob, and Mary Overturff.
1757, May   30, Ware, John, and Grace Stackhouse.
1787, Dec.   11, Ware, John, and Mary Albertson.
1794, Jan.   9, Ware, John B., and Frances Bakeman.
1721, Aug.   2, Ware, Mary, and Richard Humphreys.
1757, May   4, Ware, Mary, and Alexander Leech.
1720, Oct.   11, Warley, Bracey, and Lurena Ghristopher.
1791, March 26, Warner, Ann, and Christian Wiltenberger.
1795, June   11, Warner, Eliz., and John Roberts.
1728, May   15, Warner, Christian, and Sarah Hicks.
1731, Dec.   20, Warner, Christiana, and John Smith.
1731-2, Jan.   4, Warner, Christian, and Lydia Powel.
1730, Sept.   10, Warner, Jacob, and Charity Purdy.
1729, Dec.   7, Warner, Joanna, and Wm Pratt.
1802, Nov.   10, Warner, John, and Margaret Ellison.
1748, Jan.   2, Warner, Joseph, and Anne Greesbury.
1765, Dec.   14, Warner, Mary, and John West.
1739, March   5, Warner, Mary, and Robert Dawson.
1804, Nov.   8, Warner, Mary, and Daniel Eaton.
1784, June   23, Warner, Samuel, and Margaret Crohan.
1785, June   16, Warner, Swaine, and Eley Edwards.
1799, Jan.   17, Warner, Swenn, and Mary Hawkins.
1765, Sept.   12, Warnick, Sarah, and Presley Blackstone.
1790, Oct.   22, Warnock, Robert, and Eliz. Shedaker.
1743, May   17, Warpole, Robert, and Eleanor Bowen.
1794, Nov.   13, Warr, John, and Mary Wiley.
1735, April   24, Warrell, Joseph, and Judith Chevalier.
1794, May   15, Warrell, Margaret, and John Major.
1736, March   9, Warren, Anne, and John Goin.
1786, Aug.   25, Warren, Daniel, and Charlotte Bouchin.
1748, Jan.   6, Warren, Hannah, and Matthew Cummings.
1749, Nov.   24, Warren, Jane, and Peter White.
1716, Feb.   14, Warren, John, and Ann Stephens.
1720, Jan.   31, Warren, Mary, and William Lawton.
1748, Aug.   28, Warren, Robert, and Elizabeth Spencer.

1744, Sept.　　8, Warren, Sarah, and Michael Cranfield.
1784, Aug.　　1, Warren, William, and Rosanna Grove.
1714, Dec.　　30, Warring, Samuel, and Sarah Willcoxe.
1760, Nov.　　22, Warthington, Isaac, and Martha Carver.
1771, Dec.　　9, Washington, Michael, and Mary Cloud.
1728, June　　7, Waterfield, John, and Elizabeth Saxbye.
1802, April　　3, Waterford, Joseph, and Sarah Penington.
1743, July　　2, Waterman, Eliz., Thomas Horner.
1801, Nov.　　12, Waterman, Isaac, and Mary Tallman.
1798, March 22, Waters, Abraham, and Sarah Levallean.
1767, April　　1, Waters, Eleanor, and John Britton.
1775, Nov.　　18, Waters, Eliz., and William Thomas.
1772, June　　1, Waters, James, and Lydia Anderson.
1737, Nov.　　4, Wathell, Rachel, and Joseph Baldwin.
1743, May　　28, Watts, Ann, and Adam Leister.
1728, Sept.　　6, Watkins, Dan., and Eliza Large.
1781, Nov.　　1, Watkins, Eliz., and Thomas Pitt.
1750, Feb.　　1, Watkins, Jane, and John Baley.
1717, May　　13, Watkins, Jonathan, and Ann Carpenter.
1720, June　　7, Watkins, Mary, and Cornelius Collins.
1767, July　　3, Watkins, William, and Ann Fisher.
1784, March　4, Watmough, James Horatio, and Anna Carmick.
1805, June　　15, Watmough, Maria, and Joseph Reid.
1758, April　　6, Watson, Anna, and Samuel Howe.
1776, May　　16, Watson, Eliz., and Samuel Fletcher.
1729, Oct.　　12, Watson, Eliz., and Thomas Davis.
1794, Dec.　　9, Watson, Isaac, and Sarah Simpson.
1793, April　　11, Watson, John, and Hannah Paul.
1796, Aug.　　22, Watson, Matthew, and Mary Ferguson.
1790, Nov.　　3, Watson, Thomas, and Ann Moore.
1743, July　　24, Watson, Thomas, and Margaret Mather.
1761, Dec.　　2, Watson, William, and Margaret Boggs.
1785, Jan.　　4, Watt, Grace, and John Steinmitz.
1784, Dec.　　14, Watts, Eliz., and David Harding.
1711, Feb.　　8, Watts, Elizabeth, and Harmanus Yerkes.
1756, Feb.　　9, Watts, Jane, and Patrick Kelly.
1767, March 10, Watts, Stephen, and Frances Asheton.
1796, Jan.　　24, Wauck, Eve, and John Pierie.
1796, May　　26, Way, George, and Sarah Clarke.
1728, Dec.　　2, Way, James, and Ann Towsend.
1803, Nov.　　16, Way, Margaretta, and Thomas Hewitt.
1729-30, Feb.10, Wayn, Edward, and Mary Ryall.
1754, Feb.　　27, Wayn, William, and Sarah Gilingham.
1753, Oct.　　6, Wayne, Abraham, and Mary Holland.
1766, March 25, Wayne, Anthony, and Mary Penrose.
1804, Jan.　　19, Wayne, Caleb Parry, and Mary Stokes.

1773, June   1, Wayne, Eliz., and David Wilkin.
1795, Feb.   14, Wayne, Esther, and Benjamin Clarke.
1774, June   2, Wayne, Hannah, and James Justice.
1784, Dec.   28, Wayne, Samuel, and Eliz. Curtain.
1795, Jan.   8, Wayne, William, and Mary Hawke.
1756, Nov.   18, Weaver, Catharine, and John Saunders.
1804, March 15, Weaver, Hannah, and Joseph Wigfall.
1741, May   1, Weaver, Joyce, and William Felstoad.
1798, Jan.   20, Weaver, Kezia, and Dominick Devine.
1806, Aug.   9, Weaver, Mary, and George Thorn.
1803, Feb.   5, Weaver, Michael, and Margaret Kurtz.
1751, Aug.   25, Weaver, Susannah, and Andrew Murray.
1757, Jan.   3, Weaver, Thomas, and Abigail Chever.
1728, June   12, Webb, Ann, and Wm Gurling.
1799, Dec.   16, Webb, Lydia Frances, and Thomas Marshall.
1798, March 10, Webb, James, and Eleanor Seymer.
1796, Dec.   22, Webb, Jacob, and Sarah Nicola.
1760, Dec.   27, Webb, John, and Margaret Lington.
1731, Dec.   8, Webb, Lydia, and John Edgar.
1759, July   14, Webb, Mary, and John Powell.
1731, Oct.   21, Webb, Samuel, and Jane Wyer.
1787, March 27, Webb, Thomas, and Rachel Faulkner.
1800, April 12, Webb, Thomas, and Rebecca Betterton.
1775, June   1, Webb, William, and Martha Ord.
1759, Feb.   16, Webber, William, and Catharine Knowson.
1743, Feb.   22, Weber, Tobias, and Margaret Listrin.
1743, Dec.   17, Webster, George, and Eliz. Leuellin.
1777, July   16, Webster, John, and Eleanor Fitzgerald.
1764, Nov.   4, Webster, Lewis, and Sarah Freeman.
1771, March 24, Webster, Mary, and William Kearney.
1769, March 21, Webster, Samuel, and Margaret Adams.
1799, June   17, Webster, William, and Rebecca Edwards.
1768, Jan.   12, Weed, George, and Elizabeth Dickinson.
1737, Jan.   1, Weekings, Sarah, and John Taylor.
1749, April 20, Weeks, Mary, and James Hutton.
1767, Jan.   14, Weighter, Jacob, and Hannah Fester.
1798, April   5, Weisenfels, Harriet, and John Martin Baker.
1761, Aug.   29, Weiss, Lewis, and Mary Clugh.
1760, Oct.   4, Weist, Elizabeth and John W. Hoffman.
1804, March   5, Weistram, Samuel, and Eliz. Meredith.
1737, Jan.   6, Welch, Agnes, and John Willis.
1770, Nov.   20, Welch, Hannah, and Hugh Thompson.
1728, May   1, Welsh, James, and Ann Irish.
1741, Sept.   9, Welch, Thomas, and Ann Clark.
1730, May   26, Weld, Joseph, and Sarah Hatton.
1761, Aug.   30, Welding, Hannah, and Nathaniel Wright.

1734, March 25, Weldon, Anne, and Joseph Gregory.
1748, Dec. 6, Weldon, Lydia, and Isaac Hughes.
1764, Feb. 2, Weldon, Mary, and Samuel Read.
1774, July 25, Weldon, Raworth and Eliz. Davis.
1739, Sept. 17, Weldon, Sarah, and William Vaughan.
1749, April 27, Weldon, William, and Ann Boyd.
1742, Dec. 4, Weldon, William, and Mary Murphey.
1748, Dec. 1, Welkin, Hannah, and John Callahan.
1769, June 17, Welldon, Joseph, and Mary Kenton.
1761, Feb. 10, Wellman, William, and Elizabeth Richardson.
1785, Nov. 8, Wells, Benjamin, and Mary Nash.
1749, Dec. 12, Wells, George, and Mary Prisgy.
1780, Oct. 5, Wells, Hannah, and Absalom Reeves.
1757, April 12, Wells, Hannah, and Jacob Huggard.
1798, April 24, Wells, James, and Sarah Croscup.
1746, Feb. 17, Wells, James, and Mary Price.
1747, Feb. 14, Wells, Jehosheba Wells, and Joseph Bryan.
1801, May 23, Wells, John Craig, and Mary Wright Sontag.
1772, Dec. 12, Wells, John, and Mary Hillbourne.
1761, March 11, Wells, Jonathan, and Ruth Morris.
1716, Nov. 19, Wells, Joseph, and Ann Pugh.
1797, July 31, Wells, Lydia Ann, and William Vaughan.
1768, Aug. 2, Wells, Mary, and Edward Gottier.
1774, Feb. 23, Wells, Peter, and Margaret Crozires.
1759, Dec. 6, Wells, Rebecca, and Charles Coxe.
1712, Feb. 11, Wells, Samuel, and Joanna Saylor.
1742, Jan. 23, Wells, Thomas, and Sarah Cowley.
1790, Oct. 9, Wells, William, and Eliz. Dagworthy.
1785, Oct. 2, Welsel, Godfrey, and Ruth Burgess.
1729, June 15, Welsh, Ann, and Wm Bruce.
1747, June 11, Welsh, Catherine, and Robert Farrel.
1798, June 7, Welsh, James, and Ann McCormick.
1784, Oct. 7, Welsh, James, and Mary Land.
1758, March 25, Welsh, Jonathan, and Sarah Williamson.
1781, Dec. 6, Welsh, Margaret, and Randolph McCarty.
1771, Feb. 17, Welsh, Mary, and Richard Hartley.
1747, March 8, Welsh, Mathew, and Mary Calahan.
1734, April 16, Welsh, Rebecca, and Isaac Janvier.
1729, June 10, Welsh, Shedack, and Jane Warding.
1773, Sept. 18, Wentworth, William, and Lydia Hinton.
1787, Dec. 18, Wescott, Ruth, and John Whitehead.
1748, Aug. 15, Wessel, John, and Sarah McCarth.
1760, Jan. 11, Wessell, Godfrey, and Christina Smith.
1720, Sept. 10, Wessels, Catherine, and John Knowles.
1780, Sept. 19, Wessels, John, and Ann Fell.
1794, Sept. 13, West, Ann, and Nabro Frazer.

1744, Dec. 31, West, Deborah, and John Gooding.
1786, July 18, West, Edmond, and Amey Stinnyard.
1780, Nov. 2, West, Eliz., and Edmund Beach.
1761, Oct. 8, West, Elizabeth, and Joseph Hill.
1785, Jan. 20, West, Esther, and William Rodman.
1793, Jan. 10, West, Francis, and Mary Nixon.
1771, May 5, West, George, and Mary Wallington.
1799, July 2, West, Helen, and John Stewart.
1798, Feb. 6, West, James, and Maria Blodget.
1782, April 11, West, James. and Margaret Gilmore.
1776, April 10, West, John, and Sarah Kethcart.
1773, June 9, West, John, and Mary Reèves.
1765, Dec. 14, West, John, and Mary Warner.
1775, Sept. 27, West, Joseph, and Eliz. Lawrence.
1790, Dec. 17, West, Mark, and Ann Farrel.
1729, Dec. 26, West, Martha, and Thomas Jones.
1785, April 7, West, Mary, and Curtis Greble.
1767, March 28, West, Richard, and Sarah Hammon.
1733, Dec. 13, West, Richard, and Elizabeth Moon.
1779, Dec. 18, West, Sarah, and Col. Joseph Coperthwaite.
1774, Aug. 16, West, Sarah, and John Hugg.
1768, March 17, West, Thomas, and Mary Kithcart.
1784, Jan. 29, West, William, and Eliz. Hillbourne.
1733, Jan. 4, West, W^m, and Elizabeth Hall.
1731-2, Jan. 16, West, William, and Abigail Carwithen.
1791, March 2, Westcott, Mary, and Thomas Hockley.
1803, Nov. 28, Westen, Eliz., and George Smith.
1768, July 9, Weston, Joseph, and Ann Dixon.
1731, July 22, Weston, Mary, and James Ashby.
1805, Nov. 30, Weston, Rachel, and William Fiss.
1770, May 9, Weston, William, and Ann Davis.
1804, Dec. 4, Westray, Eleanor, and John Darley.
1804, Jan. 30, Westray, Julia, and William Burke Wood.
1742, June 16, Wetherby, Edmund, and Martha Jerman.
1762, July 21, Wetley, Henry, and Mary Dangan.
1757, March 31, Wey, Susannah, and Josiah Harper.
1751, July 5, Weyman, Edward, and Rebecca Breintnal.
1743, Feb. 12, Weyman, Mary, Jr., and Jacob Le Gay.
1770, March 15, Whale, Evan, and Catharine Campbell.
1799, Nov. 25, Wharton, Rev^r Charles H., and Ann Kinsey.
1771, April 13, Wharton, Carpenter, and Eliz. Davis.
1772, March 12, Wharton, Charles, and Jemima Edwards.
1795, May 7, Wharton, Deborah C., and Isaak H. Jackson.
1804, May 10, Wharton, Fishbourn, and Susan Shoemaker.
1800, Oct. 1, Wharton, Franklin, and Mary Cliston.
1790, June 24, Wharton, Hannah, and William Chancellor.

1795, Nov.   11, Wharton, Kearney, and Maria Salter.
1773, Sept. 14, Wharton, James, and Christiana Redd.
1714, Jan.   9, Wharton, John, and Sarah Kelley.
1751, April 23, Wharton, Joseph, and Mary Carr.
1732, July   10, Wharton, Mary, and Richard Grafton.
1788, Dec.   23, Wharton, Mary, and Joseph Baxter.
1804, Aug.   13, Wharton, Moore, and Deborah Shoemaker.
1768, April 14, Wharton, Phoebe, and John Hanna.
1781, Dec.   13, Wharton, Rachel, and William Lewis.
1789, Dec.   17, Wharton, Robert, and Salome Chancellor.
1782, May   30, Wharton, Samuel Lewis, and Rachel Musgrove.
1795, Jan.   29, Wharton, Sarah, and Jonathan Robeson.
1762, Nov.   4, Wharton, Thomas, and Susannah Lloyd.
1806, June   21, Wharton, Thomas, and Ann Green.
1728, Sept. 12, Wharton, Thomas, and Mary Curry.
1774, Dec.   7, Wharton, Thomas, and Eliz. Fishbourne.
1736, Sept. 16, Whartonby, Mary, and Bryan Hughes.
1735, Oct.   27, Whatnell, John, and Catherine Davis.
1716, March   1, Wheatly, John, and Abigail Ashton.
1806, July   1, Wheaton, Enoch, and Mary Murphy.
1801, Nov.   19, Wheeland, Cath., and Gerrat Ruscaman.
1721, Feb.   1, Wheeler, Ann, and Charles Cox.
1729–30, Jan. 13, Wheeler, Edy, and John Frost.
1765, Nov.   28, Wheeler, Samuel, and Ann Flower.
1779, Oct.   20, Wheeler, Samuel, and Eliz. Jones.
1767, July   5, Wheeler, Sarah, and George Leadbetter.
1795, Nov.   30, Wheelock, James, and Mary Ann Morony.
1774, Jan.   5, Wheely, Cleary, and John Smith.
1748, Oct.   19, Wheely, Sarah, and John Williams.
1791, Feb.   10, Wheelen, Eliz., and Joseph T. Miller.
1776, May   13, Whelline, Edward, and Catherine Vandernine.
1796, April 16, Whetcroft, Ann, and Alexander Kerr.
1752, Oct.   2, Whilding, Mercy, and Thomas Hand.
1763, Oct.   19, Whiley, Sarah, and Jacob Williams.
1763, Sept. 14, Whitby, Christopher, and Martha Tanner.
1798, April 16, Whitby William, and Isabella Orr.
1743, May   29, White, Ann, and Henry Griffith.
1772, Dec.   14, White, Ann, and Frances Daymon.
1790, Oct.   22, White, Ann, and John France.
1796, March 13, White, Ann, and Michael Clarke.
1782, Feb.   28, White, Ann, and William Constable.
1800, Nov.   24, White, Brittain, and Eliz. Gray.
1745, Aug.   1, White, Catherine, and William Poor.
1741, Oct.   28, White, Daniel, and Mary Boggs.
1757, April   7, White, Elizabeth, and Edward Green.
1769, June   22, White, Elizabeth, and John Juckness.

1803, March   9, White, Eliz., and William McPherson.
1773, Nov.   16, White, Esther, and Nathan Huddleston.
1757, March   3, White, James, and Jane Price.
1740, April 12, White, James, and Mary Ransted.
1794, Nov.   27, White, James, and Isabella Humes.
1786, July   15, White, James, and Ann Curl.
1781, April 18, White, Jesse, and Sarah Oldfield.
1737, May   13, White, John, and Jane McCurry.
1760, May   6, White, John, and Margaret Hamilton.
1758, Sept.   7, White, John, and Margaret Gregg.
1769, June   23, White, Josiah, and Catherine McCool.
1757, Dec.   1, White, Joshua, and Mary Staleop.
1801, May   3, White, Joseph, and Eliz. Wilkie.
1732, March 21, White, Martha, and Daniel McKebb.
1735, Sept. 16, White, Mary, Francis Richey.
1769, March   2, White, Mary, and Robert Morris.
1804, Dec.   4, White, Mary, and Enos Bronson.
1771, Sept. 11, White, Mary, and Isaac Harris.
1800, Dec.   26, White, Mary, and John Rice.
1786, Sept. 13, White, Michael, and Mary Brownlow.
1749, Nov.   24, White, Peter, and Jane Warren.
1730, April   8, White, Philip and Mary Anderson.
1742, May   24, White, Rebecca, and James Claypole.
1767, Jan.   31, White, Rebeccah, and John Ridge.
1710, Feb.   11, White, Richard, and Jane Parsons.
1763, Aug.   2, White, Richard, and Margaret Vivers.
1758, March 18, White, Robert, and Jane Richardson.
1796, July   4, White, Sarah, and William Cox.
1768, March 17, White, Sarah, and Moore Furman.
1759, May   26, White, Susannah, and Samuel Banks.
1747, May   7, White, Thomas, and Ester Newman.
1760, Oct.   1, White, Thomas, and Mary Connard.
1763, Dec.   28, White, Thomas, and Ann Read.
1783, Dec.   11, White, Thomas, and Magdalen Dempey.
1741, July   13, White, Townsend, and Ann Renenedet.
1740, Oct.   31, White, William, and Ruth Lambeth.
1739, Oct.   10, White, William, and Rebecca Forneaman.
1728, June   8, White, W^m, and Elizabeth Harlinge.
1730, June   30, White, William, and Laetitia Reese.
1771, Aug.   12, White, William, and Sarah Kinnard.
1773, Feb.   11, White, W^m, and Mary Harrison.
1734, June   24, Whiteacar, John, and Naomi Hulm.
1771, Jan.   24, Whitebread, Ann, and William Bellamy.
1789, Oct.   28, Whitefield, Elector, and William Matthews.
1727, Dec.   15, Whitehall, Cath., and John Boiden.
1728, March 30, Whitehead, Elizabeth, and Wm Painter.
          18—VOL. VIII.

1800, April 8, Whitehead, Hannah, and Samuel B. Eyre.
1803, July 20, Whitehead, John, and Phoebe Lewis.
1787, Dec. 18, Whitehead, John, and Ruth Wescott.
1792, June 6, Whitehead, Joseph, and Jane Hutchinson.
1769, Nov. 18, Whitehead, Margaret, and John Atkinson.
1785, Jan. 22, Whitehead, Martha, and Samuel Wooden.
1772, Nov. 18, Whitehead, Matthew, and Eliz. Pine.
1715, Nov. 27, Whitehead, Oliver, and Frances Hobart.
1746, March 17, Whitehead, Robert, and Hannah Prichard.
1762, Jan. 13, Whitehead, Thomas, and Mary Huffman.
1792, July 19, Whitehill, James, and Mary Silerue.
1795, Sept. 9, Whiteley, Daniel, and Eliz. Williams.
1752, Dec. 13, Whitelock Thomas, and Anne Taylor.
1757, Aug. 17, Whiten, Caleb, and Margaret Boyer.
1742, July 28, Whitepain, Zachariah, and Sarah Henzey.
1796, Aug. 25, Whiteside, Harriet, and Richard Bayley.
1795, March 26, Whitesides, John, and Sarah Miercken.
1794, June 1, Whitewell, William, and Christiana Mitchell.
1792, July 14, Whiteman, Anna, and James Cowan.
1776, March 21, Whiteman, Cath., and William Davis.
1784, Nov. 17, Whiteman, Eliz., and John Dubarree.
1758, Feb. 13, Whitman, Lydia, and Joseph Ashmead.
1770, April 28, Whitepaine, Ann, and Thomas Forrest.
1755, June 28, Whitepain, Sarah, and Joseph Dodd.
1740, Feb. 17, Whitterance, Francis, and Bathsheba Butler.
1728, Nov. 17, Whittington, Mary, and John Davall.
1773. March 25, Whittle, Charlotte, and John Reynolds.
1776, March 29, Whright, Sarah, and Edward Miles.
1801, April 2, Wiall Eliz., and Dell Noblit.
1737, Sept. 3, Wiar, John, and Elizabeth Holmes.
1803, March 24, Wickham, William, and Cath. Christian.
1773, Sept. 9, Wicksted, Timothy, and Eve Shobel.
1748, Aug. 6, Wickward, Samuel, and Charity Ford.
1792, June 16, Wicoff, Jacob, and Charlotte Phyle.
1762, July 9, Widowfield, John, and Elizabeth Hayman.
1770, July 9, Wier, Mary, and James Barker.
1794, May 29, Wigfall, Cath., and Edward Bowlby.
1804, March 15, Wigfall, Joseph, and Hannah Weaver.
1804, Sept. 26, Wiggins, Ann, and Peter De Forrest.
1796, May 13, Wiggins, Mary, and William Hallat.
1797, Nov. 18, Wigglesworth, John, and Mary Dixon.
1767, March 31, Wigmore, Ann, and William Carncross.
1803, Jan. 1, Wignell, Thomas, and Ann Merry.
1766, Jan. 9, Wikoff, Isaac, and Martha Cox.
1798, Feb. 7, Wikoff, Peter, and Ann Tharp.
1758, Dec. 27, Wikoff, Peter, and Grace Worrall.

1769, March 30, Wikoff, Peter, and Altha Cox.
1779, Dec.   23, Wilcocks, Ann, and William Poyntell.
1805, March 14, Wilcocks, Mary, and William Walm.
1804, Oct,   18, Wilcocks, Mary, and Charles Ingersoll.
1783, Sept.   18, Wilcocks, Samuel, and Eliz. Bella Gale.
1806, April   17, Wilcox, Eliz. Bella, and Thomas Calender.
1772, June   4, Wilcox, John, and Mary Hockley.
1761, Sept.   2, Wilcox, Mary, and Simon Guest.
1765, Jan.   1, Wild, William, and Elizabeth Barry.
1755, Dec.   4, Wilday, Thomas, and Garthenia Humphray.
1742, June   29, Wildey, Coopman, and Mary Gregory.
1763, May   16, Wildman, Mary, and Henry Cordery.
1776, Feb.   1, Wiles, William, and Ann Hyder.
1752, April   18, Wiley, Anne, and Edward Vaughan.
1773, Sept.   18, Wiley, Cath., and Thomas Bennet.
1771, Sept.   5, Wiley, James, and Catharine Benjar.
1794, Nov.   13, Wiley, Mary, and John Warr.
1752, Dec.   6, Wiley, Phœbe, and Alexander Soley.
1757, Oct.   29, Wiley, Susannah, and William Palmer.
1772, Jan.   16, Wiley, Thomas, and Jane Thompson.
1791, March 26, Wiltenberger, Christian, and Ann Warner.
1790, Dec.   4, Wiltenburger, Christiana, and Thomas Smith.
1790, June   3, Wilton, Sarah, and Aaron Palmer.
1767, June   28, Wiltshire, Mary, and Timothy Davis.
1801, May   3, Wilkie, Eliz., and Joseph White.
1773, June   1, Wilkin, David, and Eliz. Wayne.
1761, June   30. Wilkins, Azuba, and Isaac Zane.
1762, April   15, Wilkins, James, and Elizabeth Ward.
1791, Jan.   17, Wilkins, Thomas, and Priscilla Harrison.
1773, Aug.   21, Wilkins, William, and Eliz. Oxford.
1772, Aug.   6, Wilkinson, Amos, and Mercy Carpenter.
1744, May   19, Wilkinson, Ann, and Thomas Cuthbert.
1750, Oct.   11, Wilkinson, Anne, and James Seth.
1764, July   30, Wilkinson, Elizabeth, and James Craig.
1773, Sept.   27, Wilkinson, Eliz., and Nathaniel Sharpless.
1752, June   20, Wilkinson, Elizabeth, and Peter Knight.
1730, Dec.   23, Wilkinson, Gabriel, and Sarah Ridge.
1778, Nov.   12, Wilkinson, Genl. James, and Ann Biddle.
1749, Sept.   13, Wilkinson, James, and Sarah Coxe.
1737, Nov.   15, Wilkinson, Jane, and John Verlin.
1755, May   10, Wilkinson, John, Jr., and Mary Anderson.
1740, June   12, Wilkinson, Josiah, and Rose Kemble.
1716, Feb.   2, Wilkinson, Margaret, and Edward Mankin.
1733, Aug.   15, Wilkinson, Mary, and Henry Huddleston.
1743, June   16, Wilkinson, Mary, and Sam. Dowthaite.
1756, Oct.   13, Wilkinson, Mary, and Joseph Claypole.

1773, Sept. 25, Wilkinson, Rebecca, and David Harrow.
1733, Oct. 9, Wilkinson, Rebecca, and Martin Ball.
1751, Aug. 1, Wilkinson, Sarah, and Joseph Donaldson.
1795, Nov. 17, Wilkinson, Sophia, and Henry Cash.
1743, June 11, Wilkinson, Thomas, and Elizabeth Carr.
1802, Jan. 23, Wilkinson, Thomas, and Hannah Reynolds.
1716, March 1, Will, David, and Hannah ———.
1759, Feb. 21, Willard, Benjamin, and Rebecca Walker.
1800, Feb. 26, Willard, Eliz., and John South.
1766, Dec. 10, Willard, Elizabeth, and Thomas Wakefield.
1756, Feb. 17, Willard, Elizabeth, and Abraham Vandergrift.
1722, Dec. 9, Willard, James, and Rebecca Bellos.
1722, Feb. 4, Willard, John, and Margaret Morgan.
1752, Nov. 16, Willard, Margaret, and Hezekiah Kemble.
1754, Nov. 20, Willard, Thomas, and Mary Par.
1782, Oct. 27, Willard, Thomas, and Sarah Brickell.
1768, May 18, Wilcox, Alexander, Esq', and Mary Chew.
1714, Dec. 30, Wilcoxe, Sarah, and Samuel Warring.
1746, March 27, Willis, Elizabeth, and Israel Real.
1794, Feb. 7, Willet, Esther, and John Vretenburg.
1800, Jan. 18, Willet, Sarah, and James Murray.
1785, April 12, Willett, Euphemia, and Samuel Gibbs.
1782, Dec. 9, Willett, John, and Esther Robinson.
1784, Jan. 15, Willey, Robert, and Cath. Dean.
1783, Dec. 29, Williams, Ambrose, and Sarah Roberts.
1805, May 19, Williams, Andrews, and Ann Barnes.
1741, Nov. 10, Williams, Ann, and David Hogben.
1777, Oct. 9, Williams, Ann, and Robert Hogg.
1796, July 30, Williams, Ann, and James Humphreys.
1800, Sept. 14, Williams, Ann, and Sylvanus Hicks.
1734, May 31, Williams, Anne, and Alexander Gundey.
1755, May 26, Williams, Anne, and David Williams.
1753, March 20, Williams, Anne, and Lasdrass Lowry.
1784, Jan. 18, William, Baptist, and Eliz. Ford.
1781, Mar. 8, Williams, Bedford, and Anne Greenaway.
1761, Dec. 8, Williams, Catherine, and William Dunwick.
1755, May 26, Williams, David, and Anne Williams.
1766, Nov. 29, Williams, Deborah, and John David.
1758, March 27, Williams, Dorothy, and William Elberson.
1748, Sept. 4, Williams, Edward, and Mary Brown.
1736, May 31, Williams, Edward, and Jane Shaw.
1761, Feb. 18, Williams, Edward, and Ann Sweatman.
1772, May 30, Williams, Eleanor, and John Dalrymple.
1772, June 18, Williams, Elias, and Hannah Zane.
1780, Feb. 5, Williams, Eliz., and Nicholas Avery.
1800, May 28, Williams, Eliz., and Charles McGee.

1796, Nov.　12, Williams, Eliz., and John Renshaw.
1796, Nov.　29, Williams, Eliz., and John Baptist Grasse.
1797, April　6, Williams, Eliz., and Robert Clay.
1795, Sept.　9, Williams, Eliz., and Daniel Whiteley.
1761, June　20, Williams. Elizabeth, and William Boon.
1713, Dec.　18, Williams, Elizabeth, and John Meredith.
1732, Aug.　19, Williams, Elizabeth, and Alexander Edgar.
1749, Nov.　1, Wiliiams, Elizabeth, and Henry Stiles.
1767, Dec.　1, Williams, George, and Elizabeth Talbot.
1763, Feb.　25, Williams, Henry, and Mary Talbot.
1744, April　9, Williams, Henry, and Sarah Rice.
1764, Feb.　9, Williams, Hugh, and Louisa Grew.
1739, Feb.　17, Williams, Hugh, and Jane Fullerton.
1759, Dec.　29, Williams, Isabella, and John Townsend.
1790, Dec.　28, Williams, Jacob, and Ann Smollett.
1763, Oct.　19, Williams, Jacob, and Sarah Whiley.
1801, Sept.　23, Williams, James, and Mary Sears.
1728, Dec.　25, Williams, James, and Margt. Morgan.
1751, Dec.　7, Williams, James and Deborah Fisher.
1745, Oct.　16, Williams, Jane, and William Wosdel.
1753, Oct.　6, Williams, Jane, and Robert Colton.
1722, Nov.　28, Williams, Job, and Lydia Bowyer.
1805, May　26, Williams, John, and Ann Fleming.
1769, May　23, Williams, John, and Patience Chew.
1743, May　29, Williams, John, and Susannah Hodge.
1749, March　7, Williams, John, and Honour Haley.
1748, Oct.　19, Williams, John, and Sarah Wheely.
1710, Jan.　5, Williams, John, and Mary Carman.
1740, July　30, Williams, John, and Mary Gregory.
1768, Feb.　20, William, Jonathan, and Elizabeth Tew.
1786, June　10, Williams, Joseph, and Christiana Ramshaw.
1770, Nov.　24, William, Joshua, and Martha Anderson.
1739, Aug.　4, Williams, Leah, and John Saunders.
1748, Jan.　16, Williams, Margaret, and Spencer Trotter.
1725, Sept.　30, Williams, Margt., and Wm Kinman.
1728, Jan.　10, Williams, Margt., and Richd Jones.
1711, June　11, Williams, Martha, and Thomas Francis.
1780, Nov.　3, Williams, Mary, and David Cattell.
1742, Jan.　10, Williams, Mary, and William Nicholson.
1774, March 24, Williams, Mary, and John Little.
1738, Nov.　27, Williams, Mary, and William Dixsy.
1735, July　8, Williams, Oliver, and Jane Hawkins.
1733, Oct.　25, Williams, Phoebe, and John Goodwin.
1747, June　25, Williams, Priscilla, and John Carter.
1714, Jan.　10, Williams, Rachel, and Nicholas Putt.
1800, March 14, Williams, Robert, and Amelia Gray.

1721, May 4, Williams, Rose, and Joseph Shipping.
1768, March 30, Williams, Samuel, and Esther Sherlock.
1776, Oct. 10, Williams, Samuel, and Esther Ball.
1768, Feb. 7, Williams, Samuel and Elizabeth Aymes.
1754, Aug. 10, Williams, Samuel, and Sarah Morrison.
1782, Dec. 5, Williams, Sarah, and Joseph Harvey.
1797, July 13, Williams, Sarah, and Charles Mitchell.
1762, May 19, Williams, Sarah Ann, and Samuel Flower.
1727, Aug. 10, Williams, Sarah, and George Gurling.
1717, Nov. 23, Williams, Sarah, and Joseph Harwood.
1804, Aug. 18, Williams, Sarah, and John Taylor.
1753, Nov. 4, Williams, Sarah, and Robert Singer.
1752, Aug. 4, William, Stephen, and Euphemia Manypenny.
1795, July 7, Williams, Thomas, and Christian Finnix.
1800, April 20, Williams, Thomas, and Dorcas Reed.
1728, April 21, Williams, Thomas, and Sarah Tennant.
1797, Jan. 5, Williams, William, and Sarah Wingfield.
1786, May 9, Williams, William, and Margaret Davis.
1792, May 24, Wiiliams, William, and Eliz. Hulings.
1727, Dec. 13, Williams, W^m and Ann Jones.
1712, April 27, Williams, William, and Catherine Davis.
1752, Aug. 24, Williams, William, and Mary Stewart.
1755, June 12, Williams, William, and Margaret Clare.
1740, June 16, Williams, William, and Margaret McGrew.
1733, May 30, Williams, Zachariah, and Anne Ellitt.
1744, March 22, Williamson, Abraham, and Hannah Dunn.
1797, Jan. 5, Williamson, Cath., and Henry Vining.
1743, May 18, Williamson, Charles, and Mary Burk.
1755, April 23, Williamson, Elizabeth, and Thomas Fisher.
1804, May 3, Williamson, Eliz., and John Barnes.
1784, March 11, Williamson, Hannah, and Patrick Hanlon.
1733, March 29, Williamson, Henry, and Lydia Wisdom.
1737, Dec. 28, Williamson, Jacob, and Martha Boyer.
1761, Aug. 18, Williamson, John, and Hannah Oldfield.
1734, Aug. 19, Williamson, Lawrence, and Phoebe Folkers.
1765, April 11, Williamson, Mary, and Peter Bell.
1770, Dec. 5, Williamson, Mary, and William Egglestone.
1777, May 19, Williamson, Mary, and James Elliott.
1797, Dec. 3, Williamson, Rebecca, and David Flickwir.
1741, July 11, Williamson, Sarah, and Henry Rigby.
1758, March 25, Williamson, Sarah, and Jonathan Welsh.
1753, Oct. 9, Williamson, William, and Mary Howel.
1804, March 1, Willing, Abigail, and Richard Peters.
1762, Feb. 8, Willing, Ann, and Tench Francis.
1768, May 9, Willing, Ann, and Luke Morris.
1780, Oct. 26, Willing, Ann, and William Bingham.

1730-1, Jan. 21, Willing, Charles, and Anne Shippen.
1794, Sept. 25, Willing, Dorothy, and Thomas W. Francis.
1769, Aug. 7, Willing, Elizabeth, and Samuel Powel.
1795, Nov. 11, Willing, Eliz., and William Jackson.
1795, Oct. 7, Willing, George, and Maria Benezet.
1800, Nov. 26, Willing, George, and Rebecca Blackwell.
1775, Nov. 16, Willing, Margaret, and Robert Hare.
1794, July 9, Willing, Mary, and Henry Clymer.
1761, Jan. 29, Willing, Mary, and Honble William Byrd.
1804, Feb. 1, Willing, Richard, and Eliza Moore.
1763, June 9, Willing, Thomas, and Ann McCall.
1795, July 30, Willing, Thomas Mayne, and Jane Nixon.
1802, Jan. 6, Willing, William, and Maria Wilhelmina Peters.
1801, June 18, Willington, Thomas, and Cath. Reynolds.
1795, April 2, Willis, Isaac, and Mary Affleck.
1737, Jan. 6, Willis, John, and Agnes Welch.
1752, March 29, Willis, Mary, and John Taylor.
1783, Nov. 16, Willis, William, and Mary Cain.
1772, Aug. 17, Willkly, Henry, and Eliz. Rivett.
1784, Aug. 5, Willoughby, Eliz., and Joseph Martin.
1735, Sept. 8, Willoughby, Solomon, and Sarah Crawford.
1730, Aug. 25, Wills, Catherine, and Owen Thomas.
1750, Dec. 26, Wills, Elizabeth, and James Hemphill.
1746, April 17, Wills, Noah, and Mary Harrison.
1803, Sept. 8, Wills, Sarah, and Charles Godfrey.
1783, Aug. 21, Wills, Thomas, and Ann Martin.
1715, June 26, Willsear, Mary, and John Husbands.
1782, April 23, Willson, Ann, and Capt. William Hall.
1727, Sept. 14, Willson, Ann, and Francis Gerrack.
1772, Dec. 14, Willson, George, and Margaret Burrows.
1773, June 17, Willson, Jacob, and Sarah Walker.
1772, July 1, Willson, Joseph, and Margaret Windram.
1729, Feb. 27, Willson, Mary, and John Heatcot.
1769, June 17, Willson, Thomas, and Catherine Katon.
1732, Oct. 24, Wilmerton, Hannah, and Jos. Cottman.
1743, April 26, Wilmington, John, and Mary Leech.
1790, Jan. 3, Wilson, Abraham, and Sarah Pickerin.
1766, Aug. 5, Wilson, Ann, and Edward Hunt.
1754, April 9, Wilson, Anne, and Bryan Rowland.
1795, June 29, Wilson, Anthony, and Margaret Ross.
1737, Jan. 8, Wilson, Barthia, and Peter Soumans.
1745, Jan. 21, Wilson, David, and Eliz. Stackhouse.
1798, Oct. 18, Wilson, Eliz., and William Smith.
1779, Jan. 18, Wilson, George, and Frances Palmer.
1796, March 1, Wilson, Hamilton, and Mary Swasy McDonald.
1799, April 15, Wilson, Hester, and Weldon Brinton.

1768, July   7, Wilson, James, and Mary Plumsted.
1770, Aug.   2, Wilson, James, and Eliz. Singer.
1793, May   16, Wilson, Jane, and Patrick Ford.
1746, Dec.   18, Wilson, Jane, and Stephen Durham.
1779, March 4, Wilson, Capt. John, and Mary Long.
1714, Oct.   10, Wilson, John, and Mary Green.
1743, July   30, Wilson, John, and Mary Night.
1803, Oct.   20, Wilson, John, and Maria Ann Magnus.
1758, June   5, Wilson, Margaret, and Patrick Cooper.
1750, July   28, Wilson, Mary, and Owen Thomas.
1754, July   26, Wilson, Mary, and William Honeyman.
1750, July   30, Wilson, Mary, and Peter Buffington.
1750, Oct.   15, Wilson, Mary, and William Davis.
1757, Aug.   26, Wilson, Mary, and John Anderson.
1767, June   25, Wilson, Mary, and James Dougherty.
1757, May   20, Wilson, Mary, and Jonathan Downs.
1761, Dec.   11, Wilson, Mary, and Thomas Rogers.
1795, March 30, Wilson, Mary, and Alexander Philips.
1720, May   4, Wilson, Mary, and Thomas Glentworth.
1801, March 25, Wilson, Mary, and Robert Cook.
1712, Aug.   6, Wilson, Rachel, and John Kinsey.
1737, Sept.   4, Wilson, Rachel, and James Draper.
1768, May   27, Wilson, Rachel, and Abraham Nathan.
1798, April   29, Wilson, Rebecca, and John Donaldson.
1756, Jan.   2, Wilson, Robert, and Jane Ayre.
1772, Feb.   17, Wilson, Robert, and Sarah Neill.
1801, Jan.   4, Wilson, Robert, and Eliz. Connor.
1767, Nov.   14, Wilson, Samuel, and Ann Clark.
1792, Jan.   7, Wilson, Samuel, and Tabitha Thomas.
1758, Feb.   18, Wilson, Sarah, and George Abington.
1804, April   10, Wilson, Thomas, and Mary Jones.
1769, Dec.   30, Wilson, Thomas, and Ann Price.
1783, Nov.   3, Wilson, Thomas, Martha Taylor.
1793, July   7, Wilson, William, and Martha Hartrick.
1754, Jan.   15, Wilson, William, and Charity Lovett.
1781, July   12, Winchester, Rev^r Elhanon, and Mary Morgan.
1748, April   5, Windel, John, and Rebeccak Bay.
1799, May   30, Winder, Bartholomew, and Susannah Creed.
1772, July   1, Windram, Margaret, and Joseph Willson.
1744, May   5, Windridge, John, and Martha Sylas.
1757, June   20, Winekoop, Eleanor, and Fernandus von Seeler.
1767, April   16, Wing, John, and Sarah Hibbs.
1780, April   29, Wingfield, Jane, and Philip Kollock.
1797, Jan.   5, Wingfield, Sarah, and William Williams.
1744, Feb.   5, Winkle, William, and Susannah Duchet.
1752, March 23, Winn, Mary, and Henry Iddings.

1772, Feb.   11, Winn, Sarah, and James Hall.
1728, June   16, Winright, Samuel, and Esther Boieles.
1739, May   17, Wint, Elizabeth, and Edward Cooke.
1768, April   25, Winter, John, and Mary Barret.
1785, Dec.   25, Winter, Samuel, and Sarah Vansciver.
1786, May   28, Winters, Hannah, and Isaac Davis.
1805, July   6, Winters, John, and Mary Mumford.
1783, May   28, Winters, Mary, and Allen Kennedy.
1768, May   29, Winterton, Rebecca, and James Coffee.
1763, May   9, Wintmore, Mary, and Ralph Marshall.
1802, Dec.   18, Winton, Francis, and Mary Brown.
1805, Aug.   1, Wirling, George, and Margaret Greer.
1733, March 29, Wisdom, Lydia, and Henry Williamson.
1797, Nov.   28, Wistar, Cath., and William Bache.
1803, Dec.   15, Wistar, Charles, and Rebecca Bullock.
1755, Dec.   11, Wistar, Rebecca, and Samuel Morris.
1796, March 10, Wistar, Susan, and John Morgan Price.
1785, May   24, Witchill, Sarah, and Joseph Kimble.
1726, Dec.   22, Withers, Elizabeth, and Richd Adams.
1775, Sept.   21, Withey, James, and Sarah Claypoole.
1798, Jan.   2, Withy, Mary, and Daniel P. Knight.
1727, April   17, Wittiker, Sarah, and Roger Carry.
1712, Jan.   1, Wivell, Mary, and James Brendly.
1709, July   31, Wivell, William, and Mary Boldwin.
1798, April   12, Wolahorn, Sarah, and Francis Howard.
1758, Sept.   9, Wolf, Patrick, and Elizabeth Edwards.
1772, July   2, Wolfe, Mary, and George Kidd.
1781, Sept.   24, Wollard, Ann, and Henry King.
1747, May   7, Wollaston, Joshua, and Priscilla Jones.
1759, Jan.   20, Wolleby, Mary, and John Wright.
1748, Dec.   20, Womeldorfe, Mary, and Samuel Head.
1796, Feb.   27, Winters, Jacob, and Eleanor Mudge.
1765, Oct.   6, Wood, Abigail, and Jacob Marshall.
1792, March 13, Wood, Ann, and George Gass.
1781, Sept.   23, Wood, Ann, and Elias Taylor.
1756, Jan.   1, Wood, Anne, and Thomas Price.
1802, April   5, Wood, Apheus, and Sarah Davis.
1796, May   26, Wood, Frances, and Thomas Shaw.
1722, Aug.   10, Wood, Gabriel, and Martha Mason.
1785, Oct.   2, Wood, George, and Mary Marshall.
1766, Aug.   7, Wood, Hannah, and Joseph Norris.
1732, Aug.   19, Wood, James, and Catherine Davies.
1766, Dec.   18, Wood, James, and Chlotilda Hagerty.
1783, Oct.   5, Wood, Jane, and Josiah Potter.
1731-2, Feb.   12, Wood, John, and Mary Dixon.
1771, Oct.   26, Wood, John, and Mary Cannon.

1787, Aug.   30, Wood, John, and Mary Miley.
1747, Oct.   8, Wood, Joseph, and Mary Scull.
1768, Nov.   3, Wood, Margaret, and Curtis Clay.
1737, Nov.   16, Wood, Mary, and Thomas Howard.
1767, Dec.   24, Wood, Mary, and Thomas Olson.
1755, Jan.   16, Wood, Mary, and James Tull.
1757, May   30, Wood, Mary, and John Norris.
1794, May   27, Wood, Mary, and Joseph Lunden.
1757, Oct.   2, Wood, Percilla, and Henry Dawkins.
1751, Nov.   7, Wood, Richard, and Sarah Blackfan.
1759, Dec.   11, Wood, Sacheverell, and Mary Hawkins.
1799, April 15, Wood, Samuel, and Cath. Dugan.
1795, Nov.   19, Wood, Susan, and John Clifton.
1774, Nov.   10, Wood, Susannah, and Thomas Elton.
1767, Nov.   12, Wood, Thomas, and Mary Hughes.
1804, Jan.   30, Wood, William Burke, and Julian Westray.
1727, May   17, Wood, W^m, and Ann King.
1796, Jan.   13, Wood, William, and Mary Sharp.
1801, Dec.   21, Wood, Zachariah, and Hannah Lewellen.
1748, Oct.   15, Woodal, Tracy, and Rachel Likens.
1805, Sept.   3, Woodby, Sarah, and Moses Bantom.
1800, Nov.   23, Wooddruff, David, and Mary Porter.
1785, Jan.   22, Wooden, Samuel, and Martha Whitehead.
1772, June   16, Woodfield, Joseph, and Mary Rambo.
1767, May   5, Woodfield, Joseph, and Martha Holston.
1731-2, Jan. 31, Woodfield, Thomas, and Mary Eagleton.
1796, Oct.   27, Woodfield, Thomas, and Sarah Vandyke.
1802, Oct.   17, Woodhouse, John, and Margaret McCracken.
1735, May   13, Woodoth, John, and Sarah Smith.
1739, Dec.   29, Woodrop, Anne, and Joseph Sims.
1743, Aug.   20, Woodrop, Elizabeth, and Hugh Davey.
1756, Aug.   17, Woodrop, Sarah, and Peter Turner, jr.
1794, Oct.   26, Woodruff, Abraham, and Phoebe McGinnis.
1802, May   5, Woodruff, Mary, and Thomas Anderson.
1763, March   3, Woods, John, and Hannah Churchman.
1757, Aug.   21, Woods, John, and Jane Carley.
1757, Nov.   4, Woods, Margaret, and Joseph Kelly.
1751, Aug.   4, Woods, Mary, and George Fox.
1743, May   11, Woods, Susannah, and William Reley.
1751, Oct.   26, Woodside, James, and Mary Anderson.
1757, Jan.   22, Woodward, Abigail, and John Gilham.
1748, Aug.   15, Woodward, Anne, and Thomas Fox.
1796, Nov.   21, Woodward, Cath., and John O'Neal.
1796, June   15, Woodward, Eliz., and William Gartley.
1766, Dec.   26, Woodward, Francis, and Mary Ballard.
1740, May   13, Woodward, Japhet, and Elizabeth Morgan.

1772, May   14, Woodward, Mary, and John Perkins.
1796, Sept.   19, Woodward, Thomas, and Sarah Stephenson.
1737, April   27, Woodworth, Susannah, and Robert Crosier.
1742, Jan.   27, Wooleby, Henry, and Margaret Sparker.
1729, Aug.   2, Wooley, Thomas, and Sarah Coppack.
1741, Jan.   31, Wooling, Mary, and Samuel Farmer.
1771, May   29, Woollis, Nicholas, and Hannah Haycock.
1750, Nov.   16, Woolman, Esther, and Zebulon Gaunt.
1759, Dec.   24, Woolsall, Charles, and Sarah Garrigues.
1726, Dec.   27, Wordie, Alexander, and Susannah Borden.
1770, April   26, Workman, Samuel, and Mary Robinson.
1749, May   18, Worley, Mary, and George Ryall.
1756, Oct.   16, Worral, Elizabeth, and Samuel Worral.
1756, Oct.   16, Worral, Samuel, and Elizabeth Worral.
1743, Sept.   15, Worrall, Jacob, and Eliz. Ford.
1758, Dec.   27, Worrall, Grace, and Peter Wikoff.
1794, Jan.   4, Worrall, William, and Ann Log.
1775, May   24, Worrell, Esther, and Philip Kirk.
1775, April   2, Worrell, Isaac, and Eliz. Rambo.
1749, Oct.   11, Worrell, James, and Hannah Parsons.
1757, April   24, Worrell, James, and Mary Stuart.
1803, March 12, Worrell, John, and Margaret Erben.
1757, April   30, Worrell, Mary, and James Lee.
1780, June   6, Worrell, Patience, and Reynold Keen.
1731, Dec.   21, Worrel, Peter, and Mary Powel.
1801, Oct.   4, Worrel, Sarah, and John Baker.
1770, Sept.   26, Worthington, Sarah, and William Kemble.
1745, Oct.   16, Wosdel, William, and Jane Williams.
1773, Jan.   19, Wrench, Margaret, and Charles Mayer.
1741, Aug.   29, Wright, Eleanor, and William Miller.
1794, July   28, Wright, Eleanor, and George Clarke.
1761, Jan.   15, Wright, Elizabeth, and Dennis Callahan.
1800, Sept.   21, Wright, George, and Anna May.
1763, Oct.   31, Wright, George, and Mary Edwards.
1748, Aug.   13, Wright, Henry, and Elizabeth McGee.
1759, June   6, Wright, James, and Elizabeth Holmes.
1730-1, Feb. 25, Wright, Jane, and Joshua Giffin.
1774, Feb.   28, Wright, John, and Ann Agnes Carr.
1759, Jan.   20, Wright, John, and Mary Wolleby.
1757, Sept.   27, Wright, John, and Anna Maria Barbold.
1771, Dec.   28, Wright, Leonard, and Sabina Bowen.
1794, May   21, Wright, Lydia, and George Summers.
1761, Dec.   28, Wright, Lydia, and Jehu Eyre.
1803, Feb.   26, Wright, Margaret, and William Carson.
1731, May   13, Wright, Martha, and Anthony Furnis.
1720, Feb.   12, Wright, Mary, and Archibald Mickle.

1761, Jan.   8, Wright, Mary, and Manuel Eyre.
1750, Oct.   14, Wright, Mary, and Isaac Dutton.
1761, Aug.   30, Wright, Nathaniel, and Hannah Welding.
1758, Aug.   16, Wright, Rachel, and William Moore.
1733, Jan.   11, Wright, Rebecca, and George Sturk.
1746, Sept.   6, Wright, Rebecca, and Elias Hughes.
1786, Nov.   11, Wright, Rhody, and Richard Chamberlain.
1798, May   2, Wright, Sarah, and Samuel Tillyer.
1776, May   23, Wright, Thomas, and Margaret Mouch.
1772, May   25, Wright, William, and Isabel Bullock.
1726, Nov.   17, Wright, Wm, and Reb. Gillinam.
1804, March 18, Wright, William E., and Mary Kite.
1753, Dec.   2, Wright, William, and Susannah Camel.
1777, March   3, Wrightson, Eliz., and Charles Thierry.
1720, June   7, Wyatt, Arabella, and Arthur Melville.
1731, Oct.   21, Wyer, Jane, and Samuel Webb.
1740, Jan.   1, Wyers, Simon, and Hannah Pearson.
1755, Aug.   20, Wyncoop, Eleanor, and Robert Fulton.
1773, July   29, Wynkoop, Abraham, and Rachel Sharp.
1767, May   18, Wynkoop, Benjamin, and Sarah Wooddrop Sims.
1802, Oct.   21, Wynkoop, Nicholas, and Sarah Campbell.
1741, Sept.   9, Yanily, Joannah Elizabeth, and George Turner.
1765, Jan.   7, Yarborough, Elizabeth, and James Irwin.
1741, May   11, Yarbury, Martha, and Walter Goodman.
1802, Oct.   21, Yard, Edward, and Lucy Bowen.
1791, Jan.   12, Yard, Eliz., and James Yard.
1785, Jan.   30, Yard, George, and Ann Bridges.
1791, Jan.   12, Yard, James, and Eliz. Yard.
1768, April   4, Yardley, Enoch, and Mary Lambwood.
1759, Nov.   16, Yardley, Richard, and Lucy Stackhouse.
1754, Nov.   28, Yardley, Samuel, and Jane Logan.
1747, March   6, Yarkes, Sarah, and David Evans.
1781, Jan.   4, Yarnall, Deborah, and William Davis.
1758, June   3, Yarnall, Dorothy, and Ephriam Yarnall.
1858, June   3, Yarnall, Ephriam, and Dorothy Yarnall.
1804, Dec.   24, Yater, Henry, and Mary McLane.
1750, Feb.   20, Yates, Sarah, and John Ewing.
1713, April   26, Yeakum, Andrew, and Elizabeth Trollup.
1713, June   21, Yealdall, Anthony, and Eleanor Edwards.
1754, Nov.   6, Yeandal, Henry, and Susannah Hunt.
1755, Oct.   15, Yeates, Elizabeth, and David Fulton.
1736, Feb.   26, Yeates, Joseph, and Elizabeth Newberry.
1750, Dec.   15, Yeates, Joseph, and Jane Morris.
1721, Nov.   30, Yeates, Joseph, and Margaret Pearce.
1761, Dec.   23, Yeates, Mary, and Jonathan Dillon.
1711, Feb.   8, Yerkes, Harmanus, and Elizabeth Watts.

1758, June　22, Yetton, Elizabeth, and Robert Carson.
1733, March 20, Yoacum, Judith, and Aaron Hewit.
1715, Aug.　26, Yoakhum, Jonas, and Juliana Enochson.
1732, June　 3, Yacham, Christian, and Thomas Miles.
1804, Dec.　14, Yocum, George, and Ann Tennent.
1710, Feb.　 7, Yokam, Swan, and Joanna Collins.
1762, Jan.　22, York, Edward, and Sarah Stille.
1789, Oct.　 5, York, Eliz., and John Cole.
1801, Sept.　3, York, Laetitia, and John Henry.
1794, Oct.　11, Yorke, Peter, and Mary Claypole.
1798, Aug.　15, York, Peter, and Mary Haynes.
1765, Jan.　15, York, Robert, and Jane Cochran.
1781, Oct.　11, York, Sarah, and Thomas Pilkington.
1764, April 31, York, Thomas, and Margaret Forbes.
1768, July　14, Yorkson, Frances, and Alexander Hale.
1800, Sept.　18, Yorkson, Mary Ann, and Amos Marshal.
1793, April 25, Yost, Cath., and William Greble.
1757, Dec.　23, Yozen, Catherine, and Hugh Law.
1757, Dec.　24, Young, Ann, and Benjamin Lownsberry.
1772, Aug.　 5, Young, Ariadne, and Llewellin Young.
1779, July　22, Young, Edward, and Mary Gilbert.
1729, April 23, Young, Ed., and Hannah Dodd.
1783, April 29, Young, Eleanor, and William Jones.
1802, June　 1, Young, Eliz., and Samuel Gray.
1781, July　 9, Young, Eliz., and James Connor.
1781, May　18, Young, Conrad, and Mary Hayes.
1785, Sept.　28, Young, Hannah, and John Mason.
1729-30, Jan. 29, Young, Hannah, and Thomas Browne.
1767, Dec.　11, Young, Hannah, and Barzillai Haines.
1733, March 26, Young, Harrie, and Mary Taylor.
1753, Nov.　10, Young, James, and Jane Graeme.
1734, July　 2, Young, Jane, and Jacob Pyatt.
1757, April 12, Young, John, and Mary McCloud.
1797, Feb.　 2, Young, John, and Frances Holiday.
1771, Aug.　29, Young, John, and Eliza Taylor.
1712, April　8, Young, John, and Catharine Marcarty.
1737, April　9, Young, John, and Anne Boyte.
1772, Aug.　 5, Young, Llewellin, and Ariadne Young.
1805, Dec.　 5, Young, Mary, and Matthias Coarse.
1794, Feb.　 7, Young, Mary, and Frederick Mayst.
1792, Oct.　20, Young, Mary, and Isaac Hicks.
1770, Aug.　22, Young, Mary, and Thomas Mitchell.
1794, May　24, Young, Mary, and James Campbell.
1726, Sept.　20, Young, Osilla, and Walter Lewis.
1804, Aug.　 3, Young, Phoebe, and Henry Platt.
1793, Jan.　 3, Young, Phoebe, and Thomas Ryan.

1781, May   28, Young, Rosanna, and Richard Shaffis.
1742, Dec.   22, Young, Sarah, and Francis Cheyney.
1758, Aug.   24, Young, Sarah, and Jonathan Paul.
1775, May   29, Young, Thomas, and Barbara Clingham.
1795, June   25, Young, Thomas, and Eliz. McCredan.
1783, Oct.   23, Young, William, and Margaret Murray.
1724, Jan.   29, Young, William, and Joanna Humphrey.
1758, July   23, Young, William, and Grace Price.
1797, Aug.   12, Young, William and Cath. Parker.
1757, Aug.   24, Younger, Brian, and Elizabeth Deykin.
1758, Dec.   9, Younger, Robert, and Catherine Johnson.
1765, March 20, Younger, Watson, and Elizabeth Slator.
1788, Dec.   15, Zane, Abigail, and Adam Pease.
1726, Dec.   17, Zean, Elizabeth, and Wm Wade.
1772, June   18, Zane, Hannah, and Elias Williams.
1761, June   30, Zane, Isaac, and Azuba Wilkins.
1766, Oct.   1, Zane, Joel, and Hester Scull.
1766, June   20, Zane, Mary, and Thomas Vaughan.
1720, Oct.   30, Zanes, Ann, and Edward Hughs.
1754, Aug.   3, Zanes, Esther, and Richard Collins.

MARRIAGE RECORD

OF THE

SWEDES' CHURCH,

(GLORIA DEI.)

1750-1810.

SWEDES' CHURCH, PHILADELPHIA.

1755, Sept. 9, Abardean, George, and Barbara Philips.
1780, Feb. 22, Abberdeen, Susannah, and William Sawyer.
1800, Jan. 12, Abbett, Mary, and William Forpaugh.
1800, May 4, Abbet, Nelly, and John Miers.
1760, July 14, Abbet, Perthenea, and Robert McCallister.
1774, Nov. 3, Abbot, Ezekiel, and Elizabeth Williams.
1777, June 9, Abbot, Henry, and Elizabeth Marshall.
1789, June 28, Abel, Elizabeth, and Henry Rohrman.
1758, Nov. 7, Abel, Henry, and Susanna Lock.
1774, Feb. 6, Abelin, Christiana, and John Zipherhealth.
1795, Feb. 26, Abenetty, Ester, and Lawrence Cashin.
1763, April 18, Abercomby, Elizabeth, and Hugh Bowes.
1761, Nov. 9, Aborn, Jonathan, and Hannah Smith.
1762, Nov. 9, Aborn, Jonathan, and Hannah Smith.
1789, June 8, Aborn, Rebecca, and Daniel Goodwin.
1776, Sept. 15, Abram, Margaret, and George Callicken.
1799, Aug. 15, Abram, Margaret, and Joseph Armstrong Eglestone.
1766, May 23, Abrams, Elizabeth, and Joseph Lancaster.
1767, May 16, Aburn, Hannah, and Richard Hughes.
1793, June 30, Aby, John, and Nancy Williams.
1794, Aug. 8, Ace, Daniel, and Elizabeth Harrington.
1757, June 28, Ackley, John, and Elizabeth Lewzley.
1769, May 27, Adair, John, and Catharine Stamper.
1782, Dec. 23, Adamofski, Joseph, and Catherine Smith.
1759, Nov. 21, Adam, George, and Sarah Loyd.
1766, June 30, Adam, Susannah, and John Jacob Phoffhanser.
1793, July 9, Adams, Alexander, and Susannah Wallace.
1778, Sept. 9, Adams, Ann, and James Glenn.
1791, May 1, Adams, Bartholomy, and Jane Jemmison.
1785, July 12, Adams, Catherine, and John Beck.
1780, Sept. 6, Adams, Catherine, and William Rolph.
1785, March 22, Adams, Ebenezer, and Hannah Coock.
1781, Oct. 5, Adams, Eliizbeth, and Alexander Hyens.
1782, Aug. 7, Adams, Elizabeth, and Derrick Wade.

1781, Sept. 17, Adams, Elizabeth, and George Rine.

1780, March 8, Adams, Elizabeth, and John Hinan.

1790, April 1, Adams, Elizabeth, and Samuel Hinderson.

1751, Aug. 20, Adams, George, and Catreen Devire.

1795, Jan. 2, Adams, George, and Sina Boice.

1790, Aug. 26, Adams, Jacob, and Jane McCulloch.

1778, March 5, Adams, James, and Frances Bright.

1799, June 15, Adams, Jane, and James Sullender.

1794, July 20, Adams, Jane, and John Sharp.

1751, Dec. 9, Adams, John, and Anne Stephens.

1797, May 26, Adams, John, and Eleonore Davis.

1780, May 4, Adams, John, and Margaret Shippen.

1756, Feb. 1, Adams, John, and Mary Morgan.

1783, Nov. 2, Adams, Jonathan, and Elizabeth Wright.

1769, Dec. 31, Adams, Jonathan, and Susannah Flower.

1785, July 6, Adams, Margaret, and George Grays.

1776, Nov. 29, Adams, Margaret, and James Calley.

1768, Nov. 1, Adams, Margarett, and Timothy Kiesse.

1780, Jan. 30, Adams, Mary, and Andrew Tenick.

1780, April 7, Adams, Mary, and Arminius Thornton.

1778, June 4, Adams, Mary, and John Lawson.

1793, April 26, Adams, Mary, and John Sims.

1755, April 14, Adams, Nathan, and Aurelia Rush.

1796, Dec. 29, Adams, Peter, and Barbara Cousler.

1766, April 23, Adams, Peter, and Mary Rich.

1800, Dec. 21, Adams, Samuel, and Elizabeth Watkins.

1779, Jan. 7, Adams, Samuel, and Margaret McCook.

1791, Jan. 3, Adams, Sarah, and James McConnell.

1800, Aug. 3, Adams, Sarah, and John Harmon.

1790, Nov. 4, Adams, Sidney, and Nathaniel Miers.

1780, Aug. 11, Adams, Thomas, and Mary Coats.

1796, Oct. 4, Adams, Thomas, and Peggy Leaman.

1797, June 22, Adams, Thomas, and Phebe Till.

1754, July 11, Adamson, David, and Elizabeth Pyton.

1781, Feb. 19, Adare, Catharine, and Francis Brooks.

1782, Dec. 22, Adare, Daniel, and Mary Church.

1776, Dec. 1, Adam, Thomas, and Rachel Elwes.

1798, May 5, Adcock, William, and Elizabeth Smith.

1762, July 24, Addidle, Charity, and George Elliot.

1791, Nov. 30, Addison, Nancy, and Adam Smith.

1782, July 31, Ades, William, and Eleonor Dickeson.

1780, Aug. 9, Adington, Jane, and John Donhaven.

1759, Oct. 21, Adkison, Elizabeth, and Henery Lenny.

1795, April 11, Aeger, Sarah, and James Altemus.

1782, Jan. 16, Affrey Calon, and Eliza Anne Litshworth.

1780, Sept. 16, Agar, Peter, and Elizabeth Ellet.

1792, Aug.   9, Agard, Stephen, and Margret Lewis.
1800, June   8, Agea, Mary, and John Robinson.
1784, July   7, Agnew, Jane, and Andrew Morris.
1791, Aug. 10, Agnew, Lydia, and Jean Lomprez.
1765, Jan. 22, Agricola, Ludowick, and Mariah Burchard.
1771, May   12, Aberam, John, and Mary Ridding.
1797, May   10, Aiken, John, and Prudence Shelly.
1780, March 13, Aine, John, and Mary Evans.
1768, Oct. 30, Airs, Penelope, and William Danolds.
1757, Aug. 17, Airs, Richard, and Elizabeth Brownin.
1771, Oct.   9, Airs, Sarah, and John Shuts.
1779, Dec.   1, Airy, Ann, and John Eferson.
1783, April 21, Aitken, John, and Elizabeth Swiver.
1780, April 1, Akins, William, and Rachel Roberts.
1791, May   26, Aklin, Elizabeth, and Michael Williams.
1766, Aug. 26, Alback, Christian, and Mary Granin.
1779, July 18, Albah, Catharine, and John Gwillin.
1797, Dec.   3, Alberger, Henry, and Ann Kurtz.
1800, May   17, Alberger, John, and Elizabeth Tryon.
1792, Aug.   9, Albertis, Lewis, and Nancy Harned.
1760, March 28, Albertson, Enoch, and Elizabeth Chanart.
1755, Jan. 23, Albertson, Geziah, and Richard Cheesman.
1759, March 16, Albertson, Jacob, and Sebrow Redin.
1789, May   31, Albertson, Kezia, and Robert Thompson.
1795, Aug. 23, Albertson, Mathias, and Hannah Webber.
1790, Aug. 18, Albertson, Rebecca, and Amos Simpson.
1792, Sept. 22, Albertson, Sarah, and Isaac Phipps.
1793, Dec.   4, Albertson, Sarah, and William Bass.
1754, Aug. 11, Albrectson, Jacob, and Sary Banks.
1778, Dec. 24, Albuert, John, and Hannah Uhl.
1792, Jan. 22, Alcorn, Ann, and Robert Clark.
1792, June 29, Alcorn, Sarah, and Hugh Smith.
1794, May   25, Aldridge, Thomas, and Barbara Witty.
1760, Nov.   9, Aldritsh, Sarah, and Abel Pand.
1799, Dec. 22, Alexander, Adam, and Mary Saville.
1795, Feb. 22, Alexander, Ann, and Agnew Campbell.
1795, July   2, Alexander, James, and Jane Wasson.
1775, Nov. 19, Alexander, John, and Eleanor Robason.
1790, May   9, Alexander, Joseph, and Ann Cryder.
1759, Nov.   9, Alexander, Margeth, and James McKean.
1792, Jan.   3, Alexander, Mary, and Joseph Burden.
1791, June 15, Alexander, Mary, and Samuel Haslet.
1752, Dec. 12, Alexander, Nally, and William Farorre.
1766, Dec. 18, Alexander, Sarah, and Jeanings Stevenson.
1767, June 16, Alford, Samuel, and Elizabeth Freeman.
1781, Aug. 27, Alford, Samuel, and Mary Burnam.

1789, April   28, Alison, Mary, and Thomas Beesly.
1774, Jan.   10, Alkin, William, and Mary Points.
1780, April   19, Allan, Ann, and William Porters,
1771, April   29, Allan, Elizabeth, and Patrick Rue.
1778, March 27, Allan, James, and Levaney Brown.
1778, Feb.   8, Allan, Mary, and David Dymon.
1773, June   28, Allan, Mary, and William Price.
1780, June   13, Allan, Samuel, and Mary Tucker.
1777, April   20, Allan, Thomas, and Letty Collins.
1778, May   7, Allan, William, and Ann McKinney.
1777, April   24, Allcock, John, and Mary Miller.
1792, Nov.   9, Allen, Barzilla, and Sarah Plum.
1794, May   4, Allen, Diana, and Philip Will.
1780, Jan.   27, Allen, Elizabeth, and John West.
1774, Nov.   2, Allen, Hannah, and William Little.
1782, Dec.   25, Allen, Henery, and Eve Hanighan.
1759, Aug.   20, Allen, John, and Catharine Anderson.
1799, Jan.   7, Allen, Joseph, and Hannah Cleva.
1797, July   10, Allen, Louis, and Margret MacMullen.
1791, Dec.   26, Allen, Marget, and Charles Moser.
1790, Nov.   1, Allen, Mary, and Robert Rhea.
1775, Aug.   22, Allen, Mary, and Zachariah Goforth.
1781, Aug.   25, Allen, Mathew, and Elizabeth Vanhorne.
1773, April   21, Allen, Jr., Nathaniel, and Mary Dean.
1787, July   5, Allen, Richard, and Mary Parks.
1756, May   9, Allen, Richmond, and Mary Vandyke.
1792, April   12, Allen, Robert, and Margret Melzard.
1798, Dec.   6, Allen, Samuel, and Elizabeth Dubbelbarr.
1798, Nov.   12, Allen, Sarah, and Andrew Jones.
1791, July   21, Allen, Susanna, and Robert Merric.
1791, Aug.   16, Allen, Thomas, and Ann Homes.
1792, Oct.   29, Allen, Thomas Casdort, and Cathrine Lacy.
1791, April   28, Allen, Thomas, and Elizabeth Cassel.
1752, June   24, Allen, William, and Sarah Wittiker.
1764, Dec.   27, Allen, William, and Susannah Bowers.
1797, June   24, Allibone, Thomas, and Sarah Yeoman.
1775, Jan   3, Allice, John, and Mary Evans.
1791, Dec.   19, Allison, Elizabeth, and Thomas Daniel.
1759, Dec.   12, Allison, James, and Ann McClellin.
1790, May   30, Allison, Jane, and Daniel Karrigan.
1793, March 17, Allison, Rachel, and Edmund Connor.
1791, Aug.   4, Allison, Susanna, and Patric Fowler.
1778, Feb.   14, Allkins, Thomas, and Martha Webb.
1755, March 31, Alloms, Mary, and John Dougharty.
1767, July   5, Allyn, Adam, and Ann Scott.
1760, Jan.   7, Allyn, Adam, and Sarah Goulgeuir.

1770, Feb.   10, Alston, Joseph, and Mary Berry.
1795, April   11, Altemus, James, and Sarah Aeger.
1783, June   24, Alters, Jacob, and Mary Rogers.
1790, July   12, Altmore, John, and Sara Marshall.
1798, May   21, Amman, Anthony, and Elizab. Mullen.
1777, July   31, Ammey and Cadju, (negroes.)
1782, Dec.   14, Amos, Catherine, and Richard Clark Ellis Brown.
1779, Dec.   28, Amos, Jacob, and Elizabeth Perkins.
1783, May   14, Amos, John, and Elizabeth Levering.
1775, Oct.   2, Amos, John, and Rachel Benjamin.
1786, Aug.   20, Amrey, Javis, and Anne Russel.
1778, March   31, Amrick, Catharine, and Thomas Field.
1799, Feb.   25, Amy, Mary, and Francis Ritchie.
1791, June   1, Anderson, Abel, and Rachel Middleton.
1751, May   7, Andreson, Andrew, and Anne Jonston.
1764, Sept.   23, Anderson, Andrew, and Elizabeth Toy.
1751, Feb.   2, Anderson, Andrew, and Susanna Bellows.
1752, May   26, Anderson, Ann, and Anthony Martin.
1794, Sept.   20, Anderson, Ann, and Hugh Maxwell.
1791, Feb.   15, Anderson, Ann, and John Land.
1774, Nov.   1, Anderson, Ann, and John Patterson.
1778, May   27, Anderson, Catharine, and Archibald Patterson.
1800, Oct.   3, Anderson, Catharine, and Benjamin Runian.
1759, Aug.   20, Anderson, Catharine, and John Allen.
1755, Sept.   22, Anderson, Christiana, and Day Branson.
1770, June   13, Anderson, Christian, and Mary Baron.
1797, Nov.   26, Anderson, Elizabeth, and Christian Heckla.
1780, Feb.   7, Anderson, Elizabeth, and James Forster.
1755, Dec.   16, Anderson, Elizabeth, and Thomas Boggs.
1757, April   28, Anderson, Hannah, and Thomas Brooks.
1776, June   10, Anderson, Isaac, and Elizabeth Hitrick.
1767, July   25, Anderson, Isaac, and Mary Valentine.
1781, Feb.   15, Anderson, James, and Anne Williams.
1792, Nov.   25, Anderson, James, and Mary Rhodz.
1794, Feb.   17, Anderson, John, and Sarah Brown.
1771, Jan.   2, Anderson, John, and Sarah Jenkins.
1778, Feb.   25, Anderson, Margarett, and Timothy Boddington.
1775, June   20, Anderson, Mary, and Alexander Henderson.
1781, Nov.   5, Anderson, Mary, and Charles McDonald.
1795, Feb.   8, Anderson, Mary, and Frederic Quigley.
1793, July   18, Anderson, Mary, and Isaac Timbers.
1787, Oct.   27, Anderson, Mary, and Jacob Wine.
1791, Sept.   18, Anderson, Nancy, and James Davison.
1777, Feb.   1, Anderson, Peter, and Isabella McLean.
1772, May   4, Anderson, William, and Martha Clark.
1799, Dec.   12, Anderson, William, and Sarah Siddons.

1752, Sept. 17, Andewood, Elizabeth, and Richard Webb.
1751, July 1, Andover, Joseph, and Mary Reanes.
1757, Aug. 3, Andreas, James, and Ann Luttin.
1795, June 9, Andre, John Baptiste, and Cathrine Macquire.
1800, May 23, Andres, Peter, and Mary Lapat.
1794, Oct. 12, Andrews, Ann, and John Milles.
1779, May 27, Andrews, Elizabeth, and John Delley.
1794, Oct. 2, Andrews, Lydia, and David Roe.
1797, July 23, Andrews, Margret, and John Thomas.
1798, May 12, Andrews, Martha, and Daniel McKew.
1787, Nov. 16, Andrews, Martha, and John Orner.
1784, Oct. 27, Andrews, Mary, and Joel Westcoat.
1794, Aug. 23, Andrews, Mary, and Robert Lee.
1759, Sept. 30, Andrew, Nicholas, and Eve Low.
1776, Nov. 22, Andrews, Paul, and Hannah Pierce.
1771, April 4, Andrews, Rachel, and Jacob Rias.
1787, May 31, Andrews, Samuel, and Elizabeth Payne.
1792, May 10, Andrews, Susanna, and Abel Wilbanc.
1777, Oct. 30, Andrews, Thomas, and Sarah Colley.
1776, Jan. 21, Andrews, William, and Ann Lewas.
1765, Oct. 21, Angella, Sarah, and Josuah Hemmenway.
1752, Sept. 2, Annlyth, Mary, and John Chapman.
1780, Jan. 17, Annesley, Thomas, and Esther Thomson.
1791, May 29, Anthony, Christiana, and Peter Kucher.
1790, April 25, Anthony, John, and Eleonore Yater.
1792, March 29, Antrim, John, and Mary Bradshaw.
1800, Sept. 4, Antrim, Parnell, and Harriet Williams.
1792, Jan. 29, Appel, Henry, and Mary Smith.
1794, Dec. 21, Apple, George, and Sarah Smith.
1774, July 17, Apple, Henry, and Christina Sartoriusin.
1760, July 5, Appleton, William, and Mary Repton.
1769, Dec. 16, Archbold, John, and Mary Armitage.
1754, March 25, Archbold, Stephen, and Christiana Ohara.
1767, Oct. 26, Archer, Abel, and Amey Caston.
1783, Sept. 15, Archer, Elizabeth, and Thomas Webster.
1752, May 10, Archer, John, and Sarah Emerson.
1765, May 24, Archer, Martha, and James Cherry.
1793, Dec. 21, Archer, Mary, and William Parmer.
1766, Aug. 25, Archer, Rachel, and Edward Middleton.
1776, Aug. 8, Archer, Sarah, and David Cahill.
1765, May 1, Archer, William, and Margaret Trapnel.
1775, June 14, Archibald, Elizabeth, and John McGee.
1783, March 11, Archibald, Margaret, and John Melzerd.
1775, Oct. 31, Archibold, Stephen, and Sarah Jones.
1780, July 24, Archwold, Bartholomew, and Mertha Baker.
1776, June 3, Arella, Philip, and Barbarah White.

1759, Nov.   22, Arendt, Philip, and Elizabeth Reinhardt.
1769, Dec.   16, Armitage, Mary, and John Archbold.
1775, July   20, Armitage, Susannah, and William Sally.
1791, April 28, Armitt, Frances, and Aaron Morton.
1775, Dec.   27, Armon, Mary, and James Barns.
1780, Feb.   19, Armon, Philip, and Jane Negr.
1767, Dec.   29, Armour, John, and Mary Read.
1759, Aug.   11, Armstrem, Nancy, and John Richards.
1793, Oct.   7, Armstrong, Andrew, and Rachel Davey.
1787, Feb.   28, Armstrong, Bridget, and John Mathiney.
1800, Dec.   4, Armstrong, Britta, and John Cuban.
1778, March 29, Armstrong, Eleanor, and Timothy Langley.
1791, July   7, Armstrong, Elizabeth, and Martin Bardell.
1796, June   21, Armstrong, John, and Rachel Robeson.
1758, Dec.   6, Armstrong, Joseph, and Debra Burrough.
1799, Dec.   19, Armstrong, Nancy, and Nathaniel Reas Glascoe.
1793, Aug.   22, Armstrong, Sarah, and John Mills.
1770, July   8, Arnam, Frances, and William Sheehan.
1783, April 16, Arnest, Catherine, and John Drake.
1764, March 31, Arney, John, and Martha Paxton.
1779, May   6, Arnold, Jonathan, and Mertha Martin.
1800, Jan.   25, Arnold, Stephen, and Mary Sutherland.
1780, May   15, Arnold, Thomas, and Ann Thomson.
1788, Feb.   20, Arnold, Thomas, and Catharine Mophet.
1759, April 11, Aronson, Rebecca, and —— Nicholson.
1793, Oct.   14, Arragon, Jesse, and Elizabeth Lang.
1787, Feb.   8, Arrans, Patience, and Robert Freeman.
1799, June   4, Art, William, and Martha Condon.
1761, March 19, Arven, Cadwalader, and Elizabeth Wartenby.
1771, Aug.   22, Arvin, Hugh, and Ann Jones.
1794, Dec.   23, Ash, Mary, and Edward Duvall.
1790, June   8, Ash, Mary, and George Kinsler.
1799, Dec.   26, Ash, Thomas, and Mary O'Bryan.
1755, Aug.   26, Ashburn, Edward, and Elizabeth Skorlock.
1777, June   15, Ashburn, Joseph, and Elizabeth Ross.
1795, May   8, Ashby, Ann, and James Gillaspy.
1790, Nov.   13, Ashby, Nathaniel, and Frances Dewall.
1755, Jan.   21, Asheton, Mary, and Peter Wyatt.
1778, March   7, Ashley, William, and Elizabeth Sampell.
1751, Oct.   13, Ashmead, Ann, and Samuel Potts.
1759, April   8, Ashmead, William, and Elizabeth Robins.
1791, Oct.   27, Ashmore, John, and Jane Swangley.
1795, July   21, Ashton, Benjamin, and Martha Obrian.
1792, Aug.   23, Ashton, Cathrine, and Robert Harrison.
1792, June   20, Ashton, John, and Margret Melchor.
1780, June   23, Ashton, Ruth, and Henry Wester.

1778, Jan. 15, Ashton, Ruth, and Richard Lambert.
1767, April 16, Ashton, Susannah, and John Johnson.
1792, Nov. 11, Ashton, Timothy, and Barbara King.
1774, Feb. 20, Askon, Sarah, and Kenedey Hogen.
1782, Oct. 10, Asling, Frederic, and Mary Cook.
1779, March 11, Aslin, Mary, and John Smith.
1760, March 28, Aspen, Hannah, and Mathias Hope.
1772, Feb. 9, Aston, James, and Susannah Madan.
1755, Dec. 1, Atherton, William, and Jane Mersor.
1784, Aug. 5, Atkeson, Charity, and Francis Saunders.
1788, Sept. 18, Atkin, Thomas, and Elizabeth Cribben.
1792, May 21, Atkins, Mary, and Thomas Reynolds.
1755, April 11, Atkins, William, and Rachel Pullen.
1791, May 26, Atkinson, George, and Mary Moss.
1778, May 26, Atkinson, Margaret, and Jonathan Brewer.
1767, Oct. 12, Atwell, William, and Lydia Watson.
1776, March 21, Aubrey, Luke, and Margaret Joiner.
1773, Jan. 5, Auderton, Mary, and James Longden.
1779, Nov. 19, Augustus, Manasse, and Mary Sharanger.
1799, Oct. 2, Aukerman, Elizab., and Casper Sollinger.
1794, Oct. 5, Aull, Jacob, and Margret Howard.
1771, July 15, Austin, Eleanor, and Edward Dorlan.
1784, March 29, Austin, Mary, and William Parrish.
1797, Feb. 12, Austin, Thomas, and Rosetta Birmingham.
1790, Sept. 10, Avis, Rachel, and Matthias Carnes.
1795, May 9, Awll, Dorothy, and Guy Stone.
1792, Dec. 20, Axley, Andrew, and Helena Bignel.
1792, April 1, Baach, Marget, and Jacob Lang.
1783, March 10, Baar, Barbara, and Adam Britell.
1792, Dec. 7, Babby, William, and Jane Hunter.
1779, May 15, Babe, Rebecca, and William Rushworm.
1772, Dec. 6, Babington, Richard, and Martha Shevier.
1760, Oct. 11, Baby, William, and Mary Haggens.
1760, Sept. 26, Bacher, ———, and Daniel Thomson.
1785, Nov. 6, Backer, Jacob, and Catherine White.
1757, June 13, Backhouse, Isabell, and James Dexter.
1766, Nov. 1, Bacon, Elizabeth, and Morton O'Brian.
1771, Dec. 21, Badcock, John, and Christiana King.
1794, April 2, Bagly, James, and Margery Black.
1789, Oct. 5, Bahn, Luke, and Mary Stillman.
1775, Jan. 22, Bailee, Henry, and Jean Stoyle.
1756, July 22, Bailey, Elizabeth, and William Wagstaff.
1778, May 19, Bailey, Mary, and William Key.
1777, Oct. 8, Bailey, Phoebe, and Benjamin Corney.
1794, April 19, Bailey, Simon Coley, and Sarah Molton.
1782, Feb. 11, Baily, Arthur, and Ely Benton.

1754, Jan.   16, Baily, Richard, and Elizabeth Bould.
1783, July   18, Bakeoven, Sarah, and George Miller.
1759, Nov.   12, Baker, Abigail, and Edward Gressel.
1789, Nov.   25, Baker, Adam, and Ann Linn.
1756, March 30, Baker, Ann, and Jonathan Clinkin.
1795, May   17, Baker, Cathrine, and Jacob Richler.
1781, July   21, Baker, Catharine, and John Copel.
1780, June   13, Baker, Christina, and Mathias Riffet.
1794, July   29, Baker, Daniel, and Elizabeth Sickle.
1793, Sept.   9, Baker, Debora, and Thomas Shepard.
1772, Sept.   3, Baker, Elizabeth, and Nathan Baker.
1777, Dec.   17, Baker, Francis, and Margaret Christie.
1778, Oct,   19, Baker, Henery, and Catharine Kooken.
1774, Feb.   18, Baker, Henry, and Sarah Jones.
1786, April   10, Baker, Jacob, and Abigail Loughberry.
1761, April   6, Baker, Jacob, and Catharine March.
1778, Oct.   15, Baker, Jacob, and Mary Taylor.
1779, April   7, Baker, James, and Mary Roberson.
1764, Sept.   9, Baker, John, and Barbarah Brant.
1764, Jan.   16, Baker, John, and Eleonore Wheeler.
1777, Dec.   28, Baker, Joseph, and Catherine Griffey.
1765, Dec.   2, Baker, Lydiah, and John Ottey.
1780, March 14, Baker, Margaret, and Henry Dewer.
1795, Sept.   20, Baker, Mary, and Christopher Minfie.
1780, July   24, Baker, Mertha, and Bartholomew Archwold.
1779, Oct.   23, Baker, Mary, and James Sutton.
1772, Sept.   3, Baker, Nathan, and Elizabeth Baker.
1755, Oct.   22, Baker, Rachel, and James Cannaday.
1778, April   1, Baker, Rebecca, and Miles Swiney.
1754, Nov.   27, Baker, Bichard, and Christiana Wills.
1796, April   3, Baker, Sarah, and Ruben Hope.
1785, Aug.   17, Baker, Sarah, and Thomas Egan.
1778, June   7, Balderick, Martha, and Benjamin Berey.
1764, June   23, Balderston, Bartholomew, and Sarah Johnson.
1782, Aug.   9, Baldesgoi, Joseph, and Anne Bray.
1782, Aug.   29, Baldin, John, and Elizabeth Deverax.
1763, April   18, Baldwin, Catharine, and Patrick Cashaday.
1783, July   6, Baldwin, Jacob, and Susannah Gayen.
1773, Nov.   30, Baldwin, Joel, and Mary Tew.
1753, Oct.   31, Balenger, Susanna, and James Simons.
1798, Aug.   16, Balert, Marget, and Jonathan Quicksaw.
1750, Oct.   12, Baley, Anne, and William Salter.
1778, June   1, Baley, Zachariah, and Mary Rambo.
1791, July   20, Balfour, Jane, and Dennis Deny.
1797, Nov.   30, Balk, William, and Mary Booth.
1772, July   19, Ball, Michael, and Elizabeth Grace.

1756, Nov.   5, Ballard, William, and Ann McCullough.
1791, July,   5, Ballentine, William, and Cathrine Morrison.
1775, Oct.   14, Balley, William, and Margaret Shrack.
1773, Oct.   31, Bamford, Joseph, and Elizabeth Rollins.
1792, Sept. 25, Bancs, Joseph, and Nancy Fox.
1779, Jan.   17, Banden, William, and Ruth McGee.
1788, Aug.   19, Bane, Anne, and Samuel Lelew.
1775, June   12, Banford, Mary, and George Shepherd.
1754, Aug.   11, Banks, Sary, and Jacob Albrecteon.
1751, June   8, Bankson, Deborah, and John Lord.
1753, June   14, Bankson, Jacob, and Elesnor Cox.
1752, Sept. 14, Bankson, John, and Mary Holland.
1758, Oct.   10, Bankson, Mary, and Peter Cap.
1766, April 17, Bankson, Mary, and Samuel Taylor.
1759, March 26, Bankson, Peter, and Rachel Williamson.
1778, Sept. 13, Bannah, Isabella, and Hugh Philips.
1759, Sept. 30, Banner, John, and Catherine Lions.
1753, May   17, Bannett, Elizabeth, and Alexander Hill.
1770, May   7, Bant, James, and Mary Madding.
1794, Jan.   20, Barajon, Bonaventure, and Marget Magravi.
1799, Jan.   31, Barber, Jane, and John Wilmert.
1794, Sept. 16, Barber Robert, and Jane More.
1787, July   10, Barbesat, Jacob, and Mary Halberstadt.
1794, Nov.   12, Barclay, Maria, and John Young.
1754, Feb.   21, Bard, John, and Elizabeth Sweeting.
1777, April   7, Bardack, George, and Catharine Reinholds.
1791, July   7, Bardell, Martin, and Elizabeth Armstrong.
1791, March 30, Bare, Cathrine, and James Makamson.
1752, Dec.   5, Bare, Robhard, and Hanna Lin.
1790, March   1, Baremore, James, and Eunice Leeds.
1791, Dec.   11, Barepo, Thomas, and Mary Motley.
1788, Oct.   4, Barford, John, and Rachel Ward.
1769, Feb.   2, Bark, Mary, and George Ensor.
1750, Sept. 11, Bark, William, and Eleonor Gill.
1777, April   8, Barker, Ann, and Thomas Howell.
1770, Sept. 20, Barker, Dolly, and William Graves.
1778, May   24, Barker, Thomas, and Evis Kirk.
1792, May   22, Barkerd, Adam, and Abigail Grafey.
1759, Jan.   1, Barket, Jehu, and Mary Ivery.
1791, July   24, Barkley, John, and Mary Miller.
1793, Dec.   12, Barley, Henry, and Marget Summers.
1797, June   19, Barlow, Rebecca, and William Curden.
1778, March 19, Barnard, Barbarah, and William Cotton.
1760, March 11, Barnard, Mary, and Benjamin Lusher.
1796, Dec.   8, Barnard, Rachel, and James Symonds.
1780, Aug.   15, Barnes, Elizabeth, and William Keder.

1790, July   24, Barnes, James, and Sarah Robeson.
1783, May   24, Barnes, John, and Madlin Walheimer.
1792, Sept. 15, Barnes, Nancy, and Joseph Brase.
1794, May   11, Barnet, Cathrine, and James Haines.
1754, Sept.   7, Barnet, Catharine, and Robert Richardson.
1800, April 21, Barnet, Mary, and James Martin.
1783, Nov.   13, Barnet, Rebecca, and Thomas Ross.
1766, Oct.   27, Barnett, William, and Elizabeth Taylor.
1772, July   7, Barnewell, Mathew, and Elizabeth Mackey.
1769, Oct.   30, Barney, Andrew, and Anne Daill.
1780, Sept.   6, Barnheizel, Elizabeth, and Peter Christman.
1757, June   26, Barnhill, Jane, and John McGrager.
1785, May   21, Barnhill, John, and Elizabeth Lusk.
1770, Dec.   23, Barnhill, Margarett, and Samuel Henry.
1770, Oct.   21, Barnhouse, Edward, and Julia Holshan.
1775, Dec.   27, Barnes, James, and Mary Armon.
1763, April 26, Barns, James, and Sarah Carter.
1764, Jan.   1, Barns, John, and Elizabeth Fisher.
1776, Feb.   19, Barnwell, Phoebe, and John Brownley.
1794, Dec.   15, Baron, Hannah, and Edward Bolton.
1770, June   13, Baron, Mary, an Christian Anderson.
1763, Nov.   11, Baron, Mary, and Joseph Brown.
1761, Dec.   26, Barr, Ann, and John Casper de Muralt.
1796, Dec.   1, Barr, Daniel, and Barbara White.
1796, Oct.   11, Barr, Daniel, and Marget Loury.
1792, Oct.   25, Barr, Joseph, and Mary White.
1782, Jan.   3, Barr, Levite, and Esther Nailor, (negroes.)
1775, May   18, Barr, Margaret, and Henry Krips.
1782, June   2, Barren, Catherine, and Valentine Gelasby.
1783, April 10, Barret, Anne, and John McLane.
1781, Nov.   26, Barret, Nancy, and Fridric Benjamin Kinsell.
1770, Dec.   22, Barret, Richard, and Elizabeth Trapnal.
1797, Aug.   25, Barret, Thomas, and Deborah Dawson.
1782, Dec.   7, Barroner, Christiana and William Rose.
1795, Feb.   22, Barry, Ann, and William Barry.
1759, April 15, Barry, Catharine, and William Barry.
1782, Dec.   13, Barry, David, and Mary Loyd.
1797, Feb.   2, Barry, Eleonore, and William Rodney.
1784, Dec.   1, Barry, John, and Anne Tullack.
1790, Dec.   6, Barry, John, and Marget Noll.
1799, May   23, Barry, John, and Mary Miller.
1789, March 24, Barry, Mary, and Joshua Elkinton.
1790, May   10, Barry, Mary, and Michael Hogan.
1795, Feb.   22, Barry, William, and Ann Barry.
1759, April 15, Barry, William, and Catharine Barry.
1778, June   2, Barstow, Joseph, and Margaret Keyer.

1798, July   30, Bartel, Daniel, and Jemimah Lyel.
1753, July   14. Bartell, Elizabeth, and Thomas Hickenbottom.
1759, Nov.   1, Bartelson, Margeth, and David Francis.
1796, Sept.   23, Barthleson, Jane, and William McGlathery.
1766, Aug.   21, Bartholomew, Gaynor, and David Kinsey.
1794, Feb.   1, Bartholomew, Rudolph, and Alsey Levering.
1781, Oct.   17, Bartholomew, Joseph, and Mary Hines.
1789, Nov.   3, Bartim, Sara, and Mordecai More.
1796, July   7, Bartle, George, and Cathrine Lier.
1792, Dec.   26, Bartle, Mary, and Joseph Williams.
1758, Sept.   1, Bartelson, Mary, and James Fox.
1759, Feb.   9, Bartelson, Nicolas, and Jane May Hollan.
1796, Oct.   9, Bartleson, Peter, and Catherine Sell.
1757, May   3, Bartlet, Catharine, and James Furrett.
1774, Feb.   23, Bartlet, James, and Mary Bryon.
1770, Aug.   23, Bartlet, John, and Anne Bushard.
1795, Dec.   20, Bartley, John, and Mary Crevis.
1779, Jan.   15, Bartley, Margaret, and Hugh McKegney.
1798, April   28, Bartley, Mary, and Archibald McDonel.
1791, May   27, Bartlow, Sara, and John Ennis.
1754, July   16, Barton, James, and Elizabeth Bound.
1755, Nov.   5, Barton, James, and Hannah Collins.
1798, July   28, Barton, John, and Mary Benler.
1782, March   20, Barton, Margaret, and William Roney.
1753, Dec.   8, Barton, Thomas, and Esther Rittenhouse.
1764, Dec.   6, Bartram, Ann, and George Bartram.
1776, Dec.   8, Bartram, Eleanor, and Joel Wright.
1764, Dec.   6, Bartram, George, and Ann Bartram.
1795, Feb.   17, Bartram, James Alexander, and Ann Nicholson.
1769, Oct.   1, Bary, Mary, and Henry Wahlberg.
1770, Jan.   14, Bary, Theodorus, and Margarett Matley.
1773, March   15, Bary, Theodorus, and Rebecca Knowls.
1778, Dec.   13, Bary, Thomas, and Ann Lucky.
1780, May   18, Bash, Catharine, and Henry Miller.
1760, Sept.   18, Bashfull, Joseph, and Elizabeth Stuard.
1794, April   19, Baslington, Richard, and Martha Gooden.
1781, June   28, Bason, John, and Mary Eden.
1793, Dec.   4, Bass, William, and Sarah Albertson.
1777, Dec.   18, Bastian, Magdalene, and John Kinsley.
1754, May   7, Bastian, Sibyela, and John Rex.
1798, May   21, Bastian William, and Sarah Lorket.
1797, May   8, Bates, Elizabeth, and John Phillips.
1790, May   4, Bates, George, and Rachel Roney.
1793, June   15, Bates, Mary, and John Jingelson.
1782, Jan.   31, Bathsket, Catherine, and Daniel Robinson.
1771, April   7, Bathurst, John, and Elizabeth Styar.

1770, Sept. 23, Bathurst, Mary, and Isaac Cannon.
1767, Feb. 27, Bathust, Allan, and Jeane Kane.
1759, Sept. 29, Batine, Nicolas, and Magdaline Steer.
1796, Sept. 10, Batist, Peter, and Margaret Green.
1771, Oct. 21, Bats, Edward, and Elizabeth Risner.
1767, Aug. 9, Batson, Mary, and George Locke.
1791, June 21, Batt, John, Rebecca Plum.
1759, April 14, Battle, Sibilla, and James Warner.
1756, Nov. 4, Battman, Martha, and Abraham Hamor.
1784, May 22, Batton, Elizabeth, and George Keil.
1794, Sept. 18, Batton, Jemimah, and Thomas Bois.
1791, April 29, Batts, John, Hanna Edwards.
1797, Nov. 30, Bauer, Mary, and Thomas Lippencot.
1796, March 27, Baughman, Rachel, and Joseph Carr.
1778, Jan. 20, Baught, Elizabeth, and Alexander McDonal.
1791, April 11, Baum, Elizabeth, and John Teel.
1787, July 4, Bauman, Mary Margreta, and Albright Vogel.
1799, April 17, Baun, Mary, and Jacob Young.
1796, Dec. 15, Bavade, John, and Eleonore Dougan.
1765, Oct. 20, Bavington, Jonathan, and Jeane Van Dyke.
1798, June 4, Baxter, Hannah, and Patrick Gunn.
1793, Aug. 25, Baxter, John, and Elizabeth Morrow.
1778, June 14, Bay, Edward, and Ann Painter.
1781, Aug. 16, Bay, Hugh, and Elizabeth Bell.
1793, June, 30, Bayard, Eliza Juliana, and Joseph Wills.
1799, Dec. 1, Bayard, Mary, and Thomas Nevel.
1793, Nov, 17, Bayerly, Elizabeth, and Michael Kapper.
1767, April 26, Bayman, John, and Caterine McCallister.
1763, Nov. 12, Bays, Ann, and Nathaniel Mercer.
1778, Aug. 13, Bazeley, Elizabeth, and Peter Merret.
1796, Oct. 4, Bazing, John, and Hester Thomas.
1767, Aug. 16, Beach, Edmund, and Elizabeth Osborn.
1780, May 20, Beakley, Christian, and Mary Stroud.
1754, Oct. 29, Beaks, Joseph, and Jane Mayers.
1751, May 8, Bean, Joshua, and Catrenah Cothbert.
1799, July 17, Bean, Thomas Hanson, and Mary Todd.
1799, Dec. 26, Bear, Elizab., and William Supplee.
1780, March 9, Bear, Jacob, and Rachel Loid.
1797, Dec. 31, Beard, Alexander, and Cathrine McClennan.
1766, Oct. 1, Beard, Ann, and James Fitsimmons.
1776, Nov. 11, Beard, Elizabeth, and Francis Bell.
1797, July 16, Beard, Jane, and John Champagne.
1794, May 24, Beard, Robert, and Elizabeth McCall.
1792, Dec. 2, Beard, Sarah, and John Fisher.
1789, Jan. 15, Bearly, Henry, and Mary Schyller.
1774, July 28, Bearsticker, Andrew, and Mary Gravel.

1781, Jan.　16, Beary, Sarah, and Michael Munks.
1778, Jan.　12, Beattie, Arthur, and Mary Martin.
1759, Feb.　26, Beaty, James, and Ann Lewis.
1767, Feb.　31, Beaty, James, and Catharine Smith.
1784, July　7, Beauveau, John Peter, and Elizabeth Brown.
1757, Sept.　27, Beaver, Nicholas, and Mary Walhkin.
1791, Nov.　4, Beck, Elizabeth, and John Ott.
1791, March 10, Beck, Henry, and Hanna Isborn.
1769, Dec.　5, Beck, Jacob, and Elizabeth Santerling.
1785, July　12, Beck, John, and Catherine Adams.
1800, July　3, Becket, Joseph, and Elizab. Price.
1762, Sept.　21, Beckstraw, Hannah, and William Hall.
1777, March 31, Bedford, Mary, and Philip Henry.
1795, March 18, Bee, Elenore, and Esaiah Hunt.
1791, Nov.　2, Bee, Jonathan, and Sarah Dicks.
1775, June　5, Beeby, William, and Sarah Smith.
1758, Oct.　6, Beech, Mary, and Edward Morphey.
1782, July　1, Beehman, Elizabeth, and John Horss.
1762, July　18, Beeker, Jacob, and Regina Shumaker.
1762, Aug.　19, Been, Elizabeth, and Thomas Smith Callaghane.
1762, April　18, Beere, Marg. and Nicholas Sonce.
1760, Jan.　2, Bees, Oliver, and Hannah Deeleplan.
1789, April　28, Beesey, Thomas, and Mary Alison.
1776, June　2, Beetey, Mary, and Christian Keen.
1797, July　16, Belin, Augustus, and Mary Alatta Hederick.
1760, Jan.　3, Bell, Amos, and Ann Milles.
1761, March 22, Bell, Ann, and John Roth.
1776, Sept.　26, Bell, Charles, and Ann Woodburn.
1777, July　31, Bell, Deborah, and Joseph Page.
1781, Aug.　16, Bell, Elizabeth, and Hugh Bay.
1776, Nov.　11, Bell, Francis, and Elizabeth Beard.
1789, July　6, Bell, Hanna, and Thomas Jones.
1777, Feb.　25, Bell, James, and Mary Forel.
1795, July　21, Bell, Jane, and Daniel Boyle.
1793, Sept.　23, Bell, Jane, and George Burdy.
1773, June　23, Bell, Jemima, and John Bell.
1792, Nov.　20, Bell, John, and Jane Kil Patrick.
1773, June　23, Bell, John, and Jemima Bell.
1791, May　25, Bell, John, and Mary Reed.
1779, May　8, Bell, Margaret, and Edward Pashal.
1799, March　7, Bell, Maria, and William Robeson.
1770, Feb.　18, Bell, Mary Carter, and Henry Bovee.
1797, Feb.　2, Bell, Mary, and William Camp.
1755, Nov.　30, Bell, Robert, and Barbara Hanan.
1757, Jan.　3, Bell, Susannah, and John Davis.
1765, Sept.　7, Bell, Thomas, and Rosannah Shirley.

1778, Sept. 17, Bell, William, and Jane Richardson.
1753, Sept. 28, Bell, William, and Martha Thomas.
1782, Feb.   24, Bell, William, and Mary Mattis.
1774, Nov.   2, Bellingee, John, and Hannah Bonsall.
1758, July   11, Bellinger, Sarah, and Joseph Ward.
1776, Dec.   10, Bellford, Sarah, and Robert Harper.
1751, Feb.   2, Bellows, Susanna, and Andrew Anderson.
1788, Dec.   28, Bellrose, Ann, and Claire Francis Reynault.
1756, Jan.   3, Belony, Jane, and John Hoare.
1760, Aug.   22, Bely, Diana, and John Willson.
1759, Oct.   15, Bely, Rebeccah, and Robert Bely.
1759, Oct.   15, Bely, Robert, and Rebeccah Bely.
1770, Nov.   16, Bely, Thomas, and Mary Hamilton.
1774, Feb.   28, Bemford, George, and Mary Dawson.
1781, Sept. 19, Bendel, Benjamin, and Mary Packstone.
1782, May   11, Bendor, Godfrid, and Sarah Raybold.
1757, Aug.   28, Beneth, Philip, and Jane Johnson.
1781, Dec.   25, Benhysel, Elizabeth, and Jonathan Newton.
1773, Oct.   30, Benington, Robert, and Elizabeth Rambo.
1775, Oct.   2, Benjamin, Rachel, and John Amos.
1768, May   16, Benjan, Estar, and Edward Diggin.
1798, July   28, Benler, Mary, and John Barton.
1799, Sept. 14, Bennet, Ann, and John Murray.
1725, Aug.   25, Bennet, Elizabeth, and John Carell.
1753, April 23, Bennet, Elizabeth, and Patrick Mahney.
1789, Aug.   12, Bennet, Elizabeth and Thomas Riley.
1799, June   9, Bennet, Henry, and Elizab. Loan.
1793, Dec.   10, Bennet, James, and Mary Laton.
1784, Dec.   20, Bennet, Jane, and Jacob Stillwell.
1779, July   15, Bennet, John, and Eleanor Davis.
1794, Jan.   16, Bennet, Thomas, and Mary Robertson.
1783, Jan.   17, Bennit, Richard, and Elsey Meany.
1779, May   31, Benney, James, and Jane Parker.
1769, Nov.   20, Benson, Benjamin, and Hannah Scotts.
1777, March   7, Benson, Isabella, and John Cammel.
1777, Nov.   2, Benson, John, and Abella Sharp.
1763, Dec.   6, Benson, Margaret, and Charles Prior.
1782, Feb.   11, Benton, Ely, and Arthur Baily.
1767, May   9, Berchman, John, and Caterine Cranin.
1766, Jan.   12, Bereshrim, Elizabeth, and George Peter Schneider.
1778, June   12, Berey, Benjamin, and Martha Balderick.
1764, Dec.   30, Berg, Theodorah, and Francis Coatam.
1767, Oct.   23, Bergan, Dennis, and Elizabeth Blake.
1785, Aug.   13, Bergen, Dennis, and Ann Billings.
1795, April 25, Bermike, George Charles, and Marget Shoemaker.
1793, Sept. 11, Bernard, Francis, and Zilla Vankirk.

1782, April   16, Bernet, Conrad, and Barbara Burck.
1782, June   15, Bernet, Elizabeth, and John Long.
1782, June   6, Bernhard, Ruben, and Sarah Power.
1800, Aug.   25, Berriman, Jacob, and Mary Scull.
1778, Feb.   19, Berry, Benjamin, and Elizabeth Feagon.
1765, Feb.   25, Berry, Catharine, and John Smith.
1795, March 12, Berry, Hannah, and Thomas Cummans.
1789, Nov.   13, Berry, James, and Cathrine Stiles.
1778, Sept.   6, Berry, John, and Eleanor Kane.
1770, Feb.   10, Berry, Mary, and Joseph Alston.
1784, May   5, Berry, Rachel, and Charles Connard.
1782, July   5, Berry, Robert, and Sarah Jones.
1758, March 23, Bery, Walter, and Margaret Connelly.
1777, Feb.   26, Berrys, John, and Sarah Dorwill.
1779, March   8, Bersin, Elizabeth, and Friederick Sharral.
1799, Nov.   14, Berthelson, Mary, and John Blaney.
1777, Feb.   27, Bertley, Samuel, and Grace Knoles.
1783, Nov.   10, Besayade, Lewis, and Margret Miller.
1779, Jan.   28, Best, Abraham, and Elizabeth Dixson.
1764, March   3, Best, Catharine, and Enoch Woodard.
1791, Dec.   22, Best, Elizabeth, and Robert Macbeth.
1772, July   6, Best, Mary, and James Donaldson.
1795, Sept.   8, Best, Robert, and Ann Rollstone.
1781, April   9, Bethell, Rosemund, and James White.
1767, Aug.   3, Bethel Ruth, and James Heartshorn.
1751, Dec.   24, Betridge, Martha, and John Dwight.
1774, May   30, Betsey and Zanche, (negroes.)
1778, Sept.   13, Bettersby, Isabel, and John Turner.
1754, April   6, Bettle, Josiah, and Elizabeth Richey.
1786, March 30, Betton, Sidney, and Michael Steed.
1792, May   22, Betzel, Mary, and Daniel McLawrin.
1793, July   11, Bevans, John, and Cathrine Wols.
1771, Oct.   6, Beveridge, David, and Mary Plant.
1758, June   24, Bewan, Tacy, and Thomas Prior.
1789, June   21, Beydinan, Daniel, and Elizabeth Stuart.
1784, May   3, Beymouth, Martha, and Thomas Channon.
1758, Aug.   13, Bezley, Edith, and John Dresley.
1782, April   5, Bicker, Catherine, and John Gibson.
1800, Jan.   30, Bickerton, Ann, and John Johnson.
1799, Oct.   5, Bickerton, Benjamin, and Ann Earonfighter.
1792, Aug.   11, Bickerton, Benjamin, and Susanna Reno.
1791, Nov.   10, Bickham, Hanna, and Thomas Sutton.
1787, April   5, Bickin, David, and Mary Underwood.
1789, Feb.   3, Bicknell, Robert, and Rachel Pepperly.
1752, Aug.   20, Biddason, Catharine, and William Gordon.
1782, Aug.   17, Biddes, Margret, and George Wintercast.

1793, Nov. 22, Biddle, Ann, and John Fimple.
1793, Nov. 25, Biddle, Barbara, and John Cole.
1793, Nov. 25, Biddle, John, and Keziah Cole.
1764, Oct.   7, Biddle, Sarah, and David Welch.
1778, Feb. 25, Bidgood, Joseph, and Ann Thomson.
1767, Nov. 21, Bigello, Warren, and Hannah Parsons.
1781, Nov.   8, Bigelow, Warren, and Elizabeth Casten.
1753, Aug. 25, Bigford, Richard, and Elizabeth Tire.
1759, April 13, Biggs, John, and Isabella Nilleaus.
1780, April 9, Biggs, Sarah, and John Rud.
1778, Nov. 26, Bigley, Thomas, and Eleanor Larkin.
1792, Dec. 20, Bignel, Helena, and Andrew Axley.
1781, Aug. 17, Bignell, Thomas, and Lenah Fister.
1767, Nov. 12, Biles, Jonathan, and Latitia Galbreath.
1796, Feb. 18, Biley, Charles, and Judith Jones.
1785, Aug. 13, Billings, Ann, and Dennis Bergen.
1789, Aug. 30, Bingham, Alexander, and Mary Richardson.
1782, July 16, Bingham, Charles, and Anne Green.
1791, Jan.   1, Bingaman, Rosanna, and Reinhold Stein.
1758, March 24, Binns, Elizabeth, and Sampson Handkins.
1778, April 25, Binns, Samuel, and Mary Fetton.
1777, April 23, Biran, Jean, and Lawrence Willson.
1799, Dec. 26, Birch, Elsa, and Hugh Durborow.
1778, May   22, Birch, Isaac, and Margaret Lang.
1788, March 10, Bird, Joseph, and Mary Phips.
1780, March 4, Bird, William, and Rachel Edwards.
1773, Dec. 25, Birdside, Mary, and Jacob Sink.
1794, May   2, Birmingham, James, and Rosetta Obrien.
1797, Feb. 12, Birmingham, Rosetta, and Thomas Austin.
1756, Aug.   7, Bishop, George, and Mary Hawse.
1800, Sept. 24, Bishop, John, and Mary Higgins.
1757, Oct. 13, Bishop, John, and Mary Marshall.
1794, March 9, Bishop, Mary, and James Heron.
1797, Feb. 16, Bishopberry, Hannah, and Christian Flowers.
1755, May   5, Bisnet, Catharine, and Richard Goheen.
1778, Jan. 22, Bittle, Barbarah, and Joshua Peyat.
1766, May   25, Bitterworth, William, and Rebeccah Glover.
1799, Dec.   4, Bittle, David, and Eliza Townsend.
1777, March 6, Black, Benjamin, and Elizabeth Clark.
1778, Feb.   5, Black, Donald, and Jane Dyer.
1775, Aug.   9, Black, Elizabeth, and Charles Scoby.
1766, April 15, Black, Ester, and James McGill.
1796, Dec. 24, Black, Furman, and Sarah Giberson.
1783, Sept. 28, Black, Hannah, and James Lowell.
1781, June 11, Black, Hannah, and John Thomas.
1781, Feb. 12, Black, Hannah, and Robert Wolson.
      20—VOL. VIII.

1800, Nov. 13, Black, Henry, and Nancy Kyle.
1781, March 27, Black, James, and Rachel James.
1775, March 13, Black, John, and Magdalena Hollsten.
1794, April 2, Black, Margery, and James Bagly.
1780, April 5, Black, Mary, and Hugh Garley.
1772, April 22, Black, Mary, and John Fanan.
1778, June 10, Black, Mary, and Thomas Sample.
1776, Sept. 8, Black, Thomas, and Jean Sweaney.
1777, Sept. 14, Blackburn, John, and Mary Donally.
1777, Jan. 31, Blackin, Ann, and John Ford.
1757, Nov. 23, Blacklidge, Thomas, and Mary Pitts.
1780, Sept. 20, Blackney, William, and Lea Richardson.
1774, Aug. 7, Blackwood, John Sibson, and Mary White.
1770, July 15, Bladerwik, Ann, and Thomas Nangle.
1779, June 13, Blair, Sarah, and James Duffy.
1791, Aug. 21, Blair, Sarah, and James Thomas.
1778, Dec. 2, Blair, William, and Elizabeth Riley.
1761, July 4, Blak, Margaret, and Joseph Duchee.
1783, Aug. 20, Blake, Charlotte, and Hugh McCaughan.
1767, Oct. 23, Blake, Elizabeth, and Dennis Bergan.
1781, July 30, Blake, Elizabeth, and John Steal.
1754, Jan. 21, Blake, John, and Sarah Eastlike.
1762, July 4, Blake, Margaret, and Joseph Duchee.
1793, Nov. 15, Blake, Susannah, and William Cooper.
1777, Nov. 17, Blake, William, and Elizabeth Fifer.
1788, Oct. 11, Blake, William, and Hester McCorkel.
1781, Aug. 17, Blakeney, Leah, and Hugh Dole.
1792, Nov. 11, Blakney, Martha, and James Laighan.
1766, Aug. 12, Blanch, Mary, and David Houlton.
1783, Oct. 30, Blandford, John, and Maria Millner.
1780, Aug. 7, Blane, John, and Elizabeth Russell.
1799, Nov. 14, Blaney, John, and Mary Berthelson.
1762, July 3, Blankfield, Mary, and John Poskett.
1790, July 12, Blankley, Elizabeth, and Edward Towls.
1774, March 19, Blankley, John, and Mary Pouge.
1772, Oct. 11, Blankly, Elizabeth, and Nicolas McCardy.
1782, Oct. 26, Blankny, John, and Sarah Patterson.
1794, May 1, Bleachington, Alice, and Samson Davis.
1778, Feb. 14, Blakewell, Catharine, and John Skelton.
1786, Nov. 30, Blenet, Rebecca, and John Fontallet.
1779, June 5, Bleney, John, and Hagaret Jones.
1760, June 24, Blesinger, Elizabeth, and William Jacob Knight.
1759, Sept. 26, Blewer, Joseph, and Sarah Lindenmeyer.
1769, June 21, Blewett, James, and Elizabeth Dawson.
1775, July 16, Blickley, Martha, and Joshua Wint.
1770, March 8, Blid, David, and Margarett Smith.

1793, July   30, Blight, Hannah, and William Hammond.
1775, Aug.   28, Blikley, George, and Catharine Richardson.
1792, Dec.   27, Block, John Christian, and Sarah Dibert.
1789, March 17, Bloom, Adam, and Mary Roads.
1788, July   15, Bloomey, John Nicholas, and Catharine Fulman.
1758, Aug.   30, Blowne, Jane, and Michael Thornton.
1780, Sept.   13, Bloxham, John, and Mary Renshammer.
1782, March 18, Blunt, Anne, and William Riley.
1784, June   6, Blunt, Arabella, and Joseph Hammond.
1796, March 22, Blunt, Thomas, and Arabella Maria.
1755, Dec.   29, Boardman, Jacob, and Mary Rambo.
1775, May   30, Boardman, Philip, and Mary Guy.
1763, Dec.   28, Boatman, Philip, and Burges Bromingham.
1776, May   5, Boberg, Nicholas, and Elizabeth Grubb.
1778, Feb.   25, Boddington, Timothy, and Margarett Anderson.
1800, March 24, Bodet, Sim, and Nancy Simony.
1783, Feb.   6, Boehnen, Mary, and John Leech.
1757, Sept.   28, Boggs, Alexander, and Margaret Loyd.
1783, Feb.   6, Boggs, Daniel, and Elizabeth Lentner.
1795, Feb.   7, Boggs, John, and Biddy Devine.
1755, Dec.   16, Boggs, Thomas, and Elizabeth Anderson.
1793, Feb.   3, Boggs, Walter, and Christina Mackensy.
1795, Nov.   6, Bogs, Jane, and David English.
1759, May   20, Bohanon, Margaretta, and John Booth.
1755, Nov.   20, Boice, Mary, and Jonathan Wormsley.
1795, Jan.   2, Boice, Sina, and George Adams.
1751, Dec.   8, Boid, Anne, and Neal Mac Farland.
1797, Dec.   21, Boid, Eleonore, and James Lougheed.
1779, March 1, Boil, Mary, and James Doil.
1794, Sept.   18, Bois, Thomas, and Jemimah Batton.
1781, April   7, Boland, Daniel, and Mary Jaw.
1790, May   17, Bolling, Charlotte, and William Rogers.
1790, Aug.   5, Bolston, Rachel, and Seth Mead.
1782, Aug.   1, Bolter, Catherine, and Adam Hover.
1772, May   2, Bolton, Ann, and Isaac Cooper.
1794, Dec.   15, Bolton, Edward, and Hannah Baron.
1795, March 24, Bolton, Joseph, and Hester James.
1778, April   15, Bombrgy, Ann, and George Wadsworth.
1787, March 31, Bond, Elizabeth, and Gabriel Hanger.
1751, April   14, Bond, Joseph, and Margaret Giffin.
1764, May   13, Bond, Susannah, and Thomas Groves.
1765, Oct.   10, Bones, Elizabeth, and James Bruce.
1786, May   18, Boneson, Sarah, and George Danehower.
1781, Jan.   30, Bonnel, Mary, and Nathias Jantz.
1777, April   23, Bonsall, Clement, and Ann Roberts.
1774, Nov.   2, Bonsall, Hannah, and John Bellingee.

1753, Oct.   28, Bonsall, John, and Febe Willcox.
1758, Dec.   7, Bonsall, Joseph, and Lydia Bonsall.
1758, Dec.   7, Bonsall, Lydia, and Joseph Bonsall.
1788, April   12, Bonsillis, Judith, and Rebecca Heritage.
1783, Aug.   4, Bonus, Mary, and Herbert Hayes.
1785, July   17, Book, Elizabeth, and George Hardin.
1758, April   23, Book, John, and Catharine Rose.
1768, March   1, Book, Joseph, and Hannah Rigin.
1765, Feb.   25, Booker, Thomas, and Catharine Paxton.
1774, Dec.   25, Boome, Susannah, and William Nichols.
1763, July   25, Boon, Ann, and Henry Link.
1779, Dec.   15, Boon, Barbara, and James McGiltin.
1798, May   28, Boon, Elizabeth, and Joshua Merric.
1775, July   23, Boon, Elizabeth, and Samuel Brad.
1788, May   16, Boon, Hannah, and Jacob Robinson.
1763, Aug.   25, Boon, Garret, and Ellenor Morton.
1785, Feb.   17, Boon, Lydia, and Caleb Davis.
1758, Aug.   7, Boon, Mary, and Morton Morton.
1794, Dec.   7, Boon, Nancy, and John Hewson.
1790, June   21, Boon, Rebecca, and Charles Willman.
1778, Feb.   12, Boon, Solomon, and Sarah Oldfield.
1764, Dec.   18, Boon, William, and Rebeccah Morton.
1782, March   14, Boone, Michael, and Jeany McPhearson.
1764, Nov.   21, Boore, Hannah, and Thomas Davis.
1755, Dec.   6, Boor, Peter, and Mary Hall.
1780, Feb.   7, Booth, Catharine, and John Curry.
1759, May   20, Booth, John, and Margaretta Bohanon.
1797, Nov.   30, Booth, Mary, and William Balk.
1777, Oct.   19, Bop, Catharine, and Philip Fries.
1780, May   10, Borden, Joseph, and Hannah Moore.
1794, May   17, Bordenave Pierre, and Mary Oliveres.
1782, Feb.   24, Bore, Mary, and Thomas Coock.
1766, Jan.   10, Bore, Sophy, and Jacob Caster.
1767, April   7, Boris, Thomas, and Margaret Meyers.
1794, Sept.   4, Borkloe, Mary, and Murdoch Degourd.
1770, Nov.   26, Bornett, Robert, and Hannah Richeson.
1790, April   29, Bornhill, Sara, and Zedechia Needham.
1792, Aug.   16, Borroder, Elizabeth, and Thomas Pritchett.
1781, Nov.   16, Borroughs, Mary, and Peter Starkhouse.
1799, Oct.   20, Bosken, Cathrine, and Andrew Wiesman.
1800, Sept.   21, Boslock, James, and Mary Piper.
1770, Nov.   26, Bossons, Benjamin, and Susannah York.
1797, March   19, Boston, Sarah, and Jerome Souchet.
1777, Dec.   17, Boswell, John, and Jean Clark.
1757, Jan.   13, Bothman, Ann Mary, and John Rose.
1782, April   29, Botler, Daniel, and Margret Marll.

1784, June   13, Botler, Rachel, and Archiles Parker.
1767, Oct.   5, Botteweth, Elizabeth, and Joseph Conneley.
1758, Nov.   6, Bottom, Thomas, and Anne Shilslich.
1751, Dec.   8, Boucher, Mary, and Bartholomew Murphy.
1781, March   6, Bouden, Mary, and Anthony Flory.
1757, March   3, Bouer, Mary, and Andrew Woard.
1754, Jan.   16, Bould, Elizabeth, and Richard Baily.
1796, April   19, Boullay, Lewis, and Sophia Delor.
1773, Dec.   16, Boulter, Patience, and Thomas Rees.
1783, Dec.   22, Boulter, Thomas, and Sarah Holmes.
1754, July   16, Bound, Elizabeth, and James Barton.
1779, July   31, Bourcheir, James, and Elizabeth Trippe.
1786, Oct.   18, Bourcher, James, and Sarah Dawson.
1764, Jan.   2, Bourne, William, and Elizabeth Harrison.
1797, June   22, Boutcher, Mary, and John Livezly.
1777, April   17, Boutton, Sarah, and John Kello.
1770, Feb.   18, Bovee, Henry, and Mary Carter Bell.
1763, Aug.   9, Bowd, Sarah, and Daniel Wilkinson.
1783, Jan.   9, Bowen, Elizabeth, and Edward Lithgon.
1777, Jan.   29, Bowen, Elizabeth, and James Perkins.
1786, Dec.   24, Bowen, Richard, and Catherine Mittear.
1778, ·Jan.   1, Bowen, Seth, and Ann Owen.
1756, Jan.   14, Bowen, William, and Elizabeth Cannaday.
1799, Jan.   17, Bowers, Ann, and John Lockart.
1795, Nov.   15, Bowers, Dorothy, and William Parker.
1780, Jan.   25, Bowers, Elizabeth, and George Ervin.
1796, Nov.   23, Bowers, Mary, and Luke Love.
1781, April   13, Bowers, Mary, and Michael Green.
1764, Dec.   27, Bowers, Susannah, and William Allen.
1794, Feb.   22, Bowers, William, and Rebecca Soonning.
1763, April   18, Bowes, Hugh, and Elizabeth Abercomby.
1799, Jan.   24, Bowhen, Cathrine, and Vance Deford.
1797, Feb.   25, Bowles, Margret, and John Middagh.
1779, March   3, Bowles, Rebecca, and Andrew Burkill.
1784, Dec.   5, Bowls, Elizabeth, and Joseph Taft.
1797, Nov.   13, Bowls, Jonathan, and Mary Wilson.
1770, May   5, Bowman, Charles, and Mary Nerry.
1777, May   20, Bowman, Elijah, and Margaret Sunney.
1759, April   29, Bowman, George, and Elizabeth Murin.
1766, May   21, Bowman, Roger, and Margret Johnson.
1759, July   12, Bown, Charles, and Rachel Heaton.
1793, Feb.   11, Bowren, Elizabeth, and Benjamin S·ag.
1756, June   1, Bowyer, Richard, and Margaret Standley.
1782, Oct.   12, Boxon, Elizabeth, and John McMasters.
1780, July   26, Boyce, Sarah, and Arthur Higgins.
1779, May   2, Boyce, William, and Catharine Conway.

1773, July   1, Boyd, Adam, and Catharine Jenkins.
1793, Dec.   13, Boyd, Andrew, and Cathrine McQuillin.
1779, June   14, Boyd, Elizabeth, and James Mayn.
1758, Aug.   12, Boyd, John, and Elizabeth Soluvan.
1779, May   16, Boyd, John, and Judith Linch.
1777, Nov.   23, Boyd, Margaret, and Robert Merret.
1779, July   7, Boyd, Mary, and William Coles.
1779, June   3, Boyd, Thomas, and Ann Shaw.
1794, April   8, Boyde, Robert, and Elizabeth Cahan.
1794, Sept.   1, Boyel, William, and Jane Hemphill.
1788, July   30, Boyer, Catharine, and William Isaac.
1796, Sept.   13, Boyer, Mary, and Peter Rose.
1767, Oct.   17, Boyes, Samuel, and Mary Granvill.
1795, July   21, Boyle, Daniel, and Jane Bell.
1792, April   29, Boyles, Rachel, and Jacob Staeb.
1791, Jan.   28, Boy, Sara, and George Esvin.
1768, April   16, Boys, Andrew, and Catharine Ranen.
1759, May   21, Boys, John, and Mertha Graham.
1775, July   23, Brad, Samuel, and Elizabeth Boon.
1772, Jan.   23, Bradford, James, and Ann Turner.
1765, Oct.   18, Bradford, Martha, and Samuel Hall.
1760, March 17, Bradford, Mary, and Sampson Harvey.
1773, Jan.   17, Bradgin, Christopher, and Elizabeth Ceim.
1787, July   7, Bradley, Andrew, and Sarah Dawson.
1764, June   10, Bradley, Ann, and Joseph Dixon.
1753, March 27, Bradley, Ann, and Michael Daniley.
1775, Aug.   6, Bradley, Michael, and Rebecca Tollman.
1772, April   22, Bradley, Patrick, and Elizabeth Moore.
1774, May   4, Bradley, Patrick, and Margaret Steward.
1781, Oct.   22, Bradley, Robert, and Mary Burkhard.
1792, March 29, Bradshaw, Mary, and John Antrim.
1755, Aug.   14, Bradsheer, Mary, and Abner Clark.
1799, Nov.   18, Brady, Edward, and Marget Laudenbrun,
1797, Nov.   25, Brady, John, and Mary Patterson.
1776, Dec.   2, Brady, Mary, and Edward Cary Rrown.
1773, April   26, Brady, Mary, and Richard Russel.
1767, May   25, Brady, Patrick, and Jean Forester.
1778, May   27, Brady, Richard, and Mary Hulings.
1778, Dec.   2, Braidy, Catharine, and George Crowder.
1779, Nov.   22, Braidy, John, and Mary McPharlin.
1779, Dec.   23, Braidy, Mary, and John Gibbons.
1779, Aug.   10, Brailey, Ann, and Peter Mines.
1758, April   3, Braine, Elizabeth, and John Meshow.
1797, Dec.   30, Brake, Mary, and Pierre Chanson.
1797, March 5, Braken, James, and Patience Mann.
1779, June   11, Brambridge, Margarett, and Peter Collins.

1754, July   14, Branagen, Mary, and William Erskin.
1779, May   13, Brand, Eve, and Henry Shrupp.
1773, Jan.   10, Brand, Hannah, and John Vanhusen.
1752, May   8, Brandley, Catharine, and Leonard Freidley.
1771, May   29, Brandwood, William, and Mary Hover.
1780, June   14, Branen, James, and Jane Danal.
1796, Jan,   1, Branin, Michael, and Barbara Evans.
1792, Jan.   1, Brannan, Edward, and Mary Pascal.
1759, Aug.   27, Brannel, Elizabeth, and Thomas Rannels.
1765, April   9, Brannon, Elizabeth, and John Williams.
1799, Nov.   14, Brannon, James, and Cathrine Dieter.
1750, Dec.   31, Brannon, John, and Sarah Whaley.
1792, July   5, Brannon, Thomas, and Phebe Worrel.
1766, Jan.   16, Brannun, Edward, and Margaret Collins.
1774, Oct.   19, Branon, Charles, and Catharine Kinnedy.
1755, Sept.   22, Branson, Day, and Christiana Anderson.
1788, Aug.   20, Branson, Jonathan, and Ann Scott.
1796, Oct.   4, Branson, Marget, and Richard Landon.
1776, Jan.   13, Branson, Samuel, and Mary Wood.
1787, Jan.   29, Branson, Sarah, and Jonathan Harker.
1764, Sept.   9, Brant, Barbarah, and John Baker.
1772, Dec.   30, Brant, Catharine, and Conrad Myerly.
1790, April   12, Brant, Elizabeth, and Adam Franks.
1765, Dec.   5, Brant, John, and Elizabeth Frazier.
1790, Sept.   26, Brant, Sara, and Gersham Johnson.
1792, Sept.   15, Brase, Joseph, and Nancy Barnes.
1756, June   5, Brath, Margarett, and Michael Everly.
1759, July   8, Braun, Margeth, and James Payne.
1778, Jan.   24, Braun, Mary, and David Jordan.
1762, May   24, Brawley, Patrick, and Sarah Tompon.
1782, Aug.   9, Bray, Anne, and Joseph Baldesgoi.
1778, Nov.   5, Bray, James, and Mary Fowler.
1779, Aug.   15, Bray, Mary, and Thomas Jackson.
1766, May   13, Brayman, Elizabeth, and Richard Kenton.
1780, March 16, Bredin, James, and Margaret Kean.
1783, March 16, Breedang, John, and Lydia Handling.
1759, Aug.   9, Breen, Hannah, and Jeremiah Bresson.
1779, Feb.   15, Brelsford, John, and Mary Davis.
1773, Aug.   1, Bremagum, John, and Margaret Donavan.
1770, Dec.   30, Bremen, Elizabeth, and Christopher Reindollar.
1778, April   2, Bremer, George, and Elizabeth Lang.
1779, May   20, Breneize, Wollentine, and Elizabeth Painter.
1764, Dec.   29, Brenneman, Jacob, and Rosannah Evans.
1770, Dec.   2, Bresler, Ann Mary, and Richard Griffieth.
1759, Aug.   9, Bresson, Jeremiah, and Hannah Breen.
1778, May   26, Brewer, Jonathan, and Margaret Atkinson.

1791, Jan.   23, Brewster, Jane, and Lewis Miers.
1756, June   29, Brian, Patrick, and Margaret Smith.
1757, May   12, Brian, Timothy, and Isabella Dickinson.
1800, June   4, Brice, Elizabeth, and Edmund Nowlan.
1777, March   10, Brickel, Sarah, and Thomas Carter.
1781, Dec.   20, Brickley, Catharine, and Thomas Wilson.
1778, Sept.   15, Bride, John, and Priscilla Monyon.
1779, Feb.   13, Bride, Peter, and Eleanor Welsh.
1799, Jan.   26, Bridge, Sarah, and William Miller.
1777, March   7, Briener, Jacob, and Susannah Rex.
1797, Nov.   28, Brige, Mary Ann, and John White.
1787, Oct.   3, Briggs, Anne Harriet, and Patric Toy.
1772, Dec.   23, Bright, Barneby, and Cornelia Ellems.
1755, July   2, Bright, Edward, and Elizabeth Tiley.
1796, July   4, Bright, Edward, and Sarah Drake.
1756, June   1, Bright, Elizabeth, and Joseph Granger.
1778, March   5, Bright, Francis, and James Adams.
1792, Jan.   3, Bright, James, and Elizabeth Robinson.
1786, Jan.   19, Bright, William, and Mary Roberts.
1754, Oct.   9, Brily, Mary, and Thomas Herkless.
1790, July   24, Brimmer, Lewis, and Marget Reppolle.
1758, July   20, Bringhurst, Hester, and Artur Broades.
1758, Dec.   10, Brinkeross, Catherine, and William Weldon.
1780, Sept.   19, Brinkley, Mary, and James Gregory.
1754, April   6, Brinnow, Desire, and Robert Sparkes.
1780, Dec.   24, Brintnell, Joseph, and Margaret Stevens.
1790, Nov.   22, Brion, Mary, and John Hanson.
1795, Feb.   4, Brislin, Biddy, and John McGonnigel.
1776, Feb.   26, Bristol, Elizabeth, and James Landey.
1767, Dec.   23, Brite, Amy, and Joseph Prewet.
1783, March   10, Britell, Adam, and Barbara Baar.
1753, May   30, Briten, Martha, and Daniel Gregory.
1787, May   17, Britt, Robert, and Marget Ward.
1780, Jan.   16, Britt, Sarah, and James Gibson.
1795, Feb.   22, Britt, Thomas, and Mary Price.
1781, Feb.   17, Brittain, Benjamin, and Mary Martingiel.
1795, Nov.   19, Brittingham, Lazarus, and Christiana Macall.
1796, Nov.   10, Brittle, Isaac, and Deborah Tyson.
1799, July   22, Brittle, Maria, and William Mason.
1782, April   9, Britton, Elizabeth, and Adam Hammer.
1789, Dec.   3, Britton, Hanna, and John Smith.
1755, May   26, Britton, Sarah, and John Stise.
1785, Feb.   17, Britton, Thomas, and Susannah Madders.
1794, Sept.   23, Britton, William, and Cathrine Smith.
1774, June   18, Broad, Margaret, and Samuel Oldham.
1754, Oct.   20, Broadas, William, and Margaret Jouse.

1767, Oct.   12, Broadbelt, James, and Elizabeth Burk.
1758, July   20, Broades, Artur, and Hester Bringhurst.
1759, July   15, Broades, Peter, and Sarah Wills.
1789, July   2, Broches, Christiana, and John Pratt.
1781, Oct.   23, Brock, Hannah, and John Inskip.
1781, Oct.   30, Brock. Mary, and Andrew Fritch.
1785, July   15, Brock, William, and Ann Hackett.
1757, June   16, Brockdon, Latitia, and Silas Prior.
1768, Nov.   13, Broderick, John, and Rose Obryon.
1782, June   22, Broderick, Richard, and Sarah Hegens.
1762, May   25, Brodrick, Charles, and Diana McColleg.
1794, Aug.   4, Brogen, Roger, and Elizabeth Warren.
1793, May   27, Brogen Sarah, and Lewis Moliere.
1753, Nov.   1, Broitnall, George, and Rebecca Keen.
1756, Sept.   30, Brokering, Mary Magdalene, and William Kasfe-
                    rath.
1781, July   11, Bromegeham, Peggy, and Moses Calley.
1767, July   23, Bromery, Caterin, and John Simon.
1763, Dec.   28, Bromingham, Burges, and Philip Boatman.
1780, July   6, Bromley, John, and Ann Morphy.
1754, July   17, Broock, Elizabeth, and William Moars.
1775, Aug.   19, Brook, Frances, and Thomas Ellison.
1777, Jan.   1, Brook, Martha, and James Erwin.
1757, May   27, Brookbank, Richard, and Mary Singleton.
1798, Nov.   26, Brookfield, Eleonore, and John Collis.
1773, Aug.   8, Brooks, Alice, and John Warner.
1762, Nov.   21, Brooks, Ann, and Israel Motts.
1756, Aug.   11, Brooks, David, and Mary Hunt.
1779, March 11, Brooks, Edward, and Mary Mackey.
1779, March 1, Brooks, Eleanor, and Daniel Driscall.
1796, May   1, Brooks, Elizabeth, and David Williams.
1781, Feb.   19, Brooks, Francis, and Catharine Adare.
1774, May   3, Brooks, Hannah, and Jesse Sturges.
1757, May   15, Brooks, Isaac, and Hannah Thomas.
1798, June   23, Brooks, John, and Marget Foulk.
1767, July   25, Brooks, Joseph, and Mary Wood.
1779, July   2, Brooks, Lawrence, and Christiana Hall.
1781, Jan.   25, Brooks, Lowes, and Ruben Odell.
1755, April   21, Brooks, Margaret, and William McMullin.
1777, May   30, Brooks, Mary, and Francis Jones.
1759, Nov.   25, Broocks, Nicholas, and Ann Cadmore.
1781, Dec.   4, Brooks, Rachel, and Andrew Edwards.
1781, Sept.   6, Brooks, Rebecca, and Antony Fannan.
1789, July   9, Brooks, Rebecca, and Samuel Coats.
1781, Nov.   5, Brooks, Sarah, and Andrew Clark.
1757, April   28, Brooks, Thomas, and Hannah Anderson.

1783, Jan.   30, Brooks, William, and Elizabeth Shanen.
1778, Dec.   13, Brooks, William, and Rosanna Dwyer.
1755, Aug.   12, Broom, Mary, and Joseph Guinup.
1778, Aug.   19, Broomfield, Rosetta, and Archibald McKendrick.
1792, Sept.   13, Bross, John, and Elizabeth Field.
1766, Dec.   24, Brouster, Mary, and William Horrey.
1795, Dec.   1, Browers, Susannah, and Joseph Cole.
1773, Feb.   7, Brown, Ann, and George Filliger.
1795, Jan.   20, Brown, Ann, and John Fisher.
1781, July   14, Brown, Catharine, and Daniel Strut.
1769, July   28, Brown, Catharine, and Thomas Brown.
1780, Aug.   15, Brown, Charles, and Sarah Burr.
1796, Feb.   4, Brown, Charlott, and William Niblock.
1777, July   2, Brown, Dina, and Abel Morgan.
1781, Sept.   8, Brown, David, and Mary Howell.
1776, Dec.   2, Brown, Edward Cary, and Mary Brady.
1776, Jan.   22, Brown, Eleanor, and Gold Crickmore.
1774, April   7, Brown, Eleanor, and William Davis.
1792, Sept.   22, Brown, Eliza, and Steven Champaine.
1774, Oct.   16, Brown, Elizabeth, and Gerrard Gilbons.
1784, July   7, Brown, Elizabeth, and John Peter Beauveau.
1759, Dec.   22, Brown, Elizabeth, and Joseph Scottom.
1759, Jan.   11, Brown, Elisabet, and Robert Patterson.
1778, March 12, Brown, Elizabeth, and Thomas Sparrow.
1785, Dec.   1, Brown, Elizabeth, and William Butler.
1790, Nov.   18, Brown, Emily, and John Brown.
1790, Jan.   31, Brown, George, and Cathrine Cope.
1754, April   21, Brown, George, and Sarah Toston.
1792, Nov.   29, Brown, George, and Sarah Winters.
1756, Nov.   18, Brown, George, and Susannah Harlin.
1755, Jan.   11, Brown, Gustavus, and Mary Harbeson.
1784, March 29, Brown, Gustavus, and Elinor Gardner.
1776, June   9, Brown, Isabella, and Conrod Hanse.
1758, Dec.   22, Brown, Jacob, and Elizabeth Bryan.
1777, Aug.   28, Brown, James, and Ann Miller.
1779, May   23, Brown, James, and Catherine Jost.
1754, July   21, Brown, James, and Catharine McDanel.
1776, March 21, Brown, James, and Elizabeth Potts.
1791, Dec.   31, Brown, James, and Marget Stevens.
1752, June   18, Brown, James, and Mary Muttit.
1778, Nov.   19, Brown, Jane, and Hugh Ougherson.
1762, Nov.   11, Brown, Jane, and Hugh Tomand.
1780, Jan.   18, Brown, Jane, and Isaac Humphrey.
1790, July   20, Brown, Jane, and Martin Grame.
1759, Aug.   11, Brown, John, and Elizabeth Hamper.
1793, April   5, Brown, John, and Elizabeth Wilson.

1790, Nov.   18, Brown, John, and Emily Brown.
1752, Nov.   18, Brown, John, and Hannah Lewis.
1792, Nov.   17, Brown, John, and Lucy Haggerty.
1774, June   13, Brown, John, and Mary Chambers.
1754, April 17, Brown, John, and Mary Right.
1777, Aug.   14, Brown, John, and Sarah Slack.
1794, Dec.   18, Brown, Joseph, and Cathrine Gooden.
1763, Nov.   11, Brown, Joseph, and Mary Baron.
1778, June   16, Brown, Joseph, and Mary Home.
1754, Sept. 16, Brown, Letishey, and Samuel McConall.
1778, March 27, Brown, Levaney, and James Allan.
1785, March 22, Brown, Margaret, and Philip Scheimer.
1791, Jan.   9, Brown, Marget, and Christopher Pidgeon.
1794, Oct.   29, Brown, Marget, and Henry Allen Moore.
1797, Dec.   12, Brown, Margret, and Daniel Dietz.
1778, Aug.   12, Brown, Mary, and Ambrose Croker.
1795, Aug.   2, Brown, Mary, and Christopher Young.
1785, Aug.   11, Brown, Mary, and George Harmen.
1793, Aug.   10, Brown, Mary, and Henry Head.
1754, July   7, Brown, Mary, and Isaac Williams.
1790, Sept. 10, Brown, Mary, and James Goodall.
1757, May   18, Brown, Mary, and John Shuteer.
1759, March 21, Brown, Mary, and Samuel Cumberbitch.
1792, April   1, Brown, Michael, and Mary England.
1780, April   4, Brown, Nathaniel, and Rachel Shafer.
1784, July   25, Brown, Offris, and Elizabeth Crawford.
1752, July   13, Brown, Peter, and Sarah Farmer.
1798, June   19, Brown, Rachel, and James Shellburn.
1782, Dec.   14, Brown, Richard Clark Ellis, and Catherine Amos.
1799, Sept. 30, Brown, Samuel, and Mary Flyng.
1783, Jan.   7, Brown, Samuel Montgomery, and Mary Turney.
1793, Dec.   27, Brown, Samuel, and Susannah Cathrine Sinclair.
1796, Feb.   4, Brown, Sarah, and Charles Martin.
1755, Aug.   11, Brown, Sarah, and George Williams.
1794, Feb.   17, Brown, Sarah, and John Anderson.
1797, July   29, Brown, Sarah, and Thomas Phenix.
1790, May   23, Brown, Susanna, and Jacob Stinsman.
1794, Aug.   18, Brown, Susanna, and Patric Gallenogh.
1769, July   28, Brown, Thomas, and Catharine Brown.
1771, June   13, Brown, Thomas, and Mary Dun.
1778, Nov.   1, Brown, Thomas Pendegrass, and Ann Crawford.
1771, Feb.   13, Brown, Thustan, and Sarah Shanklin.
1759, July   30, Brown, William, and Catharine Patterson.
1766, March 17, Brown, William, and Catherine Richards.
1798, Aug.   2, Brown, William, and Elizab. Mitchel.
1791, Oct.   25, Brown, William, and Mary Matheaus.

1790, Oct. 25, Brown, William, and Marget Painter.
1786, April 21, Brown, William, and Mary Church.
1800, Sept. 4, Brown, William, and Rebecca Hawkins.
1779, June 8, Brown, William, and Sophia Hornick.
1758, March 25, Brownfield, Hannah, and David Hall.
1757, Aug. 17, Brownin, Elizabéth, and Richard Airs.
1776, Feb. 19, Brownley, John, and Phoebe Barnwell.
1765, Oct. 10, Bruce, James, and Elizabeth Bones.
1797, Dec. 28, Bruce, John, and Mary Cox.
1782, Jan. 26, Bruce, John, and Rachel Death.
1783, April 4, Bruce, Rachel, and John Haselton.
1788, Aug. 9, Bruce, Thomas, and Lydia Ireland.
1768, June 6, Bruchhauser, John Adam, and Ann Mary Houchin.
1797, June 19, Bruer, Ann, and Henrie Vessels.
1783, Jan. 16, Brunstrom, John Andrew, and Elizabeth Hassel-
                 ber.
1788, Dec. 21, Brush, Vashty, and Samuel Rinker.
1763, Oct. 29, Bruster, Samuel, and Rebecca Tabor.
1778, Dec. 27, Bryan, Barbarah, and Samuel Repman.
1794, Aug. 26, Bryan, Cathrine, and John Campbell.
1796, Aug. 2, Bryan, Cathrine, and William Harvey.
1777, May 23, Bryan, Elizabeth, and George McAllister.
1758, Dec. 22, Bryan, Elizabeth, and Jacob Brown.
1799, April 14, Bryan, James, and Cathrine Detto.
1774, Aug. 27, Bryan, Rebecca, and Samuel Tingle.
1773, April 13, Bryan, Sarah, and Peter Peters.
1777, May 5, Bryant, Elizabeth, and Richard Salthouse.
1777, June 11, Bryant, Mary, and William Duelley.
1758, Sept. 25, Bryant, Thomas, and Mary Cook.
1779, April 14, Bryce, John, and Agnes Richards.
1752, July 26, Bryemt, Rose, and Peter Dal.
1797, Sept. 23, Brynes, William, and Maria Mollicom.
1774, Feb. 23, Bryon, Mary, and James Bartlet.
1797, Dec. 6, Bucanan, Violetta, and Thomas Harrison.
1795, April 6, Buchaanan, George, and Mary Macbride.
1799, June 20, Buchanan, Cathrine, and Daniel Sutleffe.
1756, Dec. 24, Buchanan, John, and Uverrella Rakes.
1767, March 20, Buchanan, William, and Rachel Harmon.
1786, Jan. 1, Buchannan, John, and Mary McNeal.
1782, Feb. 28, Buchs, Cely, and Benjamin Philips, (negroes.)
1792, Oct. 16, Buchs, Maria, and Joseph Sutherland.
1790, July 1, Buck, Armeley, and John Nicholson.
1775, May 6, Buck, Isaac, and Hannah Hick.
1776, Oct. 3, Buckas, Godfrey, and Eve Steinfortz.
1778, July 31, Bucker, Mary, and Lewis Runner.
1790, May 24, Buckingham, John, and Jane Wilson.

1778, June   2, Buckly, John, and Rebecca Shonk.
1796, Sept.   10, Buckman, Hannah, and William Linton.
1751, Jan.   23, Buckstone, Richard, and Rachel Cotsee.
1799, May   1, Bud, Elizabeth, and Jacob Cruse.
1794, Sept.   17, Budd, Joseph, and Rachel Cox.
1800, June   4, Budd, Mary, and Charles Reed.
1779, May   12, Budden, Ann, and Joseph Golding.
1778, Feb.   12, Budden, Elizabeth, and James Willson, (Capt. 49
                   Reg⁺ of foot.)
1796, Oct.   7, Budden, Richard, and Margret Davis.
1751, June   23, Budman, Ulric, and Juliana Shitzen.
1766, April   23, Buffington, Mary, and John Snow.
1777, Sept.   18, Buharon, James, and Margaret Ford.
1776, March   11, Bukerin, Margaret, and Salmo Miland.
1757, Sept.   1, Bullard, Frances, and John Welch.
1759, July   22, Bultzer, William, and Catharine Liddineau.
1779, May   6, Buken, Charles, and Phœbe Wells, (free negroes.)
1784, Dec.   16, Bunker, Samuel, and Rachel Illingsworth.
1795, March   7, Bunnerman, Daniel, and Margret Swain.
1778, March   11, Bunten, Edward, and Elizabeth Ellis.
1780, July   30, Buntin, John, and Margaret Price.
1756, Jan.   6, Bunting, John, and Ann Saunders.
1760, Feb.   14, Burch, Mary, and John Marriage.
1785, Nov.   3, Burchall, James, and Elizabeth Wharence.
1761, Feb.   10, Burchard, Margaret, and George Seisinger.
1765, Jan.   22, Burchard, Mariah, and Ludowick Agricola.
1796, Oct.   5, Burchet, Ann, and Anthony Cane.
1770, Jan.   10, Burchet, Anne, and John Dick.
1794, July   13, Burchett, Ann, and Martin Conflatin.
1782, April   16, Burck, Barbara, and Conrad Bernet.
1758, May   27, Burckart William, and Catharine Sherin.
1792, Jan.   3, Burden, Joseph, and Mary Alexander.
1780, March   9, Burden, Pemas, and Susannah Johnson.
1797, Jan.   15, Burdon, Elizabeth, and Johnah Morss.
1793, Sept.   23, Burdy, George, and Jane Bell.
1759, Sept.   24, Bure, John, and Elizabeth Lantong.
1754, March   18, Burgain, Patrick, and Elizabeth English.
1781, March   26, Burgers, Joseph, and Dolly Canady.
1778, June   15, Burgess, Jean, and John Rowlerd.
1784, Jan.   16, Burgiss, Thomas, and Sophia Jones.
1798, Feb.   26, Burgoine, Margery, and Isaac Gourdon.
1776, Sept.   22, Burk, Ann, and Gideon Salmon.
1753, Dec.   26, Burk, Ann, and James Lamb.
1792, Jan.   1, Burk, David, and Elizabeth Gibbet.
1776, Dec.   2, Burk, Eleanor, and John Riley.
1767, Oct.   10, Burk, Elizabeth, and James Broadbelt.

1755, April 20, Burk, Hannah, and Richard Davis.
1776, Feb. 15, Burk, Jane, and James Lines.
1777, May 23, Burk, John, and Eleanor Leary.
1800, May 18, Burk, John, and Jane Henry.
1777, July 26, Burk, Mary, and John McCann.
1761, July 31, Burk, Mary, and Joseph Roberts.
1778, Aug. 12, Burk, Mary, and Robert Porter.
1779, April 17, Burk, Richard, and Ann Barbara Gorman.
1754, Dec. 14, Burk, Sarah, and John Campbell.
1798, Nov. 14, Burk, Thomas, and Sarah Shaw.
1799, July 18, Burke, Jane, and William Lowry.
1792, Dec. 14, Burke, Mary, and Jacob Anthony Petit Jean.
1797, Aug. 31, Burke, Nancy, and Patrick Ford.
1795, Jan. 7, Burke, William, and Susannah Sergeant.
1786, Dec. 19, Burket, Mary, and Oliver Hunter.
1780, June 20, Burkett, Phoebe, and Benjamin Millet.
1781, Oct. 22, Burkhard, Mary, and Robert Bradley.
1781, July 30, Burkhard, Peter, and Elizabeth Martin.
1779, March 3, Burkill, Andrew, and Rebecca Bowles.
1780, July 13, Burklow, Samuel, and Catherine Dickinson.
1766, Feb. 28, Burley, Elizabeth, and William Wild.
1757, Feb. 17, Burly, Robert, and Elizabeth McGee.
1781, Aug. 27, Burnam, Mary, and Samuel Alford.
1796, July 10, Burnell, Samuel, and Cathrine Oswald.
1783, April 10, Burnet, Elizabeth, and James Jordan.
1794, Dec. 9, Burnet, George, and Mary Needham.
1765, Dec. 11, Burnet, Henry, and Mary Reily.
1761, Dec. 29, Burnett, Susannah, and John Simson.
1778, Nov. 4, Burn, Andrew, and Sarah Dust.
1778, Oct. 13, Burn, Joshua, and Hannah Kennedy.
1779, June 11, Burn, Judith, and John Williams.
1799, Oct. 8, Burn, Patric, and Mary Shoemaker.
1787, May 26, Burn, Thomas, and Mary Coddle.
1795, July 19, Burns, Anthony, and Marget Stephen.
1797, March 23, Burns, Arthur, and Elizab. Killroy.
1777, March 2, Burns, Grace, and George Givens.
1783, Sept. 16, Burns, Jacob, and Ruth Metton.
1778, Feb. 4, Burns, Maurice, and Judith Holland.
1782, Aug. 27, Burns, Morris, and Eleonor McGill.
1777, Dec. 7, Burns, Samuel, and Ann Gray.
1777, May 12, Burns, Sarah, and Thomas Simson.
1793, July 3, Burns, William, and Ann Stitchfield.
1800, Oct. 6, Burnside, William, and Margret Clements.
1780, Aug. 15, Burr, Sarah, and Charles Brown.
1783, July 15, Burridge, Robert, and Elizabeth Pennington.
1777, July 11, Burris, Margaret, and John Thomson.

1758, Dec.   6, Burrough, Debra, and Joseph Armstrong.
1788, Oct.   2, Burroughs, Rebecca, and Joseph Ellis.
1785, Nov.   18, Burrows, John, and Ann Vansise.
1785, June   14, Burrows, Letitia, and Samuel Franklin.
1779, Nov.   18, Burrows, Martha, and Gustavus Risberg.
1785, Jan.   24, Burteloe, Susannah, and Jesse Hood.
1770, Nov.   26, Burton, Elizabeth, and Thomas Redman.
1795, May   17, Burton, George, and Cathrine Mahoney.
1778, April   12, Burton, Mary, and William Graham.
1790, Aug.   15, Burton, Sara, and John Lamb.
1778, March   29, Burton, William, and Ann Leine.
1754, Aug.   22, Busby, Abigail, and David Rose.
1762, Aug.   3, Buscark, Ann, and John Fairweather.
1761, Aug.   3, Buseark, Ann, and John Fairweather.
1771, Jan.   26, Busfield, Joseph, and Elizabeth Powell.
1769, March   27, Bush, Elizabeth, and Samuel Quat.
1793, April   —, Bush, Margret, and Jesse Turner.
1777, July   27, Bush, Sarah, and Peter Mack.
1770, Aug.   23, Bushard Anne, and John Bartlet.
1777, April   29, Bushway, Catharine, and John Warner.
1779, March   15, Butey, Jeremiah, and Mary Duck.
1777, Sept.   22, Butler, Andrew, and Sarah Wheeler.
1755, April   7, Butler, Anthony, and Barbary Miller.
1795, Sept.   26, Butler, Cathrine, and Henry Crottey.
1793, May   19, Butler, Charles Francis, and Elizabeth Martin.
1786, Aug.   20, Butler, Daniel, and Rebecca Vandigrest.
1778, Feb.   5, Butler, Elizabeth, and Thomas Dixon.
1776, May   12, Butler, Else, and Samuel More.
1758, Jan.   8, Butler, Francis, and Daniel Wigmore.
1753, July   7, Butler, Grace, and Isaac Fowler.
1772, Sept.   9, Butler, John, and Debora Douglas.
1757, June   10, Buttler, John, and Martha Coleman.
1774, Feb.   24, Butler, John, and Mary McLaughlin.
1778, Nov.   1, Butler, John, and Susannah Rose.
1779, July   7, Butter, Lydia, and Michael Thomson.
1773, June   7, Butler, Margaret, and Calop Cannady.
1778, Nov.   4, Butler, Margaret, and Stephen Reed.
1773, Jan.   3, Butler, Mary, and John Ellems.
1766, May   24, Butler, Peter, and Ann Noll.
1795, June   24, Butler, Priscilla, and Richard Hall.
1799, Dec.   1, Butler, Sarah, and John Welldon.
1798, Nov.   9, Butler, Sarah, and Joseph Wallace.
1785, Dec.   1, Butler, William, and Elizabeth Brown.
1769, Nov.   30, Butterfield Anne, and Joseph Gordon.
1772, Sept.   17, Butterworth, Ann, and Aaron Huett.
1755, April   8, Butterworth, Isaac, and Mercy Fouler.

1770, Oct.   15, Butterworth, James, and Debora Cox.
1776, Aug.   13, Butterworth, Mary, and Michael Hess.
1792, May   15, Butterworth, Moses, and Abigail Down.
1799, June   27, Button, Marget, and John White.
1792, Nov.   12, Buuker, Thomas, and Jane Stevenson.
1778, Jan.   3, Byan, Elizabeth, and Philip Thomas.
1779, March 11, Byar, Juliana, and John Shaw.
1781, Sept.   20, Byberry, Elizabeth, and David Johnson.
1759, Aug.   18, Bye, James, and Jeney Strafford.
1760, July   19, Bylith, Thomas, and Sarah Green.
1773, Sept.   28, Bywater, Elizabeth, and Nathaniel Hunter.
1795, Jan.   1, Cabellaw, Hannah, and Mathias Weaver.
1777, March 23, Cable, John, and Sarah Hindricks.
1796, April   23, Cacharin, Patric, and Gracey McNeal.
1764, Oct.   21, Cachey, Samuel, and Mary Thomson.
1777, July   31, Cadju and Ammey, (negroes.)
1759, Nov.   25, Cadmore, Ann, and Nicholas Broocks.
1794, April   8, Cahan, Elizabeth, and Robert Boyde.
1790, Dec.   5, Cahil, Debora, and James Greenough.
1776, Aug.   8, Cahill, David, and Sarah Archer.
1780, Feb.   8, Cahill, Mary, and John Hughes.
1755, Feb.   24, Cahoon, Thomas, and Mary George.
1791, May   21, Caire, James, and Sara Fifer.
1790, Oct.   23, Cain, John, and Ann White.
1788, Feb.   2, Cain, John, and Sarah Jacobs.
1781, March 23, Cain, Patrick, and Mary Collins.
1796, Aug.   3, Cain, Peter, and Mary Ellis.
1754, Nov.   17, Caisarin, Catharine, and Michael Rosh.
1791, Aug.   21, Cake, Mary, and Thomas Hazelton.
1799, Sept.   11, Calder, Jane, and John Merchant.
1780, July   30, Calder, Mary, and Hogsteed Hacker.
1791, Jan.   9, Caldovi, Elizabeth, and John Quest.
1778, Aug.   3, Caldwell, Charles, and Jane Woods.
1795, Nov.   28, Caldwell, Elizabeth, and James Scott.
1797, Feb.   12, Caldwell, Elizabeth, and Samuel Gregg.
1791, Jan.   28, Caldwell, James, and Elizabeth Riley.
1796, Sept.   4, Caldwell, Marget, and Robert Clendennan.
1779, May   20, Caldwell, Mary, and John McKinley.
1789, May   31, Cale, Ann, and Adam Geyry.
1792, Nov.   6, Calender, Mary, and John Terry.
1792, July   1, Calfrey, Joseph, and Elenore Harvey.
1765, April   15, Calfry, John, and Elizabeth Coff.
1791, April   23, Calhoon, Elizabeth, and John Morgan.
1756, July   24, Calhoone, Mary, and Humphrey Smith.
1788, May   8, Callagh, Charles, and Catharine Neal.
1761, Aug.   3, Callaghan, Edward, and Elizabeth Parker.

1772, Feb.   12, Callaghan, Edward, and Hannah Richards.
1778, Aug.   2, Callaghan, Hannah, and John McIntire.
1762, Aug.   19, Callaghane, Thomas Smith, and Elizabeth Been.
1795, Oct.   25, Callahan, Hugh, and Hannah Sims.
1760, April   12, Callahen, Mary, and Daniel Lely.
1788, Dec.   15, Callan, French, and Elizabeth Woods.
1757, June   26, Calley, Catharine, and Edward Harris.
1776, Nov.   29, Calley, James, and Margaret Adams.
1781, July   11, Calley, Moses, and Peggy Bromegeham.
1765, April   30, Calley, ———, and Susannah Ellis.
1776, Sept.   15, Callicken, George, and Margaret Abram.
1761, April   13, Calliord, Ruth, and Thomas Wachon.
1780, April   12, Calloughorn, Daniel, and Catharine Creeden.
1798, March   22, Callum, Andrew, and Mary Stuart.
1778, March   15, Callwell, Sarah, and Thomas McDonough.
1757, Oct.   20, Cally, Mary, and John Lees.
1754, April   10, Cally, Patrick, and Mary Theeth.
1774, Oct.   12, Calveley, William, and Elizabeth Reeve.
1778, June   2, Calverley, William, and Mary McMurran.
1759, July   4, Calyard, Rebecca, and Henry Miller.
1781, Feb.   17, Cambel, Patty, and George Hinderson.
1799, Nov.   17, Cambel, William, and Mary Soeny.
1775, July   2, Cambridge, Elizabeth, and Nathaniel Deverell.
1797, April   28, Cambridge, William, and Sarah Hallick.
1759, March   18, Cambrow, Margaret, and John Niccol.
1751, March   30, C—mel, Margareta, and Thomas Hall.
1774, March   6, Camel, Mary, and John Rogers.
1777, April   29, Cameran, Alexander, and Jean Thomson.
1785, Aug.   28, Cameron, Ann, and Jeremiah Fox.
1791, Feb.   3, Cameron, John, and Delinda Haney.
1750, Dec.   31, Cameron, John, and Margareta Hamilton.
1782, Dec.   24, Cameron, Robert, and Mary Wilcox.
1778, March   7, Cammel, John, and Isabella Benson.
1773, Jan.   20, Camp, Debora, and William Ottwell.
1786, Sept.   25, Camp, Hannah, and George Howard.
1797, Jan.   2, Camp, William, and Mary Bell.
1795, Feb.   22, Campbell, Agnew, and Ann Alexander.
1757, June   29, Campbell, Ann, and Barney Murphy.
1779, May   31, Campbell, Ann, and James Miller.
1787, Nov.   26, Campbell, Anne, and James Plant.
1770, April   9, Campbel, Catharine, and Henry Kreps.
1781, April   2, Campbell, Catharine, and John Collins.
1778, June   13, Campbell, Catharine, and Thomas Silbey.
1781, Feb.   22, Campbell, Catharine, and William George.
1794, Dec.   14, Campbell, Charles, and Elizabeth Justis.
1752, Oct.   4, Campbell, David, and Elizabeth Lawrence.

1778, March 28, Campbell, Duncan, and Margaret Hall.
1778, Nov.   22, Campbell, Elizabeth, and James Kavanagh.
1795, Jan.   21, Campbell, Elizabeth, and John McMullen.
1770, Dec.   18, Campbell, George, and Mary Cavert.
1760, Jan.   30, Campbell, Hugh, and Mary Hannah.
1779, July   11, Campbell, James, and Bridget Smith.
1780, Aug.   5, Campbell, Jane, and Michael Joys.
1794, Aug.   26, Campbell, John, and Catherine Bryan.
1796, Sept.   15, Campbell, John D., and Christiana McCormick.
1777, Nov.   25, Campbell, John, and Jane Willson.
1795, May   24, Campbell, John, and Mary Cooper.
1796, June   18, Campbell, John, and Margret Oliver.
1778, Nov.   25, Campbell, John, and Mary Kerr.
1757, May   28, Campbell, John, and Mary Reinhart.
1754, Dec.   14, Campbell, John, and Sarah Burk.
1777, April   21, Campbell, Joseph, and Elizabeth Clodier.
1790, Sept.   4, Campbell, Lawrence, and Jane Doherty.
1780, Jan.   2, Campbell, Margaret, and Francis Galen.
1775, Jan.   24, Campbell, Margaret, and Gabriel Willson.
1791, Dec.   1, Campbell, Margret, and Barnabas Downy.
1783, April   6, Campbell, Mary, and Charles Hamilton.
1785, Feb.   9, Campbell, Mary, and Charles Holland.
1795, Sept.   20, Campbell, Mary, and Henry Lane.
1778, Nov.   15, Campbell, Mary, and Patrick Dixson.
1779, May   8, Campbell, Mary, and Robert Connelly.
1790, July   13, Campbell, Patric, and Agnes Hunter.
1779, July   19, Campbell, Philip Shen, and Hannah Newmen.
1784, Nov.   30, Campbell, Richard, and Catherine Reily.
1794, July   23, Campbell, Samuel, and Isabella McRaa.
1779, June   1, Campbell, Sarah, and Patrick Linch.
1787, Oct.   16, Campbell, Sucky, and Patric Madan.
1796, Aug.   7, Campbell, Thomas, and Ann Welsh.
1791, Feb.   24, Campbell, William, and Susanna Mac Farlane.
1778, Feb.   3, Can, Mary, and Hugh Miller.
1767, March 31, Canaday, Elizabeth, and Hugh Hugh.
1776, Dec.   30, Canaday, William, and Eleanor Marshall.
1781, March 26, Canady, Dolly, and Joseph Burgers.
1781, June   18, Canady, Mary, and Jeremiah Chandler.
1796, Oct.   5. Cane, Anthony, and Ann Burchet.
1777, April   28, Cane, Christiana, and Thomas West.
1789, April   30, Cane, Hugh, and Hope Wilson.
1795, Aug.   —, Canely, William, and Ann Tribit.
1772, Sept.   23, Canig, Mary, and John Michael Price.
1796, April   26, Canna, Darby, and Cathrine McCormick.
1756, Jan.   14, Cannaday, Elizabeth, and William Bowen.
1755, Oct.   22, Cannaday, James, and Rachel Baker.

1773, June   7, Cannady, Calop, and Margaret Butler.
1777, July   10, Cannady, Elizabeth, and Robert Etherington.
1758, Jan.   8, Cannard, Mary, and Joseph Hill.
1753, Aug.   27, Canne, Ann, and William Tallot.
1770, Sept.   23, Cannon, Isaac, and Mary Bathurst.
1791, Aug.   16, Cannon, James, and Cathrine Worrels.
1795, July   20, Cannon, James, and Elizabeth Davis.
1793, Nov.   25, Cannon, Thomas, and Ann Dougherty.
1778, Feb.   27, Cannon, Thomas, and Margaret Tippen.
1771, Sept.   9, Cannor, Michael, and Eleanor Harben.
1782, Aug.   22, Canon, Alice, and David Wilder.
1793, April   7, Canzler, Baltes, and Margret Hazen.
1758, Oct.   10, Cap, Peter, and Mary Bankson.
1780, Sept.   26, Cape, Abigail, and Barnet Swiler.
1790, Jan.   29, Cape, Comfort, and William Stuart.
1778, Aug.   15, Capell, Sarah, and William Hannon.
1789, March 26, Cappas, Peter, and Eda Lord.
1777, March 2, Carby, Josiah, and Margaret Child.
1761, Sept.   21, Care, Henry, and Martha Gonney.
1762, Sept.   21, Care, Henry, and Martha Gonney.
1798, Aug.   25, Carrell, John, and Elizabeth Bennet.
1751, Oct.   13, Cargen, Oenn, and Margaret Fagleline.
1782, March 27, Caril, Mary, and Samuel Oaksman.
1782, July   30, Carill, Owen, and Anne Conrad.
1778, June   4, Carleton, William, and Catharine Mason.
1789, April   24, Carley, Joseph, and Rebecca Toy.
1778, May   30, Carliton, Richard, and Margaret Jones.
1784, March 22, Carman, Richard, and Sarah Hudson.
1782, July   25, Carmeton, Elizabeth, and William Nixon.
1783, Oct.   21, Carmichael, Elizabeth, and Alexander Jemmison.
1751, July   22, Carnack, John, and Sarah Ellisson.
1770, Oct.   1, Carnaghan, John, and Elizabeth Maclean.
1755, Dec.   26, Carnes, Margareth, and William Williams.
1790, Sept.   10, Carnes, Matthias, and Rachel Avis.
1799, May   6, Carnes, Thomas, and Elizab. McCally.
1794, May   19, Carney, Arthur, and Cathrine Huchill.
1773, March 1, Carney, Hugh, and Sarah Stevens.
1788, Nov.   16, Carney, James, and Ann Story.
1792, Nov.   12, Carney, Jane, and John Shields.
1792, Nov.   28, Carney, John, and Sarah McGill.
1795, Nov.   21, Carney, Mary Ann, and Thomas Crawford.
1770, Sept.   1, Carney, Patrick, and Elizabeth North.
1794, Sept.   9, Carney, Sarah, and David Cassie.
1794, Sept.   11, Carney, Sarah, and Hugh Ferguson.
1772, Feb.   18, Carney, Susannah, and William Carroll.
1781, June   18, Carol, James, and Margaret Smith.

1799, April 28, Caroll, Joseph, and Elizab. Hays.
1788, April 10, Carpenter, Esther, and George Entricken.
1795, Aug. 7, Carpenter, George, and Nancy Hess.
1776, Oct. 21, Carpenter, Mary, and John Clue.
1790, May 9, Carpenter, Phebe, and Abraham Easton.
1795, Sept. 6, Carpenter, Tobias, and Chloe Clendennan.
1754, Nov. 16, Carr, Ann, and Alexander Porry.
1777, March 6, Carr, Ann, and David Clark.
1787, Feb. 9, Carr, Anne, and Owen Melean.
1782, June 8, Carr, Benjamin, and Mary Ross.
1753, Aug. 18, Carr, Catharine, and Leonard Martin.
1773, Sept. 12, Carr, Debora, and David Lockard.
1777, Oct. 20, Carr, Dorothy, and Francis Carr.
1782, March 18, Carr, Dorothy, and George Coulter.
1792, March 31, Carr, Elizabeth, and Gideon Prior.
1777, Oct. 20, Carr, Francis, and Dorothy Carr.
1766, Feb. 24, Carr, Jeane, and William Sidden.
1793, Sept. 20, Carr, John, and Mary Collins.
1796, March 27, Carr, Joseph, and Rachel Baughman.
1795, Jan. 24, Carr, Mary, and Archibald Murray.
1770, Jan. 6, Carr, Mary, and James Young.
1798, June 9, Carr, Michael, and Sarah McGenly.
1755, Oct. 18, Carr, Michael, and Susanna Smith.
1773, July 19, Carr, Patrick, and Mary Foreman.
1795, April 12, Carr, Patric, and Mary Hogan.
1771, Dec. 8, Carr, Peter, and Elizabeth Owen.
1759, May 29, Carr, Robert, and Mary Haert.
1788, Jan. 29, Carr, Samuel, and Frances Salt.
1778, Oct. 19, Carral, Mary, and Oliver Hunter.
1777, Jan. 13, Carrie, Catharine, and Franklin Read.
1791, Nov. 13, Carrigan, Mary, and Charles Dominick.
1794, March 10, Carrol, Ann, and John McCarran.
1774, Oct. 27, Carrol, Ann, and Roger McGeary.
1770, Dec. 11, Carroll, Daniel, and Rosannah Pinshedler.
1772, Nov. 12, Carroll, Margaret, and John Dawson.
1772, Feb. 18, Carroll, William, and Susannah Carney.
1765, Feb. 24, Carrot, Jeane, and Jossuah Mitchell.
1798, March 8, Carsen, Elizab., and Nicholas Murpei.
1764, July 18, Carsen, Margaret, and Joseph Rankin.
1769, March 5, Carsenberry, Catharine, and Jonathan Redhead.
1799, May 11, Carson, Anne, and James Stuart.
1791, Oct. 13, Carson, Francis, and Martha Whiterup.
1771, Aug. 20, Carson, Jane, and William Edwards.
1794, March 21, Carson, John, and Cathrine Fullerton.
1770, Oct. 22, Carson, Mary, and Isaac Ely.
1775, Sept. 4, Carson, Mary, and Mathew Creemer.

1780, March 15, Carson, Rosannah, and William Talburt.
1795, Feb.   8, Carson, Samuel, and Sophia Hand, (Africans.)
1792, July   29, Carss, William, and Elizabeth Harrison.
1761, May   5, Cart, John, and Ruth Hellings.
1778, June   16, Cart, Sarah, and William Edger.
1757, Feb.   21, Cartbride, Joseph, and Martha Hephenson.
1791, July   2, Carter, Ann, and Samuel Johnson.
1775, Dec.   21, Carter, Catharine, and Wollentine Clemons.
1792, Dec.   4, Carter, Charles, and Judith Ralph.
1797, Nov.   30, Carter, Elizabeth, and John Finney.
1789, Oct.   30, Carter, Elvira, and Cornelius McDermat.
1782, Feb.   16, Carter, Hannah, and Jacob Sneider.
1793, Feb.   5, Carter, Isabella, and Thomas Hans Gifford.
1800, May   9, Carter, Jasper, and Ann Hughes.
1775, May   25, Carter, Mary, and George Gyer.
1779, Nov.   20, Carter, Mary, and John Keen.
1763, April   26, Carter, Sarah, and James Barnes.
1789, Oct.   22, Carter, Stephen, and Margreta Porter.
1777, March   10, Carter, Thomas, and Sarah Brickel.
1763, April   11, Cartey, Ann, and Patrick Dowen.
1774, Nov.   27, Cartwright, Charles, and Mary Wood.
1792, March   1, Cartwright, Daniel, and Melinda Page.
1795, Oct.   2, Cartwright, Rebecca, and William Derickson.
1796, June   6, Caruthers, George, and Elizabeth Peters.
1781, June   18, Carven, Catharine, and William Ware.
1792, Oct.   22, Carvener, Jane, and John Macmeen.
1778, Sept.   23, Carver, Ann, and John Carver.
1793, May   4, Carver, Jacob, and Elizabeth Laurence.
1778, Sept.   23, Carver, John, and Ann Carver.
1793, Aug.   7, Carver, John, and Sarah Murdoch.
1779, April   21, Cash, Sarah, and John Walter.
1763, April   18, Cashaday, Patrick, and Catharine Baldwin.
1754, Feb.   10, Cashaday, Patrick, and Hester Wall.
1795, Feb.   26, Cashin, Laurence, and Ester Abenetty.
1782, April   8, Caskey, Jeane, and George Edmonston.
1782, Aug.   11, Casler, Mary, and Isaac Leving.
1755, April   8, Casner, Hannah, and William Ottinger.
1765, Aug.   25, Cassaday, Hugh, and Rachel Richards.
1780, July   8, Cassel, Ann, and Dennis Leary.
1779, April   15, Cassel, Christiana, and John Wilkes.
1791, April   28, Cassel, Elizabeth, and Thomas Allen.
1759, Jan.   1, Casselberg, Margaret, and John McCanles.
1760, May   7, Casselberry, Ann, and Samuel Harris.
1760, Sept.   3, Casselberry, Elizabeth, and Arnold Vanferson.
1759, Oct.   30, Cassen, Margeth, and George Naree.
1774, Aug.   7, Cassenbury, Catharine, and John Hearby.

1792, Dec. 14, Cassidy, James, and Elizabeth Fisler.
1794, Sept. 9, Cassie, David, and Sarah Carney.
1767, June 6, Castel, Lydia, and Thomas Rhodes.
1781, Nov. 8, Casten, Elizabeth, and Warren Bigelow.
1766, Jan. 10, Caster, Jacob, and Sophy Bore.
1791, Jan. 25, Caster, Marget, and James Johnson.
1792, April 8, Caster, Mathias, and Rebecca Johnson.
1800, Aug. 3, Castle, Charlotte, and William Coles.
1767, Oct. 26, Caston, Amey, and Abel Archer.
1792, Nov. 27, Castor, Henry, and Anna Godschall.
1757, March 8, Caswell, Henry, and Mary Dayley.
1773, Oct. 2, Cato and Lilly, (negroes.)
1779, June 23, Cato and Peggy, (negroes.)
1777, Dec. 14, Cato and Polly, (negroes of Samuel Moore.)
1766, Sept. 22, Caton, Miles, and Rebecca Greenwood.
1767, Oct. 26, Cattan, George, and Mary Haynes.
1790, Dec. 28, Cattell, Amy, and Judah Heritage.
1795, July 9, Catton, Mary, and Etienne Nouge.
1751, March 10, Catzen, Catharine, and Jacob Schleih.
1794, March 5, Cauglin, Mary, and Hugh McLeroy.
1795, Sept. 3, Causey, William, and Christiana McCloud.
1791, March 10, Causley, Ann, and Murdoch Smith.
1778, April 14, Cauthery, Jonas, and Catharine Dilly.
1765, Feb. 6, Cauthorn, Martha, and John Cranston.
1800, Jan. 3, Cavenaugh, Eleonore, and William McClasky.
1795, June 20, Cavener, Ann, and Samuel Davenport.
1800, Nov. 29, Cavenough, Hugh, and Alice Williams.
1770, Dec. 18, Cavert, Mary, and George Campbell.
1767, May 7, Cavet, Susannah, and Daniel Winter.
1767, Aug. 22, Cavet, Susannah, and Daniel Winters.
1778, Sept. 3, Cay, Margaret, and Donald McCloud.
1767, Feb. 22, Cayton, Caterin, and Philip Cossell.
1783, Dec. 6, Cecil, Charles, and Alice Roberts.
1773, Jan. 17, Ceim, Elizabeth, and Christopher Bradgin.
1771, Aug. 4, Ceimm, Susannah, and Henry Sorber.
1769, July 5, Cein, Barnith, and Mary Reed.
1770, Sept. 2, Cein, Cornelius, and Elizabeth Noris.
1772, May 25, Cein, Rachel, and Richard Davis.
1794, March 9, Cerenio, Cathrine, and Jacques Servel.
1784, May 12, Cerenio, Stephen, and Catharine Hicks.
1784, Sept. 2, Chadwick, Maria, and Abraham Coursen.
1786, Nov. 16, Chadwick, William, and Rebecca Indigott.
1759, Oct. 16, Chalten, John, and Elsah Chinart.
1781, Dec. 25, Chamberlain, Charles, and Mary McDanell.
1780, April 5, Chamberlin, Ann, and Francis Standley.

1795, May   31, Chamberlin, (or lain,) Henry, and Elizabeth Sum-
                  mers.
1763, Sept.   7, Chambers, Ann, and John Mathews.
1780, March 26, Chambers, Deborah, and Mathew Conard.
1796, Feb.   28, Chambers, John, and Mary Stouse.
1774, June   13, Chambers, Mary, and John Brown.
1790, June   9, Chambers, Robert, and Ann Hasselberg.
1766, Nov.   6, Chambers, William, and Henrietta Cuzzins.
1761, June   25, Chamblis, Rebecca, and John Wharton.
1797, July   16, Champagne, John, and Jane Beard.
1792, Sept. 22, Champaine, Steven, and Eliza Brown.
1773, Jan.   3, Champion, Abigail, and Daniel Darcy.
1753, April 20, Champion, Amy, and Josiah Wood.
1760, March 28, Chanart, Elizabeth, and Enoch Albertson.
1753, Sept. 29, Chancelor, William, and Salome Wistar.
1781, June   18, Chandler, Jeremiah, and Mary Canady.
1758, Sept. 30, Change, Rebecca, and John Crosley.
1775, Dec.   31, Channon, Thomas, and Hannah Donovan.
1784, May   3, Channon, Thomas, and Martha Beymouth.
1797, Dec.   30, Chanson, Pierre, and Mary Brake.
1778, May   25, Chapman, Charles, and Elizabeth McDanold.
1791, June   10, Chapman, James, and Martha Orner.
1787, June   28, Chapman, John, and Elizabeth Thomas.
1758, Jan.   22, Chapman, John, and Elizabeth Warboy.
1752, Sept.   2, Chapman, John, and Mary Annlyth.
1792, Dec.   22, Chapman, Mary, and Trustum Flemming Jones.
1798, June   10, Chapman, Robert, and Cathrine James.
1794, April 17, Chapman, Susannah, and Archibald Owens.
1771, Dec.   10, Chapman, Susannah, and Jacob Grant.
1770, July   15, Chapman, William, and Anne Cornely.
1757, Sept. 29, Chappel, John, and Martha Duffell.
1797, July   8, Charles, Peter, and Johanna Christian Darn.
1795, March 29, Charlesworth, Mary, and Henry Spence.
1780, Jan.   15, Charlton, John, and Mary Hutton.
1756, Sept. 29, Charlton, Richard, and Elizabeth Smith.
1791, Nov.   15, Charters, Priscilla, and Philip Shaw.
1791, Sept. 20, Chase, Cathrine, and Christian Groll.
1786, Sept. 24, Chase, George, and Catherine Topham.
1767, Nov.   21, Chasey, Peirce, and Margaret Hickman.
1780, March   4, Chatfield, John, and Sarah Lea.
1775, Nov.   21, Chatham, John, and Elizabeth Willson.
1779, Sept. 24, Chattin, Abyhay, and Dilly Hait.
1760, Dec.   6, Chatwin, Sarah, and Bernard Winteringer.
1757, Dec.   20, Cheesman, Hannah, and Samuel Fluallen.
1755, Jan.   23, Cheesman, Richard, and Geziah Albertson.
1799, July   2, Cheesman, Sarah, and Jacob Spencer.

1795, March 21, Cheina, Marget, and St. John Harvey.
1778, May   3, Cheine, Robert, and Margaret Wilkinson.
1758, April 16, Cherington, John, and Mary Jones.
1791, June   8, Cherleen, Andrew, and Rachel Neeld.
1771, Jan.   12, Cherry, Elizabeth, and Adam McLean.
1765, May   24, Cherry, James, and Martha Archer.
1778, Nov.   10, Cherry, Mary, and Sampson Dimpsey.
1788, April 25, Chesman, Abigail, and Jacob Fifer.
1761, Sept. 21, Chester, Elizabeth, and Cornelius Hanson.
1762, Sept. 21, Chester, Elizabeth, and Cornelius Hanson.
1787, June   29, Chester, Judith, and Robert Haney.
1777, Dec.   29, Chester, Richard, and Mary Nattel.
1788, Oct.   7, Chester, Sarah, and David Elder.
1759, July   22, Chestney, Bassille, and John Mats.
1768, Sept. 30, Chestnut, Margarett, and William Lamont.
1777, Nov.   22, Cheur, William, and Sarah Ewin.
1791, Aug.   5, Chevalier, Peter Renaudet, and Jane Harriet Lillie.
1794, Sept. 25, Chevaliere, Susannah, and Isaac McClasky.
1791, June   13, Chevalier, Susannah, and S. Minchin Francis.
1791, Feb.   17, Chevalier, Thomas, and Susannah Evans.
1758, Feb.   1, Chew, Massy, and James Davis.
1791, Dec.   25, Chew, Michael, and Judith Heffenin.
1787, Oct.   30, Chew, Rachel, and Samuel Gibson.
1785, Oct.   15, Chew, Richard, and Susannah Temlinson.
1794, Aug.   20, Chickin, William, and Hannah Forbes.
1800, Sept. 1, Chilcott, David, and Eliza McKey.
1788, May   14, Child, Cephas, and Anne Kennedey.
1778, March 2, Child, Margaret, and Josiah Carby.
1759, Oct.   16, Chinart, Elsah, and John Chalten.
1781, May   17, Chown, Nancy, and John Johnson.
1769, Nov.   7, Chown, Samuel, and Hester House.
1778, Sept. 27, Chowne, Thomas, and Elizabeth Linch,
1751, March 12, Chrisley, Martha, and John Rose.
1799, Oct.   24, Chrisman, Samuel, and Marget Edwards.
1780, July   1, Christ, Elizabeth, Orpheus Kiemer.
1770, Jan.   29, Chriest, Mary Christine, and George Garling.
1770, Sept. 9, Christian, James, and Judith D. Cray.
1778, Oct.   7, Christian, William, and Sarah Wright.
1796, Jan.   10, Christie, James, and Christina Snellhart.
1797, Sept. 6, Christie, Jane, and Andrew Lochberry.
1768, Oct.   23, Christie, John, and Ann Donozen.
1791, Aug.   31, Christie, John William, and Cathrine White.
1777, Dec.   17, Christie, Margaret, and Francis Baker.
1785, April 7, Christie, Mary, and Patrick Glyn.
1778, June   30, Christine, Jemima, and Jonathan Stanton.
1781, April 15, Christman, Andrew, and Elizabeth Graff.

1780, Sept.   6, Christman, Peter, and Elizabeth Barnheizel.
1779, June   15, Christopher, Michael, and Mary Schyler.
1774, June   13, Christy, Elizabeth, and James Walleys.
1794, March   4, Christy, Robert, and Rebecca Curwethy.
1790, Aug.   3, Christy, Samuel, and Sarah Myers.
1765, Jan.   22, Chrocpan, Michael, and Mary Frapold.
1754, April   14, Chub, John, and Mary Harrington.
1765, April   9, Church, John, and Catharine Miller.
1752, April   28, Church, John, and Mary Davis.
1782, Dec.   22, Church, Mary, and Daniel Adare.
1786, April   21, Church, Mary, and William Brown.
1782, June   6, Church, Nathaniel, and Mary Horn.
1794, Dec.   2., Churchill, Thomas, and Ann Davis.
1777, Jan.   17, Cinnor, Eleanor, and John Johnson.
1776, May   6, Cisty, Susannah, and John Miller.
1755, Nov.   5, Claiton, Hannah, and Philip Super.
1768, April   4, Clamence, Ann, and William Patterson.
1759, Jan.   1, Clamen, Cornelius, and Elizabet Webb.
1765, Feb.   23, Clanby, Owen, and Martha Warton.
1775, Jan.   20, Clanges, John, and Rosanna Staul.
1788, Feb.   26, Clarc, Isaac, and Mary Guff.
1798, Feb.   24, Clarc, John, and Eliza Stuart.
1779, April   29, Clare, William, and Ann Gorelon.
1793, July   16, Clare, William, and Sarah Nutz.
1784, June   3, Clark, Abigail, and John Ward.
1755, Aug.   14, Clark, Abner, and Mary Bradsheer.
1783, May   17, Clark, Adriel, and Judith Hampton.
1794, May   13, Clark, Amos, and Leah Stillman.
1781, Nov.   5, Clark, Andrew, and Sarah Brooks.
1797, Feb.   25, Clark, Charlotte, and James Vanbritel.
1777, March   6, Clark, David, and Ann Carr.
1774, April   10, Clark, Eleanor, and James Neal.
1777, July   9, Clark, Eleanor, and John Hollers.
1777, Oct.   10, Clark, Eleanor, and Michael Hays.
1780, March 15, Clark, Eleanor, and William Smith.
1777, March   6, Clark, Elizabeth, and Benjamin Black.
1751, May   5, Clark, Fanny, and Dennis Commins.
1781, Nov.   19, Clark, Geffery, and Anne Molrow.
1762, Nov.   23, Clark, Isaac, and Rachel Ivans.
1799, Aug.   29, Clark, James, and Elizabeth McMichel.
1794, Sept.   11, Clark, Jane, and Robert Morset.
1796, April   23, Clark, Jane, and Thomas Myers.
1771, June   2, Clark, Jean, and David Haddon.
1777, Dec.   17, Clark, Jean, and John Boswell.
1776, Dec.   10, Clark, John, and Bridget Kenneday.
1779, Dec.   8, Clark, John, and Mary Parkeson.

1783, Nov.   10, Clark, Lidy, and James Ward.
1752, June   8, Clark, Margaret, and Charles Divine.
1786, Aug.   31, Clark, Marget, and James Dilks.
1790, Jan.   3, Clark, Martha, and Joseph Zane Cottings.
1772, May   4, Clark, Martha, and William Anderson.
1765, June   24, Clark, Mary, and Joseph Gold.
1790, Jan.   11, Clark, Mary, and Samuel Daw.
1751, Nov.   18, Clark, Mary, and William Davis.
1776, Nov.   18, Clark, Mary, and William Thomas.
1796, June   20, Clark, Nancy, and Peter Graham.
1780, July   9, Clark, Peter, and Catherine Steel.
1793, Dec.   8, Clark, Rachel, and Henry Courtney.
1758, Sept.   6, Clark, Robert, and Rebecca Sherrard.
1792, Jan.   22, Clark, Robert, and Ann Alcorn.
1778, June   15, Clark, Robert, and Ann Hannen.
1780, June   27, Clark, Robert, and Eleanor Smith.
1794, Aug.   19, Clark, Samuel, and Elizabeth Miller.
1796, Oct.   13, Clark, Sarah, and John Haley.
1772, Aug.   8, Clark, Sarah, and John Oar.
1759, Dec.   24, Clark, Stephan, and Hannah Mathew.
1794, Dec.   31, Clark, William, and Elizabeth Linsley.
1778, Aug.   13, Clark, William, and Mary Griffieth.
1777, June   16, Clark, William, and Prisilla Pierce.
1781, Feb.   13, Clark, William, and Susannah Smith.
1763, June   26, Clarke, Ann, and John Henry.
1753, March 12, Clarke, Ann, and William Luff.
1768, March   3, Clarke, Catharine, and Wollaston Redman.
1763, April   7, Clarke, Elizabeth, and Robert Wilkison.
1766, Oct.   26, Clarke, George, and Ann Sutor.
1758, Jan.   1, Clarke, Mary, and Edward Tascare.
1774, May   12, Clasor, John, and Elizabeth Tembown.
1792, Dec.   30, Clay, Elenore, and Thomas Darte.
1767, Sept.   2, Clay, Mary, and Alexander Dimlap.
1786, Dec.   31, Clay, Rev. Slater, and Hannah Hews.
1765, Oct.   10, Claypold, Thomas, and Jeane Ruth.
1791, Feb.   8, Claypool, Cathrine, and James Pratt.
1785, Sept.   29, Clayton, Hannah, and Thomas Heston.
1758, June   17, Clayton, Jane, and William Hart.
1788, Sept.   8, Clayton, John, and Mary Pritchard.
1791, Sept.   17, Clayton, Jonathan, and Elizabeth Evans.
1754, Jan.   23, Clayton, Mary, and Isaac Marshall.
1792, July   18, Clayton, Samuel, and Hester Hibs.
1778, Jan.   28, Clayton, Thomas, and Mary Lockwood.
1773, July   4, Clayton, William, and Margaret Shantz.
1757, Dec.   29, Cleany, Hana, and Andrew Cocks.
1786, Oct.   15, Cleasly, Catherine, and Frederic Godshall.

1756, May   31, Cleaton, Mary, and William Townsend.
1774, Jan.   27, Cleim, Susannah, and Israel Jonés.
1778, May   28, Cleinier, Rachel, and James Mullan.
1794, March 31, Cleland, Adam, and Lydia Francis.
1771, June 10, Clemence, Thomas, and Mary Kid.
1789, July 29, Clemens, Enoch, and Elizabeth Sims.
1767, Dec. 24, Clement, James, and Elizabeth Smith.
1757, May   28, Clement, Janey, and William Garner.
1767, June   6, Clement, Rebeccah, and George Hudson.
1800, Oct.   6, Clements, Margret, and William Burnside.
1774, Sept. 15, Clements, Mary, and Henry Leary.
1783, Nov. 23, Clemons, Catherine, and James Segerson.
1777, June 12, Clemons, Elizabeth, and James Gold.
1775, Dec. 21, Clemons, Wollentine, and Catharine Carter.
1795, Sept. 6, Clendannan, Chloe, and Tobias Carpenter.
1796, Sept. 4, Clendennan, Robert, and Marget Caldwell.
1780, Jan. 31, Clempton, Rachel Reed, and Andrew Cunning-
                 ham.
1757, Oct. 18, Clerk, Edward, and Mary Howard.
1799, Jan.   7, Cleva, Hannah, and Joseph Allen.
1751, July 16, Clever, Mary, and Christopher Rhea.
1785, April 27, Clever, Peter, and Elizabeth Earnhart.
1767, Aug.   3, Cleynold, Mertah, and James Lee.
1775, Aug. 30, Clifford, Thomas, and Eleanor Smith.
1791, Dec. 15, Clifft, Hester, and Hugh Fitzgerald.
1759, April 25, Clifton, Elizabeth, and William Thorne.
1755, Sept. 15, Clifton, Amy, and William Fowler.
1775, Aug.   6, Clime, Mary, and James Duffey.
1756, March 30, Climkin, Jonathan, and Ann Baker.
1797, Nov. 24, Cline, Elizabeth, and John Pascal.
1799, Aug. 25, Cline, Elizab., and Thomas Maxwell.
1789, April 5, Cline, Joseph, and Mary Kaiser.
1776, Jan. 28, Cline, Mary, and John Wolf.
1781, May   13, Cline, Philip, and Mary Fuller.
1791, Nov.   5, Cling, John, and Mary Smith.
1775, Oct. 14, Clingen, Charles, and Ann Smith.
1785, April 26, Clingman, Anne, and John Lewis.
1795, Aug.   6, Clingman, Jacob, and Mary Lewis.
1774, June   7, Clinton, Catharine, and Isaac Heston.
1775, Nov. 15, Clinton, John, and Ann Tivey.
1782, Jan. 17, Clinton, Samuel, and Sarah Spicer.
1800, Dec. 24, Clinton, William, and Mary Thomas.
1795, May   17, Clisby, John, and Cathrine Collins.
1773, Jan. 28, Clisforct, Ann, and Zachariah Goforth.
1779, April 22, Clisley, Sophia, and Joseph Morgan.
1776, July 21, Clockston, Elizabeth, and Charles Stockman.

1777, April   21, Clodier, Elizabeth, and Joseph Campbel.
1789, Aug.   6, Cloff, John, and Mary Ferguson.
1792, May   26, Clogher, John, and Elizabeth Shields.
1779, Aug.   29, Close, Dewald, and Mary Riece.
1791, April   7, Clothier, Gamaliel, and Marget Hill.
1798, Aug.   10, Cloud, James, and Deborah Hope.
1790, May   22, Cloud, Sylphia, and Thomas Gilbert.
1792, May   22, Clowfer, Cathrine, and John Durnell.
1764, March 27, Clue, John, and Ann Johnson.
1776, Oct.   21, Clue, John, and Mary Carpenter.
1777, March   2, Cneth, Margaret, and Cornelius Leary.
1764, Dec.   30, Coatam, Francis, and Theodorah Berg.
1763, June   9, Coates, John Henry, and Mary Robins.
1783, Jan.   20, Coates, William, and Mary Powel.
1794, Oct.   6, Coates, William, and Sarah Worrell.
1780, March 27, Coats, Grace, and George Litzenberg.
1777, Feb.   6, Coats, Lindsay, and Rachel Hollsten.
1780, Aug.   11, Coats, Mary, and Thomas Adams.
1789, July   9, Coats, Samuel, and Rebecca Brooks.
1756, Dec.   13, Coats, Susannah, and Thomas King.
1767, Feb.   22, Cobery, Elizabeth, and John Steel.
1764, March 20, Cobinton, Abraham, and Elizabeth Colton.
1759, Nov.   27, Coborn, Mary, and Robert McCloung.
1759, Sept.   20, Cobs, Thomas, and Margaret Hommon.
1775, Dec.   2, Coburn, Ann, and William Humphreys.
1784, Aug.   10, Coburn, Hannah, and James Whitehard.
1775, Jan.   23, Coburn, James, and Sarah Hayes.
1792, Oct.   20, Coburn, Rebecca, and Daniel O'Brian.
1765, Oct.   13, Cochern, Ann, and John Harrison.
1767, Dec.   10, Cochran, James, and Elizabeth Faries.
1791, Jan.   19, Cochran, Nancy or Anna, and Joseph Ribaud.
1776, Jan.   1, Cochran, Robert, and Elizabeth Russel.
1755, June   25, Cochran, Thomas, and Margarete Humphrey.
1791, Nov.   28, Cock, William, and Cathrine Koffry.
1766, Oct.   21, Cockle, Mary, and Humphrey Robinson.
1752, Nov.   14, Cockram, James, and Catharine Kynen.
1777, April   4, Cockran, David, and Elizabeth Stentin.
1776, May   21, Cockran, Mary, and Adam Watts.
1780, July   17, Cockran, Mary, and Francis Pursull.
1752, July   1, Cockrun, Henry, and Elizabeth Griffey.
1757, Dec.   29, Cocks, Andrew, and Hana Cleany.
1787, May   26, Coddle, Mary, and Thomas Burn.
1774, Oct.   18, Cofey, Peter, and Judith Stump.
1765, April   15, Coff, Elizabeth, and John Calfry.
1794, April   2, Coffe, Cathrine, and John Dun.
1791, Aug.   8, Coffey, Priscilla, and Elias Morris.

1767, Oct.   23, Coffin, Margaret, and John Nice.
1759, July   12, Coffy, Darbor, and Mary Swanoy.
1779, Dec.   12, Cogall, Daniel, and Margaret Graham.
1776, Feb.   4, Cogens, Catharine, and Benjamin Hickman.
1785, June   9, Coggle, Sarah, and Henry Miles.
1772, July   23, Cohen, Abraham, and Mary Garmen.
1774, July   24, Coil, Barbara, and Mark Doman.
1797, Feb.   11, Coinudet, Marie, and Jean Baptiste Pierson.
1755, April   6, Cokes, Thomas, and Anne Philips.
1778, Sept.   10, Colbert, Dorothy, and Lawrence Locgant.
1781, March   25, Colchet, Isabella, and John Dougherty.
1756, April   22, Colday, Ann, and Jacob Peterman.
1786, Jan.   10, Cole, Dorothy, and John Vannest.
1762, Dec.   30, Cole, Elias, and Sarah Sidley.
1782, Oct.   19, Cole, Esther, and John Millis.
1777, July   20, Cole, Hannah, and Aaron Collings.
1756, Sept.   21, Cole, Henry, and Alice Dunlap.
1793, Nov.   25, Cole, John, and Barbara Biddle.
1790, July   13, Cole, John, and Hanna Robeson.
1793, Nov.   10, Cole, John, and Jane Cummins.
1763, Dec.   4, Cole, John, and Margaret Locke.
1790, Oct.   21, Cole, John, and Nancy Shipley.
1778, Jan.   2, Cole, Joseph, and Mary Kiver.
1775, Dec.   1, Cole, Joseph, and Susannah Browers.
1793, Nov.   25, Cole, Keziah, and John Biddle.
1755, April   23, Cole, Mary, and Josiah Sheppard.
1782, Jan.   10, Cole, Richard, and Sarah Lawrence.
1782, July   30, Cole, Timothy, and Sarah Timins.
1780, March   14, Coleman, Christopher, and Lydy Thatcher.
1776, April   16, Coleman, Elizabeth, and David DeBertholt.
1766, Dec.   10, Coleman, John, and Martha Long.
1752, April   2, Coleman, Joseph, and Mary Johnson.
1757, June   10, Coleman, Martha, and John Buttler.
1778, April   22, Coleman, Mary, and Henery Stanton.
1759, June   8, Coleman, Mary, and Waltor Trappel.
1785, March   28, Coleman, Mary, and William Davis.
1765, Dec.   7, Coleman, Patience, and Frederick Tols.
1780, March   6, Coleman, Patrick, and Sarah Gargin.
1755, Aug.   28, Coles, Richard, and Mary Rigen.
1790, Feb.   12, Coles, Samuel, and Elizabeth Pim.
1800, Aug.   3, Coles, William, and Charlotte Castle.
1779, July   7, Coles, William, and Mary Boyd.
1753, May   14, Colgun, James, and Mary Flannagan.
1757, Oct.   13, Colket, Mary, and Anthony May.
1794, Jan.   13, Coll, John, and Isabella White.
1790, Dec.   27, Colladay, Abraham, and Hanna Rekstraw.

1759, Jan.   28, Collborn, Rebecca, and Patrick Monohon.
1765, March 14, Collet, Hannah, and Anthony Mahony.
1757, June   26, Collet, Judah, and George Killinger.
1777, Oct.   30, Colley, Sarah, and Thomas Andrews.
1777, July   20, Collings, Aaron, and Hannah Cole.
1791, June   2, Collings, James Alex^r, and Mary Ottenheimer.
1759, Nov.   4, Collings, James, and Eleonore Donovon.
1779, April 17, Collins, Benjamin, and Elizabeth Wilhelm.
1790, May   11, Collins, Cathrine, and David Feilder.
1795, May   17, Collins, Cathrine, and John Clisby.
1794, March   4, Collins, Cathrine, and John Stock.
1765, July   29, Collins, Edward, and Sarah Stevenson.
1792, July   22, Collins, Elizabeth, and John Watts.
1758, Nov.   14, Collins, Else, and Isaac Louis.
1783, Feb.   21, Collins, Hannah, and Daniel McKlan.
1767, Feb.   21, Collins, Hannah, and George Marshall.
1755, Nov.   5, Collins, Hannah, and James Barton.
1787, Aug.   27, Collins, Hannah, and John Keys.
1754, July   20, Collins, James, and Sarah Pines.
1781, April   2, Collins, John, and Catharine Campbell.
1778, Nov.   30, Collins, John, and Hannah King.
1777, April 20, Collins, Letty, and Thomas Allan.
1766, Jan.   16, Collins, Margaret, and Edward Brannun.
1784, April 25, Collins, Mary, and Henry Lepky.
1780, July   18, Collins, Mary, and James Green.
1793, Sept. 20, Collins, Mary, and John Carr.
1780, March 27, Collins, Mary, and Joseph Roberts.
1781, March 23, Collins, Mary, and Patrick Cain.
1779, March 30, Collins, Mary, and William Gossin.
1787, May   24, Collins, Nathan, and Elizabeth Malony.
1779, June   11, Collins, Peter, and Margarett Brambridge.
1758, Nov.   30, Collins, Rachel, and Mango Davidson.
1761, Jan.   1, Collins, Rebeccah, and Benjamin Hoggins.
1779, April 18, Collins, Robert, and Margaret Griffieth.
1786, April 14, Collins, Sarah, and James Read.
1800, April 27, Collins, Tallinghast, and Ann Gold.
1776, Dec.   12, Collins, William, and Mary Love.
1798, Nov.   26, Collis, John, and Eleanor Brookfield.
1781, Sept. 29, Collis, John, and Mary Skillinger.
1781, Aug.   23, Colloms, John, and Mary Strout.
1751, Jan.   29, Collon, Adam, and Anne MacGoun.
1753, Feb.   1, Collons, Brian, and Mary Jacobs.
1758, Nov.   28, Colloway, Jane, and Thomas Cox.
1782, Feb.   10, Collwell, Nicholas, and Eleonor Danell.
1779, Aug.   4, Colly, James, and Mary Mullan.

1759, March 30, Colmain, Mary, and Augustin Rios.
1751, Dec.   3, Colman, Anne, and Thomas Cooper.
1799, Dec.   2, Colman, John, and Christina Smith.
1780, June 22, Colman, Thomas, and Christine Hammer.
1757, Feb. 28, Coloran, Catherine, and Anthony Karn.
1759, Jan. 18, Colp, John, and Susanna Martin.
1762, June 23, Colston, William, and Ann Taylor.
1764, March 20, Colton, Elizabeth, and Abraham Cobinton.
1780, April 7, Colton, William and Elizabeth Upstreet.
1793, Jan. 29, Colwin, Robert, and Margret Gwin.
1779, April 5, Combs, Mary, and Paul Dogan.
1781, March 29, Comegys, Cornelius, and Nancy Paul.
1781, Dec. 20, Comford, Francis, and Mary Jones.
1788, Nov. 12, Comfort, Martha, and George Fox.
1754, Nov. 29, Commins, Thomas, and Catharine Weld.
1751, May   5, Commins, Dennis, and Fanny Clark.
1755, July 13, Commins, John, and Margaret Hinman.
1782, Aug. 27, Common, Emy, and William Robeson.
1781, Dec. 13, Commoren, Elizabeth, and David Steward.
1760, April 5, Commot, Elizabeth, and John Davis.
1800, Dec. 30, Compass, Ann, and Henry Harvey.
1777, Dec.   1, Con, Robert, and Sarah Ford.
1780, March 26, Conard, Mathew, and Deborah Chambers.
1788, April 1, Conaway, Elizabeth, and Joseph Miller.
1772, April 6, Conawey, Margaret, and Cormack McCapherty.
1796, Sept. 13, Conchlin, Susannah, and Francis Peppar.
1790, Dec. 14, Condon, Cathrine, and Michael Murphy.
1799, June   4, Condon, Martha, and William Art.
1776, March 25, Condren, Patrick, and Mary Patterson.
1777, June 17, Conehey, Mary, and Benjamin Young.
1795, Aug.   5, Conelly, Ann, and Charles William Folger.
1796, Feb.   9, Conelly, Elizabeth, and Pierie Lefevre.
1790, May   9, Conelly, George, and Margret Morrison.
1753, Dec.   1, Conelly, Thomas, and Hany Griffis.
1794, July 13, Conflatin, Martin, and Ann Burchett.
1779, May   2, Conjers, Joseph, and Margaret Nixon.
1771, Feb.   7, Conn, Leurefia, and Hugh Wilson.
1777, May   4, Connar, Cornelius, and Margaret Walkins.
1788, Dec. 14, Connar, Ephriam, and Lydia White.
1753, Dec. 10, Connar, John, and Martha Franklen.
1779, Oct.   9, Connar, Mary, and John Dougherty.
1789, June 25, Connar, Mary, and John Ozias.
1779, March 10, Connar, Mary, and William Eggiar.
1784, May   5, Connard, Clarles, and Rachel Berry.
1767, Aug. 22, Connard, Margaret, and John Rittenhouse.
1756, Sept. 3, Connard, Mary, and Lewis Jones.

1799, July   14, Connard, Nicholas, and Susannah Staires.
1796, May   31, Connel, Edward, and Cathrine Farren.
1781, Dec.   13, Connel, Margaret, and Mathew Dobson.
1763, March   2, Conneley, Dennis, and Mary Hilkenny.
1767, Oct.   5, Conneley, Joseph, and Elizabeth Botteweth.
1779, May   8, Conneley, Robert, and Mary Campbell.
1767, Dec.   7, Conneley, William, and Mertah Cox.
1757, Oct.   19, Connell, Isabella, and George Price.
1758, March 23, Connelly, Margaret, and Walter Berry.
1799, Nov.   28, Connelly, Robert, and Ann Melly.
1773, Jan.   18, Conner, Catharine, and Thomas Reelen.
1753, Oct.   24, Connerly, Jane, and Manasseh Lee.
1758, Nov.   11, Connil, John, and Anne McCullough.
1766, Dec.   26, Conningham, Samuel, and Agnes Deneson.
1755, Sept.   14, Connoly, Neal, and Mary Macumtire.
1756, Jan.   11, Conner, Cornelius, and Elizabeth Willson.
1778, Jan.   19, Connor, Daniel, and Elizabeth Nailer.
1780, Dec.   15, Connor, Edmund, and Bright Donohue.
1793, March 17, Connor, Edmund, and Rachel Allison.
1777, Nov.   30, Connor, Eleanor, and Henry Rush.
1789, Dec.   2, Connor, George, and Philista Price.
1796, Nov.   20, Connor, Mary, and James McFee.
1793, May   25, Connor, Mary, and Patric Tammany.
1800, Sept.   19, Connor, Nathaniel, and Mary Drake.
1791, Jan.   22, Connor, Peter, and Elizabeth Marshall.
1766, Feb.   16, Connoway, Margaret, and Thomas Haley.
1782, July   31, Conoly, Mary, and George Gilleckan.
1782, July   30, Conrad, Anne, and Owen Carill.
1764, May   2, Conrad, John, and Susannah Hansmon.
1777, Jan.   27, Conrad, Mathias, and Catharine Fogten.
1796, Jan.   21, Conrey, Patric, and Nancy Early.
1793, Jan.   6, Consort, Steven, and Jean Williams.
1796, June   2, Convell, James, and Margery Petlow.
1779, May   2, Conway, Catharine, and William Boyce.
1790, Aug.   25, Conway, Elizabeth, and Lambert Decock.
1781, Sept.   18, Conway, Michael, and Barbara Green.
1796, March   9, Cony, John, and Elizabeth Lewis.
1795, March 23, Conyers, Stephen, and Susanna Parram.
1785, March 22, Coock, Hannah, and Ebenezer Adams.
1772, Sept.   23, Coock, John, and Mary Smith.
1782, Feb.   24, Coock, Thomas, and Mary Bore.
1794, Aug.   21, Cook, Archibald, and Cathrine Morgan.
1794, Nov.   10, Cook, Archibald, and Christina Fisher.
1797, June   1, Cook, Archibald, and Margret Farran.
1792, Dec.   12, Cook, Debora, and David Thomas.
1792, Dec.   4, Cook, Hanna, and Daniel McKinley.

1781, Sept. 9, Cook, Jacob, and Susannah Dears.
1777, Nov. 9, Cook, John, and Elizabeth, Fowler.
1776, March 28, Cook, John, and Elizabeth Huggin.
1791, Dec. 12, Cook, John, and Mary Dodd.
1783, April 26, Cook, Mary, and Andrew Van Dyke.
1782, Oct. 10, Cook, Mary, and Frederic Asling.
1758, Sept. 25, Cook, Mary, and Thomas Bryant.
1790, Nov. 18, Cook, Mary, and William Lyons.
1796, April 7, Cook, Patience, and Amos Ireland.
1779, April 11, Cook, Peter, and Martha Lebo.
1787, Feb. 6, Cook, Philip, and Jane Forest.
1795, May 31, Cook, Prudence, and James Izatt.
1761, Nov. 23, Cook, Rose, and John Rethain.
1792, Sept. 13, Cook, Sarah, and Adoniah Stanburrough.
1778, July 30, Cook, Sarah, and John McLaughlin.
1798, Jan. 18, Cook, Sarah, and Peter Hart.
1779, Nov. 16, Cook, William, and Mary Fellon.
1789, Sept. 28, Cook, Walter, and Rebecca Gilbert.
1791, May 26, Cook, William, and Sarah Evans.
1762, Nov. 23, Cooke, Ross, and John Kethain.
1778, June 11, Cookhorn, Hannah, and John M. Gill.
1756, June 30, Cookson, Thomas, and Martha Miller.
1799, Nov. 5, Cool, Elizab., and James Gummerfield.
1775, Aug. 27, Coolmannin, Anna, and Christopher Holtz.
1772, March 15, Cooly, Eve, and Samuel Leveston.
1764, April 7, Coon, Andrew, and Ester Wolles.
1756, Oct. 10, Coonely, Henry, and Rachel Strickland.
1794, May 23, Cooper, Cathrine, and William Howlind.
1768, April 18, Cooper, Elizabeth, and Isaac Lyle.
1791, June 30, Cooper, Elizabeth, and William Marley.
1787, Nov. 10, Cooper, George, and Catharine Pike.
1795, Oct. 18, Cooper, George, and Martha Denning.
1772, May 2, Cooper, Isaac, and Ann Bolton.
1772, Dec. 10, Cooper, Jacob, and Elenor Meloy.
1790, Aug. 15, Cooper, James, and Elizabeth Odonelly.
1780, July 1, Cooper, James, and Hannah Saunder.
1763, May 10, Cooper, Job, and Rebeccah Yous.
1790, April 14, Cooper, John, and Mary Toy.
1794, Aug. 3, Cooper, Mary, and Anthony Landerin.
1795, May 24, Cooper, Mary, and John Campbell.
1782, April 8, Cooper, Mary, and William Thackera.
1789, June 3, Cooper, Samuel, and Hanna Rawth.
1797, March 14, Cooper, Sarah, and John Dover.
1751, Dec. 3, Cooper, Thomas, and Anne Colman.
1793, Nov. 15, Cooper, William, and Susannah Blake.
1767, April 26, Coowgell, Martah, and Robert Hardy.

1777, April 28, Cop, John, and Mary Gasner.
1792, Dec. 4, Cop, Margret, and John King.
1790, Jan. 31, Cope, Cathrine, and George Brown.
1790, Oct. 15, Cope, Elizabeth, and James Gibson.
1777, Oct. 9, Cope, Mary, and John Fink.
1753, March 26, Cope, Nathaniel, and Rachel Prinyard.
1781, July 21, Copel, John, and Catharine Baker.
1782, Sept. 25, Copeland David, and Prudence Willis.
1796, July 10, Copner, Marget, and William Erskin Justis.
1794, Nov. 29, Coppinger, John, and Clementina Musgrove.
1769, Aug. 9, Cops, Susannah, and William More.
1776, Dec. 8, Coran, Thomas, and Ann Lindsay.
1791, April 1, Corben, John, and Jane Tilford.
1779, Jan. 28, Corbett, John, and Margary Kelly.
1781, Feb. 27, Corbit, Anne, and Robert Karr.
1780, Jan. 18, Cordill, James, and Mary Lukans.
1793, March 18, Cordley, Mary, and Jacob Walter.
1760, Jan. 7, Cordy, Mary, and James Finny.
1751, July 6, Coren, Isaac, and Ruth Jones.
1772, March 14, Cork, Rosannah, and James Morris.
1792, July 26, Corkary, John, and Alice Wright.
1780, Feb. 8, Corkran, Mary, and John McCallister.
1775, July 1, Corkvon, Ann, and John Ellot.
1762, Dec. 13, Corn, Jonathan, and Johannah Humphreys.
1762, Feb. 9, Corn, John, and Elizabeth Ornphers.
1776, July 6, Corn, Michael, and Elizabeth Davis.
1760, May 20, Cornelius, Joseph, and Christiana Gardner.
1769, Sept. 9, Cornelius, Christopher, and Elizabeth Roberts.
1783, Jan. 30, Cornelius, Sarah, and Samuel Garrett.
1770, July 15, Cornely, Anne, and William Chapman.
1174, Sept. 8, Cornetius, Elizabeth, and Samuel Litber.
1777, Oct. 8, Corney, Benjamin, and Phoebe Bailey.
1769, Nov. 8, Cornish, Catharine, and John Margerum.
1754, Jan. 31, Cornwall, Mary, and Robert Lowry.
1783, Sept. 26, Cornwell, Susannah, and Nathaniel Derrick.
1776, July 14, Corran, William, and Margaret Crast.
1782, March 2, Correy, Benjamin, and Sarah Hinderson.
1763, Nov. 8, Correy, Catharine, and Christian Rudolph.
1768, March 14, Correy, John, and Mary Holland.
1791, Dec. 23, Corridon, Philip, and Mary Dahlbo.
1781, July 30, Corrigan, Cornelius, and Catherine Flenn.
1765, March 14, Corril, James, and Margaret Haly.
1769, April 1, Corry, Elizabeth, and Alexander Fletcher.
1755, Feb. 11, Corsbit, James, and Mary Dain.
1753, Oct. 1, Corties, Mary, and John Lattemore.
1758, June 25, Cortis, Mary, and David McCollough.

1767, Feb. 22, Cossell, Philip, and Caterin Cayton.
1753, April 22, Costard, Margaret, and Isaac Torston.
1751, May 8, Cothbert, Catrenah, and Joshua Bean.
1751, Jan. 23, Cotsee, Rachel, and Richard Buckstone.
1790, Jan. 3, Cottings, Joseph Zane, and Martha Clark.
1794, Oct. 4, Cottman, Mary, and Peter Redhead.
1778, March 19, Cotton, William, and Barbarah Barnard.
1761, June 10, Cottoro, Thomas, and Eleonore Flack.
1795, July 12, Cottrill, Elizabeth, and William Langdon.
1785, July 28, Couch, Charles, and Anne Wigley.
1770, Dec. 23, Couch, Mary, and Owen Evance.
1776, Jan. 3, Couch, Samuel, and Ann Quigg.
1778, June 9, Coudon, Philip, and Lydia Hacket.
1794, March 5, Coughlin, Mary, and —— McLeroy.
1800, Nov. 16, Coulin, Mary Ann, and George Hassell.
1756, March 16, Coulston, Hannah, and William Maulsby.
1757, Jan. 27, Coulton, Margaret, and Thomas Wynn.
1782, March 18, Coulter, George, and Dorothy Carr.
1782, March 31, Couly, Elizabeth, and Adam Revel.
1784, March 22, Couly, Margret, and Richard Wastell.
1792, Nov. 21, Coupar, Mary, and John Crippin.
1778, Oct. 28, Couper, James, and Hannah Dolloson.
1754, Sept. 3, Couphmanen, Catharine, and George Hack.
1791, Oct. 13, Course, Hanna, and William Steward.
1784, Sept. 2, Coursen, Abraham, and Maria Chadwick.
1777, March 3, Court, Catharine, and James Young.
1780, June 12, Courter, Herman, and Hannah Drinker.
1793, Dec. 16, Courtney, Cathrine, and Peter Sares.
1793, Dec. 8, Courtney, Henry, and Rachel Clark.
1768, May 18, Courtney, Hercules, and Mary Shute.
1783, July 19, Courtney, John, and Mary Jones.
1796, Dec. 29, Cousler, Barbara, and Peter Adams.
1779, Jan. 3, Covert, Isaac, and Isabel Read.
1773, Oct. 23, Covert, Lydia, and Edward Ridgeway.
1777, May 14, Cowan, Ann, and Charles Errickson.
1792, Sept. 21, Cowan, John, and Sarah Herring.
1800, Nov. 3, Cowel, Cathrine, and Joshua Emlin.
1778, Dec. 31, Cowen, Margaret, and Michael Welsh.
1751, July 8, Cowing, Margaret, and Jeremiah Pratt.
1776, Oct. 23, Cowisten, James, and Margaret Maloney.
1788, Nov. 14, Cowper, Elizabeth, and Daniel Smith.
1767, Oct. 18, Cox, Abel, and Ann Cunningham.
1783, Sept. 6, Cox, Abram, and Hannah Thomas.
1754, June 30, Cox, Adam, and Abigail Gurling.
1795, April 21, Cox, Andrew, and Ann Currie.
1770, Oct. 15, Cox, Catharine, and Aaron Hewitt.

1780, March 27, Cox, Catherine, and Benjamin Whitlow.
1783, Dec. 30, Cox, Deborah, and Jacob Hjerty.
1770, Oct. 15, Cox, Debora, and James Butterworth.
1765, March 6, Cox, Eleanor, and Andrew Yorke.
1777, June 8, Cox, Elizabeth, and Edward Rowan.
1753, June 14, Cox, Elesnor, and Jacob Bankson.
1758, Sept. 15, Cox, Elizabeth, and James Fraiser.
1786, March 25, Cox, Hannah, and Mathew Huston.
1790, April 29, Cox, Isaac, and Mary Justis.
1751, April 6, Cox, Israel, and Christiana Holton.
1750, Dec. 3, Cox, Jacob, and Martha Rambo.
1769, Oct. 9, Cox, John, and Elizabeth Younger.
1798, Aug. 30, Cox, John, and Mary Dennis.
1782, Dec. 5, Cox, Jonathan, and Rachel Ferrel.
1780, May 15, Cox, Joseph, and Mary Davis.
1785, Jan. 24, Cox, Lettis, and James Hennesey.
1762, May 27, Cox, Magdalene, and Samuel Linchet.
1774, Oct. 26, Cox, Margaret, and Stephen Morris.
1758, May 7, Cox, Mary, and Artur Reeves.
1796, Oct. 29, Cox, Mary, and David Guin.
1797, Dec. 28, Cox, Mary, and John Bruce.
1764, Feb. 8, Cox, Mary, and John Winter.
1799, Oct. 30, Cox, Mary, and Richard Poulson.
1754, June 30, Cox, Mary, and Thomas Noble.
1778, Jan. 24, Cox, Mathew, and Elizabeth Nash.
1767, Dec. 7, Cox, Mertah, and William Conneley.
1796, Dec. 25, Cox, Peter, and Jane Roberts.
1783, May 5, Cox, Philis, and Thomas Yervis, (negroes.)
1794, Sept. 17, Cox, Rachel, and Joseph Budd.
1778, Oct. 11, Cox, Sarah, and Cadwallader Evans.
1796. March 20, Cox, Sarah, and Christopher Fredric Farnel.
1795, March 19, Cox, Sarah, and Jeremiah Mathews.
1758, Nov. 28, Cox, Thomas, and Jane Colloway.
1787, Oct. 4, Cox, Thomas, and Sarah Hudle.
1778, March 6, Coxell, Jos. Henry, and Charlotta Howell.
1767, May 24, Coyle, William, and Barbarah Pymer.
1782, Jan. 2, Coyler, John, and Priscilla Douglas, (free negroes.)
1796, Feb. 24, Cozens, Susannah, and Levi Garrish.
1792, May 3, Crabens, John, and Mary Watts.
1786, Nov. 5, Crack, Rachel, and Martin Strauss.
1774, Dec. 26, Cracker, Hannah, and Daniel Mackey.
1762, Sept. 1, Craddock, James, and Heper Price.
1762, Sept. 9, Crafford, James, and Elsa Wells.
1794, Feb, 16, Craftt, Michael, and Mary Hutchinson.
1781, April 12, Crawford, Jenny, and Nicholas Koldy.
1796, May 12, Craft, John, and Cathrine Shaffer.

1782, Oct.   16, Crag, Mary, and Mathew Foy.
1795, Aug.   3, Craig, Ann, and Lewes Humphries.
1778, Jan.   26, Craig, George, and Catharine Meroney.
1778, April 19, Craig, Isabella, and William Cunningham.
1771, June   15, Craig, Martha, and James Hanton.
1778, Sept. 14, Craig, Peter, and Mary Prescott.
1779, May   16, Craig, Sarah, and Michael Gise.
1760, Jan.   1, Craig, William, and Jane Small.
1776, Aug.   22, Craig, William, and Mary Hood.
1796, Nov.   3, Craighead, John, and Sarah Halton.
1766, Jan.   17, Craley, Ann, and Henry Hughes.
1787, Oct.   12, Cramer, Bridget, and James Fox.
1783, March 27, Cramer, Francis, and Esther Facey.
1798, Dec.   9, Cramsey, Eleonor, and John Scott.
1799, May   25, Cramsey, Lydia, and Lawrence McCormick.
1769, Aug.   25, Crane, Elizabeth, and William Faster.
1767, May   9, Cranin, Caterine, and John Berchman.
1765, Feb.   6, Cranston, John, and Martha Cauthorn.
1793, Jan.   6, Crass or Croess, John, and Sibilla Reed.
1779, Feb.   2, Crasskup, Margaret, and Conrad Miller.
1776, July   14, Crast, Margaret, and William Corran.
1759, March 13, Craughin, Jane C., and George Waters.
1780, June   23, Craus, Adam, and Ann Patterson.
1789, Sept.   7, Crause, Michael, and Susannah Gvinn.
1755, July   2, Craven, Sarah, and Thomas Saunders.
1774, Sept. 11, Cravet, Joseph, and Elizabeth McNeal.
1781, Sept. 11, Cravinger, Jesse, and Margaret Mingen.
1794, May   6, Crawford, Alexander, and Christina Shockor.
1778, Nov.   1, Crawford, Ann, and Thomas Pendegrass Brown.
1777, Sept. 24, Crawford, David, and Sarah Penny.
1794, Dec.   31, Crawford, Deborah, and John Garwood.
1799, July   15, Crawford, Deborah, and Thomas Murrey.
1789, April 17, Crawford, Elizabeth, and James Williams.
1784, July   25, Crawford, Elizabeth, and Offris Brown.
1757, April 20, Crawford, Elizabeth, and Thomas Turbett.
1752, Nov.   28, Crawford, Jacob, and Margareta Irwin.
1779, Aug.   16, Crawford, John, and Margarett Hammond.
1756, March   1, Crawford, John, and Sarah Hogg.
1778, May   26, Crawford, Peter, and Eleanor Harren.
1753, Sept.   6, Crawford, Robert, and Mary Sweetaple.
1795, Nov.   21, Crawford, Thomas, and Mary Ann Carney.
1796, May   6, Crawford, William, and Jane Elliot.
1755, Nov.   24, Crawket, John, and Jane Ritchey.
1780, July   6, Crawley, Charles, and Hannah Marshall.
1770, Sept.   9, Cray, Judith D., and James Christian.
1785, Nov.   8, Crayban, John, and Elizabeth Smith.

1785, June   23, Crean, John, and Mary Prichard.
1788, Sept.   18, Crebben, Elizabeth, and Thomas Atkin.
1784, Feb.   7, Creed, Elizabeth, and Robert Story.
1780, April   10, Creeden, Catharine, and Daniel Calloughorn.
1793, July   28, Creemer. Christopher, and Barbara Dowman.
1779, July   28, Creemer, Elizabeth, and Joseph Leblang.
1775, Sept.   4, Creemer, Mathew, and Mary Carson.
1767, May   7, Creen, Eleanor, and John Shepherd.
1785, Oct.   12, Creghard, John, and Priscilla Steelman.
1772, June   30, Creman, Mary, and John Rein.
1791, Jan.   20, Cremar, Edy, and Ludvig Sherer.
1773, April   11, Cremor, Eleanor, and Samuel Johns.
1794, April   3, Cremor, Francis, and Helena Hays.
1759, Jan.   24, Crenare, Charles, and Ann Powel.
1795, Jan.   25, Cress, Eva, and Thomas Hoy.
1766, Feb.   24, Cresson. Barbarrah, and Daniel Jonickey.
1800, Feb.   17, Cresson, Ellene, and Richard Massey.
1784, April   8, Cresson. Rebecca, and William Prichett.
1763, April   13, Cresswell, Jacob, and Mary Davis.
1794, June   3, Creswell, John, and Elizabeth McLaughlin.
1797, Aug.   1, Creutz, Johan, and Maria Dorothea Sass.
1795, Dec.   20, Crevis, Mary, and John Bartley.
1779, July   21, Crews, Edward, and Mary McDonald.
1761, Sept.   1, Cribb, John, and Sarah Twanson.
1791, Sept.   13, Cribs, Mary, and Thomas Davis.
1764, Jan.   1, Crickley, James, and Mary Dose.
1776, Jan.   22, Crickmore, Gold, and Eleanor Brown.
1792, Oct.   14, Crilly, William, and Elizabeth Cross.
1794, Nov.   2, Crim, Sarah, and Abraham Inskip.
1781, May   24, Criner, John, and Margaret Fritz.
1792, Nov.   21, Crippin, John, and Mary Coupar.
1785, Aug.   22, Crispin, Mercy, and Samuel Lanning.
1778, May   31, Criss, Mary, and Edward Rowley.
1776, Sept.   22, Critchley, Mary, and Thomas Mullin.
1756, June   5, Crockett, Andrew, and Ann Harper.
1752, March   16, Crockham, William, and Mary Philips.
1765, July   8, Croft, William, and Elizabeth Tausond.
1778, Aug.   12, Croker, Ambrose, and Mary Brown.
1781, Nov.   16, Crone, Mary, and Edward Grifferd.
1765, Oct.   14, Croney, John, and Catharine Hasand.
1780, Sept.   14, Crooks, Barbara, and Joseph Crooks.
1780, Sept.   14, Crooks, Joseph, and Barbara Crooks.
1780, June   19, Croom, Nancy, and Peter Sticker.
1785, June   14, Cropley, John, and Lamar Vickers.
1795, Oct.   29, Crosby, John, and Eliza Macall,
1758, Sept.   30, Crosley, John, and Rebecca Change.

1792, Oct.   14, Cross, Elizabeth, and William Crilly.
1779, April   5, Cross, Peter, and Elizabeth Morton.
1795, Sept.   26, Crottey, Henry, and Cathrine Butler.
1788, Jan.   20, Crotto, Henry, and Mary Tones.
1795, Feb.   16, Crotty, William, and Cathrine Furey.
1787, Nov.   27, Crouse, Elizabeth, and Thomas Richards.
1778, Dec.   2, Crowder, George, and Catharine Braidy.
1779, April   20, Crowe, Edwards, and Ann Dugan.
1795, March   26, Crowel, Ruth, and Moses Levi.
1771, Jan.   19, Crozier, Margaret, and John Ringrose.
1798, Nov.   19, Crozier, William, and Mary Leech.
1751, Nov.   17, Cruck, Susanna and Arthur Redford.
1752, Feb.   16, Crull, Mary, and Michel Walton.
1790, July   28, Crumley, Thomas, Cathrine Plum.
1780, March   19, Cruse, Eleanor, and William Hutcheson.
1799, May   1, Cruse, Jacob, and Elizabeth Bud.
1775, Nov.   6, Cruse, Paul, and Mary Ruden.
1790, May   9, Cryder, Ann, and Joseph Alexander.
1767, Nov.   9, Cryps, Edward, and Elizabeth Hephron.
1800, Dec.   4, Cuban, John, and Britta Armstrong.
1782, July   28, Cudjoe, Scipis, and Esther Grant. (negroes.)
1790, July   26, Culen, Helena, and Philip Ford.
1752, Sept.   18, Culey, Francis, and Sarah Nickloson.
1757, Aug.   17, Culin, John, and Ann Morton.
1777, Dec.   21, Culin, Joseph, and Catherine Rich.
1797, Dec.   5, Cullion, John Lewis, and Julia Young.
1786, Nov.   23, Culton, Archibald, and Mary Platt.
1771, Dec.   10, Culy, Catharine, and Peter Grost.
1759, March   21, Cumberbitch, Samuel, and Mary Brown.
1795, March   12, Cummans, Thomas, and Hannah Berry.
1784, Nov.   25, Cummings, Catherine, and Henry Debuck.
1764, Aug.   17, Cummings, Eleanore, and William Philips.
1798, July   2, Cummings, Thomas, and Sarah Fox.
1793, Aug.   5, Cummins, Bridget, and James Nixon.
1793, Nov.   10, Cummins, Jane, and John Cole.
1792, Aug.   12, Cummins, Margret, and Bryan Garret.
1769, July   9, Cunard, Henry, and Elizabeth Streeper.
1780, Jan.   29, Cunner, John, and Johannah Granger.
1780, Jan.   31, Cunningham, Andrew, and Rachel Reed Clempton.
1767, Oct.   18, Cunningham, Ann, and Abel Cox.
1779, July   8, Cunningham, Edward, and Margaret Cunningham.
1774, April   3, Cunningham, Elizabeth, and John Davis.
1752, Oct.   8, Cunningham, James, and Elizabeth Scotman.
1793, Dec,   8, Cunningham, Jane, and William Todd.
1779, July   31, Cunningham, John, and Ann Farrell.
1765, Feb.   25, Cunningham, John, and Elizabeth Reah.

1774, Sept. 1, Cunningham, Mary, and Alvery Hodgson.
1777, June 25, Cunningham, Mary, and Andrew Heran.
1779, July 8, Cunningham, Margaret, and Edward Cunningham.
1791, Nov. 15, Cunningham, Peter, and Nancy Devin.
1778, April 19, Cunningham, William, and Isabella Craig.
1797, June 19, Curden, William, and Rebecca Barlow.
1794, Oct. 5, Curin, Mary, and Samuel Johnson.
1753, Feb. 17, Curny, Thomas, and Jane Roberts.
1795, July 2, Curran, Mary, and James Humes.
1776, July 2, Currey, James, and Mary McCloud.
1770, Aug. 15, Currey, Martha, and Richard Wells.
1787, Nov. 8, Currey, Mary, and William Needham.
1791, June 23. Currey, Samuel, and Sarah Richardson.
1778, Feb. 22, Currey, Thomas, and Hester Williams.
1795, April 21, Currie, Ann, and Andrew Cox.
1759, Dec. 5, Currie, Elizabeth, and James Diemer.
1771, Nov. 25, Currie, Revd William, and Lucy Jones.
1780, Feb. 7, Curry, John, and Catharine Booth.
1781, Aug. 6, Cursain, Rebecca, and Abram Rutter.
1793, Jan. 5, Curtis, James, and Lydia Risener.
1797, Dec. 31, Curtis, Elisha Randal, and Mary Young.
1797, Oct. 16, Curtis, George, and Sarah Douglas.
1777, Feb. 2, Curtis, John, and Ann Morrey.
1794, Aug. 29, Curtis, John, and Elizabeth Rosannah Freize.
1800, Jan. 12, Curts, Elizabeth, and Robert How.
1794, March 4, Curwethy, Rebecca, and Robert Christy.
1793, Jan. 20, Cushee, Peter, and Sarah Derrick.
1793, Jan. 14, Cushin, Caleb, and Margred Hoover.
1756, March 30, Custard, John, and Mary Umsted.
1782, June 27, Cuthbert, Samuel, and Elizabeth Jackson.
1779, March 11, Cutter, Ford, and Elizabeth Smith.
1766, Nov. 6. Cuzzins, Henrietta, and William Chambers.
1786, Sept. 13, Cymon, Casper, and Mary Schneider.
1762, Oct. 31. Daceson, James, and Mary Hamilton.
1794, July 11, Dady, Mary, and Peter Foulke.
1759, May 20, Daele, Peter, and Margaretta Fodheam.
1791, Dec. 23, Dahlbo Mary, and Philip Corridon.
1769, Oct. 30, Daill, Anne, and Andrew Barney.
1755, Feb. 11, Dain, Mary, and James Corsbit.
1777, June 19, Dairs, Sarah, and Isaac Wanleer.
1752, July 26, Dal, Peter, and Rose Bryernt.
1756, March 17, Dalbo, Brigitta, and Charles Stillman.
1799, Nov. 11, Dalbo, Elizab., and Jacob Stanton.
1795, June 14, Dallas, William, and Sarah Lyons.
1769, July 26, Dallet, James, and Anne Flaniken.
1797, April 30, Daly, John, and Susanna Pickson.

1761, April   6, Daly, Owen, and Catharine McGraugh.
1797, July   8, Dam, Johanna Christian, and Peter Charles.
1796, April   13, Damling, Francis Gotlieb, and Maria Gertruid
                    Reichenberg.
1790, April   23, Damon, Mely, and John Robinson.
1786, Jan.   15, Damsey, Mary, and John George Huntzinger.
1780, June   14, Danal, Jane, and James Branen.
1761, May   28, Danaway, Mathew, and Elizabeth Scout.
1756, Jan.   10, Dane, Mary, and Jonathan Thomas.
1782, Feb.   10, Danell, Eleonor, and Nicholas Collwell.
1762, July   28, Daniel, Catharine, and Hugh Delit.
1761, July   28, Daniel, Catharine, and Hiup Delit.
1779, Feb.   17, Daniel, John, and Eleanor Strong.
1792, Aug.   28, Daniel, Margret, and Samuel Ward.
1791, Dec.   19, Daniel, Thomas, and Elizabeth Allison.
1794, April   13, Danigran, Pierre, and Mary Dickinson.
1753, March 27, Daniley, Michael, and Ann Bradley.
1766, Sept.   8, Dannison, Margaret, and John Titus.
1758, June   7, Dannly, Anne, and Joseph Town.
1768, Oct.   30, Danolds, William, and Penelope Airs.
1779, Aug.   8, Dapson, Margaret, and Charles Lean.
1758, Sept.   18, Darb, Grace, and Richard Meek.
1753, Jan.   25, Darbra, Mary, and William Donaldson.
1754, April   20, Darby, Abraham, and Letisha Maxwell.
1768, Jan.   19, Darby, John, and Mary Largat.
1777, Nov.   28, Darby, Rebecca, and William McKee.
1778, Jan.   1, Darby, Susannah, and George Shade.
1781, Sept.   12, Darby, William, and Signet Rushston.
1773, Jan.   3, Darcy, Daniel, and Abigail Champion.
1768, March 3, Darkais, Margaret, and Charles Good.
1783, Sept.   1, Darragh, John, and Anne Rea.
1776, Sept.   9, Darrah, John, and Margaret McCalister.
1773, April   4, Dart, Ann, and Andrew Scott.
1792, Dec.   30, Darte, Thomas, and Elenore Clay.
1772, Oct.   6, Daster, Mary, and James Glen.
1780, June   4, Date, Daniel, and Rebecca Peters.
1768, April   22, Daugherty, Ally, and Samuel Wessenett.
1767, Jan.   20, Daugherty, Mary, and Jacob Lobb.
1756, June   28, Davenport, Margaret, and Jeremiah Nail.
1795, April   19, Davenport, Mary, and John Tuck.
1795, June   20, Davenport, Samuel, and Ann Cavener.
1779, Feb.   14, Davern, Rose, and William Hassal.
1794, May   10, Davey, Edmund, and Cathrine Pister.
1793, Oct.   7, Davey, Rachel, and Andrew Armstrong.
1795, Oct.   14, David or Davis, David, and Elizabeth Shane.
1778, June   25, David, James, and Mary Williams.

1753, July   28, David, Peter, and Margaret Param
1758, Aug.   24, David, Thomas, and Ann Horns.
1770, Feb.   11, Davids, Anne, and James Morton.
1769, March 22, Davids, Ester, and Benjamin Griffieth.
1769, Nov.   8, Davids, Hannah, and John Gallougher.
1755, Sept.   9, Davids, Issachar, and Elizabeth Nailor.
1770, April   15, Davids, Lewis, and Elizabeth Lamb.
1771, Sept.   2, Davids, Margaret, and John Stevenson.
1769, June   18, Davids, Thomas, and Sarah Odaniel.
1758, Nov.   30, Davidson, Mango, and Rachel Collins.
1793, June   18, Davin, Dennis, and Martha Sloane.
1791, July   29, Davis, Abraham, and Mary Kigby.
1759, Nov.   29, Davis, Agnes, and William Knowles.
1752, Oct.   15, Davis, Alban, and Mary Macay.
1778, Sept.   15, Davis, Ann, and Augustine Trepentine.
1785, June   21, Davis, Anne, and Henry D. Pursell.
1794, Dec.   21, Davis, Ann, and Thomas Churchill.
1785, Feb.   17, Davis, Caleb, and Lydia Boon.
1751, April   1, Davis, Catharine, and John Greeck.
1751, April   7, Davis, Charles, and Ann Wendenhurk.
1773, Sept.   23, Davis, Curtis, and Ann Gayman.
1766, Nov.   10, Davis, David, and Susannah Preehars.
1783, Aug.   25, Davis, Dorothy, and William Pinyard.
1779, July   15, Davis, Eleanor, and John Bennet.
1797, May   26, Davis, Eleonore, and John Adams.
1760, Sept.   15, Davis, Elizabeth, and Edward Williams.
1795, July   20, Davis, Elizabeth, and James Cannon.
1791, Feb.   16, Davis, Elizabeth, and James Eniard.
1776, July   6, Davis, Elizabeth, and Michael Corn.
1768, May   3, Davis, Elizabeth, and Neal O'Dear.
1778, June   21, Davis, Elizabeth, and Patrick Kempsey.
1778, June   1, Davis, Frances, and John Reiley.
1799, Nov.   20, Davis, Francis, and Phebe Jones.
1765, Oct.   27, Davis, Isaac, and Elizabeth Right.
1752, March   7, Davis, Isabella, and John Scott.
1783, Dec.   23, Davis, Israel, and Susannah Summers.
1754, Oct.   20, Davis, James, and Barbara Primstone.
1780, May   20, Davis, James, and Margaret Miller.
1768, March   3, Davis, James, and Marget Miller.
1791, April   9, Davis, James, and Mary Ming.
1758, Feb.   1, Davis, James, and Massy Chew.
1757, March 20, Davis, James, and Rebecca Porter.
1778, Aug.   6, Davis, Jane, and Daniel Evans.
1777, May   25, Davis, Jean, and John Weaver.
1767, Oct.   29, Davis, John, and Abigail Lewis.
1760, April   5, Davis, John, and Elizabeth Commot.

1774, April   3, Davis, John, and Elizabeth Cunningham.
1753, May   17, Davis, John, and Elizabeth Johnson.
1778, May   1, Davis, John, and Elizabeth Slack.
1781, June 17, Davis, John, and Marget Deyer.
1795, Dec. 24, Davis, John, and Mary Philo.
1757, Jan.   3, Davis, John, and Susannah Bell.
1800, Dec. 27, Davis, Joseph, and Elizabeth Young.
1753, Nov. 26, Davis, Joseph, and Lydia Williams.
1776, April 30, Davis, Lucy, and William Benjamin Hacket.
1775, April 20, Davis, Lydia, and William Harp.
1753, Jan. 14, Davis, Margaret, and Alexander Kenneday.
1756, April 19, Davis, Margaret, and Joseph Wilson.
1796, Oct.   7, Davis, Marget, and Richard Budden.
1774, March 9, Davis, Martha, and William Davis.
1782, Aug. 26, Davis, Mary, and George Goodall.
1763, April 13, Davis, Mary, and Jacob Cresswell.
1780, May   20, Davis, Mary, and James Fisher.
1779, Feb. 15, Davis, Mary, and John Brelsford.
1752, April 28, Davis, Mary, and John Church.
1794, Oct. 30, Davis, Mary, and John Loe.
1774, June 25, Davis, Mary, and John McDonald.
1781, Sept. 27, Davis, Mary, and John Ryan.
1780, May   15, Davis, Mary, and Joseph Cox.
1794, May   25, Davis, Mary, and Joseph Galloway.
1800, Sept.   1, Davis, Michael, and Helena Thomas.
1785, March 2, Davis, Nathan, and Mary Morrisson.
1757, March 9, Davis, Phinias, and Elizabeth Calley.
1755, April 20, Davis, Richard, and Hannah Burk.
1772, May   25, Davis, Richard, and Rachel Cein.
1794, May   1, Davis, Samson, and Alice Bleachington.
1793, July 16, Davis, Samuel Aeneas, and Cathrine Griscum.
1771, Dec. 18, Davis, Samuel, and Hannah Prize.
1757, May   18, Davis, Samuel, and Janey Neidermark.
1799, May   20, Davis, Samuel, and Mary Smith.
1773, May   20, Davis, Sarah, and John Scarret.
1790, July 23, Davis, Sarah, and Thomas Harper.
1796, Jan.   2, Davis, Sarah, and Thomas Mullen.
1767, March 1, Davis, Sarah, and William Logan.
1778, Aug. 31, Davis, Sarah, and William Mears.
1789, Sept. 29, Davis, Susannah, and Andrew Ritter.
1773, Aug.   9, Davis, Thomas, and Elizabeth Dodd.
1764, Nov. 21, Davis, Thomas, and Hannah Boore.
1791, Sept. 13, Davis, Thomas, and Mary Cribs.
1772, April 25, Davis, Thomas, and Mary Lewis.
1755, Sept.   3, Davis, Thomas, and Mary Pinyeard.
1782, Oct. 13, Davis, Thomas, and Mary Shiny.

1766, Feb.   3, Davis, William, and Catherine Montgommery.
1754, July   11, Davis, William, and Christiana Johnson.
1774, April   7, Davis, William, and Eleanor Brown.
1777, March 10, Davis, William, and Elizabeth Grames.
1794, Dec.   31, Davis, William, and Judith Narden.
1774, March 9, Davis, William, and Martha Davis.
1794, Jan.   30, Davis, William, and Martha Leacock.
1751, Nov.   18, Davis, William, and Mary Clark.
1785, March 28, Davis, William, and Mary Coleman.
1767, Dec.   17, Davis, William, and Mary Griffith.
1791, Sept.   18, Davison, James, and Nancy Anderson.
1782, July   9, Davison, Mary, and Isaac Franks.
1757, May   12, Davison, William, and Elizabeth Dickinson,
1789, April   25, Davy, Richard, and Elizabeth Lever.
1759, Oct.   24, Davy, Richard, and Margeth Gipson.
1790, Jan.   11, Daw, Samuel, and Mary Clark.
1762, Oct.   28, Dawel, Sarah, and William Herring.
1780, June   27, Dawsey, Susannah, and John Kelan.
1771, Jan.   20, Dawson, Daniel, and Hannah Hurst.
1797, Aug.   25, Dawson, Deborah, and Thomas Barret.
1778, April   24, Dawson, Elizabeth, and George Streaton.
1794, Nov.   4, Dawson, Elizabeth, and Henry Sent.
1769, June   21, Dawson, Elizabeth, and James Blewett.
1751, April   21, Dawson, Elizabeth, and John Tenbye.
1777, April   19, Dawson, Eve, and Edward Griffith.
1766, Feb.   10, Dawson, James, and Christiana Miller.
1774, April   4, Dawson, James, and Elizabeth Neil.
1750, Dec.   10, Dawson, James, and Sarah Eagle.
1772, Nov.   12, Dawson, John and Margaret Carrol.
1775, July   10, Dawson, John, and Mary Logan.
1774, Feb.   28, Dawson, Mary, and George Bemford.
1751, Aug.   6, Dawson, Mary, and George Morrison.
1787, July   7, Dawson, Sarah, and Andrew Bradley.
1786, Oct.   18, Dawson, Sarah, and James Bourcher.
1764, Feb.   3, Dawson, William, and Elizabeth George.
1769, Jan.   7, Day, Hannah, and John Ogelbery.
1786, Sept.   25, Day, John, and Jane Highman.
1778, Jan.   1, Day, Joseph, and Elizabeth Wiley.
1775, Aug.   1, Day, Martha, and Samuel Simpsen.
1758, March 26, Day, Mary, and William Grainger.
1797, Aug.   17, Day, Mary, and William Purvis.
1781, Aug.   19, Dayley, Elizabeth, and Samuel Gosling.
1757, March 8, Dayley, Mary, and Henry Caswell.
1783, July   31, Daymon, Anne, and William McDair.
1794, Oct.   16, Days, Nelly, and Ephraim Sergeant.
1778, June   25, Deacon, John, and Rachel Midleton.

1778, June　16, Deacon, Mary Arch, and James Roch.
1794, May　13, Deal, George, and Elizabeth Nannimacker.
1185, Feb.　17, Deal, Peter, and Margaret Kinsey.
1783, Jan.　11, Deal, Sarah, and Abram Horn.
1787, Aug.　25, Deamer, Joseph, and Dulcina Graham.
1778, Feb.　16, Dean, John, and Bridget Stanton.
1779, Feb.　16, Dean, John, and Bridget Stanton.
1773, April　21, Dean, Mary, and Nathaniel Allen, jr.
1767, Sept.　14, Dear, Ann, and Thomas Marshal.
1789, April　19, Dear, John, and Bridget Fairn.
1779, May　8, Dear, Melecinte, and John Jefferson.
1793, May　9, Dear, William, and Kesiah Peed.
1793, Oct.　20, Deare, John, and Elizabeth Linch.
1781, Sept.　9, Dears, Susannah, and Jacob Cook.
1790, March 24, Death, Emilia, and Charles Smith.
1782, Jan.　26, Death, Rachel, and John Bruce.
1776, April　16, DeBertholt, David, and Elizabeth Coleman.
1784, Nov.　25, Debuck, Henry, and Catherine Cummings.
1797, July　22, Deburg, John Francis, and Rachel Richards.
1782, March 18, DeCamp, Catherine, and Thomas Paul.
1790, Aug.　25, Decock, Lambert, and Elizabeth Conway.
1798, Aug.　25, De Cruse, Manivel, and Aby Sullivan.
1796, Aug.　14, Dedy, Mary, and Nathaniel Leet.
1789, Dec.　10, Dee, Christine, and William Sheed.
1760, Jan.　2, Deeleplan, Hannah, and Oliver Bees.
1796, May　22, Defellies, Elizabeth, and Christian Moser.
1790, Dec.　31, Deford, John, and Mary Kaighn.
1797, June　4, Deford, Lydia, and Thomas Donaho.
1799, Jan.　24, Deford, Vance, and Cathrine Bowhen.
1778, June　2, Deforest, Henry, and Mary Knowdel.
1777, Sept.　10, Defrees, Joseph, and Mary Start.
1787, Oct.　18, Degan, Jacob, and Margret Smith.
1794, Sept.　4, Degourd, Murdoch, and Mary Borkloe.
1795, Sept.　3, Dehaven, Jonathan, and Mary Wistar.
1781, March 10, Deitricks, Elizabeth, and Ruben Forster Topham.
1776, Dec.　6, Deits, John Nicholas, and Catharine Strowaker.
1794, March 31, Delabare, John, and Mary Ford.
1784, Dec.　6, Delahido, Elizabeth, and John Watson.
1782, July　28, Delany, Anne, and John Rupp.
1780, Sept.　20, Delaney, Edward, and Catharine Mahon.
1799, Aug.　29, Delany, Eliza, and Mathew Kengley.
1774, Dec.　11, Delany, Mary, and Jacob Spiegel.
1786, Nov.　22, Delany, Peter, and Johanna Long.
1759, April　16, Delany, Stacy, and Finis Gettman.
1756, April　19, Delap, Nathaniel, and Mary Randelor.
1755, Oct.　14, Delaplain, Nehemiah, and Mary Marshall.

1780, Aug.　20, Deleny, Richard, and Elizabeth Slack.
1785, June　22, Deleway, Catherine, and Henry Harris.
1777, Sept.　17, Delewew, Hester, and Patrick Grogen.
1778, May　14, Deley, Eleanor, and Edward Webb.
1779, June　15, Delher, Jacob, and Eve Slaughter.
1795, Nov.　7, De Lhulier John, and Mary Tavern.
1755, Oct.　11, Delipplin, Elizabeth, and William Dickinson.
1761, July　28, Delit, Hiuh, and Catharine Daniel.
1762, July　28, Delit, Hugh, and Catharine Daniel.
1780, July　5, Delly, Ann, and Joseph Row.
1779, May　27, Delly, John, and Elizabeth Andrews.
1757, June　21, Deloa, Peter, and Margaret Halbort.
1796, April　19, Delor, Sophia, and Louis Boullay.
1756, Dec.　18, Delworth, Jonathan, and Ann Peters.
1758, Dec.　30, Dempsee, Mary, and Thomas Wager.
1778, March 19, Dempsey, Ann, and Thomas Murey.
1791, March　5, Dempsey, Barney, and Mary Pinkerton.
1777, March　7, Dempsey, Joseph, and Mary Fagan.
1799, Dec.　7, Dempsie, John, and Elizabeth Trusdel.
1761, Dec.　26, De Muralt, John Casper, and Ann Barr.
1770, Sept.　4, Denais, Hannah, and John Free.
1766, Dec.　26, Deneson, Agnes, and Samuel Conningham.
1778, June　12, Deneston, Patrick, and Susannah Watson.
1793, Sept.　9, Denham, William, and Margret Law.
1789, Sept.　1. Denike, Davis, and Elizabeth Suter.
1791, May　22, Denmark, John, and Rebecca Piniard.
1777, May　17, Denney, John, and Sarah Mourow.
1794, Dec.　17, Denney, Mary, and John Young.
1798, April　15, Denning, Jesse, and Cathrine Rosin.
1795, Oct.　18, Denning, Martha, and George Cooper.
1783, June　26, Dennis, Anne, and Archibald Fisher.
1796, Oct.　5, Dennis, Henrietta, and David Ware.
1795, Sept.　14, Dennis, Hester, and Daniel Derric.
1792, May　10, Dennis, Jane, and John Green.
1798, Aug.　30, Dennis, Mary, and John Cox.
1778, June　16, Dennis, Mary, and William Parks.
1779, Feb.　15, Dennis, Philip, and Maria Killman.
1778, April　19, Dennison, Jean, and William Leenhomes.
1799, Nov.　10, Dennison, Mary, and Caleb Sarin.
1788, Oct.　5, Denny, Jonas, and Phebe Heines.
1774, March 20, Denny, Mary, and James Long.
1779, Feb.　25, Denny, William, and Hellen Donaldson.
1782, Jan.　10, Dennys, John, and Mary Duché.
1752, June　14, Denslow, Hannah, and John Priest.
1791, July　20, Deny, Dennis, and Jane Balfour.
1782, Jan.　20, DePlumagat, Michael, and Catherine Walters.

1757, July   21, Dephute, John Philip, and Leanore Rine.
1798, Aug.   14, Deredinger, Mary, and John Lichler.
1780, April   20, Derickson, Mary, and William Job.
1795, Oct.   4, Dericson, William, and Rebecca Cartwright.
1787, Oct.   17, Dermott, Mary, and John Miller.
1795, Sept.   14, Derric, Daniel, and Hester Dennis.
1790, July   3, Derrick, Mary, and Joseph Ogleby.
1783, Sept.   26, Derrick, Nathaniel, and Susannah Cornwell.
1793, Jan.   20, Derrick, Sarah, and Peter Cushee.
1794, July   13, Derricson, Joseph, and Cathrine Gareer.
1772, Dec.   13, Derogier, John Francis, and Catharine Marks.
1777, Oct.   26, DeSilver, Robert, and Mary Owen.
1800, Nov.   22, Desire, Cudjo, and Elizabeth Murray.
1794, Aug.   2, Destrue, Jean Baptist, and Cathrine Reedy.
1775, Sept.   3, Detchevery, Bethrenel, and Hannah Rogers.
1799, April   14, Detto, Cathrine, and James Bryan.
1789, Nov.   24, Deumey, Pierre, and Agautte Pitette.
1784, July   13, Deur, Jacob, and Hannah Ketley.
1795, Jan.   22, Deurbreec, Lawrence, and Sarah Hugh.
1751, Oct.   8, Deveny, Andrew, and Lurney Griffy.
1781, Feb.   10, Dever, John, and Elizabeth Rolands.
1775, July   2, Deverell, Nathaniel, and Elizabeth Cambridge.
1782, Aug.   29, Deverax, Elizabeth, and John Baldin.
1753, Aug.   19, Deverix, Elizabeth, and Edward Fitter.
1795, Feb.   7, Devine, Biddy, and John Boggs.
1791, Nov.   15, Devin, Nancy, and Peter Cunningham.
1782, April   5, Devny, Elizabeth, and David Ramick.
1790, Nov.   13, Dewall, Frances, and Nathaniel Ashby.
1780, March   14, Dewer, Henry, and Margaret Baker.
1775, Sept.   17, Deweyer, Philip, and Rosannah Morris.
1765, July   29, Dexheimer, Catharine, and Daniel Dexheimer.
1765, July   29, Dexheimer, Daniel, and Catharine Dexheimer.
1792, Aug.   15, Dexter, Ann, and William Ramsey.
1755, Oct.   2, Dexter, Elinor, and Charles Loardan.
1757, June   13, Dexter, James, and Isabella Backhouse.
1764, July   24, Dey, Margaret, and William Hegland,
1776, Nov.   12, Deyer, Joseph, and Christine Forster.
1781, June   17, Deyer, Magret, and John Davis.
1788, Dec.   5, Diamond, Eleonor, and William German.
1759, May   7, Diamond, William, and Hariot Tew.
1776, Sept.   15, Dina and Nero, (negroes.)
1764, Sept.   9, Dibert, Dorothea, and Michael Miller.
1792, Dec.   27, Dibert, Sarah, and John Christian Block.
1761, Sept.   23, Dible, Buly, and William Sanders.
1762, Nov.   23, Dible, Buly, and William Sanders.
1780, Jan.   16, Dibley, Mary, and Stephen Rowe.

1798, Feb.   12, Dice, Hannah, and Richard Young.
1779, Sept.   1, Dice, William, and Martha Smallwood.
1783, Dec.   14, Dick, Anne, and Isaac Vannost.
1792, May   22, Dick, Jane, and John Turner.
1770, Jan.   10, Dick, John, and Anne Burchet.
1780, Sept.   21, Dick, Mary, and John Pearce.
1794, March   3, Dickenson, Lydia, and John Morris.
1798, March   16, Dickenson, Nathan, and Mary Williams.
1754, July   10, Dickenson, William, and Catharine Drury.
1782, July   31, Dickeson, Eleonor, and William Ades.
1793, Sept.   8, Dickhaut, Anna Clara, and George Schlicht.
1790, June   5, Dickinson, Ashbrook, and Amy Morgan.
1780, July   13, Dickinson, Catherine, and Samuel Burklow.
1757, May   12, Dickinson, Elizabeth, and William Davison.
1757, May   12, Dickinson, Isabella, and Timothy Brian.
1794, April   13, Dickinson, Mary, and Pierre Danigran.
1792, Dec.   19, Dickinson, Thomas, and Elizabeth St. Clair.
1793, Dec.   16, Dickinson, Thomas, and Sarah Seley.
1755, Oct.   11, Dickinson, William, and Elizabeth Delipplin.
1781, Oct.   15, Dicks, Peter, and Mary Worrall.
1791, Nov.   2, Dicks, Sarah, and Jonathan Bee.
1791, Sept.   18, Dickson, Ann, and Joseph Stilwagon.
1760, Oct.   22, Dickson, Elizabeth, and David Evans.
1765, March   7, Dickson, George, and Keskiah Harmen.
1784, Dec.   7, Dickson, John, and Ketty Rose.
1751, Sept.   15, Dickson, John, and Mary Wright.
1753, April   3, Dicky, Mary, and Jacob Smith.
1791, Oct.   24, Dicky, Samuel, and Latitia Tatham.
1798, Nov.   12, Dicson, George, and Mary Rogers.
1792, May   28, Dicson, Mary, and John Sextonset.
1772, June   16, Diegel, Barbara, and David Jones.
1770, Oct.   27, Diegel, Jacob, and Hannah Ingarm.
1772, May   19, Diegel, Ursta, and Jacob Hober.
1759, Dec.   5, Diemer, James, and Elizabeth Currie.
1760, July   21, Diemer, Jerich, and Sarah Gaul.
1799, Nov.   14, Dieter, Cathrine, and James Brannon.
1785, Oct.   6, Dietrick, Elizabeth, and Jacob Huff.
1797, July   5, Dietz, Cathrine, and Ludwig Winkler.
1797, Dec.   12, Dietz, Daniel, and Margret Brown.
1758, Aug.   6, Dietz, Frederic, and Christina Ritsler.
1792, May   17, Diffenbach, George, and Lucky Schaffer.
1781, May   10, Digel, Henry, and Rebecca Rush.
1800, May   28, Digences, James, and Mary Minter.
1768, May   16, Diggin, Edward, and Estar Benjan.
1778, April   14, Diley, Catharine, and Jonas Cauthery.
1781, Oct.   6, Diley, John, and Elizabeth Jenkins.

1781, Nov.　26, Dilkes, John, and Mary Wells.
1782, Aug.　13, Dilkes, Sarah, and David Surham.
1786, Aug.　31, Dilks, James, and Marget Clark.
1790, Feb.　7, Dill, Hugh, and Ann Pickering.
1793, Dec.　24, Dill, John, and Helena Musgrave.
1771, Oct.　24, Dillahunt, Theodocia, and Archibald McMulan.
1794, Aug.　20, Dillon, John, and Hannah Latimor.
1759, Oct.　15, Dillon, Michael, and Ann Stinson.
1799, Sept.　28, Dilmer, William, and Rachel Midelton.
1765, July　29, Dils, Peter, and Ann Mary Sciperton.
1798, Feb.　5, Dilworth, Thomas, and Letitia Pomroy.
1767, Sept.　2, Dimlap, Alexander, and Mary Clay.
1764, Dec.　19, Dimley, Mary, and William McLaughlan.
1778, Nov.　10, Dimpsey, Sampson, and Mary Cherry.
1781, Nov.　18, Dingwall, Anne, and David Zabern.
1795, Dec.　13, Disher, Daniel, and Mary Green.
1781, Oct.　21, Dison, Samuel, and Anne Jones.
1752, June　8, Divine, Charles, and Margaret Clark.
1799, May　13, Dixey, Charles, and Cathrine Young.
1755, Aug.　27, Dixon, Ann, and Joseph Wood.
1778, June　30, Dixon, Jane, and Philip Hanbury.
1764, June　10, Dixon, Joseph, and Ann Bradley.
1753, June　3, Dixon, Mary, and James Hendricks.
1773, Aug.　10, Dixon, Robert, and Jane Runney.
1762, Oct.　11, Dixon, Sarah, and Peter Spence.
1778, Feb.　5, Dixon, Thomas, and Elizabeth Butler.
1777, Oct.　22, Dixon, Thomas, and Susannah Douglas, (negroes.)
1779, Aug.　28, Dixson, Daniel, and Elizabeth Young.
1779, Jan.　28, Dixson, Elizabeth, and Abraham Best.
1778, Nov.　15, Dixson, Patrick, and Mary Campbell.
1794, Nov.　24, Dobbelare, Henry, and Rebecca Lefever.
1766, Sept.　16, Dobblebower, Frederick, and Catharine Van Ost.
1795, Feb.　22, Dobbin, Charles, and Christiana Montgomery.
1758, July　24, Dobbins, Catharine, and John Tylee.
1787, Jan.　2, Dobbins, Marget, and John Wilson.
1757, Jan.　3, Dobson, John and Anna Handerson.
1781, Dec.　13, Dobson, Mathew, and Margaret Connel.
1779, May　24, Dobson Rachel, and Thomas Winter.
1791, July　4, Docherthy, Gerry, and Ann McCleuer.
1782, May　4, Docherty, Margaret, and Patrick Loghan.
1757, Nov.　16, Dodd, Elizabeth, and Terrance McMackin.
1773, Aug.　9, Dodd, Elizabeth, and Thomas Davis.
1791, Dec.　12, Dodd, Mary, and John Cook.
1757, June　28, Dodd, Stephan, and Ann Donevan.
1779, April　5, Dogan, Paul, and Mary Combs.
1759, Feb.　26, Dogged, John, and Judith Hays.

1782, Aug. 27, Dogget, John, and Mary Smith.
1773, Feb. 16, Doharty, Constantine, and Hannah Rayman.
1790, Sept. 4, Doherty, Jane, and Lawrence Campbell.
1779, March 1, Doil, James, and Mary Boil.
1779, Feb. 10, Doil, Jane, and William Hamilton.
1780, March 26, Doil, Margaret, and Samuel Sommers.
1775, Nov. 26, Doil, William, and Margaret Ling.
1795, Sept. 13, Doile, John, and Elizabeth Downs.
1767, Dec. 24, Dolan, Everhard, and Elizabeth Hemings.
1781, Aug. 17, Dole, Hugh, and Leah Blakeney.
1794, May 4, Dole, Sarah, and Edward Higby.
1796, Sept. 18, Dollin, John, and Sophia Reeves.
1778, Oct. 28, Dolloson, Hannah, and James Couper.
1789, July 27, Doman, Margret, and William Howel.
1791, Nov. 13, Dominick, Charles, and Mary Carrigan.
1797, June 4, Donaho, Thomas, and Lydia Deford.
1776, May 30, Donal, Penelope, and Peter Rutter.
1762, March 23, Donaldson, Andrew, and Eleonor Fay.
1765, July 31, Donaldson, Elenor, and William Fullerton.
1779, Feb. 25, Donaldson, Hellen, and William Denny.
1784, Nov. 8, Donaldson, Isaac, and Jane Donaldson.
1772, July 6, Donaldson, James, and Mary Best.
1784, Nov. 8, Donaldson, Jane, and Isaac Donaldson.
1753, Jan. 25, Donaldson, William, and Mary Darbra.
1777, Sept. 14, Donally, Mary, and John Blackburn.
1755, Sept. 3, Donalson, Margaret, and Andrew Macham.
1754, Aug. 6, Donat, George, and Sarah Griefits.
1754, Nov. 28, Donat, Margaret, and John Nice.
1773, Aug. 1, Donavan, Margaret, and John Bremagun.
1794, Feb. 17, Done, Nathan, and Rachel Evans.
1786, May 18, Donehower, George, and Sarah Boneson.
1757, June 28, Donevan, Ann, and Stephan Dodd.
1800, April 12, Donevan, Marget, and Timothy Halley.
1797, Aug. 5, Doney, John, and Mary Lamb.
1780, Aug. 9, Donhaven, John, and Jane Adington.
1794, Aug. 18, Donlave, Marget, and William Higinbothom.
1764, May 7, Donn, Elizabeth, and Dennis O'Neil.
1762, Nov. 4, Donnock, Mary, and Joseph Geates.
1773, Dec. 20, Donohoo, Lawrence, and Bridget McDanal.
1781, Dec. 20, Donohow, Anne, and John Mears.
1780, Dec. 15, Donohue, Bright, and Edmund Conner.
1779, May 24, Donohue, Timothy, and Ann Frances.
1775, Dec. 31, Donovan, Hannah, and Thomas Channon.
1759, Nov. 4, Donovon, Eleonor, and James Collings.
1768, Oct. 23, Donozen, Ann, and John Christie.
1762, Nov. 12, Doomond, Catharine, and Jacob Wever.

1757, March 21, Dorad, Anne, and Henry Lawrence.
1752, Oct. 15, Doran, Patrick, and Jane Long.
1792, Jan. 31, Dorat, Jean Baptiste Dismenatin, and Mary Gill.
1761, Dec. 12, Dorell, Henry, and Ann Tuff.
1771, July 15, Dorlan, Edward, and Eleanor Austin.
1767, Jan. 19, Dorn, Susannah, and George Heidel.
1774, July 24, Dornan, Mark, and Barbara Coil.
1767, Aug. 3, Dorney, John, and Sarah Vanderhold.
1763, Dec. 1, Dorough, Ann, and Job Williams.
1793, March 10, Dorse, Mary, and John Metts.
1777, Dec. 23, Dorus, Patrick, and Lowrannah Hunter.
1777, Feb. 26, Dorwill, Sarah, and John Berrys.
1764, Jan. 1, Dose, Mary, and James Crickley.
1767, April 7, Dotchin, Ann, and Hadon Rowe.
1778, June 4, Doten, Thomas, and Ann Einson.
1766, Oct. 4, Double, James, and Sarah Reading.
1791, June 30, Doublebower, Elizab., and Mathew Doyle.
1795, April 6, Dougall, John, and Marget Wharton.
1796, Dec. 15, Dougan, Eleonore, and John Bavade.
1755, March 31. Dougharty, John, and Mary Alloms.
1750, Oct. 24, Dougharty, William, and Mary Mooer.
1769, Nov. 11, Dougherty, Anne, and John McDaniel.
1793, Nov. 25, Dougherty, Ann, and Thomas Cannon.
1780, March 7, Dougherty, Anthony, and Mary McCormish.
1798, June 18, Dougherty, Cathrine, and Joseph Watson.
1772, March 18, Dougherty, Elizabeth, and Isaac Johns.
1798, Nov. 20, Dougherty, Edward, and Elizab. Williams.
1777, Sept. 10, Dougherty, George, and Margaret Kerr.
1795, Dec. 20, Dougherty, George, and Marget Strong.
1796, Nov. 3, Dougherty, James, and Isabella McMullen.
1795, May 7, Dougherty, James, and Nancy Macbreathy.
1781, March 25, Dougherty, John, and Isabella Colchet.
1779, Oct. 9, Dougherty, John, and Mary Connar.
1790, March 11, Dougherty, Mary, and Henry Fugundus.
1796, May 7, Dougherty, Mary, and James Quarel.
1777, April 20, Dougherty, Mary, and William McClean.
1796, Oct. 6, Dougherty, Owen, and Margret Hood.
1778, June 27, Dougherty, Sarah, and Charles McCarougher.
1799, June 4, Dougherty, William, and Elizab. Nixon.
1796, Jan. 12, Dougherty, William, and Jane Linsey.
1794, May 20, Dougherty, William, and Mary Long.
1793, June 20, Doughty, Abner, and Leah Holms.
1796, Aug. 25, Douglas, Cantwell, and Ann Foster.
1777, Sept. 1, Douglas, Cophy, and Phoebe Loom, (negroes.)
1797, April 2, Douglas, Daniel and Ann Mary Lehurst.
1772, Sept. 9, Douglas, Debora, and John Butler.

1762, April 28, Douglas, Frances, and John Howard.
1793, May 5, Douglas, Mary Ann, and William Tenant.
1793, Dec. 30, Douglas, Nancy, and John Shepherd.
1782, Jan. 2, Douglas, Priscilla, and John Coyler, (free negroes.)
1797, Oct. 16, Douglas, Sarah, and George Curtis.
1796, Oct. 17, Douglas, Sarah, and Francis Doyle.
1778, Oct. 22, Douglas, Susannah, and Thomas Dixon, (negroes.)
1757, April 19, Douglas, William, and Mary Price.
1777, Oct. 25, Doulin, Mary, and Mathias Scandlin.
1768, April 7, Doulis, James, and Hannah Quanah, (free negroes,)
1762, Jan. 4, Dourley, Hagan, and John Wood.
1782, Aug. 14, Douten, Jonathan, and Anne Morris.
1782, Sept. 3, Dover, John, and Mary Nice.
1797, March 14, Dover, John, and Sarah Cooper.
1773, April 8, Dow, Elijah, and Rebecca Jones.
1773, Oct. 5, Dowald, Alexander, and Elizabeth Johnston.
1798, July 5, Dowd, John, and Rebecca Hugh.
1758, Jan. 14, Dowell, George, and Sarah Griffith.
1763, April 11, Dowen, Patrick, and Ann Cartey.
1791, May 25, Dowl, Mary, and Benjamin Thomas.
1793, Jan. 28, Dowlin, Elizabeth, and William Wearin.
1778, June 26, Dowling, Kerns, and Margaret Mathews.
1753, Jan. 7, Dowling, Mathew, and Nelly Macmakin.
1793, July 28, Dowman, Barbara, and Christopher Creemer.
1792, May 15, Down, Abigail, and Moses Butterworth.
1754, April 13, Down, Ann, and John Eastlack.
1772, Oct. 26, Down, Jemima, and Samuel Waret.
1781, Feb. 2, Downer, Anna, and George Roberts.
1778, Sept. 27, Downey, Sarah, and Joseph Wattson.
1795, Sept. 13, Downs, Elizabeth, and John Doile.
1795, July 25, Downs, John, and Marget Norman.
1777, July 17, Downs, Rebecca, and James Thomson.
1782, May 14, Downs, Robert, and Margery Ross.
1791, Dec. 1, Downy, Barnabas, and Margret Campbell.
1775, April 6, Downy, John, and Elizabeth Yeates.
1793, Feb. 23, Dowsey, Martha, and John Roberts.
1767, April 24, Doyle, Bridget, and Robert Gray.
1759, July 2, Doyle, Elizabeth, and Nicholas Hore.
1796, Oct. 17, Doyle, Francis, and Sarah Douglass.
1778, March 17, Doyle, James, and Ann Willson.
1787, July 30, Doyle, John, and Mary Goforth.
1782, Oct. 15, Doyle, John, and Mary Porter.
1751, Nov. 19, Doyle, John, and Sarah Wood.
1777, Aug. 2, Doyle, Mary, and Joseph Sharp.
1791, June 30, Doyle, Mathew, and Elizab. Doublebower.
1781, Nov. 15, Doyle, Peter, and Mary Roan.

1772, May   12, Doyls, Beedy, and John Hill.
1783, April   16, Drake, John, and Catherine Arnest.
1800, Sept.   19, Drake, Mary, and Nathaniel Conner.
1796, July   4, Drake, Sarah, and Edward Bright.
1781, Feb.   22, Drape, Martha, and John Shaw.
1776, March 14, Draper, Jonathan, and Edeth Gardner.
1783, Oct.   14, Draper, Patience, and John Stoy.
1758, Aug.   13, Dresley, John, and Edith Bezley.
1779, May   16, Dresslin, Elizabeth, and George Roman.
1757, May   31, Dribary, Robert, and Elizabeth Virgo.
1794, Jan.   2, Drille, Francis, and Elenore Maccon.
1780, June   12, Drinker, Hannah, and Herman Courter.
1779, March   1, Driscall, Daniel, and Eleanor Brooks.
1775, Dec.   25, Driver, Thomas, and Mary Shippen.
1754, July   10, Drury, Catharine, and William Dickenson.
1777, Feb.   9, Dryden, Thomas, and Mary Miller.
1798, Dec.   6, Dubbelbarr, Elizabeth, and Samuel Allen.
1775, Oct.   2, Dublin, Ruse, and John McBride.
1794, July   21, Dubrevil, Peter, and Mary Hay.
1758, Nov.   11, Duchee, Anthony, jr., and Lydia Millane.
1158, Jan.   3, Duchee, Anthony, and Sara Evans.
1761, July   4, Duchee, Joseph, and Margareth Blak.
1762, July   4, Duchee, Joseph, and Margareth Blake.
1752, Dec.   28, Duchee, Rebecca, and Thomas Janvier.
1774, July   19, Duché, Lydia, and Richard Paul.
1782, Jan.   10, Duché, Mary, and John Dennys.
1779, May   13, Duché, Peter, and Hannah Shanks.
1779, Jan.   16, Duché, William, and May Price.
1779, March 15, Duck, Mary, and Jeremiah Butey.
1752, Oct.   24, Duckett, George, and Mary Duncan.
1777, June   11, Duelley, William, and Mary Bryant.
1763, April   17, Duff, Ann, and Mathew Moore.
1756, April   29, Duff, Henry, and Ann Pickle.
1779, Jan.   27, Duff, Thomas, and Catharine Mishurt.
1794, Dec.   28, Duffel, Edward, and Ann Walker.
1757, Sept.   29, Duffell, Martha, and John Chappel.
1770, May   7, Duffey, James, and Elizabeth Lockart.
1775, Aug.   6, Duffey, James, and Mary Cline.
1776, Jan.   25, Duffey, Peter, and Phoebe Williams.
1792, Nov.   16, Duffey, Philip, and Elenore Ennecy.
1765, July   8, Duffield, Benjamin, and Elizabeth Matson.
1768, Jan.   3, Duffield, Isaac, and Deliverance King.
1793, July   2, Duffin, Barnabas, and Jane Welsh.
1780, March 26, Duffy, Absolom, and Sarah Ridock.
1791, April   17, Duffy, James, and Marget Simpson.
1779, June   13, Duffy, James, and Sarah Blair.

1794, Dec. 26, Duffy, Pierce, and Margret Montgomery.
1790, Nov. 9, Duffy, Sarah, and Richard Tinker.
1788, May 21, Duffy, Sary, and Richard Simmons.
1779, April 20, Dugan, Ann, and Edward Crowe.
1794, March 22, Dugan, Ann, and John Young.
1782, Aug. 12, Dugan, Johannah, and Thomas Writeman.
1761, May 4, Duglas, Frances, and John Howard.
1752, June 7, Dugon, Mary, and Peter Richerdson.
1798, Jan. 17, Duhaven, Hannah, and George Fosler.
1771, Jan. 20, Dukey, Mary, and John Harford.
1752, Nov. 12, Dullinty, Michael, and Manny Moor.
1757, Nov. 21, Dun, Davis, and Mary Dun.
1778, March 9, Dun, Eleanor, and John Williamson.
1780, June 29, Dun, Elizabeth, and Solomon Taylor.
1780, Feb. 3, Dun, Jane, and Dominick Lawrence.
1794, April 2, Dun, John, and Cathrine Coffe.
1773, Jan. 14, Dun, Luke, and Mary Heany.
1757, Nov. 21, Dun, Mary, and Davis Dun.
1771, June 13, Dun, Mary, and Thomas Brown.
1800, May 26, Dun, Nancy, and Thomas Grier.
1771, Feb. 3, Dun, Patrick, and Mary Senter.
1778, Dec. 25, Dunbar, David, and Ann Rey.
1791, Feb. 13, Dunbar, Mary, and John Jones.
1752, Oct. 24, Duncan, Mary, and George Duckett.
1788, Nov. 30, Dungan, Mary, and Thomas Dungan.
1788, Nov. 30, Dungan, Thomas, and Mary Dungan.
1797, July 15, Dunjoo, Henrietta, and John Phillips.
1781, Aug. 7, Dunkin, George, and Marie Noble.
1798, May 19, Dunkin, William Henry, and Rebecca Parkhill.
1756, Sept. 21, Dunlap, Alice, and Henry Cole.
1776, Dec. 10, Dunlap, Ann, and James McQuoan.
1777, May 3, Dunlap, Ann, and Moses Pidgeon.
1773, April 9, Dunlap, Ann, and Thomas Richmond.
1799, Dec. 1, Dunlap, Edward, and Mary Walters.
1778, March 6, Dunlap, Jane, and Robert MacGill.
1779, Nov. 26, Dunlap, Mary, and John McFadgin.
1762, Aug. 26, Dunlap, William, and Eleonore McCaughlin.
1799, July 19, Dunne, Bartholomew, and Elizabeth Harrison.
1781, July 11, Dunn, John, and Jenny Haney.
7994, April 29, Dunn, Mary, and John Kelly.
1783, May 5, Dunn, Mary, and John Morris.
1778, May 2, Dunn, Sarah, and John Lermant.
1765, May 29, Dunn, Thomas, and Elizabeth McLavery.
1767, Dec. 12, Dunn, Thomas, and Elizabeth Poult.
1755, Sept. 18, Dunnman, Joseph Lankett, and Rebecca Roberts.
1791, March 23, Dunscomb, Elenor, and Joseph Marten.

1768, May   3, Dunwick, Sarah, and Samuel King.
1797, Dec.   8, Dunwoody, Eliza, and George Maris.
1759, Aug.   23, Duplissis, John, and Lattice Edwards.
1767, May   7, Duppernim, Catharine Elizabeth, and Henry Pin-
                    ner.
1776, Sept.   15, Durand, Andrew, and Sarah Hartson.
1795, Jan.   18, Durand, Ann Jane, and John Peter Wright.
1782, Dec.   8, Durant, James, and Eleonor Wright.
1799, Dec.   26, Durborow, Hugh, and Elsa Birch.
1799, Dec.   26, Durborow, Lydia, and Jonathan Louderbach.
1790, Oct.   12, Durell, Jonathan, and Grace Heins.
1783, Sept.   24, Durham, Elizabeth, and William Wroth.
1792, May   22, Durnell, John, and Cathrine Clowfer.
1774, Sept.   18, DuRose, Ann, and David Lycime.
1795, March 15, Durvis, Mary, and William Durvis.
1795, March 15, Durvis, William, and Mary Durvis.
1754, May   1, Dusbery, Cumfry, and Jeremiah Power.
1788, July   30, Dusky, Leman, and Hanna Whetherby.
1778, Nov.   4, Dust, Sarah, and Andrew Burn.
1782, March 29, Duty, John, and Catherine McGuire.
1794, Dec.   23, Duvall, Edward, and Mary Ash.
1751, Dec.   24, Dwight, John, and Martha Betridg.
1751, Aug.   20, Dwire, Catreen, and George Adams.
1778, Dec.   13, Dwyer, Rosanna, and William Brooks.
1759, June   7, Dyar, Alexander, and Sarah Rice.
1778, May   29, Dyer, Andrew, and Hannah Essling.
1778, Feb.   5, Dyer, Jane, and Donald Black.
1751, Dec.   2, Dyke, Sarah, and John Nesmith.
1778, Feb.   8, Dymon, David, and Mary Allan.
1779, July   18, Dymon, Michael, and Eleanor Welsh.
1775, May   21, Dyson, Charlot, and Adam Hillerman.
1779, Feb.   21, Eads, Barbarah, and Nicholas Smith.
1795, March 17, Eagens, Deborah, and James Jockum.
1785, Nov.   10, Eager, Elizabeth, and George Wat.
1750, Dec.   10, Eagle, Sarah, and James Dawson.
1788, April   2, Eakin, David, and Susannah King.
1795, Jan.   3, Earl, Mary, and John Schnider.
1789, April   1, Earl, Mary, and Samuel Kingsley.
1796, Jan.   21, Early, Nancy, and Patric Conrey.
1777, Sept.   7, Earnest, John, and Phoebe Evans.
1785, April   27, Earnhart, Elizabeth, and Peter Clever.
1799, Oct.   5, Earonfighter, Ann, and Benjamin Bickerton.
1770, March 25, Eason, Hester, and James Savage.
1794, March 20, Eastborn, Thomas, and Hannah Fling.
1754, April   13, Eastlack, John, and Ann Down.
1763, Oct.   27, Eastlack, Ruben, and Ann Flemmings.

1754, Jan.   21, Eastlake, Sarah, and John Blake.
1790, May   9, Easton, Abraham, and Phebe Carpenter.
1798, April   30, Easton, Samuel, and Judith Hooper.
1795, July   20, Eastwick, Mary, and Henry Lott.
1765, July   29, Eaton, George, and Catharine Shewin.
1797, March   2, Eberhart, John, and Sarah Woolsleyer.
1778, July   4, Ebert, Mary, and John Shields.
1777, Nov.   20, Ebright, Elizabeth, and Joseph Franklin.
1798, Nov.   22, Eckart, Mary, and Nathaniel Richards.
1768, June   5, Eckfield, Jacob, and Mariah Magdalena Scheiderin.
1776, Sept.   16, Eddrey, Sarah, and James Richards.
1796, Feb.   22, Edel, Thomas, and Nancy McGuire.
1781, June   28, Eden, Mary, and John Bason.
1753, Aug.   10, Edgar, Mary, and John Hazelwood.
1758, Aug.   28, Edge, Else, and Joseph Hatsell.
1779, Nov.   29, Edge, Sarah, and John McKin.
1779, Jan.   26, Edgecoumbe, Nicholas, and Isabel Redman.
1778, June   16, Edger, William, and Sarah Cart.
1758, May   13, Edgerton, Anne, and Joshua Hastings.
1772, Oct.   15, Edgerton, Luke, and Mary Swim.
1753, June   11, Edmonds, Joseph, and Elizabeth Money.
1782, April   8, Edmonston, George, and Jeane Caskey.
1800, Oct.   11, Edridge, Priscilla, and Ram Golden.
1781, Dec.   4, Edwards, Andrew, and Rachel Brooks.
1765, June   23, Edwards, Bitha, and Samuel Smith.
1773, Nov.   2, Edwards, Catharine, and Jacob Bensen Tested.
1771, Jan.   29, Edwards, David, and Barbarah Shippey.
1760, June   10, Edwards, Edward, and Mary Grace.
1776, Aug.   6, Edwards, Elizabeth, and Mathew Hughes.
1764, Oct.   17, Edwards, George, and Jemima Edwards.
1791, April   29, Edwards, Hanna, and John Batts.
1794, Sept.   21, Edwards, Henry Winterton, and Mary Grossier.
1764, Oct.   17, Edwards, Jemima, and George Edwards.
1778, Oct.   28, Edwards, John, and Keziah Swards.
1797, May   31, Edwards, Joseph, and Sarah Huff.
1772, Sept.   2, Edwards, Kezia, and Samuel Haslet.
1759, Aug.   23, Edwards, Lattice, and John Duplissis.
1769, Feb.   25, Edwards, Margarett, and Robert Fintly.
1799, Oct.   24, Edwards, Marget, and Samuel Chrisman.
1796, July   26, Edwards, Mary, and Henry Peters.
1767, Sept.   2, Edwards, Mary, and Philip Goodwin.
1780, March   4, Edwards, Rachel, and William Bird.
1798, March   16, Edwards Sarah, and Peter Fiss.
1771, Aug.   20, Edwards, William, and Jane Carson.
1787, Sept.   24, Edwards, William, and Sarah Willard.
1776, July   10, Edwaris, Edward, and Susannah Triggs.

1779, Dec.   1, Eferson, John, and Ann Airy.
1765, Oct.   21, Egan, John, and Margaret McGrah.
1770, Feb.   25, Eagan, Peter, and Latitia Gisfen.
1785, Aug.   17, Egan, Thomas, and Sarah Baker.
1779, March 10, Eggiar, William, and Mary Connar.
1791, March 31, Eggman, Sarah, and John Lord,
1799, Aug.   12, Egins, Mary, and Josiah Jones.
1799, Aug.   15, Eglestone, Joseph Armstrong, and Marget Abram,
1788, May   9, Eiden, George, and Dorothy Kilmore.
1778, June   4, Einson, Ann, and Thomas Doten.
1780, June   26, Eisenack, Andrew, and Mary O'Neil.
1791, Nov.   13, Elbert, Richard, and Maria Fox.
1778, May   23, Elder, Andrew, and Bridgeth McNamara.
1778, Feb.   12, Elder Charles, and Elizabeth Nicholson.
1788, Oct.   7, Elder, David, and Sarah Chester.
1759, June   25, Elder, Robert, and Elizabeth Thomson.
1759, March   5, Elder, James, and Elisabet Maips.
1779, July   19, Eldridge, Isabel, and Edward Parker.
1789, March 24, Elkinton, Joshuah, and Mary Barry.
1796, Oct.   13, Ellemans, Johannah Margreta, and Jacob Hoffman.
1772, Dec.   23, Ellems, Cornelia, and Barneby Bright.
1773, Jan.   3, Ellems, John, aud Mary Butler.
1758, Dec.   4, Elleritz, Hannah, and John Pond.
1752, June   21, Elless, Peter, and Elizabeth Harkless.
1780, Sept.   16, Ellet, Elizabeth, and Peter Agar.
1752, May   23, Ellett, Elizabeth, and Robert Hanbest.
1773, June   13, Ellick and Kesiah, (free negroes.)
1762, July   24, Elliot, George, and Charity Addidle.
1796, May   6, Elliot, Jane, and William Crawford.
1792, April   9, Elliot, John, and Elizabeth Irvin.
1790, June   26, Elliot, Robert, and Jane Wallace.
1756, April   18, Elliott, Benjamin, and Sarah Musgrove.
1778, March 11, Ellis, Elizabeth, and Edward Bunten.
1765, April   15, Ellis, Humphrey, and Hannah Loyd.
1764, Oct.   23, Ellis, Jane, and Humphrey Loyd.
1793, May   14, Ellis, Jane, and Samuel Robeson, (Africans.)
1788, Oct.   2, Ellis, Joseph, and Rebecca Burroughs.
1796, Aug.   3, Ellis, Mary, and Peter Cain.
1795, April   2, Ellis, Rachel, and Jacob Fisher.
1782, Dec.   28, Ellis, Sebilla, and Jacob Matlack.
1765, April   30, Ellis, Susannah, and ———— Calley.
1765, March 28, Ellis, Thomas, and Sarah Hinson.
1796, Oct.   9, Ellis, Thomas, and Sarah Riner.
1751, July   22, Ellisson, Sarah, and John Carnack.
1775, Aug.   19, Ellison, Thomas, and Frances Brook.
1779, March   4, Ellot, James, and Isabella Haven.

1775, July   1, Ellot, John, and Ann Corkvon.
1790, Feb.   1, Ellot, Marget, and James Gardiner.
1778, May   8, Elly, Philip, and Mary Hamilton.
1777, Jan.   21, Elmes, Stephen, and Rebecca Oldfield.
1799, Jan.   13, Elton, Susannah, and Andrew Esler.
1795, Nov.   3, Elves, Mary, and William Jones.
1800, May   23, Elvin, William, and Mary McLaughlin.
1776, Dec.   1, Elwes, Rachel, and Thomas Adan.
1770, Oct.   22, Ely, Isaac, and Mary Carson.
1763, May   13, Emerey, William, and Elizabeth Lebon.
1767, June   15, Emerlatine, Mary Evah, and George Weidman.
1752, May   10, Emerson, Sarah, and John Archer.
1799, Aug.   27, Emerson, Susannah, and Laurence McCoy.
1776, June   9, Emert, Henry, and Mary Liperhealth.
1800, Nov.   3, Emlin, Joshua, and Cathrine Cowel.
1783, March   6, Emmester, Josiah, and Patience Hauser, (negroes.)
1770, March 25, Emmony, Elizabeth, and Benjamin Lewis.
1793, July   3, Ender, Thomas, and Mary Johnson.
1776, Oct.   20, Engel, John, and Susannah Rowem.
1791, Feb.   16, Eniard, James, and Elizabeth Davis.
1755, July   19, England, Catharine, and John Christopher Lodo-
                   vig.
1751, Feb.   19, England, Elizabeth, and William Paylin.
1792, April   1, England, Mary, and Michael Brown.
1782, June   24, Engles, Thomas, and Catherine Wilkinson.
1795, Nov.   6, English, David, and Jane Bogs.
1754, March 18, English, Elizabeth, and Patrick Burgain.
1760, Sept.   28, English, Israel, and Mary Martin.
1776, April   14, English, Sarah, and William English.
1776, April   14, English, William, and Sarah English.
1792, Nov.   16, Ennecy, Elenore, and Philip Duffey.
1766, Dec.   16, Ennis, George, and Ann Guin.
1791, May   27, Ennis, John, and Sara Bartlow.
1769, Feb.   2, Ensor, George, and Mary Bark.
1782, Oct.   6, Ent, Anne, and Jacob Myers.
1788, April   10, Entricken, George, and Ester Carpenter.
1800, March 22, Eockey, Lewis, and Mary MacDaniel.
1796, April   17, Epple, Cathrine, and John Ribbel.
1755, July   24, Erdelheit, William, and Maria Foghten.
1784, Oct.   2, Erdman, Charles, and Mary Terhorst.
1780, Jan.   12, Ereley, Ann, and Stephen Sampson.
1754, April   4, Ermgriester, John, and Elizabeth Weaver.
1788, May   16, Ernest, Elizabeth, and Gasper Shipe.
1765, Dec.   9, Ernsdorf, Henrich, and Elizabeth Mollidore.
1777, May   14, Errickson, Charles, and Ann Cowan.
1754, March 14, Erskin, Archibald, and Ann Wood.

1754, July 14, Erskin, William, and Mary Branagen.
1764, Feb. 23, Erven, Elizabeth, and Samuel Lowry.
1780, Jan. 25, Ervin, George, and Elizabeth Bowers.
1773, June 15, Ervin, James, and Debora Forder.
1773, June 20, Ervin, Mary, and Peter Hopkinson.
1779, May 2, Ervin, Samuel, and Corleneh Williams.
1780, March 15, Erwin, Elizabeth, and Hermenus Skuts.
1767, Jan. 17, Erwin, Hannah, and William Happard.
1777, Jan. 1, Erwin, James, and Martha Brook.
1791, Oct. 13, Erwin, Mary, and Charles Hamilton.
1766, July 7, Erwin, Philip, and Amelia Penny.
1798, July 25, Esdell, Robert, and Nancy Kidd.
1799, Jan. 13, Esler, Andrew, and Susannah Elton.
1755, Dec. 25, Esley, Christiana, and Charles Molbren.
1778, June 14, Esling, Christina, and Francis Ward.
1772, July 5, Esling, Mary, and· Ellick Frey.
1782, March 30, Esquire, John, and Mary Peddle.
1778, May 29, Essling, Hannah, and Andrew Dyer.
1790, April 7, Esling, Sarah, and Jacob Shroudy.
1782, Oct. 15, Establier, Paul, and Martha Mollen.
1778, Oct. 21, Estens, John, and Ann Mitchell.
1799, Nov. 29, Estlin, John, and Jane Mary Fullon.
1791, April 21, Estwick, Mary, and Abraham Wickers.
1791, Jan. 28, Esvin, George, and Sara Boy.
1755, May 29, Etherige, John, and Margarete St. John.
1777, July 10, Etherington, Robert, and Elizabeth Cannady.
1756, Oct. 17, Etter, Daniel, and Catherina Fenning.
1792, Nov. 4, Euderin, Evelina, and Peter Slough.
1773, June 22, Eustace, Charles, and Rachel Fitzrandolph.
1784, April 26, Eusty, Thomas, and Rosey Stewart.
1770, Jan. 23, Evance, Edward, and Rachel Mulling.
1776, Dec. 5, Evance, Elizabeth, and Robert Wood.
1776, Sept. 23, Evance, Mary, and Thomas Robeson.
1770, Dec. 23, Evance, Owen, and Mary Couch.
1763, May 11, Evans, Andy, and Samuel Pugh.
1796, Jan. 1, Evans, Barbara, and Michael Brainin.
1771, Oct. 6, Evans, Bernard, and Ann Kelly.
1778, Oct. 11, Evans, Cadwallader, and Sarah Cox.
1778, Aug. 6, Evans, Daniel, and Jane Davis.
1775, June 23, Evans, David, and Ann Seers.
1760, Oct. 22, Evans, David, and Elizabeth Dickson.
1775, Nov. 6, Evans, Edward, and Ann Ladd.
1790, Sept. 24, Evans, Elizabeth, and Cresswell Hunt.
1752, March 28, Evans, Elizabeth, and James Hodgskins.
1791, Sept. 17, Evans, Elizabeth, and Jonathan Clayton.
1755, May 24, Evans, Elizabeth, and William Mee.

1796, July   28, Evans, Engle, and Folkert Jeanson.
1754, April   23, Evans, Fanny, and Charles Ford.
1779, Jan.   31, Evans, John, and Barbara Hinkley.
1792, Oct.   28, Evans, John, and Elizabeth Miller.
1758, Feb.   16, Evans, John, and Elizabeth Updegrave.
1754, May   9, Evans, John, and Susanna Faulkner.
1764, Nov.   21, Evans, Jonathan, and Sarah Kirk.
1798, July   16, Evans, Joshua, and Patience Warton.
1777, July   10, Evans, Martin, and Hannah Fowler.
1780, March 13, Evans, Mary, and John Aine.
1775, Jan.   3, Evans, Mary, and John Allice.
1767, Aug.   5, Evans, Mary, and Mungrel Peters.
1763, June   14, Evans, Mary, and William Hatton.
1784, Aug.   13, Evans, Mary, and William King.
1775, July   16, Evans, Mary, and William Smith.
1760, April   12, Evans, Methusalah, and Hannah Roberts.
1783, Sept.   25, Evans, Peter, and Frances Millinor.
1777, Sept.   7, Evans, Phoebe, and John Earnest.
1752, June   11, Evans, Rachel, and James Maris.
1794, Feb.   17, Evans, Rachel, and Nathan Done.
1771, Dec.   19, Evans, Robert, and Martha Taylor.
1764, Dec.   29, Evans, Rosannah, and Jacob Brenneman.
1799, Sept.   1, Evans, Samuel, and Charlotte Sprogel.
1791, May   26, Evans, Sarah, and William Cook.
1785, March 13, Evans, Susannah, and James Pentland.
1791, Feb.   17, Evans, Susanna, and Thomas Chevalier.
1796, July   6, Evans, William, and Patty McCoy.
1755, Dec.   26, Evans, William, and Sarah Morgan.
1793, May   12, Eveans, Thomas, and Hannah Carolina Miers
1795, Dec.   24, Evel, Mary, and George McKoy.
1753, Dec.   25, Evens, Jane, and Peter Paul.
1782, Aug.   11, Evens, Lewis, and Mary Weymar.
1789, Dec.   3, Everhart, George, and Rachel Magill.
1756, June   5, Everly, Michael, and Margareth Brath.
1753, July   26, Evens, James, and Mary Price.
1758, Jan.   3, Evens, Sary, and Anthony Duchee.
1764, Aug.   13, Eves, Jane, and Moses Gurlin.
1761, Aug.   29, Evins, James, and Sarah Evins.
1762, Nov.   29, Evins, James, and Sarah Evins.
1761, Aug.   29, Evins, Sarah, and James Evins.
1762, Nov.   29, Evins, Sarah, and James Evins.
1779, May   11, Evit, Richard, and Jane Maxfield.
1766, Sept.   3, Evitt, William, and Elizabeth Palmer.
1778, Jan.   27, Ewin, Sarah, and Thomas Patterson.
1777, Nov.   22, Ewin, Sarah, and William Cheur.
1781, Nov.   9, Ewing, William, and Gazelena Lane.

1778, June   9, Excell, Christina, and Joseph Kirkbride.
1784, April   11, Eyler, Susannah and John Tutell.
1782, Feb.   21, Eyre, Anne, and Martin Jugiesz.
1791, Sept.   28, Eyre, Lewis, and Susannah Worell.
1783, March   27, Facey, Esther, and Francis Cramer.
1791, Feb. ` 10, Facundus, Margret, and Christopher Raphoon.
1777, March   7, Fagan, Mary, and Joseph Dempsey.
1790, April   1, Faggins, John, and Mary Fritts.
1751, Oct.   13, Fagleline, Margaret, and Oenn Cargen.
1777, Oct.   14, Fagon, Elizabeth, and Henry Wolf.
1760, Feb.   19, Fagon, John, and Elizabeth Holm.
1796, June   5, Fagundus, Marget, and John Henry.
1760, Aug.   26, Faires, William, and Mary Ransbury.
1766, Dec.   22, Fairwether, Catharine, and George Gold.
1762, Aug.   3, Fairweather, John, and Ann Buscark.
1761, Aug.   3, Fairweather, John, and Ann Buseark.
1777, Feb.   18, Faithful William, and Jean Farrel.
1796, Feb.   29, Falcner, James, and Jane Munce.
1778, Jan.   1, Falkner, Thomas, and Jane McPherson.
1757, July   10, Falkner, William, and Francis Hudle.
1777, June   29, Fallowalta, Benet, and Elizabeth Young.
1778, Jan.   9, Fallows, Robert, and Elizabeth Young.
1786, April   24, Falls, Sarah, and Hans Keen.
1757, March   3, Fand, Ann, and John Millor.
1762, Sept.   4, Fandeberry, Derrick Cornelius, and Hannah Led-
                   ston.
1782, Oct.   22, Fanighaus, John, and Margret McMasters.
1781, Sept.   6, Fannan, Antony, and Rebecca Brooks.
1760, Sept.   22, Farbottle, Mary, and John Whitol.
1778, March   1, Fare, Elizabeth, and William Johnston.
1777, Jan.   11, Fares, Patrick, and Elizabeth Garvey.
1767, Dec.   10, Faries, Elizabeth, and James Cochran.
1789, April   19, Farin, Bridget, and John Dear.
1778, Feb.   26, Faris, Mary, and Edward Willcox.
1760, Dec.   4, Faris, Mary, and Thomas Gordon.
1796, Dec.   11, Farley, James, and Sarah Irons.
1761, April   20, Farmer, Christianna, and Peter Wenger.
1799, April   25, Farmer, Eliza, and Samuel Milbank.
1763, Aug.   24, Farmer, George, and Ann Raisford.
1766, Jan.   26, Farmer, Martha, and William Sole.
1752, July   13, Farmer, Sarah, and Peter Brown.
1778, May   29, Farmouth, Mary, and James Hughs.
1796, March 20, Farnel, Christopher Fredric, and Sarah Cox.
1776, May   8, Farnsworth, James, and Ann Gordon.
1792, June   19, Farone, Edward, and Ann McDonald.
1752, Dec.   12, Farorre, William, and Nally Alexander.

1790, Oct.   2, Farra, Samuel, and Hester Reese.
1772, April   22, Farran, John, and Mary Black.
1797, June   1, Farran, Margret, and Archibald Cook.
1779, July   31, Farrel, Ann, and John Cunningham.
1777, Feb.   18, Farrel, Jean, and William Faithful.
1778, April   8, Farrel, Mary, and Duncan McNobb.
1798, Aug.   15, Farren, Bridget, and Mathew Marr.
1796, May   31, Farren, Cathrine, and Edward Connel.
1781, Dec.   18, Farrer, Catherine, and James Teylor.
1771, April   9, Farrier, Robert, and Mary Tibberland,
1756, April   12, Farris, Ann, and John Jones.
1758, Nov.   16, Farris, John, and Ester Steel.
1781, Feb.   1, Farver, John, and Sarah Perry.
1778, Feb.   16, Faster, Thomas, and Mary O'Bryan.
1769, Aug.   25, Faster, William, and Elizabeth Crane.
1756, Dec.   13, Fastor, Catharine, and Andrew Foley.
1762, Nov.   23, Fastor, Jane, and Thomas Thompson.
1779, Jan.   26, Fatherine, Rebecca, and Jacob Meyer.
1782, May   6, Faucet, Philip, and Jemima Scannel.
1754, May   9, Faulkner, Susanna, and John Evans.
1753, June   19, Faulkner, William, and Susanna Tate.
1792, June   24, Fawcet, Joseph, and Ann Wood.
1762, March 23, Fay, Eleonore, and Andrew Donaldson.
1788, Feb.   19, Feagon, Elizabeth, and Benjamin Berry.
1761, April   29, Fearbrother, Mary, and Lachen Mintock.
1768, Nov.   13, Featherby, Jeremiah, and Sarah Woodley.
1774, Oct,   16, Feel, Peter, and Lucretia Titus.
1779, May   23, Fees, Catherine, and Humphrey Mecumber.
1752, Oct.   1, Fegen, Brigith, and Christopher Fitzgareld.
1764, April   22, Fegerley, John, and Barbarah Hoffman.
1790, May   11, Feilder, David, and Cathrine Collins.
1761, April   13, Feites, Jeane, and Peter Phile.
1782, May   15, Fell, Anne, and John Raworth.
1779, Nov.   16, Fellon, Mary, and William Cook.
1791, July   5, Fellon, William, and Cathrine Lewis.
1776, Feb.   4, Felles, Mathew, and Catharine Wallbert.
1751, Nov.   15, Felten, Thomas, and Martha Parker.
1777, Dec.   20, Fendrick, Hannah, and John Mead.
1759, Sept.   17, Fenn, Honor, and William Harper.
1778, Sept.   27, Fennemore, Mary, and Jane McPherson.
1780, Dec.   14, Fenner, Mary, and John Foulke.
1756, Oct.   17, Fenning, Catherina, and Daniel Etter.
1781, June   11, Fennymore, Jonathan, and Sarah Watson.
1752, Oct.   9, Fenstermacher, Mary, and John Warner.
1760, June   2, Fentle, Frederick, and Elizabeth Meyer.
1794, Sept.   24, Fenwick, Joseph, and Marget Williams.

1791, Aug.   20, Ferby, Timothy, and Judith West.
1778, Jan.   13, Ferd, Pen, and John Mud.
1780, June   18, Ferguson, Alexander, and Christine McDanold.
1796, May   21, Ferguson, Ann, and George Fowler.
1772, April 21, Ferguson, Henry Hugh, and Elizabeth Grame.
1782, Jan.   10, Ferguson, Henry, and Mary Potts.
1775, Sept. 25, Ferguson, Hugh, and Elizabeth Mullan.
1794, Sept. 11, Ferguson, Hugh, and Sarah Carney.
1794, Nov.   9, Ferguson, James, and Sarah Ponder.
1796, Aug.   8, Ferguson, John, and Ann Richardson.
1789, Aug.   6, Ferguson, Mary, and John Cloff.
1795, May   26, Ferguson, Robert, and Martha Wallace.
1792, May   3, Ferguson, Samuel, and Elizabeth Stuart.
1794, July   11, Ferlan, William, and Mary Morphy.
1778, Jan.   18, Ferman, Johannah, and Thomas Greenwood.
1754, June   26, Fernal, Catharine, and Engelbert Lock.
1778, Sept.   2, Fernhaver, Jacob, and Catharine Maur.
1794, Jan.   19, Ferran, Marget, and Lewis Philly.
1795, Dec.   24, Ferrel, Mary, and William Gallagher.
1782, Dec.   5, Ferrel, Rachel, and Jonathan Cox.
1778, June   15, Ferrel, Sarah, and John Orgat.
1793, April 11, Ferrel, William, and Elizabeth Gillet.
1775, June   20, Fest, Francis, and Sarah Thomson.
1778, April 25, Fetton, Mary, and Samuel Binns.
1779, Sept.   3, Few, Elizabeth, and John G. Lang.
1773, Jan.   31, Fexon, Mary, and Ernest Forster.
1772, July   23, Fians, William, and Mary Rice.
1792, Sept. 13, Field, Elizabeth, and John Bross.
1775, Sept. 17, Field, Elizabeth, and Michael Swiser.
1778, March 31, Field, Thomas and Catharine Amrick.
1787, Nov.   17, Fifer, Elizabeth, and William Blake.
1788, April 25, Fifer, Jacob, and Abigail Chesman.
1791, May   21, Fifer, Sara, and James Caire.
1758, April   1, Fight, Susanna, and Andrew Lock.
1794, Dec.   29, Fighter, Mathew Aaron, and Ann Johnson.
1778, April 30, Filgate, Sarah, and Duncan MacWey.
1773, Feb.   7, Filliger, George, and Ann Brown.
1793, Nov.   22, Fimple, John, and Ann Biddle.
1762, July   29, Finaghan, James, and Elizabeth Steel.
1799, Oct.   27, Finch, Susannah B., and Richard Guy.
1775, Nov.   5, Findley, John, and Lucy Gamon.
1777, Oct.   9, Fink, John, and Mary Cope.
1797, June   8, Finkbine, Fredric, and Latitia McGill.
1783, June   16, Finn, Mary, and John Jordan.
1772, Aug.   9, Finn, Thomas, and Mary Roads.
1755, May   28, Finnes, Mary, and Henry Tuckness.

1777, May 4, Finney, David, and Sarah Nielson.
1784, March 11, Finney, Esther, and Adam Wetsner.
1790, Oct. 24, Finnicon, Bartley, and Barbara Washbury, (or Wasby.)
1760, Jan. 7, Finny, James, and Mary Cordy.
1797, Nov. 30, Finny, John, and Elizabeth Carter.
1799, April 24, Finny, Marget, and James Martin.
1796, Jan. 12, Finny, Rachel, and John Granville.
1769, Feb. 25, Fintly, Robert, and Margarett Edwards.
1795, June 26, Fish, Casper, and Agnes Sharp.
1800, April 26, Fish, Isaac, and Eunice Huggins.
1763, Feb. 22, Fisher, Ann, and James Reet.
1783, June 26, Fisher, Archibald and Anne Dennis.
1792, July 21, Fisher, Cathrine, and George Whethrell.
1794, Nov. 10, Fisher, Christina, and Archibald Cook.
1774, April 8, Fisher, Daniel, and Margaret Krees.
1764, Jan. 1, Fisher, Elizabeth, and John Barns.
1792, June 28, Fisher, George, and Lydia Hughs.
1799, Jan. 13, Fisher, Hannah, and David More.
1790, May 8, Fisher, Hanna, and Thomas Vear Jones.
1795, April 2, Fisher, Jacob, and Rachel Ellis.
1780, May 20, Fisher, James, and Mary Davis.
1777, Jan. 30, Fisher, Jeremiah, and Elizabeth Young.
1795, Jan. 20, Fisher, John, and Ann Brown.
1799, Oct. 31, Fisher, John, and Elizabeth Lectur.
1792, Oct. 23, Fisher, John, and Mary Kelly.
1792, Dec. 2, Fisher, John, and Sarah Beard.
1791, Nov. 19, Fisher, John, and Susanna Heney.
1755, March 17, Fisher, Margaret, and John Tomlinson.
1796, Oct. 6, Fisher, Margret, and Mathias Larson.
1766, May 23, Fisher, Mary, and Benjamin Hoster.
1755, Feb. 25, Fisher, Mary, and John Warner.
1794, April 17, Fisher, Mary, and William White.
1779, Dec. 16, Fisher, Nancy, and Stephen Pascal.
1780, Dec. 16, Fisher, Nancy, and Stephen Pascal.
1789, Feb. 7, Fisher, Robert, and Christiana Montgomery.
1771, April 14, Fisher, Sarah, and George Wance.
1780, June 29, Fisher, Thomas, and Margaret Nantz.
1799, July 22, Fisher, Walter, and Margret Jeffers.
1764, Oct. 7, Fisher, William, and Ann Stephenson.
1792, Dec. 14, Fisler, Elizabeth, and James Cassidy.
1798, March 16, Fiss, Peter, and Sarah Edwards.
1781, Aug. 17, Fister, Lenah, and Thomas Bignell.
1753, Aug. 19, Fitter, Edward, and Elizabeth Deverix.
1775, July 11, Fitzell, William, and Charlot Mary Jervis.
1752, Oct. 1, Fitzgareld, Christopher, and Brigith Fegen.

1773, Oct.   14, Fitzgerald, Alley, and Andrew Supplee.
1778, June   13, Fitzgerald, Ann, and John Nealey.
1776, Oct.   20, Fitzgerald, Ann, and Thomas Smiles.
1777, Sept.   13, Fitzgerald, Eleanor, and John Melleth.
1772, Dec.   13, Fitzgerald, Elenor, and Nathaniel Reynolds.
1794, May   13, Fitzgerald, Garet, and Jane McKew.
1791, Dec.   15, Fitzgerald, Hugh, and Hester Clifft.
1778, Jan.   12, Fitzgerald, Mary, and Edward Rogers.
1774, Sept.   29, Fitzgerald, Mary, and William Gregory.
1751, Dec.   22, Fitzgerald, Robert, and Nancy Sinjohn.
1800, July   24, Fitzgerald, Thomas, and Sarah Williams.
1777, Aug.   24, Fitzgerald, William, and Mary Harris.
1766, Oct.   1, Fitsimmons, James, and Ann Beard.
1766, July   6, Fitzjareld, James, and Mary West.
1775, June   18, Fitzomans, James, and Elizabeth Lawrence.
1778, Dec.   3, Fitzpatrick, John, and Bridget Jennin.
1781, May   30, Fitspatrick, John, and Eleonor Simson.
1775, Oct.   9, Fitzpatrick, William, and Mary Graham.
1773, June   22, Fitzrandolph, Rachel, and Charles Eustace.
1759, April   12, Fitzsimons, Philip, and Mary Goldsmith.
1761, June   10, Flack, Elenore, and Thomas Cotboro.
1779, March 10, Flaherty, John, and Mary Miller.
1769, Nov.   5, Flammen, Catharine, and Andrew Miller.
1791, April   28, Flanigan, Stephen, and Phebe Vance.
1769, July   26, Flaniken, Anne, and James Dallet.
1758, Nov.   28, Flanming, James, and Matty Hairs.
1799, Aug.   1, Flannigan, Thomas, and Mary More.
1753, May   14, Flannagan, Mary, and James Colgun.
1756, July   5, Fleming, Elizabeth, and Benjamin Pickerton.
1755, Jan.   31, Fleming, William, and Elizabeth Gordon.
1779, April   19, Flemings, Thomas, and Elizabeth Lewis.
1782, Feb.   5, Flemmans, Mary, and Savory Toy.
1759, Feb.   4, Flemming, Elisabet, and William Wright.
1796, Dec.   29, Flemming, Sterne, and Cathrine Limerick.
1763, Oct.   27, Flemmings, Ann, and Ruben Eastlack.
1776, Jan.   22, Flemond, Elizabeth, and Thomas Grannon.
1781, July   30, Flenn, Catharine, and Cornelius Corrigan.
1769, April   1, Fletcher, Alexander, and Elizabeth Corry.
1778, Dec.   3, Fletcher, Elizabeth, and Robert Lee.
1799, Nov.   6, Fletcher, Elizab., and Samuell Snell.
1776, Sept.   9, Fletcher, John, and Margaret Wanbebird.
1762, Jan.   26, Fletsher, Alexander, and Mary Long.
1777, July   31, Flick, Margaret, and John Whiteman.
1785, Sept.   29, Flick, Mary, and William Stidham.
1799, June   2, Flin, John, and Marget Howard.
1792, Feb.   14, Flinders, Mary, and Arnor Preston.

24—Vol. VIII.

1752, Sept. 27, Fling, Charles, and Ruth Reed.
1794, March 20, Fling, Hannah, and Thomas Eastborn.
1783, April 24, Fling, Sarah, and Jesse Lewis.
1794, July 13, Fling, Susannah, and John Smith.
1767, June 11, Flinn, Edward, and Sarah Johnson.
1764, Dec. 8, Flett, John, and Catharine Webber.
1757, June 6, Floid. Patrick, and Elizabeth Shales.
1782, May 5, Florence, David and Nelly Toy.
1781, March 6, Flory, Anthony, and Mary Bouden.
1778, Dec. 7, Flower, Catharine, and William Rods.
1771, April 1, Flower, Elizabeth, and Christopher Portell.
1771, Feb. 12, Flower, Hannah, and John Wall.
1779, May 15, Flower, Jemima, and John McKever.
1779, Feb. 15, Flower, Margaret, and Christian Navel.
1771, March 4, Flower, Philip, and Mary Fortuner.
1785, Sept. 8, Flower, Richard, and Henrietta Graham.
1769, Dec. 31, Flower, Susannah, and Jonathan Adams.
1792, Dec. 13, Flowers, Cathrine, and Daniel Rice.
1797, Feb. 16, Flowers, Christian, and Hannah Bishopberry.
1779, May 27, Flowers, Margarett, and Ely Fylden.
1790, Nov. 11, Flowers, Marget, and Joseph Ford.
1753, Oct. 10, Flowers, William, and Mary Powel.
1774, Sept. 26, Flowery, Mary, and Joseph Stevenson.
1793, Sept. 23, Floyd, Sarah, and Robert Wile.
1792, Dec. 8, Floyd, Solomon, and Jeremiah Loyd.
1795, Sept. 4, Floyd, William, and Jane Lindsey.
1757, Dec. 20, Fluallen, Samuel, and Hannah Cheesman.
1761, July 23, Fluellen, Eliza, and John Jacob Warnich.
1761, March 3, Fluellen, John, and Elizabeth Morton.
1779, Feb. 21, Flude, Timothy, and Martha Thomson.
1799, Sept. 30, Flyng, Mary, and Samuel Brown.
1759, May 20, Fodheam, Margaretta, and Peter Daele.
1760, Oct. 24, Fogel, Adam, and Margaretta Hommins.
1795, May 18, Fogel, Dorothy, and Ephraim Ross.
1758, May 9, Foggett, Richard, and Ann Hymn.
1755, July 24, Foghten, Maria, and William Erdelheit.
1777, Jan. 27, Fogten, Catharine, and Mathias Conrad.
1756, Dec. 13, Foley, Andrew, and Catharine Fastor.
1795, Aug. 5, Folger, Charles William, and Ann Conelly.
1796, March 23, Folk, George, and Edith Jockum.
1778, April 15, Folks, Benjamin, and Margaret Southerick.
1793, May 5, Follen, Cathrine, and Francis Nugent.
1756, Jan. 18, Foot, Richard, and Elizabeth Knight.
1761, June 25, Forbes, Ann, and James Rogers.
1762, Aug. 25, Forbes, Ann, and James Rogers.
1794, Aug. 20, Forbes, Hannah, and William Chickin.

1798, Dec.   13, Forbes, Martha, and William Thompson.
1799, July   24, Force, David, and Rebecca Goslin.
1800, May   7, Force, Mary, and Jesse Franklin.
1754, April   23, Ford, Charles, and Fanny Evans.
1777, Jan.   31, Ford, John, and Ann Blackin.
1790, Nov.   11, Ford, Joseph, and Marget Flowers.
1777, Sept.   18, Ford, Margaret, and James Buharon.
1777, Aug.   31, Ford, Margaret, and James Marshall.
1798, July   9, Ford, Maria, and William Thackury.
1752, Oct.   23, Ford, Mary, and Daniel Sircks.
1794, March   31, Ford, Mary, and John Delabare.
1781, Oct.   1, Ford, Mary, and Joseph Smith.
1778, Dec.   14, Ford, Matthew, and Sarah Jones.
1797, Aug.   31, Ford, Patrick, and Nancy Burke.
1790, July   26, Ford, Philip, and Helena Culen.
1782, Dec.   17, Ford, Rose Anne, and William McClery.
1777, Dec.   1, Ford, Sarah, and Robert Con.
1780, May   2, Ford, Susannah, and Philip Thepo.
1773, June   15, Forder, Debora, and James Ervin.
1758, Feb.   27, Fordham, Benjamin, and Eliseba Shed.
1778, Sept.   19, Fordham, George, and Mary Shippey.
1778, Dec.   13, Fordman, Mary, and Henry Wolfe.
1777, Feb.   25, Forel, Mary, and James Bell.
1773, July   19, Foreman, Mary, and Patrick Carr.
1770, Nov.   4, Forepaugh, William, and Mary Remer.
1794, May   13, Forest, James, and Mary Steel.
1787, Feb.   6, Forest, Jane, and Philip Cook.
1759, Feb.   4, Forester, Christina, and James Watson.
1767, May   25, Forester, Jeane, and Patrick Brady.
1790, March   29, Forester, Rebecca, and William Johnson.
1783, Aug.   27, Forlow, Aga, and Louis Mory.
1753, March   18, Forman, Elenor, and Philip Grandin.
1794, May   4, Forman, Sarah, and John H. Scattergood.
1800, Sept.   23, Forner, Ann, and Charles Louis Fourcroi.
1800, Jan.   12, Forpaugh, William, and Mary Abbett.
1754, June   30, Forquar, Jane, and James Godfrey.
1791, July   12, Forset, Hanna, and Andrew Mcquire.
1793, Feb.   13, Forsith, Cathrine, and Lawrence MacSheane.
1794, Aug.   14, Forster, Ann, and Samuel Pennock.
1776, Nov.   12, Forster, Christine, and Joseph Deyer.
1773, Jan.   31, Forster, Ernest, and Mary Fexon.
1780, Feb.   7, Forster, James, and Elizabeth Anderson.
1759, July   2, Forster, Mary, and Robert Johnston.
1770, Nov.   7, Forsyth, Isaac, and Sarah Williams.
1782, Oct.   27, Fortescue, Mary, and Henry Slomer.
1789, July   5, Fortner, Sarah, and Francis Tyrrel.

1799, July　　11, Fortune, Sarah, and Shandy Yard.
1771, March　　4, Fortuner, Mary, and Philip Flower.
1798, Jan.　　17, Fosler, George, and Hannah Duhaven.
1765, June　　7, Foster, Alexander, and Catharine Huffman.
1796, Aug.　　25, Foster, Ann, and Cantwell Douglas.
1771, Aug.　　11, Foster, Dorothy Mary, and Christian Fox.
1787, May　　10, Foster, Elizabeth, and Asa Shircliff.
1787, Sept.　　18, Foster, George, and Buly Quin.
1777, Jan.　　15, Foster, George, and Elizabeth Pole.
1781, Aug.　　9, Foster, Hannah, and Henry Hudson.
1754, Jan.　　15, Foster, Hannah, and William Topham.
1776, May　　21, Foster, Mary, and John Stonemetz.
1797, Dec.　　9, Foster, Mary, and William Goodfellow.
1756, Sept.　　14, Foster, Rachel, and Nicholas Helfinston.
1755, May　　3, Foster, Susanna, and Thomas Watkins.
1755, April　　8, Fouler, Mercy, and Isaac Butterworth.
1755, Nov.　　5, Foulguier, John Jacob, and Christiana Barbara Schoumacher.
1780, Dec.　　14, Foulke, John, and Mary Fenner.
1798, June　　23, Foulk, Margaret, and John Brooks.
1794, July　　11, Foulke, Peter, and Mary Dady.
1799, Oct.　　19, Fountain, William, and Sarah Phenix.
1800, Sept.　　23, Fourcroi, Charles Louis, and Ann Forner.
1758, March 26, Fouster, Daniel, and Mary Young.
1786, Nov.　　30, Fontollet, John, and Rebecca Bleuet.
1775, Feb.　　10, Fowber, Isaac, and Bridget Kiggins.
1779, Aug.　　16, Fowler, Bridget, and Hugh McClenegen.
1777, Nov.　　9, Fowler, Elizabeth, and John Cook.
1796, May　　21, Fowler, George, and Ann Ferguson.
1793, Nov.　　25, Fowler, George, and Marget Lesley.
1777, July　　10, Fowler, Hannah, and Martin Evans.
1753, July　　7, Fowler, Isaac, and Grace Butter.
1778, Nov.　　5, Fowler, Mary, and James Bray.
1756, March 23, Fowler, Morris, and Mary Sleaer.
1791, Aug.　　4, Fowler, Patric, and Susanna Allison.
1780, Sept.　　7, Fowler, Thomas, and Mary May.
1755, Sept.　　15, Fowler, William, and Amy Clifton.
1786, Dec.　　12, Fox, Adam, and Anne Winson.
1771, Aug.　　11, Fox, Christian, and Dorothy Mary Foster.
1788, Nov.　　12, Fox, George, and Martha Comfort.
1784, Oct.　　27, Fox, George, and Sarah Gosline.
1787, Oct.　　12, Fox, James, and Bridget Cramer.
1758, Sept.　　1, Fox, James, and Mary Bartelson.
1785, Aug.　　28, Fox, Jeremiah, and Ann Cameron.
1774, Dec.　　4, Fox, Joas, and Anna Shaw.
1773, Aug.　　8, Fox, John, and Mary Knees.

1791, Nov.   13, Fox, Maria, and Richard Elbert.
1761, Nov.   1, Fox, Michael, and Elizabeth Goothen.
1762, Nov.   1, Fox, Michael, and Elizabeth Goothen.
1792, Sept. 25, Fox, Nancy, and Joseph Bancs.
1795, March 12, Fox, Peter, and Elizabeth Huston.
1778, Feb.   17, Fox, Rebecca, and Arthur French.
1783, Dec.   16, Fox, Robert, and Rebecca Maxfield.
1799, June   17, Fox, Sarah, and George Lidell.
1793, April 18, Fox, Sarah, and John McConnell.
1798, July   2, Fox, Sarah, and Thomas Cummings.
1778, April 30, Fox, Thomas, and Elizabeth Steneeson.
1762, July   1, Foxin, Anna Margaretha, and Christian Galley.
1761, July   1, Foxin, Ann Margaretha and Ehnstiern Galley.
1782, Oct.   16, Foy, Mathew, and Mary Crag.
1758, Sept. 15, Fraiser, James, and Elizabeth Cox.
1759, Feb.   18, Fraley, Elisabet, and William Tustian.
1799, Aug.   14, Fraley, Mary, and Patric MacMunnigal.
1756, March   4, Frame, Ann, and William Jemison.
1761, Sept. 30, Frame, Archibald, and Mary Lohey.
1762, Nov.   30, Frame, Archibald, and Mary Lohey.
1786, Nov.   4, Frame, Isaac, and Catherine James.
1757, Oct.   12, Frame, Thomas, and Mary Williams.
1791, Oct.   6, France, John, and Catharine Rife.
1779, May   24, Frances, Ann, and Timothy Donohue.
1794, March 31, Frances, Lydia, and Adam Cleland.
1798, April 16, Francis, Christopher, and Elizabeth Marts.
1759, Nov.   1, Francis, David, and Margeth Bartelson.
1772, Oct.   29, Francis, Hannah, and Joseph Homes.
1792, June   3, Francis, Jacob, and Susanna Wilkinson.
1777, March 18, Francis, John, and Elizabeth Lowder.
1780, July   17, Francis, John, and Sophia Johnson.
1794, March 31, Francis, Lydia, and Adam Cleland.
1778, Sept. 10, Francis, Sidney, and Francis Joden.
1791, June   13, Francis, S. Minchin, and Susanna Chevalier.
1782, Aug.   12, Franckford, Magdalen, and John Kirchner.
1795, Oct.   27, Frank, Maria Elizab., and Isaac Moor.
1753, Dec.   10, Franklen, Martha, and John Connar.
1800, May   7, Franklin, Jesse, and Mary Force.
1777, Nov.   20, Franklin, Joseph, and Elizabeth Ebright.
1785, June   14, Franklin, Samuel, and Letitia Burrows.
1790, April 12, Franks, Adam, and Elizabeth Brant.
1782, July   9, Franks, Isaac, and Mary Davison.
1762, June   23, Franks, John, and Margaret Philmeyer.
1778, July   25, Frantz, Catharine, and Joseph Roberts.
1765, Jan.   22, Frapold, Mary, and Michael Chrocpan.
1779, May   13, Fraser, John, and Elizabeth Gordon.

1798, Jan.　24, Fraser, William, and Elizabeth Young.
1765, Dec.　5, Frazier, Elizabeth, and John Brant.
1777, Oct.　11, Frazier, Jean, and George Scoals.
1794, Feb.　18, Frazier, Mary, and James Hinderson.
1759, Aug.　8, Frazier, William, and Elizabeth Welteardson.
1758, May　29, Fredaway, Sarah, and John Nailor.
1791, Feb.　9, Frederic, Rebecca, and Israel Helms.
1753, Dec.　17, Frederick, Lawrence, and Elizabeth Neithermark.
1773, Jan.　17, Fredericks, Christine, and John Lycom.
1755, July　8, Fredly, Andrew, and Anna Elizabeth Levan.
1770, Sept.　4, Free, John, and Hannah Denais.
1790, May　9, Freeborn, Anthony, and Elizabeth Zimmerman.
1790, Nov.　21, Freeland, James, and Rachel Talbot.
1767, June　16, Freeman, Elizabeth, and Samuel Alford.
1759, July　12, Freeman, Elsah, and William Hayes.
1781, Dec.　28, Freeman, George, and Mely Way.
1778, June　3, Freeman, Jane, and Charles Sloane.
1793, Aug.　17, Freeman, Joshua, and Maria Mason.
1778, Dec.　15, Freeman, Martha, and Patrick Welsh.
1757, Oct.　17, Freeman, Robert, and Margaret Neeson.
1787, Feb.　8, Freeman, Robert, and Patience Arrans.
1778, April　26, Freeze, John Michael, and Sophia Leonora.
1752, May　8, Freiley, Leonard, and Catharine Brandley.
1794, Aug.　29, Freize, Elizabeth Rosannah, and John Curtis.
1796, Dec.　11, Frence, Marget, and John Luke.
1755, May　17, French, Ann, and William Gray.
1778, Feb.　17, French, Arthur, and Rebecca Fox.
1779, July　28, French, Jane, and William Knowls.
1780, March　6, French, Margaret, and William Hamilton.
1784, June　6, French, Robert, and Barbara Kinch.
1783, May　26, French, William, and Ruth Higby.
1774, Dec.　12, Fresher, Mary, and William Wallman.
1782, June　18, Fresier, Archibald, and Sarah Penn.
1781, Oct.　25, Fresier, Hugh, and Margaret McGregger.
1773, Feb.　6, Freviller, Mary, and Joseph Page.
1772, July　5, Frey, Ellick, and Mary Esling.
1758, Sept.　17, Freyer, Samuel, and Mary Glene.
1790, March　1, Frick, Mary, and Nathaniel Miles.
1799, June　19, Fried, Elizabeth, and George Taxis.
1795, Aug.　12, Friend, Elizabeth, and Stuart Simpson.
1777, Oct.　19, Fries, Philip, and Catharine Bop.
1771, Feb.　13, Frill, Daniel, and Catherine Murry.
1781, Oct.　30, Fritch, Andrew, and Mary Brock.
1775, July　24, Fritch, Daniel, and Elizabeth Owens.
1769, May　27, Frites, Casper, and Margaretta Wallis.
1781, May　24, Frits, Margaret, and John Criner.

1790, April   1, Frits, Mary, and John Faggans.
1772, Oct.   20, Frittz, Sarah, and Samuel Potts.
1779, April   1, Fritz, John, and Mary Kuhn.
1791, June   5, Fritz, John, and Sarah Young.
1780, July   17, Fritz, Peter, and Sarah Moore.
1790, Oct.   5, From, Susanna, and Michael Linn.
1781, Sept.   13, Frost, James, and Elizabeth Skinner.
1757, July   4, Frost, Thomas, and Mary Turner.
1792, April   29, Fry, Abraham, and Sarah Lewis, (Africans.)
1771, March   9, Fry, Joseph, and Elizabeth Meyers,
1788, April   13, Fry, Margery, and John Keighter.
1779, May   17, Fry, Mary, and John Stewart.
1796, Nov.   6, Fry, Michael, and Priscilla Sweeten.
1791, Nov.   24, Fry, Richard, and Mary Seely.
1789, April   8, Frys, Mary Anne, and Thomas Martin.
1769, May   11, Fuder, Catharine, and John Loesher.
1769, Sept.   2, Fudge, Mary, and John Gater.
1790, March   11, Fugundus, Henry, and Mary Dougherty.
1758, June   10, Fulderd, Thomas, and Elizabeth Harp.
1768, Dec.   18, Fullan, Daniel, and Mary Willett.
1793, June   9, Fullen, Mary, and Alexander McGriggor.
1758, June   17, Fuller, John, and Mary Solluvan.
1781, May   13, Fuller, Mary, and Philip Cline.
1794, March   21, Fullerton, Cathrine, and John Carson.
1785, Jan.   27, Fullerton, John, and Elizabeth Remick.
1765, July   31, Fullerton, William, and Elenor Donaldson.
1771, Oct.   27, Fullford, Henry, and Mary Stutting.
1770, Jan.   31, Fullinton, Patrick, and Judith Webb.
1799, Nov.   29, Fullon, Jane Mary, and John Estlin.
1788, July   15, Fulman, Catharine, and John Nicholas Bloomey.
1778, May   15, Fulton, John, and Ann Templeton.
1783, Jan.   9, Fulton, John, and Catherine Weyman.
1758, April   2, Fulton, Mary, and Joshua Moore.
1790, Oct.   9, Fults, Marget, and Henry Ramstrœm.
1795, Feb.   16, Furey, Cathrine, and William Crotty.
1777, May   18, Furguson, Jean, and John Little.
1796, Feb.   21, Furlong, John, and Elizabeth Revely.
1766, Sept.   25, Furnis, William, and Margaret Holmes.
1757, May   3, Furrett, James, and Catharine Bartlet.
1756, May   24, Furst, Jacob, and Ann Krafts.
1796, April   7, Fury, Marget, and William Huntrods.
1788, Sept.   8, Fwekes, Daniel, and Rebecca Lawrence.
1778, Jan.   7, Fyen, Eleanor, and David Kelley.
1779, May   27, Fylden, Ely, and Margarett Flowers.
1778, Dec.   22, Fylden, and Henery Harrison.
1771, Nov.   16, Gabb, John, and Mary Green.

1792, Feb.   19, Gabel, Philip, and Susanna Smith.
1760, March 23, Gahagen, Hannah, and Abraham Place.
1798, Dec.   11, Gailey, Cathrine, and David Navin.
1799, Jan.   31, Gainer, Jane, and James Tailor.
1788, July   1, Galaspey, Anne, and John McKinley.
1774, June 16, Galbreath, Archibald, and Margaret Galbreath.
1766, July   9, Galbraith, Catharine, and Charles Tenant.
1771, Nov. 16, Galbreath, Jane, and Edward Lawrence.
1767, Nov. 12, Galbreath, Latitia, and Jonathan Biles.
1774, June 16, Galbreath, Margaret, and Archibald Galbreath.
1780, Jan.   2, Galen, Francis, and Margarett Campbell.
1780, March 28, Galespey, George, and Mary King.
1777, May   4, Gallagher, James, and Mary Rush.
1795, Dec. 24, Gallagher, William, and Mary Ferrel.
1764, April 19, Gallagher, William, and Mary McCoy.
1794, Aug. 18, Gallenogh, Patric, and Susanna Brown.
1780, Feb. 26, Gallerd, John, and Elizabeth Garret.
1762, July   1, Galley, Christian, and Anna Margaretha Foxin.
1761, July   1, Galley, Ehnstiern, and Ann Margaretha Foxin.
1776, Dec. 31, Gallgey, Thomas, and Sarah Hinderson.
1798, Feb. 16, Gallon, James, and Phebe Johnson.
1780, May 24, Gallougher, Catharine, and John Lowe.
1778, Nov.   8, Gallougher, Hannah, and David McLeland.
1769, Nov.   8, Gallougher, John, and Hannah Davids.
1766, April 13, Galloway, Elizabeth, and George Wood.
1800, Dec. 27, Galloway, Jane, and John Thomson.
1794, May 25, Galloway, Joseph, and Mary Davis.
1763, April 20, Gamble, Samuel, and Elizabeth Johnson.
1775, Nov.   5, Gamon, Lucy, and John Findley.
1764, Oct.   7, Gandawill, Catharine, and Robert Way.
1759, March 26, Gandawitt, Elisabet, and Christopher Thomkins.
1761, Feb. 27, Gandy, John, and Rachel More.
1800, April 28, Ganoe, Mary, and Patrick Mullen.
1753, Oct. 18, Garaway, Prudence, and James McElhenny.
1790, Feb.   1, Gardiner, James, and Marget Ellot.
1774, Jan.   1, Gardiner, Sarah, and John Reynolds.
1758, June 18, Gardley, Thomas, and Mary House.
1760, May 20, Gardner, Christian, and Joseph Cornelius.
1776, March 14, Gardner, Edeth, and Jonathan Draper.
1779, Nov. 18, Gardner, Eleanor, and William Simpson.
1784, March 29, Gardner, Elinor, and Gustavus Brown.
1751, Sept. 22, Gardner, John, and Hannah Howard.
1792, Aug.   9, Gardner, Rachel, and James Kendall.
1787, Nov.   9, Gardner, Thomas, and Jane Henry.
1781, Jan. 30, Gardsby, Ralph, and Elizabeth Twite.
1794, July 13, Gareer, Cathrine, and Joseph Derricson.

1797, June   24, Garey, Jacob, and Charlotte Hilderman.
1780, March   6, Gargin, Sarah, and Patrick Coleman.
1751, Jan.   18, Garioch, George, and Sarah Norman.
1780, April   5, Garley, Hugh, and Mary Black.
1770, Jan.   29, Garling, George, and Mary Christine Chriest.
1772, July   23, Garmen, Mary, and Abraham Cohen.
1757, May   28, Garner, William, and Janey Clement.
1791, Aug.   4, Garnet, Jane, and James Robeson.
1790, Feb.   10, Garreau, Pierre, and Sara Limes.
1792, Aug.   12, Garret, Bryan, and Margret Cummins.
1780, Feb.   26, Garret, Elizabeth, and John Gallerd.
1773, April   18, Garret, Elizabeth, and John Shee.
1778, Jan.   5, Garret, Elizabeth, and Michael York.
1792, Sept.   14, Garret, Jane, and Jesiah Pawlding.
1782, Dec.   21, Garrett, John, and Elizabeth Jones.
1775, March   24, Garret, John, and Jemima Malluck.
1753, March   10, Garret, John, and Sarah Rortee.
1777, May   4, Garrett, George, and Barbarah Meyer.
1781, June   4, Garricks, Polly, and Abram Parker.
1766, Feb.   12, Garrigues, Elizabeth, and William Smith.
1763, July   2, Garrigues, Isaac, and Hester Taylor.
1766, Sept.   9, Garrigues, Rebecca, and Henry Robison.
1759, July   17, Garrigues, Susannah, and James Gautier.
1796, Feb.   24, Garrish, Levi, and Susanna Cozens.
1760, Sept.   16, Garrson, Elizabeth, and Lorent Wens.
1788, April   28, Garter, Frances, and Lewis Husk.
1777, Jan.   11, Garvey, Elizabeth, and Patick Fares.
1794, Dec.   31, Garwood, John, and Deborah Crawford.
1780, March   2, Garwood, Joseph, and Margaret Mosley.
1781, Sept.   1, Gary, James, and Anne Shillingsford.
1756, Jan.   23, Gascill, Ann, and Peter Haddock.
1799, March   13, Gasford, Susannah, and John Pennington.
1780, Aug.   30, Gaskin, Mertha, and Amos Sharp.
1777, April   28, Gasner, Mary, and John Cop.
1778, Dec.   4, Gass, Jane, and John Hasel.
1776, Oct.   29, Gaston, Alexander, and Eleanor McCane.
1769, Sept.   2, Gater, John, and Mary Fudge.
1791, Nov.   11, Gates, Nathaniel, and Eleonore Jack.
1753, July   9, Gaugh, James, and Catharine Gilberts.
1760, July   21, Gaul, Sarah, and Jerich Diemer.
1792, Dec.   2, Gault, Henry, and Ann Lewis.
1759, July   17, Gautier, James, and Susannah Garrigues.
1782, Aug.   20, Gautrey, Susannah, and Adam Laise.
1783, July   6, Gayen, Susannah, and Jacob Baldwin.
1766, Jan.   26, Gayer, Mary, and Johannes Kimmerly.
1773, Sept.   23, Gayman, Ann, and Curtis Davis.

1762, Nov.   4, Geates, Joseph, and Mary Donnock.
1778, June   10, Gee, Joseph, and Alice Sherlock.
1784, Jan.   26, Geel, Elizabeth, and James Morrow.
1778, March 15, Geel, Henry, and Elizabeth Howard.
1787, Oct.   31, Geen, Rachel, and William Ingeron.
1771, Nov.   16, Geen, Thomas, and Margarett More.
1766, Feb.   24, Geepen, Elizabeth, and James Johnston.
1800, May   12, Geers, Richard, and Mehilla Gore.
1767, Dec.   10, Geiger, George, and Margaret Peehine.
1782, June   2, Gelasby, Valentine, and Catherine Barren.
1775, March 13, Genger, Hannah, and William Hood.
1774, Aug.   20, Gentry, Robert, and Mary Johnson.
1772, July   19, George, Abner, and Sarah Preston.
1764, Feb.   3, George, Elizabeth, and William Dawson.
1800, July   5, George, Jane, and John Wall.
1790, May   16, George, John, and Cathrine Hamelin.
1778, Feb.   4, George, Mary, and Archibald McDonald.
1755, Feb.   24, George, Mary, and Thomas Cahoon.
1790, Oct.   7, George, Mathew, and Elizabeth Kyler.
1775, June   30, George and Prudence, (negroes.)
1781, Feb.   22, George, William, and Catharine Campbell.
1791, Aug.   5, Geoghegan, Bartholomy, and Phebe Purnell.
1757, Feb.   7, Gephart, Adam, and Eva Illerin.
1788, Dec.   5, German, William, and Eleonor Diamond.
1765, July   30, Gerold, Peter Sitz, and Hannah Turner.
1791, Oct.   9, Gery, Hanna, and Samuel Wiggins.
1777, Sept. 19, Getshins, Ann, and William McClatchil.
1759, April 16, Gettman, Finis, and Stacy Delany.
1789, May   31, Geyry, Adam, and Ann Cale.
1777, Feb.   25, Ghasslin, Ann, and Daniel Stiever.
1777, May   23, Gibbern, Knight, and Mary Gramer.
1792, Jan.   1, Gibbet, Elizabeth, and David Burk.
1779, Dec.   23, Gibbons, John, and Mary Braidy.
1795, Aug.   15, Gibbons, John, and Mary Still.
1765, Dec.   4, Gibbs, Alexander, and Ann Parker.
1776, Nov.   25, Gibbs, Ann, and Richard Newton.
1796, Dec.   24, Giberson, Sarah, and Furman Black.
1778, June   17, Gibney, Simon, and Sarah O'Nell.
1790, Oct.   15, Gibson, James, and Elizabeth Cope.
1764, Dec.   25, Gibson, James, and Isabel Serjeant.
1780, Jan.   16, Gibson, James, and Sarah Britt.
1782, April   5, Gibson, John, and Catherine Bicker.
1778, Jan.   21, Gibson, Mary, and Francis Hunt.
1787, Oct.   30, Gibson, Samuel, and Rachel Chew.
1777, Aug.   12, Giddens, Mary, and William Thomas.
1761, April 20, Gietzew, Elizabeth, and Thomas Ginkens.

1751, April   14, Giffin, Margaret, and Joseph Bond.
1793, Feb.   5, Gifford, Thomas Haps, and Isabella Carter.
1779, Aug.   9, Gift, John, and Catharine Hocrast.
1797, June   19, Gihon, John, and Ann Hays.
1799, Aug.   11, Gihon, Rosanah, and St. John Harvey.
1792, Oct.   12, Gihon, Rosanna, and Hamstead Mason.
1789, Nov.   30, Gilbert, Ann, and Peter Journey.
1779, Nov.   10, Gilbert, Calop, and Martha Stackhouse.
1785, Nov.   10, Gilbert, Elizabeth, and Lawrence Johnston.
1798, Dec.   27, Gilbert, Elizab., and William Lannigan.
1790, Oct.   7, Gilbert, Jane, and Edward Jones.
1781, Jan.   30, Gilbert, Joseph, and Anne Mash.
1789, Sept.   28, Gilbert, Rebecca, and Walter Cook.
1758, March   23, Gilbert, Sarah, and Arie Scout.
1780, Sept.   24, Gilbert, Sophia, and Peter Walters.
1790, May   22, Gilbert, Thomas, and Sylphia Cloud.
1753, July   9, Gilberts, Catharine, and James Gaugh.
1774, Oct.   16, Gilbons, Gerrard, and Elizabeth Brown.
1781, Nov.   29, Gilchrist, John, and Rachel Lom, (free negroes.)
1792, March   23, Gilchrist, William, and Elizabeth Jackson.
1795, March   1, Giles, Margret, and Andrew Maclean.
1791, Dec.   21, Gilfry, Elizabeth, and Thomas Goff.
1794, July   17, Gilfry, William, and Sarah Rodes.
1750, Sept.   11, Gill, Eleoner, and William Bark.
1778, June   11, Gill, John M., and Hannah Cookhorn.
1778, June   15, Gill, Mary, and Hugh Ross.
1792, Jan.   31, Gill, Mary, and Jean Baptiste Dismenatin Dorat.
1791, June   20, Gill, Rachel, and John Philips.
1795, May   8, Gillaspy, James, and Ann Ashby.
1791, July   22, Gillaspy, Jane, and Peter Pettit.
1778, May   29, Gillbert, Margaret, and William Higgins.
1778, May   26, Gillburn, Knight, and Elizabeth Gun.
1782, July   31, Gilleckan, George, and Mary Conoly.
1793, April   11, Gillet, Elizabeth, and William Ferrel.
1790, March   6, Gillis, Alexander, and Hannah Onor.
1783, Jan.   16, Gillis, Anne, and John Kennedy.
1790, Jan.   6, Gillmar, George, and Hanna Hutson.
1778, Feb.   17, Gillmore, Martha, and William Yendle.
1779, Dec.   5, Gillmore, Mary, and Alexander Whitelaw.
1764, Aug.   30, Gillyat, Jane, and Mathew Potter.
1784, May   4, Gilmer, James, and Elizabeth McMannan.
1779, Aug.   30, Gilmore, Elizabeth, and Edward Ryan.
1764, Jan.   2, Gilmore, Margaret, and Andrew Henery.
1779, Aug.   13, Gilmore, Mary, and Samuel Smith.
1783, Aug.   30, Gilmore, Mary, and William Hudson.
1761, April   20, Ginkens, Thomas, and Elizabeth Gietzew.

1759, Oct.   24, Gipson, Margeth, and Richard Davy.
1792, Oct.   21, Giry, Daniel, and Rosina Lints.
1779, May   16, Gise, Michael, and Sarah Craig.
1770, Feb.   25, Gisfen, Latitia, and Peter Egan.
1788, July   5, Gisler, John, and Anne Lendes.
1792, Jan.   2, Gitchrift, Andrew, and Ann Milliman.
1787, Oct.   25, Gitlens, Joseph, and Sarah Hepherd Newton.
1777, March 10, Gittar, Mary, and Joseph Williams.
1800, Sept.   5, Given, John, and Anne Peel.
1777, March   2, Givens, George, and Grace Burns.
1776, Oct.   10, Glackin, John, and Deborah Plummen.
1795, May   13, Glasco, John, and Rachel McKean.
1765, Feb.   25, Glasco, Robert, and Jeane Welch.
1758, March   2, Glascodine, Joseph, and Diana Hill.
1799, Dec.   19, Glascoe, Nathaniel Reas, and Nancy Armstrong.
1798, April   18, Glascoe, Thomas, and Jane Kelly.
1770, Aug.   24, Glass, Alexander, and Margarett Stuart.
1763, March 10, Gleen, James, and Mary Prichard.
1793, Jan.   27, Gleeson, Dennis, and Elizabeth McClasky.
1793, Jan.   22, Gleeson, Francis, and Mary Nail.
1800, Jan.   5, Glen, Cathrine, and James McDonell.
1772, Oct.   6, Glen, James, and Mary Daster.
1794, April   12, Glen, Martha, and John McMullen.
1751, July   18, Glency, Charles, and Catharine Vaugh.
1758, Sept.   17, Glene, Mary, and Samuel Freyer.
1774, Feb.   7, Glenn, Daniel, and Elizabeth Lyndall.
1778, Sept.   9, Glenn, James, and Ann Adams.
1774, July   25, Glenn, James, and Mary Lindall.
1775, Sept.   7, Glenn, Mary, and Samuel Wells.
1782, March 12, Glentworth, James, and Elizabeth Graysberry.
1792, April   8, Glide, Edward, and Elenore Washinger.
1776, Jan.   14, Glink, Gerick, and Sophia Reininger.
1782, Dec.   14, Glison, Caleb, and Sarah Wiggins.
1786, Nov.   2, Gloucester, Andrews, and Joseph Low.
1766, May   25, Glover, Rebeccah, and William Bitterworth.
1779, March 29, Glover, Sarah, and Peter Hannah.
1777, March   2, Glow, Bartholomew, and Mary Low.
1785, April   7, Glyn, Patrick, and Mary Christie.
1754, Nov.   10, Godfrey, Ann, and Evan Watkins.
1755, Aug.   29, Godfrey, Edward, and Elizabeth Johnson.
1754, June   30, Godfrey, James, and Jane Forquar.
1775, May   14, Godfrey, Jean, and John Hamilton.
1766, July   10, Godfrey, John, and Mary Montgomery.
1752, Aug.   13, Godfrey, Joseph, and Deborah Wilcox.
1792, Nov.   3, Godfrey, Margret, and Samuel Lisener.
1779, Feb.   3, Godfriedt, George, and Elizabeth Johnson.

1762, July 17, Godlove, John, and Rachel Rawford.
1792, Nov. 27, Godschall, Anna, and Henry Castor.
1786, Oct. 15, Godshall, Frederic, and Catherine Cleasly.
1795, July 12, Goetschies, Hannah, and Enoch Morgan.
1791, Dec. 21, Goff, Thomas, and Elizabeth Gilfry.
1787, Nov. 8, Goffry, Christopher, and Catherine Taylor.
1787, July 30, Goforth, Mary, and John Doyle.
1773, Jan. 28, Goforth, Zachariah, and Ann Clisforct.
1775, Aug. 22, Goforth, Zachariah, and Mary Allen.
1788, Oct. 23, Gogan, Martha, and John MacKnob.
1780, Jan. 8, Gogerty, Thomas, and Bridget Mathews.
1755, May 5, Goheen, Richard, and Catharine Bisnet.
1800, April 27, Gold, Ann, and Tallinghast Collins.
1766, Dec. 22, Gold, George, and Catharine Fairwether.
1778, June 3, Gold, George, and Jane Minzer.
1777, June 12, Gold, James, and Elizabeth Clemons.
1797, May 14, Gold, Joseph, and Juliana White.
1765, June 24, Gold, Joseph, and Mary Clark.
1795, March 1, Gold, Mathew, and Marget Muhlenberg.
1756, March 30, Goldbery, Sarah, and Daniel Helmstem.
1778, July 27, Golden, Jane, and John Hannings.
1800, Oct. 11, Golden, Ram, and Priscilla Eldridge.
1785, Jan. 18, Goldin, Margaret, and Isaac Smith.
1779, May 12, Golding, Joseph, and Ann Budden.
1759, April 12, Goldsmith, Mary, and Philip Fitzsimons.
1793, June 6, Gollaher, Charles, and Susanna Muckelwee.
1776, July 16, Gollinger, Henery, and Ann Mitslef.
1761, Sept. 21, Gonney, Martha, and Henry Care.
1762, Sept. 21, Gonney, Martha, and Henry Care.
1768, March 3, Good, Charles, and Margaret Darkais.
1790, Sept. 10, Goodall, James, and Mary Brown.
1782, Aug. 26, Goodall, George, and Mary Davis.
1794, Dec. 18, Gooden, Cathrine, and Joseph Brown.
1794, April 19, Gooden, Martha, and Richard Baslington.
1797, Dec. 9, Goodfellow, William, and Mary Foster.
1797, Nov. 28, Goodfellow, William, and Sarah Wood.
1779, Feb. 14, Goodrich, John, and Elizabeth Harris.
1789, June 8, Goodwin, Daniel, and Rebecca Aborn.
1767, Sept. 2, Goodwin, Philip, and Mary Edwards.
1764, Aug. 18, Goodwin, Sarah, and William Kerlin.
1780, May 15, Goof, Elizabeth, and Walter Long.
1761, Nov. 1, Goothen, Elizabeth, and Michael Fox.
1762, Nov. 1, Goothen, Elizabeth, and Michael Fox.
1778, Jan. 28, Gorden, Ann, and John Ogelvie.
1778, Feb. 10, Gorden, William and Mary Smith.
1776, May 8, Gordon, Ann, and James Farnsworth.

1763, Feb. 12, Gordon, Catharine, and Thomas Kerr.
1774, Feb. 1, Gordon, Elizabeth, and Humphrey Marsden.
1779, May 13, Gordon, Elizabeth, and John Fraser.
1755, Jan. 31, Gordon, Elizabeth, and William Fleming.
1783, June 5, Gordon, John, and Mary White.
1769, Nov. 30, Gordon, Joseph, and Anne Butterfield.
1776, Dec. 16, Gordon, Peter, and Catharine Hodsey.
1775, Jan. 2, Gordon, Stephen, and Mary Lock.
1764, Nov. 24, Gordon, Thomas, and Hannah Jenkis.
1760, Dec. 4, Gordon, Thomas, and Mary Faris.
1752, Aug. 20, Gordon, William, and Catharine Biddason.
1758, Aug. 24, Gore, Charles, and Ann Hinberson.
1777, Dec. 1, Gore, Elizabeth, and John Lee.
1800, May 12, Gore, Mehilla, and Richard Geers.
1781, Oct. 28, Gore, Robert, and Eleonor King.
1779, June 3, Gore, Simon, and Sarah Stephenson.
1763, June 22, Goreberin, Anna Agusta, and Anton Stiemer.
1779, April 29, Gorelon, Ann, and William Clare.
1780, Dec. 10, Gorley, Margaret, and Hopkins Walker.
1779, April 17, Gorman, Ann Barbara, and Richard Burk.
1791, Aug. 11, Gormon, Mary, and Jedediah Lyon.
1796, Feb. 28, Gorsslin, Nathaniel, and Cathrine Mitchel.
1768, Feb. 20, Gorton, Daniel, and Mary Stewart.
1799, July 24, Goslin, Rebecca, and David Force.
1784, Oct. 27, Gosline, Sarah, and George Fox.
1781, Aug. 19, Gosling, Samuel, and Elizabeth Dayley.
1780, Jan. 23, Gosnell, George, and Eleanor Shaw.
1794, Feb. 6, Gosner, Henry, and Ann Smith.
1752, Dec. 15, Gosnold, Ann, and Robert Hinshelwood.
1779, March 30, Gossin, William, and Mary Collins.
1758, Dec. 28, Gossleing, Silvanius, and Mary Howel.
1787, Oct. 12, Gotler, Christopher, and Maria Weaver.
1777, June 27, Gottier, Sarah, and John Walker.
1792, Jan. 5, Gough, Elizabeth, and James Pattison.
1754, July 23, Gough, Hugh, and Martha Rogers.
1778, May 27, Gough, William, and Rachel Ogelby.
1793, July 1, Gould, Ulary, and Robert McDavid.
1760, Jan. 7, Goulgenir, Sarah, and Adam Allyn.
1798, Feb. 26, Gourdon, Isaac, and Margery Burgoine.
1774, Sept. 1, Govier, Joseph, and Elizabeth More.
1795, Dec. 26, Gowan, Jane, and Charles Grugan.
1778, Jan. 6, Gowanlock, John, and Jane Johnson.
1779, June 18, Gowdey, William, and Elizabeth Pain.
1780, Jan. 27, Grace, Aaron, and Elizabeth Williams.
1794, Sept. 2, Grace, Elizabeth, and Frederic Piper.
1772, July 19, Grace, Elizabeth, and Michael Ball.

1794, July   28, Grace, George, and Mary Nivel.
1760, June   10, Grace, Mary, and Edward Edwards.
1782, April   20, Grady, Briget, and John Whitehead.
1788, April   3, Grady, Hanna, and John Pendergrass.
1793, Nov.   20, Grady, Mary, and Macam Maclean.
1792, May   22, Grafey, Abigail, and Adam Barkerd.
1781, April   15, Graff, Elizabeth, and Andrew Christman.
1782, June   9, Graff, John, and Mary Trenchard.
1783, Sept.   11, Graff, Samuel, and Susannah McClure.
1796, Sept.   19, Graham, Dorothea G., and William Pennece.
1787, Aug.   25, Graham, Dulcina, and Joseph Deamer.
1753, July   19, Graham, George, and Elizabeth Williams.
1785, Sept.   8, Graham, Henrietta, and Richard Flower.
1790, Dec.   14, Graham, John, and Mary Thomson.
1779, Dec.   12, Graham, Margaret, and Daniel Cogall.
1795, Dec.   29, Graham, Mary, and John McCalla.
1775, Oct.   9, Graham, Mary, and William Fitzpatrick.
1759, May   21, Graham, Mertha, and John Boys.
1796, June   20, Graham, Peter, and Nancy Clark.
1790, March   3, Graham, Thomas, and Elizabeth Jonas.
1778, April   12, Graham, William, and Mary Burton.
1752, July   23, Grahams, James, and Elizabeth MacCallow.
1758, March 26, Grainger, William, and Mary Day.
1752, Oct.   18, Graisbury, Benjamin, and Elizabeth Siddons.
1786, Aug.   21, Gram, Mary, and Francis Purreau.
1772, April   21, Grame, Elizabeth, and Henry Hugh Ferguson.
1790, July   20, Grame, Martin, and Jane Brown.
1777, March 10, Grames, Elizabeth, and William Davis.
1777, May   23, Grames, Mary, and Knight Gibbern.
1778, March 17, Granan, Peter, and Catharine Hancock.
1788, June   25, Grandel, Joseph, and Marget Smith.
1759, Jan.   18, Grandewitt, Ann, and James Lee.
1753, March 18, Grandin, Philip, and Elenor Forman.
1760, Dec.   8, Grandon, Peter, and Rose Hamford.
1780, Jan.   29, Granger, Johannah, and John Cunner.
1756, June   1, Granger, Joseph, and Elizabeth Bright.
1766, Aug.   26, Granin, Mary, and Christian Alback.
1776, Jan.   22, Grannon, Thomas, and Elizabeth Flemond.
1795, Dec.   24, Grant, Alexander, and Mary Mun.
1776, Dec.   21, Grant, Christine, and John Menice.
1782, July   28, Grant, Esther, and Scipis Cudjoe, (negroes.)
1771, Dec.   10, Grant, Jacob, and Susannah Chapman.
1799, April   1, Grant, Mary, and Thomas Robeson.
1753, Jan.   16, Grant, Sary, and Stephen Randel.
1780, March   1, Grant, William, and Margarett McCay.
1768, March 15, Grantham, Margaret, and Christopher Willson.

1784, Jan. 22, Granthom, Charles, and Elizabeth Richards.
1778, April 7, Granton, Rebecca, and Nathaniel Smith.
1757, May 4, Grantum, Charles, jr., and Elizabeth Taylor.
1754, March 13, Grantum, George, and Margaret Justice.
1796, Jan. 12, Granville, John, and Rachel Finny.
1767, Oct. 17, Granville, Mary, and Samuel Boyes.
1779, Nov. 15, Grason, Jane, and Mathew Morrey.
1777, Dec. 5, Grauch, Alexander, and Isabella McKenzie.
1758, Aug. 13, Grauer, Christian, and Elizabeth Johns.
1774, July 28, Gravel, Mary, and Andrew Bearsticker.
1789, July 5, Graves, Amy, and Thomas Padric.
1770, Sept. 20, Graves, William, and Dolly Barker.
1777, Nov. 25, Gray, Andrew, and Catharine Sinclair.
1777, Dec. 7, Gray, Ann, and Samuel Burns.
1767, Feb. 8, Gray, Elizabeth, and William Jones.
1753, Sept. 1, Gray, Henry, and Rachel Moore.
1778, Nov. 29, Gray, James, and Bridget Lairy.
1798, Jan. 28, Gray, James, and Marget Shafer.
1777, Dec. 6, Gray, Jane, and William Wordlaw.
1777, April 7, Gray, Jean, and Thomas Salmon.
1767, April 24, Gray, Robert, and Bridget Doyle.
1754, April 17, Gray, Susanna, and John Suplar.
1776, May 29, Gray, Sylvester, and Elizabeth Hamilton.
1755, May 17, Gray, William, and Ann French.
1774, Oct. 28, Gray, William, and Ann Guy.
1799, Jan. 16, Gray, William, and Sarah Morton.
1778, April 12, Grayer, Mary, and James Jackson.
1785, July 6, Grays, George, and Margaret Adams.
1782, March 12, Graysberry, Elizabeth, and James Glentworth.
1774, June 20, Graytie, Ann, and Robert McCrea.
1794, Sept. 30, Greaves, Alexander, and Mary Vance.
1789, Dec. 1, Greaves, Lydia, and Michael Lewis.
1781, Feb. 13, Greaves, Mary, and Joseph Walker.
1751, April 1, Greeck, John, and Catharine Davis.
1794, Aug. 31, Green, Andrew, and Cathrine Weaver.
1782, July 16, Green, Anne, and Charles Bingham.
1781, Sept. 18, Green, Barbara, and Michael Conway.
1791, Aug. 11, Green, Elenore, and John Lawrence.
1798, May 6, Green, Elizabeth, and Alexander Weldin.
1767, June 16, Green, Elizabeth, and John McCarty.
1778, Sept. 13, Green, Elizabeth, and Patrick Tagert.
1775, Dec. 31, Green, George, and Rosannah Yethern.
1751, Nov. 24, Green, Godfrey, and Martha Hetherington.
1776, Sept. 25, Green, Hannah, and Andrew Griffen.
1796, March 17, Green, Henry, and Ann Parris.
1782, Aug. 25, Green, Hannah, and William Petterson, (negroes.)

1780, July   18, Green, James, and Mary Collins.
1792, May   10, Green, John, and Jane Dennis.
1796, Jan.   5, Green, John, and Mary Heney.
1780, July   13, Green, John, and Mary Sheldren.
1800, Oct.   30, Green, John, and Sarah Whelen.
1791, Jan.   18, Green, John, and Susanna Rodgers.
1795, March 29, Green, John Washington, and Sarah Lone.
1796, Sept.   10, Green, Margret, and Peter Batist.
1795, Dec.   13, Green, Mary, and Daniel Disher.
1753, Aug.   23, Green, Mary, and James McDaniel.
1771, Nov.   16, Green, Mary, and John Gabb.
1791, Nov.   4, Green, Mary, and John Kish.
1793, May   25, Green, Mary, and William Reynolds.
1781, April   13, Green, Michael, and Mary Bowers.
1759, May   3, Green, Peter, and Elizabeth Gurethey.
1795, Aug.   15, Green, Peter, and Nancy Jones.
1790, Nov.   6, Green, Richard, and Priscilla Reynolds.
1764, Dec.   31, Green, Sarah, and James O'Neal.
1760, July   19, Green, Sarah, and Thomas Bylith.
1769, April   16, Green, Thomas, and Eleanor Neal.
1799, Dec.   15, Green, Thomas, and Rebecca Hardy.
1798, April   16, Green, William, and Elizabeth Millegan.
1773, May   13, Greenfield, Jesse, and Elizabeth Holliday.
1796, June   25, Greennhick, Jonathan, and Cathrine McQuittrick.
1790, Dec.   5, Greenough, James, and Debora Cahil.
1793, Nov.   17, Greenwood, Jane, and William McLochlin.
1770, Oct.   7, Greenwood, John, and Margarett Morrison.
1783, Jan.   20, Greenwood, Rebecca, and Adam Norris.
1766, Sept.   22, Greenwood, Rebeccah, and Miles Caton.
1778, Jan.   18, Greenwood, Thomas, and Johannah Ferman.
1776, June   4, Greer, Charles, and Catharine Willard.
1795, Aug.   2, Greer, James, and Martha McCrery.
1793, Nov.   7, Greer, John, and Amelia Wilson.
1797, Feb.   12, Gregg, Samuel, and Elizabeth Caldwell.
1753, May   30, Gregory, Daniel, and Martha Briten.
1785, June   7, Gregory, David, and Elizabeth Rinker.
1778, May   29, Gregory, Eleanor, and James Kenndy.
1780, Sept.   19, Gregory, James, and Mary Brinkley.
1794, May   20, Gregory, John, and Frances Mitchel.
1796, Oct.   24, Gregory, Mary, and Alexander Kernes.
1774, Sept.   29, Gregory, William, and Mary Fitzgerald.
1759, Nov.   12, Gressel, Edward, and Abigail Baker.
1758, Aug.   24, Grew, Thomas, and Lowise Parwin.
1765, May   29, Grew, Timothy, and Mary McCrape.
1775, Aug.   27, Gribble, Caspar, and Sarah Marchant.
1758, March 12, Griebs, John, and Elizabeth Rosebergin.

1754, Aug.　6, Griefits, Sarah, and George Donat.
1797, Jan.　10, Grier, Nancy, and Joseph Silva.
1800, May　26, Grier, Thomas, and Nancy Dun.
1781, Feb.　25, Griffe, Sarah, and John Ives.
1776, Sept.　25, Griffen, Andrew, and Hannah Green.
1781, Nov.　16, Grifferd, Edward, and Mary Crone.
1777, Dec.　28, Griffey, Catherine, and Joseph Baker.
1752, July　1, Griffey, Elizabeth, and Henry Cockrun.
1769, March 22, Griffieth, Benjamin, and Ester Davids.
1777, Feb.　5, Griffieth, John, and Mary Mason.
1779, April　18, Griffieth, Margarett, and Robert Collins.
1778, Aug.　13, Griffieth, Mary, and William Clark.
1770, Dec.　2, Griffieth, Richard, and Ann Mary Bresler.
1778, Jan.　29, Griffieth, Sarah, and Dunchan Quigg.
1779, June　9, Griffieth, Thomas, and Mary Shingleton.
1776, Oct.　30, Griffin, Ann, and Samuel Heritage.
1800, March　8, Griffin, John, and Susannah Roddy.
1761, Nov.　14, Griffin, Samuel, and Jane Loff.
1793, Oct.　29, Griffins, Hope, and Joseph Thomas.
1753, Dec.　1, Griffis, Hany, and Thomas Conelly.
1774, Oct.　13, Griffis, Thomas, and Mary Lodge.
1777, April　19, Griffith, Edward, and Eve Dawson.
1790, Oct.　4, Griffith, Elizabeth, and James Trump.
1798, Dec.　13, Griffith, Francis, and Hannah Spear.
1790, Sept.　23, Griffith, George, and Elizabeth Jones.
1795, March 15, Griffith, George, and Mary Truck.
1753, Aug.　22, Griffith, Isabel, and John Neesbit.
1762, April　1, Griffith, Mary, and Joseph Williamson.
1767, Dec.　17, Griffith, Mary, and William Davis.
1752, Sept.　21, Griffith, Rachel, and Thomas Prowell.
1758, Jan.　14, Griffith, Sarah, and George Dowell.
1795, May　24, Griffith, Susannah, and James Maxwell.
1795, Sept.　24, Griffiths, Mary, and William Waggener.
1751, Oct.　13, Griffy, Hannah, and Philip MacGlaclen.
1751, Oct.　8, Griffy, Lurney, and Andrew Deveny.
1780, Aug.　12, Griffy, Sarah, and William Norris.
1753, Jan.　23, Griffy, William, and Elizabeth Roads.
1765, April　30, Griggar, Patrick, and Ann Thomson.
1779, June　13, Griggery, Ann, and John McGill.
1756, April　25, Grimes, Elizabeth, and Thomas Virgo.
1781, Oct.　23, Grimes, Elizabeth, and William Nolen.
1778, May　31, Grimes, Margaret, and Edward Jones.
1779, Aug.　1, Grimes, Martha, and Michael Standley.
1780, April　12, Grimes, Noble, and Mary Morrow.
1757, Feb.　12, Grimes, Robert, and Margaret Holland.
1778, April　28, Griner, Susannah, and Andrew Lepper.

1771, April   7, Gring, Mary, and Patrick Sensord.
1785, July   28, Griscom, George, and Kitty Schreiner.
1776, Oct.   13, Griscom, Hannah, and Griffieth Levering,
1793, July   16, Griscum, Cathrine, and Samuel Aeneas Davis.
1795, Feb.   21, Grison, Marget, and Samuel Moser.
1755, Oct.   28, Griss, Richard, and Elizabeth Mitchel.
1798, Jan.   22, Grisson, Ann, and Samuel Murphey.
1780, Feb.   24, Groffe, Elizabeth, and William Key.
1798, April   10, Grogan, Mary, and Thomas O'Connor.
1777, Sept.   17, Grogen, Patrick, and Hester Delewew.
1791, Sept.   20, Groll, Christian, and Cathrine Chase,
1794, Sept.   21, Grossier, Mary, and Henry Winterton Edwards.
1771, Dec.   10, Grost, Peter, and Catharine Culy.
1764, May   13, Groves, Thomas, and Susannah Bond.
1774, March   9, Grow, Elizabeth, and John Strembeck.
1781, Dec.   17, Grub, Barbara, and John Stead.
1792, Aug.   4, Grub, Margret, and Christian Smith.
1769, Sept.   1, Grubb, Catharine, and John Richy.
1776, May   5, Grubb, Elizabeth, and Nicholas Boberg.
1761, Dec.   12, Grubb, Henry, and Sarah Wells.
1775, Nov.   27, Grubb, Mary, and William Wade.
1782, March   11, Gruden, Catherine, and John Hickey.
1787, Jan.   13, Gruff, John, and Mary Reeves.
1795, Dec.   26, Grugan, Charles, and Jane Gowan.
1791, July   19, Gryffits, Elizab., and John Hollwell.
1754, Dec.   30, Grymes, Richard, and Isabella Piles.
1797, Aug.   31, Guerin de Foncin, Jean, and Margreta Zienerin.
1777, Aug.   5, Guff, Archibald, and Mary Rook.
1788, Feb.   26, Guff, Mary, and Isaac Clarc.
1778, June   22, Guffey, Archibald, and Elizabeth Wood.
1766, Dec.   16, Guin, Ann, and George Ennis.
1796, Oct.   29, Guin, David, and Mary Cox.
1779, Dec.   23, Guinar, Sarah, and Charles Taylor.
1755, Aug.   12, Guinup, Joseph, and Mary Broom.
1783, Jan.   21, Gule, Margret, and Charles Seavoy.
1781, Feb.   8, Gullhen, Mary, and John Philips.
1770, Jan.   21, Gullifer, Hannah, and Richard Shea.
1778, May   25, Gum, Catharine, and Joseph Hart.
1778, March   26, Gumley, Jeffery, and Mary Wallentine.
1799, Nov.   5, Gummerfield, James, and Elizab. Cool.
1776, Dec.   18, Gump, Catharine, and Thomas Sartin.
1778, May   26, Gun, Elizabeth, and Knight Gillburn.
1759, Sept.   30, Guulaugher, Elizabeth, and Peter Wiseburogh.
1752, July   21, Gunn, Anthony, and Jane Kendal.
1798, June   4, Gunn, Patrick, and Hannah Baxter.
1759, May   3, Gurethey, Elizabeth, and Peter Green.

1764, Aug.   13, Gurlin, Moses, and Jane Eves.
1754, June   30, Gurling, Abigail, and Adam Cox.
1774, Oct.   28, Guy, Ann, and William Gray.
1790, June   22, Guy, Ceilia, and John Wilson.
1786, Nov.   5, Guy, Elizabeth, and Philip Schafer.
1791, Oct.   6, Guy, Jane, and George Hofner.
1775, May   30, Guy, Mary, and Philip Boardman.
1799, Oct.   27, Guy, Richard, and Susannah B. Finch.
1798, Dec.   16, Guy, Sarah, and Benjamin Huggins.
1788, Oct.   4, Guyry, Daniel, and Mary Merrin.
1789, Sept.   7, Gvinn, Susannah, and Michael Crause.
1751, July   31, Gweenup, Thomas, and Elinor Windor.
1779, July   18, Gwillin, John, and Catharine Albah.
1781, Aug.   21, Gwin, Anne, and Anges Smith.
1793, Jan.   29, Gwin, Margret, and Robert Colwin.
1782, Feb.   11, Gwinnop, Sarah, and Charles Wright.
1753, Jan.   10, Gwinup, Mary, and Friend Streeton.
1775, May   25, Gyer, George, and Mary Carter.
1762, July   15, Haas, Baltsar, and Rosinna Watsin.
1772, Dec.   21, Haas, John, and Sarah Jones.
1770, June   30, Haas, Rachel, and Samuel James.
1795, Jan.   22, Hababaker, Mary, and Isaac Mason.
1754, Sept.   3, Hack, George, and Catharine Couphmanen.
1761, April   18, Hackel, Elizabeth, and Abraham Thomas.
1780, July   30, Hacker, Hogsteed, and Mary Calder.
1778, June   9, Hacket, Lydia, and Philip Condon.
1776, April   30, Hacket, William Benjamin, and Lucy Davis.
1785, July   15, Hackett, Ann, and William Brock.
1754, June   27, Hackett, George, and Elizabeth McYoung.
1756, Jan.   23, Haddock, Peter, and Ann Gascill.
1771, June   2, Haddon, David, and Jean Clark.
1767, Sept.   3, Hadkinson, Thomas, and Honour Towle.
1772, Nov.   11, Haer, Daniel, and Elizabeth Thomas.
1759, May   29, Haert, Mary, and Robert Carr.
1787, Feb.   23, Hafferman, Margret, and William Pollard.
1789, Nov.   16, Haft, Mary, and John Eric Vanselius.
1796, Oct.   25, Hagarthy, Cathrine, and John Obrian.
1781, Nov.   26, Hagen, Rosina Dorothea, and Jacob Wintz.
1779, Nov.   27, Hagerty, James, and Jane Linch.
1760, Oct.   11, Haggens, Mary, and William Baby.
1792, Nov.   17, Haggerty, Lucy, and John Brown.
1792, Dec.   20, Haig, Elizabeth, and Samuel Hampton.
1781, April   28, Hail, John, and Elizabeth Perce.
1767, Aug.   17, Hailer, Sebastian, and Elizabeth Pillager.
1784, Aug.   30, Haines, Hannah, and Alexander Orr.
1794, May   11, Haines, James, and Cathrine Barnet.

1781, May   6, Haines, Joshua, and Hannah Shivers.
1799, Nov.   10, Haines, Sarah, and Leonard Shellcross.
1757, Dec.   1, Haines, Thomas, and Elizabeth Owens.
1792, July   15, Hains, William, and Charlott Wood.
1752, May   18, Hains, Cornelius, and Sarah Rambo.
1762, May   29, Hair, Edward, and Martha Watt.
1758, Nov.   28, Hairs, Matty, and James Flanning.
1779, Sept.   24, Hait, Dilly, and Abyhay Chattin.
1789, Oct.   18, Halberstadt, Elizabeth, and Conrad Seyfert.
1787, July   10, Halberstadt, Mary, and Jacob Barbesat.
1797, Sept.   2, Haldin, Robert, and Jane Scott.
1773, Sept.   5, Haldren, Elizabeth, and John Lee.
1765, Dec.   26, Hale, James, and Deborah Heppard.
1795, July   29, Haley, Hannah, and Richard McCoy.
1781, Feb.   8, Haley, John, and Eleanor Williams.
1775, July   16, Haley, John, and Hannah Sprouse.
1796, Oct.   13, Haley, John, and Sarah Clark.
1766, Feb.   16, Haley, Thomas, and Margaret Connoway.
1785, Dec.   1, Hall, Ann, and Michael Powers.
1767, March   26, Hall, Benjamin, and Abigail Wright.
1791, Sept.   19, Hall, Benjamin, and Elizabeth Winters.
1779, July   2, Hall, Christiana, and Lawrence Brooks.
1758, March   25, Hall, David, and Hannah Brownfield.
1796, June   11, Hall, Deborah, and Joseph Leach.
1799, Nov.   16, Hall, Edward, and Rachel Lucas.
1751, Sept.   8, Hall, Elizabeth, and George Palmer.
1782, March   7, Hall, Hannah, and William Hill.
1766, Feb.   3, Hall, Hannah, and William Simonds.
1758, March   17, Hall, James, and Margaret Soudares.
1794, April   3, Hall, Jehu, and Susanna Holman.
1762, Oct.   31, Hall, Jeremiah, and Hannah White.
1773, Sept.   8, Hall, John, and Ann Lascorn.
1782, Sept.   2, Hall, Joseph, and Elizabeth Matsinger.
1778, March   28, Hall, Margaret, and Duncan Campbell.
1781, Dec.   8, Hall, Margaret, and John Pickwith.
1797, March   18, Hall, Mary, and John Ricard.
1755, Dec.   6, Hall, Mary, and Peter Boor.
1757, March   26, Hall, Michael, and Mary Pyott.
1795, June   24, Hall, Richard, and Priscilla Butler.
1765, Oct.   18, Hall, Samuel, and Martha Bradford.
1771, Dec.   15, Hall, Sarah, and George Miesner.
1773, June   27, Hall, Susanna, and Jacob Nyre.
1751, March   30, Hall, Thomas, and Margareta C—mel.
1765, June   28, Hall, Thomas, and Susannah Oconner.
1762, Sept.   21, Hall, William, and Hannah Beckstraw.

1800, May   24, Hall, William, and Hannah Linch.
1761, Sept. 21, Hall, William, and Hannah Rekstraw.
1757, June 21, Hallbort, Margaret, and Peter Deloa.
1800, April 12, Halley, Timothy, and Marget Donevan.
1796, March 26, Hallman, George, and Sarah Mitchel.
1758, Nov.   6, Halloway, Sarah, and Robert More.
1788, Aug.   5, Hallstedt, Peter, and Sarah Page.
1792, Oct. 16, Halston, Mary, and Anthony Schollard.
1778, May   31, Haltbridge, Davis, and Jane Roguon.
1796, Nov.   3, Halton, Sarah, and John Craighead.
1799, Oct.   5, Haltric, Mathew, and Elizab. Robeson.
1765, March 14, Haly, Margaret, and James Corril.
1757, Oct. 13, Haly, Penelope, and William Sword.
1793, June 27. Hambel, Mary, and Samuel Sharp.
1763, April   4, Hambel, William, and Elizabeth Schrener.
1790, May   16, Hamelin, Cathrine, and John George.
1798, March 25, Hamelin, Cathrine, and William McCorkle.
1787, Feb.   1, Hamell, Judith, and James Morrel.
1760, Dec.   8, Hamford, Rose, and Peter Grandon.
1796, July 13, Hamill, Bethiah, and Cochran Hamill.
1796, July 13, Hamill, Cochran, and Bethiah Hamill.
1759, May   22, Hamilton, Ann, and John Morris.
1796, Oct. 11, Hamilton, Charles, and Elizabeth Hartey.
1783, April   6, Hamilton, Charles, and Mary Campbell.
1791, Oct. 13, Hamilton, Charles, and Mary Erwin.
1800, April 21. Hamilton, Eleonore, and Robert Williams.
1776, May   29, Hamilton, Elizabeth, and Sylvester Gray.
1753, May   28, Hamilton, Grace, and William Roberts.
1779, July   1, Hamilton, John, and Frances More.
1775, May   14, Hamilton, John, and Jean Godfrey.
1760, May   8, Hamilton, John, and Sarah Nicholson.
1779, Oct. 13, Hamilton, Margaret, and Joseph Parkeson.
1750, Dec. 31, Hamilton, Margereta, and John Cameron.
1762, Oct. 31, Hamilton, Mary, and James Daceson.
1778, May   8, Hamilton, Mary, and Philip Elly.
1770, Nov. 16, Hamilton, Mary, and Thomas Bely.
1771, Jan. 20, Hamilton, Mary, and Samuel More.
1779, Sept. 25, Hamilton, Rachel, and Roberick McKinnon.
1765, Oct. 10, Hamilton, Sarah, and David Hollen.
1778, May   3, Hamilton, Thomas, and Mary Williams.
1779, Feb. 10, Hamilton, William, and Jane Doil.
1780, March 6, Hamilton, William, and Margaret French.
1790, May   4, Hamilton, William, and Mary Rian.
1774, May   11, Hamled, Godfrey, and Barbara Hartranft.
1791, March 3, Hammel, Mary, and John Mackgare.
1789, Nov. 12, Hammell, Rebecca, and William Scheckels.

1782, April   9, Hammer, Adam, and Elizabeth Britton.
1780, June   22, Hammer, Christine, and Thomas Colman.
1768, Jan.   19, Hammond, Elizabeth, and Thomas Prophecy.
1781, May   31, Hammond, James, and Rachel Ward.
1784, June   6, Hammond, Joseph, and Arabella Blunt.
1779, Aug.   16, Hammond, Margarett, and John Crawford.
1793, July   30, Hammond, William, and Hannah Blight.
1756, Nov.   4, Hamor, Abraham, and Martha Battman.
1759, Aug.   11, Hamper, Elizabeth, and John Brown.
1776, July   24, Hampton, Elizabeth, and Martin Hildeburn.
1783, May   17, Hampton, Júdith, and Adriel Clark.
1792, Dec.   20, Hampton, Samuel, and Elizabeth Haig.
1794, Oct.   30, Hamrich, Christian, and Christina Koenig.
1795, May   6, Hamscher, Jacob, and Cathrine Ulrich.
1755, Nov.   30, Hanan, Barbara, and Robert Bell.
1778, June   30, Hanbury, Philip, and Jane Dixon.
1791, Nov.   1, Hancock, Benjamin, and Sarah Platt.
1778, March 17, Hancock, Catharine, and Peter Granan.
1799, Jan.   10. Hancock, Eleonore, and Samuel Tufts.
1773, Oct.   7, Hancock, Mary, and Thomas Mallinton.
1791, Dec.   31, Hancock, Rachel, and William Lindsey.
1752, May   23, Hanbest, Robert, and Elizabeth Ellett.
1788, Nov.   4, Hand, Lydia, and William Johnson.
1793, April   15, Hand, Mathew, and Elenore McClentock.
1796, Aug.   25, Hand, Nicholas, and Ruth Lewis.
1795, Feb.   8, Hand, Sophia, and Samuel Carson, (Africans.)
1787, Sept.   4, Hand, William, and Mary Likens.
1778, June   25, Handbess, Peter, and Margaret Unger.
1799, April   2, Handbest, Joseph, and Mary Morris.
1757, Jan.   3, Handerson, Anna, and John Dobson.
1792, May   12, Handy, Elizabeth, and Daniel Wall.
1783, March 16, Handling, Lydia, and John Breedang.
1793, Jan.   24, Handly, Aley, and and Joseph Mackintosh.
1771, March 19, Handworker, Dorothy, and Thomas Smith.
1780, June   5, Hanegen, John, and Eve Housman.
1787, Dec.   17, Hanes, Philip, and Zillah Thorp.
1795, Nov.   26, Haney, Aaron, and Mary Hays.
1791, Feb.   3, Haney, Delinda, and John Cameron.
1781, July   11, Haney, Jenny, and John Dunn.
1765, Sept.   14, Haney, Mary, and Edward Reynolds.
1787, June   29, Haney, Robert, and Judith Chester.
1787, March 31, Hanger, Gabriel, and Elizabeth Bond.
1782, Dec.   25, Hanighan, Eve, and Henery Allen.
1773, Sept.   12, Hankey, Ann, and William Banks Sawney.
1768, April   16, Hanlan, Ann, and John Levingston.
1799, July   2, Hanley, John, and Susannah McCahan.

1800, Aug. 3, Hanley, Timothy, and Mary Stags.
1787, Feb. 20, Hanna, Margret, and William Skelton.
1774, Nov. 24, Hannah, George, and Mary Jonket.
1760, Jan. 30, Hannah, Mary, and Hugh Campbell.
1779, March 29, Hannah, Peter, and Sarah Glover.
1794, Nov. 9, Hannas, Rebecca, and Amos Wheaton.
1768, Dec. 19, Hannats, Hannah, and Edward Wager Russel.
1778, June 15, Hannen, Ann, and Robert Clark.
1778, July 27, Hannings, John, and Jane Golden.
1790, Nov. 11, Hannis, George, and Cathrine McDaniel.
1778, Aug. 15, Hannon, William, and Sarah Capell.
1772, Sept. 30, Hanor, Ann, and George Plauzick.
1779, Sept. 23, Hansby, Thomas, and Mary Prickard.
1776, June 9, Hanse, Conrod, and Isabella Brown.
1800, Feb. 26, Hansell, Andrew, and Hannah Morris.
1795, Dec. 9, Hansel, Mary, and Daniel Kinzea.
1770, June 5, Hansey, George, and Elizabeth Hiscoat.
1761, Sept. 21, Hanson, Cornelius, and Elizabeth Chester.
1762, Sept. 24, Hanson, Cornelius, and Elizabeth Chester.
1790, Nov. 22, Hanson, John, and Mary Brion.
1766, April 23, Hanson, Jonathan, and Margret Miller.
1766, Oct. 26, Hanson, Susannah, and Jacob Weiser.
1800, April 24, Hanson, William, and Cathrine Leman.
1789, Dec. 22, Hantley, Thomas, and Abby Siddon.
1771, June 15, Hanton, James, and Martha Craig.
1779, June 10, Hantwill, Hannah, and Clements Robert.
1786, Jan. 15, Hantzinger, John George, and Mary Damsey.
1779, Sept. 1, Hany, Charles, and Mary Wear.
1785, June 13, Hanzinger, Margaret, and John Holbirt.
1767, Jan. 17, Happard, William, and Hannah Erwin.
1791, Jan. 14, Happerset, John, and Mary Saverite.
1771, Sept. 9, Harben, Eleanor, and Michel Cannor.
1777, Sept. 18, Harber, Charlotte, and William Kinslar.
1767, Aug. 3, Harbert, Michael, and Ellis Richards.
1755, Jan. 11, Harbeson, Mary, and Gustavus Brown.
1778, Feb. 27, Harcourt, Ann, and William Pullin.
1789, Aug. 7, Harden, Thomas, and Jane Price.
1758, Feb. 28, Hardford, Mary, and Henry Priest.
1796, April 23, Hardie, Mary, and William Willingsford.
1785, July 17, Hardin, George, and Elizabeth Book.
1780, Feb. 25, Hardin, James, and Mary Hawkins.
1773, April 20, Hardin, Mathias, and Sarah Pinyard.
1766, July 31, Harding, George, and Mary Nelson.
1757, Nov. 30, Harding, Jane, and John Poultney.
1778, Jan. 28, Harding, John, and Elizabeth Walker.
1779, Dec. 22, Harding, Richard, and Mary Watts.

1795, July   28, Harding, William, and Mary Teft.
1792, May   21, Hardy, George, and Susanna Macfee.
1799, Dec.   15, Hardy, Rebecca, and Thomas Green.
1767, April   26, Hardy, Robert, and Martah Coowgell.
1767, Dec.   22, Haregrave, Mary, and John Rogers.
1761, July   19, Harey, Joseph, and Margth Johnson.
1771, July   14, Harford, James, and Ann Mary Sailor.
1771, Jan.   20, Harford, John, and Mary Dukey.
1780, July   24, Hargus, Rosannah, and John Lascom.
1781, May   17, Harker, Jenny, and John Harland.
1787, Jan.   29, Harker, Jonathan, and Sarah Branson.
1798, April   18, Harkes, Sarah, and George Keck.
1752, June   21, Harkless, Elizabeth, and Peter Elless.
1781, May   17, Harland, John, and Jenny Harker.
1771, Sept,   1, Harland, William, and Mary Richardson.
1778, Dec.   28, Harley, Alexander, and Mary Joiner.
1756, Nov.   18, Harlin, Susannah, and George Brown.
1751, Aug.   14, Harman, Ann, and James MacDowell.
1761, Dec.   3, Harman, Isaac, and Rachel Stilley.
1755, Sept.   6, Harman, Mary, and Mathias Landenberger.
1777, Aug.   23, Harman, Mary, and Philip Warner.
1776, July   18, Harman, Rachel, and John Taylor.
1785, Aug.   11, Harmen, George, and Mary Brown.
1765, March   7, Harmen, Keskiah, and George Dickson.
1758, May   25, Harmer, John and Ann Sage.
1777, Nov.   2, Harmer, Joseph, and Margaret Lieston.
1784, Oct.   10, Harmer, Josiah, and Sarah Jenkins.
1800, Aug.   3, Harmon, John, and Sarah Adams.
1767, March 20, Harmon, Rachel, and William Buchanan.
1792, Aug.   9, Harned, Nancy, and Lewis Albertis.
1800, Jan.   25, Harold, Harriot, and Thomas Snowden.
1758, June   10, Harp, Elizabeth, and Thomas Fulderd.
1775, April   20, Harp, William, and Lydia Davis.
1785, Feb.   10, Harper, Alice, and William Smith.
1756, June   5, Harper, Ann, and Andrew Crocket.
1754, Jan.   21, Harper, David, and Alice Jones.
1797, Nov.   16, Harper, Elizabeth, and John Minot.
1780, Sept.   11, Harper, Joseph, and Esther Ogden.
1776, Dec.   10, Harper, Robert, and Sarah Bellford.
1800, April   26, Harper, Thomas, and Hannah Oliphant.
1790, July   23, Harper, Thomas, and Sarah Davis.
1759, Sept.   17, Harper, William, and Honor Fenn.
1768, Jan.   14, Harper, William, and Sarah Philips.
1783, June   26, Harr, Elizabeth, and John Perkins.
1754, Nov.   21, Harrard, Mary, and William Warnock.
1753, Oct.   29, Harratish, Darkes, and William Pullen.

1778, May 26, Harren, Eleanor, and Peter Crawford.
1758, Nov. 14, Harrenton, James, and Ruth Hirst.
1782, April 2, Harrer, Susannah, and Henry Maag.
1775, Jan. 15, Harrington, Ann, and William Morry.
1751, Feb. 26, Harrington, Edward, and Abigail Towfield.
1794, Aug. 8, Harrington, Elizabeth, and Daniel Ace.
1754, April 14, Harrington, Mary, and John Chub.
1792, July 10, Harris, Catharine, and Martin Null.
1794, Dec. 23, Harris, Edah, and Jacob Snader.
1779, June 2, Harris, Edmund, and Margarett McPherson.
1759, June 26, Harris, Edward, and Catharine Calley.
1779, Feb. 14, Harris, Elizabeth, and John Goodrich.
1785, June 22, Harris, Henry, and Catherine Deleway.
1795, Nov. 30, Harris, John, and Jane Kaighn.
1757, Oct. 19, Harris, Margaret, and John Thomson.
1765, April 10, Harris, Mary, and Samuel Yeats.
1777, Aug. 24, Harris, Mary, and William Fitzgerald.
1798, June 10, Harris, Peggy, and William James.
1784, Nov. 13, Harris, Peter, and Anne Jones.
1792, April 22, Harris, Rachel, and John Richards.
1760, May 7, Harris, Samuel, and Ann Casselberry.
1751, June 20, Harris, Susannah, and Moses Marshall.
1799, July 19, Harrison, Elizabeth, and Bartholomew Dunne.
1764, Jan. 2, Harrison, Elizabeth, and William Bourne.
1792, July 29, Harrison, Elizabeth, and William Carss.
1778, Dec. 22, Harrison, Henery, and —— Fylden.
1782, Jan. 8, Harrison, Jean, and Henry McKeansy.
1765, Oct. 13, Harrison, John, and Ann Cochern.
1783, March 7, Harrison, Joseph, and Jennet Lockhart.
1792, Aug. 23, Harrison, Robert, and Cathrine Ashton.
1782, Jan. 15, Harrison, Sarah, and John Herrick.
1797, Dec. 6, Harrison, Thomas, and Violetta Bucanan.
1770, June 23, Harron, James, and Anne Loremar.
1756, April 25, Harron, Susannah, and Richard McBride.
1787, July 24, Harry, Margret, and Arthur Stotesbury.
1780, Sept. 16, Harry, Mary, and Edward Ritchey.
1781, April 17, Harry, Michael, and Sibil Mark.
1787, Feb. 23, Harry, and Rose, (two negro servants.)
1759, April 8, Hart, Catharine, and John Toy.
1777, Oct. 28, Hart, Elizabeth, and James McMean.
1796, Oct. 30, Hart, Hanna, and Gilbert Stanton.
1778, March 23, Hart, James, and Christiana Mentzy.
1791, July 7, Hart, John, and Elizabeth Lincorn.
1753, Nov. 8, Hart, John, and Martha Overthrow.
1778, May 15, Hart, Joseph, and Catharine Gum.
1771, Sept. 24, Hart, Lydia, and Frederic Heince.

1798, Jan.   18, Hart, Peter, and Sarah Cook.
1758, June   17, Hart, William, and Jane Clayton.
1796, Oct.   11, Hartey, Elizabeth, and Charles Hamilton.
1777, Nov.   28, Hartley, Blekey, and Martha McKinley.
1795, Oct.   15, Hartley, George, and Nancy Myrtland.
1782, May   16, Hartley, Jeane, and Thomas Wood.
1757, Jan.   26, Hartley, Martha, and Luke Williams.
1764, July   25, Hartley, Mary, and Joseph Noblet.
1782, June   16, Harton, Thomas, and Hannah Preston.
1774, May   11, Hartranft, Barbara, and Godfrey Hamled.
1776, Sept.   15, Hartson, Sarah, and Andrew Durand.
1758, May   15, Hartz, Henry, and Christina Wise.
1777, July   1, Harvey, Alexander, and Elizabeth Patterson.
1792, July   1, Harvey, Elenore, and Joseph Calfrey.
1793, Feb.   17, Harvey, Elenore, and Sante Rivola.
1800, Dec.   30, Harvey, Henry, and Ann Compass.
1753, Nov.   22, Harvey, Mary, and Joel Willis.
1760, March 17, Harvey, Sampson, and Mary Bradford.
1765, Sept.   18, Harvey, Samuel, and Margeth Steward.
1795, March 21, Harvey, St. John, and Marget Cheina.
1799, Aug.   11, Harvey, St. John, and Rosanah Gihon.
1796, Aug.   2, Harvey, William, and Cathrine Bryan.
1765, Oct.   14, Hasand, Catharine. and John Croney.
1751, April   8, Hase, Ann, and Samuel Louns.
1796, July   10, Hase, John, and Mercy Tomlin.
1784, April   19, Hase, Michael, and Mary Watson.
1778, Dec.   4, Hasel, John, and Jane Gass.
1783, April   4, Haselton, John, and Rachel Bruce.
1787, July   11, Haselton, Rachel, and John Peters.
1779, Aug.   3, Haslet, Margaret, and Conrad Walter.
1777, March   9, Haslet, Robert, and Margaret McCollough.
1772, Sept.   2, Haslet, Samuel, and Kezia Edwards.
1791, June   15, Haslet, Samuel, and Mary Alexander.
1789, Sept.   3, Haslip, Thomas, and Rachel Preston.
1779, Feb.   14, Hassal, William, and Rose Davern.
1782, Feb.   5, Hassel, Charles, and Catherine Sanders.
1783, Jan.   16, Hasselber, Elizabeth, and John Andrew Brunstrom.
1790, June   9, Hasselberg, Ann, and Robert Chambers.
1800, Nov.   16, Hassell, George, and Mary Ann Conlin.
1784, July   8, Hasselwanger, John, and Neomy Haveloh.
1782, April   9, Hasten, Thomas, and Rebecca King.
1758, May   13, Hastings, Joshua, and Anne Edgerton.
1758, Dec.   29, Hastings, Mary, and Benjamin Olden.
1775, July   7, Hastings, William, and Mary Lusad.
1774, May   19, Hathorn, Daniel, and Martha Howell.
1782, Oct.   6, Hatline, John, and Catherine Larshen.

1779, Jan.　　7, Haton, Elizabeth, and Thomas Tweedy.
1758, Aug.　28, Hatsell, Joseph, and Else Edge.
1763, June　14, Hattan, William, and Mary Evans.
1777, July　18, Hatton, Lucy, and Jacob States.
1765, April　18, Hatton, William, and Judith Money.
1758, March 24, Haudkins, Sampson, and Elizabeth Binns.
1758, Nov.　15, Haudkins, Susanna, and Samuel Lewis.
1799, Jan.　20, Haughey, William, and Alice McCartha.
1779, Sept.　18, Haughton, George, and Christine Wallence.
1783, March　6, Hauser, Patience, and Josiah Hoffman, (negroes.)
1767, Sept.　2, Hausin, Catharine, and John Holtzel.
1764, May　2, Hausmon, Susannah, and John Conrad.
1774, May　31, Hauzeley, Hannah, and Hugh Montgomery.
1784, July　8, Haveloh, Neomy, and John Hasselwanger.
1779, March　4, Haven, Isabella, and James Ellot.
1767, Aug.　15, Hawke, Samuel, and Mary Main.
1777, Jan.　22, Hawkes, Mary, and Edmond Williams.
1780, Jan.　29, Hawkins, Anne, and John Kelly.
1800, Feb.　4, Hawkins, Ebenezer, and Sarah Nelson.
1782, Dec.　2, Hawkins, Elizabeth, and Israel Woodward.
1777, Sept.　11, Hawkins, Henry, and Rosannah Tatem.
1780, Feb.　25, Hawkins, Mary, and James Hardin.
1800, Sept.　4, Hawkins, Rebecca, and William Brown.
1799, May　25, Hawkins, Sarah, and Edward Spooner.
1762, Jan.　24, Hawkins, Thomas, and Ann Jankinson.
1756, Aug.　7, Hawse, Mary, and George Bishop.
1764, Feb.　29, Hawthorne, Mary, and Joseph Lee.
1794, July　21, Hay, Mary, and Peter Dubrevil.
1767, March 31, Hay, Prudence, and Patrick McGineys.
1757, Nov.　3, Hayes, Elizabeth, and William Johnson.
1783, Aug.　4, Hayes, Herbert, and Mary Bonus.
1780, Sept.　10, Hayes, Isabella, and William Warwick.
1775, Jan.　23, Hayes, Sarah, and James Coburn.
1759, July　12, Hayes, William, and Elsah Freeman.
1772, Oct.　15, Hayman, William, and Ann Wane.
1767, Oct.　26, Haynes, Mary, and George Cattan.
1797, June　19, Hays, Ann, and John Gihon.
1799, April　28, Hays, Elizab., and Joseph Caroll.
1794, April　3, Hays, Helena, and Francis Cremor.
1759, Feb.　26, Hays, Judith, and John Dogged.
1779, Nov.　28, Hays, Margaret, and Edward Keran.
1795, Nov.　26, Hays, Mary, and Aaron Haney.
1780, April　4, Hays, Mary, and Richard McGregor.
1777, Oct,　10, Hays, Michael, and Eleanor Clark.
1766, April　22, Hayward, Andrew, and Ann McCormick.
1797, May　9, Hayward, Shadrick, and Ann Smith.

1779, Jan. 9, Haywood, Sarah, and Thomas Jones.
1787, Oct. 8, Hazelburn, Hanna, and George Sherric.
1791, Aug. 21, Hazelton, Thomas, and Mary Cake.
1753, Aug. 10, Hazelwood, John, and Mary Edgar.
1793, April 7, Hazen, Margret, and Baltes Canzler.
1782, Feb. 18, Head, Dorothea, and William McLaine, (free negroes.)
1793, Aug. 10, Head, Henry, and Mary Brown.
1792, Dec. 17, Head, Mary, and Robert Lea, (free Africans.)
1767. Jan. 17, Headcock, John, and Sarah Thomas.
1778, Jan. 1, Heald, John, and Susannah Hudston.
1773, Jan. 14, Heany, Mary, and Luke Dun.
1774, Aug. 7, Hearby, John, and Catharine Cassenbury.
1767, Aug. 3, Heartshorn, James, and Ruth Bethel.
1758, Aug. 5, Heartshorn, John, and Sarah Shellway.
1779, Sept. 25, Heathen, Mary, and Joseph Woodfield.
1783, Dec. 20, Heating, Luke, and Catherine Hess.
1759, July 12, Heaton, Rachel, and Charles Brown.
1791, July 25, Heaton, Thomas, and Christiana Hufsey.
1797, Nov. 26, Heckla, Christian, and Elizabeth Anderson.
1784, May 26, Hector, James, and Sarah Stage.
1797, July 16, Hederick, Mary Alatta, and Augustus Belin.
1778, July 22, Hedler, Ann, and John Kraus.
1791, Dec. 25, Heffenin, Judith, and Michael Chew.
1765, Sept. 29, Heft, Catharine, and Charles Howard.
1782, June 22, Hegens, Sarah, and Richard Broderick.
1764, July 24, Hegland, William, and Margaret Dey.
1767, Jan. 19, Heidel, George, and Susannah Dorn.
1760. March 3, Heidmeyer, Andrew Jacob, and Ann Catharine Magdalene.
1773, Sept. 26, Heimback, Adam, and Mary Tonniker.
1771, Sept. 24, Heince, Frederic, and Lydia Hart.
1788, Oct. 5, Heines, Phebe, and Jonas Denny.
1798, April 29, Heinimen, Mary, and Conrad Ihre.
1790, Oct. 12, Heins, Grace, and Jonathan Durell.
1773, April 11, Heley, Thomas, and Sarah Stine.
1756, Sept. 14, Helfinston, Nicholas, and Rachel Foster.
1784, Jan. 8, Hellems, Sarah, and John Lindbay.
1760, March 3, Helligas, Albrecht, and Catharine Reichert.
1761, May 5, Hellings, Ruth, and John Cart.
1759, May 21, Hellings, William, and Mary Lenrs.
1766, July 3, Hellins, Mary, and Edward Loder.
1771, Nov. 10, Hellman, Kingynda, and John Peter Weyant.
1797, Aug. 31, Helm, Elizab., and David Painter.
1792. May 1, Helm, John, and Ann Letzinger.
1783, March 27, Helmes, Rebecca, and Jeremiah McRoulan.

1793, July   24, Helmes, Elizabeth, and William Taylor.
1790, Feb.   16, Helms, Grace, and Fergus Madan.
1791, Feb.   9, Helms, Israel, and Rebecca Frederic.
1794, May   5, Helms, John, and Ann Soley.
1795, Sept.   10, Helms, Martha, and William Streaper.
1794, Jan.   9, Helms, Nancy, and Davis Smith.
1754, July   20, Helms, Sarah, and Moses Marchil.
1756, March 30, Helmstem, Daniel, and Sarah Goldbary.
1778, Feb.   16, Helviston, Mary, and John McOwen.
1767, Dec.   24, Hemings, Elizabeth, and Everhard Dolan.
1765, Oct.   21, Hemmenway, Josuah, and Sarah Angella.
1794, Sept.   1, Hemphill, Jane, and William Boyel.
1755, Oct.   16, Hemphill, John, and Elizabeth Powel.
1778, Feb.   8, Hempstead, Mary, and Timothy Mahoney.
1797, March   7, Henckel, Ann Mary, and John Jacob Reineck.
1755, July   9, Hencock, Martha, and James Thomson.
1775, June   20, Henderson, Alexander, and Mary Anderson.
1776, Feb.   19, Henderson, Ann, and Francis Proctor.
1768, April   27, Henderson, Ann, and Nathaniel Parker.
1756, May   15, Henderson, David, and Lydia Hesselius.
1785, Nov.   21, Henderson, Elizabeth, and John Hindman.
1796, Sept.   4, Henderson, Sarah, and Leonard Richard.
1793, May   30, Henderson, Thomas, and Mary Sleeth.
1788, Jan.   20, Henderson, William, and Ann Mary Phiffer.
1791, Oct.   19, Henderson, William, and Nancy McCog.
1753, June   3, Hendricks, James, and Mary Dixon.
1787, Sept.   24, Hendricks, John, and Rebecca Wilt.
1753, April   16, Hendrickson, John, and Ellen Stilly.
1764, Jan.   2, Henery, Andrew, and Margaret Gilmore.
1778, April   12, Henery, James, and Rebecca Yeates.
1776, June   9, Henery, John, and Jean McGihan.
1794, Dec.   30, Heney, John, and Elenore Midleton.
1796, Jan.   5, Heney, Mary, and John Green.
1791, Nov.   19, Heney, Susanna, and John Fisher.
1786, April   26, Heneywill, John, and Elizabeth Prusian.
1778, Nov.   19, Henin, Catharine, and Joseph Sharp.
1761, March 17, Heninton, ——, and Samuel Mour.
1771, Jan.   7, Henley, Eleanor, and John Hogan.
1772, Aug.   9, Henly, Mary, and John Scott.
1785, Jan.   24, Hennesey, James, and Lettis Cox.
1761, April   29, Henrich, Charles Sigismund, and Elizabeth Rod-
                     hefer.
1785, Oct.   27, Henricson, Patience, and John Skinner.
1791, Sept.   15, Henry, George, and Mary Pitt.
1792, Nov.   7, Henry, Jacob, and Letitia Maxwell.
1794, Sept.   18, Henry, James, and Abigail Lester.

1800, May   18, Henry, Jane, and John Burk.
1787, Nov.   9, Henry, Jane, and Thomas Gardner.
1763, June   26, Henry, John, and Ann Clarke.
1796, June   5, Henry, John, and Marget Fagundus.
1795, Sept. 20, Henry, Nancy, and James Scott.
1777, March 31, Henry, Philip, and Mary Bedford.
1770, Dec.   23, Henry, Samuel, and Margarett Barnhill.
1795, Nov.   10, Henry, Sophia, and William Silence.
1758, Feb.   6, Hensell, Lewis, and Mary Mills.
1757, Feb.   21, Hephenson, Martha, and Joseph Cartbride.
17/6, Oct.   20, Hepher, Catharine, and William Leeman.
1767, Nov.   9, Hephron, Elizabeth, and Edward Cryps.
1765, Dec.   26, Heppard, Deborah, and James Hale.
1791, Aug.   14, Heppard, Thomas, and Sarah Otto.
1777, June   25, Heran, Andrew, and Mary Cunningham.
1779, April   3, Heritage, Daniel, and Mary Swain.
1790, Dec.   28, Heritage, Judah, and Amy Cattell.
1788, April 12, Heritage, Rebecca, and Judith Bonsillis.
1776, Oct.   30, Heritage, Samuel, and Ann Griffin.
1754, Oct.   9, Herkless, Thomas, and Mary Brily.
1794, March   9, Heron, James, and Mary Bishop.
1781, March   1, Herren, Thomas, and Hetty Lock,
1782, Jan.   15, Herrick, John, and Sarah Harrison.
1792, Sept. 21, Herring, Sarah, and John Cowan.
1762, Oct.   28, Herring, William, and Sarah Dawel.
1772, Nov.   8, Herrity, Cornelius, and Catherine Thomson.
1798, Jan.   20, Hertzog, Joseph, and Catharine Wilt.
1790, April 20, Hervey, Sara, and William Hervey.
1790, April 20, Hervey, William, and Sara Hervey.
1792, June   9, Herzog, Balzar, and Jane Williams.
1783, Dec.   20, Hess, Catharine, and Luke Keating.
1776, Aug.   13, Hess, Michael, and Mary Butterworth.
1795, Aug.   7, Hess, Nancy, and George Carpenter.
1756, May   15, Hesselius, Lydia, and David Henderson.
1774, June   7, Heston, Isaac, and Catharine Clinton.
1777, Dec.   27, Heston Mary, and Thomas Tolly.
1785, Sept. 29, Heston, Thomas, and Hannah Clayton.
1751, Nov.   24, Hetherington, Martha, and Godfrey Green.
1753, Aug.   12, Hetherington, Perthenia, and Robert Porter.
1756, March   7, Heulings, Elizabeth, and Jacob Perkins.
1767, May   7, Heuman, Margret, and George Wosky.
1796, April   4, Hewes, Margret, and Terence McCann.
1775, Oct.   14, Hewes, Mary, and Thomas Morling.
1792, May   15, Hewet, Cathrine, and William McCan.
1770, Oct.   9, Hewett, Charles, and Anne Pierce.
1770, Oct.   12, Hewitt, Aaron, and Catharine Cox.

1779, Nov.   25, Hewlet, William, and Kesiah Newport.
1759, April 11, Hewlings, Israel, and Jane Sharp.
1786, Dec.   31, Hews, Hannah, and Rev. Slater Clay.
1790, Nov.   15, Hews, Henry, and Rebecca Murray.
1794, Dec.   7, Hewson, John, and Nancy Boon.
1773, Sept. 28, Hewster, Mary, and John Howe.
1792, July   18, Hibs, Hester, and Samuel Clayton.
1775, May   6, Hick, Hannah, and Isaac Buck.
1754, Dec.   14, Hickenbottom, Mary, and Richard Taylor.
1753, June   14, Hickenbottom, Thomas, and Elizabeth Bartell.
1782, March 11, Hickey, John, and Catherine Gruden.
1766, Feb.   4, Hickman, Benjamin, and Catharine Cogens.
1767, Nov.   21, Hickman, Margaret, and Peirce Chasey.
1782, Sept. 25, Hicks, Augustine, and Hannah Lawrence.
1784, May   12, Hicks, Catharine, and Stephen Ceronio.
1793, April 3, Hicks, Charlotte, and William Pitt Parvin.
1772, May   17, Hickson, Mary Ann, and Peter Jones.
1755, May   25, Hickst, William, and Barbary Ottinger.
1771, June   2, Hicky, Andrew, and Rachel Murre.
1775, Aug.   6, Hicky, Mary, and Andrew McConal.
1791, May   4, Hicky, Mary Ann, and Mathew Powers.
1780, July   2, Hide, John, and Mertha Mattis.
1790, Dec.   28, Hider, Hanna, and Daniel Hillman.
1792, April 13, Hider, Samuel, and Blancha Corsa Lea.
1797, Jan.   12, Hielan, William, and Sarah Warner.
1779, March 5, Hifes, Mary, and Thomas Price.
1794, May   4, Higby, Edward, and Sarah Dole.
1783, May   26, Higby, Ruth, and William French.
1779, March 10, Higens, Price, and Lydy Wade.
1799, Nov.   25, Higginbotham, Marget, and Patrick Williams.
1780, July   26, Higgins, Arthur, and Sarah Boyce.
1781, Aug.   23, Higgins, Jenny, and Richard Stacy.
1800, Sept. 24, Higgins, Mary, and John Bishop.
1792, Sept. 16, Higgins, Thomas, and Sarah Lucas.
1778, May   29, Higgins, William, and Margaret Gillbert.
1783, Nov.   24, Higgs, Mahlin, and Anne Weaver.
1786, Sept. 25, Highman, Jane, and John Day.
1772, Feb.   4, Hight, Walentine, and Barbary Krienerin.
1787, Aug.   14, Hights, Martin, and Rachel Simson.
1794, Aug.   18, Higinbothom, William, and Marget Donlave.
1776, July   24, Hildeburn, Martin, and Elizabeth Hampton.
1797, June   24, Hilderman, Charlotte, and Jacob Garey.
1789, May   4, Hilger, Henry, and Christina Messersmith.
1763, March 2, Hilkenny, Mary, and Dennis Conneley.
1753, May   17, Hill, Alexander, and Elizabeth Bannett.
1756, Aug.   20, Hill, Catharine, and Ezeckel Sheppard.

1752, July   1, Hill, Catharine, and John Lee.
1795, Sept. 11, Hill, Charles, and Rachel Kaufman.
1758, March 2, Hill, Diana, and Joseph Glascodine.
1794, Sept. 24, Hill, Elizabeth, and Jacques Honore.
1791, Oct.   13, Hill, Elizabeth, and John George Kahle.
1772, May   12, Hill, John, and Beedy Doyls.
1789, June   25, Hill, John, and Helena McGinnis.
1758, Jan.   8, Hill, Joseph, and Mary Cannard.
1775, April 17, Hill, Margaret, and Jacob Kriss.
1791, April   7, Hill, Marget, and Gamaliel Clothier.
1800, April 27, Hill, Mary, and Daniel Olson.
1774, March 27, Hill, Mary, and George Hoffman.
1770, July   1, Hill, Robert, and Hannah Wateheson.
1799, July   4, Hill, Robert, and Mary Minton.
1752, Nov.   10, Hill, Thomas, and Christiana Mecleland.
1755, March 1, Hill, Thomas, and Diana Spencer.
1782, March 7, Hill, William, and Hannah Hall.
1796, April 10, Hillen, Andrew, and Mary Powel.
1775, May   21, Hillerman, Adam, and Charlot Dyson.
1792, June   28, Hillerman, John, and Mary Keech.
1790, Dec.   28, Hillman, Daniel, and Hanna Hider.
1787, Oct.   16, Hillman, Lydia, and Henry Zilke.
1796, Oct.   23, Hillyer, Jane, and Richard Murthwait.
1777, June   9, Hilton, John, and Elizabeth Page.
1796, Dec.   19, Himes, John, and Margret Palmer.
1780, March   8, Hinan, John, and Elizabeth Adams.
1758, Aug.   24, Hinberson, Ann, and Charles Gore.
1792, Sept.   6, Hincle, Elizabeth, and Daniel Kerr.
1780, March 19, Hincle, Judy, and Joseph Benjamin Pettit.
1794, Feb.   18, Hinderson, James, and Mary Frazier.
1777, Oct.   25, Hinderson, John, and Judith Price.
1777, Nov.   30, Hinderson, Margaret, and William McKinzie.
1800, Dec.   13, Hinderson, Mary, and John McCoy.
1790, April   1, Hinderson, Samuel, and Elizabeth Adams.
1782, March   2, Hinderson, Sarah, and Benjamin Correy.
1776, Dec.   31, Hinderson, Sarah, and Thomas Gallgey.
1795, June   2, Hinderson, Susannah, and John Morgan.
1785, Nov.   21, Hindman, John, and Elizabeth Henderson.
1777, March 23, Hindricks, Sarah, and John Cable.
1796, Nov.   12, Hindricson, Anders, and Louisa Charlotta Mel-
                 choa.
1751, June   15, Hindricson, Elizabeth, and John Stephenson.
1758, July   6, Hindrickson, Israel, and Susanna Peterson.
1752, Nov.   8, Hindrickson, Mary, and Ezechiel Rambo.
1759, Feb.   6, Hindrickson, Rebecca, and Mathias Netsellius.
1782, May   16, Hineman, Henry, and Charlot Kolikbreuner.
        26—VOL. VIII.

1765, Feb.   24, Hines, Ann, and Mathias Toy.
1781, Oct.   17, Hines, Mary, and Joseph Bartholomey.
1772, Sept.   11, Hines, Rachel, and William Polen.
1781, Dec.   13, Hiney, Friedric, and Anne Miller.
1778, Oct.   25, Hiney, Jacob, and Margaret Scheffer.
1779, Jan.   31, Hinkley, Barbara, and John Evans.
1755, July   13, Hinman, Margaret, and John Commins.
1777, March   19, Hinshaw, Moses, and Martha White.
1778, April   21, Hinshelwood, Euphemia, and George Johnson.
1752, Dec.   15, Hinshelwood, Robert, and Ann Gosnold.
1765, March   28, Hinson, Sarah, and Thomas Ellis.
1758, Nov.   14, Hirst, Ruth, and James Harrenton.
1770, June   5, Hiscoat, Elizabeth, and George Hansey.
1755, Oct.   12, Hitchings, William, and Margaret Stedman.
1775, Feb.   17, Hithal, John, and Margaret Huston.
1777, April   3, Hitner, Frederick, and Rebecca Tuckey.
1776, June   10, Hitrick, Elizabeth, and Isaac Anderson.
1754, Jan.   13, Hives, William, and Mary Thomas.
1783, Dec.   30, Hjerty, Jacob, and Deborah Cox.
1756, Jan.   3, Hoare, John, and Jane Belony.
1776, Nov.   4, Hobbert, Anthony, and Mary Rebolt.
1772, May   19, Hober, Jacob, and Ursta Diegel.
1779, May   18, Hobert, Christian, and Margarett Walker.
1762, May   26, Hobs, Elizabeth, and William Nails.
1782, Sept.   17, Hobson, John, and Barbara Spelmennen.
1758, March   8, Hock, John, and Barbara Powell.
1786, April   20, Hockins, John, and Mary Klein.
1755, Oct.   15, Hockley, Abigail, and John Patrick.
1796, Jan.   28, Hocter, John, and Sarah Vincent.
1794, Sept.   13, Hodges, Joseph, and Jane Walbern.
1777, April   29, Hodgkinson, Honor, and George McCarty.
1780, April   10, Hodgkinson, Peter, and Ester Hollock.
1752, March   28, Hodgskins, James, and Elizabeth Evans.
1774, Sept.   1, Hodgson, Alvery, and Mary Cunningham.
1776, Dec.   16, Hodsey, Catharine, and Peter Gordon.
1781, June   27, Hoen, Anne, and George Miller.
1779, Aug.   9, Hoerast, Catharine, and John Gift.
1794, Dec.   20, Hoest, Christopher, and Rebecca Matson.
1782, Dec.   24, Hoey, Benjamin, and Anne Horn.
1780, April   22, Hoey, Sarah, and Evan James.
1797, Sept.   21, Hoffa, Margret, and William Wilson.
1764, April   22, Hoffman, Barbarah, and John Fegerley.
1781, July   5, Hoffman, Christian, and Mary Wernes.
1761, June   22, Hoffman, Christopher, and Ester Macles.
1762, July   22, Hoffman, Christopher, and Ester Marles.
1774, March   27, Hoffman, George, and Mary Hiil.

1783, Feb.   27, Hoffman, Henry, and Mary Kaver.
1796, Oct.   13, Hoffman, Jacob, and Johannah Marg[a] Ellemans.
1794, Nov.   9, Hoffman, Mary, and Simon Miller.
1795, Oct.   3, Hoffman, Susannah, and Robert McQuillen.
1791, Oct.   6, Hofner, George, and Jane Guy.
1778, March 18, Hogan, John, and Elizabeth Sheerman.
1771, Jan.   7, Hogan, John, and Eleanor Henley.
1795, April   12, Hogan, Mary, and Patric Carr.
1790, May   10, Hogan, Michael, and Mary Barry.
1764, Jan.   22, Hogan, Nicholas, and Margareth Jones.
1774, Feb.   20, Hogen, Kenedey, and Sarah Askon.
1756, May   31, Hogg, Francis, and Abigail Smith.
1756, March   1, Hogg, Sarah, and John Crawford.
1792, Nov.   15, Hoggard, Thomas, and Elizabeth Lang.
1761, Jan.   1, Hoggins, Benjamin, and Rebeccah Collins.
1785, June   13, Holbirt, John, and Margaret Hanzinger.
1789, Nov.   13, Holden, Abigail, and John Shaw.
1759, Feb.   9, Hollan, Jane Mary, and Nicolas Bartelson.
1777, Dec.   4, Holland, Bridget, and William Keyne.
1785, Feb.   9, Holland, Charles, and Mary Campbell.
1796, June   12, Holland, Christian, and Sarah Miers.
1773, Nov.   21, Holland, Elizabeth, and John Skinner.
1778, Feb.   4, Holland, Judith, and Maurice Burns.
1778, June   13, Holland, Margaret, and John Price.
1757, Feb.   12, Holland, Margaret, and Bobert Grimes.
1752, Sept.   14, Holland, Mary, and John Bankson.
1768, March 14, Holland, Mary, and John Correy.
1786, Oct.   20, Holland, Mathias, and Mary Patty.
1765, Oct.   10, Hollen, David, and Sarah Hamilton.
1776, June   23, Holler, Juliana, and Barney Showow.
1794, Dec.   25, Holler, Mary, and George Nunemaker.
1777, July   9, Hollers, John, and Eleanor Clark.
1797, April   28, Hollick, Sarah, and William Cambridge.
1773, May   13, Holliday, Elizabeth, and Jesse Greenfield.
1751, Dec.   19, Holliday, Elizabeth, and John Sitch.
1792, July   6, Holliday, Peter, and Nancy Woodworth.
1799, June   23, Holliday, Sarah, and Henry Johnson.
1780, April   10, Hollock, Ester, and Peter Hodgkinson.
1792, July   22, Hollscamp, Elizabeth, and John Roland.
1789, Nov.   24, Hollstein, Matthias, and Jane Johnson.
1775, March 13, Hollsten, Magdalena, and John Black.
1777, Feb.   6, Hollsten, Rachel, and Lindsay Coats.
1791, July   19, Hollwell, John, and Elizab. Gryffits.
1778, Sept.   23, Holly, Eve, and George Teace.
1796, May   23, Holly, James, and Sarah Springer.
1760, Feb.   19, Holm, Elizabeth, and John Fagon.

1794, April   3, Holman, Susanna, and Jehu Hall.
1794, March 5, Holmberg, Maria Christina, and Eric Johan Stenman.
1767, March 16, Holmes, Ann, and Isaac Vanible.
1768, May   5, Holmes, John, and Patience Roshell.
1768, April 16, Holmes, John, and Patience Rossell.
1766, Sept. 25, Holmes, Margaret, and William Furnis.
1773, Oct.   6, Holmes, Samuel, and Elizabeth Warwick.
1783, Dec. 22, Holmes, Sarah, and Thomas Boulter.
1754, July 31, Holms, Hannah, and William Mathew.
1793, June 20, Holms, Leah, and Abner Doughty.
1794, Dec. 21, Holmstadt, Marget, and Francis Wilson.
1770, Oct. 21, Holshan, Julia, and Edward Barnhouse.
1753, Jan. 20, Holstein, Friedrich, and Magdalene Jonse.
1766, April 24, Holstein, Peter, and Abigail Jones.
1789, May 21, Holt, Edy, and Robert Poke.
1780, Aug. 19, Holt, Samuel, and Margaret Warnick.
1775, Jan. 26, Holton, Benjamin, and Ann Smith.
1751, April   6, Holton, Christiana, and Israel Cox.
1787, May 12, Holton, Mary, and Solomon Marache.
1758, May 19, Holton, Peter, and Sarah Pearce.
1775, Aug. 27, Holtz, Christopher, and Anna Coolmannin.
1767, Sept.   2, Holtzel, John, and Catharine Hausin.
1778, June 16, Home, Mary, and Joseph Brown.
1780, Jan. 10, Homer, Mary, and Isaac Reyon.
1791, Aug. 16, Homes, Ann, and Thomas Allen.
1790, Oct. 21, Homes, Dorothy, and Philip Seward.
1777, Oct. 25, Homes, Henry, and Elizabeth Patterson.
1772, Oct. 29, Homes, Joseph, and Hannah Francis.
1795, July 28, Homes, Marget, and Richard Homes.
1781, July 21, Homes, Mary Anne, and George McCloud.
1795, July 28, Homes, Richard, and Marget Homes.
1771, Jan.   8, Homes, Susselia, and Thomas Rollin.
1753, Feb. 12, Homes, Thomas, and Ann Morgan.
1760, Oct. 24, Hommins, Margaretta, and Adam Fogel.
1759, Sept. 20, Hommon, Margaret, and Thomas Cobs.
1777, Dec. 21, Homs, William, and Judith Lawrence.
1794, Sept. 24, Honore, Jacques, and Elizabeth Hill.
1754, April 11, Hood, James, and Catharine Sinclair.
1788, May 26, Hood, Elizabeth, and David January.
1794, Jan. 30, Hood, George, and Cathrine Mullen.
1785, Jan. 24, Hood, Jesse, and Susannah Burteloe.
1796, Oct.   6, Hood, Margret, and Owen Dougherty.
1776, Aug. 22, Hood, Mary, and William Craig.
1790, July   8, Hood, Susanna, and John Morphy.
1755, Jan.   6, Hood, William, and Elizabeth Huddle.

1775, March 13, Hood, William, and Hannah Genger.
1756, Dec. 6, Hooff, Peter, and Abigail Thomson.
1780, April 1, Hooker, Thomas, and Catherine Jones.
1767, Feb. 23, Hooks, Ann, and John Thoming.
1793, Feb. 10, Hoope, Ann, and Mathew Waring.
1773, Jan. 6, Hooper, Ann, and Richard Pike.
1755, Dec. 21, Hooper, Hanna, and Joseph Smith.
1798, April 30, Hooper, Judith, and Samuel Easton.
1792, Oct. 30, Hooper, Sarah, and John Treadway.
1792, Aug. 16, Hooper, Thomas, and Ruth Merion.
1752, Oct. 23, Hoops, Margaret, and George Taylor.
1790, Oct. 20, Hoover, Fanny, and James Nichols.
1789, March 28, Hoover, Hanna, and Jacob Shermer.
1791, Jan. 11, Hoover, John, and Mary Metts.
1800, Nov. 13, Hoover, Latitia, and John Jackson.
1793, Jan. 14, Hoover, Margret, and Caleb Cushin.
1795, Sept. 27, Hoover, Nancy, and Samuel Pierce.
1759, Dec. 23, Hope, Adam, and Abigail Wheat.
1798, Aug. 10, Hope, Deborah, and James Cloud.
1760, March 28, Hope, Mathias, and Hannah Aspen.
1796, April 3, Hope, Ruben, and Sarah Baker.
1796, June 30, Hopkins, Alexander, and Cathrine McCanna.
1779, Jan. 17, Hopkins, Catharine, and Samuel Smith.
1754, Sept. 29, Hopkins, Peter, and Florella Williams.
1777, Aug. 10, Hopkins, William, and Sarah Ward.
1773, June 20, Hopkinson, Peter, and Mary Ervin.
1797, July 5, Hopper, Zephania, and Sarah Miers.
1775, Oct. 29, Hopple, John, and Margaret Lee.
1755, Oct. 1, Horditch, Ann, and Thomas Sylvester.
1759, July 2, Hore, Nicholas, and Elizabeth Doyle.
1764, Sept. 10, Horech, George, and.Margaret Robbeson.
1764, Dec. 19, Horley, Maurice, and Margaret Joiles.
1783, Jan. 11, Horn, Abram, and Sarah Deal.
1782, Dec. 24, Horn, Anne, and Benjamin Hoey.
1768, June 5, Horn, John Adam, and Elizabeth Polin.
1782, June 6, Horn, Mary, and Nathaniel Church.
1779, June 8, Hornick, Sophia, and William Brown.
1759, April 3, Horn, Mary, and Rev. Frederic Niemeyer.
1758, Aug. 24, Horns, Anne, and Thomas David.
1766, Dec. 24, Horrey, William, and Mary Brouster.
1766, Feb. 16, Horrin, Magdalene, and John Rosher.
1778, May 14, Horsefall, Joseph, and Anna Mary Margarett Hotfam.
1782, July 1, Horss, John, and Elizabeth Beehman.
1796, Aug. 4, Horton, Humphrey, and Elizabeth Robbins.
1756, Aug. 11, Hoskins, Mary, and William Warner.

1765, Feb.   25, Hossey, Margaret, and Richard Tolley.
1766, May   23, Hoster, Benjamin, and Mary Fisher.
1778, May   14, Hotfam, Anna Mary Margarett, and Joseph Horse-
      fall.
1761, Oct.   29, Hotzheimer, Jacob, and Hannah Walker.
1768, June   6, Houchin, Ann Mary, and John Adam Bruchhauser.
1766, Aug.   12, Houlton, David, and Mary Blanch.
1755, Feb.   22, Houlton, Lydia, and George Wells.
1780, Aug.   8, Hours, Elizabeth, and George Houser.
1774, June   10, House, Elizabeth, and Nicholas Trist.
1769, Nov.   7, House, Hester, and Samuel Chown.
1758, June   18, House, Mary, and Thomas Gardley.
1767, Dec.   24, House, Susannah, and Edmund Power.
1780, Aug.   8, Houser, George, and Elizabeth Hours.
1780, June   5, Housman, Eve, and John Hanegen.
1795, Feb.   26, Houston, Cathrine, and Jacob Smith.
1782, Aug.   21, Hover, Adam, and Catherine Bolter.
1771, May   29, Hover, Mary, and William Branawood.
1800, Jan.   12, How, Robert, and Elizabeth Curts.
1793, July   7, Howard, Cathrine, and Benjamin Wallis.
1765, Sept.   29, Howard, Charles, and Catharine Heft.
1778, March 15, Howard, Elizabeth, and Henry Geel.
1786, Sept.   25, Howard, George, and Hannah Camp.
1751, Sept.   22, Howard, Hannah, and John Gardner.
1762, April   28, Howard, John, and Fraces Douglas.
1761, May   4, Howard, John, and Francis Duglas.
1752, Dec.   7, Howard, Lawrence, and Nanny James.
1799, June   2, Howard, Marget, and John Flin.
1794, Oct.   5, Howard, Margret, and Jacob Aull.
1778, April   10, Howard, Mary, and Bryan Swaney.
1757, Oct.   18, Howard, Mary, and Edward Clerk.
1777, Nov.   25, Howard, Neomey, and Michael Knowles.
1793, April   20, Howard, Samuel, and Hanna Jeffries.
1764, July   2, Howater, Michael, and Catharine Pidgeon.
1773, Sept.   28, Howe, John, and Mary Hewster.
1789, May   2, Howel, Abigail, and Edward Phillips.
1766, Aug.   16, Howel, James Michael, and Elizabeth Russel.
1796, Feb.   26, Howel, Marget, and William McLean.
1758, Dec.   28, Howel, Mary, and Silvanius Gossleing.
1789, Jan.   7, Howel, Sarah, and William Isley.
1754, Aug.   8, Howel, William, and Hannah Wrissband.
1789, July   27, Howel, William, and Margret Doman.
1778, March   6, Howell, Charlotta, and Jos. Henry Coxell.
1774, March 19, Howell, Martha, and Daniel Hathorn.
1781, Sept.   8, Howell, Mary, and David Brown.
1751, June   2, Howell, Mary, and Gilbert Ronnells.

1777, April   8, Howell, Thomas, and Ann Barker.
1773, March   4, Howels, Mary, and Samuel Scott.
1794, May   23, Howlind, William, and Cathrine Cooper.
1792, April   17, Hoxworth, William, and Sarah Paine.
1766, Feb.   10, Hoy, John, and Elenor Ward.
1795, Jan.   25, Hoy, Thomas, and Eva Cress.
1795, Jan.   10, Hozier, Samuel, and Letitia Warren.
1787, Feb.   3, Hubbard, Ebenezer, and Eleonore Sheerwood.
1759, Nov.   12, Hubs, Abigail, and William Rechester.
1794, May   19, Huchill, Cathrine, and Arthur Carney.
1794, June   2, Huddell, Samuel, and Sarah Wolf.
1755, Jan.   6, Huddle, Elizabeth, and William Hood.
1757, July   10, Hudle, Frances, and William Falkner.
1787, Oct.   2, Hudle, Rachel, and John Vandusen.
1787, Oct.   4, Hudle, Sarah, and Thomas Cox.
1792, July   31, Hudson, Elizabeth, and Walter Mitchel.
1767, June   6, Hudson, George, and Rebeccah Clement.
1781, Aug.   9, Hudson, Henry, and Hannah Foster.
1784, March   22, Hudson, Sarah, and Richard Carman.
1783, Aug.   30, Hudson, William, and Mary Gilmore.
1768, June   24, Hudson, William, and Phebe Lowdher.
1773, Oct.   21, Hudstedler, Margaret, and William Villey.
1790, Aug.   28, Hudston, Mary, and George Oliver.
1778, Jan.   1, Hudston, Susannah and John Heald.
1757, March   3, Hues, Hennery, and Ealce Nolberry.
1792, Jan.   8, Huet Fanny, and Solomon Kelly.
1772, Sept.   17, Huett, Aaron, and Ann Butterworth.
1785, Oct.   6, Huff, Jacob, and Elizabeth Dietrick.
1759, Sept.   11, Huff, Mary, and Joseph Miller.
1797, May   31, Huff, Sarah, and Joseph Edwards.
1778, April   5, Huffey, John, and Kesia West.
1765, June   7, Huffman, Catharine, and Alexander Foster.
1791, July   25, Hufsey, Christiana and Thomas Heaton.
1773, Oct.   16, Hugel, Juddy, and Joseph Jackson, (negroes.)
1784, Oct.   28, Hugg, Elizabeth, and Samuel Kennard.
1789, March   28, Hugg, William, and Anne Widdifield.
1776, March   28, Huggin, Elizabeth, and John Cook.
1798, Dec.   16, Huggins, Benjamin, and Sarah Guy.
1800, April   26, Huggins, Eunice, and Isaac Fish.
1767, March   31, Hugh, Hugh, and Elizabeth Canaday.
1777, Nov.   22, Hugh, Hugh, and Sarah Parson.
1790, Oct.   23, Hugh, Rachel, and William Scott.
1798, July   5, Hugh, Rebecca, and John Dowd.
1795, Jan.   22, Hugh, Sarah, and Lawrence Deurbreec.
1800, May   9, Hughes, Ann, and Jasper Carter.
1755, March   2, Hughes, Elizabeth, and Joseph Watkince.

1766, Jan.　17, Hughes, Henry, and Ann Craley.
1799, Aug.　18, Hughs, Henry, and Mary Walter.
1780, Feb.　8, Hughes, John, and Mary Cahill.
1778, Jan.　11, Hughes, Judith, and John Power.
1778, Sept.　20, Hughes, Margaret, and James McDonalds.
1793, June　8, Hughes, Margery, and Johnson McClanichen.
1776, Aug.　6, Hughes, Mathew, and Elizabeth Edwards.
1773, Jan.　18, Hughes, Prudence, and John Ruth.
1767, May　16, Hughes, Richard, and Hannah Aburn.
1790, Oct.　20, Hughs, James, and Elenore Macbride.
1778, May　29, Hughs, James, and Mary Farmouth.
1767, Aug.　17, Hughs, James, and Mary Martin.
1792, June　28, Hughs, Lydia, and George Fisher.
1755, Aug.　23, Hughs, Mary, and Daniel Watkins.
1759, April　1, Hughs, Mary, and John McCoy.
1795, Jan.　11, Hughs, Rebecca, and Thomas McCoughley.
1787, Dec.　6, Hulet, William, and Sarah Malony.
1782, Aug.　15, Hulin, Mary, and William Turner.
1755, July　8, Hulings, Abraham, and Hesther Prath.
1752, Oct.　12, Hulings, Andrew, and Catharine Moriss.
1794, May　19, Hulings, David, and Abia Legg.
1784, May　4, Hulings, Elizabeth, and William Shillingsford.
1778, May　27, Hulings, Mary, and Richard Brady.
1751, Dec.　31, Hulins, Joseph, and Elizabeth Valleygate.
1777, June　20, Hullon, Elizabeth, and John Tull.
1783, Oct.　25, Hultgren, Swen, and Elizabeth Thomas.
1770, Dec.　25, Humbley, George, and Elizabeth Owens.
1795, July　2, Humes, James, and Mary Curran.
1794, April　5, Humphord, Hester, and Michael Stowe.
1780, Jan.　18, Humphrey, Isaac, and Jane Brown.
1784, March 17, Humphreys, Anne, and John Lowden.
1796, Dec.　10, Humphreys, David, and Sarah Mase.
1783, Oct.　30, Humphreys, Elizabeth, and Andrew Urian.
1767, Feb.　24, Humphreys, Elizabeth, and John Willson.
1774, Oct.　2, Humphreys, Elizabeth, and Joshua Johnson.
1762, Dec.　31, Humphreys, Johannah, and Jonathan Corn.
1756, July　27, Humphreys, Mary, and Humphrey Jones.
1766, April　22, Humphreys, Priscillah, and Joshua Stephens.
1775, Sept.　12, Humphreys, Susannah, and Samuel Jesserys.
1775, Dec.　2, Humphreys, William, and Ann Coburn.
1795, Aug.　3, Humphries, Lewes, and Ann Craig.
1755, June　25, Humphry, Margarete, and Thomas Cochran.
1793, Nov.　2, Hunt, Cathrine, and Andrew Swanson.
1790, Sept.　24, Hunt, Cresswell, and Elizabeth Evans.
1795, March 18, Hunt, Esaiah, and Elenore Bee.
1778, Jan.　21, Hunt, Francis, and Mary Gibson.

1791, Jan.   28, Hunt, Joseph, and Cathrine More.
1756, Aug.   11, Hunt, Mary, and David Brooks.
1787, Oct.   7, Hunt, Mary, and William Thomas.
1795, June   7, Hunt, Michael, and Johanna Lambert.
1752, Dec.   25, Hunt, Susanna, and Henry Peers.
1790, July   13, Hunter, Agnes, and Patric Campbell.
1798, June   18, Hunter, James, and Rachel Nuttle.
1792, Dec.   7, Hunter, Jane, and William Babby.
1777, Dec.   23, Hunter, Lowrannah, and Patrick Dorus.
1773, March   14, Hunter, Margaret, and Robert Needon.
1751, Oct.   16, Hunter, Margaret, and William Scarf.
1792, Aug.   11, Hunter, Martha, and Christian Young.
1777, Feb.   11, Hunter, Mary, and Hugh Jones.
1795, Sept.   16, Hunter, Nancy, and Joseph Lee.
1773, Sept.   28, Hunter, Nathaniel, and Elizabeth Bywater.
1786, Dec.   19, Hunter, Oliver, and Mary Burket.
1778, Oct.   19, Hunter, Oliver, and Mary Carral.
1780, March   14, Hunter, Robert, and Rachel Parker.
1799, Oct.   25, Hunter, William, and Mary Hutson.
1796, April   7, Huntrods, William, and Marget Fury.
1783, March   27, Huntsman, Elizabeth, and John Morris.
1796, Feb.   28, Hurley, John, and Ann Schuyler.
1794, Nov.   16, Hurley, Thomas, and Mary Rogers.
1771, Jan.   20, Hurst, Hannah, and Daniel Dawson.
1788, April   28, Husk, Lewis, and Frances Garter.
1790, Oct.   7, Hussey, Hanna, and Isaac Morris.
1775, Jan.   26, Husted, Catharine, and Jonathan Jones.
1795, March   12, Huston, Elizabeth, and Peter Fox.
1767, Oct.   10, Huston, James, and Catharine Quig.
1775, Feb.   17, Huston, Margaret, and John Hithal.
1786, March   25, Huston, Mathew, and Hannah Cox.
1756, May   22, Huston, Sarah, and John Stasy.
1778, May   25, Hutcheson, George, and Ann Price.
1799, Feb.   22, Hutcheson, Mary, and Wm Sinclair.
1780, March   19, Hutcheson, William, and Eleanor Cruse.
1790, May   29, Hutchins, Thomas, and Hanna Morgan.
1762, Dec.   10, Hutchinson, Ann, and John Mikesner.
1780, Sept.   21, Hutchinson, Hannah, and Samuel Moss.
1766, July   3, Hutchinson, Hezekiah, and Eleanor Miller.
1778, Jan.   16, Hutchinson, Mary, and Duncan Mackentash.
1794, Feb.   16, Hutchinson, Mary, and Michael Crafft.
1790, Jan.   6, Hutson, Hanna, and George Gillmar.
1781, March   24, Hutson, Hannah, and Isaac Millener.
1799, Oct.   25, Hutson, Mary, and William Hunter.
1784, July   1, Hutton, Eletter, and Thomas Smith.
1772, May   12, Hutton, John, and Jean Turner.

1790, June   26, Hutton, John, and Roseana Stout.
1780, Jan.   15, Hutton, Mary, and John Charlton.
1795, June   28, Huy, (or Hugh,) Samuel, and Cathrine McPollin.
1778, Oct.   19, Hybands, Nathan, and Mary Lowry.
1799, Jan.   17, Hyberg, Mary, and George McDonel.
1785, Sept.   15, Hyde, Andrew, and Mary Kammer.
1759, March   5, Hyde, William, and Elisabet Webb.
1781, Oct.   5, Hyens, Alexander, and Elizabeth Adams.
1796, Nov.   9, Hylaus, Jane, and John McCusick.
1764, Oct.   14, Hyman, Peter, and Ann Marchants.
1758, May   8, Hymn, Ann, and Richard Foggett.
1796, July   3, Hyneman, Cathrine, and George Murphy.
1796, Oct.   25, Hyzer, Margret, and Thomas White.
1763, April   13, Ibbison, William, and Phibiah Smith.
1702, Sept.   4, Idere, Mary, and Michael Kennedy.
1789, April   29, Ihre, Conrad, and Mary Heinimen.
1757, Feb.   7, Illerin, Eva, and Adam Gephert.
1784, Dec.   16, Illingsworth, Rachel, and Samuel Bunker.
1795, May   24, Immel, John, and Mary Tally.
1786, Nov.   16, Indigott, Rebecca, and William Chadwick.
1790, April   9, Infel, John, and Jane Kennedy.
1798, March   15, Inflefried, Christopher, and Mary Morgan.
1770, Oct.   27, Ingarm, Hannah, and Jacob Diegel.
1778, June   25, Ingells, Mary, and John Martin Korspach.
1787, Oct.   31, Ingeron, William, and Rachel Geen.
1797, June   16, Ingle, Hannah, and Peter Triant.
1758, July   30, Ingle, John, and Grace Smith.
1792, Dec.   15, Ingram, Elizabeth, and William Montgomery.
1776, Nov.   25, Ingram, George, and Catharine Kenney.
1785, Sept.   3, Ingram, John, and Mary Walton.
1767, Oct.   23, Innes, Robert, and Elizabeth Moore.
1794, Nov.   2, Inskip, Abraham, and Sarah Crim.
1784, July   14, Inskip, Hope, and Parr Willard.
1781, Oct.   23, Inskip, John, and Hannah Brock.
1789, Sept.   7, Insworth, James, and Isabel Mills.
1796, April   7, Ireland, Amos, and Patience Cook.
1788, Aug.   9, Ireland, Lydia, and Thomas Bruce.
1785, July   3, Irick, Christina, and Benjamin Thomas.
1779, April   18, Irish, Abraham, and Ann Maddicks.
1796, Dec.   11, Irons, Sarah, and James Farley.
1791, Sept.   17, Irvin, Ann, and James Magrote.
1792, April   9, Irvin, Elizabeth, and John Elliot.
1756, Feb.   5, Irwin, Isabella, and Richard Renshaw.
1775, Jan.   27, Irwin, Jennet, and Hugh Johnston.
1752, Nov.   28, Irwin, Margareta, and Jacob Crawford.
1750, Nov.   17, Irwin, Ruth, and William Ward.

1788. July   30, Isaac, William, and Catharine Boyer.
1791, March 10, Isborn, Hanna, and Henry Beck.
1789, Jan.   7, Isley, William, and Sarah Howel.
1781, Jan.   18, Israel, Joseph, and Susannah Pusey.
1778, Nov.   5, Isralo, Casper, and Jane McLaughlin.
1770, Sept.   17, Ister, George, and Mary McKensey.
1762, Nov.   21, Ivans, Mary, and Joseph Smith.
1762, Nov.   23, Ivans, Rachel, and Isaac Clark.
1761, Nov.   21, Ivens, Mary, and Joseph Smith.
1768, April   31, Ivery, Douglas, and Mary Powell.
1759, Jan.   1, Ivery, Mary, and Jehu Barket.
1781, Feb.   25, Ives, John, and Sarah Griffe.
1795, May   31, Izatt, James, and Prudence Cook.
1791, Nov.   11, Jack, Eleonore, and Nathaniel Gates.
1778, Jan.   26, Jack, Margaret, and John Padgie.
1798, Dec.   3, Jackson, Benjamin, and Mary Multy.
1780, Feb.   28, Jackson, Elizabeth, and Nicholas Selrant.
1782, June   27, Jackson, Elizabeth, and Samuel Cuthbert.
1792, March 23, Jackson, Elizabeth, and William Gilchrist.
1754, Nov.   2, Jackson, Elizabeth, and William Williams.
1778, April   12, Jackson, James, and Mary Grayer.
1793, Feb.   14, Jackson, John, and Ann Latter.
1800, Nov.   13, Jackson, John, and Latitia Hoover.
1767, Feb.   10, Jackson, John, and Rebeccah Jackson.
1773, Oct.   16, Jackson, Joseph, and Juddy Hugel, (negroes.)
1794, Oct.   31, Jackson, Lydia, and Joseph Milberry.
1777, June   18, Jackson, Lydia, and William North.
1794, March 7, Jackson, Marget, and Frederick Tryon.
1767, Feb.   10, Jackson, Rebeccah, and John Jackson.
1772, April   15, Jackson, Richard, and Margaret Stackhouse.
1794, Sept.   9, Jackson, Robert, and Judith Jones, (Africans.)
1798, Dec.   29, Jackson, Sarah, and Daniel Loid.
1779, Aug.   15, Jackson, Thomas, and Mary Bray.
1763, June   13, Jackson, William, and Margareth Lawiston.
1780, Feb.   1, Jackson, William, and Susannah Jorden.
1753, Feb.   1, Jacobs, Mary, and Brian Collons.
1774, Nov.   7, Jacobs, Rachel, and Robert Otway.
1788, Feb.   2, Jacobs, Sarah, and John Cain.
1752, Nov.   26, Jacobs, Thomas, and Susannah Templing.
1794, April   15, Jacobs, William, and Jane Row.
1799, Nov.   27, Jacobson, Hans, and Lettice Toms.
1799, Feb.   17, Jacques, William, and Ann Reeze.
1778, June   4, Jager, Mary, and Pierce Neal.
1777, Jan.   19, Jagerin, Elizabeth, and John McKnear.
1786, Nov.   4, James, Catherine, and Isaac Frame.
1798, June   10, James, Cathrine, and Robert Chapman.

1771, June   22, James, Elizabeth, and Samuel Hannah Roynel.
1780, April   22, James, Evan, and Sarah Hoey.
1794, April   27, James, Hanna, and Solomon, Steelman.
1773, March 27, James, Hannah, and Thomas Jones.
1795, March 24, James, Hester, and Joseph Bolton.
1797, April   20, James, John, and Mary Ray.
1759, Aug.   31, James, Joseph, and Sarah Torlor.
1789, Oct.   20, James, Mary, and Joseph Parmer.
1752, Dec.   7, James, Nanny, and Lawrence Howard.
1781, March 27, James, Rachel, and James Black.
1794, Dec.   24, James, Rachel, and Joseph Robins.
1763, June   22, James, Rebeceah, and John Smith.
1770, June   30, James, Samuel, and Rachel Haas.
1764, Nov.   6, James, Thomas, and Ann Page.
1788, Nov.   22, James, Thomas, and Elizabeth Loughberry.
1798, June   10, James, William, and Peggy Harris.
1767, Dec.   15, Jamison, Thomas, and Jane Long.
1762, Jan.   24, Jankinson, Ann, and Thomas Hawkins.
1755, March 31, Janny, Abel, and Elizabeth Maridith.
1760, Dec.   18, Janson, Christiana, and John Wachon.
1761, April   9, Janson, Jacob, and Elsah Roberts.
1781, Jan.   30, Jantz, Nathias, and Mary Bonnel.
1788, May   26, January, David, and Elizabeth Hood.
1763, April   14, Janvier, Isaac, and Elizabeth Renshaw.
1752, Dec.   28, Janvier, Thomas, and Rebecca Duchee.
1756, May   9, Jarsey, Henry, and Elizabeth Walker.
1781, April   7, Jaw, Mary, and Daniel Boland.
1796, July   28, Jeanson, Folkert, and Engle Evan
1778, April   9, Jefferies, John, and Mary Staiger.
1799, July   22, Jeffers, Margret, and Walter Fisher.
1787, May   8, Jefferson, John, and Melecinte Dear
1761, Sept.   28, Jefferys, Sarah, and Alexander McKey.
1766, April   28, Jeffrey, James, and Ann Seyler.
1793, April   20, Jeffries, Hanna, and Samuel Howard.
1756, March   4, Jemison, William, and Ann Frame.
1798, May   29, Jemmington, Elizab., and Thomas Miller.
1783, Oct.   21, Jemmison, Alexander, and Elizabeth Carmichael.
1791, May   1, Jemmison, Jane, and Bartholomy Adams.
1791, June   23, Jemmison, Margret, and Alexander MacDonald.
1793, July   13, Jemmison, Nathan, and Elenore Wilson.
1773, July   1, Jenkins, Catharine, and Adam Boyd.
1781, Oct.   6, Jenkins, Elizabeth, and John Diley.
1768, Oct.   24, Jenkins, Hannah, and William Kendley.
1759, Sept.   10, Jenkins, Isack, and Jane Thomson.
1776, Dec.   3, Jenkins, John, and Mary Leech.
1771, Jan.   2, Jenkins, Sarah, and John Anderson.

1784, Oct.   10, Jenkins, Sarah, and Josiah Harmer.
1772, Nov.   13, Jenkins, William, and Sarah McLouglan.
1764, Nov.   24, Jenkis, Hannah, and Thomas Gordon.
1766, March 16, Jennings, Mary, and John Need.
1778, Dec.   3, Jennins, Bridget, and John Fitzpatrick.
1775, July   11, Jervis, Charlot Mary, and William Fitzell.
1791, Aug.   20, Jervis, Mary, and Thomas MacMahon.
1798, July   22, Jesperson, Hans, and Henrietta Dorothea Livortin.
1775, Sept. 12, Jesserys, Samuel, and Susannah Humphreys.
1761, March 21, Jewel, Ann, and Samuel Roberts.
1781, Dec.   12, Jewelson, Eliah, and Elizabeth Warwick.
1767, Dec.   16, Jewery, Jacob, and Elizabeth McCarty.
1793, June   15, Jingcison, John, and Mary Bates.
1751, Oct.   6, Joachim, Judy, and Nicholas Jonce.
1780, April 20, Job, William, and Mary Derickson.
1762, April 29, Jobs, Richard, and Mary Ward.
1781, Oct.   25, Jobson, James, and Sarah Shaw.
1775, June   8, Jobson, Samuel, and Catharine Rairy.
1796, March 23, Jockum, Edith, and George Folk.
1798, Nov.   29, Jockum, Enoch, and Isabella Robeson.
1795, March 17, Jockum, James, and Deborah Eagens.
1791, Oct.   4, Jocum, John, and Martha Thomas.
1791, Dec.   2, Jocum, Peter, and Elizabeth Wilson.
1778, Sept. 10, Joden, Frances, and Sidney Francis.
1761, Jan.   21, John, Mary, and William Smith.
1782, Dec.   27, John, Rachel, and Thomas Sutton.
1753, Aug.   13, Johns, Elizabet, and Christian Grawer.
1772, March 18, Johns, Isaac, and Elizabeth Dougherty.
1752, June   18, Johns, Joseph, and Elinor Parry.
1773, April 11, Johns, Samuel, and Eleanor Cremor.
1791, May   26, Johnson, Alexander, and Susanna McCleese.
1791, March 30, Johnson, Ann, and Andrew Murrie.
1790, Feb.   25, Johnson, Ann, and Jacob Siters.
1764, March 27, Johnson, Ann, and John Clue.
1794, Dec.   29, Johnson, Ann, and Mathew Aaron Fighter.
1774, Nov.   11, Johnson, Ann, and Thomas William.
1798, Jan.   17, Johnson, Benjamin, and Rachel Shallcross.
1754, July   11, Johnson, Christiana, and William Davis.
1781, Sept. 20, Johnson, David, and Elizabeth Byberry.
1771, Sept. 12, Johnson, Deborah, and Deen Jones.
1797, Oct.   26, Johnson, Edward, and Martha Keats.
1794, Jan.   7, Johnson, Elenore, and Joseph Woodman.
1796, June   23, Johnson, Eleonore, and Thomas Starr.
1800, June   30, Johnson, Elias, and Sarah Rickey.
1755, Aug.   29, Johnson, Elizabeth, and Edward Godfrey.
1779, Feb.   3, Johnson, Elizabeth, and George Godfriedt.

1759, June 21, Johnson, Elizabeth, and Henry Rice.
1751, Jan. 3, Johnson, Elizabeth, and James Whitton.
1753, May 17, Johnson, Elizabeth, and John Davis.
1778, Dec. 2, Johnson, Elizabeth, and John Whitaker.
1785, April 14, Johnson, Elizabeth, and Nicholas Traves.
1763, April 20, Johnson, Elizabeth, and Samuel Gamble.
1790, Sept. 26, Johnson, Garsham, and Sara Brant.
1778, April 21, Johnson, George, and Euphemia Hinshelwood.
1795, June 7, Johnson, Hannah, and William Wood.
1778, Oct. 18, Johnson, Harman, and Elizabeth Roethofer.
1776, April 8, Johnson, Henry, and Elizabeth Saurey.
1796, Oct. 28, Johnson, Henry, and Mary Johnson.
1799, June 23, Johnson, Henry, and Sarah Holliday.
1755, May 7, Johnson, James, and Ann Lee.
1791, Jan. 25, Johnson, James, and Marget Caster.
1778, Jan. 6, Johnson, Jane, and John Gowanlock.
1789, Nov. 24, Johnson, Jane, and Matthias Hollstein.
1757, Aug. 28, Johnson, Jane, and Philip Beneth.
1800, Jan. 30, Johnson, John, and Ann Bickerton.
1777, Jan. 17, Johnson, John, and Eleanor Cinnor.
1754, Feb. 19, Johnson, John, and Elizabeth McMollin.
1758, July 17, Johnson, John, and Hannah Pritchard.
1781, May 17, Johnson, John, and Nancy Chown.
1767, April 16, Johnson, John, and Susannah Ashton.
1791, Aug. 17, Johnson, Jonas, and Margret Ransel.
1793, April 2, Johnson, Joseph, and Elizabeth Rogers.
1776, May 19, Johnson, Joseph, and Ruth Lewis.
1774, Oct. 2, Johnson, Joshua, and Elizabeth Humphreys.
1757, June 7, Johnson, Lydia, and Thomas Rusle.
1781, Feb. 1, Johnson, Margaret, and Henry Roberts.
1757, Oct. 29, Johnson, Margaret, and Job Wattson.
1795, Sept. 3, Johnson, Marget, and Samuel Taper.
1793, March 27, Johnson, Margret, and Joseph Russel.
1766, May 21, Johnson, Margret, and Roger Bowman.
1761, July 19, Johnson, Margth, and Joseph Harey.
1766, Sept. 10, Johnson, Martha, and Alexander McMichael.
1759, Feb. 11, Johnson, Mary, and John Simson.
1794, May 27, Johnson, Mary, and John Weeks.
1752, April 2, Johnson, Mary, and Joseph Coleman.
1774, Aug. 20, Johnson, Mary, and Robert Gentry.
1793, July 3, Johnson, Mary, and Thomas Ender.
1778, Dec. 1, Johnson, Mary, and Thomas McKinsey.
1796, April 21, Johnson, Mary, and William Leary.
1796, May 22, Johnson, Nancy Valkert, and Henry Thomas.
1798, Feb. 16, Johnson, Phebe, and James Gallon.
1792, April 8, Johnson, Rebecca, and Mathias Caster.

1794, May   17, Johnson, Robert, and Elizabeth Rihl.
1791, July   2, Johnson, Samuel, and Ann Carter.
1794, Oct.   5, Johnson, Samuel, and Mary Curin.
1764, June   23, Johnson, Sarah, and Bartholomew Balderston.
1777, June   11, Johnson, Sarah, and Edward Flinn.
1780, July   17, Johnson, Sophia, and John Francis.
1780, March   9, Johnson, Susannah, and Pemas Burden.
1790, Oct.   4, Johnson, Violet, and George Rodgers.
1757, Nov.   3, Johnson, William, and Elizabeth Hayes.
1788, Nov.   4, Johnson, William, and Lydia Hand.
1790, March 29, Johnson, William, and Rebecca Forester.
1775, Sept.   19, Johnston, Christiana, and George McKeag.
1794, July   17, Johnston, Dorcas, and William Middleton.
1773, Oct.   5, Johnston, Elizabeth, and Alexander Dowald.
1773, Oct.   1, Johnston, Elizabeth, and James Rowland.
1785, Feb.   20, Johnston, Elizabeth, and John Scanlan.
1766, April   21, Johnston, Francis, and Mary Strutton.
1775, Jan.   27, Johnston, Hugh, and Jennet Irwin.
1766, Feb.   24, Johnston, James, and Elizabeth Geepen.
1785, Nov.   10, Johnston, Lawrence, and Elizabeth Gilbert.
1753, Aug.   7, Johnston, Mary, and Alexander Withron.
1796, Oct.   28, Johnston, Mary, and Henry Johnson.
1757, Nov.   29, Johnston, Mary, and Samuel Watson.
1773, March   2, Johnston, Paul, and Johanna Stennard.
1759, July   2, Johnston, Robert, and Mary Forster.
1784, April   5, Johnston, Samuel, and Mary Riddle.
1778, March   1, Johnston, William, and Elizabeth Fare.
1782, May   27, Joice, Hannah, and Richard Thomas.
1793, Sept.   23, Joie, Patrick, and Mary Power.
1764, Dec.   19, Joiles Margaret, and Maurice Horley.
1776, March 21, Joiner, Margaret, and Luke Aubrey.
1778, Dec.   28, Joiner, Mary, and Alexander Harley.
1781, June   17, Joiner, Mary, and James O'Brayne.
1774, Sept.   4, Jolly, Margaret, and John Lang.
1766, Oct.   20, Jomaster, William, and Mary Stinson.
1790, March   3, Jonas, Elizabeth, and Thomas Graham.
1758, Jan.   29, Jonasson, Peter, and Sarah Justis.
1751, Oct.   6, Jonce, Nicholas, and Judy Joachim.
1776, April   24, Jones, Abigail, and Peter Holstein.
1754, Jan.   21, Jones, Alice, and David Harper.
1789, May   2, Jones, Alice, and John Magor.
1798, Nov.   12, Jones, Andrew, and Sarah Allen.
1771, Aug.   22, Jones, Ann, and Hugh Arvin.
1790, May   20, Jones, Ann, and James Lewis.
1764, April   6, Jones, Ann, and John Stanford.
1789, Dec.   2, Jones, Ann and Marc Titt.

1784, Nov   13, Jones, Anne, and Peter Harris.
1781, Oct.   21. Jones. Anne, and Samuel Dison.
1770, Oct.   15, Jones, Anne, and Thomas Shearman.
1770, April   9, Jones, Benjamin, and Hannah Kark.
1780, April   1, Jones, Catherine, and Thomas Hooker.
1780, Aug.   5, Jones, Charity, and Jesse Serran.
1772, June   16, Jones, David, and Barbara Diegel.
1784, Oct.   12, Jones, David, and Fanny Russler.
1771, Sept.   12, Jones, Deen, and Deborah Johnson.
1757, Dec.   4, Jones, Edward, and Ann Scotton.
1778, Nov.   25, Jones, Edward, and Dorothy Kelly.
1790, Oct.   7, Jones, Edward, and Jane Gilbert.
1778, May   31, Jones, Edward, and Margaret Grimes.
1752, Jan.   12, Jones, Elinor, and John Sitel.
1790, Sept.   23, Jones, Elizabeth, and George Griffith.
1788, Sept.   5, Jones, Elizabeth, and George Steel.
1782, Dec.   21, Jones, Elizabeth, and John Garrett.
1789, June   5, Jones, Elizabeth, and John Williams.
1798, July   25, Jones, Elizab. and Uriah Lott.
1792, Oct.   7, Jones, Elizabeth, and William Mathews.
1754, Feb.   26, Jones, Evan, and Sarah Mutchins.
1777, May   30, Jones, Francis, and Mary Brooks.
1779, June   5, Jones, Hagaret, and John Bleney.
1777, Feb.   11, Jones, Hugh, and Mary Hunter.
1756, July   27, Jones, Humphrey, and Mary Humphreys.
1774, Jan.   27, Jones, Israel, and Susannah Cleim.
1799, Aug.   12, Jones, Jesiah, and Mary Egins.
1756, April   12, Jones, John, and Ann Farris.
1799, Jan.   27, Jones, John, and Ann Short.
1778, Sept.   13, Jones, John, and Barbarah Piper.
1797, July   6, Jones, John G., and Rebecca Vanhook.
1791, Feb.   13, Jones, John, and Mary Dunbar.
1751, Dec.   5, Jones, John, and Mary Nettle.
1775, Jan.   26, Jones, Jonathan, and Catherine Husted.
1796, Feb.   18, Jones, Judith, and Charles Biley.
1794, Sept.   9, Jones, Judith, and Robert Jackson, (Africans.)
1756, Sept.   3, Jones, Lewis, and Mary Connard.
1771, Nov.   25, Jones, Lucy, and Revd William Currie.
1764, May   30, Jones, Margaret, and John Shagmessy.
1765, Jan.   22, Jones, Margareth, and Nicholas Hogan.
1778, May   30, Jones, Margaret, and Richard Carleton.
1798, Jan.   20, Jones, Marget, and Fredric Loudon.
1792, March 18, Jones, Margret, and George Allinsore Simon Si-
                   monson.
1766, April   23, Jones, Margret, and James Morris.
1795, May   31, Jones, Martha, and William Kelly.

1781, Dec.   20, Jones, Mary, and Francis Comford.
1776, May   19, Jones, Mary, and George Ray.
1778, June   1, Jones, Mary, and Jacob Rogers.
1758, April   16, Jones, Mary, and John Cherington.
1783, July   19, Jones, Mary, and John Courtney.
1789, Dec.   2, Jones, Mary, and John Miers.
1780, Jan.   31, Jones, Mary, and John Willson.
1782, June   23, Jones, Mary, and Joseph Patterson.
1784, April   14, Jones, Mary, and Thomas Lukemeyer.
1782, March   17, Jones, Mathy, and James Smith.
1795, Aug.   15, Jones, Nancy, and Peter Green.
1777, May   4, Jones, Olivia, and William Jones.
1764, Sept.   24, Jones, Paul, and Phabeah Robins.
1772, May   17, Jones, Peter, and Mary Ann Hickson.
1773, April   8, Jones, Rebecca, and Elijah Dow.
1785, Sept.   3, Jones, Rebecca, and George Sheed.
1782, Jan.   31, Jones, Robert, and Hannah Thomas.
1751, July   6, Jones, Ruth, and Isaac Coren.
1797, Dec.   17, Jones, Sarah, and Cymon Phillips.
1788, Nov.   17, Jones, Sarah, and David Schytterly.
1774, Feb.   18, Jones, Sarah, and Henry Baker.
1772, Dec.   21, Jones, Sarah, and John Haas.
1771, May   27, Jones, Sarah, and John O'Harra.
1794, Dec.   14, Jones, Sarah, and John Smith.
1778, Dec.   14, Jones, Sarah, and Matthew Ford.
1782, July   5, Jones, Sarah, and Robert Berry.
1775, Oct.   31, Jones, Sarah, and Stephen Archibold.
1792, Aug.   12, Jones, Sarah, and William Richardson.
1784, Jan.   16, Jones, Sophia, and Thomas Burgiss.
1766, Oct.   27, Jones, Thomas, and Ann Mellinix.
1761, Sept.   19, Jones, Thomas, and Ann Mersdy.
1780, March   13, Jones, Thomas, and Elizabeth Lancaster.
1789, July   6, Jones, Thomas, and Hanna Bell.
1773, March   27, Jones, Thomas, and Hannah James.
1782, April   30, Jones, Thomas, and Magdalen Wall.
1779, Jan.   9, Jones, Thomas, and Sarah Haywood.
1790, May   8, Jones, Thomas Vear, and Hanna Fisher.
1792, Dec.   22, Jones, Trustum Flemming, and Mary Chapman.
1768, Feb.   8, Jones, William, and Elizabeth Gray.
1784, July   6, Jones, William, and Elizabeth Lewis.
1758, May   17, Jones, William, and Hannah Marshall.
1766, Sept.   4, Jones, William, and James Kunney.
1795, Nov.   3, Jones, William, and Mary Elves.
1796, May   28, Jones, William, and Mary Miller.
1758, Dec.   18, Jones, William, and Mary Savage.
1776, Aug.   6, Jones, William, and Mary Sturgis.
        27—VOL. VIII.

1777, May　　4, Jones, William, and Olivia Jones.
1781. Feb.　21, Jones, William, and Rebecca Willard.
1766, Feb.　24, Jonickey, Daniel, and Barbarah Cresson.
1774, Nov.　24, Jonket, Mary, and George Hannah.
1753, Jan.　16, Jonse, Aby, and John Kenor.
1757, Sept.　27, Jonse, Elizabeth, and Felix Queen.
1760, Aug.　10, Jons, Elizabeth, and Paul Williams.
1753, Oct.　16, Jonse, Jane, and John McKinley.
1754, Jan.　23, Jonse, John, and Rachel Zane.
1753, Jan.　20, Jonse, Magdalene, and Friederick Holstein.
1754, Oct.　20, Jonse, Margaret, and William Broadas.
1752, Nov.　7, Jonse, Mary, and David Lewis.
1756, March　7, Jonse, Mary, and William McCay.
1799, Nov.　20, Jonse, Phebe, and Francis Davis.
1756, Jan.　1, Jonse, Phebe, and Richard Palmer.
1766, May　　8, Jonsson, Samuel, and Jemima Langley.
1751, May　　7, Jonston, Anne, and Andrew Androson.
1751, March 18, Jonston, Sary, and Henry Wood.
1778, Jan.　24, Jordan, David, and Mary Braun.
1783, April　10, Jordan, James, and Elizabeth Burnet.
1796, June　　2, Jordan, John, and Hester Kite.
1783, June　16, Jordan, John, and Mary Finn.
1765, Feb.　6, Jordan, Mary, and James McKinney.
1758, Jan.　26, Jordan, Mary, and Samuel Robenetts.
1799, Nov.　24, Jordan, Nela, and Catherine Rozen.
1792, Feb.　7, Jordan, Robert Gore, and Hannah Linton.
1791, Sept.　1, Jordan, Samuel, and Cathrine Maag.
1780, Feb.　1, Jorden, Susannah, and William Jackson.
1795, Sept.　5, Joseph, John, and Hester Tomkins.
1769, April　31, Joseph, Thomas, and Anne Winslow.
1792, Nov.　15, Josephson, Rachel, and William Svanson.
1777, April　1, Josiah, James, and Sarah Reynolds.
1779, May　23, Jost, Catherine, and James Brown.
1789, Nov.　30, Journey, Peter, and Ann Gilbert.
1780, Aug.　5, Joys, Michael, and Jane Campbell.
1793, March　8, Judge, Margret, and William More.
1782, Feb.　21, Jugiess, Martin, and Anne Eyre.
1764, May　13, Juley, Martha, and Thomas Kerneley.
1759, Aug.　12, Junkins, Margareth, and David Welsh.
1778, June　12, Jurden, Sarah, and Ralph Young.
1781, Dec.　16, Justes, Anne, and Reinold Schroder.
1779, Oct.　27, Justes, Sarah, and James Trowland.
1750, Nov.　7, Justice, John, and Mary Morton.
1785, Jan.　4, Justice, Lawrence, and Elizabeth Smith.
1754, March 13, Justice, Margaret, and George Granturn.
1794, Dec.　2, Justice, Nancy, and James More.

1794, Dec.   14, Justis, Elizabeth, and Charles Campbell.
1790, April   29, Justis, Mary, and Isaac Cox.
1758, Jan.   29, Justis, Sarah, and Peter Jonasson.
1796, July   10, Justis, William Erskin, and Marget Copner.
1761, Jan.   19, Justy, Elizabeth, and Peter Main.
1793, Jan.   20, Kaasfe, John, and Elenore Ridge.
1781, Dec.   13, Kafer, Catharine, and Cornelius O'Hagerty.
1791, Oct.   13, Kahl, John George, and Elizabeth Hill.
1795, Nov.   30, Kaighn, Jane, and John Harris.
1790, Dec.   31, Kaighn, Mary, and John Deford.
1792, May   10, Kaign, John, and Elizabeth Willson.
1781, Aug.   9, Kain, Edward, and Emely Starkey.
1789, April   5, Kaiser, Mary, and Joseph Cline.
1782, Oct.   27, Kalley, Sarah, and John Wilson.
1781, Sept.   4, Kalley, William, and Jenny McLochlaine.
1785, Sept.   15, Kammer, Mary, and Andrew Hyde.
1778, Sept.   6, Kane, Eleanor, and John Berry.
1767, Feb.   27, Kane, Jeane, and Allan Bathust.
1782, June   18, Kant, Mary, and James McCon.
1793, Nov.   17, Kapper, Michael, and Elizabeth Bayerly.
1796, Aug.   11, Karcher, John, and Deborah King.
1770, April   9, Kark, Hannah, and Benjamin Jones.
1781, Dec.   13, Karn, Adam, and Rebecca Printenell.
1751, Feb.   28, Karn, Anthony, and Catharine Coloran.
1782, June   13, Karr, Gotleib, and Elizabeth Keyser.
1781, March   27, Karr, Robert, and Anne Corbit.
1790, May   30, Karrigan, Daniel, and Jane Allison.
1756, Sept.   30, Kasferath, William, and Mary Magdalene Brok-
                    ering.
1795, Sept.   11, Kaufman, Rachel, and Charles Hill.
1778, Nov.   22, Kavanagh, James, and Elizabeth Campbell.
1783, Feb.   27, Kaver, Mary, and Henry Hoffman.
1781, May   1, Karvy, Samuel and Mary Munyan.
1784, Nov.   7, Kays, Mary and William Lloyd.
1759, March   13, Keain, Rachel, and Casper Klain.
1778, Nov.   25, Kean Judy, and Providence. (Free negroes.)
1780, March   16, Kean, Margaret, and James Bredin.
1799, June   30, Kean, Mary, and Charles Ramsey.
1762, Sept.   6, Keappack, Mary, and Samuel Sterrat.
1772, Dec.   24, Kearnes, Rosannah, and James Pyott.
1773, May   2, Keaton, Johannah, and John McKnary.
1794, Feb.   3, Keaton, Mary, and Philip Milligan.
1793, Sept.   18, Keaton, Michael, and Mary Mullen.
1797, Oct.   26, Keats, Martha, and Edward Johnson.
1798, April   18, Keck, George, and Sarah Harkes.
1780, Aug.   15, Keder, William, and Elizabeth Barnes.

1792, June   28, Keech, Mary, and John Hillerman.
1777, April   8, Keen, Andrew, and Margaret Toy.
1776, June   2, Keen, Christian, and Mary Beettey.
1786, April   24, Keen, Hanis, and Sarah Falls.
1783, Jan.   4, Keen, John, and Catherine Owner.
1779, Nov.   20, Keen, John, and Mary Carter.
1797, Nov.   15, Keen, Marget, and James Simkins.
1153, Nov.   1, Keen, Rebecca, and George Broitnall.
1782, April   8, Keen, Rebecca, and Hamilton Warren.
1782, May   30, Keen, Reynold, and Anne Lawrence.
1762, Oct.   21, Keen, Reynold, and Christiana Stilley.
1777, Dec.   4, Keen, Sarah, and William Sanders.
1783, June   5, Keene, Lawrence, and Gaymor Lukens.
1767, June   6, Keeper, Elizabeth, and John Warthenwy.
1772, Nov.   15, Kees, John, and Mary Watson.
1778, Nov.   27, Kees, John, and Mary Young.
1772, Dec.   31, Keeth, Margareth, and Henry Prill.
1755, Nov.   5, Kefot, Sarah, and Thomas Stroembeck.
1792, May   27, Keighler, Jacob, and Ann Moses.
1788, April   13, Keighter, John, and Margery Frey.
1784, May   22, Keil, George, and Elizabeth Batton.
1791, Jan.   2, Keillman, Christopher, and Anna Elizabeth Lig-
                     gin.
1790, March   4, Keiser, Michael, and Barbara Riggi.
1772, Aug.   11, Keiser, Sarah, and Christopher Will.
1777, March   10, Keith, Ann, and Thomas Kelley.
1777, May   4, Keith, Margaret, and Nicholas Sherdan.
1793, March   17, Keith, William, and Margret Jane Steuart.
1780, June   27, Kelan, John, and Susannah Dawsey.
1759, Jan.   29, Keley, Elisabet, and Robert King.
1757, Sept.   16, Kellen, Honor, and George Lay.
1797, June   7, Keller, Elizabeth, and Johan Wenk.
1778. Jan.   7, Kelley, David, and Eleanor Fyen.
1776, March   4, Kelley, Sarah, and George Shinn.
1779, Nov.   26, Kelley, Susannah, and Patrick Robeson.
1777, March   10, Kelley, Thomas, and Ann Keith.
1777, April   17, Kello, John, and Sarah Boutton.
1771, Oct.   6, Kelly, Ann, and Bernard Evans.
1753, Oct.   20, Kelly, Bryon, and Guany Maguire.
1778, Nov.   25, Kelly, Dorothy, and Edward Jones.
1787, May   10, Kelly, Hannah, and James Woollard.
1794, Aug.   26, Kelly, Henry, and Sarah Mullen.
1794, March   27, Kelly, James, and Jane Mackamson.
1799, Aug.   15, Kelly, Jane, and Richard Smith.
1798, April   18, Kelly, Jane, and Thomas Glascoe.
1780, Jan.   29, Kelly, John, and Anne Hawkins.

1762, April   31, Kelly, John, and Eleonore Longacre.
1794, April   29, Kelly, John, and Mary Dunn.
1779, Jan.   28, Kelly, Margary, and John Corbett.
1800, April   24, Kelly, Mary, and Christopher Linnier.
1792, Oct.   23, Kelly, Mary, and John Fisher.
1767, July   21, Kelly, Mary, and John Long.
1751, April   29, Kelly, Mary, and William Newman.
1792, Jan.   8, Kelly, Solomon, and Fanny Huet.
1795, May   31, Kelly, William, and Martha Jones.
1781, Oct.   17, Kemer, Elizabeth, and George Molledore.
1790, July   26, Kemp, Henry, and Rachel Thomas.
1770, Aug.   14, Kemp, William, and Hannah Williams.
1778, June   21, Kempsey, Patrick, and Elizabeth Davis.
1752, July   21, Kendal, Jane, and Anthony Gunn.
1792, Aug.   9, Kendall, James, and Rachel Gardner.
1768, Sept.   24, Kendley, William, and Hannah Jenkins.
1799, Aug.   29, Kengley, Mathew, and Eliza Delany.
1795, Sept.   16, Kenley, William, and Cathrine Kumius.
1784, Feb.   26, Kenly, Mary, and Mathias Landell.
1759, Dec.   16, Kennady, Isabellah, and George Sille.
1784, Oct.   28, Kennard, Samuel, and Elizabeth Hugg.
1778, May   29, Kenndy, James, and Eleanor Gregory.
1753, Jan.   14, Kenneday, Alexander, and Margaret Davis.
1776, Dec.   10, Kenneday, Bridget, and John Clark.
1788, May   14, Kennedey, Anne, and Cephas Child.
1778, Jan.   11, Kennedy, Dugal, and Mary Ann McWilliams.
1778, Oct.   13, Kennedy, Hannah, and Joshua Burn.
1790, June   12, Kennedy, Honor, and Simon Markis.
1790, April   9, Kennedy, Jane, and John Infel.
1783, Jan.   16, Kennedy, John, and Anne Gillis.
1799, June   30, Kennedy, Lucy, and William Wooton.
1794, March   31, Kennedy, Margret, and John White.
1790, Feb.   24, Kennedy, Mary, and John Toben.
1792, Sept.   4, Kennedy, Michael, and Mary Idere.
1795, Nov.   22, Kennedy, Patrick, and Mary Smith.
1776, Nov.   25, Kenney, Catharine, and George Ingram.
1777, May   10, Kenney, Lorannah, and William Patterson.
1753, Jan.   16, Kenor, John, and Abby Jonse.
1780, Sept.   18, Kentis, Anne, and Kingsmell Wells.
1782, Dec.   3, Kenton, Jenny, and Hugh Ross.
1766, May   13, Kenton, Richard, and Elizabeth Brayman.
1761, Sept.   5, Kenty, Mary, and John Williams.
1793, July   24, Kenvis, Robert, and Debora Kite.
1796, Sept.   4, Keor, Cathrine, and Henry Tauhse.
1778, Oct.   15, Kephe, Dorothea, and Justice Schaeffer.
1778, Jan.   23, Ker, Robert, and Hannah Nix.

1779, Nov. 28, Keran, Edward, and Margaret Hays.
1757, Dec. 14, Kerkpatrick, John, and Rachel Lewis.
1791, May 12, Kerlin, George, and Margret Odenheimer.
1764, Aug. 18, Kerlin, William, and Sarah Goodwin.
1790, Sept. 9, Kerlock, Mary, and John Stanley.
1764, May 13, Kerneley, Thomas, and Martha Juley.
1796, Oct. 24, Kerns, Alexander, and Mary Gregory.
1769, Aug. 1, Kerns, James, and Catharine Poet.
1791, Oct. 8, Kerr, Ann, and Thomas White.
1792, Sept. 6, Kerr, Daniel, and Elizabeth Hincle.
1793, April 9, Kerr, James, and Curtes Marshal.
1798, June 8, Kerr, James, and Jane White.
1777, Sept. 10, Kerr, Margaret, and George Dougherty.
1790, Oct. 21, Kerr, Mary, and George Moser.
1778, Nov. 25, Kerr, Mary. and John Campbell.
1763, Feb. 12, Kerr, Thomas, and Catharine Gordon.
1779, April 13, Kerr, William, and Margaret Willson.
1773, June 13, Kesiah and Ellick, (free negroes.)
1762, Nov. 23, Kethain, John, and Ross Cooke.
1778, June 13, Ketler, Sarah, and John Map.
1784, July 13, Ketley, Hannah, and Jacob Deur.
1789, May 5, Kevlin, Sarah, and Henry Oatenheimer.
1799, May 25, Key, Mary, and Jonas Matson.
1780, Feb. 24, Key, William, and Elizabeth Groffe.
1778, May 19, Key, William, and Mary Bailey.
1778, June 2, Keyer, Margaret, and Joseph Barstow.
1789, Dec. 12, Keyl, Mary, and Bernard Praser.
1785, Nov. 14, Keyly, John, and Mary Walker.
1777, Dec. 4, Keyne, William, and Bridget Holland.
1772, Feb. 16, Keys, Ann, and Michael McGratch.
1778, Aug. 27, Keys, John, and Hannah Collins.
1781, March 20, Keys, Sarah, and George Stoots.
1780, June 12, Keyser, Dorothea, and Nathaniel Mullan.
1784, Jan. 29, Keyser, Elizabeth, and Benjamin Lehman.
1782, June 13, Keyser, Elizabeth, and Gotleib Karr.
1795, May 17, Kichler, Jacob, and Cathrine Baker.
1771, June 10, Kid, Mary, and Thomas Clemence.
1800, Jan. 1, Kid, Sarah, and John Means.
1773, April 29, Kidd, Alexander, and Edeth Taylor.
1773, April 26, Kidd, Hugh, and Jane Rankin.
1779, May 7, Kidd, John, and Mary Rodgers.
1798, July 25, Kidd, Nancy, and Robert Esdell.
1780, July 1, Kiemer, Orpheus, and Elizabeth Christ.
1768, Nov. 1, Kiesse, Timothy, and Margarett Adams.
1791, July 29, Kigby, Mary, and Abraham Davis.
1775, Feb. 10, Kiggins, Bridget, and Isaac Fowber.

1757, Jan.   28, Kile, Mary, and Benjamin Oxson.
1779, Feb.   15, Killman, Maria, and Philip Dennis.
1757, June   26, Killinger, George, and Judah Collet.
1782, Sept. 18, Killpatrick, Anny, and Thomas Stiles.
1797, March 23, Killroy, Elizab , and Arthur Burns.
1788, May   9, Kilmore, Dorothy, and George Eiden.
1792, Nov.   20, KilPatric, Jane, and John Bell.
1755, May   19, Kimley, Mary, and James Rider.
1766, Jan.   26, Kimmerly, Johannes, and Mary Gayer.
1773, Oct.   10, Kimmous, Hannah, and Philip Redmond.
1795, March 19, Kinch, Barbara, and Moses Lincoin.
1784, June   6, Kinch, Barbara, and Robert French.
1766, March 20, Kinch, Mary, and Gabriel Rambo.
1794, Sept. 24, Kinche, Susannah, and Jacob Yocum.
1777, Oct.   20, Kindley, Elizabeth, and Francis Smith.
1780, Aug.   6, King, Ann, and Thomas Towzey.
1792, Nov.   11, King, Barbara, and Timothy Ashton.
1859, April   2, King, Catharine, and John Lales.
1771, Dec.   21, King Christiana, and John Badcock.
1796, Aug.   11, King, Deborah, and John Karcher.
1768, Jan.   3, King, Deliverance, and Isaac Duffield.
1781, Oct.   28, King, Eleonor, and Robert Gore.
1794, July   28, King. Elizabeth, and Foulk Pritchard.
1771, Aug.   11, King, George, and Catharine Relof.
1778, Nov.   30, King, Hannah, and John Collins.
1795, July   3, King, James, and Mary Miller.
1778, March 30, King, Jean, and John Stevens.
1792, Dec.   4, King, John, and Margret Cop.
1778, Dec.   21, King, John, and Martha Sullivan.
1780, March 28, King, Mary, and George Galespey.
1788, Oct.   4, King, Mary, and Richard Miles.
1789, March 5, King, Rachel and David Thomas.
1782, April   9, King, Rebecca, and Thomas Hasten.
1759, Jan.   29, King, Robert, and Elizabet Keley.
1768, May   3, King, Samuel, and Sarah Dunvick.
1788, April   2, King, Susannah, and David Eakin.
1769, Aug.   28, King, Thomas, and Anne Nell.
1756, Dec.   13, King, Thomas, and Susannah Coats.
1784, Aug.   13, King, William, and Mary Evans.
1789, April   1, Kingsley, Samuel, and Mary Earl.
1792, June   17, Kinnard, Thomas, and Nancy Lee.
1774, Oct.   19, Kinnedy, Catharine, and Charles Branon.
1781, Nov.   26, Kinsell, Fridric Benjamin, and Nancy Barrett.
1780, June   10, Kinsey, Barbara, and James Wood.
1766, Aug.   21, Kinsey, David, and Gaynor Bartholomew.
1785, Feb.   17, Kinsey, Margaret, and Peter Deal.

1767, Jan.　19, Kinsey, Mary, and James Land.
1777, Sept.　18, Kinslar, William, and Charlotte Harber.
1796, April　18, Kinsler, Baltes, and Mary Shaw.
1790, June　8, Kinsler, George, and Mary Ash.
1795, May　18, Kinsley, Charlotte, and James Mullen.
1777, Dec.　18, Kinsley, John, and Magdalene Bastian.
1800, Oct.　25, Kinsley, Mary, and Joseph Willis.
1795, Dec.　9, Kinzea, Daniel, and Mary Hansel.
1778, March　5, Kips, Mary, and Thomas Price.
1798, May　29, Kirbin, Mary, and Joseph Munyan.
1782, Aug.　12, Kirchner, John, and Magdalen Franckford.
1754, June　27, Kirk, Catharine, and Thomas Lewis.
1778, May　24, Kirk, Evis, and Thomas Barker.
1759, Nov.　28, Kirk, Jesse, and Elizabeth Strangel.
1754, April　10, Kirk, Jesse, and Hannah Pyott.
1764, Nov.　21, Kirk, Sarah, and Jonathan Evans.
1778, June　9, Kirkbride, Joseph, and Christina Excell.
1764, Nov.　7, Kirks, Martha, and Seth Thomas.
1787, Nov.　12, Kirkpatric, Andrew, and Hanna Scanlin.
1759, Feb.　20, Kirkpatrick, Jane, and Archibald Stuart.
1790, Dec.　16, Kirkpatrick, Marget, and Isaac Lord.
1780, May　16, Kirkwood, William, and Christine Taylor.
1791, Nov.　4, Kish, John, and Mary Green.
1796, May　1, Kissler, John, and Martha Shriver.
1793, July　24, Kite, Debora, and Robert Kenvis.
1796, June　2, Kite, Hester, and John Jordan.
1777, Dec.　20, Kitner, Sophia, and John McDaniel.
1777, Dec.　17, Kitts, George, and Margaret Nash.
1774, Dec.　6, Kittson, Sarah, and Ellis Morgan.
1778, Jan.　2, Kiver, Mary, and Joseph Cole.
1759, March　3, Klain, Casper, and Rachel Keain.
1765, Jan.　22, Klein Johan Nicholas, and Anna Margaretta On-
　　　　　clerin.
1786, April　20, Klein, Mary, and John Hockins.
1796, Feb.　24, Knaus, Mary, and Francis Thompson.
1759, Nov.　25, Knausin, Catherine, and Jacob Nayer.
1775, March 19, Knees, Catharine, and John Specht.
1773, Aug.　8, Knees, Mary, and John Fox.
1777, Aug.　18, Kneis, Michael, and Susannah Young.
1783, Sept.　8, Knight, Charles, and Sabina Wright.
1756, Jan.　18, Knight, Elizabeth, and Richard Foot.
1755, May　5, Knight, John, and Ann Parker.
1760, June　24, Knight William Jacob, and Elizabeth Blesinger.
1799, Aug.　14, Knight, William Watson, and Nancy MacDonald.
1777, Feb.　27, Knoles, Grace, and Samuel Bertley.
1783, March 13, Knorr, Barbara, and Henry Spiehl.

1783, Jan.   9, Knorr, Jacob, and Jemima Warner.
1790, Sept.   2, Knorr, Mary, and John Lohra.
1780, April   23, Knorr, Susannah, and Zachariah Poulson.
1778, June   2, Knowdel, Mary, and Henry Deforest.
1751, Jan.   29, Knowland, Jane, and John Neese.
1752, July   19, Knowles, Edward, and Sarah Pugh.
1777, Nov.   25, Knowles, Michael, and Neomey Howard.
1759, Nov.   29, Knowles, William, and Agnew Davis.
1773, March 15, Knowls, Rebecca, and Theodorus Bary.
1779, July   28, Knowls, William, and Jane French.
1783, Jan.   7, Knox, Eleonor, and Patrick Owens.
1794, Nov.   9, Knox, Henry, and Susannah Wiser.
1781, March 22, Knox, Jenny, and George Park.
1796, Nov.   8, Knox, John, and Anne Wilson.
1794, Oct.   30, Koenig, Christina, and Christian Hamrich.
1791, Nov.   28, Koffry, Cathrine, and William Cock.
1781, April, 12, Koldy, Nicholas, and Jenny Craford.
1782, May   16, Kolikbreuner, Charles, and Henry Hineman.
1778, Oct.   19, Kooken, Catharine, and Henery Baker.
1757, Nov.   5, Koon, Phinserie, and Elizabeth Rush.
1759, Jan.   10, Korns, Hugh, and Anne Lewiston.
1778, June   25, Korspach, John Martin, and Mary Ingells.
1756, May   26, Kostor, Hannah, and Jonathan Oldfield.
1763, Nov.   25, Kraft, Mary, and Thomas Wilkinson.
1756, May   24, Krafts, Ann, and Jacob Furst.
1779, Feb.   18, Krast, Joseph, and Barbarah Stille.
1778, Dec.   3, Krunear, James, and Else Neel.
1778, July   22, Kraus, John, and Ann Hedler.
1774, April   8, Krees, Margaret, and Daniel Fisher.
1770, April   9, Kreps, Henry, and Catharine Campbel.
1772, Feb.   4, Krienerin, Barbary, and Walentine Hight.
1775, May   18, Krips, Henry, and Margareth Barr.
1775, April   17, Kriss, Jacob, and Margaret Hill.
1791, May   29, Kucher, Peter, and Christiana Anthony.
1790, Nov.   6, Kugler, Adam, and Agnes McClannegan.
1778, Aug.   12, Kuhn, Catharine, and William Steward.
1773, Sept.   5, Kuhn, Christian, and Susannah Matters.
1779, April   1, Kuhn, Mary, and John Fritz.
1795, Sept.   16, Kumius, Catharine, and William Kenley.
1766, Sept.   4, Kunney, James, and William Jones.
1797, Dec.   3, Kurtz, Ann, and Henry Alberger.
1794, June   1, Kurtz, Jacob, and Rebecca Wood.
1772, Nov.   28, Kusick, Mary, and Frederis Saullers.
1790, Dec.   9, Kyger, Marget, and John Webber.
1800, Nov.   13, Kyle, Nancy, and Henry Black.
1779, June   16, Kyle, Sarah, and Walter McAlpin,

1790, Oct.   7, Kyler, Elizabeth, and Matthew George.
1793, July   3, Kyler, Susannah, and Christopher Ramsey.
1791, April 21, Kymer, Mary Hargus, and John Tanner.
1752, Nov.   14, Kynen, Catharine, and James Cockram.
1790, Dec.   25, Kyser, Daniel, and Hanna Smith.
1795, Oct.   11, Kyser, Mary, and John George Maze.
1788, Nov.   2, Lackey, Marmaduke, and Sarah Smith.
1777, March 19, Lackie, James, and Ann Roy.
1754, Sept. 15, Lacock, Richard, and Catharine Welldone.
1789, Oct.   18, Lacroon, Flora, and George Wright, (Mulattoes.)
1792, Oct.   29, Lacy, Cathrine, and Thomas Casdort Allen.
1775, Nov.   6, Ladd, Ann, and Edward Evans.
1797, Nov.   8, Lady, Jacob, and Maria Price.
1789, May   31, Laffarty, Daniel, and Martha Thompson.
1792, Sept.   8, Lafferty, Elizabeth, and Francis Dominique Vallce.
1790, July   8, Lafferty, James, and Elizabeth Masters.
1793, Oct.   17, Lafferty, Mary, and George Weaver.
1776, April 22, Lahugh, James, and Mary Lewis.
1792, Nov.   11, Laighan, James, and Martha Blakney.
1778, Nov.   29, Lairy, Bridget, and James Gray.
1782, Aug.   20, Laise, Adam, and Susannah Gantrey.
1759, April   2, Lales, John, and Catharine King.
1777, July   27, Lalley, John, and Elizabeth Linch.
1770, April 15, Lamb, Elizabeth, and Lewis Davids.
1753, Dec.   26, Lamb, James, and Ann Burk.
1790, Aug.   15, Lamb, John, and Sarah Burton.
1762, Aug.   31, Lamb, Joseph, and Elizabeth Morrison.
1797, Aug.   5, Lamb, Mary, and John Doney.
1762, Sept. 13, Lambart, Richard, and Elizabeth Pammer.
1795, June   7, Lambert, Johanna, and Michael Hunt.
1778, Jan.   15, Lambert, Richard and Ruth Ashton.
1769, June   30, Lambert, Zachariah, and Hannah Miller.
1768, Sept. 30, Lamont, William, and Margarett Chestnut.
1757, Nov.   4, Lamplay, Mary, and John Ross.
1751, May   24, Lamplugh, Mary, and Richard Mosely.
1780, March 13, Lancaster, Elizabeth, and Thomas James.
1799, Dec.   2, Lancaster, John, and Mary McDonald.
1766, May   23, Lansaster, Joseph, and Elizabeth Abrams.
1795, Aug.   27, Lancaster, Thomas, and Susannah Paul.
1767, Jan.   19, Land, James, and Mary Kinsey.
1791, Feb.   15, Land, John, and Ann Anderson.
1772, May   14, Land, Mary, and John Potts.
1793, Dec.   16, Land, Philip, and Mary White.
1784, Feb.   26, Landell, Mathias, and Mary Kenly.
1771, Sept. 27, Landen, Anne, and Alexander Morrow.
1789, Nov.   30, Landenberg, Jacob, and Mary Steel.

1755, Sept. 6, Landenberger, Mathias, and Mary Harman.
1766, Nov. 6, Landerbrunn, Frederick, and Elenor Thomson.
1793, Aug. 3, Landerin, Anthony, and Mary Cooper.
1776, Feb. 26, Landey, James, and Elizabeth Bristol.
1796, Oct. 4, Landon, Richard, and Marget Branson.
1781, Nov. 9, Lane, Gazelena, and William Ewing.
1795, Sept. 20, Lane, Henry, and Mary Campbell.
1778, April 2, Lang, Elizabeth, and George Bremer.
1793, Oct. 14, Lang, Elizabeth, and Jesse Arragon.
1792, Nov. 15, Lang, Elizabeth, and Thomas Hoggard.
1792, April 1, Lang, Jacob, and Marget Baach.
1779, Sept. 3, Lang, John G., and Elizabeth Few.
1774, Sept. 4, Lang, John, and Margaret Jolly.
1778, May 22, Lang, Margaret, and Isaac Birch.
1795, April 12, Lang, Nathaniel, and Hannah Mumford.
1798, April 19, Lang, Susannah, and John Williams.
1795, July 12, Langdon, William, and Elizabeth Cottrill.
1756, May 8, Langley, Jemima, and Samuel Jonsson.
1778, March 29, Langley, Timothy, and Eleanor Armstrong.
1798, Dec. 27, Lannigan, William, and Elizab. Gilbert.
1785, Aug. 22, Lanning, Samuel, and Mercy Crispin.
1799, Feb. 14, Lanten, Ann, and Mathew Manning.
1759, Sept. 24, Lantong, Elizabeth, and John Bure.
1800, May 23, Lapat, Mary, and Peter Andres.
1773, Aug. 8, Laperty, Daniel. and Martha Lucas.
1773, March 12, Larey, Mary, and Elijah Reeves.
1768, Jan. 19, Largat, Mary, and John Darby.
1778, Nov. 26, Larkin, Eleanor, and Thomas Bigley.
1779, April 29, Larner, Elizabeth, and Rudolph Mitchell,
1794, Sept. 1, Laroux, Mary, and James Wilson.
1782, Oct. 6, Larshen, Catherine, and John Hatline.
1796, Oct, 6, Larson, Mathias, and Margret Fisher.
1774, March 4, Larter, Barbarah, and Simon O'Bryon.
1780, July 24, Lascom, John, and Rosannah Hargus.
1773, Sept. 8, Lascorn, Ann, and John Hall.
1790, Oct. 25, Latch, David, and Susanna West.
1794, Aug. 20, Latimor, Hannah, and John Dillon.
1797, July 22, Latimore, Marget, and John McCollom.
1759, April 13, Latimore, Rowe, and —— Thomson.
1793, Dec. 10, Laton, Mary, and James Bennet.
1753, Oct. 1, Lattemore, John, and Mary Corties.
1793, Feb. 14, Latter Ann, and John Jackson.
1799, Nov. 18, Laudenbrun, Marget, and Edward Brady.
1800, May 27, Laughlin, William, and Latitia Murphy.
1785, Aug. 9, Lauke, John, and Hannah Yeaker.
1793, May 4, Laurence, Elizabeth, and Jacob Carver.

1794, Dec.   28, Laurence, Thomas, and Mary Mason.
1791, July   26, Laussin, Hanna, and Mathieu Reper.
1794, Dec.   14, Lavalla, Sarah, and Tobias Toby.
1782, Aug.   10, Laviers, Mary, and Abram Storms.
1782, March 31, Laver, Mary, and Zacheriah Summers.
1757, July   23, Lavers, Richard, and Mary Willson.
1771, Feb.   3, Lavery, Catharine, and John Ragusin.
1793, Sept.   9, Law, Margret, and William Denham.
1781, Sept.   6, Lawder, John, and Priscilla Reighley.
1763, June   13, Lawiston, Margareth, and William Jackson.
1781, Aug.   27, Lawluer, Patrick, and Winnyford Wright.
1782, May   30, Lawrence, Anne and Reynold Keen.
1780, Feb.   3, Lawrence, Dominick, and Jane Dun.
1771, Nov.   16, Lawrence, Edward, and Jane Galbreath.
1752, Oct.   4, Lawrence, Elizabeth, and David Campbell.
1775, June   18, Lawrence, Elizabeth, and James Fitzomens.
1771, May   27, Lawrence, Elizabeth, and John Lenord.
1782, Sept.   25, Lawrence, Hannah, and Augustine Hicks.
1770, May   28, Lawrence, Hannah, and Joseph Smith.
1757, March 21, Lawrence, Henry, and Anne Dorad.
1758, Nov.   7, Lawrence, Isabella, and Daniel Lewis.
1764, April   4, Lawrence, Jane, and Isaac Vaughan.
1791, Aug.   11, Lawrence, John, and Elenore Green.
1752, Jan.   19, Lawrence, John, and Mary Miller.
1782, June   27, Lawrence, John, and Sophy Piniard.
1777, Dec.   21, Lawrence, Judith, and William Homs.
1778, April   24, Lawrence, Lydia, and John Gock Rodgers.
1788, Sept.   8, Lawrence, Rebecca, and Daniel Twekes.
1758, Sept.   30, Lawrence, Sarah, and Jacob Wanculen.
1782, Jan.   10, Lawrence, Sarah, and Richard Cole.
1763, Jan.   1, Lawrence, Thomas, and Hannah Williamson.
1781, Nov.   1, Lawrence, Thomas, and Juley Mongan.
1778, June   4, Lawson, John, and Mary Adams.
1773, Oct.   27, Lawson, John, and Mary Ann McCormick.
1757, Sept.   16, Lay, George, and Honor Kellen.
1778, Dec.   31, Laycock, John, and Eleanor Nixson.
1757, Sept.   11, Layman, Catharine, and Franecies Sanders.
1792, April   13, Lea, Blancha Corsa, and Samuel Hider.
1792, Dec.   17, Lea, Robert, and Mary Head, (free Africans.)
1780, March   4, Lea, Sarah, and John Chatfield.
1796, June   11, Leach, Joseph, and Deborah Hall.
1794, Jan.   30, Leacock. Martha, and William Davis.
1762, July   15, Leaconey, James, and Elizabeth McCay.
1756, Aug.   30, Leahy, Tobia, and Jane Williams.
1796, Oct.   4, Leaman, Peggy, and Thomas Adams.
1792, Jan.   2, Leaming, Jacob, and Ruth Stephenson.

1779, Aug.   8, Lean, Charles, and Margarett Dapson.
1790, Sept.   26, Lear, John, and Agnes White.
1777, March   2, Leary, Cornelius, and Margaret Cneth.
1780, July   8, Leary, Dennis, and Ann Cassel.
1777, May   23, Leary, Eleanor, and John Burk.
1774, Sept.   15, Leary, Henry, and Mary Clements.
1796, April   21, Leary, William, and Mary Johnston.
1777, Aug.   5, Leaver, William, and Mary Ramburg.
1779, July   28, Leblang, Joseph, and Elizabeth Creemer.
1779, April   11, Lebo, Martha, and Peter Cook.
1763, May   13, Lebou, Elizabeth, and William Emerery.
1799, Oct.   31, Lectur, Elizabeth, and John Fisher.
1762, Sept.   4, Ledston, Hannah, and Derrick Cornelius Fande-
                  berry.
1755, May   7, Lee, Ann, and James Johnson.
1778, July   21, Lee, Hannah, and James McAneney.
1775, June   3, Lee, Henry, and Rachel Ramsey.
1775, July   4, Lee, Henry, and Rachel Ramsey.
1759, Jan.   18, Lee, James, and Ann Granderwitt.
1792, Aug.   2, Lee, James, and Debora West.
1777, April   24, Lee, James, and Hannah Marriett.
1767, Aug.   3, Lee, James, and Mertah Cleynold.
1751, Aug.   1, Lee, John, and Anne MacDanell.
1752, July   1, Lee, John, and Catharine Hill.
1777, Dec.   1, Lee, John, and Elizabeth Gore.
1773, Sept.   5, Lee, John, and Elizabeth Haldren.
1776, April   4, Lee, John, and Patience Toy.
1798, Nov.   10, Lee, Joseph, and Fanny Roggester.
1764, Feb.   29, Lee, Joseph, and Mary Hawthorne.
1795, Sept.   16, Lee, Joseph, and Nancy Hunter.
1752, May   10, Lee, Lady, and John Ogilby.
1780, July   8, Lee, Lydia, and Joseph Nicholson.
1753, Oct.   24, Lee, Manasseh, and Jane Connerly.
1775, Oct.   29, Lee, Margaret, and John Hopple.
1763, Jan.   31, Lee, Mary, and Charles West.
1792, June   17, Lee, Nancy, and Thomas Kinnard.
1780, July   2, Lee, Robert, and Ann Williams.
1778, Dec.   3, Lee, Robert, and Elizabeth Fletcher.
1794, Aug.   23, Lee, Robert, and Mary Andrews.
1779, Nov.   9, Lee, Thomas, and Rachel Powell.
1778, March 22, Leech, Elizabeth, and William Williams.
1767, Sept.   1, Leech, Henry, and Ann Neess.
1767, July   23, Leech, Henry, and Ann Richardson.
1756, July   17, Leech, James, and Deborah Tomlinson.
1777, Jan.   19, Leech, James, and Elizabeth Ward.
1783, Feb.   6, Leech, John, and Mary Boehnen.

1776, Dec.   3, Leech, Mary, and John Jenkins.
1798, Nov. 19, Leech, Mary, and William Crozier.
1794, Oct.   2, Leech Robert, and Mary Vaughn.
1778, March 19, Leechman, Charles, and Elizabeth McCandley.
1790, March 1, Leeds, Eunice, and James Baremore.
1776, Oct. 20, Leeman William, and Catharine Hepher.
1778, June   2, Leench, Alexander, and Mary Teatz.
1778, April 19, Leenhomes, William, and Jean Dennison.
1778, Sept. 6, Leer, Eve, and George Piper.
1757, Oct. 20, Lees, John, and Mary Cally.
1756, March 23, Lees, Mary, and Samuel Lonon.
1759, July 15, Lees, William, and Hannah Ogdon.
1757, April 13, Leeson, Elizabeth, and Robert Taylor.
1796, Aug. 14, Leet, Nathaniel, and Mary Dedy.
1793, March 4, Lefebure, Louis Philip, and Ann Williams.
1794, Nov. 24, Lefever, Rebecca, and Henry Dobbelare.
1765, April 20, Lefever, Sarah, and John Snowdon.
1796, Feb.   9, Lefevre, Pierie, and Elizabeth Conelly.
1794, May 19, Legg, Abia, and David Hulings.
1797, Dec. 12, Legrand, Samuel David, and Eleonore McFarden.
1784, Jan. 29, Lehman, Benjamin, and Elizabeth Keyser.
1778, March 29, Leine, Ann, and William Burton.
1778, June 14, Leking, Charles, and Sibila Stagg.
1788, Aug. 19, Lelew, Samuel, and Anne Bane.
1760, April 12, Lely, Daniel, and Mary Callahen.
1800, April 24, Leman, Cathrine, and William Hanson.
1795, Nov.   2, Lemmon, William, and Mary Lindsey.
1789, April 5, Lemon, John, and Catharine Petruis.
1797, Aug. 26, Lemont, Jane, and John Patterson.
1788, July   5, Lendes, Anne, and John Gisler.
1759, Oct. 21, Lenny, Heneny, and Elizabeth Adkison.
1771, May 27, Lenord, John, and Elizabeth Lawrence.
1783, Feb.   6, Lentner, Elizabeth, and Daniel Boggs.
1795, Sept. 13, Lents, Mary, and William Steeth.
1771, April 11, Leonard, James, and Margaret Rigger.
1778, April 26, Leonora, Sophia, and John Michael Freeze.
1784, April 25, Lepky, Henry, and Mary Collins.
1778, April 28, Lepper, Andrew, and Susannah Griner.
1750, Sept. 31, Leppert, Mary, and John Murchent.
1778, May   2, Lermant, John, and Sarah Dunn.
1795, May 19, Lesley, Hugh, and Mary Van Culen.
1793, Nov. 25, Lesley, Marget, and George Fowler.
1794, Sept. 18, Lester, Abigail, and James Henry.
1757, May   9, Lester, John, and Mary Whitefield.
1774, Sept. 8, Letber, Samuel, and Elizabeth Conetius.
1795, Oct. 22, Lets, Christina, and John Silvis.

1792, May   1, Letzinger, Ann, and John Helm.
1759, May   21, Leurs, Mary, and William Hellings.
1755, July   8, Levan, Anna Elizabeth, and Andrew Fredly.
1790, May   3, Levan, Isaac, and Mary Racer.
1778, April 20, Lever, Elizabeth, and John Plummer.
1789, April 25, Lever, Elizabeth, and Richard Davy.
1794, Feb.   1, Levering, Alsey, and Rudolph Bartholomew.
1754, April   2, Levering, Benjamin, and Catharine Righter.
1783, May   14, Levering, Elizabeth, and John Amos.
1776, Oct. 13, Levering, Griffith, and Hannah Griscom.
1794, Nov.   5, Levering, Hannah, and William McIntire.
1774, Sept. 6, Levering, Sebiah, and Isaac Martin.
1772, March 15, Leviston, Samuel, and Eve Cooly.
1795, Sept. 29, Levi, Joseph, and Mary Ploum.
1795, March 26, Levi, Moses, and Ruth Crowel.
1782, Aug. 11, Leving, Isaac, and Mary Casler.
1768, April 16, Levington, John, and Ann Hanlan.
1771, Jan.   13, Levis, Ann, and William L. Loyd.
1767, April 22, Leviston, Elizabeth, and Aaron Lockerd.
1766, Oct. 14, Leviston, Neal, and Catharine McMolley.
1753, Nov.   3, Levy, Samson, and Martha Thompson.
1776, Jan.   21, Lewas, Ann, and William Andrews.
1765, Dec. 26, Lewellin, Jacob, and Elenor Tou.
1767, Oct. 29, Lewis, Abigail, and John Davis.
1776, Oct. 13, Lewis, Abner, and Christina McDonald.
1792, Dec.   2, Lewis, Ann, and Henry Gault.
1759, Feb. 26, Lewis, Ann, and James Beaty.
1770, March 25, Lewis, Benjamin, and Elizabeth Emmony.
1793, Oct. 27, Lewis, Cathrine, and John Rogers.
1791, July   5, Lewis, Cathrine, and William Fellon.
1800, Jan. 14, Lewis, Cathrine, and William Mathews.
1758, Nov.   7, Lewis, Daniel, and Isabella Lawrence.
1752, Nov.   7, Lewis, David, and Mary Jonse.
1790, May   18, Lewis, Edward, and Mary Wrighter.
1796, March 9, Lewis, Elizabeth, and John Cony.
1779, April 19, Lewis, Elizabeth, and Thomas Flemings.
1784, July   6, Lewis, Elizabeth, and William Jones.
1794, Jan.   11, Lewis, Eve, and James Rosbottom.
1752, Nov. 18, Lewis, Hannah, and John Brown.
1753, July 15, Lewis, Isaac, and Catharine Pennystone.
1781, Dec. 20, Lewis, Jacob, and Mary Oats.
1790, May   20, Lewis, James, and Ann Jones.
1783, April 24, Lewis, Jesse, and Sarah Fling.
1785, April 26, Lewis, John, and Anne Clingman.
1757, May   9, Lewis, Margaret, and John McCalwey.
1792, Aug.   9, Lewis, Margret, and Stephen Agard.

1795, Aug. 6, Lewis, Mary, and Jacob Clingman.
1776, April 22, Lewis, Mary, and James Lahugh.
1799, June 2, Lewis, Mary, and Joseph Thompson.
1752, May 24, Lewis, Mary, and Samuel Reeve.
1772, April 25, Lewis, Mary, and Thomas Davis.
1789, Dec. 1, Lewis, Michael, and Lydia Greaves.
1758, April 26, Lewis, Rachel, and James McCollough.
1757, Dec. 14, Lewis, Rachel, and John Kerkpatrick.
1759, Jan. 8, Lewis, Rachel, and Joseph Marlow.
1794, April 21, Lewis, Rosamon, and Samuel Miles.
1776, May 19, Lewis, Ruth, and Joseph Johnson.
1796, Aug. 25, Lewis, Ruth, and Nicholas Hand.
1758, Nov. 15, Lewis, Samuel, and Susanna Handkins.
1792, April 29, Lewis, Sarah, and Abraham Fry, (African.)
1752, July 12, Lewis, Sarah, and Patrick Wheeler.
1754, June 27, Lewis, Thomas, and Catharine Kirk.
1754, Sept. 19, Lewis, William, and Elizabeth Morgan.
1752, Nov. 4, Lewis, William, and Ruth Miles.
1759, Jan. 10, Lewiston, Anne, and Hugh Korns.
1757, June 28, Lewzley, Elizabeth, and John Ackley.
1759, Sept. 27, Ley, Marthar, and Patrick Ogilby.
1769, Sept. 5, Libertin, Anne Eve, and Nicolas Ulric.
1798, Aug. 14, Lichler, John, and Mary Deredinger.
1752, Nov. 29, Licon, Hance, and Margareta Morten.
1759, July 22, Liddineau, Catharine, and William Bultzer.
1796, Aug. 23, Liddle, Jane, and Andrew McFarlane.
1799, June 17, Lidell, George, and Sarah Fox.
1752, Dec. 2, Lidenius, John Abraham, and Brigitta Rinberg.
1777, Feb. 27, Liebey, David, and Margaret Russel.
1796, June 7, Lier, Cathrine, and George Bartle.
1777, Nov. 2, Lieston, Margaret, and Joseph Harmer.
1778, Aug. 18, Lietch, George, and Margaret Smith.
1791, Jan. 2, Liggin, Anna Elizabeth, and Christopher Keillman.
1769, Jan. 22, Lightfoot, Rachel, and John Warner.
1753, Oct. 9, Lightholn, Barbara, and Benjamin Pollard.
1787, June 28, Lighton, Anne, and Joseph Robinson.
1788, July 21, Lighton, John, and Anne Miles.
1787, Sept. 4, Likins, Mary, and William Hand.
1791, Aug. 5, Lillie, Jane Harriet, and Peter Renaudet Cheva-
        lier.
1780, Sept. 20, Lilly, Elizabeth, and Lawrence Parsons.
1796, Dec. 29, Limerick, Cathrine, and Sterne Flemming.
1790, Feb. 10, Limes, Sara, and Pierre Garreau.
1752, Dec. 5, Lin, Hanna, and Robhard Bare.
1776, Aug. 9, Linager, Deborah, and William Plowman.
1793, Oct. 20, Linch, Elizabeth, and John Deare.

1777, July   27, Linch, Elizabeth, and John Lalley,
1797, March 19, Linch, Elizab., and John Norris.
1778, Sept.   27, Linch, Elizabeth, and Thomas Chowne.
1800, May   24, Linch, Hannah, and William Hall.
1752, Aug.   30, Linch, James, and Anne Meedwinter.
1777, June   28, Linch, James, and Elizabeth Wollaston.
1779, Nov.   27, Linch, Jane, and James Hagerty.
1779, May   16, Linch, Judith, and John Boyd.
1779, June   1, Linch, Patrick, and Sarah Campbell.
1779, Feb.   1, Linch, Peter, and Elizabeth Smith.
1762, May   27, Linchet, Samuel, and Magdalene Cox.
1795, March 19, Lincoin, Moses, and Barbara Kinch.
1792, April   11, Lincoln, Jacob, and Mary Taylor.
1791, July   7, Lincorn, Elizabeth, and John Hart.
1774, July   25, Lindall, Mary, and James Glenn.
1784, Jan.   8, Lindbay, John, and Sarah Hellems.
1762, June   6, Lindberg, Eric, and Catharine Urien.
1760, June   2, Lindemeyer, Christiana, and George Mellin.
1759, Sept.   26, Lindemeyer, Sarah, and Joseph Blewer.
1759, June   21, Lindmeyer, Mary, and Eric Nordenlind.
1767, Jan.   13, Lindmire, Rebeccah, and George Ord.
1776, Dec.   8, Lindsay, Ann, and Thomas Coran.
1771, June   10, Lindsay, Charles, and Ann Moore.
1753, Aug.   10, Lindsay, Elizabeth, and George Smith.
1795, Sept.   4, Lindsey, Jane, and William Floyd.
1795, Nov.   2, Lindsey, Mary, and William Lemmon.
1792, Nov.   20, Lindsey, Samuel, and Sarah Taylor.
1781, Sept.   29, Lindsey, William, and Elizabeth Mays.
1791, Dec.   31, Lindsey, William, and Rachel Hancock.
1776, Feb.   15, Lines, James, and Jane Burk.
1775, Nov.   26, Ling, Margaret, and William Doil.
1763, July   25, Link, Henry, and Ann Boon.
1781, Oct.   8, Linkholn, John, and Elizabeth O'Neal.
1756, Oct.   21, Linloy, John, and Ann Vooknigs.
1800, April   24, Linnier, Christopher, and Mary Kelly.
1789, Nov.   25, Linn, Ann, and Adam Baker.
1790, Oct.   5, Linn, Michael, and Susanna Frem.
1758, Oct.   8, Linn, Rosannah, and Charles Neel.
1799, June   6, Linnard, Garner, and Sarah Neuzum.
1759, April   19, Linnochs, Ester, and John Willson.
1753, May   24, Linnon, Thomas, and Ann Rhods.
1794, Jan.   12, Linnot, Timothy, and Cathrine McGrigger.
1775, July   21, Linord, Edward, and Mary Wallis.
1796, Jan.   12, Linsey, Jane, and William Dougherty.
1796, Sept.   25, Linten, Jacob, and Marget Shepard.
1792, Feb.   7, Linton, Hannah, and Robert Gore Jordan.

1796, Sept.　10, Linton, William, and Hannah Buckman.
1792, Oct.　21, Lints, Rosina, and Daniel Giry.
1759, Sept.　30, Lions, Catharine, and John Banner.
1776, June　9, Liperhealth, Mary, and Henry Emert.
1758, July　2, Lippencott, Mary, and Thomas Parent.
1797, Nov.　30, Lippencot, Thomas, and Mary Bauer.
1792, Nov.　3, Lisener, Samuel, and Margret Godfrey.
1751, Dec.　15, Lisle, Hannah, and Robert Steel.
1799, Jan.　17, Litham, John, and Mary More.
1783, Jan.　9, Lithgon, Edward, and Elizabeth Bowen.
1774, Sept.　4, Litler, Mary, and Jacob Row.
1782, Jan.　16, Litshworth, Eliza Anne, and Calon Affrey.
1777, May　18, Little, John, and Jean Furguson.
1756, April　12, Little, Michael, and Deboraw Williams.
1793, May　14, Little, Susannah, and Jacob Vigstroem.
1795, Sept.　3, Little, Thomas, and Sarah Parr.
1774, Nov.　2, Little, William, and Hannah Allen.
1754, April　15, Little, William, and Jane Reay.
1762, Oct.　26, Littleby, Richard, and Ann Murphy.
1780, March 27, Litzenburg, George, and Grace Coats.
1794, Dec.　31, Linsley, Elizabeth, and William Clark.
1797, June　22, Livezly, John, and Mary Boutcher.
1798, July　23, Livortin, Henrietta Dorothea, and Hans Jesper-
　　　　　　　son.
1783, April　9, Llewellyn, Elizabeth, and John Young.
1784, March　5, Lloyd, Philip, and Mary Parker.
1784, Nov.　7, Lloyd, William, and Mary Kays.
1752, Aug.　2, Loacock, John, and Hannah MacCally.
1799, June　9, Loan, Elizab., and Henry Bennet,
1755, Oct.　2, Loardan, Charles, and Elinor Dexter.
1782, Sept.　24, Loashe, Christopher, and Susannah Sneider.
1767, Jan.　20, Lobb, Jacob, and Mary Daugherty.
1778, Sept.　10, Locgant, Lawrence, and Dorothy Colbert.
1797, Sept.　6, Lochberry, Andrew, and Jane Christie.
1772, Dec.　22, Lock, Andrew, and Catharine Mickell.
1758, April　1, Lock, Andrew, and Susannah Fight.
1754, June　26, Lock, Engelbert, and Catharine Fernal.
1781, March　1, Lock, Hetty, and Thomas Herren.
1757, Nov.　3, Lock, Mary, and Philip Warns.
1775, Jan.　2, Lock, Mary, and Stephen Gordon.
1758, Nov.　7, Lock. Susannah, and Henry Abel.
1773, Sept.　12, Lockard, David, and Debora Carr.
1779, June　6, Lockart, Christopher, and Catharine More.
1770, May　7, Lockart, Elizabeth, and James Duffey.
1799, Jan.　17, Lockart, John, and Ann Bowers.
1767, Aug.　9, Locke, George, and Mary Batson.

1763, Dec.   4, Locke, Margaret, and John Cole.
1778, Feb.   1, Locked, Jane, and William Winter.
1751, May   29, Locker, George, and Cattron Loiance.
1767, April   22, Lockerd, Aaron, and Elizabeth Leviston.
1783, March   7, Lockhart, Jennet, and Joseph Harrison.
1778, Jan.   28, Lockwood, Mary, and Thomas Clayton.
1780, March   5, Loddell, Elizabeth, and Isaac Pearson.
1776, May   3, Loder, Edward, and Ann Tustin.
1766, July   3, Loder, Edward, and Mary Hellins.
1793, May   29, Lodge, John, and Elizabeth Reed.
1776, June   22, Lodge, Mary, and John Stephens.
1774, Oct.   13, Lodge, Mary, and Thomas Griffis.
1797, Jan.   24, Lodge, William, and Martha Parkinson.
1755, July   19, Lodovig, John Christopher, and Catharine Eng-
                 land.
1794, Oct.   30, Loe, John, and Mary Davis.
1769, May   11, Loesher, John, and Catharine Tuder.
1782, June   20, Loesher, Mary, and James Mathews.
1795, Dec.   8, Loesly, Jonathan, and Barbara Myers.
1761, Jan.   15, Lofftes, Rachel, and Ephraim Sharold.
1781, Jan.   29, Logan, James, and Mary Ward.
1798, Feb.   3, Logan, John, and Jane O'Connor.
1775, July   10, Logan, Mary, and John Dawson,
1772, July   12, Logan, Samuel, and Mary Oor.
1767, March   1, Logan, William, and Sarah Davis.
1782, May   4, Loghan, Patrick, and Margaret Docherty.
1751, May   29, Loiance, Cattron, and George Locker.
1798, Dec.   29, Loid, Daniel, and Sarah Jackson.
1779, Oct.   15, Loid, Jeptha, and Margaret Smith.
1770, Oct.   14, Loid, Margarett, and Edmond McDonnell.
1780, March   9, Loid, Rachel, and Jacob Bear.
1761, Sept. 30, Lohey, Mary, and Archibald Frame.
1762, Nov.   30, Lohey, Mary, and Archibald Frame.
1790, Sept.   2, Lohra, John, and Mary Knorr.
1799, June   20, Lollar, Alexander, and Hannah Walter.
1781, Nov.   29, Lom, Rachel, and John Gilchrist, (free negroes.)
1791, Aug.   10, Lomprez, Jean, and Lydia Agnew.
1795, March 29, Lone, Sarah, and John Washington Green.
1782, March   5, Long, James, and Jeane Moyel.
1774, March 20, Long, James, and Mary Denny.
1752, Oct.   15, Long, Jane, and Patrick Doran.
1767, Dec.   15, Long, Jane, and Thomas Jamison.
1786, Nov.   22, Long, Johanna, and Peter Delany.
1782, June   15, Long, John, and Elizabeth Bernet.
1767, July   21, Long, John, and Mary Kelly.
1766, Dec.   10, Long, Martha, and John Coleman.

1762, Jan.   26, Long, Mary, and Alexander Fletsher.
1794, May   20, Long, Mary, and William Dougherty.
1794, April   10, Long, Sarah, and Jacob Philip.
1780, May   15, Long, Walter, and Elizabeth Goof.
1787, June   27, Longacre, Andrew, and Martha Slide.
1762, April   31, Longacre, Eleonore, and John Kelly.
1762, July   29, Longacre, Phebe, and Paul Pastoley.
1773, Jan.   5, Longden, James, and Mary Anderton.
1797, Feb.   23, Longstreth, Joseph, and Marget Mackey.
1800, Aug.   25, Longstreth, Mary, and Robert Tea.
1756, March 23, Lonon, Samuel, and Mary Lees.
1777, Sept.   1, Loom, Phœbe, and Cophy, Douglas.
1793, June   8, Loper, Rebecca, and William Stow.
1755, Feb.   1, Lord, Deborah, and Thomas Wells.
1789, March 26, Lord, Eda, and Peter Cappas.
1780, April   10, Lord, Elizabeth, and David Vanneman.
1790, Dec.   16, Lord, Isaac, and Marget Kirkpatric.
1751, June   8, Lord, John, and Deborah Banskon.
1787, Aug.   14, Lord, Jonn, and Margaret McCloud.
1791, March 31, Lord, John, and Sarah Eggman.
1765, June   24, Lord, Margaret, and Robert Robbeson.
1785, July   12, Lord, Mary, and Rueben Munyan.
1779, May   18, Lore, Henry, and Catharine Wharton.
1767, Nov.   5, Loreman, John George, and Ann Rensill.
1770, July   23, Loremar, Anne, and James Harron.
1792, April   19, Lorener, Ralph, and Sarah Orr.
1798, May   21, Lorket, Sarah, and William Bastian.
1774, Nov.   27, Lost Richard, and Mary Wathers.
1780, Jan.   8, Lott, Ely, and Eleanor Smith.
1795, July   20, Lott, Henry, and Mary Eastwick.
1795, Sept.   23, Lott, Hugh Riley, and Rachel Maquire.
1798, July   25, Lott, Uriah, and Elizab. Jones.
1799, Dec.   26, Louderbach, Jonathan, and Lydia Durborow.
1791, Feb.   7, Louderback, Elizabeth, and William Wood.
1798, Jan.   20, Loudon, Fredric, and Marget Jones.
1786, April   10, Loughberry, Abagail, and Jacob Baker.
1788, Nov.   22, Loughberry, Elizabeth, and Thomas James.
1786, May   2, Loughberry, Sarah, and William Reemer.
1797, Dec.   21, Lougheed, James, and Eleonore Boid.
1796, Nov.   7, Loughery, Magee, and Patrick McDavid.
1758, Nov.   24, Louis, Isaac, and Else Collins.
1775, June   12, Louney, Peter, and Jean McColly.
1751, April   8, Louns, Samuel, and Ann Hase.
1796, Oct.   12, Loury, Bridget, and James McLaughlin.
1796, Oct.   11, Loury, Marget, and Daniel Barr.
1796, Nov.   23, Love, Luke, and Mary Bowers.

1776, Dec.　12, Love, Mary, and William Collins.
1779, May　20, Lovel, Daniel, and Elizabeth Lucas.
1777, May　23, Loveley, Eleanor, and James Ward.
1783, Oct.　11, Loveman, Elizabeth. and James Shillingford.
1793, Nov.　6, Lovemore, Ralph, and Mary Sodon.
1765, April　30, Low, Edward, and Rebeccah McCarty.
1759, Sept.　30, Low, Eve, and Nicholas Andrew.
1769, Feb.　18, Low, George, and Sarah Morris.
1779, April　27, Low, James, and Susanna Noble.
1753, July　19, Low, John, and Rebecca Windal.
1736, Nov.　2, Low, Joseph, and Andrews Gloucester.
1777, March　2, Low, Mary, and Bartholomew Glou.
1774, March 17, Lowden, John, and Anne Humphreys.
1777, March 18, Lowder, Elizabeth, and John Francis.
1768, June　24, Lowdher, Phebe, and William Hudson.
1780, May　24, Lowe, John, and Catharine Gallougher.
1783, Sept.　28, Lowell, James, and Hannah Black.
1796, Feb.　21, Lownsburg, Carpenter, and Druilla Smiley.
1777, Nov.　24, Lowrey, Ann, and James McMullan.
1778, Feb.　5, Lowry, Mary, and Charles Whenwright.
1796, Feb.　28, Lowry, Daniel, and Mary Maloy.
1795, Dec.　7, Lowry, Elizabeth, and John White.
1767, Aug.　12, Lowry, Jacob, and Newill Quicksall.
1778, Oct.　19, Lowry, Mary, and Nathan Hybands.
1754, Jan.　31, Lowry, Robert, and Mary Cornwall.
1764, Feb.　23, Lowry, Samuel, and Elizabeth Erven.
1793, Dec.　30, Lowry, Sarah, and William Mullen.
1799, July　18, Lowry, William, and Jane Burke.
1797, June　25, Loyd, Cathrine, and Patric McGerthy.
1779, Aug.　10, Loyd, Elizabeth, and John Williams.
1765, April　15, Loyd, Hannah, and Humphrey Ellis.
1798, March 14, Loyd Hannah, and James Parker.
1796, June　23, Loyd, Hugh, und Phebe Moore.
1764, Oct.　23, Loyd, Humphrey, and Jane Ellis.
1792, Dec.　8, Loyd, Jeremiah, and Solomon Floyd.
1757, Sept.　28, Loyd, Margaret, and Alexander Boggs.
1782, Dec.　13, Loyd, Mary, and David Barry.
1759, Nov.　21, Loyd, Sarah, and George Adam.
1771, Jan.　13, Loyd, William L., and Ann Levis.
1779, May　20, Lucas, Elizabeth, and Daniel Lovel.
1767, Oct.　28, Lucas, George, and Mary Polley,
1773, Aug.　8, Lucas, Martha, and Daniel Laperty.
1799, Nov.　16, Lucas, Ràchel, and Edward Hall.
1792, Sept.　16, Lucas, Sarah, and Thomas Higgins.
1765, Oct.　10, Luce, Elizabeth, and Zachariah Van Dyke.
1790, Aug.　31, Ludley, Watson, and Cathrine Pritsmon.

1778, Nov.   17, Ludwick, Martin, and Elizabeth Strep.
1773, Aug.   22, Ludwick, Otilla, and John Wilson.
1753, March 12, Luff, William, and Ann Clarke.
1780, Jan.   18, Lukans, Mary, and James Cordill.
1796, Dec.   11, Luke, John, and Marget Frence.
1780, Aug.   4, Luke, Thomas, and Elizabeth Mary Rives.
1784, April 14, Lukemeyer, Thomas, and Mary Jones.
1783, June   5, Lukens, Gaymor, and Lawrence Keene.
1778, Jan.   16, Lukens, James, and Mary Lukens.
1778, Jan.   16, Lukens, Mary, and James Lukens.
1792, Dec.   15, Lum, Hanna, and William Price.
1778, July   31, Lunn, Mary, and Richard Robeson.
1774, Nov.   10, Lunt, Sarah, and John Many.
1764, Dec.   11, Lupton, Elizabeth, and Daniel Stillwell.
1775, July   7, Lusad, Mary, and William Hastings.
1761, March 11, Lusher, Benjamin, and Mary Barnard.
1785, May   21, Lusk, Elizabeth, and John Barnhill.
1782, June   8, Luts, Conrad, and Susannah Turner.
1757, Aug.   3, Luttin, Ann, and James Andreas.
1774, Sept. 18, Lycime, David, and Ann DuRose.
1773, Jan.   17, Lycom, John, and Christine Fredericks.
1798, July   30, Lyel, Jemimah, and Daniel Bartel.
1768, April 18, Lyle, Isaac, and Elizabeth Cooper.
1774, Feb.   7, Lyndall, Elizabeth, and Daniel Glenn.
1774, Nov.   26, Lynn, Mary, and Josiah Monger.
1791, Aug.   11, Lyon, Jedediah, and Mary Gormon.
1770, Aug.   26, Lyons, John, and Ester Mosfet.
1795, June   14, Lyons, Sarah, and William Dallas.
1771, July   25, Lyons, Sophia, and Ceasor Preston.
1790, Nov.   18, Lyons, William, and Mary Cook.
1791, Sept.   1, Maag, Cathrine, and Samuel Jordan.
1781, Dec.   20, Maag, Francise, and John Shetsline.
1782, April   2, Maag, Henry, and Susannah Harrar.
1795, Nov.   19, Macall, Christiana, and Lazarus Brittingham.
1795, Oct.   29, Macall, Eliza, and John Crosby.
1799, May   14, MacAlpin, Mary, and Joseph Oat.
1790, Aug.   17, Macarmick, Bridget, and George Wagener.
1752, Oct.   15, Macay, Mary, and Alban Davis.
1791, Dec.   22, Macbeth Robert, and Elizabeth Best.
1791, Jan.   1, Macbicker, Jennet, and John O'Lary.
1795, May   7, Macbreathy, Nancy, and James Dougherty.
1790, Oct.   20, Macbride, Elenore, and James Hughs.
1795, April   6, Macbride, Mary, and George Buchaanan.
1752, July   23, MacCallow, Elizabeth, and James Grahams.
1752, Aug.   2, MacCally, Hannah, and John Loacock.
1794, Jan.   2, Maccon, Elenore, and Francis Drille.

1786, Dec.   25, MacConnel, Arthur, and Catherine Macky.
1792, July   29, MacCurdy, Alexander, and Sara Weeks.
1751, Aug.   1, MacDanell, Anne, and John Lee.
1800, March   22, MacDaniel, Mary, and Lewis Eockey.
1791, June   23, MacDonald, Alexander, and Margret Jemmison.
1796, Nov.   21, MacDonald, Mary, and James Wallace.
1799, Aug.   14, MacDonald, Nancy, and William Watson Knight.
1751, Jan.   28, MacDonnell, Constantine, and Elizabeth Willson.
1751, Aug.   14, MacDowell, James, and Ann Harman.
1792, Nov.   11, Macfall, Bridget, and Stephen Steel.
1751, Dec.   8, MacFarland, Neal, and Anne Boid.
1791, Feb.   24, MacFarlane, Susanna, and William Campbell.
1792, Dec.   9, Macfee, Sarah, and Joseph Proctor.
1792, May   21, Macfee, Susanna, and George Hardy.
1790, June   3, Macfee, Susanna, and John Owens.
1778, March   6, MacGill, Robert, and Jane Dunlap.
1797, Aug.   5, MacGiven, William, and Hannah Wright.
1751, Oct.   13, MacGlaclen, Philip, and Hannah Griffy.
1751, Jan.   29, MacGoun, Anne, and Adam Collon.
1800, Sept.   23, MacGuire, Francis, and Elizabeth Murphey.
1755, Sept.   3, Macham, Andrew, and Margaret Donalson.
1777, July   27, Mack, Peter, and Sarah Bush.
1768, June   9, Mack, Robert, and Mary Potter.
1794, March   27, Mackamson, Jane, and James Kelly.
1778, Jan.   30, Mackdue, Eleanor, and James Whenright.
1793, Feb.   3, Mackensy, Christina, and Walter Boggs.
1778, Jan.   16, Mackentush, Duncan, and Mary Hutchinson.
1772, Dec.   3, Mackenzie, Colin, and Elizabeth Sutton.
1800, Dec.   11, Mackey, Bernard, and Cathrine Moses.
1774, Dec.   26, Mackey, Daniel, and Hannah Cracker.
1772, July   7, Mackey, Elizabeth, and Mathew Barnewell.
1791, May   20, Mackey, Jane, and James Neath.
1797, Feb.   23, Mackey, Marget, and Joseph Longstreth.
1779, March   11, Mackey, Mary, and Edward Brooks.
1772, Nov.   25, MackFarlein, Isabel, and Philip Neal.
1791, March   3, Mackgare, John, and Mary Hammel.
1795, Dec.   24, Mackie, Sarah, and Michael Seatman.
1797, Nov.   24, MacKimson, Ann, and Philip Morris.
1788, Nov.   22, Mackintire, Gustavus, and Mary White.
1799, July   16, Mackintire, John, and Eleonore Macmullen.
1798, Jan.   30, Mackintosh, Isabella, and John Stuart.
1793, Jan.   24, Mackintosh, Joseph, and Alcy Handly.
1771, Sept.   1, Macklane, Catharine, and John White.
1788, Oct.   23, Macknob, John, and Martha Gogan.
1786, Dec.   25, Macky Catherine, and Arthur MacConnel.
1795, March   1, Maclean, Andrew, and Margret Giles.

1770, Oct.　　1, Maclean, Elizabeth, and John Carnaghan.
1793, Nov.　20, Maclean, Macam, and Mary Grady.
1793, Nov.　25, Maclean, Mary, and David Merrey.
1792, July　28, Maclean, William, and Isabella Maglochlin.
1761, June　22, Macles, Ester, and Christopher Hoffman.
1754, March 10, MacMahan Hannah, and John Rathwell.
1792, July　7, Macmahon, Hugh, and Cathrine Wright.
1791, Aug.　20, MacMahon, Thomas, and Mary Jervis.
1753, Jan.　7, Macmakin, Nelly, and Mathew Dowling.
1799, July　16, MacMullen, Eleonore, and John McIntire.
1797, July　10, MacMullen, Margret, and Louis Allen.
1774, Sept.　8, MacMullen, William, and Ann Martin.
1792, Oct.　22, Macmun, John, and Jane Carvener.
1799, Aug.　14, MacMunnigal, Patric, and Mary Fraley.
1792, May　5, MacNeal, Nancy, and William O'Brian.
1790, Aug.　23, MacPherson, John, and Susanna Shaw.
1795, June　9, Macquire, Cathrine, and John Baptiste Andre.
1798, Feb.　15, MacSheane, Lawrence, and Cathrine Forsith.
1755, Sept.　14, Macumtire, Mary, and Neal Connoly.
1778, April　30, MacWey, Duncan, and Sarah Filgate.
1790, Feb.　16, Madan, Fergus, and Grace Helms.
1800, Sept.　25, Madan, John, and Lydia Taylor.
1790, Jan.　31, Madan, Patric, and Mary McCollister.
1787, Oct.　16, Madan, Patric, and Sucky Campbell.
1772, Feb.　9, Madan, Susannah, and James Aston.
1757, March 24, Madden, Elizabeth, and Benjamin Peel.
1778, April　5, Madden, Nicholas, and Mary McCarty.
1785, Feb.　17, Madders, Susannah, and Thomas Britton.
1781, Sept.　27, Madders, Susannah, and Thomas Wilson.
1779, April　18, Maddicks, Ann, and Abraham Irish.
1770, May　7, Madding, Mary, and James Bant.
1761, Jan.　7, Madlock, Patience, and John Wattson.
1751, Nov.　19, Maffet, James, and Susannah Willson.
1781, Dec.　20, Maffey, James, and Mary Parkes.
1760, March 3, M gdalene, Ann Catharine, and Andrew Jacob
　　　　　　　　Heidmeyer.
1758, Sept.　8, Magdalen, Ann, and Peter Stricker.
1758, Nov.　12, Magee, Elizabeth, and David Richard.
1757, Feb.　17, Magee, Elizabeth, and Robert Burly.
1789, Dec.　3, Magill, Rachel, and George Everhart.
1792, July　28, Maglochlin, Isabella, and William Maclean.
1789, May　2, Magor, John, and Alice Jones.
1765, April　9, MaGown, Onera, and Michael McLarkey.
1794, Jan.　20, Magravi, Marget, and Bonaventure Barajon.
1791, Sept.　17, Magrote, James, and Ann Irvin.
1783, June　21, Maguire, Catherine, and John Rodgers.

1753, Oct.   20, Maguire, Guany, and Bryon Kelly.
1796, April   21, Maguire, William, and Ann Roff.
1790, Sept.   5, Maholn, Marget, and James McDaniel.
1780, Sept.   20, Mahon, Catharine, and Edward Delaney.
1795, May   17, Mahoney, Cathrine, and George Burton.
1753, April   23, Mahney, Patrick, and Elizabeth Bennet.
1794, May   8, Mahoney, Patric, and Mary McIlvoy.
1778, Feb.   8, Mahoney, Timothy, and Mary Hempsted.
1765, March   14, Mahony, Anthony, and Hannah Collet.
1767, Aug.   15, Main, Mary, and Samuel Hawke.
1761, Jan.   19, Main, Peter, and Elizabeth Justy.
1759, March   5, Maips, Elisabet, and James Elder.
1787, Sept.   18, Maires, Sarah, and Patric Taggard.
1765, May   5, Maisner, Mary, and William Watson.
1792, Jan.   5, Makamson, Deborah, and John Ware.
1791, March   30, Makamson, James, and Catharine Bare.
1780, Aug.   24, Makenison, Sarah, and Jacob Netsel.
1770, Feb.   21, Maley, Mary, and Luke Morphey.
1773, Oct.   7, Mallinton, Thomas, and Mary Hancock.
1770, July   1, Mallobey, Jane, and John Paul.
1775, March   24, Malluck, Jemima, and John Garret.
1776, Oct.   23, Maloney, Margaret, and James Cowlsten.
1787, May   24, Malony, Elizabeth, and Nathan Collins.
1798, March   6, Malony, Michael, and Marion Overman.
1787, Dec.   6, Malony, Sarah, and William Hulet.
1796, Feb.   28, Maloy, Mary, and Daniel Lowry.
1778, June   2, Man, Sarah, and Thomas Morton.
1777, Sept.   24, Manderson, George, and Catharine Supplee.
1773, Oct.   5, Manin, John, and Elizabeth Martin.
1797, March   5, Mann, Patience, and James Braken.
1799, Feb.   14, Manning, Mathew, and Ann Lanten.
1790, March   5, Mannon, Catharine, and James Rushton.
1753, Oct.   2, Mannon, Daniel, and Margret McMahonh.
1762, April   12, Manse, Charlotte, and Leonard Rost.
1772, May   27, Manuel, Elizabeth, and George Smith.
1774, Nov.   10, Many, John, and Sarah Lunt.
1778, June   13, Map, John, and Sarah Ketler.
1795, Sept.   23, Maquire, Rachel, and Hugh Riley Lott.
1787, May   12, Marache, Solomon, and Mary Holton.
1761, April   6, March, Catharine, and Jacob Baker.
1770, Oct.   1, Marchant, Philip, and Martha Saunders.
1775, Aug.   27, Marchant Sarah, and Caspar Gribble.
1764, Oct.   14, Marchants, Ann, and Peter Hyman.
1788, April   22, Marcher, John, and Elizabeth Rambo.
1750, Sept.   31, Marchent, John, and Mary Seppert.
1754, July   20, Marchil, Moses, and Sarah Helms.

1760, July 19, Marefield, Edward, and Sarah Walker.
1769, Nov. 8, Margerum, John, and Catharine Cornish.
1796, March 22, Maria, Arabella, and Thomas Blunt.
1755, March 31, Maridith, Elizabeth, and Abel Janny.
1796, Jan. 14, Mariner, Cornelius Leary, and Elizabeth Steel.
1797, Dec. 8, Maris, George, and Eliza Dunwoody.
1752, June 11, Maris, James, and Rachel Evans.
1793, July 28, Marjory, Thomas, and Cathrine Wolvin.
1781, April 17, Mark, Sibil, and Michael Harry.
1790, June 12, Markis, Simon, and Honor Kennedy.
1778, Feb. 8, Marklow, George, and Mercy Snowden.
1772, Dec. 13, Marks, Catharine, and John Francis Derogier.
1760, Jan. 7, Marks, Mary, and Bernard Reed.
1762, July 22, Marles, Ester, and Christopher Hoffman.
1791, June 30, Marley, William, and Elizabeth Cooper.
1782, April 29, Marll, Margret, and Daniel Botler.
1759, Jan. 8, Marlow, Joseph, and Rachel Lewis.
1767, April 6, Marlpool, Sarah, and John Ware.
1794, Aug. 10, Marns, John, and Susannah Pyle.
1784, Sept. 8, Marot, Joseph, and Elizabeth Woodcock.
1767, April 6, Marpool, George, and Doey Rossel.
1798, Aug. 15, Marr, Mathew, and Bridget Farren.
1760, Feb. 14, Marriage, John, and Mary Burch.
1777, April 24, Marriett, Hannah, and James Lee.
1792, Dec. 6, Marriner, Fenwick, and Marget Wright.
1782, Aug. 12, Marriott, Samuel, and Elizabeth Wright.
1781, Dec. 4, Marschalk, Francis, and Mary Ryan.
1774, Feb. 1, Masden, Humphrey, and Elizabeth Gordon.
1793, April 9, Marshal, Curtes, and James Kerr.
1767, Sept. 14, Marshal, Thomas, and Ann Dear.
1756, March 6, Marshall, Aaron, and Hannah Zeans.
1776, Nov. 19, Marshall, Abraham, and Phœbe Shea.
1782, Aug. 3, Marshall, David, and Barbara Morrison.
1776, Dec. 30, Marshall, Eleanor, and William Canaday.
1777, June 9, Marshall, Elizabeth, and Henry Abbot.
1791, Jan. 22, Marshall, Elizabeth, and Peter Connor.
1767, Feb. 21, Marshall, George, and Hannah Collins.
1780, July 6, Marshall, Hannah, and Charles Crawly.
1758, May 17, Marshall, Hannah, and William Jones.
1754, Jan. 23, Marshall, Isaac, and Mary Clayton.
1777, Aug. 31, Marshall, James, and Margaret Ford.
1780, June 16, Marshall, John, and Elizabeth Robeson.
1784, April 27, Marshall, Joseph, and Prudence Pusey.
1757, Oct. 13, Marshall, Mary, and John Bishop.
1755, Oct. 14, Marshall, Mary, and Nehemiah Delaplain.
1751, June 20, Marshall, Moses, and Susanna Harris.

1790, July   12, Marshall, Sara, and John Attmore.
1791, March 23, Marten, Joseph, and Elenore Dunscomb.
1774, Sept.   8, Martin, Ann, and William MacMullen.
1752, May   26, Martin, Anthony, and Ann Anderson.
1789, July   16, Martin, Anthony, and Elenore Waters.
1798, Dec.   31, Martin, Augustin, and Christina Ott.
1759, Oct.   19, Martin, Catharine, and William Wright.
1796, Feb.   14, Martin, Charles, and Sarah Brown.
1782, July   28, Martin, Daniel, and Mary Megee.
1796, Dec.   5, Martin, Eleonor, and John Trenor.
1799, May   25, Martin, Eleonore, and John Williams.
1793, May   19, Martin, Elizabeth, and Charles Francis Butler.
1773, Oct.   5, Martin, Elizabeth, and John Manin.
1796, Feb.   7, Martin, Elizabeth, and John Willington.
1781, July   30, Martin, Elizabeth, and Peter Burkhard.
1774, Sept.   6, Martin, Isaac, and Sebiah Levering.
1799, April   24, Martin, James, and Marget Finney.
1800, April   21, Martin, James, and Mary Barnet.
1797, Aug.   13, Martin, John, and Cathrine Peck.
1794, Sept.   3, Martin, John, and Jane Miller.
1793, Dec.   23, Martin, John, and Marget Power.
1787, Oct.   24, Martin, John, and Sarah McLease.
1784, June   1, Martin, John, and Tamor Sharp.
1780, Sept,   10, Martin, Joseph, and Ann Pounder.
1753, Aug.   18, Martin, Leonard, and Catharine Carr.
1778, Jan.   12, Martin, Mary, and Arthur Beattie.
1760, Sept.   28, Martin, Mary, and Israel English.
1767, Aug.   17, Martin, Mary, and James Hughs.
1791, May   29, Martin, Mary, and John Souders.
1794, April   7, Martin, Mary, and Richard Porter.
1779, May   6, Martin, Mertha, and Jonathan Arnold.
1759, Jan.   18, Martin, Susannah, and John Colp.
1777, Jan.   13, Martin, Susannah, and Joseph Ogleby.
1789, April   8, Martin, Thomas, and Mary Anne Frys.
1777, April   30, Martin, Thomas, and Susannah Worrall.
1781, Feb.   17, Martingiel, Mary, and Benjamin Brittain.
1798, April   16, Marts, Elizabeth, and Christopher Francis.
1798, March   5, Marts, Tobitha, and Jonathan Wilden.
1796, Dec.   10, Mase, Sarah, and David Humphreys.
1781, Jan.   30, Mash, Anne, and Joseph Gilbert.
1778, June   4, Mason, Catharine, and William Carleton.
1772, Feb.   24, Mason, Elizabeth, and Francis Neeson.
1792, Oct.   12, Mason, Hamstead, and Rosanna Gihon.
1795, Jan.   22, Mason, Isaac, and Mary Hababaker.
1793, Aug.   17, Mason, Maria, and Joshua Freeman.
1778, April   24, Mason, Mary, and Isaac Sevey.

1777, Feb.　　5, Mason, Mary, and John Griffieth.
1783, April　19, Mason, Mary, and Samuel Scott.
1794, Dec.　28, Mason, Mary, and Thomas Laurence.
1790, Dec.　21, Mason, Tanton, and Sara Scott.
1799, July　22, Mason, William, and Maria Brittle.
1785, Oct.　18, Mason, William, and Mary Stiles.
1800, Feb.　17, Massey, Richard, and Ellene Cresson.
1778, Sept.　17, Massy, John, and Elizabeth Smith.
1790, July　　8, Masters, Elizabeth, and James Lafferty.
1776, July　　2, Masters, George, and Susannah Nightlinger.
1753, Nov.　15, Masters, Margaret, and David Nicholson.
1791, Oct.　25, Matheaus, Mary, and William Brown.
1790, Nov.　11, Mather, Thomas, and Margret Ross.
1796, Nov.　17, Matheus, Bridget, and Peter Quin.
1759, Dec.　24, Mathew, Hannah, and Stephan Clark.
1769, Feb.　13, Mathew, Robert, and Eleanor Young.
1754, July　31, Mathew, William, and Hannah Holms.
1780, June　28, Mathews, Ann, and Robert Rowle.
1780, Jan.　　8, Mathews, Bridget, and Thomas Gogerty.
1789, May　10, Mathews, Bridget, and Thomas Wright.
1792, Oct.　18, Mathews, George, and Elizabeth Phillips.
1782, June　20, Mathews, James, and Mary Loesher.
1795, March 19, Mathews, Jeremiah, and Sarah Cox.
1763, Sept.　7, Mathews, John, and Ann Chambers.
1778, June　26, Mathews, Margaret, and Kerns Dowling.
1786, Dec.　31, Mathews, Mary, and William Williams.
1787, May　18, Mathews, Mary, and William Williams.
1800, Jan.　14, Mathews, William, and Cathrine Lewis.
1792, Oct.　7, Mathews, William, and Elizabeth Jones.
1787, Feb.　28, Mathiney, John, and Bridget Armstrong.
1795, July　4, Matlack, Caleb, and Hannah Wilson.
1789, May　30, Matlack, Caleb, and Mary Williams.
1790, Oct.　17, Matlack, Elizabeth, and Robert Wilson.
1782, Dec.　28, Matlack, Jacob, and Sebilla Ellis.
1797, April　27, Matlack, Melon, and Mary Matlack.
1797, April　27, Matlack, Mary, and Melon Matlack.
1770, Jan.　14, Matley, Margarett, and Theodorus Bary.
1759, July　22, Mats, John, and Basille Chestney.
1782, Sept.　2, Matsinger, Elizabeth, and Joseph Hall.
1752, Sept.　20, Matson, Catharine, and Erick Muleken.
1765, July　8, Matson, Elizabeth, and Benjamin Duffield.
1799, May　25, Matson, Jonas, and Mary Key.
1761, Nov.　9, Matson, Peter, and Christiana Peterson.
1762, Nov.　9, Matson, Peter, and Christiana Peterson.
1767, Sept.　2, Matson, Peter, and Elizabeth Supply.
1794, Dec.　20, Matson, Rebecca, and Christopher Hoest.

1775, Aug.   6, Matters, Robert, and Margaret Patton.
1773, Sept.   5, Matters Susanna, and Christian Kuhn.
1777, Feb.   4, Matthews, Catharine, and William Patterson.
1782, Feb.   24, Mattis, Mary, and William Bell.
1780, July   2, Mattis, Mertha, and John Hide.
1780, March   16, Mattson, Israel, and Catherine Moffin.
1756, Oct.   29, Matzon, Israel, and Mary Padrick.
1765, Dec.   23, Matzon, Margaret, and Abraham Varnam.
1756, March   16, Maulsby, William, and Hannah Coulston.
1778, Sept.   2, Maur, Catharine, and Jacob Fernhaver.
1751, June   10, Mauren, Elizabeth, and Christopher Rose.
1794, Sept.   10, Maux, Constant, and Mary Rigley.
1779, May   11, Maxfield, Jane, and Richard Evit.
1777, Aug.   24, Maxfield, Mary, and James Reynolds.
1783, Dec.   16, Maxfield, Rebeeca, and Robert Fox.
1793, July   7, Maxwell, Anthony, and Cath.rine Seckel.
1794, Sept.   20, Maxwell, Hugh, and Ann Anderson.
1795, May   24, Maxwell, James, and Susannah Griffith.
1754, April   20, Maxwell, Letisha, and Abraham Darby.
1792, Nov.   7, Maxwell, Letitia, and Jacob Henry.
1780, Sept.   14, Maxwell, Ruth, and Edward Williams.
1799, Aug.   25, Maxwell, Thomas, and Elizab. Cline.
1784, Nov.   16, May, Agnes, and James Ross.
1757, Oct.   13, May, Anthony, and Mary Colket.
1767, April   26, May, Charles, and Mary McCallister.
1789, May   7, May, Elizabeth, and Martin Wise.
1780, Sept.   7, May, Mary, and Thomas Fowler.
1778, May   31, May, Samuel, and Margaret Smith.
1781, March   8, May, Thomas, and Mary Wheeler.
1779, July   15, Mayas, Hannah, and Philip Waggoner.
1800, Feb.   1, Maybury, Jonathan, and Eleonore Skeen.
1762, July   19, Mayer, Lorentz, and Anna Margaret Workinger.
1754, Oct.   29, Mayers, Jane, and Joseph Beaks.
1779, June   14, Mayn, James, and Elizabeth Boyd.
1790, Oct.   30, Mayris, Mary, and William Purdon.
1781, Sept.   29, Mays, Elizabeth, and William Lindsey.
1795, Oct.   11, Maze, John George, and Mary Kyser.
1786, Nov.   30, McAckinsy, Daniel, and Marget White.
1777, May   23, McAllister, George, and Elizabeth Bryan.
1778, July   21, McAneney, James, and Hannah Lee.
1778, May   20, McArthur Duncan, and Sarah Smart.
1779, June   16, McBea, Isabell, and Daniel Wingate.
1779, May   28, McBean, Jane, and Alexander McDonald.
1765, May   29, McBreid, Marchery, and Archibald McCorkel.
1781, March   13, McBrian, Elonor Johnson, and Thomas McCams.
1763, May   13, McBride, Andrew, and Esther Sommers.

1775, Oct.   2, McBride, John, and Rose Doubin.
1756, April   25, McBride, Richard, and Susannah Harron.
1776, June   2, McCahan, John, and Susannah Shidels.
1799, July   2, McCahan, Susanna, and John Hanley.
1878, Jan.   15, McCale, Alexander, and Hannah Thomson.
1775, Sept.   9, McCalister, Margaret, and John Darrah.
1794, May   24, McCall, Elizabeth, and Robert Beard.
1785, Nov.   22, McCall, James, and Margaret McCloskey.
1795, Jan.   21, McCalla, Charles, and Sarah McGloghlin.
1795, Dec.   29, McCalla, John, and Mary Graham.
1794, Aug.   3, McCalla, Rosanna, and Thomas Thales Peters.
1764, March   20, McCalley, Jane, and Walter McMichal.
1790, June   25, McCalley, Rosana, and Joseph Stephens.
1767, April   26, McCallister, Caterine, and John Bayman.
1791, July   25, McCallister, Elizab., and John Reed.
1781, Nov.   16, McCallister, James, and Mary Wenhook.
1780, Feb.   8, McCallister, John, and Mary Corkran.
1799, Oct.   6, McCallister, John, and Mary Smith.
1767, April   26, McCallister, Mary, and Charles May.
1797, May   17, McCally, Alexander, and Rebecca McKean.
1799, May   6, McCally, Elizab., and Thomas Carnes.
1779, June   16, McCalpin, Walter, and Sarah Kyle.
1780, Jan.   20, McCalton, Andrew, and Mary McKelher.
1757, May   9, McCalwey, John, and Margaret Lewis.
1781, March   13, McCams, Thomas, and Eleonor Johnson McBrian.
1792, May   15, McCan, William, and Cathrine Hewet.
1778, March   19, McCandley, Elizabeth, and Charles Leechman.
1776, Oct.   29, McCane, Eleanor, and Alexander Gaston.
1800, March   23, McCaney, James, and Grace McCany.
1759, Jan.   1, McCanles, John, and Margaret Casselberg.
1777, July   26, McCann, John, and Mary Burk.
1796, April   4, McCann, Terence, and Margret Hewes.
1796, June   30, McCanna, Cathrine, and Alexander Hopkins.
1799, May   2, McCannan, Rebecca, and John Mumford.
1800, March   23, McCany, Grace, and James McCaney.
1772, April   6, McCapherty, Cormack, and Margaret Conawey.
1772, Oct.   11, McCardy, Nicolas, and Elizabeth Blankly.
1778, June   27, McCarougher, Charles, and Sarah Dougherty.
1794, March   10, McCarran, John, and Ann Carrol.
1778, Sept.   8, McCarter, John, and Margaret McCloud.
1799, Jan.   20, McCartha, Alice, and William Haughey.
1777, May   1, McCarty, Catharine, and Edward Shippey.
1765, July   23, McCarty, Catharine, and Jeremiah Smith.
1771, Feb.   11, McCarty, Catharine, and Samuel Walters.
1791, April   30, McCarty, Daniel, and Mary McKy.
1778, Dec.   1, McCarty, Dennis, and Ann Morris.

1776, June   27, McCarty, Dennis, and Jean Wood.
1767, Dec.   16, McCarty, Elizabeth, and Jacob Jewery.
1764, March   3, McCarty, Elleonore, and Thomas Sinnot.
1777, April 29, McCarty, George, and Honor Hodgkinson.
1760, July   14, McCarty, Hannah, and Peter String.
1766, Nov.   19, McCarty, James, and Grace Morris.
1767, June   16, McCarty, John, and Elizabeth Green.
1779, April 17, McCarty, Margarett, and Rudolph Write.
1784, Dec.   24, McCarty, Margaret, and William Smith.
1788, Oct.   8, McCarty, Mary, and Gordon O'Neal.
1778, April   5, McCarty, Mary, and Nicholas Madden.
1765, April 30, McCarty, Rebeccah, and Edward Low.
1778, Sept.   2, McCartney, Lelia, and James Quarrel.
1795, Nov.   25, McCaslin, Mary, and Claude Vionnex.
1783, Aug.   20, McCaughan, Hugh, and Charlotte Blake.
1762, Aug.   26, McCaughin, Eleonore, and William Dunlap.
1786, June   5, McCauley, Jane, and Michael Welsh.
1791, Nov.   9, McCay, Alexander, and Ann McCay.
1776, Nov.   9, McCay, Ann, and Alexander McCay.
1752, July   15, McCay, Elizabeth, and James Leaconey.
1778, July   27, McCay, James, and Sarah McYoke.
1779, April 19, McCay, John, and Catharine Nicholson.
1780, March   1, McCay, Margarett, and William Grant.
1756, March   7, McCay, William, and Mary Jonse.
1770, July   8, McCeagne, Hugh, and Mary Roads.
1794, Feb.   9, McClan, Elizabeth, and Daniel Thornton.
1793, June   8, McClanichen, Johnson, and Margery Hughes.
1790, Nov.   6, McClanigan, Agnes, and Adam Kugler.
1793, Jan.   27, McClasky, Elizabeth, and Dennis Gleeson.
1794, Sept. 25, McClasky, Isaac, and Susannah Chevaliere.
1766, July   31, McClasky, Jeane, and Jacob Walter.
1800, Jan.   3, McClasky, William, and Eleonore Cavenaugh.
1777, Sept. 19, McClatchie, William, and Ann Getshins.
1776, Sept. 10, McClean, Daniel, and Else Power.
1784, April 28, McClean, Isabella, and Alexander McGregor.
1793, July   21, McClean, Thanet and Hannah Myers.
1777, April 20, McClean, William, and Mary Dougherty.
1767, Oct.   18, McClear, James, and Mary Sinkler.
1791, May   26, McCleese, Susanna, and Alexander Johnson.
1795, May   26, McClellan, James, and Marget Snider.
1759, Dec.   12, McClellin, Ann, and James Allison.
1779, Aug.   16, McClenegen, Hugh, and Bridget Fowler.
1797, Dec.   31, McClennan, Cathrine, and Alexander Beard.
1793, April 15, McClentock, Elonore, and Mathew Hand.
1782, Dec.   17, McClery, William, and Rose Anne Ford.
1791, July   4, McCleuer Ann, and Gerry Docherthy.

1772, Feb. 27, McCleve, George, and Johannah Notter.
1782, April 16, McClish, John, and Eve Sharp.
1785, Nov. 22, McCloskey, Margaret, and James McCall.
1760, Dec. 8, McCloskey, Barbara, and John McMichael.
1779, Aug. 15, McClosky, Patrick, and Mary Wolfe.
1780. Jan. 10, McCloud, Anges, and Mary McLean.
1795, Oct. 3, McCloud, Ann, and William Power.
1780, March 9, McCloud, Catharine, and John Smith.
1795, Sept. 3, McCloud, Christiana, and William Causey.
1779, Sept. 27, McCloud, Daniel, and Mary McCloud.
1778, Sept. 3, McCloud, Donald, and Margaret Cay.
1779, Aug. 25, McCloud, Eleanor, and James Mitchelson.
1777, Dec. 10, McCloud, Eleanor, and Malcolm McDoffee.
1781, July 21, McCloud, George, and Mary Anne Homes.
1778, July 1, McCloud, John, and Hannah McKenzie.
1781, July 22, McCloud, John, and Mary Warner.
1780, Feb. 8, McCloud, Malcolm, and Margaret McCloud.
1787, Aug. 14, McCloud, Margaret, and John Lord.
1778, Sept. 8, McCloud, Margaret, and John McCarter.
1780, Feb. 8, McCloud, Margaret, and Malcolm McCloud.
1779, Sept. 27, McCloud, Mary, and Daniel McCloud.
1776, July 2, McCloud, Mary, and James Currey.
1751, Feb. 18, McCloud, Thomas, and Mary Sullivan.
1759, Nov. 27, McCloung, Robert, and Mary Coborn.
1778, May 24, McCloy, Bridget, and Robert Mills.
1795, Dec. 13, McCluer, Samuel, and Cathrine McMahon.
1783, Sept. 11, McClure, Susannah, and Samuel Graff,
1791, Oct. 19, McCoy, Nancy, and William Henderson.
1762, May 25, McColleg, Diana, and Charles Brodrick.
1775, June 12, McColley, Jean, and Peter Louney.
1790, Jan. 31, McCollister, Mary, and Patric Madan.
1760, July 14, McCollister, Robert, and Perthenea Abbet.
1777, Dec. 25, McCollock, Sarah, and John Nicoll.
1797, July 22, McCollom, John, and Marget Latimore.
1778, Feb. 1, McCollom, Mary, and James Saunders.
1758, June 25, McCollough, David, and Mary Cortis.
1758, April 26, McCollough, James, and Rachel Lewis.
1777, March 9, McCollough, Margaret, and Robert Haslet.
1800, Nov. 5, McCombe, Richard, and Sarah Peterson.
1794, Dec. 28, McCombs, Elenore, and William Wilson.
1782, July 26, McCombs, William, and Mary Wilson.
1778, Oct. 6, McCome, Jane, and Dennis McPoil.
1782, June 18, McCon, James, and Mary Kant.
1779, July 28, McConn, Frederick, and Isabella Taylor.
1775, Aug. 6, McConal, Andrew, and Mary Hicky.
1777, April 23, McConal, Elizabeth, and James Simpson.

1778, Aug.   28, McConal, Patrick, and Mary More.
1754, Sept. 16, McConall, Samuel, and Letishey Brown.
1769, Oct.   9, McConet, William, and Eleanor Sands.
1798, April   5, McConnachy, John, and Cathrine McNolche.
1791, Jan.   3, McConnel, James, and Sarah Adams.
1783, April   18, McConnel, John, and Sarah Fox.
1779, Jan.   7, McCook, Margaret, and Samuel Adams.
1765, May   29, McCorkel, Archibald, and Marchery McBreid.
1788, Oct.   11, McCorkel, Hester, and William Blake.
1798, March   25, McCorkle, William, and Cathrine Hamelin.
1757, March   8, McCormack, John, and Hannah Williams.
1775, July   29, McCormick, Andrew, and Agnes Race.
1766, April   22, McCormick, Ann, and Andrew Hayward.
1796, April   26, McCormick, Cathrine, and Darby Canna.
1796, Sept.   15, McCormick, Christiana, and John D. Campbell.
1794, May   19, McCormick, Hannah, and John Semple.
1796, June   20, McCormick, John, and Elizabeth Monney.
1799, May   25, McCormick, Laurence, and Lydia Cramsey.
1773, Oct.   27, McCormick, Mary Ann, and John Lawson.
1779, Aug.   5, McCormish, Margaret, and James McDanold.
1780, March   7, McCormish, Mary, and Anthony Dougherty.
1775, March   28, McCormish, Mary, and John Peeton.
1795, Jan.   11, McCoughley, Thomas, and Rebecca Hughs.
1794, Nov.   26, McCoumb, Charlott, and Angus McDaneeld.
1781, Oct.   5, McCowan, John, and Elizabeth Young.
1777, March   7, McCowen, Felix, and Elizabeth Yeas.
1779, March   30, McCown, James, and Margaret McFee.
1783, June   26, McCoy, Christiana, and John McKenzie.
1800, July   3, McCoy, Jane, and Jehu Springer.
1800, Dec.   13, McCoy, John, and Mary Hinderson.
1759, April   1, McCoy, John, and Mary Hughs.
1764, Nov.   7, McCoy, John, and Mary Strowd.
1799, Aug.   27, McCoy, Laurence, and Susannah Emerson.
1764, April   19, McCoy, Mary, and William Gallagher.
1796, July   6, McCoy, Patty, and William Evans.
1795, July   29, McCoy, Richard, and Hannah Haley.
1780, Jan.   25, McCoy, Sarah, and John Steward.
1767, Aug.   17, McCracken, James, and Elizabeth Morray.
1765, May   29, McCrape, Mary, and Timothy Grew,
1774, June   20, McCrea, Robert, and Ann Graytie.
1784, June   5, McCrea, William A., and Margaret Norwood.
1795, Aug.   2, McCrery, Martha, and James Greer.
1790, Sept.   20, McCuen, Ann, and Morris Quinlin.
1787, Sept.   8, McCuen, John, and Sarah Williams.
1778, Oct,   24, McCullock, Joseph, and Elizabeth Reynolds.
1758, Nov.   11, McCollough, Anne, and John Counil.

1756, Nov.   5, McCullough, Ann, and William Ballard.
1758, Dec.   12, McCullough, Barbara, and John Wayton.
1759, May   28, McCullough, Diana, and Nathaniel Petty.
1790, Aug.   26, McCullough, Jane, and Jacob Adams,
1762, Nov.   9, McCunnel, Sarah, and William West.
1788, April   1, McCurdy, Brion, and Cathrine Shafferne.
1796, Nov.   9, McCusick, John, and Jane Hylans.
1795, June   28, McCutcheon, Elizabeth, and Philip Sickle.
1795, Aug.   12, McCutcheon, James, and Eleonore McKarcher.
1783, July   31, McDair, William, and Anne Daymon.
1773, Dec.   20, McDanal, Bridget, and Lawrence Donohoo.
1779, July   19, McDanal, Elizabeth, and John Polson.
1771, Nov.   14, McDanal, Mary, and George Webster.
1774, Oct.   2, McDanal, Rebecca, and William Weekings.
1780, Feb.   17, McDanald, Catharine, and John Morrison.
1776, Oct.   13, McDanald, Christine, and Abner Lewis.
1794, Nov.   29, McDaneeld, Angus, and Charlott McCoumb.
1754, July   21, McDanel, Catharine, and James Brown.
1781, Dec.   25, McDanell, Mary, and Charles Chamberlain.
1780, March 30, McDaniel, Ann, and John Plunket.
1790, Nov.   11, McDaniel, Cathrine, and George Hannis.
1780, May   18, McDaniel, Daniel, and Catharine McGregier.
1780, April 27, McDaniel, Daniel, and Margaret McPhersin.
1767, Dec.   25, McDaniel, James, and Elizabeth McGill.
1790, Sept.   5, McDaniel, James, and Marget Maholn.
1753, Aug.   23, McDaniel, James, and Mary Green.
1769, May   15, McDaniel, James, and Mary Stead.
1773, Nov.   6. McDaniel, James, and Susanna William.
1769, Nov.   11, McDaniel, John, and Anne Dougherty.
1777, Dec.   20, McDaniel, John, and Sophia Kitner.
1763, Oct.   7, McDaniel, Rose, and Oliver Williams,
1774, Aug.   29, McDaniel, Susannah, and William More.
1780, June   18, McDanold, Christine, and Alexander Ferguson.
1780, June   22, McDanold, Daniel, and Margarett McGill.
1778, May   25, McDanold, Elizabeth, and Charles Chapman.
1778, Jan.   1, McDanold, Elizabeth, and Thomas Russel.
1779, Aug.   5, McDanold, James, and Margaret McCormish.
1754, Oct.   20, McDarmat, John, and Elizabeth Price.
1776, Sept.   8, McDarmott, Edward, and Mary Philips.
1778, March 31, McDarmouth, Catharine, and James Smith.
1780, June   12, McDarmouth, Mary, and John Strow.
1796, Nov.   7, McDavid, Patrick, and Magee Loughery.
1793, July   1, McDavid, Robert, and Mary Gould.
1789, Oct.   30, McDermat, Cornelius, and Elvira Carter.
1775, March 26, McDemond, (McDarmut,) Mary, and Joshua
                O'Hara.

1777, Dec.   10, McDoffee, Malcolm, and Eleanor McCloud.
1777, June   6, McDole, James, and Eleanor Russel.
1778, Jan.   20, McDonal, Alexander, and Elizabeth Baught.
1779, April   27, McDonald, Agnus. and —— McKever.
1779, May   28, McDonald, Alexander, and Jane McBean.
1792, June   19, McDonald, Ann, and Edward Farone.
1778, Feb.   4, McDonald, Archibald, and Mary George.
1766, Feb.   5, McDonald, Caterine, and Duncan Montgommery.
1781, Nov.   5, McDonald, Charles, and Mary Anderson.
1778, May   23, McDonald, Christine, and Alexander McKenzie.
1773, April   19, McDonald, Hugh, and Hannah Sheppard.
1778, Nov.   17, McDonald, Hugh, and Mary Revel.
1778, June   8, McDonald, Isabella, and Alexander McKenzie.
1774, June   25, McDonald, John, and Mary Davis.
1751, Feb.   18, McDonald, John, and Mary Orane.
1779, July   21, McDonald, Mary, and Edward Crews.
1799. Dec.   2, McDonald, Mary, and John Lancaster.
1778, April   28, McDonald, Mary, and Peter McLaughlin.
1765, Sept.   17, McDonald, William, and Elizabeth Sterling.
1778, Sept.   20, McDonalds, James, and Margaret Hughes.
1777, Nov.   5, McDondlet, Benjamin, and Bridget Watts.
1792, Oct.   10, McDonegh, Mary, and Daniel Murphey.
1800, Jan.   5, McDonell, James, and Cathrine Glen.
1770, Oct.   14, McDonnell, Edmond, and Margarett Loid.
1764, Dec.   19, McDonold, Patrick, and Sarah Scutt.
1778, June   2, McDonold, Sidney, and John Palfrey.
1790, April   5, McDonough, Cathrine, and William Starrett.
1778, March   15, McDonough, Thomas, and Sarah Callwell.
1798, April   28, McDouel, Archibald, and Mary Bartley.
1799, Jan.   17, McDouel, George, and Mary Hyberg.
1791, Dec.   29, McDougal, Elenore, and Michael Toy.
1794, Aug.   14, McDougan, Mary, and Francis Moore.
1798, June   21, McDowel, Hugh, and Mary Sutton.
1794, Nov.   21, McDowel, Robert, and Cathrine Morrow.
1753, Oct.   18, McElhenny, James, and Prudence Garaway.
1757, May   12, McEmson, George, and Deborah Yocum.
1779, Nov.   26, McFadgin, John, and Mary Dunlap.
1782, May   27, McFall, Catherine, and James Neagle.
1780, Sept.   10, McFall, James, and Mary Williams.
1797, Dec.   12, McFarden, Eleonore, and Samuel David Legrand.
1782, March   26, McFarland, Alexander, and Martha Young.
1778, Oct.   13, McFarland, Alexander, and Mary Onie.
1796, Aug.   23, McFarlane, Andrew, and Jane Liddle.
1795, May   11, McFarlane, Robert, and Hannah Sutton.
1793, June   8, Mcfarlen, Abigail, and David Napier.
1755, Dec.   16, McFarlin, Abigael, and John Rivo.

1796, Nov. 20, McFee, James, and Mary Connor.
1779, March 30, McFee, Margaret, and James McCown.
1779, Nov. 10, McFelin, Mary, and Nicholas Meyer.
1779, April 2, McFerson, John, and Margarett McKensey.
1778, Oct. 15, McGahey, Mary, and Paul McGowring.
1778, Aug. 16, McGard, William, and Sarah Young.
1782, Aug. 13, McGarn, Anne, and James Mills.
1774, Oct. 27, McGeary, Roger, and Ann Carrol.
1800, Aug. 27, McGee, Dennis, and Biddy McGown.
1794, Dec. 8, McGee, John, and Ann Monc.
1775, June 14, McGee, John, and Elizabeth Archibald.
1799, Jan. 1, McGee, Richard, and Elizabeth McKenzie.
1779, Jan. 17, McGee, Ruth, and William Banden.
1778, Sept. 19, McGee, Sarah, and John Smith.
1798, June 9, McGenley, Sarah, and Michael Carr.
1797, June 25, McGerthy, Patric, and Cathrine Loyd.
1776, June 9, McGihan, Jean, and John Henery.
1794, Sept. 9, McGill, Ann, and Jeremiah Stow.
1775, Oct. 14, McGill, Ann, and William Williams.
1782, Aug. 27, McGill, Eleonor, and Morris Burns.
1767, Dec. 25, McGill, Elizabeth, and James McDaniel.
1780, Jan. 12, McGill, Elizabeth, and John Tayler.
1766, April 15, McGill, James, and Ester Black.
1779, June 13, McGill, John, and Ann Griggery.
1797, June 8, McGill, Latitia, and Fredrick Finkbine.
1780, June 22, McGill, Margarett, and Daniel McDanold.
1780, April 1, McGill, Margaret, and Patrick Riley.
1782, Sept. 15, McGill, Margret, and Samuel Wallerade.
1792, Nov. 28, McGill, Sarah, and John Carney.
1779, Dec. 15, McGiltin, James, and Barbara Boon.
1782, June 3, McGilton, George, and Anne Shaw.
1795, June 23, McGindel, Fanny, and William Norris.
1767, March 31, McGineys, Patrick, and Prudence Hay.
1778, May 31, McGinn, Sarah, and James Stokes.
1789, June 25, McGinnis, Helena, and John Hill.
1777, March 12, McGinnis, James, and Mary Noble.
1777, March 6, McGinnis, John, and Margaret Woodbridge.
1789, July 23, McGinnis, Mary Ann, and Michael Tailor.
1778, May 11, McGlaghney, Mary, and Henry Monroe.
1796, Sept. 23, McGlathery, William, and Jane Barthelson.
1795, Jan. 21, McGloghlin, Sarah, and Charles McCalla.
1781, Nov. 22, McGloughlin, Anne, and Michael Morrison.
1761, Jan. 18, McGloughling, Mary, and John Shafford.
1758, May 20, McGochene, Mary, and James Rosk.
1795, Feb. 4, McGonnigel, John, and Biddy Brislin.
1775, Aug. 7, McGoveren, Mary, and William Wood.

1800, Aug.   27, McGowen, Biddy, and Dennis McGee.
1795, May   5, McGowen, Jane, and John O'Connor.
1792, Oct.   2, McGowen, John, and Jane Smith.
1778, Oct.   15, McGowring, Paul, and Mary McGahey.
1757, June   26, McGrager, John, and Jane Barnhill.
1783, March 11, McGragger, Mary, and John White.
1777, Jan.   11, McGrah, Ann, and Jacob Nathan.
1765, Oct.   21, McGrah, Margaret, and John Egan.
1772, Feb.   16, McGratch, Michael, and Ann Keys.
1761, April   6, McGraugh, Catharine, and Owen Daly.
1782, May   1, McGraw, Alexander, and Eleonor Smith.
1780, Feb.   8, McGray, Margaret, and Canady McPharlin.
1781, Oct.   25, McGregger, Margaret, and Hugh Fresier.
1780, May   18, McGregier, Catharine, and Daniel McDaniel.
1784, April 28, McGregor, Alexander, and Isabella McClean.
1780, April   4, McGregor, Richard, and Mary Hays.
1794, Jan.   12, McGrigger, Cathrine, and Timothy Linnot.
1793, June   9, McGriggor, Alexander, and Mary Fullen.
1788, April 18, McGrigree, Marget, and William Nicoll.
1793, Oct.   26, McGroty, James, and Sarah Moss.
1782, March 29, McGuire, Catherine, and John Duty.
1796, Feb.   22, McGuire, Nancy, and Thomas Edel.
1794, May   8, McIlvoy, Mary, and Patric Mahoney.
1800, Oct.   3, McIlwan, Thomas, and Christiana Stuart.
1770, Sept.   2, McIntire, Hugh, and Elizabeth Pierce.
1772, July   5, McIntire, Jean, and Mathew Shaw.
1778, Aug.   2, McIntire, John, and Hannah Callaghan.
1794, Nov.   5, McIntire, William, and Hannah Levering.
1767, Feb.   27, McIntosh, Robert, and Margret Roseby.
1766, April 28, McJine, Isabella, and James O'Dannil.
1790, June   27, McKagghan, Elizabeth, and George Rudolph.
1779, April   1, McKaige, Edward, and Sarah White.
1778, April   1, McKalop, John, and Latitia Rue.
1796, Aug.   12, McKarcher, Eleonore, and James McCutcheon.
1775, Sept. 19, McKeag, George, and Christiana Johnston.
1795, Feb.   6, McKean, Ann, and William Whetherly.
1796, July   10, McKean, Hannah, and William Ryan.
1759, Nov.   9, McKean, James, and Margeth Alexander.
1799, Feb.   23, McKean, Nancy, and Thomas Robertson.
1795, May   13, McKean, Rachel, and John Glasco.
1797, May   17, McKean, Rebecca, and Alexander McCally.
1782, Jan.   8, McKeansy, Henry, and Jean Harrison.
1793, Oct.   8, McKechin, John, and Nancy Simson.
1786, Sept. 24, McKee, Mary, and Hugh McKillep.
1777, Nov.   28, McKee, William, and Rebecca Darby.
1779, Jan.   15, McKegney, Hugh, and Margaret Bartley.

1785, Nov. 28, McKeicken, Jane, and George Rudolph.
1780, Jan. 20, McKelher, Mary, and Andrew McCalton.
1778, Aug. 19, McKendrick, Archibald, and Rosetta Broomfield.
1754, Oct. 15, McKenmin, Mary Ann, and Robert Park.
1794, Jan.   8, McKenna, Michael, and Mary Morris.
1777, Jan. 19, McKenney, Kenneday, and Catharine Toy.
1779, April 2, McKensey, Margaret, and John McFerson.
1770, Sept. 17, McKensey, Mary, and George Ister.
1776, Nov. 26, McKenzie, Alexander, and Ann Smith.
1778, May   23, McKenzie, Alexander, and Christine McDonald.
1778, June   8, McKenzie, Alexander, and Isabella McDonald.
1780, May   11, McKenzie, Alleck, and Margery McKenzie.
1799, Jan.   1, McKenzie, Elizabeth, and Richard McGee.
1778, July   1, McKenzie, Hannah, and John McCloud.
1777, Dec.   5, McKenzie, Isabella, and Alexander Grauch.
1783, June 26, McKenzie, John, and Christiana McCoy.
1780, May   11, McKenzie, Margery, and Alleck McKenzie.
1792, Oct. 10, McKenzy, Cathrine, and Alexander McKy, or Mc-
                Coy.
1781, Aug.   2, McKetrick, Anne, and John Usher.
1779, April 27, McKever, ——, and Agnus McDonald.
1779, May   15, McKever, John, and Jemima Flower.
1798, May   12, McKew, Daniel, and Martha Andrews.
1794, May   13, McKew, Jane, and Garet Fitzgerald.
1761, Sept. 28, McKey, Alexander, and Sarah Jefferys.
1800, Sept. 1, McKey, Eliza, and David Chilcott.
1799, June 10, McKicken, Jane, and John Wallington.
1786, Sept. 24, McKillep, Hugh, and Mary McKee.
1779, Nov. 29, McKim, John, and Sarah Edge.
1763, June   1, McKinlay, William, and Mary Siplin.
1792, Dec.   4, McKinley, Daniel, and Hanna Cook.
1788, July   1, McKinley, John, and Anne Galaspey.
1753, Oct. 16, McKinley, John, and Jane Jonse.
1779, May   20, McKinley, John, and Mary Caldwell.
1777, Nov. 28, McKinley, Martha, and Blekey Hartley.
1778, May   7, McKinney, Ann, and William Allan.
1765, Feb.   6, McKinney, James, and Mary Jordan.
1779, Sept. 25, McKinnon, Roderick, and Rachel Hamilton.
1778, Dec.   1, McKinsey, Thomas, and Mary Johnson.
1796, March 3, McKintosh, Neal, and Isabella McQuin.
1777, Nov. 30, McKinzie, William, and Margaret Hinderson.
1783, Feb. 23, McKlan, Daniel, and Hannah Collins.
1763, Aug. 25, McKleen, Samuel, and Hannah Scull.
1773, May   2, McKnary, John, and Johannah Keaton.
1777, Jan. 19, McKnear, John, and Elizabeth Jagerin.
1795, Dec. 24, McKoy, George, and Mary Evel.

1792, Oct.   10, McKy or McCoy, Alexander, and Catherine Mc Kenzy.

1791, April   30, McKy, Mary, and Daniel McCarty

1782, Feb.   18, McLaine, William, and Dorothea Head. (Free negroes.)

1764, June   13, McLanachan, Samuel, and Agnes Young.

1783, April   10, McLane, John, and Anne Barret.

1764, April   22, McLarhan, John, and Margaret Williamson.

1765, April   9, McLarkey, Michael, and Onera Magown.

1764, Dec.   19, McLaughlan, William, and Mary Dimley.

1794, June   3, McLaughlin, Elizabeth, and John Creswell.

1796, Oct.   12, McLaughlin, James, and Bridget Loury.

1778, Nov.   5, McLaughlin, Jane, and Casper Isralo.

1778, July   30, McLaughlin, John, and Sarah Cook.

1774, Feb.   24, McLaughlin, Mary, and John Butler.

1778, April   28, McLaughlin, Peter, and Mary McDonald.

1792, May   22, McLawrin, Daniel, and Mary Betzel.

1765, May   29, McLavery, Elizabeth, and Thomas Dunn.

1771, Jan.   12, McLean, Adam, and Elizabeth Cherry.

1777, May   19, McLean, Allan, and Elizabeth Stockman.

1777, Feb.   1, McLean, Isabella, and Peter Anderson.

1778, June   4, McLean, Laughlin, and Elizabeth Power.

1780, Jan.   11, McLean, Mary, and Anges McCloud.

1796, Feb.   26, McLean, William, and Marget Howel.

1787, Oct.   24, McLease, Sarah, and John Martin.

1778, Nov.   8, McLeland, David, and Hannah Gallougher.

1781, July   10, McLeod, Jenny, and Norman McLeod.

1781, July   10, McLeod, Norman, and Jenny McLeod.

1794, March   5, McLeroy, Hugh, and Mary Cauglin.

1794, March   5, McLeroy, Hugh, and Mary Coughlin.

1781, Sept.   4, McLocklaine, Jenny, and William Kalley.

1793, Nov.   17, McLochlin, William, and Jane Greenwood.

1772, Nov.   13, McLouglan, Sarah, and William Jenkins.

1798, July   4, McLoughlin, Daniel, and Susanna McLouglin.

1789, July   19, McLoughlin, John, and Anne O'Hara.

1798, July   4, McLoughlin, Susanna, and Daniel McLoughlin.

1778, May   24, McLouglen, John, and Elizabeth Ross.

1757, Nov.   16, McMackin, Terrance, and Elizabeth Dodd.

1776, Oct.   14, McMaham, Elizabeth, and Nicholas Tudor.

1780, Jan.   17, McMahan, Sarah, and William Ponder.

1795, Dec.   13, McMahon, Cathrine, and Samuel McCluer.

1753, Oct.   2, McMahonh, Margret, and Daniel Mannon.

1767, March   23, McMan, Armas, and Mary Packet.

1784, May   4, McMannan, Elizabeth, and James Gilmer.

1782, Oct.   12, McMasters, John, and Elizabeth Boxon.

1782, Oct.   22, McMasters, Margret, and John Fanighans.

1777, Oct.   28, McMean, James, and Elizabeth Hart.
1766, Sept.   10, McMichael, Alexander, and Martha Johnson.
1759, July   9, McMichael, Jeane, and James Smith.
1760, Dec.   8, McMichal, John, and Barbara McCloskoy.
1764, March 20, McMichal, Walter, and Jane McCalley.
1799, Aug.   29, McMichel, Elizabeth, and James Clark.
1758, Nov.   8, McMin, Joseph, and Prudence More.
1766, Oct.   14, McMolley, Catharine, and Neal Leviston.
1754, Feb.   19, McMollin, Elizabeth, and John Johnson·
1771, Oct.   24, McMulan, Archibald, and Theodocia Dillahunt.
1777, Nov.   24, McMullan, James, and Ann Lowrey.
1796, Nov.   3, McMullen, Isabella, and James Dougherty.
1795, Jan.   21, McMullen, John, and Elizabeth Campbell.
1794, April   12, McMullen, John, and Martha Glen.
1798, July   29, McMullen, Susannah, and William Stuart.
1777, April   30, McMullen, Thomas, and Ann Regem.
1755, April   21, McMullin, William, and Margaret Brooks.
1778, June   2, McMurren, Mary, and William Calverley.
1777, Dec.   23, McNail, Mary, and Michael Ryan.
1781, Oct.   19, McNair, Christiane, and John Stephens.
1777, Dec.   19, McNair, William, and Ann Pierce.
1778, May   23, McNarnara, Bridgeth, and Andrew Elder.
1774, Sept.   11, McNeal, Elizabeth, and Joseph Cravet.
1796, April   23, McNeal, Gracey, and Patric Cacharin.
1758, Nov.   22, McNeal, John, and Mary Taylor.
1786, Jan.   1, McNeal, Mary, and John Buchannan.
1766, July   29, McNeel, Lydia, and John Vaughn.
1777, June   17, McNeil, Lawrence, and Susannah Tillman.
1778, April   8, McNobb, Duncan, and Mary Farrel.
1798, April   5, McNolche, Cathrine, and John McConnachy.
1791, Oct.   9, McNourghton, Alexander, and Jane Watson.
1778, Feb.   16, McOwen, John, and Mary Helviston.
1789, July   7, McPhale, Jennet, and John Monroe.
1780, Feb.   8, McPharlin Canady, and Margaret McGray.
1780, Jan.   13, McPharlin, John, and Susannah Thompson.
1779, Nov.   22, McPharlin, Mary, and John Braidy.
1782, April   3, McPharson, Jeaney, and John Stag.
1782, March 14, McPhearson, Jeany, and Michael Borne.
1780, April   27, McPhersin, Margaret, and Daniel McDaniel.
1778, Sept.   27, McPherson, Jane, and Mary Fennemore.
1778, Jan.   1, McPherson, Jane, and Thomas Falkner.
1773, Oct.   25, McPherson, Jean, and James Stewart.
1779, June   2, McPherson, Margarett, and Edmund Harris.
1778, Oct.   6, McPoil, Dennis, and Jane McCome.
1795, June   28, McPollin, Cathrine, and Samuel Huy, (or Hugh.)
1795, Oct.   3, McQuillen, Robert, and Susannah Hoffman.

1793, Dec. 13, McQuillin, Cathrine, and Andrew Boyd.
1772, March 2, McQuiln, Rolind, and Eleanor Reardon.
1796, March 3, McQuin, Isabella, and Neal McKintosh.
1791, July 12, McQuire, Andrew, and Hanna Forset.
1772, Sept. 27, McQuire, William, and Elizabeth Thomas.
1796, June 25, McQuittrich, Cathrine, and Jonathan Greenuhick.
1776, Dec. 10, McQuoan, James, and Ann Dunlap.
1794, July 23, McRan, Isabella, and Samuel Campbell.
1778, May 11, McRacken, Archibald, and Margaret Morgan.
1783, March 27, McRoulan, Jeremiah, and Rebecca Helmes.
1775, Nov. 19, McServey, Thomas, and Mary Philips.
1757, June 29, McVaugh, Catharine, and Job Walton.
1779, Aug. 9, McWecker, Patrick, and Elizabeth Turner.
1775, Aug. 17, McWigans, Michael, and Mary Philips.
1778, Jan. 11, McWilliams, Mary Ann, and Dugal Kennedy.
1778, July 27, McYoke, Sarah, and James McCay.
1764, June 27, McYoung, Elizabeth, and George Hackett.
1766, Dec. 16, Mea, Hannah, and Richard Reyl.
1765, Feb. 6, Meacock, Edward, and Mary Wilson.
1777, Dec. 20, Mead, John, and Hannah Feudrick.
1763, Dec. 22, Mead, Mary, and Nicholas Nienus.
1790, Aug. 5, Mead. Seth, and Rachel Bolston.
1772, Dec. 6, Meady Rodgerd, and Elizabeth Tolbert.
1800, Jan. 1, Means, John, and Sarah Kid.
1783, Jan. 17, Meany, Elsey, and Richard Bennit.
1776, Aug. 26, Mearess, Mary, and James Stevenson.
1766, Sept. 28, Mearit, Henry, and Dianah Queen.
1781, Dec. 20, Mears, John, and Anne Donohow.
1778, Aug. 31, Mears, William, and Sarah Davis.
1787, Sept. 24, Meckelburg, Charles, and Elizabeth Zeames.
1752, Nov. 10, Mecleland, Christiana, and Thomas Hill.
1779, May 23, Mecumber, Humphrey, and Catherine Fees.
1792, Oct. 3, Mee, Hannah, and Thomas Musgrove.
1755, May 24, Mee, William, and Elizabeth Evans.
1755, July 29, Meed, Henry, and Mary Smith.
1752, Aug. 30, Meedwinter, Anne, and James Linch.
1758, Sept. 18, Meek, Richard, and Grace Darb.
1782, July 28, Megee, Mary, and Daniel Martin.
1777, Aug. 4, Megomery, Mary, and Jeremiah Thomson.
1770, Sept. 24, Mejer, Jacob, and Mary Stenson.
1768, Sept. 24, Mejer, Lewis, and Mary Scott.
1796, Nov. 12, Melchoa, Louisa Charlotta, and Anders Hindricson.
1792, June 20, Melchor, Margret, and John Ashton.
1787, Feb. 9, Melean, Owen, and Anne Carr.
1777, Sept. 13, Melleth, John, and Eleanor Fitzgerald.

1793, Jan.   8, Mellin, Elizabeth, and Robert Moody.
1760, June   2, Mellin, George, and Christiana Lindemeyer.
1766, Oct.   27, Mellinnix, Ann, and Thomas Jones.
1799, Nov.   28, Melly, Ann, and Robert Connelly.
1772, Dec.   10, Meloy, Elenor, and Jacob Cooper.
1792, April 12, Melrard, Margret, and Robert Allen.
1783, March 11, Melzerd, John, and Margret Archibald.
1783, Oct.   16, Meng, Dorothy, and Hugh Ogden.
1776, Dec.   21, Menice, John, and Christine Grant.
1768, Nov.   17, Menon, Grace, and Jacob Wagner.
1798, March 23, Mentzy, Christiana, and James Hart.
1763, Nov.   12, Mercer, Nathaniel, and Ann Bays.
1791, Oct.   18, Merchant, John, and Ann Mitchel.
1799, Sept. 11, Merchant, John, and Jane Calder.
1790, June   7, Meredith, Daniel, and Ann Turner.
1792, Aug.   16, Merion, Ruth, and Thomas Hooper.
1778, Jan.   26, Meroney, Catharine, and George Craig.
1778, Aug.   13, Merret, Peter, and Elizabeth Bazeley.
1777, Nov.   23, Merret, Robert, and Margaret Boyd.
1793, Nov.   25, Merrey, David, and Mary Maclean.
1790, Feb.   25, Merric, Joshua, and Ann Porter.
1798, May   28, Merric, Joshua, and Elizabeth Boon.
1791, July   21, Merric, Robert, and Susanna Allen.
1788, Oct.   4, Merrin, Mary, aud Daniel Guyry.
1796, Aug.   18, Merriot, Stacy, and Elizabeth Turner.
1792, Feb.   15, Merrywhether, Elizabeth, and Abraham Smith.
1761, Sept. 19, Mersdy, Ann, and Thomas Jones.
1755, Dec.   1, Mersor, Jane, and William Atherton.
1789, May   4, Messersmith, Christina, and Henry Hilger.
1798, July   22, Metch, John, and Eleonore Olenberg.
1782, June   20, Metier, John, and Catharine Taylor.
1795, April 13, Metsger, Cathrine, and Elisha Morris.
1783, Sept. 16, Metton, Ruth, and Jacob Burns.
1793, March 10, Metts, John, and Mary Dorse.
1791, Jan.   11, Metts, Mary, and John Hoover.
1766, May   13, Meyer, Albert, and Barbara Stanberry.
1777, May   4, Meyer, Barbarah, and George Garrett.
1760, June   2, Meyer, Elizabeth, and Frederick Fentle.
1779, Jan.   26, Meyer, Jacob, and Rebecca Fatherine.
1761, July   19, Meyer, Lorentz, and Ann Margeth Werkingen.
1775, Dec.   27, Meyer, Margaret, and Frederick Miller.
1779, Nov.   10, Meyer, Nicholas, and Mary McFelin.
1766, April 23, Meyers, Deborrah, and John Power.
1771, March   9, Meyers, Elizabeth, and Joseph Fry.
1771, March 10, Meyers, Jacob, and Mary Preston.
1767, April   7, Meyers, Margaret, and Thomas Boris.

1780, March 17, Meyers, Mary, and William Shepherd.
1779, Aug. 15, Meyers, Sarah, and John Schrack.
1795, Jan. 10, Michael, John, and Ann Mary Musgrove.
1776, Nov. 14, Michelson, James, and Grissel Smith.
1772, Dec. 22, Mickell, Catharine, and Andrew Lock.
1776, Oct. 21, Micker Rosannah, and Jacob Stow.
1792, Nov.   1, Micklin, George, and Cathrine Rowland.
1772, Aug. 13, Middagh, George, and Rachel Romberg.
1797, Feb. 25, Middagh, John, and Margret Bowles.
1776, Aug. 25, Middleton, Edward, and Rachel Archer.
1786, Nov.   3, Middleton, Nathan, and Mary Turner.
1791, June   1, Middleton, Rachel, and Abel Anderson.
1762, May   27, Middleton, Rebecca, and Robert Nixon.
1767, Sept. 21, Middleton, Rebeccah, and William Milligan.
1794, July 17, Middleton, William, and Dorcas Johnston.
1799, Sept. 28, Middleton, Rachel, and William Dilmer.
1796, Oct. 29, Middleton, Dorcas, and John Reed.
1794, Dec. 30, Middleton, Elenore, and John Heney.
1764, Jan.   1, Midleton, ——, and Jonathan Ward.
1795, March 6, Midleton, Mary, and Philip Lance.
1778, June 25, Midleton, Rachel, and John Deacon.
1799, Jan. 22, Miedskie, Johan Sam, and Ann Obermüller.
1798, April 17, Mier, Henry, and Mary Zeller.
1793, May   12, Miers, Hanna Carolina, and Thomas Eveans.
1789, Dec.   2, Miers, John, and Mary Jones.
1800, May   4, Miers, John, and Nelly Abbet.
1791, Jan. 23, Miers, Lewis, and Jane Brewster.
1790, Nov.   4, Miers, Nathaniel, and Sidney Adams.
1796, June 12, Miers, Sarah, and Christian Holland.
1797, July   5, Miers, Sarah, and Zephania Hopper.
1771, Dec. 15, Miesner, George, and Sarah Hall.
1762, Dec. 10, Mikesner, John, and Ann Hutchinson.
1776, March 11, Miland, Salmo, and Margaret Bukerin.
1799, April 25, Milbank, Samuel, and Elisa Farmer.
1794, Oct. 31, Milberry, Joseph, and Lydia Jackson.
1778, May   1, Mildrid, Richard, and Eleanor Morphey.
1788, July 21, Miles, Anne, and John Lighton.
1785, June   9, Miles, Henry, and Sarah Coggle.
1778, April 13, Miles, Isabella, and John Whittham.
1750, Dec.   3, Miles, Joseph, and Anne Nesmith.
1754, Sept. 14, Miles, Joseph, and Susanna Moore.
1782, May   23, Miles, Marassah, and Catherine Wilson.
1790, March 1, Miles, Nathaniel, and Mary Frick.
1788, Oct.   4, Miles, Richard, and Mary King.
1752, Nov.   4, Miles, Ruth, and William Lewis.
1794, April 21, Miles, Samuel, and Rosamon Lewis.

1783, Feb. 21, Miles, Sarah, and George Siders.
1758, Nov. 11, Millane, Lydia, and Anthony Duchee, Jr.
1773, Dec. 19, Millburn, Mary, and Adam Stone.
1798, April 16, Millegan, Elizabeth, and William Green.
1781, March 24, Millener, Isaac, and Hannah Hutson.
1780, June 20, Millet, Benjamin. and Phoebe Burkett.
1759, Feb. 7, Miller, Alexander, and Ann Scott.
1769, Nov. 5, Miller, Andrew, and Catharine Flammen.
1781, Dec. 13, Miller, Anne, and Friedric Hiney.
1777, Aug. 28, Miller, Ann, and James Brown.
1791, March 10, Miller, Ann, and Samuel Reed.
1777, Nov. 20, Miller, Ann, and William Rex.
1755, April 7, Miller, Barbara, and Anthony Butler.
1796, July 28, Miller, Barbara. and John Still.
1765, April 9, Miller, Catharine, and John Church.
1779, Feb. 23, Miller, Catherine, and Daniel Yoman.
1776, Dec. 1, Miller, Charles, and Barbara Shrank.
1800, Dec. 1, Miller, Charles, and Margret More.
1766, Feb. 10, Miller, Christiana, and James Dawson.
1776, July 14, Miller, Christiana, and William Purdey.
1779, Feb. 2, Miller, Conrad, and Margaret Crasskup.
1779, Oct. 15, Miller, David, and Ann Reading.
1766, July 3, Miller, Eleanor, and Hezekiah Hutchinson.
1792, Oct. 28, Miller, Elizabeth, and John Evans.
1795, June 15, Miller, Elizabeth, and John Rogers.
1794, Aug. 19, Miller, Elizabeth, and Samuel Clark.
1775, Dec. 27, Miller, Frederick, and Margaret Meyer.
1781, June 27, Miller, George, and Anne Hoen.
1783, July 18, Miller, George, and Sarah Bakeoven.
1769, June 30, Miller, Hannah, and Zachariah Lambert.
1755, Nov. 23, Miller, Hennery, and Catharine Quig.
1780, May 18, Miller, Henry, and Catharine Bash.
1759, July 4, Miller, Henry, and Rebeccah Calyard.
1778, Feb. 3, Miller, Hugh, and Mary Cau.
1779, May 31, Miller, James, and Ann Campbell.
1788, May 21, Miller, James, and Sarah Stream.
1794, Sept. 3, Miller, Jane, and John Martin
1772, March 1, Miller, John, and Catharine Wellsin.
1796, April 17, Miller, John, and Eleonore O'Donnel.
1758, Feb. 19, Miller, John, and Judith Smith.
1787, Oct. 17, Miller, John, and Mary Dermott.
1778, April 29, Miller, John, and Mary Robeson.
1774, Aug. 8, Miller, John, and Mary Savage.
1798, April 17, Miller, John, and Rebecca Morton.
1776, May 6, Miller, John, and Susannah Cisty.
1788, April 1, Miller, Joseph, and Elizabeth Conaway.

1759, Sept. 11, Miller, Joseph, and Mary Huff.
1780, May 20, Miller, Margaret, and James Davis.
1768, March 3, Miller, Marget, James Davis.
1766, April 23, Miller, Margret, and Jonathan Hanson.
1783, Nov. 10, Miller, Margret, and Lewis Besayade.
1756, June 30, Miller, Martha, and Thomas Cookson.
1781, June 28, Miller, Martin, and Catharine Misher.
1764, Nov. 22, Miller, Martin, and Susannah Peihin.
1778, May 19, Miller, Mary, and Alexander Thomson.
1795, July 3, Miller, Mary, and James King.
1777, April 24, Miller, Mary, and John Allcock.
1791, July 24, Miller, Mary, and John Barkley.
1799, May 23, Miller, Mary, and John Barry.
1779, March 10, Miller, Mary, and John Flaherty.
1752, Jan. 19, Miller, Mary, and John Lawrence.
1790, Oct. 25, Miller, Mary, and Peter Smith.
1777, Feb. 9, Miller, Mary, and Thomas Dryden.
1796, May 28, Miller, Mary, and William Jones.
1764, Sept. 9, Miller, Michael, and Dorothea Dibert.
1783, May 16, Miller, Peter, and Martha Wright.
1794, Aug. 23, Miller, Rebecca, and Ezeckiel Simkins.
1766, April 28, Miller, Ruth, and Jehu Ward.
1796, Feb. 16, Miller, Sarah, and John Robertson.
1795, May 20, Miller, Sarah, and Thomas Wood.
1794, Nov. 9, Miller, Simon, and Mary Hoffman.
1779, Feb. 20, Miller, Susannah, and Benjamin Snodgrass.
1784, April 13, Miller, Susannah, and Stephen Pater.
1798, May 29, Miller, Thomas, and Elizab. Jemmington.
1799, Jan. 26, Miller, William, and Sarah Bridge.
1760, Jan. 3, Milles, Ann, and Amos Bell.
1794, Oct. 12, Milles, John, and Ann Andrews.
1794, Feb. 3, Milligan, Philip, and Mary Keaton.
1767, Sept. 21, Milligan, William, and Rebeccah Middleton.
1792, Jan. 2, Milliman, Ann, and Andrew Gilchrist.
1783, Sept. 25, Millinor, Frances, and Peter Evans.
1782, Oct. 19, Millis, John, and Esther Cole.
1783, Oct. 30, Millner, Maria, and John Blandford.
1757, March 3, Millor, John, and Ann Fand.
1789, Sept. 7, Mills, Isabel, and James Insworth.
1782, Aug. 13, Mills, James, and Anne McGarn.
1793, Aug. 22, Mills, John, and Sarah Armstrong.
1758, Feb. 6, Mills, Mary, and Lewis Hensell.
1778, May 24, Mills, Robert, and Bridget McCloy.
1775, May 27, Millward, Samuel, and Ann Waters.
1763, Nov. 30, Millward, Thomas, and Elizabeth Sears.
1754, Jan. 19, Milner, Mary, and William Peters.

1789, April	30, Milnor, Martha, and Anthony Van Mannierch.
1796, June	9, Mincer, Joseph, and Elizabeth Rigley.
1779, April	22, Minch, Margaret, and John Winents.
1779, Aug.	10, Mines, Peter, and Ann Brailey.
1795, Sept.	20, Minfie, Christopher, and Mary Baker.
1791, April	9, Ming, Mary, and James Davis.
1781, Sept.	11, Mingen, Margaret, and Jesse Cravinger.
1759, May	16, Minister, Nicholas, and Olive Titus.
1796, July	24, Mink, Eliza, and Casper Iser Svan.
1794, Aug.	13, Mink, Hanna, and Andrew Penton.
1797, Nov.	16, Minot, John, and Elizabeth Harper.
1800, May	28, Minter, Mary, and James Digences.
1761, April	29, Min Tock, Lachen, and Mary Fearbrother.
1799, July	4, Minton, Mary, and Robert Hill.
1778, June	3, Minzer, Jane, and George Gold.
1789, March 23, Minzey, Alexander, and Catharine West.
1781, June	28, Misher, Catharine, and Martin Miller.
1758, April	3, Mishow John, and Elizabeth Braine.
1779, Jan.	27, Mishurt, Catharine, and Thomas Duff.
1791, Oct.	18, Mitchel, Ann, and John Merchant.
1796, Feb.	28, Mitchel, Cathrine, and Nathaniel Gorsslin.
1793, June	27, Mitchel, Edah, and Abraham Yocum.
1755, Oct.	28, Mitchel, Elizabeth, and Richard Griss.
1798, Aug.	2, Mitchel, Elizab. and William Brown.
1794, May	20, Mitchel, Frances, and John Gregory.
1792, Nov.	12, Mitchel, Francis, (free black,) and Ruth Vendine,
		(free mulatto.)
1794, Oct.	13, Mitchel James, and Maria Elizab. Walker.
1796, Nov.	5, Mitchel, Rosanna, and Lewis Yard.
1797, July	16, Mitchel Samuel, and Hannah Parsons.
1796, March 26, Mitchel, Sarah, and George Hallman.
1773, Aug.	9, Mitchel, Simon and Rosanna Pates.
1792, July	31, Mitchel, Walter, and Elizabeth Hudson.
1778, Oct.	21, Mitchell, Ann, and John Estens.
1765, Feb.	24, Mitchel, Jossuah, and Jeane Carrot.
1779, April	29, Mitchell, Rudolph, and Elizabeth Larner.
1779, Aug.	25, Mitchelson, James, and Eleanor McCloud.
1776, July	16, Mitslef, Ann, and Henery Gollinger.
1786, Dec.	24, Mittear, Catherine, and Richard Bowen.
1754, July	17, Moars, William, and Elizabeth Brooks.
1778, Sept.	11, Mock, Rosannah, and Henry Zipeley.
1776, Dec.	31, Mockeston, Dorothy, and John Scott.
1776, Oct.	22, Modlin, Mary, and Francis Stewart.
1799, Nov.	31, Moeller, John, and Elizabeth Shillingsford.
1769, Dec.	1, Moffet, Thomas, and Sarah Willson.
1780, March 16, Moffin, Catherine, and Israel Mattson.

1759, Feb.   5, Mogrow, Sarah, and George Speer.
1793, Nov.   17, Mohollin, Mary, and James Sergeant.
1788, March 10, Moines, Thomas, and Catharine More.
1794, April   10, Moist, John, and Elizabeth Powel.
1755, Dec.   25, Molhren, Charles, and Christiana Esley.
1793, May   27, Moliere, Lewis, and Sarah Brogen.
1781, Oct.   17, Molledore, George, and Elizabeth Kemer.
1782, Jan.   3, Mollen, Anne, and Henry Whiteman.
1782, Oct.   15, Mollen, Martha, and Paul Establier.
1783, Jan.   7, Mollen, Mary, and Thomas Wilkins.
1797, Sept.   23, Mollicom, Maria, and William Brynes.
1765, Dec.   9, Mollidore, Elizabeth, and Henrich Ernsdorf.
1754, Aug.   18, Mollin, Daniel, and Catharine White.
1778, March   8, Molly, John, and Mary Williams.
1781, Nov.   19, Molrow, Anne, and Gefferey Clark.
1757, Sept.   21, Molton, Benjamin, and Catharine Shellock.
1794, April   19, Molton, Sarah, and Simon Coley Bailey.
1797, Dec.   10, Momas, Eleonore, and Nicholas Andrew Schrope.
1794, Dec.   8, Monc Ann, and John McGee.
1776, Aug.   29, Monery, John, and Catharine Springer.
1753, June   11, Money, Elizabeth, and Joseph Edmonds.
1781, Nov.   1, Mongan, Juley, and Thomas Lawrence.
1774, Nov.   26, Monger, Josiah, and Mary Lynn.
1775, July   2, Monney, Ann, and Jacob Rhods.
1796, June   20, Monney, Elizabeth, and John McCormick.
1765, July   8, Monney, John, and Margaret Smith.
1759, Jan.   28, Monohon, Patrick, and Rebecca Collborn.
1792, July   9, Monro, Mary, and William Peel.
1792, Sept.   24, Monro, Susanna, and John Spence.
1775, May   7, Monro, William, and Elly Scott.
1778, May   11, Monroe, Henry, and Mary McGlaghney.
1789, July   7, Monroe, John, and Jennet McPhale.
1777, May   17, Monrow, Sarah, and John Denney.
1798, Aug.   27, Montgomery, Andrew, and Agnes Smith.
1795, Feb.   22, Montgomery, Christiana, and Charles Dobbin.
1789, Feb.   7, Montgomery, Christiana, and Robert Fisher.
1773, Nov.   25, Montgomery, Elizabeth, and David Ridder.
1774, May   31, Montgomery, Hugh, and Hannah Hanzeley.
1794, Dec.   26, Montgomery, Margret, and Pierce Duffy.
1766, July   10, Montgomery, Mary, and John Godfrey.
1783, March 27, Montgomery, Robert, and Catherine Philips.
1792, Dec.   15, Montgomery, William, and Elizabeth Ingram.
1799, June   23, Montgomery, William, and Marget Wilson.
1766, Feb.   3, Montgommery, Catherine, and William Davis.
1766, Feb.   5, Montgommery, Duncan, and Caterine McDonald.
1767, May   25, Montgommery, Mary, and James Philips.

1780, March 2, Monyen, Priscilla, and Peter Thought.
1778, Sept. 15, Monyon, Priscilla, and John Bride.
1782, July 25, Mood, Catherine, and Jacob Reyderman.
1793, Jan. 8, Moody, Robert, and Elizabeth Mellin.
1750, Oct. 24, Mooer, Mary, and William Dougharty.
1789, Feb. 16, Mooney, Martha, and Elias Richards.
1795, Oct. 27, Moor, Isaac, and Maria Elizab. Frank.
1790, April 1, Moor, John, and Marget Oldenbrooks.
1752, Nov. 12, Moor, Manny, and Michael Dulinty.
1771, June 10, Moore, Ann, and Charles Lindsay.
1778, July 14, Moore, Christopher, and Catharine Wenttinger.
1772, April 22, Moore, Elizabeth, and Patrick Bradley.
1767, Oct. 23, Moore, Elizabeth, and Robert Innes.
1778, June 22, Moore, Frances, and Henry Pratt.
1794, Aug. 14, Moore, Francis, and Mary McDougan.
1792, Aug. 20, Moore, Hanna, and Pattens Savage.
1780, May 10, Moore, Hannah, and Joseph Borden.
1794, Oct. 29, Moore, Henry Allen, and Marget Brown.
1755, Oct. 16, Moore, Hugh, and Rachel Thomas.
1779, Aug. 11, Moore, John, and Hannah Smith.
1758, April 2, Moore, Joshua, and Mary Fulton.
1763, April 17, Moore, Mathew, and Ann Duff.
1763, July 26, Moore, Nathan, and Elizabeth Trayge.
1783, Feb. 6, Moore, Peter, and Jeany Murtland.
1796, June 23, Moore, Phebe, and Hugh Loyd.
1753, Sept. 1, Moore, Rachel, and Henry Gray.
1785, Jan. 15, Moore, Robert, and Mary Wilson.
1780, July 17, Moore, Sarah, and Peter Fritz.
1751, July 5, Moore, Susanna, and Christopher Smith.
1754, Sept. 14, Moore, Susanna, and Joseph Miles.
1788, Feb. 20, Mophet, Catharine, and Thomas Arnold.
1795, Jan. 30, Moran, Mathew, and Sarah Page.
1793, April 26, Moraty, Timothy, and Ann Pettit.
1789, Nov. 28, More, Cathrine, and Benjamin Rowlins.
1779, June 6, More, Catharine, and Christopher Lockart.
1791, Jan. 28, More, Cathrine, and Joseph Hunt.
1788, March 10, More, Catharine, and Thomas Moines.
1799, Jan. 13, More, David, and Hannah Fisher.
1774, Sept. 1, More, Elizabeth, and Joseph Govier.
1792, April 21, More, Francis, and Cathrine Slaughter.
1779, July 1, More, Frances, and John Hamilton.
1780, Jan. 29, More, Frances, and Thomas Perris.
1769, Sept. 2, More, Hugh, and Elizabeth Roads.
1794, Dec. 2, More, James, and Nancy Justice.
1794, Sept. 16, More, Jane, and Robert Barber.
1791, March 6, More, John, and Hanna Price.

1800, Feb. 9, More, John, and Johannah Wright.
1791, Nov. 29, More, John, and Priscilla Stinmets.
1752, May 18, More, Judy, and Joseph Siles.
1771, Nov. 16, More, Margarett, and Thomas Geen.
1800, Dec. 1, More, Margret, and Charles Miller.
1791, July 17, More, Mary, and Daniel Strang.
1799, Jan. 17, More, Mary, and John Litham.
1777, March 7, More, Mary, and John Thomson.
1778, Aug. 28, More, Mary, and Patrick McConal.
1780, Jan. 8, More, Mary, and Richard Woodward.
1799, Aug. 1, More, Mary, and Thomas Flannigan.
1789, Nov. 3, More, Mordecai, and Sara Bartim.
1758, Nov. 8, More, Prudence, and Joseph McMin.
1761, Feb. 27, More, Rachel, and John Gandy.
1758, Nov. 6, More, Robert, and Sarah Halloway.
1776, May 12, More, Samuel, and Else Butler.
1771, Jan. 20, More, Samuel, and Mary Hamilton.
1793, March 8, More, William, and Margret Judge.
1769, Aug. 9, More, William, and Susannah Cops.
1774, Aug. 29, More, William, and Susannah McDaniel.
1776, May 20, Mores, William, and Eleanor Morrow.
1777, July 2, Morgan, Abel, and Dinah Brown.
1790, June 5, Morgan, Amy, and Ashbrook Dickinson.
1753, Feb. 12, Morgan, Ann, and Thomas Homes.
1763, Feb. 12, Morgan, Ann, and Thomas Robins.
1794, Aug. 21, Morgan, Cathrine, and Archibald Cook.
1798, March 15, Morgan, Mary, and Christopher Inflefried.
1794, Dec. 30, Morgan, Elizabeth, and Lewis Richards.
1754, Sept. 19, Morgan, Elizabeth, and William Lewis.
1774, Dec. 6, Morgan, Ellis, and Sarah Kittson.
1795, July 12, Morgan, Enoch, and Hannah Goetschies.
1759, April 16, Morgan, George, and Sarah Rimseey.
1800, April 24, Morgan, Hannah, and John Rose.
1790, May 29, Morgan, Hanna, and Thomas Hutchins.
1791, April 23, Morgan, John, and Elizabeth Calhoon.
1762, Aug. 22, Morgan, John, and Jeansey Tailor.
1779, April 22, Morgan, Joseph, and Sophia Clisley.
1795, June 2, Morgan, John, and Susannah Hinderson.
1778, May 11, Morgan, Margaret, and Archibald McRacken.
1790, Oct. 19, Morgan, Rachel, and Nathan Stuart.
1785, Jan. 3, Morgan, Ruth, and Thomas Pond.
1755, Dec. 26, Morgan, Sarah, and William Evans.
1791, Dec. 11, Morgan, Sophia, and Peter Rose.
1797, Nov. 25, Morgan, Thomas, and Mary Turner.
1754, July 2, Morgan, William, and Priscilla Wells.
1776, June 9, Moriarty, Timothy, and Jean Willson.

1775, Oct.   14, Morling, Thomas, and Mary Hewes.
1780, July   6, Morphey, Ann, and John Bromley.
1776, Jan.   7, Morphey, Edward, and Jane Tenton.
1758, Oct.   6, Morphey, Edward, and Mary Beech.
1778, May   1, Morphey, Eleanor, and Richard Mildrid.
1758, Dec.   16, Morphey, John, and Mary Warings.
1790, July   8, Morphey, John, and Susanna Hood.
1770, Feb.   21, Morphey, Luke, and Mary Maley.
1794, June   3, Morphey, Timothy, and Hannah Mortimer.
1782, Dec.   7, Morphy, Anne, and Adam Tripp.
1794, July   11, Morphy, Mary, and William Ferlan.
1767, Aug.   17, Morray, Elizabeth, and James McCracken.
1787, Feb.   1, Morrel, James, and Judith Hamell.
1783, Jan.   8, Morrell, Robert, and Mary Price.
1765, April   18, Morrey, Judith, and William Hatton.
1779, Nov.   15, Morrey, Mathew, and Jane Grason.
1780, July   9, Morrey, Simon, and Jane Norris.
1759, Nov.   1, Morrin, Joseph, and Sarah Thomson.
1784, July   7, Morris, Andrew, and Jane Agnew.
1778, Dec.   1, Morris, Ann, and Dennis McCarty.
1782, Aug.   14, Morris, Anne, and Jonathan Douten.
1791, Aug.   8, Morris. Elias, and Priscilla Coffey.
1791, June   13, Morris, Elihu, and Martha Patterson.
1795, April   13, Morris, Elisha, and Cathrine Metsger.
1791, Jan.   28, Morris, George, and Hanna Ward.
1766, Nov.   19, Morris, Grace, and James McCarty.
1800, Feb.   26, Morris, Hannah, and Andrew Hansell.
1790, Oct.   7, Morris, Isaac, and Hanna Hussey.
1766, April   23, Morris, James, and Margret Jones.
1772, March 14, Morris, James, and Rosannah Cork.
1759, May   22, Morris, John, and Ann Hamilton.
1783, March 27, Morris, John, and Elizabeth Huntsman.
1794, March   3, Morris, John, and Lydia Dickenson.
1783, May   5, Morris, John, and Mary Dunn.
1792, Nov.   15, Morris, Jonathan, and Rachel Pearson.
1799, April   2, Morris, Mary, and Joseph Handbest.
1794, Jan.   8, Morris, Mary, and Michael McKenna.
1754, Feb.   20, Morris, Moris, and Cruise Robert.
1797, Nov.   24, Morris, Philip, and Ann MacKimson.
1775, Sept.   17, Morris, Rosannah, and Philip Deweyer.
1796, Feb.   18, Morris, Sarah, and George Low.
1774, Oct.   26, Morris, Stephen, and Margaret Cox.
1796, March 21, Morris, William, and Cathrine Wyman.
1784, Aug.   3, Morrisson, Barbara, and David Marshall.
1791, July   5, Morrison, Cathrine, and William Ballentine.
1782, Jan.   3, Morrisson, Daniel, and Mary Steward.

1793, Oct.   2, Morrison, Elizabeth, and Andrew Ruper.
1762, Aug.   31, Morrison, Elizabeth, and Joseph Lamb.
1751, Aug.   6, Morrison, George, and Mary Dawson.
1795, April   14, Morrison, James, and Genice (or Geenia) Munian.
1780, Feb.   17, Morrison, John, and Catharine McDonald.
1761, July   30, Morrison, John, and Frances Wallacut.
1770, Oct.   7, Morrison, Margarett, and John Greenwood.
1790, May   9, Morrison, Margret, and George Connelly.
1785, March   2, Morrison, Mary, and Nathan Davis.
1766, Sept.   3, Morrison, Mary, and Simon Taylor.
1795, Dec.   19, Morrison, Mathew, and Mary Vastine.
1781, Nov.   22, Morrison, Michael, and Anne McGloughlin.
1767, March 12, Morrison, Philip, and Elizabeth Sherrin.
1773, Nov.   18, Morriston, Thomas, and Deborah Ward.
1781, Sept.   27, Morrow, Alexander, and Anne Landen.
1794, Nov.   21, Morrow, Cathrine, and Robert McDowel.
1776, May   20, Morrow, Eleanor, and William Mores.
1793, Aug.   25, Morrow, Elizabeth, and John Baxter.
1784, Jan.   26, Morrow James, and Elizabeth Geel.
1757, Nov.   10, Morrow, Jenet, and David Ralston.
1780, April   12, Morrow, Mary, and Noble Grimes.
1777, Feb.   2, Morry, Ann, and John Curtis.
1773, March 23, Morry, Enis, and Susannah Yordon.
1777, Feb.   4, Morry, Mary, and Daniel Rowen.
1779, June   24, Morry, Mary, and Thomas Woodfind.
1779, Aug.   15, Morry, Robert, and Ann Stempson.
1775, Jan.   15, Morry, William, and Ann Harrington.
1794, Sept.   11, Morset, Robert, and Jane Clark.
1797, Jan.   15, Morss, Johnah, and Elizabeth Burdon.
1752, Nov.   29, Morten, Margareta, and Hance Licon.
1794, June   3, Mortimer, Hannah, and Timothy Morphey.
1891, April   28, Morton, Aaron, and Francis Armitt.
1757, Aug.   17, Morton, Ann, and John Culin.
1784, July   8, Morton, Christiana, and Robert Towers.
1767, Dec.   24, Morton, Everhard, and Elizabeth Syales.
1761, March   3, Morton, Elizabeth, and John Fluellen.
1779, April   5, Morton, Elizabeth, and Peter Cross.
1763, Aug.   25, Morton, Ellenor, and Garret Boon.
1766, Jan.   17, Morton, George, and Ann Robinson.
1770, Feb.   11, Morton, James, and Anne Davids.
1750, Nov.   7, Morton, Mary, and John Justice.
1758, Aug.   7, Morton, Morton, and Mary Boon.
1798, April   17, Morton, Rebecca, and John Miller.
1764, Dec.   18, Morton, Rebeccah, and William Boon.
1799, Jan.   16, Morton, Sarah, and William Gray.
1773, June   21, Morton, Sketckley, and Rebecca Taylor.

1778, June   2, Morton, Thomas, and Sarah Man.
1783, Aug.   27, Mory, Louis, and Aga Forlow.
1751, May   24, Mosely, Richard, and Mary Lamplugh.
1791, Dec.   26, Moser, Charles, and Marget Allen.
1796, May   22, Moser, Christian, and Elizabeth Defellies.
1790, Oct.   21, Moser, George, and Mary Kerr.
1782, Dec.   8, Moser, Henry, and Christiana Stinsman.
1795, Feb.   21, Moser, Samuel, and Marget Grison.
1792, May   27, Moses, Ann, and Jacob Keighler.
1800, Dec.   11, Moses, Cathrine, and Bernard Mackey.
1753, Sept.   8, Moses, William, and Sarah Stephens.
1770, Aug.   26, Mosfet, Ester, and John Lyons.
1780, March   2, Mosley, Margaret, and Joseph Garwood.
1778, June   7, Moss, Charles, and Catharine Smith.
1791, May   26, Moss, Mary, and George Atkinson.
1780, Sept. 21, Moss, Samuel, and Hannah Hutchinson.
1793, Oct.   26, Moss, Sarah, and James McGroty.
1772, Dec.   15, Moss, Thomas, and Jean Riller.
1796, April 10, Motley, Jane, and Thomas Vade.
1791, May   11, Motley, Mary, and Thomas Barepo.
1762, Nov.   21, Motts, Israel, and Ann Brooks.
1783, April 20, Mount, Adam, and Elizabeth Rawford.
1798, Jan.   24, Mount, Elizabeth, and William Sheed.
1761, March 17, Mour, Samuel, and ——— Heninton.
1766, Oct.   4, Mour, Samuel, and Margaret Roty.
1752, Nov.   27, Mourin, Mary, and Jacob Reindaler.
1781, May   9, Mours, John, and Anne Roberts.
1752, Oct.   12, Moriss, Catharine, and Andrew Hulings.
1782, March   5, Moyel, Jeane, and James Long.
1759, March 13, Moyer, Hanna, and George Oyster.
1775, June   5, Mucklarein, Christiana, and William Stein.
1798, April 19, Muck, Philip, and Amelia Willis.
1793, June   6, Muckelwee, Susanna, and Charles Gollaher.
1778, Jan.   13, Mud, John, and Pen Ferd.
1791, Sept. 26, Muff, Nicholas, and Elizabeth Warren.
1795, March   1, Muhlenberg, Marget, and Mathew Gold.
1752, Sept. 20, Muleken, Erick, and Catharine Matson.
1768, Dec.   5, Mullan, Dennis, and Martha Porter.
1775, Sept. 25, Mullan, Elizabeth, and Hugh Ferguson.
1778, May   28, Mullan, James, and Rachel Cleiner.
1779, Aug.   4, Mullan, Mary, and James Colly.
1780, June   12, Mullan, Nathaniel, and Dorothea Keyser.
1778, May   19, Mullan, Sarah, and James Ratchford.
1780, March 26, Mullan, William, and Elizabeth Shanks.
1794, Jan.   30, Mullen, Cathrine, and George Hood.
1798, May   21, Mullen, Elizab., and Anthony Amman.

1795, May   18, Mullen, James, and Charlotte Kinsley.
1793, Sept.   18, Mullen, Mary, and Michael Keaton.
1777, April   12, Mullen, Patrick, and Lydia Or.
1800, April   28, Mullen, Patrick, and Mary Ganoe.
1794, Aug.   26, Mullen, Sarah, and Henry Kelly.
1796, Jan.   2, Mullen, Thomas, and Sarah Davis.
1793, Dec.   30, Mullen, William, and Sarah Lowry.
1759, Jan.   27, Muller, Elizabeth, and Philip Sherer.
1776, Sept.   22, Mullin, Thomas, and Mary Critchley.
1770, Jan.   23, Mulling, Rachel, and Edward Evance.
1798, Dec.   3, Multy, Mary, and Benjamin Jackson.
1795, April   12, Mumford, Hannah, and Nathaniel Lang.
1799, May   2, Mumford, John, and Rebecca McCannan.
1795, Dec.   24, Mun, Mary, and Alexander Grant.
1796, Feb.   29, Munce, Jane, and James Falcner.
1795, April   14, Munian, Genice (or Geenia,) and James Morrison.
1781, Jan.   16, Munks, Michael, and Sarah Beary.
1798, May   29, Munyan, Joseph, and Mary Kirbin.
1785, July   12, Munyan, Reuben, and Mary Lord.
1793, Aug.   7, Murdoch, Sarah, and John Carver.
1781, March   7, Murdock, Robert, and Mary Christine Shoemaker.
1789, July   9, Murdock, William, and Catharine Urquhart.
1778, March 19, Murey, Thomas, and Ann Dempsey.
1791, May   29, Murfin, Isaac, and Mary Pearcey.
1756, Feb.   1, Murgan, Mary, and John Adams.
1759, April   29, Murin, Elizabeth, and George Bowman.
1798, March   8, Murpei, Nicholas, and Elizab. Carson.
1757, May   1, Murphey, Ann, and Patrick Pheagan.
1792, Oct.   10, Murphey, Daniel, and Mary McDonegh.
1800, Sept.   23, Murphey, Elizabeth, and Francis MacGuire.
1796, June   19, Murphey, John, and Margret Toland.
1800, May   27, Murphey, Latitia, and William Laughlin.
1777, June   8, Murphey, Martin, and Hannah Smith.
1799, March 31, Murphey, Mary, and Edward Ryan.
1798, Jan.   22, Murphey, Samuel, and Ann Grisson.
1782, Aug.   2, Murphis, John, and Elizabeth O'Neal.
1762, Oct.   26, Murphy, Ann, and Richard Littleby.
1757, June   29, Murphy, Barney, and Ann Campbell.
1751, Dec.   8, Murphy, Bartholomew, and Mary Boucher.
1796, July   3, Murphy, George, and Cathrine Hyneman.
1790, Dec.   14, Murphy, Michael, and Cathrine Condon.
1795, Jan.   24, Murray, Archibald, and Mary Carr.
1800, Nov.   22, Murray, Elizabeth, and Cudjo Desire.
1799, Sept.   14, Murray, John, and Ann Bennet.
1770, Dec.   8, Murray, John, and Mary M. Phartin.
1767, Aug.   20, Murray, John, and Sarah Rankin.

1790, Nov. 15, Murray, Rebecca, and Henry Hews.
1771, June   2, Murre, Rachel, and Andrew Hicky.
1787, Nov. 24, Murrey, Hannah, and Isaac Perkins.
1799, July 15, Murrey, Thomas, and Deborah Crawford.
1791, March 30, Murrie, Andrew, and Ann Johnson.
1771, Feb. 13, Murry, Catherine, and Daniel Frill.
1779, May   3, Murthwaik, Richard, and Jane Roderick.
1796, Oct. 23, Murthwait, Richard, and Jane Hillyer.
1796, Sept. 24, Murthwaith, Susannah, and Thomas Neward.
1783, Feb.   6. Murtland, Jeany, and Peter Moore.
1764, Nov. 24, Muschett, Thomas, and Sarah Trumbet.
1793, Dec. 24, Musgrave, Helena, and John Dill.
1795, Jan. 10, Musgrove, Ann Mary, and John Michael.
1794, Nov. 29, Musgrove, Clementina, and John Coppinger.
1754, Nov. 21, Musgrove, Mary, and Godfrey Rheemer.
1756, April 18, Musgrove, Sarah, and Benjamin Elliott.
1792, Oct.   3, Musgrove, Thomas, and Hanna Mee.
1754, Feb. 26, Mutchins, Sarah, and Evans Jones.
1752, June 18, Muttit, Mary, and James Brown.
1781, May   1, Munyan, Mary, and Samuel Karvy.
1754, Oct. 26, Myer, Appilloney, and Jacob Sullingar.
1772, Dec. 30, Myerly, Conrad, and Catharine Brant.
1795, Dec.   8, Myers, Barbara, and Jonathan Loesly.
1798, July 21, Myers, Hannah, and Thanet McClean.
1782, Oct.   6, Myers, Jacob, and Anne Ent.
1790, Aug.   3, Myers, Sarah, and Samuel Christy.
1788, June 18, Myers, Susannah, and John Taylor.
1796, April 23, Myers, Thomas, and Jane Clark.
1795, Oct. 15, Myrtland, Nancy, and George Hartley.
1765, March 18, Nageler, Mary, and John Bartholomew Shoe.
1774, Feb. 21, Nagle, Mary Agnes, and Anthony Seufert.
1756, June 28, Nail, Jeremiah, and Margaret Davenport.
1793, Jan. 22, Nail, Mary, and Francis Gleeson.
1797, Nov. 24, Nail, Phebe, and Isaac Zanes.
1778, Jan. 19, Nailer, Elizabeth, and Daniel Connor.
1755, Sept. 9, Nailor, Elizabeth, and Issachar Davids.
1782, Jan.   3, Nailor, Esther, and Levite Barr. (Negroes.)
1772, July 12, Nailor, Jean, and John Shee.
1758, May   29, Nailor, John, and Sarah Tredaway.
1762, May   26, Nails, William, and Elizabeth Hobs.
1770, July 15, Nangle, Thomas, and Ann Bladerwik.
1794, May   13, Nannimackar, Elizabeth, and George Deal.
1780, June 29, Nantz, Margaret, and Thomas Fisher.
1793, June   8, Napier, David, and Abigail McFarlen.
1790, April 1, Napier, Margret A., and Cornelius O'Neal.
1794, Dec. 31, Narden, Judith, and William Davis.

1759, Oct.   30, Naree, George, and Margeth Cassen.
1762, July   26, Narridge, Elizabeth, and John Stator.
1778, Jan.   24, Nash, Elizabeth, and Mathew Cox.
1777, Dec.   17, Nash, Margaret, and George Kitts.
1790, Dec.   8, Nash, Rosanna, and Thomas Wright.
1777, Jan.   11, Nathan, Jacob, and Ann McGrah.
1791, Nov.   6, Nathery, Martha, and Ben Steel.
1777, Dec.   29, Nattel, Mary, and Richard Chester.
1779, Feb.   15, Navel, Christian, and Margaret Flower.
1798, Dec.   11, Navin, David, and Cathrine Gaily.
1759, Nov.   25, Nayer, Jacob, and Catherine Knausin.
1766, Sept. 15, Naylor, John, and Margaret Roberts.
1767, May   25, Neadham, John, and Elizabeth Sims.
1782, May   27, Neagle, James, and Catherine McFall.
1788, May   8, Neal, Catharine, and Charles Callagh.
1769, April 16, Neal, Eleanor, and Thomas Green.
1774, April 10, Neal, James, and Eleanor Clark.
1778, June   4, Neal, Pierce, and Mary Jager.
1772, Nov.   25, Neal, Philip, and Isabel Mack Farlein.
1778, June   13, Nealey, John, and Ann Fitzgerald.
1783, Jan.   8, Nealy, William, and Catherine Runnels.
1791, May   20, Neath, James, and Jane Mackey.
1762, Dec.   2, Nebel, Frederick, and Dorethea Rose.
1766, March 16, Needham, John, and Mary Jennings.
1794, Dec.   9, Needham, Mary, and George Burnet.
1787, Nov.   8, Needham, William, and Mary Currey.
1790, April 29, Needham Zedechia, and Sara Barnhill.
1773, March 14, Needon, Robert, and Margaret Hunter.
1758, Oct.   8, Neel, Charles, and Rosannah Linn.
1775, Dec.   3, Neel, Else, and James Krunear.
1776, Sept.   9, Neeland, Alexander, and Rachel Radileff.
1791, June   8, Neeld, Rachel, and Andrew Cherleen.
1751, Jan.   29, Neese, John, and Jane Knowland.
1772, Feb.   24, Neeson, Francis, and Elizabeth Mason.
1757, Oct.   17, Neeson, Margaret, and Robert Freeman.
1767, Sept.   1, Neess, Ann, and Henry Leech.
1780, Feb.   19, Negr, Elizabeth, and George Rodger.
1780, Feb.   19, Negr, Jane, and Philip Armon.
1757, May   18, Neidermark, Janey, and Samuel Davis.
1774, April   4, Neil, Elizabeth, and James Dawson.
1753, Dec.   17, Neithermark, Elizabeth, and Lawrence Frederick.
1769, Aug.   28, Nell, Anne, and Thomas King.
1791, May   8, Nelson, John, and Elizabeth Stout.
1766, July   31, Nelson, Mary, and George Harding.
1800, Feb.   4, Nelson, Sarah, and Ebenezer Hawkins.
1777, Nov.   12, Nerdel, John, and Elizabeth Ludrick.

1776, Sept. 5, Nero and Diana, (negroes.)
1770, May 5, Nerry, Mary, and Charles Bowman.
1754, Dec. 3, Nesbett, James, and Margaret Young.
1753, Aug. 22, Nesbit, John, and Isabel Griffith.
1750, Dec. 3, Nesmith, Anne, and Joseph Miles.
1751, Dec. 2, Nesmith, John, and Sarah Dyke.
1759, Feb. 6, Netsellius, Nathias, and Rebecca Hindrickson.
1751, Dec. 5, Nettle, Mary, and John Jones.
1780, Aug. 24, Netzel, Jacob, and Sarah Makenison.
1799, June 6, Neuzum, Sarah, and Garner Linnard.
1782, Jan. 15, Nevel, John, and Elizabeth Ward.
1799, Dec. 1, Nevel, Thomas, and Mary Bayard.
1796, Sept. 24, Newark, Thomas, and Susannah Murthwaith.
1780, July 16, Newbound, Rachel, and Alexander Whitelow.
1783, Aug. 7, Newcom, John, and Elizabeth Campbell.
1777, Oct. 20, Newland, John, and Hannah More.
1757, Nov. 30, Newlin, Nathaniel, and Jane Woodward.
1783, Oct. 30, Newman, John, and Elizabeth Pinyard.
1751, April 29, Newman, William, and Mary Kelly.
1779, July 19, Newmen, Hannah, and Philip Shen Campbell.
1779, Nov. 25, Newport, Kesiah, and William Hewlet.
1792, April 27, Newton, Benjamin, and Rosanna Stuart.
1781, Dec. 25, Newton, Jonathan, and Elizabeth Benhysel.
1776, Nov. 25, Newton, Richard, and Ann Gibbs.
1787, Oct. 25, Newton, Sarah Hepherd, and Joseph Gitlens.
1782, Dec. 6, Newton, Simon, and Jenny Small.
1780, June 21, Newton, Susannah, and Stephen Thomson.
1788, Oct. 9, Newzum, Thomas, and Marget Robinson.
1787, Jan. 2. Niblin, Mary, and John Pollard.
1796, Feb. 4, Niblock, William, and Charlott Brown.
1759, March 18, Niccol, John, and Margaret Cambron.
1767, Oct. 23, Nice, John, and Margaret Coffin.
1754, Nov. 28, Nice, John, and Margaret Donat.
1782, Sept. 3, Nice, Mary, and John Dover.
1776, Nov. 20, Nicholls, John Thomas, and Jean Peterson.
1776, July 20, Nichols, Ann, and William Prowes.
1790, Oct. 20, Nichols, James, and Fanny Hoover.
1761, March 19, Nichols Latitia, and James Thomson.
1774, Dec. 25, Nichols, William, and Susannah Boome.
1795, Feb. 17, Nicholson, Ann, and James Alexander Bartram.
1790, May 20, Nicholson, Cathrine, and James Parkinson.
1779, April 19, Nicholson, Catharine, and John McCay.
1753, Nov. 15, Nicholson, David, and Margaret Masters.
1778, Feb. 12, Nicholson, Elizabeth, and Charles Elder.
1790, July 1, Nicholson, John, and Ameley Buck.
1780, July 8, Nicholson, Joseph, and Lydia Lee.

1773, July   27, Nicholson, Rachel, and John Teis.
1759, April 11, Nicholson, ——, and Rebecca Aronson.
1760, May   8, Nicholson, Sarah, and John Hamilton.
1752, Sept. 18, Nickloson, Sarah, and Francis Culey.
1795, July   26, Niclas, Sarah, and John William, (Africans.)
1777, Dec.   25, Nicoll, John, and Sarah McCollock.
1788, April 18, Nicoll, William, and Marget McGrigree.
1756, Nov.   1, Nidermark, Rebecca, and Thomas Taylor.
1777, May   4, Nielson, Sarah, and David Finney.
1759, April   3, Niemeyer, Frederic, and Mary Hoin.
1763, Dec.   22, Nienns, Nicholas, and Mary Mead.
1776, July   2, Nightlinger, Susannah, and George Masters.
1779, Jan.   26, Nihel, Lawrence, and Nancy Wier.
1759, April 13, Nilleaus, Isabella, and John Biggs.
1752, April 13, Nionerty, Sylvester, and Hannah White.
1787, Aug.   30, Nisbet, Jane, and Nicholas Nosvaldy.
1755, March 31, Nisbett, David, and Elinor Young.
1794, July   28, Nivel, Mary, and George Grace.
1778, Jan.   23, Nix, Hannah, and Robert Ker.
1778, Dec.   31, Nixson, Eleanor, and John Laycock.
1799, June   4, Nixon, Elizab., and William Dougherty.
1793, Aug.   5, Nixon, James, and Bridget Cummins.
1779, May   2, Nixon, Margaret, and Joseph Conjers.
1762, May   27, Nixon, Robert, and Rebecca Middleton.
1782, July   25, Nixon, William, and Elizabeth Carmeton.
1797, Jan.   19, Noble, Christian, and Nancy Ort.
1781, Aug.   7, Noble, Marie, and George Dunkin.
1777, March 12, Noble, Mary, and James McGinnis.
1779, April 27, Noble, Susanna, and James Low.
1754, June   30, Noble, Thomas, and Mary Cox.
1764, July   25, Noblet, Joseph, and Mary Hartley.
1755, Aug.   12, Noblit, Joseph, and Margaret Rirnan.
1757, March 3, Nolberry, Ealce, and Hennery Hues.
1781, Oct.   23, Nolen, William, and Elizabeth Grimes.
1766, May   24, Noll, Ann, and Peter Butler.
1790, Dec.   6, Noll, Marget, and John Barry.
1759, June   21, Nordenlind, Eric, and Mary Lindmeyer.
1770, Sept.   2, Noris, Elizabeth, and Cornelius Cein.
1795, July   25, Norman, Marget, and John Downs.
1751, Jan.   18, Norman, Sarah, and George Garioch.
1783, Jan.   20, Norris, Adam, and Rebecca Greenwood.
1780, July   9, Norris, Jane, and Simon Morrey.
1797, March 19, Norris, John, and Elizab. Linch.
1758, May   28, Norris, Mary, and John Row.
1782, Dec.   17, Norris, Robert, and Charlotte Sellers.
1795, June   23, Norris, William, and Fanny McGindel.

1787, Aug. 31, Norris, William, and Margaret Scott.
1780, Aug. 12, Norris, William, and Sarah Griffy.
1786, June 6, Norrman, Joseph, and Margret Snyder.
1780, Dec. 24, North, Eleanor, and Simon Owens.
1770, Sept. 1, North, Elizabeth, and Patrick Carney.
1778, March 10, North, Mary, and Elisha Parker.
1777, June 18, North, William, and Lydia Jackson.
1778, March 10, North, Winneford, and John Wright.
1759, Nov. 28, Norton, John, and Ester Whit.
1784, June 5, Norwood, Margaret, and William A. McCrea.
1787, Aug. 30, Nosvaldy, Nicholas, and Jane Nisbet.
1772, Feb. 27, Notter, Johannah, and George McCleve.
1795, July 9, Nouge, Etienne, and Mary Catton.
1800, June 4, Nowlan, Edmund, and Elizabeth Brice.
1793, May 5, Nugent, Prancis, and Cathrine Follen.
1766, March 24, Nugent, Richard, and Hannah Stoy.
1792, July 10, Null, Martin, and Catharine Harris.
1776, July 21, Numan, John, and Jean Thomson.
1774, July 7, Nun, Martha, and Ralph Smith.
1794, Dec. 25, Nunemaker, George, and Mary Holler.
1777, Oct. 20, Nure, Hannah, and John Newland.
1763, April 11, Nutter, Henry, and Mary Sang.
1798, June 18, Nuttle, Rachel, and James Hunter.
1793, July 16, Nutz, Sarah, and William Clare.
1790, Nov. 4, Nuzum, James, and Sarah Robinson.
1773, June 27, Nyre, Jacob, and Susanna Hall.
1782, March 27, Oaksman, Samuel, and Mary Caril.
1772, Aug. 8, Oar, John, and Sarah Clark.
1799, May 14, Oat, Joseph. and Mary MacAlpin.
1789, May 5, Oatenheimer, Henry, and Sarah Kevlin.
1778, June 13, Oats, Mary, and George Reed.
1781, Dec. 20, Oats, Mary, and Jacob Lewis.
1799, Jan. 22, Obermüller, Ann, and Johan Sam. Miedskie.
1762, Sept. 29, Oberftegan, Rosina, and Jacob Schweighart.
1781, June 17, O'Brayne, James, and Mary Joiner.
1793, June 25, O'Brian, Cornelius, and Margret Worrell.
1792, Oct. 20, O'Brian, Daniel, and Rebecca Coburn.
1796, Oct. 25, Obrian, John, and Cathrine Hagarthy.
1795, July 21, Obrian, Martha, and Benjamin Ashton.
1766, Nov. 1, O'Brian, Morton, and Elizabeth Bacon.
1757, March 22, O'Brian, William, and Catharine Williams.
1792, May 4, Obrian, William, and Nancy MacNeal.
1794, May 2, Obrien, Rosetta, and James Birmingham.
1762, April 28, Obrine, Brigitta, and Thomas Pointer.
1778, Jan. 29, O'Bryan, Bridget, and Peter Rutlidge.
1778, March 18, O'Bryan, Juliana, and John Thomson.

1799, Dec. 26, O'Bryan, Mary, and Thomas Ash.
1778, Feb. 16, O'Bryan, Mary, and Thomas Faster.
1768, Nov. 13, Obryon, Rose, and John Broderic.
1774, March 4, O'Bryon, Simon, and Barbarah Larter.
1765, June 28, Oconner, Susannah, and Thomas Hall.
1795. Nov. 29, O'Connor, David, and Hannah Stark.
1798, Feb. 3, O'Connor, Jane, and John Logan.
1795, May 5, O'Connor, John, and Jane McGowen.
1798, April 10, O'Connor, Thomas, and Mary Grogan.
1769, June 18, Odaniel, Sarah, and Thomas Davids.
1766, April 28, O'Dannil, James, and Isabella McJine.
1768, May 3, O'Dear, Neal, and Elizabeth Davis.
1781, Jan. 25, Odell, Ruben, and Lowes Brooks.
1791, May 12, Odenheimer, Margret, and George Kerlin.
1790, Aug. 15, Odonelly, Elizabeth, and James Cooper.
1796, April 17, O'Donnel, Eleonore, and John Miller.
1759, June 7, Oeans, Mathew, and James Watts.
1794, Sept. 9, Offrej, Maturin, and Marget Repjohn.
1780, Sept. 11, Ogden, Esther, and Joseph Harper.
1783, Oct. 16, Ogden, Hugh, and Dorothy Meng.
1759, July 15, Ogdon, Hannah, and William Lees.
1759, April 1, Ogelbe, George, and Elizabeth Waters.
1769, Jan. 7, Ogelbery, John, and Hannah Day.
1775, Oct. 2, Ogelby, Mary, and James Sturges.
1778, May 27, Ogelby, Rachel, and William Gough.
1767, Oct. 30, Ogelby, Sarah, and William Whitefield.
1778, Jan. 28, Ogelvie, John, and Ann Gorden.
1752, May 10, Ogilby, John, and Lady Lee.
1759, Sept. 27, Ogilby, Patrick, and Marthar Ley.
1791, Jan. 19, Ogle, Thomas, and Patience Thomson.
1790, July 3, Ogleby, Joseph, and Mary Derrick.
1777, Jan. 13, Ogleby, Joseph, and Susannah Martin.
1781, Dec. 13, O'Hagerty, Cornelius, and Catharine Kafer.
1789, July 19, O'Hara, Anne, and John McLoughlin.
1754, March 25, Ohara, Christianna, and Stephen Archbold.
1775, March 26, O'Hara, Joshua, and Mary McDemond, (Darmut.)
1771, May 27, O'Harra, John, and Sarah Jones.
1778, June 27, O'Harra, Mary, and John Whideaker.
1791, Jan. 1, O'Lary, John, and Jennet Macbicker.
1758, Dec. 20, Olden, Benjamin, and Mary Hastings.
1752, Nov. 17, Olden, Jeremiah, and Elinor Smith.
1790, April 1, Oldenbrooks, Marget, and John Moor.
1781, Oct. 29, Oldfield, Hannah, and William Taylor.
1756, May 26, Oldfield, Jonathan, and Hannah Kostor.
1777, Jan. 21, Oldfield, Rebecca, and Stephen Elmes.
1778, Feb. 12, Oldfield, Sarah, and Solomon Boon.

1774, June   18, Oldham, Samuel, and Margaret Broad.
1775, Dec.   7, Oldling, Miriam, and Jacob Plankinton.
1775, Nov.   16, Oleles, Ann, and David Twells.
1798, July   22, Olenberg, Eleonore, and John Metch.
1800, April 26, Oliphant, Hannah, and Thomas Harper.
1756, Aug.   3, Oliver, Alexander, and Mary Russell.
1790, Aug.   28, Oliver, George, and Mary Hudston.
1796, June   18, Oliver, Margret, and John Campbell.
1751, Nov.   28, Oliver, Samuel, and Elizabeth Penrows.
1794, May   17, Oliveres, Mary, and Pierre Bordenave.
1778, May   26, Ollivant, Mark, and Catharine Rough.
1800, April 27, Olson, Daniel, and Mary Hill.
1759, Aug.   16, Oltey, Ann, and Daniel Young.
1765, Jan.   22, Onclerin, Anna Margaretta, and Johan Nicholas
                 Klein.
1790, April   1, O'Neal, Cornelius, and Margret A. Napier.
1774, Feb.   11, O'Neal, Daniel, and Elizabeth Welch.
1781, Oct.   8, O'Neal, Elizabeth, and John Linkholn.
1782, Aug.   2, O'Neal, Elizabeth, and John Marphis.
1788, Oct.   8, O'Neal, Gordon, and Mary McCarty.
1764, Dec.   31, O'Neal, James, and Sarah Green.
1796, July   5, Oneal, Laurence, and Margret Stafford.
1764, May   7, O'Neil, Dennis, and Elizabeth Donn.
1776, March 13, O'Neil, Ester, and Charles Riggen.
1780, June   26, O'Neil, Mary, and Andrew Eisenack.
1778, June   17, O'Nell, Sarah, and Simon Gibney.
1778, Oct.   13, Onie, Mary, and Alexander McFarland.
1783, Jan.   4, Owner, Catharine, and John Keen.
1790, March   6, Onor, Hannah, and Alexander Gillis.
1772, July   12, Oor, Mary, and Samuel Logan.
1793, April 16, Optigrove, Sarah, and William Wainwright.
1754, Sept. 19, Or, Grace, and Robert Owan.
1777, April 12, Or, Lydia, and Patrick Mullen.
1751, Feb.   18, Orane, Mary, and John McDonald.
1767, Jan.   13, Ord, George, and Rebeccah Lindmire.
1789, Nov.   27, Organ, Timothy, and Sara Wisham.
1778, June   15, Orgat, John, and Sarah Ferrel.
1794, Dec.   2, Orner, Anna Maria, and Solomon Sell.
1787, Nov.   16, Orner, John, and Martha Andrews.
1791, June   10, Orner, Martha, and James Chapman.
1784, Aug.   30, Orr, Alexander, and Hannah Haines.
1792, April 19, Orr, Sarah, and Ralph Lorener.
1797, Jan.   19, Ort, Nancy, and Christian Noble.
1790, Dec.   24, Orum, William, and Mary Robins.
1762, Feb.   9, Ornphers, Elizabeth, and John Corn.
1767, Aug.   16, Osborn, Elizabeth, and Edmund Beach.

1791, March 26, Osborn, Elizabeth, and John Springer.
1797, March 23, Osborn, Elizabeth, and John Tull.
1795, Aug. 14, Osborn, James, and Elizabeth Wilkins.
1791, March 17, Osey, John Francis, and Roda Taylor.
1782, Jan. 15, Orborne, Henry, and Sarah Stewart.
1796, July 10, Oswald, Cathrine, and Samuel Burnel.
1798, Dec. 31, Ott, Christina, and Augustin Martin.
1798, Dec. 31, Ott, Jacob, and Nancy Schroeder.
1791, Nov. 4, Ott, John, and Elizabeth Beck.
1791, June 2, Ottenheimer, Mary, and James Alex^r Collings.
1782, July 24, Ottenstein, Margret, and Henry Rittenhausen.
1765, Dec. 2, Ottey, John, and Lydiah Baker.
1799, Feb. 24, Otting, Johanna Maria, and John Baptiste Shel-
         link.
1755, May 25, Ottinger, Barbary, and William Hickst.
1755, April 8, Ottinger, William, and Hannah Casner.
1791, Aug. 14, Otto, Sarah, and Thomas Heppard.
1773, Jan. 20, Ottwell, William, and Debora Camp.
1774, Nov. 7, Otway, Robert, and Rachel Jacobs.
1778, Nov. 19, Ougherson, Hugh, and Jane Brown.
1798, March 6, Overman, Marion, and Michael Malony.
1773, Jan. 2, Overthrow, Elizabeth, and James Penderbury.
1753, Nov. 8, Overthrow, Martha, and John Hart.
1754, Sept. 19, Owan, Robert, and Grace Or.
1778, Jan. 1, Owen, Ann, and Seth Bowen.
1777, Aug. 8, Owen, Edward, and Elizabeth Owen.
1777, Aug. 8, Owen, Elizabeth, and Edward Owen.
1771, Dec. 8, Owen, Elizabeth, and Peter Carr.
1777, Oct. 26, Owen, Mary, and Robert DeSilver.
1780, June 22, Owen, Sarah, and Andrew Patton.
1794, April 17, Owens, Archibald, and Susannah Chapman.
1775, July 24, Owens, Elizabeth, and Daniel Fritch.
1770, Dec. 25, Owens, Elizabeth, and George Humbley.
1757, Dec. 1, Owens, Elizabeth, and Thomas Haines.
1790, June 3, Owens, John, and Susanna Macfee.
1783, Jan. 7, Owens, Patrick, and Eleonor Knox.
1779, July 21, Owens, Robert, and Catherine Robeson.
1780, Dec. 24, Owens, Simon, and Eleanor North.
1792, Jan. 2, Owens, Susanna, and Michael Walsh.
1790, Aug. 29, Owings, Cassandra Deje, and Benedict Francis
         Van Pradelles.
1759, Feb. 10, Owner, Marmaduke, and Lydia Potts.
1757, Jan. 28, Oxson, Benjamin, and Mary Kile.
1759, March 13, Oyster, George, and Hanna Moyer.
1789, June 25, Ozias, John, and Mary Connar.
1767, March 23, Packet, Mary, and Armas McMan.

1781, Sept. 19, Packstone, Mary, and Benjamin Bendel.
1778, Jan. 28, Padgie, John, and Margaret Jack.
1789, July 5, Padric, Thomas, and Amy Graves.
1756, Oct. 29, Padrick, Mary, and Israel Matzon.
1758, June 8, Padrick, Thomas, and Sarah Roseneth.
1764, Nov. 6, Page, Ann, and Thomas James.
1777, June 9, Page, Elizabeth, and John Hilton.
1777, July 31, Page, Joseph, and Deborah Bell.
1773, Feb. 6, Page, Joseph, and Mary Freviller.
1792, March 1, Page, Melinda, and Daniel Cartwright.
1777, May 27, Page, Richard, and Mary Winters.
1795, Jan. 30, Page, Sarah, and Mathew Moran.
1788, Aug. 5, Page, Sarah, and Peter Hallstedt.
1794, May 11, Page, Susannah, and Benjamin Sermon.
1779, June 18, Pain, Elizabeth, and William Gowdey.
1792, April 17, Paine, Sarah, and William Hoxworth.
1778, June 14, Painter, Ann, and Edward Bay.
1790, Nov. 4, Painter, Cathrine, and Joseph Smith.
1797, Aug. 31, Painter, David, and Elizab. Helm.
1792, Feb. 23, Painter, Elizabeth, and Jonathan Smith.
1779, May 20, Painter, Elizabeth, and Wollentine Breneize.
1787, Sept. 20, Painter, Jacob, and Sarah Simes.
1757, May 9, Painter, John, and Ann Gartrout Spece.
1790, Oct. 25, Painter, Marget, and William Brown.
1778, June 2, Palfrey, John, and Sidney McDonald.
1766, Sept. 3, Palmer, Elizabeth, and William Evitt.
1751, Sept. 8, Palmer, George, and Elizabeth Hall.
1796, Dec. 19, Palmer, Margret, and John Himes.
1756, Jan. 1, Palmer, Richard, and Phebe Jonse.
1762, Sept. 13, Pammer, Elizabeth, and Richard Lambart.
1760, Nov. 9. Pand, Abel, and Sarah Aldritsh.
1794, July 18, Pape, Ann, and William Stuart Skinner.
1753, July 28, Param, Margaret, and Peter David.
1758, July 2, Parent, Thomas, and Mary Lippencott.
1781, March 22, Park, George, and Jenny Knox.
1754, Oct. 15, Park, Robert, and Mary Ann McKenmin.
1792, April 8, Park, Walter, and Elizabeth Rian.
1781, June 4, Parker, Abram, and Polly Garricks.
1765, Dec. 4, Parker, Ann, and Alexander Gibbs.
1755, May 5, Parker, Ann, and John Knight.
1784, June 13, Parker, Archiles, and Rachel Botler.
1779, July 19, Parker, Edward, and Isabel Eldridge.
1761, Aug. 3, Parker, Elizabeth, and Edward Callaghan.
1778, March 10, Parker, Elisha, and Mary North.
1798, March 14, Parker, James, and Hannah Lloyd.
1779, May 31, Parker, Jane, and James Benney.

1758, Sept. 26, Parker, Judith, and Edward Reese.
1751, Nov. 15, Parker, Martha, and Thomas Felten.
1784, March 5, Parker, Mary, and Philip Lloyd.
1779, Sept. 27, Parker, Mary, and Thomas Paufield.
1768, April 27, Parker, Nathaniel, and Ann Henderson.
1780, March 14, Parker, Rachel, and Robert Hunter.
1771, June 11, Parker, Rebecca, and William Riggens.
1796, Sept. 5, Parker, Sarah, and Thomas Prior.
1778, May 21, Parker, Thomas, and Mary Yarnell.
1795, Nov. 15, Parker, William, and Dorothy Bowers.
1781, Dec. 6, Parkes, Mary Anne, and Humphrey Wayne.
1781, Dec. 20, Parkes, Mary, and James Maffey.
1779, Oct. 13, Parkeson, Joseph, and Margaret Hamilton.
1779, Dec. 8, Parkeson, Mary, and John Clark.
1779, June 3, Parkhill, John, and Sarah Smith.
1798, May 19, Parkhill, Rebecca, and William Henry Dunkin.
1790, May 20, Parkinson, James, and Cathrine Nicholson.
1797, Jan. 24, Parkinson, Martha, and William Lodge.
1776, Oct. 20, Parkinson, Mary, and Thomas Porter.
1787, July 5, Parks, Mary, and Richard Allen.
1778, June 16, Parks, William, and Mary Dennis.
1781, Nov. 12, Parmer, Joseph, and Catharine Ralley.
1789, Oct. 20, Parmer, Joseph, and Mary James.
1763, Nov. 30, Parmer, Margaret, and John Stant.
1793, Dec. 21, Parmer, William, and Mary Archer.
1795, Sept. 3, Parr, Sarah, and Thomas Little.
1795, March 23, Parram, Susanna, and Stephen Conyers.
1796, March 17, Parris, Ann, and Henry Green.
1784, March 29, Parrish, William, and Mary Austin.
1752, June 18, Parry, Elinor, and Joseph Johns.
1786, June 2, Parry, John, and Fanny Weaver.
1777, Nov. 22, Parson, Sarah, and Hugh Hugh.
1797, July 16, Parsons, Hannah, and Samuel Mitchel.
1767, Nov. 21, Parsons, Hannah, and Warren Bigello.
1780, Sept. 20, Parsons, Lawrence, and Elizabeth Lilly.
1776, Dec. 13, Parsons, Richard, and Mary Peacock.
1793, April 3, Parvin, William Pitt, and Charlotte Hicks.
1758, Aug. 24, Parwin, Lowise, and Thomas Grew.
1797, Nov. 24, Pascal, John, and Elizabeth Cline.
1792, Jan. 1, Pascal, Mary, and Edward Brannan.
1779, Dec. 16, Pascal, Stephen, and Nancy Fisher.
1780, Dec. 16, Pascal, Stephen, and Nancy Fisher.
1779, May 8, Pashal, Edward, and Margarett Bell.
1780, Jan. 30, Pashall, Benjamin, and Sarah Woods.
1762, July 29, Pastoley, Paul, and Phebe Longacre.
1784, April 13, Pater, Stephen, and Susannah Miller.

1773, Aug.   9, Pates, Rosanna, and Simon Mitchell.
1755, Oct.   15, Patrick, John, and Abigail Hockley.
1789, April   5, Patruis, Catharine, and John Lemon.
1765, Aug.   31, Patterson, Andrew, and Mary Williams.
1780, June   23, Patterson, Ann, and Adam Craus.
1778, May   27, Patterson, Archibald, and Catharine Anderson.
1759, July   30, Patterson, Catharine, and William Brown.
1777, June   1, Patterson, Elizabeth, and Alexander Harvey.
1777, Oct.   25, Patterson, Elizabeth, and Henry Horner.
1774, Nov.   1, Patterson, John, and Ann Anderson.
1797, Aug.   26, Patterson, John, and Jane Lamont.
1782, June   23, Patterson, Joseph, and Mary Jones.
1791, June   13, Patterson, Martha, and Elihu Morris.
1797, Nov.   25, Patterson, Mary, and John Brady.
1776, March 25, Patterson, Mary, and Patrick Condren.
1791, Sept.   22, Patterson, Patty, and Samuel White.
1759, Jan.   11, Patterson, Robert, and Elisabet Brown.
1782, Oct.   26, Patterson, Sarah, and John Blankny.
1778, Jan.   27, Patterson, Thomas, and Sarah Ewin.
1768, April   4, Patterson, William, and Ann Clamance.
1777, Feb.   4, Patterson, William, and Catharine Matthews.
1777, May   10, Patterson, William, and Lorannah Kenney.
1757, Dec.   5, Pattin, Margaret, and James, Young.
1782, Aug.   4, Pattinger, James, and Margret Rogers.
1792, Jan.   5, Pattison, James, and Elizabeth Gough.
1780, June   22, Patton, Andrew, and Sarah Owen.
1775, Aug.   6, Patton, Margaret, and Robert Matters.
1787, April   11, Patton, Thomas, and Marget Tryet.
1786, Oct.   20, Patty, Mary, and Mathias Holland.
1779, Sept.   27, Paufield, Thomas, and Mary Parker.
1764, June   21, Paul, Ann, and George Peppar.
1775, Oct.   5, Paul, Hannah, and Francis Young.
1797, Nov.   23, Paul, James, and Elizabeth Rodman.
1770, July   1, Paul, John, and Jane Mallobey.
1781, March 29, Paul, Nancy, and Cornelius Comegys.
1753, Dec.   25, Paul, Peter, and Jane Evens.
1774, July   19, Paul, Richard, and Lydia Duché.
1776, March 7, Paul, Susanna, and Bevan Rakestraw.
1795, Aug.   27, Paul, Susannah, and Thomas Lancaster.
1782, March 18, Paul, Thomas, and Catherine DeCamp.
1784, Feb.   19, Paul, Thomas, and Elizabeth Stadleman.
1792, Sept.   14, Pawlding, Jesiah, and Jane Garret.
1794, April   18, Pawling, Jeremiah, and Elizabeth Thomson.
1765, Feb.   25, Paxton, Catharine, and Thomas Booker.
1764, March 31, Paxton, Martha, and John Arney.
1751, Feb.   19, Paylin, William, and Elizabeth England.

1765, Oct.   10, Payn, Joseph, and Ann Thomson.
1787, May   31, Payne, Elizabeth, and Samuel Andrews.
1759, July   8, Payne, James, and Margeth Braun.
1782, Aug.   13, Peace, Elizabeth, and Andrew Pearce.
1776, Dec.   13, Peacock, Mary, and Richard Parsons.
1783, March 19, Peak, Philip, and Jane Weskot.
1782, Aug.   13, Pearce, Andrew, and Elizabeth Peace.
1780, Sept.   21, Pearce, John, and Mary Dick.
1758, May   19, Pearce, Sarah, and Peter Holton.
1791, May   29, Pearcey, Mary, and Isaac Murfin.
1757, June   30, Pearson, Elias, and Ann Wiseley.
1780, March   5, Pearson, Isaac, and Elizabeth Loddell.
1796, Feb.   8, Pearson, Joseph G., and Margret Pilloe.
1792, Nov.   15, Pearson, Rachel, and Jonathan Morris.
1780, March   9, Pearson, Susannah, and Samuel Preston.
1752, Nov.   30, Peart, Bryan, and Elizabeth Walton.
1797, Aug.   13, Peck, Cathrine, and John Martin.
1782, March 30, Peddle, Mary, and John Esquire.
1794, May   10, Pedric, Thomas, and Mary Story.
1797, July   6, Pedrick, Susannah, and Godwin Peirce.
1793, May   9, Peed, Kesiah, and William Dear.
1794, Dec.   10, Peehine, Margaret, and George Geiger.
1800, Sept.   5, Peel, Anne, and John Given.
1757, March 24, Peel Benjamin, and Elizabeth Madden.
1775, Dec.   19, Peel, John, and Mary Shippen.
1773, Nov.   4, Peel, William, and Margaret Wilson.
1792, July   9, Peel, William, and Mary Monro.
1752, Dec.   25, Peers, Henry, and Susanna Hunt.
1775, March 28, Peeton, John, and Mary McCormish.
1779, June   23, Peggy, and Cato, (negroes.)
1764, Nov.   22, Peihin, Susannah, and Martin Miller.
1797, July   6, Peirce, Godwin, and Susannah Pedrick.
1781, April   30, Peirey, Thomas, and Catherine Frump.
1773, Jan.   2, Penderburg, James, and Elizabeth Overthrow.
1788, April   3, Pendergrass, John, and Hanna Grady.
1763, May   10, Pendergast, Thomas, and Mary Sesrin.
1779, Feb.   21, Pendleton, John, and Agnes Trotter.
1782, June   18, Penn, Sarah, and Archibald Fresier.
1796, Sept.   19, Pennece, William, and Dorothea G. Graham.
1783, July   15, Pennington, Elizabeth, and Robert Burridge.
1799, March 13, Pennington, John, and Susannah Gasford.
1794, Aug.   14, Pennock, Samuel, and Ann Forster.
1766, July   7, Penny, Amelia, and Philip Erwin.
1780, Jan.   30, Penny, Catharine Many, and Benjamin Soden.
1777, Sept.   24, Penny, Sarah, and David Crawford.
1753, July   15, Pennystone, Catharine, and Isaac Lewis.

1777, Aug. 24, Penrose, James, and Abigail Perry.
1751, Nov. 28, Penrows, Elizabeth, and Samuel Oliver.
1785, March 13, Pentland, James, and Susannah Evans.
1794, Aug. 13, Penton, Andrew, and Hanna Mink.
1796, Sept. 15, Peppar, Francis, and Susannah Conchlin.
1764, June 21, Peppar, George, and Ann Paul.
1777, Nov. 2, Pepper, George, and Mary Powell.
1789, Feb. 3, Pepperly, Rachel, and Robert Bicknell.
1781, April 23, Perce. Elizabeth, and John Hail.
1779, Sept. 24, Perkeson, Elizabeth, and John Shoman.
1779, Dec. 28, Perkins, Elizabeth, and Jacob Amos.
1787, Nov. 24, Perkins, Isaac, and Hannah Murrey.
1756, March 7, Perkins, Jacob, and Elizabeth Heulings.
1777, Jan. 29, Perkins, James, and Elizabeth Bowen.
1783, June 26, Perkins, John, and Elizabeth Harr.
1783, Sept. 6, Perkins, John, and Elizabeth Skill.
1793, July 11, Perkins, Marget, and John Tailor.
1780, May 20, Perkins, Mary, and Enoch Welsh.
1792, June 3, Perkins, Sarah, and Owen Shields.
1780, Jan. 29, Perris, Thomas, and Frances More.
1777, Aug. 24, Perry, Abigail, and James Penrose.
1780, March 15, Perry, Charles, and Elizabeth Semphton.
1798, June 14, Perry, Mary, and John Spenser.
1780, March 21, Perry, Richard, and Elizabeth Smith.
1781, Feb. 1, Perry, Sarah, and John Farver.
1772, May 2, Perry, William, and Mary Slyhoof.
1764, June 13, Persey, Christopher, and Mary Smith.
1778, Jan. 11, Peten, John, and Hannah Ward.
1777, June 17, Peterman, Elizabeth, and David Wyse.
1756, April 22, Peterman, Jacob, and Ann Colday.
1756, Dec. 18, Peters, Ann, and Jonathan Delworth.
1796, June 6, Peters, Elizabeth, and George Caruthers.
1764, May 19, Peters, Elizabeth, and Robert Warnack.
1796, July 26, Peters, Henry, and Mary Edwards.
1787, July 11, Peters, John, and Rachel Haselton.
1767, Aug. 5, Peters, Mungrel, and Mary Evans.
1773, April 13, Peters, Peter, and Sarah Bryan.
1780, June 4, Peters, Rebecca, and Daniel Date.
1794, Aug. 3, Peters, Thomas Thales, and Rosanna McCalla.
1754, Jan. 19, Peters, William, and Mary Milner.
1761, Nov. 9, Peterson, Christiana, and Peter Matson.
1762, Nov. 9, Peterson, Christiana, and Peter Matson.
1776, Nov. 20, Peterson, Jean, and John Thomas Nicholls.
1800, Jan. 5, Peterson, Peter, and Mary Souders.
1783, July 1, Peterson, Rodey, and George Ross.
1800, Nov. 5, Peterson, Sarah, and Richard McCombe.

1758, July   6, Peterson, Susanna, and Israel Hendrickson.
1792, Dec.   14, Petit Jean, Jacob Anthony, and Mary Burke.
1796, June   2, Petlow, Margery, and James Convell.
1782, Aug.   25, Petterson, William, and Hannah Green, (negroes.)
1793, April   26, Pettit, Ann, and Timothy Moraty.
1792, May   27, Pettit, Jane, and Martin Servent.
1780, March 19, Pettit, Joseph Benjamin, and Judy Hinele.
1791, July   22, Pettit, Peter, and Jane Gillaspy.
1759, May   28, Petty, Nathaniel, and Diana McCullough.
1778, Jan.   22, Peyat, Joshua, and Barbarah Bittel.
1756, March 25, Pfeipher, Francis Joseph, and Margarete Wallter.
1760, Sept.   22, Phagon, Charles, and Sarah Phagon.
1760, Sept.   22, Phagon, Sarah, and Charles Phagon.
1770, Dec.   8, Phartin, Mary M., and John Murray.
1762, April   12, Phaval, Frederick, and Mary Wheeler.
1757, May   1, Pheagan, Patrick, and Ann Murphey.
1799, Oct.   19, Phenix, Sarah, and William Fountain.
1797, July   29, Phenix, Thomas, and Sarah Brown.
1788, Jan.   20, Phiffer, Anne Mary, and William Henderson.
1761, April   13, Phile, Peter, and Jeane Feites.
1794, April   10, Philip, Jacob, and Sarah Long.
1752, April   6, Philips, Anne, and Thomas Cokes.
1755, Sept.   9, Philips, Barbara, and George Abardean.
1782, Feb.   28, Philips, Benjamin, and Cely Buchs, (negroes.)
1783, March   2, Philips, Catherine, and Robert Montgomery.
1778, Sept.   13, Philips, Hugh, and Isabella Bannah.
1767, May   25, Philips, James, and Mary Montgommery.
1781, Feb.   8, Philips, John, and Mary Gullhen.
1791, June   20, Philips, John, and Rachel Gill.
1776, Sept.   8, Philips, Mary, and Edward McDarmott.
1775, Nov.   19, Philips, Mary, and Thomas McServey.
1752, March 16, Philips, Mary, and William Crockham.
1775, Aug.   17, Philips, Mary, and Michael McWigans.
1768, Jan.   14, Philips, Sarah, and William Harper.
1764, Aug.   17, Philips, William, and Eleanore Cummings.
1780, April   30, Philipson, Hannah, and William Price.
1797, Dec.   17, Phillips, Cymon, and Sarah Jones.
1789, May   2, Phillips, Edward, and Abigail Howel.
1792, Oct,   18, Phillips, Elizabeth, and George Mathews.
1797, May   8, Phillips, John, and Elizabeth Bates.
1797, July   15, Phillips, John, and Henrietta Dunjoo.
1791, Nov.   19, Phillis and Samuel, (free blacks.)
1794, Jan.   19, Philly, Lewis, and Marget Ferran.
1762, June   23, Philmeyer, Margaret, and John Franks.
1795, Dec.   24, Philo, Mary, and John Davis.
1787, June   12, Philpot, Mary, and Richard Smith.

1792, Sept. 22, Phipps, Isaac, and Sarah Albertson.
1788, March 10, Phips, Mary, and Joseph Bird.
1766, June 30, Phoffhanser, John Jacob, and Susannah Adam.
1790, Feb. 7, Pickering, Ann, and Hugh Dill.
1799, July 16, Pickering, Thomas, and Marget Vandel.
1756, July 5, Pickerton, Benjamin, and Elizabeth Fleming.
1756, April 29, Pickle, Ann, and Henry Duff.
1797, April 30, Pickson, Susanna, and John Daly.
1799, Sept. 15, Pickwert, Mary, and George Wagener.
1781, Dec. 8, Pickwith, John, and Margaret Hall.
1781, June 20, Piddrick, Isaac, and Patience Skill.
1780, Sept. 23, Piddrick, John, and Mary Ward.
1764, July 2, Pidgeon, Catharine, and Michael Howater.
1791, Jan. 9, Pidgeon, Christopher, and Marget Brown.
1788, Aug. 5, Pidgeon, Hjob, and Hanna Robeson.
1777, May 3, Pidgeon, Moses, and Ann Dunlap.
1770, Oct. 9, Pierce, Anne, and Charles Hewett.
1770, Sept. 2, Pierce, Elizabeth, and Hugh McIntire.
1776, Nov. 22, Pierce, Hannah, and Paul Andrews.
1780, Sept. 20, Pierce, John, and Hannah Steen.
1777, Dec. 19, Pierce, John, and William McNair.
1795, Feb. 18, Pierce, Peter, and Mary Smith.
1777, June 16, Pierce, Prisilla, and William Clark.
1795, Sept. 27, Pierce, Samuel, and Nancy Hoover.
1794, May 11, Piercy, George, and Eve Turner.
1783, Nov. 20, Piercy, Henry, and Mary Sherlock.
1797, Feb. 11, Pierson, Jean Baptiste, and Marie Coinudet.
1764, May 20, Pierson, John, and Sarah Pulin.
1754, Jan. 25, Pierson, Sarah, and James Pray.
1787, Nov. 10, Pike, Catharine, and George Cooper.
1778, Jan. 6, Pike, Richard, and Ann Hooper.
1781, Jan. 16, Pilen, Sarah, and Philip Thomas.
1754, Dec. 30, Piles, Isabella, and Richard Grymes.
1767, Aug. 17, Pellager, Elizabeth, and Sebastian Hailer.
1796, Feb. 8, Pilloe, Margret, and Joseph G. Pearson.
1790, Feb. 12, Pim, Elizabeth, and Samuel Coles.
1770, Nov. 18, Pines, Elizabeth, and Samuel Staut.
1754, July 20, Pines, Sarah, and James Collins.
1791, May 22, Piniard, Rebecca, and John Denmark.
1782, June 27, Piniard, Sophy, and John Lawrence.
1777, Oct. 26, Pink, Francis, and Mary Wear.
1797, March 9, Pinkard, Mary, and Charles Purpur.
1778, May 28, Pinker, James, and Elizabeth Turner.
1791, March 5, Pinkerton, Mary, and Barney Dempsey.
1767, May 9, Pinkney, Mary, and John Platt.

1767, May   7, Pinner, Henry, and Catharine Elizabeth Dupper-
                  nim.
1770, Dec.   11, Pinshedler, Rosannah, and Daniel Carroll.
1773, Aug.   17, Pinyard, Ann, and John Smith.
1783, Oct.   30, Pinyard, Elizabeth, and John Newman.
1773, April   20, Pinyard, Sarah, and Mathias Hardin.
1783, Aug.   25, Pinyard, William, and Dorothy Davis.
1755, Sept.   3, Pinyeard, Mary, and Thomas Davis.
1778, Sept.   13, Piper, Barbarah, and John Jones.
1794, Sept.   2, Piper, Fredric, and Elizabeth Grace.
1778, Sept.   6, Piper, George, and Eve Leer.
1800, Sept.   21, Piper, Mary, and James Boslock.
1794, May   10, Pister, Cathrine, and Edmund Davey.
1789, Nov.   24, Pitette. Agautte, and Pierre Deumey.
1791, Sept.   15, Pitt, Mary, and George Henry.
1757, Nov.   23, Pitts, Mary, and Thomas Blacklidge.
1760, March   23, Place, Abraham, and Hannah Gahagen.
1775, Dec.   7, Plankintom, Jacob, and Miriam Olding.
1787, Nov.   26, Plant, James, and Anne Campbell.
1771, Oct.   6, Plant, Mary, and David Beveridge.
1772, Sept.   30, Planzick, George, and Ann Hanor.
1767, May   9, Platt, John, and Mary Pinkney.
1786, Nov.   23, Platt, Mary, and Archibald Culton.
1791, Nov.   1, Platt, Sarah, and Benjamin Hancock.
1751, June   6, Pleadwell, Sarah, and John Priest.
1757, Dec.   1, Plom, Peter, and Mary Shrieler.
1795, Sept.   29, Ploum, Mary, and Joseph Levi.
1776, Aug.   9, Plowman, William, and Deborah Linager.
1793, Nov.   26, Plucher, Margret, and Jacob Schlosser.
1790, July   28, Plum, Cathrine, and Thomas Crumley.
1791, June   21, Plum, Rebecca, and John Batt.
1792, Nov.   9, Plum, Sarah, and Barzilla Allen.
1791, June   15, Plumley, Jemima, and Israel Urian.
1776, Oct.   10, Plummen, Deborah, and John Glackin.
1778, April   20, Plummer, John, and Elizabeth Lever.
1780, March   30, Plunket, John, and Ann McDaniel.
1769, Aug.   1, Poet, Catharine, and James Kerns.
1762, April   28, Pointer, Thomas, and Brigitta Obrine.
1774, Jan.   10, Points, Mary, and William Alkin.
1789, May   21, Poke, Robert, and Edy Holt.
1777, Jan.   15, Pole, Elizabeth, and George Foster.
1772, Sept.   11, Polen, William, and Rachel Hines.
1768, June   5, Polin, Elizabeth, and John Horn.
1753, Oct.   9, Pollard, Benjamin, and Barbara Lightholn.
1778, March   30, Pollard, John, and Catherine Sousth.
1787, Jan.   2, Pollard, John, and Mary Niblin.

1782, July   15, Pollard, Mary, and James Wright.
1787, Feb.   23, Pollard, William, and Margret Hafferman.
1767, Oct.   28, Polley, Mary, and George Lucas.
1777, Dec.   14, Polly and Cato, (negroes of Samuel Moore.)
1779, July   19, Polson, John, and Elizabeth McDanal.
1780, April   17, Polson, Robert, and Eleanor Rodgers.
1796, Feb.   27, Polston, Cathrine, and Alexander Wood.
1756, July   1, Polyard, Jacob, and Elizabeth Price.
1798, Feb.   5, Pomroy, Latitia, and Thomas Dilworth.
1758, Dec.   4, Pond, John, and Hannah Elleritz.
1785, Jan.   3, Pond, Thomas, and Ruth Morgan.
1794, Nov.   9, Ponder, Sarah, and James Ferguson.
1780, Jan.   17, Ponder, William, and Sarah McMahan.
1774, March   19, Ponge, Mary, and John Blankley.
1775, April   23, Pool, Maria, and Thomas Smith.
1793, May   1, Port, Henry, and Mary Taylor.
1754, Nov.   16, Porry, Alexander, and Ann Carr.
1771, April   1, Portell, Christopher, and Elizabeth Flower.
1790, Feb.   25, Porter, Ann, and Joshua Merric.
1789, Oct.   22, Porter, Margreta, and Stephen Carter.
1768, Dec.   5, Porter, Martha, and Dennis Mullan.
1782, Oct.   15, Porter, Mary, and John Doyle.
1783, Sept.   30, Porter, Rebecca, and Isaac Vannost.
1757, March   20, Porter, Rebecca, and James Davis.
1794, April   7, Porter, Richard, and Mary Martin.
1778, Aug.   12, Porter, Robert, and Mary Burk.
1753, Aug.   12, Porter, Robert, and Perthenia Hetherington.
1778, Jan.   25, Porter, Susannah, and Thomas Wilkison.
1776, Oct.   20, Porter, Thomas, and Mary Parkinson.
1780, April   19, Porters, William, and Ann Allan.
1762, July   3, Poskett, John, and Mary Blankfield.
1792, April   23, Pothin, Eve, and Conrad Renzel.
1753, Feb.   6, Pots, Rachel, and Jacob Torsten.
1785, April   1, Potter, Margaret, and Leonard Sayre.
1768, June   9, Potter, Mary, and Robert Mack.
1764, Aug.   30, Potter, Mathew, and Jane Gillyat.
1776, March   21, Potts, Elizabeth, and James Brown.
1792, Sept.   20, Potts, Jane, and John Sommerfield.
1772, May   14, Potts, John, and Mary Land.
1759, Feb.   10, Potts, Lydia, and Marmaduke Owner.
1782, Jan.   10, Potts, Mary, and Henry Ferguson.
1751, Oct.   13, Potts, Samuel, and Ann Ashmead.
1772, Oct.   20, Potts, Samuel, and Sarah Frittz.
1788, April   18, Poulson, Anne, and Newberry Smith.
1799, Oct.   30, Poulson, Richard, and Mary Cox.
1780, April   23, Poulson, Zachariah, and Susannah Knorr.

1767, Dec.   12, Poult, Elizabeth, and Thomas Dunn.
1757, Nov.   30, Poultney, John, and Jane Harding.
1785, Dec.   13, Poultney, William, and Catherine Richey.
1780, Sept.   10, Pounder, Ann, and Joseph Martin.
1782, May   2, Pouponnot, Peter Charles, and Barbara Rowan.
1759, Jan.   24, Powel, Ann, and Charles Crenare.
1787, Nov.   18, Powel, Biddy, and Peter Traner.
1786, Nov.   22, Powel, Catherine, and John Williams.
1793, Dec.   1, Powel, Elizabeth, and John Gotlieb Sillich.
1755, Oct.   16, Powel, Elizabeth, and John Hemphill.
1794, April   10, Powel, Elizabeth, and John Moist.
1756, April   28, Powel, John, and Elinor Wilson.
1796, April   10, Powel, Mary, and Andrew Hillen.
1783, Jan.   20, Powel, Mary, and William Coates.
1753, Oct.   10, Powel, Mary, and William Flowers.
1779, Nov.   9, Powel, Rachel, and Thomas Lee.
1778, May   19, Powel, Sarah, and Ezechiel Shaldrake.
1758, March   8, Powell, Barbara, and John Hock.
1771, Jan.   26, Powell, Elizabeth, and Joseph Busfield.
1768, April   31, Powell, Mary, and Douglas Ivery.
1777, Nov.   2, Powell, Mary, and George Pepper.
1784, July   14, Powell, Mary, and Thomas Statten.
1773, Aug.   21, Powell, William, and Barbara Rodin.
1785, July   27, Powell, William, and Eleanor Welch.
1767, Dec.   24, Power, Edmund, and Susannah House.
1778, June   4, Power, Elizabeth, and Laughlin McLean.
1776, Sept.   10, Power, Else, and Daniel McClean.
1754, May   1, Power, Jeremiah, and Cumfry Dusbery.
1766, April   23, Power, John, and Deborrah Meyers.
1778, Jan.   11, Power, John, and Judith Hughes.
1793, Dec.   23, Power, Margret, and John Martin.
1793, Sept.   23, Power, Mary, and Patric Joie.
1759, Aug.   30, Power, Richard, and Abigail Pugh.
1782, June   6, Power, Sarah, and Ruben Bernhard.
1799, Jan.   17, Power, Tobitha, and William Smith.
1795, Oct.   3, Power, William, and Ann McCloud.
1791, May   4, Powers, Mathew, and Mary Ann Hicky.
1785, Dec.   1, Powers, Michael, and Ann Hall.
1789, Dec.   12, Praser, Bernard, and Mary Keyl.
1755, July   8, Prath, Hesther, and Abraham Hulings.
1778, June   22, Pratt, Henry, and Frances Moore.
1791, Feb.   8, Pratt, James, and Cathrine Claypool.
1751, July   8, Pratt, Jeremiah, and Margaret Cowing.
1789, July   2, Pratt, John, and Christiana Broches.
1787, Oct.   16, Pratt, Mary, and Zalthu Treadaway.
1754, Jan.   25, Pray, James, and Sarah Pierson.

1766, Nov. 10, Preehars, Susannah, and David Davis.
1767, April 24, Preel, Ludwig, and Sophy Margett Stansin.
1795, May 21, Prentiss, Benjamin, and Hannah Van Neaman.
1798, April 3, Prentiss, John, and Ann Woodroff.
1778, Sept. 14, Prescott, Mary, and Peter Craig.
1792, Feb. 14, Preston, Amor, and Mary Flinders.
1779, July 30, Preston, Catherine, and Jacob Trump.
1771, July 25, Preston, Ceasar, and Sophia Lyons, (negroes.)
1782, June 16, Preston, Hannah, and Thomas Harton.
1771, March 10, Preston, Mary, and Jacob Meyers.
1784, Jan. 25, Preston, Mary, and Jacob Smith.
1789, Sept. 3, Preston, Rachel, and Thomas Haslip.
1780, March 9, Preston, Samuel, and Susannah Pearson.
1772, July 19, Preston, Sarah, and Abner George.
1767, Dec. 23, Prewet, Joseph, and Amy Brite.
1778, May 25, Price, Ann, and George Hutcheson.
1756, July 1, Price, Elizabeth, and Jacob Polyard.
1754, Oct. 20, Price, Elizabeth, and John McDarmat.
1800, July 3, Price, Elizab., and Joseph Becket.
1757, Oct. 19, Price, George, and Isabella Connall.
1791, March 6, Price, Hanna, and John More.
1772, June 18, Price, Hannah, and Michael Reyan.
1762, Sept. 1, Price, Heper, and James Craddock.
1789, Aug. 7, Price, Jane, and Thomas Harden.
1778, June 13, Price, John, and Margaret MelHolland.
1772, Sept. 23, Price, John Michael, and Mary Canig.
1778, Nov. 17, Price, John, and Sarah Whittle.
1777, Oct. 25, Price, Judith, and John Hinderson.
1780, July 30, Price, Margaret, and John Buntin.
1797, Nov. 8, Price, Maria, and Jacob Lady.
1753, July 26, Price, Mary, and James Evens.
1783, Jan. 8, Price, Mary, and Robert Morrell.
1795, Feb. 22, Price, Mary, and Thomas Britt.
1757, April 19, Price, Mary, and William Douglas.
1797, Jan. 16, Price, Mary, and William Duché.
1789, Dec. 2, Price, Philista, and George Connor.
1779, March 5, Price, Thomas, and Mary Hifes.
1778, March 5, Price, Thomas, and Mary Kips.
1792, Dec. 15, Price, William, and Hanna Lum.
1780, April 30, Price, William, and Hannah Philipson.
1777, Oct. 31, Price, William, and Jane Taylor.
1773, June 28, Price, William, and Mary Allan.
1763, March 10, Prichard, Mary, and James Gleen.
1785, June 23, Prichard, Mary, and John Crean.
1784, April 8, Prichett, William, and Rebecca Cresson.
1779, Sept. 23, Prickard, Mary, and Thomas Hansby.

1794, Dec.   5, Pride, Amelia, and Edward Sinnet.
1791, Nov.   12, Priest, Cathrine, and William Wood.
1758, Feb.   28, Priest, Henry, and Mary Hardford.
1752, June   14, Priest, John, and Hannah Denslow.
1751, June   6, Priest, John, and Sarah Pleadwell.
1779, April   10, Prik, Marcus, and Magdalena Zack.
1772, Dec.   31, Prill, Henry. and Margareth Keeth.
1754, Oct.   20, Primstone, Barbara, and James Davis.
1773, Dec.   16, Prince, Jean, and Abraham Thomas.
1775, June   18, Pringle, George, and Mary Sampell.
1781, Dec.   13, Printenell, Rebecca, and Adam Karn.
1753, March   26, Prinyard, Rachel, and Nathaniel Cope.
1763, Dec.   6, Prior, Charles, and Margaret Benson.
1792, March   31, Prior, Gideon, and Elizabeth Carr.
1757, June   16, Prior, Silas, and Latitia Brockdon.
1796, Sept.   5, Prior, Thomas, and Sarah Parker.
1758, June   24, Prior, Thomas, and Tacy Bewan.
1794, July   28, Pritchard, Foulk, and Elizabeth King.
1758, July   17, Pritchard, Hannah, and John Johnson.
1788, Sept.   8, Pritchard, Mary, and John Clayton.
1792, Aug.   16, Pritchett, Thomas, and Elizabeth Bonader.
1790, Aug.   31, Pritsmon, Cathrine, and Watson Ludley.
1770, April   30, Prize, Elizabeth, and Samuel Ridlay.
1771, Dec.   18, Prize, Hannah, and Samuel Davis.
1779, Feb.   6, Probant, Margaret, and John Riheback.
1776, Feb.   19, Proctor, Francis, and Ann Henderson.
1792, Dec.   9, Proctor, Joseph, and Sarah Macfee.
1768, Jan.   19, Prophecy, Thomas, and Elizabeth Hammond.
1768, March   14, Proud, Charles, and Alley Fitzgerald Smith.
1778, Nov.   25, Providence, and Judy Kean, (free negroes.)
1752, Sept.   21, Prowell, Thomas, and Rachel Griffith.
1776, July   20, Prowes, William, and Ann Nichols.
1775, June   30, Prudence and George, (negroes.)
1770, Sept.   13, Prue, Joseph, and Hannah Thomson.
1786, April   26, Prusian, Elizabeth, and John Heneywill.
1778, Aug.   22, Puddle, Elizabeth, and John Salter.
1759, Aug.   30, Pugh, Abigail, and Richard Power.
1791, Jan.   8, Pugh, Mary, and Jonas Simonds.
1792, Feb.   28, Pugh, Ruth, and John Snyder.
1763, May   11, Pugh, Samuel, and Andy Evans.
1752, July   19, Pugh, Sarah, and Edward Knowles.
1764, May   20, Pulin, Sarah, and John Pierson.
1755, April   11, Pullen, Rachel, and William Atkins.
1753, Oct.   29, Pullen, William, and Darkes Harratish.
1778, Feb.   27, Pullin, William, and Ann Harcourt.
1776, July   14, Purdey, William, and Christiana Miller.

1790, Oct.   30, Purdon, William, and Mary Mayris.
1791, Aug.   5, Purnell, Phebe, and Bartholomy Geoghegan.
1797, March   9, Purpur, Charles, and Mary Pinkard.
1786, Aug.   21, Purreau, Francis, and Mary Gram.
1772, Dec.   18, Pursell, Ann, and Thomas Rue.
1785, June   21, Pursell, Henry D., and Anne Davis.
1780, July   17, Pursull, Francis, and Mary Cockran.
1777, April 20, Purtal, Christopher, and Elizabeth White.
1797, Aug.   17, Purvis, William, and Mary Day.
1784, April 27, Pusey, Prudence, and Joseph Marshall.
1781, Jan.   18, Pusey, Susannah, and Joseph Israel.
1763, April 27, Pyatt, Jane, and Thomas Roberts.
1774, Feb.   16, Pyatt, Sarah, and William Vanderman.
1788, Sept.   6, Pyle, Nathan, and Rachel Walter.
1794, Aug.   10, Pyle, Susannah, and John Marns.
1767, May   24, Pymer, Barbarah, and William Coyle.
1773, Feb.   11, Pyott, Abraham, and Ann Warner.
1754, April 10, Pyott, Hannah, and Jesse Kirk.
1772, Dec.   24, Pyott, James, and Rosannah Kearnes.
1757, March 26, Pyott, Mary, and Michael Hall.
1754, July   11, Pyton, Elizabeth, and David Adamson.
1768, April   7, Quanah, Hannah, and James Doulis, (free ne-
                 groes.)
1796, May   7, Quarel, James, and Mary Dougherty.
1776, Aug.   13, Quarll, Joseph, and Susannah Wright.
1778, Sept.   2, Quarrel, James, and Lelia McCartney.
1769, March 27, Quat, Samuel, and Elizabeth Bush.
1766, Sept. 28, Queen, Dianah, and Henry Mearit.
1757, Sept. 27, Queen, Felix, and Elizabeth Jonse.
1782, March 28, Queen, Rebecca, and Samuel Studden.
1791, Jan.   9, Quest, John, and Elizabeth Caldovi.
1767, Aug.   12, Quicksall, Newill, and Jacob Lowry.
1798, Aug.   16, Quicksaw, Jonathan, and Marget Balert.
1755, Nov.   23, Quig, Catharine, and Hennery Miller.
1767, Oct.   10, Quig, Catharine, and James Huston.
1776, Jan.   3, Quigg, Ann, and Samuel Couch.
1778, Jan.   29, Quigg, Dunchan, and Sarah Griffieth.
1778, June   4, Quigg, Elizabeth, and George Smith.
1795, Feb.   8, Quigley, Frederic, and Mary Anderson.
1787, Sept. 18, Quinn Buly, and George Foster.
1796, Nov.   17, Quin, Peter, and Bridget Mathews.
1790, Sept. 20, Quinlin, Morris, and Ann McCuen.
1751, Dec.   10, Rabb, Mary, and Hugh Travers.
1782, March 31, Rabloy, Michael, and Mary Robeson.
1775, July   29, Race, Agnes, and Andrew McCormick.
1760, Nov.   5, Race, Elizabeth, and John Serett.

1790, May 3, Racer, Mary, and Isaac Levan.
1786, Oct. 16, Racks, Mary, and John Wise.
1776, Sept. 9, Radileff, Rachel, and Alexander Neeland.
1758, March 29, Radley, Joseph, and Catharine Uplin.
1777, Sept. 9, Rafert, Mary, and Robert Woldridge.
1777, Feb. 3, Ragusin, John, and Catharine Lavery.
1775, Sept. 26, Rainer, Sarah, and Samuel Warren.
1759, March 11, Rainniels, Alexander, and Mary Sheredin.
1775, June 8, Rairy, Catharine, and Samuel Jobson.
1763, Aug. 24, Raisford, Ann, and George Farmer.
1791, Nov. 15, Rajal, Mary, and Cornelius Woods.
1756, Dec. 24, Rakes, Uverrella, and John Buchanan.
1776, March 7, Rakestraw, Bevan, and Susannah Paul.
1781, Nov. 12, Ralley, Catharine, and Joseph Parmer.
1792, Dec. 4, Ralph, Judith, and Charles Carter.
1757, Nov. 10, Ralston, David, and Jenet Morrow.
1774, Jan. 15, Rambo, Ann, and Joseph Taylor.
1757, Nov. 30, Rambo, Benjamin, and Rachel Reeves.
1776, Aug. 5, Rambo, Christian, and Israel Tonkin.
1797, Feb. 28, Rambo, Elizab., and James Simpson.
1788, April 22, Rambo, Elizabeth, and John Marcher.
1773, Oct. 30, Rambo, Elizabeth, and Robert Benington.
1752, Nov. 8, Rambo, Ezechiel, and Mary Hindrickson.
1766, March 20, Rambo, Gabriel, and Mary Kinch.
1759, June 9, Rambo, ————, and George Rambo.
1759, June 9, Rambo, George, and ———— Rambo.
1792, March 29, Rambo, Jonathan, and Elizabeth Sturges.
1750, Dec. 3, Rambo, Martha, and Jacob Cox.
1755, Dec. 29, Rambo, Mary, and Jacob Boardman.
1778, June 1, Rambo, Mary, and Zachariah Baley.
1759, April 21, Rambo, Nicholas, and Mertha Sharp.
1751, Dec. 26, Rambo, Peter, and Rachel Tomson.
1754, Aug. 21, Rambo, Rachel, and John Walters.
1752, May 18, Rambo, Sarah, and Cornelius Hains.
1777, Aug. 5, Ramburg, Mary, and William Leaver.
1757, Feb. 17, Ramesy, Mary, and William Spense.
1782, April 5, Ramick, David, and Elizabeth Deony.
1799, June 30, Ramsey, Charles, and Mary Kean.
1793, July 3, Ramsey, Christopher, and Susannah Kyler.
1800, Feb. 17, Ramsey, Marget, and James Ray.
1755, June 3, Ramsey, Rachel, and Henry Lee.
1775, July 4, Ramsey, Rachel, and Henry Lee.
1792, Aug. 15, Ramsey, William, and Ann Dexter.
1790, Oct. 9, Ramstrœm, Henry, and Marget Fults.
1753, June 14, Randall, Jacob, and Rebecca Walton.
1753, Jan. 16, Randel, Stephen, and Sary Grant.

1756, April 19, Randelor, Mary, and Nathaniel Delap.
1768, April 16, Ranen, Catharine, and Andrew Boys.
1773, April 26, Rankin, Jane, and Hugh Kidd.
1764, July 18, Rankin, Joseph, and Margaret Carsen.
1767, Aug. 20, Rankin, Sarah, and John Murray.
1759, Aug. 27, Rannels, Thomas, and Elizabeth Brannel.
1760, Aug. 26, Ranbury, Mary, and William Faires.
1791, Aug. 17, Ransel, Margret, and Jonas Johnson.
1792, April 27, Ranz, Christopher, and Margret Schnobin.
1791, Feb. 10, Raphoon, Christopher, and Margret Facundus.
1794, Sept. 16, Raphoon, John, and Christiana Rhoads.
1778, May 19, Ratchford, James, and Sarah Mullan.
1754, March 10, Rathwell, John, and Hannah MacMahan.
1779, Aug. 18, Rauilson, Richard, and Sarah Wiggs.
1783, April 20, Rawford, Elizabeth, and Adam Mount.
1762, July 17, Rawford, Rachel, and John Godlove.
1782, May 15, Raworth, John, and Anne Fell.
1789, June 3, Rawth, Hanna, and Samuel Cooper.
1763, Sept. 9, Ray, Christopher, and Elenore Ross.
1776, May 19, Ray, George, and Mary Jones.
1800, Feb. 17, Ray, James, and Marget Ramsey.
1779, Nov. 19, Ray, John, and Mary Robert.
1797, April 20, Ray, Mary, and John James.
1781, March 22, Ray, Rebecca, and Harvey Stone.
1783, Dec. 10, Raybold, George, and Elizabeth Summers.
1782, May 11, Raybold, Sarah, and Godfrid Bendor.
1773, Feb. 16, Rayman, Hannah, and Constantine Doharty.
1752, Dec. 29, Rayn, Margaret, and William Shealan.
1783, Sept. 1, Rea, Anne, and John Darragh.
1756, Aug. 9, Read, Dorothy, and Hugh Williams.
1777, Jan. 13, Read, Franklin, and Catharine Carrie.
1779, Jan. 3, Read, Isabel, and Isaac Covert.
1786, April 14, Read, James, and Sarah Collins.
1754, Feb. 28, Read, John, and Margaret Watson.
1767, Dec. 29, Read, Mary, and John Armour.
1799, Oct. 15, Reading, Ann, and David Miller.
1794, May 15, Reading, Marget, and Samuel Walton.
1766, Oct. 4, Reading, Sarah, and James Double.
1765, Feb. 25, Reah, Elizabeth, and John Cunningham.
1751, July 1, Reanes, Mary, and Joseph Andover.
1772, March 2, Reardon, Eleanor, and Rolind McQuiln.
1754, April 15, Reay, Jane, and William Little.
1776, Nov. 4, Rebolt, Mary, and Anthony Hobbert.
1778, May 29, Rebson, Elizabeth, and Jonathan Wade.
1759, Nov. 12, Rechester, William, and Abigail Hubs.
1751, Nov. 17, Redford, Arthur, and Susanna Cruck.

1766, April 15, Redgrove, Ann, and John Taylor.
1769, March 5, Redhead, Jonathan, and Catharine Carsenberry.
1794, Oct.   4, Redhead, Peter, and Mary Cottman.
1759, March 16, Redin, Sebrow, and Jacob Albertson.
1782, May   7, Reding, Elizabeth, and James Toy.
1777, Nov. 10, Redler, Edward, and Jane Ware.
1779, Jan. 26, Redman, Isabel, and Nicholas Edgecoumbe.
1770, Nov. 26, Redman, Thomas, and Elizabeth Burton.
1768, March 3, Redman, Wollaston, and Catharine Clarke.
1773, Oct. 10, Redmond, Philip, and Hannah Kimmons.
1760, Jan.   7, Reed, Bernard, and Mary Marks.
1800, June   4, Reed, Charles, and Mary Budd.
1753, Aug. 28, Reed, Elenor, and Robert Williamson.
1793, May   29, Reed, Elizabeth, and John Lodge.
1772, March 1, Reed, Elizabeth, and Thomas Whiler.
1799, Oct. 17, Reed, Gabriel, and Hannah Spears.
1778, June 13, Reed, George, and Mary Oats.
1796, Oct. 29, Reed, John, and Dorcas Midleton.
1791, July 25, Reed, John, and Elizab. McCallister.
1763, Dec. 14, Reed, John, and Jane Row.
1765, June 24, Reed, Margaret, and Thomas Willson.
1769, July   5, Reed, Mary, and Barnith Cein.
1791, May   25, Reed, Mary, and John Bell.
1752, Sept. 27, Reed, Ruth, and Charles Fling.
1791, March 10, Reed, Samuel, and Ann Miller.
1793, Jan.   6, Reed, Sibilla, and John Crass or Croess.
1778, Nov.   4, Reed, Stephen, and Margaret Butler.
1778, June 15, Reed, Thomas, and Deborah Wintour.
1794, Aug.   2, Reedy, Cathrine, and Jean Baptist Destrue.
1773, Jan. 18, Reelen, Thomas, and Catharine Conner.
1759, June 30, Reely, Elizabeth, and William Steel.
1780, Aug.   1, Reemer, Mary, and John Shrave.
1786, May   2, Reemer, William, and Sarah Loughberry.
1789, June   2, Rees, Barbara, and William Tully.
1751, Aug. 20, Rees, John, and Mary Robeson.
1757, Feb.   6, Rees, John and Susannah Richards.
1773, Dec. 16, Rees, Thomas, and Patience Boulter.
1758, Sept. 26, Reese, Edward, and Judith Parker.
1790, Oct.   2, Reese, Hester, and Samuel Farra.
1763, Feb. 22, Reet, James, and Ann Fisher.
1774, Oct. 12, Reeve, Elizabeth, and William Calveley.
1752, May   24, Reeve, Samuel, and Mary Lewis.
1758, May   7, Reeves, Arthur, and Mary Cox.
1773, March 12, Reeves, Elijah, and Mary Larey.
1787, Jan. 13, Reeves, Mary, and John Gruff.
1757, Nov. 30, Reeves, Rachel, and Benjamin Rambo.

1796, Sept. 18, Reeves, Sophia, and John Dollin.
1799, Feb. 17, Reeze, Ann, and William Jacques.
1777, April 30, Regem, Ann, and Thomas, McMullen.
1788, Dec. 28, Regnault, Claire Francis, and Ann Bellrose.
1789, May 16, Reib, Henry, and Mary Stoger.
1796, April 13, Reichenberg, Maria Gertruid, and Francis Gotleib Damling.
1760, March 3, Reichert, Catharine, and Albrecht Helligas.
1781, Sept. 6, Reighley, Priscilla, and John Lawder.
1778, June 1, Reiley, John, and Frances Davis.
1784, Nov. 30, Reily, Catherine, and Richard Campbell.
1765, Dec. 11, Reily, Mary, and Henry Burnet.
1772, June 30, Rein, John, and Mary Creman.
1752, Nov. 27, Reindaler, Jacob, and Mary Mourin.
1770, Dec. 30, Reindollar, Christopher, and Elizabeth Bremen.
1774, Jan. 2, Reinhardin, Catharine, and Adam Warner.
1759, Nov. 22, Reinhardt, Elizabeth, and Philip Arendt.
1757, May 28, Reinhart, Mary, and John Campbell.
1777, April 7, Reinholds, Catharine, and George Bardack.
1797, March 7, Reineck, John Jacob, and Ann Mary Henckel.
1776, Jan. 14, Reininger, Sophia, and Gerick Glink.
1765, Dec. 5, Reiser, Andrew, and Barbara Shunk.
1790, Dec. 27, Rekstraw, Hanna, and Abraham Colladay.
1761, Sept. 21, Rekstraw, Hannah, and William Hall.
1771, Aug. 11, Relof, Catharine, and George King.
1770, Nov. 4, Remer, Mary, and William Forepaugh.
1785, Jan. 27, Remick, Elizabeth, and John Fullerton.
1779, Sept. 26, Renahan, Daniel, and Catharine Thomson.
1776, Jan. 3, Rench, James, and Deborah Stubbs.
1791, May 12, Reninger, Cathrine, and Jacob Zimmerman.
1793, May 29, Renn, Frederic, and Elizabeth Slight.
1792, Aug. 11, Reno, Susanna, and Benjamin Bickerton.
1780, Sept. 13, Renshammer, Mary, and John Bloxham.
1763, April 14, Renshaw, Elizabeth, and Isaac Janvier.
1756, Feb. 5, Renshaw, Richard, and Isabella Irwin.
1767, Nov. 5, Rensill, Ann, and John George Loreman.
1792, April 23, Renzel, Conrad, and Eve Pothin.
1791, July 26, Reper, Mathieu, and Hannah Laussin.
1794, Sept. 9, Repjohn, Marget, and Maturin Offrey.
1778, Dec. 27, Repman, Samuel, and Barbarah Bryan.
1790, July 24, Reppolle, Marget, and Lewis Brimmer.
1760, July 5, Repton, Mary, and William Appleton.
1759, May 29, Rester, George, and Elizabeth Stahl.
1761, Nov. 23, Rethain, John, and Rose Cook.
1758, Aug. 6, Retsler, Christina, and Frederick Dietz.
1782, March 31, Revel, Adam, and Elizabeth Conly.

1777, Nov. 28, Revel, Margaret, and Joseph Stevens.
1778, Nov. 17, Revel, Mary, and Hugh McDonald.
1777, Nov.   8, Revel, Mary, and John Wheeler.
1796, Feb. 21, Reveley, Elizabeth, and John Furlong.
1754, May   7, Rex, John, and Sibyele Bastian.
1777, March 7, Rex, Susannah, and Jacob Briener.
1777, Nov. 20, Rex, William, and Ann Miller.
1788, Dec. 25, Rey, Ann, and David Dunbar.
1772, June 18, Reyan, Michael, and Hannah Price.
1782, July 25, Reyderman, Jacob, and Catharine Mood.
1766, Dec. 16, Reyl, Richard, and Hannah Mea.
1765, Sept. 14, Reynolds, Edward, and Mary Haney.
1778, Oct. 24, Reynolds, Elizabeth, and Joseph McCullock.
1777, Aug. 24, Reynolds, James, and Mary Maxfield.
1774, Jan.   1, Reynolds, John, and Sarah Gardiner.
1772, Dec. 13, Reynolds, Nathaniel, and Elenor Fitsgerald.
1790, Nov.   6, Reynolds, Priscilla, and Richard Green.
1777, April 1, Reynolds, Sarah, and James Josiah.
1792, May   21, Reynolds, Thomas, and Mary Atkins.
1793, May   25, Reynolds, William, and Mary Green.
1780, Jan. 10, Reyon, Isaac, and Mary Homer.
1751, July 16, Rhea, Christopher, and Mary Clever.
1790, Nov.   1, Rhea, Robert, and Mary Allen.
1754, Nov. 21, Rheemer, Sodfrey, and Mary Musgrove.
1794, Sept. 16, Rhoads, Christiana, and John Raphoon.
1790, March 29, Rhoads, Rachel, and Abel Worrell.
1767, June   6, Rhodes, Thomas, and Lydia Castel.
1753, May   24, Rhods, Ann, and Thomas Linnon.
1775, July   2, Rhods, Jacob, and Ann Monney.
1792, Nov. 25, Rhodz, Mary, and James Anderson.
1792, April 8, Rian, Elizabeth, and Walter Park.
1790, May   4, Rian, Mary, and William Hamilton.
1771, April 4, Rias, Jacob, and Rachel Andrews.
1791, Jan. 19, Ribaud, Joseph, and Nancy or Anna Cochran.
1796, April 17, Ribbel, John, and Cathrine Epple.
1774, Oct. 12, Ribley, Michael, and Margaret White.
1797, March 18, Ricard, John, and Mary Hall.
1797, April 19, Rice, Anna, and Silas Richards.
1792, Dec. 13, Rice, Daniel, and Cathrine Flowers.
1759, June 21, Rice, Henry, and Elizabeth Johnson.
1776, Oct. 29, Rice, Mary, and Henry Wisemiller.
1772, July 23, Rice, Mary, and William Fians.
1798, June 20, Rice, Rebecca, and Thomas Wilkey.
1779, Jan. 25, Rice, Robert, and Mary Steward.
1759, June   7, Rice, Sarah, and Alexander Dyar.
1777, Dec. 21, Rich, Catherine, and Joseph Culin.

1756, July   1, Rich, Henry, and Anne Smith.
1766, April 23, Rich, Mary, and Peter Adams.
1758, Nov.   12, Richard, David, and Elizabeth Magee.
1798, Nov.   22, Richard, Nathaniel, and Mary Eckart.
1779, April 14, Richards, Agnus, and John Bryce.
1766, March 17, Richards, Catherine, and William Brown.
1789, Feb.   16, Richards, Elias, and Martha Mooney.
1784, Jan.   22, Richards, Elizabeth, and Charles Granthom.
1767, Aug.   3, Richards, Ellis, and Michael Harbert.
1778, Feb.   12, Richards, Hannah, and Edward Callaghan.
1776, Sept. 16, Richards, James, and Sarah Eddrey.
1759, Aug.   11, Richards, John, and Nanay Armstrem.
1792, April 22, Richards, John, and Rachel Harris.
1794, Dec.   30, Richards, Lewis, and Elizabeth Morgan.
1778, Nov.   9, Richards, Margaret, and James Stephens.
1797, July   22, Richards, Rachel, and Francis Deburg.
1765, Aug.   25, Richards, Rachel, and Hugh Cassaday.
1797, Jan.   11, Richards, Richard, and Mary West.
1782, May   27, Richards, Sarah, and Joseph Sharp.
1797, April 19, Richards, Silas, and Anna Rice.
1757, Feb.   6, Richards, Susannah, and John Rees.
1787, Nov.   27, Richards, Thomas, and Elizabeth Crouse.
1767, July   23, Richardson, Ann, and Henry Leech.
1796, Aug.   8, Richardson, Ann, and John Ferguson.
1775, Aug.   28, Richardson, Catharine, and George Blikley.
1728, Sept. 17, Richardson, Jane, and William Bell.
1780, Sept. 20, Richardson, Lea, and William Blackney.
1794, March 23, Richardson, Margret, and Isaac Williams.
1789, Aug.   30, Richardson, Mary, and Alexander Bingham.
1767, Dec.   12, Richardson, Mary, and Bernard Van Horn.
1771, Sept.   1, Richardson, Mary, and William Harland.
1796, Jan.   23, Richardson, Nehemiah, and Sarah Smith.
1754, Sept.   7, Richardson, Robert, and Catharine Barnet.
1791, June   23, Richardson, Sarah, and Samuel Currey.
1778, Jan.   28, Richardson, William, and Ann Russel.
1792, Aug.   12, Richardson, William, and Sarah Jones.
1752, June   7, Richerdson, Peter, and Mary Dugon.
1770, Nov.   26, Richeson, Hannah, and Robert Bornett.
1757, June   18, Richeson, Susanna, and James Tilley.
1785, Dec.   13, Richey, Catherine, and William Poultney.
1754, April   6, Richey, Elizabeth, and Josiah Bettle.
1781, Sept. 20, Richmond, John, and Margaret Wright.
1773, April   9, Richmond, Thomas, and Ann Dunlap.
1769, Sept.   1, Richy, John, and Catharine Grubb.
1797, Dec.   24, Richy, Samuel, and Christian Sheller.
1796, Sept.   4, Rickard, Leonard, and Sarah Henderson.

1800, June   30, Rickey, Sarah, and Elias Johnson.
1773, Nov.   25, Ridder, David, and Elizabeth Montgomery.
1771, May   12, Ridding, Mary, and John Aheran.
1784, April   5, Riddle, Mary, and Samuel Johnston.
1755, May   19, Rider, James, and Mary Kimley.
1793, Jan.   20, Ridge, Elenore, and John Kaasfe.
1773, Oct.   23, Ridgeway, Edward, and Lydia Covert.
1790, Aug.   24, Ridgway, Charles, and Marget Robeson.
1770, April   30, Ridlay, Samuel, and Elizabeth Prize.
1780, March 26, Ridock, Sarah, and Absolam Duffy.
1779, Aug.   29, Riece, Mary, and Dewald Close.
1791, Oct.   6, Rife, Cathrine, and John France.
1780, Jan.   13, Riffet, Mathias, and Christina Baker.
1779, Feb.   6, Riheback, Jonn, and Margaret Probant.
1755, Aug.   28, Rigen, Mary, and Richard Coles.
1776, March 13, Riggen, Charles, and Ester O'Neil.
1771, June   11, Riggens, William, and Rebecca Parker.
1771, April   11, Rigger, Margaret, and James Leonard.
1790, March   4, Riggi, Barbara, and Michael Keiser.
1765, Oct.   27, Right, Elizabeth, and Isaac Davis.
1754, April   17, Right, Mary, and John Brown.
1754, April   2, Righter, Catharine, and Benjamin Levering.
1754, Feb.   26, Righter, John, and Hannah Tanes.
1768, March   1, Rigin, Hannah, and Joseph Book.
1796, June   9, Rigley, Elizabeth, and Joseph Mincer.
1794, Sept.   10, Rigley, Mary, and Constant Maux.
1794, May   17, Rihl, Elizabeth, and Robert Johnson.
1789, Sept.   22, Riley, Edward, and Eleonore Willson.
1791, Jan.   28, Riley, Elizabeth, and James Caldwell.
1778, Dec.   2, Riley, Elizabeth, and William Blair.
1776, Dec.   2, Riley, John, and Eleanor Burk.
1780, April   1, Riley, Patrick, and Margaret McGill.
1789, Aug.   12, Riley, Thomas, and Elizabeth Bennet.
1782, March 18, Riley, William, and Anne Blunt.
1772, Dec.   15, Riller, Jean, and Thomas Moss.
1759, April   16, Rimsey, Sarah, and George Morgan.
1752, Dec.   2, Rinberg, Brigitta, and John Abraham Lidenius.
1781, Sept.   17, Rine, George, and Elizabeth Adams.
1757, July   21, Rine, Leanore, and John Philip Dephute.
1796, Oct.   9, Riner, Sarah, and Thomas Ellis.
1781, Jan.   23, Ringelman, John, and Kitty Woolff.
1771, Jan.   19, Ringrose, John, and Margaret Crozier.
1785, June   7, Rinker, Elizabeth, and David Gregory.
1795, Dec.   20, Rinker, Samuel, and Cathrine Seyfert.
1788, Dec.   21, Rinker, Samuel, and Vashty Brush.
1759, March 30, Rios, Augustin, and Mary Colmain.

1767, Sept.   1, Riper, Jeane, and Daniel Wheel.
1755, Aug. 12, Rirnan, Margaret, and Joseph Noblit.
1779, Nov. 18, Risberg, Gustavus, and Martha Burrows.
1793, Jan.   5, Risener, Lydia, and James Curtis.
1799, June 27, Riser, George, and Calia Wilson.
1760, Dec. 26, Risley, Sarah, and Thomas Wiggins.
1771, Oct. 21, Risner, Elizabeth, and Edward Bats.
1780, Sept. 16, Ritchey, Edward, and Mary Harry.
1755, Nov. 24, Ritchey, Jane, and John Crawket.
1799, Feb. 25, Ritchie, Francis, and Mary Amy.
1782, July 24, Rittenhausen, Henry, and Margret Ottenstein.
1756, Aug. 25, Rittenhouse, Ann, and George Shoemaker.
1753, Dec.   8, Rittenhouse, Esther, and Thomas Barton.
1767, Aug. 22, Rittenhouse, John, and Margaret Connard.
1789, Sept. 29, Ritter, Andrew, and Susannah Davis.
1780, Aug.   4, Rives, Elizabeth Mary, and Thomas Luke.
1755, Dec. 16, Rivo, John, and Abigael McFarlin.
1793, Feb. 17, Rivola, Sante, and Elenore Harvey.
1769, Sept.   2, Roads, Elizabeth, and Hugh More.
1753, Jan. 23, Roads, Elizabeth, and William Griffy.
1789, March 17, Roads, Mary, and Adam Bloom.
1770, July   8, Roads, Mary, and Hugh McCeagne.
1772, Aug.   9, Roads, Mary, and Thomas Finn.
1781, Nov. 15, Roan, Mary, and Peter Doyle.
1800, Sept. 23, Roat, Elizabeth, and John Torr.
1775, Nov. 19, Robason, Eleanor, and John Alexander.
1764, Sept. 10, Robbeson, Margaret, and George Horech.
1765, June 24, Robbeson, Robert, and Margaret Lord.
1796, Aug.   4, Robbins, Elizabeth, and Humphrey Hooton.
1758, Jan. 26, Robenetts, Samuel, and Mary Jordan.
1779, April 7, Roberson, Mary, and James Baker.
1779, June 10, Robert, Clements, and Hannah Hantwill.
1754, Feb. 20, Robert, Cruise, and Moris Morris.
1779, Nov. 19, Robert, Mary, and John Ray.
1781, Jan. 18, Roberts, Algernow, and Tacey Warner.
1783, Dec.   6, Roberts, Alice, and Charles Cecil.
1777, April 23, Roberts, Ann, and Clement Bonsall.
1781, May   9, Roberts, Anne, and John Mours.
1790, May 10, Roberts, Ann, and William Warner.
1757, June 27, Roberts, Elinor, and John Siddons.
1769, Sept.   9, Roberts, Elizabeth, and Christopher Cornelius.
1756, May 28, Roberts, Elizabeth, and George Vanleer.
1761, April 9, Roberts, Elsah, and Jacob Janson.
1781, Feb.   2, Roberts, George, and Anna Downer.
1760, April 12, Roberts, Hannah, and Methusalah Evans.
1781, Feb.   1, Roberts, Henry, and Margaret Johnson.

1800, April 21, Roberts, Isaac, and Frances Stone.
1796, Dec. 25, Roberts, Jane, and Peter Cox.
1753, Feb. 17, Roberts, Jane, and Thomas Curny.
1774, June 27, Roberts, Jemima, and Joseph Roberts.
1793, Feb. 23, Roberts, John, and Martha Dowsey.
1778, July 25, Roberts, Joseph, and Catharine Frantz.
1796, Oct. 29, Roberts, Joseph, and Hannah Stoneburner.
1774, June 27, Roberts, Joseph, and Jemima Roberts.
1761, July 31, Roberts, Joseph, and Mary Burk.
1780, March 27, Roberts, Joseph, and Mary Collins.
1776, Sept. 15, Roberts, Margaret, and John Naylor.
1786, Jan. 19, Roberts, Mary, and William Bright.
1799, July 1, Roberts, Owen, and Margret Wesby.
1755, Nov. 23, Roberts, Paul, and Ann Williams.
1794, March 22, Roberts, Rachel, and John Spence.
1780, April 1, Roberts, Rachel, and William Akins.
1755, Sept. 18, Roberts, Rebecca, and Joseph Lankett Dunnman.
1761, March 21, Roberts, Samuel, and Ann Jewel.
1754, March 22, Roberts, Susanna, and Jacob Zimmerman.
1763, April 27, Roberts, Thomas, and Jane Pyatt.
1752, Oct. 20, Roberts, William, and Elizabeth Siddons.
1753, May 28, Roberts, William, and Grace Hamilton.
1788, Feb. 5, Roberts, Zilla, and John Shivers.
1782, Sept. 19, Robertson, George, and Johannah Shaw.
1759, Oct. 24, Robertson, John, and Catharine Rods.
1796, Feb. 16, Robertson, John, and Sarah Miller.
1794, Jan. 16, Robertson, Mary, and Thomas Bennet.
1799, Feb. 23, Robertson, Thomas, and Nancy McKean.
1779, June 1, Robeson, Alexander, and Margarett Shaw.
1771, June 17, Robeson, Ann, and John Conrad Thish.
1769, Sept. 2, Robeson, Anne, and John Welsh.
1798, Feb. 17, Robeson, Ann, and Joseph Robeson.
1779, July 21, Robeson, Catherine, and Robert Owens.
1753, Dec. 24, Robeson, Elinor, and Cornelius Robin.
1780, June 16, Robeson, Elizabeth, and John Marshall.
1799, Oct. 5, Robeson, Elizab., and Mathew Haltrick.
1759, July 5, Robeson, Elizabeth, and William Vanderspiegel.
1788, Aug. 5, Robeson, Hanna, and Hjob Pidgeon.
1790, July 13, Robeson, Hanna, and John Cole.
1790, Dec. 7, Robeson, Hugh, and Elenore Still.
1798, Nov. 29, Robeson, Isabella, and Enoch Jockum.
1791, Aug. 4, Robeson, James, and Jane Garnet.
1776, Oct. 7, Robeson, John, and Margaret Robeson.
1798, Feb. 17, Robeson, Joseph, and Ann Robeson.
1779, June 7, Robeson, Margarett, and Francis Winstanley.
1776, Oct. 7, Robeson, Margaret, and John Robeson.

1790, Aug. 24, Robeson, Marget and Charles Ridgway.
1778, April 29, Robeson, Mary, and John Miller.
1751, Aug. 20, Robeson, Mary, and John Rees.
1782, March 31, Robeson, Mary, and Michael Rabloy.
1779, Nov. 26, Robeson, Patrick, and Susannah Kelley.
1796, June 21, Robeson, Rachel, and John Armstrong.
1778, July 31, Robeson, Richard, and Mary Lunn.
1793, May 14, Robeson, Samuel, and Jane Ellis, (Africans.)
1790, July 24, Robeson, Sarah, and James Barnes.
1776, Sept. 23, Robeson, Thomas, and Mary Evance.
1799, April 1, Robeson, Thomas, and Mary Grant.
1782, Aug. 27, Robeson, William, and Emy Common.
1799, March 7, Robeson, William, and Maria Bell.
1774, Oct. 31, Robesson, Thomas, and Catharine Woolley.
1753, Dec. 24, Robin, Cornelius, and Elinor Robeson.
1759, April 8, Robins, Elizabeth, and William Ashmead.
1794, Dec. 24, Robins, Joseph, and Rachel James.
1763, June 9, Robins, Mary, and John Henry Coates.
1790, Dec. 24, Robins, Mary, and William Orum.
1764, Sept. 24, Robins, Phabeah, and Paul Jones.
1763, Feb. 12, Robins, Thomas, and Ann Morgan.
1767, Nov. 17, Robinson, Aaron, and Jane Young.
1766, Jan. 17, Robinson, Ann, and George Morton.
1782, Jan. 31, Robinson, Daniel, and Catherine Bathsket.
1792, Jan. 3, Robinson, Elizabeth, and James Bright.
1787, Aug. 22, Robinson, Hanna, and Henry Townson.
1766, Sept. 9, Robinson, Henry, and Rebeccah Garrigues.
1766, Oct. 21, Robinson, Humphrey, and Mary Cockle.
1788, May 16, Robinson, Jacob, and Hanna Boon.
1798, July 22, Robinson, James, and Anne Ziegler.
1800, June 8, Robinson, John, and Mary Agea.
1790, April 23, Robinson, John, and Mely Damon.
1787, June 28, Robinson, Joseph, and Anne Lighton.
1788, Oct. 9, Robinson, Marget, and Thomas Newzum.
1787, June 19, Robinson, Ralph Nugent, and Tasy Wood.
1790, Nov. 4, Robinson, Sarah, and James Nuzum.
1775, July 10, Robinson, Susannah, and Daniel Shew.
1787, March 14, Robinson, William, and Mary Sherman.
1781, Oct. 18, Robnet, Joseph, and Eleonor Walker.
1783, March 30, Robson, John, and Anne Tunney.
1778, June 16, Roch, James, and Mary Arch Deacon.
1787, June 7, Rockenberry, Samuel, and Catherine Van Nosten.
1778, Oct. 18, Rocthofer, Elizabeth, and Harman Johnson.
1800, March 8, Roddy, Susannah, and John Griffin.
1779, May 3, Roderick, Jane, and Richard Murthwaik.
1794, July 17, Rodes, Sarah, and William Gilfry.

1780, Feb.   19, Rodger, George, and Elizabeth Negr.
1776, Sept.   15, Rodgers, Bridget, and John West.
1780, April   17, Rodgers, Eleanor, and Robert Polson.
1790, Oct.   4, Rodgers, George, and Violet Johnson.
1783, June   21, Rodgers, John, and Catherine Maguire.
1778, April   24, Rodgers, John Gock, and Lydia Lawrence.
1774, March   6, Rodgers, John, and Mary Camel.
1798, Nov.   12, Rodgers, Mary, and George Dicson.
1779, May   7, Rodgers, Mary, and John Kidd.
1784, Aug.   17, Rodgers, Mary, and Nathaniel Smith.
1791, Jan.   18, Rodgers, Susanna, and John Green.
1761, April   29, Rodhefer, Elizabeth, and Charles Sigismund Hen-
                  rick.
1780, Jan.   27, Rodhey, Augustus, and Barbara Smith.
1773, Aug.   21, Rodin, Barbara, and William Powell.
1797, Nov.   23, Rodman, Elizabeth, and James Paul.
1797, Feb.   2, Rodney, William, and Eleonore Barry.
1759, Oct.   24, Rods, Catharine, and John Robertson.
1778, Dec.   7, Rods, William, and Catharine Flower.
1794, Oct.   2, Roe, David, and Lydia Andrews.
1795, Nov.   1, Roe, Elizabeth, and William Tribit.
1796, April   21, Roff, Ann, and William Maguire.
1778, Jan.   12, Rogers, Edward, and Mary Fitzgerald.
1793, April   2, Rogers, Elizabeth, and Joseph Johnson.
1775, Sept.   3, Rogers, Hannah, and Bethenel Detchevery.
1778, June   1, Rogers, Jacob, and Mary Jones.
1761, June   25, Rogers, James, and Ann Forbes.
1762, Aug.   25, Rogers, James, and Ann Forbes.
1793, Oct.   27, Rogers, John, and Cathrine Lewis.
1795, June   15, Rogers, John, and Elizabeth Miller.
1759, Oct.   23, Rogers, John, and Latice Stevenson.
1767, Dec.   22; Rogers, John, and Mary Haregrave.
1782, Aug.   4, Rogers, Margret, and James Pattinger.
1754, June   23, Rogers, Martha, and Hugh Gough.
1783, June   24, Rogers, Mary, and Jacob Alters.
1794, Nov.   16, Rogers, Mary, and Thomas Hurley.
1790, May   17, Rogers, William, and Charlotte Bolling.
1798, Nov.   10, Roggester, Fanny, and Joseph Lee.
1778, May   31, Roguon, Jane, and Davis Haltbridge.
1789, June   28, Rohrman, Henry, and Elizabeth Abel.
1754, March   11, Roiley, Edward, and Catharine Shiffer.
1792, July   22, Roland, John, and Elizabeth Hollscamp.
1796, May   29, Roland, William, and Tracy Sooter.
1781, Feb.   18, Rolands, Elizabeth, and John Dever.
1771, Jan.   8, Rollin, Thomas, and Susselia Homes.
1773, Oct.   31, Rollins, Elizabeth, and Joseph Bamford.

1795, Sept.   8, Rollstone, Ann, and Robert Best.
1780, Sept.   6, Rolph, William, and Catherine Adams.
1779, May   16, Roman, George, and Elizabeth Dresslin.
1782, Aug.   13, Romberg, Rachel, and George Middagh.
1790, May   4, Roney, Rachel, and George Bates.
1782, March 20, Roney, William, and Margaret Barton.
1751, June   2, Ronnells, Gilbert, and Mary Howell.
1777, Aug.   5, Rook, Mary, and Archibald Guff.
1794, Nov.   29, Root, Mary, and William Ross.
1753, March 10, Rortee, Sarah, and John Garret.
1794, Jan.   11, Rosbottom, James, and Eve Lewis.
1758, April 23, Rose, Catharine, and John Bork.
1751, June   10, Rose, Christopher, and Elizabeth Mauren.
1754, Aug.   22, Rose, David, and Abigail Busby.
1762, Dec.   2, Rose, Dorothea, and Frederick Nebel.
1787, Feb.   23, Rose and Harry, (two negro servants.)
1757, Jan.   13, Rose, John, and Ann Mary Bothman.
1800, April 24, Rose, John, and Hannah Morgan.
1751, March 12, Rose, John, and Martha Chrisley.
1798, March 30, Rose, John, and Mary Weaver.
1784, Dec.   7, Rose, Ketty, and John Dickson.
1791, Nov.   16, Rose, Mary, and James Thomas.
1796, Sept.   13, Rose, Peter, and Mary Boyer.
1791, Dec.   11, Rose, Peter, and Sophia Morgan.
1782, Dec.   7, Rose, William, and Christiana Barroner.
1758, March 12, Rosebergin, Elizabeth, and John Greebs.
1767, Feb.   27, Roseby, Margret, and Robert McIntosh.
1758, June   8, Roseneth, Sarah, and Thomas Padrick.
1754, Nov.   17, Rosh, Michael, and Catharine Caisarin.
1768, May   5, Roshell, Patience, and John Holmes.
1766, Feb.   16, Rosher, John, and Magdaline Horrin.
1798, April 15, Rosin, Cathrine, and Jesse Denning.
1758, May   20, Rosk, James, and Mary McGockene.
1763, Sept.   9, Ross, Elenore, and Christopher Ray.
1778, May   24, Ross, Elizabeth, and John McLouglen.
1777, June   15, Ross, Elizabeth, and Joseph Ashburn.
1795, May   18, Ross, Ephraim, and Dorothy Fogel.
1763, Dec.   15, Ross, Esther, and Whitefield Smith.
1783, July   1, Ross, George, and Rodey Peterson.
1776, April 15, Ross, Henry, and Elizabeth Tucker.
1776, Sept.   5, Ross, Hugh, and Elizabeth Ware.
1782, Dec.   3, Ross, Hugh, and Jenny Kenton.
1778, June   15, Ross, Hugh, and Mary Gill.
1784, Nov.   16, Ross, James, and Agnes May.
1757, Nov.   4, Ross, John, and Mary Lamplay.
1759, March 26, Ross, Joseph, and Sarah Russel.

1782, May   14, Ross, Margary, and Robert Downs.
1790, Nov.   11, Ross, Margret, and Thomas Mather.
1782, June   8, Ross, Mary, and Benjamin Carr.
1779, July   8, Ross, Richard, and Mary Vaughn.
1763, Nov.   30, Ross, Sarah, and David Sims.
1795, June   28, Ross, Stephen, and Marget Thompson.
1778, Nov.   1, Ross, Susannah, and John Butler.
1783, Nov.   13, Ross, Thomas, and Rebecca Barnet.
1794, Nov.   29, Ross, William, and Mary Root.
1799, July   8, Rossbottom, Eve, and James Steel.
1767, April   6, Rossell, Doey, and George Margool.
1768, April 16, Rossell, Patience, and John Holmes.
1795, Dec.   3, Rosseter, John, and Elizabeth Smith.
1761, April 28, Rossetor, John, and Elizabeth Shaw.
1762, April 12, Rost, Leonard, and Charlotte Manse.
1761, March 22, Roth, John, and Ann Bell.
1798, Nov.   24, Rothwell, Jacob, and Mary Vandike.
1766, Oct.   4, Roty, Margaret, and Samuel Mour.
1778, May   26, Rough, Catharine, and Mark Ollivant.
1774, Sept.   4, Row, Jacob, and Mary Litler.
1763, Dec.   14, Row, Jane, and John Reed.
1794, April 15, Row, Jane, and William Jacobs.
1758, May   28, Row, John, and Mary Norris.
1780, July   5, Row, Joseph, and Ann Delly.
1782, May   2, Rowan, Barbara, and Peter Charles Pouponnot.
1777, June   8, Rowan, Edward, and Elizabeth Cox.
1770, May   9, Rowan, James, and Mary Shaw.
1767, April   7, Rowe, Hadon, and Ann Dotchin.
1780, Jan.   16, Rowe, Stephen, and Mary Dibley.
1777, Feb.   4, Rowen, Daniel, and Mary Morry.
1761, Nov.   9, Rowen, Mathew, and Elizabeth Wiver.
1762, Nov.   9, Rowen, Mathew, and Elizabeth Wiever.
1776, Oct.   20, Rowen, Susannah, and John Engel.
1790, Nov.   22, Rowend, Isaac, and Lydia Watson.
1783, Jan.   6, Rowland, Alexander, and Rachel Wallington.
1792, Nov.   1, Rowland, Cathrine, and George Micklin.
1773, Oct.   1, Rowland, James, and Elizabeth Johnston.
1780, June   28, Rowle, Robert, and Ann Mathews.
1778, June   15, Rowlerd, John, and Jean Burgess.
1778, May   31, Rowley, Edward, and Mary Criss.
1789, Nov.   28, Rowlins, Benjamin, and Cathrine More.
1777, March 19, Roy, Ann, and James Lackie.
1771, June   22, Roynel, Samuel Hannah, and Elizabeth James.
1799, Nov.   24, Rozen, Catherine, and Nela Jordan.
1780, April   9, Rud, John, and Sarah Biggs.
1785, Nov.   20, Rudd, John, and Sarah Wright.

1775, Nov.   6, Ruden, Mary, and Paul Cruse.
1763, Nov.   8, Rudolph, Christian, and Catharine Correy.
1790, June   27, Rudolph, George, and Elizabeth McKagghan.
1785, Nov.   28, Rudolph, George, and Jane McKeicken.
1794, March 17, Rudolph, John, and Mary Wells.
1792, Dec.   18, Rudolph, Mary, and George Stuart.
1797, Dec.   31, Rudolp, Michael, and Elizabeth Young.
1777, May   29, Rue, Benjamin, and Mary Taylor.
1778, April   1, Rue, Latitia, and John McKalop.
1771, April 29, Rue, Patrick, and Elizabeth Allan.
1772, Dec.   18, Rue, Thomas, and Ann Pursell.
1800, Aug.   13, Rumsey, Charles, and Sarah Town.
1773, Aug.   10, Runey, Jane, and Robert Dixon.
1800, Oct.   3, Runian, Benjamin, and Cathrine Anderson.
1783, Jan.   8, Runnels, Catherine, and William Nealy.
1778, July   31, Runner, Lewis, and Mary Bucker.
1793, Oct.   2, Ruper, Andrew, and Elizabeth Morrison.
1782, July   28, Rupp, John, and Anne Delany.
1755, April 14, Rush, Aurelia, and Nathan Adams.
1757, Nov.   5, Rush, Elizabeth, and Phinserie Koon.
1777, Nov.   30, Rush, Henry, and Eleanor Connor.
1796, Jan.   2, Rush, Magdalena, and John Schnider.
1777, May   4, Rush, Mary, and James Gallagher.
1781, May   10, Rush, Rebecca, and Henry Digel.
1775, Sept. 30, Rush, William, and Mary Stoneburner.
1790, March   5, Rushton, James, and Catharine Mannon.
1781, Sept. 12, Rushton, Signet, and William Darby.
1779, May   15, Rushworm, William, and Rebecca Babe.
1757, June   7, Rusle, Thomas, and Lydia Johnson.
1773, Nov.   27, Russel, Ann, and Hugh Smith.
1786, Aug.   20, Russel, Anne, and Javis Amrey.
1778, Jan.   28, Russel, Ann, and William Richardson.
1768, Dec.   19, Russel, Edward Wager, and Hannah Hannats.
1777, June   6, Russel, Eleanor, and James McDole.
1766, Aug.   16, Russel, Elizabeth, and James Michael Howel.
1776, Jan.   1, Russel, Elizabeth, and Robert Cochran.
1793, March 27, Russel, Joseph, and Margret Johnson.
1769, Oct.   5, Russel, Latitia, and William Stewart.
1777, Feb.   27, Russel, Margaret, and David Liebey.
1773, June   2, Russel, Mary, and Jacob Vennoble.
1773, April 26, Russel, Richard, and Mary Brady.
1759, March 26, Russel, Sarah, and Joseph Ross.
1766, March 24, Russel, Thomas, and Abigail Williams.
1778, Jan.   1, Russel, Thomas, and Elizabeth McDanold.
1780, Aug.   7, Russell, Elizabeth, and John Blane.
1756, Aug.   3, Russell, Mary, and Alexander Oliver.

1758, Aug.   23, Russell, Thomas, and Margaret Wodkints.
1784, Oct.   12, Russler, Fanny, and David Jones.
1765, Oct.   10, Ruth, Jeane, and Thomas Claypold.
1773, Jan.   18, Ruth, John, and Prudence Hughes.
1793, Feb.   26, Ruthwen, James, and Margret Walker.
1778, Jan.   29, Rutlidge, Peter, and Bridget O'Bryan.
1781, Aug.   6, Rutter, Abram, and Rebecca Cursain.
1776, May   30, Rutter, Peter, and Penelope Donal.
1795, Aug.   2, Ruven, Margret, and Jacob Springer.
1780, May   15, Ryain, James, and Biddy Sullivan.
1769, Dec.   12, Ryan, Anne, and John Smith.
1754, May   9, Ryan, Ann, and Robert Tate.
1779, Aug.   30, Ryan, Edward, and Elizabeth Gilmore.
1799, March 31, Ryan, Edward, and Mary Murphey.
1781, Sept. 27, Ryan, John, and Mary Davis.
1781, June   20, Ryan, Margaret, and David Williams.
1781, Dec.   4, Ryan, Mary, and Francis Marschalk.
1777, Dec.   23, Ryan, Michael, and Mary McNail.
1796, July   10, Ryan, William, and Hannah McKean.
1791, June   2, Ryburn, Elenore, and John Templar.
1771, Dec.   8, Sadlers, Bridget, and John Smith.
1758, May   25, Sage, Ann, and John Harmer.
1771, July   14, Sailor, Ann Mary, and James Harford.
1752, Sept. 17, Sailor, Elizabeth, and Patrick Slavin.
1760, Aug.   14, Sales, Joseph, and Mary Stuart.
1775, July   20, Sally, William, and Susannah Armitage.
1776, Sept. 22, Salmon, Gideon, and Ann Burk.
1777, April   7, Salmon, Thomas, and Jean Gray.
1783, Feb.   1, Salsbery, John, and Abigail Wiley.
1788, Jan.   29, Salt, Frances, and Samuel Carr.
1778, Aug.   22, Salter, John, and Elizabeth Puddle.
1750, Oct.   12, Salter, William, and Anne Baley.
1777, May   5, Salthouse, Richard, and Elizabeth Bryant.
1778, March   7, Sampell, Elizabeth, and William Ashley.
1775, June   18, Sampell, Mary and George Pringle.
1778, June   10, Sample, Thomas, and Mary Black.
1780, Jan.   12, Sampson, Stephen, and Ann Ereley.
1800, April   5, Samuel, Alexander, and Elizabeth Taylor.
1791, Nov.   19, Samuel, and Phillis, (free blacks.)
1782, Feb.   5, Sanders, Catherine, and Charles Hassel.
1757, Sept. 11, Sanders, Francies, and Catharine Layman.
1768, June   6, Sanders, James, and Marget Stickham.
1761, Sept. 23, Sanders, William, and Buly Dible.
1762, Nov.   23, Sanders, William, and Buly Dible.
1778, May   27, Sanders, William, and Mary Sink.
1777, Dec.   4, Sanders, William, and Sarah Keen.

1778, April 9, Sands, Abraham, and Rachel Scott.
1769, Oct.   9, Sands, Eleanor, and William McConet.
1763, April 11, Sang, Mary, and Henry Nutter.
1800, May 18, Sansom, Benjamin, and Juliana Till.
1760, June 27, Sant, Sarah, and Patrick Sinnof.
1769, Dec. 5, Santerling, Elizabeth, and Jacob Beck.
1755, Dec. 11, Sarah, Sarah, and Jacob Writer.
1793, Dec. 16, Sares, Peter, and Cathrine, Courtney.
1780, March 8, Sargant, William, and Catharine Toner.
1799, Nov. 10, Sarin, Caleb, and Mary Dennison.
1776, Dec. 18, Sartin, Thomas, and Catharine Gump.
1774, July 17, Sartoriusin, Christina, and Henry Apple.
1797, Aug. 1, Sass, Maria Dorothea, and John Creutz.
1779, Jan. 21, Satchwell, Jeremiah, and Susannah Young.
1785, April 9, Satterfield, John, and Margaret Sharp.
1772, Nov. 28, Saullers, Frederis, and Mary Kusick.
1780, July 1, Saunder, Hannah, and James Cooper.
1756, Jan. 6, Saunders, Ann, and John Bunting.
1784, Aug. 5, Saunders, Francis, and Charity Atkeson.
1778, Feb. 1, Saunders, James, and Mary McCollum.
1770, Oct. 1, Saunders, Martha, and Philip Marchant.
1755, July 2, Saunders, Thomas, and Sarah Craven.
1794, May 21, Saunders, William, and Sarah Wiley.
1776, April 8, Saurey, Elizabeth, and Henry Johnson.
1770, March 25, Savage, James, and Hester Eason.
1774, Aug. 8, Savage, Mary, and John Miller.
1758, Dec. 18, Savage, Mary, and William Jones.
1792, Aug. 20, Savage, Pattens, and Hanna Moore.
1791, Jan. 14, Saverite, Mary, and John Happerset.
1799, Dec. 22, Saville, Mary, and Adam Alexander.
1773, Sept. 12, Sawrey, William Banks, and Ann Hankey.
1773, Jan. 3, Sawyer, John, and Margarett Steward.
1780, Feb. 22, Sawyer, William, and Susannah Abberdeen.
1785, April 1, Sayre, Leonard, and Margaret Potter.
1771, Jan. 1, Scandlin, Dennis, and Elizabeth Wagoner.
1777, Oct. 25, Scandlin, Mathias, and Mary Doulin.
1785, Feb. 20, Scanlan, John, and Elizabeth Johnston.
1795, Feb. 26, Scanlin, Cornelius, and Mary Williams.
1787, Nov. 12, Scanlin, Hanna, and Andrew Kirkpatric.
1782, May 6, Scannel, Jemima, and Philip Faucet.
1751, Oct. 16, Scarf, William, and Margaret Hunter.
1776, Dec. 23, Scarlet, Rachel, and James Shea.
1773, May 20, Scarret, John, and Sarah Davis.
1794, May 4, Scattergood, John H., and Sarah Forman.
1778, Oct. 15, Schaeffer, Justus, and Dorothea Kephe.
1786, Nov. 5, Schafer, Philip, and Elizabeth Guy.

1792, May   17, Schaffer, Lucky, and George Diffenbach.
1789, Nov.   12, Scheckels, William, and Rebecca Hammell.
1778, Oct.   25, Scheffer, Margaret, and Jacob Hiney.
1755, Feb.   2, Schegy, Oschel, and Adam Taylor.
1768, June   5, Scheiderin, Mariah Magdalena, and Jacob Eckfield.
1785, March 22, Scheimer, Philip, and Margaret Brown.
1751, March 10, Schleih, Jacob, and Catharine Catzen.
1793, Sept.   8, Schlicht, George, and Anna Clara Dickhaut.
1793, Nov.   26, Schlosser, Jacob, and Margaret Plucher.
1776, Aug.   26, Schnech, George, and Barbarah Shepherd.
1776, Jan.   12, Schneider, George Peter, and Elizabeth Beresheim.
1786, Sept. 13, Schneider, Mary, and Casper Cymon.
1796, Jan.   2, Schnider, John, and Magdalena Rush.
1795, Jan.   3, Schnider, John, and Mary Earl.
1792, April 27, Schnobin, Margret, and Christopher Ranz.
1792, Oct.   16, Schollard, Anthony, and Mary Halston.
1755, Nov.   5, Schoumacher, Christiana Barbara, and John Jacob
                   Foulguier.
1779, Aug.   15, Schrack, John, and Sarah Meyers.
1797, Dec.   10, Schrape, Nicholas Andrew, and Eleonore Momas.
1785, July   28, Schreiner, Kitty, and George Griscom.
1763, April   4, Schrener, Elizabeth, and William Hamble.
1782, July   22. Schroder, Philip, and Catherine Stinsman.
1781, Dec.   16, Schroder, Reinold, and Anne Justes.
1798, Dec.   31, Schroeder, Nancy, and Jacob Ott.
1796, Feb.   28, Schuyler, Ann, and John Hurley.
1762, Sept. 29, Schweighart, Jacob, and Rosina Oberftegen.
1794, May   24, Schweris, Cathrine, and George Stealy.
1779, June   15, Schyler, Mary, and Michael Christopher.
1789, Jan.   15, Schyller, Mary, and Henry Bearly.
1788, Nov.   17, Schytterly, David, and Sarah Jones.
1765, July   29, Sciperton, Ann Mary, and Peter Dils.
1777, Oct.   11, Scoals, George, and Jean Frazier.
1775, Aug.   9, Scoby, Charles, and Elizabeth Black.
1752, Oct.   8, Scotman, Elizabeth, and James Cunningam.
1773, April   4, Scott, Andrew, and Ann Dart.
1767, July   5, Scott, Ann, and Adam Allyn.
1759, Feb.   7, Scott, Ann, and Alexander Miller.
1788, Aug.   20, Scott, Ann, and Jonathan Branson.
1775, May   7, Scott, Elly, and William Monro.
1771, Feb.   3, Scott, George, and Margarett Smarts.
1795, Nov.   28, Scott, James, and Elizabeth Caldwell.
1795, Sept. 20, Scott, James, and Nancy Henry.
1797, Sept.   2, Scott, Jane, and Robert Haldin.
1776, Dec.   31, Scott, John, and Dorothy Mockeston.
1798, Dec.   9, Scott, John, and Eleonore Cramsey.

1752, March 7, Scott, John, and Isabella Davis.
1772, Aug. 9, Scott, John, and Mary Henly.
1787, Aug. 31, Scott, Margaret, and William Norris.
1768, Sept. 24, Scott, Mary, and Lewis Meyer.
1778, April 9, Scott, Rachel, and Abraham Sands.
1773, March 4, Scott, Samuel, and Mary Howels.
1783, April 19, Scott, Samuel, and Mary Mason.
1800, Dec. 30, Scott, Sarah, and Alexander Whiteside.
1790, Dec. 21, Scott, Sara, and Tanton Mason.
1790, Oct. 23, Scott, William, and Rachel Hugh.
1757, Dec. 4, Scotton, Ann, and Edward Jones.
1759, Dec. 22, Scottorn, Joseph, and Elizabeth Brown.
1769, Nov. 20, Scotts, Hannah, and Benjamin Benson.
1758, March 23, Scout, Arie, and Sarah Gilbert.
1761, May 28, Scout, Elizabeth, and Mathew Danaway.
1794, Sept. 10, Scudder, Eby, and Thomas Stewart.
1763, Aug. 25, Scull, Hannah, and Samuel McKleen.
1766, Aug. 2, Scull, Jemima, and Isaac Sharp.
1784, April 28, Scull, Margaret, and John Shields.
1800, Aug. 25, Scull, Mary, and Jacob Berriman.
1764, Dec. 19, Scutt, Sarah, and Patrick McDonald.
1780, Jan. 27, Seaman, Mary, and William Stone.
1780, March 5, Search, Lydy, and Edward, Stricklin.
1763, Nov. 30, Sears, Elizabeth, and Thomas Millward.
1783, Jan. 21, Seavoy, Charles, and Margret Gule.
1783, Jan. 21, Seavoy, Charles, and Sarah Cornelius.
1793, July 7, Seckel, Cathrine, and Anthony Maxwell.
1781, Feb. 21, Seed, James, and Lydia Tew.
1791, Nov. 24, Seely, Mary, and Richard Fry.
1755, June 23, Seers, Ann, and David Evans.
1783, Nov. 23, Segerson, James, and Catherine Clemons.
1781, Jan. 28, Seibert, Casper, and Elizabeth Weidman.
1778, May 3, Seils, Elizabeth, and John Taylor.
1761, Feb. 10, Seisinger, George, and Margaret Burchard.
1793, Dec. 16, Seley, Sarah, and Thomas Dickinson.
1796, Oct. 9, Sell, Cathrine, and Peter Bartleson.
1794, Dec. 2, Sell, Solomon, and Anna Maria Orner.
1782, Dec. 17, Sellers, Charlotte, and Robert Norris.
1780, Feb. 28, Selrant, Nicholas, and Elizabeth Jackson.
1780, March 15, Semphton, Elizabeth, and Charles Perry.
1794, May 19, Semple, John, and Hannah McCormick.
1792, Oct. 14, Senecson, Isaac, and Cathrine Wonderly.
1771, April 7, Sensord, Patrick, and Mary Gring.
1794, Nov, 4, Sent, Henry, and Elizabeth Dawson.
1771, Feb. 3, Senter, Mary, and Patrick Dun.
1795, Dec. 24, Sentman, Michael, and Sarah Mackie.

1775, Sept.   9, Septem, Mary Lampel, and Richard Wall.
1760, Nov.   5, Serett, John, and Elizabeth Race.
1794, Oct.   16, Sergeant, Ephraim, and Nelly Days.
1793, Nov.   17, Sergeant, James, and Mary Mohollin.
1795, Jan.   7, Sergeant, Susannah, and William Burke.
1764, Dec.   25, Sergeant, Isabel, and James Gibson.
1794, May   11, Sermon, Benjamin, and Susanna Page.
1780, Aug.   5, Serran, Jesse, and Charity Jones.
1794, March   9, Servel, Jacques, and Cathrine Ceronio.
1792, May   27, Servent, Martin, and Jane Pettit.
1763, May   10, Sesrin, Mary, and Thomas Pendergast.
1774, Feb.   21, Seufert, Anthony, and Mary Agnes Nagle.
1778, April   24, Sevey, Isaac, and Mary Mason.
1790, Oct.   21, Seward, Philip, and Dorothy Homes.
1792, May   28, Sextonset, John, and Mary Dicson.
1795, Dec.   20, Seyfert, Cathrine, and Samuel Rinker.
1789, Oct.   18, Seyfert, Conrad, and Elizabeth Halberstadt.
1766, April   28, Seyler, Ann, and James Jeffrey.
1777, Aug.   18, Seymour James, and Ann Walker.
1778, Jan.   1, Shade, George, and Susannah Darby.
1789, Aug.   4, Shade, Peter, and Susannah Warner.
1798, Jan.   28, Shafer, Marget, and James Gray.
1780, April   4, Shafer, Rachel, and Nathaniel Brown.
1796, May   12, Shaffer, Cathrine, and John Craft.
1788, April   1, Shafferene, Catharine, and Biron McCurdy.
1761, Jan.   18, Shafford, John, and Mary McGloughling.
1764, May   30, Shagmessy, John, and Margaret Jones.
1778, May   19, Shaldrake, Ezekiel, and Sarah Powel.
1757, June   6, Shales, Elizabeth, and Patrick Floid.
1798, Jan.   17, Shallcross, Rachel, and Benjamin Johnson.
1779, Nov.   19, Shananger, Mary, and Manasse Augustus.
1795, Oct.   14, Shane, Elizabeth, and David David, (or Davis.)
1783, Jan.   30, Shanen, Elizabeth, and William Brooks.
1771, Feb.   13, Shanklin, Sarah, and Thustan Brown.
1780, March 26, Shanks, Elizabeth, and William Mullan.
1779, May   13, Shanks, Hannah, and Peter Duché.
1798, Aug.   2, Shannon, Jane, and William Shaw.
1773, July   4, Sharntz, Margaret, and William Clayton.
1761, Jan.   15, Sharold, Ephriam, and Rachel Lofftes.
1777, Nov.   2, Sharp, Abella, and John Benson.
1795, June   26, Sharp, Agnes, and Casper Fish.
1780, Aug.   30, Sharp, Amos, and Mertha Gaskin.
1795, May   2, Sharp, Cathrine, and John Whelan.
1782, April   16, Sharp, Eve, and John McClish.
1799, April   5, Sharp, Hannah, and William Sharp.
1766, Aug.   2, Sharp, Isaac, and Jemima Scull.

1759, April 11, Sharp, Jane, and Israel Hewlings.
1794, July 20, Sharp, John, and Jane Adams.
1778, Nov. 19, Sharp, Joseph, and Catharine Henin.
1777, Aug. 2, Sharp, Joseph, and Mary Doyle.
1782, May 27, Sharp, Joseph, and Sarah Richards.
1784, June 1, Sharp, Tamor, and John Martin.
1785, April 9, Sharp, Margaret, and John Satterfield.
1759, April 21, Sharp, Mertha, and Nicholas Rambo.
1771, Nov. 25, Sharp, Peter, and Ann Wright.
1792, Oct. *28, Sharp, Rachel and John Stancliff.
1793, June 27, Sharp, Samuel, and Mary Hambel.
1766, Jan. 10, Sharp, Silvester, and Ann Willson.
1799, April 5, Sharp, William, and Susannah Sharp.
1790, Feb. 23, Sharpless, Elizabeth, and John Vernon.
1796, Feb. 28, Sharpley, William, and Elizabeth Stow.
1779, March 8, Sharral, Friederick, and Elizabeth Bersin.
1777, June 23, Shaw, Alexander, and Jean Smith.
1774, Dec. 4, Shaw, Anna, and Joas Fox.
1782, June 3, Shaw, Anne, and George McGilton.
1779, June 3, Shaw, Ann, and Thomas Boyd.
1775, July 10, Shaw, Daniel, and Susannah Robinson.
1780, Jan. 23, Shaw, Eleanor, and George Gosnel.
1761, April 28, Shaw, Elizabeth, and John Rossetor.
1776, April 3, Shaw, George, and Mary Toplin.
1795, March 5, Shaw, James, and Rebecca Smith.
1782, Sept. 19, Shaw, Johannah, and George Robertson.
1789, Nov. 13, Shaw, John, and Abigail Holden.
1779, March 11, Shaw, John, and Juliana Byar.
1781, Feb. 22, Shaw, John, and Martha Drape.
1779, June 1, Shaw, Margarett, and Alexander Robeson.
1796, April 18, Shaw, Mary, and Baltes Kinsler.
1770, May 9, Shaw, Mary, and James Rowan.
1722, July 5, Shaw, Mathew, and Jean McIntire.
1791, Nov. 15, Shaw, Philip, and Priscilla Charters.
1781, Oct. 25, Shaw, Sarah, and James Jobson.
1798, Nov. 14, Shaw, Sarah, and Thomas Burk.
1790, Aug. 23, Shaw, Susanna, and John MacPherson.
1798, Aug. 2, Shaw, William, and Jane Shannon.
1777, Aug. 8, Shea, Elizabeth, and John Young.
1776, Dec. 23, Shea, James, and Rachel Scarlet.
1776, Nov. 19, Shea, Phoebe, and Abraham, Marshall.
1770, Jan. 21, Shea, Richard, and Hannah Gullifer.
1752, Dec. 29, Shealan, William, and Margaret Rayn.
1784, April 16, Shearman, Mary, and William Worsdell.
1770, Oct. 15, Shearman, Thomas, and Anne Jones.
1758, Feb. 27, Shed, Eliseba, and Benjamin Fordham.

1763, July   5, Shee, Jeremiah, and Elizabeth Stator.
1773, April   18, Shee, John, and Elizabeth Garret.
1772, July   12, Shee, John, and Jean Nailor.
1785, Sept.   3, Sheed, George, and Rebecca Jones.
1789, Dec.   10, Sheed, William, and Christine Dee.
1798, Jan.   24, Sheed, William, and Elizabeth Mount.
1770, July   8, Sheehan, William, and Frances Arnam.
1779, Feb.   14, Sheehin, Jeremiah, and Ann Catharine Strover.
1778, March 18, Sheerman, Elizabeth, and John Hogan.
1787, Feb.   3, Sheerwood, Eleonore, and Ebenezer Hubbard.
1753, Dec.   18, Sheirtlyst, Susanna, and Archibald Tharp.
1780, June   10, Sheldern, Ann, and Enos Worral.
1780, July   13, Sheldren, Mary, and John Green.
1798, June   19, Shellburn, James, and Rachel Brown.
1799, Nov.   10, Shellcross, Leonard, and Sarah Haines.
1797, Dec.   24, Sheller, Christian, and Samuel Richy.
1779, May   9, Sheller, Friederick, and Christina Shepherd.
1799, Feb.   24, Shellink, John Baptiste, and Johanna Maria Otting.
1757, Sept.   21, Shellock, Catharine, and Benjamin Molton.
1758, Aug.   5, Shellway, Sarah, and John Heartshorn.
1797, May   10, Shelly, Prudence, and John Aiken.
1778, Jan.   25, Shelver, Thomas, and Jane Slone.
1796, Sept.   25, Shepard, Marget, and Jacob Linten.
1793, Sept.   9, Shepard, Thomas, and Debora Baker.
1766, Aug.   26, Shepherd, Barbarah, and George Schnech.
1773, Sept.   5, Shepherd, Charles, and Agnes Wools.
1779, May   9, Shepherd, Christina, and Friederick Sheller.
1775, June   12, Shepherd, George, and Mary Banford.
1767, May   7, Shepherd, John, and Eleanor Creen.
1793, Dec.   30, Shepherd, John, and Nancy Douglas.
1779, May   20, Shepherd, Sarah, and Alexander Willson.
1780, March 17, Shepherd, William, and Mary Meyers.
1763, Sept.   30, Shepherds, Benjamin, and Rachel Thomas.
1756, Aug.   20, Sheppard, Ezeckel, and Catharine Hill.
1773, April   19, Sheppard, Hannah, and Hugh McDonald.
1755, April   23, Shepperd, Josiah, and Mary Cole.
1777, May   4, Sherdan, Nicholas, and Margarett Keith.
1759, March 11, Sheredin, Mary, and Alexander Rainniels.
1791, Jan.   20, Sherer, Ludvig, and Edy Cremar.
1759, Jan.   27, Sherer, Philip, and Elizabeth Muller.
1778, Oct.   19, Sheriden, James, and Mary Walker.
1758, May   27, Sherin, Catharine, and William Burchart.
1778, June   10, Sherlock, Alice, and Joseph Gee.
1783, Nov.   20, Sherlock, Mary, and Henry Piercy.
1787, March 14, Sherman, Mary, and William Robinson.
1789, March 28, Shermer, Jacob, and Hanna Hoover.

1758, Sept.   6, Sherrard, Rebecca, and Robert Clark.
1787, Oct.   8, Sherric, George, and Hannah Hazelburn.
1767, March 12, Sherrin, Elizabeth, and Philip Morrison.
1781, Dec.   20, Shetsline, John, and Francise Maag.
1772, Dec.   6, Shevier, Martha, and Richard Babington.
1765, July   29, Shewin, Catharine, and George Eaton.
1764, Dec.   7, Shey, Christiana, and John Smith.
1776, June   2, Shidels, Susannah, and John McCahan.
1794, Jan.   4, Shield, John, and Margret Wells.
1792, May   26, Shields, Elizabeth, and John Clogher.
1780, March 25, Shields, Francis, and Isabel Smith.
1792, Nov.   12, Shields, John, and Jane Carney.
1784, April 28, Shields, John, and Margaret Scull.
1778, July   4, Shields, John, and Mary Ebert.
1792, June   3, Shields, Owen, and Sarah Perkins.
1754, March 11, Shiffer, Catharine, and Edward Roiley.
1783, Oct.   11, Shillingford, James, and Elizabeth Loveman.
1781, Feb.   18, Shillingford, Thomas, and Rose Shyts.
1781, Sept.   1, Shillingsford, Anne, and James Gary.
1799, Nov.   31, Shillingsford, Elizabeth, and John Moeller.
1784, May   4, Shillingsford, William, and Elizabeth Hulings.
1758, Nov.   6, Shilslich, Anne, and Thomas Boltom.
1776, June   9, Shingleton, Mary, and Thomas Griffieth.
1776, March   4, Shinn, George, and Sarah Kelley.
1782, Oct.   13, Shiny, Mary, and Thomas Davis.
1788, May   16, Shipe, Gasper, and Elizabeth Ernest.
1790, Oct.   21, Shipley, Nancy, and John Cole.
1780, May   4, Shippen, Margaret, and John Adams.
1775, Dec.   19, Shippen, Mary, and John Peel.
1775, Dec.   25, Shippen, Mary, and Thomas Driver.
1771, Jan.   29, Shippey, Barbarah, and David Edwards.
1777, May   1, Shippey, Edward, and Catharine McCarty.
1778, Sept. 19, Shippey, Mary, and George Fordham.
1787, May   10, Shircliff, Asa, and Elizabeth Foster.
1765, Sept.   7, Shirley, Rosannah, and Thomas Bell.
1751, June   23, Shitzen, Juliana, and Ulric Budman.
1781, May   6, Shivers, Hannah, and Joshua Haines.
1788, Feb.   5, Shivers, John, and Zilla Roberts.
1759, Jan.   3, Shmids, Elizabet, and James Stapelton.
1794, May   6, Shockor, Christina, and Alexander Crawford.
1765, March 18, Shoe, John Bartholomew, and Mary Nageler.
1756, Aug.   25, Shoemaker, George, and Ann Rittenhouse.
1795, April 26, Shoemaker, Marget, and George Charles Bermike.
1781, March   7, Shoemaker, Mary Christine, and Robert Murdock.
1799, Oct.   8, Shoemaker, Mary, and Patric Burn.
1779, Sept. 24, Shoman, John, and Elizabeth Perkeson.

1778, June   2, Shonk, Rebecca, and John Buckly.
1799, Jan.   27, Short, Ann, and John Jones.
1776, June   23, Showow, Barney, and Juliana Holler.
1775, Oct.   14, Shrack, Margaret, and William Balley.
1776, Dec.   1, Shrank, Barbara, and Charles Miller.
1780, Aug.   1, Shrave, John, and Mary Reemer.
1776, Dec.   3, Shreyer, Elizabeth, and John Spots.
1757, Dec.   1, Shrieler, Mary, and Peter Plom,
1796, May   1, Shriver, Martha, and John Kissler.
1790, April   7, Shroudy, Jacob, and Sara Esling.
1779, May   13, Shrupp, Henry, and Eve Brand.
1762, July   18, Shumaker, Regina, and Jacob Beeker.
1765, Dec.   5, Shunk, Barbarah, and Andrew Reiser.
1768, May   18, Shute, Mary, and Hercules Courtney.
1771, Oct.   9, Shuts, John, and Sarah Airs.
1757, May   18, Shutur, John, and Mary Brown.
1781, Feb.   18, Shyts, Rose, and Thomas Shillingford.
1789, June   28, Sickes, Rachel, and McCall Wilson.
1794, July   29, Sickle, Elizabeth, and Daniel Baker.
1795, June   28, Sickle, Philip, and Elizabeth McCutcheon.
1766, Feb.   24, Sidden, William, and Jeane Carr.
1789, Dec.   22, Siddon, Abby, and Thomas Hantley.
1752, Oct.   18, Siddons, Elizabeth, and Benjamin Graisbury.
1752, Oct.   20, Siddons, Elizabeth, and William Roberts.
1757, June   27, Siddons, John, and Elinor Roberts.
1799, Dec.   12, Siddons, Sarah, and William Anderson.
1783, Feb.   21, Siders, George, and Sarah Miles.
1762, Dec.   30, Sidley, Sarah, and Elias Cole.
1778, June   13, Silbey, Thomas, and Catharine Campbell.
1795, Nov.   10, Silence, William, and Sophia Henry.
1752, May   18, Siles, Joseph, and Judy More.
1759, Dec.   16, Sille, George, and Isabellah Kennady.
1793, Dec.   1, Sillich, John Gotlieb, and Elizabeth Powell.
1773, Oct.   2, Silly, and Cate, (negroes.)
1797, Jan.   10, Silva Joseph, and Nancy Grier.
1790, Oct.   14, Silver, Mary, and James Welch.
1792, Sept.   20, Silvin, Nicholas, and Jane Wright.
1795, Oct.   22, Silvis, John, Christina Lets.
1785, July   7, Simens, Ann, and Edward Williams, (negroes.)
1787, Sept.   20, Simes, Sarah, and Jacob Painter.
1794, Aug.   23, Simkins, Ezechiel, and Rebecca Miller.
1797, Nov.   15, Simkins, James, and Marget Keen.
1785, March 15, Simmonds, Mary, and Joseph Stewart.
1755, Oct.   11, Simmons, Catharine, and John Stamper.
1777, July   24, Simmons, Nathan, and Ann Towers.
1788, May   21, Simmons, Richard, and Sary Duffy.

1755, June   17, Simms, Samuel, and Hannah White.
1767, July   23, Simon, John, and Caterin Bromery.
1791, Jan.   8, Simonds, Jonas, and Mary Pugh.
1766, Feb.   3, Simonds, William, and Hannah Hall.
1753, Oct.   31, Simons, James, and Susanna Balenger.
1792, March 18, Simonson, George Allimore Simon, and Margret
                 Jones.
1800, March 24, Simony, Nancy, and Sim Bodet.
1775, Aug.   1, Simpsen, Samuel, and Martha Day.
1790, Aug.   18, Simpson, Amos, and Rebecca Albertson.
1796, April 10, Simpson, Elizabeth, and Henry Lewis Wiederholt.
1777, April 23, Simpson, James, and Elizabeth McConal.
1797, Feb.   28, Simpson, James, and Elizab. Rambo.
1791, April 17, Simpson, Marget, and James Duffy.
1795, Aug.   12, Simpson, Stuart, and Elizabeth Friend.
1779, Nov.   18, Simpson, William, and Eleanor Gardner.
1763, Nov.   30, Sims, David, and Sarah Ross.
1789, July   29, Sims, Elizabeth, and Enoch Clemens.
1767, May   25, Sims, Elizabeth, and John Neadham.
1795, Oct.   25, Sims, Hannah, and Hugh Callahan.
1793, April 26, Sims, John, and Mary Adams.
1781, May   30, Simson, Eleonor, and John Fitspatrick.
1759, Feb.   11, Simson, John, and Mary Johnson.
1761, Dec.   29, Simson, John, and Susannah Burnett.
1793, Oct.   8, Simson, Nancy, and John McKechin.
1787, Aug.   14, Simson, Rachel, and Martin Hights.
1777, May   12, Simson, Thomas, and Sarah Burns.
1767, Feb.   24, Sincocks, Hannah, and Evan Evans.
1777, Nov.   25, Sinclair, Catharine, and Andrew Gray.
1754, April 11, Sinclair, Catharine, and James Hood.
1792, Dec.   19, Sinclair, Elizabeth, and Thomas Dickinson.
1793, Dec.   27, Sinclair, Susanna Cathrine, and Samuel Brown.
1799, Feb.   22, Sinclair, W^m, and Mary Hutcheson.
1757, May   27, Singleton, Mary, and Richard Brookbank.
1778, March 24, Singleton, Sarah, and John Snell.
1783, May   12, Singlewood, Stephen, and Anne Stroup.
1751, Dec.   22, Sinjohn, Nancy, and Robert Fitzgerald.
1773, Dec.   25, Sink, Jacob, and Mary Birdside.
1778, May   27, Sink, Mary, and William Sanders.
1767, Oct.   18, Sinkler, Mary, and James McClear.
1794, Dec.   5, Sinnet, Edward, and Amelia Pride.
1760, June   27, Sinnof, Patrick, and Sarah Sant.
1764, March   3, Sinnot, Thomas, and Elleonor McCarty.
1754, Feb.   7, Sinnott, Peter, and Frances Symmons.
1763, June   1, Siplin, Mary, and William McKinlay.
1752, Oct.   23, Sircks, Daniel, and Mary Ford.

1775, Nov. 12, Sisle, Mary, and Francis Sleigh.
1751, Dec. 19, Sitch, John, and Elizabeth Holliday.
1752, Jan. 12, Sitel, John, and Elinor Jones.
1790, Feb. 25, Siters, Jacob, and Ann Johnson.
1778, March 24, Size, John, and Christine Smith.
1800, Feb. 1, Skeen, Eleonore, and Jonathan Maybury.
1761, April 9, Skeen, Rachel, and Arnold Van Fossen.
1778, Feb. 14, Skelton, John, and Catharine Blekewell.
1787, Feb. 20, Skelton, William, and Margret Hanna.
1783, Sept. 6, Skill, Elizabeth, and John Perkins.
1781, June 20, Skill, Patience, and Isaac Piddrick.
1781, Sept. 29, Skillinger, Mary, and John Collis.
1787, June 22, Skillings, Elizabeth, and Edward Toms.
1781, Sept. 13, Skinner, Elizabeth, and James Frost.
1773, Nov. 21, Skinner, John, and Elizabeth Holland.
1785, Oct. 27, Skinner, John, and Patience Henricson.
1794, July 18, Skinner, William Stuart, and Ann Pape.
1755, Aug. 26, Skorlock, Elizabeth, and Edward Ashburn.
1794, Nov. 25, Skott, John, and Mary Stuart.
1780, March 15, Skuts, Hermenus, and Elizabeth Erwin.
1779, March 14, Slack, David, and Ann Span.
1778, May 1, Slack, Elizabeth, and John Davis.
1780, Aug. 20, Slack, Elizabeth, and Richard Deleny.
1777, Aug. 14, Slack, Sarah, and John Brown.
1792, April 21, Slaughter, Cathrine, and Francis More.
1779, June 15, Slaughter, Eve, and Jacob Delher.
1782, Dec. 29, Slaughter, Mary, and Lewis Wolf.
1752, Sept. 17, Slavin, Patrick, and Elizabeth Saelor.
1793, Aug. 22, Slawter, Mary, and William Wills.
1756, March 23, Sleaer, Mary, and Morris Fowler.
1793, May 30, Sleeth, Mary, and Thomas Henderson.
1775, Nov. 12, Sleigh, Francis, and Mary Lisle.
1771, Sept. 5, Sleigh, Sarah, and James Young.
1787, June 27, Slide, Martha, and Andrew Longacre.
1793, May 29, Slight, Elizabeth, and Frederic Renn.
1778, June 3, Sloane, Charles, and Jane Freeman.
1799, Dec. 17, Sloane, John, and Sarah VanNeaman.
1793, June 18, Sloane, Martha, and Dennis Davin.
1782, Oct. 27, Slomer, Henry, and Mary Fortescue.
1778, Jan. 25, Slone, Jane, and Thomas Shelver.
1792, Nov. 4, Slough, Peter, and Evelina Eulerin.
1772, May 2, Slyhoof, Mary, and William Perry.
1793, Aug. 6, Small, Elizabeth, and Thomas White.
1760, Jan. 1, Small, Jane, and William Craig.
1782, Dec. 6, Small, Jenny, and Simon Newton.
1779, Sept. 1, Smallwood, Martha, and William Dice.

1767, Jan. 19, Smallwood, Thomas, and Ann Ten.
1782, June 24, Smart, Anne, and John Smith,
1778, May 20, Smart, Sarah, and Duncan McArthur.
1771, Feb. 3, Smarts, Margarett, and George Scott.
1781, Nov. 4, Smerris, Mandy, and Samuel Walters, (Free negroes.)
1776, Oct. 20, Smiles, Thomas, and Ann Fitzgerald.
1796, Feb. 21, Smiley, Druilla, and Carpenter Lownsburg.
1756, May 31, Smith, Abigail, and Francis Hogg.
1792, Feb. 15, Smith, Abraham, and Elizabeth Merrywhether.
1791, Nov. 30, Smith, Adam, and Nancy Addison.
1798, Aug. 27, Smith, Agnes, and Andrew Montgomery.
1768, March 14, Smith, Alley Fitzgerald, and Charles Proud.
1781, Aug. 21, Smith, Agnes, and Anne Gwin.
1776, Nov. 26, Smith, Ann, and Alexander McKenzie.
1775, Jan. 26, Smith, Ann, and Benjamin Holton.
1775, Oct. 14, Smith, Ann, and Charles Clingen.
1770, Jan. 28, Smith, Anne, and Charles Young.
1794, Feb. 6, Smith, Ann, and Henry Gosner.
1756, July 1, Smith, Anne, and Henry Rich.
1764, July 31, Smith, Ann, and James Winter.
1769, Jan. 9, Smith, Anne, and Samuel Taylor.
1797, May 9, Smith, Ann, and Shadrick Hayward.
1780, Jan. 27, Smith, Barbara, and Augustus Rodhey.
1779, July 11, Smith, Bridget, and James Campbell.
1778, June 7, Smith, Catharine, and Charles Moss.
1767, Feb. 31, Smith, Catharine, and James Beaty.
1754, Aug. 7, Smith, Catharine, and John Wise.
1782, Dec. 23, Smith, Catherine, and Joseph Adamofski.
1794, Sept. 23, Smith, Cathrine, and William Britton.
1790, March 24, Smith, Charles, and Emilia Death.
1792, Aug. 4, Smith, Christian, and Margret Grub.
1799, Dec. 2, Smith, Christina, and John Colman.
1778, March 24, Smith, Christine, and John Size.
1751, July 5, Smith, Christopher, and Susanna Moore.
1788, Nov. 14, Smith, Daniel, and Elizabeth Cowper.
1794, Jan. 9, Smith, Davis, and Nancy Helms.
1782, May 1, Smith, Eleonor, and Alexander McGraw.
1780, Jan. 8, Smith, Eleanor, and Ely Lott.
1780, June 27, Smith, Eleanor, and Robert Clark.
1775, Aug. 30, Smith, Eleanor, and Thomas Clifford.
1752, Nov. 17, Smith, Elinor, and Jeremiah Olden.
1779, March 11, Smith, Elizabeth, and Ford Cutter.
1767, Dec. 24, Smith, Elizabeth, and James Clement.
1785, Nov. 8, Smith, Elizabeth, and John Crayban.
1778, Sept. 17, Smith, Elizabeth, and John Massy.

1795, Dec.   3, Smith, Elizabeth, and John Rosseter.
1780, Aug.   26, Smith, Elizabeth, and John Strizer.
1785, Jan.   4, Smith, Elizabeth, and Lawrence Justice.
1779, Feb.   1, Smith, Elizabeth, and Peter Linch.
1756, Sept.   29, Smith, Elizabeth, and Richard Charlton.
1780, March 21, Smith, Elizabeth, and Richard Perry.
1798, May   5, Smith, Elizabeth, and William Adcock.
1778, May   11, Smith, Francis, and Catharine Taylor.
1777, Oct.   20, Smith, Francis, and Elizabeth Kindley.
1753, Aug.   10, Smith, George, and Elizabeth Lindsay.
1772, May   27, Smith, George, and Elizabeth Manuel.
1778, June   4, Smith, George, and Elizabeth Quigg.
1758, July   30, Smith, Grace, and John Ingle.
1776, Nov.   14, Smith, Grissel, and James Michelson.
1763, Aug.   9, Smith, Hannah, and Andrew Yocum.
1790, Dec.   25, Smith, Hanna, and Daniel Keyser.
1779, Aug.   11, Smith, Hannah, and John Moore.
1761, Nov.   9, Smith, Hannah, and Jonathan Aborn.
1762, Nov.   9, Smith, Hannah, and Jonathan Aborn.
1777, June   8, Smith, Hannah, and Martin Murphey.
1797, July   9, Smith, Henry, and Jemima Stanton.
1773, Nov.   27, Smith, Hugh, and Ann Russell.
1792, June   29, Smith, Hugh, and Sarah Alcorn.
1756, July   24, Smith, Humphry, and Mary Calhoone.
1785, Jan.   18, Smith, Isaac, and Margaret Goldin.
1780, March 25, Smith, Isabel, and Francis Shields.
1795, Feb.   26, Smith, Jacob, and Cathrine Houston.
1791, Sept.   8, Smith, Jacob, and Cathrine Stine.
1753, April   3, Smith, Jacob, and Mary Dicky.
1784, Jan.   25, Smith, Jacob, and Mary Preston.
1778, March 31, Smith, James, and Catharine McDarmouth.
1759, July   9, Smith, James, and Jeane McMichael.
1782, March 17, Smith, James and Mathy Jones.
1792, Oct.   2, Smith, Jane, and John McGowen.
1777, June   23, Smith, Jean, and Alexander Shaw.
1765, July   23, Smith, Jeremiah, and Catharine McCarty.
1773, Aug.   17, Smith, John, and Ann Pinyard.
1769, Dec.   12, Smith, John, and Anne Ryan.
1782, June   24, Smith, John, and Anne Smart.
1771, Dec.   8, Smith, John, and Bridget Sadlers.
1765, Feb.   25, Smith, John, and Catharine Berry.
1780, March   9, Smith, John, and Catharine McCloud.
1764, Dec.   7, Smith, John, and Christiana Shey.
1767, Oct.   23, Smith, John, and Elizabeth Taylor.
1779, Aug.   18, Smith, John, and Fanny Wilson.
1789, Dec.   3, Smith, John, and Hannah Britton.

1779, March 11, Smith, John, and Mary Aslin.
1763, June 22, Smith, John, and Rebeccah James.
1794, Dec. 14, Smith, John, and Sarah Jones.
1778, Sept. 19, Smith, John, and Sarah McGee.
1794, July 13, Smith, John, and Susannah Fling.
1792, Feb. 23, Smith, Jonathan, and Elizabeth Painter.
1790, Nov. 4, Smith, Joseph, and Cathrine Painter.
1784, Sept. 21, Smith, Joseph, and Catherine Taylor.
1755, Dec. 21, Smith, Joseph, and Hanna Hooper.
1770, May 28, Smith, Joseph, and Hannah Lawrence.
1781, Oct. 1, Smith, Joseph, and Mary Ford.
1761, Nov. 21, Smith, Joseph, and Mary Ivens.
1762, Nov. 21, Smith, Joseph, and Mary Ivans.
1758, Feb. 19, Smith, Judith, and John Miller.
1778, Aug. 18, Smith, Margaret, and George Lietch.
1781, June 18, Smith, Margaret, and James Carol.
1779, Oct. 15, Smith, Margaret, and Jephta Loid.
1765, July 8, Smith, Margaret, and John Monney.
1756, June 29, Smith, Margaret, and Patrick Brian.
1778, May 31, Smith, Margaret, and Samuel May.
1770, March 8, Smith, Margarett, and David Blid.
1780, Sept. 16, Smith, Margarett, and Hugh Steward.
1788, June 25, Smith, Marget, and Joseph Grandel.
1787, Oct. 18, Smith, Margret, and Jacob Degan.
1782, Jan. 22, Smith, Mary Anne, and William Williams.
1764, June 13, Smith, Mary, and Christopher Persey.
1792, Jan. 29, Smith, Mary, and Henry Appel.
1755, July 29, Smith, Mary, and Henry Meed.
1791, Nov. 5, Smith, Mary, and John Cling.
1772, Sept. 23, Smith, Mary, and John Coock.
1782, Aug. 27, Smith, Mary, and John Dogget.
1799, Oct. 6, Smith, Mary, and John McCallister.
1795, Nov. 22, Smith, Mary, and Patrick Kennedy.
1795, Feb. 18, Smith, Mary, and Peter Pierce.
1799, May 20, Smith, Mary, and Samuel Davis.
1778, Feb. 10, Smith, Mary, and William Gorden.
1782, April 3, Smith, Meomy, and John Wigmore.
1781, Feb. 9, Smith, Michael, and Catherine Texter.
1791, March 10, Smith, Murdoch, and Ann Causley.
1784, Aug. 17, Smith, Nathaniel, and Mary Rodgers.
1778, April 7, Smith, Nathaniel, and Rebecca Granton.
1788, April 18, Smith, Newberry, and Anne Poulson.
1779, Feb. 21, Smith, Nicholas, and Barbarah Eads.
1790, Oct. 25, Smith, Peter, and Mary Miller.
1763, April 13, Smith, Phibiah, and William Ibbison.
1774, July 7, Smith, Ralph, and Martha Nun.

1795, March   5, Smith, Rebecca and James Shaw.
1799, Aug.   15, Smith, Richard, and Jane Kelly.
1787, June   12, Smith, Richard, and Mary Philpot.
1757, Dec.   4, Smith, Richard, and Mary Stuard.
1782, May   5, Smith, Samuel, and Anne Turner.
1765, June   23, Smith, Samuel, and Bitha Edwards.
1779, Jan.   17, Smith, Samuel, and Catharine Hopkins.
1755, March 31, Smith, Samuel, and Jane Wright.
1779, Aug.   13, Smith, Samuel, and Mary Gilmore.
1794, Dec.   21, Smith, Sarah, and George Apple.
1779, June   3, Smith, Sarah, and John Parkhill.
1788, Nov.   2, Smith, Sarah, and Marmaduke Lackey.
1796, Jan.   23, Smith, Sarah, and Nehemiah Richardson.
1775, June   5, Smith, Sarah, and William Beeby.
1755, Oct.   18, Smith, Susanna, and Michael Carr.
1792, Feb.   19, Smith, Susanna, and Philip Gabel.
1781, Feb.   13, Smith, Susannah, and William Clark.
1755, Nov.   27, Smith, Susanna, and William Staddon.
1771, March 19, Smith, Thomas, and Dorothy Handwooker.
1784, July   1, Smith, Thomas, and Eletter Hutton.
1775, April 23, Smith, Thomas, and Maria Pool.
1763, Dec.   15, Smith, Whitefield, and Esther Ross.
1785, Feb.   10, Smith, William, and Alice Harper.
1780, March 15, Smith, William, and Eleanor Clark.
1766, Feb.   12, Smith, William, and Elizabeth Garrigues.
1793, Feb.   10, Smith, William, and Jane Wilson.
1784, Dec.   24, Smith, William, and Margaret McCarty.
1775, July   16, Smith, William, and Mary Evans.
1761, Jan.   21, Smith, William, and Mary John.
1799, Jan.   17, Smith, William, and Tobitha Power.
1794, Dec.   23, Snader, Jacob, and Edah Harris.
1782, Sept. 24, Sneider, Susannah, and Christopher Loashe.
1782, Feb.   16. Sneider, Jacob, and Hannah Carter.
1778, March 24, Snell, John, and Sarah Singleton.
1799, Nov.   6, Snell, Samuel, and Elizab. Fletcher.
1796, Jan.   10, Snellhart, Christiana, and James Christie.
1792, March 31, Snethen, Wajtel, and Mary Steel.
1795, May   26, Snider, Marget, and James McClellan.
1779, Feb.   20, Snodgrass, Benjamin, and Susannah Miller.
1766, April 23, Snow, John, and Mary Buffington.
1778, Feb.   8, Snowden, Mercy, and George Marklow.
1800, Jan.   25, Snowden, Thomas, and Harriot Harold.
1765, April 20, Snowdon, John, and Sarah Lefever.
1793, Nov.   12, Snyder, Jacob, and Sophia Wiley.
1792, Feb.   28, Snyder, John, and Ruth Pugh.
1786, June   6, Snyder, Margaret, and Joseph Norrman.

1780, Jan.   30, Soden, Benjamin, and Catharine ManyPenny.
1793, Nov.   6, Sodon, Mary, and Ralph Lovemore.
1799, Nov.   17, Soeny, Mary, and William Cambel.
1766, Jan.   2ᶠ, Sole, William, and Martha Farmer.
1758, June   17, Sollewan, Mary, and John Fuller.
1794, May   5, Soley, Ann, and John Helms.
1799, Oct.   2, Sollinger, Casper, and Elizab. Aukerman.
1758, Aug.   12. Soluvan. Elizabeth, and John Boyd.
1792, Sept. 20, Sommerfield, John, and Jane Potts.
1783, May   13, Sommers, Esther, and Andrew McBride.
1757, Aug.   18, Sommers, Mary, and Nathan Woolson.
1780, March 26, Sommers, Samuel, and Margaret Doil.
1762, April 18, Sonce, Nicholas, and Marg. Beere.
1782, Aug.   11, Sonntag, Wᵐ Lewis, and Hannah Wright.
1796, May   29, Sooter, Tracy, and William Roland.
1771, Aug.   4, Sorber, Henry, and Susannah Ceimm.
1767, Feb.   22, Sorg, Valentine, and Ann Mary Thessin.
1797, March 19, Souchet, Jerome, and Sarah Boston.
1758, March 17, Souderes, Margaret, and James Hall.
1799, Aug.   14, Souders, Mary, and Charles Williams.
1791, May   29, Souders, John, and Mary Martin.
1800, Jan.   5, Souders, Mary, and Peter Peterson.
1778, March 30, Sousth, Catherine, and John Pollard.
1778, April 15, Southerick, Margaret, and Benjamin Folks.
1779, March 14, Span, Ann, and David Slack.
1788, Aug.   28, Spangenberg, Conrad, and Barbara Taxis.
1777, Dec.   4, Spanigel, Catherine, and Francis Weyman.
1754, April   6, Sparkes, Robert, and Desire Brinnow.
1762, July   26, Sparrow. Hannah, and Samuel Tew.
1778, March 12, Sparrow, Thomas, and Elizabeth Brown.
1767, Aug.   3, Spear, Ester, and John Wills.
1798, Dec.   13, Spear, Hannah, and Francis Gryffith.
1799, Oct.   17. Spears, Hannah, and Gabriel Reed.
1757, May   9, Spece, Ann Gartrout, and John Painter.
1775, March 19, Specht, John, and Catharine Knees.
1759, Feb.   5, Speer, George, and Sarah Mogrow.
1782, Sept. 17, Spelmennew, Barbara, and John Hobson.
1793, Dec.   19, Spence, Gilbert, and Priscilla Turner.
1795, March 29, Spence, Henry, and Mary Charlesworth.
1794, March 22, Spence, John, and Rachel Roberts.
1792, Sept. 24, Spence, John, and Susanna Monro.
1762, Dec.   11, Spence, Peter, and Sarah Dixon.
1755, March   1, Spencer, Diana, and Thomas Hill.
1779, Dec.   14, Spencer, Mary, and Samuel Williams.
1791, Nov.   17, Spend, John, and Juliana Sullivan.
1757, Feb.   17, Spense, William, and Mary Ramesy.

1799, July   2, Spenser, Jacob, and Sarah Cheesman.
1798, June   14, Spenser, John, and Mary Perry.
1782, Jan.   17, Spicer, Sarah, and Samuel Clinton.
1774, Dec.   11, Spiegel, Jacob, and Mary Delany.
1777, March   23, Spiegel, Margaret, and Michael Wester.
1783, March   13, Spiehl, Henry, and Barbara Knorr.
1799, May   25, Spooner, Edward, and Sarah Hawkins.
1776, Dec.   1, Spooner, Ward, and Margaret Thomson.
1776, Dec.   3, Spots, John, and Elizabeth Shreyer.
1765, March   18, Springer, Andrew, and Elizabeth Stiner.
1776, Aug.   29, Springer, Catharine, and John Monery.
1795, Aug.   2, Springer, Jacob, and Margret Ruben.
1800, July   3, Springer, Jehu, and Jane McCoy.
1791, March   26, Springer, John, and Elizabeth Osborn.
1794, Aug.   31, Springer, Joseph, and Sarah Tommelson.
1796, May   23, Springer, Sarah, and James Holly.
1799, Sept.   1, Sprogel, Charlotte, and Samuel Evans.
1780, Jan.   6, Sprogel, John, and Elizabeth Town.
1775, July   16, Sprouse, Hannah, and John Haley.
1772, April   15, Stackhouse, Margaret, and Richard Jackson.
1779, Nov.   10, Stackhouse, Martha, and Calop Gilbert.
1758, March   30, Stackhouse, Rachel, and Thomas Thomson.
1797, Aug.   19, Stacy Ann, and Obadiah Stillwell.
1761, Sept.   24, Stacy, Mathew, and Ann Walker.
1781, Aug.   23, Stacy, Richard, and Jenny Higgins.
1755, Nov.   27, Staddon, William, and Susanna Smith.
1784, Feb.   19, Stadleman, Elizabeth, and Thomas Paul.
1792, April   29, Staeb, Jacob, and Rachel Boyles.
1796, July   5, Stafford, Margret, and Laurence Oneal.
1793, Feb.   11, Stag, Benjamin, and Elizabeth Bowren.
1782, April   3, Stag, John, and Jeaney McPharson.
1784, May   26, Stage, Sarah, and James Hestor.
1778, June   14, Stagg, Sibila, and Charles Leking.
1800, Aug.   3, Stags, Mary, and Timothy Hanley.
1759, May   29, Stahl, Elizabeth, and George Rester.
1778, April   9, Staiger, Mary, and John Jefferies.
1799, July   14, Staires, Susannah, and Nicholas Connard.
1769, May   27, Stamper, Catharine, and John Adair.
1755, Oct.   11, Stamper, John, and Catharine Simmons.
1766, May   13, Stanberry, Barbara, and Albert Meyer.
1792, Sept.   13, Stanburrough, Adoniah, and Sarah Cook.
1792, Oct.   28, Stancliff, John, and Rachel Sharp.
1780, April   5, Standley, Francis, and Ann Chamberlin.
1756, June   1, Standley, Margaret, and Richard Bowyer.
1779, Aug.   1, Standley, Michael, and Martha Grimes.
1764, April   6, Stanford, John, and Ann Jones.

1780, July   19, Stanhop, Hannah, and James Welsh.
1790, Sept.   9, Stanley, John, and Mary Kerlock.
1795, July   29, Stanley, Sarah, and Benjamin Soane.
1767, April   24, Stansin, Sophy Margett, and Ludwig Preel.
1763, Nov.   30, Stant, John, and Margaret Parmer.
1778, Feb.   16, Stanton, Bridget, and John Dean.
1779, Feb.   16, Stanton, Bridget, and John Dean.
1764, Nov.   7, Stanton, George, and Ann Tussey.
1796, Oct.   30, Stanton, Gilbert, and Hanna Hart.
1778, April   22, Stanton, Henry, and Mary Coleman.
1799, Nov.   11, Stanton, Jacob, and Elizab. Dalbo.
1797, July   9, Stanton, Jemima, and Henry Smith.
1778, June   30, Stanton, Jonathan, and Jemima Christine.
1759, Jan.   3, Stapelton, James, and Elizabet Shmids.
1795, Nov.   29, Stark, Hannah, and David O'Connor.
1781, Aug.   9, Starkey, Emely, and Edward Kain.
1781, Nov.   16, Starkhouse, Peter, and Mary Borroughs.
1796, June   23, Starr, Thomas, and Eleonore Johnson.
1790, April   5, Starrett, William, and Cathrine McDonough.
1777, Sept.   10, Start, Mary, and Joseph Defrees.
1756, May   22, Stasy, John, and Sarah Huston.
1762, Sept.   24, Stasy, Mathew, and Ann Walker.
1777, July   18, States, Jacob, and Lucy Hatton.
1763, July   5, Stator, Elizabeth, and Jeremiah Shee.
1762, July   26, Stator, John, and Elizabeth Norridge:
1784, July   14, Statten, Thomas, and Mary Powell.
1770, Nov.   18, Staub, Samuel, and Elizabeth Pines.
1775, Jan.   20, Staul, Rosanna, and John Clanges.
1781, Dec.   17, Stead, John, and Barbara Grub.
1769, May   15, Stead, Mary, and James McDaniel.
1781, July   30, Steal, John, and Elizabeth Blake.
1794, May   24, Stealy, George, and Catharine Schweris.
1755, Oct.   12, Stedman, Margaret, and William Hitchings.
1786, March 30, Steed, Michael, and Sidney Betton.
1758, Dec.   5, Steedon, Benjamin, and Margaret Williamson.
1791, Nov.   6, Steel, Ben, and Martha Nathery.
1780, July   9, Steel, Catherine, and Peter Clark.
1796, Jan.   14, Steel, Elizabeth, and Cornelius Leary, (mariner.)
1762, July   29, Steel, Elizabeth, and James Finaghan.
1758, Nov.   16, Steel, Ester, and John Farris.
1788, Sept.   5, Steel, George, and Elizabeth Jones.
1756, Sept.   16, Steel, James, and Ann Williams.
1799, July   8, Steel, James, and Eva Rossbottom.
1767, Feb.   22, Steel, John, and Elizabeth Cobery.
1789, Nov.   30, Steel, Mary, and Jacob Landenberg.
1794, May   13, Steel, Mary, and James Forest.

1792, March 31, Steel, Mary, and Wajtel Snethen.
1751, Dec.   15, Steel, Robert, and Hanna Lisle.
1792, Nov.   11, Steel, Stephen, and Bridget McFall.
1759, June   30, Steel, William, and Elizabeth Reely.
1791, July   7, Steell, John, and Martha Truck.
1782, May   21, Steelman, Andrew, and Susannah Stiles.
1785, Oct.   12, Steelman, Priscilla, and John Creghard.
1794, April 27, Steelman, Solomon, and Hanna James.
1780, Sept. 20, Steen, Hannah, and John Pierce.
1759, Sept. 29, Steer, Magdaline, and Nicolas Batine.
1795, Sept. 13, Steeth, William, and Mary Lents.
1791, Jan.   1, Stein, Reinhold, and Rosanna Binghaman.
1775, June   5, Stein, William, and Christiana Muchlarein.
1776, Oct.   3, Steinfortz, Eve, and Godfrey Buckas.
1760, June   2, Stemand, Frederick, and Hannah Timberman.
1779, Aug.   15, Stempson, Ann, and Robert Morry.
1778, April 30, Steneeson. Elizabeth, and Thomas Fox.
1794, March   5, Stenman, Eric Johan, and Maria Christina Holm-
                    berg.
1773, March   2, Stennard, Johannah, and Paul Johnston.
1759, Oct.   15, Stenson, Ann, and Michael Dillon.
1770, Sept. 24, Stenson, Mary, and Jacob Myer.
1777, April   4, Stentin, Elizabeth, and David Cockran.
1757, March 22, Stephans, Patience, and John Stuart.
1795, July   19, Stephen, Marget, and Anthony Burns.
1752, Dec.   9, Stephens, Anne, and John Adams.
1778, Nov.   9, Stephens, James, and Margaret Richards.
1781, Oct.   19, Stephens, John, and Christiane McNair.
1776, June   22, Stephens, John, and Mary Lodge.
1790, June   25, Stephens, Joseph, and Rosana McCalley.
1766, April 22, Stephens, Joshua, and Priscillah Humphreys.
1753, Sept.   8, Stephens, Sarah, and William Moses.
1764, Oct.   7, Stephenson, Ann, and William Fisher.
1751, June   15, Stephenson, John, and Elizabeth Hindrickson.
1792, Jan.   2, Stephenson, Ruth, and Jacob Leaming.
1779, June   3, Stephenson, Sarah, and Simon Gore.
1765, Sept. 17, Sterling, Elizabeth, and William McDonald.
1781, June   19, Sterling, Robert, and Elizabeth Wens.
1762, Sept.   6, Sterrat, Samuel, and Mary Keappack.
1759, Feb.   20, Steuart, Archibald, and Jane Kirkpatrick.
1793, March 17, Steuart, Margret Jane, and William Keith.
1778, March 30, Stevens, John, and Jean King.
1777, Nov.   28, Stevens, Joseph, and Margaret Revel.
1780, Dec.   24, Stevens, Margaret, and Joseph Brintnell.
1791, Dec.   31, Stevens, Marget, and James Brown.
1773, March   1, Stevens, Sarah, and Hugh Carney.

1776, Aug. 26, Stevenson, James, and Mary Mearess.
1792, Nov. 12, Stevenson, Jane, and Thomas Bunker.
1766, Dec. 18, Stevenson, Jeanings, and Sarah Alexander.
1771, Sept. 2, Stevenson, John, and Margaret Davids.
1774, Sept. 26, Stevenson, Joseph, and Mary Flowery.
1759, Oct. 23, Stevenson, Latice, and John Rogers.
1765, July 29, Stevenson, Sarah, and Edward Collins.
1781, Dec. 31, Steward, David, and Elizabeth Cammoren.
1777, Feb. 7, Steward, Dorothy, and William Tucker.
1780, Sept. 16, Steward, Hugh, and Margarett Smith.
1780, Jan. 25, Steward, John, and Sarah McCoy.
1773, Jan. 3, Steward, Margarett, and John Sawyer.
1774, May 4, Steward, Margaret, and Patrick Bradley.
1765, Sept. 18, Steward, Margeth, and Samuel Harvey.
1782, Jan. 3, Steward, Mary, and Daniel Morrisson.
1779, July 28, Steward, Mary, and Edward Stroud.
1779, Jan. 25, Steward, Mary, and Robert Rice.
1778, June 4, Steward, Mary, and William Warlow.
1778, Aug. 12, Steward, William, and Catharine Kuhn.
1791, Oct. 13, Steward, William, and Hanna Course.
1778, March 25, Stewart, Alexander, and Jean Stewart.
1776, Oct. 22, Stewart, Francis, and Mary Madlin.
1773, Oct. 25, Stewart, James, and Jean McPherson.
1778, March 25, Stewart, Jean, and Alexander Stewart.
1773, Feb. 7, Stewart, Jean, and James Tanton.
1779, May 17, Stewart, John, and Mary Fry.
1785, March 15, Stewart, Joseph, and Mary Simmonds.
1768, Feb. 20, Stewart, Mary, and Daniel Gorton.
1792, July 4, Stewart, Nancy, and William Taylor.
1784, April 26, Stewart, Rosey, and Thomas Ensty.
1782, Jan. 15, Stewart, Sarah, and Henry Osborne.
1794, Sept. 10, Stewart, Thomas, and Eby Scudder.
1769, Oct. 5, Stewart, William, and Latitia Russel.
1768, June 6, Stickham, Marget, and James Sanders.
1785, Sept. 29, Stidham, William, and Mary Flick.
1763, June 22, Stiemer, Anton, and Anna Augusta Goreberin.
1777, Feb. 25, Stiever, Daniel, and Ann Ghasslin.
1789, Nov. 13, Stiles, Cathrine, and James Berry.
1785, Oct. 18, Stiles, Mary, and William Mason.
1782, May 21, Stiles, Susannah, and Andrew Steelman.
1782, Sept. 18, Stiles, Thomas, and Anny Killpatrick.
1790, Dec. 7, Still, Elenore, and Hugh Robeson.
1796, July 28, Still, John, and Barbara Miller.
1795, Aug. 15, Still, Mary, and John Gibbons.
1779, Feb. 18, Stille, Barbara, and Joseph Krast.
1762, Oct. 21, Stilley, Christiana, and Reynold Keen.

1761, Dec. 3, Stilley, Rachel, and Isaac Harman.
1756, March 17, Stillman, Charles, and Brigitta Dalbo.
1794, May 13, Stillman, Leah, and Amos Clark.
1789, Oct. 5, Stillman, Mary, and Luke Bahn.
1764, Dec. 11, Stillwell, Daniel, and Elizabeth Lupton.
1784, Dec. 20, Stillwell, Jacob, and Jane Bennet.
1797, Aug. 19, Stillwell, Obadiah, and Ann Stacy.
1794, April 15, Stillwell, Obadiah, and Ann White.
1753, April 16, Stilly, Ellen, and John Hendrickson.
1791, Sept. 18, Stilwagon, Joseph, and Ann Dickson.
1791, Aug. 20, Stimbel, Peter, and Elizabeth Syng.
1773, Dec. 19, Stimbel, Philip, and Ann Tommos.
1782, Dec. 4, Stimlerin, Elizabeth, and Francis Warner.
1791, Sept. 8, Stine, Cathrine, and Jacob Smith.
1773, April 11, Stine, Sarah, and Thomas Heley.
1765, March 18, Stiner, Elizabeth, and Andrew Springer.
1782, July 22, Stinsman, Catherine, and Philip Schroder.
1782, Dec. 8, Stinsman, Christiana, and Henry Moser.
1790, May 23, Stinsman, Jacob, and Susannah Brown.
1766, Oct. 20, Stinson, Mary, and William Jomaster.
1753, Nov. 12, Stirling, Walter, and Dorothy Witting.
1755, May 26, Stise, John, and Sarah Britton.
1793, July 3, Stitchfield, Ann, and William Burns.
1794, Nov. 1, Stites, Joshua, and Elizabeth Whelen.
1755, May 29, St. John, Margarete, and John Etherige.
1794, March 4, Stock, John, and Cathrine Collins.
1800, Jan. 9, Stockdale, Joseph, and Barbara Wolf.
1776, July 21, Stockman, Charles, and Elizabeth Clockston.
1777, May 19, Stockman, Elizabeth, and Allan McLean.
1778, May 27, Stocks, Elizabeth, and James Greenwood.
1757, Dec. 10, Stocky, George, and Catharine Wanderin.
1789, May 16, Stoger, Mary, and Henry Reib.
1778, May 31, Stokes, James, and Sarah McGinn.
1773, Dec. 19, Stone, Adam, and Mary Millburn.
1778, Dec. 10, Stone, Elizabeth, and William Willson.
1800, April 21, Stone, Frances, and Isaac Roberts.
1795, May 9, Stone, Guy, and Dorothy Awll.
1794, March 22, Stone, Harvey, and Rebecca Ray.
1781, Nov. 3, Stone, William, and Abigail Williard.
1780, Jan. 27, Stone, William, and Mary Seaman.
1796, Oct. 29, Stoneburner, Hannah, and Joseph Roberts.
1775, Sept. 30, Stoneburner, Mary, and William Rush.
1791, Nov. 29, Stonmets, Priscilla, and John More.
1776, May 21, Stonemetz, John, and Mary Foster.
1781, March 20, Stoots, George, and Sarah Keys.
1788, Nov. 16, Story, Ann, and James Carney.

1780, June 15, Story, Elizabeth, and Alexander Tindall.
1794, May 10, Story, Mary, and Thomas Pedric.
1784, Feb. 7, Story, Robert, and Elizabeth Creed.
1794, Nov. 1, Story, Thomas, and Mary Winters.
1782, Aug. 10, Storms, Abram, and Mary Laveirs.
1787, July 24, Stotesbury, Arthur, and Margret Harry.
1790, Oct. 17, Stotsenberg, Christopher, and Eliza Wilder.
1792, Sept. 27, Stotsenburgh, Margret, and Joseph Wood.
1765, May 24, Stous, Mary, and Melchior Weysinger.
1796, Feb. 28, Stouse, Mary, and John Chambers.
1791, May 8, Stout, Elizabeth, and John Nelson.
1790, June 26, Stout, Roseana, and John Hutton.
1796, Feb. 28, Stow, Elizabeth, and William Sharpley.
1776, Oct. 21, Stow, Jacob, and Rosannah Micker.
1794, Sept. 9, Stow, Jeremiah, and Ann McGill.
1793, June 8, Stow, William, and Rebecca Loper.
1794, April 5, Stowe, Michael, and Hester Humphord.
1766, March 24, Stoy, Hannah, and Richard Nugent.
1783, Oct. 14, Stoy, John, and Patience Draper.
1775, Jan. 22, Stoyle, Jean, and Henry Bailee.
1783, Sept. 28, Stradling, Catherine, and John Wells.
1759, Aug. 18, Strafford, Jeney, and James Bye.
1791, July 17, Strang, Daniel, and Mary More.
1759, Nov. 28, Strangel, Elizabeth, and Jesse Kirk.
1786, Nov. 5, Strauss, Martin, and Rachel Crack.
1788, May 21, Stream, Sarah, and James Miller.
1795, Sept. 10, Streaper, William, and Martha Helms.
1778, April 24, Streaton, George, and Elizabeth Dawson.
1751, March 19, Street, Rachel, and Thomas Testin.
1753, Jan. 10, Streeton, Friend, and Mary, Gwinup.
1774, March 9, Strembeck, John, and Elizabeth Grow.
1778, Nov. 17, Strep, Elizabeth, and Martin Ludwick.
1758, Sept. 8, Stricker, Peter, and Ann Magdalen.
1795, Sept. 24, Strickland, Hugh, and Sarah Woods.
1753, June 14, Strickland, Margaret, and John Thomas.
1756, Oct. 10, Strickland, Rachel, and Henry Cornely.
1780, June 19, Strickler, Peter, and Nancy Croom.
1780, March 5, Stricklin, Edward, and Lydy Search.
1800, March 11, Strickling, John, and Rebecca Wells.
1760, July 14, String, Peter, and Hannah McCarty.
1780, Aug. 26, Strizer, John, and Elizabeth Smith.
1775, Nov. 28, Strobey, Catharine, and William Wright.
1755, Nov. 5, Stroembeck, Thomas, and Sarah Kefot.
1779, Feb. 17, Strong, Eleanor, and John Daniel.
1795, Dec. 20, Strong, Marget, and George Dougherty.
1779, July 28, Stroud, Edward, and Mary Steward.

1780, May   20, Stroud, Mary, and Christian Beakley.
1783, May   12, Stroup, Anne, and Stephen Singlewood.
1774, Oct.   16, Strouse, Elizabeth, and William Wiley.
1781, Aug.   23, Strout, Mary, and John Colloms.
1779, Feb.   14, Strover, Ann Catharine, and Jeremiah Sheehin.
1780, June   12, Strow, John, and Mary McDarmouth.
1776, Dec.   6, Strowaker, Catharine, and John Nicholas Deits.
1764, Nov.   7, Strowd, Mary, and John McCoy.
1769, July   9, Streeper, Elizabeth, and Henry Cunard.
1781, July   14, Strut, Daniel, and Catharine Brown.
1766, April 21, Strutton, Mary, and Francis Johnston.
1787, June   12, Stuard, Elizabeth, and Humphrey Vane.
1760, Sept. 18, Stuard, Elizabeth, and Joseph Bashfull.
1757, Dec.   4, Stuard, Mary, and Richard Smith.
1800, Oct.   3, Stuart, Christiana, and Thomas McIlwan.
1798, Dec.   24, Stuart, Eliza, and John Clarc.
1789, June   21, Stuart, Elizabeth, and Daniel Beydiman.
1785, March 24, Stuart, Elizabeth, and Doyle Sweeny.
1792, May   3, Stuart, Elizabeth, and Samuel Furguson.
1797, July   17, Stuart, George, and Hannah Wright.
1792, Dec.   18, Stuart, George, and Mary Rudolph.
1799, May   11, Stuart, James, and Anne Carson.
1798, Jan.   30, Stuart, John, and Isabella MacKintosh.
1757, March 22, Stuart, John, and Patience Stephans.
1770, Aug.   24, Stuart, Margarett, and Alexander Glass.
1798, March 22, Stuart, Mary, and Andrew Callum.
1794, Nov.   25, Stuart, Mary, and John Skott.
1760, Aug.   14, Stuart, Mary, and Joseph Sales.
1790, Oct.   19, Stuart, Nathan, and Rachel Morgan.
1792, April 27, Stuart, Rosanna, and Benjamin Newton.
1790, Jan.   29, Stuart, William, and Comfort Cape.
1798, July   29, Stuart, William, and Susannah McMullen.
1776, Jan.   3, Stubbs, Deborah, and James Rench.
1759, July   26, Stubbs, Sarah, and William Whitebread.
1782, March 28, Studden, Samuel, and Rebecca Queen.
1774, Oct.   18, Stump, Judith, and Peter Cofey.
1792, March 29, Sturges, Elizabeth, and Jonathan Rambo.
1775, Oct.   2, Sturges, James, and Mary Ogelby.
1774, May   3, Sturges, Jesse, and Hannah Brooks.
1796, Feb.   18, Sturges, John, and Rebecca Thompson.
1776, Aug.   6, Sturgis, Mary, and William Jones.
1771, Oct.   27, Stutting, Mary, and Henry Fullford.
1771, April   7, Styar, Elizabeth, and John Bathurst.
1777, Nov.   12, Sudrick, Elizabeth, and John Nerdel.
1780, Jan.   6, Sugars, William, and Mary Tilsey.
1799, June   15, Sullender, James, and Jane Adams.

1778, Dec.   2, Sullevan, Rebecca, and John Williams.
1754, Oct.   26, Sullingar, Jacob, and Appilloney Myer.
1798, Aug.   25, Sullivan, Aby, and Manivel DeCruse.
1780, May   15, Sullivan, Biddy, and James Ryain.
1794, May   4, Sullivan, John, and Abigail Wade.
1777, March   27, Sullivan, John, and Margarett Weaver.
1791, Nov.   17, Sullivan, Juliana, and John Spend.
1778, Dec.   21, Sullivan, Martha, and John King.
1751, Feb.   18, Sullivan, Mary, and Thomas McCloud.
1777, Dec.   10, Sullivan, Timothy, and Bridget West.
1783, Dec.   10, Summers, Elizabeth, and George Raybold.
1795, May   31, Summers, Elizabeth, and Henry Chamberlin, (or
                  lain.)
1793, Dec.   12, Summers, Marget, and Henry Barley.
1783, Dec.   23, Summers, Susannah, and Israel Davis.
1782, March   31, Summers, Zacheriah, and Mary Laver.
1790, June   27, Sundstrœm, Andrew, and Brita Svanson.
1777, May   20, Sunney, Margaret. and Elijah Bowman.
1791, Feb.   3, Super, Joseph, and Cathrine White.
1755, Nov.   5, Super, Philip, and Hannah Claiton.
1754, April   17, Suplar, John, and Susanna Gray.
1773, Oct.   14, Supplee, Andrew, and Alley Fitzgerald.
1777, Sept.   24, Supplee, Catharine, and George Manderson.
1799, Dec.   26, Supplee, William, and Elizab. Bear.
1763, Dec.   1, Supplie, Deborah, and Christopher Timmerman.
1767, Sept.   2, Supply, Elizabeth, and Peter Matson.
1782, Aug.   13, Surham, David, and Sarah Dilkes.
1789, Sept.   1, Suter, Elizabeth, and Davis Denike.
1792, Oct.   16, Sutherland, Joseph, and Maria Buchs.
1800, Jan.   25, Sutherland, Mary, and Stephen Arnold.
1799, June   20, Sutleffe, Daniel, and Catharine Buchanan.
1766, Oct.   26, Sutor, Ann, and George Clarke.
1772, Dec.   3, Sutton, Elizabeth, and Colin Mackenzie.
1795, May   11, Sutton, Hannah, and Robert MacFarlane.
1779, Oct.   23, Sutton, James, and Mary Baker.
1767, Oct.   26, Sutton, Joshua, and Ann Wells.
1798, June   21, Sutton, Mary, and Hugh McDowell.
1791, Nov.   10, Sutton, Thomas, and Hanna Bickham.
1782, Dec.   27, Sutton, Thomas, and Rachel John.
1796, July   24, Svan, Casper Iser, and Eliza Mink.
1795, July   29, Svane, Benjamin, and Sarah Stanley.
1790, June   27, Svanson, Brita, and Andrew Sundstrœm.
1792, Nov.   15, Svanson, William, and Rachel Josephson.
1794, Feb.   22, Svinning, Rebecca, and William Bowers.
1781, Aug.   19, Swain, Joseph, and Martha Wade.
1795, March   7, Swain, Margret, and Daniel Bunneman.

1779, April   3, Swain, Mary, and Daniel Heritage.
1778, April   10, Swayney, Bryan, and Mary Howard.
1791, Oct.   27, Swangley, Jane, and John Ashmore.
1759, July   12, Swanoy, Mary, and Darbor Coffy.
1793, Nov.   2, Swanson, Andrew, and Cathrine Hunt.
1778, Oct.   28, Swards, Keziah, and John Edwards.
1776, Sept.   8, Sweaney, Jean, and Thomas Black.
1785, March 24, Sweeny, Doyle, and Elizabeth Stuart.
1782, June   7, Sweet, Francis, and Mary Watson.
1753, Sept.   6, Sweetaple, Mary, and Robert Crawford.
1796, Nov.   6, Sweeten, Priscilla, and Michael Fry.
1754, Feb.   21, Sweeting, Elizabeth, and John Bard.
1780, Sept.   26, Swiler, Barnet, and Abigail Cape.
1790, July   15, Swim, Cathrine, and Charles White.
1772, Oct.   15, Swim, Mary, and Luke Edgerton.
1778, April   1, Swiney, Miles, and Rebecca Baker.
1775, Sept.   17, Swiser, Michael, and Elizabeth Field.
1791, Nov.   6, Switcher, Gerry, and Ann Taylor.
1783, April   21, Swiver, Elizabeth, and John Aitken.
1757, Oct.   13, Sword, William, and Penelope Haly.
1767, Dec.   24, Syales, Elizabeth, and Everhard Morton.
1755, Oct.   1, Sylvester, Thomas, and Ann Horditch.
1754, Feb.   7, Symmons, Frances, and Peter Sinnott.
1796, Dec.   8, Symonds, James, and Rachel Barnard.
1791, Aug.   20, Syng, Elizabeth, and Peter Stimbel.
1755, Jan.   30, Syng, Mary, and John Withy.
1763, Oct.   29, Tabor, Rebeccah, and Samuel Bruster.
1784, Dec.   5, Taft, Joseph, and Elizabeth Bowls.
1778, Sept.   13, Tagert, Patrick, and Elizabeth Green.
1787, Sept.   18, Taggard, Patric, and Sarah Maires.
1770, June   23, Taggart, Sarah, and George Thomson.
1799, Jan.   31, Tailor, James, and Jane Gainer.
1797, Sept.   23, Tailor, Jane, and Anthony Young.
1762, Aug.   22, Tailor, Jeansey, and John Morgan.
1793, July   11, Tailor, John, and Marget Perkins.
1789, July   23, Tailor, Michael, and Mary Ann McGinnis.
1753, Oct.   29, Tailor, Peter, and Elinor Whartonbay.
1799, Oct.   27, Talbor, Mary, and Peter William.
1790, Nov.   21, Talbot, Rachel, and James Freeland.
1780, March 15, Talburt, William, and Rosannah Carson.
1753, Aug.   27, Tallot, William, and Ann Canne.
1795, May   24, Tally, Mary, and John Immel.
1793, May   25, Tammany, Patric, and Mary Connor.
1770, June   27, Tammon, Christine, and George Way.
1754, Feb.   26, Tanes, Hannah, and John Righter.
1791, April   21, Tanner, John, and Mary Hargus Kymer.
      34—Vol. VIII.

1773, Feb.	7, Tanton, James, and Jean Stewart.
1795, Sept.	3, Taper, Samuel, and Marget Johnson.
1761, April	20, Tarry, Rachel, and Isaak Willson.
1758, Jan.	1, Tascare, Edward, and Mary Clarke.
1776, Sept.	29, Tate, Benjamin, and Hannah Wilkison.
1754, May	9, Tate, Robert, and Ann Ryan.
1753, June	19, Tate, Susanna, and William Faulkner.
1752, Dec.	25, Tatem, Rebecca, and John Welsh.
1777, Sept.	11, Tatem, Rosannah, and Henry Hawkins.
1793, Feb.	12, Tatham, Latitia, and Jonathan Young.
1791, Oct.	24, Tatham, Latitia, and Samuel Dicky.
1796, Sept.	4, Tauhse, Henry, and Cathrine Keor.
1765, July	8, Tausond, Elizabeth, and William Croft.
1795, Nov.	7, Tavern, Mary, and John DeLhulier.
1788, Aug.	28, Taxis, Barbara, and Conrad Spangenberg.
1799, June	19, Taxis, George, and Elizabeth Fried.
1780, Jan.	12, Tayler, John, and Elizabeth McGill.
1791, Nov.	6, Taylor, Ann, and Gerry Switcher.
1778, Feb.	1, Taylor, Anne, and John Watson.
1755, Feb.	2, Taylor, Adam, and Oschel Schegy.
1762, June	23, Taylor, Ann, and William Colston.
1778, May	11, Taylor, Catharine, and Francis Smith.
1787, Nov.	8, Taylor, Catherine, and Christopher Goffry.
1782, June	20, Taylor, Catherine, and John Metier.
1774, Sept.	21, Taylor, Catherine, and Joseph Smith.
1779, Dec.	23, Taylor, Charles, and Sarah Guinar.
1780, May	16, Taylor, Christine, and William Kirkwood.
1773, April	29, Taylor, Edeth, and Alexander Kied.
1800, April	5, Taylor, Elizabeth, and Alexander Samuel.
1757, May	4, Taylor, Elizabeth, and Charles Grantum, junior.
1787, Nov.	3, Taylor, Elizabeth, and Charles Whitebread.
1767, Oct.	23, Taylor, Elizabeth, and John Smith.
1766, Oct.	27, Taylor, Elizabeth, and William Barnett.
1752, Oct.	23, Taylor, George, and Margaret Hoops.
1763, July	2, Taylor, Hester, and Isaac Garrigues.
1779, July	28, Taylor, Isabella, and Frederic McConn.
1777, Oct.	31, Taylor, Jane, and William Price.
1766, April	15, Taylor, John, and Ann Redgrove.
1778, May	3, Taylor, John, and Elizabeth Seils.
1792, June	13, Taylor, John, and Nancy Yocum.
1776, July	18, Taylor, John, and Rachel Harman.
1788, June	18, Taylor, John, and Susannah Myers.
1774, Jan.	15, Taylor, Joseph, and Anno Rambo.
1800, Sept.	25, Taylor, Lydia, and John Madan.
1771, Dec.	19, Taylor, Martha, and Robert Evans.
1777, May	29, Taylor, Mary, and Benjamin Rue.

1793, May   1, Taylor, Mary, and Henry Port.
1778, Oct.   15, Taylor, Mary, and Jacob Baker.
1792, April 11, Taylor, Mary, and Jacob Lincoln.
1758, Nov. 22, Taylor, Mary, and John McNeal.
1764, July   2, Taylor, Mary, and William Whitby.
1776, Nov. 25, Taylor, Rebecca, and Richard Trusted.
1773, June 21, Taylor, Rebecca, and Sketchley Morton.
1754, Dec. 14, Taylor, Richard, and Mary Hickenbottom.
1757, April 13, Taylor, Robert, and Elizabeth Leeson.
1791, March 17, Taylor, Roda, and John Francis Osey.
1769, Jan.   9, Taylor, Samuel, and Anne Smith.
1766, April 17, Taylor, Samuel, and Mary Bankson.
1792, Nov. 20, Taylor, Sarah, and Samuel Lindsey.
1766, Sept.   3, Taylor, Simon, and Mary Morrison.
1780, June 29, Taylor, Solomon, and Elizabeth Dun.
1777, Aug. 28, Taylor, Thomas, and Rachel Tussel.
1756, Nov.   1, Taylor, Thomas, and Rebecca Nidermark.
1793, July 24, Taylor, William, and Elizabeth Helms.
1781, Oct. 29, Taylor, William, and Hannah Oldfield.
1792, July   4, Taylor, William, and Nancy Stewart.
1800, Aug. 25, Tea, Robert, and Mary Longstreth.
1778, Sept. 23, Teace, George, and Eve Holly.
1778, June   2, Teatz, Mary, and Alexander Leench.
1791, April 11, Teel, George, and Elizabeth Baum.
1777, March 23, Teellman, Penroy, and John Vickars.
1795, July 28, Teft, Mary, and William Harding.
1797, April   2, Tehurst, Ann Mary, and Daniel Douglas.
1773, July 27, Teis, John, and Rachel Nicholson.
1774, May 12, Tembown, Elizabeth, and John Clasor.
1791, June   2, Templar, John, and Elenore Ryburn.
1791, Nov. 23, Temple, John, and Rachel Vanhorn.
1778, May 15, Templeton, Ann, and John Fulton.
1752, Nov. 26, Templing, Susannah, and Thomas Jacobs.
1767, Jan. 19, Ten, Ann, and Thomas Smallwood.
1766, July   9, Tenant, Charles, and Catharine Galbraith.
1793, May   5, Tenant, William, and Mary Ann Douglas.
1751, April 21, Tenbye, John, and Elizabeth Dawson.
1780, Jan. 30, Tenick, Andrew, and Mary Adams.
1776, Jan.   7, Tenton, Jane, and Edward Morphey.
1784, Oct.   2, Terhorst, Mary, and Charles Erdman.
1792, Nov.   6, Terry, John, and Mary Calender.
1773, Nov.   2, Tested, Jacob Bensen, and Catharine Edwards.
1751, March 19, Testin, Thomas, and Rachel Street.
1759, May   7, Tew, Hariot, and William Diamond.
1781, Feb. 21, Tew, Lydia, and James Seed.
1773, Nov. 30, Tew, Mary, and Joel Baldwin.

1762, July 26, Tew, Samuel, and Hannah Sparrow.
1781, Feb. 9, Texter, Catherine, and Michael Smith.
1781, Dec. 18, Teylor, James, and Catherine Farrer.
1798, July 9, Thackary, William, and Maria Ford.
1782, April 8, Thackera, William, and Mary Cooper.
1753, Dec. 18, Tharp, Archibald, and Susanna Sheirtlyst.
1780, March 14, Thatcher, Lydy, and Christopher Coleman.
1754, April 10, Theeth, Mary, and Patrick Cally.
1780, May 2, Thepo, Philip, and Susannah Ford.
1767, Feb. 22, Thessin, Ann Mary, and Valentine Sorg.
1771, June 17, Thish, John Conrad, and Ann Robeson.
1761, April 18, Thomas, Abram, and Elizabeth Hackel.
1773, Dec. 16, Thomas, Abraham, and Jean Prince.
1789, Sept. 7, Thomas, Ann, and Coffy Tomson, (free blacks.)
1800, June 22, Thomas, Ann, and Gilbert White.
1785, July 3, Thomas, Benjamin, and Christina Irick.
1791, May 25, Thomas, Benjamin, and Mary Dowl.
1792, Dec. 12, Thomas, David, and Debora Cook.
1789, March 5, Thomas, David, and Rachel King.
1772, Nov. 11, Thomas, Elizabeth, and Daniel Haer.
1787, June 28, Thomas, Elizabeth, and John Chapman.
1783, Oct. 25, Thomas, Elizabeth, and Swen Hultgren.
1772, Sept. 27, Thomas, Elizabeth, and William McQuire.
1783, Sept. 6, Thomas, Hannah, and Abram Cox.
1757, May 15, Thomas, Hannah, and Isaac Brooks.
1782, Jan. 31, Thomas, Hannah, and Robert Jones.
1800, Sept. 1, Thomas, Helena, and Michael Davis.
1796, May 22, Thomas, Henry, and Nancy Valkert Johnson.
1796, Oct. 4, Thomas, Hester, and John Bazing.
1791, Nov. 16, Thomas, James, and Mary Rose.
1791, Aug. 21, Thomas, James, and Sarah Blair.
1781, Dec. 1, Thomas, John, and Casander Walton.
1781, June 11, Thomas, John. and Hannah Black.
1753, June 14, Thomas, John, and Margaret Strickland.
1797, July 23, Thomas, John, and Margret Andrews.
1756, Jan. 10, Thomas, Jonathan, and Mary Dane.
1793, Oct. 29, Thomas, Joseph, and Hope Griffins.
1776, Dec. 1, Thomas. Margaret, and Ward Spooner.
1791, Oct. 4, Thomas, Martha, and John Jocum.
1753, Sept. 28, Thomas, Martha, and William Bell.
1800, Dec. 24, Thomas, Mary, and William Clinton.
1754, Jan. 13, Thomas, Mary, and William Hives.
1778, Jan. 3, Thomas, Philip, and Elizabeth Byan.
1781, Jan. 16, Thomas, Philip, and Sarah Pilen.
1763, Sept. 30, Thomas, Rachel, and Benjamin Shepherds.
1790, July 26, Thomas, Rachel, and Henry Kemp.

1755, Oct.   16, Thomas, Rachel, and Hugh Moore.
1782, May   27, Thomas, Richard, and Hannah Joice.
1767, Jan.   17, Thomas, Sarah, and John Headcock.
1764, Nov.   7, Thomas, Seth, and Martha Kirks.
1788, Nov.   18, Thomas, William, and Charlotte Warren.
1776, Nov.   18, Thomas, William, and Mary Clark.
1777, Aug.   12, Thomas, William, and Mary Giddens.
1787, Oct.   7, Thomas, William, and Mary Hunt.
1767, March 9, Thomas, William, and Mary Winters.
1767, Feb.   23, Thoming, John, and Ann Hooks.
1759, March 26, Thomkins, Christopher, and Elisabet Gandawitt.
1785, May   25, Thompson, Alexander, and Susannah Tips.
1796, Feb.   24, Thompson, Francis, and Mary Knaus.
1799, June   2, Thompson, Joseph, and Mary Lewis.
1795, June   28, Thompson, Marget, and Stephen Ross.
1789, May   31, Thompson, Martha, and Daniel Laffarty.
1753, Nov.   3, Thompson, Martha, and Samson Levy.
1784, April   27, Thompson, Philip, and Mary Vanorden.
1796, Feb.   18, Thompson, Rebecca, and John Sturges.
1789, May   31, Thompson, Robert, and Kezia Albertson.
1780, Jan.   13, Thompson, Susannah, and John McPharlin.
1798, Dec.   13, Thompson, William, and Martha Forbes.
1755, Oct.   12, Thoms, John, and Ansilla Warrington.
1756, Dec.   6, Thomson, Abigail, and Peter Hooff.
1778, May   19, Thomson, Alexander, and Mary Miller.
1778, Feb.   25, Thomson, Ann, and Joseph Bidgood.
1765, Oct.   10, Thomson, Ann, and Joseph Payn.
1765, April   30, Thomson, Ann, and Patrick Griggar.
1780, May   15, Thomson, Ann, and Thomas Arnold.
1781, Oct.   15, Thomson, Archibald, and Elizabeth Wilson.
1772, Nov.   8, Thomson, Catherine, and Cornelius Herrity.
1779, Sept.   26, Thomson, Catharine, and Daniel Renahan.
1760, Sept.   26, Thomson, Daniel, and ———— Bacher.
1766, Nov.   6, Thomson, Eleonor, and Frederick Landerbrunn.
1798, April   18, Thomson, Elizabeth, and Jeremiah Pawling.
1786, Dec.   21, Thomson, Elizabeth, and Mathew Waring.
1759, June   25, Thomson, Elizabeth, and Robert Elder.
1780, Jan.   17, Thomson, Esther, and Thomas Annesley.
1781, Nov.   21, Thomson, Frances, and Benjamin Worrall.
1770, June   23, Thomson, George, and Sarah Taggart.
1778, Jan.   15, Thomson, Hanuah, and Alexander McCale.
1770, Sept.   13, Thomson, Hannah, and Joseph Prue.
1761, March 19, Thomson, James, and Latitia Nichols.
1755, July   9, Thomson, James, and Martha Hencock.
1777, July   17, Thomson, James, and Rebecca Downs.
1761, Jan.   20, Thomson, James, and Sarah Thomson.

1759, Sept. 10, Thomson, Jane, and Isack Jenkins.
1777, April 29, Thomson, Jean, and Alexander Cameran.
1776, July   21, Thomson, Jean, and John Numan.
1777, Aug.   4, Thomson, Jeremiah, and Mary Megomery.
1775, April 13, Thomson, John, and Elizabeth Willson.
1800, Dec.   27, Thomson, John, and Jane Galloway.
1778, March 18, Thomson, John, and Juliana O'Bryan.
1777, July   11, Thomson, John, and Margaret Burris.
1757, Oct.   19, Thomson, John, and Margaret Harris.
1777, March   7, Thomson, John, and Mary More.
1779, Feb.   21, Thomson, Martha, and Timothy Flude.
1790, Dec.   14, Thomson, Mary, and John Graham.
1764, Oct.   21, Thomson, Mary, and Samuel Cachey.
1779, July   7, Thomson, Michael, and Lydia Butter.
1791, Jan.   19, Thomson, Patience, and Thomas Ogle.
1776, March 18, Thomson, Peter, and Martha Wharton.
1778, Sept.   2, Thomson, Rebecca, and Richard Ward.
1764, June   11, Thomson, Robert, and Mary Vorall.
1775, June   20, Thomson, Sarah, and Francis Fest.
1761, Jan.   20, Thomson, Sarah, and James Thomson.
1759, Nov.   1, Thomson, Sarah, and Joseph Morrin.
1780, June   21, Thomson, Stephen, and Susannah Newton.
1762, Nov.   23, Thomson, Thomas, and Jane Fastor.
1758, March 30, Thomson, Thomas, and Rachel Stackhouse.
1782, July   16, Thorington, Jenny, and William Williams.
1759, April 25, Thorne, William, and Elizabeth Cliffton.
1780, April   7, Thornton, Arminieus, and Mary Adams.
1794, Feb.   9, Thornton, Daniel, and Elizabeth McClan.
1758, Aug.   30, Thornton, Michael, and Jane Blowne.
1787, Dec.   17, Thorp, Zillah, and Philip Hanes.
1780, March   2, Thought, Peter, and Priscilla Monyen.
1771, April   9, Tibberland Mary, and Robert Farrier.
1792, May   10, Til, Hezekiah, and Rebecca Turner.
1755, July   2, Tiley, Elizabeth, and Edward Bright.
1791, April   1, Tilford, Jane, and John Corben.
1795, Jan.   29, Tilford, Mary, and William Trump.
1800, May   18, Till, Juliana, and Benjamin Sansom.
1797, June   22, Till, Phebe, and Thomas Adams.
1757, June   18, Tilley, James, and Susanna Richeson.
1777, June   17, Tillman, Susannah, and Lawrence McNeil.
1780, Jan.   6, Tilsey, Mary, and William Sugars.
1760, June   2, Timberman, Hannah, and Frederick Stemand.
1793, July   18, Timbers, Isaac, and Mary Anderson.
1782, July   30, Timmins, Sarah, and Timothy Cole.
1763, Dec.   1, Timmerman, Christopher, and Deborah Supplie.
1758, May   24, Timpler; Joseph, and Mary Weaver.

1785, March 28, Times, Sarah, and George Waddle.
1780, June   15, Tindall, Alexander, and Elizabeth Story.
1774, Aug.   27, Tingle, Samuel, and Rebecca Bryan.
1790, Nov.   9, Tinker, Richard, and Sarah Duffy.
1778, Feb.   27, Tippen, Margaret, and Thomas Cannon.
1785, May   25, Tips, Susannah, and Alexander Thompson.
1753, Aug.   25, Tire, Elizabeth, and Richard Bigford.
1789, Dec.   2, Titt, Marc, and Ann Jones.
1766, Sept.   8, Titus, John, and Margaret Dannison.
1774, Oct.   16, Titus, Lucretia, and Peter Feel.
1759, May   16, Titus, Olive, and Nicholas Minister.
1775, Nov.   15, Tivey, Ann, and John Clinton.
1790, Feb.   24, Toben, John, and Mary Kennedy.
1794, Dec.   14, Toby, Tobias, and Sarah Lavalla.
1799, July   17, Todd, Mary, and Thomas Hanson Beau.
1800, Dec.   16, Todd, Nancy, and Thomas Vassault.
1793, Dec.   8, Todd, William, and Jane Cunningham.
1760, Jan.   9, Todman, John, and Rachel Young.
1761, Nov.   14, Toff, Jane, and Samuel Griffin.
1782, Dec.   28, Toland, James, and Sarah Venemy.
1796, June   19, Toland, Margret, and John Murphy.
1772, Dec.   6, Tolbert, Elizabeth, and Rodgerd Meady.
1765, Feb.   25, Tolley, Richard, and Margaret Hossey.
1775, Aug.   6, Tollman, Rebecca, and Michael Bradley.
1778, Dec.   27, Tolly, Thomas, and Mary Heston.
1765, Dec.   7, Tols, Frederick, and Patience Coleman.
1762, Nov.   11, Tomand, Hugh, and Jane Brown.
1766, Dec.   22, Tomkins, Elizabeth, and Jacob Van Osten.
1795, Sept.   5, Tomkins, Hester, and John Joseph.
1796, July   10, Tomlin, Mercy, and John Hase.
1756, July   17, Tomlinson, Deborah, and James Leech.
1755, March 17, Tomlinson, John, and Margaret Fisher.
1785, Oct.   15, Tomlinson, Susannah, and Richard Chew.
1794, Aug.   31, Tommelson, Sarah, and Joseph Springer.
1773, Dec.   19, Tommos, Ann, and Philip Stimbel.
1762, May   24, Tompon, Sarah, and Patrick Brawley.
1787, June   22, Toms, Edward, and Elizabeth Skillings.
1799, Nov.   27, Toms, Lettice, and Hans Jacobson.
1789, Sept.   7, Tomson, Coffy, and Ann Thomas, (free blacks.)
1780, March 8, Toner, Catharine, and William Sargant.
1788, Jan.   20, Tones, Mary, and Henry Crotta.
1776, Aug.   5, Tonkin, Israel, and Christiana Rambo. "This couple was the last married by license—Independency having been declared some time."
1773, Sept. 26, Tonniker, Mary, and Adam Heimback.
1786, Sept. 24, Topham, Catherine, and George Chase.

1781, March 10, Topham, Ruben Forster, and Elizabeth Deitricks.
1754, Jan.　15, Topham, William, and Hannah Foster.
1776, April　3, Toplin, Mary, and George Shaw.
1759, Aug.　31, Torlor, Sarah, and Joseph James.
1799, April　18, Tornber, John, and Margret Valheimer.
1800, Sept.　23, Torr, John, and Elizabeth Roat.
1753, Feb.　6, Torsten, Jacob, and Rachel Pots.
1753, April　22, Torston, Isaac, and Margaret Costard.
1754, April　21, Toston, Sarah, and George Brown.
1765, Dec.　26, Tou, Elenor, and Jacob Lewellin.
1751, Dec.　26, Tounson, Rachel, and Peter Rambo.
1777, July　24, Towers, Ann, and Nathan Simmons.
1784, July　8, Towers, Robert, and Christiana Morton.
1751, Feb.　26, Towfield, Abigail, and Edward Harrington.
1767, Sept.　3, Towle, Honour, and Thomas Hadkinson.
1790, July　12, Towls, Edward, and Elizabeth Blankley.
1780, Jan.　6, Town, Elizabeth, and John Sprogel.
1758, June　7, Town, Joseph, and Ann Danuly.
1800, Aug.　13, Town, Sarah, and Charles Rumsey.
1799, Dec.　4, Townsend, Eliza, and David Bittle.
1783, Feb.　1, Townsend, Salomen, and Mathy Wilson.
1756, May　31, Townsend, William, and Mary Cleaton.
1787, Aug.　22, Townson, Henry, and Hanna Robinson.
1780, Aug.　6, Towzey, Thomas, and Ann King.
1794, April　17, Toy, Barbara, and George Wolfe.
1777, Jan.　19, Toy, Catharine, and Kenneday McKenney.
1764, Sept.　23, Toy, Elizabeth, and Andrew Anderson.
1782, May　7, Toy, James, and Elizabeth Reding.
1759, April　8, Toy, John, and Catharine Hart.
1777, April　8, Toy, Margarett, and Andrew Keen.
1790, April　14, Toy, Mary, and John Cooper.
1765, Feb.　24, Toy, Mathias, and Ann Hines.
1791, Dec.　29, Toy, Michael, and Elenore McDougal.
1782, May　5, Toy, Nelly, and David Florence.
1776, April　4, Toy, Patience, and John Lee.
1787, Oct.　3, Toy, Patric, and Anne Harriet Briggs.
1787, April　24, Toy, Rebecca, and Joseph Carley.
1782, Feb.　5, Toy, Savory, and Mary Flemmans.
1787, Nov.　18, Traner, Peter, and Biddy Powel.
1781, Feb.　18, Trapell, Mary, and Nicholas West.
1770, Dec.　22, Trapnal, Elizabeth, and Richard Banet.
1765, May　1, Trapnel, Margaret, and William Archer.
1759, June　8, Trappel, Waltor, and Mary Coleman.
1751, Dec.　10, Travers, Hugh, and Mary Rabb.
1785, April　14, Traves, Nicholas, and Elizabeth Johnson.
1763, Nov.　11, Trayel, Elizabeth, and John White.

1763, July   26, Trayge, Elizabeth, and Nathan Moore.
1787, Oct.   16, Treadaway, Zalthu, and Mary Pratt.
1792, Oct.   30, Treadway, John, and Sarah Hooper.
1786, Sept.   28, Tremells, John, and Mary White.
1782, June   9, Trenchard, Mary, and John Graff.
1789, Oct.   19, Trenkel, Michael, and Elizabeth Vade.
1796, Dec.   5, Trenor, John, and Eleonor Martin.
1778, Sept.   15, Trepentine, Augustine, and Ann Davis.
1797, June   16, Triant, Peter, and Hannah Ingle.
1795, Aug.   —, Tribit, Ann, and William Canely.
1795, Nov.   1, Tribit, William, and Elizabeth Roe.
1799, Nov.   6, Tricket, William, and Elizab. Tygart.
1776, July   10, Triggs, Susannah, and Edward Edwaris.
1782, Dec.   7, Tripp, Adam, and Anne Morphy.
1779, July   31, Trippe, Elizabeth, and James Bourcheir.
1774, June   10, Trist, Nicholas, and Elizabeth House.
1779, Feb.   21, Trotter, Agnes, and John Pendleton.
1779, Oct.   27, Trouland, James, and Sarah Justes.
1791, July   7, Truck, Martha, and John Steell.
1795, March 15, Truck, Mary, and George Griffith.
1764, Nov.   24, Trumbet, Sarah, and Thomas Muschett.
1784, April   8, Trump, Anne, and William Walker.
1781, April   30, Trump, Catharine, and Thomas Peirey.
1779, July   30, Trump, Jacob, and Catharine Preston.
1790, Oct.   4, Trump, James, and Elizabeth Griffith.
1767, Nov.   19, Trump, John, and Ann Welders.
1795, Jan.   29, Trump, William, and Mary Tilford.
1799, Dec.   7, Trusdel, Elizabeth, and John Dempsie.
1758, Dec.   8, Trusdell, John, and Hannah Hamilton.
1776, Nov.   25, Trusted, Richard, and Rebecca Taylor.
1787, April   11, Tryet, Marget, and Thomas Patton.
1800, May   17, Tryon, Elizabeth, and John Alberger.
1794, March 7, Tryon, Frederick, and Margret Jackson.
1795, April   19, Tuck, John, and Mary Davenport.
1776, April   15, Tucker, Elizabeth, and Henry Ross.
1780, June   13, Tucker, Mary, and Samuel Allan.
1777, Feb.   7, Tucker, William, and Dorothy Steward.
1755, May   28, Tuckness, Henry, and Mary Finnis.
1778, Dec.   13, Tuckey, Ann, and Thomas Bary.
1777, April   3, Tucky, Rebecca, and Frederick Hitner.
1776, Oct.   14, Tudor, Nicholas, and Elizabeth McMahan.
1761, Dec.   12, Tuff, Ann, and Henry Dorell.
1799, June   10, Tufts, Samuel, and Eleonore Hancock.
1777, June   20, Tull, John, and Elizabeth Hullon.
1797, March 23, Tull, John, and Elizabeth Osborn.
1784, Dec.   1, Tullock, Anne, and John Barry.

1789, June   2, Tully, William, and Barbara Rees.
1783, March 30, Tumey, Anne, and John Robson.
1757, April 20, Turbett, Thomas, and Elizabeth Crawford.
1790, June   7, Turner, Ann, and Daniel Meredith.
1772, Jan.   23, Turner, Ann, and James Bradford.
1782, May   5, Turner, Anne, and Samuel Smith.
1778, May   28, Turner, Elizabeth, and James Pinker.
1779, Aug.   9, Turner, Elizabeth, and Patrick McWecker.
1796, Aug.   18, Turner, Elizabeth, and Stacy Merriot.
1794, May   11, Turner, Eve, and George Piercy.
1765, July   30, Turner, Hannah, and Peter Sitz Gerold.
1756, March   7, Turner, James, and Hannah Williams.
1772, May   12, Turner, Jean, and John Hutton.
1793, April —, Turner, Jesse, and Margret Bush.
1778, Sept. 13, Turner, John, and Isabel Bettersby.
1792, May   22, Turner, John, and Jane Dick.
1786, Nov.   3, Turner, Mary, and Nathan Middleton.
1757, July   4, Turner, Mary, and Thomas Frost.
1797, Nov.   25, Turner, Mary, and Thomas Morgan.
1793, Dec.   19, Turner, Priscilla, and Gilbert Spence.
1792, May   10, Turner, Rebecca, and Hezekiah Til.
1782, June   8, Turner, Susannah, and Conrad Luts.
1782, Aug.   15, Turner, William, and Mary Hulin.
1783, Jan.   7, Turney, Mary, and Samuel Montgomery Brown.
1777, Aug.   28, Tussel, Rachel, and Thomas Taylor.
1764, Nov.   7, Tussey, Ann, and George Stanton.
1759, Feb.   18, Tustian, William, and Elisabet Fraley.
1781, April 10, Tustin, Abram, and Hannah Waters.
1776, May   3, Tustin, Ann, and Edward Loder.
1784, April 11, Tutell, John, and Susannah Eyler.
1761, Sept.   1, Twanson, Sarah, and John Cribb.
1791, May   29, Tweed, Christiane, and John Vannemen.
1779, Jan.   7, Tweedy, Thomas, and Elizabeth Haton.
1775, Nov.   16, Twells, David, and Ann Oleles.
1781, Jan.   30, Twite, Elizabeth, and Ralph Gardsby.
1799, Nov.   6, Tygart, Elizab., and William Tricket.
1758, July   24, Tylee, John, and Catharine Dobbins.
1789, July   5, Tyrrel, Francis, and Sarah Fortner.
1796, Nov.   10, Tyson, Deborah, and Isaac Brittle.
1778, Dec.   24, Uhl, Hannah, and John Albuert.
1769, Sept.   5, Ulric, Nicolas, and Anne Eve Libertin.
1795, May   6, Ulrich, Cathrine, and Jacob Hamscher.
1783, Oct.   28, Ulrich, Eve, and Andrew Weaver.
1756, March 30, Umsted, Mary, and John Custard.
1787, April   5, Underwood, Mary, and David Bickin.
1778, June   25, Unger, Margaret, and Peter Handbess.

1758, Feb. 16, Updegrave, Elizabeth, and John Evans.
1758, March 29, Uplin, Catharine, and Joseph Radley.
1780, April 7, Upstreet, Elizabeth, and William Colton.
1783, Oct. 30, Urian, Andrew, and Elizabeth Humphreys.
1791, June 15, Urian, Israel, and Jemima Plumley.
1762, June 6, Urien, Catharine, and Eric Lindberg.
1789, July 9, Urquhart, Catharine, and William Murdock.
1781, Aug. 2, Usher, John, and Anne McKetrick.
1789, Oct. 19, Vade, Elizabeth, and Michael Trenkel.
1796, April 10, Vade Thomas, and Jane Motley.
1767, July 25, Valentine, Mary, and Isaac Anderson.
1799, April 18, Valheimer, Margret, and John Tornber.
1792, Sept. 8, Vallce, Francis Dominique, and Elizabeth Lafferty.
1755, Dec. 31, Valleygate, Elizabeth, and Joseph Hulins.
1784, Feb. 19, Valoi, Susannah, and John Wattel.
1797, Feb. 25, Vanbritel, James, and Charlotte Clark.
1794, Sept. 30, Vance, Mary, and Alexander Greaves.
1791, April 28, Vance, Phebe, and Stephen Flanigan.
1795, March 6, Vance, Philip, and Mary Midleton.
1795, May 19, Van Culen, Mary, and Hugh Lesley.
1789, Nov. 7, Vandegriff, Jacob, and Ann Wharton.
1761, May 28, Vandegrift, John, and Ann Walton.
1799, July 16, Vandel, Marget, and Thomas Pickering.
1767, Aug. 3, Vanderhold, Sarah, and John Dorney.
1774, Feb. 16, Vanderman, William, and Sarah Pyatt.
1759, July 5, Vanderspiegel, William, and Elizabeth Robeson.
1786, Aug. 20, Vandigrest, Rebecca, and Daniel Butler.
1798, Nov. 24, Vandike, Mary, and Jacob Rothwell.
1787, Oct. 2, Vandusen, John, and Rachel Hudle.
1783, April 26, Van Dyke, Andrew, and Mary Cook.
1765, Oct. 20, Van Dyke, Jeane, and Jonathan Bavington.
1756, May 9, Vandyke, Mary, and Richmond Allen.
1765, Oct. 10, Van Dyke, Zachariah, and Elizabeth Luce.
1787, June 12, Vane, Humphrey, and Elizabeth Stuard.
1780, April 10, Vaneman, David, and Elizabeth Lord.
1760, Sept. 3, Vanferson, Arnold, and Elizabeth Casselberry.
1761, April 9, Van Fossen, Arnold, and Rachel Skeen.
1797, July 6, Vanhook, Rebecca, and John G. Jones.
1767, Dec. 12, Van Horn, Bernard, and Mary Richardson.
1781, Aug. 25, Vanhorne, Elizabeth, and Mathew Allen.
1799, Sept. 30, Van Horn, Garret, and Hannah Yard.
1791, Nov. 23, Vanhorn, Rachel, and John Temple.
1773, Jan. 10, Vanhusen, John, and Hannah Brand.
1767, March 16, Vanible, Isaac, and Ann Holmes.
1779, Sept. 27, Vanisten, James, and Elizabeth Younger.
1793, Sept. 11, Van Kirk, Zilla, and Francis Bernard.

1756, May   28, Vanleer, George, and Elizabeth Roberts.
1789, April   30, Van Mannierck. Anthony, and Martha Milnor.
1795, May   21, Van Neaman, Hannah, and Benjamin Prentiss.
1799, Dec.   17, Van Neaman, Sarah, and John Sloane.
1791, May   29, Vannemen, John, and Christiane Tweed.
1786, Jan.   10, Vannest, John, and Dorothy Cole.
1783, Dec.   14, Vannost, Isaac, and Anne Dick.
1783, Sept.   30, Vannost, Isaac, and Rebecca Porter.
1787, June   7, Van Nosten, Catherine, and Samuel Rockenbury.
1784, April   27, Vanorden, Mary, and Philip Thompson.
1766, Sept.   16, Van Ost. Catherine, and Frederick Dobbelbower.
1766, Dec.   22, Van Osten. Jacob, and Elizabeth Tomkins.
1790, Aug.   29, Van Pradelles, Benedict Francis, and Cassandra
                   Deje Owings.
1757, Aug.   17, Vansant, Mary, and Able Warton.
1789, Nov.   16, Vanselius John Eric, and Mary Haft.
1785, Nov.   18, Vansise, Ann, and John Burrows.
1765, Dec.   23, Varnam, Abraham, and Margaret Matzon.
1800, Dec.   16, Vassault, Thomas, and Nancy Todd.
1795, Dec.   19, Vastine, Mary, and Mathew Morrison.
1751, July   18, Vaugh, Catharine, and Charles Glency.
1764, April   4, Vaughan, Isaac, and Jane Lawrence.
1766, July   29, Vaughn, John, and Lydia McNeel.
1779, July   8, Vaughn, Mary, and Richard Ross.
1794, Oct.   2, Vaughn, Mary, and Robert Leech.
1799, July   24, Veare, Thomas, and Susannah Wall.
1792, Nov.   12, Vendine, Ruth, (free mulatto,) and Francis
                   Mitchel, (free black.)
1782, Dec.   28, Venemy, Sarah, and James Toland.
1773, June   2, Vennoble, Jacob, and Mary Russel.
1790, Feb.   23, Vernon, John, and Elizabeth Sharpless.
1797, June   19, Vessels, Henrie, and Ann Bruer.
1777, March 23, Vickars, John, and Penroy Teellman.
1785, June   14, Vickers, Tamar, and John Cropley.
1793, May   14, Vigstroem, Jacob, and Susannah Little.
1773, Oct.   21, Villey, William, and Margaret Hudstedler.
1796, Jan.   28, Vincent, Sarah, and John Hecter.
1795, Nov.   25, Vionnex, Claude, and Mary McCaslin.
1757, May   31, Virgo, Elizabeth, and Robert Dribary.
1756, April   25, Virgo, Thomas, and Elizabeth Grimes.
1787, July   4, Vogel, Albright, and Mary Margreta Bauman.
1756, Oct.   21, Voknigs, Ann, and John Linloy.
1764, June   11, Vorall, Mary, and Robert Thomson.
1760, Dec.   18, Wachon, John, and Christiana Janson.
1761, April   13, Wachon, Thomas, and Ruth Calliord.
1785, March 28, Waddle, George, and Sarah Tims.

1794, May   4, Wade, Abigail, and John Sullivan.
1782, Aug.   7, Wade, Derrick, and Elizabeth Adams.
1778, May   29, Wade, Jonathan, and Elizabeth Rebson.
1779, March 10, Wade, Lydy, and Price Higens.
1781, Aug.   19, Wade, Martha, and Joseph Swain.
1775, Nov.   27, Wade, William, and Mary Grubb.
1778, April 15, Wadsworth, George, and Ann Bombrey.
1790, Aug.   17, Wagener, George, and Bridget Macarmick.
1799, Sept. 15, Wagener, George, and Mary Pickwert.
1758, Dec.   30, Wager, Thomas, and Mary Dempsee.
1795, Sept. 24, Waggener, William, and Mary Griffiths.
1779, July   15, Waggoner, Philip, and Hannah Mayas.
1768, Nov.   17, Wagner, Jacob, and Grace Menon.
1771, Jan.   1, Wagoner, Elizabeth, and Dennis Scandlin.
1756, July   22, Wagstaff, William, and Elizabeth Bailey.
1769, Oct.   1, Wahlberg, Henry, and Mary Bary.
1793, April 15, Wainwright, William, and Sarah Optigrove.
1794, Sept. 13, Walbern, Jane, and Joseph Hodges.
1783, May   24, Walheimer, Madlin, and John Barnes.
1757, Sept. 27, Walhkin, Mary, and Nicholas Beaver.
1794, Dec.   28, Walker, Ann, and Edward Duffel.
1777, Aug.   18, Walker, Ann, and James Seymour.
1761, Sept. 24, Walker, Ann, and Mathew Stacy.
1762, Sept. 24, Walker, Ann, and Mathew Stasy.
1799, Sept. 12, Walker, Ann, and Robert Walker.
1783, April 11, Walker, Catherine, and George Wilson.
1781, Oct.   18, Walker, Eleonor, and Joseph Robnet.
1756, May   9, Walker, Elizabeth, and Henry Jarsey.
1778, Jan.   28, Walker, Elizabeth, and John Harding.
1761, Oct.   29, Walker, Hannah, and Jacob Hotzheimer.
1780, Dec.   10, Walker, Hopkins, and Margaret Gorley.
1793, Jan.   30, Walker, Jane, and George Way.
1777, June   27, Walker, John, and Sarah Gottier.
1781, Feb.   13, Walker, Joseph, and Mary Greaves.
1779, May   18, Walker, Margaret, and Christian Hobert.
1771, June   7, Walker, Margaret, and Samuel Webster.
1793, Feb.   26, Walker, Margret, and James Ruthwen.
1794, Oct.   13, Walker, Maria Elizab., and James Mitchel.
1799, July   26, Walker, Martha, and William Andrew Williamson.
1778, Oct.   19, Walker, Mary, and James Sheriden.
1785, Nov.   14, Walker, Mary, and John Keyly.
1779, Dec.   30, Walker, Ralph, and Mary West.
1799, Sept. 12, Walker, Robert, and Ann Walker.
1760, July   19, Walker, Sarah, and Edward Marefield.
1778, June   9, Walker, Sarah, and Thomas Williams.
1784, April   8, Walker, William, and Anne Trump.

1777, May   4, Walkins, Margaret, and Cornelius Connor,
1792, May   12, Wall, Daniel, and Elizabeth Handey.
1774, March 20, Wall, Elizabeth, and Richard Wallace.
1754, Feb.   10, Wall, Hester, and Patrick Cashaday.
1771, Feb.   12, Wall, John, and Hannah Flower.
1800, July   5, Wall, John, and Jane George.
1782, April 30, Wall, Magdalen, and Thomas Jones.
1775, Sept.   9, Wall, Richard, and Mary Lampel Septem.
1799, July   24, Wall, Susannah, and Thomas Veare.
1796, Nov.   21, Wallace, James, and Mary MacDonald.
1790, June   26, Wallace, Jane, and Robert Elliot.
1798, Nov.   9, Wallace, Joseph, and Sarah Butler.
1795, May   26, Wallace, Martha, and Robert Ferguson.
1774, March 20, Wallace Richard, and Elizabeth Wall.
1793, July   9, Wallace, Susannah, and Alexander Adams.
1761, July   30, Wallacut, Frances, and John Morrison.
1776, Feb.   4, Walbert, Catharine, and Mathew Felles.
1779, Sept. 18. Wallence, Christine, and George Haughton.
1778, March 26, Wallentine, Mary, and Jeffery Gumley.
1774, June   13, Walleys, James, and Elizabeth Christy.
1799, June   10, Wallington, John, and Jane McKicken.
1783, Jan.   6, Wallington, Rachel, and Alexander Roland.
1793, July   7, Wallis, Benjamin, and Cathrine Howard.
1778, Nov.   1, Wallis, James, and Lucy Wolf.
1767, May   15, Wallis, Jane, and John Wallis.
1767, May   15, Wallis, John and Jane Wallis.
1760. May   27, Wallis, Margaretta, and Casper Frites.
1775, July   21, Wallis, Mary, and Edward Linord.
1774, Dec.   12, Wallman, William, and Mary Fresher.
1756, March 25, Walter, Margarette, and Francis Joseph Pfeipher.
1792, Jan.   2, Walsh, Michel, and Susanna Owens.
1752, Feb.   16, Walten, Michael, and Mary Crull.
1779, Aug.   3, Walter, Conrad, and Margaret Haslet.
1799, June   20, Walter, Hannah, and Alexander Lollar.
1766, July   31, Walter, Jacob, and Jeane McClasky.
1793, March 18, Walter, Jacob, and Mary Cordley.
1779, April 21, Walter, John, and Sarah Cash.
1799, Aug.   18, Walter, Mary, and Henry Hughs.
1788, Sept.   6, Walter, Rachel, and Nathan Pyle.
1782, Jan.   20, Walters, Catherine, and Michael DePlumagat.
1754, Aug.   21, Walters, John, and Rachel Rambo.
1799, Dec.   1, Walters, Mary, and Edward Dunlap.
1780, Sept. 24, Walters, Peter, and Sophia Gilbert.
1771, Feb.   11, Walters, Samuel, and Catharine McCarty.
1781, Nov.   4, Walters, Samuel, and Mandy Smerris, (Free ne-
                    groes.)

1761, May   28, Walton, Ann, and John Vandegrift.
1781, Dec.   1, Walton, Casander, and John Thomas.
1752, Nov.   30, Walton, Elizabeth, and Bryan Peart.
1757, June   29, Walton, Job, and Catharine McVaugh.
1785, Sept.   3, Walton, Mary, and John Ingram.
1757, June   14, Walton, Rebecca, and Jacob Randall.
1794, May   15, Walton, Samuel, and Marget Reading.
1766, Aug.   4, Walton, Sarah, and William Wood.
1776, Sept.   9, Wanbebird, Margaret, and John Fletcher.
1771, April   14, Wance, George, and Sarah Fisher.
1758, Sept.   30, Wanculen, Jacob, and Sarah Lawrence.
1757, Dec.   10, Wanderin, Catharine, aad George Stocky.
1772, Oct.   15, Wane, Ann, and William Hayman.
1777, June   19, Wanleer, Isaac, and Sarah Dairs.
1758, Jan.   22, Warboy, Elizabeth, and John Chapman.
1773, Nov.   18, Ward, Deborah, and Thomas Morriston.
1766, Feb.   10, Ward, Elenor, and John Hoy.
1777, Jan.   19, Ward, Elizabeth, and James Leech.
1782, Jan.   15, Ward, Elizabeth, and John Nevel.
1778, June   14, Ward, Francis, and Christina Esling.
1791, Jan.   28, Ward, Hannah, and George Morris.
1778, Jan.   11, Ward, Hannah, and John Peten.
1777, May   23, Ward, James, and Eleanor Loveley.
1783, Nov.   10, Ward, James. and Lidy Clark.
1766, April   28, Ward, Jehu, and Ruth Miller.
1784, June   3, Ward, John, and Abigail Clark.
1764, Jan.   1, Ward, John, and ——— Midleton.
1758, July   11, Ward, Joseph, and Sarah Bellinger.
1787, May   17, Ward, Marget, and Robert Britt.
1781, Jan.   29, Ward, Mary, and James Logan.
1780, Sept.   23, Ward, Mary, and John Piddrick.
1762, April   29, Ward, Mary, and Richard Jobs.
1781, May   31, Ward, Rachel, and James Hammond.
1788, Oct.   4, Ward, Rachel, and John Barford.
1778, Sept.   2, Ward, Richard, and Rebecca Thomson.
1792, Aug.   28, Ward, Samuel, and Margret Daniel.
1777, Aug.   10, Ward, Sarah, and William Hopkins.
1750, Nov.   17, Ward, William, and Ruth Irwin.
1796, Oct.   5, Ware, David, and Henrietta Dennis.
1776, Sept.   5, Ware, Elizabeth, and Hugh Ross.
1777, Nov.   10, Ware, Jane, and Edward Redler.
1792, Jan.   5, Ware, John, and Debora Hakamson.
1767, April   6, Ware, John, and Sarah Marlpool.
1781, June   18, Ware, William, and Catharine Carven.
1786, Dec.   21, Wareng, Mathew, and Elizabeth Thomson.
1772, Oct.   26, Waret, Samuel, and Jemima Down.

1793, Feb. 10, Waring, Matheu, and Ann Hoope.
1758, Dec. 16, Warings, Mary, and John Morphey.
1781, July 26, Warlington, Charles, and Abigail Wood.
1778, June 4, Warlow, William, and Mary Steward.
1764, May 19, Warnack, Robert, and Elizabeth Peters.
1774, Jan. 2, Warner, Adam, and Catharine Reinhardin.
1773, Feb. 11, Warner, Ann, and Abraham Pyott.
1782, Dec. 4, Warner, Francis, and Elizabeth Stimlerin.
1757, April 14, Warner, James, and Sibilla Battle.
1783, Jan. 9, Warner, Jemima, and Jacob Knorr.
1773, Aug. 8, Warner, John, and Alice Brooks.
1777, April 29, Warner, John, and Catharine Bushway.
1752, Oct. 9, Warner, John, and Mary Fenstermacher.
1755, Feb. 25, Warner, John, and Mary Fisher.
1769, Jan. 22, Warner, John, and Rachel Lightfoot.
1781, July 22, Warner, Mary, and John McCloud.
1777, Aug. 23, Warner, Philip, and Mary Harman.
1797, Jan. 12, Warner, Sarah, and William Hielan.
1789, Aug. 4, Warner, Susannah, and Peter Shade.
1781, Jan. 18, Warner, Tacey, and Algernow Roberts.
1790, May 10, Warner, William, and Ann Roberts.
1791, June 21, Warner, William, and Hanna White.
1756, Aug. 11, Warner, William, and Mary Haskins.
1761, July 23, Warnich, John Jacob, and Eliza Huellen.
1780, Aug. 19, Warnick, Margaret, and Samuel Holt.
1754, Nov. 21, Warnock, William, and Mary Harrard.
1757, Nov. 3, Warns, Philip, and Mary Lock.
1767, Dec. 7, Warold, Rebeccah, and William Young.
1777, April 30, Warrall, Susannah, and Thomas Martin.
1788, Nov. 18, Warren, Charlotte, and William Thomas.
1791, Sept. 26, Warren, Elizabeth, and Nicholas Muff.
1794, Aug. 4, Warren, Elizabeth, and Roger Brogen.
1782, April 8, Warren, Hamilton, and Rebecca Keen.
1795, Jan. 10, Warren, Letitia, and Samuel Hozier.
1777, Aug. 16, Warren, Phebe, and Seth Warren.
1775, Sept. 26, Warren, Samuel, and Sarah Rainer.
1777, Aug. 16, Warren, Seth, and Phebe Warren.
1755, Oct. 12, Warrington, Ausilla, and John Thoms.
1761, March 19, Wartenby, Elizabeth, and Cadwalader Arven.
1767, June 6, Warthenwy, John, and Elizabeth Keeper.
1757, Aug. 17, Warton, Able, and Mary Vansant.
1765, Feb. 23, Warton, Martha, and Owen Clanby.
1798, July 16, Warton, Patience, and Joshua Evans.
1781, Dec. 12, Warwick, Elizabeth, and Eliah Jewelson.
1773, Oct. 6, Warwick, Elizabeth, and Samuel Holmes.
1780, Sept. 10, Warwick, William, and Isabella Hayes.

1790, Oct.　24, Washbury, (or Wasby,) Barbara, and Bartley Finnicon.
1792, April　8, Washinger, Elenore, and Edward Glide.
1753, Oct.　18, Wassols, Rebecca, and Mathew Wilson.
1795, July　2, Wasson, Jane, and James Alexander.
1784, March 22, Wastell, Richard, and Margret Couly.
1785, Nov.　10, Wat, George, and Elizabeth Eager.
1770, July　1, Wateheson, Hannah, and Robert Hill.
1775, May　27, Waters, Ann, and Samuel Millward.
1789, July　16, Waters, Eleonore, and Anthony Martin.
1759, April　1, Waters, Elizabeth, and George Ogelbee.
1781, April　10, Waters, Hannah, and Abram Tustin.
1759, March 13, Waters, George, and Jane C. Craughin.
1776, Nov.　27, Wathers, Mary, and Richard Lost.
1755, March　2, Watkince, Jaseph, and Elizabeth Hughes.
1755, Aug.　23, Watkins, Daniel, and Mary Hughs.
1800, Dec.　21, Watkins, Elizabeth, and Samuel Adams.
1754, Nov.　10, Watkins, Evan, and Ann Godfrey.
1755, Oct.　2, Watkins, Thomas, and Mary White.
1755, May　3, Watkins, Thomas, and Susanna Foster.
1762, July　15, Watsin, Rosinna, and Baltsar Haas.
1800, Jan.　16, Watson, Ann, and James Welsh.
1759, Feb.　4, Watson, James, and Christina Forester.
1791, Oct.　9, Watson, Jane, and Alexander McNourghton.
1778, Feb.　1, Watson, John, and Anne Taylor.
1784, Dec.　6, Watson, John, and Elizabeth Delahide.
1781, Feb.　21, Watson, John, and Elizabeth Young.
1798, June　18, Watson, Joseph, and Cathrine Dougherty.
1790, Nov.　22, Watson, Lydia, and Isaac Rowend.
1767, Oct.　12, Watson, Lydia, and William Atwell.
1754, Feb.　28, Watson, Margaret, and John Read.
1782, June　7, Watson, Mary, and Francis Sweet.
1772, Nov.　15, Watson, Mary, and John Kees.
1784, April　19, Watson, Mary, and Michael Hase.
1781, June　11, Watson, Sarah, and Jonathan Fennymore.
1765, May　5, Watson, William, and Mary Maisner.
1757, Nov.　29, Watson, Samuel, and Mary Johnston.
1778, June　12, Watson, Susannah, and Patrick Deneston.
1762, May　29, Watt, Martha, and Edward Hair.
1784, Feb.　19, Wattel, John, and Susannah Valoi.
1776, May　21, Watts, Adam, and Mary Cockran.
1777, Nov.　5, Watts, Bridget, and Benjamin McDondlet.
1759, June　7, Watts, James, and Mathew Oeans.
1792, July　22, Watts, John, and Elizabeth Collins.
1792, May　3, Watts, Mary, and John Crabens.
1779, Dec.　22, Watts, Mary, and Richard Harding.

1757, Oct.   29, Wattson, Job, and Margaret Johnson.
1761, Jan.   7, Wattson, John, and Patience Madlock.
1778, Sept.   27, Wattson, Joseph, and Sarah Downey.
1770, June   27, Way, George, and Christine Tammon.
1793, Jan.   30, Way, George, and Jane Walker.
1783, May   10, Way, Jeane, and Richard Webster.
1781, Dec.   28, Way, Mely, and George Freeman.
1764, Oct.   7, Way, Robert, and Catharine Gandawill.
1781, Dec.   6, Wayne, Humphrey, and Mary Anne Parkes.
1758, Dec.   12, Wayton, John, and Barbara McCullough.
1779, Sept.   1, Wear, Mary, and Charles Hany.
1777, Oct.   26, Wear, Mary, and Francis Pink.
1780, Sept.   15, Wearier, John, and Elizabeth Young.
1793, Jan.   28, Wearin, William, and Elizabeth Dowlin.
1781, Oct.   27, Weatherby, Joseph, and Mary Whiteall.
1783, Oct.   28, Weaver, Andrew, and Eve Ulrich.
1783, Nov.   24, Weaver, Anne, and Mahlin Higgs.
1794, Aug.   31, Weaver, Cathrine, and Andrew Green.
1754, April   4, Weaver, Elizabeth, and John Ermgriester.
1786, June   2, Weaver, Fanny, and John Parry.
1793, Oct.   17, Weaver, George, and Mary Lafferty.
1777, May   25, Weaver, John, and Jean Davis.
1777, March   27, Weaver, Margaret, and John Sullivan.
1787, Oct.   12, Weaver, Maria, and Christopher Gotler.
1798, March   30, Weaver, Mary, and John Rose.
1758, May   24, Weaver, Mary, and Joseph Timpler.
1795, Jan.   1, Weaver, Mathias, and Hannah Cabellaw.
1778, May   14, Webb, Edward, and Eleanor Deley.
1759, Jan.   1, Webb, Elizabet, and Cornelius Clamen.
1759, March   5, Webb, Elizabet, and William Hyde.
1770, Jan.   31, Webb, Judith, and Patrick Fullinton.
1778, Feb.   14, Webb, Martha, and Thomas Allkins.
1787, July   2, Webb, Mary, and John Williams.
1752, Sept.   17, Webb, Richard, and Elizabeth Anderwood.
1764, Dec.   8, Webber, Catharine, and John Flett.
1795, Aug.   23, Webber, Hannah, and Mathias Albertson.
1776, June   2, Webber, Henry, and Mary Welt.
1790, Dec.   9, Webber, John, and Marget Kyger.
1771, Nov.   14, Webster, George, and Mary McDanal.
1783, May   10, Webster, Richard, and Jeane Way.
1771, June   7, Webster, Samuel, and Margaret Walker.
1783, Sept.   15, Webster, Thomas, and Elizabeth Archer.
1774, Oct.   2, Weekings, William, and Rebecca McDanal.
1794, May   27, Weeks, John, and Mary Johnson.
1792, July   29, Weeks, Sara, and Alexander MacCurdy.
1781, Jan.   28, Weidman, Elizabeth, and Casper Seibert.

1767, June 15, Weidman, George, and Mary Evah Emerlatine.
1766, Oct. 26, Weiser, Jacob, and Susannah Hanson.
1787, April 1, Welch, Alice, and Henderson Wright.
1764, Oct. 7, Welch, David, and Sarah Biddle.
1785, July 27, Welch, Eleanor, and William Powell.
1774, Feb. 11, Welch, Elizabeth, and Daniel O'Neal.
1790, Oct. 14, Welch, James, and Mary Silver.
1765, Feb. 25, Welch, Jeane, and Robert Glasco.
1757, Sept. 1, Welch, John, and Francis Bullard.
1754, Nov. 29, Weld, Catharine, and Thomas Commings.
1798, May 6, Weldin, Alexander, and Elizabeth Green.
1758, Dec. 10, Weldon, William, and Catharine Brinkeross.
1767, Nov. 19, Wellders, Ann, and John Trump.
1799, Dec. 1, Welldon, John, and Sarah Butler.
1754, Sept. 15, Welldone, Catharine, and Richard Lacock.
1767, Oct. 26, Wells, Ann, and Jushua Sutton.
1770, July 22, Wells, Cowly, and Phabe Jackson.
1762, Sept. 9, Wells, Elsa, and James Crawford.
1755, Feb. 22, Wells, George, and Lydia Houlton.
1783, Sept. 28, Wells, John, and Catherine Straddling.
1780, Sept. 18, Wells, Kingsmell, and Ann Kentis.
1794, Jan. 4, Wells, Margret, and John Shield.
1781, Nov. 26, Wells, Mary, and John Dilkes.
1794, March 17, Wells, Mary, and John Rudolph.
1779, May 6, Wells, Phoebe, and Charles Bunken, (free negroes.)
1754, July 2, Wells, Priscilla, and William Morgan.
1800, March 11, Wells, Rebecca, and John Strickling.
1770, Aug. 15, Wells, Richard, and Martha Currey.
1775, Sept. 7, Wells, Samuel, and Mary Glenn.
1761, Dec. 12, Wells, Sarah, and Henny Grubb.
1755, Feb. 1, Wells, Thomas, and Deborah Lord.
1772, March 1, Wellsin, Catharine, and John Miller.
1796, Aug. 7, Welsh, Ann, and Thomas Campbell.
1759, Aug. 12, Welsh, David, and Margareth Junkins.
1779, July 18, Welsh, Eleanor, and Michael Dymon.
1779, Feb. 13, Welsh, Eleanor, and Peter Bride.
1800, March 20, Welsh, Elizabeth, and William Winters.
1780, May 20, Welsh, Enoch, and Mary Perkins.
1800, Jan. 16, Welsh, James, and Ann Watson.
1780, July 19, Welsh, James, and Hannah Stanhop.
1793, July 2, Welsh, Jane, and Barnabas Duffin.
1769, Sept. 2, Welsh, John, and Anne Robeson.
1752, Dec. 25, Welsh, John, and Rebecca Tatem.
1761, April 7, Welsh, Luke, and Jane White.
1786, June 5, Welsh, Michael, and Jane McCauley.
1778, Dec. 31, Welsh, Michael, and Margaret Cowen.

1778, Dec. 15, Welsh, Patrick, and Martha Freeman.
1776, June 2, Welt, Mary, and Henry Webber.
1759, Aug. 8, Welteardson, Elizabeth, and William Frazier.
1751, April 7, Wendenhurk, Ann, and Charles Davis.
1761, April 20, Wenger, Peter, and Christiana Farmer.
1781, Nov. 16, Wenhook, Mary, and James McCallister.
1797, June 7, Wenk, Johan, and Elizabeth Keller.
1781, June 19, Wens, Elizabeth, and Robert Sterling.
1760, Sept. 16, Wens, Lorent, and Elizabeth Garson.
1778, July 14, Wenttinger, Catharine, and Christopher Moore.
1761, July 19, Werkingen, Ann Margeth, and Lorentz Meyer.
1781, July 5, Wernes, Mary, and Christian Hoffman.
1795, Oct. 12, Wert, Philip, and Mary White.
1799, July 1, Wesby, Margret, and Owen Roberts.
1783, March 19, Weskot, Jane, and Philip Peak.
1768, April 22, Wessenett, Samuel, and Ally Daugherty.
1777, Dec. 10, West, Bridget, and Timothy Sullivan.
1789, March 23, West, Catharine, and Alexander Minzey.
1763, Jan. 31, West, Charles, and Mary Lee.
1792, Aug. 2, West, Debora, and James Lee.
1760, May 22, West, James, and Sarah H. West.
1776, Sept. 15, West, John, and Bridget Rodgers.
1780, Jan. 27, West, John, and Elizabest Allen.
1791, Aug. 20, West, Judith, and Timothy Ferby.
1787, April 5, West, Kesia, and John Huffey.
1766, July 6, West, Mary, and James Fitzjareld.
1779, Dec. 30, West, Mary, and Ralph Walker.
1797, Jan. 11, West, Mary, and Richard, Richards.
1781, Feb. 18, West, Nicholas, and Mary Trapell.
1760, May 22, West, Sarah H., and James West.
1790, Oct. 25, West, Susanna, and David Latch.
1777, April 28, West, Thomas, and Christiana Kane.
1762, Nov. 9, West, William, and Sarah McCunnel.
1784, Oct. 27, Westcoat, Joel, and Mary Andrews.
1780, June 23, Wester, Henry, and Ruth Ashton.
1777, March 23, Wester, Michael, and Margaret Spiegel.
1784, March 11, Wetzner, Adam, and Esther Finney.
1762, Nov. 12, Wever, Jacob, and Catharine Doomond.
1771, Nov. 10, Weyant, John Peter, and Kingynda Hellman.
1783, Jan. 9, Weyman, Catherine, and John Fulton.
1777, Dec. 4, Weyman, Francis, and Catherine Spanigel.
1782, Aug. 11, Weymar, Mary, and Lewis Evans.
1765, May 24, Weysinger, Melchior, and Mary Stows.
1750, Dec. 31, Whaley, Sarah, and John Brannon.
1759, June 9, Whalton, Ester, and Thomas Whalton.
1759, June 9, Whalton, Thomas, and Ester Whalton.

1785, Nov.   3, Wharence, Elizabeth, and James Burchall.
1753, Oct.   29, Whartenbay, Elinor, and Peter Tailor.
1789, Nov.   7, Wharton, Ann, and Jacob Vandegriff.
1779, May   18, Wharton, Catharine, and Henry Lore.
1761, June   25, Wharton, John, and Rebecca Chamblis.
1795, April   6, Wharton, Marget, and John Dougall.
1776, March 18, Wharton, Martha, and Peter Thomson.
1769, Dec.   23, Wheat, Abigail, and Adam Hope.
1794, Nov.   9, Wheaton, Amos, and Rebecca Hannas.
1767, Sept.   1, Wheel, Daniel, and Jeane Riper.
1764, Jan.   16, Wheeler, Eleonore, and John Baker.
1777, Nov.   8, Wheeler, John, and Mary Revel.
1762, April 12, Wheeler, Mary, and Frederic Phaval.
1781, March   8, Wheeler, Mary, and Thomas May.
1752, July   12, Wheeler, Patrick, and Sarah Lewis.
1777, Sept. 22, Wheeler, Sarah, and Andrew Butler.
1795, May   2, Whelan, John, and Cathrine Sharp.
1794, Nov.   1, Whelen, Elizabeth, and Joshua Stites.
1800, Oct.   30, Whelen, Sarah, and John Green.
1778, Feb.   5, Whenright, Charles, and Mary Lowrey.
1778, Jan.   30, Whenright, James, and Eleanor Mackdue.
1788, July   30, Whetherby, Hanna, and Leman Dusky.
1792, July   21, Whetherell, George, and Cathrine Fisher.
1795, Feb.   6, Whetherly, William, and Ann McKean.
1778, June   27, Whideaker, John, and Mary O'Harra.
1772, March   1, Whiler, Thomas, and Elizabeth Reed.
1759, Nov.   28, Whit, Ester, and John Norton.
1759, July   8, Whit, Samuel, and Ann Willson.
1778, Dec.   2, Whitater, John, and Elizabeth Johnson.
1759, July   26, Whitbread, William, and Sarah Stubbs.
1764, July   2, Whitby, William, and Mary Taylor.
1790, Sept. 26, White, Agnes, and John Lear.
1790, Oct.   23, White, Ann, and John Cain.
1794, April 15, White, Ann, and Obadiah Stillwell.
1796, Dec.   1, White, Barbara, and Daniel Barr.
1776, June   3, White, Barbara, and Philip Arella.
1785, Nov.   6, White, Catherine, and Jacob Backer.
1791, Aug.   31, White, Cathrine, and John William Christie.
1791, Feb.   3, White, Cathrine, and Joseph Super.
1790, July   15, White, Charles, and Cathrine Swim.
1777, April 20, White, Elizabeth, and Christopher Purtal.
1779, April   4, White, Elizabeth, and William Williams.
1800, June   22, White, Gilbert, and Ann Thomas.
1762, Oct.   31, White, Hannah, and Jeremiah Hall.
1755, June   17, White, Hannah, and Samuel Simms.
1752, April 13, White, Hannah, and Sylvester Nionerty.

1791, June   21, White, Hanna, and William Warner.
1794, Jan.   13, White, Isabella, and John Coll.
1781, April   9, White, James, and Rosemund Bethell.
1798, June   8, White, Jane, and James Kerr.
1761, April   7, White, Jane, and Luke Welsh.
1771, Sept.   1, White, John, and Catharine Macklane.
1795, Dec.   7, White, John, and Elizabeth Lowry.
1763, Nov.   11, White, John, and Elizabeth Trayal.
1799, June   27, White, John, and Marget Button.
1794, March 31, White, John, and Margret Kennedy.
1797, Nov.   28, White, John, aud Mary Ann Brige.
1783, March 11, White, John, and Mary McGragger.
1797, May   14, White, Juliana, and Joseph Gold.
1788, Dec.   14, White, Lydia, and Ephraim Connar.
1774, Oct.   12, White, Margaret, and Michael Ribley.
1786, Nov.   30, White, Marget, and Daniel McAckinsy.
1777, March 19, White, Martha, and Moses Hinshaw.
1788, Nov.   22, White, Mary, and Gustavus Mackintire.
1783, June   5, White, Mary, and John Gordon.
1774, Aug.   7, White, Mary, and John Sibson Blackwood.
1786, Sept.   28, White, Mary, and John Tremells.
1792, Oct.   25, White, Mary, and Joseph Barr.
1793, Dec.   16, White, Mary, and Philip Land.
1795, Oct.   12, White, Mary, and Philip Wert.
1755, Oct.   2, White, Mary, and Thomas Watkins.
1791, Sept.   22, White, Samuel, and Patty Patterson.
1779, April   1, White, Sarah, and Edward McKaige.
1791, Oct.   8, White, Thomas, and Ann Kerr.
1793, Aug.   6, White, Thomas, and Elizabeth Small.
1796, Oct.   25, White, Thomas, and Margret Hyzer.
1794, April 17, White, William, and Mary Fisher.
1781, Oct.   27, Whiteall, Mary, and Joseph Weatherby.
1787, Nov.   3, Whitebread, Charles, aud Elizabeth Taylor.
1757, May   9, Whitefield, Mary, and John Lester.
1767, Oct.   39, Whitefield, William, and Sarah Ogelby.
1784, Aug.   10, Whitehard, James, and Hannah Coburn.
1782, April 20, Whitehead, John, and Bridget Grady.
1784, Aug.   13, Whitehead, John, and Penelope Whitehead.
1784, Aug.   13, Whitehead, Penelope, and John Whitehead.
1779, Dec.   5, Whitelaw, Alexander, and Mary Gillmore.
1780, July   16, Whitelow, Alexander, aud Rachel Newbound.
1782, Jan.   3, Whiteman, Henry, and Anne Mollen.
1777, July   31, Whiteman, John, and Margaret Flick.
1791, Oct.   13, Whiterup, Martha, and Francis Carson.
1800, Dec.   30, Whiteside, Alexander, and Sarah Scott.
754, Aug.   18, Whitle, Catharine, and David Mollin.

1780, March 27, Whitlow, Benjamin, and Catherine Cox.
1760, Sept. 22, Whitol, John, and Mary Farbottel.
1786, March 12, Whittall, Hannah, and John Wills.
1778, April 13, Whittham, John, and Isabella Miles.
1778, Nov. 17, Whittle, Sarah, and John Price.
1751, Jan. 3, Whitton, James, and Elizabeth Johnson.
1791, April 21, Wickers, Abraham, and Mary Estwick.
1789, March 28, Widdifield, Anne, and William Hugg.
1796, April 10, Widerholt, Henry Lewis, and Elizabeth Simpson.
1779, Jan. 26, Wier, Nancy, and Lawrence Nihel.
1799, Oct. 20, Wiesman, Andrew, and Cathrine Bosken.
1762, Nov. 9, Wiever, Elizabeth, and Mathew Rowen.
1757, June 8, Wigerly, Abigal, and Richard Wright.
1791, Oct. 9, Wiggins, Samuel, and Hanna Gery.
1782, Dec. 14, Wiggins, Sarah, and Caleb Glison.
1760, Dec. 26, Wiggins, Thomas, and Sarah Risley.
1779, Aug. 18, Wiggs, Sarah, and Richard Rauilson.
1785, July 28, Wigley, Anne, and Charles Couch.
1758, Jan. 8, Wigmore, Daniel, and Francis Butler.
1782, April 3, Wigmore, John, and Meomy Smith.
1792, May 10, Wilbanc, Abel, and Susanna Andrews.
1752, Aug. 13, Wilcox, Deborah, and Joseph Godfrey.
1782, Dec. 24, Wilcox, Mary, and Robert Cameron.
1769, Feb. 28, Wild, William, and Elizabeth Burley.
1798, March 5, Wilden, Jonathan, and Tobitha Marts.
1782, Aug. 22, Wilder, David, and Alice Canon.
1790, Oct. 17, Wilder, Eliza, and Christopher Stotsenberg.
1793, Sept. 23, Wile, Robert, and Sarah Floyd.
1783, Feb. 1, Wiley, Abigail, and John Salsbery.
1778, Jan. 1, Wiley, Elizabeth, and Joseph Day.
1794, May 21, Wiley, Sarah, and William Saunders.
1793, Nov. 12, Wiley, Sophia, and Jacob Snyder.
1774, Oct. 16, Wiley, William, and Elizabeth Strouse.
1779, April 17, Wilhelm, Elizabeth, and Benjamin Collins.
1779, April 15, Wilkes, John, and Christiana Cassel.
1798, June 20, Wilkey, Thomas, and Rebecca Rice.
1795, Aug. 14, Wilkins, Elizabeth, and James Osborn.
1783, Jan. 7, Wilkins, Thomas, and Mary Mollen.
1782, June 24, Wilkinson, Catherine, and Thomas Engles.
1763, Aug. 9, Wilkinson, Daniel, and Sarah Bowd.
1778, May 3, Wilkinson, Margaret, and Robert Cheine.
1792, June 3, Wilkinson, Susanna, and Jacob Francis.
1763, Nov. 25, Wilkinson, Thomas, and Mary Kraft.
1776, Sept. 29, Wilkison, Hannah, and Benjamin Tate.
1763, April 7, Wilkison, Robert, and Elizabeth Clarke.
1778, Jan. 25, Wilkison, Thomas, and Susannah Porter.

1772, Aug.   11, Will, Christopher, and Sarah Keiser.
1794, May   4, Will, Philip, and Diana Allen.
1776, June   4, Willard, Catharine, and Charles Greer.
1776, May   29, Willard, Hannah, and George Willson.
1784, July   14, Willard, Parr, and Hope Inskip.
1781, Feb.   21, Willard, Rebecca, and William Jones.
1787, Sept.   24, Willard, Sarah, and William Edwards.
1778, Feb.   26, Willcox, Edward, and Mary Faris.
1753, Oct.   28, Willcox, Febe, and John Bonsall.
1768, Dec.   18, Willett, Mary, and Daniel Fullan.
1773, Jan.   6, William, Jean, and Steven Consort.
1795, July   26, William, John, and Sarah Niclas, (Africans.)
1799, Oct.   27, William, Peter, and Mary Talbor.
1773, Nov.   6, William, Susanna, and James McDaniel.
1766, March 24, Williams, Abigail, and Thomas Russel.
1800, Nov.   29, Williams, Alice, and Hugh Cavenough.
1770, Nov.   26, Williams, Alice, and Michael Williamson.
1781, Feb.   15, Williams, Anne, and James Anderson.
1756, Sept.   16, Williams, Ann, and James Steel.
1793, March   4, Williams, Ann, and Louis Philip Lefebure.
1755, Nov.   23, Williams, Ann, and Paul Roberts.
1780, July   2, Williams, Ann, and Robert Lee.
1780, Jan.   1, Williams, Ann, and Thomas Woodford.
1757, March 22, Williams, Catharine, and William O'Brian.
1789, Sept.   30, Williams, Catharine, and William Witel.
1799, Aug.   14, Williams, Charles, and Mary Souder.
1779, May   2, Williams, Corleneh, and Samuel Ervin.
1796, May   1, Williams, David, and Elizabeth Brooks.
1781, June   20, Williams, David, and Margaret Ryan.
1756, April   12, Williams, Deborow, and Michael Little.
1777, Jan.   22, Williams, Edmond, and Mary Hawkes.
1785, July   7, Williams, Edward, and Ann Simens, (negroes.)
1760, Sept.   15, Williams, Edward, and Elizabeth Davis.
1780, Sept.   14, Williams, Edward, and Ruth Maxwell.
1781, Feb.   8, Williams, Eleanor, and John Haley.
1780, Jan.   27, Williams, Elizabeth, and Aaron Grace,
1798, Nov.   20, Williams, Elizab., and Edward Dougherty.
1774, Nov.   3, Williams, Elizabeth, and Ezekiel Abbot.
1753, July   19, Williams, Elizabeth, and George Graham.
1754, Sept.   29, Williams, Florella, and Peter Hopkins.
1755, Aug.   11, Williams, George, and Sarah Brown.
1756, March   7, Williams, Hannah, and James Turner.
1757, March   8, Williams, Hannah, and John McCormack.
1770, Aug.   14, Williams, Hannah, and William Kemp.
1800, Sept.   4, Williams, Harriot, and Parnell Antrim.
1778, Feb.   22, Williams, Hester, and Thomas Currey.

1756, Aug.   9, Williams, Hugh, and Dorothy Read.
1794, March 23, Williams, Isaac, and Margret Richardson
1754, July   7, Williams, Isaac, and Mary Brown.
1789, April 17, Williams, James, and Elizabeth Crawford.
1792, June   9, Williams, Jane, and Balzar Herzog.
1756, Aug.   30, Williams, Jane, and Tobia Leahy.
1763, Dec.   1, Williams, Job, and Ann Dorrough.
1786, Nov.   22, Williams, John, and Catherine Powel.
1799, May   25, Williams, John, and Eleonore Martin.
1765, April   9, Williams, John, and Elizabeth Brannon.
1789, June   5, Williams, John, and Elizabeth Jones.
1779, Aug.   10, Williams, John, and Elizabeth Loyd.
1779, June   11, Williams, John, and Judith Burn.
1761, Sept.   5, Williams, John, and Mary Kenty.
1787, July   2, Williams, John, and Mary Webb.
1778, Dec.   2, Williams, John, and Rebecca Sullevan.
1798, April 19, Williams, John, and Susannah Lang.
1792, Dec.   26, Williams, Joseph, and Mary Bartle.
1777, March 10, Williams, Joseph, and Mary Gittar.
1757, Jan.   26, Williams, Luke, and Martha Hartley.
1753, Nov.   26, Williams, Lydia, and Joseph Davis.
1794, Sept. 24, Williams, Marget, and Joseph Fenwick.
1765, Aug.   31, Williams, Mary, and Andrew Patterson.
1789, May   30, Williams, Mary, and Caleb Matlack.
1795, Feb.   26, Williams, Mary, and Cornelius Scanlin.
1778, June   25, Williams, Mary, and James David.
1780, Sept. 10, Williams, Mary, and James McFall.
1778, March   8, Williams, Mary, and John Molly.
1798, March 16, Williams, Mary, and Nathan Dickenson.
1757, Oct.   12, Williams, Mary, and.Thomas Frame.
1778, May   3, Williams, Mary, and Thomas Hamilton.
1791, May   26, Williams, Michael, and Elizabeth Aklin.
1793, June   30, Williams, Nancy, and John Aby.
1763, Oct.   7, Williams, Oliver, and Rose McDaniel.
1799, Nov.   25, Williams, Patrick, and Marget Higginbotham.
1760, Aug.   10, Williams, Paul, and Elizabeth Jones.
1776, Jan.   25, Williams, Phœbe, and Peter Duffey.
1800, April 21, Williams, Robert, and Eleonore Hamilton.
1779, Dec.   14, Williams, Samuel, and Marg. Spencer.
1770, Nov.   7, Williams, Sarah, and Isaac Forsyth.
1787, Sept.   8, Williams, Sarah, and John McCuen.
1800, July   24, Williams, Sarah, and Thomas Fitzgerald.
1774, Nov.   11, Williams, Thomas, and Ann Johnson.
1778, June   9, Williams, Thomas, and Sarah Walker.
1775, Oct.   14, Williams, William, and Ann McGill.
1754, Nov.   2, Williams, William, and Elizabeth Jackson.

1778, March 22, Williams, William, and Elizabeth Leech.
1779, April 4, Williams, William, and Elizabeth White.
1782, July 16, Williams, William, and Jenny Thorington.
1755, Dec. 26, Williams, William, and Margareth Carnes.
1782, Jan. 22, Williams, William, and Mary Anne Smith.
1786, Dec. 31, Williams, William, and Mary Mathews.
1787, May 18, Williams, William, and Mary Mathews.
1763, Jan. 1, Williamson, Hannah, and Thomas Lawrence.
1778, March 9, Williamson, John, and Eleanor Dun.
1762, April 1, Williamson, Joseph, and Mary Griffith.
1758, Dec. 5, Williamson, Margaret, and Benjamin Steedon.
1764, April 22, Williamson, Margaret, and John McLarhan.
1770, Nov. 26, Williamson, Michael, and Alice Williams.
1759, March 26, Williamson, Rachel, and Peter Baukson.
1753, Aug. 28, Williamson, Robert, and Elenor Reed.
1799, July 26, Williamson, William Andrew, and Martha Walker.
1781, Nov. 3, Williard, Abigail, and William Stone.
1796, April 23, Willingsford, William, and Mary Hardie.
1796, Feb. 7, Willington, John, and Elizabeth Martin.
1798, April 19, Willis, Amelia, and Philip Mück.
1753, Nov. 22, Willis, Joel, and Mary Harvey.
1800, Oct. 25, Willis, Joseph, and Mary Kinsley.
1782, Sept. 25, Willis, Prudence, and David Copeland.
1790, June 21, Willman, Charles, and Rebecca Boon.
1754, Nov. 27, Willis, Christiana, and Richard Baker.
1767, Aug. 3, Wills, John, and Ester Spear.
1786, March 12, Wills, John, and Hannah Whittall.
1793, June 30, Wills, Joseph, and Eliza Juliana Bayard.
1759, July 15, Wills, Sarah, and Peter Broades.
1793, Aug. 22, Wills, William, and Mary Slawter.
1779, May 20, Willson, Alexander, and Sarah Shepherd.
1778, March 17, Willson, Ann, and James Doyle.
1759, July 8, Willson, Ann, and Samuel Whit.
1766, Jan. 10, Willson, Ann, and Silvester Sharp.
1768, March 15, Willson, Christopher, and Margaret Grantham.
1751, Jan. 28, Willson, Elizabeth, and Constantine MacDonnel.
1756, Jan. 11, Willson, Elizabeth, and Cornelius Connor.
1775, Nov. 21, Willson, Elizabeth, and John Chatham.
1792, May 10, Willson, Elizabeth, and John Kaign.
1775, April 13, Willson, Elizabeth, and John Thompson.
1775, Jan. 24, Willson, Gabriel, and Margaret Campbell.
1776, May 29, Willson, George, and Hannah Willard.
1761, April 20, Willson, Isaak, and Rachel Tarry.
1778, Feb. 12, Willson, James, (Capt. 49th reg^t of foot,) and Elizabeth Budden.
1777, Nov. 25, Willson, Jane, and John Campbell.

1776, June   9, Willson, Jean, and Timothy Moriarty.
1760, Aug.   22, Willson, John, and Diana Bely.
1767, Feb.   24, Willson, John, and Elizabeth Humphreys.
1759, April 19, Willson, John, and Ester Linnochs.
1780, Jan.   31, Willson, John, and Mary Jones.
1777, April 23, Willson, Lawrence, and Jean Biran.
1779, April 13, Willson, Margaret, and William Kerr.
1757, July   23, Willson, Mary, and Richard Lavers.
1769, Dec.   1, Willson, Sarah, and Thomas Moffet.
1751, Nov.   19, Willson, Susannah, and James Maffet.
1765, June   24, Willson, Thomas, and Margaret Reed.
1778, Dec.   10, Willson, William, and Elizabeth Stone.
1799, Jan.   31, Wilmert, John, and Jane Barber.
1793, Nov.   7, Wilson, Amelia, and John Greer.
1796, Nov.   8, Wilson, Anne, and John Knox.
1799, June   27, Wilson, Calia, and George Riser.
1782, May   23, Wilson, Catherine, and Narassah Miles.
1786, Sept. 22, Wilson, Eleonore, and Edward Riley.
1793, July   13, Wilson, Elenore, and Nathan Jemmison.
1756, April 28, Wilson, Elinor, and John Powel.
1781, Oct.   15, Wilson, Elizabeth, and Archibald Thomson.
1793, April   5, Wilson, Elizabeth, and John Brown.
1791, Dec.   2, Wilson, Elizabeth, and Peter Jocum.
1799, Aug.   18, Wilson, Fanny, and John Smith.
1794, Dec.   21, Wilson, Francis, and Marget Holmstadt.
1783, April 11, Wilson, George, and Catherine Walker.
1788, Feb.   7, Wilson, Hannah, and Agvilla Wollaston.
1795, July   4, Wilson, Hannah, and Caleb Matlack.
1789, April 30, Wilson, Hope, and Hugh Cane.
1771, Feb.   7, Wilson, Hugh, and Lewrefia Conn.
1794, Sept.   1, Wilson, James, and Mary Laroux.
1790, May   24, Wilson, Jane, and John Buckingham.
1793, Feb.   10, Wilson, Jane, and William Smith.
1790, June   22, Wilson, John, and Ceilia Guy.
1787, Jan.   2, Wilson, John, and Marget Dobbins.
1773, Aug.   22, Wilson, John, and Otilla Ludwick.
1782, Oct.   27, Wilson, John, and Sarah Kalley.
1756, April 19, Wilson, Joseph, and Margaret Davis.
1773, Nov.   4, Wilson, Margaret, and William Peel.
1799, June   23, Wilson, Marget, and William Montgomery.
1765, Feb.   6, Wilson, Mary, and Edward Meacock.
1797, Nov.   13, Wilson, Mary, and Jonathan Bowls.
1785, Jan.   15, Wilson, Mary, and Robert Moore.
1782, July   26, Wilson, Mary, and William McCombs.
1753, Oct.   18, Wilson, Mathew, and Rebecca Wassols.
1783, Feb.   1, Wilson, Mathy, and Salomen Townsend.

1789, June 28, Wilson, McCall, and Rachel Sickes.
1790, Oct. 17, Wilson, Robert, and Elizabeth Matlack.
1781, Dec. 20, Wilson, Thomas, and Catharine Brickley.
1781, Sept. 27, Wilson, Thomas, and Susannah Madders.
1794, Dec. 28, Wilson, William, aud Elenore McCombs.
1797, Sept. 21, Wilson, William, and Margret Hoffa.
1798, Jan. 30, Wilt, Cathrine, and Joseph Hertzog.
1787, Sept. 24, Wilt, Rebecca, and John Hendricks.
1753, July 19, Windal, Rebecca, and John Low.
1751, July 31, Windor, Elinor, and Thomas Giveenup.
1787, Oct. 27, Wine, Jacob, and Mary Anderson.
1779, April 22, Winents, John, and Margaret Minch.
1779, June 16, Wingate, Daniel, and Isabell McBea.
1797, July 5, Winkler, Ludwig, and Cathrine Dietz.
1769, April 31, Winslow, Anne, and Thomas Joseph.
1786, Dec. 12, Winson, Anne, and Adam Fox.
1779, June 7, Winstanley, Francis, and Margarett Robeson.
1775, July 16, Wint, Joshua, and Martha Blickley.
1767, May 7, Winter, Daniel, and Susannah Cavet.
1764, July 31, Winter, James, and Ann Smith.
1764, Feb. 8, Winter, John, and Mary Cox.
1779, May 24, Winter, Thomas, and Rachel Dobson.
1778, Feb. 1, Winter, William, and Jane Locked.
1782, Aug. 17, Wintercast, George, and Margret Biddes.
1760, Dec. 6, Winteringer, Bernard, and Sarah Chatwin.
1767, Aug. 22, Winters, Daniel, and Susannah Cavet.
1791, Sept. 19, Winters, Elizabeth, and Benjamin Hall.
1777, May 27, Winters, Mary, and Richard Page.
1794, Nov. 1, Winters, Mary, and Thomas Story.
1767, March 9, Winters, Mary, and William Thomas.
1792, Nov. 29, Winters, Sarah, and George Brown.
1800, March 20, Winters, William, and Elizabeth Welsh.
1778, June 15, Wintour, Deborah, and Thomas Reed.
1781, Nov. 26, Wintz, Jacob, and Rosina Dorothea Hagen.
1758, May 15, Wise, Christina, and Henry Hartz.
1754, Aug. 7, Wise, John, and Catharine Smith.
1786, Oct. 16, Wise, John, and Mary Racks.
1789, May 7, Wise, Martin, and Elizabeth May.
1759, Sept. 30, Wiseburogh, Peter, and Elizabeth Gunlaugher.
1757, June 30, Wiseley, Ann, and Elias Pearson.
1776, Oct. 29, Wisemiller, Henery, and Mary Rice.
1794, Nov. 9, Wiser, Susannah, and Henry Knox.
1789, Nov. 27, Wisham, Sara, and Timothy Organ.
1795, Sept. 3, Wistar, Mary, and Jonathan Dehaven.
1753, Sept. 29, Wistar, Salome, and William Chancelor.
1789, Sept. 30, Witel, William, and Catharine Williams.

1753, Aug.   7, Withron, Alexander, and Mary Johnston.
1755, Jan.   30, Withy, John, and Mary Syng.
1752, June   24, Wittiker, Sarah, and William Allen.
1753, Nov.   12, Witting, Dorothy, and Walter Stirling.
1794, May   25, Witty, Barbara, and Thomas Aldridge.
1761, Nov.   9, Wiver, Elizabeth, and Mathew Rowen.
1757, March 3, Woard, Andrew, and Mary Boder.
1758, Aug.   23, Wodkints, Margaret, and Thomas Russel.
1777, Sept.   9, Woldridge, Robert, and Mary Rafert.
1800, Jan.   9, Wolf, Barbara, and Joseph Stockdale.
1794, April   17, Wolf, George, and Barbara Foy.
1777, Oct.   14, Wolf, Henry, and Elizabeth Fagon.
1776, Jan.   28, Wolf, John, and Mary Cline.
1782, Dec.   29, Wolf, Lewis, and Mary Slaughter.
1778, Nov.   1, Wolf, Lucy, and James Wallis.
1794, June   2, Wolf, Sarah, and Samuel Huddell.
1778, Dec.   13, Wolf, Henry, and Mary Fordman.
1779, Aug.   15, Wolf, Mary, and Patrick McClosky.
1788, Feb.   7, Wallaston, Agvilla, and Hannah Wilson.
1777, June   28, Wollaston, Elizabeth, and James Linch.
1782, Sept.   15, Wollerade, Samuel, and Margaret McGill.
1764, April   7, Wolles, Ester, and Adrew Coon.
1793, July   11, Wols, Cathrine, and John Bevans.
1781, Feb.   12, Wolson, Robert, and Hannah Black.
1793, July   28, Wolvin, Cathrine, and Thomas Marjory.
1792, Oct.   14, Wonderly, Cathrine, and Isaac Senecson.
1771, July   26, Wood, Abigail, and Charles Warlington.
1796, Feb.   27, Wood, Alexander, and Cathrine Polston.
1754, March 14, Wood, Ann, and Archibald Erskin.
1792, June   24, Wood, Ann, and Joseph Fawcet.
1792, July   15, Wood, Charlott, and William Haino.
1778, June   22, Wood, Elizabeth, and Archibald Guffey.
1766, April   13, Wood, George, and Elizabeth Galloway.
1751, March 18, Wood, Henry, and Sary Jonson.
1780, June   10, Wood, James, and Barbara Kinsey.
1776, June   27, Wood, Jean, and Dennis McCarty.
1778, March 8, Wood, John, and Elizabeth Wright.
1762, Jan.   4, Wood, John, and Hagan Dourley.
1755, Aug.   27, Wood, Joseph, and Ann Dixon.
1792, Sept.   27, Wood, Joseph, and Margret Stotsenburgh.
1753, April   20, Wood, Josiah, and Amy Champion.
1774, Nov.   27, Wood, Mary, and Charles Cartwright.
1767, July   25, Wood, Mary, and Joseph Brooks.
1776, Jan.   13, Wood, Mary, and Samuel Branson.
1794, June   1, Wood, Rebecca, and Jacob Kurtz.
1776, Dec.   5, Wood, Robert, and Elizabeth Evance.

1751, Nov.   19, Wood, Sarah, and John Doyle.
1797, Nov.   28, Wood, Sarah, and William Goodfellow.
1787, June   19, Wood, Tasy, and Ralph Nugent Robinson.
1782, May   16, Wood, Thomas, and Jeane Hartley.
1795, May   20, Wood, Thomas, and Sarah Miller.
1791, Nov.   12, Wood, William, and Cathrine Priest.
1791, Feb.   7, Wood, William, and Elizabeth Louderback.
1795, June   7, Wood, William, and Hannah Johnson.
1775, Aug.   7, Wood, William, and Mary McGoveren.
1766, Aug.   4, Wood, William, and Sarah Walton.
1764, March   3, Woodard, Enoch, and Catharine Best.
1777, March   6, Woodbridge, Margaret, and John McGinnis.
1776, Sept.   26, Woodburn, Ann, and Charles Bell.
1784, Sept.   8, Woodcock, Elizabeth, and Joseph Marot.
1779, Sept.   25, Woodfield, Joseph, and Mary Heathen.
1779, June   24, Woodfind, Thomas, and Mary Morry.
1780, Jan.   1, Woodford, Thomas, and Ann Williams.
1768, Nov.   13, Woodley, Sarah, and Jeremiah Featherby.
1794, Jan.   7, Woodman, Joseph, and Elenore Johnson.
1798, April   3, Woodroff, Ann, and John Prentiss.
1791, Nov.   15, Woods, Cornelius, and Mary Rajal.
1788, Dec.   15, Woods, Elizabeth, and French Callam.
1778, Aug.   3, Woods, Jane, and Charles Caldwell.
1780, Jan.   30, Woods, Sarah, and Benjamin Pashall.
1795, Sept.   24, Woods, Sarah, and Hugh Strickland.
1782, Dec.   2, Woodward, Israel, and Elizabeth Hawkins.
1757, Nov.   30, Woodward, Jane, and Nathaniel Newlin.
1780, Jan.   8, Woodward, Richard, and Mary More.
1792, July   6, Woodworth, Nancy, and Peter Holliday.
1781, Jan.   23, Woolff, Kitty, and John Ringelman.
1787, May   10, Woollard, James, and Hannah Kelly.
1774, Oct.   31, Woolley, Catharine, and Thomas Robesson.
1773, Sept.   5, Wools, Agnes, and Charles Shepherd.
1797, March   2, Woolsleyer, Sarah, and John Eberhart.
1757, Aug.   18, Woolson, Nathan, and Mary Sommers.
1755, Nov.   20, Woomsly, Jonathan, and Mary Boice.
1793, June   25, Worrell, Margret, and Cornelius O'Brian.
1799, June   30, Wooten, William, and Lucy Kennedy.
1777, Dec.   6, Wordlaw, William, and Jane Gray.
1791, Sept.   28, Worell, Susanna, and Lewis Eyre.
1762, July   19, Workinger, Anna Margaret, and Lorentz Mayer.
1780, June   10, Worral, Enos, and Ann Sheldern.
1781, Nov.   21, Worrall, Benjamin, and Frances Thomson.
1781, Oct.   15, Worrall, Mary, and Peter Dicks.
1790, March 29, Worrell, Abel, and Rachel Rhoads.
1790, Oct.   25, Worrell, John, and Sarah Wort.

1792, July   5, Worrel, Phebe, and Thomas Brannon.
1794, Oct.   6, Worrell, Sarah, and William Coates.
1791, Aug.   16, Worrels, Catharine, and James Cannon.
1784, April 16, Worsdell, William, and Mary Shearman.
1790, Oct.   25, Wort, Sarah, and John Worrell.
1767, May   7, Wosky, George, and Margret Heuman.
1767, March 26, Wright, Abigail, and Benjamin Hall.
1792, July   26, Wright, Alice, and John Corkary.
1771, Nov.   25, Wright, Ann, and Peter Sharp.
1792, July   7, Wright, Cathrine, and Hugh Macmahon.
1782, Feb.   11, Wright, Charles, and Sarah Gwinnop.
1782, Dec.   8, Wright, Eleonor, and James Durant.
1778, March   8, Wright, Elizabeth, and John Wood.
1783, Nov.   2, Wright, Elizabeth, and Jonathan Adams.
1782, Aug.   12, Wright, Elizabeth, and Samuel Marriott.
1790, Oct.   18, Wright, George, and Flora Lacroon, (mulatoes.)
1797, July   17, Wright, Hannah, and George Stuart.
1782, Aug.   11, Wright, Hannah, and Wm. Lewis Sonntag.
1797, Aug.   5, Wright, Hannah, and William MacGiven.
1787, April   1, Wright, Henderson, and Alice Welch.
1782, July   15, Wright, James, and Mary Pollard.
1792, Sept. 20, Wright, Jane, and Nicholas Silvin.
1755, March 31, Wright, Jane, and Samuel Smith.
1776, Dec.   8, Wright, Joel, and Eleanor Bartram.
1800, Feb.   9, Wright, Johannah, and John More.
1795, Jan.   18, Wright, John Peter, and Ann Jane Durand.
1778, March 10, Wright, John, and Winneford North.
1781, Sept. 20, Wright, Margaret, and John Richmond.
1792, Dec.   6, Wright, Marget, and Fenwick Marriner.
1783, May   16, Wright, Martha, and Peter Miller.
1751, Sept. 15, Wright, Mary, and John Dickson.
1757, June   8, Wright, Richard, and Abigal Wigerly.
1783, Sept.   8, Wright, Sabina, and Charles Knight.
1785, Nov.   20, Wright, Sarah, and John Rudd.
1778, Oct.   7, Wright, Sarah, and William Christian.
1776, Aug.   13, Wright, Susannah, and Joseph Tuarll.
1752, Jan.   11, Wright, Susannah, and Nathan Yearsley.
1789, May   10, Wright, Thomas, and Bridget Mathews.
1790, Dec.   8, Wright, Thomas, and Rosanna Nash.
1759, Oct.   19, Wright, William, and Catharine Martin.
1775, Nov.   28, Wright, William, and Catharine Strobey.
1759, Feb.   4, Wright, William, and Elisabet Flamming.
1781, Aug.   27, Wright, Winnyford, and Patrick Lawluer.
1790, May   18, Wrighter, Mary, and Edward Lewis.
1754, Aug.   8, Wrissband, Hannah, and William Howel.
1779, April 17, Write, Rudolph, and Margarett McCarty.

1782, Aug. 21, Writeman, Thomas, and Johannah Dugan.
1755, Dec. 11, Writer, Jacob, and Sarah Sarah.
1783, Sept. 24, Wroth, William, and Elizabeth Durham.
1755, Jan. 21, Wyatt, Peter, and Mary Asheton.
1796, March 21, Wyman, Cathrine, and William Morris.
1757, Jan. 27, Wynn, Thomas, and Margaret Coulton.
1777, June 17, Wyse, David, and Elizabeth Peterman.
1799, Sept. 30, Yard, Hannah, and Garret Van Horn.
1796, Nov. 5, Yard, Lewis, and Rosanna Mitchel.
1799, July 11, Yard, Shandy, and Sarah Fortune.
1778, May 21, Yarnell, Mary, and Thomas Parker.
1790, April 25, Yater, Eleonore, and John Anthony.
1785, Aug. 9, Yeaker, Hannah, and John Lauke.
1752, Jan. 11, Yearsley, Nathan, and Susanna Wright.
1777, March 7, Yeas, Elizabeth, and Felix McCowen.
1775, April 6, Yeates, Elizabeth, and John Downy.
1778, April 12, Yeates, Rebecca, and James Henery.
1765, April 10, Yeats, Samuel, and Mary Harris.
1778, Feb. 17, Yendle, William, and Martha Gillmore.
1797, June 24, Yeoman, Sarah, and Thomas Allibone.
1783, May 5, Yervis, Thomas, and Philis Cox, (negroes.)
1775, Dec. 31, Yethern, Rosannah, and George Green.
1779, Sept. 27, Yoanger, Elizabeth, and James Vanisten.
1793, Jan. 27, Yocum, Abraham, and Edah Mitchel.
1763, Aug. 9, Yocum, Andrew, and Hannah Smith.
1757, May 12, Yocum, Deborah, and George McEmson.
1794, Sept. 24, Yocum, Jacob, and Susannah Kinche.
1792, June 13, Yocum, Nancy, and John Taylor.
1779, Feb. 23, Yoman, Daniel, and Catherine Miller.
1773, March 23, Yordon, Susannah, and Enis Morry.
1777, July 6, York, Bethinia, and Robert Young.
1778, Jan. 5, York, Michael, and Elizabeth Garret.
1790, Nov. 26, York, Susannah, and Benjamin Bossons.
1765, March 6, Yorke, Andrew, and Eleanor Cox.
1764, June 13, Young, Agnes, and Samuel McLanachan.
1797, Sept. 23, Young, Anthony, and Jane Tailor.
1777, June 17, Young, Benjamin, and Mary Conehey.
1799, May 13, Young, Cathrine, and Charles Dixey.
1770, Jan. 28, Young, Charles, and Anne Smith.
1792, Aug. 11, Young, Christian, and Martha Hunter.
1795, Aug. 2, Young, Christopher, and Mary Brown.
1759, Aug. 16, Young, Daniel, and Ann Oltey.
1769, Feb. 13, Young, Eleanor, and Robert Mathew.
1755, March 31, Young, Elinor, and David Nisbett.
1777, June 29, Young, Elizabeth, and Benet Fallowolta.
1779, Aug. 28, Young, Elizabeth, and Daniel Dixson.

1777, Jan.   30, Young, Elizabeth, and Jeremiah Fisher.
1781, Oct.   5, Young, Elizabeth, and John McCowan.
1781, Feb.   21, Young, Elizabeth, and John Watson.
1780, Sept. 15, Young, Elizabeth, and John Wearier.
1800, Dec.   27, Young, Elizabeth, and Joseph Davis.
1797, Dec.   31, Young, Elizabeth, and Michael Rudolp.
1778, Jan.   9, Young, Elizabeth, and Robert Fallows.
1798, Jan.   24, Young, Elizabeth, and William Fraser.
1775, Oct.   5, Young, Francis, and Hannah Paul.
1799, April 17, Young, Jacob, and Mary Baum.
1777, Feb.   3, Young, James, and Catherine Court.
1757, Dec.   5, Young, James, and Mary Pattin.
1770, Jan.   6, Young, James, and Mary Carr.
1771, Sept.   5, Young, James, and Sarah Sleigh.
1761, Nov.   17, Young, Jane, and Aaron Robinson.
1794, March 22, Young, John, and Ann Dugan.
1783, April   9, Young, John, and Elizabeth Llewellyn.
1777, Aug.   8, Young, John, and Elizabeth Shea.
1794, Nov.   12, Young, John, and Maria Barclay.
1794, Dec.   17, Young, John, and Mary Denney.
1793, Feb.   12, Young, Jonathan, and Latitia Tatham.
1797, Dec.   5, Young, Julia, and John Lewis Cullion.
1754, Dec.   3, Young, Margaret, and James Nesbett.
1782, March 26, Young, Martha, and Alexander McFarland.
1797, Dec.   31, Young, Mary, and Elisha Randal Curtis.
1778, Nov.   27, Young, Mary, and John Kees.
1760, Jan.   9, Young, Rachel, and John Todman.
1778, June 12, Young, Ralph, and Sarah Jurden.
1798, Feb.   12, Young, Richard, and Hannah Dice.
1777, July   6, Young, Robert, and Bethinia York.
1791, June   5, Young, Sara, and John Fritz.
1778, ·Aug. 16, Young, Sarah, and William McGard.
1779, Jan.   21, Young, Susannah, and Jeremiah Satchwell.
1777, Aug.   18, Young, Susannah, and Michael Kneis.
1767, Dec.   7, Young, William, and Rebeccah Warold.
1769, Oct.   9, Younger. Elizabeth, and John Cox.
1763, May   10, Yous, Rebecca, and Job Cooper.
1758, March 26, Yung, Mary, and Daniel Fouster.
1781, Nov.   18, Zabern, David, and Anne Dingwall.
1779, April 10, Zach, Magdalena, and Marcus Prik.
1774, May   30, Zanche and Betsey, (negroes.)
1754, Jan.   23, Zane, Rachel, and John Jonse.
1797, Nov.   14, Zanes, Isaac, and Phebe Nail.
1787, Sept. 24, Zeams, Elizabeth. and Charles Meckelburg.
1756, March 6, Zeans, Hannah, and Aaron Marshall.
1798, April 17, Zeller, Mary, and Henry Mier.

1798, July   22, Ziegler, Anne, and James Robinson.
1797, Aug.   31, Zienerin, Margareta, and Jean Guerin-de-Foncin.
1787, Oct.   16, Zilke, Henry, and Lydia Hillman.
1790, May   9, Zimmerman, Elizabeth, and Anthony Freeborn.
1791, May   12, Zimmerman, Jacob, and Cathrine Reniger.
1754, March 22, Zimmerman, Jacob, and Susanna Roberts.
1778, Sept.   11, Zipeley, Henry, and Rosannah Mock.
1774, Feb.   6, Zipherhealth, John, and Christiana Abelin.

ADDENDA.

1756, Oct.   10, Comely, Henry, and Rachel Strickland.
1781, April 30, Frump, Catharine, and Thomas Peirey.
1796, Jan.   14, Leary, Cornelius, (mariner,) and Elizabeth Steel.
1780, Jan.   30, Manypenny, Catharine, and Benjamin Loden.
1778, June 13, Melholland, Margaret, and John Brice.

MARRIAGE RECORD

OF THE

FIRST PRESBYTERIAN CHURCH,

AT CARLISLE.

1785–1812.

FIRST PRESBYTERIAN CHURCH, CARLISLE.

1792, April 6, Adams, Esther, and Joseph Neily.
1793, Nov. 12, Adams, Joseph, and ——— ———.
1806, Sept. 9, Adams, Martha, and Nathaniel Jones.
1804, Jan. 12, Adams, Samuel, and Mary Porter.
1803, May 5, Agnew, Dr. Samuel, and Jane Greer.
1808, June 9, Agnew, Matthew, and Rebecca Forbes.
1793, May 6, Alcorn, James, and Isabella Cochran.
1806, April 22, Alexander, Byers, Esq., and Sidney Smith.
1796, Oct. 18, Alexander, Isabella, and Robert Evans.
1798, April 12, Alexander, James, and Jane Sanderson.
1792, Oct. 18, Alexander, John, and Elizabeth McCleary.
1800, Sept. 25, Alexander, Joseph, and Mary Young.
1809, March 30, Alexander, Nancy, and Thomas Weakley.
1785, Sept. 13, Alexander, Samuel, and Isabella Creigh.
1792, Dec. 18, Alexander, William, and Jean Miller.
797, Dec. 9, Allen, Agnes, and John Day.
1788, Nov. 14, Allen, Catharine, and Samuel Gray.
1794, Feb. 20, Allen, Elizabeth, and Henry Rumble.
1794, Sept. 16, Allen, Jenny, and John Barr.
1806, Nov. 25, Allen, Jacob, and Jane Spottswood.
1789, Sept. 16, Allen, Margaret, and William McAlevy.
1798, Jan. 4, Allen, W^m, and Jenny McCammon.
1807, April 2, Anderson, Elizabeth, and William Edmint.
1788, Dec. 11, Anderson, James, and Margaret Brownlee.
1791, Jan. 5, Anderson, James, and Margaret Smith.
1798, March 22, Anderson, James, and Mary McQueen.
1807, Jan. 6, Anderson, Jane, and Samuel Lamb.
1812, Feb. 27, Anderson, Jane, and Wm Anderson.
1789, Dec. 2, Anderson, John, and Margaret McClure.
1793, Aug. 8, Anderson, John, and Polley Neil.
1792, Nov. 22, Anderson, Joseph, and Betsey Walker.
1793, April 11, Anderson, Letitia, and David Duncan.
1798, May 14, Anderson, Mary, and Alexander Beers.
1807, Oct. 26, Anderson, Mary, and Thomas Kernan.
1812, Feb. 27, Anderson, W^m, and Jane Anderson.

1785, March 24, Andrew, Margaret, and John Campbell.
1807, April 2, Armor, William, and Nancy Herwick.
1809, March 14, Armstrong, Charles, and Agness Blackwood.
1789, June 18, Armstrong, Dr. James, and Polley Stephenson.
1788, May 24, Armstrong, James, and Eleanor Pollock.
1798, Sept. 24, Armstrong, Robert, and Polly Landrum.
1799, Dec. 17, Armstrong, Thomas, and Isabella Stephenson.
1789, May 26, Arnold, Peter, and Susanna Eakard.
1792, Oct. 19, Arthurs, John, and Peggy Smith.
1785, May 11, Aspell, Margaret, and Henry Miller.
1797, Dec. 27, Augney, Mary, and Robert Mason Uroth.
1792, June 26, Aull, Jean, and Alexander Clinton.
1810, Oct. 23, Ayres, David, and Rachel Bailey.
1789, Oct. 27, Bailey, Elizabeth, and Jesse Kennedy.
1810, Oct. 23, Bailey, Rachel, and David Ayres.
1801, July 30, Baker, William, and Polly Moore.
1812, March 26, Barber, Elizabeth, and Hugh Walker.
1807, Dec. 8, Barber, Mary, and Jacob Heller.
1789, April 16, Barker, Martha, and Francis White.
1794, Sept. 16, Barr, John, and Genny Allen.
1800, July 17, Bayles, Betsey, and Wm Cascadon.
1804, May 3, Bayles, Moses, and Isabella Wallace.
1792, June 26, Beard, Margaret, and David Kilgore.
1794, Feb. 10, Beatty, Samuel, and Catharine Caswell.
1798, June 21, Beckwith, Ann, and Joseph Watson.
1798, May 14, Beers, Alexander, and Mary Anderson.
1788, July 18, Bell, Agness, and Joseph Young..
1800, Oct. 21, Bell, Catharine, and John McCune.
1803, March 17, Bell, Elizabeth, and Robert Dunlap.
1803, Jan. 1, Bell, James, and Hannah Wilson.
1794, June 10, Bell, James, and Jane Milligan.
1796, Jan. 12, Bell, James, and Nancy Haggerty.
1796, May 12, Bell, Samuel, and Eleanor Campbell.
1802, Sept. 6, Biegle, George, and Mary Rheinhart.
1794, Oct. 9, Black, Margaret, and Gilbert Wade.
1809, March 14, Blackwood, Agness, and Charles Armstrong.
1802, Aug. 17, Blackwood, John, and Mary Trotter.
1812, March 26, Blackwood, Wm, and Rebecca Boileau.
1795, Jan. 16, Blaine, James, and Peggy Lyon.
1797, Nov. 7, Blaine, Jean, and John Endsley.
1812, March 31, Blair, Andrew, and Elizabeth Hays.
1806, Nov. 7, Blair, James, and Mary McCartney.
1795, May 16, Blair, John, (son of Randel,) and Isabella Hall.
1794, June 10, Blair, Mary, and John Mitchell.
1805, Sept. 12, Boden, Andrew, and Mary King.
1809, June 8, Boileau, John, and Margaret Pollock.

1812, March 26, Boileau, Rebecca, and Wm Blackwood.
1800, Oct. 1, Bollinger, Conrad, and Sarah Stewart.
1790, Nov. 24, Bovard, Charles, and Rachel Wallace.
1793, May 8, Bow, Catharine, and George Hamilton.
1788, July 30, Bow, Catharine, and John Gaw.
1792, Feb. 2, Bow, Nancy, and Jared Carothers.
1793, July 23, Boyd, John, and Margaret Johnson.
1796, Feb. 12, Boyd, Joseph, and Elizabeth Jourdan.
1792, March 22, Boyd, William, and Abigail Robeson.
1805, Aug. 8, Boyer, Nancy, and George Philips.
1793, July 25, Bradley, Margery, and Francis McCollum.
1796, June 7, Bradley, Mary, and John Glenn.
1804, Jan. 8, Brady, Joseph, and Elizabeth Foster.
1801, Feb. 26, Brandon, Elizabeth, and Archibald McGrue.
1799, April 17, Brandon, Sarah, and Robert Moorehead.
1795, June 8, Brandt, Christopher, and Eve Douy.
1809, May 30, Breden, John, and Mary Philips.
1792, May 23, Brice, Mary, and Alexander Moore.
1800, Feb. 13, Briggs, Mary, and Jared Pollock.
1788, Nov. 6, Brisland, Sarah, and Lancelot Mollan.
1795, Jan. 1, Broadley, Daniel, and Hannah Jameson.
1800, July 11, Brooks, James, and Rachel McCart.
1792, Feb. 9, Brown, Alexander, and Elizabeth Logue.
1806, Dec. 17, Brown, Alexander, and Mary Weakley.
1799, Oct. 31, Brown, Betsey, and Henry Wilson.
1788, Jan. 17, Brown, Isabella, and Lewis Foulke.
1806, Dec. 31, Brown, John, and Betsey Finley.
1797, Feb. 9, Brown, John, and Mary Irwin.
1807, Jan. 16, Brown, John, and Polly McPherson.
1789, Oct. 27, Brown, Joseph, and Polly McFee.
1808, Oct. 10, Brown, Lettitia, and Samuel Thompson.
1786, Feb. 2, Brown, Moses, and Jean Donaldson.
1796, Feb. 23, Brown, Rebecca, and Robert Brown.
1796, Feb. 23, Brown, Robert, and Rebecca Brown.
1801, May 28, Brown, Sarah, and Christopher Lees.
1798, March 15, Brown, William, and Nancy Buchannan.
1797, Jan. 12, Brown, W^m, and Nancy Loughridge.
1788, Dec. 11, Brownlee, Margaret, and James Anderson.
1796, Feb. 16, Bryan, Patrick, and Margery Davis.
1792, March 1, Buchanan, Robert, and Mary McKay.
1799, March 5, Buchannan, Arthur, and Agness Graham.
1798, March 15, Buchannan, Nancy, and William Brown.
1792, Nov. 16, Burke, Elizabeth, and Archibald Cambell.
1790, Sept. 20, Burkholder, Elizabeth, and Peter Latchsha.
1802, Jan. 16, Burkholder, Henry, and Eliz Laird.
1808, Jan. 26, Burkholder, Jacob, and Sarah Welch.

1790, Sept.   20, Burkholder, John, and Elizabeth Latchsha.
1812, Jan.   30, Burney, Jane, and David Sterrett.
1796, Dec.   22, Caldwell, Samuel, and Jenny Wilson.
1785, April   28, Calendar, Pattey, and Thomas Duncan.
1792, Nov.   16, Cambell, Archibald, and Elizabeth Burke.
1796, March   29, Cambell, William, and Jenny Grier.
1789, March   2, Camble, Nancy, and John Tongue.
1807, Aug.   19, Camblin, John, and Elizabeth Neily.
1796, May   12, Campbell, Eleanor, and Samuel Bell.
1785, March   24, Campbell, John, and Margaret Andrew.
1793, June   28, Canning, Charles, and Jean Huston.
1812, June   11, Carothers, Andrew, and Catharine Loudon.
1809, March   14, Carothers, Eliz., and Erasmus Holzapel.
1800, Sept.   17, Carothers, James, Jun., and Johanna Maria Kline.
1792, Feb.   2, Carothers, Jared, and Nancy Bow.
1808, Sept.   13, Carothers, John, and Patty Quigley.
1788, Jan.   10, Carothers, John, and Polly Holmes.
1803, Nov.   10, Carothers, Polly, and James Grayson.
1789, Sept.   29, Carothers, Rogers, and Sarah Penwell.
1812, March   31, Carothers, W^m, and Fanny Clark.
1809, March   14, Carter, Esther, and James Dundas.
1800, July   17, Cascadon, W^m, and Betsy Bayles.
1794, Feb.   10, Caswell, Catharine, and Samuel Beatty.
1807, Sept.   10, Cauffman, George, and Elizabeth Smith.
1792, Nov.   8, Chambers, Betsey, and William Kelso.
1810, March   6, Chambers, Geo., Esq., and Ally Lyon.
1797, April   6, Chambers, Margaret, and John Logan.
1789, May   26, Chambers, Mary, and John Davidson.
1801, Oct.   27, Chambers, Nancy, and John Sterret.
1795, June   17, Chambers, Polly, and Mordecai McKinney.
1799, June   25, Chapman, James, and Nancy Fleming.
1801, Sept.   24, Chapman, Sarah, and John Duff.
1789, Feb.   16, Christie, Mary, and Edward Williams.
1809, Feb.   18, Christy, Jane, and James Oriswell.
1807, Oct.   15, Christy, Mary, and William McCoy.
1809, Oct.   10, Clark, Catharine, and Robert Montgomery.
1812, March   31, Clark, Fanny, and Wm Carothers.
1796, April   19, Clark, Sarah, and Thomas White.
1793, May   10, Clawson, Elsie, and Archibald Kelly.
1789, May   13, Clayton, John, and Elizabeth Miller.
1791, Jan.   20, Clendenan, Isabella, and Archibald McCullogh.
1794, May   8, Clendenan, Jean, and Jehu Woodward.
1807, Dec.   31, Clendenen, John, and Martha Waugh.
1809, Jan.   24, Clendenon, Ann, and William Murdock.
1803, Sept.   28, Clendenon, Elizabeth, and John Hannah.
1792, June   26, Clinton, Alexander, and Jean Aull.

1793, May   6, Cochran, Isabella, and James Alcorn.
1806, April   3, Conelly, Thomas, and Nancy Johnston.
1799, May   7, Connelly, Jane, and Robert McCormick.
1801, Nov.   5, Connor, Francis, and Elizabeth Montgomery.
1795, Oct.   13, Cook, Jacob, and Elizabeth Right.
1805, Feb.   18, Cooney, Mary, and Edward White.
1786, Feb.   13, Cooper, Adam, and Elizabeth Foster.
1805, Feb.   14, Cooper, John, and Rachel Craighead.
1801, Feb.   19, Cooper, Polly, and James Noble.
1786, May   31, Coots, Margaret, and Thomas Ruggles.
1795, April   30, Coover, Henry, and Elizabeth Stair.
1796, Feb.   1, Copely, Samuel, and Jane Sibbet.
1800, Dec.   18, Coulter, Henry, and Amelia Postlethwaite.
1806, Feb.   22, Coulter, William, and Jane Steen.
1790, Oct.   21, Cowher, Agness, and Samuel Reed.
1792, Oct.   9, Craft, Gershom, and Jean Steel.
1790, Sept.   30, Craighead, Gilson, and Nancy White.
1812, April   9, Craighead, Isabella, and Andrew Stewart.
1788, March 11, Craighead, John, and Jean Lamb.
1809, July   4, Craighead, Mary, and Thomas Geddes.
1805, Feb.   14, Craighead, Rachel, and John Cooper.
1789, March 26, Craighead, Rachel, and Samuel Lightcap.
1796, Nov.   15, Craighead, Thomas, and Rebecca Weakley.
1805, Feb.   5, Crain, Jane, and Matthew Williams.
1794, April   22, Crane, Richard, and Sally Flemming.
1794, May   29, Crawford, Agnes, and Robert Herron.
1796, Feb.   11, Crawford, Joseph, and Ann Davidson.
1811, March 13, Crawford, Robert, and Jane Seaton.
1800, March   6, Creigh, Betsey, and Samuel Duncan.
1785, Sept.   13, Creigh, Isabella, and Samuel Alexander.
1796, May   12, Creigh, John, and Eleanor Dunbar.
1801, April   2, Creigh, Polly, and John Kennedy.
1791, March   3, Crochet, Elizabeth, and David McGowan.
1808, Feb.   4, Crocket, Catharine, and Philip Miller.
1789, Dec.   18, Crocket, Elsie, and Stephen Keepers.
1798, Jan.   2, Crocket, James, and Sarah Nimmon.
1793, Dec.   19, Crocket, Sarah, and Alexander Trindle.
1797, Nov.   16, Crocket, Thomas, and Esther Johnson.
1791, May   17, Cromley, John, and Mary Robeson.
1793, May   27, Crosson, Mary, and William Douds.
1793, April   4, Culbertson, Joseph, and Polley McCune.
1809, June   22, Culbertson, Margaret, and John Johnston.
1807, Dec.   1, Culbertson, Sally, and James Dunlap.
1806, March 15, Culbertson, Samuel, and Rebecca Officer.
1803, May   4, Culens, Betsey, and James Pinkerton.
1804, March 29, Cummins, John, and Rebecca Moore.

1802, May 25, Cunningham, Benj., and Elizabeth Smiley.
1792, Sept. 29, Cunningham, Mary, and John Urie.
1798, Oct. 25, Daniel, Thomas, and Agnes Dugan.
1785, May 31, Daugherty, Eleanor, and Matthew Hart.
1796, Feb. 11, Davidson, Ann, and Joseph Crawford.
1807, April 30, Davidson, Dr. Robert, and Margaret Montgomery.
1811, Oct. 22, Davidson, George, and Mary Woods.
1801, Jan. 28, Davidson, George, and Polly Nimmons.
1812, April 30, Davidson, Isabella, and John Nisbet.
1789, May 26, Davidson, John, and Mary Chambers.
1787, Jan. 30, Davidson, Mary, and Samuel Davidson.
1804, Feb. 6, Davidson, Peggy, and Samuel Herrick.
1810, April 17, Davidson, Rev. Rob., D. D., and Jane Harris.
1787, Jan. 30, Davidson, Samuel, and Mary Davidson.
1810, Feb. 15, Davidson, William, and Ann McWilliams.
1800, June 12, Davis, Elizabeth, and Edwin Putnam, Esq.
1786, Sept. 7, Davis, Elizabeth, and John Smith.
1796, April 5, Davis, Elizabeth, and John Smith.
1796, Feb. 16, Davis, Margery, and Patrick Bryan.
1801, Dec. 10, Davis, Polly, and Doctor Watson.
1796, Nov. 14, Davis, Polly, and Robert Kenny.
1796, Dec. 9, Davis, Rachel, and George Kirkenluber.
1809, May 3, Dawson, William, and Betsey Dunn.
1797, Dec. 9, Day, John, and Agnes Allen.
1789, Feb. 27, Decker, Mary, and Sam¹ Galbreath.
1787, April 23, Dederick, Magdalina, and George Swingel.
1810, May 30, Delzell, John, and Jane McClure.
1789, May 21, Denney, William, and Polley Fleming.
1793, July 25, Denny, David, and Peggy Lyon.
1800, Oct. 2, Denny, Dennis, and Unity McLaughlin.
1793, April 11, Denny, Peggy, and Samuel Simison.
1804, June 21, Denny, Polly, and George Murray.
1796, Feb. 10, Deyrmond, Elizabeth, and John Love.
1795, April 2, Dickson, Andrew, and Mary Ramsay.
1805, Aug. 8, Dimcy, Jenny, and Robert Haney.
1787, Dec. 24, Dimsey, Fergus, and Salley Johnson.
1795, Sept. 23, Dimsey, Mary, and James Edmiston.
1789, Nov. 24, Dodds, Thomas, and Polley Guthrie.
1786, Feb. 2, Donaldson, Jean, and Moses Brown.
1794, June 24, Donaldson, John, and Rebecca Tremble.
1798, Sept. 6, Donelly, John, and Dorothy Smith.
1791, July 21, Donnell, Francis, and Jean McDonald.
1793, May 27, Douds, William, and Mary Crosson.
1787, Nov. 6, Douglass, Jane, and Alexander Logan.
1800, March 27, Douglass, John, and Margaret Sexton.
1795, June 8, Douy, Eve, and Christopher Brandt.

1799, Jan.   24, Dowds, Andrew, and Sarah Russel.
1803, May   5, Drennen, John, and Peggy Ross.
1801, Sept.   24, Duff, John, and Sarah Chapman.
1799, Oct.   8, Duffy, Catharine, and Hugh Sweney.
1798, Oct.   25, Dugan, Agnes, and Thomas Daneel.
1796, May   12, Dunbar, Eleanor, and John Creigh.
1790, Sept.   9, Dunbar, Elizabeth, and Allen Means.
1802, Feb.   9, Dunbar, Margaret, and James Hamilton.
1793, Feb.   7, Dunbar, Margaret, and Thomas Urie.
1796, April   14, Dunbar, William, and Betsey Forbes.
1808, Oct.   4, Duncan, Ann, and Edward Stiles.
1792, June   2, Duncan, Anne, and Samuel Mahon.
1793, April   11, Duncan, David, and Letitia Anderson.
1805, March   28, Duncan, Eleanor, and Robert Duncan.
1788, Dec.   30, Duncan, James, and Margaret Johnson.
1808, April   5, Duncan, Mary Ann, and Dr. James Gustine.
1797, Sept.   20, Duncan, Mrs., and Ephraim Polaine.
1805, March   28, Duncan, Robert, and Eleanor Duncan.
1800, March   6, Duncan, Samuel, and Betsey Creigh.
1811, Feb.   12, Duncan, Stephen, Esq., and Margaret Stiles.
1802, Nov.   16, Duncan, Stephen, and Harriet Elliot.
1785, April   28, Duncan, Thomas, and Pattey Calendar.
1809, March   14, Dundas, James, and Esther Carter.
1804, April   11, Dundass, Mary, and John Hasty.
1795, Oct.   26, Dunlap, Betsey, and James Smith.
1807, Dec.   1, Dunlap, James, and Sally Culbertson.
1808, June   13, Dunlap, John, and Rebecca McCafferty.
1803, March   17, Dunlap, Robert, and Elizabeth Bell.
1809, May   3, Dunn, Betsey, and William Dawson.
1811, Jan.   17, Dunn, Jane, and James Elliot.
1795, July   3, Eagolf, Polly, and Thomas Matheson.
1789, May   26, Eakard, Susanna, and Peter Arnold.
1785, March   1, Eaken, Mary, and William Work.
1787, Dec.   25, Earls, William, and Sarah Redman.
1790, Jan.   26, Eckles, Deborah, and James McCullogh.
1807, April   2, Edmint, William, and Elizabeth Anderson.
1795, Sept.   23, Edmiston, James, and Mary Dimsey.
1787, Nov.   15, Edmiston, Samuel, and Jenny Montgomery.
1809, Oct.   17, Ege, Capt. Geo., and Elizabeth Miller.
1810, Feb.   13, Ege, Michael, and Mary Galbreath.
1802, Nov.   16, Elliot, Harriet, and Stephen Duncan.
1794, July   14, Elliott, James, and Agnes Gregg.
1811, Jan.   17, Elliot, James, and Jane Dunn.
1796, Oct.   7, Elliot, Martha, and James Giffin.
1801, Nov.   24, Elliot, Mary, and John Goudy.
1801, Dec.   22, Elliot, Patience, and Capt. Calender Irvine.

1796, Nov.	22, Elliot, Peggy, and Francis McCullogh.
1798, Dec.	13, Elliot, Robert, and Rebecca Fleming.
1797, Nov.	7, Endsley, John, and Jean Blaine.
1804, April	12, Epright, Philip, and Mary Hunter.
1796, Oct.	18, Evans, Robert, and Isabella Alexander.
1787, March 27, Ewings, Jane, and William Lindsey.
1789, Sept.	12, Fee, Patrick, and Margaret McGoldrick.
1791, Jan.	13, Ferguson, Geo., and Isabella (alias Peggy) Sharon.
1794, Nov.	18, Ferguson, Margaret, and William Hardy.
1802, Nov.	2, Ferguson, Nancy, and Henry Miller.
1803, Sept.	22, Feyerabend, Christiana, and Jacob Seiler.
1796, April	26, Fields, Rebecca, and Benjamin Jones.
1806, Dec.	31, Finley, Betsey, and John Brown.
1790, March	8, Fish, Elizabeth, and Michael McCall.
1789, April	8, Fisher, Tobias, and Polley Irwin.
1807, Aug.	20, Flannigan, Elizabeth, and William Parks.
1793, May	14, Fleming, James, and Fanny Randolph.
1795, Feb.	24, Fleming, Nancy, and Charles Gregg.
1799, June	25, Fleming, Nancy, and James Chapman.
1789, May	21, Fleming, Polley, and William Denney.
1798, Dec.	13, Fleming, Rebecca, and Robert Elliot.
1796, Nov.	24, Fleming, Susanna, and Paul Randolph.
1794, April	22, Flemming, Sally, and Richard Crane.
1796, April	14, Forbes, Betsey, and William Dunbar.
1808, June	9, Forbes, Rebecca, and Matthew Agnew.
1804, Jan.	2, Forbs, Robert, and Catharine Wood.
1788, Aug.	6, Forsyth, Isbel, and William Webster.
1786, Feb.	13, Foster, Elizabeth, and Adam Cooper.
1804, Jan.	8, Foster, Elizabeth, and Joseph Brady.
1796, Feb.	25, Foster, James, and Elizabeth Hutchison.
1804, May	1, Foulk, Dr. Geo., and Polly Steel.
1788, Jan.	17, Foulke, Lewis, and Isabella Brown.
1811, March 14, Foulke, Priscilla, and James Weakley.
1809, July	25, Foulke, Sarah, and James Hunter.
1812, April	23, Franks, Sarah, and James Reily.
1796, June	9, Frazer, Emelia, and John Sterrett.
1800, Oct.	19, Frazer, Isabella, and Samuel Funk.
1787, April	9, Frazer, Nancy, and Robert Hunter.
1802, May	20, Freeland, Jane, and Michael Hoover.
1700, Oct.	16, French, Martha, and ―――― Thompson.
1788, April	26, French, Wᵐ, and Jean Gordon.
1793, April	19, Fullerton, Eliza, and Hugh McCormick.
1800, Oct.	19, Funk, Samuel, and Isabella Frazer.
1794, March 27, Gabby, William, and Amelia McCormick.
1808, July	26, Galbreath, Juliana, and Capt. Wᵐ Irvine.
1810, Feb.	13, Galbreath, Mary, and Michael Ege.

1793, July   18, Galbreath, Rebecca, and David Herron.
1789, Feb.   27, Galbreath, Sam[l], and Mary Decker.
1798, Jan.   9, Galbreath, Samuel, and Nancy Moore.
1789, Nov.   26, Gamble, Elizabeth, and Francis Jameson.
1793, April   23, Gass, James, and Rebecca Rowan.
1788, July   30, Gaw, John, and Catherine Bow.
1793, March   2, Geach, Ann, and John Lane.
1809, July   4, Geddes, Thomas, and Mary Craighead.
1795, Dec.   1, George, Nancy, and Samuel Hay.
1805, Nov.   1, Gerhart, Peter, and Polly Wallace.
1790, March   26, Gest, Anna, and Thomas Eliot Kennedy.
1797, Dec.   25, Gibbon, John, and Sarah White.
1794, June   3, Gibson, Elizabeth, and Hugh McCullogh.
1796, March   22, Gibson, Jane, and James Hall.
1804, Sept.   4, Gibson, Rebecca, and George Richison.
1786, March   9, Giffen, Gennet, and W[m] Hunter.
1796, Oct.   7, Giffen, James, and Martha Elliot.
1788, March   20, Gillespie, George, and Sarah Young.
1794, April   4, Gillmor, Margaret, and William Smith.
1794, Feb.   4, Given, James, and Omelia Steel.
1791, July   7, Gladney, William, and Mary Ann Woods.
1788, Jan.   9, Glenn, John, and Genny Hunter.
1796, June   7, Glenn, John, and Mary Bradley.
1793, Oct.   23, Gold, Joseph, and Margaret Rowan.
1800, March   6, Goorley, Sarah, and Stephen Ligget.
1788, July   1, Gordon, Ann, and Joseph Hays.
1788, April   26, Gordon, Jean, and W[m] French.
1801, Nov.   24, Goudy, John, and Mary Elliot.
1795, Aug.   31, Gourley, Samuel, and Agnes Sibbet.
1799, March   5, Graham, Agness, and Arthur Buchannan.
1800, Aug.   12, Graham, Jane, and William Greer.
1793, June   20, Graham, Margaret, and W[m] Nixon.
1803, May   19, Gray, John, and Nancy Henry.
1788, Nov.   14, Gray, Samuel, and Catharine Allen.
1791, Feb.   24, Gray, Samuel, and Elizabeth McDowel.
1803, Nov.   10, Grayson, James, and Polly Carothers.
1791, July   15, Grayson, Jean, and Samuel Waugh.
1792, Nov.   16, Grayson, William, and Agness Nimmons.
1795, May   11, Green, Adam, and Jane Moore.
1799, Sept.   —, Green, Mary, and Alexander McBride.
1803, May   5, Greer, Jane, and Dr. Samuel Agnew.
1794, Sept.   22, Greer, Patrick, and Elizabeth Wilson.
1800, Aug.   12, Greer, William, and Jane Graham.
1794, July   14, Gregg, Agnes, and James Elliott.
1795, Feb.   24, Gregg, Charles, and Nancy Fleming.
1798, Nov.   1, Gregg, Elizabeth, and George McKee.

1787, April 19, Gregg, Jane, and Francis McEwen.
1793, March 29, Gregory, Elizabeth, and Samuel Lindsey.
1812, Aug. 13, Grier, George, and Elizabeth Woods.
1796, March 29, Grier, Jenny, and William Cambell.
1800, March 31, Grier, Polly, and Lieut. David Offly.
1795, April 13, Griffin, Mary, and Charles Sweney.
1808, April 5, Gustine, Dr. James, and Mary Ann Duncan.
1792, May 24, Gustin, Sally, and Nathanael Snowden.
1789, Nov. 24, Guthrie, Polley, and Thomas Dodds.
1707, Oct. 26, Guthrie, Samuel, and Jane Wilson.
1807, Dec. 22, Hackett, Plunkett, and Hannah Kirkpatrick.
1796, Jan. 12, Hagerty, Nancy, and James Bell.
1800, May 10, Hague, Elizabeth, and Sergt. Benj. Woodward.
1795, May 16, Hall, Isabella, and John (son of Randel) Blair.
1796, March 22, Hall, James, and Jane Gibson.
1793, May 8, Hamilton, George, and Catharine Bow.
1802, Feb. 9, Hamilton, James, and Margaret Dunbar.
1805, Aug. 8, Haney, Robert, and Jenny Dimcy.
1803, Sept. 28, Hannah, John, and Elizabeth Clendenon.
1804, April 6, Hannon, John, and Mary Miller.
1798, Nov. 22, Hardy, Catharine, and Isaac Hoffer.
1794, Nov. 18, Hardy William, and Margaret Ferguson.
1798, Nov. 13, Harris, David, and Sally Montgomery.
1810, April 17, Harris, Jane, and Rev. Rob. Davidson, D. D.
1785, May 31, Hart, Matthew, and Elenor Daugherty.
1785, April 5, Harwick, Elizabeth, and John Isset.
1796, Oct. 14, Hasson, Samuel, and Polly Mauson.
1804, April 11, Hasty, John, and Mary Dundass.
1811, Nov. 12, Hatton, Maria, and Robert Parkinson.
1795, Dec. 1, Hay, Samuel, and Nancy George.
1788, July 1, Hayes, Joseph, and Ann Gordon.
1793, Sept. 16, Hayes, Margaret, and —— ——.
1788, Feb. 1, Hayes, Mary, and John Rosebury.
1786, May 11, Hayes, Mary, and William Logue.
1812, March 31, Hays, Elizabeth, and Andrew Blair.
1802, Oct. 14, Hazleton, Hugh, and Mary Mickey.
1807, Dec. 8, Heller, Jacob, and Mary Barber.
1803, April 28, Henderson, Benjamin, and Nancy Rose.
1803, May 19, Henry, Nancy, and John Gray.
1791, June 28, Herren, Reuben, and Martha Laird.
1804, Feb. 6, Herrick, Samuel, and Peggy Davidson.
1793, July 18, Herron, David, and Rebecca Galbreath.
1794, May 29, Herron, Robert, and Agnes Crawford.
1803, July 26, Hertzel, Susanna, Christian Sensabaugh.
1807, April 2, Herwick, Nancy, and William Armor.
1799, Jan. 31, Hewes, Caleb, and Sarah Magaw.

1798, Nov.   22, Hoffer, Isaac, and Catharine Hardy.
1789, Jan.   27, Hoffer, Melchor, and Matty McClellan.
1811, Aug.   15, Hoge, Fanny, and Robert Shaddin.
1791, March 22, Hoge, James Read, and Polley McKinney.
1798, April 12, Hoge, William, and Belle Lyon.
1791, Sept.   22, Hogg, Martha, and John McHaffey.
1798, Oct.   18, Hogg, Thomas, and Betsey Holmes.
1796, Nov.   17, Holcham, Hannah, and Archibald Loudon.
1800, Oct.   30, Holmes, Abraham, and Rebecca Weakley.
1798, Nov.   20, Holmes, Agness, and Robert Wright.
1798, Oct.   18, Holmes, Betsey, and Thomas Hogg.
1793, Aug.   23, Holmes, Daniel, and Peggy Woods.
1807, March 26, Holmes, Jane, and John McCague.
1789, March 26, Holmes, Jenny, and Jesse Kilgore.
1785, May   31, Holmes, John, and Nancy Stephenson.
1787, April   19, Holmes, Jonathan, and Jane Laird.
1802, Nov.   25, Holmes, Margaret, and John Thompson.
1792, Nov.   23, Holmes, Nancy, and George Patterson.
1788, Jan.   10, Holmes, Polly, and John Carothers.
1794, Dec.   15, Holtzoppel, Peggy, and James Sloane.
1809, March 14, Holzapel, Erasmus, and Eliz. Carothers.
1802, May   20, Hoover, Michael, and Jane Freeland.
1793, May   22, Houk, Adam, and Salome Live.
1803, Feb.   1, Houtz, Rev. Mr., and Catharine Keller.
1800, June   26, Hughes, Betsey, and Hugh H. Potts.
1788, Oct.   30, Hunt, Letitia, and Michael Marshall.
1788, Jan.   9, Hunter, Genny, and John Glenn.
1809, July   25, Hunter, James, and Sarah Foulke.
1809, March 7, Hunter, Mary, and Christopher Quigley.
1804, April   12, Hunter, Mary, and Philip Epright.
1791, Aug.   21, Hunter, Mary, and William Love.
1787, April   9, Hunter, Robert, and Nancy Frazer.
1806, March 1, Hunter, Sarah, and James McGlachin.
1809, Feb.   2, Hunter, Thomas, and Anna Quigley.
1790, Feb.   1, Hunter, Thomas, and Margaret Mathis.
1786, March 9, Hunter, W^m, and Gennet Giffin.
1793, May   14, Huston, Andrew, and Elizabeth Simund.
1798, Aug.   16, Huston, Elizabeth, and Andrew Miller.
1793, June   28, Huston, Jean, and Charles Canning.
1879, April   26, Hutchinson, Francis, and Ann Searight.
1796, Feb.   25, Hutchison, Elizabeth, and James Foster.
1801, Dec.   22, Irvine, Capt. Calender, and Patience Elliot.
1808, July   26, Irvine, Capt. W^m, and Juliana Galbreath.
1802, Nov.   23, Irvine, Elenor, and Samuel McKinney.
1811, Dec.   19, Irvine, Robert, and Eleanor Mitchell.
1792, Feb.   16, Irwine, Polley, and Thomas McCartney.

1789, Sept. 23, Irwin, Catharine, and James Ross.
1797, Feb. 9, Irwin, Mary, and John Brown.
1788, June 26, Irwin, Polley, and Joseph McClellan.
1789, April 8, Irwin, Polley, and Tobias Fisher.
1790, March 15, Isett, Henry, and Lydia Roath.
1785, April 5, Isset, John, and Elizabeth Harwick.
1803, May 26, Jackson, Ann, and James Jackson.
1803, May 26, Jackson, James, and Ann Jackson.
1794, May 8. Jackson, Samuel, and Margaret Ramsey.
1789, Nov. 26, Jameson, Francis, and Elizabeth Gamble.
1796, July 27, Jameson, Francis, and Margaret Melligan.
1795, Jan. 1, Jameson, Hannah, and Daniel Broadley.
1786, Aug. 1, Jameson, Rachel, and Morton McDonald.
1797, Nov. 16, Johnson, Esther, and Thomas Crocket.
1803, Feb. 16, Johnson, John, and Ann McFarlan.
1787, Feb. 7, Johnston, Adam, and Elizabeth Johnston.
1787, Feb. 7, Johnston, Elizabeth, and Adam Johnston.
1793, Jan. 24, Johnston, George, and Nancy Maxwell.
1801, Jan. 12, Johnston, Jane, and George McKeehan.
1809, June 22, Johnston, John, and Margaret Culbertson.
1788, Dec. 30, Johnston, Margaret, and James Duncan.
1793, July 23, Johnston, Margaret, and John Boyd.
1804, July 3, Johnston, Mary, and Philip Wareham.
1806, April 3, Johnston, Nancy, Thomas Conelly.
1788, April 1, Johnston, Rev. John, and Jean McBeth.
1787, Dec. 24, Johnston, Salley, and Fergus Dimsey.
1795, Dec. 22, Johnston, Samuel, and Rachel Love.
1796, April 26, Jones, Benjamin, and Rebecca Fields.
1806, Sept. 9, Jones, Nathaniel, and Martha Adams.
1803, Dec. 16, Jordan, Samuel, and Eleanor McGowan.
1796, Feb. 12, Jourdan, Elizabeth, and Joseph Boyd.
1802, Feb. 11, Jumper, Ann, and Joseph Logue.
1789, Jan. 15, Jumper, Jean, and George Logue.
1803, Nov. 1, Kean, Elizabeth, and John Skyles.
1789, Dec. 18, Keepers, Stephen, and Elsie Crocket.
1803, Feb. 1, Keller, Catharine, and Rev. Mr. Houtz.
1793, May 10, Kelly, Archibald, and Elsie Clawson.
1793, Nov. 17, Kelly, Grace, and Richard Price.
1795, Oct. 22, Kelly, Patrick, and Martha McKinley.
1792, May 9, Kelly, Samuel, and Elizabeth Kilgore.
1792, Nov. 8, Kelso, William, and Betsey Chambers.
1790, March 26, Kenedy, Thomas Eliot, and Anna Gest.
1803, May 2, Kennedy, Catharine, and John Wise.
1794, July 26, Kennedy, Harris, and Margaret Mercer.
1789, Oct. 27, Kennedy, Jesse, and Elizabeth Bailey.
1801, April 2, Kennedy, John, and Polly Creigh.

1785, July   23, Kenny, Eleanor, and Brice Smith.
1796, Nov.   14, Kenny, Robert, and Polly Davis.
1807, Oct.   26, Kernan, Thomas, and Mary Anderson.
1807, April   30, Kerrau, John, and Mary Rayny.
1787, Dec.   27, Kidd, ——, and —— Love.
1796, June   26, Kilgore, David, and Margaret Beard.
1792, May   9, Kilgore, Elizabeth, and Samuel Kelly.
1789, March   26, Kilgore, Jesse, and Jenny Holmes.
1805, May   2, Kilgore, Margaret, and James Wilson.
1805, Sept.   12, King, Mary, and Andrew Boden.
1796, April   27, Kinkead, John, and Mary Lee.
1785, Sept.   13, Kirk, Mary, and Oliver Ramsey.
1796, Dec.   9, Kirkenluber, George, and Rachel Davis.
1806, April   1, Kirkpatrick Guinthlen and William Mitchell.
1807, Dec.   22, Kirkpatrick, Hannah, and Plunkett Hackett.
1800, Sept.   17, Kline, Johanna Maria, and James Carothers, jun.
1798, May   16, Knittle, Henry, and Hannah Walker.
1812, Aug.   25, Knox, Joseph, and Mary McClure.
1789, Nov.   25, Lackey, Robert, and Mary Shortie.
1802, Jan.   16, Laird, Eliz., and Henry Burkholder.
1787, April   19, Laird, Jane, and Jonathan Holmes.
1791, June   28, Laird, Martha, and Reuben Herren.
1785, April   19, Lamb, Jane, and Stewart Rowan.
1788, March   11, Lamb, Jean, and John Craighead.
1785, March   1, Lamb, Mary, and Samuel Reed.
1807, Jan.   6, Lamb, Samuel, and Jane Anderson.
1793, March   2, Lane, John, and Ann Geach.
1807, March   19, Lang, William, and Eleanor Smith.
1805, Oct.   3, Latcha, Mary, and Robert Walker.
1790, Sept.   20, Latchsha, Elizabeth, and John Burkholder.
1790, Sept.   20, Latchsha, Peter, and Elizabeth Burkholder.
1799, Nov.   21, Latshaw, Joseph, and Mary Riddle.
1801, Jan.   22, Latta, Thomas, and Martha McGrew.
1798, Sept.   24, Laudrum, Polly, and Robert Armstrong.
1811, April   15, Laughlin, W^m, and Jane Oliver.
1810, April   5, Lee, Jane, and Geo. Matthews.
1796, April   27, Lee, Mary, and John Kinkead.
1801, May   28, Lees, Christopher, and Sarah Brown.
1798, Dec.   13, Lefevre, Barbara, and John Lyne.
1807, March   19, Lefevre, John, and Elizabeth Line.
1809, June   15, Lefevre, Samuel, and Hannah Winger.
1793, April   23, Lemmon, Jeane, and Daniel Morrison.
1787, March   20, Leviston, William, and Nancy Shaw.
1806, Dec.   2, Lewis, Francis, and Peggy Stansbury.
1800, March   6, Ligget, Stephen, and Sarah Goorley.
1804, Nov.   27, Lightcap, Godfrey, and Jane McElheny.

1789, March 26, Lightcap, Samuel, and Rachel Craighead.
1800, June 16, Linch, Robert, and Elizabeth Peeling.
1793, March 29, Lindsey, Samuel, and Elizabeth Gregory.
1787, March 27, Lindsey, William, and Jane Ewings.
1807, March 19, Line, Elizabeth, and John Lefevre.
1807, April 28, Line, Mary, and Philip Spangler.
1809, Aug. 17, Line, Rachel, and Henry Snyder.
1806, Nov. 14, Line, Sally, and Peter Frit.
1805, April 30, Lisle, David, and Mary Neilan.
1791, Aug. 25, Little, Eleanor, and William Wilson.
1793, May 22, Live, Salome, and Adam Houk.
1804, Nov.. 15, Lobaugh, Elizabeth, and Alex^r Searight.
1787, Nov. 6, Logan, Alexander, and Jane Douglass.
1797, April 6, Logan, John, and Margaret Chambers.
1792, June 28, Logue, Adam, and Nancy Sterrett.
1792, Feb. 9, Logue, Elizabeth, and Alexander Brown.
1789, Jan. 15, Logue, George, and Jean Jumper.
1802, Feb. 11, Logue, Joseph, and Ann Jumper.
1786, May 11, Logue, William, and Mary Hayes.
1801, March 17, Long, Bailey, and Margaret Weaver.
1796, Nov. 17, Loudon, Archibald, and Hannah Holcham
1812, June 11, Loudon, Catharine, and Andrew Carothers
1804, Jan. 12, Loudon, Miss, and David Woods.
1797, Jan. 12, Loughridge, Nancy, and Wm Brown.
1787, Dec. 27, Love, ——, and —— Kidd.
1789, Dec. 18, Love, James, and Mary Passel.
1796, Feb. 10, Love, John, and Elizabeth Deyrmond.
1795, Dec. 22, Love, Rachel, and Samuel Johnston.
1791, Aug. 21, Love, William, and Mary Hunter.
1789, Oct. 22, Lutz, Margaret, and Samuel Wilson.
1798, Dec. 13, Lyne, John, and Barbara Lefevre.
1791, May 12, Lyne, Susanna, and Robert Smith.
1810, March 6, Lyon, Ally, and Geo. Chambers, Esq.
1798, April 12, Lyon, Belle, and William Hoge.
1809, Oct. 5, Lyon, Mary, and Robert McPherson.
1793, July 25, Lyon, Peggy, and David Denny.
1795, Jan. 16, Lyon, Peggy, and James Blaine.
1803, Nov. 8, Maffit, Hugh, and Elizabeth McKnight.
1799, Jan. 31, Magaw, Sarah, and Caleb Hewes.
1797, Jan. 3, Magee, George, and Elizabeth McElwain.
1796, Jan. 26, Magee, Polly, and John Rhinehart.
1792, June 2, Mahon, Samuel, and Anne Duncan.
1798, Sept. 28, Marchbanks, James, and Ann Ralston.
1788, Oct. 30, Marshall, Michael, and Letitia Hunts.
1798, Aug. 29, Martin, James, and Margaret Walker.
1808, March 22, Martin, Jane, and William Martin.

1810, March 15, Martin, Margaret, and Francis Noble.
1789, June   3, Martin, Rosanna, and Archibald McKay.
1803, Oct.   13, Martin, Sarah, and Samuel Wilson.
1808, March 22, Martin, William, and Jane Martin.
1803, Nov.   3, Mather, James, and Ruth Wilson.
1801, May   26, Mathers, John, and Mary Rippeth.
1795, July   3, Matheson, Thomas, and Polly Eagolf.
1790, Feb.   1, Mathis, Margaret, and Thomas Hunter.
1810, April   5, Matthews, Geo., and Jane Lee.
1793, June   5, Matthews, Polley, and Roger McGee.
1796, Oct.   14, Mauson, Polly, and Samuel Hasson.
1793, Jan.   24, Maxwell, Nancy, and George Johnston,
1795, April   9, McAdams, Ann, and William Murray.
1788, March 18, McAfee, Letty, and George Sparr.
1789, Sept.   16, McAlevy, William, and Margaret Allen.
1801, Jan.   8, McAlister, Mary, and Thomas McAntire.
1801, Jan.   8, McAntire, Thomas, and Mary McAlister.
1793, April   9, McAnulty, Hugh, and Rachel Spottswood.
1790, July   8, McBeth, Alex^r, and Rachel Whitehill.
1788, April   1, McBeth, Jean, and Rev. John Johnston.
1798, April   3, McBeth, Peggy, and James Neely.
1799, Sept.   —, McBride, Alexander, and Mary Green.
1798, Aug.   8, McCabe, Jane, and Robert Seetin.
1789, June   29, McCabe, Patrick, and Sarah Power.
1808, June   13, McCafferty, Rebecca, and John Dunlap.
1807, March 26, McCague, John, and Jane Holmes.
1790, March   8, McCall, Michael, and Elizabeth Fish.
1786, Nov.   6, McCallister, Elizabeth, and James Parker.
1788, Feb.   26, McCallister, Jean, and Joseph Pierce.
1800, July   11, McCart, Rachel, and James Brooks.
1796, April   20, McCartney, John and Elizabeth Wilson.
1806, Nov.   7, McCartney, Mary, and James Blair.
1792, Feb.   16, McCartney, Thomas, and Polley Irwine.
1792, Nov.   20, McClain, Dr. James, and Patty Sanderson.
1792, Oct.   18, McCleary, Elizabeth, and John Alexander.
1790, Feb.   17, McCleland, Ann, and David Murray.
1788, June   26, McClellan, Joseph, and Polley Irwin.
1789, Jan.   27, McClellan, Matty, and Melchor Hoffer.
1792, March   1, McClintock, Rachel, and Robert Read.
1788, Nov.   3, McCloud, Kitty, and Hercules Murphy.
1797, March   9, McClure, Charles, and Rebecca Parker.
1810, May   30, McClure, Jane, and John Delzell.
1789, Dec.   2, McClure, Margaret, and John Anderson.
1812, Aug.   25, McClure, Mary, and Joseph Knox.
1793, July   25, McCullum, Francis, and Margery Bradley.
1798, Jan.   4, McCommon, Jenny, and William Allen.

1792, Feb.   29, McCord, Mary, and John Scott.
1794, March 27, McCormick, Amelia, and William Gabby.
1808, Oct.   4, McCormick, David, and Jane Thompson.
1793, April 19, McCormick, Hugh, and Eliza Fullerton.
1799, May   7, McCormick, Robert, and Jane Connelly.
1807, Oct. 15, McCoy, William, and Mary Christy.
1791, Jan. 20, McCullogh, Archibald, and Isabella Clendenan.
1796, Nov. 22, McCullogh, Francis, and Peggy Elliot.
1797, Nov. 29, McCullogh, George, and Elizabeth Thompson.
1794, June   3, McCullogh, Hugh, and Elizabeth Gibson.
1790, Jan. 26, McCullogh, James, and Deborah Eckles.
1798, Jan. 11, McCullough, John, and Polly Williamson.
1800, Oct. 21, McCune, John, and Catharine Bell.
1793, April 4, McCune, Polley, and Joseph Culbertson.
1793, April 17, McCune, Rosanna, and Robert Stewart.
1792, May 24, McDaniel, Daniel, and Jean Simonds.
1791, July 21, McDonald, Jean, and Francis Donnell.
1786, Aug.   1, McDonald, Martin, and Rachel Jameson.
1791, Feb. 24, McDowel, Elizabeth, and Samuel Gray.
1786, May   3, McDowel, Lydia, and Thomas Parker.
1796, April 14, McDowel, Nancy, and Charles Rainey.
1804, Nov. 27, McElheny, Jane, and Godfrey Lightcap.
1795, Oct. 22, McElravy, Mary, and Matthew Murdack.
1797, Jan.   3, McElwain, Elizabeth, and George Magee.
1787, April 19, McEwen, Francis, and Jane Gregg.
1803, Feb. 16, McFarlan, Ann, and John Johnson.
1785, Nov. 24, McFarlane, Jean, and William Thompson.
1789, Oct. 27, McFee, Polley, and Joseph Brown.
1803, April 21, McFeely, Eleanor, and John McKinley.
1807, June 18, McFeely, Salome, and George Reighter.
1806, Nov. 20, McFeely, William, and Mary Smith.
1793, June   5, McGee, Roger, and Polley Matthews.
1806, March 1, McGlachin, James, and Sarah Hunter.
1789, Sept. 12, McGoldrick, Margaret, and Patrick Fee.
1788, Jan.   7, McGonagle, Edward, and Sally Turner.
1798, May   3, McGovern, Catharine, and John McJunkins.
1791, March 3, McGowan, David, and Elizabeth Crochet.
1803, Dec. 16, McGowan, Eleanor, and Samuel Jordan.
1789, May 15, McGranahan, W^m, and Mary Roach.
1786, Sept. 22, McGrew, Archibald, and Ruth Miller.
1794, April 10, McGrew, Elizabeth, and Philip Shaw.
1801, Jan. 22, McGrew, Martha, and Thomas Latta.
1801, Feb. 26, McGrue, Archibald, and Elizabeth Brandon.
1791, Sept. 22, McHaffey, John, and Martha Hogg.
1792, April 17, McIntyre, Elizabeth, and W^m McIntyre.
1792, April 17, McIntyre, W^m, and Elizabeth McIntyre.

1798, May   3, McJunkins, John, and Catharine McGovern.
1789, June   3, McKay, Archibald, and Rosanna Martin.
1792, March   1, McKay, Mary, and Robert Buchanan.
1793, Feb.   13, McKee, Daniel, and Mary Stewart.
1798, Nov.   1, McKee, George, and Elizabeth Gregg.
1801, Jan.   12, McKeehan, George, and Jane Johnson.
1808, Jan.   14, McKimm, James, and Catharine Miller.
1791, Nov.   29, McKimmon, Michael, and Mary Patton.
1791, Jan.   4, McKinley, Daniel, and Sarah Smith.
1799, Jan.   3, McKinley, Henry, and Eleanor Stevens.
1800, June   26, McKinley, James, and Margaret Robeson.
1803, April   21, McKinley, John, and Eleanor McFeely.
1795, Oct.   22, McKinley, Martha, and Patrick Kelly.
1793, Nov.   28, McKinney, Jean, and John Wills.
1795, June   17, McKinney, Mordecai, and Polly Chambers.
1801, Nov.   5, McKinney, Nancy, and Mathew Thompson.
1791, March   22, McKinney, Polley, and James Read Hoge.
1802, Nov.   23, McKinney, Samuel, and Eleanor Irvine.
1803, Nov.   8, McKnight, Elizabeth, and Hugh Maffit.
1787, Nov.   14, McKnight, John, and Grifey Sanderson.
1810, April   5, McKown, John, and Margaret Porter.
1802, Oct.   21, McLaughlin, Neal, and Piety Porter.
1800, Oct.   2, McLaughlin, Unity, and Dennis Denny.
1789, April   28, McMichael, Daniel, and Jean Orvan.
1798, Feb.   27, McMullen, William, and Mary White.
1805, June   13, McMurray, Ann, and Jacob Miller.
1792, Feb.   2, McNealans, William, and Polley Reaugh.
1807, Jan.   16, McPherson, Polly, and John Brown.
1809, Oct.   5, McPherson, Robert, and Mary Lyon.
1798, March   22, McQueon, Mary, and James Anderson.
1793, March   21, McQueon, Rosanna, and Alexander Work.
1810, Feb.   15, McWilliams, Ann, and William Davidson.
1790, Sept.   9, Means, Allen, and Elizabeth Dunbar.
1798, Feb.   12, Mehaffy Bridget, and Thomas Mehaffy.
1798, Feb.   12, Mehaffy, Thomas, and Bridget Mehaffy.
1794, July   26, Mercer, Margaret, and Harris Kennedy.
1802, Oct.   14, Mickey, Mary, and Hugh Hazleton.
1798, Aug.   16, Miller, Andrew, and Elizabeth Huston.
1808, Jan.   14, Miller, Catharine, and James McKimm.
1809, Oct.   17, Miller, Elizabeth, and Capt. Geo. Ege.
1789, May   13, Miller, Elizabeth, and John Clayton.
1785, May   11, Miller, Henry, and Margaret Aspel.
1802, Nov.   2, Miller, Henry, and Nancy Ferguson.
1805, June   13, Miller, Jacob, and Ann McMurray.
1792, Dec.   18, Miller, Jean, and William Alexander.
1794, April   15, Miller, John, and Jean Temple.

1804, April   6, Miller, Mary, and John Hannon.
1808, Feb.   4, Miller, Philip, and Catharine Crocket.
1786, Sept. 22, Miller, Ruth, and Archibald McGrew.
1791, Jan.   6, Miller, William, and Eleanor Styles.
1794, June 10, Milligan, Jane, and James Bell.
1796, July 27, Milligan, Margaret, and Francis Jameson.
1785, April 19, Milligan, W^m, and Margaret Sweeney.
1811, Dec. 19, Mitchell, Eleanor, and Robert Irvine.
1794, June 10, Mitchell, John, and Mary Blair.
1806, April   1, Mitchell, William, and Guinthlen Kirkpatrick.
1788, Nov.   6, Mollan, Lancelot, and Sarah Brisland.
1801, Nov.   5, Montgomery, Elizabeth, and Francis Connor.
1791, Sept. 28, Montgomery, Hetty, and John Morrison.
1787, Nov. 15, Montgomery, Jenny, and Saml Edmiston.
1807, April 30, Montgomery, Margaret, and Dr. Robert Davidson.
1809, Oct. 10, Montgomery, Robert, and Catharine Clark.
1798, Nov. 13, Montgomery, Sally, and David Harris.
1793, May   1, Montgomery, Samuel, and Polley Ramsey.
1807, Nov.   5, Montgomery, Sarah, and William Porter.
1792, May 23, Moore, Alexander, and Mary Brice.
1795, May 11, Moore, Jane, and Adam Green.
1798, Jan.   9, Moore, Nancy, and Samuel Galbreath.
1801, July 30, Moore, Polly, and William Baker.
1804, March 29, Moore, Rebecca, and John Cummins.
1799, April 17, Moorehead, Robert, and Sarah Brandon.
1796, March 15, Moorhead, Edward. and Sarah Passel.
1793, April 23, Morrison, Daniel, and Jeane Lemmon.
1795, Nov. 12, Morrison, Hans, (of Pittsburgh,) and Peggy Pol-
              lock.
1791, Sept. 28, Morrison, John, and Hetty Montgomery.
1795, Oct. 22, Murdack, Matthew, and Mary McElravy.
1809, Jan. 24, Murdock, William, and Ann Clendenon.
1788, Nov.   3, Murphy, Hercules, and Kitty McCloud.
1790, Feb. 17, Murray, David, and Ann McCleland.
1804, June 21, Murray, George, and Polly Denny.
1795, April   9, Murray, William, and Ann McAdams.
1798, April   3, Neely, James, and Peggy McBeth.
1793, Aug.   8, Neil, Polley, and John Anderson.
1805, April 30, Neilan, Mary, and David Lisle.
1793, Sept. 13, Neilson, Polley, and William Powers.
1807, Aug. 19, Neily, Elizabeth, and John Camblin.
1792, April   6, Neily, Joseph, and Esther Adams.
1798, Jan.   2, Nimmon, Sarah, and James Crocket.
1792, Nov. 16, Nimmons, Agness, and William Grayson.
1801, Jan. 28, Nimmons, Polly, and George Davidson.
1812, April 30, Nisbet, John, and Isabella Davidson.

1793, June   20, Nixon, W^m, and Margaret Graham.
1810, March 15, Noble, Francis, and Margaret Martin.
1801, Feb.   19, Noble, James, and Polly Cooper.
1800, June   25, Norton, Elizabeth, and Wm Shields.
1793, Oct.   31, Officer, David, and Elizabeth Walker.
1796, May   31, Officer, John, and Margaret Officer.
1796, May   31, Officer, Margaret, and John Officer.
1806, March 15, Officer, Rebecca, and Samuel Culbertson.
1800, March 31, Offly, Lieut. David, and Polly Grier.
1790, May   4, Oliver, Elizabeth, and James Thompson.
1811, April 15, Oliver, Jane, and Wm Laughlin.
1792, Feb.   14, Oliver, Thomas, and Isabella Smith.
1806, Feb.   18, Oriswell, James, and Jane Christy.
1798, Oct.   9, Orr, ——, and Adam Simonton.
1794, Jan.   31, Orr, David, and Rebecca Stephenson.
1797, Dec.   1, Orr, James, and Margaret Thompson.
1789, April 28, Orvan, Jean, and Daniel McMichael.
1786, Nov.   6, Parker, James, and Elizabeth McCallister.
1797, March   9, Parker, Rebecca, and Charles McClure.
1786, May   3, Parker, Thomas, and Lydia McDowel.
1788, Oct.   28, Parker, William, and Elizabeth Templeton.
1811, Nov.   12, Parkinson, Robert, and Maria Hatton.
1807, Aug.   20, Parks, William, and Elizabeth Flannigan.
1793, May   1, Passel, John, and Mary Rowen.
1789, Dec.   18, Passel, Mary, and James Love.
1796, March 15, Passel, Sarah, and Edward Moorhead.
1792, Nov.   23, Patterson, George, and Nancy Holmes.
1794, April   8, Patterson, Jean, and James Walker.
1806, July   24, Patterson, Mrs. ——, and William Patton.
1796, April 19, Patterson, William, and Eva Pense.
1791, Nov.   29, Patton, Mary, and Michael McKimmon.
1787, May   30, Patton, William, and Margaret Silvers.
1806, July   24, Patton, William, and Mrs. —— Patterson.
1800, June   16, Peeling, Elizabeth, and Robert Linch.
1796, April 19, Pense, Eva, and William Patterson.
1789, Sept. 29, Penwell, Sarah, and Rogers Carothers.
1805, Aug.   8, Philips, George, and Nancy Boyer.
1809, May   30, Philips, Mary, and John Breden.
1807, May   10, Phillips, Martha, and Hugh Rodey.
1788, Feb.   26, Pierce, Joseph, and Jean McCallister.
1803, May   4, Pinkerton, James, and Betsey Culens.
1797, Sept. 20, Polaine, Ephraim, and Mrs. —— Duncan.
1788, May   24, Pollock, Eleanor, and James Armstrong.
1800, Feb.   13, Pollock, Jared, and Mary Briggs.
1809, June   8, Pollock, Margaret, and John Boileau.

1795, Nov.   12, Pollock, Peggy, and Hans Morrison, (of Pittsburgh.)
1808, Nov.   24, Pollock, Susanna, and James Scott.
1810, April   5, Porter, Margaret, and John McKown.
1804, Jan.   12, Porter, Mary, and Samuel Adams.
1802, Oct.   21, Porter, Piety, and Neal McLaughlin.
1807, Nov.   5, Porter, William, and Sarah Montgomery.
1800, Dec.   18, Postlethwaite, Amelia, and Henry Coulter.
1799, April 10, Postlethwaite, Dr. James, and Elizabeth Smith.
1787, Jan.   3, Postlethwaite, Joseph, and Mary Wilkins.
1800, June   26, Potts, Hugh H., and Betsey Hughes.
1789, June   29, Power, Sarah, and Patrick, McCabe.
1793, Sept. 13, Powers, William, and Polley Nelson.
1793, Nov.   17, Price, Richard, and Grace Kelly.
1790, Feb.   13, Provens, Charles, and Mary Ann Provens.
1790, Feb.   13, Provens, Mary Ann, and Charles Provens.
1800, June   12, Putman, Edwin, Esq., and Elizabeth Davis.
1809, Feb.   2, Quigley, Anna, and Thomas Hunter.
1809, March   7, Quigley, Christopher, and Mary Hunter.
1811, Sept.   5, Quigley, James. and Elizabeth Wise.
1808, Sept. 13, Quigley, Patty, and John Carothers.
1796, April 14, Rainey, Charles, and Nancy McDowel.
1798, Sept. 28, Ralston, Ann, and James Marshbanks.
1798, April 24, Ramsay, Agnes, and Richard Weston.
1795, April   2, Ramsay, Mary, and Andrew Dickson.
1804, June   14, Ramsay, William, and Eliz. Sneider.
1794, May   8, Ramsey, Margaret, and Samuel Jackson.
1785, Sept. 13, Ramsey, Oliver, and Mary Kirk.
1793, May   1, Ramsey, Polley, and Samuel Montgomery.
1796, Nov.   24, Randolph, Paul, and Susanna Fleming.
1786, Dec.   26, Randolph, Rebecca, and Wm Sanderson.
1793, May   14, Randolph, Tanny, and James Fleming.
1807, April 30, Rayny, Mary, and John Kerrau.
1792, March   1, Read, Robert, and Rachel McClintock.
1792, Feb.   2, Reaugh, Polley, and William McNealans.
1787, Dec.   25, Redman, Sarah, and William Earls.
1812, March 17, Reece, Hannah, and Jonathan Walker.
1786, Oct.   30, Reed, Geo., (of N. Castle,) and Maria Thompson.
1790, Oct.   21, Reed, Samuel, and Agness Cowher.
1785, March   1, Reed, Samuel, and Mary Lamb.
1807, June   18, Reighter, George, and Salome McFeely.
1812, April 23, Reily, James, and Sarah Franks.
1802, Sept.   6, Rheinhart, Mary, and George Biegle.
1796, Jan.   26, Rhinehart, John, and Polly Magee.
1804, Sept.   4, Richison, George, and Rebecca Gibson.
1811, Nov.   12, Riddle, James M., and Elizabeth Weaver.

1799, Nov.   21, Riddle, Mary, and Joseph Latshaw.
1795, Oct.   13, Right, Elizabeth, and Jacob Cook.
1801, March 12, Rippet, Hannah, and Joseph Shaw.
1801, May   26, Rippeth, Mary, and John Mathers.
1789, May   15, Roach, Mary, and W^m McGranahan.
1790, March 15, Roath, Lydia, and Henry Isett.
1792, March 22, Robeson, Abigail, and William Boyd.
1792, April 12, Robeson, Alexander, and Jane Sanderson.
1800, June   26, Robeson, Margaret, and James McKinley.
1791, May   17, Robeson, Mary, and John Cromley.
1807, May   10, Rodey, Hugh, and Martha Phillips.
1809, April 17, Rogers, William, and Margaret Scott.
1803, April 28, Rose, Nancy, and Benjamin Henderson.
1788, Feb.   1, Rosebury, John, and Mary Hayes.
1789, Sept. 23, Ross, James, and Catharine Irwin.
1803, May   5, Ross, Peggy, and John Drennen.
1793, Oct.   22, Rowan, Margaret, and Joseph Gold.
1793, Nov.   14, Rowan, Peggy, and John Stewart.
1793, April 23, Rowan, Rebecca, and James Gass.
1785, April 19, Rowan, Stewart, and Jane Lamb.
1793, May   1, Rowen, Mary, and John Passel.
1786, May   31. Ruggles, Thomas, and Margaret Coots.
1794, Feb.   20, Rumble, Henry, and Elizabeth Allen.
1806, Dec.   23, Rupert, Michael, and Nancy Smith.
1799, Jan.   24, Russel, Sarah, and Andrew Dowds.
1808, June   31, Rutledge, William, and Peggy Waugh.
1787, Nov.   14, Sanderson, Grifey, and John McKnight.
1792, April 12, Sanderson, Jane, and Alexander Robeson.
1798, April 12, Sanderson, Jane, and James Alexander.
1789, June   30, Sanderson, Margaret, and Samuel Smiley.
1792, Nov.   20, Sanderson, Patty, and Dr. James McClain.
1786, Dec.   26, Sanderson, W^m, and Rebecca Randolph.
1792, Feb.   2. Scott, Alexander, and Martha Stewart.
1804, April 19, Scott, James, and Polly Scott.
1808, Nov.   24, Scott, James, and Susanna Pollock.
1792, Feb.   29, Scott, John, and Mary McCord.
1809, April 17, Scott, Margaret, and William Rogers.
1804, April 19, Scott, Polly, and James Scott.
1792, April 23, Scroggs, Miriam, and William Work.
1804, Nov.   15, Searight, Alex^r, and Elizabeth Lobaugh.
1789, April 26, Searight, Ann, and Francis Hutchinson.
1798, Aug.   8, Seetin, Robert, and Jane McCabe.
1811, March 13, Seeton, Jane, and Robert Crawford.
1808, Nov.   3, Seidle, Elizabeth, and Samuel Waugh.
1803, Sept. 22, Seiler, Jacob, and Christiana Feyerabend.
1801, Oct.   27, Selander, Christian, and Eliz. Wunderlich.

1791, Feb.   10, Semple, Sarah, and John Sterrett.
1803, July   26, Sensabough, Christian, and Susanna Hertzel.
1800, March 27, Sexton, Margaret, and John Douglass.
1811, Aug.   15, Shaddin, Robert, and Fanny Hoge.
1788, Nov.   4, Sharon, Elizabeth, and William Steel.
1791, Jan.   13, Sharon, Isabella, (alias Peggy,) and Geo. Ferguson.
1792, Oct.   10, Sharp, Elizabeth, and John Smith.
1801, March 12, Shaw, Joseph, and Hannah Rippet.
1787, March 20, Shaw, Nancy, and William Leviston.
1794, April 10, Shaw, Philip, and Elizabeth McGrew.
1800, June   25, Shields, W^m, and Elizabeth Norton.
1789, Nov.   25, Shortie, Mary, and Robert Lackey.
1795, Aug.   31, Sibbet, Agnes, and Samuel Gourley.
1796, Feb.   1, Sibbet, Jane, and Samuel Copely.
1787, May   30, Silvers, Margaret, and William Patton.
1793, April 11, Simison, Samuel, and Peggy Denny.
1802, Feb.   18, Simmons, Nancy, and Joseph Turner.
1792, May   24, Simonds, Jean, and Daniel McDaniel.
1798, Oct.   9, Simonton Adam, and ——— Orr.
1793, May   14, Simund, Elizabeth, and Andrew Huston.
1803, Nov.   1, Skyles, John, and Elizabeth Kean.
1794, Dec.   15, Sloane, James, and Peggy Holtzopple.
1802, May   25, Smiley, Elizabeth, and Benj. Cunningham.
1789, June   30, Smiley, Samuel, and Margaret Sanderson.
1789, March 23, Smiley, Thomas, and Genny Sterret.
1785, July   23, Smith, Brice, and Eleanor Kenny.
1798, Sept.   6, Smith, Dorothy, and John Donelly.
1807, March 19, Smith, Eleanor, and William Lang.
1799, April 10, Smith, Elizabeth, and Dr. James Postlethwaite.
1807, Sept. 10, Smith, Elizabeth, and George Cauffman.
1785, Nov.   21, Smith, George, and Isabella Stevens.
1792, Feb.   14, Smith, Isabella, and Thomas Oliver.
1795, Oct.   26, Smith, James, and Betsey Dunlap.
1786, Sept.   7, Smith, John, and Elizabeth Davis.
1796, April   5, Smith, John, and Elizabeth Davis.
1792, Oct.   10, Smith, John, and Elizabeth Sharp.
1791, Jan.   5, Smith, Margaret, and James Anderson.
1806, Nov.   20, Smith, Mary, and William McFeely.
1806, Dec.   23, Smith, Nancy, and Michael Rupert.
1792, Oct.   19, Smith, Peggy, and John Arthurs.
1791, May   12, Smith, Robert, and Susanna Lyne.
1791, Jan.   4, Smith, Sarah, and Daniel McKinley.
1806, April 22, Smith, Sidney, and Byers Alexander, Esq.
1789, Sept. 10, Smith, Thomas, and Rebecca Watson.
1794, April   4, Smith, William, and Margaret Gillmor.
1804, June   14, Sneider, Eliz., and William Ramsay.

1792, May   24, Snowden, Nathanael, and Sally Gustin.
1809, Aug.   17, Snyder, Henry, and Rachel Line.
1807, April   28, Spangler, Philip, and Mary Line.
1788, March 18, Sparr, George, and Letty McAfee.
1806, Nov.   25, Spottswood, Jane, and Jacob Allen.
1793, April   9, Spottswood, Rachel, and Hugh McAnulty.
1795, April   30, Stair, Elizabeth, and Henry Coover.
1806, Dec.   2, Stansbury, Peggy, and Francis Lewis.
1792, Oct.   9, Steel, Jean, and Gershom Craft.
1794, Feb.   4, Steel, Omelia, and James Given.
1804, May   1, Steel, Polly, and Dr. Geo. Foulk.
1788, Nov.   4, Steel, William, and Elizabeth Sharon.
1806, Feb.   22, Steen, Jane, and William Coulter.
1799, Dec.   17, Stephenson, Isabella, and Thomas Armstrong
1785, July   5, Stephenson, Jean, and Edward West.
1785, May   31, Stephenson, Nancy, and John Holmes.
1789, June   18, Stephenson, Polley, and Dr. James Armstrong.
1794, Jan.   31, Stephenson, Rebecca, and David Orr.
1812, Jan.   30, Sterrett, David, and Jane Burney.
1789, March 23, Sterrett, Genny, and Thomas Smiley.
1796, June   9, Sterrett, John, and Emelia Frazer.
1801, Oct.   27, Sterrett, John, and Nancy Chambers.
1791, Feb.   10, Sterrett, John, and Sarah Semple.
1792, June   28, Sterrett, Nancy, and Adam Logue.
1799, Jan.   3, Stevens, Eleanor, and Henry McKinley.
1785, Nov.   21, Stevens, Isabella, and George Smith.
1812, April   9, Stewart, Andrew, and Isabella Craighead.
1793, Nov.   14, Stewart, John, and Peggy Rowan.
1792, Feb.   2, Stewart, Martha, and Alexander Scott.
1791, Nov.   8, Stewart, Martha, and Jacob Walters.
1793, Feb.   13, Stewart, Mary, and Daniel McKee.
1793, April   17, Stewart, Robert, and Roseanna McClune.
1800, Oct.   1, Stewart, Sarah, and Conrad Bollinger.
1792, Sept.   13, Stewart, Sarah, and John Walker.
1808, Oct.   4, Stiles, Edward, and Ann Duncan.
1811, Feb.   12, Stiles, Margaret, and Stephen Duncan, Esq.
1793, Oct.   29, Stone, Ann, and Isaac Williams.
1796, July   26, Stone, John, and Martha Wilson.
1791, Jan.   6, Styles, Eleanor, and William Miller.
1785, April   19, Sweeney, Margaret, and Wᵐ Milligan.
1791, Aug.   3, Sweiner, Barbara, and George Warner.
1795, April   13, Sweney, Charles, and Mary Griffin.
1799, Oct.   8, Sweney, Hugh, and Catharine Duffey.
1787, April   23, Swingel, George, and Magdalina Dederick.
1794, April   15, Temple, Jean, and John Miller.
1788, Oct.   28, Templeton, Elizabeth, and William Parker.

1804, April   19, Thompson, Abraham, and Leah Wolf.
1797, Nov.   29, Thompson, Elizabeth, and George McCullogh.
1790, May   4, Thompson, James, and Elizabeth Oliver.
1808, Oct.   4, Thompson, Jane, and David McCormick.
1802, Nov.   25, Thompson, John, and Margaret Holmes.
1797, Dec.   1, Thompson, Margaret, and James Orr.
1786, Oct.   30, Thompson, Maria, and George Reed, of N. Castle.
1790, Oct.   16, Thompson, ———, and Martha French.
1801, Nov.   5, Thompson, Matthew, and Nancy McKinney.
1808, Oct.   10, Thompson, Samuel, and Lettitia Brown.
1788, June   10, Thompson, William, and Hannah Wallace.
1775, Nov.   24, Thompson, William, and Jean McFarlane.
1789, March   2, Tongue, John, and Nancy Camble.
1794, June   24, Tremble, Rebecca, and John Donaldson.
1790, Nov.   4, Trimble, George, and Martha Waugh.
1811, March   28, Trimble, Thomas, and Mary Woods.
1793, Dec.   19, Trindle, Alexander, and Sarah Crocket.
1795, April   8, Trindle, John, and Margaret Waddel.
1806, Nov.   14, Trit, Peter, and Sally Line.
1802, Aug.   17, Trotter, Mary, and John Blackwood.
1802, Feb.   18, Turner, Joseph, and Nancy Simmons.
1788, Jan.   7, Turner, Sally, and Edward McGonagle.
1792, Sept.   29, Urie, John, and Mary Cunningham.
1793, Feb.   7, Urie, Thomas, and Margaret Dunbar.
1797, Dec.   27, Uroth, Robt. Mason, and Mary Augney.
1795, April   8, Waddel, Margaret, and John Trindle.
1794, Oct.   9, Wade, Gilbert, and Margaret Black.
1792, Nov.   12, Walker, Betsey, and Joseph Anderson.
1793, Oct.   31, Walker, Elizabeth, and David Officer.
1798, May   16, Walker, Hannah, and Henry Knittle.
1812, March   26, Walker, Hugh, and Elizabeth Barber.
1794, April   8, Walker, James, and Jean Patterson.
1792, Sept.   13, Walker, John, and Sarah Stewart.
1812, March   17, Walker, Jonathan, and Hannah Reece.
1798, Aug.   29, Walker, Margaret, and James Martin.
1805, Oct.   3, Walker, Robert, and Mary Latcha.
1788, June   10, Wallace, Hannah, and William Thompson.
1804, May   3, Wallace, Isabella, and Moses Bayles.
1805, Nov.   1, Wallace, Polly, and Peter Gerhart.
1790, Nov.   24, Wallace, Rachel, and Charles Bovard.
1791, Nov.   8, Walters, Jacob, and Martha Stewart.
1804, July   3, Wareham, Philip, and Mary Johnston.
1791, Aug.   3, Warner, George, and Barbara Sweiner.
1801, Dec.   10, Watson, Doctor, and Polly Davis.
1798, June   21, Watson, Joseph, and Ann Beckwith.
1789, Sept.   10, Watson, Rebecca, and Thomas Smith.

1790, Nov.   4, Waugh, Martha, and George Trimble.
1807, Dec.   31, Waugh, Martha, and John Clendenen.
1808, June   31, Waugh, Peggy, and William Rutledge.
1808, Nov.   3, Waugh, Samuel, and Elizabeth Seidle.
1791, July   15, Waugh, Samuel, and Jean Grayson.
1811, Mareh 14, Weakley, James, and Priscilla Faulke.
1796, May   31, Weakley, Jane, and Nathan Woods.
1809, Oct.   16, Weakley, Jane, and Rev. John Wright.
1806, Dec.   17, Weakley, Mary, and Alexander Brown.
1800, Oct.   30, Weakley, Rebecca, and Abraham Holmes.
1796, Nov.   15, Weakley Rebecca, and Thomas Craighead.
1809, March 30, Weakley Thomas, and Nancy Alexander.
1811, Nov.   12, Weaver, Elizabeth, and James M. Riddle.
1801, March 17, Weaver, Margaret, and Bailey Long.
1788, Aug.   6, Webster, William, and Isabel Forsyth.
1808, Jan.   26, Welsh, Sarah, and Jacob Burkholder.
1785, July   5, West, Edward, and Jean, Stephenson.
1798, April 24, Weston, Richard, and Agnes Ramsay.
1805, Feb.   18, White, Edward, and Mary Cooney.
1789, April 16, White, Francis, and Martha Barker.
1798, Feb.   27, White, Mary, and William McMullen.
1790, Sept. 30, White, Nancy, and Gilson Craighead.
1797, Dec.   25, White, Sarah, and John Gibbon.
1796, April 19, White, Thomas, and Sarah Clark.
1790, July   8, Whitehill, Rachel, and Alex^r McBeth.
1787, Jan.   3, Wilkins, Mary, and Joseph Postlethwaite.
1789, Feb.   16, Williams, Edward, and Mary Christie.
1793, Oct.   29, Williams, Isaac, and Ann Stone.
1805, Feb.   5, Williams, Matthew, and Jane Crain.
1798, Jan.   11, Williamson, Polly, and John McCullough.
1793, Nov.   28, Wills, John and Jean McKinney.
1796, April 20, Wilson, Elizabeth, and John McCartney.
1794, Sept. 22, Wilson, Elizabeth, and Patrick Greer.
1803, Jan.   1, Wilson, Hannah, and James Bell.
1791, Oct.   31, Wilson, Henry, and Betsey Brown.
1805, May   2, Wilson, James, and Margaret Kilgore.
1807, Oct.   26, Wilson, Jane, and Samuel Guthrie.
1796, Dec.   22, Wilson, Jenny, and Samuel Caldwell.
1796, July   26, Wilson, Martha, and John Stone.
1803, Nov.   3, Wilson, Ruth, and James Mather.
1789, Oct.   22, Wilson, Samuel, and Margaret Lutz.
1803, Oct.   13, Wilson, Samuel, and Sarah Martin.
1791, Aug.   25, Wilson, William, and Eleanor Little.
1809, June   15, Winger, Hannah, and Samuel Lefevre.
1811, Sept.   5, Wise, Elizabeth, and James Quigley.
1803, May   2, Wise, John, and Catharine Kennedy.

1804, April 19, Wolf, Leah, and Abraham Thompson.
1804, Jan.   2, Wood, Catharine, and Robert Forbs.
1804, Jan.   12, Woods, David, and Miss Loudon.
1812, Aug.   13, Woods, Elizabeth, and George Grier.
1804, June   1, Woods, John, and Mary Woods.
1791, July   7, Woods, Mary Ann, and William Gladney.
1811, Oct.   22, Woods, Mary, and George Davidson.
1804, June   1, Woods, Mary, and John Woods.
1811, March 28, Woods, Mary, and Thomas Trimble.
1796, May   31, Woods, Nathan, Jane Weakley.
1793, Aug.   23, Woods, Peggy, and Daniel Holmes.
1794, May   8, Woodward, Jehu, and Jean Clendenan.
1800, May   10, Woodward, Sergt. Benj., and Elizabeth Hague.
1793, March 21, Work, Alexander, and Rosanna McQueen.
1785, March 1, Work, William, and Mary Eaken.
1792, April 23, Work, William, and Miriam Scroggs.
1809, Oct.   16, Wright, Rev. John, and Jane Weakley.
1798, Nov.   20, Wright, Robert, and Agness Holmes.
1801, Oct.   27, Wunderlich, Eliz., and Christian Selander.
1788, July   18, Young, Joseph, and Agness Bell.
1800, Sept. 25, Young, Mary, and Joseph Alexander.
1788, March 20, Young, Sarah, and George Gillespie.

MARRIAGE RECORD

OF

ST. PAUL'S EPISCOPAL CHURCH,

CHESTER,

1704–1733.

1732–3, Feb. 2, Aaron, John, and Sarah Keyser.
1704, Nov. 21, Adams, William, and Sarah Hall.
1704, May 6, Addams, Samuel, and Elizabeth Allen.
1704, May 6, Allen, Elizabeth, and Samuel Addams.
1730–1, Mar. 24, Anderson, Henry, aud Sarah Evans.
1704–5, Jan. 15, Andree, Joanna, and John Langford.
1729, Aug. 31, Atkinson, Michael, and Susannah Weston.
1713, Dec. 21, Bainton, Rebecca, and Thomas Weston.
1705, May 15, Baker, Nathan, and Sarah Collet.
1730, May 8, Baker, Sarah, and Philip Ottey.
1712–13, Feb. 6, Baldwin, Joseph, and Elizabeth Mealis.
1713–14,Mar. 29, Baldwin, Thomas, and Mary Beel.
1705, Dec. 20, Bane, Mordecai, and Naomi Medley.
1730, Oct. 12, Barker, Mary, and John Young.
1706, Sept. 25, Barker, Mary, and William Richardson.
1731–2, Feb. 20, Barnet, Sarah, and Greg. Cook.
1730, Nov. 4, Barnett, Margaret, and John Wood.
1730, Oct. 8, Barton, Thomas, and Sarah Mather.
1733, July 11, Baufort, Ann, and John Taylor.
1729, May 18, Bear, Samuel, and Katherine Rowland.
1713–14,Mar. 29, Beel, Mary, and Thomas Baldwin.
1729–30, Feb. 2, Beg, James, and Elizabeth Hartnet.
1731–2, Feb. 25, Bell, Mary, and Jeremiah Garraway.
1732, July 25, Bertram, Jane, and Richard Colse.
1730, Oct. 20, Best, John, and Martha Jones.
1711, Nov. 27, Bever, William, and Mary Rodes.
1729–30, Jan. 5, Bishop, Mary, and Andrew Cox.
1704, Dec. 7, Bony, Mary, and Joseph Collins.
1829–30, Jan. 15, Boon, Ann, and John Rawson.
1731–2, Feb. 10, Boris, Nicholas, and Mary Yeates.
1730, Dec. 21, Bound, Katherine, and Andrew Heydon.
1730, July 27, Bourn, Benjamin, and Katherine Parker.
1732, July 25, Boyd, Patrick, and Rachel Grimson.
1730, June 15, Bradley, James, and Elizabeth Till.
1705–6, Jan. 15, Broom, Ann, and Nathaniel Tucker.
1711, Dec. 4, Broom, Thomas, and Elizabeth Hanum.
1729, Aug. 21, Broomeil, Jane, and Aaron Thompson.
1730–1, Jan. 17, Broydon, Prudence, and John Moore.

1732, June　11, Burns, Elizabeth, and Charles Reynolds.
1705, June　 5, Carel, Margaret, and Robert Jones.
1733, May　 1, Carr, Ann, and George Machiel.
1731-2, Feb. 28, Carte, Patrick, and Margaret Skelton.
1730, Sept. 29, Chaffin, Solomon, and Ann Jefferys.
1729-30, Mar.15, Chest, Hannah, and William Wright.
1730, Dec.　20, Clifft, Edward, and Mary Pouton.
1730, June　 8, Colburn, Dinah, and Edward Russell.
1732, July　22, Coleburn, Roger, and Eleanor Higgins.
1705, May　15, Collet, Sarah, and Nathan Baker.
1704, Dec.　 7, Collins, Joseph, and Mary Bony.
1732, July　25, Colse, Richard, and Jane Bertram.
1731-2, Feb. 20, Cook, Greg., and Sarah Barnet.
1712, Aug.　12, Cook, Catherine, and Richard Willatson.
1705, Nov,　 8, Cooper, James, and Mary Ludurdge.
1704, March 24, Cornish, Mary, and James Mills.
1733, June　 3, Cornwell, Mary, and Christ. Hemmings.
1729-30, Jan. 5, Cox, Andrew, and Mary Bishop.
1743, April　12, Cox, Jonathan, and Susannah ———.
1706, June　 7, Crafts, Robert, and Hilsha Vannemmon.
1731, April　28, Cranesbury, Margaret, and Shelsto Moony.
1739,-1 March 7, Culbertson, Margaret, and Robert Jackson.
1730-1, March 9, Culin, Barbara, and Joseph Robinet.
1733, May　 1, Culin, Margaret, and Titus Dinnsie.
1730, Dec.　31, Curry, John, and Mary Jenkins.
1730, Nov.　10, Danger, Annabal, and Benjamin Manifold.
1728, Dec.　23, Davil, Evan, and Rachel Messer.
1729, Sept.　15, Davis, Ann, and William Evans.
1704, Aug.　 4, Davis, James, and Martha Jones.
1706-7, Mar. 13, Davis, John, and Mary Jones.
1706-7, Feb. 13, Davis, Margaret, and Thomas Waters.
1729, Nov.　24, Davis, Mary, and James Summers.
1729-30, Mar.18, Davis, Rachel, and Jonathan Smith.
1733, May　 1, Dinnsie Titus, and Margaret Culin.
1729-30, Feb. 4, Dirrick, Lidda, and Allen Robinet.
1730, Dec.　25, Donaldson, Patrick, and Elizabeth Philips.
1743, April　 5, Evans, Marg^t, and John ———.
1730-1, Mar. 24, Evans, Sarah, and Henry Anderson.
1729, Sept.　15, Evans, William, and Ann Davis.
1730-1, Mar. 28, Fell, William, and Ann Thompson.
1733, May　27, Fitsher, John, and Mary Jones.
1731, April　 5, Flemins, Martha, and James Webb.
1706, Sept.　24, Foresithe, Elizabeth, and Thomas Gale.
1731, May　30, France, Ellin, and John Wallace.
1731-2, Feb. 14, Francis, Jane, and Lewis Lloyd.
1705, Nov.　10, Friend, Barbara, and Peter Longacre.

1706, Sept.   24, Gale, Thomas, and Elizabeth Foresithe.
1731, April   21, Garrat, Thomas, and Katherine Lancaster.
1731-2, Feb. 25, Garraway, Jeremiah, and Mary Bell.
1731, April   20, Garren, Paul, and Mary Hopman.
1707, April   17, Gatchell, Elizabeth, and Henry Nichols.
1729, Aug.   3, Gill, Margaret, and John Patterson.
1729, May   5, Godfrey, Eliz., and Chris. Ottey.
1730, Nov.   22, Graham, William, and Jenet Morgan.
1733, June   3, Gregory, Esther, and Robert Skien.
1732, July   25, Grimson, Rachel, and Patrick Boyd.
1729-30, Jan. 5, Hall, Hannah, and Patrick MacMannus.
1708, May   10, Hall, Sarah, and George Robertson.
1704, Nov.   21, Hall, Sarah, and William Adams.
1731, April   23, Hall, William, and Hannah Richardson.
1711, Dec.   4, Hanum, Elizabeth, and Thomas Broom.
1707, Dec.   1, Hardwick, Mary, and William Loyd.
1730-1, Feb. 17, Hart, George, and Elizabeth Lyon.
1729-30, Feb. 2, Hartnet, Elizabeth, and James Beg.
1733, June   3, Hemmings, Christ., and Mary Cornwell.
1729, Dec.   2, Hendrickson, Peter, and Anna Robinson.
1713, Dec.   30, Hersden, Richard, and Ann Simons.
1730, Dec.   21, Heydon, Andrew, and Katherine Bound.
1706, Nov.   13, Hift, Ruth, and James Lloyd.
1732, July   22, Higgins, Eleanor, and Roger Coleburn.
1730-1, Mar. 25, Hine, Jacobus, and Margaret Morton.
1731, April   20, Hopman, Mary, and Paul Garren.
1730-1, Feb. 27, Hoskins, Mary, and John Mather.
1730, July   1, Howell, Ann, and Richard Hues.
1729, July   1, Howell, Ann, and Richard Huet.
1705, June   6, Howell, Barbara, and Walter Martin.
1704, June   8, Howell, Mary, and Joseph Powell.
1704, June   8, Howell, Mary, and Walter Martin.
1732, April   10, Howman, Katherine, and George Newlin.
1730, Aug.   24, Huddston, Sarah, and John Van Culand.
1730, July   1, Hues, Richard, and Ann Howell.
1731, June   18, Hues, Sarah, and Samuel Ourn.
1729, July   1, Hult, Richard, and Ann Howell.
1729, April   24, Hunter, Sarah, and Henry Peirce,
1705, Aug.   18, Iddings, Richard, and Margaret Philips.
1730-1, Mar.   7, Jackson, Robert, and Margaret Culbertson.
1730, Sept.   29, Jefferys, Ann, and Solomon Chaffin.
1705, March   29, Jeffreys, Mary, and William Latton.
1730, Dec.   31, Jenkins, Mary, and John Curry.
1731, May   4, Johnson, Henry, and Dinah Stedham.
1730, Nov.   5, Johnson, Mary, and William Oliver.
1712, April   24, Jones, Charles, and Sara Peterson.

1730-1, Feb. 3, Jones, David, and Jane Thomas.

1706, Dec. 12, Jones, Hugh, and Jane Pugh.

1704, Aug. 4, Jones, Martha, and James Davis.

1730, Oct. 20, Jones, Martha, and John Best.

1706-7, Mar. 13, Jones, Mary, and John Davis.

1733, May 27, Jones, Mary, and John Fitsher.

1705, June 5, Jones, Robert, and Margaret Carel.

1731-2, Feb. 10, Kelly, Patrick, and Rachel Wineas.

1712-13, Feb. 3, Keyse, Sarah, and Thomas Powel.

1732-3, Feb. 2, Keyser, Sarah, and John Aaron.

1730, Aug. 5, Lack, John, and Elizabeth Martin.

1731, April 21, Lancaster, Katherine, and Thomas Garrat.

1704-5, Jan. 15, Langford, John, and Joanna Andree.

1705, May 29, Latton, William, and Mary Jeffreys.

1713-14, Feb. 9, Linvel, Thomas, and Dinah Richards.

1706, Nov. 13, Lloyd, James, and Ruth Hift.

1731-2, Feb. 14, Lloyd, Lewis, and Jane Francis.

1729, Nov. 17, Lloyd, Margaret, and Thomas Wilkinson.

1730-1, Jan. 22, Lloyd, Thomas, and Ann Thomas.

1731, May 30, Loaden, Peter, and Elizabeth Parry.

1730-1, Mar. 27, Long, Abraham, and Ann Rumsey.

1729, Sept. 15, Longacre, Briget, and Joseph Tetlow.

1705, Nov. 10, Longacre, Peter, and Barbara Friend.

1707, Dec. 1, Loyd, William, and Mary Hardwick.

1705, Nov. 8, Ludurdge, Mary, and James Cooper.

1730-1, Feb. 17, Lyon, Elizabeth, and George Hart.

1712, May 10, MacDaniel, John, and Mary Robinson.

1733, May 1, Machiel, George, and Ann Carr.

1731, May 13, Mackgee, Richard, and Ann Sandeland.

1729-30, Jan. 5, McMannus, Patrick, and Hannah Hall.

1730, Nov. 10, Manifold, Benjamin, and Annabal Danger.

1730, Aug. 5, Martin, Elizabeth, and John Lack.

1705, June 6, Martin, Walter, and Barbara Howell.

1704, June 8, Martin, Walter, and Mary Howell.

1730-1, Feb. 27, Mather, John, and Mary Hoskins.

1730, Oct. 8, Mather, Sarah, and Thomas Barton.

1704-5, Jan. 2, Maurice, James, and Ann Taylor.

1712-13, Feb. 6, Mealis, Elizabeth, and Joseph Baldwin.

1705, Dec. 20, Medley, Naomi, and Mordecai Bane.

1704-5, Jan. 3, Meredith, David, and Sarah ———.

1732-3, Feb. 2, Meredith, James, and Mary Nicholas.

1728, Dec. 23, Messer, Rachel, and Evan Davil.

1731, May 1, Miller, Margaret, and Edward Nicholas.

1731, April 6, Miller, Richard, and Eliz. Willson.

1703-4, Mar. 24, Mills, James, and Mary Cornish.

1731, April 28, Moony, Shelsto, and Margaret Cranesbury.

1730–1, Jan. 17, Moore, John, and Prudence Broydon.
1730, Nov. 22, Morgan, Jenet, and William Graham.
1730–1, Mar. 25, Morton, Margaret, and Jacobus Hine.
1704, Dec. 20, Moulder, Elizabeth, and Thomas Pedrick.
1730–1, Feb. 25, Nevill, Ann, and Isaac Tunniclift.
1731, April 10, Newlin, George, and Katherine Howman.
1731, May 1, Nicholas, Edward, and Margaret Miller.
1732–3, Feb. 2, Nicholas, Mary, and James Meredith.
1707, April 17. Nichols, Henry, and Elizabeth Gatchell.
1731, April 13, Norrys, John, and Katherine Willdson.
1730, Nov. 5, Oliver, William, and Mary Johnson.
1729, May 5, Ottey, Chris., and Eliz. Godfrey.
1730, May 8, Ottey, Philip, and Sarah Baker.
1731, June 18, Ourn, Samuel, and Sarah Hues.
1730, July 27, Parker, Katherine, and Benjamin Bourn.
1731, May 30, Parry, Elizabeth, and Peter Loaden.
1729, Aug. 3, Patterson, John, and Margaret Gill.
1704, Dec. 20, Pedrick, Thomas, and Elizabeth Moulder.
1729, April 24, Peirce, Henry, and Sarah Hunter.
1730–1, Mch. 22, Penrose, Ann, and Thomas Wills.
1712, April 24, Peterson, Sara, and Charles Jones.
1730, Dec. 25, Philips, Elizabeth, and Patrick Donaldson.
1705, Aug. 18, Philips, Margaret, and Richard Iddings.
1729, April 24, Pierce, Henry, and Sarah Hunter.
1732, May 28, Porter, Margaret, and John Sterrill.
1730, Dec. 20, Pouton, Mary, and Edward Clifft.
1704, June 8, Powell, Joseph, and Mary Howell.
1712–13, Feb. 3, Powell, Thomas, and Sarah Keyse.
1730, Sept. 20, Price, Mary, and John Wyburn.
1730–1, Mch. 25, Pue, Margaret, and John Smith.
1706, Dec. 12, Pugh, Jane, and Hugh Jones.
1729–30, Jan. 15, Rawson, John, and Ann Boon.
1732, June 11, Reynolds, Charles, and Elizabeth Burns.
1713–14, Feb. 9, Richards, Dinah, and Thomas Linvel.
1730–1, Apl. 23, Richardson, Hannah, and William Hall.
1730–1, Feb. 28, Richardson, Richard, and Ann ———.
1706, Sept. 25, Richardson, William, and Mary Barker.
1707, Nov. 3, Roberts, David, and Susanna Tudor.
1708, May 10, Robertson, George, and Sarah Hall.
1729–30, Feb. 4, Robinet, Allan, and Lidda Dirrick.
1730–1, Mar. 9, Robinet, Joseph, and Barbarah Culin.
1729, Dec. 2, Robinson, Anna, and Peter Hendrickson.
1712, May 10, Robinson, Mary, and John MacDaniel.
1733, June 3, Rockafette, Eve, and John Smith.
1711, Nov. 27, Rodes, Mary, and William Bever.
1729, May 18, Rowland, Katherine, and Samuel Bear.

1730-1, Mar. 27, Rumsey, Ann, and Abraham Long.
1730, June   8, Russell, Edward, and Dinah Colburn.
1731, May   13, Sandeland, Ann, and Richard Mackgee.
1713, Dec.   30, Simons, Ann, and Richard Hersden.
1731-2, Feb. 28, Skelton, Margaret, and Patrick Carte.
1733, June   2, Skien, Robert, and Esther Gregory.
1733, June   3, Smith, John, and Eve Rockafette.
1730-1, Mar. 25, Smith, John, and Margaret Pue.
1729-30, Mar.18, Smith, Jonathan, and Rachel Davis.
1731, May   4, Stedham, Dinah, and Henry Johnson.
1733, May   28, Stephens, Sarah, and Edward Thomas.
1732, May   28, Sterrill, John, and Margaret Porter.
1729, Nov.   24, Summers, James, and Mary Davis.
1713-14, Mar.29, Tate, Magnes, and Honer Williams.
1704-5, Jan.   2, Taylor, Ann, and James Maurice.
1733, July   11, Taylor, John, and Ann Baufort.
1729, Sept.   15, Tetlow, Joseph, and Briget Longacre.
1730-1, Jan.   22, Thomas, Ann, and Thomas Lloyd.
1733, May   28, Thomas, Edward, and Sarah Stephens.
1730-1, Feb.   3, Thomas, Jane, and David Jones.
1729, Aug.   21, Thompson, Aaron, and Jane Broomell.
1730-1, Mar. 28, Thompson, Ann, and William Fell.
1729, Aug.   25, Thompson, Esther, and Edward Young.
1730, June   15, Till, Elizabeth, and James Bradley.
1705-6, Jan. 15, Tucker, Nathaniel, and Ann Broom.
1707, Nov.   3, Tudor, Susanna, and David Roberts.
1730-1, Feb. 25, Tunniclift, Isaac, and Ann Nevill.
1730, Aug.   30, Van Culand, John, and Sarah Huddston.
1706, June   7, Vannemmon, Hilsha, and Robert Crafts.
1731, May   30, Wallace, John, and Ellin France.
1706-7, Feb. 13, Waters, Thomas, and Margaret Davis.
1731, April   5, Webb, James, and Martha Flemins.
1729, Aug.   31, Weston, Susannah, and Michael Atkinson.
1713, Dec.   21, Weston, Thomas, and Rebecca Bainton.
1729, Nov.   17, Wilkinson, Thomas, and Margaret Lloyd.
1712, Aug.   12, Willatson, Richard, and Katherine Cook.
1731, April 13, Willdson, Katherine, and John Norrys.
1713-14, Mar. 29, William, Honer, and Magnes Tate.
1730-1, Mar. 22, Wills, Thomas, and Ann Penrose.
1731, April   6, Willson, Eliz., and Richard Miller.
1731-2, Feb. 10, Wineas, Rachel, and Patrick Kelly.
1730, Nov.   4, Wood, John, and Margaret Barnett.
1729-30, Mar. 15, Wright, William, and Hannah Chest.
1730, Sept.   20, Wyburn, John, and Mary Price.
1731-2, Feb. 10, Yeates, Mary, and Nicholas Boris.
1729, Aug.   25, Young, Edward, and Esther Thompson.
1730, Oct.   12, Young, John, and Mary Barker.

MARRIAGE RECORD

OF

THE REFORMED CHURCH,

FALKNER SWAMP, MONTGOMERY COUNTY, PA.

1748–1800.

REFORMED CHURCH, FALKNER SWAMP.

1783, June 24, Ache, Cathrina, and Adam Andreas.
1794, Nov. 6, Achy, Johanes, and Barbara Jung.
1792, May 9, Acker, Magdalena, and Jacob Buchwalter.
1772, May 19, Acker, Philip, and Elizabeth Fedel.
1798, May 8, Aker, Maria, and Josep Schmid.
1794, May 6, Albrecht, Catharina, and Johannes Bender.
1782, Nov. 5, Andrau, Susanna, and Samuel Hirsch.
1783, June 24, Andreas, Adam, and Cathrina Ache.
1783, May 20, Antes, Elizabeth, and Philip Bernhard.
1775, Aug. 17, Antes, Friedrich, and Catharina Schuhler.
1795, Aug. 23, Apt, Wilhelm, and Anna Wolfinger.
1790, Oct. 26, Bädmann, Johannes, and Hanna Brand.
1789, Nov. 30, Bar, Bernhard, and Margrith Langbein.
1791, Sept. 27, Baret, Johannes, and Margrith Sell.
1781, May 2, Barringer, Elisabeth, and John Jakson.
1775, Dec. 6, Bauer, Christian, and Catharina Seibert.
1790, Dec. 14, Bauer, Jacob, and Anna Fried.
1791, Aug. 23, Bauer, Margrith, and Samuel Davis.
1792, Oct. 30, Bechtel, Georg, and Henna Schweinhart.
1797, March 5, Bechtel, Johannes, and Maria Misemer.
1781, Jan. 2, Beck, Dorthea, and Johannes Restschneider.
1781, Dec. 4, Beck, Sophia, and Henrich Reifschneider.
1769, March 17, Becker, Daniel, and Anna Huber.
1798, Aug. 19, Beckers, Isaac, and Elizabeth Zeigler.
1783, March 27, Becker, Wilhelm, and Maria Reiffschneider.
1798, March 20, Beiteman, Catharina, and Friderich Delliker.
1797, Aug. 31, Bejer, Catharina, and Heinrich Kihly.
1791, Sept. 1, Bejer, Elizabeth, and Johannes Cunz.
1793, Sept. 29, Bejer, Johannes, and Barbara Zigler.
1793, Sept. 24, Bejer, Maria, and Jacob Kihly.
1798, Aug. 19, Bejer, Sara, and Jacob Groll.
1796, Feb. 23, Bejer, William, and Catharina Groll.
1794, March 25, Beker, Christina, and Johannes Livegood.
1785, Dec. 10, Bender, Anna Maria, and Heinrich Freyer.
1781, Nov. 20, Bender, Cathrina, and Conrad Neuman.
1790, Jan. 26, Bender, Elizabeth, and George Huber.
1794, May 6, Bender, Johannes, and Catharina Albrecht.
1785, Sept. 20, Bender, Ludwig, and Rosina Schik.

1787, Oct. 9, Bender, Margrith, and Abraham Bleüler.
1798, Dec. 4, Benjamin, Pahly and Mahlon Long.
1788, April 1, Benner, Daniel, and Anna Maria Schöner.
1792, June 24, Beringer, Ester, and Peter Bock.
1790, Aug. 17, Berger, Hannes, and Christina Faust.
1781, April 17, Bernhard, Elizabeth, and Henrich Gratzer.
1774, Nov. 1, Bernhard, Jacob, and Anna Dotter.
1791, Nov. 3, Bernhard, Maria, and Matthew Deker.
1783, May 20, Bernhard, Phillip, and Elizabeth Antes.
1790, Jan. 26, Bertoly, Samuel, and Elizabeth Frey.
1793, Aug. 13, Betto, Chtistian, and Barbara Schik.
1789, March 10, Betz, Margrith, and Daniel Koch.
1772, March 17, Betz, Maria, and Johannes Jahn.
1780, May 16, Biedel, Andreas, and Barbara Neumen.
1798, Nov. 29, Bikhard, Conrad, and Elizabeth Schneisforth.
1796, April 5, Bikhard, Maria, and Peter Schweitzford.
1790, Sept. 14, Bikhards, Christian, and Anna Schlotten.
1755, Feb. 25, Bleiler, Jacob, and Agnes Engel.
1787, Oct. 9, Bleüler, Abraham, and Margrith Bender.
1796, April 5, Bock, Jacob, and Dorathea Weiseisen.
1789, Oct. 20, Bock, Magdalena, and Johanes Scheid.
1792, June 24, Bock, Peter, and Ester Beringer.
1791, Dec. 20, Bohlich, Thomas, and Elisabeth Kehl.
1749, March 27, Böhmer, Adam, and Anna Margaretha Seiwel.
1798, Nov. 9, Bolton, Nathan, and Susanna Updegräf.
1752, April 21, Born, Maria Catharina, and Sylvester Otho.
1784, April 20, Boshard, Heinrich, and Gertraud Jung.
1779, Jan. 13, Boyer, Valentine, ——— Gorst.
1794, Nov. 18, Brand, Benjamin, and Elisabeth Mejer.
1748, Nov. 8, Brand, Christina, and Jacob Liebegut.
1790, Feb. 2, Brand, Elisabeth, and Niclas Pfuhl.
1790, Oct. 26, Brand, Hanna Johannes Bädmann.
1782, April 16, Brand, Jacob, and Elisabeth Weiss.
1779, Nov. 23, Brand, Maria, and Franz Picany.
1787, Oct. 30, Brand, Philip, and Catharina Schaff.
1789, March 17, Brand, Susanna, and Johanes Ritterman.
1780, Nov. 7, Breiniger, Jacob, and Salome Jost.
1776, Feb. 20, Brendel, Elisabeth, and Adam Miller.
1797, June 4, Broks, Thomas, and Elisabeth Misemer.
1792, Nov. 20, Brooks, John, and Mary Keppener.
1798, Jan. 28, Bruch, Catharina, and Philip Kreis.
1793, Oct. 29, Bruch, David, and Anna Kihler.
1779, Dec. 14, Bruer, Christina, and John Nagel.
1794, Aug. 3, Bucher, Christina, and Heinrich Schmid.
1791, April 2, Bucher, Conrad, and Anna Maria Engel.
1783, Aug. 19, Bucher, Elisabeth, and Jacob Engle.

1788, Dec.   16, Bucher, Georg, and Christina Schneider.
1796, Nov.   29. Bucher, Johannes, and Elisabeth Schöner.
1785, April 12, Bucher, Maria Cath., and Heinrich Gotz.
1790, March 15, Bucher, Maria, and Samuel Vedder.
1782, May   9, Buchwalter, Jacob, and Magdalena Acker.
1791, Aug.   21, Buff, Johannes, and Christina Scheufely.
1799, Aug.   4, Bull, Martha, and James McClintuck.
1772, Aug.   11, Busch, Peter, and Mary Costert.
1779, Nov.   11, Butterweck, Joseph, and Margaretha Striecker.
1775, April 30, Carl, Elisabeth, and Phillip Seeler.
1799, Dec.   24, Carl, Jacob, and Elisabeth Hippel.
1773, May   11, Carl, Johannes, and Catharina Wagener.
1773, Dec.   19, Clauss, Christophel, and Catharina Hang.
1779, March 18, Clayfield, John, and Cathrina Eichelberger.
1778, March 3, Clears. Elisabeth, and Andrew Maccason.
1798, May   5, Cohl, Conrad, and Henna Werly.
1791, Sept. 18, Cohl, Heinrich, and Barbara Eichelberger.
1797, April 17, Conell, Edward, and Susanna Keyser.
1783, Feb.   18, Conrad, Friedrich, and Cathrina Schneider.
1753, July   —, Corper, Johann Julius, and Catharina Reimer.
1772, Aug.   11, Costert, Mary, and Peter Busch.
1749, Sept. 11, Coulston, Levi, and Sarah Evans.
1794, Jan.   2, Cozens, Dr. Wilhelm Arch, and Charlotte Maus.
1792, Jan.   3, Craw, Heinrich, and Sophia Zollir.
1749, Feb.   14, Crebill, Philippina, and Joh. Georg Vogle.
1788, June   3, Creider, Anna Barbara, and Joh. Jacob Roschong.
1793, Dec.   24, Cresch, Maria, and Andreas Schmid.
1749, Dec.   —, Christinann, Anna Ella, and Johannes Grobb.
1785, May   19, Christmann, Elizabeth, and George Neiss.
1792, March 13, Crumrein, Johannes, and Elisabeth Martin.
1791, Sept.   1, Cunz, Johannes, and Elisabeth Bejer.
1796, March 22, Cunz, Sara, and John Hohlenbusch.
1791, Aug.   23, Davis, Samuel, and Margrith Bauer.
1782, Dec.   25, Decker, Michel, and Elisabeth Ferbig.
1775, March 14, Defrehn, Anna Maria, and Henrich Laubach.
1779, July   11, Dehlinger, Eva, and Joh. Conrad Devitz.
1790, May   18, Deising, Isaac, and Sara Frey.
1791, Nov.   3, Deker, Matthew, and Maria Bernhard.
1798, March 20, Delliker, Friderich, and Catharina Beiteman.
1786, Oct.   12, Delliker, Friderick, and Maria Magdalena Schu-
                    vena.
1798, Sept. 16, Delliker, Maria Cath., and Johannes Thomas.
1791, March 17, Dengeler, Catharina, and Johannes Schneider.
1779, Aug.   17, Dengeler, Georg, and Anna Maria Spigle.
1785, Aug,   30, Dengeler, Jacob, and Catharina Walder.
1784, April 20, Dengeler, Johanes, and Magdalena Schmid.

1787, Sept. 18, Dering, Jacob, and Catharina Ekelmann.
1789, April   7, Dettweyler, Johannes, and Magdalena Gugger.
1788, Jan.   1, Devertshausers, Catharina, and Jacob Reifschnei-
            der.
1779, July   11, Devitz, Joh. Conrad, and Eva Dehlinger.
1773, May   9, Diener, Joh. Peter, and Margareth Mayer.
1787, Jan.   30, Dieterich, Conrad, and Elizabeth Sussholz.
1798, Dec.   6, Dieterick, Georg, and Catharina Kehr.
1750, Jan.   9, Dietz, Peter, and Catharina Frohnbach.
1792, Dec.   18, Doderer, Abraham, and Elisa Reifschneider.
1787, April 12, Doderer, Daniel, and Barbara Muthard.
1786, Feb.   23, Doderer, Magdalena, and Peter Osterlein.
1789, April 28, Doderer, Maria, and George Freyer.
1774, Oct.   25, Dorr, Barbara, and Friedrich Losch.
1774, Nov.   1, Dotter, Anna, and Jacob Bernhard.
1774, Oct.   25, Dotter, Barbara, and Jost Freyer.
1779, Nov. 16, Dotter, Benigna, and John Jost.
1772, April 23, Dotter, Elizabeth, and N. Pomp.
1781, July   3, Dotter, Phillipina, and Henrich Maurer.
1772, Dec.   22, Dotterer, Johannes, and Anna Maria Schmid.
1780, April 24, Drees, Georg, and Cathrina Schloind.
1750, Aug.   7, Eberle, Johannes, and Cath. Hempel.
1795, April 26, Edinger, Abraham, and Elisabeth Lichtly.
1791, May   10, Edward, Elisabeth, and Conrad Kihler.
1791, Sept. 18, Eichelberger, Barbara, and Heinrich Cohl.
1779, March 18, Eichelberger, Cathrina, and John Clayfield.
1784, Oct.   16, Eichelberger, Susanna, and Jacob Freyer.
1787, Sept. 18, Eckelmann, Catharina, and Jacob Dering.
1798, Feb.   14, Ekelman, Heinrich, and Elisabeth Roschong.
1755, Feb.   25, Engel, Agnes, and Jacob Bleiler.
1791, April   2, Engel, Anna Maria, and Conrad Bucher.
1783, Aug.   19, Engel, Jacob, and Elisabeth Bucher.
1776, April   2, Engel, John, and Anna Margareth Georg.
1751, Oct.   31, Engle, Gertraudt, and Johann Philipp Lauterbach.
1787, May   22, Erb, Casper, and Catharina Reinheim.
1786, April 11, Erb, Peter, and Christina Renninger.
1782, March 19, Erbach, Ann, and John Huber.
1780, June   6, Erhard, Magdalena, and Jacob Schneider.
1784, Nov.   9, Ernes, Anna Barbara, and Adam Luckharts.
1795, Nov.   3, Eschenfelder, Catharina, and Mattheas Schilich.
1769, April   2, Eschenfelder, Peter and Elisabeth Rieser.
1782, Jan.   29, Esterlein, Michael, and Elisabeth Faust.
1794, Sept. 11, Evans, Sarah, and Levi Coulston.
1788, April 22, Evny, Anna Maria, and Johannes Zoller.
1750, Aug.   7, Faass, Philipp, and Margaretha Barbara Mom-
            bauer.

1790, Aug. 17, Faust, Christina, and Hannes Berger.
1782, Jan. 29, Faust, Elizabeth, and Michael Esterlein.
1789, Oct. 20, Faust, Han Neikel, and Elisabeth Walbert.
1772, May 19, Fedel, Elizabeth, and Philip Acker.
1786, Jan. 26, Felix, Elisabeth, and Peter Schmid.
1782, Dec. 25, Ferbig, Elisabeth, and Michel Decker.
1798, June —, Feyer, Maria, and Rasmus Lever.
1791, March 2, Fillman, Christiana, and Christian Freyer.
1780, May 23, Fillman, Phillip, and Elisabeth Sehner.
1779, May 18, Finck, Peter, and Cathrina Jung.
1787, March 7, Firer, Johannes, and Margrith Gorchy.
1752, Feb. 13, Fischer, Anna Barbara, and Melchior Hubner.
1790, May 18, Fischer, Eva, and George Langbein.
1799, Dec. 30, Fischer, Jacob, and Eliz. Weidner.
1778, May 12, Frehn, Elisabeth, and Gosteph Serben.
1776, May 7, Fren, Catharina, and Peter Schnack.
1790, Jan. 26, Frey, Elisabeth, and Samuel Bertoly.
1788, Dec. 30, Frey, Jacob, and Catharina Reifschneider.
1792, Nov. 5, Frey, Magdalena, and Johannes Schlichter.
1780, Nov. 14, Frey, Maria, and Michael Schwartz.
1790, May 18, Frey, Sara, and Isaac Deising.
1750, Sept. 4, Freyer, Anna Maria, and Johann Christian Hahn.
1791, March 2, Freyer, Christian, and Christiana Fillman.
1789, April 28, Freyer, George, and Maria Doderer.
1783, March 16, Freyer, Georg, and Maria Schneider.
1785, Dec. 10, Freyer, Heinrich, and Anna Maria Bender.
1784, Oct. 16, Freyer, Jacob, and Susanna Eichelberger.
1774, Oct. 25, Freyer, Jost and Barbara Dotter.
1787, Aug. 11, Freyer, Philip, and Elisabeth Reinheim.
1794, Feb. 27, Freyer, Philip, and Elisabeth Schneider.
1790, Dec. 14, Fried, Anna, and Jacob Bauer.
1794, Dec. 25, Fritz, Peter, and Susanna Schöner.
1750, Jan. 9, Frohnbach, Catharina, and Peter Dietz.
1786, May 23, Fup, Catharina, and Conrad Vogely.
1797, Nov. 3, Gabel, Philip, and Catharina Schneider.
1784, Nov. 23, Gaukler, Joh. Georg, and Dorathea Zink.
1781, May 15, Gehry, Jacob, and Elisabeth Lauer.
1797, Oct. 17, Geist, Elisabeth, and Daniel Kraz.
1793, Sept. 17, Gejer, Anna Maria, and Michael Wien.
1796, Aug. 14, Gejer, Carl, and Margrith Specht.
1793, Nov. 26, Gejer, Johannes, and Margrith Jeger.
1776, April 2, Georg, Anna Margareth, and John Engel.
1799, Oct. 15, Gerling, Hanna, and David Lubold.
1778, Oct. 22, Geyer, Elisabeth, and Johannes Schulz.
1789, May 17, Geyer, Johannes, and Anna Maria Hillegass.
1795, June 21, Gilbert, Maria, and Johan Schik.

1779, Feb.　9, Gilbert, Nicolaus, and Mary Neiss.
1787, March　7, Gorchy, Margrith, and Johanes Firer.
1779, Jan.　13, Gorst, ————, and Valentine Boyer.
1785, April　12, Gotz, Heinrich, and Maria Cath. Bucher.
1774, April　4, Gotz, Johannes, and N. N.
1772, Dec.　6, Gotzelmann, Anna Maria, and Peter Schmid.
1786, April　4, Graff, Georg, and Christina Johns.
1753, Dec.　18, Graf, Maria Christina, and Sebastian Schales.
1781, April　17, Gratzer, Henrich, and Elizabeth Bernhard.
1791, April　14, Greder, Johannes, and Christina Neumann.
1792, June　19, Grob, Abraham, and Margrith Zoller.
1778, May　21, Grob, Annella, and Conrad Grob.
1778, May　21, Grob, Conrad, and Annella Grob.
1786, May　30, Grob, Jacob, and Elizabeth Kalb.
1749, Dec.　—, Grobb, Johannes, and Anna Ella Christmann.
1797, Dec.　31, Groll, Anna, and Benjamin Reif.
1796, Feb.　23, Groll, Catharina, and William Bejer.
1798, Aug.　19, Groll, Jacob, and Sara Bejer.
1785, Jan.　30, Grote, Heinrich, and Elizabeth Wood.
1790, Oct.　20, Grub, Margrith, and Abraham Huber.
1789, March 10, Gugger, Georg, and Christina Spiess.
1789, April　7, Gugger, Magdalena, and Johannes Dettweyler.
1793, July　18, Gugger, Susanna, and Heinrich Seyler.
1795, April　2, Guker, Barbara, and Abraham Sell.
1788, April　22, Haag, Georg, and Anna Weyermann.
1788, March 11, Haas, Sara, and Heinrich Stetler.
1784, Oct.　7, Hahn, Catharina, Johannes Meyer.
1750, Sept.　4, Hahn, Johann Christian, and Anna Maria Freyer.
1795, Oct.　15, Hahn, Margrith, and Wilhelm Handel.
1787, July　24, Hahs, Elisabeth, and Johannes Steiper.
1796, Feb.　13, Hakley, Anna, and William Mebbeny.
1795, Oct.　15, Handel, Wilhelm, and Margrith Hahn.
1773, Dec.　19, Hang, Catharina, and Christophel Clauss.
1753, Nov.　20, Happel, Henrich, and Catharina Müller.
1753, Dec.　25, Happel, Johann George, and Maria Elizabeth Lan-
　　　　　　　　tess.
1784, Dec.　30, Hartenstein, Heinrich, and Magdalena Ren.
1780, Nov.　14, Hartranft, Maria, and Conrad Mayer.
1788, March 13, Haven, Elisabeth, and Jacob Weyermann.
1791, Jan.　23, Heinrich, Hanna, and Johannes Lee.
1798, Oct.　1, Heist, Georg, and Susanna Kihler.
1772, April　7, Hellwich, Elisabeth, and Johannes Schmid.
1779, Aug.　10, Hellwich, Magdalena, and Nicolaus Mack.
1750, Aug.　7, Hempel, Cath., and Johannes Eberle.
1780, April　24, Herb, Abraham, and Sibilla Wachst.
1748, Nov.　17, Herb, Susanna, and Johann Conrad Lorsbach.

1782, April   2, Herbst, Georg, and Elisabeth Wiebel.
1796, April   12, Hildenbentel, Maria, and Heinrich Hohlenbusch.
1789, May   17, Hillegass, Anna Maria, and Johannes Geyer.
1786, Feb.   7, Hillegass, Barbara, and Daniel Jost.
1780, May   30, Hillegass, Cathrina, and Johannes Maurer.
1780, May   30, Hillegass, Elisabeth, and Michel Huber.
1789, May   17, Hillegass, Susanna, and Adam Jost.
1779, Sept.   12, Hippel, Cathrina, and Adam Steim.
1779, Dec.   24, Hippel, Elisabeth, and Jacob Carl.
1781, June   19, Hippel, Henrich, and Hanna Schneider.
1773, Nov.   23, Hippel, Johannes, and Anna Maria Jager.
1774, Jan.   25, Hippel, Lorentz, and Margaretha Stein.
1782, Nov.   5, Hirsch, Samuel, and Susanna Andrau.
1796, April   12, Hohlenbusch, Heinrich, and Maria Hildenbentel.
1796, March 22, Hohlenbusch, John, and Sara Cunz.
1750, Aug.   21, Holb, Anna Marg., and Johann Jacob Reinhard.
1791, June   2, Hornbeck, Elisabeth, and Elias Wats.
1774, Oct.   18, Huben, Sara, and Daniel Meias.
1789, April   14, Hubener, Friderick, and Christina Roschong.
1790, Oct.   20, Huber, Abraham, and Margrith Grub.
1769, March 17, Huber, Anna, and Daniel Becker.
1782, Jan.   15, Huber, Anna Maria, and Henrich Pfaltzgrast.
1783, March 25, Huber, Elisabeth, and Matheiss Regener.
1790, Jan.   26, Huber, George, and Elizabeth Bender.
1785, Oct.   9, Huber, Hannes, and Magdalena Sorg.
1782, March 19, Huber, John, and Ann Erbach.
1780, May   30, Huber, Michel, and Elizabeth Hillegass.
1752, Feb.   13, Hubner, Melchior, and Anna Barbara Fischer.
1773, Nov.   23, Jager, Anna Maria, and Johannes Hippel.
1782, April   18, Jager, Johan, and Magdalena Renar.
1772, March 17, Jahn, Johannes, and Maria Betz.
1781, May   2, Jakson, John, and Elisabeth Barringer.
1782, March 19, James and Mulatto, (mulatto girl.)
1795, Dec.   1, Jeger, Catharina, and Jacob Lik.
1793, Nov.   26, Jeger, Margrith, and Johannes Gejer.
1781, March 13, Jodde, Georg, and Anna Maria Neumann.
1786, April   4, Johns, Christina, and Georg Graff.
1795, Sept.   17, Johns, Magdalena, and Johannes Rorchong.
1793, Nov.   4, Jolly, Charles, and Sophia Mebbery.
1796, March   3, Jolly, John, and Rebecca Mebbery.
1785, Oct.   25, Jorger, Jacob, and Catharina Schmid.
1789, May   17, Jost, Adam, and Susanna Hillegass.
1785, Oct,   13, Jost, Christina, and Jacob Schellenberger.
1786, Feb.   7, Jost, Daniel, and Barbara Hillegass.
1798, July   25, Jost, Heinrich, and Margrith Rikert.
1798, July   10, Jost, Jacob, and Henna Schwarzlender.

1793, July   23, Jost, Johannes, and Maria Seipel.
1779, Nov.   16, Jost, John, and Benigna Dotter.
1798, Nov.   18, Jost, Joseph, and Elisabeth Kepler.
1780, Nov.   7, Jost, Salome, and Jacob Breoniger.
1794, Nov.   6, Jung, Barbara, and Johanes Achy.
1779, May   18, Jung, Cathrina, and Peter Finck.
1795, May   25, Jung, Elisabeth, and Heinrich Schuey.
1784, April   20, Jung, Gertraud, and Heinrich Boshard.
1776, May   12, Jung, Peter, and Cathrina Schneider.
1749, July   18, Jups, Friederica Cath., and Jacob Krem.
1797, March   14, Jus, Maty, and Samuel Potts.
1794, Oct.   12, Kalb, Anna Cath., and Johannes Reninger.
1786, May   30, Kalb, Elisabeth, and Jacob Grob.
1791, Dec.   20, Kehl, Elisabeth, and Thomas Bohlich.
1788, Oct.   20, Kehl, Magdalena, and Abraham Zarn.
1775, Nov.   7, Kehl, Mose, and Catharina Spies.
1798, Dec.   6, Kehr, Catharina, and George Dieterick.
1796, Aug.   10, Kehr, Johannes, and Maria Kemel.
1786, Dec.   3, Kember, Henna, and Heinrich Kihly.
1796, Aug.   10, Kemel, Maria, and Johannes Kehr.
1777, Aug.   24, Kendel, Benjamin, and Elizabeth Kendel.
1777, Aug.   24, Kendel, Elizabeth, and Benjamin Kendel.
1798, Nov.   18, Kepler, Elisabeth, and Joseph Jost.
1796, Sept.   11, Kepler, Hanna, and Benjamin Stetler.
1792, Nov.   20, Keppener, Mary, and John Brooks.
1792, June   28, Key, Edmund, (lawyer,) and Ruth Anna Potts.
1794, Oct.   28, Keyser, Georg, and Eva Speidlin.
1797, April   17, Keyser, Susanna, and Edward Conell.
1785, Aug.   28, Kiechelein, Catharina, and Martin Zieler.
1799, Dec.   31, Kiehler, Susanna, and Frederic March.
1785, April   14, Kieler, Magdalena, and Heinrich Neuman.
1793, Oct.   29, Kihler, Anna, and David Bruch.
1791, May   10, Kihler, Conrad, and Elizabeth Edward.
1796, April   5, Kihler, Michel, and Elizabeth Ziegler.
1798, Oct.   1, Kihler, Susanna, and Georg Heist.
1797, Aug.   31, Kihly, Heinrich, and Catharina Bejer.
1786, Dec.   3, Kihly, Heinrich, and Henna Lember.
1793, Sept.   24, Kihly, Jacob, and Maria Bejer.
1789, July   6, King, George, and Catharina Langbein.
1781, May   9, Knauss, Henrich, and Elisabeth Ried.
1789, March   10, Koch, Daniel, and Margrith Betz.
1788, Dec.   14, Kolb, Elisabeth, and Wilhelm Stillwagen.
1780, Feb.   17, Kolb, Michel, and Magdalena Leidig.
1775, June   5, König, Magdalena, and Johannes Moses.
1779, April   25, Konig, ——, and son of Johannes Schneider.
1797, Oct.   17, Kraz, Daniel, and Elisabeth Geist.

1798, Jan.   28, Kreis, Philip, and Catharina Bruch.
1749, July   18, Krem, Jacob, and Friederica Cath. Jups.
1779, Aug.   17, Kuhly, Jacob, and Cathrina Sassemanshausen.
1799, May   26, Kurtz, Barbara, and Friderich Weiss.
1796, March 27, Kurz, Magdalena, and Valentin Stelz.
1792, July   8, Lachmund, Barbara, and Peter Reifschneider.
1796, Aug.   21, Lachmund, Catharina, and Johannes Sebold.
1794, April   13, Lachmund, Niclas, and Catharina Thomas.
1796, May   16, Lacy, Andree, and Beky Williams.
1784, May   9, Langbein, Barbara, and George Moor.
1789, July   6, Langbein, Catharina, and George King.
1790, May   18, Langbein, George, and Eva Fischer.
1789, Nov.   30, Langbein, Margrith, and Bernhard Bar.
1753, Dec.   25, Lantes, Maria Elizabeth, and Johann George
                       Happel.
1775, March 14, Laubach, Henrich, and Anna Maria Defrehn.
1781, May   15, Lauer, Elisabeth, and Jacob Gehry.
1749, Jan.   17, Laugenbeis, Gottfried, and Anna Margaretha
                       Schnied.
1755, Feb.   25, Lautenschlager; Johann Michael, and Anna Eliza-
                       beth Saler.
1751, Oct.   31, Lauterbach, Johann Philipp, and Gertraudt Engle.
1796, Dec.   5, Lee, Heinrich, and Catharina Mud.
1791, Jan.   23, Lee, Johannes, and Hanna Heinrich.
1791, Dec.   11, Lee, Maria, and Jacob Oberdorff.
1780, Feb.   17, Leidig, Magdalena, and Michel Kolb.
1793, Dec.   26, Leidner, Johannes, and Catharina Misemer.
1798, June   —, Lever, Rasmus, and Maria Feyer.
1795, April   26, Lichtly, Elisabeth, and Abraham Edinger.
1748, Nov.   9, Liebegut, Jacob, and Christina Brand.
1783, Jan.   28, Liebegut, Matheis, and Cathrina Schuster.
1749, Jan.   23, Liebegut, Peter, and Christina Mohn.
1795, Dec.   1, Lik, Jacob, and Catharina Jeger.
1792, Feb.   7, Linzenbügler, Catharina, and Peter Livegood.
1798, March 13, Livegood, Catharina, and Johannes, Willauer.
1794, March 25, Livegood, Johannes, and Christina Beker.
1791, Aug.   23, Livegood, Johannes, and Elisabeth Reifschneider.
1792, Feb.   7, Livegood, Peter, and Catharina Linzenbügler.
1792, Oct.   2, Livegood, Philip, and Elisabeth Mebbery.
1798, Dec.   4, Long, Mahlon, and Phaly Benjamin.
1787, Dec.   27, Lord, Maria, and Friderich Schwarts.
1785, Oct.   9, Lorg, Magdalena, and Hannes Huber.
1748, Nov.   17, Lorsbach, Johann Conrad, and Susanna Herb.
1774, Oct.   25, Lösch, Friedrich, and Barbara Dorr.
1777, Feb.   25, Löwenberg, Peter, and Justinia Sherrard.
1799, Oct.   15, Lubold, David, and Hanna Gerling.

1784, Nov.   9, Luckharts, Adam, and Anna Barbara Evnes.
1778, March   3, Maccason, Andrew, and Elisabeth Clears.
1779, Aug.   10, Mack, Nicolaus, and Magdalena Hellwich.
1796, May   1, Major, Anna, and Jacob Roschong.
1795, Oct.   26, Major, John, and Elisabeth Neunzehnholtzer.
1794, Oct.   19, Major, Maria, and Heinrich Roschong.
1799, Dec.   31, March, Frederic, and Susanna Kiehler.
1792, March 13, Martin, Elisabeth, and Johannes Crumrein.
1775, May   30, Matthew, Susanna, and Henrich Schneider.
1779, Oct.   24, Maurer, Henrich, and Magdalena Vollmer.
1781, July   3, Maurer, Henrich, and Phillipina Dotter.
1780, May   30, Maurer, Johannes, and Cathrina Hillegass.
1794, Jan.   2, Maus, Charlotte, and Dr. Wilhelm Arch Cozens.
1780, Nov.   14, Mayer, Conrad, and Maria Hartranft.
1781, May   7, Mayer, Jacob, and Sara Mayer.
1773, May   9, Mayer, Margareth, and John Peter Diener.
1781, May   7, Mayer, Sara, and Jacob Mayer.
1791, June   8, McClintik, Maly Maria, and Dr. Joseph Rass.
1799, Aug.   4, McClintuck, James, and Martha Bull.
1793, June   23, Mebbeny, Catharina, and Christoph Scheffy.
1793, Nov.   4, Mebbeny, Sophia, and Charles Jolly.
1796, Feb.   13, Mebbeny, William, and Anna Hakley.
1792, Oct.   2, Mebbery, Elizabeth, and Philip Livegood.
1796, March   3, Mebbery, Rebecca, and John Jolly.
1792, May   12, Mechlein, Catharina, and Johan Michael Müller.
1774, Oct.   18, Meias, Daniel, and Sara Huben.
1794, Nov.   18, Meyer, Elizabeth, and Benjamin Brand.
1786, April   4, Meyer, Eva, and Jacob Stoffeleth.
1784, Nov.   16, Mekleins, Philip, and Margrith Barbara Schmid.
1772, Dec.   3, Melcker, Margareth, and William Rittenhauser.
1772, June   9, Mercke, Elizabeth, and John Neumann.
1772, March 17, Merckle, Elizabeth, and John Sieber.
1792, Feb.   21, Merz, Elizabeth, and Wilhelm Schmid.
1784, Oct.   7, Meyer, Johannes, and Catharina Hahn.
1776, Feb.   20, Miller, Adam, and Elizabeth Brendel.
1778, April 14, Miller, Cathrina, and Nicolaus Niebel.
1775, March 21, Miller, Nicolaus, and Maria Schmid.
1790, Dec.   14, Minner, Conrad, and Elisabeth Schmid.
1793, Dec.   26, Misemer, Catharina, and Johannes Leidner.
1797, June   4, Misemer, Elisabeth, and Thomas Broks.
1797, March   5, Misemer, Maria, and Johannes Bechtel.
1799, Dec.   31, Missemer, George, and Eliz. Thomas.
1749, Jan.   23, Mohn, Christina, and Peter Liebegut.
1750, Aug.   7, Mombauer, Margaretha Barbara, and Philip Faass.
1784, May   9, Moor, George, and Barbara Langbein.
1793, Sept. 29, Moser, Johannes, and Henna Weidner.

1775, June　5, Moses, Johannes, and Magdalena König.
1796, Dec.　5, Mud, Catharina, and Henrich Lee.
1753, Nov.　20, Müller, Catharina, and Henrich Happel.
1792, May　12, Müller, Johan Michael, and Catharina Mechlein.
1787, April　12, Muthard, Barbara, and Daniel Doderer.
1779, Dec.　14, Nagel, John, and Christina Bruer.
1785, May　19, Neiss, George, and Elisabeth Christmann.
1788, Feb.　26, Neiss, Johannes, and Henna Reinert.
1779, Feb.　9, Neiss, Mary and Nicolaus Gilbert.
1788, April　22, Neiss, Nenci, and Abraham Zimermann.
1779, June　22, Neuman, Cathrina, and Johannes Specht.
1781, Nov.　20, Neuman, Conrad, and Cathrina Bender.
1785, April　14, Neuman, Henrich, and Magdalena Kieler.
1781, March 13, Neumann, Anna Maria, and Georg Jodde.
1791, April　14, Neumann, Christina, and Johannes Greder.
1793, April　2, Neumann, Johannes, and Elisabeth Schilchy.
1772, June　9, Neumann, John, and Elisabeth Mercke.
1779, April　6, Neumann, Margareth, and Peter Specht.
1780, May　16, Neumen, Barbara, and Andreas Biedel.
1795, Oct.　26, Neunzehnholtzer, Elisabeth, and John Major.
1789, June　23, Newmauer, Elisabeth, and Johannes Vander
　　　　　　　　Schleiss.
1778, April　14, Niebel, Nicolaus, and Cathrina Miller.
1791, Dec.　11, Oberdorff, Jacob, and Maria Lee.
1796, March 27, Obryen, Elisabeth, and Georg Pfeihl.
1786, Feb.　23, Osterlein, Peter, and Magdalena Doderer.
1752, April　21, Otho, Sylvester, and Maria Catharina Born.
1784, March　2, Ovenshane, Georg, and Mary Taylor.
1782, Jan.　15, Pfaltzgrast, Henrich, and Anna Maria Huber.
1796, March 27, Pfeihl, Georg, and Elisabeth Obryen.
1790, Feb.　2, Pfuhl, Niclas, and Elisabeth Brand.
1779, Nov.　23, Picany, Franz, and Maria Brand.
1752, Feb.　13, Pieters, Warner, and Catharina Van-der Sleys.
1772, April　23, Pomp, N., and Elisabeth Dotter.
1797, March 14, Potts, Samuel, and Maty Jus.
1792, June　28, Potts, Ruth Anna, and Lawyer Edmund Key.
1791, June　8, Rass, Dr. Joseph, and Maly Maria McClintik.
1783, March 25, Regener, Matheiss, and Elisabeth Huber.
1797, Dec.　31, Reif, Benjamin, and Anna Groll.
1788, Dec.　30, Reifschneider, Catharina, and Jacob Frey.
1794, Nov.　27, Reifschneider, Conrad, and Elisabeth Wien.
1792, Dec.　18, Reifschneider, Elisa, and Abraham Doderer.
1791, Aug.　23, Reifschneider, Elisabeth, and Johannes Livegood.
1781, Dec.　4, Reifschneider, Henrich, and Sophia Beck.
1788, Jan.　1, Reifschneider, Jacob, and Catharina Devertshaus-
　　　　　　　　ers.

1796, Feb.　9, Reifschneider, Johannes, and Catharina Schöner.
1783, March 27, Reiffschneider, Maria, and Wilhelm Becker.
1792, July　8, Reifschneider, Peter, and Barbara Lachmund.
1772, June　4, Reil, Nicolaus, and Margaret Schuhler.
1753, July　—, Reimer, Catharina, and Johann Julius Corper.
1783, April　10, Reimer, Elisabeth, and Jacob Schwenck.
1752, Nov.　28, Reimer, Johann Peter, and Rahel Ziber.
1788, Feb.　26, Reinert, Henna, and Johannes Neiss.
1750, Aug.　21, Reinhard, Johann Jacob, and Anna Marg. Holb.
1787, May　22, Reinheim, Catharina, and Casper Erb.
1787, Aug.　11, Reinheim, Elisabeth, and Philip Freyer.
1784, Dec.　30, Ren, Magdalena, and Heinrich Hartenstein.
1751, Dec.　19, Renar, Catharina, and Johann Henrich Schneider.
1782, April　18, Renar, Magdalena, and Johan Jager.
1794, Oct.　12, Reninger, Johannes, and Anna Cath. Kalb.
1786, April　11, Renninger, Christina, and Peter Erb.
1781, Jan.　2, Restschneider, Johannes, and Dorothea Beck.
1781, May　9, Ried, Elisabeth, and Henrich Knauss.
1769, April　2, Rieser, Elisabeth, and Peter Eschenfelder.
1798, July　25, Rikert, Margrith, and Heinrich Jost.
1784, June　29, Rill, Anna Margrith, and Frederich Wilhelm Van den Sclett.
1795, Nov.　19, Rittenhauser, Maria, and Jacob Schmid.
1772, Dec.　3, Rittenhauser, William, and Margareth Melcker.
1789, March 17, Ritterman, Johanes, and Susanna Brand.
1789, March 31, Roscher, Jacob, and Henna Weiss.
1784, May　25, Roschong, Catharina, and Christoph Scheffy.
1789, April　14, Roschong, Christina, and Friderick Hubener.
1798, Feb.　14, Roschong, Elisabeth, and Heinrich Eckelman.
1784, April' 13, Roschong, Heinrich, and Catharina, Trumbauer.
1794, Oct.　19, Roschong, Heinrich, and Maria Major.
1796, May　1, Roschong, Jacob, and Anna Major.
1795, Sept.　17, Roschong, Johannes, and Magdalena Johns.
1788, June　3, Roschong, Joh. Jacob, and Anna Barbara Creider.
1783, April　22, Roschon, Peter, and Maria Wolfang.
1790, Feb.　2, Rudy, Jacob, and Cath. Scheid.
1777, May　4, Rupranst, Anna Maria, and Peter Seibert.
1775, May　30, Ryly, Anna Maria, and John Stuven.
1755, Feb.　25, Saler, Anna Elizabetha, and Johann Michael Lautenschlager.
1779, Aug.　17, Sassemanshausen, Cathrina, and Jacob Kuhly.
1795, Oct.　25, Sassemann, Maria, and Michel Ziegler.
1787, Oct.　30, Schaff, Catharina, and Philip Brand.
1753, Dec.　18, Schales, Sebastian, and Maria Christina Graf.
1793, June　23, Scheffy Christoph, and Catharina Mebbeny.
1784, May　25, Scheffy Christoph, and Catharina Roschong.

1790, Feb.   2, Scheid Cath., and Jacob Rudy.
1798, Oct.   20, Scheid, Johannes, and Magdalena Bock.
1786, Nov.   21, Schellenberger, Heinrich, and Barbara Schmid.
1785, Oct.   13, Schellenberger, Jacob, and Christina Jost.
1795, May   5, Schellkopf, Catharina, and Georg Schmid.
1777, May   28, Scheste, Georg, and Anna Margareth Weinrich.
1791, Aug.   21, Scheufely, Christina, and Johannes Buff.
1793, Aug.   13, Schik, Barbara, and Christian Betto.
1795, June   21, Schik, Johan, and Maria Gilbert.
1785, Sept.   20, Schik, Rosina, and Ludwig Bender.
1795, Nov.   3, Schilich, Mattheis, and Catharina Eschenfelder.
1793, April   2, Schilchy, Elizabeth, and Johannes Neumann.
1792, Nov.   5, Schlichter, Johannes, and Magdalena Frey.
1780, April   24, Schloind, Cathrina, and Georg Drees.
1790, Sept.   14, Schlotten, Anna, and Christian Bikhards.
1793, Dec.   24, Schmid, Andreas, and Maria Cresch.
1772, Dec.   22, Schmid, Anna Maria, and Johannes Dotterer.
1786, Nov.   21, Schmid, Barbara, and Heinrich Schellenberger.
1785, Oct.   25, Schmid, Catharina, and Jacob Jorger.
1783, May   27, Schmid, Conrad, and Margareth Spiess.
1790, Dec.   14, Schmid, Elizabeth, and Conrad Minner.
1794, May   25, Schmid, Elizabeth, and Johannes Spengler.
1772, March 17, Schmid, Fronia, and Gottfried Seeler.
1795, May   5, Schmid, Georg, and Catharina Schellkopf.
1794, Aug.   3, Schmid, Heinrich, and Christina Bucher.
1795, Nov.   19, Schmid, Jacob, and Maria Rittenhauser.
1772, April   7, Schmid, Johannes, and Elizabeth Hellwich.
1783, April   22, Schmid, Johannes, and Maria Schner.
1798, May   8, Schmid, Josep, and Maria Aker.
1784, April   20, Schmid, Magdalena, and Johanes Dengeler.
1784, Nov.   16, Schmid, Margrith Barbara, and Philip Mekleins.
1775, March 21, Schmid, Maria, and Nicolaus Miller.
1772, Dec.   6, Schmid, Peter, and Anna Maria Gotzelmann.
1786, Jan.   26, Schmid, Peter, and Elizabeth Felix.
1784, Dec.   14, Schmid, Susanna, and Johannes Schneider.
1792, Feb.   21, Schmid, Wilhelm, and Elisabeth Merz.
1799, Sept.   3, Schmidt, Catharina, and Christian Steltz.
1776, May   7, Schnack, Peter, and Catharina Fren.
1776, Jan.   7, Schneider, Andreas, and Magdalina Schneider.
1776, March 26, Schneider, Catharina, and Chas. Werner.
1783, Feb.   18, Schneider, Cathrina, and Friedrich Conrad.
1776, May   12, Schneider, Cathrina, and Peter Jung.
1797, Nov.   3, Schneider, Catharina, and Philip Gabel.
1788, Dec.   16, Schneider, Christina, and Georg Bucher.
1794, April   15, Schneider, Christina, and Samuel Ziegler.
1794, Feb.   27, Schneider, Elisabeth, and Philip Freyer.

1781, June   19, Schneider, Hanna, and Henrich Hippel.
1775, May   30, Schneider, Henrick, and Susanna Matthew.
1780, June   6, Schneider, Jacob, and Magdalena Erhard.
1791, March 17, Schneider, Johannes, and Catharina Dengeler.
1784, Dec.   14, Schneider, Johannes, and Susanna Schmid.
1780, Dec.   5, Schneider, Johannes, and Susanna Stein.
1751, Dec.   19, Schneider, Johann Henrich, and Catharina Renar.
1776, Jan.   7, Schneider, Magdalena, and Andreas Schneider.
1772, Aug.   11, Schneider, Margaret, and Bastian Wagener.
1783, March 16, Schneider, Maria, and Georg Freyer.
1779, April   25, Schneider, son of Johannes, and daughter of Konig.
1798, Nov.   29, Schneisforth, Elisabeth, and Conrad Bikhard.
1797, April   20, Schnell, Catharina, and Johannes Stelz.
1780, May   23, Schner, Elisabeth, and Phillip Fillman.
1783, April   22, Schner, Maria, and Johannes Schmid.
1749, Jan.   17, Schnied, Anna Margaretha, and Gottfried Laugen-
                      beis.
1788, April   1, Schöner, Anna Maria, and Daniel Benner.
1796, Feb.   9, Schöner, Catharina, and Johannes Reifschneider.
1792, Nov.   6, Schöner, Catharina, and Johannes Sens.
1796, Nov.   29, Schoner, Elisabeth, and Johannes Bucher.
1794, Dec.   25, Schöner, Susanna, and Peter Fritz.
1783, May   8, Schönholtz, Elisabeth, and Jacob Steger.
1795, May   25, Schuey, Heinrich, and Elisabeth Jung.
1775, Aug.   17, Schuhler, Catharina, and Friedrich Antes.
1772, June   4, Schuhler, Margaret, and Nicolaus Reil.
1778, Oct.   22, Schulz, Johannes, and Elisabeth Geiger.
1797, March 5, Schunk, Abraham, and Patty Thomas.
1783, Jan.   28, Schuster, Cathrina, and Matheis Leibegut.
1786, Oct.   12, Schuvena, Maria Magdalena, and Friderick Delli-
                      ker.
1787, Dec.   25, Schwarts, Friderich, and Maria Lord.
1780, Nov.   14, Schwartz, Michel, and Maria Frey.
1798, July   10, Schwarzlender, Henna, and Jacob Jost.
1796, April   5, Schweitzford, Peter, and Maria Bikhard.
1792, Oct.   30, Schweinhart, Henna, and Georg Bechtel.
1783, April   10, Schwenck, Jacob, and Elisabeth Reimer.
1796, Aug.   21, Sebold, Johannes, and Catharina Lachmund.
1772, March 17, Seeler, Gottfried, and Fronia Schmid.
1775, April   30, Seeler, Phillip, and Elisabeth Carl.
1775, Dec.   6, Seibert, Catharina, and Christian Bauer.
1777, May   4, Seibert, Peter, and Anna Maria Rupranst.
1703, July   23, Seipel, Maria, and Johannes Jost.
1749, March 27, Seiwel, Anna Margaretha, and Adam Böhmer.
1795, April   2, Sell, Abraham, and Barbara Guker.
1791, Sept.   27, Sell, Margrith, and Johannes Baret.

1792, Nov.   6, Sens, Johannes, and Catharina Schöner.
1778, May   12, Serben, Gosteph, and Elisabeth Frehn,
1793, July   18, Seyler, Heinrich, and Susanna Gugger.
1777, Feb.   25, Sherrard, Justinia, and Peter Löwenberg.
1772, March 17, Sieber, John, and Elizabeth Merckle.
1786, May   9, Sinzendorfer, Barbara, and Christian Specht.
1786, May   9, Specht, Christian, and Barbara Sinzendorfer.
1779, June   22, Specht, Johannes, and Cathrina Neuman.
1796, Aug.   14, Specht, Margrith, and Carl Gejer.
1779, April   6, Specht, Peter, and Margareth Neumann.
1791, March 17, Speidlin, Barbara, and Johannes Viery.
1792, Jan.   24, Speidlin, Elisabeth, and Johannes Wilson.
1794, Oct.   28, Speidlin, Eva, and Georg Keyser.
1794, May   25, Spengler, Johannes, and Elisabeth Schmid.
1775, Nov.   7, Spies, Catharina, and Mose Kehl.
1789, March 10, Spiess, Christina, and Georg Gugger.
1783, May   27, Spiess, Margareth, and Conrad Schmid.
1779, Aug.   17, Spigle, Anna Maria, and Georg Dengeler.
1777, April   8, Steger, Catharine, and Jacob Steger.
1777, April   1, Steger, Elisabeth, and Johannes Steger.
1777, April   8, Steger, Jacob, and Catharine Steger.
1783, May   8, Steger, Jacob, and Elisabeth Schönholtz.
1777, April   1, Steger, Johannes, and Elisabeth Steger.
1779, Sept.   12, Stein, Adam, and Cathrina Hippel.
1774, Jan.   25, Stein, Margaretha, and Lorentz Hippel.
1780, Dec.   5, Stein, Susanna, and Johannes Schneider.
1787, July   24, Steiper, Johannes, and Elisabeth Hahs.
1799, Sept.   3, Steltz, Christian, and Catharina Schmidt.
1796, Sept.   11, Stetler, Benjamin, and Hanna Kepler.
1788, March 11, Stetler, Heinrich, and Sara Haas.
1797, April   20, Stelz, Johannes, and Catharina Schnell.
1796, March 27, Stelz, Valentin, and Magdalena Kurz.
1788, Dec.   14, Stillwagen, Wilhelm, and Elisabeth Kolb.
1786, April   4, Stoffeleth, Jacob, and Eva Mejer.
1779, Nov.   11, Striecker, Margaretha, and Joseph Butterweck.
1775, May   30, Stuven, John, and Anna Maria Ryly.
1787, Jan.   30, Sussholz, Elisabeth, and Conrad Dietrich.
1794, March   2, Taylor, Mary, and Georg Ovenshane.
1794, April   13, Thomas, Catharina, and Niclas Lachmund.
1799, Dec.   31, Thomas, Eliz., and George Missemer.
1798, Sept.   16, Thomas, Johannes, and Maria Cath. Delliker.
1797, March   5, Thomas, Patty, and Abraham Schunk.
1789, March   3, Tris, Anna Margrith, and Friderich Zarn.
1784, April   13, Trumbauer, Catharina, and Heinrich Roschong.
1798, Nov.   9, Updegräf, Susanna, and Nathan Bolton.

1784, June 29, Vanden Sclett, Frederich Wilhelm, and Anna Margrith Rill.

1752, Feb. 13, Vander Sleys, Catharina, and Warner Pieters.

1789, June 23, Vander Schleiss, Johannes, and Elisabeth Newmauer.

1790, March 15, Vedder, Samuel, and Maria Bucher.

1791, March 17, Viery, Johannes, and Barbara Speidlin.

1786, May 23, Vogely, Conrad, and Catharina Fup.

1749, Feb. 14, Vögel, Joh. Georg, and Philippina, Crebill.

1779, Oct. 24, Volmer, Magdalena, and Henrich Maurer.

1780, April 24, Wachst, Sibilla, and Abraham Herb.

1772, Aug. 11, Wagener, Bastian, and Margaret Schneider.

1773, May 11, Wagener, Catharina, and Johannes Carl.

1789, Oct. 20, Walbert, Elisabeth, and Han Nikel Faust.

1785, Aug. 30, Walder, Catharina, and Jacob Dengeler.

1791, June 2, Wats, Elias, and Elisabeth Hornbeck.

1799, Dec. 30, Weidner, Eliz., and Jacob Fischer.

1793, Sept. 29, Weidner, Henna, and Johannes Morer.

1777, May 28, Weinrich, Anna Margareth, and Georg Scheste.

1796, April 5, Weiseisen, Dorathea, and Jacob Bock.

1782, April 16, Weiss, Elisabeth, and Jacob Brand.

1799, May 26, Weiss, Friderich, and Barbara Kurtz.

1789, March 31, Weiss, Henna, and Jacob Roscher.

1798, May 5, Werly, Henna, and Conrad Cohl.

1776, March 26, Werner, Chas., and Catharina Schneider.

1788, April 22, Weyerman, Anna, and Georg Haag.

1788, March 13, Weyermann, Jacob, and Elisabeth Haven.

1782, April 2, Wiebel, Elisabeth, and Georg Herbst.

1794, Nov. 27, Wien, Elisabeth, and Conrad Reifschneider.

1793, Sept. 17, Wien, Michel, and Anna Maria Gejer.

1798, March 13, Willauer, Johannes, and Catharina Livegood.

1796, May 16, Williams, Beky, and Andree Lacy.

1792, Jan. 24, Wilson, Johannes, and Elisabeth Speidlin.

1783, April 22, Wolfang, Maria, and Peter Roschon.

1795, Aug. 23, Wolfinger, Anna, and Wilhelm Apt.

1790, March 2, Wolfinger, Cath., and Franz Zoller.

1785, Jan. 30, Wood, Elisabeth, and Heinrich Grote.

1788, Oct. 20, Zarn, Abraham, and Magdalena Kehl.

1789, March 3, Zarn, Friderich, and Anna Margrith Tris.

1752, Nov. 28, Ziber, Rachel, and Johann Peter Reimer.

1798, Aug. 19, Ziegler, Elisabeth, and Isaac Bekers.

1796, April 5, Ziegler, Elisabeth, and Michel Kihler.

1795, Oct. 25, Ziegler, Michel, and Maria Sassemann.

1794, April 15, Ziegler, Samuel, and Christina Schneider.

1785, Aug. 28, Zieler, Martin, and Catharina Kiechelein.

1793, Sept. 29, Zigler, Barbara, and Johannes Bejer.

1788, April 22, Zimmermann, Abraham, and Nenci Neiss.
1784, Nov. 23, Zinc, Dorathea, and Joh. Georg Gaukler.
1790, March 2, Zoller, Franz, and Cath. Wolfinger.
1788, April 22, Zoller, Johannes, and Anna Maria Evny.
1792, June 19, Zoller, Margrith, and Abraham Grob.
1792, Jan. 3, Zoller, Sophia, and Heinrich Craw.

MARRIAGE RECORD

OF

THE LUTHERAN CHURCH,

NEW HANOVER, MONTGOMERY COUNTY, PA.

1745–1809.

LUTHERAN CHURCH, NEW HANOVER.

1776, Feb.   12, Abendson, Sam¹, and Phoebe Daler.
1769, Nov.   14, Acker, Catharine, and Michael Ickes.
1769, April   28, Acker, John Christian, and Elizabeth Fuchs.
1808, Jan.   3, Acker, Peter, and Elizabeth Bickel.
1772, Feb.   25, Albrecht, Maria, and Jacob Eisehauer.
1769, Aug.   1, Albrecht, Michael, and Elizabeth Gorger.
1805, Dec.   14, Albrecht, Michael, and Susanna Kurz.
1800, Oct.   12, Albrecht, Tobias, and Catharine Gilbert.
1800, Dec.   30, Allebach, ——, and Magda. Langenbach.
1783, May   20, Altendorfer, Michael, and Anna Maria Schwein-
                     hard.
1770, April   1, Amborn, Catharine, and Thomas Wilkson.
1772, Dec.   22, Ammerman, Anna Maria, and Ludwig Francken-
                     berger.
1769, May   14, Andrae, Elizabeth, and John Peter Moses.
1770, May   29, Appel, Catharine, and John Reier.
1774, Jan.   18, Appel, Elizabeth, and Michael Schupp.
1777, Jan.   7, Armbruster, Peter, and Margaret Gilbert.
1807, Oct.   1, Arms, Jacob, and Susanna Weinland.
1807, May   17, Arms, Magdalena, and Jacob Spatz.
1775, Oct.   15, Arnd, John Geo., and Magdalena Wengert.
1770, Nov.   15, Arnd, Maria Margaret, and Jacob Loeber.
1774, Feb.   24, Aschenbach, Anna, and Francis Turner.
1769, Feb.   12, Ashenfelder, Thomas, and Anna Hennrich.
1753, Oct.   8, Austein, John Geo., and Catharine Burger.
1765, Jan.   29, Baer, Fred'k, and Elizabeth Gilbert.
1772, Nov.   10, Baer, Peter, and Elizabeth Beideman.
1779, June   1, Baiteman, Fred'k, and Maria Reichert.
1748, Jan.   14, Bakon, Sara, and John Ulen.
1770, June   21, Balde, John, and Catharine Marstaller.
1763, Oct.   25, Baltner, Philip, and —— Wolst.
1807, July   3, Bar, John, and Catharine Bechtel.
1764, Nov.   25, Bard, John Geo., and Catharine Glantz.
1768, Dec.   23, Barker, Mary, and Conrad Schunck.
1779, Oct.   4, Barnet, Mary, and Adam Hartman.
1795, Oct.   29, Barrall, Jacob, and Margaret Eckbrett.
1807, Nov.   3, Bartman, Christina, and Henry Rumfield.
1807, Nov.   22, Basleres, Solomon, and Eliz. Schlonecker.

1769, March 7, Batz, John, and Elizabeth Kebner.
1772, April 21, Bauer, Michael, and Regina Tuerr.
1764, Dec. 27, Bauersax, Valentine, and Barbara Schlonecker.
1807, March 26, Baum, Margaret, and John Tyson.
1782, Dec. 17, Bauman, Isaac, and Susanna Schirmin.
1748, April 14, Bauman, Margaret, and Simon Wolffer.
1776, Nov. 18, Bausman, Fronica, and Andrew Lauck.
1808, May 22, Bayer, Andrew, and Catharine Jacob.
1799, May 12, Bayer, Elizabeth, and Jacob Krebs.
1800, March 1, Bayer, Henry, and Salome Krebs.
1799, Dec. 24, Bayer, Jacob, and Elizabeth Schmidt.
1750, April 17, Bayer, John, and Elizabeth Speicht.
1769, May 7, Bayer, Maria, and George Freund.
1749, Aug. 1, Becholt, Maria Eva, and Paul Moser.
1807, July 3, Bechtel, Catharine, and John Bar.
1768, Aug. 19, Bechtel, Samuel, and Margaret Colson.
1807, July 19, Bechtel, Susanna, and William Janson.
1774, Dec. 27, Beck, Balthaser Henry, and Marga Wollfart.
1775, Jan. 31, Beck, Catharine, and Jacob Elgert.
1753, Sept. 25, Beck, Hans, Geo., and Catharine Schlagel.
1801, Sept. 20, Beck, Henry, and Hannah Ludwig.
1804, Nov. 11, Beck, Mary, and Stephen Glaze.
1745, Oct. 31, Becker, John Fred'k, and Widow Schlagel.
1772, March 8, Becker, Peter, and Elizabeth Kugler.
1804, Aug. 25, Becktel, Hanna, and Math. Gilbert.
1733, April 29, Beideman, Adam, and Veronica Bender.
1772, Nov. 10, Beideman, Elizabeth, and Peter Baer.
1785, Jan. 18, Beiteman, Christina, and Jacob Stichter.
1773, April 13, Beiteman, Marga., and John Emmerich.
1807, July 12, Beitenman, Henry, and Susanna Hoerner.
1801, Oct. 11, Beitenman, John Geo., and Cath. Reiher.
1764, Dec. 18, Bell, Lawrence, and Rebecca Yocum.
1800, March 30, Benkus, Peter, and Elizabeth Kolb.
1772, Dec. 15, Bender, Anton, and Catharine Lober.
1783, April 29, Bender, Veronica, and Adam Beideman.
1804, Dec. 25, Berlinger, Philip, and Mary More.
1803, Jan. 9, Bernhard, Eliz., and Jacob Loh.
1776, Dec. 17, Berninger, Eva, and John Ehrhard.
1752, Feb. 11, Berninger, Philip, and Anna Margaret Schaefer.
1807, Nov. 29, Bernt, Jacob, and Cath. Sechler.
1807, Sept. 20, Bernt, Magda., and Jacob Sussholz.
1795, Oct. 13, Berritt, Jacob, and Rachel Reifschneider.
1748, Aug. 30, Besner, John, and Mary Barbara Meyer.
1801, April 28, Bettman, Joseph, and Hanna Kalb.
1796, April 10, Betz, Hanna, and Henry Krebs.
1804, June 26, Beuteler, Mally, and Andreas Hoffman.

1752, Nov.   9, Beuterman, Geo. Freiderich, and Anna Margaret Gilbert.
1748, May   24, Beyer, Catharine, and John Greiner.
1783, Aug.   19, Beyer, Elizabeth, and Henry Landes.
1796, Jan.   26, Beyer, Henry, and Maria Netz.
1749, April   10, Beyer, Michael, and Marga. Eliz Wartmann.
1796, March   1, Beyer, Susanna, and Peter Kelchune.
1808, Jan.   3, Bickel, Elizabeth, and Peter Acker.
1801, May   5, Bickel, Henry, and Maria Voegely.
1776, May   7, Bickel, Jacob, and Eliz Schidler.
1801, May   3, Bickel, John, and Elizabeth Stelz.
1784, June   1, Bickel, Magdalena, and Samuel Mecklin.
1805, July   14, Bierbrauer, Christina, and Jacob Bowman.
1906, Feb.   18, Bierman, Hanna, and Christopher Frey.
1807, July   25, Bilger, John, and Catharine Newman.
1807, Aug.   2, Binder, Elizabeth, and Paul Linzenbichler.
1795, Feb.   22, Binder, Geo. Michael, and Maria Christina Herbel.
1806, Nov.   2, Binder, Geo., and Susanna Palsgraf.
1803, Aug.   7, Binder, Henry, and S. Palsgraf.
1800, Sept.   14, Binder, Jacob, and Eliz Friederich.
1795, April   5, Bitling, Magdalena, and Jacob Schnell.
1798, March   25, Bitting, Peter, and Elizabeth Burkert.
1806, April   20, Bitting, Sarah, and George Sensendorfer.
1776, March   31, Blecklie, Catharine, and Thomas Lord.
1768, Jan.   26, Boehme, Daniel, and Margaret Jaus.
1806, March   9, Boehm, John, and Susanna Slagenhaupt.
1775, Dec.   5, Boldo, Elizabeth, and Henry Huben.
1782, Sept.   —, Bolich, Barbara, and Peter de Frohn.
1775, Jan.   10, Bolich, George, and Catharine Mecklin.
1767, Aug.   2, Borck, Catharine, and David Friederich.
1746, March   16, Boreth, George Michael, and Ursula Miller.
1753, May   15, Boretz, Philip, and Margaret Diel.
1807, July   25, Borleman, Marga., and Abrah. Hildebentel.
1774, March   22, Born, Anna, and Christoph Klein.
1765, April   1, Bossert, John, and Catharine Heinrig.
1747, June   10, Bossert, Maria, and Andreas Eschenbach.
1773, Feb.   2, Boughter, Barbara, and James Bowen.
1773, Feb.   2, Bowen, James, and Barbara Boughter.
1747, Feb.   11, Bower, Conrad, and Phillippina Keylwein.
1805, July   14, Bowman, Jacob, and Christina Bierbrauer.
1804, June   3, Boyer, Daniel, and Sara Burkert.
1808, March   20, Boyer, Elizabeth, and Jacob Knetz.
1804, July   29, Boyer, Susanna, and —— Hauck.
1752, June   2, Brauningen, Gertrude, and John Geo. Wisner.
1765, July   2, Braus, John Adam, and Cath. Rothermel.
1771, May   27, Brautigam, Cath., and Geo. William Lindeman.

1776, Nov. 12, Brand, Maria, and Henry Kebler.
1802, Feb. 28, Brant, Jacob, and Elizabeth Krauss.
1799, Feb. 14, Brendlinger, Jacob, and Maria Kurz.
1767, Dec. 15, Brendlinger, Joseph, and Ann Rosina Lober.
1804, May 6, Brendlinger, Peter, and Maria Burkert.
1764, April 10, Brenholz, Fred'k, and Eva Kraik.
1806, April 20, Brey, Magdalena, and William Hartranft.
1779, July 27, Breyer, Eva Cath., and Jacob Detweiler.
1769, Jan. 5, Brook, Mary, and David Jones.
1774, Jan. 11, Brotzman, ———, and Hanna Mercklin.
1804, Dec. 25, Brotzman, John, and Hanna Mohr.
1773, April 11, Bruge, Anna Dorothea, and George Schnell.
1776, June 18, Bruthard, Christn William, and Elizabeth Oehlgatte.
1797, Feb. 7, Bucher, Sara, and Math. Reicherd.
1796, March 27, Buckel, Elizabeth, and Henry Staffler.
1806, May 29, Bugger, Diederich, and Cath. Christman.
1771, April 30, Bull, Thomas, and Sara Grono.
1745, Oct. 3, Bullinger, Martin, and Widow de Hohsin.
1770, May 22, Burckard, Sara, and John Jacob Hartman.
1753, Oct. 8, Burger, Catharine, and John Geo. Austein.
1798, March 25, Burkert, Elizabeth, and Peter Bitting.
1804, May 6, Burkert, Maria, and Peter Brendlinger.
1804, June 3, Burkert, Sara, and Daniel Boyer.
1764, March 15, Buskirk, Jacob, and Mary Hollebach.
1749, May 22, Buttebinder, Christoph., and Anna Eliz. Mayer.
1767, Nov. 8, Calb, Catharine, and Henry Kunstman.
1771, Aug. 27, Cambe, Anna Marga., and Valentine Voigt.
1801, Aug. 30, Candle, Joseph, and Margaret Ludwig.
1753, Oct. 9, Cangler, Jacob, and Cath. Kohler.
1750, Dec. 18, Chapman, Sarah, and Jeremiah Hickes.
1806, May 29, Christman, Cath., and Diederich Bugger.
1804, May 13, Christman, Gertrude, and Peter Vogely.
1767, Aug. 6, Christman, Henry, and Susanna Kiehl.
1764, Oct. 27, Clauser, Gertrude, and John Geo. Eirich.
1799, June 16, Clayfield, John, and Marg. McGeby.
1807, Feb. 27, Clemence, Abrah., and Mally Miller.
1751, Sept. 22, Collins, Patrick, and Sara Miller.
1764, Dec. 20, Collman, Katy, and John Shute.
1755, Oct. 23, Colman, Margaret, and John Geo. Michael.
1768, Aug. 19, Colson, Margaret, and Samuel Bechtel.
1799, May 14, Colton, Hanna, (widow,) and Andrew Maurer.
1745, May 28, Conrad, Catharine, and John Andrew Jurger.
1755, March 31, Conrad, John, and Susanna Kohler.
1746, Aug. 19, Conrad, Mary Magdalena, and Adam Muller.
1748, Aug. 30, Conrad, Peter, and Anna Maria Grabiler.

1768, Dec.   20, Cor, Christian, and Hanna Miller.
1784, Dec.   12, Corbett, Michael, and Elizabeth Harvey.
1767, Nov.   22, Cox, Peter, and Anna Hughes.
1775, Sept. 26, Crebiel, Nicolaus, and Barbara Decker.
1776, June   30, Crebiel, Philippina, and John Michael Gebhard.
1747, Nov.   17, Crump, Philip Tobias, and Marga. Eliz. Wartman.
1775, June   6, Dachebach, John, and Maria Graf.
1776, Feb.   12, Daler, Phoebe, and Sam¹ Abendson.
1764, March 17, Dampman, Catharine, and John Fritz.
1806, April   7, Daub, Henry, and Maria Schwenk.
1771, Oct.   16, Dauberman, Andreas, and Eliz. Himmelre.
1799, May   14, Davidshauser, Henry, and An. Maria Weitner.
1799, Oct.   22, Davidshauser, John, and Barbara Meister.
1775, Sept. 26, Decker, Barbara, and Nicolaus Crebiel.
1782, Sept. —, De Frohn, Peter, and Barbara Bolich.
1769, May   23, de Hart, Catharine, and Conrad Loefler.
1776, Feb.   5, De Hart, Jacob, and Salome Well.
1769, Feb.   25, 'de Hauen, Mary, and Nicholas Schneider.
1745, Oct.   3, de Hohsin, Widow, and Martin Bullinger.
1796, Sept. 18, Dennis, Andrew, and Margaret Stark.
1769, May   30, Derr, Elizabeth, and Ulrich Stalp.
1796, Feb.   28, Deters, Hanna, and John Seeger.
1799, May   13, Detter, Eliz., and Carl Ellenberger.
1779, July   27, Detweiler, Jacob, and Eva Cath. Breyer.
1807, May   12, Detweiler, Jacob, and Magdalena Heist.
1805, Dec.   14, Detweiler, Maria, and Daniel Miller.
1804, July   15, Dewalt, Philip, and Polly Underhofler.
1763, May   3, Diel, Geo. Philip, and Eliz. Cath. Fuchs.
1753, May   15, Diel, Margaret, and Philip Boretz.
1805, Jan.   3, Diener, Christina, and John Koch.
1769, Feb.   14, Dieter, John, and Catharine Reifschneider.
1774, July   5, Dieterich, Michael, and Catharine Meier.
1802, May   9, Doerr, Henry, and Catharine Schneider, (widow.)
1799, June   16, Dotter, An. Maria, and Jacob Schmidt.
1796, May   10, Dotterer, Eliz., and Peter Henry.
1763, Dec.   28, Dotterer, Margaret, and Joseph Thomson.
1764, Sept.   3, Dottinger, Regina, and Diederich Geiger.
1806, June   29, Dress, Cath., and Math. Hase.
1807, April 19, Drollinger, Peter, and Cath. Reitenauer.
1752, Dec.   26, Duckert, Sybilla, and Michael Satler.
1774, Sept. 20, Dull, Caspar, and Hanna Mathews.
1802, Sept.   5, Dumig, Jacob, and Maria Schmidt.
1755, April 26, Durr, Andrew, and Magdalena Rieger.
1745, Nov.   20, Durr, Jacob, and Marga. Barbara Schlagel.
1745, Nov.   20, Durr, Melchior, and Anna Barbara Hilbart.
1796, Nov.   22, Eberhard, Matheus, and Catharine Miller.

1752, May   25, Eberhardt, John Caspar, and Christina Schmidt.
1748, May   15, Ebhard, Cath. Sybilla, and John Schaut.
1747, Nov.   10, Ebli, Mary Marga., and John Jacob Loeser.
1763, May   23, Ebly, Jacob, and Christina Mann.
1806, May   4, Eckbrett, Henry, and Catharine Fuchs.
1795, Oct.   29, Eckbrett, Margarett, and Jacob Barrall.
1797, Jan.   21, Eckbrett, Susanna, and George Kolb.
1799, Sept.   9, Edelman, John, and Magda. Friede.
1799, Nov.   5, Egold, Catharine, and Fred'k Herb.
1805, June   19, Egolf, Eliz., and Philip Voegely.
1771, April   23, Ehrhard, Barbara, and Adam Wartman.
1777, Dec.   17, Ehrhard, John., and Eva Berninger.
1764, Oct.   27, Eirich, John Geo., and Gertrude Clauser.
1772, Feb.   25, Eisehauer, Jacob, and Maria Albrecht.
1755, Oct.   23, Ekel, John Henry, and Margaret Horner.
1775, Jan.   31, Elgert, Jacob, and Catharine Beck.
1799, May   13, Ellenberger, Carl, and Eliz. Detler.
1799, July   7, Ellenberger, George, and Eliz. Hilpart.
1808, March   13, Emmerich, Geo., and Eliza Jago.
1773, April   13, Emmerich, John, and Marga. Beiteman.
1773, Dec.   14, Engers, Maria, and Jacob Schuman.
1807, Dec.   6, Erb, John Geo., and Cath. Hartman.
1785, Feb.   15, Erb, John George, and Catharine Renninger.
1765, April   2, Erhart, Margaret, and Michael Joerger.
1764, June   5, Erne, Jacob, and Anna Barbara Linzenbigler.
1778, April   7, Ernst, John Fred'k, and Eliz. Jaeger.
1747, June   10, Eschenbach, Andreas, and Maria Bossert.
1796, March   26, Essig, Susanna, and John Remby.
1745, June   5, Ethes, Elizabeth, and Martin Orner.
1806, Nov.   20, Ewald, Catharine, and William Miller.
1807, May   21, Ewald, Geo., and Magdalena Hillegass.
1745, June   23, Fager, Frederica Dorothea, and Philip Gras.
1804, May   1, Feather, Maria, and Henry Schmidt.
1774, Jan.   9, Febinger, Adam, and Elizabeth Hubert.
1795, Sept.   15, Febinger, Maria, and Peter Lehman.
1776, July   9, Fedele, Magdalena, and Nicholas Pfuhl.
1751, Nov.   26, Fedele, Michael, and Cath. Wartman.
1754, April   4, Fedele, Sarah, and Jacob Krebs.
1764, Feb.   21, Fertig, Elizabeth, and Jacob Geringer.
1764, Feb.   21, Fertig, Margaret, and Henry Millhahn.
1764, June   10, Fertig, Michael, and Anna Maria Ries.
1774, Feb.   8, Finckbeiner, Philip Jacob, and Mary Magdalena
                  Schilley.
1772, June   23, Fischer, Catharine, and Henry Thieme.
1763, Oct.   18, Fischer, Jacob, and Mary Cath. Schmidt.
1795, April   5, Fisher, Barbara, and Geo. Griessinger.

1767, April 20, Fisher, Eva, and Veit Wolf.
1755, Jan. 26, Flegel, Anna Maria, and Christian Seitz.
1807, March 30, Flicker, Susanna, and John Reichert.
1771, Jan. 8, Frack, Anna Maria, and Michael Hellebard.
1768, May 24, Francke, John Dan'l, and Elizabath Long.
1769, Oct. 31, Franck, Maria Salome, and Hans Adam Lude.
1774, Aug. 23, Franckenberger, Cath., and John Sackman.
1772, Dec. 22, Franckenberger, Ludwig, and Anna Maria Ammerman.
1809, March 26, Frankenberger, Magdalena,and Andrew Hartranft.
1804, Nov. 18, Frede, Maria, and Jonah Merklay.
1775, March 5, Freed, Sam¹, and Maria Meyer.
1769, May 7, Freund, George, and Maria Bayer.
1806, Feb. 18, Frey, Christopher, and Hanna Burman.
1795, April 2, Frey, Elizabeth, and Daniel Traumbeller.
1776, April 9, Frey, Joshua, and Eliz. Wittman.
1801, April 14, Freyer, Barbara, and Henry Nus.
1772, Feb. 18, Fried, John, and Margaret Grafe.
1799, Sept. 9, Friede, Magda., and John Edelman.
1796, July 24, Friederich, Caspar, and Maria Eliz. Hassmann.
1767, Aug. 2, Friederich, David, and Catharine Borck.
1794, Nov. 2, Friederich, Eliz., and Isaac Meyer.
1800, Sept. 14, Friederich, Eliz., and Jacob Binder.
1805, Jan. 27, Friederich, Geo., and Sara Kurz.
1804, Feb. 12, Friederich, Magda., and Fred'k Schick.
1804, Jan. 1, Friederich, Magdalena, and Jacob Gilbert.
1802, Jan. 17, Friederich, Maria, and Daniel Miller.
1771, March 12, Friederich, Peter, and Margaret Krause.
1764, Oct. 16, Fritz, Anna Maria, and John Hofman.
1767, June 16, Fritz, Anna Regina, and George Lutz.
1763, June 20, Fritz, Balthasar, and Susanna Cath. Raeder.
1767, March 31, Fritz, Catharine, and Simon Kachel.
1798, Nov. 25, Fritz, Fred'k Gottlieb, and Margaret Vogel.
1764, March 17, Fritz, John, and Catharine Dampman.
1807, Dec. 20, Fritz, Maria, and John Fuss.
1774, July 19, Frohn, Barbara, and Martin Kieler.
1773, Dec. 25, Frohn, Jacob, and Regina Joerger.
1807, Feb. 3, Fronhauser, John, and Cath. Herb.
1804, Nov. 13, Fronhauser, Mary, and John Schodder.
1795, April 5, Fruy, Elizabeth, and Jacob Mohr.
1806, May 4, Fuchs, Catharine, and Henry Eckbrett.
1763, May 3, Fuchs, Eliz. Cath., and Geo. Philip Diel.
1769, April 28, Fuchs, Elizabeth, and John Christian Acker.
1775, Dec. 26, Fuchs, Eva Maria, and Peter Hassinger.
1769, April 11, Fuchs, Henry, and Anna Maria Moser.
1807, May 17, Fuchs, Jacob, and Catharine Huber.

1746, Nov.   25, Fuchs, John Christopher, and Rosina Eliz. Linking.
1806, Nov.   30, Fuchs, Maria, and Henry Zink.
1795, April 19, Füllman, Fred'k, and Nancy Reichert.
1796, June   12, Fullman, Jacob, and Margaret Lober.
1767, June   21, Fullman, Jost, and Elizabeth Hartt.
1807, Dec.   20, Fuss, John, and Maria Fritz.
1763, Nov.   2, Fuss, Valentine, and Rosina Henrich.
1775, April   6, Galger, Joseph, and Elizabeth Huben.
1799, April 21, Gauchler, John, and Elizabeth Renninger.
1776, June   30, Gebhard, John Michael, and Philippina Crebiel.
1769, April   2, Geider, Adam, and Magdalen Scheratti.
1746, Nov.   25, Geiger, Anthony, and Barbara Geiger.
1746, Nov.   25, Geiger, Barbara, and Anthony Geiger.
1764, Sept.   3, Geiger, Diederich, and Regina Dottinger.
1808, March 29, Geiger, Elizabeth, and Jacob Stadtler.
1747, March 10, Geiger, Mary Marga., and John Stapleton.
1770, Sept. 18, Genie, John, and Anna Barbara Keller.
1764, July   31, Genter, Anna Maria, and Jacob Roller.
1772, Oct.   27, George, Magdalena, and John Hartsill.
1795, Nov.   1, Gerber, John, and Magdalena Kien.
1764, Feb.   21, Geringer, Jacob, and Elizabeth Fertig.
1779, June   5, Gerlin, David, and Margaret Stophelet.
1796, March 27, Gilbert, Andrew, and Anna Makary.
1752, Nov.   9, Gilbert, Anna Margaret, and Geo. Freiderich Beu-
                  terman.
1802, Feb.   28, Gilbert, Barbara, and John Adam Muller.
1752, Nov.   21, Gilbert Bernhard, and Mary Eliz. Meyer.
1800, Oct.   12, Gilbert, Catharine, and Tobias Albrecht.
1795, March   3, Gilbert, Christina, and Michael Sweinhard.
1800, May   20, Gilbert, David, and Maria Merklay.
1774, May   23, Gilbert, Elias, and Magdalena Sorgen.
1765, Jan.   29, Gilbert, Elizabeth, and Fred'k Baer.
1805, April   7, Gilbert, Henry, and Salome Kaiser.
1784, Dec.   14, Gilbert, Jacob, and Barbara Schinlein.
1804, Jan.   1, Gilbert, Jacob, and Magdalena Friederich.
1777, Jan.   7, Gilbert, Margaret, and Peter Armbruster.
1804, Aug.   12, Gilbert, Maria, and Henry Renninger.
1748, Jan.   5, Gilbert, Mathias, and Christina Dorothy Huber.
1804, Aug.   25, Gilbert, Math., and Hanna Becktel.
1776, Nov.   19, Gilbert, Samuel, and Catharine Saule.
1769, Feb.   7, Gilhelm, Thomas, and Hanna Kandel.
1764, Nov.   25, Glantz, Catharine, and John Geo. Bard.
1765, Jan.   6, Glas, Martinus, and Elizabeth Huber.
1804, Sept. 27, Glaze, John Adam, and Catharine Weiss.
1804, Nov.   11, Glaze, Stephen, and Mary Beck.
1770, June   28, Glouse, Barbara, and Christoph Mintz.

1776, Feb. 13, Goetze, Christian, and Maria Barbara Petrie.

1763, Nov. 6, Goetzelman, An. Maria, and Adam Rau.

1768, Feb. 2, Goetzelman, Dorothea, and Adam Thieme.

1769, Aug. 1, Gorger, Elizabeth, and Michael Albrecht.

1804, Oct. 2, Gottschall, John, and Maria Neidig.

1808, March 13, Gottschall, Margaret, and Andr. Honetler.

1808, Jan. 31, Gottshall, Philip, and Cath. Neuman.

1774, Oct. 18, Gottschaler, Ernst, and Maria Klein.

1773, Nov. 16, Gottwald, Christina, and William Reeh.

1748, Aug. 30, Grabiler, Anna Maria, and Peter Conrad.

1805, Jan. 15, Graf, Jacob, and Catharine Reiff.

1774, June 21, Graf, Margaret, and Paul Joerger.

1775, June 6, Graf, Maria, and John Dachebach.

1772, Feb. 18, Grafe, Margaret, and John Fried.

1763, Feb. 20, Gras, Catharine, and David Hebbenheimer.

1745, June 23, Gras, Philip, and Frederica Dorothea Fager.

1796, Aug. 30, Grauss, Abraham, and Eliz. Ziegler.

1802, April 19, Gray, Anna Elizabeth, (widow,) and Christian Miller.

1748, May 24, Greiner, John, and Catharine Beyer.

1771, Nov. 12, Gresson, Math., and Elizabeth Maurer.

1763, May 15, Gretler, Regina, and Solomon Westle.

1801, Dec. 12, Griesinger, Maria, and Adam Neidig.

1795, April 5, Griessinger, Geo., and Barbara Fisher.

1800, Aug. 31, Grissinger, Magdalena, and John Lang.

1795, Sept. 30, Groll, Catharine, and George Herpel.

1771, April 30, Grono, Sara, and Thomas Bull.

1808, March 3, Grote, Jacob, and Elizath Shumacher.

1807, March 23, Grove, Jacob, and Cath. Underhofler

1786, Oct. 25, Grub, Caspar, and Eva Schweitzer.

1770, July 24, Grube, Peter, and Susanna Schweitzer.

1795, May 31, Guldin, Daniel, and Margaret Joerger.

1772, April 7, Haacke, Gottfried, and Johanna Mozer.

1750, March 28, Haag, An. Maria, and Math. Walter.

1751, Sept. 24, Haarim, Tobias, and Elizabeth Possert.

1796, April 16, Haas, Benj., and Eliz. Liebeguth, (widow.)

1772, June 9, Haberlin, Barbara, and Nicholas Schneider.

1775, Jan. 24, Hagen, Anton, and Catharine Joerger.

1769, Dec. 3, Hahlman, Margaret, and Melchior Rieser.

1745, June 23, Hahns, Anna Maria, and Jacob Hauch.

1803, April 14, Hanberger, Peter, and Christina Kepner.

1752, Feb. 2, Hanselman, Hans Geo., and Maria Christina Macherlin.

1779, Sept. 14, Hartlein, Lorenz, and Magdalena Seibert.

1750, April 23, Hartlein, Margaret, and John Wit.

1779, Oct. 4, Hartman, Adam, and Mary Barnet.

1807, Dec.   6, Hartman, Cath., and John Geo. Erb.
1796, Dec.   11, Hartman, Fred'k, and Sophia Weiss.
1770, May   22. Hartman, John Jacob, and Sara Burckard.
1809, March 26, Hartranft,Andrew,and Magdalena Frankenberger.
1806, Nov.   17, Hartranft, John, and Maria Roth.
1806, April 20, Hartranft, William, and Magdalena Brey.
1767, June   21, Hartt, Elizabeth, and Jost Fullman.
1772, Oct.   27. Hartsill, John, and Magdalena George.
1784, Dec.   12, Harvey, Elizabeth, and Michael Corbett.
1806, June   29, Hase, Math., and Cath. Dress.
1775, Dec.   26, Hassinger, Peter, and Eva Maria Fuchs.
1796, July   24, Hassmann, Maria Eliz., and Caspar Friederich.
1745, June   23, Hauch, Jacob, and Anna Maria Hahns.
1806, Aug.   24, Hauck, Daniel, and Cath. Trumheller.
1806, May   13, Hauck, Jacob, and An. Maria Minninger.
1773, Jan.   12, Hauck, John Henry, and Eva Rosina Heinzelman.
1804, July   29, Hauck, ——, and Susanna Boyer.
1808, March 20, Haws. Margaret, and Sam'l Schnell.
1763, Feb.   20, Hebbenheimer, David, and Catharine Gras.
1767, Oct.   20, Heibst, Nicholas, and Appolonia Wamser.
1765, Jan.   10, Heil, Christian, and Cath. Wambold.
1749, March 26. Heilig, An. Maria, and John Mich. Schlouecker.
1773, Nov.   18, Heilman, Catharine, and Isaac Schunck.
1747, April   9, Heimbach, Math., and Susanna Weske.
1765, April   1, Heinrig, Catharine, and John Bossert.
1773, Jan.   12, Heinzelman, Eva Rosina, and John Henry Hauck.
1807, May   12, Heist, Magdalena, and Jacob Detweiler.
1771, Jan.   8, Hillebard, Michael, and Anna Maria Frack.
1805, April 16, Heller, John, and Maria Wagner.
1774, Sept. 20, Hellm, Catharine, and Jacob Ruff.
1804, Oct.   7, Helm, Daniel, and Susanna Ludwig.
1807, Oct.   12, Hellpart, Barbara, and Jacob Hillegass.
1747, April   6, Henckle, Maria Eliz., and John Theobald Schultz.
1745, Sept. 10, Henckel, Mary Marga., and John Geo. Jond.
1752, Nov.   19, Henkel, Susanna Margaret, and Henry Muller.
1769, Feb.   12, Hennrich, Anna, and Thomas Ashenfelder.
1769, Feb.   23, Hennrich, Elizabeth, and Mathew Kugler.
1763, Nov.   2, Henrich, Rosina, and Valentine Fuss.
1800, Oct.   19, Henry, Jacob, and Nancy Landes.
1796, May   10, Henry, Peter, (widower,) and Eliz. Dotterer.
1796, Feb.   11, Herb, Barbara, and Andreas Nester.
1795, April   2, Herb, Catharine, and Jacob Huter.
1807, Feb.   3, Herb, Cath., and John Frohnhauser.
1799, Nov.   5, Herb, Fred'k, and Catharine Egold.
1796, June   23, Herb, Peter, and Elizabeth Hillegas.
1795, Feb.   22, Herbel, Maria Christina,and Geo. Michael Binder.

1775, Nov. 14, Herbst, Anna Barbara, and Geo. Henry Wertz.
1808, Feb. 14, Herbst, Elizabeth, and John Stofelet.
1776, Nov. 12, Herbst, George, and Barbara Kelly.
1805, July 7, Herp, Anna, and Daniel Popp.
1795, Sept. 30, Herpel, George, and Catharine Groll.
1750, Dec. 18, Hickes, Jeremiah, and Sarah Chapman.
1745, Nov. 20, Hilbart, Anna Barbara, and Melchior Durr.
1807, July 25, Hildebentel, Abrah., and Marga. Borleman.
1803, Sept. 10, Hildebentel, Daniel, and Elizabeth Reiter.
1797, May 15, Hildebentel, John, and Catharine Schittler.
1748, April 26, Hill, Catharine, and John Christoph Weichel.
1808, March 19, Hill, Catharine, and John Hill.
1808, March 19, Hill, John, and Catharine Hill.
1748, March 29, Hill, Susanna, and Christian Moser.
1796, June 23, Hillegas, Elizabeth, and Peter Herb.
1807, Oct. 12, Hillegass, Jacob, and Barbara Hellpart.
1807, May 21, Hillegass, Magdalena, and Geo. Ewald.
1799, July 7, Hilpart, Eliz., and George Ellenberger.
1771, Oct. 16, Hommelre, Eliz., and Andreas Dauberman.
1804, April 23, Hoch, Abrah, and Cath. Muthhard.
1785, May 4, Hockley, Nancy, and Thomas Walker.
1801, Oct. 4, Hoerner, Sara, and David Mayer.
1807, July 12, Hoerner, Susanna, and Henry Beitenman.
1804, June 26, Hoffman, Andreas, and Mally Beuteler.
1798, April 1, Hoffman, Andrew, and Elizabeth Knetz.
1749, Nov. 5, Hoffman, Anna Barbara, and John Kneiper.
1764, Oct. 16, Hofman, John, and Anna Maria Fritz.
1764, March 15, Hollebach, Mary, and Jacob Buskirk.
1808, March 13, Honetler, Andr., and Margaret Gottshall.
1799, Jan. 22, Honetler, Catharine, and Henry Schweinhard.
1785, May 19, Hoover, Jacob, and Maria Semple.
1785, July 5, Hoover, Maria, and John Witman.
1747, Sept. 6, Hopkin, Mathew, and Leah Johns.
1806, Dec. 7, Horn, Catharine, and Solomon Swarz.
1755, Oct. 23, Horner, Margaret, and John Henry Ekel.
1763, March 13, Horning Benedick, and Elizabeth Miller.
1773, March 24, Hotteman, Sara, and Christn Steinman.
1775, April 6, Huben, Elizabeth, and Joseph Galger.
1775, Dec. 5, Huben, Henry, and Elizabeth Boldo.
1807, May 17, Huber, Catharine, and Jacob Fuchs.
1803, March 27, Huber, Catharine, and John Sell.
1748, Jan. 5, Huber, Christina Dorothea, and Mathias Gilbert.
1765, Jan. 6, Huber, Elizabeth, and Martinus Glas.
1749, Feb. 21, Huber, Margaret, and Philip Wirts.
1794, Jan. 9, Hubert, Elizabeth, and Adam Febinger.
1767, Nov. 22, Hughes, Anna, and Peter Cox.

1753, March 25, Hummel, Jacob, and Anna Maria Stichter.
1808, March 20, Hummel, Jonathan, and Magda. Walter.
1795, April   2, Huter, Jacob, and Catharine Herb.
1769, Nov. 14, Ickes, Michael, and Catharine Acker.
1771, Dec. 10, Ickes, Peter, and Dorothea Kebner.
1755, Jan. 27, Ide, Henry, and Ilse Dorothea Pless.
1795, March 18, Imbos, Catharina, and Abraham Muthard.
1772, March 30, Ingerson, Magdalena, and John Kohler.
1768, April   5, Jacob, Anna Catharine, and Caspar Meier.
1808, May   22, Jacob, Catharine, and Andrew Bayer.
1778, April   7, Jaegar, Eliz., and John Fred'k Ernst.
1808, March 13, Jago, Eliz., and Geo. Emmerich.
1807, July   19, Janson, William, and Susanna Bechtel.
1768, Jan. 26, Jaus, Margaret, and Daniel Boehme.
1764, Jan. 24, Jenkin, Anna, and Nicholas Kurtz.
1774, Dec.   6, Joerger, Adam, and Elizabeth Neuman.
1783, Dec. 23, Joerger, Andreas, and Anna Stauffer.
1775, Jan. 24, Joerger, Catharine, and Anton Hagen.
1795, May   24, Joerger, David, and Elizabeth Krebs.
1768, July   5, Joerger, Dewald, and Mary Margaret Kreiner.
1782, Dec. 17, Joerger, Eliz., and John Stauffer.
1796, April   3, Joerger, Eva, and Jacob Yauser.
1795, May   25, Joerger, Jacob, and Margaret Lude.
1795, May   31, Joerger, Margaret, and Daniel Guldin.
1801, March 16, Joerger, Margaret, and John Reifschneider.
1765, April   2, Joerger, Michael, and Margaret Erhart.
1774, June   21, Joerger, Paul, and Margaret Graf.
1796, Nov.   1, Joerger, Philip, and Maria Soldin.
1773, Dec. 25, Joerger, Regina, and Jacob Frohn.
1747, Sept.   6, Johns, Leah, and Mathew Hopkin.
1745, Sept. 10, Jond, John Geo., and Mary Marga. Henckel.
1769, Jan.   5, Jones, David, and Mary Brook.
1772, June   25, Jones, Hanna, and Henry Moore.
1784, Dec.   6, Jones, Rachel, and Jacob Mathai.
1773, Dec.   7, Jost, John Henry, and Susanna Kieler.
1745, May   28, Jurger, John Andrew, and Catharine Conrad.
1747, March 17, Jurger, John Thomas, and An. Maria Miller.
1794, Nov.   20, Jurger, Veit, and Sybilla Renninger.
1767, March 31, Kachel, Simon, and Catharine Fritz.
1764, Sept.   5, Kaebler, Abraham, and Cath. Miller.
1805, April   7, Kaiser, Salome, and Henry Gilbert.
1801, April   28, Kalb, Hanna, and Joseph Bettman.
1746, June   3, Kallbach, Anna Maria, and Geo. Bernard Renn.
1769, Feb.   7, Kandel, Hanna, and Thomas Gilhelm.
1772, July   21, Kanner, David, and Appollonia Roth.
1776, Nov. 12, Kebler, Henry, and Maria Brand.

1752, Dec.   5, Kebner, David, and Hanna Singer.
1771, Dec.   10, Kebner, Dorothea, and Peter Ickes.
1769, March   7, Kebner, Elizabeth, and John Batz.
1769, March 28, Kebner, William, and Catharine Liebegath.
1794. Nov.   9, Kehl, John, and Eliz. Renninger.
1747, Sept.   30, Keil, Elizabeth, and John Benedict Muntz.
1802, March 19, Keiler, Eliz., (widow,) and Jacob Schnell.
1765, July   9, Keiser, Mary Magda., and Dan¹ Rothermel.
1796, March   1, Kelchune, Peter, and Susanna Beyer.
1770, Sept.   18, Keller, Anna Barbara, and John Genie.
1774, May   29, Keller, Magdalena, and Henry Reidelsdorfer.
1776, Nov.   12, Kelly, Barbara, and George Herbst.
1785, April   5, Kelly, Peter, (widower,) and Susanna Schneider,
                     (widow.)
1808, Jan.   31, Kepler, Henry, and Cath. Schell.
1755, April   13, Kepner, Bernard, and Eva Meyer.
1755, April   14, Kepner, Catharine, and Melchior Knople.
1803, April   14, Kepner, Christina, and Peter Hanberger.
1752, March   18, Kepperling, Caspar, and Litz Stemple.
1806, March   30, Kerber, Jacob, and Elizabeth Kuter.
1795, April   7, Kerper, Maria, and Isaac Merckel.
1776, May   7, Ketler, Barbara, and John Knauer.
1747, Feb.   11, Keylwein, Philippina, and Conrad Bower.
1771, Nov.   12, Kiehle, Catharine, and Andreas Kuhn.
1771, Dec.   10, Kiehle, Susanna, and Fred'k Schonleber.
1767, Aug.   6, Kiehl, Susanna, and Henry Christman.
1795, March   17, Kiel, Nicholas, and Eliz. Setzler.
1774, July   19, Kieler, Martin, and Barbara Frohn.
1773, Dec.   7, Kieler, Susanna, and John Henry Jost.
1795, Nov.   1, Kien, Magdalena, and John Gerber.
1761, March   3, Kitterer, An. Maria, and John Schoener.
1806, March   16, Klein, Barbara, and Philip Schulz.
1802, Sept.   7, Klein, Carl, and Sara Lutz.
1768, May   10, Klein, Catharine, and John Stuard.
1775, Jan.   23, Klein, Christina, and Valentine Knochen.
1774, March   22, Klein, Christoph, and Anna Born.
1784, Sept.   21, Klein, Elizabeth, and Jacob Tormayer.
1773, Dec.   14, Klein, Elizabeth, and John Knodel.
1748, May   8, Klein, Hans Geo., and Mary Catharine Kunz.
1806, May   15, Klein, Geo., and Louise Wagner.
1806, March   23, Klein, Jacob, and Susanna Kropp.
1767, Jan.   1, Klein, Lewis, and Sara Thale.
1774, Oct.   18, Klein, Maria, and Ernst Gottschaler.
1776, May   7, Knauer, John, and Barbara Ketler.
1767, June   16, Knaus, William, and Lydia Miller.
1749, Nov.   5, Kneiper, John, and Anna Barbara Hoffman.

1798, April 1, Knetz, Elizabeth, and Andrew Hoffman.
1808, March 20, Knetz, Jacob, and Elizabeth Boyer.
1774, Jan. 23, Knochen, Valentine, and Christina Klein.
1773, Dec. 14, Knodel, John, and Elizabeth Klein.
1755, April 14, Knople, Melchior, and Catharine Kepner.
1807, April 19, Knous, William, and Hanna Krebs.
1784, Dec. 14, Koch, John Carl, and Maria Reinheimer.
1805, Jan. 3, Koch, John, and Christina Diener.
1769, Aug. 1, Koerner, Cath., and Nicholas Lachmund.
1753, Oct. 9, Kohler, Cath., and Jacob Cangler.
1772, March 30, Kohler, John, and Magdalena Ingersen.
1747, July 14, Kohler, Margaret, and Conrad Mohr.
1755, March 31, Kohler, Susanna, and John Conrad.
1804, Jan. 15, Kolb, Catharine, and Abrah. Reifschneider.
1800, March 30, Kolb, Elizabeth, and Peter Benkus.
1796, Jan. 21, Kolb, George, and Susanna Eckbrett.
1764, April 10, Kraik, Eva, and Fred'k Brenholz.
1753, Dec. 11, Krause, George, and Christina Singer.
1771, March 12, Krause, Margaret, and Peter Friederich.
1754, April 18, Krause, Salome, and John Michael Renn.
1772, May 12, Kraus, Henry, and Mary Magdalene Schwenk.
1802, Feb. 28, Krauss, Elizabeth, and Jacob Brant.
1802, June 6, Krauss, Jacob, and Elizabeth Voegely.
1801, Nov. 14, Krauss, Maria, and Frederick Walt.
1801, Feb. 16, Krebs, Catharine, (widow,) and John Reichert.
1795, May 24, Krebs, Elizabeth, and David Joerger.
1807, April 19, Krebs, Hanna, and William Knous.
1796, April 10, Krebs, Henry, and Hanna Betz.
1799, May 12, Krebs, Jacob, and Elizabeth Bayer.
1754, April 4, Krebs, Jacob, and Sarah Fedele.
1771, June 25, Krebs, Michael, and Catharine Kunz.
1800, March 1, Krebs, Salome, and Henry Bayer.
1768, July 5, Kreiner, Mary Margaret, and Dewald Joerger.
1748, May 15, Kressler, Philip, and Anna Margaret Miller.
1761, Jan. 6, Kretzler, Jacob, and Elizabeth Nied.
1795, Oct. 11, Krieg, Catharine, and Henry Moser.
1775, Dec. 26, Kropp, Cath., and Jacob Leininger.
1806, March 23, Kropp, Susanna, and Jacob Klein.
1773, July 27, Kropp, Susanna, and Jno. Geo. Schneider.
1772, March 8, Kugler, Elizabeth, and Peter Becker.
1769, Feb. 23, Kugler, Mathew, and Elizabeth Hennrich.
1771, Nov. 12, Kuhn, Andreas, and Catharine Kiehle.
1767, Nov. 8, Kunstman, Henry, and Catharine Calb.
1749, Sept. 26, Kunz, Cath. Barbara, and Geo. Adam Leibers-
            berger.
1771, June 25, Kunz, Catharine, and Michael Krebs.

1748, May   8, Kunz, Mary Catharine, and Hans Geo. Klein.
1747, Dec.   9, Kurtz, H., and Anna Eliz. Seidel.
1764, Jan.   24, Kurtz, Nicolas, and Anna Jenkin.
1764, Sept.   11, Kurtz, Susanna, and Ludwig Reimer.
1767, March 29, Kurz, Anna, and Mathew Tagebach.
1802, June   6, Kurz, John, and Hanna Scheelkopf.
1799, Feb.   14, Kurz, Maria, and Jacob Brendlinger.
1805, Jan.   27, Kurz, Sara, and Geo. Freiderich.
1799, Feb.   25, Kurz, Susanna, and Henry Roy.
1805, Dec.   14, Kurz, Susanna, and Michael Albrecht.
1806, March 30, Kuter, Elizabeth, and Jacob Kerber.
1770, Sept.   18, Lachmund, Anna Cath., and Henry Rohrman.
1769, Aug.   1, Lachmund, Nicholas, and Cath Koerner.
1775, April   3, Lachmund, Regina, and Christoph Steinrock.
1806, Dec.   20, Lachmund, Valentine, and Cath. Pott.
1764, Nov.   29, Land, Conrad, and Catharine Mack.
1784, Nov.   2, Landes, Catharine, and Gilleon Weiss.
1783, Aug.   19, Landes, Henry, and Elizabeth Beyer.
1807, Sept.   21, Landes, Jesse, and Veronica Langenecker.
1800, Oct,   19, Landes, Nancy, and Jacob Henry.
1800, Aug.   31, Lang, John, and Magdalena Grissinger.
1800, Oct.   12, Langenbach, Elizabeth, and John Reiher.
1800, Dec.   30, Langenbach, Magda., and ———— Allebach.
1795, May   7, Langenecker, Jacob, and Cath. Zimmerman.
1807, Sept.   21, Langenecker, Veronica, and Jesse Landes.
1776, Nov.   18, Lauck, Andrew, and Fronica Bausman.
1772, June   9, Leber, Barbara, and Fred'k Zimmerman.
1807, March 30, Lehen, Elizabeth, and John Yoerger.
1795, Sept.   15, Lehman, Peter, and Maria Febinger.
1749, Sept.   26, Leibersberger, Geo. Adam, and Cath. Barbara
                  Kunz.
1775, May   30, Leininger, Catharine, and Philip Rieseman.
1775, Dec.   26, Leininger, Jacob, and Cath. Kropp.
1750, April   21, Lerch, Anna Rosina, and John Michael Pfrang.
1771, March   5, Lessig, John Christian, and Eliz. Reifschneider.
1808, March 20, Lewis, Elizabeth, and Jacob Schwenk.
1767, Dec.   15, Liben, Henry, and Mary Magdalena Stauch.
1769, March 28, Liebegath, Catharine, and William Kebner.
1796, April   16, Liebeguth, Eliz., (widow,) and Benj. Haas.
1771, May   27, Lindeman, Geo. William, and Cath. Brautigam.
1747, May   24, Lindermann, John, and Miss Uhl.
1746, Nov.   25, Linking, Rosina Eliz., and John Christoph. Fuchs.
1804, Jan.   22, Linzenbichler, Eliz., and Michael Weigel.
1808, Jan.   31, Linzenbichler, Magda., and Jacob Strohman.
1807, March   8, Linzenbichler, Margaret, and Jacob Stauffer.
1807, Aug.   2, Linzenbichler, Paul, and Elizabeth Binder.

1795, Sept. 15, Linzenbigler, Abrah., and Christina Miller.
1764, June 5, Linzenbigler, Anna Barbara, and Jacob Erne.
1800, Feb. 4, Liser, Elizabeth, and Jacob Sussholz.
1770, Dec. 25, Lober, Anna Maria, and George Volck.
1795, Nov. 10, Lober, Anna, and Henry Süssholz.
1772, Dec. 15, Lober, Catharine, and Anton Bender.
1796, June 12, Lober, Margaret, and Jacob Fullman.
1767, Dec. 15, Lober, Anna Rosina, and Joseph Brendlinger.
1806, Oct. 2, Loch, Sally, and Henry Maurer.
1770, Nov. 15, Loeber, Jacob, and Maria Margaret Arnd.
1769, May 23, Loefler, Conrad, and Catharine de Hart.
1747, Nov. 10, Loeser, John Jacob, and Mary Marga. Ebli.
1803, Jan. 9, Loh, Jacob, and Eliz. Bernhard.
1768, May 24, Long, Elizabeth, and John Dan'l Francke.
1806, Jan. 7, Loopold, John, and Barbara Spatz.
1776, March 31, Lord, Thomas, and Catharine Blecklie.
1804, Sept. 2, Low, Elizabeth, and Peter Vogely.
1764, March 27, Loyer, Michael, and Catharine Ritter.
1769, Oct. 31, Lude, Hans Adam, and Maria Salome Franck.
1795, May 25, Lude, Margaret, and Jacob Joerger.
1801, Sept. 20, Ludwig, Hanna, and Henry Beck.
1801, Aug. 30, Ludwig, Margaret, and Joseph Candle.
1804, Oct. 7, Ludwig, Susanna, and Daniel Helm.
1750, April 22, Luser, Barbara, and Fred'k Moser.
1767, June 16, Lutz, George, and Anna Regina Fritz.
1767, April 19, Lutz, Michael, and Anna Regina Mercklin.
1802, Sept. 7, Lutz, Sara, and Carl Klein.
1752, Feb. 2, Macherlin, Maria Christina, and Hans Geo. Hanselman.
1752, Feb. 23, Machnert, Michael, and Widow Symmerey.
1764, Nov. 29, Mack, Catharine, and Conrad Land.
1796, March 27, Mackary, Anna, and Andrew Gilbert.
1763, May 23, Mann, Christina, and Jacob Ebly.
1770, June 21, Marstaller, Catharine, and John Balde.
1796, March 22, Marstaller, Fred'k, and Hannah Peterson.
1764, Dec. 20, Marsteller, Dan'l, and Elizabeth Umstat.
1784, Dec. 6, Mathai, Jacob, and Rachel Jones.
1775, June 25, Matthai, John, and Catharine Wendel.
1774, Sept. 20, Mathews, Hanna, and Caspar Dull.
1783, March 10, Mauck, Conrad, and Catharine Zoller.
1799, May 14, Maurer, Andrew, and Hanna Colton, (widow.)
1771, Nov. 12, Maurer, Elizabeth, and Math. Gresson.
1806, Oct. 2, Maurer, Henry, and Sally Loch.
1770, Sept. 23, Maurer, Peter, and Catharine Schweitzer.
1768, March 3, May, Hanna, and Henry Moore.

1807, May   17, Maybury, William, and Marga. Scheuren.
1749, May   22, Mayer, Anna Eliz., and Christophe Buttebinder.
1799, Aug.   4, Mayer, Carl, and Eliz. Muller.
1801, Oct.   4, Mayer, David, and Sara Hoerner.
1808, Jan.   3, Mayer, Maria, and Jacob Sehler.
1807, Oct.   1, McCarly, James, and Margaret Staufer.
1799, June   16, McGeby, Marg., and John Clayfield.
1775, Jan.   10, Mecklin, Catharine, and George Bolich.
1784, Nov.   16, Mecklin, Philip, and Barbara Smith.
1784, June   1, Mecklin, Samuel, and Magdalena Bickel.
1768, April   5, Meier, Caspar, and Anna Catharine Jacob.
1774, July   5, Meier, Catharine, and Michael Dieterich.
1772, Dec.   1, Meisenheimer, Marga., and John Schuck.
1799, Oct.   22, Meister, Barbara, and John Davidshauser.
1775, April   3, Melick, John, and Anna Marga. Steinrock.
1795, April   7, Merckel, Isaac, and Maria Kerper.
1767, April   19, Mercklin, Anna Regina, and Michael Lutz.
1804, Nov.   18, Merklay, Jonah, and Maria Frede.
1800, May   20, Merklay, Maria, and David Gilbert.
1774, Jan.   11, Mercklin, Hanna, and —— Brotzman.
1771, June   25, Meyer, Catharine, and John Fred'k Miller.
1795, Nov.   3, Meyer, Catharine, and John Muthardt.
1755, April   13, Meyer, Eva, and Bernard Kepner.
1794, Nov.   2, Meyer, Isaac, and Eliz. Frederick.
1775, March   5, Meyer, Maria, and Saml. Freed.
1748, Aug.   30, Meyer, Mary Barbara, and John Besner.
1752, Nov.   21, Meyer, Mary Eliz., and Bernhard Gilbert.
1770, April   1, Meyer, Philippina, and John Stoltzenberg.
1755, Oct.   23, Michael, John Geo., and Margaret Colman.
1747, March   17, Miller, An. Maria, and John Thomas Jurger.
1764, Sept.   5, Miller, Cath., and Abraham Kaebler.
1768, Dec.   20, Miller, Catharine, and Leonhard Schneider.
1796, Nov.   22, Miller, Catharine, and Matheus Eberhard.
1795, Sept.   15, Miller, Christina, and Abrah. Linzenbigler.
1802, April   19, Miller, Christian, and Anna Elizabeth Gray, (widow.)
1806, Oct.   4, Miller, Daniel, and Catharine Voegely.
1805, Dec.   14, Miller, Daniel, and Maria Detweiler.
1802, Jan.   17, Miller, Daniel, and Maria Friederich.
1763, March   13, Miller, Elizabeth, and Benedick Horning.
1807, May   3, Miller, Esaias, and Susanna Sehler.
1768, Dec.   20, Miller, Hanna, and Christian Cor.
1775, Dec.   5, Miller, John, and Cath. Schleider.
1771, June   25, Miller, John Fred'k, and Catharine Meyer.
1767, June   16, Miller, Lydia, and William Knaus.
1807, Feb.   27, Miller, Mally, and Abrah. Clemence.
1748, May   15, Miller, Margaret, and Philip Kressler.

1771, March 26, Miller, Maria, and Christopher Schmid.
1806, June　8, Miller, Maria, and Jacob Staufer.
1767, Feb.　24, Miller, Martha, and Philip Told.
1768, Aug.　16, Miller, Michael, and Anna Maria Roshman.
1751, Sept.　22, Miller, Sara, and Patrick Collins.
1746, March 16, Miller, Ursula, and Geo. Michael Boreth.
1769, June　13, Miller, Valentine, and Cath. Reifschneider.
1806, Nov.　20, Miller, William, and Catharine Ewald.
1764, Feb.　21, Millhahn, Henry, and Margaret Fertig.
1802, Nov.　9, Milz, John, and Margaret Weiss.
1806, Nov.　23, Minner, Rosina, and Philip Rumfield.
1806, May　13, Minninger, An. Maria. and Jacob Hauck.
1770, June　28, Mintz, Christopher, and Barbara Glouse.
1769, Nov.　5, Moennichinger, Andreas, and Eliz. Moritz.
1747, July　14, Mohr, Conrad, and Margaret Kohler.
1804, Dec.　25, Mohr, Hanna, and John Brotzman.
1795, April　5, Mohr, Jacob, and Elizabeth Fruy.
1774, March　8, Mollen, Michael, and Esther Wollfert.
1772, June　25, Moore, Henry, and Hanna Jones.
1768, March　3, Moore, Henry, and Hanna May.
1748, Feb.　24, Morea, John, and Christina Straten.
1807, Nov.　29, More, John, and Catharine Wyand.
1804, Dec.　25, More, Mary, and Philip Berlinger.
1769, Nov.　5, Moritz, Eliz., and Andreas Moennichinger.
1769, April 11, Moser, Anna Maria, and Henry Fuchs.
1748, March 29, Moser, Christian, and Susanna Hill.
1763, Dec.　18, Moser, Eva, and Baltzer Traut.
1750, April 22, Moser, Fred'k, and Barbara Luser.
1803, Jan.　23, Moser, George, and Maria Schmidt.
1795, Oct.　11, Moser, Henry, and Catharine Krieg.
1749, Aug.　1, Moser, Paul, and Maria Eva Becholt.
1808, Jan.　31, Moser, Rebecca, and Leonhard Neidig.
1769, May　14, Moses, John Peter, and Elizabeth Andrae.
1772, April　7, Mozer, Johanna, and Gottfried Haacke.
1764, Dec.　18, Muckevus, Helena, and George Peck.
1799, March 19, Muhlhoff, John, and Cath. Schweinfort.
1746, Aug.　19, Muller, Adam, and Mary Magdalena Conrad.
1799, Aug.　4, Muller, Eliz., and Carl Mayer.
1802, Feb.　28, Muller, John Adam, and Barbara Gilbert.
1752, Nov.　19, Muller, Henry, and Susanna Margaret Henkel.
1747, Sept.　30, Muntz, John Benedict, and Elizabeth Keil.
1808, Feb.　10, Muskschalk, Sara Brown, and John Christopher
　　　　　　　　Strebel.
1795, March 18, Muthard, Abraham, and Catharine Imbos.
1804, April 23, Muthard, Cath., and Abrah. Hock.
1795, Nov.　3, Muthardt, John, and Catharine Meyer.

1764, Sept. 19, Myller, Henry, and Hanna Winters.
1801, Dec.   12, Neidig, Adam, and Maria Griesinger.
1808, Jan.   31, Neidig, Leonhard, and Rebecca Moser.
1804, Oct.   2, Neidig, Maria, and John Gottschall.
1796, Feb.   11, Nester, Andreas, and Barbara Herb.
1807, Jan.   13, Nester, Daniel, and Esther Wagner.
1796, Jan.   26, Netz, Maria, and Henry Beyer.
1807, July   25, Neuman, Catharine, and John Bilger.
1808, Jan.   31, Neuman, Cath., and Philip Gottshall.
1774, Dec.   6, Neuman, Elizabeth, and Adam Joerger.
1794, Dec.   16, Neuman, Maria, and Jacob Schoener.
1806, June   29, Niece, Abraham, and Elizabeth Ryer.
1761, Jan.   6, Nied, Elizabeth, and Jacob Kretzler.
1801, April 14, Nies, Henry, and Barbara Freyer.
1748, March 29, Niss, Anna Maria, and John Ringer.
1764, March 16, Oberholser, Mary, and William Springer.
1773, Feb.   2, O'Brian, Brian, and Anna Mary Thomas.
1776, June   18, Oehlgatte, Elizabeth, and Christn. William Bru-
                 thard.
1754, June   3, Oesterlein, Jeremiah, and Mary Cath. Weitner.
1745, June   5, Orner, Martin, and Elizabeth Ethes.
1803, Aug.   7, Palsgraf, S., and Henry Binder.
1806, Nov.   2, Palsgraf, Susanna, and Geo. Binder.
1771, Oct.   10, Pawli, Rachel, and Wm Ludwig Truckenmiller.
1764, Dec.   18, Peck, George, and Helena Muckevus.
1796, March 22, Peterson Hanna, and Fred'k Marstaller.
1776, Feb.   13, Petrie, Maria Barbara, and Christian Goetze.
1750, April 21, Pfrang, John Michael, and Anna Rosina Lerch.
1754, April 14, Philips, John, and Esther Rees.
1795, April 26, Pfonnebecker, Eliz., and William Pfonnebecker.
1795, April 26, Pfonnebecker, William, and Eliz. Pfonnebecker.
1776, July   9, Pfuhl, Nicholas, and Magdalena Fedele.
1770, Aug.   16, Phull, John, and Barbara Rothermal.
1751, Sept. 24, Pickel, Ludwig, and Eva Barbara Schweinhard.
1755, Jan.   27, Pless, Ilse Dorothea, and Henry Ide.
1805, July   7, Popp, Daniel, and Anna Herp.
1751, Sept. 24, Possert, Elizabeth, and Tobias Haarim.
1806, Dec.   20, Pott, Cath., and Valentine Lachmund.
1763, June   20, Raeder, Susanna Cath., and Balthasar Fritz.
1806, Feb.   23, Rahn, Joseph, and Elizabeth Schnell.
1763, March   1, Ramsteir, John Henry, and Eliz. Schmidt.
1763, Nov.   6, Rau, Adam, and An. Maria Goetzelman.
1804, June   19, Rautenbush, Sara, and Geo. Roeller.
1784, Dec.   21, Rawn, Samuel, and Hanna Sleiss.
1773, Nov.   16, Reeh, William, and Christina Gottwald.
1754, April 14, Rees, Esther, and John Philips.

1770, Nov. 13, Reicherd, Christina, and Philip Vetterrolf.
1797, Feb. 7, Reicherd, Math., and Sara Bucher.
1801, Feb. 16, Reichert, John, and Catharine Krebs, (widow.)
1807, March 30, Reichert, John, and Susanna Flicker.
1779, June 1, Reichert, Maria, and Fred'k Baiteman.
1795, April 19, Reichert, Nancy, and Fred'k Füllman.
1774, May 29, Reidelsdorfer, Henry, and Magdalena Keller.
1764, Jan. 24, Reidennauer, Elizabeth, and John Sommer.
1770, May 29, Reier, John, and Catharine Appel.
1805, Jan. 15, Reiff, Catharine, and Jacob Graf.
1804, Jan. 15, Reifschneider, Abrah., and Catharine Kolb.
1764, Feb. 14, Reifschneider, Catharine, and John Dieter.
1769, June 13, Reifschneider, Cath., and Valentine Miller.
1771, March 5, Reifschneider, Eliz., and John Christian Lessig.
1801, March 16, Reifschneider, John, and Margaret Joerger.
1746, Dec. 9, Reifschneider, John W^m, and Eva Catharine Schweinhard.
1771, May 21, Reifschneider, Juliana, and Andreas Schoener.
1795, Oct. 13, Reifschneider, Rachel, and Jacob Berritt.
1801, Oct. 11, Reiher, Cath., and John Geo. Beitenman.
1804, Jan. 29, Reiher, George, and Cath. Wambold.
1800, Oct. 12, Reiher, John, and Elizabeth Langenbach.
1763, Sept. 11, Reimer, Ludwig, and Susanna Kurtz.
1805, March 19, Reiner, Philip, and Sara Rittenhouse.
1784, Dec. 14, Reinheimer, Maria, and John Clark Koch.
1807, April 19, Reitenauer, Cath., and Peter Drollinger.
1803, Sept. 10, Reiter, Elizabeth, and Daniel Hildebentel.
1796, March 26, Remby, John, and Susanna Essig.
1746, June 3, Renn, Geo. Bernard, and Anna Maria Kallbach.
1754, April 18, Renn, John Michael, and Salome Krause.
1785, Feb. 15, Renninger, Catharine, and John George Erb.
1804, Dec. 24, Renninger, Eliz., (widow,) and George Renninger.
1799, April 21, Renninger, Elizabeth, and John Gauchler.
1794, Nov. 9, Renninger, Eliz., and John Kehl.
1804, Dec. 24, Renninger, George, and Eliz. Renninger, (widow.)
1804, Aug. 12, Renninger, Henry, and Maria Gilbert.
1749, Nov. 20, Renninger, Sybilla, and Veit Jurger.
1796, March 22, Reyher, Christina, and Michael Schupp.
1796, Dec. 11, Reyher, Michael, and Eva Schweinhard.
1804, Nov. 25, Reyer, Rebecca, and George Spatz.
1775, Dec. 26, Rickerd, John, and Cath. Eliz. Thein.
1807, March 23, Rickert, Susanna, and Henry Ritter.
1755, April 26, Rieger, Magdalena, and Andrew Durr.
1764, June 10, Ries, Anna Maria, and Michael Fertig.
1775, May 30, Riesman, Philip, and Catharine Leininger.
1748, March 29, Ringer, John, and Anna Mary Niss.

1708, March 13, Ritter, Math., and Catharine Roads.
1805, March 19, Rittenhouse, Sara, and Philip Reiner.
1807, March 23, Ritter, Henry, and Susanna Rickert.
1764, March 27, Ritter, Catharine, and Michael Loyer.
1808, March 13, Roads, Catharine, and Math. Ritter.
1804, June 19, Roeller, Geo. and Sara Rautenbush.
1770, Sept. 18, Rohrman, Henry, and Anna Cath. Lachmund.
1768, Feb. 28, Roller, Barbara, and John Goe. Weymar.
1764, July 31, Roller, Jacob, and Anna Maria Genter.
1769, Jan. 4, Rose, Conrad, and Maria Winzenheiler.
1768, Aug. 16, Roshman, Anna Maria, and Michael Miller.
1772, July 21, Roth, Appollonia, and David Kanner.
1801, April 6, Roth, David, and Catharine Stelz, (widow.)
1806, Nov. 16, Roth, Maria, and John Hartranft.
1804, March 3, Roth, Peter, and Maria Stuter.
1770, Aug. 16, Rothermal, Barbara, and John Phull.
1765, July 2, Rothermel, Cath., and John Adam Braus.
1765, July 9, Rothermel, Dan'l, and Mary Magda. Keiser.
1799, Feb. 25, Roy, Henry, and Susanna Kurz.
1764, April 24, Royer, Michael, and Rosina Seybert.
1774, Sept. 20, Ruff, Jacob, and Catharine Hellm.
1807, Nov. 3, Rumfield, Henry, and Christina Bartman.
1806, Nov. 23, Rumfield, Philip, and Rosina Minner.
1798, Nov. 25, Rurz, Valentine, and Elizabeth Weiss.
1769, Dec. 3, Ruser, Melchoir, and Margaret Hahlman.
1806, June 29, Ryer, Elizabeth, and Abram Niece.
1806, Feb. 23, Ryer, Maria, and Jacob Thomas.
1774, Sept. 13, Sackman, Henry, and Anna Maria Saule.
1774, Aug. 23, Sackman, John, and Cath. Franckenberger.
1747, Sept. 24, Saem, Maria Cath., and John Geo. Voegely.
1752, Dec. 26, Satler, Michael, and Sybilla Duckert.
1774, Sept. 13, Saule, Anna Maria, and Henry Sackman.
1776, Nov. 19, Saule, Catharine, and Samuel Gilbert.
1750, Dec. 16, Savage, Anna, and Lewis Walker.
1764, March 13, Savage, Elizabeth, and Thomas Williams.
1752, Feb. 11, Schaefer, Anna Margaret, and Philip Berninger.
1804, April 29, Schanz, John, and Maria Walt.
1748, May 15, Schaut, John, and Cath. Sybilla Ebhard.
1802, June 6, Scheelkopf, Hanna, and John Kurz.
1808, Jan. 31, Schell, Cath., and Henry Kepler.
1769, Nov. 12, Schell, Lois, and John Martin Schletzer.
1764, Jan. 31, Schener, Rebecca, and John Van Der Schleis.
1769, April 2, Scheratti, Magdalen, and Adam Geider.
1763, May 3, Scherer, Conrad, and Eva Young.
1807, May 17, Scheuren, Marga., and William Maybury.
1804, Feb. 12, Schick, Fred'k, and Magda. Friederich.

1761, Jan.   6, Schick, Rosina, and Leonard Wiessner.
1776, May   7, Schidler, Eliz., and Jacob Bickel.
1776, Aug.   20, Schidler, Ludwig, and Susanna Catharine Wam-
                   bold.
1774, Feb.   8, Schilley, Mary Magdalena, and Philip Jacob Finck-
                   beiner.
1784, Dec.   14, Schinlein, Barbara, and Jacob Gilbert.
1782, Dec.   17, Schirmin, Susanna, and Isaac Bauman.
1797, May   15, Schittler, Catharine, and John Hildebentel.
1753, Sept.   25, Schlagel, Catharine, and Hans Geo. Beck.
1745, Nov.   20, Schlagel, Marga. Barbara, and Jacob Durr.
1745, Oct.   31, Schlagel, Widow, and John Fred'k Becker.
1775, Dec.   5, Schleider, Cath., and John Miller.
1769, Nov.   12, Schletzer, John Martin, and Lois Schell.
1764, Dec.   27, Schlonecker, Barbara, and Valentine Bauersax.
1763, March 13, Schlonecker, Geo. Adam, and Dorothea Barbara
                   Wister.
1784, May   9, Schlonecker, Henry, and Eliz. Steinbrenner.
1807, Nov.   22, Schlonecker, Eliz., and Solomon Basleres.
1749, March 26, Schlonecker, John Mich., and An. Maria Heilig.
1771, March 26, Schmid Christoph, and Maria Miller.
1753, May   25, Schmidt, Christina, and John Caspar Eberhardt.
1799, Dec.   24, Schmidt, Elizabeth, and Jacob Bayer.
1799, June   16, Schmidt Jacob, and An. Maria Dotler.
1763, March   1, Schmidt, Eliz., and John Henry Ramstein.
1804, May   1, Schmidt, Henry, and Maria Feather.
1803, Jan.   23, Schmidt, Maria, and George Moser.
1802, Sept.   5, Schmidt, Maria, and Jacob Dumig.
1763, Oct.   18, Schmidt, Mary Cath., and Jacob Fischer.
1796, Oct.   2, Schmidt, Peter, and Sara Zueber.
1750, Nov.   19, Schmied, John Martin, and Anna Gertrude Stutsh.
1802, May   9, Schneider, Catharine, (widow,) and Henry Doerr.
1773, July   27, Schneider, John Geo., and Susanna Kropp.
1768, Dec.   20, Schneider, Leonhard, and Catharine Miller.
1772, June   9, Schneider, Nicholas, and Barbara Haberlin.
1769, Feb.   25, Schneider, Nicholas, and Mary de Haven.
1795, March 17, Schneider, Nicholas, and Nancy Wartmiller.
1785, April   5, Schneider, Susanna, (widow,) and Peter Kelly,
                   (widower.)
1806, Feb.   24, Schnell, Elizabeth, and Joseph Rahn.
1773, April   11, Schnell, George, and Anna Dorothea Bruge.
1802, March 19, Schnell, Jacob, and Eliz. Keiler, (widow.)
1795, April   5, Schnell, Jacob, and Magdalena Bitling.
1808, March 20, Schnell, Sam'l, and Margaret Haws.
1804, Nov.   13, Schodder, John, and Mary Frohnhauser.
1771, May   21, Schoener, Andreas, and Juliana Reifschneider.

1795, Dec.   27, Schoener, Elizabeth, and John Trumheller.
1794, Dec.   16, Schoener, Jacob, and Maria Neumam.
1761, March   3, Schoener, John, and An. Maria Kitterer.
1771, Dec.   10, Schonleber, Fred'k, and Susanna Kiehle.
1774, June   28, Schrack, John, and Elizabeth Weber.
1772, Dec.   1, Schuck, John, and Marga. Meisenheimer.
1747, April   6, Schultz, John Theobald, and Maria Eliz. Henckel
1806, March 16, Schultz, Philip, and Barbara Klein.
1776, April   30, Schuman, Eliz., and John Stophelet.
1773, Dec.   14, Schuman, Jacob, and Maria Engers.
1768, Dec.   23, Schunck, Conrad, and Mary Barker.
1773, Nov.   18, Schunck, Isaac, and Catharine Heilman.
1807, May   1, Schunk, Henry, and Sarah Sehler.
1796, March 22, Schupp, Michael, and Christina Reyher.
1774, Jan.   18, Schupp, Michael, and Elizabeth Appel.
1799, March 19, Schweinfort, Cath., and John Muhlhoff.
1783, May   20, Schweinhard, Anna Maria, and Michael Alten
                     dorfer.
1751, Sept.   24, Schweinhard, Eva Barbara, and Ludwig Pickel.
1746, Dec.   9, Schweinhard, Eva Catharine, and John Wm Reif-
                     schneider.
1796, Dec.   11, Schweinhard, Eva, and Michael Reyher.
1805, Oct.   20, Schweinhard, George, and Susanna Sehler.
1799, Jan.   22, Schweinhard, Henry, and Catharine Honetter.
1770, Sept.   23, Schweitzer, Catharine, and Peter Maurer.
1768, Oct.   25, Schweitzer, Eva, and Caspar Grub.
1770, July   24, Schweitzer, Susanna, and Peter Grube.
1799, Oct.   27, Schwenk, Elizabeth, and Andrew Walt.
1804, Aug.   12, Schwenk, Henry, and M. Trombor.
1808, March 20, Schwenk, Jacob, and Elizabeth Lewis.
1799, March 26, Schwenk, Maria, and George Walt.
1806, April   7, Schwenk, Maria, and Henry Daub.
1772, May   12, Schwenk, Mary Magdalena, and Henry Kraus.
1801, March 24, Schwenkand, John, and Salome Stadtler.
1807, Nov.   29, Sechler, Cath., and Jacob Bernt.
1771, June   30, Seebold, David, and Elizabeth Weichel.
1796, Feb.   28, Seeger, John, and Hanna Deters.
1808, Jan.   3, Sehler, Jacob, and Maria Mayer.
1807, May   1, Sehler, Sara, and Henry Schunk.
1802, Jan.   31, Sehler, Sara, and Henry Walt.
1807, May   3, Sehler, Susanna, and Esaias Miller.
1805, Oct.   20, Sehler, Susanna, and George Schweinhard.
1779, Sept.   14, Seibert, Magdalena, and Lorenz Hartlein.
1747, Dec.   9, Seidel, Anna Eliz., and H. Kurtz.
1755, Jan.   26, Seitz, Christian, and Anna Maria Flegel.
1803, March 27, Sell, John, and Catharine Huber.

1785, May 19, Semple, Maria, and Jacob Hoover.
1806, April 20, Sensendorfer, Geo., and Sara Bitting.
1795, March 17, Setzler, Eliz., and Nicholas Kiel.
1764, April 24, Seybert, Rosina, and Michael Royer.
1808, March 3, Shumacher, Elizabeth, and Jacob Grote.
1764, Dec. 20, Shute, John, and Katy Collman.
1753, Dec. 11, Singer, Christina, and Geo. Krause.
1752, Dec. 5, Singer, Hanna, and David Kebner.
1806, March 9, Slagenhaupt, Susanna, and John Boehm.
1784, Dec. 21, Sleiss, Hanna, and Samuel Rawn.
1784, Nov. 16, Smith, Barbara, and Philip Mecklin.
1796, Nov. 1, Soldin, Maria, and Philip Joerger.
1764, Jan. 24, Sommer, John, and Elizabeth Reidennauer.
1774, May 23, Sorgen, Magdalena, and Elias Gilbert.
1806, Jan. 7, Spatz, Barbara, and John Loopold.
1804, Nov. 25, Spatz, George, and Rebecca Reyer.
1807, May 17, Spatz, Jacob, and Magdalena Arms.
1750, April 17, Speicht, Elizabeth, and John Bayer.
1764, March 16, Springer, William, and Mary Oberholser.
1808, March 29, Stadtler, Jacob, and Elizabeth Geiger.
1801, March 24, Stadtler, Salome, and John Schwenkand.
1796, March 27, Staffler, Henry, and Elizabeth Buckel.
1807, Dec. 20, Stahl, Susanna, and John Weller.
1769, May 30, Stalp, Ulrich, and Elizabeth Derr.
1747, March 10, Stapleton, John, and Mary Marga. Geiger.
1797, April 16, Stark, Ludwig, and Maria Zoller.
1796, Sept. 18, Stark, Margaret, and Andrew Dennis.
1801, June 7, Stattler, Abraham, and Eliz. Voegely.
1767, Dec. 15, Stauch, Mary Magdalena, and Henry Liben.
1806, June 8, Staufer, Jacob, and Maria Miller.
1807, Oct. 1, Stauffer, Margaret, and James McCarly.
1804, May 3, Stauffer, Abraham, and Esther Stauffer.
1783, Dec. 23, Stauffer, Anna, and Andreas Joerger.
1804, May 3, Stauffer, Esther, and Abraham Stauffer.
1807, March 8, Stauffer, Jacob, and Margaret Linzenbichler.
1782, Dec. 17, Stauffer, John, and Eliz. Joerger.
1784, May 9, Steinbrenner, Eliz., and Henry Schlonecker.
1773, March 24, Steinman, Christ[n], and Sara. Hotleman.
1775, April 3, Steinrock, Anna Marga., and John Melich.
1775, April 3, Steinrock, Christoph., and Regina Lachmund.
1801, April 6, Stelz, Catharine, (widow,) and David Roth.
1801, May 3, Stelz, Elizabeth, and John Bickel.
1752, March 18, Stemple, Litz, and Caspar Kepperling.
1753, March 25, Stitchter, Anna Maria, and Jacob Hummel.
1785, Jan. 18, Stichter, Jacob, and Christina Beiteman.
1807, Jan. 25, Stofelet, Geo., and Maria Werthain.

1808, Feb.   14, Stofelet, John, and Elizabeth Herbst.
1770, April   1, Stoltzenberg, John, and Philippina Meyer.
1776, April   30, Stophelet, John, and Eliz. Schuman.
1775, June   9, Stophelet, Margaret, and David Gerlin.
1748, Feb.   24, Straten, Christina, and John Morea.
1808, Jan.   31, Strohman, Jacob, and Magda. Linzenbichler.
1808, Feb.   10, Strebel, John Christopher, and Sarah Brown
                      Muskschalk.
1768, May   10, Stuard, John, and Catharine Klein.
1750, Nov.   19, Stutsh, Anna Gertrude, and John Martin Schmied.
1804, March   3, Stuter, Maria, and Peter Roth.
1795, Nov.   10, Süssholz, Henry, and Anna Lober.
1800, Feb.   4, Sussholz, Jacob, and Elizabeth Liser.
1807, Sept.   20, Sussholz, Jacob, and Magda. Bernt.
1806, Dec.   7, Swarz, Solomon, and Catharine Horn.
1795, March   3, Swinehard, Michael, and Christina Gilbert.
1752, Feb.   23, Symmerey, Widow, and Michael Machnert.
1767, March   29, Tagebach, Mathew, and Anna Kurz.
1767, Jan.   1, Thale, Sara, and Lewis Klein.
1768, Feb.   2, Thieme, Adam, and Dorothea Goetzelman.
1772, June   23, Thieme, Henry, and Catharine Fischer.
1775, Dec.   26, Thien, Cath. Eliz., and John Rickerd.
1773, Feb.   2, Thomas, Anna Mary, and Brian O'Brian.
1806, Feb.   23, Thomas, Jacob, and Maria Ryer.
1767, Feb.   24, Told, Philip, and Martha Miller.
1763, Dec.   28, Tomson, Joseph, and Margaret Dotterer.
1748, Sept.   21, Tormayer, Jacob, and Elizabeth Klein.
1795, April   2, Traumbeller, Daniel, and Elizabeth Frey.
1763, Dec.   18, Traut, Baltzer, and Eva Moser.
1804, Aug.   12, Trombor, M., and Henry Schwenk.
1771, Oct.   10, Truckenmiller, Wm Ludwig, and Rachel Pawli.
1806, Aug.   24, Trumheller, Cath., and Daniel Hauck.
1795, Dec.   27, Trumheller, John, and Elizabeth Schoener.
1772, April   21, Tuerr, Regina, and Michael Bauer.
1774, Feb.   24, Turner, Francis, and Anna Aschenbach.
1807, March   26, Tyson, John, and Margaret Baum.
1806, Nov.   6, Tyson, William, and Barbara, Uriny.
1747, May   24, Uhl, Miss, and John Lindermann.
1748, Jan.   14, Ulen, John, and Sara Bakon.
1764, Dec.   20, Umstat, Elizabeth, and Dan'l Marsteller.
1807, March   23, Underhofler, Cath., and Jacob Grove.
1804, July   15, Underhofler, Polly, and Philip Dewalt.
1806, Nov.   6, Uriny, Barbara, and William Tyson.
1764, Jan.   31, Van Der Schleis, John, and Rebecca Schener.
1770, Nov.   13, Vetterrolf, Philip, and Christina Reicherd.
1806, Oct.   4, Voegely, Catharine, and Daniel Miller.

1801, June   7, Voegely, Eliz., and Abraham Stattler.
1802, June   6, Voegely, Elizabeth, and Jacob Krauss.
1747, Sept. 24, Voegely, John Geo., and Maria Cath. Saem.
1801, May   5, Voegely, Maria, and Henry Bickel.
1805, June 19, Voegely, Philip, and Eliz. Egolf.
1798, Nov. 25, Vogel, Margaret, and Fred'k Gottlieb Fritz.
1804, Sept. 2, Vogely, Peter, and Elizabeth Low.
1804, May 13, Vogely, Peter, and Gertrude Christman.
1771, Aug. 27, Voigt, Valentine, and Anna Marga. Cambe.
1754, April 15, Volck, Anna Eliz., and Anthon Walter.
1770, Dec. 25, Volck, George, and Anna Maria Lober.
1807, Jan, 13, Wagner, Esther, and Daniel Nester.
1806, May 15, Wagner, Louise, and Geo. Klein.
1805, April 16, Wagner, Maria, and John Heller.
1750, Dec. 16, Walker, Lewis, and Anna Savage.
1785, May   4, Walker, Thomas, and Nancy Hockley.
1799, Oct. 27, Walt, Andrew, and Elizabeth Schwenk.
1801, Nov. 14, Walt, Frederick, and Maria Krauss.
1799, March 26, Walt, George, and Maria Schwenk.
1802, Jan. 31, Walt, Henry, and Sara Sehler.
1804, April 29, Walt, Maria, and John Schanz.
1754, April 15, Walter, Anthon, and Anna Eliz. Volck.
1808, March 20, Walter, Magda, and Jonathan Hummel.
1750, March 28, Walter, Math., and An. Maria Haag.
1765, Jan. 10, Wambold, Cath., and Christian Heil.
1804, Jan. 29, Wambold, Cath., and George Reiher.
1776, Aug. 20, Wambold, Susanna Catharine, and Ludwig Schidler.
1767, Oct. 20, Wamser, Appolonia, and Nicholas Heibst.
1771, April 23, Wartman, Adam, and Barbara Ehrhard.
1751, Nov. 26, Wartman, Cath., and Michael Fedele.
1749, April 10, Wartmann, Marga. Eliz., and Michael Beyer.
1747, Nov. 17, Wartman, Marga. Eliz., and Philip Tobias Crump.
1795, March 17, Wartmiller, Nancy, and Nicholas Schneider.
1774, June 28, Weber, Elizabeth. and John Schrack.
1771, June 30, Weichel, Elizabeth, and David Seebold.
1748, April 26, Weichel, John Christoph., and Catharine Hill.
1764, Nov. 15, Weidner, David, and Hanna Wumeldorf.
1804, Jan. 22, Weigel, Michael, and Eliz. Linzenbichler.
1807, Oct.   1, Weinland, Susanna, and Jacob Arms.
1804, Sept. 27, Weiss, Catharine, and John Adam Glaze.
1798, Nov. 25, Weiss, Elizabeth, and Valentine Rurz.
1784, Nov.   2, Weiss, Gilleon, and Catharine Landes.
1802, Nov.   9, Weiss, Margaret, and John Milz.
1796, Dec. 11, Weiss, Sophia, and Fred'k Hartman.
1799, May 14, Weitner, An Maria, and Henry Davidshauser.
1754, June   3, Weitner, Mary Cath., and Jeremiah Oesterlein.

1761, Feb.   3, Weldin, Margaret, and Thomas Weston.
1776, Feb.   5, Well, Salome, and Jacob de Hart.
1807, Dec.   20, Weller, John, and Susanna Stahl.
1775, June   25, Wendel, Catharine, and John Matthai.
1775, Oct.   15, Wengert, Magdalena, and John Geo. Arnd.
1808, Jan.   10, Wenner, Geo., and Eliz. Wyand.
1807, Jan.   25, Werthain, Maria, and Geo. Stofelet.
1775, Nov.   14, Werty, Geo. Henry, and Anna Barbara Herbst.
1747, April   9, Weske, Susanna, and Math. Heimbach.
1763, May   15, Westle, Solomon, and Regina Gretler.
1761, Feb.   3, Weston, Thomas, and Margaret Weldin.
1768, Feb.   28, Weymar, John Geo., and Barbara Roller.
1761, Jan.   6, Weissner, Leonard, and Rosina Schick.
1770, April   1, Wilkson, Thomas, and Catharine Amborn.
1764, March 13, Williams, Thomas, and Elizabeth Savage.
1764, Sept. 19, Winters, Hanna, and Henry Myller.
1769, Jan.   4, Winzenheiler, Maria, and Conrad Rose.
1749, Feb.   21, Wirts, Philip, and Margaret Huber.
1752, June   2, Wisner, John Geo., and Gertrude Brauningen.
1763, March 13, Wister, Dorothea Barbara, and Geo. Adam Schlo-
                 necker.
1750, April   23, Wit, John, and Margaret Hartlein.
1785, July   5, Witman, John, and Maria Hoover.
1776, April   9, Wittman, Eliz., and Joshua Frey.
1767, April   20, Wolf, Veit, and Eva Fisher.
1748, April   14, Wolffer, Simon, and Margaret Bauman.
1774, Dec.   27, Woolfart, Marga., and Balthaser Henry Beck.
1774, March   8, Woolfert, Esther, and Michael Mollen.
1763, Oct.   25, Wolst, ———, and Philip Baltner.
1808, Jan.   10, Wonnemacher, Maria, and Dan'l Yoerger.
1764, Nov.   15, Wumeldorf, Hanna, and David Weidner.
1807, April   26, Wyand, An. Elizabeth, and Sam'l Wyand.
1807, Nov.   29, Wyand, Catharine, and John More.
1808, Jan.   10, Wyand, Eliz., and Geo. Wenner.
1807, April   26, Wyand, Sam'l, and An. Elizabeth Wyand.
1796, April   3, Yauser, Jacob, and Eva Joerger.
1764, Dec.   18, Yocum, Rebecca, and Lawrence Bell.
1808, Jan.   10, Yoerger, Dan'l, and Maria Wonnemacher.
1807, March   30, Yoerger, John, and Elizabeth Lehen.
1763, May   3, Young, Eva, and Conrad Scherer.
1796, Aug.   30, Ziegler, Eliz., and Grauss Abraham.
1795, May   7, Zimmerman, Cath., and Jacob Langenecker.
1772, June   9, Zimmerman, Fred'k, and Barbara Leber.
1806, Nov.   30, Zink, Henry, and Maria Fuchs.
1783, March   10, Zoller, Catharine, and ConradMauck.
1797, April   16, Zoller, Maria, and Ludwig Stark.
1796, Oct.   2, Zueber, Sara, and Peter Schmidt.

MARRIAGE RECORD

OF

THE GERMAN REFORMED CHURCH,

AT PHILADELPHIA,

1748–1802.

GERMAN REFORMED CHURCH, PHIL'A.

1794, April 29, Abel, George, and Dorothea Koch.
1749, July 13, Abel, Joh. Mattias, and Anna Margaret Velt.
1761, Jan. 1, Adam, Johannes, and Verena Ebereht.
1777, Sept. 9, Adams, Anna Barbara, and Martin Tschudy.
1801, Feb. 27, Adams, Fred., and Cath. Hail.
1783, May 29, Adams, John, and Cath. Oberdorff.
1778, April 28, Adams, Salome, and Heinrich Hasler.
1779, March 23, Ailkils, George, and Barbara Downs.
1779, July 29, Ainger, Thomas, and Abigail Fairies.
1779, July 29, Albach, Elizabeth, and Hienerich Schneider.
1800, Oct. 27, Albach, Joh., and Maria Rosenberger.
1787, Oct. 4, Alberger, Adam, and Mary Colloday.
1782, June 30, Alberger, Christian, and Cath. Hoover.
1786, May 14, Alberger, Christian, and Susanna Meng.
1759, Sept. 9, Alberger, Christiana, and Johann Peter Lorie.
1785, July 19, Albert, Caspar, and Nancy Counen.
1769, Feb. 19, Albert, Johannes, and Maria Gertdorffer.
1783, March 13, Albert, Elizabeth, and Lorenz Foth.
1799, July 4, Alberry, Elizabeth, and Christian Bobschel.
1776, Sept. 17, Albrecht, John Jacob, and Mary Barbara Kubler·
1789, Sept. 15, Alburgen, Philip, and Doroth. Betsch.
1795, April 5, Alburger Jacob, and Margaretha Gassmann.
1784, March 4, Alburger, Johannes, and Dorothea Scherreden.
1799, March 6, Alburger, Philip, and Dolly Snyder.
1801, March 15, Alentrue, Francis, and Lydia Lee.
1786, Sept. 12, Alhausen, John Theis, and Anna Agite Kinry.
1753, Feb. 6, Allen, Ann, and John Grimwood.
1780, May 4, Allen, Elizabeth, and John Stimson.
1768, May 5, Allenbach, Friedenrich, and Maria Schmidt.
1785, March 15, Allin, Mary, and David Archer.
1786, June 22, Allioth Jerm. and Hannah Clear.
1779, Aug. 19, Allison, Sarah, and Edmund Edmunds.
1754, Oct. 23, Alloway, Mechelemiah, and Rebecca Rogers.
1750, Jan. 18, Aloway, Margaret, and John Johnson.
1750, July 29, Alowey, Elizabeth, and Lorentz Vetter.
1761, Aug. 13. Alster, Conrad, and Maria Froelich.
1775, July 15, Andersee, Conrad, and Maria Fischer.

1802, March 26, Anderson, Zebedee, and Cath. Zerns.
1784, April   27, Andressen, Eliz., and George Klein.
1775, April   4, Antes, Elizabeth, and John Shuler.
1767, Dec.   8, Antes, Henry, and Sophia Schnyder.
1785, May   19, Anthony, Magd. and Philip Maus.
1787, Sept.   6, Appel, Henry, and Anna Eliz. Danecker.
1759, June   26, Appenzeller, Jacob, and Eliz. Henrica Seifert.
1790, April   15, Applin, Jane, and Benjamin Inglis.
1785, March   15, Archer, David, and Mary Allin.
1781, March   29, Arenbold, Sarah, and Daniel Shea.
1786, May   14, Aris, James, and Cath. Thresscher.
1779, July   29, Armat, Thomas, and Mary McCutcheon.
1770, Aug.   8, Armbruster, Johann, and Cath. Gelbert.
1797, Jan.   26, Armstrong, Polly, and Valentine Schweitzer.
1785, Nov.   16, Arn, Daniel, and Dorothy Streeper.
1773, Oct.   17, Arnold, Margaretha, and Johann Sandor.
1765, Aug.   1, Arpiengast, Johann George, and Maria Magdalena
                    Pleininger.
1785, March   1, Ascher, Margaret, and Conrad Axs.
1783, April   7, Ashener, Maria, and Adam Roth.
1795, Nov.   1, Ashton, William, and Susanna Munch.
1779, Jan.   28, Aspey, Jane, and Alexander Parry.
1780, Nov.   28, Aspey, Rachel, and Henry Berrit.
1778, Sept.   20, Assmus, Joh. Christopher, and Cath. Hunt.
1750, July   7, Atkinson, John, and Elizabeth Radley.
1794, Aug.   10, Auffahrt, Sophia, and Moses Williams.
1791, Dec.   25, Aufforth, Charlotta, and Heinrich Jobst.
1801, Sept.   19, Auner, Mary, and Charles Harford.
1802, March   16, Auner, Jun., Peter, and Maria Will.
1785, March   1, Axs, Conrad, and Margaret Ascher.
1799, June   8, Bach, Jacob Berckel, and Philippina Hein.
1750, Feb.   19, Bachmaen, Maria Sophia, and Peter Kurlz.
1784, Feb.   15, Bachman, Conrad, and Susanna Bridges.
1787, Oct.   28, Bachman, Sarah, and Henry Schmidt.
1796, July   9, Bachofew, Johannes, and Maria Hoffman.
1788, March   9, Bachoff, Eliz., and Jacob Hill.
1775, Sept.   28, Bachtle, Daniel, and Margaretha Fotin.
1777, Feb.   13, Backer, Johann, and Mercy Griffith.
1796, April   21, Backer, Peter, and Comfort Higins.
1779, Dec.   5, Baechtel, Susanna, and Peter Schneider.
1748, Aug.   23, Baechtold, Joh. Veit, and Susanna Maria Erusin.
1796, May   29, Baer, Johannes, and Elizabeth Conrad.
1787, April   10, Baerdt, John Mich., and Cath. Scherer.
1790, June   25, Baerth, Magd., and Peter Nannetter.
1765, Jan.   17, Baertling, Emanuel, and Elizabeth Etter.
1779, Nov.   25, Bailey, Henry, and Agnes Tyger.

1777, March 4, Baily, Sophia, and Andrew Mullon.
1778, Nov. 24, Baker, Charles, and Mary Ritts.
1784, Feb. 29, Baker, Mary, and John Wagoner.
1802, April 10, Baker, Michael, and Eliz. Wilt.
1799, April 18, Bakins, Joh., and Hannah Downing.
1787, Feb. 13, Balde, Anthon, aud Christ. Ohlin.
1753, Dec. —, Balteweyn, Nicol., and Cath. Donber.
1784, Aug. 5, Bamberger, Anna Marg., and Heinrich Hildebrand
1801, Oct. 2, Bank, Joh., and Cath. Miller.
1800, Oct. 28, Banks, Joh., and Cath. Willow.
1801, Dec. 20, Bannin, Johannes, and Susannah Hoch.
1778, June 22, Bantzer, Johannes, and Christina Barb. Donner.
1762, Sept. 25, Barber, Hannah, and Daniel White.
1801, April 13, Bard, Eliz., and Joh. George Panekuchen.
1791, April 19, Bard, Sarah, and Michael Reader.
1799, May 5, Barn, Cath., and Caspar Zollinder.
1777, June 19, Barnes, Frances, and Gotfried Minney.
1785, July 18, Barnet, George, and Sara Fisher.
1778, Sept. 22, Barnhill, Robert, and Elizabeth Potts.
1802, Feb. 25, Barnoleger, Eliz., and William Bautelon.
1753, Oct. 26, Barns, John, and Rachel Ramsey.,
1791, May 22, Baron Philip, and Helena Schopp.
1801, July 25, Barr, Joh., and Polly Karmer.
1750, Aug. 6, Barry, Rowland, and Hannah Evans.
1790, Dec. 8, Barrye, Jeremiah, and Mary Clinton.
1706, Nov. 11, Bart, Margaretha, and Nicholaus Knauf.
1771, Jan. 24, Bart, Peter, and Magdalena Huntzel.
1778, April 20, Bartholmai, Benedick, and Marg. Kohler.
1797, Jan. 17, Barton, Anthony, and Charity Cook.
1788, Nov. 29, Bartram, Sarah, and Claudius Antomies Betier.
1784, Jan. 14, Baselman, Sybilla, and Philip Schuck.
1776, Feb. 20, Bathorn, Hugh, and Elizabeth Scheed.
1791, Feb. 17, Bating, Sarah, and Peter Schreiber.
1778, July 26, Batiste, John, and Anna Blum.
1790, Nov. 11, Bauen, Barbara, and Ludwig Schill.
1790, June 1, Bauer, Paul, and Polly Roun.
1760, Feb. 25, Baumaenn, Susanna, and Rudolph Friess.
1771, Jan. 29, Bauman, Margaret, and Johannes Becker.
1797, Jan. 5, Baumgart, Magdalena, and Johannes Pfau.
1786, Feb. 12, Baumgarth, Jacob, and Catherine Weiler.
1748, Oct. —, Baur, Heinrick, and Anna Catharine Ries.
1802, Feb. 25, Bautelon, William, and Eliz. Barnoleger.
1783, Oct. 23, Bautz, George, and Isabella McMollen.
1794, Sept. 28, Baxter, Elizabeth, and Christopher Schreiner.
1802, May 23, Bayer, Hen., and Beve Meyer.
1790, April 15, Bayer, Reb., and Joh. Marers.
1780, April 16, Bayer, Sarah, and John Meyer.

1778, June 11, Beyer, Susanna, and Peter Laub.
1788, April 1, Bayer, Doroth., and Conrad Scherer.
1788, June 6, Beaumies, Bartholomeus, and Maria Frances Lombard.
1762, Dec. 2, Bebler, Anna Cath., and George Wilhelm Friedrich.
1795, Sept. 6, Beck, Barbara, and Friedrich Wolf.
1797, Dec. 7, Beck, George, and Lydia Fullerton.
1777, Dec. 25, Beck, Joh. Diehlman, and Susanna Roth.
1779, July 15, Beck, John, and Mary Stumpf.
1779, April 8, Beck, Marg., and John Schmidt.
1786, Oct. 4, Bechtle, David, and Priscilla Hurff.
1767, March 24, Becker, Catherine, and Wendel Zerbau.
1790, Feb. 2, Becker, Cath., and Joseph Bennet.
1790, Jan. 21, Becker, Conrad, and An. Mar. Sorgen.
1796, Nov. 13, Becker, Conrad, and Susanna Fraely.
1789, March 10, Becker, Joh. George, and Sophia Milefeld.
1767, Dec. 22, Becker, Peter, and Marlena Dermin.
1798, April 26, Becker, Elizabeth, and George Schaed.
1794, Aug. 28, Becker, Elizabeth, and Johannes Reil.
1777, Feb. 2, Becker, Elizabeth, and Thomas Rooke.
1796, Aug. 14, Becker, Elizabeth, and George Janey.
1774, April 9, Becker, Jacob, and Hannah Schmidt.
1786, March 9, Becker, Jacob, and Elizabeth Mielefeld.
1771, Jan. 29, Becker, Johannes, and Margaret Bauman.
1793, March 10, Becker, Johannes, and Barbara Milforth.
1775, March 2, Becker, John, and Elizabeth Schreiner.
1760, Feb. 17, Becker, Lorenz, and Anne Margaretha Suter.
1794, Aug. 24, Becker, Magdalena, and Heinrich Bender.
1773, Jan. 25, Becker, Maria, and John Souder.
1790, ——— —, Becker, Marl., and John Rummel.
1776, Aug. 22, Becker, Peter, and Eliz. Flick.
1760, June 28, Becker, Wilhelm, and Rachel Fiesler.
1775, June 13, Becker, Barbara, and Gotfried Birchenbeul.
1778, Aug. 13, Becker, Cath., and Michael Schneider.
1766, June 9, Becker, Margaretha, and Johann George Horner.
1786, Oct. 26, Becker, Mary, and Christopher Muller.
1772, March 26, Becker, Susanna, and Johannes Freyburg.
1796, Oct. 11, Beckers, Maria, and Oart Van Vreen.
1783, June 3, Beckman, Zacharias, and Barbara Berckenbeil.
1781, March 16, Bedelion, Isaac, and Magdalena Daun.
1781, May 10, Bedellion, Cath. and Isaac Jones.
1788, April 1, Bedellion, Isaac, and Ursula Rohe.
1783, Nov. 9, Bedford, Cath., and Ludwig Hammer.
1769, Feb. 2, Beer, Conrad, and Cath. Staht.
1773, Jan. 10, Beer, Jacob, and Anna Marg. Rimin.
1782, March 21, Beezley, Johnston, and Maria Virgin.

1790, Oct.   12, Behns, John, and Sophia Rosenbusch.
1770, April   16, Behringer, Jacob, and Anna Stiber.
1794, Oct.   12, Behrt, Margaretha, and Wilhelm Schneider.
1753, March   6, Beker, George Bernard, and Anna Eliz. Frank.
1761, April   24, Beker, Hans Adam, and Dorothea Bomin.
1759, Dec.   30, Beker, Catharina, and Joh. Heinrich Winkler.
1761, June   25, Beker, Eliz. Margaretha, and Nicolas Hahn.
1749, Nov.   —, Beker, Susanna, and Peter Diel.
1753, Oct.   2, Bell, Elizabeth, and John Lindsey.
1770, March   4, Bell, William, and Margareth Steinmetz.
1789, June   9, Belsterling, Joh. Jac., and Maria Magdalena Bol-
                  leck.
1789, March   5, Beltz, George, and Cath. Zahner.
1797, Oct.   1, Beltz, Hannah, and Weygard Miller.
1799, Aug.   1, Bencil, Margaretha, and Valentine Bert.
1797, Nov.   11, Bender, Barbara, and Thomas Lorentz Huttman.
1794, Aug.   24, Bender, Heinrich, and Magdalena Becker.
1762, March   9, Bender, Anna Maria, and George Scheid.
1795, Jan.   8, Benedick, Christian, and Juliana Sturges.
1768, April   9, Bener, Isaac, and Laetitia Helton.
1787, May   5, Bener, Rachel, and John Boutcher.
1750, Sept.   18, Bengler, Juliana Eliz., and Christian Jaentzer.
1768, Jan.   17, Benjamin, Jacob, and Jane Fluck.
1797, June   13, Benners, Christian, and Elizabeth Weller.
1798, May   28, Benners, George, and Susanna Urweiler.
1790, Feb.   2, Bennet, Joseph, and Cath. Becker.
1780, Jan.   20, Bense, Christian Peter, and Anna Christina Kan-
                  ten.
1799, July   4, Benser, Cath., and Jacob Hell.
1797, Oct.   2, Benson, Henry, and Elizabeth Wissauer.
1777, March   13, Benther, Barbara, and George Madoery.
1775, Oct.   9, Bentz, Hannah, and Johannes Adam Meyer.
1779, June   24, Berckemeyer, Daniel, and Margaretha Schnyder.
1783, June   3, Berckenbeil, Barbara, and Zacharias Beckman.
1784, Aug.   19, Berckenbeil, George, and Elizabeth Omensetter.
1765, Dec.   3, Berckenbeul, Antony, and Barbara Mueller.
1767, Jan.   17, Berclin, Elizabeth, and Simon Schellenberger.
1792, April   22, Berg, Jacob, and Maria Protzman.
1785, Nov.   28, Bergendahler, Cath., and William Rup.
1788, May   4, Bergman, John, and Eliz. Buddy.
1794, Feb.   25, Bergmayer, Daniel, and Christina Gaulin.
1785, Dec.   8, Berner, Eliz., and John Meibert.
1755, April   17, Bernhol, Dorothea Magdalena, and John George
                  Reith.
1780, Nov.   28, Berrit, Henry, and Rachel Aspey.
1779, May   20, Berry, Mary, and Henry Matthews.

1799, Aug.　1, Bert, Valentine, and Margretha Bencil.
1762, Feb.　15, Beruth, Elizabeth, and Thomas Labeker.
1765, May　4, Bestlie, William, and Barbara Kulin.
1788, Nov.　29, Betier, Claudius Antomies, and Sarah Bartram.
1789, Sept.　15, Betsch, Doroth., and Philip Alburger.
1768, July　28, Bettman, Anna, and Jacob Wollenschleger.
1751, Jan.　22, Betz, Christian, and Christian Gerhard.
1787, March　6, Beumer, George, and Cath. Scholl.
1778, Nov.　5, Bevan, Evan, and Marg. Scott.
1778, Oct.　11, Beyer, Frederick, and Cath. Frey.
1773, May　11, Bickley Catharina, and George Taylor.
1780, June　4, Bieber, Magdalena, and Gottlieb Mayer.
1786, April　6, Biel, Susanna, and John Seiler.
1789, Sept.　22, Biesle, Susanna, and Jac. Wentz.
1801, Jan.　30, Bigg Mary, and Geo. Spumenberg.
1785, Oct.　25, Binder, Barbara, and Abraham Pohl.
1780, May　30, Binder, Jacob, and Barbara Kennedy.
1783, July　13, Bingel, John, and Jacobina Warner.
1785, Nov.　30, Bingeman, Catharina, and Michael Pfifer.
1775, June　13, Birckenbeul, Catharina, and Daniel Gilbert.
1775, June　13, Birckenbeul, Gotfried, and Barbara Becker.
1776. Sept.　8, Birckenbeul, Jacob, and Anna Marg. Bronner.
1784, May　16, Birckenbeul, Joh. Died., and Amalia Kremer.
1788, March 25, Bischhoven, Gerhard, and Eliz. Jamissen.
1783, March　9, Bischoffberger, Anna Cath, and Andreas Scholl.
1796, Aug.　1, Bischoffsberger, Christina, and George Trump.
1796, May　5, Bischoffsberger, Elizabeth, and Valentin Ulrich.
1787, Oct.　17, Bischoffberger, Jac., and Susanna Miller.
1783, April　29, Bischoffberger, Jacob, and Eliz Tschudy.
1780, Feb.　29, Bischofberger, Eliz., and Christian Meyland.
1801, May　14, Bitting, Maria, and Enoch Koller.
1776, April　21, Black, Elizabeth, and Robert Johnston.
1795, July　16, Black, Elizabeth, and David Hall.
1799, March　7, Blais, Peter, and Barbara Sherrer.
1769, Jan.　1, Blanckenban, Michael, and Marlena Therri.
1771, May　19, Blaise, Rosina, and Andreas Theis.
1794, March　6, Blattberger, Elizabeth, and Johannes Lehmann.
1767, May　3, Blecked, Elizabeth, and Immanuel Joins.
1795, April　16, Blecker Catharine, and Heinrich Lang.
1750, July　10, Bleikenstorffer, Jacob, and Priscilla Rudy,
1798, July　29, Blocher, Elizabeth, and Conrad Weigand.
1784, Sept.　7, Bloom, George, and Catharine Schaffery.
1778, July　26, Blum Anna, and John Batiste.
1799, March 21, Blum, Joh. Harry, and An. Gertrude ———.
1791, May　5, Blum, Maria, and John Leeish.
1784, Sept.　30, Blum, Margaret, and Fried. Kehleheffer.

1799, July 4, Bobschel, Christian, and Elizabeth Alberry.
1798, Feb. 28, Boch, Wilhelm, and Maria Diehl.
1766, Feb. 20, Bocked, Joseph, and Sara Dick.
1765, June 11, Bocked, Johann, and Regina Hehl.
1778, March 17, Boch, Susanna, and Matthias Krehmer.
1799, Aug. 8, Bockius, Jno., and Hannah ———.
1785, Oct. 6, Bockius, Mary, and George Herford.
1786, Jan. 10, Bockius, Peter, and Rosina Hessin.
1785, April 24, Bockius, Peter, and Elizabeth Etter.
1784, Nov. 24, Bockius, Peter, and Hannah Lehman.
1799, Aug. 4, Bockius, Philip, and Maria Desny.
1776, Jan. 28, Bocklin, Eliz., and Peter Simon.
1750, July 8, Boehler, Esther, and Samuel Neidtlinger.
1792, Dec. 2, Beohm, Daniel, and Catharina Peltz.
1753, Aug. 2, Boehm, Joh. Philip, and Anna Maria Jostin.
1784, April 15, Boehm, Kitty, and James Steel.
1784, May 25, Boehm, Maria, and Wilhelm Peltz.
1760, Dec. 7, Boetker, Joh. Wilhelm, and Anna Veronica Sorber.
1772, Feb. 5, Bohme, Charles Lewis, and Catharina Moser.
1792, Aug. 23, Bolebacher, Margaretha, and William Dietz.
1789, June 9, Bolleck, Maria Magdalena, and Joh. Jac. Belsterling.
1778, Nov. 17, Bolton, John, and Hannah Pretsman.
1761, April 24, Bomin, Dorothea, and Hans Adam Beker.
1750, Oct. 27, Bond, Joseph, and Esther Jenes.
1786, May 16, Bond, Mary, and Lewis Hansal.
1797, Aug. 10, Bonden, Stephen, and Rachel Finck.
1780, March 6, Bonecker, Fanny, and Frederick Kreider.
1782, Oct. 4, Bonenacker, Elizabeth, and George Flauers.
1772, March 5, Bonner, Jacob, and Elizabeth Moser.
1768, Aug. 30, Bonner, Johann, and Eliz. Stadelman.
1788, Sept. 30, Bonnet, An., and Peter Forest.
1787, May 5, Boutcher, John, and Rachel Bener.
1792, Dec. 9, Boog, Jacob, and Anna Schneider.
1771, June 20, Boon, Maria Elizabeth, and Peter Diehl.
1750, June 9, Boon, Rachel, and Barry Mullonney.
1748, Dec. 23, Boone, Esther, and Christian Eickler.
1767, Nov. 1, Born, Edward, and Charity Ewins.
1795, Oct. 15, Born, Johannes, and Elizabeth Freund.
1778, Sept. 29, Borner, Adam, and Maria Muller.
1784, Nov. 11, Bornhaus, George, and Elizabeth Zinck.
1774, June 16, Bornin, Cath., and Johann Michel Reinhard.
1775, June 29, Borstel, Fried., and Cath. Fotin.
1778, June 14, Borstell, Cath., and Samuel Stern.
1777, Dec. 18, Boscho, George, and Anna Cath. Ernst.
1794, July 19, Boss, Friedrich, and Wilhelmina Weber.

1784, March 23, Bottom, Catharina, and Frederick Moyerley.
1785, May   28, Boutler, James, and Hannah Rees.
1786, Jan.   26, Bowen, John, and Maria Swoop.
1783, Dec.   4, Bowle, Elizabeth, and Nicolaus Eisenmenger.
1778, Nov.   16, Boyd, James, and Doroth. Zuben.
1761, July   3, Boyd, Margaret, and David Harrald.
1785, May   16, Boyer, Adam, and Rebecca Thomson.
1786, Feb.   17, Boyer, Eliz., and Caspar Petzlar.
1760, Nov.   17, Brach, Anna Christina, and Johann Jacob Velz.
1788, Oct.   12, Braderick, Andreas, and Clara Reble.
1780, June   26, Braderick, Andreas, and Maria Mueller.
1771, June   13, Bradshaw, David, and Patience Farmer.
1759, Oct.   1, Brand, Jacob, and Elizabeth Sinner.
1750, Oct.   8, Brands, Maria, and Joseph Wills.
1778, Oct.   17, Brannill, Eliz., and William Bush.
1794, July   17, Brauer, Jacob, and Maria Festinger.
1792, Sept.   8, Braun, Arant, and Catharina Zerbahn.
1797, Dec.   10, Braun, Esther, and Wilhelm ———.
1794, Dec.   26, Braun, Heinrich, and Christina Pfeiffer.
1748, April 17, Brechly, Joh. Daniel, and Cath. Gertrude Klein.
1751, Feb.   1, Brecht, Jacob, and Susanna Rittenhouse.
1785, Oct.   4, Breda, Henry, and Anna Gilbert.
1788, Jan.   1, Breding, Margaretha, and Heinrich Wever.
1801, Feb.   6, Breeding, Mary, and Wᵐ Hibbs.
1768, Oct.   25, Brennen, Maria, and Frederick Simon.
1778, Oct.   6, Breutigam, Eliz.. and George Eisenring.
1790, Oct.   31, Bretz, Heinrich, and Eva Espy.
1784, Feb.   15, Bridges, Susanna, and Conrad Bachman.
1799, April 18, Bringhurst, Eliz., and Christopher Ottinger.
1753, Aug.   23, Brit, John, and Sarah Fletscher.
1768, Aug.   7, Briton, Anna, and William Sintelton.
1795, Nov.   5, Britton, Sarah, and Benage Brown.
1763, Feb.   20, Brob, Barbara, and Jacob Vollenweider.
1785, Dec.   17. Brock, Anna, and John Sproson.
1783, Oct.   19, Brockman, Chresselly, and Franz Wilh. Troemner.
1776, Sept.   8, Bronner, Anna Marg., and Jacob Birckenbeul.
1774, Aug.   18, Bronner, Johannes, and Cath. Jaeger.
1778, July   1, Bronner, Maria, and John McWrath.
1750, Sept. 29, Brooks, Elizabeth, and Daniel Newton.
1769, Dec.   19, Brown, Alexander, and Mary Shoklard.
1795, Nov.   5, Brown, Benage, and Sarah Britton.
1767, Jan.   8, Brown, Cornelius, and Elizabeth Schesnut.
1771, Oct.   22, Brown, Cornelius, and Maria, Magdalena Haffner.
1767, May   12, Brown David, and Elizabeth Higgins.
1784, Jan.   20, Brown Elizabeth, and Henry Maag.
1785, Feb.   16, Brown, George, and Maria Lubrian.

1788, April 29, Brown, Jacob, and Maria Fling.
1781, May 17, Brown, John, and Abia Withmer.
1750, March 15, Brown, John, and Priscilla Warren.
1750, March 25, Brown, John, and Priscilla Warren.
1785, Jan. 13, Brown, Maria, and Wilhelm Pidgeon.
1789, Feb. 3, Brown, Rebecca, and Philip Peltz.
1775, March 8, Brown, Richard, and Rachel Wickward.
1784, Feb. 19, Brown, Sara, and George Richner.
1769, June 22, Brown, Valentin, and Regina Heimberg.
1779, Dec. 14, Brownig, Jacob, and Marg. Lorentz.
1760, June 30, Brunner, Anna Maria, and Christian Schmid.
1781, July 15, Bryen, Mary, and Benjamin Loxley.
1776, March 21, Buchard, Paul, and Anna Eliz. Buzel.
1797, Oct. 20, Bucher, Jacob, and Maria Magdalena Veit.
1795, Dec. 22, Buchhammer, Johannes, and Eliz. Heissler.
1801, Oct. 13, Buchholtz, Joh. Andreas, and Barbara Trout.
1779, Sept. 19, Buck, Francis, and Cath. Grubb
1753, Oct. 21, Buck, Joh. Philip, and Elizabeth Schynlin.
1799, Dec. 11, Buckingham, Hannah, and Richard Hickham.
1780, July 27, Buckius, Cath., and Christian Russ.
1788, May 4, Buddy, Eliz., and John Bergman.
1748, Aug. 14, Buecky, Rudolph, and Anna Cath. Ekin.
1779, Feb. 25, Bullman, Eliz., and John Pfau.
1753, June 11, Burckard, Philip, and Anna Margareth Lind.
1760, July 22, Burckhard, Anna, and Joh. Ludwig Kling.
1782, July 4, Burckardt, Margaret, and Conrad Rush.
1781, Nov. 8, Burck, Elizabeth, and Jac. Himpelman.
1782, Dec. 8, Burghart, Anna Maria, and John George Gerster.
1774, June 9, Burgy, Henry, and Elizabeth Kryder.
1801, Sept. 22, Burkhart, Eliz., and John Singers.
1769, Aug. 29, Burkey, Henry, and Mary Chamberlain.
1792, Nov. 29, Burth, Maria, and George Schwartz.
1781, May 12, Busch, Christian, and Eliz. Senft.
1798, Feb. 22, Busch, Elizabeth, and Bernhard Rothhaar.
1790, Feb. 4, Bush, Edward, and Barbara Eakele.
1778, Oct. 17, Bush, William, and Eliz. Brannill.
1779, June 16, Buskirk, Mary, and Thomas Gray.
1793, Sept. 14, Buth, Diederich, and Susanna Krafft.
1765, July 28, Butterfass, Barbara, and Peter Care.
1784, Feb. 26, Button, Elizabeth, and John Ebert.
1776, March 21, Buzel, Anna Eliz., and Paul Buchard.
1779, Jan. 21, Byins, Lewis, and Rody Scott.
1797, July 1, Byram, Mary, and John Ryan.
1777, March 17, Callanan, John, and Nancy O'hera.
1751, Jan. 2, Calle, Anna Maria, and Fridenrich Haene.
1752, Dec. 31, Cameron, Jane, and John Kiddie.

1774, March 27, Camper, Maria, and William Saunders.
1784, Nov. 30, Capp, John, and Catherine Schamberlaine.
1779, March 31, Carden, Jane, and Jacob Eyler.
1765, July 28, Care, Peter, and Barbara Butterfass.
1769, Jan. 10, Carlan, Mary and Michael Blanckenhan.
1791, May 27, Carlsen, Margaretha Maria, and Christian Kuck.
1748, Nov. 25, Carmatt, Jonathan, and Elizabeth Stenton.
1779, Oct. 27, Carr, James, and Kath. Lark.
1798, April 18, Carrigan, Christina, and Joseph Good.
1791, Dec. 24, Cart, Catharina, and Heinrich Plenn.
1753, Feb. 21, Carter, Sarah, and David Clayton.
1779, Oct. 23, Casey, Alice, and Charles Rosengrandt.
1779, April 6, Cassoph, Magd., and John Luver.
1797, April 8, Catharina, Johannes, and George Karstens.
1801, Jan. 14, Caul, Wilhelm, and Frederica Foebel.
1784, Feb. 19, Cave, Thomas, and Catharina Meyer.
1794, March 11, Cerisier, Jean Baptiste, and Maria Ursula Lapostolait.
1789, Feb. 26, Cerral, Dinah, and James Geary.
1801, April 10, Chamberlain, Joh., and Eliz. Sellers.
1769, Aug. 29, Chamberlain, Mary, and Henry Burkey.
1785, July 14, Chamberlein, Maria, and Conrad Ronw.
1786, Nov. 17, Chamberlein, Susanna, and Garret Hughes.
1755, July 22, Chapman, Daniel, and Esther Edwards.
1777, April 13, Cherry, Cath., and Thomas Hustler.
1772, Nov. 16, Chressman, Nicolaus, and Susanna Shanholtz.
1762, Sept. 19, Christeiny, Catharina, and Anthony Hen.
1787, July 24, Ciprian, Heinrich, and Elizabeth Scherer.
1789, April 19, Ciss, Henry, and Cath. Schmidt.
1769, March 30, Clampfer, Anna, and William Will.
1789, May 15, Clark, Marg., and Francis Lynn.
1780, April 29, Clark, Thomas, and Eliz. Mellin.
1748, Dec. 14, Clarke, Anne, and William Raworth.
1796, Feb. 4, Clarkson, Johannes, and Elizabeth Stetzenbach.
1796, Jan. 9, Claudy, Christopher, and Maria Valentin.
1753, Feb. 21, Clayton, David, and Sarah Carter.
1786, June 22, Clear, Hannah, and Jerm. Allioth.
1763, May 17, Cleaver, Joshua, and Marg. Nelson.
1760, June 24, Cleland, James, and Jane McCallough.
1768, May 17, Clemen, Elizabeth, and Christian Kehr.
1777, Sept. 2, Cline, Hannah, and Thomas Hall.
1767, Oct. 31, Cline, Rosina, and John Hai.
1790, Dec. 8, Clinton, Mary, and Jeremiah Barryl.
1769, Aug. 21, Cliwer, Marlena, and George Gangever.
1787, July 19, Cloedy, Cath., and Jacob Erwin.
1772, Jan. 5, Cloethy, Mary, and Johann Jaeger.

1750, June 25, Clowser, Peter, and Elizabeth Spedin.
1789, Sept. 15, Cloyer, Anna, and Adam Seibert.
1776, Oct. 10, Clunn, Charles, and Rachel Mercelus.
1795, Nov. 4, Clunn, Johannes, and Susanna Keiler.
1780, Aug. 24, Clumberg, Mary, and Peter Lohra.
1777, March 6, Coeleman, Jacob, and ——— George.
1768, Oct. 13, Coeleman, Maria, and Johann George Zeller or Teller.
1787, Sept. 27, Coffin, Jac., and Katy Jerkis.
1789, April 2, Coffin, Marg., and James Middleton.
1781, Oct. 30, Coldflesh, Henry, and Eliz. Davis.
1775, April 24, Collett, Anna, and John Wormington.
1780, July 13, Colliday, Sarah, and James Seloover.
1753, Jan. 21, Collings, William, and Susannah Yard.
1753, June 23, Collins, Catharina, and Thomas Foster.
1753, Nov. 20, Collins, Hannah, and Nathaniel Moore.
1787, Oct. 4, Colloday, Mary, and Adam Alberger.
1764, July 30, Colp, Barbara, and Wilhelm Will.
1782, Dec. 19, Colp, Catharina, and John Suter.
1798, Feb. 1, Comeley, Isaac, and Maria Jetter.
1750, June 9, Commons, John, and Maria Simons.
1797, Oct. 20, Connelly, Francis, and Philippina Knaus.
1785, July 19, Connen, Nancy, and Caspar Albert.
1773, April 26, Connoly, Robert, and Bridget Dunn.
1766, Oct. 10, Connwy, Eleanora, and Johann Ross.
1787, May 2, Conrad, Anna, and John Wiltfang.
1796, May 29, Conrad, Elizabeth, and Johannes Baer.
1753, Aug. 26, Conrad, George, and Maria Barbara Neuhausen.
1796, Oct. 30, Conrad, Johannes, and Hannah Williams.
1786, Sept. 14, Conrad, Marg., and John Sturtzebach.
1783, Feb. 22, Conrad, Wilhelm, and Maria Genthener.
1788, Feb. 13, Conrad, Wilhelm, and Eva Kochenberger.
1748, April 14, Consul, Stephan, and Anna Vandersberg.
1784, April 1, Conver, Anna, and George Hess.
1764, Oct. 11, Conver, Johann Peter, and Anna Catharina Ernstdorff.
1797, Jan. 17, Cook, Charity, and Anthony Barton.
1755, ——— —, Cook, George, and Hannah Lawton.
1785, July 21, Coop, Nelly, and Daniel Kuhn.
1801, Jan. 22, Cooper, Math., and Dolly Merkel.
1785, March 13, Cope, Anne, and Francis Curtis.
1777, Sept. 15, Copia, Cath., and David Rischong.
1750, Dec. 1, Coppok, John, and Sarah Harris.
1793, Jan. 31, Cornelius, William, and Margaretha Diess.
1788, Sept. 4, Cortis, John, and Eliz. Von der Halt.
1794, Aug. 19, Covert, Elizabeth, and Andreas Von Weiler.

1796, Feb.　4, Cowan, Sarah, and Adam Heller.
1797, March 21, Cowan, Susanna, and Friedrich Zahn.
1793, Sept.　19, Cox, Albion, and Maria Anna Harmstadt.
1752, Aug.　12, Cox, Ann, and William Honeyman.
1785, Oct.　20, Cox, Mary, and Frederick Meyer.
1787, May　24, Cox, Polly, and George Lauris.
1777, March　2, Craig, Daniel, and Maria Lacy.
1789, June　26, Crames, Maria Christina, and Conrad Pfaffhausen.
1775, Feb.　28, Cran, John, and Sarah Souder.
1764, June　25, Crason, Eva, and Christopher Grafley.
1762, March　2, Crawford, James, and Catharina Howel.
1796, Oct.　6, Creaghead, Job, and Mary Harford.
1770, Dec.　18, Creamer, Rachel, and John Lange.
1785, Jan.　20, Cress, John, and Marg. Kintzler.
1793, April　1, Creukeri, Jenny, and Jacob Stoll.
1781, June　4, Cripps, Sarah, and Conrad Steiger.
1785, Jan.　13, Crombie, Mary, and John Rudy.
1773, March　8, Crommy, W^m, and Cath. Glam.
1770, Dec.　11, Cronsen, Barbara, and George Orffar.
1775, March　5, Croockham, Deborah, and Jonathan Edwards.
1785, April　11, Cross, Hannah, and Benjamin Hancock.
1785, July　24, Cross, James, and Margaret Eliz. Koch.
1783, June　30, Cullman, Adam, and Susanna Weidlinger.
1763, Jan.　25, Cumben, Maria Magdalena, and Johannes Wagner.
1783, Sept.　9, Cunningham, James, and Kather McCord.
1798, April　25, Curren, Nancy, and Daniel Wilkeson.
1790, April　15, Curry, Jane, and Christopher Rarah.
1768, May　24, Custer, Maria, and Mathias Pennybecker.
1785, March 13, Curtis, Francis, and Anne Cope.
1787, Sept.　6. Danecker, Anna Eliz., and Henry Appel.
1791, July　10, Dannecker, Anna, and Johann George Mill.
1790, May　25, Dannecker, Eliz., and John Schreiner.
1779, Feb.　23, Danock, Thomas, and Elizabeth Miller.
1769, Aug.　13, Daub, Catherine, and Heinrich Schreiber.
1768, Feb.　25, Daubendistel, Jacob, and Barbara Schneider.
1796, Dec.　3, Daubendistel, Sarah, and Jacob Miller.
1762, Oct.　5, Daubentischler, Wilhelmina, and Casper Suter.
1785, Dec.　6, Dauber, Fried., and Eliz. Edel.
1801, Feb.　26, Dauberman, Susanna, and Joh. Huber.
1781, March 16, Daun, Magdalena, and Isaac Bedelion.
1801, Nov.　30, Davenport, W^m, and Eliz. Sohenhollingshead.
1767, Aug.　26, Davi, Catharina, and Jacob Wurgeler.
1799, June　24, David, Nancy, and Charles Meder.
1789, Jan.　13, Davids, Nathaniel, and Ann Thomas.
1792, Nov.　4, Davis, Benjamin, and Jemima Roberts.
1784, July　13, Davis, Elizabeth, and Henry Schearer.

1781, Oct.　30, Davis, Eliz., and Henry Coldflesh.
1753, Sept.　9, Davis, Mary, and John Drummon.
1794, March 26, Davis, Noah, and Catharina Lies.
1762, Oct.　18, Davis, Thomas, and Lidie Waterman.
1789, May　12, Dawn, John, and Mary Kartrieth.
1784, April　4, Dawson, Joseph, and Martha Schoen.
1781, June　2, Day, Mary, and David Turner.
1777, March 20, Daylershaedts, Sarah, and Michael Redman.
1785, Aug.　11, Deaberger, Charlotte, and Philip Fritz.
1750, May　29, Dean, William, and Jean Turner.
1772, March 19, Deaney, Marg., and Henry Reinhard.
1771, June　2, Decon, Hannah, and John McBride.
1764, April　23, Dees, Johannes Peter, and Catharina Muellern.
1793, Nov.　16, Degenhard, George, and Elizabeth List.
1781, Nov.　28, Degenhardt, George, and Wilhelmina Von Obstrand.
1786, Oct.　12, Delliker, Fried., and Maria Juvenal.
1785, April　7, Delwich, Maria, and Jacob Frey.
1778, June　24, Demand, Joh. Jacob, and Eliz. Wentzel.
1779, Feb.　23, Dempsey, Richard, and Magd. Hauer.
1772, Aug.　22, Denham, Elizabeth, and Matthias Garret.
1788, June　5, Denn, Maria Clara, and Philip Fred. Mischodt.
1788, Sept.　30, Dennis, Sally, and Christian Groh.
1778, July　19, Denny, Henry, and Mary Kline.
1774, Nov.　19, Depperwin, Adam, and Elizabeth Swaine.
1788, March 13, Derick, Betsy, and Michael Grub.
1773, July　5, Derland, Catharina, and James Scott.
1802, May　23, Derland, Mary, and Alexander Hamton.
1767, Dec.　22, Dermin, Marlena, and Peter Becker.
1765, May　3, Derri, Michael, and Hannah Pielin.
1794, April　15, Descamps, Jean, and Sarah Pluncket.
1779, June　10, Descheler, Maria, and William Haberstig.
1767, Feb.　2, Deschong, Frederick, and Margaretha Gobler.
1767, Oct.　27, Deschong, Heinrich, and Catharina Teith.
1774, Dec.　15, Deschong, Peter, and Susanna Gilman.
1799, Aug.　4, Desny, Maria, and Philip Bockius.
1772, July　30, Dettingen, Anna Marg., and Reuben Kerbe,
1794, Oct.　7, Dettweiler, Johannes, and Margaretha Diehl.
1766, March 18, Dettweller, Johann Adam, and Dorotha Senck.
1782, June　20, Deufflinger, Heinrich, and Sarah Supper.
1791, Aug.　—, Deusing, Anthon, and Elizabeth Graf.
1792, May　8, Deuss, Anna Margaretha, and Christian Stiebel.
1775, Jan.　24, Dewald, Marlena, and Mathias Gucker.
1794, April　2, Dewees, Jonathan, and Rebecca Johnson.
1780, Sept.　28, Dexter, Mary, and John Mueller.
1760, Aug.　9, Dibo, Cath. Eliz., and Andreas Thiss.

1787, March 4, Dick, Catharina, and Thomas Hueter.
1766, Feb. 20, Dick, Sara, and Joseph Bocked.
1799, July 20, Dickel, Joh. and J. Wilhelme Smith.
1787, March 29, Dickes, John Fried., and Catharine Herr.
1779, Sept. 29, Dickins, George, and Cath. Starck.
1774, May 11, Diedrich, Margaretha, and Adam Schneider.
1786, June 15, Diederich, Susanna, and Nich. Weierich.
1779, July 25, Diehl, Cath., and George Duer.
1783, Oct. 9, Diehl, Cath., and Adam May.
1789, April 14, Diehl, Maria, and Philip Mieser.
1766, June 3, Diehl, Caspar, and Juliana Seller.
1798, March 25, Diehl, Catharina, and Joh. Friederich D———.
1796, May 19, Diehl, Catharina, and Jacob Tag.
1797, April 20, Diehl, Elizabeth, and Ulrich Weckerle.
1787, Nov. 22, Diehl, Henry, and Maria Eberth.
1737, April 22, Diehl, Jacob, and Eliz. Knies.
1769, May 15, Diehl, Johannes, and Catherina Fritz.
1776, Feb. 11, Diehl, Johannes, and Cath. Freyman.
1784, Feb. 26, Diehl, Margaret, and William Fusselbach.
1794, Oct. 7, Diehl, Margaretha, and Johannes Dettweiler.
1798, Feb. 28, Diehl, Maria, and Wilhelm Bock.
1771, June 20, Diehl, Peter, and Maria Elizabeth Boon.
1796, Nov. 15, Diehm, Hannah, and George Lutz.
1762, April 14, Diel, Johannes, and Regina Catharina Gross.
1749, Nov. —, Diel, Peter, and Susanna Beker.
1750, April 1, Dielin, Maria Eliz., and Simon Pilanus.
1780, June 6, Diemel, Heinrich and Marg. Messerschmid.
1781, June 26, Diemern, Maria, and Christian Kauck.
1784, June 8, Dies, Maria, and Philip Gosser.
1792, Jan. 31, Diess, Margaretha, and William Cornelius.
1798, April 12, Dietrich, Johannes, and Maria Doernberger.
1783, Feb. 11, Dietz, Ketty, and Adam Wever.
1777, Aug. 13, Dietz, William, and Cath. Susabeth.
1792, Aug. 23, Dietz, William, and Margaretha Bolebacher.
1787, May 2, Dinges, John, and Cath. Wilky.
1790, March 4, Dinges, Jul., and Joh. Ewald Ellenberger.
1772, June 28, Dirman, Joseph, and Anna Maur.
1790, Dec. 21, Dishong, Matthias, and Elizabeth Mogy.
1792, Dec. 2, Dithmar, Johannes, and Rebecca Riester.
1787, March 21, Ditzer, James, and Abigail Worrall.
1794, Nov. 11, Dix, Abraham, and Catharina Sattler.
1798, Feb. 11, Dixon, Elizabeth, and Jacob Hill.
1750, April 4, Dixon, Sarah, and Abraham Russell.
1762, May 17, Diz, Wilhelm, and Margaret Cath. Zigler.
1777, Sept. 9, Dobson, Thomas, and Jane Gray.
1793, June 29, Doerffer, George, and Rachel Rubsam.

1801, Oct.　24, Doering, Joh. and Christina Freshern.
1792, Aug.　5, Doeringer, Susanna, and George Weiser.
1798, April　12, Doernberger, Maria, and Johannes Dietrich.
1798, March　4, Doerr, Elizabeth, and Alexander Johnson.
1777, July　9, Dolbon, Jona. and Sarah Hendrickson.
1770, July　10, Dollman, Maria Marg., and Jacob Niderer.
1773, July　1, Dollman, Rosina, and Solomon Merckele.
1796, Sept.　24, Doman, Ann, and Peter Angel Stottenwork.
1751, Jan.　2, Dombaer, Thomas, and Rebecca King.
1779, Feb.　4, Domenick, Mary, and Lewis Micke.
1768, Dec.　11, Dominick, Heinrich, and Eleanoras Welsh.
1762, Oct.　19, Dommen, Marx, and Louise Hartin.
1753, Dec.　—, Donber, Cath., and Nicol. Balteweyn.
1797, Aug.　30, Donneberg, David, and Eva Reiner.
1783, Aug.　19, Donnel, Gratis, and Henry Oberman.
1778, June　22, Donner, Christina Barb., and Johannes Bautzer.
1792, July　25, Dorffer, Catharina, and Joseph Gally.
1796, Jan.　14, Dorffer, George, and Susanna Rubsam.
1783, June　19, Dorffer, Christina, and Michael Rummel.
1768, Nov.　4, Dorneck, Rosina, and Johannes Schenck.
1797, Oct.　27, Dorr, Elizabeth, and Joseph Robinson.
1794, Dec.　7, Dorr, Elizabeth, and Johannes Montgomery.
1781, March 29, Dorsius, Cornelia, and John McMachtane.
1760, Nov.　30, Dosey, Anna, and Castar Nipp.
1798, Jan.　21, Dougherty, Charles, and Fanny Lee.
1778, Aug.　3, Dougherty, Edward, and Mary Stalferd.
1789, March 25, Dougherty, Joseph, and Mary Long.
1801, Sept.　10, Douglass, Abraham, and Eliz. Sheyder.
1796, Sept.　6, Douglas, Sarah, and Johannes Keiler.
1792, April　19, Dowel, Johannes, and Barbara Eschman.
1799, April　18, Downing, Hannah, and Joh. Bakins.
1779, March 23, Downs, Barbara, and George Ailkils.
1750, Jan.　13, Draeson, Matteis, and Sarah Powel.
1753, May　29, Drake, James, and Mary Parsons.
1791, Sept.　—, Drangenstein, Johannes, and Maria Schlatter.
1753, Nov.　10, Drescher, Joh. George, and Anna Eliz. Schmiedlin.
1753, Sept.　9, Drummon, John, and Mary Davis.
1750, Nov.　—, Du Bois, Anna, and David Marinus.
1796, Dec.　8, Dubs, Martin, and Sarah Jones.
1783, Dec.　19, Duche, Maria, and John Pollard.
1759, June　12, Duchmaennier, Maria Salome, and Johann Wilhelm Nagel.
1779, July　25, Duer, George, and Cath. Diehl.
1788, Dec.　25, Duerr, George, and Veronica Jentzer.
1795, July　31, Duffs, Samuel, and Mary Hancock.
1770, Feb.　4, Dugan, Samuel, and Elizabeth Robarts.

1801, Aug. 28, Dunbar, David, and Phoebe Organd.
1779, Feb. 25, Duncan, Mary, and Peter Sevitt.
1773, April 26, Dunn, Bridget, and Robert Connoly.
1796, May 24, Dupuy, Samuel, and Anna Musch.
1800, Dec. 23, Dutill, Gerhard, and A. Cath. Hess.
1800, Dec. 24, Duvall, Maria, and Fred. Troll.
1790, Feb. 4, Eakele, Barbara, and Edward Bush.
1750, Feb. 12, Eakins, Henry, and Margaret Greenfield.
1777, March 6, Eakon, Mary, and George Wilson.
1781, Feb. 24, Earl, Christian, and Anne Harrison.
1769, Feb. 14, Eastend, Anna, and Heinrich Van Ried.
1794, June 5, Eckstein, Jacob, and Elizabeth Root.
1775, July 27, Eckstein, Johannes, and Anna Cath. Mayer.
1796, Oct. 30, Ebel, Jacob, and Margaretha Engel.
1761, Jan. 1, Ebereht Varena, and Johannes Adam.
1797, April 20, Eberhard, Abraham, and Margaretha More.
1786, March 5, Eberhard, Maria, and John Schutz.
1784, Feb. 26, Ebert, John, and Elizabeth Button.
1793, Feb. 16, Eberth, Elizabeth, and Isaac Hough.
1787, Nov. 22, Eberth, Maria, and Henry Diehl.
1762, Jan. 20, Ebert, Magdalena, and Conrad Steinmez.
1785, Dec. 6, Edel, Eliz., and Fried Dauber.
1788, May 1, Edenborn, Jacob, and Maria Schreiber.
1753, July 3, Edger, Catharina, and David Patterson.
1748, Dec. 19, Edgar, John, and Mary Owen.
1749, Nov. —, Edinbonn, Anna Cath., and Philip Lorenz Walter.
1785, Nov. 14, Edman, Martha, and Joh. William Stetzer.
1779, Aug. 19, Edmunds, Edmund, and Sarah Allison.
1794, June 19, Edridge, Richoff, and Elizabeth Keischel.
1755, July 22, Edwards, Esther, and Daniel Chapman.
1775, March 5, Edwards, Jonathan, and Deborah Croockham.
1794, Aug. 21, Ehringer, Philip, and Magdalena Peltzner.
1799, April 15, Ehrman, Wilhelm, and Elizabeth Hoff.
1748, Dec. 23, Eickler, Christian, and Esther Boone.
1762, Nov. 23, Eidler, Johanna Margaret, and Christian Hahn.
1784, Feb. 13, Einwachter, George, and Elizabeth Keblehauser.
1753, Jan. 2, Eisenmayer, Catharina Dorothea, and Johann Heinrich Gaertner.
1783, Dec. 4, Eisenmenger, Nicholaus, and Elizabeth Bowle.
1778, Oct. 6, Eisenring, George, and Eliz. Brentigam.
1748, Aug. 14, Ekin, Anna Cath., and Rudolph Buecky.
1780, July 6, Elies, Lyddy, and Thomas Simpson.
1753, Sept. 15, Eliot, Mary, and Jonathan Tagart.
1790, March 4, Ellenberger, Joh. Ewald, and Jul. Dinges.
1750, April 7, Elliot Rachel, and Thomas Logan.
1779, June 5, Elliott, Hannah, and Jacob Williams.

1767, Aug.   29, Ellis, Mary, and Henry McBride.
1785, Dec.   15, Emig, Peter, and Susanna Steuerwald.
1771, May   20, Empson, Judith, and Nicholaus Rash.
1749, April —, Emsin, Anna Eliz., and Joh. George Moeklin.
1750, April   3, Emsin, Anna Cath., and Thomas Loudon.
1767, July   9, Enek, Johann Jacob, and Catharine Hahn.
1797, Nov.   14, Engel Johannes, and Catharina Rickstein.
1780, June   8, Engel, Maria, and Heinerich Huber.
1760, Oct.   30, Engel, Margaretha, and Jacob Ebel.
1785, May   6, Engelhard, George, and Maria Schutz.
1781, April 25, Engle, Margaret, and Jacob Schnyder.
1760, April 12, Entees, Margaretha, and Peter Lang.
1781, Dec.   17, Erl, Elizabeth, and Jacob Wisseler.
1798, Aug.   5, Ernst, Catharina, and Bernhard Nailer.
1797, Aug.   20, Ernst, Heinerich, and Henrietta Simons.
1764, Oct.   11, Ernstdorff, Anna Catharine, and Johann Peter
                 Conver.
1783, June   19, Ernstdorff, Eliz., and John Milles.
1777, Dec.   18, Ernst, Anna Cath., and George Boscho.
1774, Feb.   8, Ernst, Maria Magdalena, and Heinrich Fiehter.
1785, May   24, Erringer, Jacob, and Marl. Jaeglen.
1787, July   19, Erwin, Jacob, and Cath. Cloedy.
1765, Sept. 16, Eschelman, Isaac, and Catharina Schmidt.
1774, April   5, Eschenfelder, Cath., and Philip May.
1780, Aug.   29, Esch, Eliz., and Nicolaus Kayser.
1792, April 19, Eschman, Barbara, and Johannes Dowel.
1797, June   29, Eschman, Peter, and Helena ——.
1772, Oct.   5, Eshinbaugh, John, and Rebecca Simmerman.
1788, Dec.   25, Espey, Maria, and Stephen Gerlach.
1790, Oct.   31, Espy, Eva, and Heinrich Bretz.
1779, Sept. 30, Esseler, Jacob, and Susanna Peters.
1797, Jan.   3, Esseler, Esther, and Pierre Savoy.
1763, Dec.   8, Eteborn, Jacob, and Elizabeth Haan.
1792, Jan.   29, Etrir, Barbara, and Jacob Muench.
1785, April 24, Etter, Elizabeth, and Peter Bockius.
1765, Jan.   17, Etter, Elizabeth, and Emanuel Baertling.
1798, Jan.   2, Euler, Anna Maria, and Johannes Gamber.
1792, Sept. 21, Euler, Wilhelm, and Anna Gertrude Rupert.
1775, June   7, Ennis, Richard, and Mary Rinedollar.
1755, Dec.   3, Eustace, Charles, and Catherine Sutten.
1750, Oct.   1, Evans, Edward, and Jane Hamilton.
1766, April   8, Evans, Elizabeth, and Daniel Pheila.
1750, Aug.   6, Evans, Hannah, and Rowland Barry.
1750, May   7, Evans, Jonathan, and Sarah Swen.
1755, Dec.   18, Evans, Joshua, and Elizabeth Howell.
1769, Aug.   6, Evans, Ruth, and John Scotton.

1781, April   30, Everman, Eliz., and William Ogelbie.
1769, April   16, Evingen, Eliz. Marg., and Fred[k] Hupertus Fuchs.
1770, Nov.   26, Evy, Mary, and Johann Williams.
1767, Nov.   1, Ewins, Charity, and Edward Brown.
1779, March 31, Eyler, Jacob, and Jane Carden.
1793, Feb.   7, Faans, Jacob, and Phoebe Tomblenson.
1797, Feb.   28, Faber, Catharine, and John Kelly.
1759, Nov.   1, Fackret, Matthias, and Maria Marg. Schaeffer.
1777, Aug.   21, Facundes, Eliz., and William Ritter.
1780, July   6, Faerling, Maria, and Henricus Rosker.
1769, Jan.   10, Faeundy, Fridenrich, and Mary Carlan.
1783, Jan.   14, Fahns, Fanny, and Peter Paris.
1797, Jan.   2, Fahns, (or Jahns,) Jacob, and Catharina Klein.
1779, July   29, Fairies, Abigail, and Thomas Ainger.
1795, Feb.   5, Falbirr, Johannes, and Anna Stillyes.
1766, Nov.   14, Falckenstein, Veronica, and William Lohman.
1775, Nov.   16, Fans, Christian, and Christina Steiger.
1769, May   30, Fans, Michael, and Marg. Mueller.
1779, Aug.   26, Faries, Jane, and William Oackley Lock.
1762, Nov.   7, Fariss, Johannes, and Barbara Haert.
1760, Nov.   17, Farly, James, and Catharina Vatterly.
1786, Feb.   2, Farmer, Lewis, and Eliz. Fohrer.
1768, March   7, Farmer, Martha, and John Vance.
1771, June   13, Farmer, Patience, and David Bradshaw.
1768, June   5, Farner, Michael, and Maria Süz.
1766, Dec.   25, Faun, George, and Eliz. Rau.
1783, June   30, Fauth, Cath., and Heinrich Riegeler.
1776, March 31, Feichtel, John, and Anna Maria Schnell.
1765, June   6, Feil, Magdalena, and Jacob Pfister.
1770, June   12, Feit, Jacob, and Anna Maag.
1750, July   2, Fenimose, Thomas, and Mary Harker.
1782, Aug.   11, Fenner, Heinrich, and Elizabeth Vonder Halt.
1784, Oct.   7, Fenner, Peter, and Cath. Schneider.
1799, April   14, Fering, Samuel, and Sarah Worl.
1790, June   2, Ferringer, Eliz., and Christopher Meyer.
1794, July   17, Festinger, Maria, and Jacob Bauer.
1767, March 29, Fibo, Johann Philip, and Eliz. Spitznagel.
1774, Feb.   8, Fiechter, Heinrich, and Maria Magdalena Ernst.
1775, May   23, Fiegener, Paul, and Rebecca Vonder Halt.
1760, June   28, Fiesler, Rachel, and Wilhelm Becker.
1780, Jan.   4, Finck, Jacob, and Maria Marg. Hanin.
1797, Aug.   10, Finck, Rachel, and Stephen Bonden.
1782, April   14, Fis, George, and Mary Stenerwald.
1770, Aug.   30, Fis, Peter, and Elizabeth Riel.
1797, July   27, Fischbach, Elizabeth, and Joseph Muntzer.
1779, Jan.   3, Fischer, ———, and Christopher Logner.

1784, Sept. 21, Fischer, Adam, and Elizabeth Gamber.
1770, June 2, Fischer, Benjamin, and Wilhelmina Schippen.
1796, April 2, Fischer, Christina, and Richard Hemer.
1785, June 2, Fischer, Elizabeth, and William Kalhmer.
1796, Dec. 8, Fischer, Heinrich, and Maria Haut.
1775, July 15, Fischer, Maria, and Conrad Andersee.
1797, Feb. 16, Fischer, Maria, and Daniel Stellwagen.
1773, Nov. 7, Fischer, Martin, and Cath. Schallus.
1796, July 13, Fischer, Sebastian, and Elizabeth ———.
1801, Sept. 8, Fisher, Barbara, and Wᵐ Schaefer.
1799, March 21, Fisher, David, and ——— Smith.
1772, Feb. 20, Fisher, Mary, and Hermanus Johnston.
1802, Feb. 20, Fisher, Sally, and Peter Rice.
1785, July 18, Fisher, Sara, and George Barnet.
1784, Sept. 17, Fismeier, Marg., and Philip Losch.
1780, June 4, Fiss, Jacob, and Anna Funck.
1767, Nov. 3, Fisteler, Ludwick, and Margaretha Rapin.
1802, Jan. 18, Fite, Margaretha, and Hen. Murr.
1782, April 11, Fitler, Maria, and Jacob Loscher.
1783, Feb. 11, Flachs, John, and Marlena Schnyder.
1782, Oct. 4, Flauers, George, and Elizabeth Bonenacker.
1786, Feb. 12, Fleck, William, and Maria Scheaf.
1748, Dec. 5, Flek, Johanna Philipila, and Michael Lawler.
1750, ——— —, Flerin, Anna Eliz., and Christian Guggart.
1753, Aug. 23, Fletscher, Sarah, and John Brit.
1751, Jan. 24, Flex, Anna, and John Peon.
1776, Aug. 22, Flick, Eliz., and Peter Becker.
1778, Oct. 5, Flick, William, and Eliz. Hoffman.
1796, Jan. 26, Flicker, Petronella, and Jacob Reus.
1788, April 29, Fling, Maria, and Jacob Brown.
1784, June 22, Flock, Justus, and Marg. Stuertzen.
1797, Feb. 20, Flowers, Christian, and Catharina Daubert.
1768, Jan. 17, Fluck, Jane, and Jacob Benjamin.
1801, Jan. 14, Foebel, Frederica, and Wilhelm Caul.
1769, Nov. 24, Foering, Christian Frederick, and Margareth Mueller.
1796, May 1, Foering, Johannes, and Catharina Knorr.
1782, Nov. 1, Foering, Margaret, and George Janus.
1786, Feb. 2, Fohrer, Eliz., and Lewis Farmer.
1797, July 1, Fohringer, Maria, and Johann Carl Preis.
1782, Jan. 15, Foller, Eliz., and John Adam Steiner.
1759, Aug. 4, Folweiler, Johannes, and Maria Stitter.
1801, May 18, Fouse, Fanny, and Thomas Palmer.
1761, March 21, Ford, Ann, and Philip Lawrence.
1788, Sept. 30, Forest, Peter, and An. Bonnet.
1782, Aug. 15, Forster, Hannah, and Richard Gray.

1775, Jan.   12, Fortune, Richard, and Amelia Maxwell.
1788, March 30, Foster, Diana, and Alexander Square.
1753, June   23, Foster, Thomas, and Catharina Collins.
1783, March 13, Foth, Lorentz, and Elizabeth Albert.
1775, June   29, Fotin, Cath., and Fried. Borstel.
1775, Sept.   28, Fotin, Margaretha, and Daniel Bachtle.
1797, Dec.   14, Fotteral, Stephen, and Catharina Knault.
1776, Jan.   25, Fought, Maria, and Gottfried Hanger.
1776, Feb.   1, Foulckrod, Elizabeth, and Christian Troutman.
1783, May   27, Fox, Abraham, and Dorothea Rhodt.
1774, Sept.   25, Fox, Abraham, and Sophia Wassernan.
1796, May   17, Fox, Anna, and Heinrich Schell.
1796, Nov.   13, Fraely, Susanna, and Conrad Becker.
1762, Aug.   25, Fraily, Regina, and Jacob Gardner.
1769, May   14, Fraley, Heinrich, and Susanna Rice.
1779, Aug.   13, Franck, Johann Spalter, and Eliz. Klappar.
1799, June   9, Frank, Christian, and Margaretha Stoll.
1750, Oct.   2, Franker, Anna Cath., and Johann Straub.
1753, March   6, Frankin, Anna Eliz., and George Bernard Beker.
1759, June   25, Fraser, George, and Dorothea Cath. Saenmaenn.
1777, Feb.   11, Frick, Heinrich, and Barbara Schnyder.
1762, May   27, Frick, Barbara, and Jacob Vollenweider.
1773, Jan.   26, Friebel, Cath., and Frederick Frolig.
1748, Oct.   —, Friedenrich, Joh., and Susanna Maria Nig.
1786, March   9, Friederich, John Andreas, and Cath. Schaeff.
1784, June   8, Friederich, Margaret, and John Walter.
1762, Dec.   2, Friedrich, George Wilhelm, and Anna Cath.
                  Bebler.
1768, May   1, Fries, Margaretha, and Simon Lauder.
1760, Feb.   25, Friess, Rudolph, and Susanna Baumaenn.
1750, Dec.   6, Frik, John, and Gertrude Hiesten.
1787, Oct.   28, Frioth, Eliz., and William Jones.
1783, June   13, Frisseler, Philip, and Mary Stubert.
1783, April   10, Fritz, Eliz.. and John Steel.
1785, Aug.   11, Fritz, Philip, and Charlotte Deaberger.
1769, May   15, Fritz, Catherina, and Johannes Diehl.
1774, March   3, Freed, Salome, and Gabriel Schwartzlander.
1793, Sept.   8, Freier, Johannes, and Eva Frollinger.
1749, March —, Frenger, Maria Cath. Eliz., and Joh. Peter Schmeid.
1790, ——   —, Frescher, Ludwig, and Christina Peiffer.
1801, Oct.   24, Freshern, Christian, and Joh. Doering.
1795, Oct.   15, Freund, Eliz., and Johannes Born.
1785, April   7, Frey, Jacob, and Maria Delwick.
1750, Nov.   14, Frey, Johann Andrew, and Cath. Strohoner.
1786, Dec.   10, Frey, Veronica, and John Stuber.
1760, April   24, Frey, William, and Elizabeth Gor.

1772, March 26, Freyburg, Johannes, and Susanna Becker.
1778, Oct. 11, Frey, Cath., and Frederick Beyer.
1776, Feb. 11, Freyman, Cath., and Johannes Diehl.
1797, April 30, Freytag, Michael, and Christina Gerrit.
1762, March 16, Froehlich, Christian, and Elizabeth Rueng.
1759, Aug. 13, Froehlich, Magdalena, and Johann George Reichly.
1761, Aug. 13, Froelich, Maria, and Conrad Alster.
1784, June 10, Froelig, John, and Marsey Thomas.
1773, Jan. 26, Frolig, Frederick, and Cath. Friebel.
1793, Sept. 8, Frollinger, Eva, and Johannes Freier.
1777, Dec. 7, Froman, Conrad, and Marg. Meyer.
1772, Oct. 17, Fry, Mary, and Henry Hook.
1769, April 16, Fuchs, Frederick Hupertus, and Eliz. Marg. Ev-
　　　　　ingen.
1777, March 4, Fuchs, Johannes, and Maria Weil.
1794, April 13, Fuchs, Margaretha, and Andreas Roth.
1785, Feb. 24, Fuller, Elizabeth, and Manly Smallwood.
1782, May 30, Fuller, Hannah, and Jacob Schlemer.
1797, Dec. 7, Fullerton, Lydia, and George Beck.
1750, ———, Fuls, Christina, and Barnt Van Leer.
1780, June 4, Funck, Anna, and Jacob Fiss.
1801, Sept. 10, Furr, Jacob, and Eliz. Kinseler.
1784, Feb. 26, Fusselbach, William, and Margaret Diehl.
1798, Feb. 4, Fynn, Jane, and John Lyons.
1776, Jan. 18, Gachoh, Jacob, and Anna Eliz. Kretzer.
1753, Jan. 2, Gaertner, Joh. Heinrich, and Catharina Dorothea
　　　　　Eisenmayer.
1755, Jan. 14, Gahler, George, and Maria Barbara Kress.
1760, Jan. 10, Galadin, Sara, and Ulrich Meng.
1796, March 10, Galle, Sarah, and Friederich ———.
1750, March 13, Gallmann, Magdalena, and Daniel Scheible.
1750, Dec. 29, Gallohon, Margareth, and James Rody.
1768, April 5, Gally, Jacob, and Lydia Hollenswordt.
1792, July 25, Gally, Joseph, and Catharina Dorffer.
1785, June 16, Gamber, Catharine, and Robert Richerton.
1798, Jan. 2, Gamber, Johannes, and Anna Maria Euler.
1791, April 7, Gamber, Maria Magdalena, and Johannes Hof-
　　　　　staedler.
1796, Oct. 6, Gamber, Philip Jacob, and Christina Rosk.
1773, March 11, Gambleman, Jacob, and Philippina Schraen.
1784, Sept. 21, Gamber, Elizabeth, and Adam Fischer.
1771, Sept. 26, Gamberlein, Catharina, and Nicolaus Kayser.
1753, Oct. 4, Gamper, Joh. Heinrich, and Maria Magdalena Rup.
1773, Oct. 19, Gamper, Michael, and Susanna Gilbert.
1760, Jan. 6, Gampert, Anna Maria, and Nicholas Schreiner.
1769, Aug. 21, Gangever, George, and Marlena Cliwer.

1799, March 13, Garde, Johannes, and Maria Christina R———.
1762, Aug. 25, Gardner, Jacob, and Regina Fraily.
1775, Feb. 23, Garret, Adam, and Christina Hysel.
1772, Aug. 22, Garret, Matthias, and Elizabeth Denham.
1762, July   4, Gassert, Maria Esther, and Wilhelm Schneider.
1796, March 15, Gassmann, Dorothea, and Johannes Laury.
1795, April   5, Gassmann, Margaretha, and Jacob Alburger.
1770, March 20, Gattwaltz, Elizabeth, and Henrick Wilhelm.
1787, May   1, Gauel, John Abrah., and Elizabeth Lotz.
1788, July 27, Gaul, Fried, and Clara Walten.
1786, Feb. 19, Gaul, George, and Cath. Mitschet.
1783, June 24, Gaul, Joh. Fried., and Marg. Metzinger.
1775, Nov. 12, Gaul, Valentine, and Sabina Pest.
1794, Feb. 25, Gaul, Christina, and Daniel Bergmeyer.
1782, April 16, Gaul, Elizabeth, and John Martin Liest.
1787, March 27, Gawin, John, and Meine Richardson.
1789, Feb. 26, Geary, James, and Dinah Cerral.
1781, Sept.   9, Gebhard, John, and Regina Warner.
1773, June   3, Gebhardt, Gabriel, and Mary Gerber.
1762, May   18, Geier, Elizabeth, and Johannes Mueller.
1750, Jan.   1, Geiger, Wolf Caspar, and Joh. Eliz. Schmied.
1787, May   10, Geiss, Francis, and Regina Schussler.
1791, May   9, Geissel, Christian George, and Hannah Crist. Jett.
1768, May   23, Geitz, Rosina Dorothea, and Jacob Petry.
1770, Aug.   8, Gilbert, Cath., and Johann Armbruster.
1792, Aug.   7, Gelersen, Maria Magdalena, and Johann Gottlieb
                  Wichor.
1783, Aug. 14, Gemeinbauers, Anna Maria Eliz., and John Krei-
                  mer.
1766, Nov.   4, Gensel, Catherina, and Peter Kupper.
1783, Feb. 22, Genthener, Maria, and Wilhelm Conrad.
1777, March 6, George, ———, and Jacob Coeleman.
1778, June 11, George, Maria, and Nicholas Oliver.
1774, Nov. 17, George, Susanna, and Heinrich Strup.
1789, Aug.   4, Gerbach, Anna Maria, and Gerhard Huhn.
1773, June   3, Gerber, Mary, and Gabriel Gebhardt.
1779, May   16, Gerber, Charlotta, and Charles Seitz.
1772, Oct. 15, Gerber, Maria, and Jacob Uttree.
1761, Sept. 24, Gerckes, Conrad, and Maria Philippina Sesam-
                  bach.
1782, April   4, Gerhard, Conrad, and Elizabeth Jung.
1760, Jan.   21, Gerhard, Catharina, and Jacob Maag.
1751, Jan.   22, Gerhard, Christian, and Christian Betz.
1792, April   3, Gerhardt, Jacob, and Magdalena Mullern.
1779, Jan.   10, Gerlach, Eliz., and Philip Reybold.
1788, Dec.   25, Gerlach, Stephen, and Maria Espay,

1796, Nov.   7, German, James, and Victory Maillard.
1791, April 26, Garreth, John, and Catharina Goebler.
1797, April 30, Gerrit, Christina, and Michael Freytag.
1779, July   8, Gerrith, Johannes, and Margaretha Jung.
1788, June   9, Gerstener, Maria, and George Lampater.
1787, March 22, Gerster, George, and Marg. Jung.
1782, Dec.   2, Gerster, John George, and Anna Maria Burghart.
1787, March 27, Gerster, Marg., and Jacob Meyer.
1769, Feb.   19, Gertdorffer, Maria, and Johannes Albert.
1769, Aug.   1, Gertner, Anna Cath., and Daniel Suder.
1775, April   4, Gesting, Frederick, and Elizabeth Seffrons.
1769, March 16, Geyer, Apollonia, and Julius Rebele.
1788, March 18, Giebert, Christian, and Marg. Lafarty.
1765, Oct.   27, Giel, Johann Heinrich, and Anna Sophia Volck-
                 marr.
1796, Jan.   31, Giffin, Mary, and Johannes Marshall.
1775, June   13, Gilbert, Daniel, and Catharina Birckenbeul.
1795, July   19, Gilbert, David, and Maria Schwartz.
1777, Jan.   1, Gilbert, Marg., and Ludwick Krauer.
1788, May   25, Gilbert, Susanna, and Christopher Kinsle.
1785, Oct.   4, Gilbert, Anna, and Henry Breda.
1773, Oct.   19, Gilbert, Susanna, and Michael Gamper.
1782, Jan.   17, Gillman, Eva, and Henry William Guize.
1787, June   19, Gillmore, Frances, and George Hetton.
1774, Dec.   15, Gilman, Susanna, and Peter Deschong.
1783, May   10, Gilyard, Eliz., and Leonh. Rothar.
1785, April 14, Ginder, John, and Marg. Wack.
1798, Feb.   1, Givin, David, and Elizabeth Grimes.
1773, March 8, Glam, Cath., and Wm Crommy.
1801, Dec.   10, Glan, Daniel, and Mary Humphreys.
1773, Dec.   12, Glasky, Simon, and Elizabeth Grickory.
1787, Feb.   11, Glentworth, Maria, and George Hansell.
1781, Oct.   30, Glockener, Christian, and Cath. Lartsch.
1760, Feb.   12, Gloeler, Maria Cath., and Johannes Messmer.
1753, Aug.   13, Glosmeyer, Joh. Peter, and Anna Cath. Thilman.
1771, April   2, Gobler, Gottfried, and Cath. Tischong.
1796, Oct.   13, Gobler, Matthaeus, and Anna Scholl.
1775, March 2, Goddart, Nicolaus, and Barbara Stroble.
1791, April 26, Goebler, Catharina, and John Gerreth.
1782, June   13, Goebler, Elizabeth, and John Maag.
1801, Oct.   24, Goebler, Fred., and Abigail Kitts.
1798, April 18, Good, Joseph, and Christina Carrigan.
1769, Nov.   11, Goodshius, Jacob, and Mary Schmidt.
1760, April 24, Gor, Elizabeth, and William Frey.
1755, May   26, Gorges, Mary, and William Van Aken.
1784, June   8, Gosser, Philip, and Maria Dies.
        43—VOL. VIII.

1789, June 11, Gotter, Joh. Christopher, and Christina Zimmerman.
1760, Oct. 20, Gottfried, George, and Maria Margaretha Lind.
1783, May 23, Gottschalck, Hannah, and Charles Riste.
1753, July 8, Goz, Maria, and Jacob Hooneker.
1753, Oct. 2, Graaf, Cleovea, and Joh. Ulrich Soudereker.
1778, Aug. 18, Graeff, Maria, and Joh. Christoph. Meining.
1779, June 10, Graefling, Hannah, and Lorentz Reichard.
1791, Aug. —, Graf, Elizabeth, and Anthon Deusing.
1784, May 31, Graff, Caspar, and Rebecca Lindley.
1786, April 17, Graff, Thomas, and Hester Kunck.
1764, June 25, Grafley, Christopher, and Eva Carson.
1788, Oct. 5, Graft, John, and Eliz. Kart.
1787, Aug. 23, Graham, Edward, and Margaretha Stenerwald.
1783, Oct. 14, Gramlich, Eliz., and Jacob Kreider.
1778, July 28, Gramlich, Susanna, and John Justus Koch.
1786, Dec. 19, Grauel, John, and Eliz. Grub.
1799, April 5, Grave, Fred., and Cath. Mum.
1777, Sept. 9, Gray, Jane, and Thomas Dobson.
1782, Aug. 15, Gray, Richard, and Hannah Forster.
1779, June 16, Gray, Thomas, and Mary Buskirk.
1802, March 17, Green, Cath., and John O'Keen.
1776, Feb. 19, Green, Mary, and John Turner.
1787, June 28, Green, Samuel, and Mary White.
1789, May 28, Green, Stephen, and Cath. Henry.
1776, Aug. 18, Greene, Juliana Eliz., and Bernhard Michel.
1750, Feb. 12, Greenfield, Margaret, and Henry Eakins.
1755, Aug. 17, Gregery, Sarah, and Heinrich Gross.
1779, Oct. 26, Greis, Eliz., and George Umback.
1773, Dec. 12, Grickory, Elizabeth, and Simon Glasky.
1761, June 16, Grible, David, and Susanna Reinwalt.
1770, July 17, Grienwat, Alexander, and Sabina Steiber.
1766, Sept. 14, Griessie, Margretha, and Matthews Jacobs.
1783, Oct. 15, Griffith, Mary, and Benjamin Tunis.
1785, June 21, Griffith, Maria, and John Jung.
1777, Feb. 13, Griffith, Mercy, and Johann Backer.
1760, Sept. 24, Griffiths, Sarah, and James Helton.
1785, Aug. 16, Grim, Elizabeth, and John Henry Runipf.
1774, Sept. 13, Grim, Joh. Jacob, and Dinah Meason.
1798, Feb. 1, Grimes, Elizabeth, and David Givin.
1753, Feb. 6, Grimwood, John, and Ann Allen.
1764, Oct. 25, Grob, Heinrich, and Anna Margaretha Heller.
1749, Dec. 26, Grob, Joh., and Anna Maria Haens.
1769, May 28, Groener, Dorothea, and Johann Adam Schifferes.
1779, Feb. 12, Groff, Eliz., and Jacob Kichele.
1780, Aug. 2, Groff, Sam., and Mary Pinjard.

1781, June   16, Grogan, Patrick, and Cath. Southam.
1788, Sept. 30, Groh, Christian, and Sally Dennis.
1794, July   24, Gros, Jacob, and Rosina Valentin.
1797, March 16, Gros, Philip, and Christina Kraus.
1754, Oct.   28, Gross, Anna Maria, and George Lingenfeld.
1755, Aug.   17, Gross, Heinrich, and Sarah Gregery.
1755, March 31, Gross, Johann, and Anna Spitler.
1790, Nov.   23, Gross, Maria, and Thomas Watson.
1762, April 14, Gross, Regina Catharina, and Johannes Diel.
1771, April   7, Grothausen, Dorothea, and Johannes Kranapf.
1779, Jan.   11, Grove, Eliz., and Bernhard Mool.
1786, Dec.   19, Grub, Eliz., and John Grauel.
1770, May   26, Grub, Henry, and Barbara Kinsley.
1788, March 13, Grub, Michael, and Betsy Derick.
1784, June   6, Grubb, Catharina, and Nicolaus Wirich.
1779, Sept. 19, Grubb, Cath., and Francis Buck.
1801, Feb.   6, Grubb, Mary, and Peter Zambo.
1792, Sept. 27, Gruninger, Susanna, and Daniel Pelz.
1782, May   9, Gunckel, Maria, and John Neimand.
1777, Oct.   1, Gucker, Christian, and Dorothea Keyler.
1784, Sept. 22, Gucker, Jacob, and Maria Heith.
1796, April   7, Gucker, Jacob, and Mary Horton.
1784, July   6, Gucker Martin, and Cath. Souder.
1775, Jan.   24, Gucker, Mathias, and Marlena Dewald.
1750, ——   —, Guggart, Christian, and Anna Eliz. Flerin.
1782, Jan.   17, Guize, Henry William, and Eva Gillman.
1767, Oct.   6, Gulman, Daniel, and Christina Schuetz.
1797, Oct.   20, Gummy, Johannes, and Maria Molitor.
1774, Feb.   10, Gummy, Johann, and Catharina Mueller.
1799, May   9, Gunderman, Joh., and Elizabeth Truber.
1798, April 23, Gunther, Catharina, and James Tate.
1797, Aug.   10, Gunther, Friedericka, and Friedrick Weber.
1794, Sept. 18, Gut, Christina, and Wilhelm Stoltz.
1750, Jan.   24, Gutt, Heinrich, and Catharina Nuesset.
1780, March 14, Gwillim, John, and Mary Oberdorff.
1753, April 13, Gwin, Evan, and Hannah, Johns.
1765, Sept.   3, Gwin, John, and Maria Sevgerdt.
1765, Jan.   27, Haan, Joseph, and Maria Knodler.
1771, June   6, Haan, Peter, and Catharina Lohry.
1766, Oct.   26, Haan, Catharine, and Michael Kreider.
1763, Dec.   8, Haan, Elizabeth, and Jacob Eteborn.
1796, May   26, Haas, Catharina, and George Lambert.
1785, Aug.   14, Haas, Elizabeth, and Joh. George Kehr.
1787, Dec.   27, Haas, Friederick, and Eliz. Friederick.
1793, July   14, Haas, Martin, and Anna Kehr.
1779, June   10, Haberstig, William, and Maria Descheler.

1796, March 8, Hackedy, Maria, and Matthias Heineberg.
1779, July   15, Hackemuller, Jacob, and Maria Mullen.
1766, Dec.   9, Haen, Johannes, and Elizabeth Lotz.
1751, Jan.   2, Haene, Fridenrich, and Anna Maria Calle.
1762, Nov.   7, Haert, Barbara, and Johannes, Fariss.
1784, Nov.   18, Haerth, Mary, and Caleb Hughes.
1782, Jan.   31, Hafener, Catherina, and Michael Worn.
1787, Jan.   4, Hafener, Anna Maria, and Henry Jungst.
1777, Feb.   2, Haffner, Heinrich, and Anna Marg. Termoelen.
1771, Oct.   22, Haffner, Maria Magdalena, and Cornelius Brown.
1762, Nov.   23, Hahn, Christian, and Johann Margaret Eidler.
1777, June   10, Hahn, Christina, and Arnold Krehmer.
1785, May   7, Hahn, Elizabeth, and Anthony Weiss.
1761, June   25, Hahn, Nicolas, and Eliz. Margaretha Beker.
1801, May   14, Hahn, Susannah, and Joh. Wille.
1767, July   9, Hahn, Catherine, and Johann Jacob Enek.
1794, June   29, Hahns, George, and Maria Schaffer.
1767, Oct.   31, Hai, John, and Rosina Cline.
1801, March 15, Hail, Cath., and Fred. Adams.
1798, June   7, Hains, Anton, and Margaretha Koster.
1788, June   24, Hains, Jacob, and Eva Miller.
1776, Aug.   28, Haines, Millicent, and Thomas Newe.
1801, Sept.   7, Hainback, Maria, and Sylvanius Simons.
1801, Nov.   5, Hains, Maria, and Peter Stein.
1786, April   6, Hainy, Nicol., and R——— Wilson.
1768, Feb.   14, Hair, Anna, and Jeremiah Leahr.
1750, Aug.   29, Hairs, Elizabeth, and Anthony McKneel.
1784, Feb.   4, Hald auf der Heide, Johannes, and Eliz. Schlechter.
1787, March 31, Haley, John, and Deborah Thomas.
1795, July   16, Hall, David, and Elizabeth Black.
1768, July   31, Hall, James, and Marg. Ryan.
1795, Dec.   3, Hall, Salome, and Friedrich Schinckel.
1777, Sept.   2, Hall, Thomas, and Hannah Cline.
1785, Aug.   14, Haller, Jacob, and Maria Ravans.
1785, Feb.   1, Haller, Philip, and Maria Threyer.
1784, Oct.   28, Haller, Anna Barb., and Nicolaus Rummel.
1779, Aug.   31, Halter, Johann Jacob, and Christina Laub.
1784, Jan.   5, Halvilson, Philippina, and Daniel Von der Schleis.
1779, Dec.   30, Hamerly, Fabian, and Cath. Rigel.
1755, July   12, Hamilton, David, and Margaret Ponwel.
1750, Oct.   1, Hamilton, Jane, and Edward Evans.
1750, Oct.   13, Hamilton, William, and Elizabeth Roul.
1783, Nov.   9, Hammer, Ludwig, and Cath. Bedford.
1775, May   6, Hammer, Mary, and Isaac Thomas.
1769, May   15, Hammerstane, Juliane, and Martin Lantze.
1771, Feb.   19, Hammerick, Elizabeth, and Adam Schutz.

1802, May   23, Hamton, Alexander, and Mary Derland.
1785, April 11, Hancock, Benjamin, and Hannah Cross.
1795, July   31, Hancock, Mary, and Samuel Duffs.
1796, Oct.   30, Handschuh, Christina, and Simon Sorg.
1776, Sept. 21, Handschuh, Elizabeth, and Henry Rudy.
1790, Feb.   9, Handschuk, Mary, and Thomas Ried.
1779, Feb.   23, Haner, Magd., and Richard Dempsey.
1777, April 12, Haneson, Mary, and James Johnston.
1793, April 24, Hange, Johannes, and Susanna Remholdt.
1776, Jan.   25, Hanger, Gottfried, and Maria Fought.
1780, Jan.   4, Han, Maria Marg., and Jacob Finck.
1766, Aug.   17, Hanley, Thomas, and Margaretha Mathews.
1793, Feb.   16, Hanlon, John, and Catharina Heller.
1786, May   16, Hansal, Lewis, and Mary Bond.
1787, Feb,   11, Hansell, George, and Maria Glentworth.
1795, June   14, Hansen, Andreas, and Anna Maria Sieberick.
1796, Oct.   20, Hansen, C. Maria, and Joh. George Tan.
1775, June   14, Hans, Charlotte, and Peter Walter.
1773, Jan.   21, Hansman, Elizabeth, and Michael Schreiber.
1778, Nov.   29, Hardwick, Joh. Heinr., and Philip Schuhen.
1801, Sept. 19, Harford, Charles, and Mary Auner.
1796, Oct.   6, Harford, Mary, and Job Creaghead.
1750, July   2, Harker, Mary, and Thomas Fenimose.
1768, Jan.   24, Harmer, Jane, and Josiah Harned.
1793, Sept. 19, Harmstadt, Maria Anna, and Albion Cox.
1768, Jan.   24, Harned, Josiah, and Jane Harmer.
1767, Aug.   6, Harper, Francis, and Martha Margen.
1760, July   4, Harper, William, and Eleanor Smith.
1762, Dec.   18, Hart, Felix, and Elizabeth Hesson.
1762, Oct.   19, Hart, Louise, and Marx Dommen.
1774, Feb.   15, Hartman, Catharina, and Theodore Hartman.
1801, April 12, Hartman, Christian, and Eliz. Jost.
1773, July   27, Hartman, Heinrich, and Cath. Weising.
1774, Feb.   15, Hartman, Theodore, and Catharina Hartman.
1798, June   3, Hartneck, M. Christina, and Andreas Tan.
1775, May   2, Hartramphret, Christopher, and Cathrina Kuntz.
1761, July   3, Harrald, David, and Margaret Boyd.
1750, Dec.   1, Harris, Sarah, and John Coppok.
1750, Aug.   30, Harrison, Ann, and James Simpson.
1781, Feb.   24, Harrison, Anne, and Christian Earl.
1752, May   17, Hartwig, John George, and Anna Cath. West-
                  hov.
1770, Nov.   28, Has, Hannah, and Philip Walter.
1772, Nov.   22, Hasencleaver, Francis Caspar, and Maria Mel-
                  chior.
1778, April 28, Hasler, Heinrich, and Salome Adams.

1801, June 13, Hasselton, Eliz., and Joh. Sleyhoff.
1762, Jan. 24, Hassert Aaron, and Catharina Stitschert.
1766, April 27, Hassert, Catherina, and Peter Rasber.
1782, April 22, Hastings, Clarissa, and James Trimble.
1785, Sept. 27, Haubt, Elizabeth, and Peter Weiel.
1801, Dec. 24, Haushalter, Christina, and William Palmer.
1796, Nov. 3, Hausler, Jacob, and Catharina Hut.
1796, Dec. 8, Haut, Maria, and Heinrich Fischer.
1798, May 27, Hays, Addis, and Catharina Cambert.
1750, Nov. 15, Hays, James, and Maria Stark.
1787, Jan. 25, Healy, Edward, and Mary Mathews.
1792, Aug. 4, Hecht, Johann Christina Henrietta, and Gottlieb M——.
1768, Oct. 15, Heck, Barbara, and Frederick Locker.
1767, April 10, Heckman, Maria, and Andreas Longecker.
1792, Dec. 14, Heehr, Susanna, and Heinrich Schee.
1775, Dec. 26, Heffter, Anna Barbara, and Nicholaus Staad.
1761, Sept. 10, Hegelgans, Sigmund, and Margaretha Truckenmuller.
1792, June 24, Heher, Catharina, and Johannes Schneider.
1765, June 11, Hehl, Regina, and Johann Bocked.
1760, June 17, Heid, Daniel, and Catharina Schmid.
1761, Jan. 6, Heid, Magdalena Elizabeth, and Mehael Peter.
1783, June 13, Heidle, Anna, and David Muller.
1750, Aug. 9. Heidt, Anna Eliz., and Carl Ludwig Weiss.
1783, Dec. 1, Heimberger, Fried, and Mary Stimmel.
1770, Feb. 18, Heimberger, Dorothea, and Johannes Sommer.
1769, June 22, Heimberger, Regina, and Valentine Brown.
1783, April 3, Heimer, John, and Eliz. Henrich.
1795, April 15, Hein, Catharina, and Philip Rossel.
1799, June 8, Hein, Philippina, and Jacob Berchel Bach.
1796, March 8, Heineberg, Matthias, andMaria Hackedy.
1793, March 17, Heineman, George and Maria Klein.
1767, March 22, Heing, Maria Rosina, and Johannes Meyer.
1762, Dec. 4, Henricks, Rachel, and Jacob Metz.
1761, Aug. 12, Heinricus, Anna Maria, and Jos Philip Sensfelder.
1787, Feb. 20, Heiser, Adam, and Eva Wirth.
1795, Dec. 22, Heissler, Eliz., and Johannes, Buchhammer.
1784, Sept. 22, Heith, Mary, and Jacob Gucker.
1761, Dec. 15, Heker, Anna Eliz., and Js Jacob Stud.
1797, Dec. 7, Held, Johannes, and Margaretha Wentz.
1797, Aug. 17, Held, Peter, and Maria Schneider.
1783, Sept. 25, Held, Rebecca, and Philip Rummel.
1773, Feb. 11, Helffenstein, Albertus, and Cath. Karcher.
1799, July 4, Hell, Jacob, and Cath. Benser.
1750, Nov. 27, Hellebrand, Elizabeth, and Henrich Lynbaker.

1796, Feb.   4, Heller, Adam, and Sarah Cowan.
1764, Oct. 25, Heller, Anna Margareth, and Heinrich Grob.
1793, Feb. 16, Heller, Catharina, and John Hanlon.
1773, May   3, Heller, Friedrich, and Cath. Wilhelmina Juengst.
1775, Sept. 19, Heller, John, and Mary Jones.
1762, Jan. 14, Heller, Catharina, and Gottfried Wilk.
1767, Dec. 13, Helm, Christian, and Margaretha Pennington.
1771, Jan. 1, Helm, Peter, and Elizabeth Schlemmer.
1750, May   7, Helsby, Ralph, and Sarah Willey.
1787, Sept. 2, Helt, Eliz., and Joh. Philip Petry.
1787, Sept. 2, Helt, Peter, and An. Eliz. Petry.
1768, April 9, Helton, Laetitia, and Isaac Bener.
1760, Sept. 24, Helton, James, and Sarah Griffiths.
1786, Oct. 3, Helwig, Marg., and Samuel Forten.
1774, Nov. 6, Helwig, Cath., and Valentin Klages.
1796, April 2, Hemer, Richard, and Christina Fischer.
1766, June 10, Hemsing, Heinrich, and Christina Petrien.
1762, Sept. 19, Hen, Anthony, and Catharina Christeiny.
1779, March 21, Henckel, Conrad, and Marg. Mueller.
1790, May   3, Henckel, Cornelius, and Maria Lotz.
1801, Oct. 24, Hendel, Eliz., and —— ——.
1777, July 9, Hendrickson, Sarah, and Jona. Dolbon.
1794, April 22, Henrich, Magdalena, and Daniel Miller.
1783, April 3, Henrich, Eliz., and John Heimer.
1772, Nov. 29, Henrick, Margaretha, and Ludwick Reith.
1789, May 28, Henry, Cath., and Stephen Green.
1777, May 29, Henry, George, and Mary Housman.
1783, Sept. 28, Henry, Maria, and John Eberman.
1797, June 11, Hensel, Maria, and Martin Waters.
1769, April 4, Hensler, Susanna, and Jacob Muller.
1767, Jan. 20, Hensman, Maria, and Peter Schreiber.
1784, March 22, Henssen, Matthews, and Mary Meier.
1797, Feb. 23, Hentz, Elizabeth, and Sebastian Hoffmann.
1785, Oct. 6, Herford, George, and Mary Bockius.
1760, April 27, Hergert, Magdalena, and Peter Osias.
1767, Jan. 27, Herguth, Cath., and Christian Petz.
1794, Nov. 19, Herman, Catharine, and Conrad Kuppel.
1767, May 4, Herman, Maria, and Ernest Schlosser.
1765, Oct. 23, Hermann, Johannes, and Cath. Mueller.
1797, Aug. 5, Heron, Anne Blondel, and Paul Randon.
1787, March 29, Herr, Catharine, and John Fried. Dickes.
1787, Nov. 4, Hertzog, Rachel, and Abraham Wilt.
1794, April 30, Hertzog, Rebecca, and Philip Mittmann.
1782, April 11, Hertzog, Susanna, and Wilhelm Miller.
1780, Nov. 23, Hess, Anne, and Jacob Warden.
1786, Oct. 12, Hess, Eliz., and John Christian Ziegeler.

1784, April 1, Hess, George, and Anna Conver.
1748, Aug. 23, Hess, Jacob, and Elizabeth Lam.
1753, Oct. 27, Hess, Joh. Ludwig, and Anna Maria Swabb.
1775, Jan. 21, Hess, Maria, and James Jakson.
1798, Dec. 7, Hess, Peter Martin, and Veronica Reis.
1800, Dec. 23, Hess, A. Cath., and Gerhard Dutill.
1785, Nov. 16, Hess, Cath., and Mich. Kaiser.
1779, Aug. 31, Hess, Elizabeth, and Christian Weyard.
1785, April 24, Hess, Marg., and Christian Jacob.
1786, Jan. 10, Hess, Rosina, and Peter Bockius.
1787, Sept. 30, Hess, Wilhelmina, and Jac. Zible.
1762, Dec. 18, Hesson, Elizabeth, and Felix Hart.
1787, June 19, Hetton, George, and Frances Gillmore.
1779, April 8, Heuman, Eliz., and Nicolaus Stimmel.
1782, June 3, Hey, Rosina, and Andreas Schuster.
1771, Sept. 18, Heyl, John, and Mary Stricker.
1771, Nov. 7, Heyl, Maria, and Philip Worn.
1779, April 15, Heyler, Johannes, and Susanna Walter.
1801, Feb. 6, Hibbs, Wᵐ, and Mary Breeding.
1799, Dec. 11, Hickham, Richard, and Hannah Buckingham.
1750, Dec. 6, Hiester, Gertrude, and John Frick.
1767, May 12, Higgins, Elizabeth, and David Brown.
1796, April 21, Higins, Comfort, and Peter Backer.
1784, Aug. 5, Hildebrand, Heinrich, and Anna Maria Bamberger.
1779, Aug. 19, Hiler, George, and Elizabeth King.
1769, May 20, Hill, Elizabeth, and Hugh King.
1789, July 5, Hill, Eliz., and Joh. Philip Reis.
1798, Feb. 11, Hill, Jacob, and Elizabeth Dixon.
1788, March 9, Hill, Jacob, and Eliz. Backoff.
1749, Nov. —, Hill, Jacob, and Anna Maria Paul.
1753, Aug. 27, Hill, Rachel, and John Schey.
1799, May 29, Hill, William, and Katy Wagner.
1760, July 27, Himpelmaenn, Christina, and Hans Heinrick Rigg.
1781, Nov. 8, Himpelman, Jac., and Elizabeth Burck.
1784, Aug, 1, Hinckel, George, and Ruth Owen.
1761, Feb. 17, Hinz, Gottfried, and Cath. Eliz. Schmid.
1801, Aug. 13, Hippensteil, Justina, and Jacob Ristein.
1760, May 6, Hirsch, Anna Barbara, and Johann Martin Klein.
1749, April —, Hitwohl, Mathaeus, and Maria Magdalena Schaeffer.
1801, Dec. 20, Hoch, Susannah, and Johannes Bann.
1760, Aug. 14, Hoch, Catherine, and Christian Hoffmann.
1792, May 15, Hoeffly, Maria, and George Roebsamen.
1774, June 26, Hoehser, Regina Catharina, and Johann Wilhelm Schneider.
1769, Aug. 26, Hoerlimann, Felix, and Maria Appolonia Schrott.

1794, Oct.   26, Hoff, Catharina, and George Mill.
1799. April 15, Hoff, Elizabeth, and Wilhelm Ehrman.
1790, March 30, Hoffman, Cath. and Jac. ·Siegmund.
1787, Feb.   1, Hoffman, Charlotte, and George Weybel.
1778, Sept. 15, Hoffman, Christian, and Cath. Kerner.
1778, Oct.   5, Hoffman, Eliz., and William Flick.
1786, Dec.   31, Hoffman, Lorentz, and Maria Schling.
1776, May   6, Hoffman, Jacob, and Catharina Jung.
1775, April 17, Hoffman, Johannes, and Dorothea Zervass.
1767, March 12, Hoffman, Johann Wilhelm, and Maria Wormly.
1769, June   29, Hoffman, Mary, and Heinrich Mueller.
1760, Aug.   14, Hoffmann, Christian, and Catherina Hoch.
1756, May   20, Hoffman, Joh. George, and Anna Nuescheler.
1797, Feb.   23, Hoffmann, Sebastian, and Elizabeth Hentz.
1796, July   9, Hoffmann, Maria, and Johannes Bachofen.
1750, Nov.   13, Hofman, Joh. Ulrich, and Sarah Powel.
1770, July   10, Hofsess, Eva Cath., and Johannes Jacob Jud.
1791, April   7, Hofstaedler, Johannes, and Maria Magdalena Gam-
                 ber.
1755, Jan.   30, Hogermuth, Anna, and Jacob Rubb.
1768, April   5, Hollenswordt, Lydia, and Jacob Gally.
1770, Feb.   22, Holton, William, and Mary Schmidt.
1752, Aug.   12, Honeyman, William, and Ann Cox.
1782, July   31, Hood, Thomas, and Sarah Lambeth.
1772, Oct.   17, Hook, Henry, and Mary Fry.
1753, July   8, Hooneker, Jacob, and Maria Goz.
1802, Feb.   4, Hoot, ———, and ——— ———.
1782, June   30, Hoover, Cath, and Christian Alberger.
1769, Aug.   29, Hope, Gottfried, and Anna Maria Mielin.
1766, June   9, Horner, Johann George, and Margaretha Becker.
1781, April   8, Horning, Elizabeth, and John Keyser.
1791, Jan.   24, Horning, Jacob, and Nancy North.
1773, Oct.   4, Horst, Elizabeth, and George Peeling.
1796, April   7, Horton, Mary, and Jacob Gucker.
1774, Oct.   12, Hough, Eliz., and Samuel Lyons.
1793, Feb.   16, Hough, Isaac, and Elizabeth Eberth.
1773, July   21, Housard, Elizabeth, and John McAfee.
1777, May   29, Housman, Mary, and George Henry.
1783, April 13, Housman, Sophia, and Martin Runner.
1762, March   2, Howell, Catharina, and James Crawford.
1755, Dec.   18, Howell, Elizabeth, and Joshua Evans.
1801, Aug.   28, Huben, Caspar, and Cath. Rath.
1780, June   8, Huber, Heinrich, and Maria Engel.
1801, Feb.   26, Huber, Joh., and Susanna Dauberman.
1799, March 12, Huber, Joseph, and Anna Maria Tise.
1787, Sept. 23, Huber, Maria, and Henry Tepes.

1788, Jan.   1, Huck, Anna Marg., and Christian Schaeffer.
1779, Feb.   14, Hudd, Thomas, and Christina Noldin.
1787, March   4, Hueter, Thomas, and Catharina Dick.
1784, Nov.   18, Hughes, Caleb, and Mary Haerth.
1786, Nov.   17, Hughes, Garret, and Susanna Chamberlein.
1781, Feb.   13, Hughes, Jane, and Griffith Owen.
1784, Aug.   21, Hughes, Uriah, and Phebe Rennard.
1802, April   8, Hughs, Mary, and Sam'l Kaflay.
1788, April   8, Huhn, Cath., and Samuel Walker.
1789, Aug.   4, Huhn, Gerhard, and Anna Maria Gerbach.
1782, Aug.   29, Huhn, Johannes, and Christina Milsin.
1789, Sept. 22, Huhn, Susanna, and Michael Weitener.
1750, April   3, Humphreys, Maria, and Robert Roberts.
1801, Dec.   10, Humphreys, Mary, and Daniel Glan.
1770, Dec.   25, Hunsigger, Maria, and Herman Leck.
1778, Sept. 20, Hunt, Cath., and Joh. Christopher Assmus.
1771, Jan.   24, Huntzel, Magdalena, and Peter Bart.
1786, Oct.   4, Hurff, Priscilla, and David Bechtle.
1798, May   22, Huss, (or Heiss,) Catharina, and Jacob ——.
1777, April 13, Hustler, Thomas and Cath. Cherry.
1796, Nov.   3, Hut, Catharina, and Jacob Hausler.
1792, Jan.   10, Huth, Peter, and Barbara Kriger.
1797, Nov.   11, Huttman, Thomas Lorentz, and Barbara Bender.
1801, July   4, Hutts, Eliz., and George Ozeas.
1775, Feb.   23, Hysel, Christina, and Adam Garret.
1789, May   25, Immel, Peter, and An. Mar. Philipan.
1790, April 15, Inglis, Benjamin, and Jane Applin.
1759, Aug.   19, Isser, Cath. Marg., and Johann Reinhard Mueller.
1790, June   12, Istwick, Charles, and Mary Taylor.
1773, July   27, Jackquart, Peter, and Anna Odilia Karcher.
1778, May   31, Jackson, Maria, and David Sutter.
1784, Sept. 20, Jackson, Rebecca, and Joseph Smallwood.
1792, May   8, Jacob, Christian, and Barbara Rheily.
1785, April 24, Jacob, Christian, and Marg. Hess.
1766, Sept. 14, Jacobs, Matthews, and Margretha Griessie.
1772, Jan.   5, Jaeger, Johann, and Mary Cloethy.
1778, Oct.   11, Jaeger, Maria, and John Schreiber.
1774, Aug.   18, Jaeger, Cath., and Johannes Bronner.
1785, May   24, Jaeglin, Marl., and Jacob Erringer.
1750, Sept. 18, Jaentzer, Christina, and Juliana Eliz. Bengler.
1797, Jan.   2, Jahns, (or Fahns,) Jacob, and Catharina Klein.
1748, Oct.   —, Jakly, Ulrich, and Susanna Somerauer.
1775, Jan.   21, Jakson, James, and Maria Hess.
1778, March 25, Jamissen, Eliz., and Gerhard Bischhoven.
1796, Aug.   14, Janey, George, and Elizabeth Becker.
1770, Nov.   15, Jansson, Anna Maria, and Christian Schneider

1782, Nov.   1, Janus, George, and Margaret Foering.
1748, Sept.   23, Jay, Franciscus, and Anna Elizabeth Leinweber.
1798, May   18, Jefferys, Mary, and Samuel Perrot.
1750, Oct.   27, Jenes, Esther, and Joseph Bond.
1792, Feb.   27, Jenser, Clara, and Lorentz Schuessler.
1792, Aug.   7, Jentzen, Anna Catharina, and Joachim Lorentz.
1786, June   13, Jentzer, Fried., and Jacobina Wengen.
1788, June   10, Jentzer, Jac., and Barb. Tschudy.
1778, Sept.   20, Jentzer, Susanna, and Feter Muller.
1788, Dec.   25, Jentzer, Veronica, and George Duerr.
1782, April   16, Jentzer, Anna Marg., and Johannes Pello.
1782, June   20, Jerger, Cath., and Martin Worn.
1787, Sept.   27, Jerkis, Katy, and Jac. Coffin.
1801, April   14, Jerymy, Eliz., and Augustus Reichel.
1798, Feb.   1, Jetter, Maria, and Isaac Comeley.
1791, May   9, Jettin, Hannah Christ, and Christian George Geis-
                  sel.
1789, July   26, Jobst, Joh. Mich., and Cath. Kep.
1791, Dec.   25, Jobst, Johannes, and Charlotta Anfforth.
1753, Sept.   9, Johnes, Martha, and Peter Luken.
1756, Feb.   11, Johnes, Mary, and William Jones.
1753, April   13, Johns, Hannah, and Even Gwin.
1760, Nov.   2, Johns, Martha, and Johannes Krauss.
1798, March   4, Johnson, Alexander, and Elizabeth Doerr.
1791, Sept.   25, Johnson, Anna Maria, and Johann George Rieger.
1750, Nov.   12, Johnson, Esther, and George Fridenrich Moschel.
1750, Jan.   18, Johnson, John, and Margaret Aloway.
1768, April   20, Johnson, Margaretha, and Joseph Wild.
1794, April   2, Johnson, Rebecca, and Jonathan Dewees.
1784, Oct.   28, Johnson, Robert, and Mary Krouse.
1772, Feb.   20, Johnston, Hermanus, and Mary Fisher.
1783, March   4, Johnston, Jacob, and Eliz. Weierman.
1777, April   12, Johnston, James, and Mary Haneson.
1776, April   21, Johnston, Robert, and Elizabeth Black.
1787, Feb.   22, Johnston, Sarah, and Jacob Lehn.
1750, Nov.   17, Johnstown, Margareth, and John McMichael.
1767, May   3, Joins, Immanuel, and Elizabeth Blecked.
1781, Feb.   2, Jones Cath., and Adam Lapp.
1801, Nov.   15, Jones, Debby, and David Wilfahn.
1779, Sept.   2, Jones, Enos, and Elizabeth Potts.
1802, Jan.   4, Jones, Hannah, and George Wharton.
1781, May   10, Jones, Isaac, and Cath. Bedellion.
1776, March   26, Jones, Isaac, and Anna Watkins.
1801, May   10, Jones, Jacob, and Marg. Lowery.
1771, Aug.   8, Jones, Janes, and Jacob Peters.
1784, Sept.   2, Jones, John, and Elizabeth Weithman.

1775, Sept.   19, Jones, Mary, and John Heller.
1796, Dec.   8, Jones, Sarah, and Martin Dubs.
1756, Feb.   11, Jones, William, and Mary Johnes.
1787, Oct.   28, Jones, William, and Eliz. Frioth.
1768, March   1, Jonwenal, David, and Dorothea Lander.
1801, April   12, Jost, Eliz., and Christian Hartman.
1748, Oct.   —, Jost, Nicholans, and Catherina Klason.
1792, April   3, Jost, Peter, and Elizabeth Zigler.
1753, Aug.   2, Jost, Anna Maria, and Joh. Philip Boehm.
1773, Jan.   31, Jonch, Christian, and Maria Otto.
1789, Nov.   15, Jonch, Cath., and William Schmidt.
1785, May   10, Jonch, Elizabeth, and Nicolaus Meyers.
1770, July   10, Jud, Johannes Jacob, and Eva Cath. Hofsess.
1773, May   3, Juengst, Cath. Wilhelmia, and Frekerich Heller
1799, June   12, Jund, Eliz., and Conrad Keller.
1786, May   30, Junck, Joseph, and Mary Schneider.
1797, April   9, Juncker, George, and Maria ———.
1796, May   1, Juncker, Joseph, and Maria Schutz.
1780, Oct.   2, Jung, Andrew, and Cath. Meyers.
1774, May   5, Jung, Carl Christian, and Eliz. Magdalena Stetz-
                   erin.
1773, June   10, Jung, Catharine, and Archibald McFaggart.
1753, Nov.   25, Jung, Christina, and John Liesch.
1767, April   28, Jung, Christopher, and Rebecca Keisel.
1797, March   21, Jung, Jacob, and Magdalena Zahn.
1785, June   21, Jung, John, and Maria Griffith.
1803, April   23, Jung, Joh. Geo., and Susanna Macklin.
1777, Dec.   21, Jung, Ludwick, and Carolina Kehler.
1779, June   10, Jung, Maria, and Jacob Kreiger.
1765, May   21, Jung, Maria, and Johannes Ritz.
1765, Aug.   15, Jung, Maria Eliz, and Conrad Scheller.
1788, Aug.   21, Jung, Peter, and Rebecca Werntz.
1762, Jan.   20, Junger, Anna Maria, and Johann Adam Stock
1776, May   6, Jung, Catharina, and Jacob Hoffman,
1781, April   4, Jung, Elizabeth, and Conrad Gerhard.
1787, March   22, Jung, Marg., and George Gerster.
1779, July   8, Jung, Margaretha, and Johannes Gerrith.
1787, Jan.   4, Jungst, Henry, and Anna Maria Haffener.
1776, Oct.   27, Juvenal, John, and Maria Schmidt.
1786, Oct.   12, Juvenal, Maria, and Fried. Delliker.
1798, April   11, Kaestenbach, Johannes, and Christina Sinck.
1802, April   8, Kaffiay, Samuel, and Mary Hughs.
1780, Nov.   12, Kahmer, Eliz., and John Worckin.
1785, June   2, Kahmer, William, and Elizabeth Fischer.
1785, Nov.   16, Kaiser, Mich., and Cath. Hessin.
1784, April   8, Kalbfleisch, John, and Maria Lorentz.

1782, July   25, Kalbfleisch, Maria, and Lorentz Sandman.
1761, Sept.   15, Kamenz, Maria, and Johannes Laap.
1794, Oct.   19, Kammer, Elizabeth, and Mitschet Kort.
1780, Jan.   20, Kanten, Anna Christiana, and Christian Peter Bense.
1784, June   13, Kanwertz, Conrad, and Anna Douglish.
1782, Jan.   22, Kappel, Marg., and Johannes Latsch.
1773, Feb.   11, Karcher, Cath., and Albertus Helffenstein.
1755, Feb.   6, Karcher, Ludwig Heinrich, and Maria Anna Cath. Rein.
1773, July   27, Karcher, Anna Odilia, and Peter Jackquart.
1801, July   25, Karmer, Polly, and Joh. Barr.
1797, April   8, Karstens, George, and Johannes Catharina.
1788, Oct.   5, Kart, Eliz., and John Graft.
1789, May   12, Kartrieth, Mary, and John Dawn.
1784, April   4, Katz, Michael, and Marg. Keller.
1779, Dec.   19, Katz, Michael, and Elizabeth Schaub.
1781, June   26, Kauck, Christian, and Maria Diemern.
1796, Oct.   11, Kauffman, Heinrich, and Catharina Kort.
1771, Sept.   26, Kayser, Nicholaus, and Catharina Gamberlein.
1780, Aug.   29, Kayser, Nicolaus, and Eliz. Eschin.
1784, Feb.   13, Keblehauser, Elizabeth, and George Einwachter.
1801, Dec.   24, Kehl, Jacob, and Maria Rietnel.
1777, Dec.   21, Kehler, Carolina, and Ludwick Jung.
1784, Sept.   30, Kehlheffer, Fried., and Margaret Blum.
1796, Dec.   3, Kehr, Catherina, and Abraham Pollebacker.
1768, April   17, Kehr, Christian, and Elizabeth Clemen.
1790, June   18, Kehr, Eliz., and John Kuhn.
1760, July   27, Kehr, George, and Margaret Scheid.
1785, Aug.   14, Kehr, Joh. George, and Elizabeth Haas.
1765, March 31, Kehr, Johann, and Anna Schmid.
1767, March   4, Kehr, Barbara, and John Wenostine.
1767, Feb.   3, Kehrt, Bernhard, and Catharina Mitshed.
1785, Sept.   25, Keiler, Barbara, and Frederick Miley.
1794, June   19, Keischel, Elizabeth, and Richoff Edridge.
1796, Sept.   6, Keiler, Johannes, and Sarah Douglas.
1782, July   16, Keiler, Margaretha, and Jacob Miley.
1795, Nov.   4, Keiler, Susanna, and Johannes Clunn.
1767, April   28, Keisel, Rebecca, and Christopher Jung.
1777, April   12, Keiser, Lydia, and Matthias Roop.
1801, Dec.   —, Keller, Anna, and Moses Pierse.
1797, Aug.   29, Keller, Christina, and Joh. Kraft Weber.
1799, June   12, Keller, Conrad, and Eliz. Jund.
1780, Nov.   26, Keller, Conrad, and An. Eliz. Kramer.
1795, April   19, Keller, George, and Margaretha Pfeiffer.
1792, Sept.   16, Keller, Johannes, and Maria Magdalena Pfeifer.

1771, Oct. 31, Keller, Maria, and Philip Wager.
1761, Jan. 13, Keller, Elizabeth, and Daniel Klein.
1784, April 4, Keller, Marg., and Michael Katz.
1765, July 16, Kell, Cath., and Johann Wilhelm Schneider.
1785, April 6, Kelly, Elizabeth, and Daniel McCoy.
1750, May 16, Kelly, Erasmus, and Hannah Vastine.
1779, Oct. 14, Kelly, Esther, and Isaac Stats.
1797, Feb. 28, Kelly, John, and Catharine Faber.
1783, June 26, Kempert, Eliz., and John Kempert.
1783, June 26, Kempert, John, and Eliz. Kempert.
1780, May 30, Kennedy, Barbara, and Jacob Binder.
1789, July 26, Kep, Cath., and Joh. Mich. Jobst.
1768, April 11, Kephasting, Rachel, and Jno. Strupe.
1772, July 30, Kerbe, Reuben, and Anna Marg. Dettingen.
1781, Feb. 2, Kerby, Charles, and Hannah Sellers.
1782, April 11, Kerch, Maria, and Conrad Scholl.
1768, May 24, Kern, Jacob, and Anna Elizabeth Mueller.
1775, June 4, Kern, Johann, and Eliz. Mayer.
1778, Sept. 15, Kerner, Cath., and Christian Hoffman.
1784, April 12, Kesen, Barbara, and Johannes Zehner.
1774, Oct. 13, Ketcham, Mary, and Jacob Strickler.
1777, Oct. 1, Keyler, Dorothea, and Christian Gucker.
1789, Aug. 11, Keyser, Eliz., and Conrad Weiel.
1781, April 8, Keyser, John, and Elizabeth Horning.
1779, Feb. 12, Kichelein, Jacob, and Eliz. Groff.
1752, Dec. 31, Kiddie, John, and Jane Cameron.
1785, Nov. 3, Kiegbert, Christian, and Marlena Loesch.
1765, May 27, Kiehl, George Jacob, and Christina Raucshen.
1796, Jan. 21, Kiesle, Jacob, and Hannah Weber.
1748, Nov. 20, Kiewith, John Valentin, and Cath. Elizabeth Steine.
1779, Oct. 14, Kiler, Cath., and John Miley.
1779, Aug. 19, King, Elizabeth, and George Hiler.
1769, May 20, King, Hugh, and Elizabeth Hill.
1751, Jan. 2, King, Rebecca, and Thomas Dombaer.
1786, Sept. 12, Kinry, Anna Agita, and John Theis Alhausen.
1801, Sept. 10, Kinseler, Eliz., and Jacob Furr.
1793, March 17, Kinsinger, Michael, and Elizabeth Potey or Poti.
1788, May 25, Kinsle, Christopher, and Susanna Gilbert.
1770, May 26, Kinsley, Barbara, and Henry Grub.
1776, Oct. 24, Kinsley, Jacob, and Cath. Rumelin.
1785, Jan. 20, Kintzlerin, Marg., and John Cress.
1778, Nov. 5, Kirchhoff, Christian, and Maria Riedlinger.
1774, Aug. 25, Kisselman, Friedrich, and Susannah VanReed.
1801, Dec. 27, Kittel, Joh., and Cath. Yeattern.
1801, Oct. 24, Kitts, Abigail, and Fred Goebler.

1785, March 3, Kitts, Charles, and Biddy Welch.
1798, April 3, Kitts, Christina, and George Schneider.
1783, May 27, Klages, Daniel, and Maria Rohrman.
1774, Nov. 6, Klages, Valentin, and Cath. Helwig.
1781, Dec. 22, Klark, Rachel, and James Stats.
1778, Dec. 31, Klang, Maria, and Heinrich Stetzer.
1785, Aug. 11, Klap, John, and Maria Stucky.
1779, Aug. 13, Klapfar, Eliz., and Johann Spalter Franck.
1748, Oct. —, Klason, Catherina, and Nicolaus Jost.
1797, June 10, Klein, Abraham, and Maria Ottinger.
1784, Oct. 28, Klein, Cath., and Martin Schuster.
1748, April 17, Klein, Cath. Gertrude, and Joh. Daniel Brechly.
1797, Jan. 2, Klein, Catharina, and Jacob Jahns or Fahns.
1761, Jan. 13, Klein, Daniel, and Elizabeth Keller.
1785, April 27, Klein, George, and Eliz. Andressen.
1760, May 6, Klein, Johann Martin, and Anna Barbara Hirsch.
1793, March 17, Klein, Maria, and George Heineman.
1790, Jan. 1, Klein, Maria, and Wilh. Pret.
1773, April 13, Klemmer, Anna Veronica, and Adam Mayer.
1782, Aug. 22, Kline, Elizabeth, and Peter Krim.
1778, July 19, Kline, Mary, and Henry Denny.
1784, June 3, Kline, Mary, and John Painter.
1760, July 22, Kling, Joh. Ludwig, and Anna Burckhard.
1773, May 16, Kliver, Jacob, and Anna Margaretha Weinheimer.
1769, Oct. 8, Kloh, Jacob, and Catherina Werner.
1784, June 27, Klosbach, Maria, and John George Ries.
1796, Nov. 11, Knauf, Nicolaus, and Margaretha Bart.
1794, Nov. 23, Knauf, Nicolaus, and Maria Mason.
1797, Dec. 14, Knault, Catharina, and Stephen Fotteral.
1797, Oct. 20, Knaus, Philippina, and Francis Connelly.
1780, July 16, Kneil, Barbara, and Frederick Mangold.
1801, June 8, Knes, Wilhelme, and Joh. Witers.
1787, April 22, Knies, Eliz., and Jacob Diehl.
1761, Feb. 24, Knies, Friderick, and Margaretha Ulmaennin.
1802, Feb. 20, Knipe, Barbara, and James Cogan Warren.
1786, Sept. 29, Knochel, John Bern., and Anna Cath. Zacher.
1765, Jan. 27, Knodler, Maria, and Joseph Haan.
1796, May 1, Knorr, Catharina, and Johannes Foering.
1779, May 16, Kobeler, Jacob, and Maria Magd. Souder.
1798, Feb. 6, Koch, Catharine, and Samuel Schaaf.
1794, April 29, Koch, Dorothea, and George Abel.
1751, Jan. 2, Koch, Elsie, and Dirk Lefferts.
1777, Aug. 10, Koch, Eva Marg., and George Schmidt.
1776, March 24, Koch, George, and Cath. Parish.
1779, May 27, Koch, George, and Maria Cath. Mueller.
1778, July 28, Koch, John Justus, and Susanna Gramlich.

1785, July   24, Koch, Margaret Eliz., and James Cross.
1788, Feb.   13, Kochenberger, Eva, and Wilhelm Conrad.
1776, May   27, Kocher, Nancy, and John Zampel.
1792, Jan.   27, Kochard, Paul, and Maria Elizabeth Young.
1748, July   10, Koenig, Anna Elizabeth, and Alexander Satler.
1791, Jan.   13, Kohl, Johannes, and Elizabeth Kuhly.
1778, April 20, Kohler, Marg., and Benedick Bartholmai.
1779, Feb.   21, Kolbenhoffer, Christ,, and John Barndt Simon.
1801, May   14, Koller, Enoch, and Maria Bitting.
1786, Oct.   26, Konser, Marg., and Jacob Souder.
1773, July   22, Kopfer, Cath., and Heinrich Ritter.
1797, Nov.   21, Kopp, Jacob, and Johanna Maria Krafft.
1751, Jan.   15, Kopp, Joh. Jacob, and Maria Eliz. Wynhold.
1786, May   8, Korck, An. Maria, and George Mueller.
1796, Oct.   11, Kort, Catharina, and Heinrich Kauffmann.
1794, Oct.   19, Kort, Jacob Mitschet, and Elizabeth Kammer.
1785, Sept. 17, Korterman, John, and Susanna Sutten.
1798, June   7, Koster, Margaretha, and Anton Hains.
1784, Dec.   23, Koyser, John, and Pamelia Price.
1797, April   3, Krafft, Charlotte, and Johannes Spangenberg.
1797, Nov.   21, Krafft, Johanna Maria, and Jacob Kopp.
1793, Sept. 14, Krafft, Susanna, and Diederick Buth.
1798, June   11, Kramer, Catharina, and Philip Kramer.
1798, June   11, Kramer, Philip, and Catharina Kramer.
1761, July   7, Kramer, Samuel, and Ottilia Ludwig.
1780, Nov.   26, Kramer, Ann Eliz., and Conrad Keller.
1771, April   7, Krampf, Johannes, and Dorothea Grothausen.
1801, Nov.   15, Kraun, George, and Eliz. Weyer.
1777, Jan.   1, Krauer, Ludwick, and Marg. Gilbert.
1797, March 16, Kraus, Christina, and Philip Gros.
1750, Sept. 11, Kraus, Jacob, and Ursula Stel.
1784, Oct.   14, Krautz. Jacob, and Cath. Wilhelm.
1801, Dec.   20, Krapp, Eliz., and Joh. Lebkin.
1760, Nov.   2, Krauss, Johannes, and Martha Johns.
1777, June   10, Krehmer, Arnold, and Christina Hahn.
1778, March 17, Krehmer, Matthias, and Susanna Bock.
1791, Dec.   18, Kreider, Christian, and Anna Eliz. Pigler.
1788, June   22, Kreider, Daniel, and Marl. Williams.
1780, March   6, Kreider, Frederick, and Fanny Bonecker.
1783, Oct.   14, Kreider, Jacob, and Eliz. Gramlich.
1766, Oct.   26, Kreider, Michael, and Catharina Haan.
1789, April   5, Kreider, Wilhelm, and Mary Schreiner.
1775, April   4, Kreider, Marl., and Michel Steiber.
1776, Feb.   8, Kreider, Susanna, and Paul Caspar Preton.
1784, May   16, Kremer, Amalia, and Joh. Died. Birckenbeul.

1783, Aug. 14, Kreimer, John, and Anna Maria Eliz. Gemeinbauers.
1784, Dec. 23, Kremer, Michael, and Maria Miller.
1755, Jan. 14, Kress, Jacob, and Margaret Paul.
1755, Jan. 14, Kress, Maria Barbara, and George Gahler.
1776, Jan. 18, Kretzer, Anna Eliz., and Jacob Gachoh.
1779, June 10, Krieger, Jacob, and Maria Jung.
1792, Jan. 10, Kriger, Barbara, and Peter Huth.
1782, Aug. 22, Krim, Peter, and Elizabeth Kline.
1774, Oct. 11, Krohin, Eliz. Cath., and Hartman Winck.
1751, Jan. 24, Krouse, Elsie, and Simon Van Asdaalen.
1784, Oct. 28, Krouse, Mary, and Robert Johnson.
1773, June 27, Krug, Johann Gerhardt, and Maria Magdalena
Lelentel.
1780, July 23, Krug, Anna Christ., and John Heinr. Raber.
1795, Oct. 29, Krumbach, Christina, and Johannes Metzgar.
1766, Nov. 2, Krum, Maria, and Jacob Weber.
1799, Aug. 1, Kruse, Cornelius, and Molly Race.
1795, Aug. 20, Kruse, Elizabeth, and James McCauly.
1774, June 9, Kryder, Elizabeth, and Henry Burgy.
1776, Sept. 17, Kuber, Mary Barbara, and John Jacob Albrecht.
1791, May 27, Knck, Christian, and Margaretha Maria Carlsen.
1798, March 6, Kuebler, Johannes, and Esther Stauffer.
1785, Nov. 1, Kuemmel, Sarah, and William Spade.
1772, April 26, Kuhlemann, Christopher, and Anna Maria Strom.
1783, Dec. 2, Kuhl, Cath., and Joh. George Streith.
1791, Jan. 13, Kuhly, Elizabeth, and Johannes Kohl.
1785, July 21, Kuhn, Daniel, and Nelly Coop.
1790, June 18, Kuhn, John, and Eliz. Kehr.
1796, Dec. 31, Kuhn, Maria, and Johann Rudolph Stamm.
1765, May 4, Kul, Barbara, and William Bestlie.
1786, April 17, Kunck, Hester, and Thomas Graff.
1755, March 18, Kuntz, Anna Barbara, and Joh. Bohner.
1748, July 26, Kunzen, Anna Maria, and Joh. Heinrich Wyn
heimer.
1775, May 2, Kuntz, Cathrina, and Christopher Hartramphret.
1794, Nov. 19, Kuppel, Conrad, and Catharine Herman.
1791, July 3, Kupper, Jacob, and Catharina Trauth.
1766, Nov. 4, Kupper, Peter, and Catherina Gensel.
1750, Feb. 19, Kurlz, Peter, and Maria Sophia Bachmaen.
1768, March 6, Kurtz, Cath., and Conrad Stoltz.
1761, Sept. 15, Laap, Johannes, and Maria Kamenz.
1762, Feb. 15, Labeker, Thomas, and Elizabeth Beruth.
1777, March 2, Lacy, Maria, and Daniel Craig.
1788, March 18, Lafarty, Marl., and Christian Giebert.
1789, April 7, Lair, Eliz., and George Westenberger.
44—VOL. VIII.

1750, Sept. 27, Lakin, Anna Christian, and John Jacob Latch.
1796, May 26, Lambert, George, and Catharina Haas.
1782, July 31, Lambeth, Sarah, and Thomas Hood.
1798, May 27, Lambert, Catharina, and Addis Hays.
1788, June 9, Lampater, George, and Maria Gerstener.
1786, March 7, Land, John, and Phoebe Nobel.
1768, May 1, Lander, Simon, and Margaretha Fries.
1768, March 1, Lander, Dorothea, and David Jouwenal.
1764, Aug. 12, Landgraf, Jacob, and Eva Stueber.
1796, March 27, Lane, James, and Hannah Rittenhouse.
1796, May 17, Lane, William, and Susanna Vansciver.
1795, April 16, Lang, Heinrich, and Catharina Blecker.
1760, April 12, Lang, Peter, and Margaretha Entees.
1770, Dec. 18, Lange, John, and Rachel Creamer.
1767, April 10, Langecker, Andreas, and Maria Heckman.
1778, Aug. 26, Langecker, Mary, and Caleb Rassel.
1774, March 17, Lang, Salome, and Nicolaus Ruebel.
1769, May 17, Lantze, Martin, and Juliane Hammerstane.
1794, March 11, Lapostolait, Marja Ursula, and Jean Baptiste Cerisier.
1781, Feb. 2, Lapp, Adam, and Cath. Jones.
1786, July 23, Large, Peter, and Jane Williams.
1779, Oct. 27, Lark, Kath., and James Carr.
1781, Oct. 30, Lartsch, Cath., and Christian Glockener.
1782, Dec. 24, Latch, Jacob, and Jane Rose.
1750, Sept. 27, Latch, Joh. Jacob, and Anna Christian Lakin.
1780, May 15, Latch, Nancy, and Matthias Schnider.
1796, Nov. 17, Latour, Franz, and Margaretha Smith.
1782, Jan. 22, Latsch, Johannes, and Marg. Kappel.
1779, Aug. 31, Laub, Christina, and Johann Jacob Halter.
1778, June 11, Laub, Peter, and Susanna Bayer.
1781, Dec. 18, Laub, Peter, and Maria Leim.
1783, Aug. 5, Laubach, Maria, and David Seltenreich.
1779, Jan. 17, Laub, Cath., and Michael Lehnhard.
1769, Sept. 3, Laurer, Michael, and Barbara Redelbach.
1790, Nov. 18, Lauri, Johannes, and Maria Barbara Wiltfang.
1787, May 24, Lauris, George, and Polly Cox.
1796, March 15, Laury, Johannes, and Dorothea Gassmann.
1797, July 6, Laury, Philip, and Margaretha Meisterschriver.
1748, Dec. 5, Lawler, Michael, and Johanna Philipila Flek.
1748, Dec. 23, Lawrence, Elizabeth, and John Rees.
1761, March 21, Lawrence, Philip, and Ann Ford.
1755, —— —, Lawton, Hannah, and George Cook.
1782, Feb. 21, Lawyer, Christian, and Maria Orlob.
1767, Feb. 14, Leahr, Jeremiah, and Anna Hair.
1781, Aug. 24, Leap, Peter, and Sarah Wills.

1801, Dec.   20, Lebkin, Joh., and Eliz. Krapp.
1792, May   5, Leck, Heinrich, and Maria Schnell.
1770, Dec.   25, Leck, Herman, and Maria Hunsigger.
1780, Jan.   7, Leck, Herman, and Anna Maria Thiel.
1797, April   25, Leck, Johannes, and Catharina Tessle.
1796, Nov.   14, Leck, Maria, and Samuel Park.
1787, Nov.   1, Lecherom, Maria Cath., and Conrad Scherer.
1798, Jan.   21, Lee, Fanny, and Charles Dougherty.
1801, March   15, Lee, Lydia, and Francis Alentrue.
1791, May   5, Leeish, John, and Maria Blum.
1775, Dec.   20, Leek, Herman, and Maria Barbara Wolff.
1778, Dec.   6, Lees, George, and Cath. Zimmerman.
1751, Jan.   2, Lefferts, Dirk, and Elsie Koch.
1782, July   4, Lehman, Anna, and George Loscher.
1788, April   5, Lehman, Eliz., and Melchior Meng.
1784, Nov.   24, Lehman, Hannah, and Peter Bockius.
1771, March   12, Lehman, Jacob, and Anna Maria Stump.
1794, March   6, Lehmann, Johannes, and Elizabeth Blattberger.
1798, July   19, Lehmann, Sarah, and Philip Muellen.
1779, Jan.   17, Lehnhard, Michael, and Cath. Laub.
1782, Sept.   12, Lehr, Adam, and Rebecca Schwartz.
1786, March   2, Lehr, Henry, and Eliz. Nannetter.
1780, Oct.   19, Lehr, John, and Cath. Scheibler.
1787, Feb.   22, Lehn, Jacob, and Sarah Johnston.
1781, Dec.   18, Leim, Maria, and Peter Laub.
1773, June   27, Lelentel, Maria Magdalena, and Johann Gerhardt
                   Krug.
1799, Aug.   8, Lenord, Hannah, and Joh. Geo. Walter.
1787, March   8, Lentz, John, and Sarah Reinhard.
1800, Aug.   4, Leonard, Hannah, and Joh. George Walter.
1761, May   14, Leonard, Nicolas, and Catharina Schweizer.
1787, Sept.   8, Leonhard, James, and Mary McClain.
1781, March   8, Leonhard, John, and Cath. Unkle.
1781, April   19, Lesher, George, and Elizabeth Schmidt.
1786, June   2, Le Telier, John, and Sarah Withpain.
1762, Dec.   7, Levan, Eve, and Peter Yoder.
1801, Feb.   10, Levill, Zacharias, and Mary Wood.
1769, Oct.   26, Lewer, Rachel, and Johann Ludwig Schmick.
1785, Nov.   8, Lewis, Jonas, and Nancy Tschudy.
1775, Oct.   31, Lex, Andreas, and Maria Vockenhaus.
1764, July   2, Liblischen, Elizabeth, and Hannes Mundschaner.
1767, Feb.   7, Lichtendehler, Anna Regina, and Johnes Mengen.
1760, Nov.   19, Lichtmaenn, Maria, and Johannes Wilemeier.
1794, March 26. Lies, Catharina, and Noah Davis.
1753, Nov.   25, Liesch, John, and Christina Jung.
1782, April   16, Liest, John Martin, and Elizabeth Gaul.

1784, Feb.   19, Limeburner, Philip, and Mary Botz.
1798, July   8, Linck, Rosina, and Wilhelm Mueller.
1760, Oct.   20, Lind, Maria Margaretha, and George Gottfried.
1753, June   11, Lind, Anna Margareth, and Philip Burchard.
1784, May   31, Lindley, Rebecca, and Caspar Graff.
1753, Oct.   2, Lindsey, John, and Elizabeth Bell.
1754, Oct.   28, Lingenfeld, George, and Anna Maria Gross.
1792, Nov.   16, List, Elizabeth, and George Degenhard.
1779, Aug.   26, Lock, William Oackley, and Jane Faries.
1768, Oct.   15, Locker, Frederick, and Barbara Heck.
1785, Nov.   3, Loesch, Marlena, and Christian Kiegbert.
1748, Oct.   17, Loersch, Valentin, and Anna Margaret Mayer.
1793, Jan.   17, Loescher, Catharina, and Conrad Pfaffhausen.
1776, Sept.   28, Loeck, Anna Cath., and Caspar Paetzler.
1750, April   7, Logan, Thomas, and Rachel Elliot.
1779, Jan.   3, Logner, Christopher, and —— Fischer.
1766, Nov.   14, Lohman, William, and Veronica Falckenstein.
1780, Aug.   24, Lohra, Peter, and Mary Clumberg.
1771, June   6, Lohry, Catharina, and Peter Haan.
1788, June   6, Lombard, Maria Frances, and Bartholomeus Beau-
                  mies.
1750, April   3, Loudon, Thomas, and Anna Cath. Emsin.
1789, March 25, Long, Mary, and Joh. George Becker.
1799, April   7, Lono, Christmas, and Eleonora Micdermott.
1768, Nov.   22, Lora, George, and Eliz. Roads.
1786, June   29, Lorah, An. Mary, and George Pet. Stondt.
1779, Jan.   3, Lorche, Hannah, and Johannes Wickhard.
1792, Aug.   7, Lorentz, Joachim, and Anna Catharina Jentzen.
1784, April   8, Lorentz, Maria, and John Kalbfleisch.
1779, Dec.   14, Lorentz, Marg., and Jacob Brounig.
1779, Feb.   2, Lorentz, Marlena, and Michael Rummel.
1759, Sept.   9, Lorie, Johann Peter, and Christina Alberger.
1778, June   20, Lory, Eliz. Cath., and George Zahner.
1784, Sept.   17, Losch, Philip, and Marg. Fismeier.
1782, July   4, Loscher, George, and Anna Lehman.
1782, April   11, Loscher, Jacob, and Maria Fitler.
1784, Nov.   26, Loston, Anna Mary, and Joh. Caspar Toeletz.
1794, May   23, Lotz, Adam, and Margaretha Schober.
1787, May   1, Lotz, Elizabeth, and John Abrah. Gauel.
1790, May   3, Lotz, Maria, and Cornelius Henckel.
1766, Dec.   9, Lotz, Elizabeth, and Johannes Haen.
1801, May   10, Lowery, Marg., and Jacob Jones.
1781, July   15, Loxley, Benjamin, and Mary Bryen.
1801, Dec.   24, Loyd, John, and Susannah Weaver.
1785, Feb.   16, Lubrian, Maria, and George Brown.
1786, April   27, Luchard Christian, and Elizabeth Vergondern.

1768, Dec.   15, Ludwick, Heinrich, and Elizabeth Wilmen.
1760, Nov.   28, Ludwig, Anna Barbara, and Friedrick Vogel.
1761, July   7, Ludwig, Ottilia, and Samuel Kramer.
1762, March 22, Luezelberger, Barbara, and Heinrich Meyer.
1753, Sept. 9, Luken, Peter, and Martha Johnes.
1756, Jan.   7, Lukens, Joseph, and Sarah Powel.
1801, Jan.   18, Lutts, Joh., and A, Rusk.
1786, March 30, Luty, Mark, and Marg. Schmitt.
1796, Nov.   16, Lutz, George, and Hannah Diehm.
1782, Dec.   5, Lutz, Jacob, and Rosina Schlemmer.
1762, Sept. 13, Lutz, Anna Maria, and Johann Conrad Schmid.
1779, April 6, Luver, John, and Magd. Cassoph.
1750, Nov.   27, Lynbaker, Heinrich, and Eliz. Hellebrand.
1789, May   15, Lynn, Francis, and Marg. Clark.
1899, May   23, Lyon, Polly, and Joh. Watson.
1798, Feb.   4, Lyons, John, and Jane Fynn.
1774, Oct.   12, Lyons, Samuel, and Eliz. Hough.
1797, Aug.   2, Lyons, Susanna, and Peter Schneider.
1770, June   12, Maag, Anna, and Wilhelm Runckel.
1764, Jan.   17, Maag, Barbara, and Samuel Sevirt.
1784, Jan.   20, Maag, Henry, and Elizabeth Brown.
1773, April 6, Maag, Jacob, and Maria Peltz.
1760, Jan.   21, Maag, Jacob, and Catharina Gerhard.
1782, June   13, Maag, John, and Elizabeth Goebler.
1787, Nov.   11, Maag. William, and Eliz. Schumacher.
1799, July   21, Mack, Anna, and Joh. Smith.
1801, April 23, Macklin, Susanna, and Joh. Geo. Jung.
1777, March 13, Madoery, George, and Barbara Benther.
1753, April 8, Maenin, Daniel, and Maria Sarah Rein.
1748, Jan.   2, Magoldt, Petrus, and Maria Elizabeth Stern.
1796, Nov.   7, Maillard, Victory, and James German.
1797, June   11, Manger, Catharine, and Johannes Melcher.
1780, July   16, Mangold, Frederick, and Barbara Kneil.
1780, Feb.   22, Mann, William, and Eliz. Tomkin.
1764, Jan.   24, Mannebach, Maria Cath., and John Christian Min-
             nen.
1774, May   22, Mans, Charles, and Maria Sadler.
1773, April 12, Marcker, George, and Margaret Stillwagen.
1777, March 31, Marcks, Robert, and Eliz. Weckers.
1790, April 15, Marers, Joh., and Reb. Boyer.
1767, Aug.   6, Margen, Martha, and Francis Harper.
1750, Nov.   —, Marinus, David, and Anna DuBois.
1796, Jan.   31, Marshall, Johannes, and Mary Giff.
1794, June   29, Martin, Catharina, and George Picard.
1785, March 28, Martin, Daniel, and Eliz. Wine.
1787, March 14, Martin, John, and Anna Matlack.

1766, Oct. 　30, Marton, Anna, and William Woodhouse.
1759, Oct. 　29, Marvin, Margareth, and David Stryner.
1797, June 　5, Marx, Margaretha, and Herman Sander.
1776, Sept. 　1, Mash, Mary, and Thomas Smales.
1794, Nov. 　23, Mason, Maria, and Nicolaus Knauf.
1761, Sept. 　9, Massey, Assley, and Jane Skidmore.
1762, April 20, Master, Maria, and Christoph. Reinwald.
1779, May 　20, Matthews, Henry, and Mary Berry.
1766, Aug. 　17, Mathews, Margaretha, and Thomas Hanley.
1787, Jan. 　25, Mathews, Mary, and Edward Healy.
1787, March 14, Matlack, Anna, and John Martin.
1772, June 　28, Maur, Anna, and Joseph Dirman.
1785, May 　19, Maus, Philip, and Magd. Anthony.
1775, Jan. 　12, Maxwell, Amelia, and Richard Fortune.
1783, Oct. 　9, May, Adam, and Cath. Diehl.
1798, Jan. 　25, May, Bernhard, and Agnes Monscheher.
1774, April 　5, May, Philip, and Cath. Eschenfelder.
1773, April 13, Mayer, Adam, and Anna Veronica Klemmer.
1775, May 　4, Mayer, Eliz., and Johann Kern.
1792, July 　22, Mayer, Elizabeth, and Johannes Tuttel.
1791, Dec. 　25, Mayer, Elizabeth, and Johannes Schnyder.
1780, June 　4, Mayer, Gottlieb, and Magdalena Bilber.
1798, June 　10, Mayer, Hannah, and Andreas Strohl.
1795, April 16, Mayer, Joh. Philip, and Wilhelmina Steiner.
1800, Oct. 　27, Mayer, Nicolas, and Cath. Walker.
1775, June 　27, Mayer, Anna Cath., and Johannes Eckstein.
1773, July 　21, McAfee, John, and Elizabeth Housard.
1767, Aug. 　29, McBride, Henry, and Mary Ellis.
1775, June 　27, McBride, John, and Maria Cath. Miller.
1771, June 　2, McBride, John, and Hannah Decon.
1787, Sept. 　8. McClain, Mary, and James Leonhard.
1778, June 　17, McCall, Agnes, and John McCall.
1778, June 　17, McCall, John, and Agnes McCall.
1760, June 　24, McCallough, Jane, and James Clelland.
1771, June 　15, McCannon, Martha, and Adam Von Erden.
1779, Nov. 　3, McCan, Catharine, and George Walker.
1795, Aug. 　20, McCauly, James, and Elizabeth Kruse.
1771, Jan. 　19, McCleland, Margaret, and Daniel Montgomery.
1785, Jan. 　5, McCluer, John, and Mary Steiger.
1783, Sept. 　9, McCord, Kather, and James Cunningham.
1785, April 　6, McCoy, Daniel, and Elizabeth Kelly.
1767, April 25, McCoy, Mary, and John Murray.
1772, Nov. 　6, McCullough, John, and Margaret Peters.
1794, Dec. 　31, McCully, Hugh, and Willy Nottenius.
1801, May 　27, McClure, Thomas, and Sally Redlay.
1779, July 　29, McCutcheon, Mary, and Thomas Armat.

1773, June 10, McFaggart, Archibald, and Catharina Jung.

1780, Dec. 13, McGraw, Mich., and Lydia Reine.

1750, Aug. 29, McKneel, Anthony, and Elizabeth Hairr.

1750, Oct. 3, McKnollen, Ann, and Thomas Robinson.

1750, Nov. 17, McMichael, John, and Margareth Johnstown.

1783, Oct. 23, McMollen, Isabella, and George Bantz.

1781, March 29, McNachtane, John, and Cornelia Dorsius.

1780, March 21, McSparran, William, and Christina Walter.

1778, July 1, McWrath, John, and Maria Bronner.

1774, Sept. 13, Meason, Dinah, and Joh. Jacob Grim.

1799, June 24, Meder, Charles, and Nancy David.

1797, Jan. 8, Meffener, Johannes, and Maria Reichard.

1750, Jan. 28, Meffort, Maria Margaret, and Wilhelm Tonber.

1785, Dec. 8, Meibert, John, and Eliz. Berner.

1784, March 22, Meier, Mary, and Matthews Heussen.

1788, Oct. 16, Meile, Sarah, and William Reude.

1778, Aug. 18, Meining, Joh. Christoph., and Maria Graeff.

1761, May 25, Meininger, Anna Margaretha, and Samuel Schneider.

1797, July 6, Meisterschriver, Margaretha, and Philip Laury.

1771, Sept. 22, Melcher, Elizabeth, and Jacob Schallus.

1797, June 11, Melcher, Johannes, and Catharine Mauger.

1772, Nov. 22, Melchior, Maria, and Francis Caspar Hasenclever

1780, April 29, Mell, Eliz., and Thomas Clark.

1788, April 5, Meng, Melchior, and Eliz. Lehman.

1786, May 14, Meng, Susanna, and Christian Alberger.

1760, Jan. 10, Meng, Ulrich, and Sara Galad.

1768, Feb. 7, Mengen, Johnes, and Anna Regina Lichtendehler.

1780, June 22, Mennen, Eliz., and George Raush.

1784, June 6, Mensch, Peter, and Christina Muller.

1776, Oct. 10, Mercelus, Rachel, and Charles Clunn.

1772, Aug. 30, Merchant, Anna, and George Poff.

1801, Jan. 22, Merkel, Dolly, and Math. Cooper.

1798, Feb. 22, Mercker, Godfried, and Maria Schmid.

1798, May 14, Merckel, Margaretha, and Francis ———.

1773, July 1, Merckele, Solomon, and Rosina Dollman.

1773, Feb. 23, Mertens, Joh., and Eliz. Schubart.

1780, June 6, Messerschmid, Marg., and Heinrich Diemel.

1760, Feb. 12, Messmer, Johannes, and Maria Cath. Gloelner.

1762, Dec. 4, Metz, Jacob, and Rachel Heinricks.

1787, March 29, Metzgar, Francis Anthony, and Hannah Will.

1795, Oct. 29, Metzger, Johannes, and Christina Krumbach.

1783, June 24, Metzinger, Marg., and Joh. Fried. Gaul.

1793, Jan. 25, Mey, Sarah, and Heinrich Wattles.

1772, Jan. 30, Meyer, Adam, and Catherina Schneider.

1790, May 27, Meyer, Andreas, and Cath. Strupt.

1802, May 23, Meyer, Beve, and Hen. Bayer.
1790, June 2, Meyer, Christopher, and Eliz. Ferringer.
1785, Oct. 20, Meyer, Frederick, and Maria Cox.
1762, March 22, Meyer, Heinrich, and Barbara Luezelberger.
1779, July 13, Meyer, Jacob, and Eliz. Walker.
1787, March 27, Meyer, Jacob, and Marg. Gerster.
1767, March 22, Meyer, Johannes, and Maria Rosina Heing.
1775, Oct. 9, Meyer, Johannes Adam, and Hannah Bentz.
1790, Jan. 1, Meyer, John, and Cath. Schmidt.
1780, April 16, Meyer, John, and Sarah Bayer.
1801, Dec. —, Meyer, Joh. Julius Vollgang, and M. Mollekays.
1791, Sept. —, Meyer, Margaretha, and Thomas Wolpert.
1785, May 10, Meyer, Nicolaus, and Elizabeth Jonch.
1760, Dec. 7, Meyer, Rudolph, and Catharina Oberlin.
1784, Feb. 19, Meyer, Catharina, and Thomas Cave.
1777, Dec. 17, Meyer, Eliz., and Johannes Schultz.
1777, Dec. 7, Meyer, Marg., and Conrad Froman.
1783, Aug. 19, Meyers, Cath., and Henry Stroud.
1780, Oct. 2, Meyers, Cath., and Andrew Jung.
1780, Feb. 29, Meyland, Christian, and Eliz. Bischofberger.
1799, April 7, Micdermott, Eleonora, and Christmas Lono.
1797, Nov. 8, Michaelis, Johannes, and Maria Schaaf.
1792, Aug. 7, Michaelzen, Maria Elizabeth, and Daniel Friederick Seifferth.
1779, Feb. 4, Micke, Lewis, and Mary Domenick.
1789, April 2, Middleton, James, and Marg. Coff.
1786, March 9, Mielefeld, Elizabeth, and Richard Shaugh.
1786, March 9, Mielefeld, Elizabeth, and Jacob Becker.
1769, Aug. 29, Miel, Anna Maria, and Gottfried Hope.
1789, April 14, Mieser, Philip, and Maria Diehl.
1789, March 10, Milefeld, Sophia, and Joh. George Becker.
1785, Sept. 25, Miley, Frederick, and Barbara Keiler.
1782, July 16, Miley, Jacob, and Margaretha Keiler.
1779, Oct. 14, Miley, John, and Cath. Kiler.
1793, March 10, Milforth, Barbara, and Johannes Becker.
1794, Oct. 26, Mill, George, and Catharina Hoff.
1791, July 10, Mill, Johann George, and Anna Dannecker.
1784, May 6, Miller, Benjamin, and Hannah Stimmel.
1801, Oct. 2, Miller, Cath., and Joh. Bank.
1797, Oct. 2, Miller, Catharina, and William Woodman.
1794, April 22, Miller, Daniel, and Magdalena Henrich.
1765, Aug. 30, Miller, Eliz., and Johannes Wilhelm Mueller.
1779, Feb. 23, Miller, Elizabeth, and Thomas Danoch.
1788, June 24, Miller, Eva, and Jacob Hains.
1770, Oct. 16, Miller, Frederick, and Catharina Rasber.
1776, Oct. 6, Miller, Heinrich, and Anna Montgomery.

1796, Dec.   3, Miller, Jacob, and Sarah Daubendistel.
1793, April 19, Miller, Jonathan, and Catharina Peffer.
1788, July   10, Miller, Joh., and Hannah Willet.
1782, April 21, Miller, Marg., and Lewis Price.
1784, Dec. 23, Miller, Maria, and Michael Kremer.
1755, April 27, Miller, Michael, and Maria Ursula Reibels.
1796, March 13, Miller, Philip, and Susanna Sinck.
1785, Jan. 12, Miller, Phoebe, and Henry Wetzler.
1775, April 6, Miller, Veronica, and Heinrich Zimmerman.
1797, Oct.   1, Miller, Weygand, and Hannah Beltz.
1782, April 11, Miller, Wilhelm, and Susanna Hertzog.
1775, June 27, Miller, Maria Cath., and John McBride.
1787, Oct. 17, Miller, Susanna, and Jac. Bischoffberger.
1783, June 19, Milles, John, and Eliz. Ernstdorff.
1782, Aug. 29, Mils, Christina, and Johannes Huhn.
1776, Oct. 14, Miltenberg, Michael, and Eliz. Schmidt.
1787, June 18, Minck, John, and Christina Senderik.
1764, Jan. 24, Minnen, Joh. Christian, and Maria Cath. Manne-
              bach.
1777, June 19, Minney, Gotfried, and Frances Barness.
1761, July   7, Minz, Rosina, and Peter Oberstein.
1788, June   5, Mischodt, Philip Fred., and Maria Clara Deun.
1794, April 30, Mitmann, Philip, and Rebecca Hertzog.
1767, Feb.   3, Mitsched, Catharina, and Bernhard Kehrt.
1786, Feb. 19, Mitschet, Cath., and George Gaul.
1749, April —, Moeklin, Joh. George, and Anna Eliz. Ems.
1790, Dec. 21, Mogy, Elizabeth, and Matthias Dishong.
1799, July 29, Mohr, Maria, and Ernst Snider.
1797, Oct. 20, Molitor, Maria, and Johannes Gummy.
1796, Feb. 23, Moll, Simon, and Maria Wilt.
1801, Dec. —, Mollekays, M., and Joh. Julius Vollgang Meyer.
1782, March 28, Mollohon, William, and Charlotte Moser.
1798, Jan. 25, Monschehr, Agnes, and Bernhard May.
1798, May 31, Monsers, Catharina, and George ———.
1776, Oct.   6, Montgomery, Anna, and Heinrich Miller.
1771, Jan. 19, Montgomery, Daniel, and Margaret McCleland.
1794, Dec.   7, Montgomery, Johannes, and Elizabeth Dorr.
1756, May 28, Montgomery, John, and Mary Rose.
1779, Jan. 11, Mool, Bernhard, and Eliz. Grove.
1801, Feb. 26, Moore, Cath., and Geo. Rechern.
1779, May   3, Moore, Eve, and Archibald Steward.
1801, Oct. 25, Moore, Joh., and Sarah Witherstein.
1753, Nov. 20, Moore, Nathaniel, and Hannah Collins.
1795, May 31, More, James, and Eleanor ———.
1797, April 20, More, Margareth, and Abraham Eberhard.
1753, Nov. —, More, Rachel, and Henry Titter.

1774, Dec. 17, More, Sarah, and David Sharpless.
1750, March 17, Morfy, Darby, and Abigail Simmins.
1784, Aug. 5, Morgan, Elizabeth, and Samuel Muschell.
1786, Feb. 22, Morris, Catherine, and Christian Stahl.
1800, Oct. 27, Morris, Mary, and Abraham Rosenberger.
1775, Dec. 26, Morton, John, and Sophia Sims.
1750, Nov. 12, Moschel, George Fridenrich, and Esther Johnson.
1782, March 28, Moser, Charlotte, and William Mollohon.
1772, Feb. 5, Moser, Catharina, and Charles Lewis Bohme.
1772, March 5, Moser, Elizabeth, and Jacob Bonner.
1783, March 23, Moyerley, Frederick, and Catharina Bottom.
1779, July 15, Mullen, Maria, and Jacob Hackemuller.
1760, Jan. 13, Mueller, Adam, and Anna Maria Schneider.
1768, May 24, Mueller, Anna Elizabeth, and Jacob Kern.
1791, Sept. —, Mueller, Christopher, and Susanna Statelman.
1786, May 8, Mueller, George, and An. Maria Korck.
1769, June 29, Mueller, Heinrich, and Mary Hoffman.
1785, Feb. 22, Mueller, Jacob, and Elizabeth Roos.
1765, Aug. 30, Mueller, Johannes Wilhelm, and Eliz. Miller.
1762, May 18, Mueller, Johannes, and Elizabeth Geier.
1764, Aug. 28, Mueller, Johannes, and Philipina Scheerenberger.
1759, Aug. 19, Mueller, Johann Reinhard, and Cath. Marg. Isser.
1780, Sept. 28, Mueller, John, and Mary Dexter.
1780, June 26, Mueller, Maria, and Andreas Braderick.
1798, July 19, Mueller, Philip, and Sarah Lehmann.
1795, Jan. 31, Mueller, Susanna, and Daniel Sutter, senior.
1764, Feb. 9, Mueller, Wilhelm, and Maria Schouffleth.
1763, Dec. 6, Mueller, Wilhelm Ludwig, and Cath. Walcker.
1798, July 8, Mueller, Wilhelm, and Rosina Linck.
1765, Dec. 3, Mueller, Barbara, and Antony Berckenbeul.
1768, May 23, Mueller, Catharina, and George Rubel.
1774, Feb. 10, Mueller, Catharina, and Johann Gummy.
1765, Oct. 23, Mueller, Catherina, and Johannes Hermann.
1790, Dec. 2, Mueller, Dorotha, and Adam Widerstein.
1776, Feb. 26, Mueller, Dorothea, and Heinrich Sebalt.
1779, March 21, Mueller, Marg., and Conrad Henckel.
1769, Nov. 24, Mueller, Margareth, and Christian Frederick Foer-
     ing.
1769, May 30, Mueller, Marg., and Michael Faus.
1779, May 27, Mueller, Maria Cath., and George Koch.
1761, April 21, Mueller, Maria Magdalena, and Nicholaus Rupp.
1764, April 23, Muellern, Catharine, and Johannes Peter Dees.
1792, Jan. 29, Muench, Jacob, and Barbara Etrir.
1772, May 21, Muller, Andreas, and Apollonia Vonder Halt.
1784, June 6, Muller, Christiana, and Peter Mensch.
1786, Oct. 26, Muller, Christopher, and Mary Becker.

1783, June 13, Muller, David, and Anna Heidle.
1775, Oct. 26, Muller, George, and Charlotta Vorster.
1784, Aug. 8, Muller, George, and Maria Magd. Wentzel.
1769, April 4, Muller, Jacob, and Susanna Hensler.
1750, Jan. 28, Muller, Johann, and Catherine Vex.
1786, March 26, Muller, Martin, and Eliz. Sharky.
1778, Sept. 20, Muller, Peter, and Susanna Jentzer.
1798, Feb. 22, Muller, Peter, and Elizabeth Sanders.
1778, Sept. 29, Muller, Maria, and Adam Borner.
1777, Sept. 4, Muller, Regina, and Jacob Steinmetz.
1792, April 3, Mullern, Magdalena, and Jacob Gerhardt.
1777, March 4, Mullon, Andrew, and Sophia Baily.
1750, June 9, Mullouney, Barry, and Rachel Boon.
1795, Nov. 1, Munch, Susanna, and William Ashton.
1764, July 2, Mundschauer, Hannes, and Elizabeth Liblischen.
1799, April 5, Mum, Cath., and Fred. Grave.
1797, July 27, Muntzer, Joseph, and Elizabeth Fischbach.
1801, July 4, Murphy, Danl., and Han. Wizzurd.
1802, Jan. 18, Murr, Hen., and Margaretha Fite.
1767, April 25, Murray, John, and Mary McCoy.
1778, Sept. 27, Murren, Mary, and Christopher Patterson.
1796, May 24, Musch, Anna, and Samuel Dupuy.
1784, Aug. 5, Muschell, Samuel, and Elizabeth Morgan.
1785, May 10, Muth, Anthony, and Rebecca Neuman.
1795, Aug. 24, Muth, Dorothea, and Heinrich Siebert.
1748, March 23, Naeff, Rachel, and Johannes Rudy.
1762, Aug. 24, Naegle, Johannes, and Anna Margareth Peterson.
1759, June 12, Nagel, Johann Wilhelm, and Maria Salome Duch-
maurnier.
1769, June 27, Nail, Christian, and Elizabeth Taylor.
1798, Aug. 5, Nailer, Bernhard, and Catharina Ernst.
1750, June 28, Nanna, Ann, and John Roberts.
1790, June 25, Nannetter, Peter, and Magd. Baerth.
1786, March 2, Nannetter, Eliz., and Henry Lehr.
1795, Jan. 4, Neefis, (Napheys,) Sarah, and Franz Ries.
1779, July 18, Neff, Barbara, and Adam Stricker.
1797, April 18, Nehs, Elizabeth, and Heinrich Nehs.
1797, April 18, Nehs, Heinrich, and Elizabeth Nehs.
1783, June 30, Neidlinger, Susanna, and Adam Cullman.
1750, July 8, Neitlinger, Samuel, and Esther Boehler.
1770, June 5, Neiz, Catharina, and Wilhelm Runckel.
1773, May 17, Nelson, Marg., and Joshua Cleaver.
1796, Nov. 14, Neu, Christina, and Hugh Quigley.
1753, Aug. 26, Neuhausen, Maria Barbara, and George Conrad.
1788, Dec. 9, Neu, Cath., and Jacobus Tethers.
1788, Dec. 9, Neu, Eliz., and Anthony Redissen.

1785, May   10, Neuman, Rebecca, and Anthony Muth.
1776, Aug.   28, Newe, Thomas, and Millicent Haines.
1750, Sept.   29, Newton, Daniel, and Elizabeth Brooks.
1780, July   13, Newton, Mary, and Daniel Van Voorhis.
1796, Aug.   18, Nichel, Bernhard, and Juliana Eliz. Grene.
1794, March 8, Nicholson, Sarah, and Johannes Sieffeld.
1784, Jan.   26, Nick, Marg., and Franz Joseph Uss.
1801, Dec.   20, Nickim, Joh., and Cath. Smok.
1770, July   10, Niderer, Jacob, and Maria Marg. Dollman.
1785, March 15, Niederhaus, Daniel, and Elizabeth Reinhold.
1782, May   9, Niemand, John, and Maria Gunckel.
1748, Oct.   —, Nig, Susanna Maria, and Joh. Friedenrich.
1760, Nov.   30, Nipp, Castar, and Anna Dosey.
1786, March 7, Nobel, Phoebe, and John Land.
1779, Feb.   14, Nold, Christina, and Thomas Hudd.
1756, Feb.   9, Norris, Elizabeth, and Griffith Vaughan.
1791, March 24, North, Nancy, and Jacob Horning.
1752, Nov.   2, Norton, Ann, and James Riky.
1794, Dec.   31, Nottenius, Willy, and Hugh McCully.
1756, May   20, Nuescheler, Anna, and Joh. George Hoffman.
1750, Jan.   24, Nuesset, Catharina, and Heinrich Gutt.
1783, May   29, Oberdorff, Cath., and John Adams.
1780, March 14, Oberdorff, Mary, and John Gwillim.
1760, Dec.   7, Oberl, Catharina, and Rudolph Meyer.
1783, Aug.   19, Oberman, Henry, and Gratia Donnel.
1761, July   7, Oberste, Peter, and Rosina Minz.
1796, Dec   25, Odenheimer, Philip, and Barbara Schreiber.
1772, June   11, Odenheimer, Philip, and Catharina Uttree.
1773, Sept.   12, Odenkirchen, Eva Margaretha, and Johann Adam
                Reichel.
1774, Feb.   22, Oelgerd, Jacob, and Catharina Rump.
1767, Aug.   29, Ogborn, Mary, and Michel Purr.
1781, April   30, Ogelbie, William, and Eliz. Everman.
1777, March 17, Ohera, Nancy, and John Callanan.
1787, Feb.   13, Ohlin, Christ., and Anthon Balde.
1796, Nov.   27, Ohman, Johannes, and Eva Trippel.
1794, March 30, Ohnenseller, Maria Magdalena, and Sebastian
                Schade.
1802, March 17, O'Keen, John, and Cath. Green.
1778, June   11, Oliver, Nicholas, and Maria George.
1771, Sept.   26, Omen, Maria, and Ludwick Valckenstein.
1784, Aug.   19, Omensetter, Elizabeth, and George Berckenbeil.
1784, April   22, Orefgen, John, and Elizabeth Scheffer.
1770, Dec.   11, Orffar, George, and Barbara Cronsen.
1801, Aug.   28, Organd, Phoebe, and David Dunbar.
1782, Feb.   21, Orlob, Maria, and Christian Lawyer.

1787, Feb.   27, Orner, Jacob, and Sarah Schmidt.
1782, Aug.   20, Orner, Margaretha, and Lorentz Werntz.
1786, Jan.   24, Orth, Ludwig, and Margaretha Romer.
1762, April   25, Osbeck, Johannes Peter, and Margaretha Seller.
1760, April   27, Osias, Peter, and Magdalena Hergert.
1798, April   10, Osler, Anna Catharina, and Jacob Sinck.
1776, Feb.   29, Osmon, John, and Elizabeth Seller.
1799, April   18, Ottinger, Christopher, and Eliz. Bringhurst.
1797, June   10, Ottinger, Maria, and Abraham Klein.
1772, Feb.   6, Otto, Bodo, and Cath. Schweighauser.
1773, Jan.   31, Otto, Maria, and Christian Jonch.
1787, Jan.   20, Overstake, Jacob, and Sarah Procter.
1781, Feb.   13, Owen, Griffith, and Jane Hughes.
1748, Dec.   19, Owen, Mary, and John Edgar.
1784, Aug.   1, Owen, Ruth, and George Hinckel.
1771, May   11, Oxley, Edward, and Margaretha Steltz.
1801, July   4, Ozeas, George, and Eliz. Hutts.
1763, Feb.   22, Pacquet, Sarah, and James Thompson.
1750, Dec.   27, Paerson, Sarah, and Robert Smith.
1776, Sept.   28, Paetzler, Caspar, and Anna Cath. Loeck.
1784, June   3, Painter, John, and Mary Kline.
1801, May   18, Palmer, Thomas, and Fanny Fouse.
1801, Dec.   24, Palmer, William, and Christina Haushalter.
1801, April   13, Panekuch, Joh. George, and Eliz. Bard.
1750, April   17, Pantly, Jacob, and Barbara Wiots.
1802, March   9, Paris, Fanny, and Simeon Robinson.
1783, Jan.   14, Paris, Peter, and Fanny Fahns.
1776, March   24, Parish, Cath., and George Koch.
1796, Nov.   14, Park, Samuel, and Maria Leck.
1777, Aug.   3, Parker, George, and Eliz. Rebo.
1777, April   2, Parks, John, and Cath. Schnider.
1777, May   9, Parish, Eliz., and Conrad VonHoldt.
1779, Jan.   28, Parry, Alexander, and Jane Aspey.
1753, May   29, Parsons, Mary, and James Drake.
1760, Jan.   1, Passach, Catharina, and Jacob Steinmez.
1787, Sept.   26, Patissen, Sarah, and Jacob Penther.
1778, Sept.   27, Patterson, Christopher, and Mary Murren.
1753, July   3, Patterson, David, and Catharina Edger.
1755, Jan.   14, Paul, Margaret, and Jacob Kress.
1795, Feb.   17, Paulus, Esther, and Ludwig Thomas.
1784, April   7, Pawling, Rachel, and George Reif.
1797, April   6, Pearson, Sally, and Charles Stewart.
1783, Nov.   6, Peddle, George, and Marg. Potts.
1773, Oct.   4, Peeling, George, and Elizabeth Horst.
1753, March   6, Peen, Anna Barbara, and John Wilhelm Strobel.
1793, April   19, Peffer, Catharina, and Jonathan Miller.

1790, —— —, Peiffer, Christina, and Ludwig Frescher.
1782, April 16, Pello, Johannes, and Anna Marg. Jentzer.
1792, Dec.   2, Peltz, Catharina, and Daniel Boehm.
1792, Sept. 27, Pelz, Daniel, and Susanna Gruninger.
1773, April   6, Peltz, Maria, and Jacob Maag.
1789, Feb.   3, Peltz, Philip, and Rebecca Brown.
1769, Jan.   19, Peltz, Wilhelm, and Catherina Witman.
1784, May   25, Peltz, Wilhelm, and Maria Boehm.
1794, Aug.   21, Peltzner, Magdalena, and Philip Ehringer.
1775, Jan.   9, Penn, Mary, and James Schmith.
1774, April 19, Penner, Magd., and Albanus Weidenmeyer.
1767, Dec.   13, Pennington, Margaretha, and Christian Helm.
1768, May   24, Pennybecker, Mathias, and Maria Custer.
1773, March 18, Penther, Christopher, and Catharina Schuetz.
1781, Jan.   30, Penther, Doroth., and Philip Werth.
1785, Feb.   23, Penther, Elizabeth, and John Tolcker.
1770, Sept.   8, Penther, George, and Anna Marg. Will.
1787, Sept. 26, Penther, Jacob, and Sarah Patissen.
1787, Nov.   29, Penther, Maria, and Jacob Schmidt.
1788, Aug.   21, Penther, Nicolaus, and Marg. Schwab.
1751, Jan.   24, Peon, John, and Anna Flex.
1788, June   1, Pepper, Rebecca, and Daniel Whils.
1782, March 12, Pepperley, Mary, and Jacob Woodward.
1798, May   18, Perrot, Samuel, and Mary Jeffreys.
1775, Nov.   12, Pest, Sabina, and Valentine Gaul.
1761, March 9, Peter, Abraham, and ——Sulzbach.
1761, Jan.   6, Peter, Mehael, and Magdalena Elizabeth Heid.
1771, Aug.   8, Peters, Jacob, and Jane Jones.
1772, Nov.   6, Peters, Margaret, and John McCullough.
1788, Jan.   24, Peters, Marg., and John Pope.
1776, May   6, Peters, Maria, and Adam Zap.
1773, June   16, Peters, Mary, and Matthias Turner.
1788, May   8, Peters, Rosina, and Martin Souerman.
1779, Sept. 30, Peters, Susanna, and Jacob Esseler.
1762, Aug.   24, Peterson, Anna Margaret, and Johannes Naegle.
1762, Aug.   24, Peterson, Heinrich Jacob, and Maria Elizabeth
                 Margaret Schmidt.
1783, May   4, Peterson, Martha, and Henry Schmidt.
1766, June   10, Petrien, Christina, and Heinrich Hemsing.
1787, Sept.   2, Petry, An. Eliz., and Peter Helt.
1768, May   23, Petry, Jacob, and Rosina Dorothea Geitz.
1787, Sept.   2, Petry, Joh. Philip, and Eliz. Helt.
1767, Jan.   27, Petz, Christian, and Cath. Herguth.
1786, Feb.   17, Petzlar, Caspar, and Eliz. Boyer.
1795, Sept.   9, Pfaff, George, and Catharina Pfaffhauser.
1793, Jan.   17, Pfaffhausen, Conrad, and Catharina Loescher.

1789, June   26, Pfaffhausen, Conrad, and Maria Christina Crames.
1795, Sept.   9, Pfaffhauser, Catharina, and George Pfaff.
1774, Sept.   27, Pfaffhauser, Eliz., and Johann David Stetzer.
1797, Jan.   5, Pfau, Johannes, and Magdalena Baumgart.
1779, Feb.   25, Pfau, John, and Eliz. Bullman.
1778, Nov.   19, Pfau, William, and Barbara Strampfholtz.
1794, Dec.   26, Pfeiffer, Christina, and Heinrich Braun.
1786, Dec.   28, Pfeiffer, Citty, and Reinhard Schneltz.
1798, Aug.   26, Pfeiffer, Jean, and George Schmid.
1776, Oct.   24, Pfeiffer, Heinrich, and Christina Threis.
1795, April   19, Pfeiffer, Margaretha, and George Keller.
1792, Sept.   16, Pfeifer, Maria Magdalena, and Johannes Keller.
1777, Aug.   26, Pfeiffer, Anna Eva, and John Wever.
1785, Nov.   30, Pfifer, Michael, and Catharina Bingeman.
1759, Aug.   8, Pfirman, Christoph, and Catharina Schmith.
1765, June   6, Pfister, Jacob, and Magdalena Feil.
1761, July   20, Pfohlenz, Heinrick, and Maria Sibilla Stamm.
1766, April   8, Pheila, Daniel, and Elizabeth Evans.
1789, May   25, Philipan, An. Mar., and Peter Immel.
1756, May   9, Philips, Abraham, and Catharina Rees.
1794, June   29, Picard, George, and Catharina Martin.
1785, Jan.   13, Pidgeon, Wilhelm, and Maria Brown.
1765, May   3, Piel, Hannah, and Michael Derri.
1801, Dec.   —, Pierse, Moses, and Anna Keller.
1795, Oct.   18, Pieter, Catharina, and Adam Schmid.
1791, Dec.   18, Pigler, Anna Eliz., and Christian Kreider.
1750, April   1, Pilanus, Simon, and Maria Eliz. Diel.
1748, Oct.   —, Pilanus, Simon, and Catharina Schneider.
1780, Aug.   2, Pinjard, Mary, and Sam. Groff.
1770, May   20, Pinus, Wilhelm, and Maria Eliz. Schweitzer.
1801, April   12, Piper, Sally, and John Wiser.
1797, Nov.   30, Pitt, Jun., John, and Mary Sharp.
1765, Aug.   1, Pleininger, Maria Magdalena, and Johann George Arpiengast.
1791, Dec.   24, Plenn, Heinrich, and Catharina Cart.
1776, June   25, Pluck, George, and Catharina Wentz.
1794, April   15, Pluncket, Sarah, and Jean Descamps.
1772, Aug.   30, Poff, George, and Anna Merchant.
1785, Oct.   25, Pohl, Abraham, and Barbara Binder.
1785, March   31, Point, Sarah, and Leonhard Schuster.
1783, Dec.   19, Pollard, John, and Maria Duche.
1769, Dec.   3, Pollebacker, Abraham, and Catherina Kehr.
1755, July   12, Ponwel, Margaret, and David Hamilton.
1779, Dec.   5, Poor, Rebecca, and Bernhard Wentz.
1788, Jan.   24, Pope, John, and Marg. Peters.
1784, Jan.   15, Porter, John, and Cath. Ritter.

1793, March 17, Potey, (or Poti,) Elizabeth, and Michael Kinsinger.
1779, Sept. 2, Potts, Elizabeth, and Enos Jones.
1778, Sept. 22, Potts, Elizabeth, and Robert Barnhill.
1783, Nov. 6, Potts, Marg., and George Peddle.
1785, March 9, Powel, Hannah, and Martin Worn.
1756, Jan. 7, Powel, Sarah, and Joseph Lukens.
1750, Jan. 13, Powel, Sarah, and Matteis Draeson.
1750, Nov. 13, Powell, Sarah, and Joh. Ulrich Hofman.
1783, Feb. 18, Praupert, Wilhelm, and Barbara Schneider.
1788, June 5, Praupert, Cath., and Joseph Shafley.
1781, March 5, Praupert, Anna, and Heinrich Ritter.
1773, May 5, Pree, Anna Elizabeth. and Peter Vannetter.
1793, May 23, Preh, Johannes, and Catharina Weid.
1777, Aug. 28, Preh, Cath., and Jacob Vanneter.
1797, July 1, Preis, Johann Carl, and Maria Fohringer.
1790, Jan. 1, Pret, Wilh., and Maria Klein.
1776, Feb. 8, Preton, Paul Caspar, and Susannah Kreider.
1778, Nov. 17, Pretsman, Hannah, and John Bolton.
1782, April 21, Price, Lewis, and Marg. Miller.
1784, Dec. 19, Price, Margaret, and William Wever.
1784, Dec. 23, Price, Pamelia, and John Koyser.
1787, Jan. 20, Procter, Sarah, and Jacob Overstake.
1792, April 22, Protzman, Maria, and Jacob Berg.
1766, June 8, Purfel, Selle, and Christian Ruch.
1767, Aug. 29, Purr, Michael, and Mary Ogborn.
1796, Nov. 14, Quigley, Hugh, and Christian Neu.
1780, July 23, Raber, Joh. Heinr., and Anna Christ. Krug.
1799, Aug. 1, Race, Molly, and Cornelius Kruse.
1750, July 7, Radley, Elizabeth, and John Atkinson.
1756, May 18, Raessler, Johannes, and Anna Maria Tillbou.
1750, June 7, Raester, Elizabeth, and Abraham Scot.
1753, Oct. 26, Ramsey, Rachel, and John Barns.
1779, March 16, Randolph, Edward, and Juliana Steltz.
1797, Aug. 5, Randon, Paul, and Aime Blondel Heron.
1765, May 27, Rauschen, Christina, and George Jacob Kiehl.
1767, Nov, 3, Rap, Margaretha, and Ludwick Fisteler.
1790, April 15, Rarah, Christopher, and Jane Curry.
1789, Jan. 30, Rasber, Eliz., and John Zinck.
1766, March 27, Rasber, Peter, and Catherina Hassert.
1770, Oct. 16, Rasber, Catharina, and Frederick Miller.
1771, May 20, Rash, Nicolaus, and Judith Empson.
1784, Oct. 7, Rash, Nicholas, and Catherina Summers.
1778, Aug. 26, Rassel, Caleb, and Mary Langecker.
1801, Aug. 28, Rath, Cath., and Caspar Huben.
1791, March 8, Rauh, Dorothea, and Johannes Rubert.
1766, Feb. 13, Rau, Anna Margaretha, and Carl Stolz.

1766, Dec.　25, Rau, Eliz., and George Faun.
1780, June　22, Raush, George, and Eliz. Mennen.
1785, Aug.　14, Ravaus, Maria, and Jacob Haller.
1748, Dec.　14, Raworth, William, and Anna Clarke.
1791, April　19, Reader, Michael, and Sarah Bard.
1769, March 16, Rebele, Julius, and Apollonia Geyer.
1788, Oct.　12, Reble, Clara, and Andreas Braderick.
1777, Aug.　3, Rebo, Eliz., and George Parker.
1801, Feb.　26, Rechern, Geo., and Cath. Moore.
1769, Sept.　3, Redelbach, Barbara, and Michael Laurer.
1785, Feb.　8, Reder, William, and Anna Maria Rummer.
1788, Dec.　9, Redissen, Anthony, and Eliz. Neu.
1801, May　27, Redlay, Sally, and Thomas McClure.
1765, June　10, Redman, Antony, and Catherine Robinson.
1777, March 20, Redman, Michael, and Sarah Daylershaedts.
1750, June　30, Reed, Ann, and John Titermarry.
1756, May　9, Rees, Catharina, and Abraham Philip.
1785, May　28, Rees, Hannah, and James Boutler.
1748, Dec.　23, Rees, John, and Elizabeth Lawrence.
1802, May　23, Rees, Joh., and Mary Zeller.
1755, April　27, Reibels, Maria Ursula, and Michael Miller.
1779, June　10, Reichard, Lorentz, and Hannah Graefling.
1797, Jan.　8, Reichard, Maria, and Johannes Meffener.
1801, April　14, Reichel, Augustus, and Eliz Jerymy.
1773 Sept.　12, Reichel, Johann Adam, and Eva Margaretha Oden-
　　　　　　kirchen.
1759, Aug.　13, Reichly, Johann George, and Magdalena Froeh-
　　　　　　lich.
1783, April　3, Reide, Johannes, and Margaret Wisper.
1787, Dec.　6, Reide, Maria, and William Schmidt.
1784, April　7, Reif, George, and Rachel Pawling.
1794, Aug.　28, Reil, Johannes. and Elizabeth Becker.
1774, Dec.　22, Reinan, Anna Margretha, and George Theiss.
1755, Feb.　6, Rein, Maria Anna Cath., and Ludwig Heinrich
　　　　　　Karcher.
1753, April　8, Rein, Maria Sarah, and Daniel Maenin.
1780, Oct.　13, Reine, Lydia, and Mich. McGraw.
1797, Aug.　30, Reiner, Eva, and David Donneberg.
1790, April　8, Reiner, Maria Tauen, and Henry Weisbrod.
1773, March 19, Reinhard, Henry, and Marg. Deaney.
1774, June　16, Reinhard, Johann Michel, and Cath. Bornin.
1787, March　8, Reinhard, Sarah, and John Lentz.
1779, March 18, Reinhard, Susanna, and George Shultheis.
1793, March 23, Reinhardt, Christian, and Christina Scheller.
1760, Dec.　15, Reinhold, Charlotta, and Heinrick Schmid.
1785, March 15, Reinhold, Elizabeth, and Daniel Niederhaus.

1762, April 20, Reinwald, Christoph, and Maria Master.
1761, June 16, Reinwalt, Susanna, and David Grible.
1774, Dec.   4, Reis, Johannes, and Anna Maria Wager.
1789, July —, Reis, Joh. Philip, and Eliz. Hill.
1794, Dec.   7, Reis, Veronica, and Peter Martin Hess.
1765, April   8, Reiss, Johann Philip, and Catharina Schneider.
1755, April 17, Reith, John George, and Dorothea Magdalena
             Bernhol.
1772, Nov. 29, Reith, Ludwick, and Margaretha Henrick.
1784, June   8, Reitlinger, Jacob, and Elizabeth Schwam.
1793, April 24, Reinholdt, Susanna, and Johannes Hange.
1784, Aug. 21, Rennard, Phebe, and Uriah Hughes.
1753, Feb.   2, Rense, Charles, and Patience Warrell.
1788, Oct. 16, Reude, William, and Sarah Meile.
1796, Jan. 26, Reus, Jacob, and Petronella Flicker.
1761, July 29, Reuter George, and Catharina Rieder.
1787, April 10, Reuter, John, and Maria Tolck.
1802, Feb. 10, Rewell, George, and Justina Smith.
1777, March 23, Rewle, Nicolaus, and Christina Schellenberger.
1796, April 24, Reybold, Elizabeth, and Albertus Schilock.
1779, Jan. 10, Reybold, Philip, and Eliz. Gerlach.
1792, Dec. 18, Reyli, Maria, and Frederick Rieser.
1792, May   8, Rheily, Barbara, and Christian Jacob.
1784, May   2, Rhinhardt, Sophia, and Abraham Schmidt.
1798, April 19, Rhoads, Susanna and Christopher Schreiner.
1783, May   27, Rhodt, Dorothea, and Abraham Fox.
1781, Sept. 10, Ridge, Mary, and George Streeton.
1802, Feb. 20, Rice, Peter, and Sally Fisher.
1787, March 27, Richardson, Meine, and John Gawin.
1785, June 16, Richerton, Robert, and Catherine Gamber.
1784, Feb. 19, Richner, George, and Sara Brown.
1797, Nov. 14, Richstein, Catharina, and Johannes Engel.
1794, Nov. 28, Rickets, Joseph, and Elizabeth Schallus.
1790, Feb.   9, Ried, Thomas, and Mary Handschuh.
1761, July 29, Rieder, Catharina, and George Reuter.
1767, Jan.   1, Riedlinger, Hannah, and Thomas Wind.
1778, Nov.   5, Riedlinger, Maria, and Christian Kirchhoff.
1783, June 30, Riegeler, Heinrich, and Cath. Fauth.
1791, Sept. 25, Rieger, Johann George, and Anna Maria Johnson.
1798, May   23, Riehm, Elizabeth, and Peter Rudolph.
1770, Aug. 30, Riel, Elizabeth, and Peter Fis.
1795, Jan.   4, Ries, Franz, and Sarah Neefis, [Napheys.]
1784, June 27, Ries, John George, and Maria Klosbach.
1792, Dec. 18, Rieser, Frederick, and Maria Reyli.
1769, June   4, Ries, Margaretha, and Philip Zeller.
1792, Dec.   2, Riester, Rebecca, and Johannes Dithmar.

1801, Dec. 24, Rietnel, Maria, and Jacob Kehl.
1787, May 28, Rifferth, Peter, and Maria Tries.
1788, April 10, Riffert, Cath., and Joh. Ludwig Taber.
1780, April 17, Riffet, Philip, and Orschal [Ursula] Sheng.
1779, Dec. 30, Riegel, Cath., and Fabian Hamerly.
1760, July 27, Rigg, Hans Heinrich, and Christina Himplemaenn.
1752, Nov. 2, Riky, James, and Ann Norton.
1773, Jan. 10, Rimin, Anna Marg., and Jacob Beer.
1775, June 7, Rinedollar, Mary, and Richard Ennis.
1777, Sept. 19, Rischong, David, and Cath. Copia.
1783, May 23, Riste, Charles, and Hannah Göttschalck.
1801, Aug. 13, Riste, Jacob, and Justina Hippensteil.
1762, Nov. 25, Ritchie, Rachael, and William Skinner.
1796, March 27, Rittenhouse, Hannah, and James Lane.
1751, Feb. 1, Rittenhouse, Susanna, and Jaccb Brecht.
1784, Jan. 15, Ritter, Cath., and John Porter.
1801, Nov. 18, Ritter, Geo., and Eliz. Taylor.
1773, July 22, Ritter, Heinrich, and Cath. Kopfer.
1781, March 5, Ritter, Heinrich, and Anna Praupert.
1764, June 22, Ritter, Nicolaus Wilhelm, and Anna Sophia Spaeth.
1777, Aug, 21, Ritter, William, and Eliz. Facundes.
1778, Nov. 24, Ritts, Mary, and Charles Baker.
1765, May 21, Ritz, Johannes, and Maria Jung.
1762, April 20, Rizin, Christina, and Hans Ulrich Ronner.
1770, Feb. 4, Robarts, Elizabeth, and Samuel Dugan.
1778, Sept. 24, Roberts, Cath., and James Robinson.
1750, June 28, Roberts, John, and Ann Nanna.
1792, Nov. 4, Roberts, Jemima, and Benjamin Davis.
1750, April 3, Roberts, Robert, and Maria Humphreys.
1765, June 10, Robinson, Catherine, and Antony Redman.
1778, Sept. 24, Robinson, James, and Cath. Roberts.
1797, Oct. 27, Robinson, Joseph, and Elizabeth Dorr.
1802, March 9, Robinson, Simeon, and Fanny Paris.
1750, Oct. 3, Robinson, Thomas, and Ann McKmollen.
1750, Dec. 29, Rody, James, and Margareth Gallahon.
1792, May 15, Roebsamen, George, and Maria Haeffly.
1802, Jan. 15, Roehl, George, and Justina Mary Serid.
1754, Oct. 23, Rogers, Rebecca, and Mechelemiah Alloway.
1788, April 1, Rohe, Ursula, and Isaac Bedellion.
1755, March 18, Rohner, Joh., and Anna Barbara Kuntz.
1796, March 22, Rohe, Elizabeth, and Carl Zollner.
1783, May 27, Rohrman, Maria, and Daniel Klages.
1786, Jan. 24, Romer, Margaretha, and Ludwig Orth.
1762, April 20, Ronner, Hans Ulrich, and Christina Rizin.
1785, July 14, Rouw, Conrad, and Maria Chamberlein.
1768, Nov. 22, Roods, Eliz., and George Lora.

1777, Feb.   9, Rooke, Thomas, and Elizabeth Becker.
1777, April   12, Roop, Matthias, and Lydia Keiser.
1785, Feb.   22, Roos, Elizabeth, and Jacob Mueller.
1794, June   5, Root, Elizabeth, and Jacob Eckstein.
1750, March   25, Ros, Hannah, and John Steers.
1780, July   30, Rosch, Cath., and Andreas Von Willer.
1782, Dec.   24, Rose, Jane, and Jacob Latch.
1756, May   28, Rose, Mary, and John Montgomery.
1780, June   15, Rose, Peter, and Maria Rup.
1777, June   7, Rose, William, and Hannah Sellers.
1800, Oct.   27, Rosenberger, Abraham, and Mary Morris.
1800, Oct.   27, Rosenberger, Maria, and Joh. Albach.
1790, Oct.   12, Rosenbusch, Sophia, and John Behns.
1779, Oct.   23, Rosengrandt, Charles, and Alice Casey.
1755, Dec.   18, Rosewater, Rachel, and Samuel Winkel.
1779, March   7, Rosh, Maria, and John Schmidt.
1796, Oct.   6, Rosk, Christina, and Philip Jacob Gamber.
1780, July   6, Roskes, Henricus, and Maria Faerling.
1766, Oct.   10, Ross, Johann, and Eleanora Cownny.
1768, May   12, Rossel, Maria, and George Stoudtinger.
1795, April   15, Rossel, Philip, and Catharina Hein.
1783, April   7, Roth, Adam, and Maria Ashener.
1794, April   13, Roth, Andreas, and Margaretha Fuchs.
1778, Sept.   17, Rothar, Anna Maria, and Conrad Verclas.
1783, May   10, Rothar, Leonh., and Eliz. Gilyard.
1798, Feb.   22, Rothhaar, Bernhard, and Elizabeth Busch.
1791, July   17, Rothhaar, Martin, and Anna Maria Weissman.
1777, Dec.   25, Roth, Susanna, and Joh. Diehlman.
1750, Oct.   13, Roul, Elizabeth, and William Hamilton.
1790, June   1, Roun, Polly, and Paul Bauer.
1750, Oct.   13, Rowell, Jane, and James Westcott.
1750, Oct.   13, Rowell, Jane, and James Westkett.
1794, June   16, Rozell, Charles, and Mary White.
1755, Jan.   30, Rubb, Jacob, and Anna Hogermuth.
1768, May   23, Rubel, George, and Catharina Mueller.
1791, March   8, Rubert, Johannes, and Dorothea Rauh.
1796, Jan,   14, Rubsam, Susanna, and George Dorffer.
1784, May   16, Rubsamen, Anna, and Johannes Walter.
1771, March   14, Rubsamen, Henrich, and Elizabeth Vander Halt.
1793, June   29, Rubsamen, Rachel, and George Doerffer.
1769, May   14, Rice Susanna, and Heinrich Fraley.
1766, June   8, Ruch, Christian, and Selle Purfel.
1798, Jan.   22, Rudel, Johannes, and Carolina Mariana Schlag-
                    mueller.
1798, May   23, Rudolph, Peter, and Elizabeth Riehm.
1784, June   24, Rudolph, William, and Mary Schmidt.

1798, May 13, Rudy, Fanny, and John ———.
1776, Sept. 21, Rudy, Henry, and Elizabeth Handschuh.
1748, March 23, Rudy, Johannes, and Rachel Naeff.
1785, Jan. 13, Rudy, John, and Mary Crombie.
1750, July 10, Rudy, Priscilla, and Jacob Bleikenstorffer.
1784, Jan. 4, Rudybach, Marg., and Charles Schakar.
1774, March 17, Ruebel, Nicolaus, and Salome Lang.
1753, Jan. 23, Ruebsamen, Regula, and Johannes Waspy.
1762, March 16, Rueugin, Elizabeth, and Christian Froehlich.
1776, Oct. 24, Rumel, Cath., and Jacob Kinsley.
1790, ——— ——, Rummel, John, and Marl. Becker.
1783, June 19, Rummel, Michael, and Christina Dorffer.
1779, Feb. 2, Rummel, Michael, and Marlena Lorentz.
1784, Oct. 28, Rummel, Nicolaus, and Anna Barb. Haller
1783, Sept. 25, Rummel, Philip, and Rebecca Held.
1785, Feb. 8, Rummer, Anna Maria, and William Reder.
1785, Aug. 16, Rumpf, John Henry, and Elizabeth Grim.
1774, Feb. 22, Rump, Catharina, and Jacob Oelgerd.
1770, June 5, Runckel, Wilhelm, and Catharina Neiz.
1761, Feb. 10, Runig, Eliz. Magdalena, and Franz Schaftner.
1783, April 13, Runner, Martin, and Sophia Housman.
1753, Oct. 4, Rup, Maria Magdalena, and Joh. Heinrich Gamper.
1780, June 15, Rup, Maria, and Peter Rose.
1785, Nov. 28, Rup, William, and Cath. Bergendahler.
1792, Sept. 21, Rupert, Anna Gertrude, and Wilhelm Euler.
1765, Dec. 1, Rup, Maria Eliz., and Caspar Schuffelberg.
1760, Nov. 4, Rupp, Kilian, and Catharine Taumueller.
1793, July 13, Rupp, (or Roop,) Maria, and Reinhard Scholl.
1761, April 21, Rupp, Niclaus, and Maria Magdalena Mueller.
1782, July 4, Rush, Conrad, and Margaret Burckhardt.
1801, Jan. 18, Rusk, A., and Joh. Lutts.
1750, April 4, Russell, Abraham, and Sarah Dixon.
1780, July 27, Russ, Christian, and Cath. Buckius.
1797, Feb. 27, Ryan, Jean, and Peter Slesman.
1797, July 1, Ryan, John, and Mary Byram.
1768, July 31, Ryan, Marg., and James Hall.
1775, July 23, Ryeholt, Philip, and Francisca Tuckney.
1770, Dec. 6, Ryning, Mary, and Adam Taylor.
1794, March 28, Sackreuter, Catharina, and George Wilhelm Stein-
              hauer.
1774, May 22, Sadler, Maria, and Charles Mans.
1759, June 25, Saenmaenn, Dorothea Cath., and George Fraser.
1801, April 14, Salder, Jacob, and Cath. Sneider.
1755, April 27, Sammet, Christian, and Maria Stahlern.
1797, June 5, Sander, Herman, and Margaretha Marx.
1798, Feb. 22, Sanders, Elizabeth, and Peter Muller.

1782, July   25, Sandman, Lorentz, and Maria Kalbfleisch.
1773, Oct.   17, Sandor, Johann, and Margaretha Arnold.
1748, Oct.   —, Sasemanshaus, Herman, and Maria Amalina Spiess.
1748, July   10, Satler, Alexander, and Anna Elizabeth Koenig.
1794, Nov.   11, Sattler, Catharina, and Abraham Dix.
1787, March 12, Sattler, John, and Sarah Seibert.
1797, March 23, Sauerheber, George, and Philippina ———.
1774, March 27, Saunders, William, and Maria Camper.
1797, Jan.   3, Savoy, Pierre, and Esther Essler.
1797, Nov.   8, Schaaf, Maria, and Johannes Michaelis.
1798, Feb.   6, Schaaf, Samuel, and Catharine Koch.
1783, Aug.   8, Schaaff, Catharine, and Nicholaus Schultz.
1794, March 30, Schade, Sebastian, and Maria Magdalena Ohmen-
                    seller.
1798, April   26, Schaed, George, and Elizabeth Becker.
1796, Sept.   19, Schaed, George, and A. Maria Weber.
1778, Sept.   17, Schaed, Hein., and Marg. Weingard.
1801, Sept.   8, Schaefer, W^m, and Barbara Fisher.
1786, March   9, Schaeff, Cath., and John Andreas Friederick.
1786, Sept.   10, Schaeffer, Catharina, and Melchior Schaeffer.
1788, Jan.   1, Schaeffer, Christian, and Anna Marg. Huck.
1796, Aug.   13, Schaeffer, Christian, and Jemima Stanton.
1786, Sept.   10, Schaeffer, Melchior, and Catharina Schaeffer.
1749, April   —, Schaeffer, Maria Magdalena, and Mathaeus Hit-
                    wohl.
1759, Nov.   1, Schaeffer, Maria Margaretha, and Matthias Fackret.
1761, June   19, Schaefter, Maria, and Johannes Zeller.
1795, March   4, Schaffer, Carl, and Elizabeth Strohman.
1794, June   29, Schaffer, Maria. and George Hahns.
1784, Sept.   7, Schaffery, Catharina, and George Bloom.
1761, Feb.   10, Schaftner, Franz, and Eliz. Magdalena Runig.
1772, May   5, Schakar, Barbara, and Heinrich Schnider.
1784, Jan.   8, Schakar, Charles, and Marg. Rudybach.
1780, April   20, Schal, Cath., and Christian Weierich.
1773, Nov.   7, Schallus, Cath., and Martin Fischer.
1794, Nov.   28, Schallus, Elizabeth, and Joseph Rickets.
1771, Sept.   22, Schallus, Jacob, and Elizabeth Nelcher.
1784, Nov.   30, Schamberlaine, Catherine, and John Capp.
1779, Dec.   19, Schaub, Elizabeth, and Michael Katz.
1765, Dec.   1, Schauffelberg, Caspar, and Maria Eliz. Rup.
1796, Oct.   11, Schaup, Barbara, and David Wissauer.
1786, Feb.   12, Scheaf, Maria, and William Fleck.
1784, July   13, Schearer, Henry, and Elizabeth Davis.
1792, Dec.   14, Schee, Henrich, and Susanna Heehr.
1776, Feb.   20, Scheed, Elizabeth, and Hugh Bathorn.
1764, Aug.   28, Scheerenberger, Philipina, and Johannes Mueller

1779, Oct.   14, Scheff, John Peter, and Eliz. Schiel.
1784, April 23, Scheffer, Elizabeth, and John Orefgen.
1778, Dec.   13, Scheibeler, Marg., and John Schneider.
1750, March 13, Scheible, Daniel, and Magdalena Gallman.
1780, Oct.   19, Scheibler, Cath., and John Lehr.
1762, March 9, Scheid, George, and Anna Maria Bender.
1760, July   27, Scheid, Margaretha, and George Kehr.
1796, May   17, Schell, Heinrich, and Anne Fox.
1777, March 23, Schellenberger, Christina, and Nicolaus Rewle.
1773, July   28, Schellenberger, Simon, and Dorothea Zimmerman.
1767, Jan.   17, Schellenberger, Simon, and Elizabeth Berclin.
1793, March 23, Scheller, Christina, and Christian Reinhardt.
1765, Aug.   15, Scheller, Conrad, and Maria Eliz. Jung.
1768, Nov.   4, Schenck, Johannes, and Rosina Dorneck.
1785, Feb.   17, Scherer, Barbara, and Sirach Tschudi.
1787, April 10, Scherer, Cath., and John Mich. Baerdt.
1787, Nov.   1, Scherer, Conrad, and Maria Cath. Lecherom.
1788, April   1, Scherer, Conrad, and Doroth. Bayer.
1787, July   24, Scherer, Elizabeth, and Heinrich Ciprian.
1796, March 24, Scherr, Catharina, and Johannes Traut.
1784, March   4, Scherreden, Dorothea, and Johannes Alburger.
1767, Jan.   8, Schesnut, Elizabeth, and Cornelius Brown.
1789, April 23, Schet, George, and Maria Schubart.
1753, Aug.   27, Schey, John, and Rachel Hill.
1779, Oct.   14, Schiel, Eliz., and John Peter Scheff.
1748, May   1, Schietel, Joh. Henrich, and Margaret Barbara
                   Wagner.
1769, May   28, Schifferes, Johann Adam, and Dorothea Groener.
1796, April 24, Schilock, Albertus, and Elizabeth Reybold.
1790, Nov.   11, Schill, Ludwig, and Barbara Bauen.
1795, Dec.   3, Schinckel, Friedrich, and Salome Hall.
1766, Feb.   11, Schiple, Frederick, and Maria Laplin.
1770, June   2, Schippen, Wilhelmina, and Benjamin Fischer.
1790, Nov.   10, Schlachter, Elizabeth, and George Schreier.
1798, Jan.   22, Schlagmueller, Carolina Mariana, and Johannes
                   Rudel.
1791, Sept. —, Schlater, Maria, and Johannes Drangestein.
1776, May   7, Schlatter, Maria, and Adam Schnyder.
1784, Feb.   4, Schlechterin, Eliz., and Johannes Hald auf der
                   Heide.
1782, May   30, Schlemer, Jacob, and Hannah Fuller.
1782, Dec.   5, Schlemmer, Rosina, and Jacob Lutz.
1771, Jan.   1, Schlemmer, Elizabeth, and Peter Helm.
1786, Dec.   31, Schling, Maria, and Lorentz Hoffman.
1767, May   4, Schlosser, Ernest, and Maria Herman.
1766, April 30, Schmallwood, Margaret, and Robert Stiles.

1792, May   17, Schmaltz, Heinrich, and Elizabeth Spatz.
1776, Sept.   1, Schmaltz, Heinrich, and Marg. Schneck.
1777, April 17, Schmaltz, Anna, and Hein. Sutter.
1769, Oct.   26, Schmick, Johann Ludwig, and Rachel Lewer.
1749, March —, Schmeid, Joh. Peter, and Maria Cath. Eliz. Fren-
                 ger.
1795, Oct.   18, Schmid, Adam, and Catharina Pieter.
1765, March 31, Schmid, Anna, and Johann Kehr.
1760, June   30, Schmid, Christian, and Anna Maria Brunner.
1798, July   26, Schmid, George, and Jean Pfeffer.
1795, Nov.   5, Schmid, George, and Elizabeth Simpson.
1760, Dec.   15, Schmid, Heinrick, and Charlotta Reinhold.
1762, Sept. 13, Schmid, Johann Conrad, and Anna Maria Lutz.
1798, Aug.   16, Schmid, Joh. Heinrich, and Catharina Tauenheim.
1798, Feb.   22, Schmid, Maria, and Godfried Mercker.
1762, Jan.   14, Schmid, Anna Maria, and J⁸ George Wilk.
1760, June   17, Schmid, Catherina, and Daniel Heid.
1761, Feb.   17, Schmid, Cath. Eliz., and Gottfried Hinz.
1762, May   8, Schmid, Catharina, and Johannes Simon.
1761, Sept.   8, Schmid, Maria, and Johann Christoph Siel.
1784, May   2, Schmidt, Abraham, and Sophia Rhinhardt.
1789, April 19, Schmidt, Cath., and Henry Ciss.
1790, Jan.   1, Schmidt, Cath, and John Meyer.
1773, March 25, Schmidt, Christopher, and Anna Cath. Schu-
                 macher.
1776, Oct.   14, Schmidt, Eliz., and Michal Miltenberg.
1781, April 19, Schmidt, Elizabeth, and George Lesher.
1777, Aug.   10, Schmidt, George, and Eva Marg. Koch.
1786, Aug.   20, Schmidt, Gottfried Ernst, and ——— ———.
1774, April   9, Schmidt, Hannah, and Jacob Becker.
1783, May   4, Schmidt, Henry, and Martha Peterson.
1787, Oct.   28, Schmidt, Henry, and Sarah Backman.
1787, Nov.   29, Schmidt, Jacob, and Maria Penther.
1779, March   7, Schmidt, John, and Maria Rosh.
1779, April   8, Schmidt, John, and Marg. Beck.
1787, Feb.   22, Schimidt, John, and Eliz. Stondt.
1762, Aug.   24, Schmidt, Maria Elizabeth Margaret, and Heinrich
                 Jacob Peterson.
1776, Oct.   27, Schmidt, Maria, and John Juvenal.
1784, June   24, Schmidt, Mary, and William Rudolph.
1769, Nov.   11, Schmidt, Mary, and Jacob Goodshius.
1770, Feb.   22, Schmidt, Mary, and William Holton.
1772, July   28, Schmidt, Sarah, and Thomas Simpson.
1787, Feb.   27, Schmidt, Sarah, and Jacob Orner.
1787, Dec.   6, Schmidt, William, and Maria Reide.
1789, Nov.   15, Schmidt, William, and Cath. Jonch.

1765, Sept. 16, Schmidt, Catharina, and Isaac Eschelman.
1778, Aug. 3, Schmidt, Christina, and Kraft Weyand.
1768, May 5, Schmidt, Maria, and Friedenrich Allenbach.
1748, Aug. 23, Schmied, John, and Margaret Stroman.
1753, Nov. 10, Schmiedlin, Anna Eliz, and John George Drescher.
1759, Aug. 8, Schmith, Catharina, and Christoph Pfirman.
1775, Jan. 9, Schmith, James, and Mary Penn.
1788, Jan. 29, Schmith, Anna Maria, and John Philip Volckrath.
1786, March 30, Schmitt, Marg., and Mark Luty.
1783, July 18, Schneck, Eliz., and Fried. Tschudy.
1776, Sept. 1, Schneck, Marg., and Heinrich Schmaltz.
1774, May 11, Schneider, Adam, and Margaretha Diederich.
1792, Dec. 9, Schneider, Anna, and Jacob Boog.
1768, Feb. 25, Schneider, Barbara, and Jacob Daubendistel.
1765, April 8, Schneider, Catharina, and Johann Philip Reiss.
1772, Jan. 30, Schneider, Catharina, and Adam Meyer.
1777, April 2, Schnider, Cath., and John Parks.
1770, Nov. 15, Schneider, Christian, and Anna Maria Jansson.
1798, April 3, Schneider, George, and Christina Kitts.
1795, Feb. 12, Schneider, Heinrich, and Elizabeth Stubert.
1779, July 29, Schneider, Heinrich, and Elizabeth Albach.
1761, March 24, Schneider, Jacob, and Dorothea Sehambach.
1774, June 26, Schneider, Johann Wilhelm, and Regina Catharina Hoeaser.
1765, July 16, Schneider, Johann Wilhelm, and Cath. Kell.
1762, May 8, Schneider, Johannes, and Susanna ———.
1792, June 24, Schneider, Johannes, and Catharina Heher.
1778, Dec. 13, Schneider, John, and Marg. Scheibeler.
1797, Aug. 17, Schneider, Maria, and Peter Held.
1780, Jan. 13, Schneider, Mary, and Paul Slottman.
1786, May 30, Schneider, Mary, and Joseph Junck.
1780, May 15, Schneider, Matthias, and Nancy Latch.
1778, Aug. 13, Schneider, Michael, and Cath. Becker.
1778, Sept. 10, Schneider, Peter, and Maria Uttre.
1797, Aug. 2, Schneider, Peter, and Susanna Lyons.
1779, Dec. 5, Schneider, Peter, and Susanna Baechtel.
1761, May 25, Schneider, Samuel, and Anna Margaretha Meininger.
1762, July 4, Schneider, Wilhelm, and Maria Esther Gassert.
1794, Oct. 12, Schneider, Wilhelm, and Margaretha Behrt.
1760, Jan. 13, Schneider, Anna Maria, and Adam Mueller.
1783, Feb. 18, Schneider, Barbara, and Wilhelm Praupert.
1760, Aug. 11, Schneider, Catherine, and Mattheus Schuz.
1784, Oct. 7, Schneider, Cath., and Peter Fenner.
1778, Sept. 30, Schneider, Juliana and Fried. Winter.
1761, July 9, Schneider, Magdalena Sophia, and Philip Jacob Wack.

1796, Feb.　7, Schneit, Catharina, and Johannes Tuston.
1774, Aug.　14, Schnell, Jacob, and Maria Ziegler.
1776, March 31, Schnell, Anna Maria, and John Feichtel.
1792, May　5, Schnell, Maria, and Heinrich Leck.
1772, May　5, Schnider, Heinrich and Barbara Schakar.
1776, May　7, Schnyder, Adam, and Maria Schlatter..
1785, March 31, Schnyder, Cath., and Johann Herman Winckhaus.
1781, April　25, Schnyder, Jacob, and Margaret Engle.
1791, Dec.　25, Schnyder, Johannes, and Elizabeth Mayer.
1779, June　24, Schnyder, Margaretha, and Daniel Berckemeyer.
1767, Dec.　8, Schnyder, Sophia, and Henry Antes.
1777, Feb.　11, Schnyder, Barbara, and Heinrich Frick.
1783, Feb.　11, Schnyder, Marlena, and John Flachs.
1793, May　23, Schober, Margaretha, and Adam Lotz.
1782, June　16, Schober, Barbara, and Martin Sigismund Zibolt.
1784, April　4, Schoen, Martha, and Joseph Dawson.
1783, March　9, Scholl, Andreas, and Anna Cath. Bischoffberger.
1796, Oct.　13, Scholl, Anna, and Matthaeus Gobler.
1787, March　6, Scholl, Cath., and George Beumer.
1782, April　11, Scholl, Conrad, and Maria Kerch.
1793, July　13, Scholl, Reinhard, and Maria Rupp or Roop.
1791, May　22, Schopp, Helena, and Philip Baron.
1764, Feb.　9, Schouffleth, Maria, and Wilhelm Mueller.
1773, March　8, Schraen, Philippina, and Jacob Gambelman.
1796, Dec.　25, Schreiber, Barbara, and Philip Odenheimer.
1769, Jan.　13, Schreiber, Heinrich, and Catherina Daub.
1778, Oct.　11, Schreiber, John, and Maria Jaeger.
1788, May　1, Schreiber, Maria, and Jacob Edenborn.
1773, Jan.　21, Schreiber, Michael, and Elizabeth Hansman.
1791, Feb.　17, Schreiber, Peter, and Sarah Bating.
1767, Jan.　20, Schreiber, Peter, and Maria Hensman.
1790, Nov.　10, Schreier, George, and Elizabeth Schlachter.
1798, April　19, Schreiner, Christopher, and Susanna Rhoads.
1794, Sept.　28, Schreiner, Christopher, and Elizabeth Baxter.
1786, June　4, Schreiner, Christoph., and Eliz. Stucky.
1775, March　2, Schreiner, Elizabeth, and John Becker.
1783, Nov.　2, Schreiner, Jacob, and Eliz. Stillwagen.
1789, Aug.　29, Schreiner, Jacob, and Eliz. Stillwagen.
1790, May　25, Schreiner, John, and Eliz. Dannecker.
1789, April　5, Schreiner, Mary, and Wilhelm Kreider.
1760, Jan.　6, Schreiner, Nicolaus, and Anna Maria Gampert.
1760, Aug.　26, Schrott, Maria Appolonia, and Felix Hoerlimann.
1773, Feb.　23, Schubart, Eliz., and Joh. Mertens.
1789, April　23, Schubart, Maria, and George Schet.
1784, Jan.　14, Schuck, Philip, and Sybilla Baselman.
1793, March 19, Schuck, Catharina, and Daniel Vonder Schleuss.

1786, Dec.　28, Schueltz, Reinhard, and Citty Pfeiffer.

1792, Feb.　27, Schuessler, Lorentz, and Clara Jenser.

1773, March 18, Schuetz, Catharina, and Christopher Penther.

1767, Oct.　6, Schuetz, Christina, and Daniel Gulman.

1789, July　26, Schuf, Maria, and Daniel Walter.

1778, Nov.　29, Schuhen, Philip, and Joh. Heinr. Hardwick.

1801, Aug.　15, Schuller, Eliz., and ——— ———.

1779, March 18, Schultheis, George, and Susanna Reinhard.

1777, Dec.　17, Schultz, Johannes, and Eliz. Meyer.

1783, Aug.　8, Schultz, Nicolaus, and Catharina Schaaff.

1771, July　15, Schumacker, Catharina, and Martin Schuster.

1787, Nov.　11, Schumacher, Eliz., and William Maag.

1785, May　3, Schumacher, Marg., and John Wester.

1777, Oct.　12, Schumacher, Michael, and Eliz. Weiss.

1773, March 25, Schumacker, Anna Cath., and Christopher Schmidt.

1780, July　13, Schuman, Gertrude Eliz., and Philip Peter Walter.

1787, May　10, Schussler, Regina, and Francis Geiss.

1782, June　3, Schuster, Andreas, and Rosina Hey.

1785, March 31, Schuster, Leonhard, and Sarah Point.

1784, Oct.　28, Schuster, Martin, and Cath Klein.

1771, July　15, Schuster, Martin, and Catharina Schumacker.

1771, Feb.　19, Schutz, Adam, and Elizabeth Hammerick.

1786, March 5, Schutz, John, and Maria Eberhard.

1796, May　1, Schutz, Maria, and Joseph Juncker.

1785, May　6, Schutz, Maria, and George Engelhard.

1760, Aug.　11, Schuz, Mattheus, Catherine Schneider.

1788, Aug.　21, Schwab, Marg., and Nicolaus Penther.

1784, June　8, Schwam, Elizabeth, and Jacob Restlinger.

1792, Nov.　29, Schwartz, George, and Maria Burth.

1795, July　19, Schwartz, Maria, and David Gilbert.

1782, Sept.　12, Schwartz, Rebecca, and Adam Lehr.

1774, March 3, Schwartzlander, Galbriel, and Salome Freed.

1772, Feb.　6, Schweighauser, Cath., and Bodo Otto.

1797, Jan.　26, Schweitzer, Valentin, and Polly Armstrong.

1770, May　20, Schweitzer, Maria Eliz., and Wilhelm Pinns.

1761, May　14, Schweizer, Catharina, and Nicolas Leonard.

1792, Sept.　20, Schwob, Elizabeth, and Daniel Zeller.

1753, Oct.　21, Schynlin, Elizabeth, and Joh. Philip Buch.

1750, June　7, Scot, Abraham, and Elizabeth Raester.

1773, July　5, Scott, James, and Catharina Derland.

1778, Nov.　5, Scott, Marg., and Evan Bevan.

1779, Jan.　21, Scott, Rody, and Lewis Byins.

1769, Aug.　6, Scotton, John, and Ruth Evans.

1776, Feb.　26, Sebalt, Heinrich, and Dorothea Mueller.

1796, March 31, Seeright, James, and Mary Starkey.

1775, April　4, Seffrons, Elizabeth, and Frederick Gesting.

1761, March 24, Sehambach, Dorothea, and Jacob Schneider.
1789, Sept. 15, Seibert, Adam, and Anna Cloyer.
1787, March 12, Seibert, Sarah, and John Sattler.
1759, June 26, Seifert, Eliz. Henrica, and Jacob Appenzeller.
1792, Aug. 7, Seiffert, Daniel Frederick, and Maria Elizabeth Michaelzen.
1796, Jan. 3, Seiler, Heinrich, and Maria Wundert.
1786, April 6, Seiler, John, and Susanna Biel.
1779, May 16, Seitz, Charles, and Charlotta Gerber.
1786, April 18, Sell, Henry, and Mary Weith.
1776, Feb. 29, Seller, Elizabeth, and John Osmon.
1766, June 3, Seller, Juliana, and Caspar Diehl.
1762, April 25, Seller, Margaretha, and Johann Peter Osbeck.
1801, April 10, Sellers, Eliz., and Joh. Chamberlain.
1781, Feb. 2, Sellers, Hannah, and Charles Kerby.
1777, June 7, Sellers, Hannah, and William Rose.
1785, Aug. 18, Sellers, Sarah, and John Strecker.
1780, July 13, Seloover, James, and Sarah Colliday.
1783, Aug. 5, Seltenreich, David, and Maria Laubach.
1766, March 18, Senck, Dorothea, and Johann Adam Dettweller.
1787, June 18, Senderik, Christina and John Minck.
1768, Aug. 23, Sender, Maria Magdalena, and George Therri.
1781, May 12, Senft, Eliz., and Christian Busch.
1761, Aug. 12, Sensfelder, Jos. Philip, and Anna Maria Heinricus.
1802, Jan. 15, Serid, Justina Mary, and George Roehl.
1761, Sept. 24, Sesambach, Maria Philippina, and Conrad Gercker.
1765, Sept. 3, Sevgerdt, Maria, and John Gwin.
1764, Jan. 17, Sevirt, Samuel, and Barbara Maag.
1779, Feb. 25, Sevitt, Peter, and Mary Duncan.
1788, June 5, Shafley, Joseph, and Cath. Praupert.
1784, Feb. 10, Shambough, Joseph, and Catherine Shephard.
1786, March 9, Shaugh, Richard, and Elizabeth Mielefeld.
1772, Nov. 16, Shauholtz, Susanna, and Nicolaus Chressman.
1786, March 26, Sharky, Eliz., and Martin Muller.
1797, Nov. 30, Sharp, Mary, and John Pitt, Jun.
1774, Dec. 17, Sharpless, David, and Sarah More.
1781, March 29, Shea, Daniel, and Sarah Arenbold.
1780, April 17, Sheng, Orschal, [Ursula,] and Philip Riffet.
1784, Feb. 10, Shephard, Catherine, and Joseph Shambough.
1781, Dec. 16, Sheridan, Paul, and Hannah Tedders.
1799, March 7, Sherrer, Barbara, and Peter Blais.
1801, Sept. 10, Sheyder, Eliz., and Abraham Douglass.
1787, April 17, Shlottery, William, and Catharina Wierman.
1800, Nov. 6, Shoemacker, Heinrich, and Cath. Streinehn.
1769, Dec. 19, Shokland, Mary, and Alexander Brown.
1787, April 16, Shone, John, and Mary Skinner.

1775, April   4, Shuler, John, and Elizabeth Antes.
1795, June   14, Sieberick, Anna Maria, and Andreas Hansen.
1795, Aug.   24, Siebert, Heinrich, and Dorothea Muth.
1794, March 8, Sieffeld, Johannes, and Sarah Nicholson.
1790, March 30, Siegmund, Jac., and Cath. Hoffman.
1761, Sept.   8, Siel, Johann Christoph, and Maria Schmid.
1772, Oct.   5, Simmerman, Rebecca, and John Eshinbaugh.
1750, March 17, Simmins, Abigail, and Darby Morfy.
1768, Oct.   25, Simon, Frederick, and Maria Brennen.
1762, May   8, Simon, Johannes, and Catharina Schmid.
1779, Feb.   21, Simon, John Barndt, and Christ. Kolbenhoffer.
1776, Jan.   28, Simon, Peter, and Eliz. Bocklin.
1797, Aug.   20, Simons, Henrietta, and Heinrich Ernst.
1750, June   9, Simons, Maria, and John Commons.
1801, Sept.   7, Simons, Sylvanius, and Maria Hainback.
1795, Nov.   5, Simpson, Elizabeth, and George Schmid.
1750, Aug.   30, Simpson, James, and Ann Harrison.
1780, July   6, Simpson, Thomas, and Lyddy Elies.
1772, July   28, Simpson, Thomas, and Sarah Schmidt.
1775, Dec.   26, Sims, Sophia, and John Morton.
1798, April 11, Sinck, Christina, and Johannes Kaestenbach.
1798, April 10, Sinck, Jacob, and Anna Catharina Osler.
1796, March 13, Sinck, Susanna, and Philip Miller.
1801, Sept.   22, Singers, John, and Eliz. Burkart.
1859, Oct.   1, Sinner, Elizabeth, and Jacob Brand.
1799, June   9, Sinniff, Elizabeth, and Henry Sommers.
1768, Aug.   7, Sintelton, William, and Anna Briton.
1771, Sept.   9, Skidmore, Jane, and Assley Massey.
1787, April 16, Skinner, Mary, and John Shone.
1786, June   22, Skinner, William, and Eliz. Williams.
1762, Nov.   25, Skinner, William, and Rachel Ritchie.
1770, Sept.   23, Skinner, Christian Maria, and Johannes Werner.
1768, May   27, Steininetz, Susanna, and Jacob Swope.
1797, Feb.   27, Slesman, Peter, and Jean Ryan.
1801, June   13, Sleyhoff, Joh., and Eliz. Hasselton.
1785, Dec.   23, Slide, William, and Maria Sullivan.
1780, Jan.   13, Slottman, Paul, and Mary Schneider.
1776, Sept.   1, Smales, Thomas, and Mary Mash.
1785, Feb.   24, Smallwood, Isaac, and Priscilla Stiles.
1784, Sept.   20, Smallwood, Joseph, and Rebecca Jackson.
1785, Feb.   24, Smallwood, Manly, and Elizabeth Fuller.
1799, March 21, Smith, ——, and David Fisher.
1777, Jan.   1, Smith, Alexander, and Christina Strasburger.
1760, July   4, Smith, Eleanor, and William Harper.
1750, March 25, Smith, Elizabeth, and Samuel Wap.
1799, July   21, Smith, Joh., and Anna Mack.

1802, Feb. 10, Smith, Justina, and George Rewell.
1799, March 17, Smith, Margaretha, and James White.
1796, Nov. 17, Smith, Margaretha, and Franz Latour.
1801, Feb. 23, Smith, Melia, and Geo. Vanderslice.
1750, Dec. 27, Smith, Robert, and Sarah Paerson.
1801, Sept. 19, Smith, W^m, and Cathy. Trayley.
1799, July 20, Smith, J. Wilhelme, and Joh. Dickel.
1801, Dec. 20, Smok, Cath., and Joh. Nickim.
1799, July 29, Snider, Ernst, and Maria Mohr.
1802, March 13, Snider, John, and —— ——.
1801, April 14, Snider, Cath., and Jacob Salder.
1799, March 6, Snyder, Dolly, and Philip Alburger.
1801, Nov. 30, Sohenhollingshead, Eliz., and Wm Davenport.
1748, Oct. —, Someraurer, Susanna, and Ulrich Jakly.
1770, Feb. 18, Sommer, Johannes, and Dorothea Heimberger.
1767, March 19, Sommers, Elizabeth, and Adam Stricker.
1799, June 9, Sommers, Henry, and Elizabeth Sinniff.
1760, Dec. 7, Sorber, Anna Veronica, and Joh. Welhelm Boetker.
1791, Aug. —, Sorck, Jacob, and Elizabeth ——.
1796, Oct. 30, Sorg, Simon, and Christina Handschuh.
1790, Jan. 21, Sorgen, An. Mar., and Conrad Becker.
1786, Oct. 26, Souder, Jacob, and Marg. Konser.
1773, Jan. 25, Souder, John, and Maria Becker.
1768, April 11, Souder, Peter, and Eva Gretha Weisserbach.
1775, Feb. 28, Souder, Sarah, and John Cran.
1753, Oct. 2, Soudereker, Joh. Ulrich, and Cleovea Graaf.
1784, July 6, Souder, Cath., and Martin Gucker.
1779, May 16, Souder, Maria Magd.. and Jacob Kobeler.
1788, May 8, Souerman, Martin, and Rosina Peters.
1781, June 16, Southam, Cath., and Patrick Grogan.
1785, Nov. 1, Spade, William, and Sarah Kuemmel.
1764, June 23, Spheth, Anna Sophia, and Nicolaus Wilhelm Ritter.
1797, April 3, Spangenberg, Johannes, and Charlotte Krafft.
1792, May 17, Spatz, Elizabeth, and Heinrich Schmaltz.
1750, June 25, Sped, Elizabeth, and Peter Clowser.
1796, Feb. 7, Spengler, Catharina, and Wilhelm ——.
1748, Oct. —, Spiess, Maria Amalina, and Herman Sasemanshaus.
1755, March 31, Spitler, Anna, and Johann Gross.
1767, March 29, Spitznagel, Eliz., and Johann Philip Fibo.
1785, Dec. 17, Sproson, John, and Anna Brock.
1801, Jan. 30, Spumenberg, Geo., and Mary Bigg.
1788, March 30, Square, Alexander, and Diana Foster.
1775, Dec. 26, Staad, Nicolaus, and Anna Barbara Heffter.
1768, Aug. 30, Stadelman, Eliz., and Johann Bonner.
1769, Jan. 24, Stadler, George, and Eliz. Strunck.
1767, Dec. 17, Stager, Jacob, and Eliz., Titelsen.

1784, Aug. 16, Staggart, Sarah, and Robert Steward.
1786, Feb. 22, Stahl, Christian, and Catherine Morris.
1755, April 27, Stahlern, Maria, and Christian Sammet.
1769, Feb. 2, Staht, Cath., and Conrad Beer.
1778, Aug. 3, Stalferd, Mary, and Edward Dougherty.
1750, June 4, Stamen, Louis, and Anna Maria Steinhiller.
1791, July 21, Stamm, Elizabeth, and Abraham Ziegler.
1796, Dec. 31, Stamm, Johann Rudolph, and Maria Kuhn.
1761, July 20, Stamm, Maria Sibilla, and Heinrick Pfohlen z.
1760, Dec. 17, Stand, William, and Margaretha Zink.
1796, Aug. 13, Stanton, Jemima, and Christian Schaeffer.
1786, April 7, Starck, Andras, and Veronica Mercker.
1779, Sept. 29, Starck, Cath., and George Dickins.
1750, Nov. 15, Stark, Maria, and James Hays.
1796, March 31, Starkey, Mary, and James Seeright.
1796, Sept. —, Statelman, Susanna, and Christopher Mueller.
1779, Oct. 16, Stats, Isaac, and Esther Kelly.
1781, Dec. 22, Stats, James, and Rachel Klark.
1798, March 6, Stauffer, Esther, and Johannes Kuebler.
1785, Dec. 24, Stayger, Hannah, and John David Waelpper.
1784, April 15, Steel, James, and Kitty Boehm.
1782, April 10, Steel, John, and Eliz. Fritz.
1750, March 25, Steers, John, and Hannah Ros.
1769, Feb. 28, Steffel, Sophia, and Michael Taylor,
1775, April 4, Steiber, Michael, and Marl. Kreider.
1770, July 17, Steiber, Sabina, and Alexander Grienwat.
1785, Jan. 5, Steiger, Mary, and John McCluer.
1781, June 4, Steiger, Conrad, and Sarah Cripps.
1775, Nov. 16, Steiger, Christina, and Christian Fans.
1801, Nov. 5, Stein, Peter, and Maria Hains.
1859, Sept. 13, Stein, Philip, and Margaretha Weger.
1782, Jan. 15, Steiner, John Adam, and Eliz. Foller.
1789, Sept. 4, Steiner, Melchior, and Susanna ——.
1795, April 16, Steiner, Wilhelmina, and Joh. Philip Mayer.
1794, March 28, Steinhauer, George Wilhelm, and Catharina Sack-
                renter.
1750, June 4, Steinhiller, Anna Maria, and Louis Stamen.
1777, Sept. 4, Steinmetz, Jacob, and Regina Muller.
1770, March 4, Steinmetz, Margareth, and William Bell.
1762, Jan. 20, Steinmez, Conrad, and Magdalena Ebert.
1760, Jan. 1, Steinmez, Jacob, and Catharina Passach.
1750, Sept. 11, Stel, Ursula, and Jacob Kraus.
1797, Feb. 16, Stellwager, Daniel, and Maria Fischer.
1787, March 8, Steltz, Marg., and Jac. Whitman.
1771, May 11, Steltz, Margaretha, and Edward Oxley.
1779, March 16, Steltz, Juliana, and Edward Randolph.

1787, Aug. 23, Stenerwald, Margaretha, and Edward Graham.
1782, April 14, Stenerwald, Mary, and George Fis.
1785, Dec. 15, Stenerwald, Susanna, and Peter Emig.
1778, June 14, Stern, Samuel, and Cath. Borstell.
1748, Jan. 2, Stern, Maria Elizabeth, and Petrus Magoldt.
1796, Feb. 4, Stetzenbach, Elizabeth, and Johannes Clarkson.
1778, Dec. 31, Stetzer, Heinrich, and Maria Klang.
1785, Nov. 14, Stetzer, Joh. William, and Martha Edman.
1777, Feb. 27, Stetzer, Johannes, and Eliz. Stimmel.
1774, Sept. 27, Stetzer, Johann David, and Elizabeth Pfaffhauser.
1774, May 5, Stetzer, Eliz. Magdalena, and Carl Christian Jung.
1779, May 3, Steward, Archibald, and Eve Moore.
1797, April 6, Steward, Charles, and Sally Pearson.
1797, Dec. 10, Stewart, Joanna, and John ———.
1784, Aug. 16, Steward, Robert, and Sarah Staggart.
1789, Aug. 29, Stillwagen, Eliz., and Jacob Schreiner.
1770, April 16, Stiber, Anna, and Jacob Behringer.
1792, May 8, Stiebel, Christian, and Anna Margaretha Deuss.
1785, Feb. 24, Stiles, Priscilla, and Isaac Smallwood.
1766, April 30, Stiles, Robert, and Margaret, Smallwood.
1780, June 20, Still, John, and Hannah Williamson.
1783, Nov. 2, Stillwagen, Eliz., and Jacob Schreiner.
1773, April 12, Stillwagen, Margaret, and George Marcker.
1795, Feb. 5, Stillyes, Anna, and Johannes Falbirr.
1784, May 6, Stimmel, Hannah, and Benjamin Miller.
1783, Dec. 1, Stimmel, Mary, and Fried. Heimberger.
1779, April 8, Stimmel, Nicolaus, and Eliz. Henman.
1777, Feb. 27, Stimmel, Eliz., and Johannes Stetzer.
1780, May 4, Stimson, John, and Elizabeth Allen.
1762, Jan. 24, Stitschert, Catharina, and Aaron Hassert.
1759, Aug. 4, Stitter, Maria, and Johannes Folweiler.
1762, Jan. 20, Stock, Johann Adam, and Anna Maria Junger.
1793, April 1, Stoll, Jacob, and Jenny Creukeri.
1799, June 9, Stoll, Margaretha, and Christian Frank.
1768, March 6, Stoltz, Conrad, and Cath. Kurtz.
1794, Sept. 18, Stoltz, Wilhelm, and Christina Gut.
1766, Feb. 13, Stolz, Carl, and Anna Margaretha Rau.
1791, Jan. 23, Stolz, Maria, and William Whitman.
1796, Sept. 24, Stottenwork, Peter Angel, and Ann Doman.
1764, Feb. 7, Stouder, Maria, and Christian Taylor.
1787, Feb. 22, Stoudt, Eliz., and John Schmidt.
1786, June 29, Stoudt, George Pet., and An. Mary Lorah.
1768, May 12, Stoudtinger, George, and Maria Rossel.
1773, May 6, Stow, Charles, and Mercy Willard.
1777, Jan. 1, Strasburger, Christina, and Alexander Smith.
1750, Oct. 2, Straub, Johann., and Ann Cath. Franken.

1785, Nov. 16, Streeper, Dorothy, and Daniel Arn.
1781, Sept. 10, Streeton, George, and Mary Ridge.
1783, Dec. 2, Streith, Joh. George, and Cath. Kuhl.
1800, Nov. 6, Stremehn, Cath., and Heinrich Shoemacker.
1767, March 19, Stricker, Adam, and Elizabeth Sommers.
1779, July 18, Stricker, Adam, and Barbara Neff.
1785, Aug. 18, Stricker, John, and Sarah Sellers.
1771, Sept. 18, Stricker, Mary, and John Hyel.
1752, Sept. 19, Strickler, Anna, and Cerak Tites.
1774, Oct. 13, Strickler, Jacob, and Mary Kitcham.
1775, March 2, Stroble, Barbara, and Nicholaus Goddart.
1753, March 6, Strobel, Johann Wilhelm, and Anna Barbara Peen.
1798, June 10, Strohl, Andreas, and Hannah Mayer.
1795, March 4, Strohman, Elizabeth, and Carl Schaffer.
1750, Nov. 14, Strohoner, Cath., and Johann Andrew Frey.
1748, Aug. 23, Stroman, Margaret, and John Schmied.
1750, Sept. 16, Strombek, Ulrich, and Juliana Wild.
1772, April 26, Strom, Anna Maria, and Christopher Kuhlemann.
1783, Aug. 19, Stroud, Henry, and Cath. Meyers.
1778, Nov. 19, Strumpfholtz, Barbara, and William Pfau.
1769, Jan. 24, Strunck, Eliz., and George Stadler.
1774, Nov. 17, Strup, Heinrich, and Susanna George.
1768, April 11, Strupe, Jno., and Rachel Kephasting.
1790, May 27, Strupt, Cath., and Andreas Meyer.
1759, Oct. 29, Stryner, David, and Margareth Marvin.
1777, July 2, Stuard, Elizabeth, and Walter Tipp.
1786, Dec. 10, Stuber, John, and Veronica Frey.
1797, Feb. 12, Stubert, Elizabeth, and Heinrich Schneider.
1783, June 13, Stubert, Mary, and Philip Frisseler.
1786, June 4, Stucky, Eliz., and Christoph. Schreiner.
1785, Aug. 11, Stucky, Maria, and John Klap.
1761, Dec. 15, Stud, J^s Jacob, and Anna Elizabeth Tleker.
1764, Aug. 12, Stueber, Eva, and Jacob Landgraf.
1784, June 22, Stuertzen, Marg., and Justus Flock.
1779, July 15, Stumpf, Mary, and John Beck.
1771, March 12, Stump, Anna Maria, and Jacob Lehman.
1795, Jan. 8, Sturges, Juliana, and Christian Benedick.
1786, Sept. 14, Sturtzebach, John, and Marg. Conrad.
1769, Aug. 1, Suder, Daniel, and Anna Cath. Gertner.
1785, Dec. 23, Sullivan, Maria, and William Slide.
1761, March 9, Sultzbach, ———, and Abraham Peter.
1784, Oct. 7, Summers, Catherine, and Nicholas Rash.
1782, June 20, Supper, Sarah, and Heinrich Deufflinger.
1777, Aug. 13, Susabeth, Cath., and William Dietz.
1762, Oct. 5, Suter, Caspar, and Willhelmina Daubentischler.
1782, Dec. 19, Suter, John, and Catharina Colp.

1760, Feb.	17, Suter, Anne Margaretha, and Lorenz Becker.
1750, Dec.	3, Sutten, Catherine, and Charles Eustace.
1785, Sept.	17, Sutten, Susanna, and John Korterman.
1776, Oct.	20, Sutter, Barbara, and Philip Witz.
1795, Jan.	31, Sutter, Sen., Daniel, and Susanna Mueller.
1778, May	31, Sutter, David, and Maria Jackson.
1777, April	17, Sutter, Heinr., and Anna Schmaltz.
1768, June	5, Suz, Maria, and Michael Farner.
1753, Oct.	27, Swabb, Anna Maria, and Joh. Ludwig Hess.
1774, Nov.	19, Swaine, Elizabeth, and Adam Depperwin.
1768, Dec.	29, Swan, Peter, and Elizabeth Taney.
1750, May	7, Swen, Sarah, and Jonathan Evans.
1786, Jan.	26, Swoop, Maria, and John Bowen.
1768, May	27, Swope, Jacob, and Snsanna Steinmetz.
1788, April	10, Taber, Joh. Ludwig, and Cath Riffert.
1796, May	19, Tag, Jacob, and Catharina Diehl.
1753, Sept.	15, Tagart, Jonathan, and Mary Eliot.
1798, June	3, Tan, Andreas, and M. Christina Hartneck.
1796, Oct.	20, Tan, Joh. George, and C. Maria Hausen.
1768, Dec.	29, Taney, Elizabeth, and Peter Swan.
1766, Feb.	11, Taplin, Maria, and Frederick Schiple.
1798, April	23, Tate, James, and Catharina Gunther.
1798, Aug.	16, Tauenheim, Catharina, and Joh. Heinrich Schmid.
1760, Nov.	4, Taumueller, Catharina, and Kilian Rupp.
1798, Aug.	13, Tay Elias, and Elizabeth Wallis.
1770, Dec.	6, Taylor, Adam, and Mary Ryning.
1764, Feb.	7, Taylor, Christian, and Maria Stouder.
1769, June	27, Taylor, Elizabeth, and Christian Nail.
1801, Nov.	18, Taylor, Eliz., and Geo. Ritter.
1773, May	11, Taylor, George, and Catharina Bickley.
1790, June	12, Taylor, Mary, and Charles Istwick.
1769, Feb.	28, Taylor, Michael, and Sophia Steffel.
1781, Dec.	16, Tedders, Hannah, and Paul Sheridan.
1767, Oct.	27, Teith, Catharina, and Heinrich Deschong.
1768, Oct.	13, Teller, Johann George, and Maria Coeleman.
1787, Sept.	23, Tepes, Henry, and Maria Huber.
1777, Feb.	2, Termoelen, Anna Marg. and Heinrich Haffner.
1797, April	25, Tessle, Catharina, and Johannes Leck.
1788, Dec.	9, Tethers, Jacobus, and Cath. Neu.
1771, May	19, Theis, Andreas, and Rosina Blase.
1774, Dec.	22, Theiss, George, and Anna Margretha Reiman.
1768, Aug.	23, Therri, George, and Maria Magdalena Sender.
1769, Jan.	1, Therri, Marlena, and Michel Blanckenhan.
1780, Jan.	7, Thiel, Anna Maria, and Herman Leck.
1753, Aug.	13, Thilman, Anna Cath., and Joh. Peter Glosmeyer.
1760, Aug.	9, Thiss, Andreas, and Cath. Eliz. Dibo.

1771, Aug.   29, Thoma, Anna, and John Wister.
1789, Jan.   13, Thomas, Ann, and Nathaniel Davids.
1787, March 31, Thomas, Deborah, and John Haley.
1775, May   6, Thomas, Isaac, and Mary Hammer.
1795, Feb.   17, Thomas, Ludwig, and Esther Paulus.
1784, June   10, Thomas, Marsey, and John Froelig.
1797, Nov.   9, Thomas, Peter, and Elizabeth Widerstein.
1785, May   16, Thompson, Rebecca, and Adam Boyer.
1776, Oct.   24, Threis, Christian, and Heinrich Pfeiffer.
1786, May   14, Thresscher, Cath., and James Aris.
1785, Feb.   1, Threyer, Maria, and Philip Haller.
1785, March   2, Thuye, Catherina, and Jeremia Vielmalter.
1756, May   18, Tillbon, Anna Maria, and Johannes Raessler.
1777, July   2, Tipp, Walter, and Elizabeth Stuard.
1769, May   15, Tips, Abraham, and Magd. Sop.
1771, April   2, Tischong, Cath., and Gottfried Tischong.
1799, March 12, Tise, Anna Maria, and Joseph Huber.
1767, Dec.   17, Titelsen, Eliz., and Jacob Stager.
1750, June   30, Titermary, John, and Ann Reed.
1752, Sept. 19, Tites, Cerak, and Anna Strickler.
1753, Nov.   —, Titter, Henry, and Rachel More.
1761, Dec.   15, Tleker, Anna Elizabeth, and Y^n Jacob Stud.
1784, Nov.   26, Toeletz, Joh. Caspar, and Anna Mary Loston.
1787, April 10, Tolck, Maria, and John Reuter.
1785, Feb.   23, Tolcker, John, and Elizabeth Penther.
1793, Feb.   7, Tomblenson, Phoebe, and Jacob Faans.
1780, Feb.   22. Tomkin, Eliz., and William Mann.
1763, Feb.   22, Thompson, James, and Sarah Pacquet.
1750, Jan.   28, Tonber, Wilhelm, and Maria Margaret Meffort.
1781, Nov.   20, Toplift, Sarah, and John Warner.
1786, Oct.   3, Torter, Samuel, and Marg. Helwig.
1759, Dec.   23, Trauck, Joh. Peter, and Anna Maria Zwirn.
1796, March 24, Traut, Johannes, and Catharina Scherr.
1791, July   3, Trauth, Catharina, and Jacob Kupper.
1801, Sept. 19, Trayley, Cathy, and Wm Smith.
1787, May   28, Tries, Maria, and Peter Rifferth.
1765, Feb.   14, Trimber, Elizabeth, and Johann Jacob Weber.
1782, April 22, Trimble, James, and Clarissa Hastings.
1791, Dec.   17, Trimper, Heinrich, and Elizabeth Weaver.
1796, Nov.   27, Trippel, Eva, and Johannes Ohman.
1783, Oct.   19, Troemner, Franz. Wilh., and Chresselly Brockman.
1800, Dec.   24, Troll, Fred., and Maria Duvall.
1801, Oct.   13, Trout, Barbara, and Joh. Andreas Buchholtz.
1776, Feb.   1, Troutman, Christian, and Elizabeth Foulckrod.
1799, May   9, Truber, Elizabeth, and Joh. Gunderman.
1761, Sept. 10, Truckenmueller, Maria Margaretha, and Sigmund
                 Hegelgaus.

1796, Aug.   1, Trump, George, and Christina Bischoffsberger.
1785, Feb.   17, Tschudi Sirach, and Barbara Scherer.
1788, June   10, Tschudy, Barb., and Jac. Jentzer.
1783, April   29, Tschudy, Eliz., and Jacob Bischoffberger.
1783, July   18, Tschudy, Fried., and Eliz. Schneck.
1777, Sept.   9, Tschudy, Martin, and Anna Barbara Adams.
1785, Nov.   8, Tschudy, Nancy, and Jonas Lewis.
1775, July   23, Tuckney, Francisca, and Philip Ryeholt.
1783, Oct.   15, Tunis, Benjamin, and Mary Griffith.
1781, June   2, Turner, David, and Mary Day.
1750, May   29, Turner, Jean, and William Dean.
1776, Feb.   19, Turner, John, and Mary Green.
1773, June   16, Turner, Matthias, and Mary Peters.
1796, Feb.   7, Tuston, Johannes, and Catharina Schneit.
1792, July   22, Tuttel, Johannes, and Elizabeth Mayer.
1779, Nov.   25, Tyger, Agnes, and Henry Bailey.
1761, Feb.   24, Ulmaenn, Margaretha, and Friderick Knies.
1792, Sept.   27, Ulrich, Valentin, and Elizabeth Weiss.
1796, May   5, Ulrich, Valentin, and Elizabeth Bischoffsberger.
1750, Feb.   19, Umas, Maria Eliz., and Fridenrick Wynhold.
1779, Oct.   26, Umbach, George, and Eliz. Greis.
1781, March   8, Unkle, Cath., and John Leonhard.
1798, May   28, Urweiler, Susanna, and George Benners.
1784, Jan.   26, Uss, Franz Joseph, and Marg. Nick.
1778, Sept.   10, Uttre, Maria, and Peter Schneider.
1772, June   11, Uttre, Catharina, and Philip Odenheimer.
1772, Oct.   15, Uttree, Jacob, and Maria Gerber.
1775, Oct.   31, Vackenhaus, Maria, and Andreas Lex.
1760, Nov.   17, Vaetterly, Catherina, and James Farly.
1771, Sept.   26, Valckenstein, Ludwick, and Maria Oman.
1796, Jan.   9, Valentin, Maria, and Christopher Claudy.
1794, July   24, Valentin, Rosina, and Jacob Gros.
1755, May   26, Van Aken, William, and Mary Gorges.
1751, Jan.   24, Van Asdaalen, Simon, and Elsie Krouse.
1768, March   7, Vance, John, and Martha Farmer.
1771, March   14, Vanderhalt, Elizabeth, and Henrich Rubsamen.
1748, April   14, Vandersberg, Anna, and Stephan Consul.
1801, Feb.   23, Vanderslice, Geo., and Melia Smith.
1789, Dec.   5, Vandervoordt, Sarah, and Joseph Wright.
1750, ——   —, Van Leer, Barnt, and Christina Fuls.
1777, Aug.   28. Vanneter, Jacob, and Cath. Preh.
1773, May   5, Vannetter, Peter, and Anna Elizabeth Pree.
1774, Aug.   25, Van Reed, Susanna, and Friedrich Kisselman.
1769, Feb.   14, Van Ried, Heinrich, and Anna Eastend.
1796, May   17, Vansciver, Susanna, and William Lane.
1796, Oct.   11, Van Vreen, Oart, and Maria Beckers.

1780, July   12, Van Voorhis, Daniel, and Mary Newton.
1750, May   16, Vastine, Hannah, and Erasmus Kelly.
1756, Feb.   9, Vaughan, Griffith, and Elizabeth Norris.
1797, Oct.   20, Veit, Maria Magdalena, and Jacob Bucher.
1782, June   25, Velbach, Marg. Henrietta, and Nicolaus Zes-
                   singer.
1749, July   13, Velt, Anna Margaret, and Joh. Matthias Abel.
1760, Nov.   17, Velz, Johann Jacob, and Anna Christina Brach.
1778, Sept.   17, Verclas, Conrad, and Anna Maria Rothar.
1786, April   27, Vergondern, Elizabeth, and Christian Luchard.
1750, July   29, Vetter, Lorentz, and Elizabeth Alowey.
1750, Jan.   28, Vex, Catherine, and Johann Muller.
1785, March   2, Vielmalter, Jeremia and Catherine Thuye.
1782, March 21, Virgin, Maria, and Johnston Beezley.
1760, Nov.   28, Vogel, Friedrick, and Anna Barbara Ludwig.
1765, Oct.   27, Volckmarr, Anna Sophia, and Johann Heinrich
                   Giel.
1788, Jan.   29, Volckrath, John Philip, and Anna Maria Schmith.
1763, Feb.   20, Vollenweider, Jacob, and Barbara Brob.
1762, May   27, Vollenweider, Jacob, and Barbara Frick.
1782, Aug.   11, Von der Halt, Elizabeth, and Heinrich Fenner.
1788, Sept.   4, Von der Halt, Eliz., and John Cortis.
1775, May   23, Von der Halt, Rebecca, and Paul Fiegener.
1772, May   21, Von der Halt, Apollonia, and Andreas Muller.
1793, March 19, Von der Schleuss, Daniel, and Catharina Schuck.
1784, Jan.   5, Von der Schleis, Daniel, and Philippina Havilson.
1771, June   15, Von Erden, Adam, and Martha McCannon.
1777, May   9, Von Holdt, Conrad, and Eliz. Parrish.
1780, Nov.   28, Von Obstrand, Wilhelmina, and George Degen-
                   hardt.
1794, Aug.   19, Von Weiler, Andreas, and Elizabeth Covert.
1780, July   30, Von Willer, Andreas, and Cath. Rosch.
1775, Oct.   26, Vorster, Charlotta, and George Muller.
1759, Nov.   15, Waber, Daniel, and Catharina Weh.
1761, July   9, Wack, Philip Jacob, and Magdalena Sophia Schnei-
                   der.
1798, Aug.   19, Wadlow, Moses, and Jane Wright.
1763, Jan.   25, Wagner, Johannes, and Maria Magdalena Cumben.
1784, Feb.   29, Wagoner, John, and Mary Baker.
1799, May   29, Wagner, Katy, and William Hill.
1771, Oct.   31, Wager, Philip, and Maria Keller.
1774, Dec.   4, Wager, Anna Maria, and Johannes Reis.
1763, Dec.   6, Walcker, Cath., and Wilhelm Ludwig Mueller.
1800, Oct.   27, Walker, Cath., and Nicolas Mayer.
1779, July   13, Walker, Eliz., and Jacob Meyer.
1779, Nov.   3, Walker, George, and Catharine McCan.

1784, June   8, Walker, John, and Margaret Friederick.
1788, April   8, Walker, Samuel, and Cath. Huhn.
1707, Nov.   23, Wallauer, Peter, and Margaretha Walton.
1798, Aug.   13, Wallis, Elizabeth, and Elias Tay.
1788, July   27, Walten, Clara, and Fried Gaul.
1780, March 21, Walter, Christian, and William McSparran.
1789, July   26, Walter, Daniel, and Maria Schuf.
1750, June   9, Walter, Job, and Elizabeth Warner.
1784, May   16, Walter, Johannes, and Anna Rubsamen.
1799, Aug.   8, Walter, Joh. Geo., and Hannah Lenord.
1800, Aug.   4, Walter, Joh. George, and Hannah Leonard.
1775, June   14, Walter, Peter, and Charlotte Hans.
1749, Nov.   —, Walter, Philip Lorenz, and Anna Cath. Edinbonn.
1780, July   13, Walter, Philip Peter, and Gertrude Eliz. Schuman.
1770, Nov.   28, Walter, Philip, and Hannah Has.
1779, April   15, Walter, Susanna, and Johannes Heyler.
1797, Nov.   23, Walton, Harrietta, and Daniel Zahner.
1797, Nov.   23, Walton, Margaretha, and Peter Wallauer.
1750, March 25, Wap, Samuel, and Elizabeth Smith.
1780, Nov.   23, Warden, Jacob, and Anne Hess.
1750, June   9, Warner, Elizabeth, and Job Walter.
1783, July   13, Warner, Jacobina, and John Bingel.
1781, Nov.   20, Warner, John, and Sarah Toplift.
1781, Sept.   9, Warner, Regina, and John Gebhard.
1753, Feb.   2, Warrell, Patience, and Charles Rense.
1802, Feb.   20, Warren, James Cogan, and Barbara Knipe.
1750, March 15, Warren, Priscilla, and John Brown.
1750, March 25, Warren, Priscilla, and John Brown.
1802, Jan.   4, Warton, George, and Hannah Jones.
1753, Jan.   23, Waspy, Johannes, and Regula Ruebsamen.
1774, Sept.   25, Wasseman, Sophia, and Abraham Fox.
1762, Oct.   18, Waterman, Lidie, and Thomas Davis.
1797, June   11, Waters, Martin, and Maria Hensel.
1776, March 26, Watkins, Anna, and Isaac Jones.
1799, May   23, Watson, Joh., and Polly Lyon.
1799, July   17, Watson, Matthew, and Rachel Gehman.
1790, Nov.   23, Watson, Thomas, and Maria Gross.
1793, Jan.   25, Wattles, Heinrick, and Sarah Mey.
1791, Dec.   17, Weaver, Elizabeth, and Heinrich Trimper.
1801, Dec.   24, Weaver, Susannah, and John Loyd.
1787, May   20, Weber, Alexander, and Catharina Zeuner.
1796, Sept.   19, Weber, A. Maria, and George Schaed.
1797, Aug.   10, Weber, Friedrich, and Friedericka Gunther.
1796, Jan.   21, Weber, Hannah, and Jacob Kiesle.
1766, Nov.   2, Weber, Jacob, and Maria Krum.
1765, Feb.   14, Weber, Johann Jacob, and Elizabeth Trimber.

1797, Aug. 29, Weber, Joh. Kraft, and Christina Keller.
1748, Feb.   2, Weber, Maria Magdalena, and Christian Zueder.
1794, July 19, Weber, Wilhelmina, and Friedrich Boss.
1797, April 20, Weckerle, Ulrich, and Elizabeth Diehl.
1777, March 31, Weckers, Eliz., and Robert Marcks.
1778, March 1, Weeks, Samuel, and Rosina Wendel.
1759, Sept. 13, Weger, Margaretha, and Philip Stein.
1759, Nov. 15, Weh, Catharina, and Daniel Waber.
1774, April 19, Weidenmeyer, Albanus, and Magd. Penner.
1793, May   23, Weid, Catharina, and Johannes Preh.
1789, Aug. 11, Weiel, Conrad, and Eliz. Keyser.
1785, Sept. 27, Weiel, Peter, and Elizabeth Haubt.
1780, April 20, Weierich, Christian, and Cath. Schal.
1786, June 15, Weierich, Nich., and Susanna Diederich.
1776, Sept. 3, Weiermann, Mary, and Jacob Wismer.
1783, March 4, Weiermann, Eliz., and Jacob Johnson.
1798, July 29, Weigand, Conrad, and Elizabeth Blocher.
1786, Feb. 12, Weiler, Catherine, and Jacob Baumgarth.
1777, March 4, Weil, Maria, and Johannes Fuchs.
1791, April 28, Weingaertner, Elizabeth, and Wilhelm Wolffknehl.
1778, Sept. 17, Weingard, Marg., and Heinr. Schaed.
1773, May   16, Weinheimer, Anna Marg., and Jacob Kliver.
1761, Feb. 15, Weinhold, Barbara, and Peter Wolf.
1776, Nov.   9, Weini, Joh. Jacob, and Susanna Zimmer.
1790, April 8, Weisbrod, Henry, and Maria Tauen Reiner.
1792, Aug.   5, Weiser, George, and Susanna Doeringer.
1773, July 27, Weising, Cath., and Heinrich Hartman.
1785, May   7, Weiss, Anthony, and Elizabeth Hahn.
1750, Aug.   9, Weiss, Carl Ludwig. and Anna Eliz. Heidt.
1792, Sept. 27, Weiss, Elizabeth, and Valentin Ulrich.
1777, Oct. 12, Weiss, Eliz., and Michael Schumacher.
1768, April 11, Weisserbach, Eva Gretha, and Peter Souder.
1791, July 17, Weissman, Anna Maria, and Martin Rothhaar.
1789, Sept. 22, Weitener, Michael, and Susanna Huhn.
1786, April 18, Weith, Mary, and Henry Sell.
1784, Sept. 2, Weithman, Elizabeth, and John Jones.
1779, Nov. 23, Weithman, Hannah, and Heinrich Wever.
1785, March 3, Welch, Biddy, and Charles Kitts.
1779, Aug. 22, Welchs, Aaron, and Hannah Worrell.
1797, June 13, Weller, Elizabeth, and Christian Benners.
1768, Dec. 11, Welsh, Eleanoras, and Heinrich Dominick.
1778, March 1, Wendel, Rosina, and Samuel Weeks.
1786, June 13, Wengen, Jacobina, and Fried. Jentzer.
1766, March 4, Wenostine, John, and Barbara Kehr.
1779, Dec.   5, Wentz, Bernhard and Rebecca Poor.
1776, June 25, Wentz, Catharina, and George Pluck.

1789, Sept. 22, Wentz, Jac., and Susanna Biesle.
1797, Dec. 7, Wentz, Margaretha, and Johannes Held.
1778, June 24, Wentzel, Eliz., and Joh. Jacob Demand.
1784, Aug. 8, Wentzel, Maria Magd., and George Muller.
1770, Sept. 23, Werner, Johannes, and Christian Maria Skinner.
1769, Oct. 8, Werner, Catherina, and Jacob Kloh.
1782, Aug. 20, Werntz, Lorentz, Margaretha Orner.
1788, Aug. 21, Werntz, Rebecca, and Peter Jung.
1781, Jan. 30, Werth, Philip, and Doroth. Penther.
1795, June 16, West, George, and Catharina B———.
1750, Oct. 13, Westcott, James, and Jane Rowell.
1789, April 7, Westenberger, George, and Eliz. Lair.
1785, May 3, Wester, John, and Marg. Schumacker.
1752, May 17, Westhov, Anna Cath., and John George Hartwig.
1750, Oct. 13, Westkett, James, and Jane Rowell.
1785, Jan. 12, Wetzler, Henry, and Phoebe Miller.
1783, Feb. 11, Wever, Adam, and Kitty Dietz.
1779, Nov. 23, Wever, Heinrich, and Hannah Weithman.
1788, Jan. 1, Wever, Heinrich, and Margaretha Breding.
1777, Aug. 26, Wever, John, and Anna Eva Pfeiffer.
1784, Dec. 19, Wever, William, and Margaret Price.
1778, Aug. 3, Weyand, Kraft, and Christina Schmidt.
1779, Aug. 31, Weyard, Christian and Elizabeth Hess.
1787, Feb. 1, Weybel, George, and Charlotte Hoffman.
1801, Nov. 15, Weyer, Eliz., and Geo. Krame.
1762, Sept. 25, White, Daniel, and Hannah Barber.
1799, March 17, White, James, and Margaretha Smith.
1794, June 16, White, Mary, and Charles Rozell.
1787, June 28, White, Mary, and Samuel Green.
1787, March 8, Whitman, Jac., and Marg. Steltz.
1791, Jan. 23, Whitman, William, and Maria Stolz.
1788, June 1, Whils, Daniel, and Rebecca Pepper.
1792, Aug. 7, Wichor, Johann Gottlieb, and Maria Magdalena Gelersen.
1785, April 14, Wick, Marg., and John Ginder.
1779, Jan. 3, Wickhard, Johannes, and Hannah Lorche.
1775, March 8, Wickward, Rachel, and Richard Brown.
1790, Dec. 2, Widerstein, Adam, and Dorotha Mueller.
1797, Nov. 9, Widerstein, Elizabeth, and Peter Thomas.
1787, April 17, Wierman, Catharina, and William Shlottery.
1768, April 20, Wild, Joseph, and Margaretha Johnson.
1750, Sept. 16, Wild, Juliana, and Ulrich Strombek.
1760, Nov. 19, Wilemeier, Johannes, and Maria Lichtmaenn.
1801, Nov. 15, Wilfahn, David, and Debby Jones.
1784, Oct. 7, Wilhelm, Cath., and Jacob Krantz.
1770, March 20, Wilhelm, Heinrich, and Elizabeth Gattwaltz.

1798, April   25, Wilkeson, Daniel, and Nancy Curren.
1762, Jan.   14, Wilkin, Gottfried, and Catharina Heller.
1762, Jan.   14, Wilkin, Jˢ George, and Anna Maria Schmid.
1787, May   2, Wilky, Cath., and John Dinges.
1770, Sept.   8, Will, Anna Marg., and George Penther.
1787, March 29, Will, Hannah, and Francis Anthony Metzgar.
1802, March 16, Will, Maria, and Peter Auner, Junr.
1764, July   30, Will, Wilhelm, and Barbara Colp.
1769, March 30, Will, William, and Anna Clampfer.
1773, May   6, Willard, Mercy, and Charles Stow.
1801, May   14, Wille, Joh., and Susannah Hahn.
1788, July   10, Willet, Hannah, and Joh. Miller.
1750, May   7, Willey, Sarah, and Ralph Helsby.
1786, June   22, Williams, Eliz., and William Skinner.
1796, Oct.   30, Williams, Hannah, and Johannes Conrad.
1779, June   5, Williams, Jacob, and Hannah Elliott.
1786, July   23, Williams, Jane, and Peter Large.
1770, Nov.   26, Williams, Johann, and Mary Evy.
1788, June   22, Williams, Marl., and Daniel Kreider.
1794, Aug.   10, Williams, Moses, and Sophia Auffahrt.
1780, June   20, Williamson, Hannah, and John Still.
1800, Oct.   28, Willow, Cath., and Joh. Banks.
1750, Oct.   8, Wills, Joseph, and Maria Brands.
1781, Aug.   24, Wills, Sarah, and Peter Leap.
1768, Dec.   15, Wilmen, Elizabeth, and Heinrich Ludwick.
1786, April   6, Wilson, R———, and Nicol. Hainy.
1777, March   6, Wilson, George, and Mary Eakon.
1787, Nov.   4, Wilt, Abraham, and Rachel Hertzog.
1802, April   10, Eliz., and Michael Baker.
1796, Feb.   23, Wilt, Maria, and Simon Moll.
1787, May   2, Wiltfang, John, and Anna Conrad.
1790, Nov.   18, Wiltfang, Maria Barbara, and Johannes Lauri.
1774, Oct.   11, Winck, Hartman, and Eliz. Cath. Kroh.
1785, March 31, Winckhaus, Johann Herman, and Cath. Schnyder.
1767, Jan.   1, Wind, Thomas, and Hannah Riedlinger.
1785, March 28, Wine, Eliz., and Daniel Martin.
1755, Dec.   18, Winkel, Samuel, and Rachel Rosewater.
1859, Dec.   30, Winckler, Joh. Heinrich, and Catharina Beker.
1778, Sept.   30, Winter, Fried., and Juliana Schneider.
1750, April   17, Wiots, Barbara, and Jacob Pautly.
1784, June   6, Wirick, Nicolaus, and Catherine Grubb.
1787, Feb.   20, Wirth, Eva, and Adam Heiser.
1801, April   12, Wiser, John, and Sally Piper,
1776, Sept.   3, Wismer, Jacob, and Mary Weiermann.
1783, April   3, Wisper, Margaret, and Johannes Reide.
1796, Oct.   11, Wissauer, David, and Barbara Schaup.

1797, Oct.   2, Wissauer, Elizabeth, and Henry Benson.
1781, Dec. 17, Wisseler, Jacob, and Elizabeth Erl.
1771, Aug. 29, Wister, John, and Anna Thoma.
1801, June   8, Witers, Joh., and Wilhelme Knes.
1301, Oct. 25, Witherstein, Sarah, and Joh. Moore.
1781, May 17, Withmer, Abia, and John Brown.
1786, June   2, Withpain, Sarah, and John Le Telier.
1769, Jan. 19, Witman, Catherina, and Wilhelm Peltz.
1776, Oct. 20, Witz, Philip, and Barbara Sutter.
1778, Sept. 17, Witzel, Philip, and A. Marg. Wolff.
1801, July   4, Wizzurd, Han., and Dan'l Murphy.
1785, Dec. 24, Woelpper, John David, and Hannah Stayger.
1795, Sept. 6, Wolf, Friedrich, and Barbara Beck.
1761, Feb. 15, Wolf, Peter, and Barbara Weinhold.
1778, Sept. 17, Wolff, An. Marg., and Philip Witzel.
1775, Dec. 20, Wolff, Maria Barbara, and Herman Leek.
1791, April 28, Wolffknehl, Wilhelm, and Elizabeth Weingaertner.
1768, July 28, Wollenschleger, Jacob, and Anna Bettman.
1791, Sept. —, Wolpert, Thomas, and Margaretha Meyer.
1801, Feb. 10, Wood, Mary, and Zacharias Levill.
1766, Oct. 30, Woodhouse, William, and Anna Marton.
1797, Oct.   2, Woodman, William, and Catharina Miller.
1782, March 12, Woodward, Jacob, and Mary Pepperly.
1780, Nov. 12, Worck, John, and Eliz. Kahmer.
1799, April 4, Worl, Sarah, and Samuel Fering.
1775, April 25, Wormington, John, and Anna Collett.
1767, March 12, Wormly, Maria, and Johann Wilhelm Hoffman.
1782, June 20, Worn, Martin, and Cath. Jerger.
1785, March 9, Worn, Martin, and Hannah Powel.
1782, Jan. 31, Worn, Michael, and Catherina Hafener.
1771, Nov.   7, Worn, Philip, and Maria Heyl.
1787, March 21, Worrall, Abigail, and James Ditzer.
1779, Aug. 22, Worrell, Hannah, and Aaron Welchs.
1798, Aug. 19, Wright, Jane, and Moses Wadlow.
1789, Dec.   5, Wright, Joseph, and Sarah Vander Voordt.
1796, Jan.   3, Wundert, Maria, and Heinrich Seiler.
1767, Aug. 26, Wurgeler, Jacob, and Catherina Davi.
1748, July 26, Wynheimer, Joh. Heinrich, and Anna Maria Kun-
              zen.
1750, Feb. 19, Wynhold, Friedenrich, and Maria Eliz. Umas.
1751, Jan. 17, Wynhold, Maria Eliz., and Joh. Jacob Kopp.
1801, Dec. 27, Yeathern, Cath., and Joh. Kittel.
1762, Dec.   7, Yoder, Peter, and Eve Levan.
1753, Jan. 21, Yard, Susannah, and Wm Collings.
1793, Jan. 27, Young, Maria Elizabeth, and Paul Kockard.
1786, Sept. 29, Zacher, Anna Cath., and John Bern. Knochel.

1797, March 21, Zahn, Friedrich, and Susanna Cowan.
1797, March 21, Zahn, Magdalena, and Jacob Jung.
1778, June   20, Zahner, George, and Eliz. Cath. Lory.
1797, Nov.   23, Zahner, Daniel, and Harrieta Walton.
1789, March 5, Zahner, Cath., and George Beltz.
1801, Feb.   6, Zambo, Peter, and Mary Grubb.
1776, May   26, Zampel, John, and Nancy Kocher.
1776, May   6, Zap, Addam, and Maria Peters.
1784, April   12, Zehner, Johannes, and Barbara Kesen.
1792, Sept.   20, Zeller, Daniel, and Elizabeth Schwob.
1761, June   19, Zeller, Johannes, and Maria Schaefter.
1768, Oct.   13, Zeller, Johann George, and Maria Coeleman.
1802, May   23, Zeller, Mary, and Joh. Rees.
1769, June   4, Zeller, Philip, and Margaretha Ries.
1792, Sept.   8, Zerbahn, Catharina, and Arant Braun.
1792, Nov.   4, Zerban, Philippina, and Wendel Zerban.
1792, Nov.   4, Zerban, Wendel, and Philippina Zerban.
1767, March 24, Zerban, Wenden, and Catherine Becker.
1802, March 26, Zerns, Cath., and Zebedee Anderson.
1775, April   17, Zerwass, Dorothea, and Johannes Hoffman.
1782, June,   25, Zessinger, Nicolaus, and Marg. Henrietta Velbach.
1787, May   20, Zenner, Catharina, and Alexander Weber.
1787, Sept.   30, Zible, Jac., and Wilhelmina Hess.
1782, June   16, Zibolt, Martin Sigismund, and Barbara Schober.
1786, Oct.   12, Ziegeler, John Christian, and Eliz. Hess.
1791, July   21, Ziegler, Abraham, and Elizabeth Stamm.
1774, Aug.   14, Ziegler, Maria, and Jacob Schnell.
1792, April   3, Zigler, Elizabeth, and Peter Jost.
1762, May   17, Zigler, Margaret Cath., and Wilhelm Diz.
1776, Nov.   9, Zimmer, Susanna, and Joh. Jacob Weini.
1778, Dec.   6, Zimmerman, Cath., and George Lees.
1789, June   11, Zimmerman, Christina and Joh. Christopher Got-
              ter.
1773, July   28, Zimmerman, Dorothea, and Simon Schellenberger.
1775, April   8, Zimmerman, Heinrich, and Veronica Miller.
1784, Nov.   11, Zinck, Elizabeth, and George Bornhaus.
1789, Jan.   30, Zinck, John, and Eliz. Rasher.
1760, Dec.   17, Zink, Margaretha, and William Stand.
1798, June   21, Zoller, Jacob, and Elizabeth Worn.
1799, May   5, Zollinder, Caspar, and Cath Barn.
1796, March 22, Zollner, Carl, and Elizabeth Rohr.
1778, Nov.   16, Zuben, Doroth., and James Boyd.
1748, Feb.   2, Zueder, Christian, and Maria Magdalena Weber.
1759, Dec.   23, Zwirn, Anna Maria, and Joh. Peter Trauck.

MARRIAGE RECORD

OF THE

FIRST BAPTIST CHURCH,

PHILADELPHIA.

1761–1803.

FIRST BAPTIST CHURCH, PHILADELPHIA.

1774, May   17, Abel, Susannah, and John Annadown.
1800, July   4, Aborn, John, and Mary Valens.
1784, July   15, Ackley, Hannah, and Samuel Talbert.
1791, July   28, Adair, William, and Mary Dougherty.
1795, May   25, Adams, Catherine, and William Pearson.
1769, March 23, Adams, Christina, and William Knowland.
1802, Dec.   10, Adams, Daniel Jeniser, and Prudence Moore.
1785, Oct.   12, Adams, John, and Elizabeth Towne.
1763, Aug.   10, Adams, Mary, and Gideon Vore.
1795, May   3, Adams, Samuel, and Mary McGuire.
1788, Oct.   25, Adgate, Andrew, and Mary Westcott.
1771, Dec.   3, Akerly, Kaziah, and William Carlisle.
1790, March 14, Alberger, Mary, and Thomas Schallcross.
1795, Dec.   3, Alexander, Ann, and Aaron Pitner.
1796, March 17, Alexander, Elizabeth, and Lewis Savoy.
1784, March 25, Alexander, John, and Anne Reynolds.
1794, Nov.   15, Allen, Charles, and Susannah Eccle.
1794, March 20, Allen, George, and Mary Ridge.
1795, Nov.   15, Allen, John, and Ann Ware.
1763, May   2, Allen, Mary, and Joseph Rodman.
1802, April   8, Alloway, Mary, and Charles Jones.
1796, Sept.   4, Anderson, Alexander, and Lydia Bryarly.
1802, April   4, Anderson, Andrew, and Hannah Levering.
1796, March   6, Anderson, Andrew, and Lydia McKean.
1769, Aug.   21, Anderson, Hannah, and Job Harvey.
1774, July   26, Anderson, Hannah, and James Morrison.
1802, Dec.   7, Anderson, Jane, and Patton McConnell.
1797, July   22, Anderson, Jane, and Daniel Waidner.
1793, Aug.   23, Anderson, Sarah, and George Green.
1792, Sept.   8, Anderson, Susannah, and George Eccle.
1794, July   30, Andrews, Jane, and William Carson.
1774, May   17, Annadown, John, and Susanna Abel.
1772, July   9, Anthony, Abigail, and William Turner.
1766, Dec.   11, Anthony, Ann, and Thomas Guy,
1795, April   9, Anthony, Martha, and Hugh Pollock.

1791, Oct.   30, Anthony, Nicholas, and Mary Burck.
1788, April   9, Applegate, William, and Jane Chester.
1794, Aug.   16, Archibald, Mary, and John Morrow.
1790, Nov.   2, Armitage, John, and Eleanor Siddons.
1794, Oct.   4, Armstrong, John, and Hannah Mitchell.
1792, April   4, Art, Bailey, and Sarah Lees.
1797, Dec.   10, Ash, Mary, and William Bethell.
1792, Oct.   30, Ashby, Hannah, and Capt. Philip Atkins.
1795, June   27, Ashmead, Ann, and William Shippen.
1789, May   24, Ashton, Susannah, and Joseph Marshall.
1792, Oct.   30, Atkins, Capt. Philip, and Hannah Ashby.
1801, April   22, Atkins, William, and Rachel Thomas.
1784, Dec.   30, Atkinson, Samuel, and Rhoda Osborne.
1770, Feb.   9, Atkinson, Samuel, and Elizabeth Conaroe.
1797, Nov.   12, Attmore, Isaac, and Margaret Stroop.
1769, Aug.   21, Atwell, Ann, and Richard Tyson.
1793, Jan.   11, Ayars, Rebecca, and Enoch Remick.
1802, Oct.   22, Baily, Abraham, and Rachel Carpenter.
1790, April   14, Baker, Catherine, and John Miller.
1790, Jan.   15, Baker, George, and Elizabeth Inglish.
1801, April   14, Baker, John, and Elizabeth Delaney.
1793, Oct.   8, Baker, Mary, and William Gibbons.
1796, April   26, Baker, Mary, and James Harkley.
1794, May   31, Baker, Sarah, and John Sharp.
1766, Jan.   27, Baker, William, and Sarah Neaves.
1793, Aug.   25, Baldesquy, Julia, and Francis Stille.
1800, Jan.   28, Ballentine, William, and Mary Morrow.
1769, April   8, Bampford, Mary, and William Dogharty.
1794, Nov.   20, Banger, Timothy, and Sarah Webb.
1795, June   27, Banigan, Thomas, and Ann Morrison.
1792, July   14, Bankson, Elizabeth, and Morgan Edwards.
1795, June   28, Barber, John, and Tacey Jones.
1794, Dec.   14, Barber, Joseph, and Isabella Todd.
1796, April   7, Barber, Robert, and Mary Ravely.
1787, June   19, Barlow, John, and Phœbe Bolton.
1797, Jan.   19, Barnes, Sarah, and William Maghee.
1801, Oct.   29, Barney, John, and Elizabeth Dunkarly.
1792, Sept.   13, Barns, Sarah, and Fincher Hellings.
1795, Dec.   10, Barret, Elizabeth, and John Downs.
1774, Jan.   3, Barrow, James, and Mary Roberts.
1790, Nov.   6, Barry, James, and Sarah Philips.
1791, Aug.   25, Bart, George, and Sarah Collier.
1786, Oct.   5, Bartholomew, Elizabeth, and Greenberry Dorsey.
1783, July   29, Bartholomew, Joseph, and Lethea Spring.
1795, Nov.   5, Bartleman, Thomas, and Elizabeth Hawker.
1799, April   1, Bartlett, James, and Mary Snyder.

1762, Sept.   8, Burton, Elizabeth, and Jonathan Ewers.
1790, April 14, Bason, John, and Jane Neal.
1790, Aug.   26, Basset, John, and Sarah Beasly.
1801, Feb.   1, Bassett, William, and Anne Morgan.
1794, Dec.   16, Batson, Esqr., John W., and Catherina Britton.
1794, May   1, Bayne, Catherine, and Ewing Wiley.
1792, Dec.   6, Bayne, Nathaniel, and Elizabeth Rodman.
1801, July   19, Beach, Jonathan, and Elizabeth Gilbert.
1769, May   4, Bearden, Sarah, and Samuel Woodbridge.
1790, Aug.   26, Beasly Sarah, and John Basset.
1792, Oct.   23, Beaumont, Hannah, and David Cornoy.
1775, April 20, Bell, Francis, and Mary Cole.
1796, Nov.   1, Bell, Samuel, and Elizabeth McGee.
1790, Jan.   24, Bennard, Peter, and Sarah Shepherd.
1784, Oct.   28, Bennet, Chanty, and John Eve.
1786, Sept. 14, Bennet, Elizabeth, and John Ely.
1795, Dec.   10, Bennet, Jeremiah, and Sarah Shellenger.
1794, Nov.   29, Bennett, William, and Lucy Wilson.
1772, Nov.   20, Bentley, Eli, and Mary Hunter.
1783, Nov.   21, Bergen, Elizabeth, and John Gray.
1798, Nov.   17, Berger, Maria, and Silas Suplee.
1785, Dec.   22, Berrett, Mary, and Robert Brown.
1791, May   18, Berry, John, and Sarah Leake.
1761, Oct.   29, Bertholt, Elizabeth, and Barnaby Neaves.
1794, Aug.   24, Bessiere, John, and Mary Greble.
1793, April   3, Bessonet, Sarah, and Joseph Carson.
1797, Dec.   10, Bethell, William, and Mary Ash.
1790, July   1, Bevans, Ann, and Philip Shiver.
1798, July   9, Bewley, Robert, and Catherine Brining.
1777, July   31, Biays, Joseph, and Mary McMullin.
1790, Aug.   1, Bible, Thomas, and Elizabeth Williams.
1799, March 24, Bickerton, Elizabeth, and Henry O'Neill.
1802, May   29, Bickley, Margaret, and Benjamin Harrison.
1799, Oct.   24, Bicknell, Rachel, and George Frank.
1770, Dec.   15, Bicton, Sarah, and John Ridge.
1777, March 4, Biddle, Ann, and William Fairis.
1791, Dec.   13, Bildervack, Lydia, and George Fox.
1777, May   25, Binney, Dr. Barnabas, and Mary Woodrow.
1791, Dec.   10, Binney, Mary, and Marshall Spring.
1795, Nov.   12, Birch, Matthias, and Anna White.
1792, Sept. 12, Bishop, Abigail, and John Barton.
1774, June   20, Blackledge, Rachel, and John Kelly.
1794, Aug.   7, Blair, Samuel, and Mary Moore.
1795, Aug,   8, Blyth, Mary, and John Turner.
1774, Nov.   24, Boggs, Elizabeth, and Isaac Githen.
1792, Feb.   9, Boggs, John, and Hannah Dewees.

1794, July   24, Boggs, Joseph, and Margaret Donaldson.
1794, Oct.   16, Boker, Aaron, and Elizabeth Stewart.
1777, March 17, Bole, James, and Katherine Weaver.
1801, July   9, Bollen, Sarah, and Joseph Thatcher.
1764, Feb.   13, Bolton, Everard, and Deborah Griscom.
1787, June   19, Bolton, Phoebe, and John Barlow.
1789, Oct.   1, Bolton, Rebecca, and Joseph Palmer.
1761, July   25, Bond, Mary, and Nathan Hendricks.
1773, Aug.   4, Bond, Sarah, and Clement Dungan.
1763, May   29, Bonsel, Phoebe, and George Brant.
1791, Nov.   27, Bonsill, Susan, and Jonathan Carson.
1802, April   4, Boon, Andrew, and Elizabeth Culin.
1790, Sept.   2, Boor, Jeremiah, and Rachel Weathery.
1792, Sept.   12, Borton, John, and Abigail Bishop.
1764, Sept.   23, Bouchier, James, and Susanna Mason.
1794, Nov.   9, Bowen, Ashley, and Hannah Moore.
1800, April   14, Bowen, Frances, and Archelaus Gardner.
1774, Aug.   29, Bowen, Rachel, and Richard Whitaker.
1803, April   9, Bowers, Sarah, and James Powers.
1792, Aug.   19, Bowker, John, and Sarah Woollard.
1801, Sept.   21, Boyle, Susan, and Thomas Carney.
1775, Jan.   25, Braddock, John, and Anna Green.
1774, May   4, Bradley, Margaret, and John Flynn.
1800, May   26, Brady, Elizabeth, and William Rourk.
1799, Dec.   12, Brady, Noah, and Mary Rees.
1793, Sept.   2, Braley, John, and Hannah Esher.
1791, Aug.   16, Braman, Isaac, and Ruth Campson.
1803, April   17, Brannan, Ann, and John Bresland.
1763, May   29, Brant, George, and Phoebe Bonsel.
1799, Dec.   26, Bratten, Telitha, and John Highland.
1796, Aug.   25, Breidenhart, Eliza, and John Frederick Gebler.
1799, May   21, Brelsford, Elizabeth, and Nathaniel Walton.
1796, April   10, Brent, Charles Phillips, and Hannah Saunders.
1803, April   17, Bresland, John, and Ann Brannan.
1773, Nov.   18, Brice, William, and Rachel Jones.
1792, Nov.   15, Bridson, Eleanor, and Mordecai Davis.
1765, April   4, Bright, Christiana, and Christopher Pechin.
1774, April   28, Bright, George, and Mary Moulder.
1782, Sept.   12, Bright, Mary, and Edward Burroughs.
1769, June   4, Bringhurst, William, and Mary Morris.
1798, July   9, Brining, Catherine, and Robert Bewley.
1790, June   6, Bristol, Sarah, and Charles McGrady.
1801, April   21, Britton, Ann, and John Cook.
1794, Dec.   16, Britton, Catherine, and John W. Batson, Esqr.
1786, Oct.   19, Britton, Catherine, and Thomas Edward.
1785, Feb.   11, Britton, Kezie, and George Sweetman.
1774, Jan.   24, Britton, Rebecca, and Thomas Fleeson.

1792, Dec.　20, Brooke, Ruth, and Job Pugh.
1800, Sept.　27, Brooks, John, and Elizabeth Weaver.
1801, May　12, Brown, Ebenezer, and Ann Johnson.
1780, April　24, Brown, Esther, and Caleb Eddy.
1790, Nov.　13, Brown, George, and Charity Hoops.
1794, Oct.　15, Brown, Isaac, and Phillis Champin.
1793, Oct.　17, Brown, Jane, and Benjamin H. Wharton.
1788, Sept.　4, Brown, John, and Sarah Sanders.
1786, Nov.　21, Brown, John, and Amelia Newton.
1792, Dec.　25, Brown, Margaret, and William Fiss.
1793, Aug.　1, Brown, Margaret, and George Johnston.
1787, April　25, Brown, Nathaniel, and Kitty Williamson.
1787, Feb.　22, Brown. Paul, and Rudith Fackery.
1781, Oct.　23, Brown, Rachel, and Charles McCarter.
1795, July　19, Brown, Rebecca, and James Rue.
1785, Dec.　22, Brown, Robert, and Mary Berrett.
1792, March 22, Brown, Samuel, and Williamina Rittenhouse.
1800, Jan.　2, Brown, William, and Elizabeth Edwards.
1793, June　13, Brown, William, and Mary Fiss.
1794, Oct.　2, Brown, William, and Ann Shepherd.
1784, April　22, Browne, William, and Joanna Burman.
1802, April　18, Brotherton, Benjamin, and Hannah Zilley.
1799, June　13, Brotherton, James, and Ann Condon.
1801, April　6, Brotherton, Reuben, and Mary Handkins.
1769, April　17, Brounfield, Mary, and Jacob Levering.
1800, May　29, Brusstar, Catherine, and William Vinyard.
1796, Feb.　26, Bryan, Livia, and Thomas Darrah.
1796, Sept.　4, Bryarly, Lydia, and Alexander Anderson.
1796, March 10, Buchanan, Alexander, and Ann Penrose.
1792, Nov.　8, Buckley, Rebecca, and James Ferguson.
1791, Oct.　30, Burck, Mary, and Nicholas Anthony.
1802, Jan.　23, Burd, Elizabeth, and Joseph Caldwell.
1791, May　12, Burkitt, John, and Kezia Friend.
1777, March 25, Burle, Henry, and Mary Conrigan.
1784, April　22, Burman, Joanna, and William Browne.
1796, April　6. Burnett, John, and Margaret Reay.
1795, May　30, Burnhouse, Elizabeth, and Forbes Newton.
1784, June　15, Burn, John, and Hannah Williams.
1785, Nov.　2, Burns, Phoebe, and John Hamilton.
1790, July　7, Burns, Samuel, and Ann McKinley.
1766, Nov.　8, Burris, Catherine, and Benjamin McLeane.
1782, Sept.　12, Burroughs, Edward, and Mary Bright.
1785, Dec.　18, Burrows, Elizabeth, and Enos Gibbs.
1791, Nov.　24, Burt, Daniel, and Abigail Harris.
1792, June　3, Busby, Mary, and Reading Howell.
1770, Oct.　30, Butcher, John, and Ann Evans.

1764, Jan.   14, Butler, Elizabeth, and Samuel Cartwright.
1763, Feb.   12, Buzzard, Mary, and John Ricks.
1768, Sept.   17, Buzerd, Barbery, and John Fryreas.
1785, June   5, Byles, Dinah, and William Ferrill.
1802, June   23, Caldwell, Joseph, and Elizabeth Burd.
1794, Sept.   25, Campbell, Christiana, and John Scott.
1765, March 25, Campbell, Elizabeth, and Thomas Wood.
1794, July   4, Campbell, James, and Mary Simpson.
1779, Sept.   16, Campbell, Robert, and Mary Hall.
1785, Dec.   1, Campbell, Sarah, and Joseph Hibbard.
1764, May   16, Cample, William, and Anna Philips.
1791, Aug.   16, Campson, Ruth, and Isaac Braman.
1797, Nov.   19, Canary, Edy, and William Gardner.
1782, Feb.   14, Canby, Sarah, and Moses Chamberlain.
1800, July   2, Carey, Catha., and Henry Smith.
1798, Dec.   18, Carl, Elizabeth, and John Humes.
1771, Dec.   3, Carlisle, William, and Kaziah Akerly.
1787, March 22, Carmalt, Hannah, and William Matlack.
1787, Aug.   16, Carmalt, Rebecca, and David Christie.
1791, Aug.   2, Carman, James, and Elizabeth Norris.
1801, Sept.   21, Carney, Thomas, and Susan Boyle.
1803, April   16, Carpenter, Jun., John, and Ann Crampton.
1765, May   11, Carpenter, Mary, and John Watson.
1802, Oct.   22, Carpenter, Rachel, and Abraham Baily.
1796, June   2, Carpenter, Samuel, and Jane Wiltbank.
1763, Feb.   5, Carpenter, Thomas, and Esther Squirrell.
1795, Dec.   6, Carr, Isaac, and and Elizabeth Kelly.
1763, Dec.   24, Carrell, Eleanor, and John Hart.
1792, July   4, Carskadan, George, and Rosanna Mounty.
1791, Nov.   27, Carson, Jonathan, and Susan Bonsill.
1793, April   3, Carson, Joseph, and Sarah Bessonet.
1794, July   30, Carson, William, and Jane Andrews.
1796, Feb.   1, Carter, Elizabeth, and Ebenezer Hickling.
1793, April   13, Carter, Esther, and Rowland Parry.
1763, March 7, Carter, James, and Rebecca Lincoln.
1764, Jan.   14, Cartwright, Samuel, and Elizabeth Butler.
1793, June   13, Caruthers, Sarah, and Peter Sutter.
1798, June   3, Cashaday, Clarissa, and Bowman Simpson.
1762, Nov.   27, Cassey, Rebecca, and John Starr.
1778, April   13, Castleburg, Catherine, and John Enox.
1798, Dec.   30, Cathcart, Allen, and Lethea Gentry.
1800, Nov.   5, Cathrell, Dr. Isaac, and Ann Hay.
1783, May   4, Caton, Phoebe, and Richard Paul.
1799, Aug.   1, Caustels, Rachel, and James Parsons.
1795, Feb.   26, Chadwick, Isaac, and Margaret Weldon.
1782, Feb.   14, Chamberlain, Moses, and Sarah Canby.

1793, June   9, Chambers, David, and Martha McCutcheon.
1794, Oct.   15, Champin, Phillis, and Isaac Brown.
1777, June   9, Champion, Mary, and John Clark.
1792, April 12, Chancellor, William, and Grace Conrow.
1777, Aug.   14, Chandler, Sybil, and Elijah Coffin.
1786, Oct.   1, Charlesworth, Hannah, and Thomas Willis.
1784, Oct.   17, Charlesworth, Jane, and Jacob Humphrey.
1792, April   1, Chatham, Margaret, and Thomas Cross.
1780, Feb.   2, Chattin, Lydia, and Robert Cook.
1795, March 16, Chatting, John, and Tabitha Morgan.
1794, Sept. 27, Cheeseman, Jacob, and Sarah Stiles.
1796, March   6, Chesnutwood, Mary, and Benjamin Tage.
1788, April   9, Chester, Jane, and William Applegate.
1801, Jan.   18, Chevalier, Samuel, and Susannah Morgan.
1794, July   26, Chew, Joseph, and Elizabeth Richardson.
1781, July   15, Childs, John, and Mary Wood.
1769, Feb.   7, Chisty, Mary, and Walter Stephens.
1787, Aug.   16, Christie, David, and Rebecca Carmalt.
1799, Jan.   27, Christie, Sarah, and William Moore.
1796, March 31, Church, Capt. Jeremiah, and Mary Schacks.
1791, April 27, Church, Jeremiah, and Ruth Wood.
1763, Feb.   3, Church, William, and Elizabeth Moore.
1764, Sept. 24, Clark, Elizabeth, and Thomas Hartley.
1790, Oct.   17, Clark, George, and Ann Glover.
1795, March 22, Clark, Israel, and Sarah Hartshorn.
1794, Nov.   20, Clark, Jane, and John Peckworth.
1777, June   9, Clark, John, and Mary Champion.
1794, March 18, Clark, Joseph, and Ann Woodard.
1795, Nov.   12, Clark, Lewis Newel, and Hannah Naylor.
1787, June   12, Clark, Robert, and Phoebe Roland.
1794, Nov.   13, Clark, Robert, and Rebecca Workman.
1790, Sept. 13, Clark, Samuel, and Jane Loxley.
1790, Aug.   5, Clay, John, and Ann McNealous.
1791, May   10, Cleaver, Joseph, and Mary Davis.
1794, Dec.   25, Cleland, Rachel, and Thomas Webb.
1795, Jan.   1, Clements, Elizabeth, and Joseph Herbert.
1793, May   2, Clunn, Elizabeth, and Samuel Hamilton.
1785, April 14, Coate, Elizabeth, and Daniel DeBenneville.
1790, Nov.   15, Coates, Elizabeth, and Benjamin Sweeten.
1796, April 28, Coates, John, and Diodema Griffith.
1801, Oct.   6, Coates, Mary, and Charles Moore.
1773, June   24, Cobourn, Elizabeth, and David Rees.
1787, July   1, Cochran, Hiran, and Susannah Walters.
1785, Aug.   8, Cochran John, and Kitty Rush.
1800, Dec.   3, Cochran, Robert, and Sarah Mallinson.
1777, Aug.   14, Coffin, Elijah, and Sybil Chandler.

1788, June   7, Cogins, Elizabeth, and Daniel Maris.
1791, Sept.   7, Colbeirt, John, and Margaret Walters.
1789, May   14, Coldter, Hannah, and Lewis Demear.
1761, July   25, Cole, Ann, and Robert Hunter.
1767, Jan.   8, Cole, John, and Rebecca Lippincott.
1775, April   20, Cole, Mary, and Francis Bell.
1771, Feb.   13, Cole, Rachel, and Joseph Rowand.
1799, July   4, Cole, Samuel, and Susan Lloyd.
1799, Dec.   31, Coleman, Keziah, and John Kirkpatrick.
1788, Oct.   18, Coles, Richard, and Hannah Sayre.
1766, April   28, Coleston, John, and Elizabeth Wentz.
1797, Oct.   26, Colgan, John, and Susannah Lewis.
1795, Sept.   23, Collard, John, and Elizabeth Klingel.
1781, Jan.   4, Collier, Mary, and Walter Charles Davids.
1791, Aug.   25, Collier, Sarah, and George Bart.
1773, Oct.   20, Collum, Mary, and Eli Hibbs.
1786, July   11, Conarroe, Thomas, and Martha Riley.
1799, June   13, Condon, Ann, and James Brotherton.
1778, April   13, Conner, Margaret, and William Hailey.
1790, Sept.   16, Connor, John, and Charlotte Davis.
1777, March   25, Conrigan, Mary, and Henry Burle.
1785, April   7, Conroe, Eunice, and Jonah Thomas.
1792, April   12, Conrow, Grace, and William Chancellor.
1801, Oct.   15, Consland, John, and Frances Rea.
1799, June   17, Coch, Francis L., and Elizabeth Maris.
1794, Nov.   23, Cook, David, and Maria Duffield.
1800, Feb.   23, Cook, Elizabeth, and John Speelman.
1801, April   21, Cook, John, and Ann Britton.
1780, Feb.   2, Cook, Robert, and Lydia Chattin.
1794, Nov.   20, Cook, Sarah, and William Perkins.
1771, Feb.   24, Coon, Catherine, and Thomas Search.
1764, Oct.   31, Cooper, William, and Eleanor Helmes.
1799, April   18, Copeland, William, and Martha Wallace.
1774, Sept.   8, Copperthwait, Mary, and John Kille.
1787, Dec.   21, Copson, Esther, and William Lucas.
1800, March   24, Coree, Samuel, and Charlotte Fithian.
1792, Oct.   23, Cornoy, David, and Hannah Beaumont.
1795, March   19, Cornoy, Jane, and Sampson Davis.
1799, Sept.   15, Covenhoven, Margaret, and Elisha Salter.
1790, July   18, Cowgill, Margaret, and David Thompson.
1769, July   4, Cowman, Atwood, and Amy Sherald.
1770, March   4, Cox, Mary, and Robert Jones.
1764, March   14, Cox, Nicholas, and Rebecca Potts.
1774, Nov.   21, Cox, Thomas, and Ruth Ellison.
1801, June   8, Coyle, Eleanor, and Solomon Robinson.
1800, Sept.   13, Craig, Robert, and Jane Royston.

1803, April 16, Crampton, Ann, and John Carpenter, Jun.
1770, Nov.   19, Crawford, Anthony, and Judith Smith.
1797, June   3, Crawford, Elizabeth, and William West.
1766, Nov.   6, Crean, Cumberland, and James McCullough.
1790, June   17, Creed, Jane, and Nathaniel Davis.
1771, Feb.   27, Cress, Elizabeth, and Robert Hugh.
1795, Jan.   8, Cressin, Mary and Joseph Lewis.
1783, June   18, Cridlin, Mary, and Nicholas Lloyd.
1769, Dec.   31, Crispin, Mary, and Warwick Hale.
1764, Sept. 29, Crispin, Paul, and Rebecca Hewlins.
1788, Oct.   12, Crispin, Silas, and Esther Dougherty.
1791, Aug.   15, Crocket, Mary, and Frederick Vanneman.
1796, May   21, Crone, John, and Mary Ann Patrick.
1792, April   1, Cross, Thomas, and Margaret Chatham.
1794, May   1, Crowell, Samuel, and Jane Stuart.
1802, April   4, Culin, Elizabeth, and Andrew Boon.
1794, May   15, Culin, Martha, and Hugh Hart.
1765, Dec.   25, Culin, Prudence, and Swan Rambo.
1802, July   27, Cummings, John, and Catherine Kelcher.
1795, July   30, Cunningham, Eleanor, and Michael Fimple.
1795, March 22, Cunnings, Elizabeth, and George Vanderslice.
1795, May   14, Curtis, Ann, and William Grant.
1796, June   23, Curwin, James, and Esther White.
1785, Dec.   20, Daniel, Elizabeth, and Elias Deal.
1796, Feb.   26, Darrah, Thomas, and Livia Bryan.
1781, April 25, David, Zebadiah, and Jane Nicholson.
1781, Jan.   4, Davids, Walter Charles, and Mary Collier.
1796, April   7, Davies, Samuel, and Rebecca Ledru.
1769, July   1, Davis, Abigail, and William Faries.
1764, May   10, Davis, Ann, and John Turk.
1790, Sept. 16, Davis, Charlotte, and John Connor.
1798, May   9, Davis, Elizebath, and Ezekiel Murphy.
1785, Jan.   20, Davis, Elizabeth, and David Shakespear.
1780, March 23, Davis, George, and Mary Yocum.
1794, Dec.   25, Davis, Hannah, and Charles Nicholson.
1777, March   7, Davis, Jane, and Colonel John Patton.
1773, May   19, Davis, Jemima, and Peter Wells.
1765, Feb.   5, Davis, Margaret, and Robert Macmullen.
1773, Dec.   7, Davis, Margaret, and Thomas Davis.
1792, March   4, Davis, Martha, and Samuel Evans.
1764, Feb.   2, Davis, Mary, and Levy Dungan.
1791, May   10, Davis, Mary, and Joseph Cleaver.
1794, May   8, Davis, Mary, and Dugle Moore.
1792, Nov.   15, Davis, Mordecai, and Eleanor Bridson.
1790, June   17, Davis, Nathaniel, and Jane Creed.
1798, July   4, Davis, Rebecca, and Samuel Garrets.

1794, Sept.   9, Davis, Rebecca, and Lemuel Shaw.
1771, June   6, Davis, Richard, and Sarah Moore.
1795, March 19, Davis, Sampson, and Jane Cornoy.
1790, Oct.   7, Davis, Jun., Samuel, and Mary Smith.
1770, March 27, Davis, Sarah, and Isaac Morgan.
1770, March 28, Davis, Sarah, and Joshua Philips.
1800, Dec.   18, Davis, Thomas, and Esther Speakman.
1763, Dec.   22, Davis, Thomas, and Mary Gayman.
1773, Dec.   7, Davis, Thomas, and Margaret Davis.
1794, April 24, Davis, William, and Mary Sink.
1764, Oct.   10, Daugherty, Susanna, and Israel Taylor.
1765, Jan.   22, Daullis, George, and Mary Vahan.
1795, Aug.   6, Dawson, Margaret, and David Paul.
1785, Dec.   20, Deal, Elias, and Elizabeth Daniel.
1785, April 14, DeBenneville, Daniel, and Elizabeth Coate.
1801, April 14, Delaney, Elizabeth, and John Baker.
1774, July   6, Delavan, John, and Barbara Kroser.
1789, May   14, Demear, Lewis, and Hannah Coldter.
1801, March   5, Deney, John, and Jerusha Oliphant.
1794, April 19, Dent, Mary, and Thomas Young.
1774, May   14, Dever, Ann, and Charles Grimes.
1796, Jan.   11, Devillers, Joseph Auguste, and Catherine Holton.
1792, Feb.   9, Dewees, Hannah, and John Boggs.
1794, Oct.   18, Dickey, Capt. Adam, and Betsy Holt.
1790, Jan.   15, Dickinson, Catherine, and James Harris.
1800, April 17, Dickinson, Mary, and Andrew Thatcher.
1788, June   8, Dickinson, Rebecca, and Harding Williams.
1796, March 30, Dickinson, Sarah, and Robert Shewel.
1794, May   2, Dicks, Job, and Rachel Powell.
1773, Oct.   21, Dilworth, John, and Hannah Hunter.
1795, Feb.   26, Doane, Jane, and James Murray.
1799, June   20, Dobbin, Justice, and Charlotte Lewis.
1797, Nov.   2, Dobson, Ann, and William Griffin.
1793, Oct.   17, Doggett, Thomas Foster, and Elizabeth Green.
1769, April   8, Dogharty, William, and Mary Bampford.
1794, July   24, Donnaldson, Margaret, and Joseph Boggs.
1794, Oct.   23, Dorrell, William, and Sylvia Richardson.
1786, Oct.   5, Dorsey, Greenberry, and Elizabeth Bartholomew.
1777, June   17, Dorsey, Sarah, and John German.
1773, Jan.   7, Dougherty, Catherine, and Fincher Hellings.
1789, June   10, Dougherty, Charles, and Jane Taylor.
1788, Oct.   12, Dougherty, Esther, and Silas Crispin.
1778, April 24, Dougherty, George, and Sarah McIntire.
1794, Sept. 18, Dougherty, John, and Susannah Grove.
1791, July   28, Dougherty, Mary, and William Adair.
1795, Jan.   24, Doughty, William, and Eleanor Wilson.

1787, Oct.   29, Douglass, Robert, and Mary Lawrence.
1780, Dec.   14, Downer, Elizabeth, and Richard Glassock.
1800, March 13, Downing, Ann, and John Williams.
1766, Dec.   25, Downing, Dennis, and Margaret Witten.
1795, Dec.   10, Downs, John, and Elizabeth Barret.
1789, July   23, Draper, Ann, and John Fraser.
1794, Nov.   23, Duffield, Maria, and David Cook.
1781, March 16, Duncan, Ann, and Robert Elliott.
1793, March 5, Duncan, James, and Rachel Guy.
1791, June   23, Duncan, Martha, and William Moulder.
1792, Oct.   31, Duncan, William, and Polly Moulder.
1773, Aug.   4, Dungan, Clement, and Sarah Bond.
1764, Feb.   2, Dungan, Levy, and Mary Davis.
1801, Oct.   29, Dunkarly, Elizabeth, and John Barney.
1802, Dec.   25, Dunkarly, Mary, and John Wigglesworth.
1800, Dec.   3, Dunlap, Catharine, and Michael McKarnas.
1782, Dec.   25, Dunn, James, and Sarah Hodges.
1799, June   10, Duon, Honore, and Elizabeth Morris.
1790, Jan.   5, Eager, Eleanor, and Matthew Mannen.
1796, Sept.   29, Eagin, Charles, and Elizabeth Stocksberry.
1774, Oct.   8, Eaminster, John, and Hannah Lum.
1766, June   14, Eaton, Edith, and John James.
1792, Sept.   8, Eccle, George, and Susannah Anderson.
1794, Nov.   15, Eccle, Susannah, and Charles Allen.
1780, April   24, Eddy, Caleb, and Esther Brown.
1786, Oct.   19, Edward, Thomas, and Catherine Britton.
1800, Jan.   2, Edwards, Elizabeth, and William Brown.
1796, Nov.   17, Edwards, George, and Jane Ferguson.
1795, April   2, Edwards, Jacob, and Lydia Stewart.
1781, June   21, Edwards, Jemima, and Thomas Pilkinton.
1771, Aug.   9, Edwards, John, and Martha Moore.
1765, April   1, Edwards, John, and Ann Griffiths.
1771, May   3, Edwards, Rev. Morgan, and Elizabeth Singleton,
1792, July   14, Edwards, Morgan, and Elizabeth Bankson.
1800, Aug.   7, Edwards, Robert, and Susannah Whartanby.
1761, June   25, Edwards, Thamar, and Thomas James, Esqr.
1793, April   13, Elkin, Angel, and Miribah Robins.
1796, Jan.   21, Elliot, Hannah, and John Moore.
1794, Oct.   16, Elliot, Margaret, and Peter Rose.
1794, July   1, Elliott, James, and Ann Hill.
1795, June   24, Elliott, John, and Susan Johnson.
1781, March 16, Elliott, Robert, and Ann Duncan.
1774, Nov.   21, Ellison, Ruth, and Thomas Cox.
1786, Sept.   14, Ely, John, and Elizabeth Bennet.
1794, Sept.   25, Engle, Elizabeth, and Abel Wiley.
1776, May   23, Engle, Hannah, and Benjamin Thaw.

1792, Feb.   22, Engle, John, and Elizabeth Winter.
1798, May   19, Engle, Mary, and Robert Maull.
1778, April   13, Enox, John, and Catherine Castleburg.
1802, Nov.   28, Ernest, Byard, and Mary Shives.
1796, Sept.   17, Erwin, Robert, and Mary Fox.
1793, Sept.   2, Esher, Hannah, and John Braley.
1795, May   25, Espey, Ann, and Loftus Noell.
1799, May   11, Espey, Elizabeth, and Cornelius McLean.
1788, Dec.   25, Esty, Eleanor, and Jacob Keene.
1786, May   25, Esty, Rebecca, and Martin Thomas.
1796, Oct.   1, Evans, Ann, and William Griffith.
1770, Oct.   30, Evans, Ann, and John Butcher.
1788, Nov.   19, Evans, Elisha, and Rebecca Jolly.
1772, April   10, Evans, Elizabeth, and Josiah James.
1783, Feb.   8, Evans, Hannah, and Samuel Roberts.
1789, June   19, Evins, John, and Margaret McQuistin.
1790, March   4, Evans, Lot, and Maria Robinson.
1794, June   1, Evans, Maria, and Samuel Williamson.
1765, May   13, Evans, Martha, and Jacob Jackson.
1772, Nov.   11, Evans, Mary, and William Patton.
1796, Dec.   29, Evans, Parthenia, and Henry Hisar.
1773, Jan.   9, Evans, Ruth, and Abraham Free.
1792, March   4, Evans, Samuel, and Martha Davis.
1765, April   24, Evans, Sarah, and James Megmegen.
1786, Jan.   12, Evans, Sarah, and George North.
1802, July   29, Evans, Susannah, and Jacob Tyson.
1795, March   3, Evans, Thomas, and Elizabeth Thornburgh.
1784, Oct.   28, Eve, John, and Chanty Bennet.
1762, Oct.   13, Ewer, John, and Sarah Glading.
1762, Sept.   8, Ewers, Jonathan, and Elizabeth Barton.
1787, Feb.   22, Fackery, Rudith, and Paul Brown.
1777, March   4, Fairis, William, and Ann Biddle.
1798, March 21, Falts, Elizabeth, and Thomas Harding.
1769, July   1, Faries, William, and Abigal Davis.
1772, April   13, Farmer, Hannah, and Ezekiel Letts.
1765, April   13, Farmer, James, and Margaret Messner.
1796, Oct.   23, Farow, John, and Catherine McGlade.
1766, May   19, Farr, Isaac, and Mary Musgrove.
1778, May   25, Farr, William, and (wid.) Martha Rees.
1794, Aug.   20, Farrady, John, and Thomasin Mills.
1791, Aug.   5, Farrell, Thomas, and Jane Grant.
1795, Oct.   17, Farren, Elizabeth, and John Louden.
1794, Nov.   25, Felty, Eleanor, and Thomas Gibbs.
1792, Nov.   8, Ferguson, James, and Rebecca Buckley.
1802, May   4, Ferguson, John, and Rebecca Jones.
1770, Nov.   1, Ferguson, Margaret, and Francis Gottier.

1785, June   5, Ferrill, William, and Dinah Byles.
1795, July   30, Fimple, Michael, and Eleanor Cunningham.
1762, May   4, Finley, John, and Mary Todd.
1786, March 19, Finney, Elizabeth, and Samuel Jobson.
1800, June   28, Finour, Joseph, and Mary Garrison.
1793, June   13, Fiss, Mary, and William Brown.
1792, Dec.   25, Fiss, William, and Margaret Brown.
1800, March 24, Fithian, Charlotte, and Samuel Coree.
1777, June   5, Fitzgerald, Thomas, and Catherine Francis.
1792, Oct.   3, Fitzpatrick, Catherine, and Alexander Frazer.
1791, Dec.   14, Flanegan, James, and Else Keys.
1774, Jan.   24, Fleeson, Thomas, and Rebecca Britton.
1797, Feb.   4, Flintham, Elizabeth, and John How.
1786, May   31, Flower, Hannah, and Edward Hannon.
1762, May   5, Flower, Rebecca, and William Young.
1775, March 20, Floyd, Henry, and Rosanna Huston.
1774, May   4, Flynn, John, and Margaret Bradley.
1791, Feb.   24, Foight, Lewis, and Sarah Ludgate.
1791, May   31, Folwell, John, and Ruth Vernon.
1799, June   20, Ford, George, and Elizabeth Montgomery.
1761, Oct.   31, Forst, Henry, and Lydia White.
1793, Dec.   23, Fortner, Leah, and William Murfin.
1786, July   10, Foster, Lydia, and Joseph Woodman.
1795, Dec.   8, Foulke, Lowry, and Samuel Miles Jun.
1773, April   8, Fowler, James, and Hannah Swanson.
1799, Aug.   18, Fox, Frances, and James Youmans.
1791, Dec.   13, Fox, George, and Lydia Bildervack.
1793, Feb.   28, Fox, Martha, and Henry Hoare.
1796, Sept.   17, Fox, Mary, and Robert Erwin.
1792, March 29, Frampton, James, and Mary Shellmire.
1794, Aug.   4, France, Margaret, and Joseph Price.
1785, Nov.   29, Francis Anne, and Nathan Thomas.
1777, June   5, Francis, Catherine, and Thomas Fitzgerald.
1796, May   4, Francis, David, and Mary Rowland.
1784, Dec.   30, Francis, Elizabeth, and Elisha Gordon.
1799, Oct.   24, Frank, George, and Rachel Bicknell.
1789, July   23, Fraser, John, and Ann Draper.
1792, Oct.   3, Frazer, Alexander, and Catherine Fitzpatrick.
1764, March   3, Freak, Rebecca, and Charles Willson.
1773, Jan.   9, Free, Abraham, and Ruth Evans.
1799, June   6, Free, Benjamin, and Amy Wolverton.
1793, April   25, Freeman, Sophia, and Richard Towne.
1774, Aug.   24, French, Jonathan, and Sarah Parsons.
1794, Jan.   12, French, Margaret, and Robert Robinson.
1795, Feb.   12, French, Sarah, and Michael O'Neal.
1791, May   12, Friend, Kezia, and John Burkitt.

1794, July   5, Froman, Margaret, and William Hutchinson.
1791, March 20, Frouance, John, and Elizabeth Roberts.
1763, July   9, Frontaine, John Papin, and Catherine Richardson.
1793, May   25, Fry, Elizabeth, and Simon Webb.
1789, Feb.   3, Fry, Jacob, and Margaret Springer.
1801, March 14, Fry, John, and Catherine Patterson.
1768, Sept.   17, Fryreas, John, and Barbery Buzerd.
1773, Feb.   16, Fulkrod, Catherine, and Godfrey Henry.
1799, Oct.   25, Fultin, Mary, and George Anthony Rogers.
1764, Dec.   9, Fulton, Hugh and Rachel Thomas.
1796, Nov.   17, Furgusen, Jane, and George Edwards.
1763, Sept.   8. Fust, Ann, and Peter Waters.
1799, April   9, Gabb, William, and Rebecca Wills.
1794, Nov.   20, Galbreath, Patrick, and Elizabeth Lynn.
1764, Jan.   15, Gallows, Sarah, and Robert Shewell.
1795, Oct.   8, Galt, Sarah, and Capt. John Harris.
1800, March 30, Gaunon, Joanna, and Hezekiah Hawk.
1800, April   14, Gardner, Archelaus, and Frances Bowen.
1798, Nov.   15, Gardner, Barzillai, and Catherine Sheppard.
1798, July   3, Gardner, Benjamin, and Elizabeth Smith.
1773, June   29, Gardner, Hannah, and William Rogers.
1774, March 31, Gardner, John, and Mary Scott.
1797, Nov.   19, Gardner, William, and Edy Canary.
1773, July   22, Gardiner, Frances, and Abraham Mitchell.
1798, July   4, Garrets, Samuel, and Rebecca Davis.
1782, Feb.   5, Garrison, Allathea, and Felix Winbert.
1800, June   28, Garrison, Mary, and Joseph Finour.
1785, Nov.   19, Garrison, Silas, and Catherine Sailor.
1763, Dec.   22, Gayman, Mary, and Thomas Davis.
1795, July   6, Geary, Thomas, and Ann Rogers.
1796, Aug.   25, Gebler, John Frederick, and Eliza Breidenhart.
1798, Dec.   30, Gentry, Lethea, and Allen Cathcart.
1798, Dec.   28, Geoghegan, Bartholomew, and Elizabeth White.
1786, Sept.   10, George, Anthony, and Elizabeth Raser.
1777, June   17, German, John, and Sarah Dorsey.
1764, Feb.   29, Gibbon, Abel, and Eleanor John.
1786, June   1, Gibbons, Ruth, and William Walker.
1793, Oct.   8, Gibbons, William, and Mary Baker.
1774, Feb.   3, Gibbs, Benjamin, and Hannah Sewell.
1785, Dec.   18, Gibbs, Enos, and Elizabeth Burrows.
1794, Nov.   25, Gibbs, Thomas, and Eleanor Felty.
——, ——   —, Gilbert, Abigail, and John Smith.
1764, March 27, Gilbert, Abigail, and John Tomkins.
1801, July   19, Gilbert, Elizabeth, and Jonathan Beach.
1770, Jan.   1, Gilbert, Elizabeth, and Joseph Hart.
1770, Dec.   6, Gilbert, Joseph, and Euphemia Rees.

1784, Oct.	18, Gilbert, Lydia, and Richard Steed.
1800, Jan.	5, Gilbert, Susanna, and John Saul.
1794, March	6, Gisty, John, and Mary Woods.
1774, Nov.	24, Githen, Isaac, and Elizabeth Boggs.
1762, Oct.	13, Glading, Sarah, and John Ewer.
1780, Dec.	14, Glassock, Richard, and Elizabeth Downer.
1791, July	3, Gloss, Ludwig, and Elizabeth Weldon.
1790, Oct.	17, Glover, Ann, and George Clark.
1801, Dec.	17, Goodrich, William, and Margaret Johnston.
1791, Nov.	27, Gordon, Abraham, and Sarah Kittera.
1784, Dec.	30, Gordon, Elisha, and Elizabeth Francis.
1787, April	22, Gordon, Elizabeth, and Nathaniel Prentis.
1797, Jan.	31, Gordon, Sarah, and James Ruxton.
1786, Sept.	21, Gosline, William, and Martha Stackhouse.
1770, Nov.	1, Gottier, Francis, and Margaret Ferguson.
1784, Oct.	27, Graham, George, and Rebecca Jackson.
1794, Oct.	1, Graham, George, and Elizabeth Wilson.
1794, May	8, Graham, Mary, and Robert Shaw.
1791, Aug.	5, Grant, Jane, and Thomas Farrell.
1795, May	14, Grant, William, and Ann Curtis.
1788, Aug.	7, Gravenstine, Peter, and Ann Kinsey.
1781, March 11, Gray, Alexander, and Hannah Having.
1783, Nov.	21, Gray, John, and Elizabeth Bergen.
1794, Aug.	24, Greble, Mary, and John Bessiere.
1775, Jan.	25, Green, Anna, and John Braddock.
1778, May	25, Green, Berryman, and Ann Pritchard.
1793, Oct.	17, Green, Elizabeth, and Thomas Foster Doggett.
1793, Aug.	23, Green, George, and Sarah Anderson.
1781, March 11, Green, Sarah, and John Jones.
1771, Nov.	12, Gregory, John, and Rachel Steward.
1796, June	2, Gregory, Clement, and Rachel Heslip.
1791, March	2, Gribbell, Mary, and Joseph McKean.
1799, March 10, Grible, Elizabeth, and William Ward.
1792, Nov.	24, Grice, Susannah, and John Taylor.
1801, June	25, Griffin, Bryan, and Elizabeth Murratt.
1762, Feb.	17, Griffin, Comfort, and James Watkins.
1797, Nov.	2, Griffin, William, and Ann Dobson.
1762, April	28, Griffith, Ann, and Edward Middleton.
1796, April	28, Griffith, Diodema, and John Coates.
1792, April	5, Griffith, Elizabeth, and Isaac Morris.
1794, Feb.	9, Griffith, Eliza, and Samuel Jodon.
1794, March 20, Griffith, Joseph, and Eliza Spears.
1796, Oct.	1, Griffith, William, and Ann Evans.
1765, April	1, Griffiths, Ann, and John Edwards.
1771, May	14, Griffiths, John, and Margaret Lewis.
1770, March 18, Griffiths, Mary, and John Middleton.

1774, May 14, Grimes, Charles, and Ann Dever.
1764, Feb. 13, Griscom, Deborah, and Everard Bolton.
1790, Sept. 5, Groff, Susanna, and John Raboteau.
1794, Sept. 18, Grove, Susannah, and John Dougherty.
1786, Feb. 9, Gullen, John, and Sarah Willdee.
1801, Nov, 23, Gusnip, Christiana, and Charles Johnston.
1794, June 28, Gustard, Richard, and Mary Ryan.
1788, April 29, Gutrage, Sarah, and Henry Towne.
1789, Feb. 28, Guttrey, Margaret, and Stephen Ogelby.
1774, June 16, Guy, Ann, (wid.,) and James Stuart.
1793, March 5, Guy, Rachel, and James Duncan.
1766, Dec. 11, Guy, Thomas, and Ann Anthony.
1800, Sept. 14, Guyger, John, and Frances Holland.
1776, June 24, Hackett, Susanna, and William Lewellin.
1801, Oct. 8, Haight, Charlotte, and Mathew Van Alstyne.
1778, April 13, Hailey, William, and Margaret Conner.
1801, March 22, Haines, Margaret, and John Sharpnack.
1799, Aug. 10, Hains, Philip, and Susannah Shoemaker.
1769, Dec. 31, Hale, Warwick, and Mary Crispin.
1766, Nov. 1, Hall, Leven, and Christiana Hopman.
1792, May 12, Hall, Mary, and Thomas Weatherby.
1794, Aug. 16, Hall, Mary, and John Maxwell.
1779, Sept. 16, Hall, Mary, and Robert Campbell.
1764, Aug. 20, Hamilton, Ann, and Patrick Johnston.
1785, Nov. 2, Hamilton, John, and Phoebe Burns.
1799, March 25, Hamilton, Robert, and Jessie McNaughton.
1772, June 11, Hamilton, Robert, and Mary Street.
1793, May 2, Hamilton, Samuel, and Elizabeth Clunn.
1773, Feb. 13, Hammett, Sarah, and John Wolohon.
1801, April 6, Handkins, Mary, and Reuben Brotherton.
1762, Dec. 26, Handy, Mary, and Joseph Richey.
1787, June 6, Hanlow, James, and Margaret McDaniel.
1786, May 31, Hannon, Edward, and Hannah Flower.
1798, March 21, Harding, Thomas, and Elizabeth Falts.
1794, Oct. 9, Hargrove, William, and Esther Reeves.
1796, April 26, Harkley, James, and Mary Baker.
1761, Oct. 29, Harmon, Hannah, and George Jenkins.
1794, June 20, Harn, Rebecca, and John Tree.
1791, Nov. 24, Harris, Abigail, and Daniel Burt.
1796, Dec. 19, Harris, Edward, and Jane Ustick.
1790, Jan. 15, Harris, James, and Catherine Dickinson.
1795, Sept. 12, Harris, John, and Eleanor Kelly.
1795, Oct. 8, Harris, Capt. John, and Sarah Galt.
1788, Dec. 7, Harris, Samuel, and Margaret Mines.
1802, May 29, Harrison, Benjamin, and Margaret Bickley.
1794, May 15, Hart, Hugh, and Martha Culin.

1763, Dec.   24, Hart, John, and Eleanor Carrel.
1788, Jan.   9, Hart, John, and Margaret Summers.
1770, Jan.   1, Hart, Joseph, and Elizabeth Gilbert.
1764, Sept.   24, Hartley, Thomas, and Elizabeth Clark.
1795, March 22, Hartshorn, Sarah, and Israel Clark.
1769, Aug.   21, Harvey, Job, and Hannah Anderson.
1795, April   30, Harvey, Mary, and Thomas Inglish.
1780, Feb.   2, Harvey, Rosanna, and James Shannon.
1781, Feb.   15, Harvey, Samuel, and Hannah Robinson.
1800, Sept.   2, Harvey, Peter, and Sarah Wharry.
1781, March 11, Having, Hannah, and Alexander Gray.
1800, March 30, Hawk, Hezekiah, and Joanna Gannon.
1795, Nov.   5, Hawker, Elizabeth, and Thomas Bartleman.
1781, June   19, Haworth, Stephanus, and Rebecca Warner.
1800, Nov.   5, Hay, Ann, and Dr. Isaac Cathrell.
1783, April   11, Hays, Joseph, and Jane Wilday.
1788, Aug.   25, Hegeman, Rebecca, and John Terry.
1794, Sept.   16, Hellings, Elizabeth, and John Roberts.
1773, Jan.   7, Hellings, Fincher, and Catherine Dougherty.
1792, Sept.   13, Hellings, Fincher, and Sarah Barns.
1800, Aug.   24, Hellings, Jacob, and Charlotte Rodman.
1801, Dec.   22, Helm, George W., and Lydia Newson.
1764, Oct.   31, Helmes, Eleanor, and William Cooper.
1787, Aug.   14, Helveston, Eleanor, and Samuel Neff.
1794, Feb.   20, Henderson, Maria, and Stephen Page.
1761, July   25, Hendricks, Nathan, and Mary Bond.
1794, Aug.   13, Hener, Elizabeth, and Capt. Silas Webb.
1789, March 19, Henneberry, Patrick, and Margaret Hilen.
1773, Feb.   16, Henry, Godfrey, and Catherine Fulkrod.
1775, Oct.   11, Henry, Philip, and Margaret Thornburn.
1795, Jan.   1, Herbert, Joseph, and Elizabeth Clements.
1794, June   5, Hergesheimer, Samuel, and Elizabeth Shubert.
1796, June   2, Heslip, Rachel, and Clement Gregory.
1798, Dec.   31, Heston, Jacob, and Patience Viall.
1764, Sept.   29, Hewlins, Rebecca, and Paul Crispin.
1785, Dec.   1, Hibbard, Joseph, and Sarah Campbell.
1773, Oct.   20, Hibbs, Eli, and Mary Collum.
1773, Jan.   28, Hickey, John, and Alice Tufft.
1796, Feb.   1, Hickling, Ebenezer, and Elizabeth Carter.
1794, June   24, Hide, Benjamin, and Mary Reedy.
1799, Dec.   26, Highland, John, and Telitha Bratten.
1789, March 19, Hilen, Margaret, and Patrick Henneberry.
1794, July   1, Hill, Ann, and James Elliott.
1801, June   25, Hill, Joseph, and Henrieth Vinyard.
1798, Nov.   13, Hiltzhimer, Hannah, and Richard E. Smith.
1796, Dec.   29, Hisar, Henry, and Parthenia Evans.

1793, Feb.   28, Hoare, Henry, and Martha Fox.
1763, Feb.   19, Hobbs, Hannah, and Anthony Wright.
1770, Dec.   9, Hobbs, Henry, and Sarah Lownes.
1782, Dec.   25, Hodges, Sarah, and James Dunn.
1787, Nov.   5, Hofner, Henry, and Sophia Omensetter.
1791, Oct.   9, Holgat, Jacob, and Elizabeth Sheitz.
1800, Sept.   14, Holland, Frances, and John Guyger.
1800, Feb.   18, Holland, Sarah, and Lewis Trimble.
1765, June   1, Holmes, James, and Helenor Lawrence.
1784, July   11, Holmes, Jonathan Stout, and Elizabeth Pintard.
1783, July   17, Holmes, Mary, and Enoch Northup.
1789, Oct.   3, Holmes, Thomas, and Mary Turner.
1796, June   13, Holmes, Thomas, and Tacey Richardson.
1790, Dec.   17, Holmes, William, and Elizabeth Miles.
1793, Nov.   12, Holmes, William, and Margaret Vollens.
1793, Feb.   16, Holston, William and Rebecca Lounsborough.
1794, Oct.   18, Holt, Betsy, and Capt. Adam Dickey.
1796, Jan.   11, Holton, Catherine, and Joseph Auguste Devillers.
1790, Oct.   14, Holton, Rebecca, and James Miles.
1790, Nov.   13, Hoops, Charity, and George Brown.
1798, April   12, Hoops, Elizabeth, and William James.
1779, April   20, Hooversack, Elizabeth, and James Street.
1794, June   12, Hopkins, Thomas, and Mary Miginnis.
1766, Nov.   1, Hopman, Christiana, and Leven Hall.
1793, Sept.   28, Hortz, Peter, and Eleanor Loper.
1795, March   12, Houch, Joseph, and Mary Gainer Roberts.
1798, April   19, Houlton, Elizabeth, and Joseph Kidder.
1799, Feb.   25, Houston, James, and Ann Watkins.
1797, Feb.   4, How, John, and Elizabeth Flintham.
1771, Feb.   7, How, William, and Christian Hutson.
1798, June   18, Howard, Ruth, and Ichabod Warner.
1794, Dec.   23, Howell, Joseph, and Hannah Kinnard.
1782, April   29, Howell, Rachel, and Benjamin Thompson.
1792, June   3, Howell, Reading, and Mary Busby.
1787, Aug.   23, Howell, Ruth, and Thomas Watkins.
1794, Nov.   13, Hozey, Isaac, and Jane Budd Jones.
1775, Jan.   25, Huff, Daniel, and Mary Sharp.
1770, April   14, Huffdale, John, and Elizabeth Yerkes.
1796, July   1, Hugg, Sarah, and James McDonald.
1770, April   15, Hugh, Nicholas, and Ann Roberts.
1771, Feb.   27, Hugh, Robert, and Elizabeth Cress.
1796, Oct.   23, Hughes, Levi, and Rebecca Thomson.
1795, Jan.   15, Hughes, Margaret, and· John Wheeler.
1792, Dec.   31, Hughes, Martha, and James Pritchard.
1798, Dec.   18, Humes, John, and Elizabeth Carl.
1784, Oct.   17, Humphrey, Jacob, and Jane Charlesworth.

1774, Sept.   5, Hunt, Esaias, and Elizabeth Statton.
1789, April   30, Hunter, Catherine, and Thomas Williams.
1773, Oct.   21, Hunter, Hannah, and John Dilworth.
1772, Nov.   20, Hunter, Mary, and Eli Bentley.
1761, July   25, Hunter, Robert, and Ann Cole.
1800, Feb.   18, Husler, Joseph, and Martha Nash.
1775, March   20, Huston, Rosanna, and Henry Floyd.
1798, July   15, Hutchinson, James, and Sarah Shubart.
1762, Dec.   28, Hutchinson, Mary, and David Thomson.
1794, July   5, Hutchinson, William, and Margaret Froman.
1771, Feb.   7, Hutson, Christian, and William How.
1764, Nov.   1, Indecot, Samuel, and Elizabeth Roberts.
1799, July   14, Iley, Mary, and Thomas Wells.
1772, Dec.   8, Inglis, Hannah, and Thomas Waterman.
1765, Jan.   2, Inglis, John, and Eleanor Yocum.
1790, Jan.   15, Inglish, Elizabeth, and George Baker.
1795, April   30, Inglish, Thomas, and Mary Harvey.
1770, May   3, Ingels, George, and Mary Rush.
1801, Oct.   22, Ingels, Hannah, and Capt. Joseph Reynolds.
1791, May   2, Ingels, Joseph, and Elizabeth Ledyard.
1801, May   14, Ingels, Mary, and John Miles.
1795, April   23, Innes, Joseph, and Rachel Warner.
1796, Jan.   31, Inskeep, Thomas, and Mary Stockton.
1795, Jan.   20, Irvine, Francis, and Mary Miller.
1762, Jan.   1, Irwin, Jerrard, and Rachel Owen.
1801, May   13, Jackson, Ann, and Edward McLaughlin.
1765, May   13, Jackson, Jacob, and Martha Evans.
1789, Dec.   31, Jackson, John, and Anne Moore.
1796, Oct.   10, Jackson, Mary, and Robert Shields.
1784, Oct.   27, Jackson, Rebecca, and George Graham.
1777, March   17, Jackson, Sarah, and John Lewis.
1794, Feb.   2, Jackway, Mary, and Alexander Whitesides.
1794, July   3, Jacobs, Jane, and David Pill.
1789, June   11, James, Elizabeth, and Isaac Oakford.
1766, June   14, James, John, and Edith Eaton.
1772, April   10, James, Josiah, and Elizabeth Evans.
1765, April   8, James, Samuel, and Anna Keslwm.
1761, June   25, James, Esqr, Thomas, and Thamar Edwards.
1798, April   12, James, William, and Elizabeth Hoops.
1775, March   16, January, Benjamin, and Hannah Langdale.
1786, Feb.   21, Jeickways, William, and Rebecca Smith.
1790, Sept.   26, Jenkins, David, and Ann Zane.
1799, Jan.   3, Jenkins, Elizabeth, and William Paul.
1761, Oct.   29, Jenkins, George, and Hannah Harmon.
1782, Dec.   17, Jenkins, Hannah, and Jonathan Zane.
1786, Jan.   11, Jenkins, Hannah, and James Spong.

1767, June　25, Jenkins, Hannah, and Thomas Middleton.
1802, Dec.　28, Jenkins, Margaret, and Lodowick Sprogell.
1795, May　7, Jenkins, Sarah, and David Ogden.
1800, May　20, Jenkins, Thomas, and Mary Weaver.
1786, March 19, Jobson, Samuel, and Elizabeth Finney.
1793, Dec.　25, Jodon, Daniel, and Anna McNeal.
1794, Feb.　6, Jodon, Samuel, and Eliza Griffith.
1764, Feb.　29, John, Eleanor, and Abel Gibbon.
1769, Jan.　4, John, Hester, and John Williams.
1801, May　12, Johnson, Ann, and Ebenezer Brown.
1802, April　11, Johnson, John, and Elizabeth Price.
1795, May　16, Johnson, Joseph, and Mary Walker.
1801, April　22, Johnson, Mary, and George Roberts Shaw.
1774, Oct.　6, Johnson, Mary, and Phineas Waterman.
1795, June　24, Johnson, Susan, and John Elliott.
1796, March 13, Johnson, William, and Sarah McKean.
1801, Nov.　23, Johnston, Charles, and Christiana Guinup.
1793, Aug.　1. Johnston, George, and Margaret Brown.
1801, Dec.　17, Johnston, Margaret, and William Goodrich.
1770, April　25, Johnstone, Mary, and Thomas Rooke.
1764, Aug.　20, Johnston, Patrick, and Ann Hamilton.
1788, Nov.　19, Jolly, Rebecca, and Elisha Evans.
1792, Dec.　19, Jones, Agnes, and Thomas Wayne.
1788, May　29, Jones, Amy, and Thomas Thompson.
1801, Oct.　18, Jones, Catherine, and James Peal.
1802, April　8, Jones, Charles, and Mary Alloway.
1779, Sept.　15, Jones, David, and Judith Ward.
1786, June　1, Jones, David, and Rosanna Reedle.
1773, Dec.　28, Jones, David, and Latitia Powell.
1771, May　4, Jones, Elizabeth, and Nathaniel Jones.
1796, Dec.　1, Jones, Evan, and Margaret Roberts.
1765, Oct.　23, Jones, Griffith, and Hannah Lloyd.
1801, April　23, Jones, Hannah, and William Richardson.
1794, Nov.　13, Jones, Jane Budd, and Isaac Hozey.
1781, March 11, Jones, John, and Sarah Green.
1764, Feb.　21, Jones, Letitia, and Joseph Roberts.
1792, Oct.　1, Jones, Capt. Lloyd, and Eliza. Loxley.
1774, April　7, Jones, Margaret, and Christian Ruscom.
1790, March 13, Jones, Mary, and Jonathan Pearson.
1776, Nov.　30, Jones, Mary, and James Naglee.
1797, Aug.　22, Jones, Mary, and Archibald McClean.
1771, May　4, Jones, Nathaniel, and Elizabeth Jones.
1796, Nov.　5, Jones, Philip, and Grace Elizabeth Smith.
1773, Nov.　18, Jones, Rachel, and William Brice.
1802, May　4, Jones, Rebecca, and John Ferguson.
1770, March　4, Jones, Robert, and Mary Cox.

1764, Nov.   10, Jones, Samuel, and Sylvia Spicer.
1795, June   28, Jones, Tacey, and John Barber.
1786, Aug.   9, Jordan, Robert, and Sarah Levis.
1796, Dec.   28, Judd, Eunice, and John Mather.
1785, Nov.   10, Junkin, Susannah, and Richard Morris.
1790, March 23, Kaign, John, and Lydia Skadan.
1774, Dec.   6, Karr, John, and Elizabeth Maddox.
1799, July   1, Keen, Jane, and Thomas Mifflin Souder.
1788, Jan.   24, Keen, Joseph, and Margaret Williams.
1785, April 22, Keen, Peter, and Rebecca Wessel.
1795, Nov.   15, Keen, Samuel, and Sarah Keiter.
1788, Dec.   25, Keene, Jacob, and Eleanor Esty.
1796, Sept. 15, Keirle, John, and Ann Murphy.
1795, Nov.   15, Keiter, Sarah, and Samuel Keen.
1802, July   27, Kelcher, Catherine, and John Cummings.
1800, Dec.   30, Kelly, Abel, and Thomasin Scattergood.
1795, Sept. 12, Kelly, Eleanor, and John Harris.
1795, Dec.   6, Kelly, Elizabeth, and Isaac Carr.
1770, Nov.   1, Kelly, Erasmus, and Mary Morgan.
1778, April   4, Kelly, Jane, and Thomas Sims.
1774, June, 20, Kelly, John, and Rachel Blackledge.
1763, Dec.   17, Kennard, Jacob, and Mary Wallis.
1797, May   2, Kennedy, Dorotha, and Patrick Welsh.
1794, July   6, Kerlin, William, and Elizabeth Patterson.
1787, June   7, Ker, Joseph, and Sarah Rush.
1765, Jan.   22, Kerr, John, and Mary Shecan.
1797, July   9, Kerr, Martha, and John Sessford.
1765, April   8, Keslwm, Anna, and Samuel James.
1791, Dec.   14, Keys, Else, and James Flanegan.
1790, Nov.   30, Keyser, Jacob, and Catherine Wise.
1792, April 26, Keyzer, William, and Rebecca Roberts.
1794, June   5, Kidd, Catherine, and Robert Wolfington.
1783, June   30, Kidd, John, and Rebecca Oldfield.
1798, April 19, Kidder, Joseph, and Elizabeth Houlton.
1772, Dec.   17, Kigings, Susanna, and James Miles.
1774, Sept.   8, Kille, John, and Mary Copperthwait.
1766, Aug.   13, Kimsey, Mary, and Jehu Wood.
1799, Oct.   22, King, Lydia, and Stephen Russel.
1794, Dec.   23, Kinnard, Hannah, and Joseph Howell.
1775, May   4, Kinnard, William, and Elizabeth Stockford.
1765, April 22, Kinnersley, Esther, and Joseph Shewell.
1788, Aug.   7, Kinsey, Ann, and Peter Gravenstine.
1793, April 27, Kinsey, Elizabeth, and John Servoss.
1800, May   25, Kinsey, Harman, and Ann Merrick.
1799, Dec.   31, Kirkpatrick, John, and Keziah Coleman.
1798, June   30, Kitfield, Nathaniel, and Elsey Oates.

1791, Nov. 27, Kittera, Sarah, and Abraham Gordon.
1794, Jan. 1, Klingel, Andrew, and Mary Lee.
1795, Aug. 23, Klingel, Elizabeth, and John Collard.
1787, Feb. 1, Knight, Elizabeth, and James Lefferts.
1769, March 23, Knowland, William, and Christina Adams.
1784, Oct. 10, Knowles, Mary, and Rev. Elhanon Winchester.
1774, July 6, Kroser, Barbara, and John Delavan.
1795, Feb. 19, Kuhnsman, Margaret, and William Stuard.
1796, May 25, Lang, John, and Sarah Ustick.
1791, July 12, Lang, Margaret, and Duncan McInnis.
1775, March 16, Langdale, Hannah, and Benjamin January.
1777, Aug. 15, Langdale, Jane, and Dr. Thomas Parke.
1795, Nov. 12, Lapess, Mary, and Capt. Stephen Parsons.
1794, Aug. 30, Larzalere, Elizabeth, and Asa Sutton.
1765, June 1, Lawrence, Helenor, and James Holmes.
1795, April 9, Lawrence, Mary, and Thomas Lees.
1787, Oct. 29, Lawrence, Mary, and Robert Douglass.
1773, Feb. 5, Lawrence, Richard, and Rebecca Lewis.
1794, May 14, Lawrenty, James, and Maria Pillar.
1799, March 7, Lawton, George R., and Ann Pole.
1791, May 18, Leake, Sarah, and John Berry.
1791, June 25, Lear, Margaret, and Henry Myers.
1796, April 7, Ledru, Rebecca, and Samuel Davis.
1795, Nov. 15, Ledrue, Catherine, and Thomas Rigden.
1791, May 2, Ledyard, Elizabeth, and Joseph Ingels.
1794, May 10, Lee, Benjamin, and Mary Wetherby.
1794, Jan. 1, Lee, Mary, and Andrew Klingel.
1792, April 4, Lees, Sarah, and Bailey Art.
1795, April 9, Lees, Thomas, and Mary Lawrence.
1787, Feb. 1, Lefferts, James, and Elizabeth Knight.
1797, Feb. 8, Leib, Hetty, and George W. Morgan.
1800, Jan. 26, Lenfesty, John, and Mary Rudolph.
1793, July 28, Leodor, Benjamin, and Lewaza Street.
1794, July 17, Lester, Mary, and William McKinsey.
1772, April 13, Letts, Ezekiel, and Hannah Farmer.
1763, May 12, Levering, Aaron, and Hannah Wrighter.
1802, April 4, Levering, Hannah, and Andrew Anderson.
1769, April 17, Levering, Jacob, and Mary Brounfield.
1792, March 23, Levering, Samuel, and Rebecca Roberts.
1786, Aug. 9, Levis, Sarah, and Robert Jordan.
1776, Jan. 24, Lewellin, William, and Susanna Hackett.
1799, June 20, Lewis, Charlotte, and Justice Dobbin.
1765, Oct. 30, Lewis, Hannah, and Levy Lloyd.
1777, March 17, Lewis, John, and Sarah Jackson.
1795, Jan. 8, Lewis, Joseph, and Mary Cressin.
1771, May 14, Lewis, Margaret, and John Griffiths.

1772, April 10, Lewis, Mary, and James Thomas.
1773, Feb. 5, Lewis, Rebecca, and Richard Lawrence.
1797, Oct. 26, Lewis, Susannah, and John Colgan.
1763, March 7, Lincoln, Rebecca, and James Carter.
1767, Jan. 8, Lippincott, Rebecca, and John Cole.
1762, Aug. 28, Lisha, Catherine, and Amos Weeton.
1793, Sept. 18, Livingston, Eve, and Edward Newton.
1781, Feb. 3, Lloyd, Elizabeth, and Andrew Ten Eyck.
1765, Oct. 23, Lloyd, Hannah, and Griffith Jones.
1765, Oct. 30, Lloyd, Levy, and Hannah Lewis.
1783, June 18, Lloyd, Nicholas, and Mary Cridlin.
1799, July 4, Lloyd, Susan, and Samuel Cole.
1798, Dec. 15, Lloyd, Susan, and Luke Tuckness.
1790, Oct. 20, Long, Margaret, and Herman Yerkes.
1793, Jan. 23, Long, Nimrod, and Sarah Stuart.
1790, Sept. 29, Long, Rebecca, and Samuel Oakford.
1793, Sept. 28, Loper, Eleanor, and Peter Hortz.
1795, Oct. 17, Louden, John, and Elizabeth Farren.
1799, Nov. 16, Loughery, John, and Esther Rush.
1793, Feb. 16, Lounsborough, Rebecca, and William Holston.
1803, Jan. 4, Lowden, Hannah, and David Lund.
1793, March 12, Lowe, Vincent, and Charlotte Palmer.
1770, Dec. 9, Lownes, Sarah, and Henry Hobbs.
1792, Oct. 1, Loxley, Eliza, and Capt. Lloyd Jones.
1790, Sept. 13, Loxley, Jane, and Samuel Clark.
1796, Feb. 22, Loxly, Ann, and Rev. Morgan John Rhees.
1787, June 26, Lucas, Esther, and Henry Molier.
1787, Dec. 21, Lucas, William, and Esther Copson.
1796, Nov. 8, Ludenburgh, Lawrence, and Christiana Slater.
1791, Feb. 24, Ludgate, Sarah, and Lewis Foight.
1774, Oct. 8, Lum, Hannah, and John Eaminster.
1803, Jan. 4, Lund, David, and Hannah Lowden.
1791, Feb. 17, Lush, Ann, and John Peckworth.
1792, March 20, Lyle, Elizabeth, and Robert Wood.
1794, Nov. 20, Lynn, Elizabeth, and Patrick Galbreath.
1763, Feb. 19, Lyon, Charles, and Ann Vaughan.
1765, Feb. 5, Macmullen, Robert, and Margaret Davis.
1774, Dec. 6, Maddox, Elizabeth, and John Karr.
1797, Jan. 19, Maghee, William, and Sarah Barnes.
1796, March 31, Maine, Mary, and Nathaniel Peirse.
1787, Sept. 23, Maines, Andrew, and Hannah Willson.
1786, Sept. 28, Malin, James, and Margaret Richards.
1800, Dec. 3, Mallinson, Sarah, and Robert Cochran.
1764, Aug. 29, Malone, Letitia, and Enoch Morgan.
1790, Jan. 5, Mannen, Matthew, and Eleanor Eager.
1803, March 17, Mannington, Elizabeth, and John Marple.

1794, Dec.   25, Mansell, John, and Elizabeth Marson.
1774, Oct.   18, Marclay, Benjamin, and Hannah Wentz.
1788, June   7, Maris, Daniel, and Elizabeth Cogins.
1799, June   17, Maris, Elizabeth, and Francis L. Cooch.
1776, April 11, Marple, David, and Ann McClean.
1785, March 26, Marple, Dorothy, and Isaac Van Horne.
1803, March 17, Marple, John, and Elizabeth Mannington.
1788, March 10, Marple, Mary, and Joseph Monrow.
1794, May   10, Marpole, William, and Elizabeth Spunninberger.
1795, Jan.   15, Marsh, Susan, and William Rogers.
1789, May   24, Marshall, Joseph, and Susannah Ashton.
1794, Dec.   25, Marson, Elizabeth, and John Mansell.
1795, Nov.   7, Martin, Ann, and John McAffer.
1791, April 18, Martin, John, and Mary Shee.
1787, Oct.   25, Martin, William, and Elizabeth Middleton.
1764, Sept. 23, Mason, Susanna, and James Bouchier.
1795, May   21, Mason, William, and Ann Tomkins.
1795, March 19, Massey, Ann, and Thomas Shoemaker.
1795, April   7, Massey, Elizabeth, and Joshua John Moore.
1796, Dec.   28, Mather, John, and Eunice Judd.
1770, Jan.   21, Mathers, Mary, and Edward Vernon.
1774, Feb.   22, Mathew Edward, and Eleanor Thomas.
1795, Dec.   15, Mathias, Mary, and John Young.
1793, April 24, Mathias, Nathan, and Catherine Miller.
1787, March 22, Matlack, William, and Hannah Carmalt.
1798, May   19, Maull, Robert, and Mary Engle.
1794, Aug.   16, Maxwell, John, and Mary Hall.
1796, May   19, Maxwell, Sarah, and Samuel Test.
1780, Oct.   2, May, Catherine, and Patrick Walsh.
1788, March 12, May, Peter, and Catherine Walters.
1795, Nov.   7, McAffer, John, and Ann Martin.
1799, Dec.   10, McCall, Jesse, and Sarah Tussey.
1792, Dec.   6, McCalley, John, and Mary Russell.
1799, April   9, McCarsnan, Ann, and Mark Thompson.
1781, Oct.   23, McCarter, Charles, and Rachel Brown.
1766, Nov.   5, McCarty, Paul, and Kissander Williams.
1789, Oct.   1, McCatten, Mary, and Nicholas Miller.
1776, April 11, McClean, Ann, and David Marple.
1797, Aug.   22, McClean, Archibald, and Mary Jones.
1798, Aug.   12, McCleland, Jane, and Joseph Wood.
1802, Dec.   7, McConnell, Patton, and Jane Anderson.
1794, June   21, McCoreal, Martha, and Jonathan Smith.
1794, June   23, McCoy, Daniel, and Ann Wilson.
1766, Nov.   6, McCullough, James, and Cumberland Crean.
1793, Nov.   21, McCutcheon, James, and Sarah Smith.
1793, June   9, McCutcheon, Martha, and David Chambers.

1787, June   6, McDaniel, Margaret, and James Hanlon.
1796, July   1, McDonald, James, and Sarah Hugg.
1790, Nov.   7, McDougall, Ann, and David Smith.
1775, April   28, McDowell, John, and Mary McSparren.
1794, July   3, McFall, Catherine, and Duncan Robertson.
1782, Oct.   10, McGannon, Deborah, and Joseph White.
1796, Nov.   1, McGee, Elizabeth, and Samuel Bell.
1796, Oct.   23, McGlade, Catherine, and John Farow.
1799, Aug.   27, McGonnegill, Elizabeth, and Hugh Miller.
1790, June   6, McGrady, Charles, and Sarah Bristol.
1795, Aug.   9, McGragar, Elizabeth, and Capt. John Thompson.
1795, Feb.   22, McGuire, Joseph, and Mary Morton.
1795, May   3, McGuire, Mary, and Samuel Adams.
1778, April   24, McIntire, Sarah, and George Dougherty.
1791, July   12, McInnis, Duncan, and Margaret Lang.
1800, Dec.   3, McKarnas, Michael, and Catharine Dunlap.
1786, April   13, McKean, Joseph Borden, and Hannah Miles.
1791, March   2, McKean, Joseph, and Mary Gribbell.
1796, March   6, McKean, Lydia, and Andrew Anderson.
1796, March   13, McKean, Sarah, and William Johnson.
1790, July   7, McKinley, Ann, and Samuel Burns.
1794, July   17, McKinsey, William, and Mary Lester.
1798, July   9, McKown, Hugh, and Hannah Neal.
1795, June   25, McKoy, Robert, and Ann Thomas.
1801, May   13, McLaughlin, Edward, and Ann Jackson.
1789, July   15, McLaughlin, Hugh, and Elizabeth Scott.
1799, May   11, McLean, Cornelius, and Elizabeth Espey.
1766, Nov.   8, McLeane, Benjamin, and Catherine Burris.
1782, Jan.   29, McLeod, John, and Margaret McNealous.
1765, March   2, McMullen, John, and Elizabeth Rhodes.
1777, July   31, McMullin, Mary, and Joseph Biays.
1799, March   25, McNaughton, Jessie, and Robert Hamilton.
1793, Dec.   24, McNeal, Anna, and Daniel Jodon.
1801, Dec.   3, McNeal, Malcolm, and Sarah Oliver.
1790, Aug.   5, McNealous, Ann, and John Clay.
1782, Jan.   29, McNealous, Margaret, and John McLeod.
1790, Dec.   22, McPherson, Daniel, and Ann Thackera.
1770, Jan.   14, McQuattiat, Margaret, and William Robinson.
1789, June   19, McQuistin, Margaret, and John Evins.
1775, April   28, McSparren, Mary, and John McDowell.
1794, Sept.   14, McSteward, John, and Elizabeth Morgan.
1774, Jan.   20, McVaugh, Edmund, and Elizabeth Taylor.
1765, April   24, Megmegen, James, and Sarah Evans.
1785, May   19, Melvin, Gregory, and Sarah Van Solingen.
1792, May   31, Meredith, Wheeler, and Sarah Singleton.
1774, Oct.   8, Merit, Mary, and William Ross.

1800, May 25, Merrick, Ann, and Harman Kinsey.
1794, Aug. 11, Merrick, Ann, and Joshua Mitchell.
1765, April 13, Messner, Margaret, and James Farmer.
1770, Dec. 11, Mettlen, Elizabeth, and Isaac Williams.
1785, March 23, Meyer, Jacob, and Esther Musgrave.
1762, April 28, Middleton, Edward, and Ann Griffith.
1787, Oct. 25, Middleton, Elizabeth, and William Martin.
1795, Nov. 25, Middleton, Hannah, and Charles Rhoads.
1770, March 18, Middleton, John, and Mary Griffiths.
1767, June 25, Middleton, Thomas, and Hannah Jenkins.
1795, Jan. 31, Middleton, William, and Mary Wood.
1794, June 12, Miginis, Mary, and Thomas Hopkins.
1788, Dec. 7, Mines, Margaret, and Samuel Harris.
1799, Dec. 5, Minster, William, and Lydia Smith.
1785, Dec. 8, Miles, Abigail, and Thomas Potts.
1790, Dec. 17, Miles, Elizabeth, and William Holmes.
1763, Sept. 3, Miles, Enos, and Sarah Pugh.
1786, April 13, Miles, Hannah, and Joseph Borden McKean.
1790, Oct. 14, Miles, James, and Rebecca Holton.
1772, Dec. 17, Miles, James, and Susanna Kigings.
1801, May 14, Miles, John, and Mary Ingels.
1795, Dec. 8, Miles, Jun. Samuel, and Lowry Foulke.
1761, Feb. 16, Miles, Samuel, and Catherine Wister.
1769, Aug. 16, Millar, Mary, and William Moulder.
1793, April 24, Miller, Catherine, and Nathan Mathias.
1796, Oct. 16, Miller, Elizabeth, and Jonas Symonds.
1764, Oct. 23, Miller, Hugh, and Frances Kilpatrick.
1799, Aug. 27, Miller, Hugh, and Elizabeth McGonegill.
1790, April 14, Miller, John, and Catherine Baker.
1794, June 19, Miller, John, and Maria Smith.
1795, Jan 20, Miller, Mary, and Frances Irvine.
1789, Oct. 1, Miller, Nicholas, and Mary McCatten.
1791, July 14, Milless, Joanna, and John Starkey.
1793, Nov. 26, Milligan, James, and Mary Thomas.
1794, Aug. 20, Mills, Thomasin, and John Farrady.
1786, Feb. 17, Milnor, Martha, and Tobias Rudolph.
1800, March 23, Mitchel, Letitia, and John Patterson.
1773, July 22, Mitchell, Abraham, and Frances Gardiner.
1794, Oct. 4, Mitchell, Hannah, and John Armstrong.
1794, Aug. 11, Mitchell, Joshua, and Ann Merrick.
1765, April 7, Mitchell, Mary, and Elijah Weed.
1787, June 26, Molier, Henry, and Esther Lucas.
1794, Oct. 23, Molony, James, and Anne Moore.
1801, Nov. 10, Monington, Christener, and William Vandergrist.
1794, Oct. 9, Monington, John, and Elizabeth Roberts.
1799, June 20, Montgomery, Elizabeth, and George Ford.

1789, Dec. 31, Moore, Anne, and John Jackson.
1794, Oct. 23, Moore, Anne, and James Molony.
1769, March 25, Moore, Anne, and Christophel Rue.
1801, Oct. 6, Moore, Charles, and Mary Coates.
1794, May 8, Moore, Dugle, and Mary Davis.
1797, Nov. 5, Moore, Elizabeth, and Levi Springer.
1763, Feb. 3, Moore, Elizabeth, and William Church.
1794, Nov. 9, Moore, Hannah, and Ashley Bowen.
1799, April 1, Moore, Isaac, and Mirian Wells.
1796, Jan. 21, Moore, John, and Hannah Elliot.
1795, April 7, Moore, Joshua John, and Elizabeth Massey.
1791, Sept. 3, Moore, Jonathan, and Sarah Thompson.
1771, Aug. 9, Moore, Martha, and John Edwards.
1791, April 13, Moore, Mary, and Arthur Vanse.
1794, Aug. 7, Moore, Mary, and Samuel Blair.
1802, Dec. 10, Moore, Prudence, and Daniel Jeniser Adams.
1771, June 6, Moore, Sarah, and Richard Davis.
1792, Aug. 30, Moore, William, and Mary Prodly.
1799, Jan. 27, Moore, William, and Sarah Christie.
1783, Jan. 2, Moore, William, and Rachel Wood.
1786, May 11, Moose, Ann, and Samuel Osler.
1762, Dec. 26, Moreton, James, and Mary Wells.
1801, Feb. 1, Morgan, Anne, and William Bassett.
1794, Sept. 14, Morgan, Elizabeth, and John McSteward.
1764, Aug. 29, Morgan, Enoch, and Letitia Malone.
1797, Feb. 8, Morgan, George W., and Hetty Leib.
1770, March 27, Morgan, Isaac, and Sarah Davis.
1770, Nov. 1, Morgan, Mary, and Erasmus Kelly.
1794, Dec. 8, Morgan, Rebecca, and Joseph Piles.
1775, Oct. 25, Morgan, Sarah, and Richard Williams.
1801, Jan. 18, Morgan, Susannah, and Samuel Chevalier.
1795, March 16, Morgan, Tabitha, and John Chatting.
1799, June 10, Morris, Elizabeth, and Honore Duon.
1792, April 5, Morris, Isaac, and Elizabeth Griffith.
1785, Nov. 10, Morris, Leah, and John Tucker.
1797, Jan. 24, Morris, Mary, and Rowland Smith.
1769, June 4, Morris, Mary, and William Bringhurst.
1785, Nov. 10, Morris, Richard, and Susannah Junkin.
1795, June 27, Morrison, Ann, and Thomas Banigan.
1774, July 26, Morrison, James, and Hannah Anderson.
1794, Aug. 16, Morrow, John, and Mary Archibald.
1800, Jan. 28, Morrow, Mary, and William Ballentine.
1795, Feb. 22, Morton, Mary, and Joseph McGuire.
1790, May 9, Mosman, Ann, and Charles Wilson.
1783, Dec. 25, Moulder, Elizabeth, and Gerard Vogels.
1774, April 28, Moulder, Mary, and George Bright.

1792, Oct.   31, Moulder, Polly, and William Duncan.
1769, Aug.   16, Moulder, William, and Mary Millar.
1791, June   23, Moulder, William, and Martha Duncan.
1792, July   4, Mounty, Rosanna, and George Carskadan.
1788, March 10, Mourow, Joseph, and Mary Marple.
1786, Nov.   7, Mulford, Martha, and Nathan Shephard.
1772, July   11, Murdock, John, and Sarah Whitsall.
1780, Nov.   22, Murell, Elizabeth, and Reuben Stiles.
1793, Dec.   23, Murfin, William, and Leah Fortner.
1770, Nov.   8, Murll, Thomas, and Lydia Reynolds.
1796, Sept.   15, Murphy, Ann, and John Keirle.
1798, May   9, Murphy, Ezekiel, and Elizabeth Davis.
1803, April   10, Murphy, James, and Prudense Wood.
1794, Sept.   3, Murphy, Mary, and Peter Pope.
1801, June   25, Murratt, Elizabeth, and Bryan Griffin.
1795, Feb.   26, Murray, James, and Jane Doane.
1785, March 23, Musgrave, Esther, and Jacob Meyer.
1769, Nov.   25, Musgrove, Jane, and Thomas Owen.
1766, May   19, Musgrove, Mary, and Isaac Farr.
1791, June   25, Myers, Henry, and Margaret Lear.
1776, Nov.   30, Naglee, James, and Mary Jones.
1800, Feb.   18, Nash, Martha, and Joseph Husler.
1795, Nov.   12, Naylor, Hannah, and Lewis Newel Clark.
1798, July   9, Neal, Hannah, and Hugh McKown.
1796, April   14, Neal, Jane, and John Bason.
1761, Oct.   29, Neaves, Banaby, and Elizabeth Bertholt.
1766, Jan.   27, Neaves, Sarah, and William Baker.
1766, May   16, Needom, Elizabeth, and Samuel Powell.
1787, Aug.   14, Neff, Samuel, and Eleanor Helveston.
1801, Dec.   22, Newson, Lydia, and George W. Helm.
1786, Nov.   21, Newton, Amelia, and John Brown.
1793, Sept.   18, Newton, Edward, and Eve Livingston.
1795, May   30, Newton, Forbes, and Elizabeth Burnhouse.
1794, Dec.   25, Nicholson, Charles, and Hannah Davis.
1781, April   25, Nicholson, Jane, and Zebadiah David.
1797, Nov.   6, Nicholson, John, and Mary Schuyler.
1795, May   25, Noell, Loftus, and Ann Espey.
1791, Aug.   2, Norris, Elizabeth, and James Carnan.
1786, Jan.   12, North, George, and Sarah Evans.
1783, July   17, Northup, Enoch, and Mary Holmes.
1798, Feb.   10, Nutters, Williamson, and Sarah Wallace.
1790, Jan.   7, Oakford, Charles, and Mary Wallington.
1789, June   11, Oakford, Isaac, and Elizabeth James.
1790, Sept.   29, Oakford, Samuel, and Rebecca Long.
1792, Feb.   9, Oakford, William, and Hannah Posey.
1798, June   30, Oates, Elsey, and Nathaniel Kitfield.

1794, June   12, Odenheimer, Polly, and Daniel Sutter, junior.
1769, July   20, Ogden, Ann, and William Siddons.
1795, May   7, Ogden, David, and Sarah Jenkins.
1789, Feb.   28, Ogelby, Stephin, and Margaret Guttrey.
1794, May   14, Ogle, Howard, and Ann Wilson.
1783, June   30, Oldfield, Rebecca, and John Kidd.
1801, March 5, Oliphant, Jerusha, and John Deney.
1801, Dec.   3, Oliver, Sarah, and Malcolm McNeal.
1787, Nov.   5, Omensetter, Sophia, and Henry Hofner.
1795, Feb.   12, O'Neal, Michael, and Sarah French.
1799, March 24, O'Neill, Henry, and Elizabeth Bickerton.
1784, Dec.   30, Osborne, Rhoda, and Samuel Atkinson.
1786, May   11, Osler, Samuel, and Ann Moose.
1762, Jan.   1, Owen, Rachel, and Jerrard Irwin.
1769, Nov.   29, Owen, Thomas, and Jane Musgrove.
1786, March 30, Ower, Sarah, and Stpehen Weeks.
1793, Nov.   23, Ozborne, Ruth, and Isaac Williams.
1794, Feb.   20, Page, Sarah, and Frederick Wing.
1785, Aug.   2, Page, Stephen, and Elizabeth Sprong.
1794, Feb.   20, Page, Stephen, and Maria Henderson.
1793, March 12, Palmer, Charlotte, and Vincent Lowe.
1789, Oct.   1, Palmer, Joseph, and Rebecca Bolton.
1762, April 15, Palmer, William, and Margaret Pew.
1794, Jan.   2, Park, James, and Margaret Robinson.
1777, Aug.   15, Parke, Dr. Thomas, and Jane Langdale.
1788, Oct.   2, Parker, Sarah, and Rev. John Stancliff.
1796, June   5, Parry, Elizabeth, and Richard Thomas.
1793, April 13, Parry, Rowland, and Esther Carter.
1799, Aug.   1, Parsons, James, and Rachel Caustels.
1774, Aug.   24, Parsons, Sarah, and Jonathan French.
1795, Nov.   12, Parsons, Capt. Stephen, and Mary Lapess.
1789, Feb.   3, Parsons, Thomas, and Hannah Scollar.
1801, June   25, Paschall, Sarah, and James Roney.
1796, May   21, Patrick, Mary Ann, and John Crone.
1801, March 14, Patterson, Catherine, and John Fry.
1794, July   6, Patterson, Elizabeth, and William Kerlin.
1799, Aug.   3, Patterson, Jane, and Malcom Wright.
1800, March 23, Patterson, John, and Letitia Mitchel.
1777, March 7, Patton, Colonel John, and Jane Davis.
1796, May   8, Patton, Mathew, and Tacey Vanwinkle.
1772, Nov.   11, Patton, William, and Mary Evans.
1795, Aug.   6, Paul, David, and Margaret Dawson.
1783, May   4, Paul, Richard, and Phoebe Caton.
1799, Jan.   3, Paul, William, and Elizabeth Jenkins.
1801, Oct.   18, Peal, James, and Catherine Jones.
1794, July   5, Pearce, Alexander, and Eleanor Roe.

1790, March 13, Pearson, Jonathan, and Mary Jones.
1795, May 25, Pearson, William, and Catherine Adams.
1765, April 4, Pechin, Christopher, and Christiana Bright.
1794, Nov. 20, Peckworth, John, and Jane Clark.
1791, Feb. 17, Peckworth, John, and Ann Lush.
1799, July 20, Peiffer, William, and Ann Skellenger.
1796, March 31, Peirse, Nathaniel, and Mary Maine.
1795, May 24, Pendleburg, William, and Margaret Ryan.
1765, Oct. 30, Pennel, Rebecca, and Thomas Walter.
1787, Dec. 18, Pennington, Ann, and Robert Smock.
1761, Aug. 3, Pennington, William, and Mary Vickerts.
1795, May 14, Pennock, Talman, and Mary Talman.
1796, March 10, Penrose, Ann, and Alexander Buchanan.
1799, Feb. 14, Perkins, Thomas, and Sarah Robinson.
1794, Nov. 20, Perkins, William, and Sarah Cook.
1794, March 6, Peterson, Thomas, and Phoebe Price.
1762, April 15, Pew, Margaret, and William Palmer.
1792, June 23, Pfeiffer, George, and Mary Williams.
1790, Sept. 7, Phileno, John, and Mary Wagner.
1764, May 16, Philips, Anna, and William Cample.
1770, March 28, Philips, Joshua, and Sarah Davis.
1790, Nov. 6, Philips, Sarah, and James Barry.
1799, May 9, Phillips, Abraham, and Mary Ryan.
1773, April 17, Phillips, Catherine, and Nathan Sturgis.
1791, April 28, Pile, Martha, and William Warnick.
1794, Dec. 8, Piles, Joseph, and Rebecca Morgan.
1781, June 21, Pilkinton, Thomas, and Jemima Edwards.
1794, July 3, Pill, David, and Jane Jacobs.
1794, May 14, Pillar, Maria, and James Lawrenty.
1796, March 15, Pinson, John, and Hannah Roland.
1784, July 11, Pintard, Elizabeth, and Jonathan Stout Holmes.
1795, Dec. 3, Pitner, Aaron, and Ann Alexander.
1793, Sept. 18, Plain, Catherine, and Jacob Trebolet.
1793, June 23, Plane, Henry, and Christiana White.
1799, March 7, Pole, Ann, and George R. Lawton.
1795, April 9, Pollock, Hugh, and Martha Anthony.
1794, Sept. 3, Pope, Peter, and Mary Murphy.
1792, Feb. 9, Posey, Hannah, and William Oakford.
1764, March 14, Potts, Rebecca, and Nicholas Cox.
1785, Dec. 8, Potts, Thomas, and Abigail Miles.
1794, Feb. 27, Powell, Hannah, and Daniel Rambow.
1768, June 23, Powell, Isaac, and Sarah Rush.
1773, Dec. 28, Powell, Latitia, and David Jones.
1794, May 2, Powell, Rachel, and Job Dicks.
1766, May 16, Powell, Samuel, and Elizabeth Needom.
1795, April 16, Powell, Sarah, and Joseph Warren.

1765, Jan.   3, Powell, William, and Mary Thomas.
1803, April   9, Powers, James, and Sarah Bower.
1762, Sept.   1, Pratt, Alleneor, and Joseph Watkins.
1787, April   22, Prentis, Nathaniel, and Elizabeth Gordon.
1795, Nov.   19, Preston, Sarah, and Thomas Tomkins.
1802, April   11, Price, Elizabeth, and John Johnson.
1793, July   7, Price, Jane, and Jonathan Walter.
1794, Aug.   4, Price, Joseph, and Margaret France.
1794, March   6, Price, Phœbe, and Thomas Peterson.
1784, Nov.   11, Pringle, Jane, and John Williamson.
1766, June   18, Prior, Samuel, and Elizabeth Gilbert.
1778, May   25, Pritchard, Ann, and Berryman Green.
1792, Dec.   31, Pritchard, James, and Martha Hughes.
1796, Nov.   12, Pritner, John, and Elizabeth Sturgis.
1792, Aug.   30, Prodly, Margaret, and James Walker.
1792, Aug.   30, Prodley, Mary, and William Moore.
1792, Dec.   20, Pugh, Job, and Ruth Brooke.
1763, Sept.   3, Pugh, Sarah, and Enos Miles.
1790, Sept.   5, Raboteau, John, and Susanna Groff.
1771, Jan.   2, Raile, John, and Ann Rowland.
1765, Dec.   25, Rambo, Swan, and Prudence Culin.
1794, Feb.   27, Rambow, Daniel, and Hannah Powell.
1786, April   29, Ramsey, Thomas Hancock, and Elizabeth Ruxby.
1786, Sept.   10, Raser, Elizabeth, and Anthony George.
1796, April   7, Ravely, Mary, and Robert Barber.
1801, Oct.   15, Rea, Frances, and John Consland.
1798, Dec.   27, Read, Charles, and Elizabeth Richley.
1796, April   6, Reay, Margaret, and John Burnett.
1785, March   24, Reed, Davis, and Elizabeth Steel.
1794, June   24, Reedy, Mary, and Benjamin Hide.
1799, Oct.   16, Reed, Samuel, and Frances Stirk.
1786, June   1, Reedle, Rosanna, and David Jones.
1773, June   24, Rees, David, and Elizabeth Cobourn.
1770, Dec.   6, Rees, Euphemia, and Joseph Gilbert.
1778, May   25, Rees, Martha, (wid.), William Farr.
1799, Dec.   12, Rees, Mary, and Noah Brady.
1794, Oct.   9, Reeves, Esther, and William Hargrove.
1799, Jan.   2, Reiley, Mary, and Peter W. Walter.
1785, May   27, Reinhard, Peter, and Sarah Taylor.
1793, Jan.   11, Remick, Enoch, and Rebecca Ayars.
1782, July   11, Renford, Catherine, and Jacob VanBurkelow.
1784, March   25, Reynolds, Anne, and John Alexander.
1801, Oct.   22, Reynolds, Capt. Joseph, and Hannah Ingels.
1770, Nov.   8, Reynolds, Lydia, and Thomas Murll.
1796, Feb.   22, Rhees, Rev. Morgan John, and Ann Loxly.
1795, Nov.   25, Rhoads, Charles, and Hannah Middleton.

1765, March 2, Rhodes, Elizabeth, and John McMullen.
1786, Sept. 28, Richards, Margaret, and James Malin.
1763, July   9, Richardson, Catherine, and John Capin Froutaine.
1799, July 13, Richardson, Catharine, and Joseph Whartnaby.
1794, July 26, Richardson, Elizabeth, and Joseph Chew.
1794, Oct. 23, Richardson, Sylvia, and William Dorrell.
1796, June 13, Richardson, Tacey, and Thomas Holmes.
1801, April 23, Richardson, William, and Hannah Jones.
1802, May   9, Richers, William, and Mary Wallace.
1762, Dec. 26, Richey, Joseph, and Mary Handy.
1798, Dec. 27, Richley, Elizabeth, and Charles Read.
1763, Feb. 12, Ricks, John, and Mary Buzzard.
1770, Dec. 15, Ridge, John, and Sarah Bicton.
1794, March 20, Ridge, Mary, and George Allen.
1785, April 28, Riffett, Mary, and John Steel.
1795, Nov. 15, Rigden, Thomas, and Catherine Ledrue.
1786, July 11, Riley, Martha, and Thomas Conarroe.
1792, March 22, Rittenhouse, Williamina, and Samuel Brown.
1788, July   8, Ritter, Sophia, and George Snowden.
1790, Nov.   4, Roads, Sarah, and Jacob Roberts.
1794, Oct.   5, Robenson, Samuel, and Mary Till.
1770, April 15, Roberts, Ann, and Nicholas Hugh.
1795, May   7, Roberts, Ann, and Jacob Walter.
1797, Jan. 25, Roberts, Elizabeth, and Mathias Smith.
1764, Nov.   1, Roberts, Elizabeth, and Samuel Indecot.
1794, Oct.   9, Roberts, Elizabeth, and John Monington.
1791, March 20, Roberts, Elizabeth, and John Fronance.
1776, July   4, Roberts, Elizabeth, and David Zell.
1794, April 16, Roberts, Hannah, and George Thomas.
1790, Nov.   4, Roberts, Jacob, and Sarah Roads.
1799, Dec. 20, Roberts, Jane, and Henry Smith.
1794, Sept. 16, Roberts, John, and Elizabeth Hellings.
1764, Dec.   1, Roberts, Jonathan, and Ann Starr.
1764, Feb. 21, Roberts, Joseph, and Letitia Jones.
1796, Dec.   1, Roberts, Margaret, and Evan Jones.
1795, March 12, Roberts, Mary Gainer, and Joseph Houck.
1774, Jan.   3, Roberts, Mary, and James Barrow.
1792, April 26, Roberts, Rebecca, and William Keyzer.
1792, March 23, Roberts, Rebecca, and Samuel Levering.
1783, Feb.   8, Roberts, Samuel, and Hannah Evans.
1794, July   3, Robertson, Duncan, and Catherine McFall.
1793, April 13, Robins, Miribah, and Angel Elkin.
1795, April 20, Robinson, Ann, and George Stout, Jun.
1781, Feb. 15, Robinson, Hannah, and Samuel Harvey.
1767, Jan.   5, Robinson, John, and Elizabeth Woolf.
1794, Jan.   2, Robinson, Margaret, and James Park.

1790, March 4, Robinson, Maria, and Lot Evans.
1794, Jan.   12, Robinson, Robert, and Margaret French.
1799, Feb.   14, Robinson, Sarah, and Thomas Perkins.
1801, June   8, Robinson, Solomon, and Eleanor Coyle.
1770, Jan.   14, Robinson, William, and Margaret McQuattiat.
1800, Aug.   24, Rodman, Charlotte, and Jacob Hellings.
1792, Dec.   6, Rodman, Elizabeth, and Nathaniel Bayne.
1763, May   2, Rodman, Joseph, and Mary Allen.
1794, July   5, Roe, Eleanor, and Alexander Pearce.
1795, July   6, Rogers, Ann, and Thomas Geary.
1799, Oct.   25, Rogers, George Anthony, and Mary Fultin.
1774, Jan.   13, Rogers, John, and Mary Trapell.
1773, June   29, Rogers, William, and Hannah Gardner.
1795, Jan.   15, Rogers, William, and Susan Marsh.
1796, March 15, Roland, Hannah, and John Pinson.
1787, June   12, Roland, Phoebe, and Robert Clark.
1801, June   25, Roney, James, and Sarah Paschall.
1800, Sept. 27, Roney, Rachel, and Robert Taylor.
1770, April 25, Rooke, Thomas, and Mary Johnstone.
1794, Oct.   16, Rose, Peter, and Margaret Elliot.
1787, June   30, Ross, Thomas, and Mary Thomas.
1774, Oct.   8, Ross, William, and Mary Merrit.
1800, May   26, Rourk, William, and Elizabeth Brady.
1771, Feb.   13, Rowand, Joseph, and Rachel Cole.
1793, Nov.   12, Rowen, Mary, and Matthew Vollens.
1771, Jan.   22, Rowland, Ann, and John Raile.
1796, May   4, Rowland, Mary, and David Francis.
1800, Sept. 13, Royston, Jane, and Robert Craig.
1765, Oct.   28, Rudolph, Jacob, and Judith Yocum.
1800, Jan.   26, Rudolph, Mary, and John Lenfesty.
1786, Feb.   14, Rudolph, Tobias, and Martha Milnor.
1769, March 25, Rue, Christophel, and Anne Moore.
1795, July   19, Rue, James, and Rebecca Brown.
1774, April   7, Ruscom, Christian, and Margaret Jones.
1799, Nov.   16, Rush, Esther, and John Loughery.
1785, Aug.   8, Rush, Kitty, and John Cochran.
1770, May   3, Rush, Mary, and George Ingels.
1768, June   23, Rush, Sarah, and Isaac Powell.
1787, June   7, Rush, Sarah, and Joseph Ker.
1780, Dec.   14, Rush, William, and Martha Wallace.
1792, Dec.   6, Russell, Mary, and John McCalley.
1799, Oct.   22, Russel, Stephen, and Lydia King.
1786, April 29, Ruxby, Elizabeth, and Thomas Hancock Ramsey.
1797, Jan.   31, Ruxton, James, and Sarah Gordon.
1795, May   24, Ryan, Margaret, and William Pendleburg.
1794, June   28, Ryan, Mary, and Richard Gustard.

1799, May   9, Ryan, Mary, and Abraham Phillips.
1771, April 28, Sadler, Susannah, and Charles Tuckenmiller.
1785, Nov.   19, Sailor, Catherine, and Silas Garrison.
1799, Sept. 15, Salter, Elisha, and Margaret Covenhoven.
1788, Sept.   4, Sanders, Sarah, and John Brown.
1794, Aug.   14, Saul, Asa, and Martha Smith.
1800, Jan.   5, Saul, John, and Susanna Gilbert.
1796, April 10, Saunders, Hannah, and Charles Phillips Brent.
1796, March 17, Savoy, Lewis, and Elizabeth Alexander.
1790, Oct.   24, Saxton, Elizabeth, and William Saxton.
1790, Oct.   24, Saxton, William, and Elizabeth Saxton.
1788, Oct.   18, Sayre, Hannah, and Richard Coles.
1796, March 22, Scaise, Ann, and Adam Scurrah.
1800, Dec.   30, Scattergood, Thomasin, and Abel Kelly.
1796, March 31, Schacks, Mary, and Capt. Jeremiah Church.
1797, Nov.   6, Schuyler, Mary, and John Nicholson.
1789, Feb.   3, Scollar, Hannah, and Thomas Parsons.
1793, May   18, Scott, Ann, and Daniel Shoemaker.
1789, July   15, Scott, Elizabeth, and Hugh McLaughlin.
1794, Sept. 25, Scott, John, and Christiana*Campbell.
1774, March 31, Scott, Mary, and John Gardner.
1788, June   11, Scott, Reuben, and Rachel Van Horne.
1796, March 22, Scurrâh, Adam, and Ann Scaise.
1771, Feb.   24, Search, Thomas, and Catherine Coon.
1793, April 27, Servoss, John, and Elizabeth Kinsey.
1797, July   9, Sessford, John, and Martha Kerr.
1774, Feb.   3, Sewell, Hannah, and Benjamin Gibbs.
1785, Jan.   20, Shakespear, David, and Elizabeth Davis.
1790, March 14, Shallcross, Thomas, and Mary Alberger.
1780, Feb.   2, Shannon, James, and Rosanna Harvey.
1794, May   31, Sharp, John, and Sarah Baker.
1775, Jan.   25, Sharp, Mary, and Daniel Huff.
1799, May   8, Sharp, Robert, and Charlotte Thompson.
1801, March 22, Sharpnack, John, and Margaret Haines.
1801, April 22, Shaw, George Roberts, and Mary Johnson.
1794, Sept.   9, Shaw, Lemuel, and Rebecca Davis.
1794, May   8, Shaw, Robert, and Mary Graham.
1801, Sept. 10, Sheaff, Mary, and Moses Taylor.
1765, Jan.   22, Shecan, Mary, and John Kerr.
1791, April 18, Shee, Mary, and John Martin.
1791, Oct.   9, Sheitz, Elizabeth, and Jacob Holgat.
1795, Dec.   10, Shellenger, Sarah, and Jeremiah Bennet.
1792, March 29, Shellmire, Mary, and James Frampton.
1786, Nov.   7, Shephard, Nathan, and Martha Mulford.
1790, Jan.   24, Shephard, Sarah, and Peter Bennard.
1794, Oct.   2, Shepherd, Ann, and William Brown.

1798, Nov. 15, Sheppard, Catherine. and Barzillai Gardner.
1769, July   4, Sherald, Amy, and Atwood Cowman.
1765, April 22, Shewell, Joseph, and Esther Kinnersley.
1796, March 30, Shewell, Robert, and Sarah Dickinson.
1764, Jan.   15, Shewell, Robert, and Sarah Gallows.
1789, May   2, Shewell, Sallows, and Mary Shields.
1789, May   2, Shields, Mary, and Sallows Shewell.
1796, Sept. 10, Shields, Rebecca, and Stephen C. Ustick.
1796, Oct.   10, Shields, Robert, and Mary Jackson.
1795, June   27, Shippen, William, and Ann Ashmead.
1790, July   1, Shiver, Philip, and Ann Bevans.
1802, Nov.   28, Shives, Mary, and Byard Ernest.
1793, May   18, Shoemaker, Daniel, and Ann Scott.
1799, Aug.   10, Shoemaker, Susannah, and Philip Hains.
1795, March 19, Shoemaker, Thomas, and Ann Massey.
1798, July   15, Shubart, Sarah, and James Hutchinson.
1794, June   5, Shubert, Elizabeth, and Samuel Hergesheimer.
1790, Nov.   2, Siddons, Eleanor, and John Armitage.
1769, July   20, Siddons, William, and Ann Ogden.
1765, Oct.   13, Simmons, Leeson, and Hannah Watkins.
1798, June   3, Simpson, Bowman, and Clarissa Cashaday.
1794, July   4, Simpson, Mary, and James Campbell.
1778, April 4, Sims, Thomas, and Jane Kelly.
1771, May   3, Singleton, Elizabeth, and Rev. Morgan Edwards.
1792, May   31, Singleton, Sarah, and Wheeler Meredith.
1794, April 24, Sink, Mary, and William Davis.
1790, March 23, Skadan, Lydia, and John Kaign.
1799, July   20, Skellenger, Ann, and William Peiffer.
1796, Nov.   8, Slater, Christiana, and Lawrence Ludenburgh.
1802, Sept. 18, Sloan, James W., and Ann Williamson.
1790, Nov.   7, Smith, David, and Ann McDougall.
1798, July   3, Smith, Elizabeth, and Benjamin Gardner.
1796, Nov.   5, Smith, Grace Elizabeth, and Philip Jones.
1799, Dec.   20, Smith, Henry, and Jane Roberts.
1800, July   2, Smith, Henry, and Catha. Carey.
1793, Sept. 12, Smith, Jannet, and Alexander Watson.
—— —— —, Smith, John, and Abigal Gilbert.
1787, Aug.   6, Smith, John, and Ann Wall.
1794, June   21, Smith, Jonathan, and Margaret McCoreal.
1770, Nov.   19, Smith, Judith, and Anthony Crawford.
1799, Dec.   5, Smith, Lydia, and William Minster.
1794, June   19, Smith, Maria, and John Miller.
1794, Aug.   14, Smith, Martha, and Asa Saul.
1790, Oct.   7, Smith, Mary, and Samuel Davis, Jun.
1797, Jan.   25, Smith, Mathias, and Elizabeth Roberts.
1795, Jan.   24, Smith, Thomas, and Elizabeth Smithson.

1786, Feb. 21, Smith, Rebecca, and William Jeickways,
1798, Nov. 13, Smith, Richard E., and Hannah Hiltzheimer.
1797, Jan. 24, Smith, Rowland, and Mary Morris.
1795, Jan. 24, Smithson, Elizabeth, and Thomas Smith.
1787, Dec. 18, Smock, Robert, and Ann Pennington.
1788, July   8, Snowden, George, and Sophia Ritter.
1799, April 1, Snyder, Mary, and James Bartlett.
1786, May   8, Soley, Obadiah, and Mary Wood.
1799, July. 1, Souder, Thomas Mifflin, and Jane Keen.
1800, Dec. 18, Speakman, Esther, and Thomas Davis.
1794, March 20, Spears, Eliza, and Joseph Griffith.
1799, March 26, Speechy, Prudense, and Philip Taylor.
1800, Feb. 23, Speelman, John, and Elizabeth Cook.
1764, Nov. 10, Spicer, Sylvia, and Samuel Jones.
1786, Jan. 11, Spong, James, and Hannah Jenkins.
1783, July 29, Spring, Lethea, and Joseph Bartholomew.
1791, Dec. 10, Spring, Marshall, and Mary Binney.
1797, Nov.   5, Springer, Levi, and Elizabeth Moore.
1789, Feb.   3, Springer, Margaret, and Jacob Fry.
1785, Aug.   2, Sprong, Elizabeth, and Stephen Page.
1802, Dec. 28, Sprogell, Lodowick, and Margaret Jenkins.
1794, May   10, Spunninberger, Elizabeth, and William Marpole.
1763, Feb.   3, Squirrell, Esther, and Thomas Carpenter.
1786, Sept. 21, Stackhouse, Martha, and William Gosline.
1788, Oct.   2, Stancliff, Rev. John, and Sarah Parker.
1789, April 30, Standaland, Tacey, and William White.
1791, July 14, Starkey, John, and Joanna Milless.
1764, Dec.   1, Starr, Ann, and Jonathan Roberts.
1762, Nov. 27, Starr, John, and Rebecca Cassey.
1774, Sept. 5, Statton, Elizabeth, and Esaias Hunt.
1784, Oct. 18, Steed, Richard, and Lydia Gilbert.
1785, April 28, Steel, John, and Mary Riffett.
1785, March 24, Steel, Elizabeth, and Davis Reed.
1769, Feb.   7, Stephens, Walter, and Mary Chisty.
1771, Nov. 12, Steward, Rachel, and John Gregory.
1794, Oct. 16, Stewart, Elizabeth, and Aaron Boker.
1795, April 2, Stewart, Lydia, and Jacob Edwards.
1780, Nov. 22, Stiles, Reuben, and Elizabeth Murell.
1794, Sept. 27, Stiles, Sarah, and Jacob Cheeseman.
1793, Aug. 25, Stille, Francis, and Julia Baldesquy.
1799, Oct. 16, Stirk, Frances, and Samuel Reed.
1775, May   4, Stockford, Elizabeth, and William Kinnard.
1796, Jan. 31, Stockton, Mary, and Thomas Inskeep.
1784, Feb. 18, Stockton, Samuel, and Ann Wood.
1796, Sept. 29, Stocksberry, Elizabeth, and Charles Eagin.
1797, Nov.   9, Stokely, Nathaniel, and Sarah Wigens.

1794, May   6, Stone, Anthony, and Eleanor Wilson.
1765, May   15, Stoneburner, Hester, and William Woodrow.
1774, Dec.   21, Stotz, Martha, and Joseph Wright.
1795, April   20, Stout, Jun., George, and Ann Robinson.
1801, June   18, Streaper, Mary, and Titus Yerkes.
1779, April   20, Street, James, and Elizabeth Hooversack.
1793, July   28, Street, Lewaza, and Benjamin Leodor.
1785, Nov.   24, Street, Mary, and Richard Wall.
1772, June   11, Street, Mary, and Robert Hamilton.
1796, Sept.   8, Strong, Dr. John, and Rebecca Young.
1797, April   30, Stroop, Catherine, and Samuel Trivit.
1797, Nov.   12, Stroop, Margaret, and Isaac Attmore.
1795, Feb.   19, Stuard, William, and Margaret Kuhnsman.
1774, June   16, Stuart, James, and Ann Guy, (widow.)
1794, May   1, Stuart, Jane, and Samuel Crowell.
1793, Jan.   23, Stuart, Sarah, and Nimrod Long.
1796, Nov.   12, Sturgis, Elizabeth, and John Pritner.
1773, April   17, Sturgis, Nathan, and Catharine Phillips.
1788, Jan.   9, Summers, Margaret, and John Hart.
1798, Nov.   17, Suplee, Silas, and Maria Berger.
1794, June   12, Sutter, Jun. Daniel, and Polly Odenheimer.
1793, June   13, Sutter, Peter, and Sarah Caruthers.
1794, Aug.   30, Sutton, Asa, and Elizabeth Larzalere.
1773, April   8, Swanson, Hannah, and James Fowler.
1790, Nov.   15, Sweeten, Benjamin, and Elizabeth Coates.
1785, Feb.   11, Sweetman, George, and Kezia Britton.
1796, Oct.   15, Symonds, Jonas, and Elizabeth Miller.
1796, March   6, Tage, Benjamin, and Mary Chestnutwood.
1784, July   15, Talbert, Samuel, and Hannah Ackley.
1786, Sept.   28, Talbert, Tabitha, and Richard Wells.
1795, May   14, Talman, Mary, and Talman Pennock.
1764, Aug.   2, Tarton, Martha, and Andrew Vandike.
1763, June   23, Taylor, Abigail, and Gerrard Vanhorn.
1774, Jan.   20, Taylor, Elizabeth, and Edward McVaugh.
1764, Oct.   10, Taylor, Israel, and Susanna Daugherty.
1789, June   10, Taylor, Jane, and Charles Dougherty.
1792, Nov.   24, Taylor, John, and Susannah Grice.
1796, March   9, Taylor, Martha, and William Tomlinson.
1776, June   21, Taylor, Mary, and Robert Willson.
1801, Sept.   10, Taylor, Moses, and Mary Sheaff.
1799, March   26, Taylor, Philip, and Prudense Speechy.
1800, Sept.   27, Taylor, Robert, and Rachel Roney.
1785, May   27, Taylor, Sarah, and Peter Reinhard.
1781, Feb.   3, Ten Eyck, Andrew, and Elizabeth Lloyd.
1788, Aug.   25, Terry, John, and Rebecca Hegeman.
1796, May   19, Test, Samuel, and Sarah Maxwell.

1790, Dec. 22, Thackera, Ann, and Daniel McPherson.
1800, April 17, Thatcher, Andrew, and Mary Dickinson.
1801, July 9, Thatcher, Joseph, and Sarah Bollen.
1776, May 23, Thaw, Benjamin, and Hannah Engle.
1794, April 2, Thomas, Amos, and Martha Thomas.
1795, June 25, Thomas, Ann, and Robert McKoy.
1775, April 18, Thomas, Ann, and Thomas Thomas.
1792, July 31, Thomas, Eber, and Zillah Thomas.
1774, Feb. 22, Thomas, Eleanor, and Edward Mathew.
1794, April 16, Thomas, George, and Hannah Roberts.
1772, April 10, Thomas, James, and Mary Lewis.
1785, April 7, Thomas, Jonah, and Eunice Conroe.
1794, April 2, Thomas, Martha, and Amos Thomas.
1786, May 25, Thomas, Martin, and Rebecca Esty.
1787, June 30, Thomas, Mary, and Thomas Ross.
1765, Jan. 3, Thomas, Mary, and William Powell.
1794, March 1, Thomas, Mary, and David Williams.
1793, Nov. 26, Thomas, Mary, and James Milligan.
1785, Nov. 29, Thomas, Nathan, and Anne Francis.
1764, Dec. 9, Thomas, Rachel, and Hugh Fulton.
1801, April 22, Thomas, Rachel, and William Atkins.
1796, June 5, Thomas, Richard, and Elizabeth Parry.
1775, April 18, Thomas, Thomas, and Ann Thomas.
1792, July 31, Thomas, Zillah, and Eber Thomas.
1782, April 29, Thompson, Benjamin, and Rachel Howell.
1799, May 8, Thompson, Charlotte, and Robert Sharp.
1794, July 22, Thompson, David, and Elizabeth Wright.
1790, July 18, Thompson, David, and Margaret Cowgill.
1795, Aug. 9, Thompson, Capt. John, and Elizabeth McGragar.
1799, April 9, Thompson, Mark, and Ann McCarsnan.
1791, Sept. 3, Thompson, Sarah, and Jonathan Moore.
1788, May 29, Thompson, Thomas, and Amy Jones.
1800, Nov. 24, Thompson, William, and Margaret White.
1762, Dec. 28, Thomson, David, and Mary Hutchinson.
1796, Oct. 23, Thomson, Rebecca, and Levi Hughes.
1798, June 14, Thomson, William, and Jenny Wilson.
1770, May 10, Thorn, Abigal, and Robert Webber.
1795, March 3, Thornburgh, Elizabeth, and Thomas Evans.
1775, Oct. 11, Thornburn, Margaret, and Philip Henry.
1773, Jan. 7, Thorne, Aaron, and Elizabeth Van.
1794, Oct. 5, Till, Mary, and Samuel Robenson.
1794, Dec. 14, Todd, Isabella, and Joseph Barber.
1762, May 4, Todd, Mary, and John Finley.
1795, May 21, Tomkins, Ann, and William Mason.
1788, March 28, Tomkins, Elizabeth, and Herman Yercas.
1764, March 27, Tomkins, John, and Abigal Gilbert.

1795, Nov.   19, Tomkins, Thomas, and Sarah Preston.
1794, May   11, Tomlinson, Richard, and Elizabeth Wheldon.
1796, March   9, Tomlinson, William, and Martha Taylor.
1792, Nov.   21, Town, Mary, and Cornelius Trimnell.
1785, Oct.   12, Towne, Elizabeth, and John Adams.
1788, April   29, Towne, Henry, and Sarah Gutrage.
1793, April   25, Towne, Richard, and Sophia Freeman.
1774, Jan.   13, Trapell, Mary, and John Rogers.
1793, Sept.   18, Trebolet, Jacob, and Catherine Plain.
1794, June   20, Tree, John, and Rebecca Harn.
1791, Dec.   8, Trenchard, Elizabeth, and John Vallance.
1800, Feb.   18, Trimble, Lewis, and Sarah Holland.
1792, Nov.   21, Trimnell, Cornelius, and Mary Town.
1797, April   30, Trivit, Samuel, and Catherine Stroop.
1771, April   28, Tuckenmiller, Charles, and Susannah Sadler.
1785, Nov.   10, Tucker, John, and Leah Morris.
1798, Dec.   15, Tuckness, Luke, and Susan Lloyd.
1773, Jan.   28, Tufft, Alice, and John Hickey.
1764, May   10, Turk, John, and Ann Davis.
1795, Aug.   8, Turner, John, and Mary Blyth.
1789, Oct.   3, Turner, Mary, and Thomas Holmes.
1772, July   9, Turner, William, and Abigail Anthony.
1799, Dec.   10, Tussey, Sarah, and Jesse McCall.
1802, July   29, Tyson, Jacob, and Susannah Evans.
1769, Aug.   21, Tyson, Richard, and Ann Atwell.
1796, Dec.   19, Ustick, Jane, and Edward Harris.
1796, May   25, Ustick, Sarah, and John Lang.
1796, Sept.   10, Ustick, Stephen C., and Rebecca Shields.
1765, Jan.   22, Vahan, Mary, and George Daullis.
1800, July   4, Valens, Mary, and John Aborn.
1791, Dec.   8, Vallance, John, and Elizabeth Trenchard.
1796, Nov.   14, Vallens, Robert Bell, and Jane Wilson.
1773, Jan.   7, Van, Elizabeth, and Aaron Thorne.
1801, Oct.   8, Van Alstyne, Mathew, and Charlotte Haight.
1782, July   11, VanBurkelow, Jacob, and Catherine Renford.
1803, Jan.   20, Vandegrist, Jane, and John Woodward.
1801, Nov.   10, Vandergrist, William, and Christener Monington.
1795, March 22, Vanderslice, George, and Elizabeth Cunnings.
1764, Aug.   2, Vandike, Andrew, and Martha Tarton.
1763, June   23, Vanhorn, Gerrard, and Abigal Taylor.
1785, March 26, VanHorne, Isaac, and Dorothy Marple.
1788, June   11, VanHorne, Rachel, and Reuben Scott.
1791, Aug.   15, Vanneman, Frederick, and Mary Crocket.
1791, April   13, Vanse, Arthur, and Mary Moore.
1785, May   19, VanSolingen, Sarah, and Gregory Melvin.
1796, May   8, Vanwinkle, Tacey, and Mathew Patton.

1763, Feb. 19, Vaughan, Ann, and Charles Lyon.
1770, Jan. 21, Vernon, Edward, and Mary Mathers.
1791, May 31, Vernon, Ruth, and John Folwell.
1798, Dec. 31, Viall, Patience, and Jacob Heston.
1761, Aug. 3, Vickers, Mary, and William Pennington.
1800, May 29, Vineyard, William, and Catherine Brusstar.
1801, June 25, Vinyard, Henrieth, and Joseph Hill.
1783, Dec. 25, Vogels, Gerard, and Elizabeth Moulder.
1793, Nov. 12, Vollens, Margaret, and William Holmes.
1793, Nov. 12, Vollens, Matthew, and Mary Rowen.
1763, Aug. 10, Vore, Gideon, and Mary Adams.
1763, Aug. 13, Wade, James, and Rebecca Weaver.
1790, Sept. 7, Wagner, Mary, and John Phileno.
1797, July 22, Waidner, Daniel, and Jane Anderson,
1798, May 16, Walbridge, Rufus, and Judith Yocum.
1792, Aug. 30, Walker, James, and Margaret Prodly.
1795, May 16, Walker, Mary, and Joseph Johnson.
1786, June 1, Walker, William, and Ruth Gibbons.
1787, Aug. 6, Wall, Ann, and John Smith.
1785, Nov. 24, Wall, Richard, and Mary Street.
1780, Dec. 14, Wallace, Martha, and William Rush.
1799, April 18, Wallace, Martha, and William Copeland.
1802, May 9, Wallace, Mary, and William Richers.
1798, Feb. 10, Wallace, Sarah, and Williamson Nutters.
1790, Jan. 7, Wallington, Mary, and Charles Oakford.
1763, Dec. 17, Wallis, Mary, and Jacob Kennard.
1780, Oct. 2, Walsh, Patrick, and Catherine May.
1795, May 7, Walter, Jacob, and Ann Roberts.
1793, July 7, Walter, Jonathan, and Jane Price.
1799, Jan. 2, Walter, Peter W., and Mary Reiley.
1765, Oct. 30, Walter, Thomas, and Rebecca Pennel.
1788, March 12, Walters, Catherine, and Peter May.
1791, Sept. 7, Walters, Margaret, and John Colbeirt.
1787, July 1, Walters, Susannah, and Hiram Cochran.
1799, May 21, Walton, Nathaniel, and Elizabeth Brelsford.
1764, Jan. 19, Walton, Samuel, and Elizabeth Willis.
1779, Sept. 15, Ward, Judith, and David Jones.
1764, Nov. 21, Ward, Mary, and Thomas Willson.
1799, March 10, Ward, William, and Elizabeth Grible.
1795, Nov. 15, Ware, Ann, and John Allen.
1798, June 18, Warner, Ichabod, and Ruth Howard.
1795, April 23, Warner, Rachel, and Joseph Innes.
1781, June 16, Warner, Rebecca, and Stephanus Haworth.
1791, April 28, Warnick, William, and Martha Pile.
1795, April 16, Warren, Joseph, and Sarah Powell.
1774, Oct. 6, Waterman, Phineas, and Mary Johnston.

1772, Dec.   8, Waterman, Thomas, and Hanna Inglis.
1763, Sept.   8, Waters, Peter, and Ann Fust.
1799, Feb.   28, Watkins, Ann, and James Houston.
1762, Feb.   17, Watkins, James, and Comfort Griffin.
1762, Sept.   1, Watkins, Joseph, and Alleneor Pratt.
1787, Aug.   23, Watkins, Thomas, and Ruth Howell.
1793, Sept.   12, Watson, Alexander, and Jannet Smith.
1765, May   11, Watson, John, and Mary Carpenter.
1762, Nov.   30, Watts, John, and Rachel Watts.
1762, Nov.   30, Watts, Rachel, and John Watts.
1792, Dec.   19, Wayne, Thomas, and Agnes Jones.
1792, May   12, Weatherby, Thomas, and Mary Hall.
1790, Sept.   2, Weathery, Rachel, and Jeremiah Boor.
1800, Sept.   27, Weaver, Elizabeth, and John Brooks.
1796, Dec.   11, Weaver, Henry, and Mary Wiley.
1777, March   17, Weaver, Katherine, and James Bole.
1800, May   20, Weaver, Mary, and Thomas Jenkins.
1763, Aug.   13, Weaver, Rebecca, and James Wade.
1794, Nov.   20, Webb, Sarah, and Timothy Banger.
1794, Aug.   13, Webb, Capt Silas, and Elizabeth Hener.
1793, May   25, Webb, Simon, and Elizabeth Fry.
1794, Dec.   25, Webb, Thomas, and Rachel Cleland.
1770, May   10, Webber, Robert, and Abigail Thorn.
1765, April   7, Weed, Elijah, and Mary Mitchell.
1786, March   30, Weeks, Stephen, and Sarah Ower.
1762, Aug.   28, Weeton, Amos, and Catherine Lisha.
1791, July   3, Weldon, Elizabeth, and Ludwig Gloss.
1795, Feb.   26, Weldon, Margaret, and Isaac Chadwick.
1802, Aug.   2, Welker, John, and Rachel Wright.
1802, Sept.   18, Williamson, Ann, and James W. Sloan.
1762, Dec.   26, Wells, Mary, and James Moreton.
1799, April   1, Wells, Miriam, and Isaac Moore.
1773, May   19, Wells, Peter, and Jemima Davis.
1786, Sept.   28, Wells, Richard, and Tabitha Talbert.
1799, July   14, Wells, Thomas, and Mary Iley.
1797, May   2, Welsh, Patrick, and Dorotha Kennedy.
1774, Sept.   15, Wentz, Abraham, and Sophia Wentz.
1766, April   28, Wentz, Elizabeth, and John Coleston.
1714, Oct.   18, Wentz, Hannah, and Benjamin Marclay.
1774, Sept.   15, Wentz, Sophia, and Abraham Wentz.
1785, April   22, Wessel, Rebecca, and Peter Keen.
1797, June   3, West, William, and Elizabeth Crawford.
1788, Oct.   25, Westcott, Mary, and Andrew Adgate.
1794, May   10, Wetherby, Mary, and Benjamin Lee.
1800, Sept.   2, Wharry, Sarah, and Peter Harvy.
1800, Aug.   7, Whartanby, Susannah, and Robert Edwards.
1799, July   13, Whartnaby, Joseph, and Catharine Richardson.

1793, Oct. 17, Wharton, Benjamin H., and Jane Brown.
1795, Jan. 15, Wheeler, John, and Margaret Hughes.
1794, May 11, Wheldon, Elizabeth, and Richard Tomlinson.
1774, Aug. 29, Whitaker, Richard, and Rachel Bowen.
1795, Nov. 12, White, Anna, and Matthias Birch.
1793, June 23, White, Christiana, and Henry Plane.
1798, Dec. 28, White, Elizabeth, and Bartholomew Geoghegan.
1796, June 23, White, Esther, and James Curwin.
1798, March 15, White, Isabella, and George Wilson.
1782, Oct. 10, White, Joseph, and Deborah McGannon.
1761, Oct. 31, White, Lydia, and Henry Forst.
1800, Nov. 24, White, Margaret, and William Thompson.
1789, April 30, White William, and Tacey Standeland.
1794, Feb. 2, Whitesides, Alexander, and Mary Jackway.
1772, July 11, Whitsall, Sarah, and John Murdock.
1797, Nov. 9, Wigens, Sarah, and Nathaniel Stockely.
1802, Dec. 25, Wigglesworth, John, and Mary Dunkarly.
1783, April 11, Wilday, Jane, and Joseph Hays.
1794, Sept. 25, Wiley, Abel, and Elizabeth Engle.
1784. May 1, Wiley, Ewing, and Catherine Bayne.
1796, Dec. 11. Wiley, Mary, and Henry Weaver.
1799, Nov. 16, Wiley, Nathaniel, and Hannah Wood.
1786, Feb. 9, Willdee, Sarah, and John Gullen.
1794, March 1, Williams, David, and Mary Thomas.
1790, Aug. 1, Williams, Elizabeth, and Thomas Bible.
1784, June 15, Williams, Hannah, and John Burn.
1788, June 8, Williams, Harding, and Rebecca Dickinson.
1770, Dec. 11, Williams, Isaac, and Elizabeth Mettlen.
1793, Nov. 23, Williams, Isaac, and Ruth Ozborne.
1769, Jan. 4, Williams, John, and Hester John.
1800, March 13, Williams, John, and Ann Downing.
1766, Nov. 5, Williams, Kissander, and Paul McCarty.
1788, Jan. 24, Williams, Margaret, and Joseph Keen.
1792, June 23, Williams, Mary, and George Pfeiffer.
1775, Oct. 25, Williams, Richard, and Sarah Morgan.
1789, April 30, Williams, Thomas, and Catherine Hunter.
1794, Nov. 2, Williamson, Jesse, and Sarah Williamson.
1784, Nov. 11, Williamson, John, and Jane Pringle.
1787, April 25, Williamson, Kitty, and Nathaniel Brown.
1794, June 1, Williamson, Samuel, and Maria Evans.
1794, Nov. 2, Williamson, Sarah, and Jesse Williamson.
1764, Jan. 19, Willis, Elizabeth, and Samuel Walton.
1786, Oct. 1, Willis, Thomas, and Hannah Charlesworth.
1799, April 9, Wills, Rebecca, and William Gabb.
1764, March 3, Willson, Charles, and Rebecca Freak.
1787, Sept. 23, Willson, Hannah, and Andrew Maines.

1776, June   21, Willson, Robert, and Mary Taylor.
1764, Nov.   21, Willson, Thomas, and Mary Ward.
1794, June   23, Wilson, Ann, and Daniel McCoy.
1794, May   14, Wilson, Ann, and Howar l Ogle.
1790, May   9, Wilson, Charles, and Ann Mosman.
1794, May   6, Wilson, Eleanor, and Anthony Stone.
1795, Jan.   24, Wilson, Eleanor, and William Doughty.
1785, March 29, Wilson, Elias, and Ruth Wright.
1794, Oct.   1, Wilson, Elizabeth, and George Graham.
1798, March 15, Wilson, George, and Isabella White.
1796, Nov.   14, Wilson, Jane, and Robert Bell Vallens.
1798, June   14, Wilson, Jenny, and William Thomson.
1794, Nov.   29, Wilson, Lucy, and William Bennett.
1796, June   —, Wiltbank, Jane, and Samuel Carpenter.
1790, Nov.   30, Wise, Catherine, and Jacob Keyser.
1782, Feb.   5, Winbert, Felix, and Allathea Garrison.
1784, Oct.   10, Winchester, Rev. Elhanon, and Mary Knowles.
1794, Feb.   20, Wing, Frederick, and Sarah Page.
1800, Nov.   16, Winner, Alice, and John Winner.
1800, Nov.   16, Winner, John, and Alice Winner.
1792, Feb.   22, Winter, Elizabeth, and John Engle.
1761, Feb.   16, Wister, Catherine, and Samuel Miles.
1766, Dec.   25, Witten, Margaret, and Dennis Downing.
1794, June   5, Wolfington, Robert, and Catherine Kidd.
1773, Feb.   13, Wolohon, John, and Sarah Hammett.
1799, June   6, Wolverton, Amey, and Benjamin Free.
1784, Feb.   18, Wood, Ann, and Samuel Stockton.
1799, Nov.   16, Wood, Hannah, and Nathaniel Wiley.
1766, Aug.   13, Wood, Jehu, and Mary Kemsey.
1798, Aug.   12, Wood, Joseph, and Jane McCleland.
1786, May   8, Wood, Mary, and Obadiah Soley.
1781, July   15, Wood, Mary, and John Childs.
1795, Jan.   31, Wood, Mary, and William Middleton.
1803, April   10, Wood, Prudense, and James Murphy.
1783, Jan.   2, Wood, Rachel, and William Moore.
1792, March 20, Wood, Robert, and Elizabeth Lyle.
1791, April   27, Wood, Ruth, and Jeremiah Church.
1765, March 25, Wood, Thomas, and Elizabeth Campbell.
1794, March 18, Woodard, Ann, and Joseph Clark.
1769, May   4, Woodbridge, Samuel, and Sarah Bearden.
1786, July   10, Woodman, Joseph, and Lydia Foster.
1777, May   25, Woodrow, Mary, and Dr. Barnabas Binney.
1765, May   15, Woodrow, William, and Hester Stoneburner.
1794, March 6, Woods, Mary, and John Gisty.
1803, Jan.   20, Woodward, John, and Jane Vandegrist.
1767, Jan.   5, Woolf, Elizabeth, and John Robinson.

1792, Aug.   19, Woolard, Sarah, and John Bowker.
1794, Nov.   13, Workman, Rebecca, and Robert Clark.
1763, Feb.   19, Wright, Anthony, and Hannah Hobbs.
1794, July   22, Wright, Elizabeth, and David Thompson.
1774, Dec.   21, Wright, Joseph, and Martha Stotz.
1799, Aug.   3, Wright, Malcom, and Jane Patterson.
1802, Aug.   2, Wright, Rachel, and John Welker.
1785, March 29, Wright, Ruth, and Elias Wilson.
1763, May   12, Wrighter, Hannah, and Aaron Levering.
1788, March 28, Yercas, Herman, and Elizabeth Tomkins.
1770, April 14, Yerkes, Elizabeth, and John Huffdale.
1790, Oct.   20, Yerkes, Herman, and Margaret Long.
1801, June   18, Yerkes, Titus, and Mary Streaper.
1765, Jan.   2, Yocum, Eleanor, and John Inglis.
1798, May   16, Yocum, Judith, and Rufus Walbridge.
1765, Oct.   28, Yocum, Judith, and Jacob Rudolph.
1780, March 23, Yocum, Mary, and George Davis.
1799, Aug.   18, Youmans, James, and Frances Fox.
1796, Dec.   15, Young, John, and Mary Mathias.
1796, Sept.   8, Young, Rebecca, and Dr. John Strong.
1794, April 19, Young, Thomas, and Mary Dent.
1762, May   5, Young, William, and Rebecca Flower.
1790, Sept. 26, Zane, Ann, and David Jenkins.
1782, Dec.   17, Zane, Jonathan, and Hannah Jenkins.
1776, July   4, Zell, David, and Elizabeth Roberts.
1802, April 18, Zilley, Hannah, and Benjamin Brotherton.

MARRIAGE RECORD

OF

PAXTANG AND DERRY CHURCHES,

1741–1810.

PAXTANG AND DERRY CHURCHES.

1801, Feb. 11, Alden, Major Roger, and Eliza Carver.
1757, Feb. 11, Allen, Samuel, and Rebecca Smith.
1772, March —, Anderson, James, and Margaret Chambers.
1788, April 22, Anderson, James, and Esther Thom.
1787, Nov. 20, Augeer, Mary, and John Culbertson.
1783, Feb. 25, Auld, Sarah, and Joseph Green.
1809, Jan. 9, Awl, James, and Ann Stricker.
1773, Nov. 1, Ayres, Margaret, and William Forster.
1741, Aug. 13, Baker, Mary, and Rev. John Elder.
1786, Dec. 19, Beatty, Mary Brereton, and Patrick Murray.
1790, Feb. 5, Beatty, Nancy, and Samuel Hill.
1773, Oct. 14, Bell, John, and Martha Gilchrist.
1774, June 24, Bell, Samuel, and Ann Berryhill.
1774, June 24, Berryhill, Ann, and Samuel Bell.
1796, July 7, Bittner, Mr., and Mrs. Charlotte King.
1784, March 2, Boal, Robert, and Mary Wilson.
1781, March 1, Boyce, ———, and James Robinson.
1766, ——— —, Boyd, Joseph, and Elizabeth Wallace.
1777, April 8, Boyd, Margaret, and Joseph Wilson, of Derry.
1783, March 11, Boyd, Margaret, and Joseph Wilson.
1785, March 15, Boyd, Mary, and Robert Templeton.
1795, June 11, Boyd, Rachael, and William Hamilton.
1807, June 4, Boyd, William, and Martha Cowden.
1879, Sept. 14, Boyd, ———, and William Moore.
1796, May 19, Brice, Alexander, and Peggy Kearsley.
1772, Jan. 2, Brisban, Margaret, and James Rutherford.
1746, Nov. 6, Brown, James, and Eleanor Mordah.
1773, ——— —, Brown, Sarah, and John Graham.
1769, Oct. 19, Brown, William, and Sarah Semple.
1774, Oct. 7, Brunson, Barefoot, and Agnes White.
1810, July 5, Buchanan, Molly, and David Stewart.
1771, Sept. 24, Buck, Elijah, and ——— ———.
1785, Jan. 3, Buck, William, and Margaret Elliott.
1783, Feb. 27, Caldwell, Matthew, and Mary Pinkerton.
1786, April 11, Calhoun, David, and Eleanor King.

1773, —— —, Calhoun, Mary, and Alexander McCullom.
1772, April 1, Campbell, Ann, and Hugh Hamilton.
1777, Dec. 23, Carothers, Eleanor, and James Kyle.
1807, Oct. 31, Carson, Dinah, and John Rodgers.
1785, April 28, Carson, Elizabeth, and Alexander Wilson.
1748, June 16, Carson, James, and Mary Espy.
1801, Feb. 11, Carver, Eliza, and Major Roger Alden.
1786, June 13, Cathcart, Sarah, and Joseph Hutchinson.
1769, April 27, Cavet, James, and —— ——.
1800, March 19, Chambers, Benjn, and Grace Stewart.
1771, Dec. 5, Chambers, Maxwell, and Elizabeth ——.
1780, Jan. 13, Chesney, John, and —— ——.
1769, Dec. 14, Christy, William, and —— ——.
1790, Oct. 14, Clark, Charles, and Elizabeth Robinson.
1783, Aug. 7, Clark, John, and Mary Smith.
1775, April 13, Clark, William, and —— ——.
1807, June 23, Clendennin, Rachel, and Samuel Robinson.
1788, June 7, Cochran, Ann, and Sankey Dixon.
1769, Sept. 12, Cochran, Martha, and James Robinson.
1810, Jan. 11, Cochran, William, and Rachel Gross.
1776, March 14, Collier, Susan, and Samuel Rutherford.
1780, —— —, Cook, William, and Sarah Simpson.
1784, Oct. 21, Cowden, Elizabeth, and Robert Keys.
1777, March 20, Cowden, James, and Mary Crouch.
1807, June 4, Cowden, Martha, and William Boyd.
1777, Jan. 23, Cowden, Mary, and David Wray.
1799, March 23, Cox, Catharine, and Thomas Elder.
1778, Jan. 22, Crain, George, and —— ——.
1781, Nov. 13, Crouch, Elizabeth, and Matthew Gilchrist.
1777, March 20, Crouch, Mary, and James Cowden.
1787, Nov. 20, Culbertson, John, and Mary Augeer.
1774, April 14, Curry, Agnes, and William Curry.
1775, March 7, Curry, Daniel, and —— ——.
1774, April 14, Curry, William, and Agnes Curry.
1799, Feb. 10, Dentzell, John, Esq., and Jean Gilchrist.
1805, Jan. 8, Detweiler, David, and Mrs. Margaret Shriner.
1780, July 13, Dickey, James, and —— ——.
1778, Jan. 13, Dickey, John, and —— ——.
1772, Dec. 1, Dickey, William, and —— ——.
1777, Dec. 4, Dixon, George, and —— ——.
1774, March 15, Dixon, Isabella, and James McCormick.
1788, June 7, Dixon, Sankey, and Anna Cochran.
1779, Dec. 14, Donaldson, James, and —— ——.
1774, Jan. 9, Dugal, Mr., and Sarah Wilson.
1795, April 21, Dugal, Mr., and Jenny Hilton.
1779, Oct. 5, Duncan, Andrew, and—— ——.

1779, Sept. 23, Elder, Ann, and ——— ———.
1766, Dec. —, Elder, Eleanor, and John Hays.
1741, Aug. 13, Elder, Rev. John, and Mary Baker.
1751, Nov. 5, Elder, Rev. John, and Mary Simpson.
1788, Jan. 18, Elder, John, jr., and Sarah Kennedy.
1773, Sept. 16, Elder, Joshua, and ——— ———.
1783, May 27, Elder, Joshua, and ——— ———.
1784, May 18, Elder, Mary, and James Wilsen.
1798, Sept. 25, Elder, Mary, and John Forster.
1795, June 4, Elder, Michael, and Nancy McKinney.
1769, Feb. 7, Elder, Robert, and ——— ———.
1787, June 19, Elder, Sarah, and James Wallace.
1799, March 23, Elder, Thomas, and Catharine Cox.
1705, Jan. 3, Elliott, Margaret, and William Buck.
1748, June 16, Espy, Mary, and James Carson.
1807, June 2, Espy, William, and Susan Gray.
1744, Sept. 16, Findlay, John, and Elizabeth Harris.
1781, March 6, Fleming, John, and Nancy Neill.
1798, Sept. 25, Forster, John, and Mary Elder.
1800, April 24, Forster, Mary, and James Kirk.
1800, May 29, Forster, Peggy, and Reuben Lockhart.
1773, Nov. 1, Forster, William, and Margaret Ayres.
1784, Dec. 14, Foster, Robert, and Esther Renick.
1777, Nov. 4. Foster, Thomas, and Jane Young.
1796, Feb. 3, Foulke, Peggy, and William Priestly.
1807, Aug. 20, Fox, Margaret, and John Phillips.
1784, June 7, Fulk, Mary, and Christopher Irwin.
1785, March 7, Fullion, Jean, and James Smith Polk.
1770, ——— —, Fulton, Jean, and Moses Wallace.
1771, Nov. 5, Fulton, Benjamin, and ——— ———.
1774, June 16, Fulton, Grizel, and Alexander Wilson.
1772, April 30, Fulton, Isabella, and Hugh Wilson.
1780, Jan. 25, Fulton, Joseph, and ——— ———.
1744, June 14, Fulton, Richard, and Isabella McChesney.
1771, Dec. 12, Galbraith, Benjamin, and ——— ———.
1781, Feb. 27, Gilchrist, Eleanor, and Richard McGuire.
1799, Feb. 10, Gilchrist, Jean, and John Dentzell, Esq.
1771, Aug. 22, Gilchrist, John, and ——— ———.
1773, Oct. 14, Gilchrist, Martha, and John Bell.
1781, Nov. 13, Gilchrist, Matthew, and Elizabeth Crouch.
1784, Nov. 9, Gillmor, Moses, and Isabella Wallace.
1781, June 21, Glen, Elizabeth, and William Trousdale.
1774, Aug. 13, Gowdie, Jane, and John Ryan.
1774, June 15, Gowdie, John, and Abigail Ryan.
1776, Nov. 28, Goorly, John, and ——— ———.
1773, ——— —, Graham, John, and Sarah Brown.

1787, March 13, Graham, Martha, and David Ramsey.
1808, May   26, Graham, Mrs. Susan, and Gen. Michael Simpson.
1779, —— —, Gray, John, and Mary Robinson.
1779, Nov. 11, Gray, Joseph, and —— ——.
1807, June   2, Gray, Susan, and William Espy.
1805, Jan.   10, Green, Elizabeth, and Major John Lytle.
1783, Feb.   25, Green, Joseph, and Sarah Auld.
1810, Jan.   11, Gross, Rachel, and William Cochran.
1772, April   1, Hamilton, Hugh, and Ann Campbell.
1804, March 15, Hamilton, Mr. and Jane Hays.
1788, Sept. 27, Hamilton, Thomas, and Mary Kyle.
1795, June   11, Hamilton, William, and Rachel Boyd.
1744, Sept. 16, Harris, Elizabeth, and John Findlay.
1749, June   3, Harris, Esther, and William Plunket.
1752, June   1, Harris, Esther (Say), and William McChesney.
1768, June   2, Harris, James, and Mary Laird.
1779, May   27, Harris, James, and —— ——.
1749, May   3, Harris, John, jr., and Elizabeth McClure,
1774, Sept. 15, Harris, Mary, and William Maclay.
1752, Oct.   4, Harris, William Augustus, and Margaret Simpson.
1804, March 15, Hays, Jane, and Mr. Hamilton.
1810, Aug. 21, Hays, Jacob, and —— Thomas.
1766, Dec. —, Hays, John, and Eleanor Elder.
1810, Jan.   30, Hays, Patrick, and Margaret Mickey.
1807, Feb. 12, Hays, Sable, and William Larned.
1778, April 9, Hays, ——, and Archibald McAllister.
1787, Nov. 20, Henderson, James, and Margaret Wiggins.
1771, Jan.   24, Hetherington, Alexander, and —— ——.
1790, Feb.   5, Hill, Samuel, and Nancy Beatty.
1795, April 21, Hilton, Jenny, and Mr. Dugal.
1776, Dec. 10, Hodge, Isaac, and Margaret Wilson.
1781, April 12, Houston, Mary, and John Maxwell.
1786, June 13, Hutchinson, Joseph, and Sarah Cathcart.
1775, April 18, Hutchinson, Margaret. and Robert Moody.
1780, June 29, Hutchinson, Samuel, and Jane Rutherford.
1799, Nov. 26, Ingram, James, and Margaret Logan.
1784, June   7, Irwin, Christopher, and Mary Fulk.
1783, May   12, Jackson, Edward, and Margaret Lewis.
1776, July   3, Jenkins, Walter, and —— ——.
1774, March 31, Johnson, Alexander, and —— ——.
1802, Dec. 23, Johnson, Elizabeth, and Thomas McCallen.
1810, April 3, Johnston, Isaac, and Lydia Philson.
1771, Aug. 15, Johnson, James, and —— ——.
1804, Aug. 23, Johnson, James, and Polly Johnson.
1781, April 3, Johnson, Jane, and John Patterson.
1804, Aug. 23, Johnson, Polly, and James Johnson.

1808, March 24, Kean, Eleanor, and Dr. William Patton.
1774, ——— —, Kearsley, Samuel, and Sarah ———.
1796, May   19, Kearsley, Peggy, and Alexander Brice.
1796, Feb.   4, Kelso, John, and Sally Morton.
1757, May   23, Kelso, William, and ——— Simpson.
1775, Jan.   17, Kennedy, David, ——— ———.
1788, Jan.   18, Kennedy, Sarah, and John Elder, jr.
1808, April   28, Kerr, Rev. William, and Mary Wilson.
1784, Oct.   21, Keys, Robert, and Elizabeth Cowden.
1796, July   7, King, Mrs. Charlotte, and Mr. Bittner.
1786, April   11, King, Eleanor, and David Calhoun.
1778, Dec.   10, King, Mary, and James McKinzie.
1782, Dec.   31, King, Richard, and Mary Wylie.
1800, April   24, Kirk, James, and Mary Forster.
1777, Dec.   23, Kyle, James, and Eleanor Carothers.
1788, Sept.   27, Kyle, Mary, and Thomas Hamilton.
1808, May   24, Kucher, Jacob, and Jane Wray.
1799, March   9, Lanning, John, and Catharine Vought.
1778, Sept.   10, Laird, James, and ——— ———.
1788, Feb.   12, Laird, James, and Mary McFarland.
1791, April   4, Laird, John, and Rachel ———.
1768, June   2, Laird, Mary, and James Harris.
1807, Feb.   12, Larned, William, and Sable Hays.
1774, Sept.   29, Lerkin, John, and ——— ———.
1782, May   6, Lewis, John, and ——— ———.
1783, May   12, Lewis, Margaret, and Edward Jackson.
1800, May   29, Lochart, Reuben, and Peggy Forster.
1780, July   20, Lytle, John, and ——— ———.
1805, Jan.   10, Lytle, Major John, and Elizabeth Green.
1796, Sept.   22, Lytle, Samuel, and Nancy Robinson.
1773, Nov.   10, Maclay, Samuel, and Elizabeth Plumket.
1774, Sept.   15, Maclay, William, and Mary Harris.
1778, April   9, McAllister, Archibald, and ——— Hays.
1776, Jan.   25, McArthur, Barbara, and James Walker.
1807, Aug.   11, McCabe, Mary, and John McElrath.
1802, Dec.   23, McCallen, Thomas, and Elizabeth Johnson.
1744, June   14, McChesney, Isabella, and Richard Fulton.
1752, June   1, McChesney, William, and Esther (Say) Harris.
1783, Jan.   23, McCleaster, James, and Sarah Roan.
1775, Jan.   31, McClure, Andrew, and ——— ———.
1749, May   3, McClure, Elizabeth, and John Harris, jr.
1782, Aug.   8, McClure, Francis, and ——— ———.
1779, Aug.   3, McClure, Joseph, and ——— ———.
1777, March 23, McClure, Richard, and ——— ———.
1797, April   6, McCord, Flora, and John Morrison, Esq.
1781, Dec.   11, McCord, Samuel, and Martha McCormick.

1774, March 15, McCormick, James, and Isabella Dixon.
1781, Dec.   11, McCormick, Martha, and Samuel McCord.
1784, March 29, McCormick, William, and Grizel Porter.
1773, —— —, McCullom, Alexander, and Mary Calhoun.
1784, June   3, McDonald, John, and Lydia Sturgeon.
1787, May   1, McElhenny, William, and Elizabeth McNeal.
1807, Aug.   11, McElrath, John, and Mary McCabe.
1772, May   7, McFadden, James, and —— ——.
1788, March 11, McFarland, Elizabeth, and Joseph Sawyer.
1788, Feb.   12, McFarland, Mary, and James Laird.
1781, Feb.   27, McGuire, Richard, and Eleanor Gilchrist.
1778, June   4, McHadden, William, and —— ——.
1782, April   8, McHargue, Margaret, and Hugh Ramsey.
1795, June   4, McKinney, Nancy, and Michael Elder.
1778, Dec.   10, McKinzie, James, and Mary King.
1108, May   22, McNair, Archibald, and Polly Miller.
1771, May   9, McNair, Thomas, and Ann Maria Wallace.
1776, May   7, McNamara, James, and —— ——.
1787, May   1, McNeal, Elizabeth, and William McElhenny.
1779, April 12, McQuown, (McEwen,) John, and —— ——.
1779, Sept. 23, McTeer, Samuel, and —— Quigley.
1781, April 12, Maxwell, John, and Mary Houston.
1770, —— —, Maxwell, Margaret, and James Monteith.
1779, April 15, Means, Adam, and —— ——.
1784, April 15, Meloy, Ann, and George Williams.
1810, Jan.   30, Mickey, Margaret, and Patrick Hays.
1810, May   22, Miller, Polly, and Archibald McNair.
1776, April 25, Miller, Thomas, and —— ——.
1787, April   3, Mitchel, David, and Susanna Wilson.
1803, Feb.   10, Mitchel, Mary, and Thomas Watson.
1770, —— —, Montieth, James, and Margaret Maxwell.
1771, May   30, Montgomery, James, and —— ——.
1775, April 18, Moody, Robert, and Margaret Hutchison.
1746, Nov.   6, Mordah, Eleanor, and James Brown.
1793, March 7, Moore, Anna, and Thomas Smith.
1796, June   7, Moore, Frances, and James Russell.
1779, Sept. 14, Moore, William, and —— Boyd.
1808, April   4, Moorhead, Col. Thomas, and Mrs. Jean Wilson.
1797, April   6, Morrison, John, Esq., and Flora McCord.
1796, Feb.   4, Morton, Sally, and John Kelso.
1776, May   7, Murray, Margaret, and John Simpson.
1786, Dec.   19, Murray, Patrick, and Mary Brereton Beatty.
1781, March 6, Neill, Nancy, and John Fleming.
1804, April 22, Orth, Peggy, and Thomas Peacock.
1762, —— —, Park, Margaret, and John Rutherford.
1781, April   3, Patterson, John, and Jane Johnston.

1776, Oct. 15, Patton, Samuel, and —— ——.
1808, March 24, Patton, Dr. William, and Eleanor Kean.
1804, April 22, Peacock, Thomas, and Peggy Orth.
1807, Aug. 20, Phillips, John, and Margaret Fox.
1810, April 3, Philson, Lydia, and Isaac Johnston.
1777, April 22, Pinkerton, David, and —— ——.
1783, Feb. 27, Pinkerton, Mary, and Matthew Caldwell.
1773, Nov. 10, Plunket, Elizabeth, and Samuel Maclay.
1749, June 3, Plunket, William, and Esther Harris.'
1785, March 7, Polk, James Smith, and Jean Fullion.
1784, March 29, Porter, Grizel, and William McCormick.
1796, Feb. 3, Priestley, William, and Peggy Foulke.
1779, Sept. 23, Quigley, ——, and Samuel McTeer.
1774, April 21, Ramsey, David, and —— ——.
1787, March 13, Ramsey, David, and Martha Graham.
1782, April 8, Ramsey, Hugh, and Margaret McHargue.
1782, March 31, Reid, James, and —— ——.
1769, Feb. 16, Reid, John, and —— ——.
1771, July 15, Reid, Thomas, and Mary West.
1784, Dec. 14, Renick, Esther, and Robert Foster.
1775, Dec. 19, Renick, Martha, and William Swan.
1771, June 27, Rhea, Robert, and —— ——.
1783, Jan. 23, Roan, Sarah, and James McCleaster.
1803, Feb. 16, Roberts, Daniel, and Polly Roberts.
1803, Feb. 16, Roberts, Polly, and Daniel Roberts.
1775, Nov. 16, Robinson, Andrew, and —— ——.
1790, Oct. 14, Robinson, Elizabeth, and Charles Clark.
1769, Sept. 12, Robinson, James, and Martha Cochran.
1781, March 1, Robinson, James, and —— Boyce.
1779, —— —, Robinson, Mary, and John Gray.
1796, Sept. 22, Robinson, Nancy, and Samuel Lytle.
1803, Jan. 20, Robinson, Peggy, and William Smith.
1807, June 23, Robinson, Samuel, and Rachel Clendennin.
1807, Oct. 31, Rodgers, John, and Dinah Carson.
1772, Feb. 6, Rodgers, William, and —— ——.
1796, June 7, Russell, James, and Frances Moore.
1782, May 14, Russell, Samuel, and —— ——.
1772, Jan. 2, Rutherford, James, and Margaret Brisban.
1780, June 29, Rutherford, Jane, and Samuel Hutchinson.
1762, —— —, Rutherford, John, and Margaret Park.
1776, March 14, Rutherford, Samuel, and Susan Collier.
1803, June 28, Rutherford, Thomas, and Mary Shulze.
1801, March 17, Rutherford, William, and Sarah Swan.
1774, June 15, Ryan, Abigail, and John Gowdie.
1774, Aug. 13, Ryan, John, and Jane Gowdie.
1778, March 11, Sawyer. Joseph, and Elizabeth McFarland.

1781, Dec.   18, Sawyer, Mary, and William Sawyer.
1781, Dec.   18, Sawyer, William, and Mary Sawyer.
1766, Oct.   19, Semple, Sarah, and William Brown.
1804, Oct.   29, Seyfert, Anthony, and Jane Sheily.
1772, May   11, Shaw, James, and ——— ———.
1781, March   8, Shearl, John, and Margaret Thom.
1804, Oct.   29, Sheily, Jane, and Anthony Seyfert.
1803, Nov.   17, Sherer, Mary, and James Stewart.
1805, Jan.   8, Shriner, Mrs. Margaret, and David Detwiler.
1801, March 22, Shulze, Mrs. Cath., and Col. George Toot.
1803, June   28, Shulze, Mary, and Thomas Rutherford.
1757, May   23, Simpson, ———, and William Kelso.
1776, May   7, Simpson, John, and Margaret Murray.
1752, Oct.   4, Simpson, Margaret, and Wm. Augustus Harris.
1751, Nov.   5, Simpson, Mary, and Rev. John Elder.
1780, ——— —, Simpson, Mary, and Robert Taggart.
1774, Feb.   10, Simpson, Mathias, and ——— ———.
1808, May   26, Simpson, Gen. Michael, and Mrs. Susan Graham
1780, ——— —, Simpson, Sarah, and William Cook.
1771, Jan.   31, Simpson, Thomas, and ——— ———.
1784, Nov.   9, Sinclair, Duncan, and Hannah Templeton.
1789, March   3, Sloan, Samuel, and Prudence Walker.
1783, Aug.   7, Smith, Mary, and John Clark.
1757, Feb.   11, Smith, Rebecca, and Samuel Allen.
1769, May   15, Smith, William, and ——— ———.
1803, Jan.   20, Smith, William, and Peggy Robinson.
1782, Jan.   31, Smiley, Thomas, and Ann Tucker.
1793, March   7, Smith, Thomas, and Anna Moore.
1776, Jan.   12, Snodgrass, John, and ——— ———.
1782, May   9, Spence, James, and ——— ———.
1788, Jan.   13, Spence, Jean, and Thomas White.
1745, April   3, Sterret, Martha, and James Wilson.
1779, Dec.   23, Sterrett, William, jr, and ——— ———.
1810, July   5, Stewart, David, and Molly Buchannan.
1800, March 19, Stewart, Grace, and Benjⁿ Chambers.
1803, Nov.   17, Stewart, James, and Mary Sherer.
1809, Jan.   9, Stricker, Ann, and James Awl.
1784, June   3, Sturgeon, Lydia, and John McDonald.
1782, April   1, Swan, Hugh, and ——— ———.
1799, Nov.   26, Swan, Margaret, and James Ingram.
1801, March 17, Swan, Sarah, and William Rutherford.
1775, Dec.   19, Swan, William, and Martha Renick.
1780, ——— —, Taggart, Robert, and Mary Simpson.
1784, Nov.   9, Templeton, Hannah, and Duncan Sinclair.
1776, June   25, Templeton, John, and ——— ———.
1785, March 15, Templeton, Robert, and Mary Boyd.

1801, Aug. 21, Thomas, ——, and Jacob Hays.
1788, April 22, Thom, Esther, and James Anderson.
1781, March 8, Thom, Margaret, and John Shearl.
1772, May 18, Thompson, James, and —— ——.
1777, June 19, Thompson, John, and —— ——.
1776, April 9, Thompson, Samuel, and —— ——.
1803, Nov. 14, Tice, Mary, and John Whitall.
1778, April 30, Todd, James, and Mary Wilson.
1807, March 22, Toot, Col. George, and Mrs. Cath. Shulze.
1774, Aug. 25, Trousdale, John, and —— ——.
1781, June 21, Trousdale, William, and Elizabeth Glen.
1782, Jan. 31, Tucker, Ann, and Thomas Smiley.
1782, Aug. 19, Vandyke, Lambert, and —— ——.
1799, March 9, Vought, Catharine, and John Lanning.
1776, Jan. 25, Walker, James, and Barbara McArthur.
1789, March 3, Walker, Prudence, and Samuel Sloan.
1771, May 9, Wallace, Ann Maria, and Thomas McNair.
1784, Nov. 9, Wallace, Isabella, and Moses Gillmor.
1776, —— ——, Wallace, Mary, and Hugh Graham.
1766, —— ——, Wallace, Elizabeth, and Joseph Boyd.
1787, June 19, Wallace, James, and Sarah Elder.
1770, —— ——, Wallace, Moses, and Jean Fulton.
1775, Sept. 19, Wallace, William, and —— ——.
1779, Nov. 15, Watson, David, and —— ——.
1803, Feb. 10, Watson, Thomas, and Mary Mitchel.
1778, June 22, Weir, Samuel, and —— ——.
1771, July 15, West, Mary, and Thomas Reid.
1803, Nov. 14, Whitall, John, and Mary Tice.
1774, Oct. 7, White, Agnes, and Barefoot Brunson.
1788, Jan. 13, White, Thomas, and Jean Spence.
1786, Dec. 19, Whitley, Sarah, and John Wylie.
1787, Nov. 20, Wiggins, Margaret, and James Henderson.
1784, April 15, Williams, George and Ann Meloy.
1774, June 16, Wilson, Alexander, and Grizel Fulton.
1785, April 28, Wilson, Alexander, and Elizabeth Carson.
1772, April 30, Wilson, Hugh, and Isabella Fulton.
1745, April 3, Wilson, James, and Martha Sterrett.
1776, Feb. 13, Wilson, James, and —— ——.
1784, May 18, Wilson, James, and Mary Elder.
1805, April 4, Wilson, Mrs. Jean, and Col. Thomas Moorhead
1777, April 8, Wilson, Joseph, and Margaret Boyd.
1783, March 11, Wilson, Joseph, and Margaret Boyd.
1776, Dec. 10, Wilson, Margaret, and Isaac Hodge.
1781, May 10, Wilson, Margaret, and William Young.
1778, April 30, Wilson, Mary, and James Todd.
1784, March 2, Wilson, Mary, and Robert Boal.

1808, April 28, Wilson, Mary, and Rev. Wm. Kerr.
1774, Jan.   9, Wilson, Sarah, and Mr. Dugal.
1787, April 3, Wilson, Susanna, and David Mitchel.
1773, ——— —, Wilson, William, and Elizabeth Robinson.
1777, Jan. 23, Wray, David, and Mary Cowden.
1808, May 24, Wray, Jane, and Jacob Kucher.
1776, April 14, Wylie, James, and ——— ———.
1786, Dec. 19, Wylie, John, and Sarah Whitley.
1782, Dec. 31, Wylie, Mary, and Richard King.
1777, July 31, Wylie, Thomas, and ——— ———.
1772, June 16, Young, Andrew, and ——— ———.
1777, Nov. 4, Young, Jane, and Thomas Foster.
1781, May 10, Young, William, and Martha Wilson.